EXECUTIVE'S GUIDE TO BUSINESS LAW

EXECUTIVE'S GUIDE TO BUSINESS LAW

WILLIAM A. HANCOCK

McGRAW-HILL BOOK COMPANY
New York   St. Louis   San Francisco   Auckland
Bogotá   Düsseldorf   Johannesburg   London   Madrid   Mexico
Montreal   New Delhi   Panama   Paris   São Paulo
Singapore   Sydney   Tokyo   Toronto

Library of Congress Cataloging in Publication Data

Hancock, William A
  Executive's guide to business law.

  Includes index.
    1. Trade regulation—United States.   2.   Labor laws
and legislation—United States.   3.   Taxation—Law and
legislation—United States.   4.   Executives—United
States—Handbooks, manuals, etc.
  II. Title.
KF1609.H36   346'.73'07   79-1350
ISBN 0-07-025978-X

1234567890   KPKP   7865432109

The editor for this book was W. Hodson Mogan,
the designer was William E. Frost, and the production supervisor was
Sally Fliess. It was set in Century Schoolbook by The Kingsport Press.
Printed and bound by The Kingsport Press.

CONTENTS

PREFACE

Executive's Guide to Business Law was written to help business executives make more effective use of legal counsel in today's highly regulated business climate. The book contains a modern discussion of the laws which concern business executives today. These laws are generally the new federal laws dealing with employee health and safety, consumer product safety, employee discrimination, product liability, warranties, environment, toxic substances, freedom of access to government information, current practices in antitrust enforcement, foreign corrupt practices, and international boycotts. In the past, books on business law have dealt not with these subjects but rather with commercial laws, including those covering the law of agency, contract, and corporations. These commercial laws are not dealt with extensively in this book because they are adequately covered elsewhere. *Executive's Guide to Business Law* also contains understandable explanations of some of the major and frequently encountered problems in the fields of securities law and federal income tax law.

Most lawyers feel that these laws are too complex and difficult to explain to business people in understandable terms and further, that they change so frequently that any such explanation would be out of date before it was published. To some extent this is true, but there is a certain baseline of information which has remained essentially unchanged in all these areas. While the details change, this baseline of information should prove useful to business executives trying to communicate effectively with their lawyers.

The book should help the reader identify situations where specific legal advice should be sought; it should facilitate communications between lawyer and business executives in talking about these problems and taking constructive actions. It is not intended to encourage business people to make their own legal decisions but instead to help them and their lawyers to communicate about these problems and to reach realistic and workable solutions.

Section 1 advocates a program of preventative legal advice—I call it positive legal help for management. The guiding thought in preparing the book is not to help you get out of trouble but to keep you from getting into trouble. Analogies can be drawn to medicine. Major responsibility for an individual's medical health rests with the individual—not with the doctor. Doctors can and should provide advice on how people can prevent illness and stay healthy. However, they cannot do it without the patient's full cooperation—indeed, the initiative almost always has to come from that individual. Certainly, doctors must treat specific illnesses as they appear, but this is not their sole function.

The same is true in business. Lawyers must deal with specific legal problems as they appear, but that should not be their sole role. They can and should provide advice on how to keep the business legally healthy, but substantial initiative on this front must come from management. Similarly, much of what is advocated herein cannot be done entirely by lawyers. To pursue the medical analogy, your doctor may advocate a program of physical exercise for you, but you are the one who must actually do the exercises.

The portion of the book which advocates this program of positive legal help for management charts a long course. Keep in mind however, that the longest journey begins with the first step, and it is neither necessary nor appropriate to do everything at once.

This book covers much, but not all, of the law relating to business. Those areas which it does cover represent the areas which are developing the most rapidly. The book is an excellent starting point for helping you and your lawyer keep your business healthy, and many lawyers will find it useful. However, it is not a substitute for specific legal advice nor for the more detailed publications which will be available to your lawyers. The book should be used to obtain a general understanding of the basic framework of the law on the subjects covered, and most of it should remain accurate for a number of years because I have tried to avoid specific discussions of fine points which might change.

The book is not intended to be critical of lawyers or of managers who use (or don't use) lawyers. However, in my judgment, the relationship between lawyers and their business clients has almost never developed into the close, constructive relationship which has developed between members of other professions. I have not attempted to assign any blame for this, but I do feel a problem is present and have therefore identified it. I hope this book contributes to the development of the lawyer/business relationship so that lawyers can continue to fulfill their obligation to be independent counselors as well as their obligation to provide positive, preventative legal advice.

An obvious question that will arise during the course of examining this book is the cost/benefit ratio of the kinds of preventative legal programs which are suggested. Almost everyone would agree in principle that all the programs I have suggested are desirable, but like many things that may be desirable, they may cost more than they are worth. This is a very important observation. It is the rare company that can justify full scale prevention/ education programs in each of the areas of law discussed in this book. However, most companies will benefit from *some* of these programs, executed in varying degrees of detail and cost. Management and its counsel should work together to achieve a program that falls somewhere between the extremes of no preventative legal advice at all and burdensome and costly preventative programs that aren't justified by the company's risks. I hope this book helps the reader make these judgments.

A note about language in this book: The generic "he" is generally used but only for the sake of simplicity, and it is always intended to refer to both sexes.

ACKNOWLEDGMENT

I would like to acknowledge the assistance of my mother, Mrs. Leona F. Hancock, in the typing of this entire manuscript through several drafts and in the preparation of the index.

EXECUTIVE'S GUIDE TO BUSINESS LAW

SECTION ONE: GENERAL MATTERS

INTRODUCTION

This book is dedicated to the proposition that business executives who are affected by the law should know something about it and about the lawyers they rely on to interpret and apply it. It is based on the belief that business executives who know the fundamentals of the laws which govern the operation of their businesses will be better able to use their lawyers, will get better performance from them, and will move ahead of those who fail to do so.

The business world is already highly legalistic and becoming more so. Federal legislators are more inclined each year to tell business executives how to run their businesses, and state legislators are following suit.

While business executives need not and should not attempt to do their own legal work, those business executives who simply abandon the whole area to their lawyers are making a sad mistake. Nothing can take a bigger chunk out of company profits than a mistake in some of these legal areas. Nothing can sap the energies of management more than a serious legal entanglement.

For this reason, this book will be devoted almost entirely to "preventive medicine." It will show the business executive how to take maximum advantage of all the competitive flexibility the law allows while complying with the necessary rules and avoiding costly and energy-draining legal confrontations. It will also show the executive how to fit lawyers into his operation in the most efficient and economical manner.

Why is it necessary for the business executive to pay more than passing attention to these laws? After all, that's what the lawyers are for. Why not let them worry about it?

The answers are simple, yet overlooked by many business executives.

These laws present both problems and opportunities. Lawyers are trained to solve problems and not to take advantage of the opportunities the law allows. Indeed, law students in any good law school are given a copy of the *Canons of Professional Ethics* at the beginning of their education, and one of the most important of these canons is the one preventing the lawyer from soliciting business. Any lawyer who violates this canon is branded an "ambulance chaser" and scorned by his professional colleagues. Recent Supreme Court rulings allowing advertising by lawyers for some routine services will not change this basic attitude in the near future. Is it any wonder that lawyers usually render advice only when problems are presented to them? To go out and find the problems and turn them into opportunities goes against their training from their very first exposure to the law. To be sure, there are many lawyers who frequently render constructive advice to their clients without requiring the client to come after it. However, the executive who depends upon this and fails to exercise his prerogative to insist upon full and complete legal advice in all appropriate areas of business is not using all the tools he has available to help him do his job and to make his business more successful.

There is another fundamental problem—the communications gap. In far too many cases, there is a tremendous communications gap between lawyers and their business clients. Business executives sometimes do not realize that they have legal problems or that their lawyers might help them solve a problem or take advantage of an opportunity. They therefore go their own ways without legal advice and, far too frequently, either get into a legal situation which is difficult, costly, or embarrassing to get out of or fail to take advantage of a business opportunity because of their own belief that there are legal problems when, in fact, competent counsel could show them how to accomplish the desired objective with little or no legal risk. Lawyers are frequently guilty of contributing to this gap. Too many times, the corporate counsel will sit in his office and write memos which will not be read and could not be followed even if they were read. Often, what he should be doing is talking to the business executives who are actually dealing with the problem and finding out the business requirements so that a practical and constructive legal contribution can be made. In short, frequently the lawyer is guilty of an overly academic approach to business problems and sometimes gives advice which is of no value to the business executive who receives it.

Whose fault is this? Does it matter? Is your physical health your responsibility or that of your doctor? If you have had regular checkups for a number of years and then find out that you have developed a serious problem which, had it been discovered sooner, could have been remedied much more easily, can you blame your doctor? The answer may depend upon your communications with the physician. If you requested complete physicals periodically and fully disclosed any abnormalities you had noticed yourself, perhaps you can and should blame the doctor. But if you went to him simply for specific problems and asked him for specific help with those problems, can you blame him if you developed an unrelated problem and he didn't discover it? To pursue the analogy further, if you asked for a "complete physical" because you had been experiencing digestive discomfort but did not tell the doctor the precise nature of your concern on the theory that he was the doctor and he would find it in the "complete" physical you requested, would you be justified in blaming your problems on anyone but yourself?

The relationship between a business executive and his lawyer is not unlike that between doctor and patient. The patient himself lives with his body constantly and knows more about it than does the doctor—at least about when and how it experiences problems. Lawyers, even business lawyers, are not business executives, and it is the rare lawyer who knows very much about the day-to-day operations of the business. It is therefore incumbent upon the business executive to make sure this information is provided if he expects the lawyer to render good service. If the executive fails to provide the necessary information, is it the lawyer's duty to pry it out of him? This is an unrealistic and unproductive argument. Communication is a two-way street, and when the one-way sign goes up there is going to be a problem.

THE QUALITY OF YOUR LAWYER

There are no two lawyers of precisely equal ability, and there are as many kinds of lawyers as there are kinds of people. Unfortunately, these include dumb ones, arrogant ones, those who are more concerned with making a buck than helping a client, and those who lack the fundamental human skills to make effective use of their legal abilities. There are also overworked lawyers who just don't have time to do the proper job for their clients. There are also an astounding number of lawyers who don't know the law. Fortunately, however, most corporate lawyers are bright, conscientious, ethical people who diligently try to do the best possible job for their clients and who maintain the highest professional standards regarding their own personal education and professional development.

There is a reason for this, and it is very simple. Most corporate law firms hire only students who have graduated very high in their classes from the best law schools and who, as the interviewers sometimes say, "have their heads screwed on right." The reason for this is, in turn, very simple. Corporate law firms need these kinds of people and can afford them. They need them because of the tremendous complexity of today's business world and because they must deal with business executives who are themselves very bright and able. They can afford them because they charge fees which will enable them to pay high salaries. Clients pay these fees because they know they need this high-quality help. Almost all corporate legal departments hire their lawyers out of these corporate law firms, and those who don't either hire the most able government lawyers they can find or use the same high recruiting standards used by the large corporate law firms. Thus, whether the corporation gets its advice from its in-house legal staff or from independent counsel, it is very likely to be getting advice from the cream of the crop and to be paying accordingly. This places a premium on using this high-priced resource efficiently.

It is true that there is a great deal of routine legal work which must be done and that it is not necessary to have the highest-paid Wall Street lawyer or the brightest Harvard Law School graduate do it. This, however, is not the kind of legal advice we are talking about at this point. We are talking about "corporate counsel," not about law clerks, and we will be talking about legal advice and not about routine legal work. This is another reason why business executives must appreciate the fundamental principles of law governing their businesses. If they do not know the difference between corporate counsel and law clerks, or between legal counsel and routine legal work, they run a high risk of either getting bad advice or wasting a great deal of money. Thus, we have a chapter titled "How to Use Your Lawyer," which will give some guidance on how business executives can get top-quality legal advice and, at the same time, not overpay for routine legal work.

THE ORGANIZATION OF THE BOOK

Chapter 1, "Positive Legal Help for Management," lists two approaches which the executive can use to get better and more cost-effective legal advice. The first approach is to list a series of sample "problems" which may be presented by today's legal climate. Each problem is then followed by a short paragraph which describes a possible "solution." Naturally, each of these problem/solution scenarios is considerably oversimplified, and in some cases the "solution" is simply to watch out for the problem. The remainder of the book will be devoted to a more detailed discussion of these and other problems and solutions.

Another approach which the executive can use to "audit" his legal function is to do it by statute. In other words, the executive simply asks his lawyers what exposure the company has under the various statutes which affect its business and what the lawyer is doing to minimize the risks and take maximum advantage of the opportunities.

Throughout this book, we will use the terms "legal counsel" or "lawyer" to refer to the company's in-house or outside counsel. However, the choice of whether to receive one's legal advice wholesale or retail is very important, and so the pros and cons of each system are discussed in Chapter 2, "Methods of Obtaining Legal Services."

A WORD ABOUT "LEGAL COMPLEXITY"

"Legal complexity" can mean a number of things:

1. It can refer to the drafting of the laws itself. The classic example is the Internal Revenue Code. The plain and simple truth, however, is that a detailed law is sometimes easier to understand and apply than is a simply worded one. Let's take two examples.

    The complexity of the Internal Revenue Code is legendary. However, the overwhelming majority of day-to-day tax problems can be solved by consulting only the Internal Revenue Code and the Internal Revenue Service regulations thereunder. These are contained in three volumes. To be sure, the print is fine and the paper is thin, but the volumes are fairly well indexed, only a relatively small number of the sections are applicable to any one problem, and most tax lawyers know which ones they are.

    Consider, on the other extreme, section 10(b)(5) of the Securities Exchange Act and section 1 of the Sherman Act. These are very simple statutes which can be quoted in a few words:

    > Section 10(b)   It shall be unlawful for any person, directly or indirectly . . . to use or employ, in connection with the purchase or sale of any security . . . any manipulative or deceptive device. . . .
    > Section 1   Every contract, combination in the form of trust or otherwise, or conspiracy, in restraint of trade or commerce . . . is hereby declared to be illegal. . . .

    However, it is submitted that the complexity of these two statutes is actually greater than that of the Internal Revenue Code. The reason is this: The Internal Revenue Code statutes and regulations—while sometimes difficult to read—usually contain an answer to the question. On the other hand, in the 10(b)(5) and Sherman Act, there simply is no *sure* answer except in the clearest of cases. Thus your lawyer may have to give you a less than certain answer, and this will involve the ultimate complexity—uncertainty. The true complexity of the law should not be measured by the wording of the statute.

2. Legal complexity can refer to the need for complex and detailed descriptions of fact situations in order to apply the law. In other words, the application of the law is so complicated that it just can't be explained simply. Further, legend has it that if one tries to simplify the law, one distorts the true picture and misleads the reader. In some cases, this is undoubtedly true—particularly in the complicated business laws we are going to be discussing in this book. However, it can be done. It is difficult. It is time consuming. Thus, the cry of complexity is sometimes raised by those lawyers who are unable or unwilling to put forth the effort to reduce the law to understandable terms for their business clients, or those business executives who will not put forth the effort to understand material which, admittedly, does not have a great deal of sex appeal.

Thus we suggest to the reader—be he business executive or lawyer—that while simplification may leave out some points which can be important, it is much better than a complete lack of understanding of the problem and complete abandonment of the area to lawyers without informed executive participation.

CHAPTER ONE

POSITIVE LEGAL
HELP FOR
MANAGEMENT

Management in modern business has learned to live with lawyers in almost all aspects of its daily affairs. In most well-run companies, top management includes a lawyer at the vice-presidential level; and in many large companies, the board of directors includes at least one practicing attorney (not necessarily the legal counsel for the company). Financial management will frequently consult with tax and securities lawyers; personnel management will generally have access to the services of labor attorneys; the procurement function, long neglected by both management and the legal profession, will today probably have access to a commercial lawyer; and marketing and sales people will have a trade-regulation lawyer as one of their resources. However, in most, if not all, of these situations, the lawyer is looked upon as a resource and expected to perform a function akin to that of the goalie in a hockey game. The lawyer is not expected, or in some cases even permitted, to initiate actions on his own.

In many companies, there is not even a formal legal audit procedure for lawyers to regularly audit the legal affairs of the company nor any procedure for management to audit the performance of the legal function.

In contrast, the financial auditing procedures of most companies are elaborate and well-documented, and management can audit the effectiveness of its financial people by some relatively standard and objective measures. (Indeed, a simple look at the balance tells quite a bit.) Manpower planning and personnel development are well-established aspects of the human-relations function and are generally well planned and organized. Furthermore, management usually carefully reviews these programs and can, at least to some extent, measure the personnel function by the quality of people in key positions and the procedures used to develop key people. Sales and marketing planning strategy are usually well-thought-out and organized on both a short- and long-term basis; and measurement of sales strategy is straightforward—the company either made its sales goals or it didn't. Even procurement is coming around to playing a more active role in the economic performance of the company, and management can measure the performance of the procurement function by fairly objective means.

In today's climate, however, it is not only proper but essential that the lawyer interject himself into all affairs regulated by a set of legal rules (which today is almost all of the affairs of the company), and it is equally essential that management evaluate the quality of advice obtained from its lawyers and audit their activity so that their performance can be measured with at least some degree of objectivity. To pursue a policy where the lawyers provide advice only when consulted (act as goalies) will, in the long run, force the company to divert a great deal of its resources toward solving the complex and potentially very costly legal problems which will undoubtedly arise; and for management to simply blindly follow the advice of its lawyers when it feels disposed to ask for it is just as potentially disastrous in the legal area as it is in the medical area.

How is management to do this? Must managers become their own lawyers? Certainly not—just as the company president doesn't have to be an auditor to evaluate his auditing system, he doesn't have to be a lawyer to evaluate his legal function. All he needs is (1) typical management skills, (2) a rudimentary knowledge of the legal area and the possible problems and solutions, and (3) a willingness to spend the time to find out what his lawyers actually do, what they should be doing, and how well they are handling problems and devising constructive programs of their own.

There are at least two ways to begin a program which will improve the legal service received by corporations and allow management to evaluate the quality of its legal services:

1. Have the lawyers prepare a list of problem areas, provide suggestions for positive legal help to avoid problems, and explain any preventive measures already taken.

2. Have the lawyers prepare a list of all of the federal laws and widely applicable state laws which affect the company in a substantial way, provide a report for management on effective legal guidance in these areas, and explain what steps have already been taken to reduce possible legal problems.

THE PROBLEM-AREA APPROACH

Affirmative and timely advice by corporate counsel before a problem arises could save the company money in the areas of trade regulation; securities and finance; taxation; labor laws; industrial property; product safety, warranty, and liability; and commercial laws.

Trade Regulation

Criminal Antitrust Violations

The Sherman Act imposes severe penalties on anticompetitive agreements among competitors, but there is widespread misunderstanding about what kind of activity comes within the proscriptions of this act.

Many executives think there must be some kind of clandestine conspiracy, complete with smoke-filled rooms and registration in hotels under fictitious names. More sophisticated executives may realize that conduct falling far short of this Hollywood scenario can create a problem, but few of them realize that the conspiracy proscribed by the Sherman Act may simply be a tacit understanding to keep, for example, wholesale prices "low" and retail prices "high." In addition, some managers don't realize the devastating effect that a criminal indictment can have on their careers even if they are proved innocent of unlawful conduct. The criminal sanctions of this act, together with the possibility for private plaintiffs to recover their attorney's fees and three times their damages, makes this one of the areas where corporate counsel *must* devote substantial efforts towards preventive measures.

The normal solution to this problem is an antitrust-compliance program conducted by the company's lawyers. This program consists generally of (1) a policy statement, (2) some kind of publication which sets forth the thrust of the antitrust laws, (3) a series of meetings and discussions between the company's lawyers and top management and (4) a series of speeches delivered by the company's lawyers to other people in the company so that the company does not inadvertently get dragged into an antitrust case. (See Chapter 7.)

Trade Associations: Antitrust

Experience has shown that trade associations play a substantial part in almost all of the "hard-core" antitrust violations which are subject to criminal penalties. It is the rare price-fixing case in which a trade association meeting is not one, if not the principal, damaging instance which serves to incriminate the defendant. The trade-association question is so troublesome that some antitrust counselors flatly recommend against their clients or their clients' representatives attending any trade-association meetings whatsoever. Other counselors adopt various procedures to assure that trade-association meetings will not become forums for price-fixing, market allocation, and so on.

Trade associations perform a useful function. They can be beneficial to companies, and the mere possibility that their meetings may also become forums for antitrust violations should not be sufficient to require counsel to make a blanket recommendation against attendance at their meetings by business executives. On the other hand, there is no denying the danger. Therefore, a program of (1) ascertaining that the trade association's formal sessions are conducted in a proper and legal manner (this generally requires that counsel do a good job of making sure that the trade association is represented by adequate counsel) and (2) educating all of the company's employees who attend the trade association meetings will generally reduce any problem to a much smaller level. (See Chapter 8.)

Distribution

Distributorship situations are perhaps the most frequent source of antitrust difficulty for a company. In some cases, antitrust issues raised by distributorship questions are not overwhelmingly serious because they are usually susceptible of a relatively amicable settlement without substantial financial cost to the manufacturer. However, the company's operations can be inhibited, the company's people can be tied up in drawn-out negotiations, and, conceivably, the problem could snowball into a very costly and troublesome lawsuit if proper legal guidance is not given in this area.

The solutions to this problem are (1) a competent legal review of all of the distributorship documents used by the company and (2) education of the sales and marketing people on the antitrust rules in the distributorship area and some of the legal rules which place a premium on having sales and marketing people conduct the proper conversations and write the proper memorandums involving distributors. For example, the appropriate people should be taught that under current legal theories the distributor is an independent businessperson and, after he purchases the products of your company he usually cannot be restricted in the later sales of those products in terms of the price that he charges, the territories in which he sells, or the customers to whom he sells. In addition, the distributor cannot be prevented from handling competitive goods.

(See Chapter 11.)

Price Discrimination

The Robinson-Patman Act is a very complicated statute, not fully understood by all lawyers and generally agreed to be an anomaly in the antitrust law because it can have the effect of prohibiting a company from competing for business by offering lower prices. The general thrust of the act is that sellers may not discriminate in price among purchasers of their products if those purchasers compete with one another. However, this relatively simple proposition creates a number of highly complex and difficult problems. Also, some of the prohibitions of the Robinson-Patman Act are governed by extremely detailed regulations promulgated by the Federal Trade Commission. For example, if a company desires to offer advertising allowances, it must comply with many pages of detailed regulations governing exactly how this must be done.

Generally, Robinson-Patman Act problems cannot be avoided by merely having the company counsel conduct meetings or write memorandums to the appropriate management people. Instead, there must be certain procedures by which management is alerted to the areas in which the Robinson-Patman Act may apply and specific legal advice then sought. In other words, the solution to this problem is the establishment of procedures whereby certain actions involving the company's advertising or the pricing of the company's goods must receive advance legal approval.

(See Chapter 12.)

Unfair Competition

The Federal Trade Commission Act generally prohibits any "unfair method of competition." Again, this seemingly simple statement generates many complex problems in actual practice. Most of the problems in this area involve advertising the company's products. In the past, this was an area where common sense would be a relatively good guide. Today, however, there are so many technical rules involved in advertising and labeling that this is no longer the case.

The company lawyers must make sure that management understands the thrust of the expanded powers of the Federal Trade Commission and the expanded scope of the prohibition against unfair and deceptive practices. Counsel must themselves keep up with this flow of new regulations and must make sure that appropriate procedures are established to disseminate this information to those who must comply with the stated rules.

Other federal laws, such as the Fair Packaging and Labelling Act and the new warranty legislation, also mean that advertising is no longer an area where common sense will be sufficient to comply with the rules. For

example, the new warranty legislation requires that certain detailed and very technical warranty statements be included in all advertising material, and the Fair Packaging and Labelling Act already requires that a great many products have certain specific disclosures contained on their packages.
(See Chapter 18.)

Mergers and Joint Ventures

Mergers and joint ventures are governed by complex antitrust rules which generally provide that it is illegal for companies to merge with one another or to enter into joint ventures with one another if there is a substantial adverse effect on competition. Again, however, this simple principle has given rise to a great many technical legal theories and some problems which are by no means obvious at first glance. The most troublesome of these is the so-called "potential-competition theory," by which not only direct competitors but potential competitors are prohibited from merging with one another or entering into certain joint ventures.

The solution is to (1) establish a procedure whereby all mergers and joint ventures are carefully reviewed by antitrust counsel, (2) do a little bit of advance education of the business people who negotiate these deals so that they don't negotiate any which will have to be renegotiated or abandoned, and (3) make sure the business executives understand the implications of the market analyses and memorandums they create.
(See Chapters 13 and 14.)

Securities and Finance

Officer and Director Liability

There are growing bodies of law which place personal liability on officers and directors who take illegitimate action in the legitimate belief that they are serving the best interests of the company. The most notable examples are in the areas of securities law. Today, any officer or director who signs a registration statement becomes personally liable for any inaccuracies or misstatements therein, and the Employee Retirement Income Security Act provides that officers and directors may be personally liable for loss or misuse of pension funds.

In order to insure that the company is managed by officers and directors who can devote substantially all of their efforts towards managing the company rather than worrying about their own personal liability, it is necessary to take steps to provide that the officers and directors of the company will be reimbursed for any personal liability.
The general solution to this problem is as follows:

1. Educate all of the directors as to their potential liabilities and duties under State Common Law and the relevant federal laws.

2. Make sure that the proper provisions are contained in the company's articles, code of regulations, or bylaws in order to make sure that they can be indemnified in case of potential personal liability.

3. Consider appropriate officers' and directors' liability insurance.

4. Establish good procedures so that the officers and directors can discharge their legal obligations to the company.

In addition, company counsel should participate in all meetings of the board of directors so that these meetings can be properly recorded. Company counsel should also be aware of any significant developments so that appropriate legal advice can be rendered in any situation where it might appear that personal liability of the officers and directors might exist.

(See Chapter 65.)

Insider Trading

Ever since the famous *Texas Gulf Sulphur* case, possible liability under the federal securities laws has been of great concern to officers and directors of companies. Basically, rule 10(b)(5) of the securities laws simply provides that no "insider" should be allowed to profit from trading in the securities of the company based upon information known by him but not known to the investing public. Again, however, this simple rule has given rise to a great deal of litigation and many technical rules which are not solved by simply having the officers and directors act in good faith in trading in the company securities. Similar rules of the New York Stock Exchange provide some guidelines in this area.

The solution to this problem is for corporate counsel to make sure that all appropriate people in the company—and for this purpose, "appropriate people" includes anyone with possession of inside information, not just officers and directors—are aware of the basic prohibition of rule 10(b)(5) and act accordingly.

(See Chapter 39.)

Misleading Information Releases

As a corollary to insider trading problems, the company itself can be liable to purchasers of its securities where there has been dissemination of information which is inaccurate or misleading—either too positive or too negative. Indeed, it was the content of two disputed news releases upon which the extensive litigation involved in the Texas Gulf Sulphur situation was based. Unfortunately, common sense is not a completely adequate guide here, and technical legal rules apply.

If company counsel adequately monitors all of the news releases of the company, this problem can be minimized. Accordingly, the solution to this problem is to:

1. Educate the public relations department about the basic problem.
2. Adopt a procedure where all news releases are cleared with company counsel before being issued.
3. Make sure that speeches by company management are within appropriate rules.
   (See Chapter 39.)

Short-Swing Profits

Section 16(b) of the securities laws provides that no officer, director, or 10 percent shareholder of the company may profit from any purchase or sale of company stock within any six-month period. Again, however, this very simple rule has given rise to a great number of complex situations, particularly where stock options, dividend-reinvestment plans, stock-savings plans, and other such programs are in effect. Unless proper guidance is given, it is possible for officers and directors of the company to incur substantial liabilities under section 16(b), even in situations where there has been no actual profit.

Short-swing profit problems can be avoided by proper education of company directors and 10 percent shareholders and by proper procedures which apply whenever any officer, director, or 10 percent shareholder desires to purchase or sell company stock. It should be remembered that these procedures have to include *all* trading, including the exercise of stock options, purchase of stock pursuant to dividend reinvestment plans, and participation in company stock-purchase programs. *All* insider transactions should be discussed beforehand with corporate counsel.

(See Chapter 40.)

Accounting Regulations

The past few years have seen a veritable blizzard of new accounting rules. This presents a significant problem because the division of responsibility between accountants and lawyers in preparation of financial statements and other matters necessary to comply with the federal securities laws sometimes becomes clouded. The general principle is very easy to state. The lawyers ought to be responsible for the narrative portion of the prospectus and registration statement, the accountants ought to be responsible for the financial statements, and the auditors ought to be responsible for the adequacy of the company's internal controls. However, this becomes complicated in practice.

It is generally considered to be good practice to have the lawyers fully aware of the content of the financial statements and the methods of preparing them to make sure that appropriate accounting principles as announced by the SEC have been followed, and it is also appropriate for the accountants to be fully aware of the narrative portion of the prospectus or registration statements so that their input into this part of the document can be obtained.

In addition, some accounting rules—like those relating to capitalization of leases and accounting for deferred compensation—are very important in the lawyer's work related to these fields. The lawyer should make sure both he and the appropriate business people understand them.

(See Chapters 41 and 42.)

Taxation

Tax-Free Reorganizations

The essential problem here is that reorganizations of all types, including particularly the acquisition of one company by another, are governed by complex and technical tax rules which, in many cases, cause the acquisition to be financially much more attractive in one form than in the other. In addition, there are certain other legal problems which may mean that the transaction should or should not be accomplished through some particular structure. On the other hand, when business executives negotiate acquisitions, they typically think only in terms of the basic business transaction and not in terms of these technicalities. If appropriate precautions have not been taken, it is possible that business executives may negotiate a deal which is much less advantageous than would be possible if another form could be used.

Generally, the solution to this problem is for the company lawyers to make sure that they have informed those people in the company who actually negotiate the initial stages of these kinds of deals of the basic alternatives which are available and cautioned them that in making the initial commitments, it would be most desirable to avoid making any kind of commitment as to the precise form of the transaction.

For example, if one company desired to acquire another through merger or exchange of stock, it would not be necessary at the initial stages of negotiation to actually decide on what kind of tax-free reorganization could be used. Instead, the appropriate procedure would simply be for the companies, upon reaching a basic agreement, to execute a letter of intent which said simply that one company had agreed to enter into negotiations with the other for the acquisition of the second company. The agreement could then go on to recite the price or stock-exchange ratio which had been agreed upon. It would be neither necessary nor appropriate at that stage to go on to say in the letter of intent that the agreement would take place as a tax-free merger or to make any other commitment. At that point, the lawyers and accountants could reevaluate the situation and consider all of the various alternative methods of acquiring the company and make a recommendation as to which would be best.

(See Chapter 32.)

The Interplay between Lawyers and Accountants

In some companies, lawyers and accountants work together as a well-organized team to handle all of the company's tax problems and do all the necessary tax planning to make sure taxes are held to a minimum. In other companies, there is some sort of division. The lawyers may do the tax planning, and the accountants may handle preparation of the tax returns and specific tax problems like IRS audits. In still other companies, there is constant bickering between the two functions, with no one really understanding what the responsibilities of the other are. Obviously in this latter case, the company's tax situation will not be good because problems will not be handled in the most effective way, and tax planning will deteriorate into conflicts between the lawyers and accountants as to "whose idea it was."

The executive doesn't care who does the tax work, but he wants it done right. However, it is not a simple problem because the accountants have some special abilities which the lawyers do not and vice versa. Therefore, if they do not work together somehow, performance will be less than optimum. Personal pride and motivation are important, and there is usually some jealousy.

There is no easy solution to this problem. However, if proper attention is given to the question—and if the company has good people in both the legal and accounting departments—a good solution is usually obtainable.

(See Chapter 31.)

Labor Laws

Union Organization Drives

In most companies which have employees represented by a union, there has been some attention given to the problems imposed by the National Labor Relations Act upon the relationship between the company and the employees. However, in companies where there is no union, there is sometimes a total lack of awareness of this problem and when the company learns of a potential union organization drive, panic sets in and a great number of wrong and illegal actions are taken. The company is then placed in a very disadvantageous position. If it loses the election it cannot complain of its own actions, and if it wins the election the union can have it set aside for unfair labor practices and have a second chance.

The solutions to this problem are (1) to make sure that the company has access to competent labor relations counsel on very short notice, and (2) to make sure that the appropriate management people in the company (generally down to the first-level supervisory people) are aware of what they may or may not do in a union organization drive. In some cases, this can be done by a seminar whereby these people are invited to hear presentations of labor lawyers as to what conduct is permissible.

(See Chapter 30.)

Pension Law

The Employee Retirement Income Security Act (ERISA) has created a great many troublesome situations, particularly for the officers and directors of companies with pension plans. The new rules are extremely technical and, even given a complete awareness of the general principles by the officers and directors, common sense and good judgment are probably not sufficient to ensure compliance. For example, directors of a company may be held personally liable for mismanagement of pension funds even when they had no part in deciding what investments would be made.

The solution to this problem is to make sure that corporate counsel has fully analyzed the situation and taken whatever steps are necessary to minimize the liability of the directors.

ERISA has been said to be one of the most important and fundamental changes in business law for many years, and this is certainly true. ERISA establishes many technical rules for pension plans and their funding. Generally, business executives, as well as general corporate attorneys, are better off leaving this aspect of ERISA to the pension experts. However, in addition to the personal liability problem, there are at least the following other implications of this new law which business executives and their general corporate counsel must consider in a wide variety of situations.

1. The new law zeros in on the so-called "defined benefit" plan. This is the kind of a plan where the company promises to pay the employee a certain amount of money—usually expressed as a percentage of his average salary over a certain period of time. The law has a serious effect on these kinds of plans but has relatively less effect on defined contribution plans. The typical defined contribution plan is a profit-sharing plan, where the company makes a given contribution and, at retirement, the employee is entitled to whatever is in his account at the time and no promises are made to him that it will be any specific amount or percentage of his average salary. The implications are obvious. Before instituting any new employee retirement plan, the new law should be examined closely. It may tip the balance in favor of a profit-sharing plan and against a pension plan.

2. The new law imposes tremendous record-keeping problems for companies with pension plans.

3. The new law imposes severe problems for terminations of pension plans and provides that the company itself may be liable to employees for up to one-third of the total assets of the company if the assets of the pension plan are not sufficient to pay off vested liabilities. Obviously this must be considered in any case involving a plant shutdown.

4. The new law establishes elaborate procedures for reporting the contents of plans to the government and giving summary plan descriptions to the participants. This has an effect on the entire company approach to the employee-benefit area and should be carefully considered.

These are but a few of the problems caused by this extremely important and burdensome legislation. This law has generated a whole new body of law—not to mention a whole new body of lawyers, accountants, and other experts. Its full implications will not be known for many years, and it is possible that while its principal objective was clearly good—making sure employees were treated fairly regarding their pensions—the entire thrust of the law may substantially erode the private pension system and make it so complicated and risky for business executives that, in the long run, it will not be in the best interests of working Americans.

(See Chapter 27.)

Discrimination in Employment

At this stage of development of federal and state legislation, almost everyone in business realizes that it is illegal to discriminate in employment against minority groups. However, sometimes the extent of the rules, together with some of the practical aspects of the problem, are not adequately dealt with by corporate counsel.

For example, in some companies the responsibility for handling a complaint filed by an employee with either the federal or state Equal Employment Opportunity agency is delegated to personnel people, and lawyers do not participate until the employee either exhausts his remedies in the federal or state agencies and institutes a lawsuit or until the case at the agency level gets to such a serious state that the personnel people call the lawyers in to participate. This is extremely unfortunate because in many situations EEO claims are filed by people who have absolutely no legitimate complaint. However, the agency investigators come into the company and because of the failure of company people to take appropriate action to limit the investigation, the EEOC goes through the company's practices with a fine-tooth comb and comes up with something which is potentially discriminatory.

The substantive content of the rules against discrimination in employment has become so elaborate and technical that even a company which exercises good faith and common sense can run afoul of some of the latest pronouncements of the federal courts or the Equal Employment Opportunity Commission.

The solution to this problem is to:

1. Make sure that appropriate procedures are established so that proper legal counsel is provided at an early stage. This will mean that a lawyer who is trained in gathering facts and presenting them in the best possible light will personally investigate a complaint situation and present the company side of the story in the best and most persuasive manner. In addition, the lawyer will assure to the maximum extent possible that the investigation does not get out of hand and develop into a general overall review of all the company's employment practices.

2. Make sure that company counsel has adequately informed himself of the personnel practices of the company and has conducted whatever educational programs are necessary to ensure that the personnel people understand enough about the general principles of law involved to know when to seek legal guidance.

    (See Chapter 25.)

Occupational Safety and Health

The Occupational Safety and Health Act of 1970 generally provides that a company is obligated to provide a safe place of employment for its employees and to comply with numerous and detailed technical standards governing such things as machine guards and noise levels. Generally, actual compliance with the technical requirements should be in the hands of competent engineers who understand the requirements. However, there are a number of legal implications which the company must keep in mind.

For example, when an inspector arrives at the plant, there are certain legal obligations on the company and, in addition, there are certain legal restrictions on the inspector's activities. In addition, when an employee files a complaint with the Occupational Safety and Health Administration alleging a safety hazard, there are certain legal restrictions on what actions the employer may take. Perhaps most important, however, there are a number of steps a company can take to prepare for an OSHA inspection and to handle it in the best way possible. This depends on prior education of the people involved. Once the inspector arrives at the door, it is too late. Further, there are substantial and drastic actions which the inspector can take (like shutting down a particular operation or even a whole plant), but there are also restrictions on how and under what circumstances these actions may be taken. Accordingly, unless there is advance planning with legal guidance, OSHA inspections may create unnecessary headaches for the company.

In addition to all of the above, there are criminal penalties for certain OSHA violations—generally willful ones which result in the death of an employee—and there are record-keeping, reporting, and posting requirements with which to comply.

The general solution to this problem is to make sure that legal counsel has drafted and circulated a memorandum which informs all managers of every plant of the basic rules of the Occupational Safety and Health Act and what to do when an inspector arrives at the door. This memorandum should cover such things as the inspector's rights, the rights of the employees to have a representative accompany the inspector, and the obligation of the company to allow the inspector, within certain bounds, to conduct a complete and thorough investigation. It should also include, however, a complete discussion of some of the practical aspects of this problem so that the plant manager is not caught by surprise at the first investigation. Also, appropriate information should be disseminated on the rights of employees so that the regulations governing their rights are not inadvertently violated.

Naturally, there should also be provision for obtaining prompt legal guidance in the event of a citation which the company feels is unjustified. Under law, there is a very short time period for complaining about a citation, and if the citation is not objected to it becomes final.

(See Chapter 26.)

Wage-and-Hour Laws

The entire body of wage-and-hour laws is extremely detailed. However, at this point in the development of the laws, most companies have adequate procedures for ensuring compliance with most of the rules.

The principal rule under the wage-and-hour laws is the requirement that a company pay time and a half for overtime, and another important requirement is that the company pay certain minimum wages. Another aspect of the wage-and-hour law which becomes important from time to time is the restriction of employment of minors in certain areas. These, however, are all relatively mechanical problems which most companies which have paid any attention at all to their payroll practices have already solved.

However, from time to time a number of practical problems arise under the wage-and-hour laws. The most frequent of these are (1) the propriety of paying bonuses and (2) the classification of certain people. The bonus problem is that in most cases, bonuses have to be considered as part of the employee's regular rate. This means that a company which pays a bonus over and above what a worker would normally get may end up having to pay an additional amount because such bonus is calculated as part of the regular rate and time and a half may have to be paid to an employee who has worked overtime. Another problem which arises with some degree of frequency is the categorization of people as either "exempt" or "nonexempt."

(See Chapter 28.)

Industrial Property

Patent Licensing Agreements

Patent licensing agreements are governed by some fairly complex antitrust rules, and in many cases the individuals in the company who actually negotiate the licenses are not aware of these rules. If the negotiators make a tentative deal on the basis of an arrangement which cannot be supported under the antitrust laws, a number of unfortunate consequences can occur. If the lawyers are eventually persuaded to draft the agreement on a doubtful basis, it is possible that it cannot be enforced and that the value of the patent will be lost. In extreme cases, if the company does try to enforce its rights under such a license, antitrust counterclaims can cause not only the loss of the patent but a substantial liability on the part of the licenser.

If, on the other hand, the lawyers find that the agreement is so clearly illegal that it cannot be drafted at all, the management people will have to go back and renegotiate the license, thus causing some embarrassment and perhaps the loss of their bargaining power.

On the other side of the coin, the licensee may raise unwarranted objections on "antitrust" principles when the real problem is that the licensee simply doesn't want to agree to the legitimate restrictions the manufacturer may impose. Here, counsel can supply the needed input to assure his company that there is no real antitrust problem.

The solution to this problem is generally to:

1. Establish a procedure whereby all patent license agreements are reviewed by company antitrust counsel and patent counsel.

2. Educate the people doing the actual negotiations for the license as to some of the basic legal principles involved so that it is easier for them to negotiate a deal which can be properly drafted and enforced and still contains legitimate restrictions.

3. Make the licensing lawyers' experience available to the business executives. This is one area where lawyers acquire a substantial amount of useful business knowledge over the years, and this knowledge should not be wasted by having the licensing lawyers relegated to the role of scrivener.
   (See Section 7.)

Patents and Trade Secrets

With today's changing technology, many companies are in a position of constant development of new products and expansion into new areas. In some cases, these new developments can generate a completely unexpected patent-infringement suit which can involve the company in costly and burdensome litigation for many years. In addition, while most companies do a pretty good job of protecting their own information and products by patents, it is possible that there may be some noticeable gaps in this patent protection, particularly in foreign countries.

Many companies have a great many items which comprise legitimate trade secrets which are very important to the company but are not properly safeguarded by legal means. High-technology companies generally have elaborate procedures for safeguarding their trade secrets. However, almost all companies have a considerable amount of more mundane knowledge and expertise which lends them a competitive advantage. This includes such things as methods of doing business, methods of organizing and scheduling plant production to achieve maximum efficiency, customer lists, lists of particularly good suppliers, and so on. These are also trade secrets, and can be lost to competitors and the company can be left without any realistic protection unless adequate safeguards are provided.

A competent patent counsel will make sure that the company's own products and processes are adequately protected in all appropriate countries. In today's worldwide economy, it is necessary that patent protection of the company's products be extended to more than just the United States, even if the company does not want to operate in foreign countries. If this is not done, a substantial source of revenue which may be obtained by licensing other companies to sell in foreign markets under the foreign patents would be lost. Counsel should also make sure at an early stage that the company's proposed new products and new developments do not infringe on other patents. The company's lawyers should understand exactly what kinds of information and procedures comprise a trade secret and then use the normal legal means for protecting these trade secrets, including confidentiality agreements for all appropriate employees and marking of all relevant documents as proprietary. In appropriate cases more extensive legal protection, such as contracts with suppliers or customers who may have access to the information, should be sought.

(See Chapters 46 and 49.)

Shop Rights and Employees' Inventions

In many cases, employees will invent an item which is clearly within the course and scope of their employment and is done on company property, on company time, and using company materials. In this event, it is absolutely clear that the corporation has a so-called "shop right," which is basically a nonexclusive license to use the invention. If the corporation has an invention-assignment form (and all corporations should have these forms), it may require the employee to assign the invention to the corporation. In other cases, an employee will invent something which is clearly unrelated to company work on his own time, using his own home and his own materials. In these cases, the corporation obviously has no right to require the employee to assign the invention to it and has no shop right in the invention. The problem arises in the gray areas.

The solution is to devise a set of procedures and a set of forms which the company can use in virtually all cases where employees develop a potentially useful invention.

(See Chapter 46.)

Trademarks

In many cases, companies spend a great deal of time, effort, and money generating a particular trademark or trade name which has substantial value. Naturally, any such trademark or trade name should be registered, and almost all business executives and lawyers understand this requirement. If the trademark or trade name is to be completely protected, however, there is a substantial amount of activity in the form of policing the use of such a trademark or trade name which must take place.

(See Chapter 48.)

Copyrights

In the course of its normal business, some companies will generate information which should be copyrighted and monitored to make sure other companies don't steal it. Other companies will see something which they realize would take them a long time to develop themselves and will simply copy it, acting on the theory that it is all public information anyway and they could have developed it themselves if they had wanted to. The documents in question could be catalogs, mailing lists, or simply descriptive literature about products.

Any manufacturing company can have copyright problems, and management should be aware of some of the dangers in taking other people's information as well as some of the techniques which it can use to protect its own catalogs or technical papers.

(See Chapter 47.)

Product Safety, Warranty, and Liability

Consumer Product Safety

Consumer product safety is closely related to product liability, but because it is governed by a specific and detailed statute, some of the affirmative legal requirements are different.

The Consumer Product Safety Act and the regulations thereunder contain detailed provisions requiring a manufacturer to notify the Consumer Product Safety Commission any time it obtains information which indicates that a consumer product might have an unreasonable risk of harm. These provisions require such notification within a relatively short time, and the items of information which must be supplied are very detailed. Accordingly, unless the company and its lawyers think about this problem in advance, it will be almost impossible to comply with this rule. Failure to comply can result in substantial civil and even criminal penalties.

The solution again is obvious. Some advance planning and some discussion of this problem between the lawyers and engineers will generally serve to establish at least enough of an awareness of the problem to institute appropriate procedures.

(See Chapter 44.)

Warranties

Warranties are another area where the law is preempting the judgment of the business executive. The Federal Warranty Law already includes general requirements for warranties covering consumer products, and regulations issued under this law have made these requirements even more detailed and complex. Product-liability problems are also tied into the warranty question.

Counsel must make sure that the people who are establishing the warranties on the company's products are aware of the detailed provisions of law governing the substantive content of warranties and comply with them. In addition, counsel should make sure that everyone realizes that warranties are worth money. Therefore, the price the company charges for its products must include an appropriate factor for warranty, and the price the company pays for items it purchases should depend on the warranties it receives. (See Chapter 43.)

Product Liability

Product liability is a subject of increasing interest to almost all companies because of the extremely large amounts of damages which have been awarded in personal injury cases recently and the greatly increased cost of insuring against these product-liability claims. If the company's lawyers merely sit back and allow the insurance company to defend product-liability cases, the following adverse results will occur:

1. Premiums will undoubtedly rise.

2. The defense might not be adequate in all cases.

3. There may be increased liability in the form of recalls or a greater number of personal injury cases.

4. The company will not be taking advantage of the various legal means at its disposal to have the product-liability burden minimized or shared with other people in the chain of distribution.

The solutions to this problem are fairly obvious and include the following:

1. The company's lawyer cannot simply abdicate all product liability questions to the insurance company lawyers. Instead he must monitor what is going on so that he is comfortable with the lawyers who are actually defending the case and with the information they get from the company's engineers and technical people.

2. The contractual arrangements of the company should be examined to see if it is possible to shift part of the product-liability burden. This may be especially appropriate where the company is supplying more or less standard products which are then incorporated into other finished goods.

3. Company counsel should point out to the appropriate people that product liability is an item of costs and therefore should be considered in pricing the company's products.
    (See Chapter 45.)

Commercial Laws

The Battle of the Forms

In most cases, legal transactions entered into by a company consist of the exchange of printed business forms. There are, however, a considerable number of legal technicalities involved in the exchange of these forms.

The basic problem in this area is that the Uniform Commercial Code contains provisions that will allow one company to impose all of its terms and conditions on another company unless the other company is on its toes and provides suitable forms for rebuttal. Generally what happens is that one company sends to another company a well-drafted and well-thought-out form which has a provision to the effect that all of the terms and conditions on that form will govern the transaction. If the other company merely sits back and does nothing, all those terms and conditions, including usually such things as burdensome warranty and indemnification provisions, will become part of the deal. If the second company has its own set of forms, it can at least accomplish the objective of having the burdensome and one-sided provisions in the first set of forms invalidated so that the deal is basically the transaction agreed upon (quantity, price, delivery, description of the goods, and so on), and then normal legal principles in the Uniform Commercial Code govern everything else. Since these provisions are basically fair between buyer and seller, this position is usually much better than simply agreeing to the other party's terms.

The solution to this problem is obviously to have good forms and to educate the appropriate people on how to use them.

(See Chapter 56.)

Purchasing Law

The combined amount of all monies expended by the company's purchasing department is generally an extremely large portion of all the monies spent by the company. It is not at all unusual to have a situation in a normal manufacturing company where the total amount expended by the purchasing agents is about equal to one-third to one-half of the entire sales of the company. Many companies have realized that it is possible to avoid some waste and potential trouble by having their purchasing agents exposed to at least a basic amount of legal information. This information should include such things as the basic law of agency, basic contract law, basic warranty provisions, and the proper use of forms. Failure to provide this legal exposure can mean trouble for the company, usually in the form of legal disputes involving some aspect of the company's procurement operation. Typical examples are procurement of items without proper safeguards to assure that the company has a right of action against the supplier if the products are not delivered on time, do not conform to specification, or infringe upon a third party's patent.

All purchasing agents should be required to have at least a basic understanding of contract law. They can acquire this understanding in a number of ways, ranging from some commercially available courses for purchasing agents through having the company's lawyers provide this information through memorandums, seminars, or a combination of the two. Management should, however, make sure that the purchasing department is aware of both the need and the availability of the legal resource and then make whatever arrangements with the lawyers seem appropriate in order to provide the necessary legal service.

(See Chapter 57.)

Leasing

Leasing transactions have become more and more common as it becomes possible to lease almost anything. Generally, whenever the company desires to procure any item of capital equipment—all the way from a typewriter to a very expensive piece of machinery—the leasing alternative is available. Unfortunately, at this point leasing is a little more complicated than a normal sales transaction, and generally speaking, it is advisable to have legal counsel involved in any substantial lease because of the following complications:

1. Generally, the documents are long and complicated. The normal purchase transaction is accomplished by the exchange of relatively standard and simple purchase-order and purchase-acknowledgement forms, but a leasing transaction is generally accomplished by individually drafted and negotiated leases.

2. The tax treatment of leasing depends to a considerable extent upon the terms of the lease. If the proper requirements are not met, the Internal Revenue Service may characterize the lease as a sale, and instead of having a deduction for the lease payments, the company will have a deduction only for the interest portion of the payment plus what would otherwise be proper depreciation. In addition, the investment credit is a very important part of the transaction, and the company should either be sure that the proper documents are exchanged so that the investment credit is passed through to it or that the lease payments are reduced so that the economic equivalent of the investment credit is achieved by the corporation.

3. The SEC became concerned about some companies' long-term lease obligations and instituted rather detailed and technical requirements for disclosure of lease obligations in the company's financial statements.
(See Chapter 57.)

Miscellaneous

State Corporation Laws

A corporation may want to loan one of its employees money. Some state corporation laws have provisions which make the directors personally liable if the employee fails to pay back such a loan. In this event, company counsel should advise management of this fact and perhaps suggest making some alternative arrangement. For example, the corporation might consider guaranteeing a bank loan to the employee rather than making a loan.

This is only one example of the problems generated by state corporation laws. This book obviously cannot discuss all of these problems because they vary tremendously among the different states. However there are a number of common threads in state corporation laws which cause problems which can and should be addressed by corporate counsel. These include various formal requirements as to how the corporation may act. For example:

1. Many laws have specific requirements which must be either approved or ratified by the board of directors. Some laws permit executive committees (subcommittees of the board of directors) to act in all respects as the full board; other laws are frankly unclear on this point.

2. Many laws require shareholder approval of certain actions, and it is necessary for company management to know precisely what things must be approved by their shareholders.

3. Many corporation laws contain certain provisions dealing with conflict of interest between the directors of the company and the company itself, and these provisions should be understood by all parties.
(See Chapter 64.)

Conflict of Interest

There are federal securities laws, antitrust laws, state corporation laws, and numerous other regulations which seek to prevent conflicts of interest between the officers and directors of a corporation and the corporation itself. Many of these regulations are based on commonsense principles and should not be a problem to any officer or director who is acting in good faith and is reasonably aware of them. However, some are extremely technical.

For example, section 8 of the Clayton Act prohibits any person from serving on the board of directors of two corporations if those corporations are competitors in any way. With today's diversified companies, this section has caused a great deal of difficulty. In some cases, companies compete in very small ways, and the competition is not even known to those who serve on the board of directors. Many companies today, for example, sell automotive parts in the after market, and most of the original-equipment manufacturers also sell parts through the after market. In some cases, the overlap is extremely small, but it would cause a prohibition of any common director among the original-equipment manufacturers and the company who sold replacement parts in the after market. A similar situation would exist in the case of many oil companies with largely diversified product lines.

The solution to the section 8 problem is relatively simple. It consists of the following:

1. Any vacancy on the board of directors should be filled only after the prospective director has listed all of his other directorships and it has been verified that there is no competition.

2. All of the directors of the company should maintain a complete list of their directorships so that company counsel can make sure there are no overlaps.

There are other technical rules in this area. For example, the Federal Reserve Board may object to a director serving on both the board of a bank and the board of a company which is a substantial borrower from the bank.

Another conflict-of-interest situation might arise where one company wants to either purchase from or sell to another company in which an officer or director of the first company has an interest. It is necessary for company counsel to educate the officers and directors of the company on this problem and make sure that all material transactions are free from any potentially embarrassing situations.

(See Chapter 23 and Section 5.)

Record Retention: Legal Aspects

Record retention is a problem which sometimes gets presented to lawyers in special fact situations. Someone may ask, for example, "How long do I have to keep these documents?" Other times, the question might arise when it would appear that it might be in the best interests of the company to discard certain documents to keep them from coming into the hands of either the government or a potential plaintiff against the company.

These kinds of questions are very difficult to answer in the context in which they are usually raised. It is, for example, very easy to destroy documents pursuant to a normal record-retention program, but it is quite another matter willfully to destroy documents which may be incriminating in the context of some government investigation or private law suit. Also, the question of how long documents *must* be kept from a legal point of view is not necessarily the same as how long they *should* be kept from a practical business point of view. Further complicating this, there are many laws—most notably the recent Employee Retirement Income Security Act—which have provisions which require a great deal of additional and more lengthy record-keeping procedures than were required in the past. Even further complicating this problem is the fact that many of the legal requirements governing record retention are not phrased in specific terms but instead are phrased in general terms. For example, most of the record-retention rules in the income tax area are phrased simply in terms of keeping the records for a period of time sufficient to calculate what the company's income tax might be. Since in many cases, the company's income tax might depend on such things as prior years' earnings and profits, it is necessary in some cases to keep records permanently in order to assure adequate records for income tax purposes.

The solution to this problem is generally a well-thought-out and administered record-retention program which the lawyers can and should draft and recommend to management.

(See Chapter 63.)

Environment

The vast body of legislation and regulation dealing with discharges into the air and water and the question of noise will affect almost all companies. Failure to evaluate and consider these detailed environmental regulations properly can be extremely costly to the company.

Adequate awareness of the problem by the company's lawyers and communication with appropriate management and engineering people will usually serve to pinpoint the areas of greatest exposure. Appropriate action can then be taken.

(See Section 8.)

Corporate Political Activity

Many corporations can and should engage in activity which results in direct contact between their people and representatives of the United States government. Examples include loaning employees to the government, allowing employees to serve the government as advisers, lobbying, and corporate political-action funds. These activities are very beneficial but fraught with both political and legal problems, and mistakes of law or judgment can be disastrous.

Competent legal advice should be obtained in the beginning and all the way through any such endeavors. Specifically, (1) corporate counsel should ascertain whether or not any company employees should be registered as lobbyists, (2) any corporate political funds should be carefully monitored by legal counsel to ensure compliance with all the new rules of the federal election laws, and (3) all of the various conflict-of-interest provisions which govern the relationship between the government and the corporation where the corporation either employs, has employed, or will employ someone who has served the government with or without pay should be carefully evaluated and all of the risks laid out for management beforehand.

(See Chapter 60.)

Privacy Law

The privacy of the American citizen is receiving more and more attention since it was revealed that during our Watergate troubles and perhaps at other times in our history, there was a great deal of domestic spying on the personal affairs of some of our citizens. However, legislation regarding protection of the privacy of individuals has, in some cases, gone to extreme lengths. The Privacy Act of 1974 affects only the government and not private corporations. However, we can be sure that in the future there will undoubtedly be substantial restrictions on not only corporate disclosure of information relating to the corporation's employees but also the very method which a corporation uses to keep this information for its own use and records. There are already some laws at the state level which allow employees to see their company personnel records. At the time of this writing this is a developing area of the law, and it is probably safe to say that by the time the book is actually printed and published there will be a great many more restrictions and regulations in the privacy area than exist at this time.

(See Chapter 61.)

Credit and Credit-Reporting

There are a great many laws regarding the granting of credit and the obtaining of credit reports. Most of these laws apply to companies engaged in the credit business, but some of them apply to ordinary companies not otherwise engaged in the business of granting credit or writing credit reports on people. For example, if a company which is considering hiring an employee obtains an investigative credit report on that employee and then, because of information contained in that report, fails to hire the employee, the company must notify the person of the fact that the report was obtained and that it was the reason for the failure to hire that person. In addition, many companies which sell goods on credit are governed by the numerous and detailed requirements for disclosing the interest rate and various other aspects of the credit transaction.

(See Chapter 59.)

Arbitration

Disenchantment with the courts has caused increased interest in the other major way of resolving disputes—arbitration. Companies should know when and how to use arbitration and when and how to stay out of it.

(See Chapter 58.)

Protection of Information Given to the Government

On many occasions, it will be necessary or appropriate to give either trade-secret or proprietary information which the company would not like released to its competitors to the federal government. In other cases, the information might reveal possible situations where the company has some legal liability (such as the company's affirmative-action plans, which might reveal areas where the company has some exposure under the Equal Employment Opportunity laws). This area is fraught with danger. Basically, the problem is that the Freedom of Information Act has made it very difficult for the government to legally restrict access to information and, in addition, the changed attitude on the part of many government agencies has removed any inclination which they may have previously had to do so. Accordingly, the government is both an unwilling and unable protector of the company's information.

The solution to this problem is to make sure that proper legal advice is obtained before any sensitive information is given to the government. There are some legal techniques that can reduce the company's exposure to a minimum. Unhappily, sometimes these legal techniques involve an inordinate expenditure of time and effort to solve what should be a simple problem. In some cases, counsel might have to go to the extreme of refusing to supply the information to the government unless the government gets a court order requiring the company to do so, and then counsel may have to go to court to get a "protective order" by which the court orders the federal agency to hold the information in confidence.

(See Chapter 62.)

THE LEGAL-STATUTE APPROACH

The specific-problem approach is only one way in which management can obtain active legal participation in the management of the company. Another approach is to list the basic statutes and groups of statutes which regulate business and then request counsel to answer certain questions about these laws. These basic areas of concern are dealt with in the various chapters and sections of this book. In summary, they are the following:

The antitrust and trade regulation laws

The securities laws

The labor laws, including ERISA, OSHA, EEO, and the "normal" labor laws, like the National Labor Relations Act and the Fair Labor Standards Act

The tax laws (both federal and state)

Certain miscellaneous laws, which include the following:

Patent, trademark, and copyright laws

The Freedom of Information Act

The federal election laws (those sections which restrict corporate political activity)

State corporate laws

Product safety laws

Product warranty laws

The Uniform Commercial Code

Environmental laws

Energy laws

Credit and credit-reporting laws

Privacy laws

One could extend the list indefinitely, but the above are the most important and frequently encountered areas of legal concern in a standard business. (As used in this book, the terms "normal" or "standard" business will refer to unregulated business. This should be contrasted with the airline, food and drug, railroad, telephone, and other businesses whose operations are governed by all of these laws and, in addition, by specific industry laws.)

Company counsel should first be requested to examine this list because, in many cases, there are specific statutes not included on the list which regulate specific businesses. Examples include the regulatory framework for public utilities and banks, the Fair Credit Reporting Act for credit companies, and the National Traffic and Motor Vehicle Safety Act for companies in the auto industry.

After a complete list of applicable laws is obtained, management should have the answers to the following questions for each of the laws:

1. How does the law specifically affect our company?

2. What is our present status of compliance with the law?

3. What is the magnitude of our present exposure, and what are our plans to come into full compliance?

4. What programs do we have to safeguard against unauthorized or inadvertent violations of these laws? These programs will fall into two categories:

    (a) Educational programs to assure that employees do not inadvertently violate the law

    (b) Audit or supervisory programs to find and correct violations

5. What policies or procedures do we have to take maximum advantage of the law to obtain a competitive advantage in the marketplace?

Following are illustrations of possible answers to these questions:

1. How does the law specifically affect our company?

    Management should know whether the law is very important and significant to the company or whether it is not. Some laws, like antitrust and tax laws, are of course important and significant to all companies. Others, however, range from very important to merely annoying. For example, occupational safety and health concerns are of prime importance in foundries, mines, and most factories, but of little importance if the business is primarily service-oriented. Environmental laws are of great importance if the business involves discharges into the air or water, but of relatively small importance if the business is "clean." The Employee Retirement Income Security Act is extremely important for companies with trusteed, defined benefit pension plans, but only annoying where the only benefits are the so-called welfare benefits or defined-contribution profit-sharing plans. Management must know which laws are really important and require significant attention and which are not in its particular operation.

2. What is our present status of compliance with the law?

    Management should know where the skeletons are. This is a delicate subject and one where counsel must be extremely careful to "let sleeping dogs lie." However, a conscientious board of directors, as well as the officers of the company, should be briefed on the posture of the company regarding compliance with at least all of the laws described in this book. In some cases, compliance should be 100 percent. For example, if there is any suspicion that there may be any hard-core antitrust violations, they must be remedied immediately. In other cases compliance will be important, but management may want to take a stronger position against possible financial detriment by taking an aggressive stance. The tax law is a primary example. There are many "grey" areas in the tax law, and management is certainly entitled to resolve legitimate questions in its own favor. On the other hand, any possibility of tax fraud is serious indeed and ranks with antitrust problems in seriousness. In still other cases, full compliance is practically impossible and it is necessary for the company to weigh risks and costs intelligently and determine a meaningful program so that it is in substantial compliance but, at the same time, does not severely damage its competitive position by going overboard. Examples are EEO and OSHA.

3. What is the magnitude of the present exposure?

    This question is particularly important in the area of equal employment opportunity. Realistically, most large employers should assume that it is only a matter of time before some employee or applicant either brings a class action himself or causes the EEOC to do so. In this event, the whole question of the company's hiring practices and existing situation regarding the employment of minorities may be opened to inspection and the company should have some advance understanding of what the total exposure is, if any.

4. What programs do we have to educate and audit?

    This is one of the most important questions. Examples of typical programs were given in the discussion of the problem-area approach and are more thoroughly discussed in subsequent chapters.

5. How do we attempt to take advantage of the law?

    This is another important question. Ways in which this can be done include the careful and proper drafting and use of forms for the company; the careful construction and evaluation of warranties; the minimization of administrative costs in all legal-related areas, especially SEC laws; and the proper handling of trade secrets and information submitted to the government.

WHICH APPROACH IS BEST?

The advantage of the problem-area approach is that it raises very specific questions and the lawyers must provide management with concrete answers. With the legal-statute approach, almost any good lawyer is going to be able to "accentuate the positive" if he desires to do so and possibly delude management into thinking that the area is well under control when, in fact, it is not. The advantage of the legal-statute approach is that it is not limited to specific problems and counsel is given a free hand to list potential problems and to suggest solutions. There is no reason why both approaches cannot be used. This would require counsel to deal with specific problem areas and, at the same time, allows him freedom to suggest other important problems or opportunities.

CHAPTER TWO

METHODS OF
OBTAINING LEGAL
SERVICES

Legal services and legal advice can be obtained by these three basic methods:

1. House counsel—a salaried attorney
2. Outside counsel—an independent practitioner who may be retained by a company on either an hourly or a retainer basis
3. A combination of the two

By far the best method is to use a combination of house counsel and outside counsel, and it is really only a matter of emphasis which is in question. However, for purposes of analysis, we will go through a description of the advantages and disadvantages of house counsel versus outside counsel so management can make a better decision on exactly how these two methods of obtaining legal services can be applied to the company. For purposes of this analysis, we will not get into the relative merits of the lawyers involved and will assume, instead, that the quality of the house counsel and the outside counsel is the same.

HOUSE COUNSEL

House counsel is a salaried full-time employee of a corporation. There are both advantages and disadvantages in employing house counsel.

Advantages

Availability

Because of the fact that the lawyer is a full-time employee, his availability will depend upon the wishes of management rather than upon his own wishes, the wishes of other clients, or previous commitments. Management can depend upon having legal advice and service available almost instantaneously.

Access

For the same reason as stated above, management can depend upon having greater access to house counsel than to outside counsel. This is true for two reasons. The first is the fact that the house counsel is on the premises. The second is a little less tangible but even more important. This is the factor of ease of access to a lawyer who is part of the management team, who is known to other managers, and whose office is located in close proximity to them. In order to have access to the company's lawyer, all management typically has to do is walk down the hall or pick up the telephone. On the other hand, access to outside counsel, particularly a good one who will almost always be busy, is restricted by that other lawyer's schedule and availability. In addition, while we are disregarding cost for the present purposes, it should be observed in this context that a manager who knows he is going to be charged anywhere from 25 dollars on up even for a short telephone call is bound to be a little more reluctant to call an outside lawyer than he is to go down the hall to consult with his house counsel.

Knowledge of the Company

Because of house counsel's full-time employment, he should have a better knowledge of the company and its business than outside lawyers. Knowledge of the company, its people, its organizational structure, the level at which decisions must be made, and company policies, are a very important part of house counsel's job. Some house counsel do not realize this and consequently don't spend enough time learning about their company, its products, its policies, and its people, but it is management's duty to insist that the lawyers undertake this responsibility.

Commitment to the Company

House counsel may be more committed to the success of the company. He is often going to be compensated on an incentive basis: perhaps he has stock options. The fact that he is employed by and identified with the company also tends to make him more committed to the success of that company than an outside lawyer who is merely providing legal services to one of many clients.

Preventive Measures More Likely

Because of house counsel's availability, because he can see what is going on, and because he has access to company people and knows which people to talk to for what problems, it is much more likely that house counsel can do an effective job of taking the preventive measures described in this book.

Particular Expertise

Some companies become involved in areas of the law which require a particular expertise. For example, a leasing company, a real estate company, a credit-reporting company, and all of the companies regulated by specific laws (like banks and public utilities) have need for lawyers with this expertise. House counsel can acquire a higher degree of expertise in this area for his company than can outside lawyers.

Disadvantages

Lack of Objectivity

After a lawyer has been employed by a company for a long period of time, it may be possible for him to lose a certain amount of his objectivity. Indeed, the very fact that he depends for his livelihood upon one client may, in itself, reduce some of his objectivity. As part of this reduction of objectivity, it may be more difficult for inside counsel to say "No" to a top management plan which involves something of questionable legality than it would be for an outside lawyer.

Reluctance to Use Outside Lawyers

If management does not carefully nip any problems in the bud, it is possible that the proper involvement of outside counsel can be hindered because house counsel may object to having his decisions checked by outside counsel, having his judgment questioned by outside counsel, or, for some other reason, feel threatened by management's asking outside counsel's opinion or advice on various subjects.

Generally, the best way to handle this problem is to have house counsel himself become the "client" for the outside law firm. This will avoid a situation where, for example, the president of the company goes to house counsel, describes a problem, gets an answer, and then goes to the outside law firm, describes the same problem, gets a different answer, and then, when faced with the question of deciding which lawyer to believe, ends up questioning the judgment of his own house counsel. Management should instead present the problem to house counsel and ask house counsel not only to give his opinion but to make sure that he gets the advice and judgment of the company's outside lawyers. This will facilitate the use of outside lawyers because house counsel will not feel threatened by them and he will not be having his advice second-guessed. At the same time, quality of his own advice will be improved by the judgment, perspective, and experience of the outside lawyers.

Management must exercise a little control here, however, because house counsel is hired to perform legal services and render legal advice and not simply to act as a postal service between management and the outside law firm. Consequently, there must be a mutual understanding between house counsel and his employer as to how outside counsel will be used and when, and management is indeed entitled to expect house counsel to operate within some kind of a budget, although it must be recognized that a legal budget, including outside counsel fees, must be subject to some flexibility because the company never knows when it is going to get sued, when it is going to have to sue someone else, or when it is going to get involved in some other kind of costly legal problem.

Costs

Cost can be either an advantage or a disadvantage as applied to either an inside or an outside counsel. The key is to make the evaluation of whether or not the legal advice or services which are going to be obtained should best be obtained by inside or outside counsel on an accurate and scientific basis. Essentially, obtaining legal advice can be thought of as either buying it wholesale from a full-time employee or retail from a law firm. Just like any other commodity, if one has a need for a great deal of it, it is obviously better to buy it wholesale. If one needs only a small amount, it will save money in the long run to buy it retail because the expenses involved in financing and storage will offset the decrease in unit cost.

The threshold question to be asked in determining whether one should have house counsel is the point at which a company should hire its first full-time lawyer. Thereafter, another decision must be made each time another person is added to the legal department.

There have been a number of yardsticks used to measure the size of a company which should justify one full-time lawyer. However, this is very misleading and not a very good way to approach the problem. Instead, the company should ask what legal services are required, what kind of legal advice is required, and at what point a full-time house counsel can be of use. As a general rule, any company whose stock is publicly traded should carefully consider hiring a full-time house counsel because the problems involved in having publicly traded stock provide enough legal work so that in conjunction with the other legal problems which are present in all companies, a lawyer can usually justify spending all of his time with one client. It is useful to go through the process of financially evaluating hiring a full-time lawyer versus using outside counsel because this evaluation is essentially the same for the first lawyer as it is for the second and the third, with the possible caveat that once one already has a rather substantial legal department, the marginal cost of hiring new lawyers might be a little smaller because one would have already built up the necessary law library, filing system, and word-processing system.

The company must compare the outside legal fees with more than the salary of the lawyer. However, a nonlawyer is likely to grossly underestimate the cost of having a full-time effective lawyer on the company payroll. Again, we must be sure to emphasize that we are "going first class" in this assumption. We are not hiring a lawyer to do some routine legal work like drafting leases or collecting bad debts. Instead, we are hiring legal counsel comparable to the partners in the larger law firms throughout the country. On this basis, the following are some of the representative costs which must be involved when a company considers the addition of a lawyer:

Lawyer's Salary

This includes fringe benefits and salary increases. If you get a good lawyer, you are going to have to increase his salary just as his income would increase if he worked for an outside law firm.

Secretary's Salary

Fringe benefits and increases must be considered here also.

Offices

In order to recruit and retain a high-quality lawyer, it is going to be necessary to provide him with offices similar to those he would have enjoyed in a private law firm, and the cost of these must be included.

Office Equipment

This includes typewriters and dictation equipment.

Law Library

A lawyer without law books is likely to be a liability rather than an asset. If a company is going to spend the money for a lawyer, his office, his secretary, and all of the other items mentioned above, it cannot afford to skimp on law books. On the other hand, law books are very expensive in terms of initial cost, storage, and upkeep. For purposes of illustration, let's assume that the company is going to hire one lawyer and that they are going to have only one legal service for each major subject. Let's further assume that the major subjects are defined to be the following:

1. Tax law

2. Securities regulation

3. Antitrust law

4. Labor law (including wage and hour, EEO, OSHA, unemployment, and compensation)

This might be considered a very minimum library. In addition, a lawyer involved in specific problems is going to desire and need a great deal more legal reference material. However, for purposes of this analysis, it is sufficient to note that the number of volumes contained in the Commerce Clearing House Services which cover the above subjects is over fifty and growing. This includes only the looseleaf volumes, which are supplemented periodically (weekly or biweekly), and does not include the many volumes of cases which are also necessary in order to make these volumes useful. The whole library could fit in the lawyer's office so space would not be too much of a problem, but one must also consider that it is supplemented very frequently and at least 2 to 3 hours per week of the lawyer's secretary's time is going to have to be spent in keeping the services up-to-date by filing the supplementary pages. If the lawyer has to generate a substantial amount of legal documentation to satisfy his other duties, his secretary may not have enough time to keep these services up-to-date, and at some point when the library expands to what would be considered a fairly adequate library for a relatively large corporation, it must be anticipated that a full-time librarian must be hired in order to simply keep these services up-to-date, pay the bills, and make sure that everything is filed properly.

Seminars and Continuing Legal Education

If you have a lawyer who has not gone to any seminars or participated in any continuing legal-education programs for the past year, you have a definite problem. The field of law is developing very rapidly, and except in certain rare cases, it is impossible for a lawyer to keep up with all of the necessary developments through reading. Instead, he must attend seminars or other continuing legal-education programs to keep his skills up-to-date. The cost of these programs in terms of the tuition, travel, and time away from work should be considered.

Filing System

This can be considered in the same way as the library. In the first case of hiring one lawyer and a secretary, it is probable that the lawyer's secretary could develop a legal filing system and maintain it. However, within a very short period of time, this legal filing system is going to grow to a stage where a secretary cannot handle it along with other normal duties.

On the other hand, in going over these costs, it becomes apparent that the company is getting a substantial amount of benefit from them. For example, having a library on the premises will make it possible to get answers to many questions in a much more rapid and economical manner than would be possible through the use of an outside law firm. If a company has a problem which has to be researched and doesn't have the law books on premises to do it, it will have to call an outside lawyer; and if the outside lawyer has to take the time to look it up, reduce his answer to writing, and communicate that back to management, it is very likely that a problem which might involve only 1 hour of actual legal work if done by a lawyer on premises will take 3 days or more. To be sure, it would be possible to say to outside counsel that the company needed the answer "right now" and have the outside counsel drop everything, look up the question, and call management back. However, in many cases this is not necessary, even though it would be convenient. In these latter situations, management is unlikely to force outside counsel to do it that quickly. Furthermore, in some cases until you look at the books, you really don't know how complicated the problem is. Sometimes, an answer appears very quickly; other times, it takes a considerable amount of research. Accordingly, the costs of the library must be offset by this substantial benefit that a company can get by having a certain amount of these answers readily obtainable in a very rapid and economical way.

The same thing can be said for the filing system. While it is likely that a filing system established by the legal department for corporate records would be somewhat costly, it would also be of benefit to the company in many cases. For example, if the company had all of its real estate, patents, and securities documents located in one central place in an easily understood, indexed, organized manner, it would be able to find these documents, use them for reference, and answer questions much more quickly than it would if the documents were located at outside counsel's offices.

OUTSIDE COUNSEL

There are also advantages and disadvantages in employing outside counsel.

Advantages

A Selected Lawyer

When one goes to an outside law firm—particularly a large one—one can select a lawyer with particular expertise in the problem at hand. On the other hand, inside counsel is going to be more of a generalist.

Greater Expertise

For the same reason as stated above, it is possible that by going to an outside counsel one can get greater technical expertise in some areas than the expertise which any inside counsel can build up himself. However, this is subject to a number of qualifications. In the first place, the opposite may be true if the company's problems are not of a "general" nature where outside counsel would have built up expertise through working on other problems. If, instead, the company's problems are rather particular because its business is unusual or because it is regulated by a set of statutes applying only to it, it is likely to be able to obtain a greater degree of expertise through inside counsel than by using outside lawyers.

Status

There is no denying that in certain cases, the status of outside counsel—particularly the larger prestigious law firms—is greater than that of some in-house lawyers. Accordingly, if one wants to impress a person (either someone you are about to sue or someone who is threatening to sue you), it is sometimes useful to have actions taken by these prestigious law firms rather than by in-house counsel. Also, in protecting the officers and directors of the company, it is sometimes useful to have opinions of the legality of certain actions obtained from outside law firms rather than from the company's own house counsel.

Knowledge of Other Companies

Because law firms—particularly the larger ones—represent a number of other companies and because the law firms themselves compare notes about various legal subjects, it can be expected that an outside law firm will generally have a better idea of what other companies are doing about particular problems than would inside counsel. It should be noted that this is not a universal truth, and inside counsel who makes it his business to join the proper organizations, meet the proper people, and keep in touch with other inside counsel, can actually obtain a better knowledge of what other companies are doing than can some outside lawyers. However, as a general proposition, one of the things that an outside law firm can contribute is a knowledge of some other approaches to problems which are frequently presented.

Continuity

The fact that lawyers on the company payroll may retire, die, quit, become ill for extended periods of time, or otherwise cease to function properly must be considered. In the case of a large company legal department, it should not be a problem. Even in the case of a small one with two or three lawyers, it should not be a problem with proper planning. However, if the company has only one house counsel, there is some danger that it will be left in an untenable position if that house counsel disappears and no one has kept up with what he was doing. This will be especially troublesome if the house counsel has been personally taking care of all the company's periodic SEC filings, pension-plan work, and other items which must continue if the company is going to avoid administrative trouble. For this reason, some companies in this position make a habit of having a certain outside law firm designated for "backup," and that firm keeps files on all litigation, keeps essentially up-to-date on what is happening, and generally remains prepared to help the company's lawyer in an emergency and to step in and take over—at least temporarily—if that lawyer leaves for any reason.

Disadvantages

The disadvantages in employing outside counsel are (1) that you are buying advice retail rather than wholesale, (2) that the outside counsel will have other clients and other commitments which may make his work for you of a lesser priority than house counsel would give it, and (3) that the outside counsel will typically be less familiar with your company and its policies, procedures, products, and business practices than will house counsel.

Large Law Firms versus Small Law Firms

We have alluded to large law firms above. However, this does not mean that the only way to use outside counsel is to hire the largest law firms. Indeed, in some situations this would not be a prudent course of action.

The decision as to whether a company should use for its outside legal advice a large law firm, a medium-sized law firm, a small law firm, or a sole practitioner, depends upon an extremely large number of variables. However, for purposes of this discussion, we will assume that the company has stock which is publicly traded and is faced with most of the problems which are discussed in this book. For all practical purposes, this will eliminate the sole practitioner and reduce the choices to a large law firm, a medium-sized law firm, or a small law firm.

While the exact lines between when the law firm is small, medium, or large are not universally agreed upon, as a general proposition a law firm with more than fifty lawyers should be considered large. A law firm with twenty to fifty lawyers can be classified as medium-sized, and one which has twenty or fewer lawyers can be classified as small.

In addition, it is not necessary to choose one law firm to handle all of the company's work which is going to be done by outside counsel. Many firms acquire particular specialties and expertise in given areas, and where necessary these specialties and expertise should be used. Typical examples are tax and patent firms and some of the firms in Washington which acquire special expertise in dealing with particular government agencies—usually because their partners are former members of those agencies. Other firms acquire particular expertise in special kinds of cases. There are, for example, firms which have specific expertise in defending cases involving airplane crashes and firms which have particular expertise in defending cases involving the various legislation governing credit-reporting practices. Where a company has these kinds of problems, it is useful to know about the smaller law firms which possess these specialties and to use them if appropriate.

Large law firms typically contain specialists in just about every conceivable area of the law where a company will need legal advice. The same can be true for a medium-sized law firm. Accordingly, the essential difference between a medium-sized and a large law firm is simply the number of lawyers involved and the size of the clients represented. Typically, the larger law firms will represent the larger corporations, the medium-sized law firms will represent the medium-sized corporations, and the smaller corporate law firms will represent the smaller corporations. There is some logic and advantage in staying within one's "pond." If a smaller corporation desires an outside law firm to do the majority of its work (recognizing that special problems may be assigned elsewhere as appropriate), it might be better to choose a smaller law firm because in a large law firm, the smaller client would not be given the same priority as some of the larger clients. This is a generalization and may not be true in all cases. However, it is a consideration which is important. If you are not sure that your business is going to be important to the law firm, you do run the risk of second-class treatment.

In the same regard, making your business important to a law firm depends at least a little on giving the law firm most of the work. It is not desirable to spread one's legal work too thin, and the general policies involved in procurement, where there should be dual sources for everything, shouldn't be carried too far in the legal area because if the legal work is spread so thin that no particular law firm feels that the client is of primary importance, it might be given second-class treatment in all of them.

Naturally, this raises the question of whether it is best to go to a large law firm (at least as large as possible given the size of the company and its legal budget) and obtain all services from that large law firm or whether it is best to use smaller law firms with specific expertise. Again, a delicate balancing is required. There are no easy answers to this. However, it is useful to divide the corporation's problems into everyday problems and "extraordinary" problems. Everyday problems would be those faced by all corporations (tax, securities, labor-law, trade-regulation, products, liability, and commercial-law problems). These can usually be very ably handled by a general corporate law firm, and it may not be in the best interests of the company to find a firm which specializes in securities work and have that firm do all of its securities work and then find another, smaller firm which specializes in tax work and give all the tax work to them, and so on. However, there are three important exceptions to this rule.

The first would be a situation where your general corporate law firm has a pronounced weakness. In almost all corporate law firms, there will be one area which is rather weak. There is no easy explanation for this, but it is a fact of life which unfortunately exists in almost all cases. Accordingly, the company, usually through its inside counsel, will have to find out whether its outside law firm is capable of handling all problems. If it has a weak link, it may be necessary to supplement the advice of the general outside law firm with a specialist.

The next exception is that even assuming that the general outside law firm has a relatively uniform degree of expertise in all areas, there may be some problems which require particular expertise, either because of their severity or because of their unusual nature. Litigation is a prime example. Once a company gets involved in a detailed and expensive lawsuit, it is necessary to have a law firm which has both the expertise and the personnel to handle it appropriately. Patent suits, antitrust suits, and some disputes with the federal government—perhaps involving government contracting—fall into this category.

The third exception is matters which arise in some other jurisdiction. For example, if a company is located in Chicago and has as its general outside counsel a Chicago law firm, it would still be necessary to retain local counsel if the company was either suing or being sued in California. This is necessary for two reasons. The first is that the Chicago law firm is likely not to be in the best position to defend or prosecute a California lawsuit because of their lack of knowledge of the local judges and procedures. The second is that there is an obvious logistical problem in paying lawyers to travel from Chicago to California and back again in a lawsuit.

ANALYZING THE WORK

In determining how best to obtain the necessary legal advice, the first step is to ascertain what that legal advice is. Here it is necessary to make a distinction between routine legal work and legal counsel. (This does not mean to say that a lawyer who has been hired to do routine legal work can never be asked to provide legal counsel or that a lawyer who is asked to be responsible for legal counsel can never be asked to "soil his hands" by preparing SEC material, drafting leases, or doing other items which may be considered routine legal work. This is a fairly complex and important distinction.

Legal counsel is the planning advice and counsel rendered by lawyers to management in order to keep the business out of legal trouble to the maximum extent possible and, when legal problems do arise, to minimize their impact upon the business and to handle them in the best way possible for the company.

Routine legal work, on the other hand, usually involves the generation of rather standard legal documents and, in many cases, involves the generation of a fairly large amount of rather routine documents.

Sometimes the rendering of legal advice and counsel involves the necessity for the performance of legal work. For example, it would be possible to divide an antitrust compliance program into the initial formative stages—where legal advice and counsel was rendered as to exactly what should be covered by the program, what documents should be examined, and what manuals or policy statements should be prepared—and the second part of the program—actually doing the work of interviewing the people, examining the documents, writing the policy statements—which could be classified as legal work. However, for purposes of this chapter, we will not make this distinction but, instead, will consider both of the above to fall within the category of legal counsel and will limit the definition of legal work to the performance of various routine tasks which should be performed by a lawyer but which do not necessarily require as high a degree of judgment and legal expertise as legal counsel.

Some examples will make the difference very clear and will show the importance of that difference. Following are all examples of rather routine legal work which can and should be done by a lawyer but which can be done by lawyers with limited experience. These kinds of legal jobs can be done by salaried attorneys. Assuming that the amount of work is sufficient to justify relatively full-time activity, the salary paid to these attorneys will usually be substantially less than the cost of having this kind of work done by outside counsel.

1. The preparation of leases in the case of any company which either leases a large number of properties from others for its own operations (a chain-store operation would be a prime example) or which has a great deal of real estate and leases it to others for their operation (companies which operate as real estate holding companies would be a prime example)

2. Companies which sell a substantial amount of goods on credit and try to protect their interest in these goods by filing appropriate security statements under the various state laws which permit a creditor to retain a security interest in the goods he sells on credit

3. Any company which engages in a substantial number of real estate transactions involving the preparation and filing of deeds or other instruments of conveyance

4. Any company which either borrows or lends in a substantial number of transactions involving the preparation of loan agreements or other similar financial arrangements, such as leasing companies

The above are only a few examples of the kinds of situations where a great deal of legal work in terms of the preparation of a large number of documents—all essentially similar but each having its own peculiar aspects—must be prepared.

In this kind of a situation, management must carefully consider hiring a lawyer full-time because to obtain this kind of service from an outside law firm may be expensive and inefficient. These kinds of jobs, however, are vastly different from the kinds of legal counsel which are referred to in the remaining chapters of this book. In addition, the broad areas of law which require a rather long time to master—labor law, federal securities law, and taxation and antitrust law—all require a substantial amount of experience and judgment. It is in these areas that management must use discretion as to whether it hires one lawyer to be responsible for the area, gets its advice from outside counsel, or uses a combination of the two.

The economics of the situation are only clear where the full-time lawyer has enough work to keep him busy. If there is not enough work to keep one lawyer busy, management is going to have to decide whether it is willing to allow this "junior" lawyer who is doing the routine legal work to get involved in some of the other areas where the potential for mistakes and misjudgment is larger. This depends on the junior lawyer's potential and initiative. If both are high, he should be worked into the company's legal affairs under the supervision of outside counsel *and with a clear understanding of everyone's role.*

Pursuing the discussion further, management then has the option of supplementing the legal counsel it might obtain from inside lawyers with legal counsel from outside counsel who may be older, have more experience, more exposure to different kinds of problems, and perhaps even better judgment.

The largest companies can afford the luxury of highly paid legal staffs and can and do recruit their lawyers from the large law firms. In these kinds of situations, management doesn't really have to be too worried about missing out on good advice from more qualified lawyers because the typical pattern is that the lawyers who work for the particular client in the law firm are the ones who go to that client as salaried attorneys later on. In essence, the client is getting the same legal advice from the same person anyway. However, in small corporations which cannot afford the luxury of a large and highly paid legal staff, this kind of balancing between the use of junior, lower-priced lawyers for the routine legal work and obtaining legal advice and counsel on a higher plane from higher-paid outside people (but using less of their time) must be considered.

There are all kinds of personnel and motivational aspects to this question. No lawyer is going to admit that he doesn't have as good judgment as outside counsel. Therefore, if the matter is not handled with some finesse and diplomacy, one is likely to wind up with a terrible mess. On the other hand, if a company establishes the position of "general counsel" and fills the position with a lawyer being paid $30,000 a year, it is going to have to ask itself whether it is getting the same quality of advice from its $30,000 lawyer as it would get from lawyers who command two or three times as much on the outside. Realistically, the answer has to be no.

The distinction between legal services and legal advice is also important to many lawyers. Many lawyers do not have either the ability or desire to keep up with a substantial amount of developing law in the broad range of subjects covered in this book. In fact, it is the rare lawyer who will have this ability and desire. Most of them want either to specialize within a certain area of the law or to progress into some kind of management role where they are supervising the work of other lawyers who, in turn, keep up with the detailed rules. Accordingly, there are many highly competent and proficient lawyers who, by their own choice, have become very efficient in doing one kind of work and desire to continue doing that kind of work. Many lawyers, for example, thoroughly enjoy the drafting of all documents related to real-estate transactions and have absolutely no desire to get tangled up in the company's antitrust problems. Other lawyers would be perfectly happy to work 40 hours a week from the age of 40 to the age of 65 completely mastering one area of the law—for example, securities law—and doing the company's security work for that entire period.

Part of the problem is matching the right people to the right job and, in some cases, matching the job to the people. Exactly which approach one takes depends upon one's general management approach. One company will define the job carefully and then find a lawyer to fit the description. Another company will hire a lawyer who works well with other people and who is an asset to the company and then will attempt to structure the legal function around the talent it has hired. Either approach will work. The first approach is a little simpler from a management point of view. However, it is generally a little less appealing from a personnel point of view and, consequently, a little more difficult to find the exact lawyer one is looking for on a permanent basis. The second approach is a little more difficult and challenging, but since it is more rewarding for the lawyers, it generally results in a more consistent legal staff with less turnover.

HOW TO MAKE THE DECISIONS

As with most legal questions, the decisions as to how to obtain legal services should be made at the recommendation of the company's lawyer. The purpose of this chapter is not to suggest that management itself evaluate the legal work which should be done for the company and then, by some process of internal contemplation, come up with the proper mixture of inside and outside counsel. The purpose is instead to show management the differing considerations and to suggest that management should periodically require their general counsel—be he presently on the payroll or an outside lawyer—to report to them on how the company should be obtaining its legal services. Laws are always changing, and the company's business is likely changing and growing (or contracting). All of these factors will make it necessary to reexamine this question periodically. Some of the questions management should get answers to are the following:

1. Has the amount of legal work been analyzed recently to see if the company is making proper use of inside counsel? Should the company be hiring additional lawyers? Should the company be looking for outside counsel to fill a particular need which is currently not being met?

2. Is the company making proper use of paralegals, administrative assistants, and secretaries in the legal department? In the past few years, the cost of legal talent has soared. When this writer graduated in 1966, the "going rate" during the fall interviews was $7800 ("going rate" being defined as the rate paid by the larger New York firms and matched by many other larger firms in other parts of the country). By the time lawyers in the class of 1966 actually started to work after passing the bar, the rate had gone up to about $9000, and within 2 years it jumped to $15,000. By 1976, it was approximately $25,000. It should be kept in mind that this $25,000 rate was for a lawyer right out of law school who, realistically, couldn't be trusted to draft a lease or write a simple contract for a client without supervision. It should also be noted that this "going rate" was for the top few percent of the country's better law schools. The rate drops substantially if the lawyer is not in the top few percent or has not attended one of the better law schools, further pointing up the need to distinguish between routine legal work and top-quality legal advice. On the other hand, rates for paralegals generally ran in the $12,000-$15,000 range in 1976, and this was for a good, experienced paralegal.

Consequently, if one has lawyers 3 to 5 years out of law school doing work which could be done by a paralegal, the company may be paying double what it would have to if paralegals were employed. Again, the point is not for management to force paralegals down the throat of the law department but to require that the lawyers assure management that they are getting the maximum possible use out of this cost-saving approach.

3. Does the company have the proper mixture of younger and more experienced attorneys? If the company is larger, it will have to keep in mind that younger lawyers must be developed to fill the shoes of the older ones. On the other hand, if the company's lawyers are all highly experienced (and presumably highly paid), it may be possible to economize by filling the next vacancy with a younger lawyer. Again, management should require its general counsel to consider this and report to it.

4. Management should get periodic reports on the balance between inside and outside counsel, how much work is being done by each, and the long-range objectives.

In summary, management should be aware that many excellent lawyers are very poor managers. While the material contained in this chapter may not be new to them, they may never have taken the time to apply it and to analyze the company's legal requirements and how they are being filled. It is management's prerogative and duty to force this analysis if it is not generated by the company's lawyers on their own initiative.

CHAPTER THREE

HOW TO USE
YOUR LAWYER

WHO IS YOUR LAWYER?

While it may sound a bit elementary, the first step toward making the best use of your lawyer is to ascertain exactly who he is. In a small business where there is a small management group and one general counsel, this is not a problem. However, once the business gets a little larger and retains the services of a law firm consisting of a number of lawyers or a legal department containing more than one lawyer, the issue becomes important because in the eyes of some business executives "a lawyer is a lawyer," and when a legal question arises, they simply stroll over to the law department and talk to the lawyer they happen to get along with best or call up the law firm and talk to the person who happens to be most conveniently accessible. In today's business world, this is a very poor approach to the use of the lawyers.

The first step in making the best use of lawyers is for the business executive to understand the structure in which legal advice is provided. In some companies, lawyers will be assigned specific tasks. For example, some companies may have a lawyer designated as a labor lawyer, and questions regarding labor contracts, EEO matters, or OSHA matters could be addressed to that lawyer with assurance that he would be the proper one to respond. In many cases, however, business executives will feel that they have a "legal problem" but not be exactly sure as to what area of law might be involved, and indeed many problems involve more than one area of the law. Therefore, just as human beings today are forced into an elementary knowledge of medicine simply in order to know what kind of a doctor to go to for various problems, business executives are forced into a basic understanding of the law and the legal structure for their company in order to understand whom to go to when they have a legal problem. The best general approach to this problem is to have all business executives instructed to present all legal questions to one general counsel, who would then assume responsibility for ascertaining which, if any, other lawyers should get into the act. Naturally, there are significant exceptions. If the personnel department presently forwards all of its questions about EEO problems to the general counsel, who in turn forwards them to the labor lawyer, there is no reason why this process could not be shortened by having the personnel department contact the labor lawyer directly on all EEO problems. Indeed, this would be the most productive way to handle this situation. A word of caution is in order, however. Business executives can get into the habit of going to a particular lawyer with *all* of their problems. For example, the personnel department may have a problem of how to divest a minority-owned business. The lawyer the department has been using for EEO purposes may or may not be the right one to handle this type of problem. Both business executives and lawyers must be aware of this situation, and both should be sure that the company's general counsel is kept informed of any problem which is at all out of the ordinary or for which there is no routine procedure already established.

Sometimes larger companies will divide legal responsibility along product or division lines rather than along legal subject matter lines. In this case, the "general counsel" for a particular business executive's purpose may be the lawyer who has been assigned responsibility for his product line or division rather than the person who has the title of "general counsel" for the company. Unfortunately, in a surprising number of cases this writer has found that in situations like this, some executives—particularly at the lower levels—do not even know who their product or division lawyer is! Obviously, in these kinds of situations there is a serious communications gap, and steps should be taken to close it up.

In the case of a company which obtains legal services from a law firm, the problems are similar, but it is even more important to find the right communication link and use it almost all the time. If outside law firms are to be used directly by company executives—a situation which is generally not recommended if there is a full-time house counsel—it is very important to have substantially all initial contacts funneled through the partner of that firm who is in charge of the company's account. There are exceptions, but this should be the general rule.

In summary, the first step in knowing how to use your lawyer is to understand exactly who your lawyer is. In some cases this will be far from obvious, and especially in larger companies with large law departments or companies represented by larger law firms, the question of which lawyer to contact can become quite complex. Logically, the burden ought to be placed completely on the legal function or law firm. If there is a mix-up and you wind up in trouble because a labor lawyer has tried unsuccessfully to shepherd the company through a divestiture, the legal function or law firm is clearly to blame. However, given the less-than-perfect world in which lawyers and everyone else live, this is not a productive attitude. We are not trying to fix blame for problems; we are trying to avoid problems.

Management should do its share by recognizing the human problems involved. The labor lawyer may think he is capable of doing a divestiture; he may be afraid to admit that he isn't; he may not realize the other problems (the latter is the usual situation). Rather than simply ignoring the problem, on the theory that the responsibility rests elsewhere, managers should themselves make sure they are seeing the right lawyer for the right problem. Generally, this is done by simply asking directly whether the lawyer you are talking to is the right person. A direct question supplemented with a little common sense, the general rule of going to the general counsel when in doubt, and a competent and reasonably well-oiled legal function should keep most problems well under control.

WHAT IS YOUR LAWYER PAID FOR?

In order to use lawyers effectively, it is necessary to understand what they get paid for. There are a number of different philosophies on this point. The first is the so-called "mouthpiece" philosophy. Under this philosophy, a lawyer is someone whom one consults when one already has a specific legal problem and wants the lawyer to "handle it." In many cases, this is unavoidable. Sometimes legal problems strike like lightning out of the blue, and management must simply consult lawyers without any advance planning because management itself didn't have any time to do any advance planning. As a general proposition, however, the philosophy that the lawyer is there only to solve specifically defined legal problems is an inefficient use of the lawyer because, in the legal context, the old proverb that "an ounce of prevention is worth a pound of cure" gets translated into "a hundred dollars' worth of advice to stay out of trouble is worth thousands of dollars in legal fees to get out of trouble."

Business executives must keep in mind that a business lawyer is fundamentally different from the old image of the general practitioner who was consulted when you needed a will or wanted to sell a house and needed a deed drawn. Today's business lawyer should be used to help management make business decisions and weigh risks involved in those business decisions. Most business decisions will involve some degree of legal risk, and it is the lawyer's duty to ascertain to the best of his ability the degree of that legal risk and inform managers of that legal risk so that a proper decision can be made. In addition, most business objectives can be accomplished in a number of ways, involving substantially different legal risks. It is the lawyer's duty to advise management of different ways to accomplish the same objective—ways which might involve a smaller legal risk. Almost all legal advice, as opposed to legal work, can be broken into these two categories: (1) risk analysis and (2) planning assistance.

Risk Analysis

Risk analysis in the legal sense must be distinguished from predictions as to the likelihood of getting caught in an illegal act. The latter is not the kind of risk we are talking about. For planning purposes, it would be, in this writer's view, entirely inappropriate for lawyers to base their advice on the risk of getting caught—and entirely inappropriate for management to either ask for or accept such advice. Instead, the risks we are talking about are—assuming that the full facts are known to all appropriate parties—the *legal* risks involved. In some cases, the legal risks are overwhelming, and there is no conceivable business objective which could justify assuming those risks. These are cases where the conduct in question clearly violates criminal statutes—such as the federal antitrust laws—or where the question involves clear *misrepresentations* (the legal term for "lies") to investigatory bodies such as federal or state grand juries. In these circumstances, the benefits to be gained cannot possibly outweigh the legal risks involved, and the lawyers must inform management in no uncertain terms that the proposed course of action violates a criminal law and cannot be undertaken.

However, in most cases, this will not be the situation, and management and the lawyers will find themselves in a "gray area," an area in which a business decision will involve some risk but there will be something to be gained (or money to be saved) from the proposed course of action. Here, a weighing of the legal risks as against the benefits will be necessary. Staying with the antitrust laws for our examples, the Robinson-Patman Act is a good illustration of a gray area. In a great many cases, it will be virtually impossible to predict with any degree of certainty what the actual legal risks involved in a violation of the Robinson-Patman Act will be because the legal risks depend upon injury to competition which is difficult to prove after the fact and even more difficult to predict before the fact. Furthermore, there are a number of widely used business practices which are probably clear technical violations of the Robinson-Patman Act. The typical volume-discount or volume-rebate practices of almost all corporations are examples. There is no exception in the Robinson-Patman Act for selling at different prices to different customers simply because one customer buys more than the other. Indeed, that was the practice the act was aimed at stopping in the context of the chain-store buying practices in 1936 when it was adopted. If there is to be any defense for such a price differential, it must be that the lower price to the person purchasing the higher quantity is granted for one of the three following reasons:

1. There is a cost savings in selling to the person who purchases the larger quantity, and this cost savings is substantially equal to the difference in price.

2. The lower price to the larger-volume buyer was granted in order to meet competition from another company.

3. The volume discounts are *functionally* available on proportionately equal terms to all customers.

The Robinson-Patman Act is a complicated area and is discussed at some length in Chapter 12. However, for purposes of this discussion, the following observations are relevant:

1. The cost justification defense is probably impossible to prove in court.

2. The "meeting competition" defense is usable *if* your company wasn't the first to adopt the volume-rebate schedule and if your schedule only meets and does not beat those of the competition.

3. The question of whether the discount is functionally available to both large and small buyers is very complicated and subjective, and, in most cases, companies do not even attempt to structure different volume-discount schedules for larger as compared to smaller customers.

As we all know, giving volume discounts is an everyday practice at many companies. Yet, as explained above, it is probable that if challenged, it would be held at least a technical violation of the Robinson-Patman Act. Thus the importance of the legal input.

What, then, is the risk? Here the lawyer must analyze the industry to see what, if any, is the likely competitive effect, must examine the magnitude of the difference in price between the larger and smaller purchasers, must determine if there is any cost savings involved, and must determine what the competition is doing. After this examination, the lawyer can present his analysis to management and make recommendations.

Obviously, the legal risks are an important factor in the final decision. Counsel should inform management of the enforcement climate for the Robinson-Patman Act (which is currently *very* low on the part of the government). The only practical risk, therefore, comes from a disadvantaged customer or competitor. Suits by competitors are hard to win under the Robinson-Patman Act because the competitor has to show some actual loss of profits. Thus, as a practical matter, this leaves suits by the smaller customers who did not get the larger discount. Robinson-Patman cases are typically not successful as "class actions" so each disadvantaged customer would have to sue in his own case. All these factors should go into the equation, and management is entitled to all of this knowledge before adopting a volume-discount schedule.

Planning Assistance

Next, the lawyer should point out that there are many ways to grant large purchasers lower prices. These range all the way from simple volume-discount schedules to annual buy arrangements where discounts for large-volume purchases are given in the form of rebates at year-end. All of this material is more fully discussed in the chapter on the Robinson-Patman Act and will not be repeated here, but the point that the various methods of granting lower prices to larger purchasers do not have the same degree of risk should be made, and management and counsel should discuss the situation fully. Management should discuss its marketing and sales requirements, and counsel should discuss the implications of the Robinson-Patman Act so that the company can accomplish its objective with a minimum of legal risk—and such legal risk as there might be should be fully explained to management *before* it undertakes an action rather than after.

YOUR LAWYER IS HUMAN

The next element of good use of lawyers is to realize that lawyers are human. They get angry when they are insulted. They generally function a lot better if you give them a little time to think about a question before you ask them for the answer. (In some cases, they need time to do some research because they don't know all the law on every point.) They make mistakes.

One sure way to get a lawyer angry is to treat him like a law clerk or technician. Some managers make the sad mistake of asking the lawyer for his legal opinion on a given question and making it perfectly clear that all they want is his opinion as to the legality or illegality of a proposed transaction or the legal implications of a proposed transaction. A business counselor gets turned off when a manager makes it quite clear from the beginning that he thinks the lawyer has absolutely no business judgment nor any comments of a general business nature which could be at all useful. A good manager will ask the lawyer for his legal input in such a way that the lawyer feels he can also give his commonsense business-judgment input—so long as he separates the two. The manager then is free to use whatever good business ideas the lawyer presents and to disregard the nonlegal input if he thinks it is wrong. This same principle holds true for all disciplines including finance, personnel, and purchasing. It seems only common courtesy and good management sense, but it is often not done—especially by managers who feel threatened by lawyers.

Another frequent misuse of lawyers is to present them with an already accomplished transaction and ask them to "draw up the papers." Lawyers like to think of themselves as a little more than technicians or law clerks and react adversely to this kind of an approach. While business executives can and should insist that the lawyer separate his legal from his business advice so that they can make their own decisions as to what weight should be accorded to his business advice, it is a waste of money to ask a highly paid business counselor to function like a law clerk.

WHAT TO ASK FOR

Some business executives don't know what to ask for when they go to a lawyer. Furthermore, they tend to fragment their questions into a number of specific, very simple questions, failing to realize that the whole is often different from the sum of its parts.

Generally, the best approach is for lawyers and management to develop a sufficient rapport where they can discuss problems and mutually decide what kind of advice must be given. In some cases, it is necessary to have a formal legal opinion. For example, if you are buying a business or entering into a merger, it might be essential to have a formal legal opinion that the proposed course of action does not violate any law. In most cases, however, this approach will not provide the best business advice. Instead, the lawyer should be approached for constructive advice on how to structure proposed transactions or how to solve specific problems in a way which will minimize legal risks.

If a manager is so insecure that he will not do anything without a letter in his file from his lawyer stating that the action is legal, he will be operating at a severe competitive disadvantage. On the other hand, if a manager is so oblivious to the legal environment that he enters into transactions without any legal advice whatsoever, he may incur legal liabilities which can also place his company at a severe competitive or financial disadvantage. The only road is the middle road. Legal risks, like financial and business risks, must be evaluated and thrown into the equation along with all other factors.

Furthermore, in many situations a lawyer will not be able to answer the question, "Is this proposed transaction legal?" The law is not an exact science. There are many transactions which cannot be analyzed in this way, and, because lawyers are generally conservative, managers who ask this kind of simple question without giving the lawyer the opportunity to respond in a constructive fashion are going to be operating at a competitive disadvantage.

Another mistake which is sometimes made is to walk into a lawyer's office, ask him for his "off-the-cuff" opinion on some rather vague fact situation, and then assume that if he responds in a way which is at all affirmative the matter has been "cleared with the legal department."

On the other side of the coin, managers are likely to be faced with lawyers who respond to questions in a way which is not particularly useful to them. For example, a manager may present a program to a lawyer and ask his legal opinion about it, and the lawyer may say that the program involves a very high degree of legal risk and should not be undertaken. The lawyer is remiss in his duty if he does not go on to explain exactly what features of the program constitute the unacceptable legal risk and how the program could be modified to accomplish the desired result within acceptable limits of legal risk. In summary, when asking for legal advice, the manager must know what he is asking for, but in order to know what he is asking for, he must first consult with the lawyer on an informal basis to discuss the situation.

If he does not do this, either he or the lawyer is likely to be put in an untenable position.

The area of occupational safety and health could serve as an example. If a manager went to a lawyer with a program for eliminating virtually all safety hazards in a plant over the next 2 years and asked for the lawyer's opinion on the legality of such a program, the lawyer would have to respond that the program was insufficient to comply with the law because the law required compliance when it was passed in 1971 and, except for certain standards where the effective date is later, any program of compliance over any period of time short of immediately does not comply with the law. On the other hand, almost all business counselors would agree that if a manufacturing facility was inspected by the plant engineer and found to be in need of certain changes in order to comply with occupational safety and health requirements, and those changes were costly and substantial, a program of making those changes so that the plant was totally in compliance with the Occupational Safety and Health Act over the period of the next few years would, as a practical matter, be the best possible way to eliminate any legal risks under the Occupational Safety and Health Act.

In summary, the best thing to ask for in most legal situations is legal counsel. If one asks, instead, for formal and simplistic legal opinions as to legality or illegality—or goes to the other extreme and merely asks for the lawyer's off-the-cuff advice in a casual manner without taking time to explain all the facts to the lawyer and allowing the lawyer time to think about the problem and do any necessary research—it will be very difficult to obtain effective legal advice.

Our occupational safety and health example deserves further elaboration. Given the same facts—engineer comes with report of deficiencies and program for compliance over the next 2 years—the lawyer should not only say that the program is technically deficient but practically all right, but he should go on to point out the legal implications of the report. After all, there are criminal penalties for willful and knowing violations which result in a death, and it is not inconceivable that the report discloses a clear violation which will not be remedied for some time. Suppose that by some remote chance, this violation causes a death? Does the generation of the report make top management or the engineer guilty of a criminal violation? The question is certainly there, and the lawyer should make the following recommendations:

1. The document in question (the engineer's report) is very sensitive and should be kept by the engineer and not duplicated.

2. It need not be shown to a compliance officer if there is an OSHA inspection and should not be shown even if it is requested. (It is unlikely that it would be requested because OSHA inspectors are generally reasonable and fair and they realize the benefits of internal company studies and the damper they would put on them if they asked for them during an inspection.)

3. The program of fixing the deficiencies should proceed, and the most serious deficiencies should be dealt with first—even if they are the most costly to remedy—in order to minimize the danger.

Accordingly, the engineer should not restrict his question—nor the lawyer his answer—to the simple proposition of legality versus illegality. Practical advice should be sought and given. If it is not given, the manager should be sure and ask for it. Questions like "Do you see any other legal implications to the program?" should elicit the above kind of counseling. Also, personal discussions are much better than memo exchanges. The report should not simply be put in the interoffice mail and addressed to the legal department with a cryptic note asking for comments. Instead, there should be a meeting where the engineers explain exactly what they did, generally what is in the report, and their program, and the lawyer should then be asked for his advice and counsel—after allowing him time to read up on OSHA if the field is new to him.

OBTAINING COST-EFFECTIVE LEGAL ADVICE

Legal advice, like anything else a company purchases, should be obtained in the most cost-effective way. The following observations are relevant:

1. It is always best to do a little thinking on your own before you go into the lawyer's office. Have the objective to be accomplished (or the problem you feel you have) clearly focused in your own mind before you spend the lawyer's time.

2. The next important step in making sure you get cost-effective legal advice is to make sure that the lawyer completely understands the stage the problem is in, the importance of the problem, and the degree of certainty which is required at the time. The remarks made about some of the disadvantages of off-the-cuff legal advice should not be construed to mean that informal legal advice obtained in the very preliminary stages of a transaction is not valuable.

Some problems business executives have with lawyers arise when they go to a lawyer with a very vague idea of some project they want to accomplish. Through a failure of full communication, the lawyer interprets this to be an assignment to analyze all of the legal implications of the program and accordingly spends a great deal of time and effort and generates a high legal fee on a project which the business executive is not sure he wants to undertake anyway.

A lawyer should be told exactly what is required at the time. If you merely want informal legal advice, tell the lawyer not to spend a great deal of time researching complicated and esoteric legal questions. In addition, since a great deal of legal time is required to change oral legal advice into written legal memorandums, do not ask for a written legal memorandum unless you need one. It will save the lawyer time and therefore save you money. There are also different kinds of legal memorandums. There is nothing wrong with asking a lawyer to commit to writing some brief observations on some of the legal implications which he has observed in a preliminary discussion about some project. This can usually be done in an economical way. Again, however, both parties should be clear as to what the end product will be. The business executive should not make the mistake of taking this preliminary legal memorandum, which may be simply dictated in rough form and passed on to him, as definitive legal advice just as the lawyer should not overkill the problem by producing a polished legal memorandum in a situation where management hasn't even decided that the program makes sense from a business point of view.

Working together with a common understanding of the project, its business importance, its status, and all of its legal and business problems is the best way to obtain cost-effective legal advice.

In many cases, having a lawyer attend a preliminary meeting to discuss a project and asking him to make observations about potential legal difficulties will provide all of the legal input necessary for planning purposes. On the other hand, if business executives hold a great many meetings and progress on a project to a considerable extent before the lawyer is brought in, two things might happen:

1. The lawyer might find some fundamental legal fault in the program which will mean that the business executives have wasted a great deal of time. This is particularly true in the acquisition context, where it is not at all unusual for business executives to spend a great deal of time contemplating an acquisition only to have the lawyers tell them it would not be permissible under antitrust laws anyway.

2. The lawyer will have to spend more time digging up facts, reading files, and interviewing people in order to bring himself up to speed than would have been necessary had he been involved in some of the preliminary meetings.

Accordingly, another element of obtaining good cost-effective legal advice is to have the lawyer involved in the early stages of planning.

MAKE SURE THE LAWYER DOES NOT ABUSE HIS POWER TO SAY "NO"

Lawyers in business have a very unusual veto power over a great many business transactions. As a practical matter, there are very few business transactions which management is going to pursue in the face of a legal opinion that they are illegal or involve unacceptable degrees of legal risk. This places tremendous power in the hands of the lawyers, and management should be sure that they do not abuse it. Lawyers should also be aware of their power in this regard and bend over backwards to give advice on how projects can be accomplished rather than to throw up roadblocks. A complete and candid discussion by management and its lawyers is called for in this area. Both should understand that the lawyer's basic function is to help management run the business, and legal advice should be rendered accordingly.

MAKE SURE YOU HAVE LAWYERS WHO CAN STAND UP TO MANAGEMENT

While it is very important that lawyers do not abuse their power to say "No," it is equally important that they have the courage to say "No" when necessary. There is nothing more useless than a lawyer who is afraid to stand up and forcefully argue against courses of conduct which are illegal or which involve substantial degrees of legal risk. While a certain amount of diplomacy is required in all business transactions, a lawyer who fails to argue either against something which is unacceptable from a legal point of view or for something which is necessary because of some legal requirement (such as OSHA, EEO, or environmental protection) is not doing his job as corporate counsel.

INSIST ON EXCELLENCE

As in any area, when one's boss or client is sloppy in his own thinking or mediocre in his own performance, the people who work for him may tend to this approach also. Business executives should demand excellence from their legal counsel and should not settle for anything less. While "excellence" may be a little hard to pin down in a neatly worded paragraph, it is a little like one judge's definition of *pornography:* "I may not be able to define it, but I know it when I see it." It takes little perception for most business executives to know if their lawyers are really interested in their problems and diligently trying to provide the kind of legal advice they deserve. If you feel you need some touchstones, following are some items which you should be receiving from your lawyer if he is doing a good job:

1. Periodic notification of new developments in the law which may affect your job or business

2. Prompt service, or at least status reports, so that you are not left in the dark about the status of matters pending between you and your lawyer

3. Clear concise memorandums. As stated many times in this book, there is generally no reason why lawyers cannot use the same English as everyone else in business. If your lawyer's memorandums to you read like sections from statutes or cases, the memorandums may well be sections from statutes or cases which your lawyer has merely copied as a short way to provide an answer without really thinking about the entire problem and constructive solutions. On the other hand, your lawyer should provide you with copies of relevant statutes or cases so that you can see for yourself the law on which the advice is based if you care to read through it. Business executives will find, in many cases, that insistence on excellence in their legal counsel will go a long way toward guaranteeing that excellence. On the other hand, satisfaction with mediocrity will, unfortunately, tend to produce that result also.

LEARN A LITTLE ABOUT THE SUBJECT

The whole thesis of this book is that you can better use your lawyer if you learn a little about the law that affects your business or job. There are many ways to do this. This book is a start, but in today's rapidly changing business and legal environment, one must be very suspect of anything at all detailed which one reads in a hardcover book. The material in hardcover books is essential as a basis for building knowledge and for providing a working knowledge on which to build, but if one's business involves any of the substantive areas of law discussed in this book—and we would be hard put to think of a business which didn't—something in the way of current information is going to be needed.

There are a multitude of services which can be purchased on just about anything. Some of these services are aimed at lawyers, but there is certainly no reason why business executives cannot receive and read them. The trouble with some of the legal services is that even for business lawyers, they provide immensely more information than is needed on a day-to-day basis and are really more like reference services than services aimed at pointing out current problems and new ideas. For the latter, business executives are usually better able to use other sources, such as trade-association publications, business magazines, and even the old standby, the *Wall Street Journal.* In any event, the business executive who makes use of these services and asks his legal counsel for amplification of anything he reads which he feels might affect his business will be well down the road towards effective use of legal counsel.

REWARD YOUR LAWYER

Just as Pavlov's dogs, lawyers, as well as all the rest of the human beings in this world, react to some fairly standard sets of stimuli. In the business-legal relationship, this generally means at least the following:

1. If your lawyer sends you a notice of some new law which may affect your job or business, tell him you appreciate it or, in some other way, react in a manner which indicates you have received the memo and appreciate your lawyer's interest. You don't need to make a big deal out of it, but if your lawyer sends you a few memorandums describing new legal developments and never hears anything back from you, he is very likely to simply quit sending you the memorandums. This will work to the detriment of both of

you because not only will you not receive notice of some possibly important development but your lawyer will not have gone through the learning process of analyzing the new development and writing the memo. He may, therefore, be unprepared if a question arises and may react by either providing incorrect legal advice or taking too long to bring his own knowledge up to an acceptable level.

2.   If your lawyer goes out of his way to do a job for you in a hurry, tell him you appreciate it. If you don't, the next time a job needs to be done in a hurry your lawyer may be busy doing some other job in a hurry for someone who appreciates it.

3.   If a lawyer does a job for you, let him know how the project turns out. This will not only be a learning experience for both of you, but it will eliminate the feeling some lawyers have about being left out of the interesting parts of the business relationship. If your lawyer drafts a lease for you or sends you a memo on some problem, drop him a short note or call to let him know how the matter finally turned out. It will do a lot to help future communications.

MANAGE YOUR LAWYER

The principle is the same as rewarding your lawyer, but the technique has to be much more polished or you will end up with a lifelong enemy from whom you will get little, if any, useful legal counsel. You cannot effectively manage your lawyer by shouting at him, threatening to tell his boss what a lousy job he did, or blaming him for an unanticipated result—even if he did, in fact, contribute towards that result. You can effectively manage your lawyer by doing the following:

1.   Explain any concerns you have to your lawyer; this is commonsense communication. If you are dissatisfied and suffer in silence, your dissatisfaction is likely to grow and your lawyer is not likely to do anything to change his ways.

2.   If you think your lawyer's work product is unsatisfactory, go over it line by line and raise a lot of questions. On occasion, your lawyer may prepare a document which doesn't do the job you think it should. It may be too short and not deal with some of the important problems, or it may be too long and contain a lot of legalese which clouds the situation rather than clarifies it. If you simply list all of the problems your lawyer may have forgotten or go through the document paragraph by paragraph and make the lawyer explain the reason for each paragraph, your lawyer will soon get the point.

     However, some words of caution are in order on this point. In order for this technique to work, there must be good communication between you and your lawyer in the first place. The subject of employment contracts makes a good case study. In the first place, there are a number of ways to practice law and to draft documents, just as there are many ways to do almost any job. Drafting employment contracts is a prime example. If you simply go to your lawyer and say that you are hiring a new vice-president for a certain division and think there should be an employment contract, your lawyer may respond in a number of ways, ranging all the way from arguing that an employment contract is not necessary to coming back with a thirty-page document which the other party is likely to have to spend $500 in legal fees just to have his own lawyer read and explain to him. There is nothing "wrong" with either approach. In fact, an employment contract is not necessary in many situations. For example, if all you want the employment contract to say is that the prospective vice-president will not disclose any of your trade secrets, you probably do not need an employment contract at all; a simple nondisclosure agreement will do. (See Chapter 49.) On the other hand, many lawyers have studied employment contracts in depth because they have to draft them frequently, and if your lawyer comes back with a thirty-page contract he probably will be able to give a convincing story on why each provision is desirable. There are a number of different approaches that fall between these two, ranging from a simple one-page letter contract to a five- or six-page document which spells out the basics. If you are sure your new employee will resent the thirty-page approach and don't tell your lawyer, you can't very well blame him when he doesn't produce the letter agreement you had in mind. On the other hand, if you have a very delicate situation and you want all the details spelled out, together with all the protection possible for your company, and you fail to tell this to your lawyer, you can't very well fault him for coming back with his one-page, letter-form agreement, which may have been used by him without any problem in the past.

However, if you are sure you have communicated your desires to your lawyer and he still delivers a product which is unsatisfactory to you, the technique of going through your requirements and his documents and examining any discrepancies is appropriate and effective.

3. Send your lawyer some samples of the kind of product you want. Sometimes this technique is effective, but again there are some important caveats.

Some of these samples may be a little hard to find, but keep in mind the Freedom of Information Act: There is a lot of good legal work free for the asking in the government's files. (See Chapter 62.) Pension plans, profit-sharing plans, merger agreements, all manner of executive-compensation arrangements, and many other excellent documents drafted by the country's finest law firms are available in these government files either by simple request or by invoking your rights under the Freedom of Information Act. Also, if you happen to run across a good-quality work product, you should send it to your lawyer for his information and files even if he is normally doing a very good job. Just as your lawyer should send you new developments which affect your job or business, you should do the same for him in areas where he does work for you.

A WORD ABOUT TIME

One of the most frequent complaints about lawyers is that they take forever to do anything. At the same time, there are very few complaints about lawyers alleging that they are lazy. Most lawyers work long and hard at their jobs. Are these complaints about lawyers taking so long to do anything justified? The answer is obvious—although less than helpful. In some cases, the complaints are justified; in others, they are not.

Business executives are entitled to insist upon prompt service from their lawyers, but lawyers are entitled to insist upon enough time to do a good job right, and if business executives don't give them enough time, it is the lawyers' duty to take it. If your lawyer lets you push him into doing a quick and sloppy job on an important project, you need a new lawyer and should reexamine your own priorities. On the other hand, projects do have varying degrees of importance and significance to the company, and the lawyer who insists upon making every memorandum a law-review article of publishable quality is wasting his time and your money. As in all things, the proper balance is what both parties should be striving to achieve. One of the prime elements of achieving this proper balance is communication. However, there are some things which business executives should keep in mind when attempting to decide whether their legal services are being rendered quickly enough.

Suppose, for example, you need a lease for a manufacturing facility calling for substantial rental payments over a number of years. You and your lawyer agree that this is an important project. The rentals are substantial, and your company wants the free and uninterrupted use of the facility during the term of the lease.

Leases are "stock" items for lawyers, and if you have an experienced lawyer, he will undoubtedly have access to prior leases and will be able to draw on his own experience to supplement these forms. Therefore, a normal lease will be one of the simplest documents your lawyer will ever be asked to prepare. On the other hand, if the lease is adequate to protect you and to spell out all of your rights, options, and duties, it will likely be a minimum of fifteen to twenty typewritten legal pages—double spaced—and perhaps longer. Assuming that your lawyer already has a form from which to work, he will have to go through this form and make the necessary adaptations to your situation, and if he does a good job and thinks about all the problems and makes a list of questions to ask you concerning the various alternatives, this is likely to take all morning, particularly when you consider that your lawyer is likely to be interrupted by telephone calls from other people and will have to read his mail. Then your lawyer will have to get in touch with you so that you can answer some questions. (This can be done after the first draft, but it will lengthen the total time involved if the first draft has to be changed substantially.) Assuming you are available when your lawyer calls (and this is a big assumption), your lawyer is going to be doing quite well to get the lease to his secretary that same day, and then you have to figure on at least one day to type and proofread the lease. After the lawyer's secretary types and proofreads the lease, the lawyer has to read it at least once more, and since human beings are less than perfect, it is not unreasonable to allow for some additional changes or improvements at this point. This reading and these changes may take another day. (In figuring days, remember that your lawyer cannot put himself in a padded cell and work on your project. He must honor previous commitments and answer telephones.) Thus when you ask your lawyer how soon he can have your lease back to you, your lawyer is probably mentally going to add up all of this time and then add a little to cover other possible unforeseen events. Therefore, it is submitted that your lawyer is not being at all unreasonable if he tells you it is going to take a week to have your lease back. If he tells you two weeks, you probably don't have much to complain about.

In considering time, remember that the mark of a good lawyer is that he is busy. Enough said on this point.

A WORD ABOUT FORMS

Many people in business have a misconception about forms. In the example above, some would have the impression that the lawyer simply took out a form lease and told the secretary to change the names. If your lawyer does this, you need a new lawyer. If you ask your lawyer to do this, your lawyer should explain to you that this is courting disaster.

On the other hand, forms are one of the most useful and time-saving devices that a lawyer can have, and properly used, they will increase the quality of his work. Therefore, many lawyers spend a great deal of time developing their own system of forms, and many law-book companies publish much material under the title "legal forms." Indeed, there are specialized form books for just about every subject, and a comprehensive set of forms can run to many thick volumes of fine print. However, a good form is a combination of two things: language and points of concern. In other words, in addition to supplying language which the lawyer or publisher thinks is adequate to make the desired point clearly, the form raises a great many possible points and operates as a kind of checklist. Not all of these points are appropriate for every transaction. It is the lawyer's duty to use these forms as guides—

taking what he needs and discarding what is not appropriate, adding what is necessary (forms do not cover everything) and changing what may be necessary in order to accomplish the desired objective. Most first drafts are negotiating documents and will have to be drafted accordingly, putting your best position forward. In short, forms save time, but they still take time to use.

Before leaving forms, another point must be made: Your lawyer is likely to have a large number of forms in his files for a great many typical transactions. These forms can be used for your transaction with some, but not extensive, modification. Leases are a prime example. If at all possible, it is a good idea to allow your lawyer to use these forms without unnecessary restrictions. For example, in most lease transactions, it really doesn't matter how long the lease is because, in the business context, both parties are going to be represented by counsel anyway.

If you think that by telling your lawyer that you want a "simple" lease not over five pages long, you are going to save time and allow him to get the lease back to you more quickly, you are probably mistaken. Instead of using the standard lease as a model, the lawyer is going to either have to develop a new five-page form or else take so much out of the standard form that in the long run, the time expended will be longer and, very importantly, it will be the lawyer's time. Since most lawyers charge a flat fee for their time and usually figure the fee high enough to cover secretarial help, office, and library, if you increase the lawyer's time you are greatly increasing the total bill while if you increase stenographic time, you probably do not affect the bill substantially. In corporate legal departments where you are not actually paying for legal help by the hour, the same principle holds true because the cost of the lawyer is obviously greater than the cost of the stenographic help. Total time is still unlikely to be reduced, and the quality of the work product could suffer. In short, it is not a good idea to place arbitrary restrictions on the length of document you expect from your lawyer unless those restrictions are important. If, in the course of your negotiations, you discover that the other party will not accept a lengthy formal document and wants a shorter, informal agreement, you are certainly entitled to require your lawyer to act accordingly. However, this should not be done on the theory that it will, in fact, speed up the process; it probably will not. In addition, simpler documents are not as comprehensive as longer ones, and there are more points for possible disagreement later on. Business executives should make these judgments and trade-offs intelligently, and their lawyers should explain any points which are not covered in the simpler document.

Another point in drafting documents is who should take the initiative. Sometimes, business executives will suggest that the other party prepare the first draft of any relevant documents on the theory that it is the first draft which takes the most time and you might as well have the other party pay for it. However, this is not a universal truth. Sometimes it takes more time to review a document thoroughly than it does to draft it.

Consider our lease example. If your lawyer has a good lease form which has been previously developed to satisfy all of your concerns and protect all of your interests and then he is asked, not to draft a lease but to review one, he must get out his form and make sure the one drafted by the other party takes care of all your concerns and does not impose any unreasonable obligations on your company. Since it is likely that a lease prepared by someone else will not satisfy your special requirements and will impose unreasonable obligations on you, you can expect your lawyer to have to write a rather lengthy letter explaining how the proposed lease should be changed. This may take more time than it would have to draft an original lease—and again it will be expensive legal time rather than stenographic time.

In summary, it is not a good idea to be too quick to let the other party take the initiative in drafting. It is not likely to save you any legal time in the long run, and the risk of your lawyer failing to notice an important omission or disadvantageous provision is greater. Again, remember that lawyers are human.

EMERGENCIES

In some cases, the lawyer will expend considerable effort to meet a deadline only to have the document he created or the work he did lie dormant for a number of days or weeks. It is not unlike the boy who cried "wolf" once too often. Some clients develop a reputation for this, and their cries of "emergency" fall on deaf ears. Other clients are quite the opposite, and when they say they have an important problem which requires prompt action, the lawyer knows that this is really the case. The business executive's job is to develop a relationship with his lawyer which will allow him to cry "wolf" when there really is an emergency but, at the same time, will allow him to transact normal business—which is usually not of the emergency variety—in a reasonable way. Sometimes, in reaction to the problem of lawyers taking too much time, clients tell the lawyer that everything is an emergency because if they do not, they are afraid that either (1) the lawyer will spend too much time on the problem—thus running up too high a bill—or (2) the job will never get done at all or will take many weeks.

On the first point—costs—two comments are in order.

1. In a corporate legal department this should not be a problem.

2. In private practice, most lawyers have a surcharge which they place on emergency projects because the time required is intensive and they must neglect their other clients. Calling everything an "emergency" may therefore be self-defeating if you do it to try and save money. Also, the old proverb "haste makes waste" has the same validity in the legal area as in any other area. Calling a project an "emergency" when it really isn't is not likely to save time or money and may, in fact, do the opposite.

The second problem, however, is much more difficult. The fact is that lawyers do tend to give the grease to the wheel that squeaks the loudest. If you remain quiet, your project may not get attention, and while it may not be an emergency, the project is undoubtedly important to you personally if for no other reason than the normal desire to finish things one starts without letting them drag on interminably.

Here is where a little finesse comes in. Instead of saying a project is really rush when it isn't, simply state what you think is a reasonable time for completion and see if your lawyer agrees. In this kind of atmosphere, it is very likely that a mutually satisfactory agreement can be reached. Lawyers tend to let second-priority projects slide, not out of malice to the people who initiate them, but simply because other matters seem more pressing at the time. If your lawyer has promised you a project in 2 weeks, at the end of a week and a half, that project should be high on his list of priorities if it still remains uncompleted. Again, however, theory is not always matched in practice, and if you do not do something, your originally stated time deadline might come and go without word from your lawyer.

Don't just sit there and stew. Call him up. You can be friendly. You can ask if there is anything you can do to help the project along; you can say simply that you are following up and want to know the status of the project. There are many different techniques that can be used, all of them requiring some kind of contact with the lawyer and none of them requiring hostility or unpleasantness. However, if you get your lawyer mad at you, or if you call everything an "emergency," your time problems from your lawyer will, in the long run, increase rather than decrease in severity.

CHAPTER FOUR

AMERICA'S
LEGAL FRAMEWORK

A basic knowledge of America's legal framework is essential to an understanding of any legal material. Without this knowledge, there is the danger of overreacting to pronouncements of lower courts which may say that a certain course of conduct is permissible or impermissible and later be overturned by a higher court. There is the danger of confusion because of the frequently differing opinions on legal questions between courts and federal agencies. Last but not least, there is the danger that really important legal pronouncements may not be placed in their proper perspective.

America's legal framework descends from English common law. It differs from the systems used in most other countries of the world, where some form of civil law is used. The essential difference between common law and civil law is that in common-law countries, the law is in the form of statutes enacted by a sovereign (in the United States, this can be either the federal or state government) and cases decided by the courts. In other words, an opinion of the Supreme Court of the United States has roughly the same status in the hierarchy of legal framework as a law enacted by Congress. In fact, because the Constitution of the United States is above every other law— and the U.S. Supreme Court has responsibility for interpreting the Constitution—a decision of the U.S. Supreme Court holding an act of Congress unconstitutional actually takes precedence over the act of Congress itself so the unconstitutional law cannot be enforced. In a civil-law country, the law is some form of code enacted by the sovereign. Cases decided by the courts have little or no precedence; they merely resolve disputes between the parties to the case.

Because America follows the common-law system of making law by cases, it is very important to understand the judicial system and to understand the importance of each court and exactly what its decisions mean and who must abide by them. Almost everyone knows that a decision by one state court does not require compliance by a company which operates only in other states. However, when the federal courts get into the picture, the scene becomes a bit more cluttered.

Since the laws dealt with in this book are mostly federal laws, a brief description of this federal system and how it works is necessary. While this system is being discussed, we will also discuss the state systems and federal preemption.

FEDERAL SYSTEM

The Constitution

The basic legal document in this country is the Constitution. However, for practical business purposes, the Constitution itself rarely becomes important as a planning document. While it is possible to argue that some of the laws your lawyer requires you to comply with are against the spirit of one or more provisions of the Constitution, such an argument is always very nebulous and uncertain at best, and to disregard a law at either the state or federal level on the assumption that it is unconstitutional usually creates more problems than it solves. However, it should be kept in mind that laws enacted by Congress and the states do have to come within the scope of the United States Constitution, and on many occasions, the Supreme Court of the United States has found that certain basic fundamental and important laws have, indeed, been unconstitutional. A recent example is the holding by the United States Supreme Court that the 1974 law establishing the Federal Election Commission was unconstitutional.

Federal Statutes

Next on the level of hierarchy are the federal statutes. These are the laws promulgated by Congress and signed by the President. These are the basic laws which this book explains. They include the tax laws, the securities laws, the labor laws, the Consumer Product Safety Act, the Civil Rights Act, and the Occupational Safety and Health Act. These laws are universally applicable to all businesses operating in the United States and the words contained in these statutes must be taken as "the law."

Regulations

Remaining at the federal level, the next piece of authority under the federal statutes consists of the regulations which interpret those statutes. These regulations are issued by the administrative agencies in charge of enforcing the statutes. The most prominent example of a federal statute and the regulations thereunder is the Internal Revenue Code of 1954 and the regulations of the Internal Revenue Service interpreting it. Virtually all of the laws discussed in this book are subject to much explanatory material in the form of regulations. The regulations typically have the advantage of being written in a little more easily understandable language. They are a little more specific, and in many cases they use examples to illustrate the point they are trying to make. However, it must constantly be kept in mind that regulations of administrative bodies are not law, and while it may be prudent to comply with them in the overwhelming majority of cases, there are situations where counsel may feel that a regulation is so inherently unreasonable or so unjustified under the basic statute that the company should be willing to run the risk involved in ignoring it. This is a risk-weighing operation which must be done by company counsel in a very careful way and explained cautiously to management.

A prime example is the Equal Employment Opportunity regulation indicating that pregnancy must for all purposes be treated as a short-term disability by corporations paying benefits for short-term disabilities. This regulation was announced by the Equal Employment Opportunity Commission under the Civil Rights Act of 1964. However, many business counselors felt that the legality of this regulation was subject to question and therefore did not comply with it. This position has since been supported by the Supreme Court. Business counselors who were thoughtful enough to create this argument and stand up for it saved their clients much money. It should be noted, however, that failure to comply with the Equal Employment Opportunity Commission's regulation on paying benefits to pregnant females was a rather modest risk. In most cases, the number of females who would have been eligible for these benefits was small. The only risk was back pay for the period when they were actually out of work because of pregnancy, and there were no criminal sanctions. Accordingly, it was relatively easy for counsel to recommend that companies who desired to do so would be justified in disregarding this dubious regulation and waiting until clarification was obtained by court action.

This, however, is an unusual situation. In most cases, company counsel will advise clients to comply with regulations issued by administrative bodies under the statutes which they are in charge of administering.

Court Cases

Remaining with the federal system as distinguished from state law, another body of authority consists of court cases.

As we all learned in our high-school political-science classes, the United States is governed by three equal bodies: the executive branch, Congress, and the courts. Accordingly, the highest decision of each of these branches is accorded roughly equal weight.

The Supreme Court

Decisions of the Supreme Court are essentially equal to federal statutes. Accordingly, when one reads a Supreme Court decision interpreting a particular law or setting forth some guidelines under the law, this Supreme Court decision must be taken as the law which applies universally throughout all fifty states.

Courts of Appeal

Immediately below the Supreme Court are various courts of appeal. The United States is divided into eleven geographic circuits. These circuits are governed by circuit courts of appeals.

Decisions of these circuit courts of appeals are binding within that circuit but not in any other circuit. In many cases, one circuit will give considerable weight to the opinion of a court from another circuit. However, it is not legally required to do so, and it is frequent that the opinions of the various circuit courts of appeals differ on rather important issues. Typically, when there is a difference of opinion among the circuits on a particular point, the point will be appealed to the Supreme Court, which will clarify the issue. From that point on, all circuits must abide by the rule adopted by the Supreme Court. However, it is important to note that circuit courts of appeals decisions are only actually binding in the particular circuit in which they are effective. Accordingly, if your company is headquartered and operates entirely in the First Circuit and a particularly troublesome rule is adopted in the Second Circuit, there is a considerable amount of legal justification for ignoring the rule in the Second Circuit until it becomes binding in the First Circuit, either by decision of the Court of Appeals for the First Circuit or by the Supreme Court of the United States.

This, however, is a rather subjective question depending upon the risks involved in ignoring the decision and the likelihood of the correctness of the Second Circuit decision. Accordingly, this matter should be carefully evaluated by legal counsel, and decisions to ignore a circuit court of appeals case and the implications thereof should be made very sparingly.

District Courts

Immediately below the circuit courts of appeals are a multitude of federal district courts governing ninety-three geographic districts.

A decision of a district court is only binding in that particular district. If two district courts in a particular circuit give different answers to the same question, the matter is usually appealed to the circuit court of appeals. From that point on, all the district courts in the circuit must abide by the rule announced by that circuit court of appeals.

However, when you get down to the decisions of district courts, companies have much more latitude in deciding whether or not to comply with the rules stated. If a company decided to comply with every rule stated by every district court in the country, it would have many conflicting directions to follow and would be unduly restricted in its operations and competitive ability because it would be operating under a number of decisions which will subsequently be reversed either by the circuit courts of appeals or by the Supreme Court. This is particularly troublesome because many business publications—and even some of the legal sources—are "hungry for news." In many situations, they will take an interesting and perhaps controversial federal district court decision and write a very good article on it, failing to point out that the rule of that case only applies in one district.

Accordingly, one of the big jobs of corporate counsel is to filter through this mass of federal district court decisions to decide which are legally binding, which it makes sense to comply with, and which are way-out. Decisions which govern the district where the corporation or plant operates are legally binding. It makes sense to comply with decisions which will probably be supported by other district courts, the circuit court of appeals, and perhaps the Supreme Court. Decisions which are way-out or "off-the-mark" need not be complied with and perhaps should not be complied with until compliance is made necessary by decree of a court having jurisdiction over the company.

This is the central point to be made by this chapter. Whenever someone says there is a case that requires a certain action to be taken or prohibits a certain action, it is necessary to ascertain what court rendered that decision. If it is the Supreme Court of the United States, the decision must be complied with by everyone. If it is a circuit court of appeals, the decision must be complied with by all those companies in that circuit. If the company is not in the circuit, an intelligent legal decision will have to be made as to whether compliance is desirable. If the decision is by a federal district court, however, considerable discretion must be used in judging what the company's compliance posture ought to be. Obviously, if the decision is from the district in which the particular company operates, the decision must be complied with at least until it is overruled or modified. However, in all other districts, it is important to avoid overreaction to a district court decision. Instead, where these out-of-line decisions are reported, it is more desirable to await further legal development before committing a company to a different policy direction.

Executive Orders

As indicated, the three branches of government are equal, and the highest pronouncements of each are given equal weight. The highest pronouncement in the executive branch is generally an executive order. For business purposes, executive orders do not usually play an important role. One very important exception is the executive order which requires government contractors to use affirmative action in hiring and promoting minority employees.

STATE SYSTEM

Shifting over to the state level, the general framework of state court decisions is similar to the federal system except, of course, that a state court decision only governs operations in that state. Most states have a state supreme court and different levels of courts below that.* The same words of caution apply to state court decisions. A state court decision must be complied with by any company in that state unless it is inconsistent with a federal rule. Sometimes, inconsistencies do arise because state supreme courts will construe a state statute in a way which is inconsistent with a federal rule. This is particularly troublesome in some of the employment-discrimination areas, where state statutes enacted many years ago to protect females are inconsistent with the new federal laws on this subject. However, except in these kinds of unusual cases, a decision of the state supreme court will be binding upon all residents of that state. Lower-court decisions, however, are another matter entirely. In some cases, lower-court decisions aren't even publicly reported. Where they are reported, it is necessary to have legal counsel carefully evaluate the weight and scope of the decision to avoid overreaction and overgeneralization.

FEDERAL PREEMPTION

Federal laws preempt state laws in certain situations. Wherever there is a definite conflict between a federal and a state statute, the state statute must give way. Typical examples include the civil rights, occupational safety and health, antitrust, securities, and federal income tax statutes. As a general proposition, however, states can adopt their own statutes dealing with essentially the same subjects as federal laws, and in the overwhelming majority of industrialized states, there are really two sets of parallel rules. In most cases, compliance with the federal rules will assure compliance with the state rules because the state rules are usually patterned after the federal rules, and where they are not, the federal rules are usually more restrictive. How-

---

* Some names can be misleading, however. In New York, for example, the highest court is the New York Court of Appeals.

ever, as a prerequisite for the application of any federal rule, there has to be interstate commerce. There are a whole host of decisions which stand for the general proposition that just about any kind of activity imaginable can be interpreted as "interstate commerce." For example, a barbershop in an airport which services interstate travelers can be said to be engaged in interstate commerce. However, there are certain situations and certain companies which operate entirely within one state. Accordingly, many states feel it appropriate to have their own laws which substantially duplicate the federal laws discussed in this book so that companies which do operate only in one state will be subject to essentially similar rules. Many states have their own antitrust laws, their own securities laws, and their own labor laws. In some cases, the federal pattern itself is to defer to the state statutes. In the employ-ment-discrimination area, any state which has employment legislation and agencies to implement it is usually given first crack at enforcement of employ-ment-discrimination complaints. In the area of occupational safety and health, the Occupational Safety and Health Act itself provides that if a state has an approved plan, the state, rather than the federal, government will have authority for enforcing the plan's provisions. In other cases, companies are subject to both sets of rules. Examples here are the areas of securities, anti-trust, and tax, where companies must not only abide by the federal antitrust rules and the federal rules regarding the purchase and sale of securities and pay federal income taxes but must also abide by the state rules covering substantially similar activities and pay state taxes. In the area of commercial law—sometimes referred to as contracts or sales—the two sets of laws do not overlap quite so much. In this area, certain subjects are governed by federal law, including the Consumer Products Safety Act and warranty legisla-tion, but the overwhelming majority of commercial-law questions are governed by state law. However, these state laws can be lumped together because they are all substantially similar.

Beginning in about 1962, states started adopting the Uniform Commercial Code, a set of statutes designed to be adopted by every state and designed to govern almost all commercial transactions. For our purposes, the most important part of the Uniform Commercial Code is the chapter on sales, which establishes the rules dealing with normal commercial contracts. The Uniform Commercial Code, as its name implies, is relatively uniform throughout the forty-nine states which have now adopted it. (The only state which has not is Louisiana, and the reason for this is that Louisiana is the only state of the Union which is governed by European civil law rather than English com-mon law.) To be sure, there are minor differences in the way various states have enacted or interpreted the Uniform Commercial Code. In the main, how-ever, commercial rules are the same throughout all states of the Union because of this code. Because of the uniformity of this law, state-court decisions inter-preting provisions of the Uniform Commercial Code take on a little more significance than do their decisions in some other cases. For example, if Illinois interprets a provision of the Uniform Commercial Code in a certain way, and that provision is identical to those in the other forty-eight states, state courts in those other forty-eight states are very likely to give considerable weight to the Illinois decision on the point even though it is not legally binding upon them. Again, however, a word of caution is in order. Business publications which report on decisions under the Uniform Commercial Code and warn business executives of emerging trends and possible problems sometimes do not make distinctions among the various states. While it is certainly true that a decision in one state involving a statute which is in existence in all of the other states has *some* persuasive value, it is not true that it is always appropriate for a company, say, in California to follow a rule adopted by an Illinois court, even when the statutes involved are identical and the reasoning of the Illinois court sounds persuasive. This is a matter for legal judgment and is important responsibility of corporate counsel. Counsel must maintain a proper balance, so that compliance, where necessary, is accomplished while overreaction and unduly restrictive practices are avoided. This book concentrates on federal laws and, because it has been adopted in almost uniform fashion throughout the country, the Uniform Commercial Code.

However, in reading the book it must always be kept in mind that there are these two parallel sets of rules, and the generalization that compliance with the federal rules will usually result in compliance with state laws does have its exceptions. Accordingly, one of the things management should insist upon from their counsel is an explanation of both federal and state rules, where appropriate. Some counsel tend to forget about state laws when they are dealing with companies which operate in interstate commerce and to rely instead upon the generalization that federal laws will govern most problems. It is appropriate for management to cross-examine counsel on this point because many state-law problems can present themselves even when a company is in full compliance with federal rules. To carry the matter a step further, it is also necessary in some cases to comply with city, county, or other local ordinances. However, the scope and applicability of these ordinances is so widely different that we have not even made an attempt to mention them except to say that they exist, and in some areas, like building code and zoning restrictions, they are obviously an important part of the legal framework in which a company must operate.

Again, however, a practical approach is required. All companies should understand the antitrust and securities laws in the states in which they operate and should make special efforts to make sure they comply with these laws. However, tax and labor rules are an entirely different matter. Naturally, when a company finds out about a particular tax or labor rule, it should immediately comply if it is not doing so. However, to go out and make a detailed examination of all the company's facilities to make certain they are complying with every state or local rule on every subject is generally a waste of corporate time and money. Even assuming it would be possible to do this—a dubious assumption—the company would barely finish with the compliance review when it might have to start over again because of changes in these laws. Instead, a more realistic approach is to adopt a position of full compliance with all federal laws, compliance with all known state and local laws, and, when a particular problem emerges on the state or local front, immediate compliance with any appropriate law or regulation without going out and making an "audit" to ascertain the state of the company's compliance with this multitude of different rules.

CHAPTER FIVE

THE ATTORNEY/CLIENT PRIVILEGE AND THE LAWYER'S OBLIGATION TO HIS CLIENT

Ever since the beginning of English common law, communications between attorney and client have been protected from disclosure against the will of the client. The attorney/client privilege is applicable in both civil and criminal matters. Thus if you are accused of a crime, consult an attorney, and tell him whether you actually committed the crime, this communication *cannot* be revealed by the attorney without your consent, even in court and even if the attorney should desire to do so. In the same manner if you are sued in a civil matter, you may freely discuss the facts with your lawyer without fear of having your communications disclosed. In legal parlance, this is known as "privileged communication." In theory, this privilege exists in business, and it exists for corporations as well as their employees. However, in the business context, the application of the privilege is complicated, and since it is so important in corporate planning, business executives should be familiar with the ground rules and make sure their lawyers pay proper attention to this problem. This chapter discusses those ground rules and other related matters.

BASIC QUESTIONS

It is clear that the attorney/client privilege exists whether the attorney is house counsel or an independent practitioner or whether the client is a corporate entity or an individual. However, in the case of a corporation, the attorney/client privilege becomes rather complicated and subject to a number of qualifications.

A good general statement of the qualifications, from one of the leading cases on the subject, is as follows:

The privilege applies only if (1) the asserted holder of the privilege is or sought to become a client; (2) the person to whom the communication was made (a) is a member of the bar of a court, or his subordinate and (b) in connection with this communication is acting as a lawyer; (3) the communication relates to a fact of which his attorney was informed (a) by his client (b) without the presence of strangers (c) for the purpose of securing primarily either (i) an opinion on law or (ii) legal services or (iii) assistance in some legal proceeding, and not (d) for the purpose of committing a crime or tort; and (4) the privilege has been (a) claimed and (b) not waived by the client. [*United States v. United Shoe Machinery*, 89 F.Supp. 35–7 (1950)]

Despite the importance of the attorney/client privilege, the question of whether it could be claimed by a corporation was not directly decided until the *Radiant Burners* case in 1963. In that case, counsel for both sides at first assumed that a corporation, like a person, had the benefit of the privilege. However, the judge expressed some doubt about this and requested the parties to brief the question. Despite extensive efforts by all of the law firms representing the multiple defendants, no one was able to turn up a single case in which it had been actually decided (rather than simply assumed) that a corporation had such a privilege, and so the trial court declared that a corporation did not have the privilege. A higher court of appeals later reversed this decision and held that as a principle of law, the privilege does exist for corporations. However, the court stated that the nature and limits of the privilege, as applied to corporations, would have to be developed on a case-by-case basis through the decisional process.

Following are the basic questions which usually arise in the context of the attorney/client privilege in the corporate area:

1. Who is the client? Is it the corporation? Is it the officers, directors, and employees of the corporation? Is it some other group?

2. Who is the attorney? Is the privilege limited to outside counsel, or does it include house counsel? Is the privilege limited to various legal communications, or does it extend to business communications?

3. What is the confidentiality requirement?

Related questions concern the mechanics of assertion of the privilege, the interaction of the privilege with the so-called "work-product doctrine," and the complication which is introduced in a derivative action where, in theory, the plaintiff in the lawsuit is the corporation.

Who Is the Client?

It seems clear, as a matter of abstract legal principle, that the corporation is entitled to claim the attorney/client privilege. However, since the corporation must act through its officers and agents, the privilege must be extended to them if it is to be meaningful. Two court decisions are important. The first is one of the electrical equipment antitrust cases,* where the court established the so-called "control-group" test for determining whether individual officers represented the corporate client. In that case, the court held that the privilege does apply to communications of an employee if the employee "is in a position to control or even to take a substantial part in a decision about any action which the corporation may take upon the advice of the

---

* *City of Phil. v. W. Elec. Corp.*, 210 F.Supp. 483 (1962)

attorney, or if he is an authorized member of a body or group which has that authority." The control-group test has been used by a number of other courts, but the *Harper & Row Publishers* case broadens it a bit. That case involved a series of debriefing memorandums prepared by attorneys after interviews with various defendants who had testified before a grand jury investigating the publishing industry. Presumably, the attorney was gathering these memorandums in anticipation of a potential antitrust action. Many of the employees involved were not in the control group, and the court said:

> We conclude that the control group test is not wholly adequate, that the corporation's attorney-client privilege protects communications of some corporate agents who are not within the control group, and that in those instances where the order here under attack must rest entirely upon the control group test, the order is unlawful. [*Harper & Row v. Decker,* 423 F.2d 487 (1970)]

The *Harper and Row* court held that the correct test was:

> We conclude that an employee of a corporation, though not a member of its control group, is sufficiently identified with the corporation so that his communication to the corporation's attorney is privileged where the employee makes the communication at the direction of his superiors in the corporation and where the subject matter upon which the attorney's advice is sought by the corporation and dealt with in the communication is the performance by the employee of the duties of his employment.

Who Is the Attorney?

The attorney/client privilege is only applicable in cases of a communication to and from an attorney regarding legal advice or services. It seems clear that corporate law departments, at least insofar as the lawyers are acting in their capacity as attorneys, are protected by the privilege. However, it is also probable that the mere fact that an employee has a law degree and is in the legal department does not establish the existence of the privilege. He must be acting in his capacity as an attorney and not in his capacity as a business adviser. There appears to be a rather broad definition of legal assistance, but there is a point at which legal advice stops and business advice begins. This line is a bit hazy when the advice comes from house counsel rather than from outside counsel. The distinction between legal advice and other advice depends upon the facts in each case.

Confidentiality Requirement

The confidentiality problem arises frequently in the corporate context where information is passed around among various employees. A typical example is contained in the case of *United States v. Aluminum Co. of America,* where the court ruled that a document which would ordinarily have been privileged because it was furnished by an executive to an attorney in response to the attorney's request for information was not privileged because a copy of that same document had been sent to the corporation's president in response to his request for the same information. Also, some situations inherently create a situation where a disclosure cannot be confidential. Examples, again, are the electrical company antitrust cases, where the court said that disclosures made to the company's general counsel were not confidential, and therefore not privileged, because the attorney advised the employee that although his disclosures were privileged, if it should turn out that they revealed a violation of written company-policy directives, the lawyer would report that fact to management.

Here, there seems to be a distinction between newly created documents and existing documents. This distinction is based on the *Radiant Burners* case, where it was said that "certainly the privilege would never be available to allow a corporation to funnel its papers and documents into the hands of its lawyers for custodial purposes and thereby avoid disclosure." Also, in the electrical equipment case, the court said that a client may not refuse to disclose any relevant fact within his knowledge merely because he incorporated a statement of such fact into his communication to his attorney. Generally, memorandums to a lawyer requesting legal advice, memorandums from a lawyer giving legal advice, or memorandums from a lawyer requesting additional facts and memorandums from the client supplying those additional facts would all clearly be privileged if the other requirements for the privilege were present. However, it is difficult to claim the privilege for any preexisting documents not prepared in conjunction with legal advice, even if such documents are in the custody of the attorney and relevant to the attorney's legal advice.

Assertion of the Privilege—Waiver

The attorney/client privilege can generally be asserted at any time and in just about any context. However, it can also be waived, and it can be waived inadvertently. Examples of such inadvertent waiver are cases where a corporation allowed government investigators to review its files, including privileged communications, and cases where a privileged communication was sent outside the control group or to a person who was in the control group but outside the attorney/client relationship. It has also been held that allowing an attorney to testify before the SEC waived a privilege which might otherwise have been claimed by the attorney's underwriter-client. The attorney/client privilege clearly applies with respect to administrative agencies, including subpoenas issued by them. In a court case, the privileged information is usually submitted *in camera* and examined by the judge. However, the privilege question may also be decided by a judge on the basis of evidence as to how the documents were prepared.

Work-Product Doctrine

In the early case of *Hickman v. Taylor,* the court held that the work product of a lawyer could not generally be obtained by opposing counsel. The court reasoned that a contrary rule would mean that much of what is now put down in writing would remain unwritten, leading to inefficiency, unfairness, and sharp practices. However, the court also held that discovery of such papers would be allowed if good cause was shown. Also, it appears that this work-product doctrine applies only to matters related to, or in anticipation of, litigation.

A further problem with the work-product doctrine would appear from the Federal Rules of Civil Procedure, which seem to substitute a substantial "need" requirement for a good "cause" requirement. At this stage, the work-product doctrine would appear to be limited to documents like file memos prepared by the attorney, directly related to the client's problems, and dealing with the attorney's conclusions, legal analysis, or other information directly obtained by the attorney pursuant to work, research, or investigation performed by the attorney in his capacity as an attorney.

Derivative Action

According to a lower-court decision in one case, the corporation cannot claim any privilege in a derivative lawsuit because the plaintiff is, in theory, the corporation itself. Fortunately, this holding has been reversed, but the current state of the law on this point is still somewhat confused. At present, the law on the point is the following from the appellate court opinion reversing the lower court in *Garner v. Wolfinbarger:*

> In summary, we say this. The attorney-client privilege still has viability for the corporate client. The corporation is not barred from asserting it merely because those demanding information enjoy the status of stockholders. But where the corporation is in suit against its stockholders, on charges of acting inimically to stockholder interests, protection of those interests as well as those of the corporation and of the public require that the availability of the privilege be subject to the right of the stockholders to show cause why it should not be invoked in the particular instance. [*Garner v. Wolfinbarger,* 430 F.2d 1093 (1970)]

Other Limitations

Another limitation on the privilege doctrine is that it does not apply to communications made by a client to his attorney during or before the commission of a crime or fraud for the purpose of being guided or assisted in its commission. Since many securities, tax, antitrust, and labor laws have criminal penalties or speak in terms of fraud, this exception is more important in the corporate context than might at first be anticipated.

THE FEDERAL RULES OF CIVIL PROCEDURE

While the state of the law regarding the attorney/client privilege is a little uncertain, the above discussion, standing alone, would probably not give rise to any great alarm on the part of either attorneys or professional business clients. However, it is necessary for one to go a little further than an analysis of when the privilege might exist and consider how the question might arise. Obviously, the question will arise in a lawsuit—usually in the federal courts—and this makes it necessary to consider the Federal Rules of Civil Procedure. These rules do contain limited protection against disclosure of privileged material.

As a practical matter, however, one side is not likely to take the other's word as to what is privileged and what is not. Accordingly, all of the material must usually be submitted to the judge, who will then decide. Considering the fact that many cases in the federal courts are tried before a judge without a jury (and even in a jury case the judge is a very important participant) it would seem a little ridiculous to place too much weight on a legal theory which protects documents from everyone except the judge. To do so would be to make an unrealistic assessment of a judge's ability or willingness to simply erase from his mind everything which he read which he deemed to be privileged. Further, it would appear to us that if the lawyer tells his client that any communications between them will be privileged from everyone except the judge, the client will take an entirely different view of the situation than if the lawyer simply says communications will be privileged without adding the qualifying phrase. This is important for counseling purposes because it has considerable effect on the weight the lawyer and client should place on the privilege in creating and sending documents between them.

LAWYERS' COMMUNICATIONS TO AUDITORS

For many years there has been considerable discussion of the duties of the accountants to present the financial statements of the company fairly and accurately versus the duties of a lawyer to represent his client as an advocate and to retain as confidential any matters which he learns in such representation.

The accountants generally feel that they should be fully informed of all existing litigation, any threatened litigation, and any liabilities which the company knows about but which have not yet been asserted—like a patent which the company knows it is infringing but which the other party has not yet discovered.

On the other hand, lawyers point out that it is imprudent, at best, to make predictions to third parties on the likely outcome of litigation because so many cases cannot be predicted with any degree of certainty, and in addition, if the company really does have some exposure, a statement to that effect to independent auditors could be deemed an admission and dragged into court by the other side. The same arguments are made for threatened litigation. As to unasserted claims, lawyers point out that in addition to all of the above-mentioned problems, there is a problem of inviting litigation if one sets forth all of the skeletons in the corporate closet.

Both sides to this argument have considerable merit, and there is no solution which is going to keep everybody completely happy. However, after considerable discussion, the lawyers and accountants have reached accord— at least in the form of a written policy statement—which essentially passes the buck to management by saying that the lawyers should provide full and complete disclosure to the accountants on all matters where management waives the attorney/client privilege by telling the auditors. The lawyer/accountant agreement does contain a statement that "the lawyer has an obligation not knowingly to participate in any violation by the client of the disclosure requirements of the securities laws. In appropriate circumstances, the lawyer also may be required under the code of professional responsibility to resign his engagement if his advice concerning disclosures is disregarded by the client."

One of the reasons behind heightened concern in this area is the Financial Accounting Standards Board's Statement No. 5, which was issued in March of 1975 and which is effective for fiscal years beginning on or after July 1, 1975.

FASB Statement No. 5 is aimed at precluding companies from playing around with their contingency reserves in order to achieve whatever trend lines they want on their earnings-per-share record. Since, by their very nature, loss contingency reserves were very subjective, it was fairly easy for a company to place larger or smaller amounts in this reserve in any given year if that was appropriate in order to increase or decrease earnings per share. The new rule, however, provides that an estimated loss from a contingency (litigation and unasserted claims are both considered contingencies) should be charged to income only if both of the following are met:

1. It is probable that a future event or events will occur confirming the likelihood that an asset has been impaired or a liability has been incurred as of the balance-sheet date.

2. The amount of the loss can be reasonably estimated.

The rule preserves the existing policy that contingencies which may result in gains should not be recorded until they are actually realized.

If a judgment is made to accrue a loss contingency, there must be some disclosure of the nature of the accrual and, under some circumstances, the amount accrued. If the contingency is not accrued, but still rises to the dignity of what is called a "reasonable possibility" of loss, there must be a disclosure of the nature of the contingency and an estimate of the possible loss or range of loss—or a statement that such an estimate cannot be made.

The statement lists the following factors to consider in determining whether accrual and/or disclosure are required for pending or threatened litigation and actual or possible claims and assessments:

1. The date of occurrence of the cause of action

2. The degree of probability of an unfavorable outcome

3. The ability to reasonably estimate the amount of the loss

In evaluating the probability of an unfavorable outcome, a company should consider the following factors set forth in the statement:

1. The nature of the litigation, claim, or assessment

2. The progress of the case

3. Opinions or views of legal counsel and other advisers

4. Experience of the company in similar cases

5. Experience of other companies

6. Any decision of the company's management as to how the company intends to respond to the lawsuit, claim, or assessment

In discussing the above factors, the statement says: "The fact that legal counsel is unable to express an opinion that the outcome will be favorable to the enterprise should not necessarily be interpreted to mean that the condition for accrual of a loss . . . is met" [*Financial Accounting Standards Board Opinion No. 5 (1975)*].

It also states: "The filing of a suit or a formal assertion of a claim or assessment does not automatically indicate that accrual of a loss may be appropriate."

Unasserted claims and assessments should be evaluated in terms of the degree of probability that a cause of action will be brought against the company, the possibility of an unfavorable outcome, and the ability to estimate any loss.

If a company has been following conservative accounting practices in the past and has not gone overboard on reserves for litigation or pending or threatened claims, the net effect of FASB Statement No. 5 on the financial statements is not likely to be significant. The statement will be of substantial effect in some other areas—like reserves for product warranties. However, by spelling out all of this material in an accounting statement and reaching agreement with the lawyers as to how they should respond and what their duties are to the client, it is submitted that corporate counsel is going to have to give substantial attention to this subject.

There would seem to be a premium placed on central control or coordination of all litigation and unasserted claims. Someone should be able to discuss with the accountants all of the claims and all of the factors listed above. It would be imprudent, at best, to require, or even allow, the accountants to go to all of the lawyers who may be handling any affair for the company and make these inquiries on their own. Instead, it should all be channeled through either the general counsel or someone under his control. Beyond that, however, there are a number of unanswered questions. Consider the following problems:

1. Company counsel, pursuant to continued antitrust compliance programs, learns about some activities of company executives which may violate the antitrust laws and which, if known to the enforcement agencies, might cause them to bring suit.

2. Company counsel, while pursuing normal counseling in the EEO area, learns of a possible inequality in pay between males and females which has existed for a long time.

3. Patent counsel happens to come across a patent which no one has noticed before but which seems to cover some of the company's major products, and the company has no license under this patent.

A list of these kinds of problems could be endless. Discussion as to exactly what to do depends upon the attorney's assessment of the magnitude of the problem if all the facts were known. In addition, it would appear that the attorney is placed in a position of having to make at least some judgment on the likelihood of his client's transgressions being found out by someone in a position to institute a lawsuit.

In summary, it appears that both attorneys and their clients should take care to couch all sensitive communications in a form which would maximize the likelihood of their being privileged. This would include at least labeling written communications as privileged and restricting the distribution of documents to persons who would most likely fit the requirements of the privilege. However, it also seems clear that the attorney/client privilege is a thin strand by which to hold incriminating documents from the liberal discovery rules and that the best cure for this problem is prevention by not creating incriminating documents in the first place.

In those situations where the matter is so complicated that possibly incriminating facts must be written down simply to keep them straight or to express them clearly, there should be a tight control of these documents.

CHAPTER SIX

THE LAWYER
AND THE
COMPANY'S ETHICS

In today's complex world, it is painfully apparent to any realistic observer—lawyer or not—that many of the grossest kinds of fraudulent, immoral, dishonest, and illegal conduct—including violations of the SEC rules, antitrust violations, gross abuses of the tax laws, and out-and-out bribes or illegal political contributions through slush funds which were laundered through elaborate financial arrangements—have had some participation by lawyers. The kinds of elaborate schemes which were designed to camouflage the illegal activity—and the very complexity of the illegal activity itself—strongly suggest the involvement of a lawyer who had, at a minimum, closed his eyes to activity which he knew or should have known was patently illegal. The organized bar is certainly not unaware of this, and there have been a number of articles and investigations dealing with the general question of the duty owed by a lawyer to his client in the corporate context.

To put the matter in perspective, it should be observed that one of the better statements of the problem was contained in the *Harvard Law Review* of the year 1934. Mr. Justice Stone, at the dedication of the University of Michigan Law Quadrangle, acknowledged that:

> [W]hen we know and face the facts we shall have to acknowledge that such departures from the fiduciary principle do not usually occur without the active assistance of some member of our profession, and that their increasing recurrence would have been impossible but for the complaisance of the Bar . . . . without the constant advice and guidance of lawyers, business would come to an abrupt halt. And whatever standards of conduct in the performance of its function the Bar consciously adopts must at once be reflected in the character of the world of business and finance. [Stone, *The Public Influence of the Bar,* 48 HARV. L. REV. 1 (1934)]

It thus appears that the problems of 1934 were little different from the problems of today. If anything, Justice Stone's comments in 1934 regarding the legal complexity of business are even more true today than they were then.

Since lawyers are faced with this internal struggle, management should know some of the things which go through the mind of a lawyer when these troublesome questions are being dealt with.

We should assume for purposes of this discussion that we are talking about "gray areas." Overt legal participation in any kind of fraudulent scheme is excluded from the discussion. Unfortunately, the legal profession has its unscrupulous members just as does any other profession, but the subject of this discussion is the conscientious, ethical lawyer who, in many cases, finds himself torn between his duty to his client, his duty to his profession, and his own sense of personal ethics.

QUESTIONS

To oversimplify a very complex problem, there are two questions which each lawyer must address and answer for himself. There is no right or wrong answer, but most competent corporate counsel have addressed these questions and have at least some parameters under which they operate. The first question concerns the role which the lawyer should play, and the second question concerns the identity of the client.

What Role Should the Lawyer Play?

On the one hand, it can be argued that there is no way in which business can be better served by conscientious corporate counsel than by that counsel rendering the best possible legal advice to his clients. It can be further argued that any attempt by counsel to impose his own set of standards or ethics on the client is completely inappropriate. In fact, some go so far as to say that it is unethical for a lawyer to attempt to impose his own ideas about social, political, or economic morality on the client.

On the other hand, it can be argued with equal persuasion that a lawyer should act as an adviser in the broadest sense of the word, telling the client not only what is legal and what is not, but giving his advice as to what is "right" and what is "wrong." Those who hold this view say that even in cases where the client attempts to force the lawyer into a narrower role, the lawyer should continue to provide the broadest possible advice on not only the strict legal but also the ethical and moral issues of the problem.

Further complicating the situation is the fact that both lawyers and their clients are going to hold views on this subject, and if the views don't match, there is likely to be friction. This is especially true today, when there is much "social" legislation which is unclear and when almost all activity has an emotional, ethical, or moral overtone. As can be imagined, the views on the above question could greatly affect a lawyer's advice in the areas of employment discrimination, employment safety, product safety, the environment, and international boycotts.

Who Is the Client?

It seems to be fairly well agreed from a legal point of view that corporate counsel's client (whether inside or outside) is the corporate entity. Unfortunately, this is another one of those legal theories which seems to make very good sense but, unless one is willing to enshrine the corporate record book in a sacred hall and render advice to the certificate of incorporation, is a little difficult for lawyers to follow. When the lawyer renders advice, he must render it to or for someone, and the only available choices in this context are the corporate officers, the board of directors, or the shareholders. One can argue about which of these three is the client. However, as a practical matter, it is abundantly clear that all three are the client and must be considered. Lawyers cannot render advice which robs the shareholders and unjustly enriches the corporate officers or directors, but legal ethics have progressed far beyond this point, and almost all of counsel's advice is going to have to take into account the well-being of all of these groups because none of them can reap long-term benefits if any of the others is unduly prejudiced.

The area of officer and director liability is a prime example. Officer and director liability insurance is very expensive; legal fees are expensive; it is very expensive for the corporation to indemnify officers and directors against legal fees and possible judgments, but if this is not done, the corporation may not be able to attract good directors and officers and the shareholders would be prejudiced.

To extend the problem further, in today's climate, counsel must consider not only his corporate constituents but a number of other groups which may be involved. These include the community, the public, the company's employees, and, in some cases, the government or government agencies. To ignore these groups is to court unnecessary disaster in the form of labor problems, adverse public sentiment reflected in lost business, and reactive government regulation or legislation.

So long as the corporate ship is sailing in friendly waters, the lawyers shouldn't have any trouble with the fact that the client may consist of several different constituencies. However, when a storm hits, there can definitely be problems. Both lawyers and management should watch out for these problems. Some examples include a Clayton Act Section 8 case alleging that a member of the board of directors of the corporation also sits on the board of a competitor, a grand jury proceeding investigating alleged price fixing, a lawsuit seeking to recover illegal short-swing profits from an executive, and a tender-offer situation where the shareholders' interest is in obtaining the highest price for their stock while the executives' interest is in retaining their highly paid jobs. These are difficult cases. Neither management nor lawyers should let themselves be put in conflict situations simply because they are and always have been friends or it might be inconvenient or costly to get additional counsel. The only workable test is that if there is any conceivable factual development which could cause two parties to have conflicting objectives, the lawyer should not represent both of them. If an executive's individual interests might differ from those of the corporation, he should get his own lawyer.

FOREIGN OPERATIONS

If the company does business in another country, the legal and ethical responsibilities become even more complicated. There is absolutely no justification for imposing U.S. legal or ethical standards on anyone else. On the other hand, the mere fact that one happens to be doing business with or in another country does not justify compromising one's own moral values. There have been many high-sounding statements on this subject to the general effect that employees should act with the highest degree of ethics and should not pay any bribes. Unfortunately, in most cases, these statements do not really handle the problem because they fail to take into account the tremendous differences in law and ethics throughout the world. These kinds of statements are generally issued with the bribe problem in mind. There are very few countries, if any, in which it is legal to bribe public officials in order to get government business or to do business in that country. However, this rule which is aimed at the "clear case" fails to take into account the tremendous difference in many other laws where there are legitimate differences in opinion as to what is legal and what is ethical.

For example, if multinational companies were to saddle their foreign subsidiaries with all of the antitrust, employment–discrimination, employment–safety, product-safety, and other laws faced here in the United States, it is probably safe to say that many of those subsidiaries would shortly go out of business. Even more to the point, if one company does it and its competitors do not, the competitors will simply take over, and the shareholders, workers, and customers of the company will suffer.

Accordingly, the first step in analyzing one's international course of conduct must be to realize that ethics and legal concepts differ among nations and that the American way may not be the only way. On the other hand, it is equally clear that companies cannot and should not violate American laws or their own codes of ethics when transacting business overseas. In the end, they will have to make the same decision in the foreign country as they have to make in this country: Either engage in the objectionable conduct or give up the business. This is an age-old problem and will undoubtedly continue to exist in one form or another so long as there is a commercial world.

POLICY STATEMENTS

In addition to recognizing the pressures, sensitivities, and concerns that lawyers are going to have when management asks for advice in some of these touchy areas, management should also solicit legal assistance in providing some guidance for the company so that they can stay out of trouble.

One of the tools with which these problems can be dealt is the policy-statement.

Government Investigations

Sometimes, government investigators who are delving into some of the practices which disturb the public come to the company's facilities and want to talk individually with many of the company's top employees, some employees further down the chain of command, and, on some occasions, even secretaries. This procedure is totally uncalled for, and there is no reason why any corporation should sit still for it. A company, like an individual, has a right to know when it is being investigated, has a right to counsel, and has a right to defend itself, including requiring all government investigators to talk with company employees only upon prior notice, the ability of that employee to have counsel present if desired, and the ability of the company to have a representative at such conversations so it can independently know what was said to the government investigators. This is in no way an attempt to restrict the government investigation, to cover up, or to say the government cannot interview the employees. On the other hand, the Constitution does guarantee the right of due process of law, and the company counsel should insist upon this right.

It is, therefore, desirable to have a company policy statement on government investigations, stating that company employees should talk to government investigators only after certain due-process safeguards have been made available. On the other hand, the policy statement must be realistic, and company counsel cannot be expected to be present every time there is a normal EEO, OSHA, income tax, or GAO audit. The policy statement should be aimed at unusual investigations, or investigations where someone has reason to believe that the government suspects illegal conduct. There is a difference between a normal tax audit and a tax audit where there is suspicion of criminal tax evasion. A suggested form follows.

"It is the policy of our company to cooperate with governmental authorities in the proper performance of their functions in conducting investigations of our company or any other company or in gathering information and preparation for making a decision on whether or not to conduct such an investigation. However, it is important that all such inquiries be properly coordinated within the company and that any inquiries in connection with such an investigation or inquiry be handled in an orderly manner. Since government investigations are normally conducted pursuant to some applicable law, the general counsel of the company should immediately be informed when any employee is approached by any person conducting a government investigation. As used in this policy, 'investigation' means any nonroutine inquiry regarding a possible violation of any law by our company or any other company. It does not include routine government audits or compliance reviews.

"In order to insure proper coordination and the furnishing of accurate and complete information, as well as to safeguard the constitutionally guaranteed rights of the company and its employees, no information, whether oral or written, and no records or files of any nature should be furnished to any outside investigator in connection with any nonroutine inquiry except upon prior advice and approval of the general counsel.

"Employees are advised that criminal sanctions can be imposed upon any person submitting false or misleading information to the government in connection with any government investigation and that full coordination of any response in connection with any such investigation is essential from both corporate and individual viewpoints."

Depending upon the organization of the company, it might be desirable to include in the policy statement a more precise description of the kinds of activity which the policy statement covers and the kinds of activity which it does not cover. If this is desired, the following might be included in the statement:

1. This policy statement includes any requests for company information or documents in connection with any investigation by the Federal Bureau of Investigation, the Department of Justice, the Federal Trade Commission, the Equal Employment Opportunity Commission, the Securities and Exchange Commission or any other government department or agency. The statement also covers any request for information or testimony from any employee of the company in connection with any investigation whether that investigation is active, pending, or contemplated by any government agency. It also includes any Congressional investigation or Congressional inquiry.

2. This policy statement does not include information which does not involve the activities of the employee in his capacity as an employee (in other words, if the government is investigating the employee individually), nor does it cover routine government audits respecting past, present, or future performance under government contracts or proposals, nor the furnishing of routine reports to representatives of the Department of Labor in conjunction with affirmative-

action requirements or job-safety requirements. The company might also want to exclude tax audits because these might be covered under a specific policy (the company should have a separate policy for tax audits).

Political Contributions

The company should make a few basic decisions on political contributions and issue a policy statement because this is a frequently recurring area of trouble. The clearest one, of course, is that the company should use no corporate funds for any political contributions whatsoever. This, however, is only required at the federal level, and some states do allow corporations to use corporate funds for political contributions at the state or local level. This gets very complicated, and if a corporation desires to engage in this kind of activity, it definitely warrants heavy legal involvement because the state laws are complex and, in most cases, require, at the very least, elaborate reporting.

Legal and Ethical Conduct

It has become fashionable for companies to issue fairly lengthy statements on the legal and ethical conduct required of employees. There are a number of these statements in existence, some very short, merely stating that it is the policy of the company to comply fully with all of the laws governing its operations and to conduct its affairs in keeping with good moral, legal, and ethical standards, and some going on at great length. It is submitted, however, that whatever approach is taken in the basic policy statement, the statement should contain provisions on responsibility and enforcement.

As to responsibility, the policy should state that there is both a corporate obligation and an individual obligation to fulfill the intent of the policy. It might then go on to say that while it is not expected that every employee or every member of management will be fully informed of all laws, it is expected that all employees with significant responsibilities will have a general knowledge of the prohibited activities involved in their work and will seek guidance from their supervisors or the company's lawyers concerning a matter where there may be a question. The policy statement then may go on to say that the legal department is responsible for constant review and interpretation of the laws.

As to enforcement, the policy statement may specify that the law department of the company is responsible for educating the employees as to their legal obligations and answering any questions which may arise as to what those legal obligations are. The policy statement should also specify that the law department can, on its own initiative, conduct such reviews or examinations as it feels should be made and make periodic reports to the chief executive officers of the company and the board of directors with respect to the status of enforcement of the policy throughout the company.

The company's managers should also be given certain responsibilities in this area, including the responsibility to communicate the policy, inform the company lawyers of any potential problems, warn employees with respect to any acts which may lead to violations, and initiate any educational programs which may be appropriate.

As a practical matter, it is a little difficult to ascertain what use a policy statement on legal and ethical conduct would have other than to facilitate reviews of company conduct and to make responsibility for the legal and ethical conduct of the company's employees a little clearer. A reissuance of a policy already stated in the past might serve to bring everyone's attention to it and might therefore help to avoid some problems. The principal motive in issuing this kind of a policy, however, seems to be political. There are so many companies coming out with these kinds of statements that it appears to be a little unpatriotic *not* to come out with one; and in today's antibusiness political atmosphere, it is sometimes feared, with some justification, that the failure to make a legal and ethical policy statement means that the company and its employees will not act legally and ethically. While this is admittedly a deplorable state of affairs, it is a practical factor which counsel should consider in deciding whether or not to recommend such a policy.

Conflicts of Interest

Another useful policy statement is one on conflict of interest. This is a legitimate concern of all employees of the company because it is unrealistic in today's liberated society to assume that all employees are going to devote their entire lives solely to their existing employer. Indeed, some of the company's best employees are likely to be the ones who are energetic and personally motivated enough to conduct activities on their own. Accordingly, a policy statement on conflict of interest which states the company's position is justified and useful.

The policy statement should deal with the question of outside business or other activity of the employees. The general approach here is to say that the company does not object to outside business activities provided that the outside activity does not lessen the efficiency of the employee or affect his impartiality or judgment in any company transactions.

The company may then want to spell out certain other activities which would be against company policy. Certainly divulging of company confidential information, purchasing or selling company stock or securities based on inside information, borrowing money from competitors or customers, and purchasing stock in competitive companies (other than minor amounts of publicly traded companies) would be against company policy. The difficult provision comes in a prohibition against the acceptance of gifts, entertainment, or other favors by an employee or members of his family from present or prospective competitors, customers, or suppliers. The easiest thing to do, of course, is to make an outright prohibition. This, however, can sometimes be a little unrealistic, and it can inhibit useful relationships as well as create embarrassing situations. Again, it is the lunches and dinners and perhaps other related entertainment which create the problem.

There should be an outright prohibition against company employees accepting any money or any tangible products from competitors or customers because there is no reason for this. Even the traditional Christmas gifts in the form of single bottles of liquor, boxes of candy, and fruit cakes are frowned upon in today's business climate, and almost all companies have policies against them. However, if a representative of a supplier comes to the plant in the morning to discuss a major transaction and the discussion progresses through lunch, it would seem unwarranted to assume that if a company employee lets the vendor pay for the lunch, his impartiality is going to be compromised. The same thing could be said with respect to dinner meetings.

A policy statement on this subject should also specify the employees to whom it applies. It does not make much sense to restrict the items which the purchasing people in the company can accept and then allow the people in the sales area to offer gifts to other companies' purchasers. This, unfortunately, is the state of affairs at most companies.

It is submitted that one reasonably palatable approach is that of the National Association of Purchasing Management, whose statement on the standards and ethics of buying and selling includes the following two provisions:

A. To provide or accept no gifts or entertainment in the guise of sales expenses where the intent or effect is to unduly prejudice the recipients in favor of the donor as against legitimate competitors.

B. To give or receive no bribes, in the form of money or otherwise, in any commercial transaction and to expose commercial bribery wherever encountered for the purpose of maintaining the highest standard of ethics in the industry.

It should be noted that the policy makes a distinction between a bribe in the form of money or otherwise (which is completely prohibited) and gifts or entertainment (which is only prohibited where there is an intent or effect to prejudice the recipient). Admittedly, this is a little imprecise because of the ambiguity of the words "intent or effect," and as a logical matter, it could probably be strongly argued that the salesman would not buy the purchaser lunch or dinner unless he felt that it would help him somehow—even if only by making the purchaser as friendly toward him as he is toward his competitor, who bought the purchaser lunch or dinner yesterday. However, a rule of reason does have to be considered, and the statement of the National Association of Purchasing Management seems to be a good one.

Foreign Policy Statements

Since it appears that much illegal or unethical activity has taken place overseas, a company should make sure that its policy statement includes all of its operations, both domestic and foreign. On the other hand, it is imprudent and perhaps misleading and illegal to draft one policy which is appropriate in this country and then simply publish it everywhere in the world. For example, a policy statement on U.S. government investigations which is at all specific would be meaningless and confusing in England or France because of the differing laws and differing enforcement agencies there. In addition, most policy statements provide for disciplinary action or dismissal if there is a clear violation, but in some countries, employees cannot be disciplined or discharged without using appropriate legal procedures or negotiating with the union. Even more fundamental, if the statement goes beyond legal requirements and is fairly stringent in the areas of moral and ethical conduct, there is always the danger of one country trying to impose its set of ethics and morals on another.

AUDIT COMMITTEE

Some years ago, it became fashionable to increase the outside director representation on boards of directors and to have one or more committees for specific tasks. In almost all situations, one of these committees was a so-called "audit committee." This committee was supposed to consist principally of outside directors and to ask the right questions of the right people to assure that the company's financial situation was presented fairly to the investing public. With the recent disclosure of illegal or immoral payments, the functions of many audit committees have been expanded to cover this area also. It would seem to be good practice for any company which has not already established such a committee to consider doing so.

EDUCATION

While the reason escapes us, it does appear that there are many people in this country occupying relatively high positions in corporations who are completely oblivious to what is going on around them in the areas discussed above. Given the amount of publicity these kinds of things have had, it is a little difficult to see how a company lawyer can further educate anybody who remains ignorant at this time. However, consideration should be given to the subject of education. Sometimes the problem may be a failure of communication where the offending people in the company do not really believe that they are not supposed to make political contributions, when requested, to candidates for federal office who may be in a position to do them some good or entertain Defense Department people lavishly when a good deal of the company's business is conducted in the area of defense. If such a failure of communication exists, it might be desirable for top people in the company to state expressly and clearly to the people involved that both the law and company policy really do mean these things.

ENFORCEMENT

If there is one single pitfall in this whole area which could cause all of the efforts of the company's lawyers and management to be of no avail, it is a significant violation of a law or principle of ethical conduct which is discovered by the company management and not acted upon. Persons who do not abide by the company's policies and the law must be disciplined. A second problem is having no provisions for auditing performance or ascertaining what is going on. The days when management and its counsel could sit in their offices and wait for problems to be presented are gone. It is necessary to have some kind of audit procedure, by whatever name the company desires to use, in order to specifically address this problem by direct questions to appropriate company people regarding fundamental legal and ethical points and further examination of the books and records and files of the company at least on a spot-check basis to ascertain that no significant violations are taking place.

RECORD KEEPING

Record keeping is always a problem when it is coupled with questions relating to business morality. There appears to be some school of thought to the general effect that there is nothing at all wrong with rather lavish entertainment of Department of Defense people so long as you do not put their names on your expense account. Counsel should address this problem and, it is submitted, take a rather hard line. If anyone is spending money which they would not like the government to find out about, they should be instructed to cease spending it. It should be noted that this is a significant problem because the general practice in industry and in the government seems to be to extend the no-name record-keeping philosophy to lunches, dinners, and all other forms of entertainment; and Department of Defense people themselves have been known to raise the question of whether or not the lunch is going to go on the contractor's expense account. As a legal proposition, however, there is absolutely no way a lawyer can justify any expenses by different criteria depending on what records are kept.

SECTION TWO: TRADE REGULATION

INTRODUCTION

Chapters 7 to 24 will deal with antitrust and trade-regulation problems. This introduction will set forth the general rules and areas of concern as an overview of the subject.

The following are the principal statutory rules involved in most antitrust problems:

1. Section 1 of the Sherman Act provides that every contract, combination in the form of trust or otherwise, or conspiracy, in restraint of trade or commerce among the several states, or with foreign nations, is illegal. Section 1 is the basic antitrust law. It prohibits any form of consensual activity between competitors or between manufacturers or sellers and their distributors which has the effect of lessening competition.

2. Section 2 of the Sherman Act provides that every person who shall monopolize, or attempt to monopolize, or combine or conspire with any other person or persons to monopolize any part of the trade or commerce among the several states or with foreign nations shall be deemed guilty of a felony.

3. Section 3 of the Clayton Act makes it unlawful to sell products on the condition that the purchaser will not purchase products of a competitor.

4. Section 4 of the Clayton Act allows a person injured by a violation of any antitrust law to collect treble damages and attorneys' fees from the violator in a private suit.

5. Section 7 of the Clayton Act provides that certain mergers are illegal where the effect of the merger may be to lessen competition in any line of commerce.

6. Section 8 of the Clayton Act makes certain interlocking directorates unlawful.

7. The Robinson-Patman Act is found in section 2 of the Clayton Act and prohibits discriminations in price.

8. The principal provision of the Federal Trade Commission Act is section 5, which prohibits any unfair method of competition. Any conduct which violates any antitrust law would also violate section 5 of the Federal Trade Commission Act. However, section 5 is much broader than the antitrust laws and is generally used in cases involving (1) conduct which violates the spirit or intention of an antitrust law but probably is not illegal under the current laws or where prosecution under existing laws would be difficult because of some technical problem, or (2) conduct which the Federal Trade Commission feels is unfair to the consumer. (False or misleading advertising cases fall into this category.)

Most antitrust questions involve a violation of more than one of the above statutes. The only significant difference in the impact of the above laws is that section 5 of the Federal Trade Commission Act is not considered an antitrust law. The significance of this is that a violation of section 5 does not give rise to any private cause of action, and a judgment in favor of the government under section 5 of the Federal Trade Commission Act is not prima facie evidence of any violation of the antitrust laws in a subsequent private suit. (Section 5 of the Clayton Act provides that any judgment in favor of the government under the antitrust laws that a defendant has violated said laws is prima facie evidence against such defendant in a subsequent civil action.)

With the exception of section 5 of the Federal Trade Commission Act, which can only be used by the government, all of the antitrust laws may be enforced by either the government or a private litigant or both. On the government side, the agencies involved are the Federal Trade Commission and the Department of Justice. If the government brings a suit, the possible remedies are fines and imprisonment. If a private litigant sues, the remedy is the collection of treble damages and attorneys' fees. An injunction or other equitable relief is also a possible remedy for both the government and a private litigant.

In a considerable number of government cases, the outcome is a consent decree, where the defendant makes no admissions of any illegal conduct but agrees on the course of action satisfactory to the government. The consent-decree procedure minimizes the exposure of the defendant in future private litigation. Recently instituted procedures have, however, complicated the process.

CHAPTER SEVEN

CRIMINAL ANTITRUST VIOLATIONS

Antitrust is one of the few areas in which a business executive's carelessness can result in criminal indictment and perhaps conviction.

The principles of antitrust law set forth in this chapter must constantly be kept in mind. A single indiscretion—perhaps after a few drinks with business executives at a trade-association meeting—can cause serious problems.

The antitrust principles discussed in subsequent chapters—those involving distributorships, the Robinson-Patman Act, mergers, and other areas of business planning—are also important; however, in almost all cases these kinds of problems will arise in a situation where the business executive can consult his lawyer and adequately plan his actions. In addition, violations of these other rules do not generally result in criminal sanctions.

Criminal antitrust violations are agreements with competitors—express or implied—which restrict competition. Sometimes they are referred to as "horizontal restraints of trade." (Vertical restraints of trade deal with the chain of distribution.) This kind of activity with a competitor—or indeed any communication between competitors—should immediately raise the red flag of antitrust.

By far the most important statute under the antitrust laws is section 1 of the Sherman Act, which states:

> Every contract, combination in the form of trust or otherwise, or conspiracy, in restraint of trade or commerce among the several states, or with foreign nations, is declared to be illegal.

The statute draws no distinction between vertical and horizontal restraints; however, this distinction is one of the most important in the antitrust laws, and most lawyers tend to make the distinction. In the area of horizontal restraints of trade—the criminal violations—by far the most important is price-fixing. This is followed by agreements relating to market division or group boycotts, or agreements among competitors allocating territories or customers or limiting production.

In order for a horizontal restraint of trade to be a violation of section 1 of the Sherman Act, certain elements must be present.

1. There must be at least two persons acting in concert. This indeed is the essence of the violation. One person acting unilaterally cannot violate section 1 of the Sherman Act.

2. The restraint involved must affect interstate trade or commerce. Under current rules, almost any conceivable form of economic activity will satisfy this requirement. It is, therefore, of little importance for planning. It should be noted that the test is only that the activity must *affect* interstate commerce. This is the most all-inclusive of all tests under the government's power under the commerce clause of the Constitution. Accordingly, business executives should assume that any activity will affect interstate commerce unless the activity in question has been clearly evaluated by legal counsel and a contrary determination has been made.

3. The restraint must be unreasonable. The Sherman Act does not forbid all trade restraints, only those which are unreasonable. However, the reasonableness question has developed its own special set of rules. There are some restraints which the courts have determined are so inherently bad that they will be deemed unlawful restraints without any inquiry by the court into whether the restraint actually had any effect on commerce, was necessary for business purposes, or was otherwise justified. It is usually said that these restraints are unreasonable "per se" or that they are "per se violations" of the Sherman Act. Generally, any activity which even remotely tampers with the price structure will fall into this category. Also included are market divisions, agreements among competitors to restrict or allocate production, and group boycotts. As to other agreements which restrain trade, the rule of reason applies. This means that if the alleged combination contract or conspiracy involves something besides a per se violation, the court will look to all of the relevant facts to determine whether or not the restraint is unlawful. The following quotation from Justice Brandeis in the *Chicago Board Trade* case (decided in 1918) illustrates the type of considerations which might be relevant and is still the best statement of the law on the rule of reason:

> Every agreement concerning trade, every regulation of trade, restrains. To bind, to restrain, is of their very essence. The true test of legality is whether the restraint imposed is such as merely regulates and perhaps thereby promotes competition or whether it is such as may suppress or even destroy competition. To determine that question the court must ordinarily consider the facts peculiar to the business to which the restraint is applied; its condition before and after the restraint was imposed; the nature of the restraint and its effect, actual or probable. The history of the restraint, the evil believed to exist, the reason for adopting the particular remedy, the purpose or end sought to be attained, are all relevant facts. This is not because a good intention will save an otherwise objectionable regulation or the reverse; but because knowledge of intent may help the court to interpret facts and to predict consequences. [*Chicago Bd. of Trade v. United States*, 246 U.S. 231 (1918)]

The rule of reason approach will not be discussed in this chapter because criminal sanctions are generally imposed only when the activities of business executives fall within the per se violations. Restrictions which are analyzed under the rule of reason approach are potentially very serious antitrust problems because they can involve extremely large lawsuits with a great deal of exposure in terms of both legal fees and monetary judgments against the company. They do not, however, usually result in criminal indictments against the individuals involved because, by its very nature, the rule of reason approach is subjective, and the courts are not going to put business executives in jail for having guessed wrong on whether or not a particular activity or agreement was "reasonable." On the other hand, the basic per se violations of the Sherman Act have been well established for 50 years or more, and the courts are not going to listen to any arguments that a business executive "did not know the activity in question was illegal."

Before proceeding to the specific kinds of conduct which can put one in jail, it is appropriate to say a few words about the central ingredient in all of them—a conspiracy.

Unfortunately, many business executives have a stereotyped image of a conspiracy as something that takes place in a smoke-filled room and is accompanied by little black books kept under lock and key at all times, registration in hotels using fictitious names, and letters containing statements like "destroy this letter immediately after reading." This misconception is one of the chief causes for trouble under the Sherman Act. A conspiracy, within the meaning of the antitrust laws, can be nothing more than a tacit agreement to go along with a suggestion. Furthermore, the agreement need not be expressed verbally or in writing; it can be implied.

Classic examples of antitrust cases involving conspiracies are cases brought by the government where the only evidence is that a trade-association meeting was held where a participant discussed prices. This may be the only hard piece of evidence in the government's case. If the government can show that a number of competitors attended a trade-association meeting where any one of the competitors discussed price, it will have enough information to get the case to the jury on whether or not the other members attending that trade-association meeting agreed on the price discussion. Furthermore, the discussion on prices does not even have to relate to specific prices. In one recent case, a number of supermarket executives were indicted for price-fixing when one member of a trade association stated at a meeting that he thought wholesale meat prices should be kept low and retail prices should be kept high. There was no evidence of any specific agreement as to specific prices, and there was not even any evidence that other members of the trade association agreed with this speaker. Many times, subsequent facts which may be totally unrelated to the discussion in question will serve to incriminate the participants. For example, if, after the trade-association meeting, wholesale meat prices tended to go down or to remain low while retail prices tended to go up or remain high, this would be a substantial piece of evidence in the government's case and would probably, along with the statement by the participant in the trade-association meeting, be enough for the government to obtain indictments.

Another source of possible conspiracies are social gatherings, golf outings, or any other setting where competitors meet. For example, golf outings where executives of competing companies play golf together can serve as the basis for a conspiracy even if the conversation among them is as general as one member of the outing suggesting that it would be in all parties' best interests to raise prices or to refrain from cutting prices. There need not be any specific agreement or specific reference to the amount of a price increase or price reduction. In the same context, a suggestion by one of the members of the group that it would be good business practice for each of the companies to stay within its own territories could also serve as the basis for a conspiracy under the antitrust laws.

PRICE-FIXING

Price-fixing includes any activity which tampers with the price structure. It includes any activity which is directed at stabilizing prices, even though downward. Fixing maximum prices is equally unlawful. A violation exists when any element of the price is agreed upon, as in the *Plymouth Dealers'** case, for example, where the sticker price was agreed upon—even though it was shown that substantial bargaining and, therefore, competition existed because the actual selling price of the automobiles was always below the sticker price. The per se rule also applies to incidentals of the price, such as trading stamps. An agreement among competitors not to give trading stamps would be a violation. An agreement not to advertise prices would also be a per se violation. The minimum-fee schedules used by many professionals, such as lawyers and real estate brokers, also are illegal price-fixing conspiracies under the antitrust laws. This latter area, however, should be distinguished because at least until someone can show an actual agreement among some specific people, it is unlikely that lawyers, real estate brokers, or anyone else adhering to a minimum-fee schedule would be thrown into jail. They would, however, be leaving themselves open to costly antitrust litigation and injunctions or civil penalties.

MARKET DIVISION

Another per se violation of the Sherman Act is the division of markets. This includes both geographic markets and product markets. Generally, it is unlawful to agree with a competitor that he will sell in one group of states and not in another or that he will sell in one group of states and you will sell in another. It has been held unlawful to agree that one company will sell in the United States and another will sell abroad. An agreement by one company to refrain from entering a particular product market is also a violation of the antitrust laws. For example, if the executives of two auto-parts manufacturers were to get together and even mention the desirability of the company that makes one part not making another part, this would probably be sufficient to get a case to a jury on whether or not there was an implied conspiracy by the companies to stay within their own product markets.

CUSTOMER ALLOCATIONS

Just as it is unlawful to divide markets, it is unlawful to divide customers. If competing companies get together and decide that one company will sell to specific customers or to specific groups of customers and the other will sell to other companies or other types of companies, a clear violation would be present.

GROUP BOYCOTTS

A group boycott can occur when, for example, someone does something "bad." (A wholesaler may sell in competition with his retailer, or a "style pirate" may take the original designs of others and mass-produce them.) Others in the industry then get upset and decide not to do business with the "maverick." It is clear, from a theoretical standpoint, that if each other corporation inde-

---

* *Plymouth Dealers' Ass'n of N. Cal. v. United States,* 279 F.2d 128 (1960). The case arose before the current practice of placing the sticker on the car by the manufacturer.

pendently and unilaterally makes the decision, there is no group boycott. However, that rarely is the case. There is usually a "blacklist" of some kind, or an agreement through the industry trade association, or some other fact which allows a finding of an agreement, which of course gives rise to a per se violation.

Another possibility in the group-boycott area is that a powerful retailer will request his suppliers to refrain from doing business with his competitors. If the suppliers go along, an unlawful group boycott arises, even if only selected products or product lines were involved in the boycott.

In summary, any activity among competitors which amounts to an agreement to refrain from vigorous competition in the area of prices, territories, customers, or products is something which, if found out by the government, is very likely to give rise to criminal antitrust indictments against the individuals involved. In today's antibusiness climate, this is indeed a serious and foreboding possibility. The possibility of trial by press is always present. The ease with which the government can get the case to a jury raises all of the problems of the present social prejudice against business. Accordingly, the brevity of this chapter should not deceive the reader as to its importance. Indeed, it is perhaps the most important chapter in the book. It should be read very carefully and reread at periodic intervals. It should also be read along with the chapter on trade associations (Chapter 8) and the chapter on antitrust compliance programs (Chapter 24), where the same message is set forth. If a business executive has even the slightest doubt as to the propriety of his actions, he should immediately consult with counsel and discuss the matter thoroughly. If the business executive has been a party to the kinds of conversations described above, he should give careful consideration to documenting his lack of any agreement with any competitor. This, however, should only be done after thorough and careful consultation with competent antitrust counsel.

CHAPTER EIGHT

TRADE ASSOCIATIONS: ANTITRUST

Trade associations perform a useful function for their members and for society in that:

1. A substantial amount of beneficial self-regulation can be done by the industry itself without cost to the taxpayer and without unwarranted government intervention in private business.
2. A substantial amount of generally beneficial standardization and safety development can be done by trade associations without taxpayer expense or government intervention.

FORUM FOR ANTICOMPETITIVE ACTIVITY

On the other hand, trade associations can also provide a forum for anticompetitive activity, including:

1. Informal discussions between competitors who gather together at trade-association meetings
2. Various kinds of formal trade-association activity which can be used anticompetitively, including anticompetitive membership restrictions, anticompetitive programs involving certification of products (generally from a safety or quality point of view) and standards setting, and joint research and development

The starting point for analysis of trade-association activity from an antitrust point of view begins with the following propositions:

1. Generally, there is no restriction against competitors joining together in a trade association to further their interests or provide service to their members.

2. Section 1 of the Sherman Act condemns any agreement between competitors which unreasonably restrains trade, and there is no exception for trade associations. That is, any agreement among competitors which unreasonably restrains trade will be a violation of the antitrust laws even if it is done under the shelter of a trade association.

Informal Discussions

The problem here involves informal discussions among members of the association either before or after the formal part of the meeting. At this stage of development of the antitrust law, most business executives are aware that they may not use trade-association get-togethers as occasions for price-fixing, territory allocation, customer allocation, or other anticompetitive agreements. The best protection here is good antitrust education for all company people who attend trade-association get-togethers. However, the problem may arise on less formal occasions, and so all company people who have occasion to meet with competitors socially should be instructed in at least the rudiments of antitrust law, especially in the hard-core area, and should have the presence of mind to know when to excuse themselves from any discussions in these areas.

It is widely known that almost all government lawyers—and many private lawyers—are suspicious of trade-association meetings and other meetings of competitors, and at the slightest hint of any kind of collusion among competitors about prices, the government will subpoena the records of all those people who might have attended various trade-association meetings. Perhaps at one of these meetings there was an after-hours party in a small room where a group of competitors got together and where some of those present discussed prices. If this matter comes to light months or even years later, it will be very difficult to recollect exactly who said what. In many cases, the only thing that will be at all clear is who attended the meeting or gathering. Here, it is possible for a business executive who was not involved in the discussion to be indicted along with a group of other people on a criminal price-fixing charge.

Recently, some supermarket executives were held to have violated the Sherman Act on the basis of a trade-association meeting where one of them made a speech to the effect that it was time to stop passing lower wholesale meat prices on to consumers. The court found a conspiracy to keep wholesale prices low and retail prices high, even though there had not been any discussion of specific prices or any overt agreement. The mere mention of prices was sufficient for the case to be presented to a jury, which found an implied agreement.

It is sobering to think that an executive may, by merely attending a trade-association meeting, wind up as a defendant in a criminal antitrust price-fixing case. However, the possibility cannot be overlooked, and counsel must advise all executives on a proper course of conduct. This advice may be a warning not to attend any trade-association meetings or it may be a suggestion that the executive spill a glass of water on the table and stomp out whenever any conversation about prices takes place. The most reasonable approach is for the executive to be aware of the problem at all times and to obtain a reputation among associates and competitors that he will, under no circumstances, engage in any conversations regarding prices or make any agreements with competitors. This will obviously not eliminate the problem, but it will minimize it. If the matter comes to light months or years later, the participants may not remember exactly who said what to whom, but they will remember that this particular executive certainly would not have been a party to any of these kinds of discussions.

Formal Trade-Association Activity

No company should permit its people to belong to any trade association which is not represented by adequate antitrust counsel. Executives should be especially careful of new associations which use unknown attorneys who may not have had a great deal of antitrust experience. Before permitting any company employee to join a trade association, it is a good idea for company counsel to look at the basic documents under which the association acts— generally articles of association and/or bylaws. Also, company counsel should have the name of the legal firm representing the association and should satisfy himself as to its antitrust capability. Company employees who belong to a trade association should be informed of the potential problems which membership may cause the company. Appropriate procedures should be provided for them to get legal advice informally at an early stage if they see anything which looks questionable to them. Employees belonging to trade associations should be allowed and encouraged to consult with company counsel directly at the first sign of any questionable activity. Most of the larger trade associations have been around for a long time and are quite adequately represented by established firms with a high degree of antitrust capability. However, it is very dangerous to assume that this fact alone makes exposure impossible.

Anticompetitive Membership Restrictions

If there are ten companies in an industry, and the membership requirements of a trade association are such that nine of them are eligible and one is not, the one that is not eligible is obviously prejudiced. This, however, is generally not a problem if the membership criteria are valid. Valid criteria include the size of the firm, the length of time the firm has been in business, the functional level—manufacturing, wholesaling, or retailing—and the geographical area.

However, all of these criteria must be applied reasonably. For example, if the company must be of a certain size to use the benefits of the association or to contribute to it, that is a valid criterion. Otherwise, size may be used to further entrench the dominant firms or impede additional competition. If used for that purpose, it would obviously not be an acceptable criterion.

Further, the degree of prejudice to the excluded member is highly relevant. In many cases, membership in a particular trade association is absolutely essential if a firm expects to compete effectively; in many other situations, membership provides such a distinct advantage as to lessen substantially the ability of a company to compete without it. An example of a very important membership is that of a realtor in a local board of realtors which allows members to participate in multiple property listings. Another example is the membership of a florist in an association which allows the filling of intercity orders.

Basically, there are two types of problems here. The first is defining the criteria for membership in such a way that even though they are applied uniformly, there is an anticompetitive effect. Again, an example would be the florist area. If membership in the association allowing the filling of inter-city orders were denied to florists who were located in supermarkets or who were not situated at street level, the requirement would be held anticompeti-tive if not otherwise justified. Generally, if the association provides an impor-tant competitive advantage, provisions which exclude those competing in the relevant market will be highly suspect and must be justified on some reason-able and legitimate business basis.

The other problem is membership requirements which specifically exclude competitors. For example, it would be questionable for a floral wire service to exclude members who belong to any other wire service, restrict its member-ship to one firm in any one city, or have restrictions against the admittance of a competitor of any of its members. Also, if competitors have jointly created a valuable property right or an organization that gives them a competitive advantage over other, nonmember, competitors, denial of membership can amount to an unreasonable restraint of trade. Furthermore, a refusal of the association or its members to make the advantage available to nonmembers has been held to be anticompetitive. A prime example is the *Associated Press* case, wherein the Supreme Court held that the refusal of the AP to make its material available to nonmember newspapers and restriction of member-ship in the AP constituted unreasonable restraints in violation of the Sherman Act.

Membership requirements should be specific and administered evenhand-edly. Problems will almost always result if membership is left to the discretion of a committee.

Seals of Approval and Standardization

The following portions of a speech by a Department of Justice official sets forth the present state of the law on seals of approval as well as the views of the Department of Justice:

> Some trade associations may also have seals of approval which are of great commercial value, because products bearing those seals are generally recognized to meet certain minimum levels of safety, quality, and the like. Also, local ordinances may prohibit the use of products which do not bear the seal or comply with a private trade association safety standard. Certainly, membership in these trade associations and access to the seals of approval may have substantial economic importance.
>
> Trade associations having this kind of economic clout should take some care to insure that the standards they set have been subjected to a wide cross-section of review by members of the industry involved. Both large and small producers should have the opportunity to participate in the standards-making process. I would also suggest that the users of a product be given the opportunity to present their views before standards are imposed.
>
> Also, access to the association's testing procedure and its seal of approval should be made available to all interested manufacturers, be they foreign or domestic, on a reasonable and non-discriminatory basis. Courts have held that where competi-tors have jointly created a valuable property right or organization that gives them a competitive advantage over other non-member competitors, and denial of that membership amounts to a significant limitation on non-member firms and their ability to compete, such denial can amount to an unreasonable restraint of trade.
>
> [Clearwaters, "Trade Associations and the Antitrust Laws—A View from the Justice Department" (March 21, 1973)]

Joint Research and Development

The current view of the Department of Justice is that joint research by com-petitors is suspect and is not any less suspect if it is done through a trade association. Generally, the views are as set forth in Chapter 9, "Other Activity between Competitors."

FORECLOSURE OF BENEFITS TO NONMEMBERS

An association which, under its bylaws, is established to promote an entire industry must, under the antitrust laws, really do so. The antitrust laws are to associations what the civil-rights laws are to individuals. Accordingly, even assuming that a trade association's membership requirements pass muster, there still must be consideration given to what benefits the trade association must make available to nonmembers. The most cited examples are the gathering and dissemination of statistical information and participation at trade shows. There is a kind of a sliding scale of legality. If the membership requirements are such that any company can join, there is less need to make the benefits available to nonmembers. On the other hand, if membership is limited, consideration must be given to allowing nonmember competitors to obtain the benefits of the trade association's statistical surveys and trade shows.

Certainly, however, the members of the association are not required to give away the benefits which they have paid money (through their dues) to obtain. It is, therefore, possible to make the benefits of the association available to nonmembers at a higher cost than to members. For example, if participation in a trade show costs members 100 dollars, nonmembers may be charged 150 dollars if that difference is reasonably justified by the administrative costs in setting up the show.

One must also be aware of possible tying problems. For example, it would probably be held illegal to attempt to force all competitors to join the association by tying association membership to participation in important association trade shows. A similar rule would be applicable to obtaining a seal of approval from an industry association. The seal would probably have to be made reasonably available to nonmembers as well as members, and it would probably be insufficient to say that membership in the association was open to all.

CHAPTER NINE

OTHER ACTIVITY
BETWEEN COMPETITORS

In addition to the criminal antitrust violations and trade-association problems discussed in the immediately preceding chapters, there are a number of activities between competitors which can give rise to antitrust problems. Indeed, any communication among competitors should raise the red flag of antitrust for business managers, and they should be sure to get proper legal advice.

COMMUNICATIONS BETWEEN COMPETITORS

Communications between competitors are always a problem, and since communication is the purpose of a trade-association meeting, trade associations provide one of the biggest single antitrust problems. Besides trade associations, however, there are a number of other areas where communications between competitors can cause a problem and where there is at least some agreement among antitrust lawyers as to the issues if not as to how to solve the problems. The best solution is to avoid unsupervised messages to competitors. This, however, is not always practical. Therefore, the persons who usually make such communications should be encouraged to check with counsel periodically and should be educated about the most significant problems.

There is a continuing debate among practitioners over whether all communications should be formal, including written memorandums of telephone conversations, or whether permanent documents should be avoided. According to one school, formal documents are best because no one can then question precisely what was said or done; according to another school, oral communications are best because written communications only serve to point up problems and sometimes come back to haunt the parties involved.

Another debate is over whether there is anything improper about exchanging price lists or catalogs containing prices with one's competitors. Such exchange is certainly improper if it takes place before the price list is announced. If it takes place *after* it is announced, it is technically not objectionable, but it can certainly give rise to the implication of an agreement or understanding relating to prices. Because of the implication and the adverse feelings the practice might create in the minds of a judge or jury, most counselors advise against these exchanges. If the price list is public and a competitor calls and asks for one, some counselors feel there is no problem in supplying it, while others object. This is not a matter of legality versus illegality, unless, of course, some larger scheme is involved. Naturally, there is no reason why a competitor should not obtain your price list (or you his) through normal channels, which might mean picking up a copy from a distributor who handles both lines.

Price-list information of a general nature should be distinguished from information on the particular prices charged individual customers. In no case should a company ask for, or divulge to a competitor, specific price information. The Supreme Court has even held that exchanging price information with a competitor in order to use the "meeting competition" defense under the Robinson-Patman Act is illegal. You must find some other way to verify the competitor's price besides direct communication.

JOINT ACTIVITY BY COMPETITORS

Another potential problem involving horizontal restraints is joint activity by competitors. The following excerpts from a letter by Thomas E. Kauper, Assistant Attorney General in charge of the Antitrust Division, illustrate the potential problems and the Department of Justice attitude in several instances of joint activity by competitors. (Letter dated March 28, 1973, written in response to inquiry from Paul W. Hallman, Deputy Director of the Bureau of Product Safety relating to the match industry.)

We are of the opinion . . . the antitrust laws in general would (not) raise any legal obstacles to a joint advertising plan limited solely to warning the public of the safety hazards connected with matches.

The second proposal contemplates that the members of the industry would jointly develop voluntary safety standards for matches and matchbooks. Section 1 of the Sherman Act prohibits concerted actions which may unreasonably restrain trade or commerce. Therefore, the critical question as to whether joint efforts by the match manufacturers to establish voluntary safety standards would violate the antitrust laws is whether the actual standards developed unreasonably restrained trade or commerce. Efforts by the match manufacturers to jointly develop safety standards, in and of themselves, would not violate the . . . antitrust laws. However, until the standards are developed, it is of course impossible for us to determine whether the standards might unreasonably restrain trade. We can, on the other hand, venture certain suggestions which, if adhered to, would lessen the likelihood that the standards would raise serious competitive problems.

The standards should not arbitrarily disadvantage any group of manufacturers. This danger may be lessened if all segments of the industry as well as interested persons outside of the industry are provided the opportunity to participate in the development of the proposed standard. Whenever possible, the standards should be drafted with reference to "performance" rather than design specifications. The use of "performance" standards allows manufacturers to innovate and seek more efficient methods of achieving the goal of the standard—in this case, improved safety. No attempt should be made to coerce compliance with any voluntary standard. Such action by manufacturers would amount to a private abrogation of public power in violation of the antitrust laws. Finally, it must be stressed that any attempt to use the voluntary standards as part of a price-fixing, market allocation, or other anticompetitive scheme, would violate . . . the antitrust laws . . .

The third course of action contemplated would involve joint industry presentations of technical information and advice to the Bureau to assist the Bureau in developing mandatory safety standards . . . The antitrust laws (do not) prevent the match manufacturers from consulting jointly with a government agency for the purpose of assisting the latter to develop safety standards. The Department believes, however, that the Bureau when attempting to determine the present state of the art or the technical feasibility of a standard should discuss such matters with the manufacturers on an individual basis rather than with the industry as a whole. By acting in this manner the Bureau might find that, by considering a variety of viewpoints, it can develop its mandatory standards from a broader database. . . .

Whether an industry-wide joint research effort would unreasonably restrain competition in innovation depends upon an assessment of a number of factual considerations particular to the specific joint research effort. The magnitude of the research problem must be assessed in relation to the individual research capabilities of the members of the industry and the structure of the industry. The effect of the joint research on the opportunities of independent inventors and the incentives of the members of the joint venture must also be considered. For example, the existence of mandatory patent or technology pooling or licensing provisions may in some circumstances reduce member and independent inventor incentives to engage in research.

Since no specific joint research proposal has been agreed upon, we of course, cannot make any determination as to whether such joint research would raise serious antitrust problems. For your guidance, however, we can make several suggestions. Potential antitrust concerns can be lessened by limiting the joint efforts to what might be considered "basic" as distinguished from "applied" research. Joint research efforts to determine the most dangerous properties of matches and to establish uniform means of testing or measuring such properties would not appear to raise significant antitrust concerns. Once the basic research knowledge has been developed, however, the members of the industry should, in most cases, be required to engage in independent efforts to reduce the basic scientific knowledge to practice.

Political Activity

When competitors join together for any reason, the antitrust laws must be considered. Joining together for political activity is certainly no exception. However, the first amendment to the Constitution guarantees citizens the right to petition the government, and three important United States Supreme Court cases have held that competitors may join in activity which is aimed at influencing the legislative, judicial, or executive branches of the government. In the two cases of *Eastern Railroad Presidents Conference v. Noerr,* and *United Mine Workers v. Pennington,* the Supreme Court established the so-called Noerr-Pennington doctrine, which generally provides that joint activities among competitors to petition Congress to enact or refuse to enact certain legislation is constitutionally protected and exempt from any of the prohibitions of the Sherman Act. In the *Noerr* case, the railroads were actively campaigning for laws and law-enforcement practices that would be detrimental to the trucking industry; the *Pennington* case involved concerted activity by large coal companies to have high minimum wages required for companies selling coal to the TVA, thus driving some smaller companies out of business.

To some extent, the Noerr-Pennington doctrine was limited by the case of *California Motor Transport Co. v. Trucking, Unlimited.* In that case, a group of trucking companies joined together to oppose administrative action which would allow competitors various routes. The plaintiffs in that case alleged that the defendants conspired to put them out of business as competitors by instituting actions in state and federal proceedings to resist and defeat the plaintiffs' applications for operating rights, thus deterring the plaintiffs from having free and unlimited access to the agencies and courts. The Supreme Court said in this case that if the plaintiffs proved their allegations, there would be a violation of the antitrust laws. However, it is important to note that the court expressly recognized the rights of the defendants to join together in administrative and adjudicative processes as well as legislative processes. The problem in the *Trucking, Unlimited* case was that the defendants went beyond merely acting jointly, and their actions amounted, in substance, to undue harassment of the plaintiff by making use of the federal administrative agencies. The language of the court is illustrative:

> One claim, which a court or agency may think baseless, may go unnoticed; but a pattern of baseless, repetitive claims may emerge which leads the factfinder to conclude that the administrative and judicial processes have been abused. That may be a difficult line to discern and draw. But once it is drawn, the case is established that abuse of those processes produced an illegal result, viz., effectively barring respondents from access to the agencies and courts. Insofar as the administrative or judicial processes are involved, actions of that kind cannot acquire immunity by seeking refuge under the umbrella of "political expression."

Other cases have made it clear, however, that the Noerr-Pennington doctrine does nothing more than protect bona fide attempts by groups of competitors to influence government policy matters.

In three cases, all involving claims of monopolization, it has been fairly well settled that:

1. The assertion of false facts to government administrative agencies is not protected.

2. The exercise of improper influence on public officials (as, for example, improperly influencing the design requirements for public swimming pools so that only the plaintiff's products could qualify) is not protected.

3. Exercise of discretionary power conferred on private companies by the government to eliminate a competitor is not protected.

The Noerr-Pennington doctrine has generated a considerable amount of writing and debate among antitrust practitioners, but most of this debate is on a theoretical level and arises out of language used in the Noerr and Pennington decisions. This language, which is probably overly broad, has been seized upon by defendants to try to immunize them from the antitrust consequences of acts which were in no way related to their constitutional right to petition the government.

The practical implications of the doctrine are that it will serve to protect good-faith joint activity by competitors aimed at influencing government policy. It will not protect that activity (at least not at the administrative or judicial level) if it is done in such a manner that the government agency is only used as an instrument in a broader scheme to limit competition, and in no event can it protect any joint activity which is simply aimed at some aspect of public procurement as opposed to policymaking.

Other Joint Activity

Sometimes it is thought that activity which would be clearly illegal if done in a straightforward manner is somehow permissible if done as part of a joint-bidding arrangement or if done for joint research and development. This is not the case at all; there is no exemption in the Sherman Act for any of these subjects. However, as a practical matter, normal antitrust principles are applied differently in these contexts. The following are some appropriate observations:

Joint Bidding

There is no exemption in the Sherman Act for team agreements to bid on government procurement matters, even if the teaming arrangement has been suggested or encouraged by a government procurement agency. Normal inter-government rivalries come to the surface here, and assertions to the Department of Justice that some other government agency approved the arrangement will fall on deaf ears.

However, team arrangements can be properly and advantageously used and, as a practical matter, are generally not challenged if their sole purpose is to prepare a responsive proposal to a government procurement agency. They are particularly useful for large, complex matters like procurement of space-related apparatus or complicated weapons systems.

Following are some useful suggestions in this area:

1. Team arrangements should be avoided where the company has the practical capability of submitting a responsive proposal by itself. The fact that the corporate resources and technology of two companies is essential to the under-taking is perhaps the most important justification for a team-bidding arrange-ment; without it, substantial antitrust implications would seem to be present.

2. The team arrangement should be limited to the specific undertaking in ques-tion and should end either on termination of the project, if the bid is accepted, or immediately, if the bid is rejected or the project abandoned.

3. Naturally, the team arrangement should be fully disclosed to the government so it could object if it desired. (Disclosure should be made to the government procurement agency; it is neither necessary nor desirable to disclose the agree-ment to the Department of Justice or to the Federal Trade Commission.)

4. The number of team members should be restricted so that only companies capable of offering something essential to the project are included.

5. As in the case of the corporate joint venture, many problems can arise from restrictions in the team arrangement. Generally, restrictions against disclosure of confidential information are proper, but restrictions on the individual com-pany's abilities to compete either during or after the joint-venture undertaking should be very carefully examined.

6. It is generally best to keep the two companies' operations as separate as possi-ble. The pooling of production facilities or the joint buying of required parts or materials causes increased exposure.

Joint Research and Development

The subject of joint research and development by competitors has received a great deal of attention lately. Generally, the Department of Justice has taken the view that such joint arrangements must have their competitive effects judged on a fairly abstract basis. That is, the agreement must be judged purely on the basis of the effect it will have on competition between those who are a part of the arrangement and their competitors or potential competitors. The fact that some social objective may be achieved by the joint research and development activities must be judged irrelevant for antitrust purposes. Even though pollution and energy shortages are a problem to our society and economy, they cannot be used as productive arguments to justify an otherwise anticompetitive joint research and development arrangement.

As in the other areas previously mentioned, the antitrust problems involved in joint research and development usually arise not out of the arrangement itself but out of some anticompetitive aspect of the arrangement. In other words, joint research and development is not illegal per se. The particular arrangement, and all of the provisions of the agreement, must be carefully analyzed to determine whether or not there is any anticompetitive effect. In this regard, the following are useful comments:

1. Risk of attack is lessened if there are two or more joint arrangements working on the same problem. That way, it can be shown that competition has not been entirely eliminated. Conversely, if all the companies in the industry are involved in the arrangement, risk of attack is increased.

2. As mentioned in the Department of Justice letter about the match industry, limiting the arrangement to basic rather than applied research lessens the risk of attack.

3. The involvement of small and medium-sized firms in the arrangement reduces the risk of a charge of antitrust violation because it helps the small and medium-sized firms to compete and avoids monopolization by the largest companies.

4. If the basic research turns out to be successful and trade secrets or patents are generated, making these innovations available to all competitors reduces the antitrust exposure—even if reasonable royalties are charged.

5. Inclusion of representatives of the public sector avoids the appearance of collusion or secret arrangements.

6. Specifically limiting the joint research and development to some specific problem or area of research, and limiting and duration of the program, reduces the risk of attack still further.

CHAPTER TEN

MONOPOLIZATION, CONSPIRACIES TO MONOPOLIZE, AND ATTEMPTS TO MONOPOLIZE

OVERVIEW

The basic statute dealing with monopolies is section 2 of the Sherman Act. This statute, which has remained unchanged (except for the penalty) since 1890, provides as follows:

> Every person who shall *monopolize*, or attempt to *monopolize*, or *combine or conspire* with any other person or persons, to monopolize any part of the trade or commerce among the several States, or with foreign nations, shall be deemed guilty of a felony, and, on conviction thereof, shall be punished by fine not exceeding one million dollars if a corporation, or, if any other person, one hundred thousand dollars, or by imprisonment not exceeding three years, or by both said punishments, in the discretion of the court.

The consequences of the "monopolist" label being attached to a corporation are quite severe. Unless the corporation has had the monopoly thrust upon it, or unless one of the other defenses hereinafter discussed applies, the corporation will have violated section 2 of the Sherman Act and will, therefore, be subject to the criminal sanctions imposed therein. In addition, private antitrust plaintiffs may recover damages.

Even if the monopoly has been lawfully acquired, the operations of the corporation will be severely restricted in the following ways:

1. Refusals to deal by a monopolist generally give rise to antitrust exposure even if the refusal is unilateral.

2. The corporation's Robinson-Patman Act problems will be aggravated because the availability of the "meeting competition" defense may be severely restricted, and activity which may not constitute a technical violation of the Robinson-Patman Act may be deemed to violate section 2 of the Sherman Act.

3. Conduct which is considered merely aggressive competition when practiced by a nonmonopolist may be considered to constitute an unreasonable maintenance or extension of a monopoly when practiced by a monopolist.

The first major monopolization case involved the Standard Oil Company of New Jersey. In this case, extensive relief was obtained by the government under sections 1 and 2 of the Sherman Act against Standard, a holding company, and the seven individuals chiefly directing it. This relief required Standard to transfer its controlling stock interests in thirty-seven oil corporations to its stockholders and prohibited subsidiaries and shareholders from combining with each other or with Standard in further violation of the Sherman Act.

In a detailed review of Standard's history, the Court stated that Standard had acquired monopoly power over refined petroleum, its pipeline transportation, and the sale of its products and, as an inevitable result, had acquired monopoly power over crude oil. To acquire and maintain this position, the Court found, Standard had engaged in a series of combinations and mergers and had utilized numerous unfair practices, such as predatory price cutting and the procurement of preferential freight rates and rebates.

SINGLE-FIRM MONOPOLIZATION

Single-firm monopolization is the acquisition of monopoly power by a single corporation or by a group of corporations which are related to each other in some way. It should be contrasted with a conspiracy to monopolize, which occurs when two unrelated corporations conspire together to acquire monopoly power, and an attempt to monopolize, which can involve one or more corporations but refers to conduct which is directed toward the acquisition of a monopoly but which falls short of it.

DEFINITION OF "MONOPOLIZATION"

The following quotation from *United States v. Grinnell Corporation* defines the offense of monopoly:

> The offense of monopoly under Section 2 of the Sherman Act has two elements; (1) the possession of monopoly power in the relevant market and (2) the wilful acquisition or maintenance of that power as distinguished from growth or development as a consequence of a superior product, business acumen, or historic accident.

This definition raises several questions:

1. What is monopoly power?

2. What is a relevant market?

3. What conduct satisfies the willful acquisition or maintenance requirement?

In *United States v. Aluminum Company of America*, it was decided that the question of the existence of a monopoly is determined by the market share held. That case said that a 90 percent market share is enough to constitute a monopoly. It also said that it is doubtful whether 60 percent or 64 percent would be enough and certainly 33 percent is not enough to create a monopoly. In the *Cellophane* case, which involved Du Pont, the allegation was that Du Pont had acquired a monopoly in the cellophane market. Du Pont controlled 75 percent of that market and important patent technology. The remaining 25 percent of the cellophane market was in the hands of just one other producer. Du Pont successfully defended the case by arguing that the relevant market included not only cellophane but other types of flexible wrapping materials, thus reducing Du Pont's share of the market to less than 20 percent. However, for the purpose of this inquiry, it is significant to note that the Court seemed to accept the fact that if the market were to be limited to cellophane, Du Pont's control of 75 percent of that market would amount to a monopoly. In the *International Boxing* case, the defendants controlled 81 percent of the relevant market; in the *Grinnell* case, the defendants controlled 87 percent of the relevant market. Both of these cases held that the defendants possessed a monopoly.

Monopoly Power

Monopoly power has been defined as "the power to control prices or exclude competition." The primary consideration in determining whether a monopoly exists is not whether prices are raised and competition actually excluded but whether the *power* to raise prices or exclude competition exists.

Relevant Market

In monopolization cases, as in many other antitrust cases, one of the most important and perhaps the most difficult determination is the determination of the relevant market. The market which one must study to determine when a company has monopoly power varies with the part of commerce under consideration. The market is composed of products which are reasonably interchangeable for the purposes for which they are produced. Price, use, and the qualities of the product are considered in making this determination.

Economists talk about the relevant market in terms of the cross-elasticity of demand. "Cross-elasticity of demand" refers to the shift from one product to another product caused by changes in price. In the cellophane context, for example, it was determined that if the price of cellophane were raised, consumers would simply switch to other forms of flexible wrapping material; thus there was a high cross-elasticity of demand between cellophane and other flexible wrapping materials, and the relevant market included those other flexible wrapping materials.

However, in determining the relevant market, there are three other factors which must be considered.

1.   There may be submarkets, which are considered to comprise the entire relevant market for purposes of the case in question. For example, in the *Grinnell* case, the defendant controlled 87 percent of insurance-accredited central-station protective devices. These devices were particular forms of burglar alarms and fire and theft alarms. There were, however, many, many other different types of arrangements which accomplished substantially the same purpose. A potential customer for Grinnell's products could also consider watchmen, watchdogs, automatic proprietary systems, alarm systems connected with some local police or fire stations, and other (accredited or unaccredited) central-station protective services. However, the Court in Grinnell said, "There are, to be sure, substitutes for the accredited central station service. But none of

them appears to operate on the same level as the central station service so as to meet the interchangeability test of the Du Pont case."

2. Even where the product or service is identical to other products or services, if one particular form of the commodity is much more lucrative or important than all of the other forms, that lucrative or important form may be considered a market in and of itself. This was the situation in *International Boxing Club of New York v. United States*, where the Court said that championship boxing is the cream of the boxing business and is a sufficiently separate part of the trade or commerce to constitute the relevant market for Sherman Act purposes.

3. The relevant market may be limited to very small geographic areas. This was evident in the *Lorain Journal* case, wherein the monopoly consisted of the dominance of mass dissemination of news and advertising in a small Ohio city, and the *Union Leader* case, which involved the daily newspaper business in a small Massachusetts city.

An examination of section 2 of the Sherman Act reveals that the mere possession of monopoly power is not a violation; rather, the statutory words are "*monopolize, . . . attempt* to monopolize, or . . . *conspire . . .* to monopolize." This has given rise to the requirement that the plaintiff in a monopolization case show not only that the defendant has a monopoly and possesses monopoly power but that he has the purpose or intent to exercise that power. However, the *DuPont* and *Grinnell* cases have, for practical purposes, all but eliminated the deliberateness requirement because the *DuPont* case said that "when alleged monopolists have power over price and competition an intention to monopolize in a proper case may be assumed," and the *Grinnell* case said that "once the government has borne the burden of proving what is the relevant market and how predominate a share of that market the defendant has, it follows that there are rebuttable presumptions that defendant has monopoly power *and has monopolized* in violation of Section 2."

Willful Acquisition

Once a monopoly has been shown in terms of the required percentage of the relevant market, the defendant has two defenses against a section 2 conviction: (1) the "thrust upon" defense, which says, in essence, that the defendant had his monopoly thrust upon him by circumstances beyond his control and (2) the defense that the monopoly was acquired by superior skill, acumen, foresight, and industry.

A firm has not monopolized if monopoly has been "thrust upon" it by the fact that demand was so limited only one firm could economically supply the demand or by the fact that change in cost or taste drove out all but one supplier. The firm has also not monopolized if it survived by virtue of superior skill, foresight, and industry. Technically, these two defenses are still valid. In the *Grinnell* case, the Supreme Court began defining the offense of *monopoly* as "the wilful acquisition or maintenance of [monopoly] power as distinguished from growth or development as a consequence of a superior product, business acumen, or historic accident." However, for practical purposes, the district court's opinion in the *Grinnell* case sums up the significance of these two defenses.

It is the highly exceptional case, the *rara avis* more often found in academic groves than in the thickets of business, where monopoly power was thrust upon an enterprise by the economic character of the industry and by what Judge L. Hand in *Aluminum* called "superior skill, foresight and industry." More than seven decades of Sherman Act enforcement leave the informed observer with the abiding conviction that durable, non-statutory monopolies (ones created without patents or licenses or lasting beyond their term), are, to a moral certainty, due to acquisitions of competitors or restraints of trade prohibited by Section 1. They are the achievement of the quiet life after the enemy's capitulation or his defeat in inglorious battle.

SHARED MONOPOLY

Some writers have suggested that where a small number (three or four) companies have a monopoly, their interdependent pricing practices or other market action might be attacked under section 2 of the Sherman Act or section 5 of the Federal Trade Commission Act. This has not been widely accepted.

SIZE

It has been said many times that mere size is not an offense under the Sherman Act. "Size" here refers to dollar volume of business, sales, or assets rather than market shares. However, it has also been said that size carries with it an opportunity for abuse that should not be ignored when the opportunity is proved to have been utilized in the past.

UNFAIR PROFITS

The offense of monopolization under the Sherman Act does not include the reaping of unfair profits. The fact that the monopoly has not been used to extract from the consumer more than a fair profit, therefore, cannot be used as a defense against the charge of monopolization.

ATTEMPTS TO MONOPOLIZE AND CONSPIRACIES TO MONOPOLIZE

The Sherman Act not only prohibits monopolization but also prohibits attempts and conspiracies to monopolize. There are not too many cases in this area, and the problems are similar to conspiracies and attempts generally. In the "attempt" area, the key elements appear to be (1) a specific intent to monopolize and (2) some conduct aimed at attaining this objective. The "attempt" area does not require any proof that monopoly was actually attained. However, it is necessary to prove the specific intent, and there must be a "dangerous probability" of success in the attempt. "Dangerous probability" has been used synonymously with "would be likely to accomplish." In order to satisfy the "dangerous probability" requirement, the defendant would have to have sufficient market or economic power to create a reasonable likelihood that he could, in time, establish a monopoly.

The "conspiracy to monopolize" problem of section 2 is less severe than the problems discussed previously under section 1 of the Sherman Act. Most questionable dealings involving two separate corporations could be attacked much more easily as conspiracies to restrain trade than as conspiracies to monopolize.

In the "attempt to monopolize" area, there is some concern that section 2 "attempt to monopolize" cases might develop into general regulation by the courts of aggressive single-firm conduct. This is clearly not intended, and many courts go out of their way to point out that aggressive conduct alone does not amount to an attempt to monopolize. A good example is the *Sears* case, which indicated as follows:

The complaint herein does recite an intent by Sears to destroy any business in which the plaintiff might engage and thereby instill fear in its other suppliers, but that allegation cannot be twisted into a charge that Sears was attempting to monopolize the market in nursery lamps. Furthermore, the complaint does not allege a dangerous probability that defendant may achieve a monopoly . . . We think the trial court stated the situation well in these words . . . The actions taken to ruin the plaintiff and discipline suppliers may be reprehensible but there is not the slightest showing of impending monopoly other than the bare assertion of the pleader.

SUMMARY

If a company has a large (70 percent or more) share of a given market, its activities—especially those which might be characterized as aggressive—should be monitored by counsel with monopolization problems in mind. (This, of course, presumes that the company has gone through the exercise of deciding where it may have monopoly power—hopefully without the creation of self-incriminating documents.)

Thereafter, the managers of these potential trouble spots should be alerted to the problem and asked to check with counsel before undertaking *any* lawsuit. Even a suit for expropriation of trade secrets or breach of contract should be weighed against the risk of an antitrust counterclaim. In addition, any pricing practices or marketing practices should be carefully checked because practices like unilateral refusals to sell or meeting price competition can create problems for a monopolist even though they are relatively risk free if done by a nonmonopolist.

In addition, the submarket and geographic market problems should be kept in mind. The fact that the company is small does not preclude a monopolization problem if the relevant market is correspondingly small. It is doubtful that before litigation, the *Lorain Journal* would have thought of itself as a monopolist along with such companies as Standard Oil, Alcoa, and Du Pont. However, because the relevant market was limited, this was indeed the case.

CHAPTER ELEVEN

DISTRIBUTION AND OTHER VERTICAL ANTITRUST PROBLEMS

The problems discussed in the previous chapters are the most serious antitrust problems, but problems relating to distributors are the most frequently encountered antitrust problems. This chapter will deal with distributorship problems and other vertical antitrust problems involving relations between a company and its suppliers and customers, as opposed to its competitors.

THE RULE OF REASON

In considering the subjects in this chapter, it is especially important to keep in mind that almost all of them are analyzed according to the rule of reason. The rule-of-reason approach is just what the name implies. The practice in question is assumed to restrict competition—almost all agreements restrict competition in some way—but the kinds of agreements discussed in this chapter have legitimate commercial purposes. The process is to weigh the legitimate business purpose against the restrictive effect on competition. Obviously, different people will look at the same situation and come to different conclusions. Furthermore, in many situations the legal consequences of an arrangement will be less than certain because the lawyer cannot be sure that the judge will look at the matter in the same way he does. Subjectivity is the common denominator in rule-of-reason problems.

The legal analysis is based on economic realities. While legal economics and classic economics may not be exactly the same, it is necessary to look at the actual economic effect of transactions as well as at the words which are used to describe them.

If two companies are actually going to get together and agree on prices, it will do no good whatsoever for management to have the lawyers draw up an agreement called a "joint management agreement" which carefully avoids expressly stating anything illegal. The facts will govern. On the other hand, words can serve to incriminate otherwise legitimate transactions. For example, if a distribution agreement contains provisions about setting prices, staying within certain territories, or allocating customers, the fact that these provisions are not enforced will not insulate the parties from legal difficulty. In short, good words will not save a bad transaction, but bad words can contaminate a good transaction.

Also, management must understand the subjectivity of this whole area and must resist pushing too strongly for clear legal advice in areas where it is simply impossible to give it. If the company's business executives are reasonably sophisticated, they can avoid clear problems, but it will still be difficult for them to draw fine lines in many cases. For example, the precise line where counseling and suggesting stop and coercion, or requiring, begins is very difficult to draw. In many cases, it is simply impossible to draw this line with any degree of certainty, and if anyone attempts to do so, he may be second-guessed by a judge or jury.

RECIPROCITY

Reciprocity is the use of the purchasing power of a corporation to promote its sales. The current feeling is that reciprocity introduces an irrelevant and alien factor into the purchasing decision, thus affecting what would otherwise be an unimpeded competitive choice based on the price, quality, and service of the corporation and its product. Consequently, the government thinks reciprocity is illegal and will challenge it wherever appropriate.

Some distinctions, however, are important. There are three kinds of reciprocal dealings: (1) coercive reciprocity, (2) voluntary agreements, and (3) mutual patronage without any kind of agreement.

Coercive reciprocity has long been established as an unfair method of competition under section 5 of the Federal Trade Commission Act. However, there does not appear to be any clear authority that it is a violation of section 1 of the Sherman Act. Since section 1 of the Sherman Act can be used by private plaintiffs to recover treble damages and attorneys' fees, while the Federal Trade Commission Act can only be used by the government and then only to stop the transaction, this distinction is far from academic. Coercive reciprocity, however, is definitely inviting trouble and should be avoided.

The distinction between voluntary agreements and mutual patronage without any agreement is very hard to draw because in the antitrust area, implied agreements are certainly sufficient to constitute a violation of the Sherman Act. This kind of reciprocity, if practiced on a relatively substantial or organized scale, is asking for trouble because of the government's feeling that it is illegal and the apparent tendency of court cases in that direction—although there appears to be no square holding on the point. Consequently, for planning purposes, any kind of organized reciprocity should be avoided. Generally, organized reciprocity may exist where a company maintains data about sales to a customer in the purchasing department, and vice versa. That is, where purchasers have access to information showing which companies their business sells to, and where sellers have access to information showing where their companies purchase, a problem may exist.

Consent Decrees

One of the problems with walking too close to the line on reciprocity is the danger of a government attack and the practical necessity of entering into a consent decree, which may go much further than merely prohibiting the reciprocity.

For example, in a case involving U. S. Steel, the decree not only prohibited coercion and voluntary reciprocity but prohibited the following conduct: (1) discussions with suppliers concerning the relationship of purchases to sales, (2) advice to suppliers that preference will be given in purchasing products from them based on their own purchases, (3) maintenance of statistical compilations comparing sales to and purchases from suppliers, and (4) issuance to purchasing personnel of lists identifying customers and their purchases.

Monopolization

If a company has a large market share, or if there are other facts suggesting a possible monopolization problem, coercive reciprocity could be held to be either an unlawful maintenance of a monopoly or an attempt to monopolize.

In summary, any kind of organized reciprocity should be discouraged. There may be some questions as to precisely which kinds of reciprocity violate which laws—and this may indeed be important in some cases—but there can be no question about the government's opinion, and prudence would dictate avoiding the problem where possible.

TYING

A tying agreement is any arrangement whereby one party refuses to sell a given product except on condition that the buyer also purchase a different (or tied) product or, at least, not purchase that product from any other supplier.

It is not necessary that the tied and tying items be furnished by the same seller. If the seller of the tying product requires the buyer to purchase the tied product from a designated third party in return for a commission, a tie-in is said to exist.

A tie-in does require the existence of two distinct products, however. It is not unlawful for a seller to include several items in a single mandatory package when the items may be reasonably considered to constitute parts of a single distinct product. The fact that the seller offers two or more products as a part of a package at a single price does not constitute an unlawful tie-in if he also sells each of the products separately. However, the seller cannot arrange the price structure so as to make it economically impractical to purchase the products separately. Generally speaking, the difference in price between purchasing the products separately and purchasing them as a package must be reasonably justified by cost considerations. There is a fundamental distinction between a seller offering one item at a discount or bargain price if a second item is also being purchased, and an unlawful tie-in. In the bargain-price situation, the effectiveness of the arrangement is based upon the inducement of a lower rate rather than upon the power to coerce purchases by controlling availability of a desired product. As a practical matter, however, it is sometimes difficult to distinguish between the inducement of a lower rate and an unlawful tie-in. The appropriate issue in a tie-in case is not whether the seller has driven a hard bargain or even imposed upon the buyer but the effect of the tie-in on the competitors of the seller. However, some cases refer to the imposition on the buyer, and it certainly has at least an emotional significance. It cannot, therefore, be ignored.

Some examples can illustrate the tying problem very clearly. One of the best-known tying cases involved IBM and the sales of its equipment using punch cards and the punch cards themselves. When this kind of equipment was originally introduced, IBM required its customers to purchase the cards used by the IBM equipment. These cards were manufactured to close tolerances and made of a specific kind of heavy paper so that they would work well in the IBM equipment and avoid failures or breakdowns of the equipment. IBM's justification for the requirement was that in order to be sure the equipment would work properly, the customers had to use these high-quality cards. On the other hand, other paper companies soon found that the market for these keypunch cards was rather large and that the IBM price could be easily met and, perhaps, beaten. In a suit brought by the government, the court held that the IBM requirement was an illegal tie-in and that IBM's argument was without merit because IBM could accomplish its objective of having its equipment work properly by simply stating specifications which the cards had to meet. In other words, IBM could require the purchasers of its machinery to use keypunch cards meeting certain specifications, but it could not require users to buy those cards from IBM.

A great many tie-in cases involve a tie-in between equipment and the supplies that that equipment uses. In most cases, the economics of the situation are that the sale of the equipment is a one-shot deal where the markup is limited, whereas the sale of supplies is a continuing business with a high profit margin. However, almost all of these cases have come to the conclusion that any kind of requirement imposed by a manufacturer of machinery that the customer purchase the supplies which are necessary to operate that equipment from the manufacturer is an illegal tie-in. The reason for the illegality is that in most cases, the products are separate, and a requirement by the manufacturer would foreclose competition from the companies in the business of making and selling the supplies.

FULL-OUTPUT AND REQUIREMENTS CONTRACTS

Full-output contracts and requirements contracts can be analyzed together because the rules are the same. From an antitrust point of view, the difficulty with requirements contracts is that if a company agrees to purchase all of its requirements from a single source, all other suppliers of that same product are foreclosed from competing for the company's business. Similarly, if a company is required to sell all of its output to a single customer, that company is effectively taken out of competition in that market for that product, to the possible detriment of competition as a whole. Accordingly, in analyzing full-output and requirements contracts, one must use the rule-of-reason approach, which simply states that the detrimental effect on competition must be outweighed by some reasonable business consideration.

Two very different types of situations must be considered. The first is the unusual business deal. This is the case where a business decides to purchase all of its requirements for a certain commodity from one source in order to assure a constant and dependable source of the product at a fixed or determinable price. The classic situation is the *Tampa Electric* case. The *Tampa* case involved a long-term contract for coal to be supplied to an electric utility company. The court held that the agreement did not violate the antitrust laws, even though quite a substantial sum of money was involved. The court said that:

To determine substantiality in a given case, it is necessary to weigh the probable effect of the contract on the relevant area of competition, taking into account (1) the relative strength of the parties, (2) the proportionate volume of commerce involved in relation to the total volume of commerce in the relevant market area, and (3) the probable immediate and future effects which preemption of that share of the market might have on effective competition therein. It follows that a mere showing that the contract itself involves a substantial number of dollars is ordinarily of little consequence.

It would appear that in this kind of case, the arrangement should be analyzed by using the rule-of-reason approach, and management should make sure that its lawyers fully understand the business necessity for the action and that all of the provisions of the agreement are analyzed for their reasonableness.

The second type of situation which must be considered is a situation where a manufacturer tells a distributor that he must purchase all of his requirements from the manufacturer. This is much more troublesome. Generally, most distribution schemes involving a trademark, a trade name, or the goodwill of the manufacturer will present this problem. These cases are much more difficult to justify, and, as a matter of fact, much of the discussion in this area revolves around the question of whether the arrangement is illegal per se or merely illegal because it is impossible to justify under the rule-of-reason approach.

The classic case in this category is *FTC v. Brown Shoe Co.* In this case, approximately 650 retail shoe stores agreed, in return for some special benefits, to purchase only one complete line of shoes—Brown's. They were permitted to handle other individual models but not the complete line of any other manufacturer. The Supreme Court said that the result of this program was to foreclose Brown Shoes' competitors from selling to a "substantial number of retail shoe dealers," and that this was sufficient to hold the arrangement to be a violation of section 5 of the Federal Trade Commission Act.

There has been much writing on this subject. Most of that writing goes into elaborate discussion of the rules of quantitative and qualitative substantiality. These terms refer to the method by which one analyzes whether the amount of competition foreclosed is substantial. Under one theory, one uses a percentage or dollar amount; under the other, one uses the rule of reason and the criteria stated in the quotation from the *Tampa Electric* case. Basically, the problem is that in 1949, the Supreme Court announced, in the *Standards Stations* case, a so-called rule of quantitative substantiality which generally said that the legality of an exclusive-dealing arrangement depended upon the quantity of commerce which might be foreclosed. In that case, 6.7 percent was held to be substantial, but this is clouded somewhat by the fact that the court emphasized the widespread use of similar exclusive-dealing contracts by all other major suppliers. In 1961, the Supreme Court decided the *Tampa Electric* case. This case is generally said to stand for the rule that exclusive-dealing arrangements are judged by a qualitative rule and one should apply the rule of reason by using the elements set forth in the decision in this case. Unfortunately, the *Tampa* case did not overrule the *Standard Stations* case, so the two are, at least on the surface, left to co-exist as best they can.

There have been literally hundreds of other cases decided since Tampa, with some of them leaning toward a qualitative rule and some toward a quantitative rule. There have been many attempts by antitrust writers to reconcile all of these cases and come to some kind of a conclusion but, at this time, it would be safe to say that their attempts have been to no avail. The best way to handle the problem, therefore, is not to try to figure out whether the rule of quantitative substantiality applies, as opposed to the rule of qualitative substantiality, but to divide the situations into the nonsystematic long-term requirements contracts and the systematic approach. The former contracts have the following characteristics: (1) They are of benefit to both parties, (2) they are economically justified, (3) the share of the relevant market is small, (4) there is no trend to concentration in the industry, and (4) there do not appear to be any anticompetitive motives on the part of either of the parties. If a requirements or full-output contract has all of these characteristics, it should not create any substantial risk. This will be true even though the particular contract in question might involve a great deal of money, as in the *Tampa* case.

However, in the case of a systematic approach, where a manufacturer requires his distributors to purchase substantially all of their requirements exclusively from him, the only question is under which theory the arrangement will be held to be illegal. It does not even appear that the fact that trademarks or goodwill are involved will provide any justification for this kind of requirements contract. Instead, the courts will say that the manufacturer or holder of the trademark can protect his goodwill by providing specifications for distributors or franchisees and requiring that only products meeting those specifications be sold.

In a classic case illustrating the point, Chicken Delight was not allowed to require its franchisees to purchase the chicken sold in their outlets solely from Chicken Delight, even though that was the only compensation Chicken Delight asked for in their franchise agreements. In other words, Chicken Delight said that the franchisees could use the "Chicken Delight" trademark free so long as they purchased the chicken from Chicken Delight. The court held that this was an illegal tie-in (between the trademark "Chicken Delight" and the chicken itself) and was, therefore, illegal. What Chicken Delight should have done was to charge a separate franchise fee for the use of the "Chicken Delight" trademark and then allow the franchisees to purchase the chicken from anybody they wanted to, subject to quality control and specification.

REFUSALS TO SELL

There are many good reasons why one business executive might refuse to sell to another. The reasons may include poor credit, improper service, or simply personality considerations. A refusal to deal for any of these reasons is certainly not a violation of antitrust laws. If one business executive finds another to be a bad credit risk, it is likely that other business executives will also find this to be the case, and these other business executives may also, independently, refuse to sell to him. This also creates no antitrust violation. However, if two business executives get together and decide that one or both of them will not deal with a third party, or if one business executive, acting unilaterally, refuses to deal for some anticompetitive purpose, there will be a definite antitrust problem. The important questions in this area are:

1. When is the anticompetitive purpose present?
2. When is there the necessary consensual action between two separate persons?

Any discussion of refusals to sell should begin with a distinction between a refusal to sell someone who was not previously a customer and the cutting off of an existing account. Theoretically, there is no difference between these two situations. However, as a practical matter, there is a big difference. If a distributor is cut off, someone is hurt—sometimes severely. Furthermore, there is a definite event which causes the problem. In addition, many cases involve a company which has a lawyer. There is, therefore, a much greater than normal chance for a lawsuit.

If a company originally decides to have only one distributor in an area, appoints one, and then refuses to deal with all others, there is no antitrust problem and very little possibility of anyone raising the issue to the extent of going to court. However, a manufacturer who has ten distributors in an area and then decides to cut back to one and terminates the other nine has a much greater potential for antitrust litigation. Because of this problem, there has developed a considerable amount of sophistication relating to distributorship terminations, and tremendous care should be taken in the initial selection of distributors.

Distinction must also be made between an action taken by a monopolist and an action taken by a nonmonopolist. As a general proposition, a monopolist may not refuse to sell to anybody except for very clear business reasons—such as poor credit. Therefore, the discussion contained herein applies only to nonmonopolists. Of course, the question of when one has a monopolistic position depends on a great many considerations, the most important and most difficult of which is the definition of the relevant market.

Anticompetitive Purpose

Some anticompetitive purposes are obvious—resale-price maintenance is the one most often encountered. Others include all of the areas of antitrust law—tying arrangements, boycotts, price-fixing, and market divisions. As usual, the problems involve the gray areas. For example, a company wants to cut off a distributor because of poor representation in an area—but it also happens that the distributor involved is a price-cutter. Documentation is important here. It is necessary to show, by independent, objective data, that the announced reason is the real reason for the refusal.

Consensual Action

As mentioned in an earlier chapter, violation of section 1 of the Sherman Act—the relevant statute in considering refusals to deal—depends upon consensual action. This was established in the early and often-cited *Colgate* case, where the Court said that a company could independently announce a policy of refusing to sell to anyone who did not abide by its retail price policies and could thereafter so refuse to sell. Theoretically, this is still the law. However, as a practical matter, courts can infer an agreement from conduct which goes very little further than an announcement and subsequent refusal to deal.

For example, if a company announced a policy, discovered that a distributor was cutting prices, talked to the distributor about the matter, and the distributor subsequently stopped discounting, the necessary consensual action between the manufacturer and distributor could be inferred. In another example, if one distributor in a city suggested that another be cut off—the necessary consensual action between the first distributor and the manufacturer could be inferred. In fact, even if a distributor is about to be cut off for a valid business purpose and another distributor approaches the manufacturer and suggests or requests the cutoff, the contact may prevent the manufacturer from taking the action because of its potential for the inference of an agreement. The more vocal the distributors who request the cutoff become, the more difficult it becomes for the manufacturer to make the cutoff, even assuming he desires to do so and has valid business reasons for his desire.

As a practical matter, the Colgate doctrine cannot be used for planning purposes because later cases make it clear that anything besides the mere announcement of a policy and subsequent refusal to deal with violators could provide the necessary consensual action. The "something plus" could be one of the following:

1. In the announcement area, deliberate and frequent explanations that a manufacturer will refuse to sell to violators are suspect, even though there is, in fact, no express agreement from the dealers. Also, continuous announcements to dealers every time one of them is cut off because of a violation can cause a problem.

2. Another problem concerns the procedures one establishes to discover whether one's policy is being violated. Certainly the requirement of reporting sales and prices is inappropriate and dangerous. On the other hand, if a manufacturer relies on his customers to police the activity, there arises immediately the question of what he can do if a customer reports a violation. If he acts on a customer complaint, there is the problem of the inference of an agreement. If the manufacturer decides to police the distributor's activity himself, the logical person to do this would be the salesperson who services the account. However, salespersons are in a somewhat difficult position because it is in their best interests to admonish the dealer but not to report him and thus require the company to cut him off.

3. Enforcement is also a big problem because assuming the manufacturer has made an appropriate announcement and has discovered a violation by appropriate means, he has little choice but to cut off the offender immediately. This may not be to anyone's best economic interest. However, if the manufacturer talks to the offender and convinces him of the error of his ways, or even if he cuts him off and then immediately reinstates him upon his promise to abide by the policy in the future, there is a definite possibility of the inference of an agreement between the manufacturer and the distributor.

The consensus of opinion seems to be that the net result of all of the above is that, for planning purposes, it is impossible to accomplish anything which may be considered a restraint of trade by the announcement of a policy and the subsequent refusal to deal with those who do not go along with the policy.

Dealing with Competitors

Occasionally a customer will become a competitor. At this point, it might be desirable, for business reasons, to refrain from future business dealings with him. An illustrative case on this point is *Deltown Foods, Inc. v. Tropicana Products, Inc.* A supplier of orange juice refused to continue to sell to a distributor who began distributing his own brand of orange juice, and the Court held that such refusal did not violate antitrust laws. The rationale was that the distributor, having his own private brand of orange juice, would treat Tropicana's brand as second best. The following points should be made in connection with the *Deltown* case:

1. The case involved Deltown's own private brand. There was a stipulation that Tropicana sell to Deltown while Deltown also distributed Minute Maid orange juice. The clear implication of the case is that the rationale only applies where the distributor is distributing his own brand or a brand in which he has some proprietary interest other than simply being a distributor. Deltown, in distributing its own private brand, was itself a competitor of Tropicana—not merely a distributor of competitive products.

2. There was a finding that there was insufficient evidence from which to infer that Tropicana had a monopolistic position in the relevant market and at least an implication that in the Court's opinion, they did not.

3. The only evidence of a conspiracy under section 1 of the Sherman Act was the plaintiff's affidavit. The affidavit was controverted by the defendant's affidavit, and the Court found that there was insufficient evidence from which to infer a conspiracy.

4. There was an express finding that section 3 of the Clayton Act was inapplicable. This section prohibits any sale or contract for the sale of goods on the condition, agreement, or understanding that the purchaser is not to use or deal in the goods of a competitor of the seller where the effect may be to lessen competition or to create a monopoly. If section 3 is applicable, the standard of proof is very low. All that need be shown is that the contract *may* lessen competition. It is not generally necessary to go into elaborate market studies to define the relevant market and the various shares of that market. However, in the refusal-to-deal case, the Court held that section 3 was inapplicable because there was no contract or sale. The clear lesson from this portion of the opinion is that if a distributor becomes a competitor, it may be all right to cut him off but it is probably more dangerous to continue to sell on condition that he refrain from marketing his competitive product in any way.

Customer's Suit

Occasionally a customer will institute an antitrust suit against a supplier. The question then arises as to whether it is permissible to refuse to deal with that customer. The general rule on this point is that the bringing of a lawsuit by a customer does provide a sound business reason for the manufacturer to terminate relations with the customer. This was the holding in the *Simplicity Pattern* case in 1962, and it is still the general rule. There are, however, some qualifications to this general rule. In *McKesson & Robbins, Inc. v. Charles Pfizer & Co., Inc.*, the Court did require the supplier to continue to deal with the distributor while the distributor's antitrust suit was pending. The Court distinguished this case from the *Deltown* case, principally on the grounds that there was no possibility of treating one product as second best when the product was sold only pursuant to prescriptions which were written by brand name 80 percent of the time. There was no discussion of the *Simplicity Pattern* case, but the Court apparently felt that it had the general equity power to require the supplier to continue to deal with the distributor, and it so decreed.

It appears that once a customer has instituted an antitrust suit against a supplier, there is very little more to be lost by refusing to deal with that customer. The refusal may be upheld under the Simplicity Pattern decision, and even if it is not, the worst that can generally happen is an injunction to force continued dealings. It is very unlikely that the refusal to sell after the antitrust suit will cause the manufacturer any more difficulties than did the original antitrust claim of the customer.

Conclusions

In the refusal-to-deal area, a premium is placed on the intelligent selection of distributors because it is much easier to refuse to sell a new account than to cut off an existing one. However, if distributors are to be cut off, it is best to do it on an objective and well-documented basis. It is also essential that the program be nondiscriminatory. Generally, it would not be illegal to refuse to continue to deal with an account which did not purchase a certain minimum quantity or which did not perform adequately in the territory, considering the territory's area and population. Also, a company which has a great many distributors located in many places may embark on a program of reducing distributorships. In this process, it is certainly entitled to keep the best accounts and cut off the others. Of course, distributors can also be cut off for any number of other valid business reasons. However, once the factual situation can be interpreted as giving rise to the inference of an agreement—either between the manufacturer and the distributor who is threatened with cutoff or between the manufacturer and another distributor—the motives of the transaction must be carefully analyzed. Of course, this includes an analysis of what a judge or jury, looking at the objective facts, might determine the motives to be.

DISTRIBUTION

Almost all of the antitrust problems discussed thus far arise frequently in a normal distribution network. A discussion of typical antitrust distribution problems can, therefore, be very helpful in understanding these concepts.

Establishing the System

The kind of distribution system which a manufacturer will use to sell his products is usually governed by business and financial, rather than legal, considerations. However, if an opportunity to counsel a manufacturer arises early in the game, lawyers can present a catalog of the kinds of distribution systems available and the legal implications of each of them. These systems include:

1. The simplest method of distribution is direct sales by the manufacturer. However, in any market where national distribution is called for and where the product must be available on short notice, the manufacturer will have to establish many branch locations to store the product pending its ultimate sale to the consumer. If this is done on a large scale, it can become extremely costly because of the very large investments in locations and inventories required. Also, the business of distributing and selling a product to the ultimate consumer is simply not the same as the business of manufacturing that product, and expertise in one area does not really give any indication of expertise or success in the other area.

2. A variation on the direct-sale approach is the use of manufacturers' representatives. These representatives simply act as salespeople for the manufacturer, except that they are not on the manufacturer's payroll but, rather, act as independent contractors. Typically, all they do is solicit orders and pass them on to the manufacturer, who fills them. The contract usually runs directly from the manufacturer to the purchaser, and the only function of the manufacturer's representative is to solicit orders. His compensation is, typically, a percentage of the sale.

    A further variation is where the representative actually purchases some of the products and carries them in a limited inventory to satisfy the emergency requirements of his clients.

3. An agent, who does no more than solicit orders, is fundamentally different from an independent distributor, who purchases and sells products for his own account. In the distributor situation, all of the rules contained herein are fully applicable. However, in the agency situation, the company can generally control the activities of the agent to a significant extent. This includes placing restrictions on pricing, territories, customers, and the handling of competitive products, restrictions which generally cannot legally be placed on an independent distributor.

    In the hybrid case of an agent who purchases some of the products for his own account to satisfy the requirements of his clients, the company should treat the sale of those products which the salesman keeps, just as if they were made to a distributor. That is, the agent should not be restricted as to price, territory, and customers in the handling of those products. If the agent is, at least as to these sales, acting, in fact, as a distributor, with all the risks of loss, storage problems, and credit problems which a distributor encounters, the labeling of him as an "agent" will not mean that he will be treated like one for antitrust purposes. On the other hand, one must take a realistic and practical approach to the problem. There is obviously a big difference between a sales agent who sells $200,000 worth of products a year through solicitation of orders and keeps $1000 worth of goods in the trunk of his car to cover special, or emergency, cases, and a sales agent who sells $200,000 worth of goods a year, $100,000 worth of which comes directly from his own inventory, which he keeps in a rented warehouse under his own name. There may be little or no practical risk in treating the first man entirely as an agent and dictating prices, territories, and customers to him, but in the second case, such a procedure would have considerable potential exposure.

4. Assuming there must be some distribution beyond the manufacturer's own agents or employees, the alternatives are basically between (1) what might be called "normal" distribution, where a manufacturer sells to a distributor who is an independent business executive and handles products of many manufacturers, and (2) a franchise system, where the manufacturer establishes various franchise locations throughout the marketing territory. These franchises are also owned by independent business executives, but they handle only products from the one manufacturer.

    Prime examples of the first type of distribution system would be the distribution of automotive parts and bearings. Here, sales are typically made to established warehouse distributors, or jobbers, who handle many parts from many manufacturers and sell them to the ultimate consumer. Examples of the second type of system are the fast-food franchises or hotel chains—e.g., Howard Johnson and Holiday Inn. However, the franchise approach can also be used for the distribution of hard goods. The typical automobile franchise and gas-station franchise are examples. Here, the franchisee is typically an independent business executive who may own both the location and the inventory but typically deals only in goods supplied by one manufacturer.

    From a legal point of view, the antitrust risks in either of these two areas are substantially similar. However, different bodies of law have grown up around them. The specific body of law dealing with the so-called "business franchise" (Chicken Delight and Holiday Inn) is discussed in Chapter 17.

5. A manufacturer may sell both directly and to independent distributors. Here, however, there are two basic problems.

    The first is the Robinson-Patman Act problem, which will be generated by sales at different prices. This will almost always come about because the manufacturer will obviously be selling his product at a lower price to a distributor than to the end customer. This may not create a legal problem because the difference in price might be justified. However, the manufacturer must be aware of this problem and exercise some diligence in maintaining appropriate records and charging prices which are not discriminatory.

    The dual-distribution arrangement can also generate problems under other antitrust laws. If, during a period of scarcity, for example, a manufacturer were to allocate all of his supplies to his own customers and none to satisfying the demands of other distributors, a problem might result. Also, if the manufacturer were to raise his prices to his distributor, while maintaining or lowering his price to his own customers, it could be alleged that this was an improper method of competition or an attempt to monopolize. The Robinson-Patman implications of dual distribution are covered in Chapter 12.

6. Sometimes the device of consignment is used to try and avoid antitrust problems. When goods are sold on consignment, title does not pass to the ultimate consumer until the sale takes place. The manufacturer merely deposits his goods at the location of the intermediary, and title remains with the manufacturer. The intermediary then makes the sale to the consumer, and at that point title passes. It has, therefore, been argued that the consignment arrangement could be used to maintain resale prices because the sales are actually those of the manufacturer, and the manufacturer is not attempting to dictate the price at which the intermediary must sell.

This was attempted in the gas-station context in the *Simpson Oil* case and very clearly struck down. The Simpson court termed the consignment a mere legalism to avoid an illegal vertical price-fixing scheme. Therefore, this device would seem at this point to have little general applicability. The *Simpson* case involved rather special facts because of the nature of the product (gasoline), which was unpatented but trademarked and was, at least supposedly, specially formulated. There was also a history of coercive regulation of the station operators by the suppliers. Nevertheless, the language of that case is so broad that most practitioners feel that a consignment arrangement is not an effective way to maintain the resale price of their articles.

In summary, the method used by a manufacturer to distribute his products will almost always be governed by business or financial considerations, and only rarely will the particular legal requirements make one system preferable to another. The most notable exception to this is the fast-food or hotel/motel type of business. In this area, it becomes extremely desirable for the manufacturer/franchisor to maintain a high degree of uniformity of product, service, and quality throughout the country. If this is one of the given facts from a business point of view, a strong legal emphasis is given to the traditional franchise because in this area, these kinds of controls are possible to attain.

Picking the Distributors

Proper initial selection of distributors is very important because of the extreme difficulty in terminating a distributor. Most lawsuits involving the distribution problem come about because a distributor is terminated by his supplier. An initial refusal to sell to a distributor who does not meet the requirements of the manufacturer, or for just about any other reason, presents few antitrust problems. Generally, it is inadvisable to select a new distributor in an area simply because he is the best one available. If the marketing plans of the company eventually call for selecting other distributors and terminating this one, it is best to either appoint the distributor with the understanding that if he performs satisfactorily, he will continue to be a distributor or to delay distribution in the affected area until a better distributor can be obtained.

Another problem frequently mishandled involves the evaluation of a company which approaches a manufacturer and asks to be a distributor.

In some cases, the typical salesperson's approach is to encourage conversations with the prospective distributor even though the salesperson may know full well that his company will not appoint that distributor. In other cases, the salesperson will even indicate that he will ask the other distributors in the area what they think of appointing the new company as an additional distributor. These two approaches cause significant problems.

The first approach of talking to the distributor may amount to leading him on and causing him to expend substantial amounts of time and perhaps even money. The proposed distributor is then rejected by company headquarters because distribution in the area is adequate, and, in many cases, there is a substantial legal question about whether or not the sales representative made an oral contract with the distributor which was subsequently breached. Merely telling the distributor that the sales representative had no authority to make such a contract will seldom remove the problem if the distributor decides to push it. Whether or not a court would eventually find a breach of an oral contract here, this procedure is not generally regarded as good business and, in some cases, is damaging to the reputation of the manufacturer. The proper approach is to make sure that all sales representatives know the company's position regarding the appointment of additional distributors. In most cases, the position is that all appointments of additional distributors will be done by company headquarters. Further, many companies have a policy of not appointing additional distributors where the distribution existing in a given area is already adequate. Sales representatives should know when they are talking to a distributor who is in an area which already has adequate distribution and, at the most, should indicate that if the distributor wants to apply to be a distributor of the company's products, he should write a letter to company headquarters. Sales representatives should not create problems by telling the distributor to be sure to send financial statements and statements of sales volume, because this implies that if all these statements are adequate, he will be appointed as a distributor.

The second approach of consulting with other distributors in the area is an even more severe problem. It may be assumed that if an existing distributor is asked whether or not the company should appoint another distributor in his area for the same product, his answer will be a resounding "no." There is, therefore, no point whatever in asking. Furthermore, consultation with the other distributor may give rise to sufficient evidence to show that an eventual refusal to deal was the result of a conspiracy between the manufacturer and other distributors in the area rather than a unilateral action of the manufacturer, and this may give rise to an antitrust problem. Sales representatives should be instructed to discuss distributorship matters only with the particular distributor involved. In no event should they be permitted to discuss a relationship between the company and one distributor with another distributor. This is especially true in the area of the appointment or termination of distributors.

There are a number of good cases which indicate that a manufacturer may consult with existing distributors about appointing a third distributor. In the event that a distributor who is refused appointment or terminated raises the problem and threatens a lawsuit, these cases should definitely be used in support of the company's bargaining position. Naturally, they should also be relied on heavily if the matter ever gets to court. However, these cases should not be used for planning purposes, and a one-on-one approach between manufacturer and distributor should be encouraged. The reason for this is that experience with a great many distributor-termination cases has shown that when all the files have been examined and all the witnesses have been deposed, it turns out that the case was very seldom pure, and some conversations concerning resale prices and territories have occurred. This, of course, makes the case much more difficult to defend. Furthermore, the practice of consulting other distributors about a termination seems to provoke litigation—whether or not the litigation has merit—and it is always best to keep out of litigious situations even if the probability of eventual success by the other side is low.

Ongoing Restraints on the Distributor

This heading covers restrictions as to (1) prices, (2) territories, (3) customers, and (4) the handling of competitive goods and purchases of separate items from a manufacturer.

Price Restrictions

If there is one thing which is abundantly clear under the antitrust laws, it is that almost all forms of agreement affecting prices are unlawful. This rule also applies to a resale price maintenance agreement between a manufacturer and an intermediary.

Once a manufacturer has sold his product to an independent wholesaler or distributor, it is illegal for him to attempt to dictate the resale price of that product. It is immaterial whether price maintenance is done in a direct or an indirect way.

It might be interesting to examine some of the motives behind a manufacturer's attempt to maintain his resale prices. It may be thought that a manufacturer who is selling only to wholesalers would welcome the wholesaler's lower price so that more of his products would be sold. Assuming that the manufacturer maintained his own price to the wholesaler, it would seem that this would increase his volume and be to his general benefit. This might be true in a limited context for a very short term. However, in the long term, price-cutting can have a substantially detrimental effect on the manufacturer for a number of reasons:

1. Other wholesalers will not be able to sell the product at the original price and will, therefore, not want to handle the product because of the low profit margins. The manufacturer's volume, therefore, will be reduced.

2. If the manufacturer himself is selling the product to others, he also will have to reduce his price to meet the competition of the price-cutting wholesaler.

3. In the long run, a substantial price-cutting program can affect the marketability of a product because if the program is extensive, the product will become known in the market as a cheap product, and later, if the prices are raised or brought back to their normal levels, the product will not sell.

A company may unilaterally suggest resale prices and may even counsel distributors as to proper resale prices which will provide the distributor a fair profit. However, this suggesting, or counseling, must not rise to the level of any kind of coercion. Technically, it is not even unlawful to do a little "jawboning" (meaning attempted persuasion of the distributor to charge the recommended price). However, this can create substantial practical problems, especially if done by inexperienced or unsophisticated sales representatives. There is always the possibility that a court may hold that even "jawboning," in the context of a large company with great bargaining power against a small independent distributor, really amounts to coercion. Most antitrust counselors, therefore, are very cautious about allowing their clients to engage in "jawboning." One approach, which seems to be the most practical, is to forbid "jawboning" by the sales force but to inform upper management—

perhaps at the level of district sales manager—that in the proper circumstances, with the proper legal guidance, some persuasion may be possible in this area. When the occasion arises, legal advice should be obtained.

Territory and Customer Restrictions

In 1967, the Supreme Court announced that territory and customer restrictions on independent distributors were per-se violations of the Sherman Act. This gave rise to a whole body of law dealing with distribution and caused antitrust counsel and their companies to reconsider their distribution methods and contracts completely to see that they did not run afoul of this new rule. There were hundreds and hundreds of cases on the point—most of them decided in favor of distributors. Manufacturers were not allowed to introduce evidence as to the reasonableness of their attempted restrictions because such evidence was considered irrelevant under this interpretation of the law.

In 1977, however, the Supreme Court reversed itself and held that restrictions on the distribution system ought to be judged on a rule-of-reason basis. Accordingly, at this time it is necessary to decide whether any restriction placed by a manufacturer on a distributor is procompetitive or anticompetitive. That is, of course, a very difficult and subjective question.

As a practical matter, it is probably best to refrain from attempting to impose on a distributor any restriction which would have been illegal under the old law until you have first described the whole situation to antitrust counsel and he has made a thorough review of the facts and the law and advised you on the legality of your proposed program.

One of the most troublesome aspects of the per-se rule was its application to territories, and that was the context in which it was reversed. There are many variations on territory restrictions. The first is simply to tell a distributor he can't sell the products outside of a defined territory. Another is to tell the distributor he can only sell from a specific location (the location clause). Another is to say that the distributor is assigned an area of primary responsibility and must use adequate efforts to develop all sales in that territory or he will be terminated. This will force him to concentrate on his assigned territory before he goes out into someone else's. The theory is that if he uses enough of his energy to develop his area of primary responsibility adequately, he will not have enough left to go out of that area, or, if he can, at least distribution in the primary area will not be adversely affected. Since the usual justification given by manufacturers for wanting restricted territories is to prevent "skimming" (a process by which a distributor sells to the good accounts in a wide area rather than using his efforts to get all of the business out of a smaller area), assigning an area of primary responsibility can be useful. A related approach is simply to require adequate representation in a given area.

Another technique which is somewhat more difficult to administer is sometimes referred to as the "profit-passover" technique. The approach here is to require a distributor who sells a product in the territory of another distributor to pay some amount to the other distributor to compensate him for his advertising and promotional work.

All of these techniques have to be justified by an analysis of the competitive situation. Obviously, the greater the restriction, the greater the justification needs to be. It is probably very difficult simply to restrict the geographical area in which a distributor will sell because one of the elements of a rule-of-reason inquiry is whether a lesser restriction would have served the same purpose, and the lesser restrictions listed above would probably serve the same purpose in many cases. However, the other restrictions mentioned above were held legal in many cases even under the old per-se law and should be even less risky under the new approach.

The law on restricting which customers a distributor can sell to is essentially the same as for territories; it is a rule-of-reason inquiry. A simple restriction against selling to a particular class of customers is probably difficult to justify. For example, a program which said that a distributor could not sell directly to any company reserved as a national account by the manufacturer would probably be difficult to justify. The manufacturer could, of course, sell national accounts directly, but he could not prevent a distributor from attempting to sell any specific customer without some rather unusual facts to offset the harshness of this restriction. Similarly, a restriction which says that a distributor can sell only to a particular class of customers would be difficult to justify.

Dealing in Goods of a Competitor

Section 3 of the Clayton Act prohibits any sale of goods on the condition, agreement, or understanding that the purchaser is not to use or deal in the goods of a competitor if such an agreement would have the effect of lessening competition or tending to create a monopoly. It is, therefore, improper for a manufacturer to sell his products to a distributor on the condition that the distributor refuse to handle competing lines.

However, the manufacturer is entitled to sell to distributors who will adequately promote his product, and to that end the manufacturer may insist that a distributor sell a reasonable number of his products. In some cases, it may even be possible for a manufacturer to sell to a distributor on condition that some fraction, say 50 percent, of the distributor's total volume consist of the manufacturer's products. If the distributor thereafter were to concentrate his sales in other lines so that of his total sales, 70 percent were of a competitive stock, the manufacturer could thereupon terminate that distributor and appoint another. The manufacturer may also require the distributor to devote "substantial efforts," "best efforts," "adequate efforts" or some other phrase indicating that the distributor is bound to promote the products actively. The manufacturer may also establish reasonable sales goals in terms of absolute dollars, and if those goals are not met, the manufacturer may terminate the distributor. The basic point is that the covenants should be affirmative rather than negative.

Tying

Tying arrangements have been discussed in the context of a maker of machinery trying to force the customer to buy supplies for the machinery from him. The same principle holds true in the distribution area. It is illegal to tie different products together so that a distributor has to purchase something he doesn't want in order to get something he does. On the other hand, the situation here is different because the manufacturer has a legitimate interest in requiring distributors to carry a reasonably representative line of the manufacturer's products and to stock a reasonable amount of inventory of those products. Accordingly, judgment and reason must govern.

Full-line forcing refers to a requirement that a distributor handle the manufacturer's full line of products. There are at least two good cases holding that full-line forcing is not a violation of the antitrust laws. However, conservative counsel will want to temper these holdings with some good judgment. First of all, even these cases make it very clear that full-line forcing cannot be used to coerce distributors into overstocking or selling only the supplier's products. Second, the horizons of section 5 of the Federal Trade Commission Act are constantly expanding.

Of course, it goes without saying that full-line forcing is only legal if substantially related products are concerned. In these days of conglomerate diversification, full-line forcing cannot be used as a justification for requiring customers to purchase substantially unrelated lines of products. It is obviously one thing for a furniture manufacturer to require a distributor to stock a full line of his office furniture and quite another for him to require a customer to purchase a certain quantity of home furnishings in order to carry the office-furniture line. In other words, full-line forcing is limited to a legitimate line.

Full-line forcing, by its very name, seems coercive in nature, and management will probably want to think very carefully about any arrangement which will have the effect of forcing distributors to purchase substantially more of the company's products than they would if they were conducting their business in a normal, efficient, and aggressive manner. However, manufacturers are certainly entitled to require their distributors to represent their lines adequately. A manufacturer does not have to sell to a distributor who only wants to spot-buy. If all the distributor wants to do is keep a very small number of fast-moving items in stock and buy anything else from the manufacturer when he gets an order, the manufacturer may either refuse to deal with that distributor or insist, as a condition of future dealings, that the distributor more adequately represent the line.

Somewhat related to full-line forcing is the concept of block-booking, which requires the distributor to purchase the products in certain groups which are put together by the seller. The concept arose in the context of movies, where Loews packaged its pictures into certain blocks which a theater had to take. Of course, the block contained both the popular films which the theater wanted and the unpopular ones which it didn't. The Supreme Court held the arrangement to be an illegal tying arrangement.

In this area, management should avoid any obvious program which involves the coercive tying of two separate lines. On the other hand, an aggressive program of requiring distributors to handle a full line of merchandise should not create substantial problems if:

1. It makes reasonable business sense for the distributor and is accepted by most distributors (if most distributors object strenuously, the program should probably be reevaluated)

2. The program is not used to prevent distributors from handling the goods of a competitor

3. The program is free of other anticompetitive implications

Exclusive Distributorships

In some situations, it is good business for a manufacturer and a distributor to agree that the manufacturer will sell his products only to a particular distributor in a given area. The essential reason for this is that the business of manufacturing is very different from the business of selling or distributing. Furthermore, the distribution process requires a substantial amount of capital. A manufacturer may not have the ability or capital to distribute his goods himself. An independent distributor can fill this need, but in order to have good distribution, the distributor must, in many cases, have some assurance from the manufacturer that his investment will produce a profit. The distributor will be very reluctant to expend a substantial amount of effort and money if there are no assurances that another distributor will not open up shortly in the next block with precisely the same products. In order for the manufacturer to induce the distributor to provide adequate service, full inventories, and a full line of products, it is often necessary for him to promise in return that he will not sell his products to anyone else in that territory.

Generally, the legality of these arrangements is governed by the rule of reason. At common law, it was lawful to agree not to compete with the buyer of products in such a way as to derogate from the value of the property or business sold, provided that the restriction was "such only as to afford a fair protection to the buyer's interest and not so large as to interfere with the interest of the public."

Under the Sherman Act, which is the principal antitrust law applicable to these types of arrangements, exclusive selling arrangements have traditionally been sustained where the manufacturer has no monopoly of the product and the restraint of trade is ancillary to a reasonable main purpose (e.g., assuring a source of supply to the distributor) and fairly protective of that distributor's interest, but not so large as to interfere with the interests of the public. Conversely, there is a violation of the Sherman Act if the seller enjoys a monopoly position or if the buyer is attempting to corner the market. The usual question in these types of cases is whether there is effective inter-brand competition in the relevant market so that there are other suppliers to whom competing buyers can turn. The following is generally accepted to be a fair statement of the law:

> A manufacturer of a product, other and equivalent brands of which are readily available in the market, may select his customers, and for this purpose he may "franchise" certain dealers to whom, alone, he will sell his goods. . . . If the restraint stops at that point—if nothing more is involved than vertical "confinement" of the manufacturer's own sales of the merchandise to selected dealers, and if competitive products are readily available to others, the restriction, on these facts alone, would not violate the Sherman Act. [*United States v. Arnold Schwinn & Co.*, 388 U.S. 365 (1967)]

If the exclusive agreement is broader than is necessary to protect the buyer, the restraint may be held unreasonable and, therefore, violative of the Sherman Act. The word "exclusive" is a troublesome one. It should not be used without a full explanation of precisely what is meant because it could have these other meanings:

1. It could mean that the manufacturer will allow only the designated distributor to distribute the goods in the exclusive territory. If other distributors encroached, the manufacturer would cut them off. This would be a very difficult restriction to justify. In most cases, it would probably be held illegal.

2. It could mean that the distributor will only be allowed to sell in the described territory. If he strayed from this territory, he would be cut off. This would also be an interpretation which would result in substantial antitrust exposure.

Terminations

Termination of distributors is one of the most troublesome areas of antitrust law. The following factors create problems:

1. Termination of a distributor is a specifically identifiable event which usually gives rise to at least the threat of a lawsuit. The terminated distributor usually

suffers a financial loss, and he is usually a business executive with a lawyer. This is a bad combination for the one causing the loss.

2. The present state of the antitrust law is not understood by many business executives and even some business counselors. They think that every refusal to deal by a manufacturer is a violation of the antitrust laws.

3. When all the facts are gathered, it frequently turns out that a sales representative or field representative has made comments which could at least be interpreted as suggesting anticompetitive reasons for the termination—usually enough to get most termination cases to a jury. This situation is always dangerous for a large manufacturer being sued by a small business executive.

Because of these factors, distributor terminations create a special class of problems for business executives and antitrust lawyers.

Look at the Trial Risks

Statistically, the manufacturer has about a sixty-to-forty chance of winning a distributor-termination suit if he just looks at past reported cases. However, there are probably 1000 cases settled for each one tried. These cases are easy to settle, and this is one fact which should be taken into consideration. Generally, a rather modest amount of money—or in some cases merely reinstatement—will settle the case. Also, counsel should keep in mind that these cases are difficult for large manufacturers because of the image created at trial when they are sued by small business executives. Further, the injury of the terminated distributor is readily apparent to the jury.

Analyze

Much of the analysis is common sense, but a thorough, systematic approach is necessary. Following is a general outline of the required considerations in the analysis:

1. Check all facts, including files, conversations, letters, and contacts or involvement of other distributors.

2. Does the distributor owe you money? Counterclaims are typical if you sue him for merchandise delivered.

3. What are the real motives for the termination?

4. What kinds of facts exist that may give your opponent an argument that the motive is anticompetitive? Are there complaints from other distributors?

5. Obtain a ball-park estimate of financial exposure if he sues you.

6. Has this distributor made investments in reliance on your line?

7. Consider the effect on your total system. Remember that others may sue and others may become militant.

8. Be certain to filter out emotions. Many times field salespeople become personally and emotionally involved in termination situations, and these emotions must be filtered out so that the facts are considered.

9. Decide whether the distributor is really hurting you—or standing in the way of a genuine opportunity for better distribution.

Conclude

Following the above analysis, one of three conclusions will usually be fairly easy to draw:

1. You don't really have to cut off the distributor because he's doing a pretty good job, or he may have some faults, but basically he's not hurting you or standing in the way of better distribution. In this event, it is probably better not to terminate him if there is any antitrust risk.

2. You would really like to terminate the distributor because he is really troublesome, but you can't because there are overriding dangers from an antitrust point of view. In this event, it is better to wait until you have a better record. Document all your problems and establish meaningful quotas for your distributors. Either make the distributor perform well or have established bona-fide and documented reasons for the termination.

3. Terminate. In this event, the procedure is important.

Terminate

The key word is "fairness." When you have decided to terminate a distributor, make sure you do the following:

1. Give longest possible notice.

2. Explain the business reasons in an honest but firm and unequivocal way.

3. Refrain from mentioning any other distributor.

4. Give the distributor a chance to minimize any financial losses.

5. Give him a chance to complete any short-term deals and retain his anticipated profit from them.

Do not rely on the contract for a short notice on termination, send a heavy-handed letter, or send a letter which includes any anticompetitive language. You might possibly give him a temporary supply of goods, but be precise here. State exactly what you will do and for how long. You might also arrange for other means to get products—as buying them from another distributor. This is especially important if you are replacing one distributor with another.

Threats of termination will generate promises of all kinds. Promises will include pricing, territory, and customers. Do not agree to any of these. Make your decision and stick to it.

Do not leave unanswered letters in your file to cloud the record, and make certain that field people send in all papers bearing on the termination and give the complete story.

Federal Trade Commission

Section 5 of the Federal Trade Commission Act prohibits any unfair method of competition. This very broad statement can be construed to apply to almost any program which unduly restrains competition or which is in any way unfair or deceptive to consumers. Fortunately, this statute can only be enforced by the Federal Trade Commission, and the remedies are generally cease-and-desist orders rather than large fines. However, section 5 should not be overlooked when considering the legality of programs involving distribution.

State Laws

Counsel dealing with distribution problems should be aware of the increased activity of state legislatures in this area. To date, most state activity has involved legislation dealing with the business franchise, where the franchisee pays some fee to the franchisor for use of the trademark or trade name.

However, this is not universally true. For example, a Wisconsin statute provides that dealership agreements entered into after the effective date of the new law cannot be terminated by the granter except with good cause, and the burden of proving the good cause is on the granter. The granter must give 90 days' notice of termination and must allow the dealer an opportunity to cure the alleged defect causing the termination. Also, some franchise statutes define the term "franchise" in such a way as to include most normal distributors (even those who do not pay a franchise fee).

CHAPTER TWELVE

THE ROBINSON-PATMAN ACT

INTRODUCTION

There are those who say that since pricing is so important to a business's profitability, the Robinson-Patman Act, which deals with price discrimination, is one of the most frequently encountered antitrust problems. There are others who say that the Robinson-Patman Act should be repealed because it is not being enforced by the government and is so complex that it is impossible to comply with anyway.

Both points of view are correct in their own way. The Robinson-Patman Act is one of the most frequently encountered problems in running a business, and it is not being enforced by the federal government. Whether or not it should be repealed is an academic discussion because it has not been repealed. The enforcement problem is a bit misleading because while it is true that the act is not being enforced by the federal government, it can be enforced by private litigants, attorneys may recover their fees, and it is one of the antitrust laws under which successful plaintiffs may recover three times their damages. As to the complexity of the act, this, also, is a two-sided coin. To be sure, there are some rather esoteric questions which make it impossible to give definitive conclusions in a number of important factual situations, but, on the other hand, there are many situations where the application of the Robinson-Patman Act is crystal clear and a violation is inviting trouble from private plaintiffs.

While the Robinson-Patman Act has its clear points, it unfortunately doesn't have many simple points. Accordingly, this chapter—even though lengthy—may be guilty of oversimplifying the problem. However, it should point out some of the problems and suggest some areas where companies should be very careful about their pricing practices. It will also suggest some situations which would technically seem to present clear violations of the Robinson-Patman Act under the decided cases and where management, along with its lawyers, is simply going to have to make a decision as to whether or not the business advantages of the contemplated transaction justify the legal risks.

BACKGROUND

The Robinson-Patman Act is the popular name for section 2 of the Clayton Act. The Clayton Act was passed in 1914, at a time when the flow of goods from manufacturers to consumers followed the relatively simple distribution pattern of manufacturers to intermediaries to retailers to consumers. By 1929, chain stores had established themselves in the retail market and had changed this traditional pattern by eliminating the intermediary. The chain stores, particularly the Great Atlantic & Pacific Tea Company, entered into many arrangements which were thought to be an abuse of their dominant buying power, and in addition, many small grocery stores were forced out of business by the lower prices charged by these chains. With the political pressures of the small grocery stores—coupled with the abuses of the large chains in getting kickbacks and other forms of under-the-table discounts—the time was right for the passage of an act aimed at protecting the small business executive and removing any advantage which a large company might be able to obtain from sellers through its mass purchasing power. Accordingly, in 1936 the Robinson-Patman Act was passed to accomplish these objectives.

While the act had its inequities and problems when passed, it has been further outmoded by additional developments in the distribution network. It is no longer unusual to find companies occupying more than one position in the chain of distribution. Manufacturing companies may have their own retail outlets; retailing companies may join together to form larger warehousing companies in order to buy in larger quantities; and even those people in the middle of the distribution line who neither manufacture nor sell to the public may occupy more than one position. Accordingly, some of the rather straightforward rules enunciated in the Robinson-Patman Act are simply impossible to apply in the modern commercial environment. Other principles, however, remain quite clear and easy to apply, and, since pricing is so important to a business's profitability, it is necessary to understand the constraints within which a company must operate—along with the opportunities and flexibility which are available with proper planning and understanding of the law.

VIOLATIONS UNDER THE ROBINSON-PATMAN ACT

The basic prohibition of the Robinson-Patman Act is against a seller charging different prices to different customers for the same product where such a price differential might injure competition.

Almost every word of the act has special significance. In order to have a violation of the Robinson-Patman Act, there must be all of the following: (1) discrimination in price, (2) sale of a commodity, (3) sale in interstate commerce, (4) goods of like grade and quality, (5) sold by the same seller, and (6) with a possible injury to competition.

If all of these elements are present, the defendant's only recourse is to use one of the following defenses: (1) meeting competition, (2) cost justification, (3) availability (saying that the lower price was available to all competing buyers—basically a rebuttal of the element of competitive injury, (4) changing market conditions (including sales made in a discontinuance of business in a particular product).

Discrimination in Price

As a general proposition, a discrimination in price means any difference in price. However, the following differences in price may not be illegal price discrimination under the Robinson-Patman Act: (1) different prices charged at substantially different times, (2) a difference between the price charged in a single transaction and the price charged under a long-term contract arrangement with a particular customer, and (3) quantity discounts, if the same discount or long-term arrangement is functionally available to all competing purchasers. However, each of these examples is a very troublesome situation which should have careful legal review. In fact, most of the decided cases go against these kinds of situations; analysis will rarely yield a clear answer, and there will be some legal risk-weighing in the process.

The act does not define the term "price," but the general approach is to determine what the buyer is required to pay and not what the seller receives. For example, consider the case of a manufacturer located in Philadelphia who sells the same merchandise to purchasers in New York and Los Angeles. Further assume that the seller grants a 2 percent discount for cash payment. Taking an example sale of 100 dollars worth of merchandise, it is conceivable that the New York purchaser will not take advantage of the 2 percent cash discount and will pay the seller 100 dollars, while the Los Angeles purchaser will take advantage of it and will pay the seller only 98 dollars. This doesn't matter—there is no illegal discrimination. Further, it has obviously cost the seller more to ship the goods to Los Angeles than to New York. However, for Robinson-Patman Act purposes, there would be no discrimination in price here, either. It would also be perfectly permissible for the seller to sell his product F.O.B. his own plant and add the freight as a separate item. The seller could also sell at a "delivered price" and make it the same for everyone, averaging the cost of freight over all the customers.

Price discriminations must be between different purchasers. It is obvious that one who buys directly from a seller is a purchaser. However, the Federal Trade Commission has developed a doctrine of the so-called "indirect purchaser" which further complicates this problem. This doctrine provides that where the purchasing entity is under the control of either the seller or someone further down the chain of distribution, the transaction might be collapsed to characterize the sale as being directly from the seller to the person further down the chain, with the result that a price discrimination is created.

The problem usually results where buyers gather together and form a cooperative buying organization for the purpose of obtaining volume discounts. A classic example of the harshness of the Robinson-Patman Act and the difficulty encountered when you try to follow all of its implications is this case of the group-buying company. Many group-buying cases have involved the automobile-parts industry, where a group of retailers got together and formed a larger buying entity to obtain a larger discount. Typically, these retailers have joined to form a warehouse distributor, who purchased in larger quantities from the automobile-parts makers. Since the warehouse distributor was not competing with the retailer, the parts makers were free to grant a lower price to the warehouse distributor without bothering to consider such defenses as cost justification or meeting competition.

In the first set of group-buying cases, the retailers had formed a paper corporation in which the warehouse distributor was nothing more than a paper entity which would buy the products from the manufacturing companies and then have them shipped throughout the area to the participating retailers. As one would suspect, the Federal Trade Commission was uniformly successful in attacking these paper corporations and holding that the retailers were indirect purchasers from the manufacturer. Accordingly, it was held that the members of the retail group were granted a lower price—the one nominally charged to the warehouse distributor—while other competing retailers who were not part of this buying group had to pay a higher price.

The second set of group-buying cases, however, were far more troublesome. After the paper-corporation scheme was shown to be legally ineffective, some automobile-parts retailers formed a legitimate, bona-fide warehouse-distributor corporation. The warehouse-distributor corporation had all the attributes of any other warehouse distributor, including a large inventory, employees, and capitalization. Furthermore, in some of these cases, the warehouse distributor serviced other people besides the member retailers. Even in these kinds of cases, however, the Federal Trade Commission was successful in having the retailers deemed to be indirect purchasers, just as in the paper-corporation cases. This is one of the many areas where it has been strongly argued that the Robinson-Patman Act does not promote competition at all but, in fact, hinders it and causes prices to the ultimate consumer to be higher than they might otherwise be.

Sale of a Commodity

The Robinson-Patman Act only applies in the case of the sale of a commodity. If the transaction is not a sale, or if the thing being sold is not a commodity, the act simply does not apply. Consequently, it has been held that the act does not apply to sales of advertising space. Similarly, the act would not apply to a leasing transaction because a lease is not the same as a sale. Also, consignment transactions or credit is not covered by the act.

Sale in Interstate Commerce

The Robinson-Patman Act only applies to goods sold *in* interstate commerce. The standard is somewhat more restrictive than the "affecting interstate commerce" test used in the Sherman Act. While any kind of a meaningful discussion of exactly what either *affects* or is *in* interstate commerce within the meaning of federal legislation can involve many pages of decisions, it is clear that if both the purchasing and selling parties operate entirely within one state, the Robinson-Patman Act will probably not apply. However, as is the case with most of the subjects discussed in this book, while the activity may not be covered by the federal statute if it takes place totally within one state, the majority of industrialized states have statutes similar to the federal statute. Therefore, the commerce requirement is really a technicality which can be used by lawyers in litigation rather than a meaningful tool for business planning.

Goods of Like Grade and Quality

In order for the Robinson-Patman Act to apply, there must be a discrimination in price for goods of like grade and quality.

The usual question here involves private brands. The law is clear that goods are of like grade and quality if they are, in fact, substantially the same, even if they have different labels or brands.

For example, where Borden produced its own well-known Borden Evaporated Milk and, in addition, produced the same product for private brands, it was held that the two products were of like grade and quality. The fact that one brand was extensively advertised on a national basis did not change this result.

On the other hand, the customer acceptance generated by the national advertising program and the lack of it in the private brand may be used to show that there is really no effect on competition because of the discriminatory price. In fact, that is exactly what happened in the *Borden* case when it was remanded on the damage issue. On remand, the Fifth Circuit Court of Appeals found no evidence to support an injury to competition either at the primary level (competitors of Borden) or at the secondary level (customers of Borden and their competitors). The court said: "We are of the firm view that where a price differential between a premium and a non-premium brand reflects no more than a customer preference for the premium brand, the price differential creates no competitive advantage to the recipient of the cheaper, private brand product. . . ." In addition, there may be a cost-justification defense if the price difference reflects only the cost of advertising a national brand.

Sold by the Same Seller

In order for the Robinson-Patman Act to apply, the different prices must be quoted by the same seller.

Generally, corporate entities are recognized in this context, and a subsidiary's price may not be deemed the parent's price unless the parent directs or participates in the subsidiary's pricing decision. The courts have been fairly liberal in applying this rule and have held that a subsidiary's corporate identity should be recognized even if it is wholly owned by the parent corporation and even if its officers, with one exception, are also officers of the parent corporation. This is another example of the inconsistency of Robinson-Patman Act decisions. Compare, for example, the holding in this case with the holdings in the group-buying cases, where the court deliberately disregarded bona-fide corporations in order to strike down the arrangement.

Injury to Competition

The Robinson-Patman Act applies only if the discrimination has the effect of lessening competition substantially or tending to create a monopoly in any line of commerce. This is definitely the most important and least understood aspect of the act.

The starting point must be a discussion of the various lines of commerce. This is important because there is a tremendous practical difference between the application of the act at the various levels. This is true even though the act itself makes no distinction between these levels and, as a matter of fact, uses the phrase "any line of commerce," which has been determined to include all of the levels of competition. The following are the three levels of commerce:

1. Competition at the primary level, or in the primary line, refers to competition between the company which grants the discriminatory price and another company competing with it.

   For example, if a seller of heavy machinery granted an illegal discount to a customer, his competition at the primary level would consist of other sellers of heavy machinery. In this situation, the other sellers—his primary-line competitors—would have a claim against the discriminating seller only if they could show injury *to competition* among them. The fact that one of them—who, in fact, did compete with the company granting the discriminatory price—was injured would not be enough. The act is designed to protect *competition*, not the individual competitor. On the other hand, in order to recover any damages, each seller would have to prove his own injury, either by showing that he lost a specific piece of business or in some other way. Thus, a complaining party in the primary line would have to show his own individual damages and some injury to competition. In addition, the history of the Robinson-Patman Act indicates that this is not the kind of problem it was supposed to solve. Accordingly, the courts have been strict in requiring proof of injury in this kind of case.

2. Competition at the secondary level refers to competition between the purchaser who is granted a discriminatory price and another company competing with him. This is the kind of problem the Robinson-Patman Act was supposed to solve. It is assumed that if a company buys a product for less, it can sell it for less, and injury to the competitor who was not favored with the lower price will thus be presumed. However, this is only true if the product is sold in substantially the same form as it is purchased. This is the typical grocery-store situation, in which so many Robinson-Patman Act cases arise, and it also applies to the automobile-parts industry.

   This situation must be distinguished from the normal purchasing of supplies which are used or consumed in the manufacturing process. Here, even assuming a particular purchaser is favored, it may not have any effect on the disfavored purchaser if the item is only a small part of the total cost of the finished product. For example, if one purchaser who manufactured heavy machinery was allowed a discriminatorily low price on office supplies, the effect on competition in the heavy-machinery market would be minimal. In fact, while some lawyers would undoubtedly dispute the logic of this statement, it would appear that the level of risk in a Robinson-Patman Act case is lowered almost to the point of insignificance in any situation which involves a commodity which is not going to be resold in substantially the same form in which it is purchased. Thus, business executives who engage in businesses which involve the creation of an item—like an automobile part—and then the sale of that item in substantially the same form down the chain of distribution have to be very concerned about the Robinson-Patman Act. Retail-oriented companies and mass merchandisers also have to be very concerned. On the other hand, companies which produce components, or which sell items which are traditionally used as a part of some other product, have a much lower risk of any Robinson-Patman Act problem and, accordingly, much greater flexibility in their pricing practices. Many companies occupy both positions. For example, bearing manufacturers will typically sell to both original-equipment manufacturers, which will use their ball bearings in other equipment, and to bearing distributors, which will sell those bearings in exactly the same form down a chain of distribution. For the sales of the ball bearings which are made to original-equipment manufacturers, the Robinson-Patman Act could be largely ignored. On the other hand, for the sales of the bearings made to bearing-distributing companies, the act must be complied with rather explicitly in order to avoid unnecessary risk of exposure from some bearing distributor who may have to pay a higher price.

3. Beyond the level of secondary competition, there are further layers of competition which may be affected by a discriminatory price. This is called the "tertiary level."

For example, the normal chain of distribution in the auto-parts field is from manufacturer to warehouse distributor to jobber to retailer to consumer, but the manufacturer who sells to a distributor may also own some retail outlets himself or sell to a large direct-buying retailer. His distributor also sells to retail outlets which compete with the manufacturer's retail outlets or with the direct-buying retailer. This, the traditional pattern of the so-called "dual-distribution" situation, can create troublesome situations from a Robinson-Patman Act standpoint. In fact, under the decided cases it is virtually impossible to counsel companies in many of these situations. If the manufacturer sells at the same price to everyone, he will have no legal problems, but he will have an almost impossible business situation because his distributor will find it impossible to find a retailer willing to purchase from him when a competing retailer is purchasing directly from the manufacturer at a price equal to the distributor's cost. On the other hand, if the manufacturer sells at different prices, he will have to justify the price discrimination in some way, and a justification is hard to find. Generally, the defense is that the wholesaler and retailer do not compete with one another but, in today's jumbled distribution network, this is often not the case.

The line-of-commerce reasoning is difficult and complex, but from a practical point of view it is often more important than any of the other aspects of the act. Accordingly, it is useful to pursue this matter by giving examples of problems on the various levels.

Primary-Level Examples

A national company sells products at a discriminatorily low price to a single purchaser in one city. The action is part of the company's attempt to gain a large market share in that city or to drive out its principal local competitor.

In this case, the local competitor would have a good case under the Robinson-Patman Act against the offending seller, even though it is in the primary line. The reason is the aggravating factor—that the lower price was offered in only one city with the express purpose of driving out the local competition. The local competitor might also have a case under section 2 of the Sherman Act (monopolization).

In another case, a national manufacturing company offers a large national retailer a very low price on a line of wood-working tools designed for the home do-it-yourself market. Another *manufacturer* of hardware hears of this and institutes suit.

This would be a very difficult case for the plaintiff to prove. In order to prove any violation of the Robinson-Patman Act at all, he would first have to prove an adverse effect on competition (not just an adverse effect on *him*), and then he would have to prove his own damages by showing actual loss of specific business. In order to show an adverse effect on competition, the plaintiff would have to introduce evidence of some kind of anticompetitive motive, which might be very difficult for him to acquire. Even assuming the plaintiff could show some anticompetitive motive, he would still have to show business lost because of the discriminatorily low price granted by his competitor. Thus, as a practical matter, the national manufacturing company which granted the lower price would not have much exposure in the primary level of competition.

Secondary-Level Example

A national retailer obtains a discriminatorily low price on hardware. This time, however, the *local hardware store* (which purchases wood-working tools from the same manufacturer) complains. His complaint is that he was not offered an equally low price; the fact that he did not buy in as large a volume as the national retailer is not relevant. The local hardware store introduces evidence to show that his store is in competition with the national retailer, their locations being only a mile apart in the same suburb.

Here, the local retailer would have a good case, even though he might not be able to show that any particular customer patronized the national retailer over his store because of the lower price. He would still have to prove his damages, but some damages could be presumed from the mere fact of the discrimination. Also, he might be entitled to an injunction, and there is a good possibility that his attorney could recover his fees from the defendant.

This, of course, is the classic problem of the mass merchandiser versus the local shop owner. Many mass merchandisers and companies who want to sell to them at a lower price have devised ways to get around this problem. From a legal point of view, the clearest way is for the mass merchandiser to have everything designed to his specifications. That way, there is no question of like grade and quality because his products are different from those sold by his competitor.

This is what Sears Roebuck has done. Many Sears Roebuck products are made by companies which sell almost identical products to competitors of Sears. However, the Sears design is just a little different, and this makes the Robinson-Patman Act inapplicable. Naturally, the precise point at which one graduates into a different product, as opposed to the same product with a minor difference, is a little ambiguous. For example, if all Sears did was have the standard products painted a different color, it is unlikely it would be able to justify a claim that the products were really different. However, when you change the basic appearance of the product—perhaps substitute some additional design specifications and have the Sears name placed on the product—it would appear that there is enough of a difference.

Retailers who are not as large as Sears Roebuck and do not have the capability of designing their own specifications have to be a little more ingenious in order to get around the Robinson-Patman Act. Here is where counseling becomes difficult, and practicalities often dictate that a particular course of action be undertaken even though, as a strictly legal proposition, it is probably not entirely free from risk.

One defense a manufacturer can use, if the retailer can convince the manufacturer to try and use it, is the cost-justification defense. However, as further explained in this chapter, cost justification is an exceedingly complex and difficult defense. Accordingly, one must view the cost-justification defense on two levels. One is whether or not it would succeed in court, where the answer is almost always going to be "no," and the other is whether or not it at least provides enough justification for the price difference to blunt any serious consequences.

The only other applicable defense under the Robinson-Patman Act is the meeting-competition defense, and this is really only good for the second seller in line. If a mass merchandiser like Penney's or K-Mart comes to a seller with a specific competitive offer and asks that seller to meet the competitive offer, there will be no problem. However, the meeting-competition defense will not be useful to the first seller.

The problem becomes even more acute when the mass merchandiser uses the manufacturer's name. If the mass merchandiser has his own name put on the product and issues his own catalog, he is assuming some of the costs of the seller and, as a practical matter, considerably lessening his exposure under the Robinson-Patman Act. On the other hand, if the mass merchandiser is the typical discount store and wants to advertise name brands, there is not going to be any question at all about like grade and quality. The products will be absolutely identical, all the way down to the trademark. In these kinds of situations, both the mass merchandiser and the seller have to use some discretion when pricing the product. One device which has been used to justify a lower price are annual contracts, where the mass merchandiser agrees to purchase all of his requirements from one seller, thus distinguishing his transaction from that of the corner hardware store, which purchases products on an as-needed basis without any annual commitment. Another device is the cost-justification study, which involves computing the savings generated by larger volume.

Warehousing services are another device which is sometimes used. The mass merchandiser will purchase a large amount, warehouse it himself, and send it out to his retailing outlets on an as-needed basis. Unfortunately, not only is there nothing in the Robinson-Patman Act which justifies a functional discount, but the group-buying cases already alluded to would certainly stand in the way of any kind of legal justification for this scheme. If a group of retailers can't get together and form a warehousing company, one retailer certainly cannot justify doing the same thing for his own stores. Therefore the warehousing approach can only be used to justify actual cost reductions to the seller.

Another argument which the mass merchandiser might make is that the seller has to maintain his own sales force and issue his own catalogs when he sells to the local hardware store, but when he sells to the mass merchandiser, he does not need a sales force or other service in the form of a manufacturer's sales representative to counsel distributors as to product performance and proper inventory levels.

The trouble with all of these justifications is that the mass merchandiser is likely to want a price which is lower than the manufacturer can justify by adding up all of the easily identified cost-savings factors. In addition, the technical rules governing a cost-justification defense would make it very difficult for anyone to give advance clearance to the transaction from a legal point of view without doing an elaborate accounting study and a legal review.

Tertiary-Level Example

The impact of the Robinson-Patman Act at levels beyond the primary and the secondary is perhaps its most complicated and troublesome aspect.

The prime example of competition at the tertiary level is the 1969 opinion of the United States Supreme Court in *Perkins v. Standard Oil Company of California.* In this case, the plaintiff operated a retail outlet and purchased directly from Standard. Standard also sold to a wholesaler at a lower price. At this point, there was no Robinson-Patman Act problem because the wholesaler did not compete with the retailer. However, Perkins alleged that the price Standard granted to the wholesaler was so low that the wholesaler could sell to Perkins' competitor, who could then undersell Perkins. The Supreme Court held that in spite of this distant removal from Standard, the Robinson-Patman Act covered injury at this level and allowed Perkins to recover over $1 million from Standard.

The *Perkins* case is factually complex because Perkins had wholesale activities in addition to its retail outlets. If the Court had indicated that the basis for its holding was the actual competition between the favored wholesaler and Perkins' wholesale operation, the case would not have created much difficulty. However, while the case is far from clear, it seems to indicate that in a dual-distribution situation, the manufacturer is responsible for the price charged by a wholesaler who sells to a retailer who happens to compete with other retailers who are buying direct from the manufacturer. Obviously, this flies in the face of the Sherman Act and, as a practical matter, is absolutely unworkable. However, no one has suggested any very clear solution to the problem. Companies which charge one price to a wholesaler and another price to a direct-purchasing retailer, therefore, have some exposure if the wholesaler sells to retailers who happen to compete with the direct-buying outlet. However, since a company has no control over the price at which the wholesaler resells the product, there is an obvious practical problem in this approach to distribution, and it makes counseling very difficult. Theoretically, the manufacturer could simply refrain from selling to anyone beyond the wholesale level. However, it would be a sad commentary on our legal framework to say that a manufacturer had to pass up business simply because he couldn't figure out a legal price to charge for the product. This, unfortunately, is just about the state of existing law. The manufacturer is going to have to either refrain from engaging in this kind of dual distribution or else realize that there is some theoretical exposure under the Perkins doctrine and make whatever management decisions seem appropriate.

Functional Discounts

Functional discounts refer to a pricing technique by which a seller sells at different prices to different levels of distribution. The Robinson-Patman Act does not have any provisions dealing with functional discounts. In considering a functional discount, therefore, it must be tested under normal Robinson-Patman Act rules, which means that it must be justified by showing that: (1) the discount will not result in any effect on competition, (2) the discount is cost-justified, or (3) The discount was granted to meet competition.

Since the cost-justification defense is very difficult to employ, the usual justification for a functional discount is that it has no effect on competition because wholesalers do not compete with retailers. In today's climate, however, this is often simply not the case.

DEFENSES

Cost Justification

The Robinson-Patman Act says that it does not prevent "differentials which make only due allowance for the differences in the cost of manufacture, sale, or delivery." The cost-justification defense, while logically very appealing, is shrouded with so much uncertainty and so many legal technicalities that some commentators have tagged it "marginally illusory." The following should be kept in mind in conducting a cost-justification study as a defense in a court case:

1. The burden of proving the defense rests upon the person claiming it.

2. It is not necessary to prove an absolute mathematical identity between the costs saved and the allowance. However, the cost differential must make only due allowance and cannot exceed greatly the actual costs saved. Thus, about the only leeway a company has is that it doesn't have to pass any mathematical-exactitude test. Beyond that, however, it is not even clear how close is close when you are trying to justify a differential, although it is clear that close is pretty close indeed, and the courts have not given any comfort to the use of approximations or estimates.

3. Volume discounts must be justified by relating the savings to manufacture, sale, or delivery through the volume transaction.

4. The cost justification must relate to the costs saved as applied to a particular *class* of purchasers, not to a particular purchaser. In other words, the cost-justification defense cannot be based upon incremental or marginal costs. For example, if a manufacturing plant is operating at 100 percent capacity without requiring overtime, there can be no price differential between previous customers and a new customer whose orders require overtime, even though the company could clearly identify what work the people would be doing on overtime and that such work would be attributable to the new customer.

5. The costs involved must be the costs of manufacture, sale, or delivery. Any cost justification must come within one of these three categories. If it does not, it is deemed a so-called indirect cost and cannot be considered. An automotive-parts manufacturer who was required to maintain an investment of over $10 million in distribution facilities which serviced only warehouse distributors and jobbers attempted to justify a differential in the price he charged original-equipment manufacturers and the price he charged warehouse distributors and jobbers on the basis of a reasonable return on this substantial investment which served only the one class of purchasers. This was denied by the Federal Trade Commission, however, because return on investment was considered by them to be not a cost of manufacture, sale, or delivery but an indirect cost.

6. Marketing and distribution costs are acceptable sources for cost-justification data.

7. Manufacturing costs must relate to differing methods or quantities in which products are sold or delivered. Typical acceptable manufacturing costs include product development and design, tooling up, employee training, and methods of production. Brokerage or commission costs savings are also acceptable cost-justification figures.

8. In most cases, the price differential will be based on elements of costs which are spread over more than a single product or a single customer, and, therefore, problems of allocation arise. In this area, one rule emerges supreme: Accounting estimates alone will, in every instance, fail to justify a cost differential. Estimates can be used, but in order to be considered, they must fall in the category of obvious and commonsense assumptions. An example of this is the commission's agreement that loaf cheese and package cheese, carried in the same truck, shared roughly equal delivery costs per unit. Generally, a plausible allocation formula should be evolved, based upon some sort of empirical data. For example, an allocation of salaries of sales and clerical personnel may be based on a time study or based on the number of orders handled. Sampling techniques may also be used in arriving at a reasonable allocation formula.

9. One cannot combine an overjustified cost differential with an underjustified cost differential and come up with the conclusion that no price differential exists.

   For example, a parts manufacturer who sold automotive parts to both original-equipment manufacturers and to warehouse distributors and jobbers attempted a cost justification by showing that the prices he charged certain original-equipment manufacturers resulted in a smaller cost differential than was justified while the prices he charged other original-equipment manufacturers resulted in a larger cost differential than was justified. The commission refused to allow the company to average out sales to all original-equipment manufacturers in such a way as to come to the conclusion that there was no price discrimination. Its reasoning was that sales to each of the original-equipment manufacturers created an area of competition, and, therefore, an injury to competition occurred even though it might be balanced out by an opposite effect on competition in another area.

In conducting a cost-justification study for purposes of justifying a proposed course of action (as opposed to conducting one as a defense in a court case), the following should be kept in mind:

1. The study should be conducted so that it looks forward and not backward.

2. It should be well documented.

3. If challenged, it will be open to discovery by the plaintiff. Considering the details which must be contained in this study, this fact alone has deterred the use of the cost-justification defense in many situations.

Changing Market Conditions

The last provision of the Robinson-Patman Act provides that the act does not prevent price changes from time to time where such price changes are in response to changing conditions affecting the market for or the marketability of the goods concerned. Examples given are the deterioration of perishable goods, obsolescence of seasonal goods, distress sales under court process, or sales in good faith in a discontinuance of business in a particular product.

Meeting Competition

Section 2(b) of the Robinson-Patman Act provides that if the seller can show that his lower price or his furnishing of special services or facilities to any purchaser or purchasers was granted in order to meet the equally low price of a competitor or the services or facilities furnished by a competitor, this shall constitute a complete defense to an otherwise valid Robinson-Patman Act complaint. While the meeting-competition defense has not suffered from the same judicial erosion as the cost-justification defense, it is nevertheless encumbered by the following technicalities:

1. The lower price must be granted in order to meet the lower price of a competitor of the company, not the lower price of a competitor of a customer of the company. This is particularly significant in an industry where dealers and manufacturers have a very close day-to-day relationship. The gasoline industry is an example.
   In one case involving the Sun Oil Company, there arose a situation where Super Test was selling gas at a lower price than that charged by Sun Oil stations in the same area. Sun Oil accordingly reduced its price to local gas stations so that they could meet Super Test's prices. The meeting-competition defense was held not to be applicable here because Sun Oil Company was meeting the lower price, not of one of *its* competitors but of the Super Test gasoline stations which were competitors of the Sun Oil stations. In this case, it was assumed that comparable price reductions were not being granted by Super Test's suppliers.

2. Competition must be met in good faith. It has been determined that the good-faith requirement will only be satisfied if the price being met is a lawful price. Therefore, if one supplier is granting an unlawful price-cut to his customers in a particular area, another company cannot respond by granting the same unlawful price-cut to its suppliers in the same area. However, the defendant does not have to show that the price he is meeting is a lawful price. If he, in good faith, *believes* it to be lawful, he may meet the price.

3. A price can be lowered only to *meet* a competitor's price, not to beat it. The one exception to this rule is in a bidding or auction situation, where the lowest bid gets all of the business. Here, one can go slightly below a competitor's bid in order to obtain the business. However, even here it is usually held that the meeting-competition proviso is a defensive measure and cannot be used offensively. Accordingly, any price which is lowered below the actual competitor's price must be examined very carefully. Some of the old Robinson-Patman Act cases make a distinction between granting a price reduction to meet competition for existing customers and granting a price reduction to meet competition for new customers. However, most business counselors rely on the later cases, which seem to indicate that this distinction has no basis in the act and that it doesn't really make any difference whether the customer is a new one or an old one in the meeting-competition setting.

4. A seller has a duty to ascertain and verify, with some degree of particularity, the nature of the price he is trying to meet. For example, the seller cannot rely on reports from his sales representatives to the effect that a competitor is offering a lower price.

    Verification of a competitor's lower prices raises another problem. Because too-energetic effort to ascertain what price a competitor is charging can violate the Sherman Act, most counselors discourage direct contact with competitors in order to verify a price. The Supreme Court has held that trying to get information for the meeting-competition defense is not a defense to illegal price-fixing. In meeting competition, the seller must make a reasonable individualized response in a given situation and must take into consideration the power of the alleged competitor as well as his own strength. Generally, it is dangerous to adopt a pricing plan or system simply because a competitor is known to have granted equivalent prices in individual cases. The Supreme Court has authorized a so-called "feathering" technique, whereby a seller can feather, or scale down, his price reductions in a given area to meet local competition.

    In the gasoline situation, for example, if there was an intense price war in one city, the seller could grant a reduction of 3 cents a gallon inside the city, a reduction of 2 cents a gallon in the near suburbs, a reduction of 1 cent a gallon in the outlying suburbs, and maintain the original price in areas beyond.

5. In the meeting-competition area, the relevant criterion for comparable commodities is a commercial test—equivalent salability—rather than the technical test of like grade and quality used in other parts of the act. This, however, can work to the detriment of a company because if one has a premium product which commands a higher price than a competitor's product, it may not be possible to disregard this premium and meet the competitor's lower prices.

6. As a kind of overriding principle, the cases have emphasized the necessity of reasonable and prudent conduct in using the meeting-competition defense.

Availability

The defense of availability is not spelled out in the Robinson-Patman Act but is alluded to in some of the court cases. The classic statement of the doctrine is in the *Borden* case, decided by the Supreme Court in 1966. Both the majority and dissenting opinions mention the concept, but the following footnote in the dissent by Justice Stewart is usually quoted: "So long as Borden makes private label brands available to all customers of its premium milk, it is unlikely that price discrimination within the meaning of 2(a) can be made out."

In order to use the availability defense, the lower price must be actually available to all competing customers. If it is limited, for example, to carload purchasers, it is not functionally available to small purchasers and therefore availability cannot be used as a defense because small purchasers will not be able to take advantage of the lower price. The availability defense has not yet been fully developed by the courts, but as a practical matter, most business counselors subscribe to the theory that if two different prices are both functionally available to all competing customers, no one is being treated unfairly and no customer is being put at a disadvantage. There is, therefore, no antitrust violation.

BROKERAGE PAYMENTS

Section 2(c) of the Robinson-Patman Act prohibits the granting of commissions, brokerage payments, or other compensation except for services actually rendered by a person on behalf of the person who is paying for the services. To illustrate, assume that an independent seller contacts an independent broker and asks him to act as his agent in finding purchasers for his product. The independent broker contacts an independent purchaser and arranges for him to buy goods from the seller. A brokerage payment is paid to the broker by the seller. This transaction is perfectly permissible. If, however, the broker involved is not independent but is either an employee or otherwise under the direct control of the purchaser, the payment of brokerage to such a person by the seller is unlawful, even if the broker performed the same duties as the independent broker. Of course, so-called "brokerage" or "commission" payments which are, in reality, kickbacks are also illegal. For example, if a purchaser buys products from a seller on the understanding that the seller will pay brokerage although there is no broker involved, the agreement constitutes a violation of section 2(c).

Most of the Robinson-Patman Act applies to either the seller or the buyer. However, section 2(c) applies to "any person," and this can include the broker. Therefore, if the broker goes to the seller and says that he will lower his commission rate so that the seller can correspondingly reduce his price to the buyer in order to make the sale, this amounts, in substance, to an unlawful payment by the seller's broker to the buyer. As the Supreme Court has observed, the powerful buyer who demands a price concession is concerned only with getting it. He does not care whether it comes from the seller, the seller's broker, or both.

Knowledge or intent are not requirements for a violation of section 2(c). There is also no need to prove any actual competitive injury under section 2(c). Accordingly, brokerage is an area where no chances should be taken. Brokerage payments should be made only for services actually rendered, and any payments in the form of brokerage which really amount to something else should be avoided at all costs because there are virtually no defenses. A company accused of making an illegal brokerage payment cannot raise the traditional defenses of lack of any kind of effect on competition or even that it had no intention of making an illegal payment. All the government has to do is show that the illegal payment was, in fact, made.

ADVERTISING AND PROMOTIONAL ALLOWANCES

Another method of engaging in price discrimination is for a large buyer's customers to demand and a seller to grant special allowances in the form of payments for advertising and other sales-promotional services. Such allowances are illegal under the Robinson-Patman Act if they are not available to all competing customers, or if the service is not rendered as agreed, or if business and is thus able to shift to the vendor substantial portions of his own advertising costs while his smaller competitor is unable to command such allowances.

The advertising-allowance problem is best illustrated by the 1968 Supreme Court decision in *FTC v. Fred Meyer*. This case held that advertising allowances granted by a seller had to be granted not only to direct customers of that seller but to any competitors of such direct customers who may have acquired the product indirectly, such as through an independent wholesaler. In 1969, the Federal Trade Commission issued a set of detailed guidelines which elaborated on this basic idea and provided the mechanics to accomplish it. These FTC advertising guidelines should be considered "must" reading for any executive engaged in this kind of activity.

The *Fred Meyer* case is another one of those areas where the application of the Robinson-Patman Act may have been carried beyond its logical extremes. However, from the point of view of the business executive, the only immediate and certain practical implication of the case is that if promotional allowances are granted, they must be granted to all competing sellers—whether or not the sellers actually purchase the product from the company granting the allowance. When you think about it for a minute, this is a large order. How do you grant promotional allowances to someone you don't know and have had no dealings with? This is where the advertising-allowance guidelines come in. They provide detailed rules on how this should be done.

Fred Meyer Inc. operated a chain of thirteen supermarkets in the Portland, Oregon, area. These supermarkets engaged in the retail sale of groceries, drugs, variety items, and a limited line of clothing. In 1957, Meyer's sales exceeded $40 million. According to its 1960 prospectus, it made one-fourth of the retail food sales in the Portland area and was the second largest seller of all goods in that area. Since 1936, Meyer had conducted an annual four-week promotional campaign in its stores based on the distribution of coupon books to customers. The books usually contained seventy-two pages, and each page featured a single product being sold by Meyer at a reduced price. The consumer bought the book for the nominal sum of 10 cents and had to surrender the appropriate coupon when making his purchase. If the customer used all of the coupons, he would save slightly over 50 dollars. These promotional campaigns were very successful. Aside from the nominal sum paid by the consumers for the coupon books, Meyer financed the promotion by charging the supplier of each featured product a fee of at least 350 dollars for each coupon page advertising his product. Some participating suppliers further underwrote the promotion by giving Meyer price reductions on its purchases of featured items, by replacing at no cost a percentage of the goods sold by Meyer during the campaign, or by redeeming coupons at an agreed rate.

Tri-Valley Packing Association and Idaho Canning Company were two companies which participated in the Meyer campaign. Both of these companies also sold their products to Hudson House and Whadhams & Company, both of which companies were wholesalers who sold to local grocery stores in competition with Meyer. Neither Hudson House nor Whadhams & Company nor their customers were granted any promotional allowances during this period.

Meyer argued that Tri-Valley and Idaho Canning could not have violated the requirement of proportional equality among "customers competing in the distribution" of their products because:

1. Meyer, a retailer, was not competing in the distribution of canned corn and peaches with the diversified wholesalers Hudson House and Whadhams.

2. The retailers found by the commission to be competing with Meyer in the resale of these products were not customers of Tri-Valley and Idaho Canning but were customers of Hudson House and Whadhams.

It is probable that most business counselors would have agreed with the analysis of Fred Meyer. However, the Supreme Court held, instead, that those competing retailers were customers of Tri-Valley and Idaho Canning. Basically, it is probably accurate to say that they did this because they thought it was called for by the intent of the act. On the facts of the *Fred Meyer* case, this is hard to argue with. The basic thrust of the act was to protect the small retailer, and the smaller retailer was generally (as here) the one who would be buying from independent wholesalers rather than directly from the manufacturer like Fred Meyer. Therefore, the Court concluded that "[T]he most reasonable construction of Section 2(d) is one which places on the supplier the responsibility for making promotional allowances available to those resellers who compete directly with the favored buyer." The Court realized that this did create a bit of a practical problem because the manufacturer often did not have any precise knowledge of the identity of many of the independent stores which acquired his products indirectly through wholesalers. The Court said:

> The Commission argues here that the view we take of section 2(d) is impracticable because suppliers will not always find it feasible to bypass their wholesalers and grant promotional allowances directly to their numerous retail outlets. Our decision does not necessitate such bypassing. We hold only that, when a supplier gives allowances to a direct-buying retailer, he must also make them available on comparable terms to those who buy his products through wholesalers and compete with the direct buyer in resales. Nothing we have said bars a supplier, consistently with other provisions of the antitrust laws, from utilizing his wholesalers to distribute payments or administer a promotional program, so long as the supplier takes responsibility, under rules and guides promulgated by the Commission for the regulation of such practices, for seeing that the allowances are made available to all who compete in the resale of his product.

The commission rose to the occasion and issued a fairly detailed set of advertising guidelines. While much has been written about these guidelines, it is probably safe to say that the writings really do not add much to the plain meaning of the guidelines themselves, and therefore anyone engaging in these kinds of programs has a pretty clear road map to follow. Basically, the guidelines establish that a seller must comply with the guidelines whenever he pays for any services or facilities or actually furnishes services or facilities to a customer. They also define "customer" to include both direct and indirect customers and provide some examples of the kinds of services covered (any kind of advertising, catalogs, demonstrations, display or storage cabinets, display materials, special packaging or package sizes, accepting returns for credit, and prizes or merchandise for conducting promotional contests).

The guidelines also specify that anyone engaging in these kinds of programs must have a plan which conforms to the following:

1. Payments or services are available on proportionally equal terms to all competing customers.

2. Sellers take action to inform all competing customers of the existence and essential features of the plan.

3. The plan furnishes alternatives if the plan is not functionally available to all competitors.

4. In informing customers of the details of the plan, the seller provides sufficient information to give a clear understanding of the exact terms of the offer, including its alternatives.

5. The seller takes reasonable precautions to see that the services are actually performed and that the buyer is not overpaying for them.

In summary, advertising and promotional allowances should raise an immediate red flag in the mind of any business executive. He should make sure that all such programs are cleared with counsel under the authority of the *Fred Meyer* case and the FTC guidelines because, again, the defenses are very limited. All the government has to show is that the advertising allowances were not provided in accordance with the guidelines. While it is true that the allowances need only be made available to customers on the same level of the distribution scheme (it is perfectly permissible to grant allowances to wholesalers and not to retailers, or vice versa), there is really nothing else to the government's case. If it shows that the advertising allowances were not provided in accordance with the guidelines, the company cannot use the defenses of good faith or lack of any effect on competition.

BUYERS ALSO SUBJECT TO THE ACT

As pointed out above, one of the principal evils which Congress sought to remedy by the Robinson-Patman Act was intimidation of small suppliers by large buyers, with the buyers seeking preferential treatment. However, even though that was the main thrust of the statute, all of the language, except for one small paragraph, deals with the seller and not with the buyer. The exception is section 2(f), which provides that it is unlawful for any person engaged in commerce to induce or receive a discrimination in price which is prohibited by the act. The discriminatory price received by the buyer must be one which is forbidden by section 2(a). Consequently, the defenses of sections 2(a) and 2(b) are available. The act provides that either the knowing inducement or the receipt of a discriminatory price is condemned. It is not necessary to show that the attempt was successful.

In the early 1970s, there was a great deal of concern over section 2(f) of the Robinson-Patman Act because the FTC had instituted a lawsuit against the Kroger Company and obtained a judgment against it holding that it knowingly induced an improper price by misrepresenting competitive offers to the seller. The seller, however, was absolved because it was held that he was protected by the meeting-competition defense, even though the competition he was meeting was fictitious—having been misrepresented by Kroger. The problem was that some people misinterpreted this case and assumed that it extended to any kind of hard bargaining by which a buyer was granted the preferential price. To be sure, there is some legal authority for the proposition that if a knowledgeable buyer obtains a low price after hard bargaining, he will be assumed to have a general knowledge of the prices prevailing in the industry and will be presumed to know a discriminatory price when he sees one. However, as a practical matter, section 2(f) of the Robinson-Patman Act should not in any way inhibit hard bargaining. The Kroger case involved misrepresentation in addition to hard bargaining. That, of course, is an entirely different matter. Furthermore, to prove that a buyer knew or should have known that his competitors were not obtaining an equally low price interjects a rather substantial burden to the government's case.

However, a further development was that some sellers seized upon the Kroger case and started to write letters to purchasers who were trying to bargain with them, saying that they were granting a low price "in response to equally low prices which we understand you have received from competitors," whether or not the purchaser had ever told the seller that he had received a low price from a competitor. In other words, the sellers were trying to put themselves in the position of placing any problem which might arise in the lap of the buyer. They were trying to make it appear as if the buyer occupied the position of the Kroger buyer who misrepresented competitive offers.

Most counselors responded to this by advising their clients not to accept any such language from their sellers unless it was true, and if the purchasers had simply sent out a request for quotations and the quotations had come back with this kind of language in them, to return them to the sellers and advise the sellers that they were interested only in the particular products and the prices, not in any of the seller's Robinson-Patman Act problems.

Generally, this problem seems to have gone away, at least for the present, and concern over section 2(f) is now back in its proper perspective.

SALES BELOW COST

Section 3 of the Robinson-Patman Act provides that it is unlawful to sell goods at an unreasonably low price for the purpose of eliminating a competitor. "An unreasonably low price" generally means a below-cost price, but it is not clear exactly which "costs" are being considered. It is dangerous to assume that the reference is to marginal costs. To be safe, one would have to consider total costs, including overhead.

CHAPTER THIRTEEN

MERGERS

GENERALLY

The principal statutory provision governing the legality of mergers from an antitrust standpoint is section 7 of the Clayton Act, which provides as follows:

> No corporation engaged in commerce shall acquire, directly or indirectly, the whole or any part of the stock or other share capital and no corporation subject to the jurisdiction of the Federal Trade Commission shall acquire the whole or any part of the assets of another corporation engaged also in commerce, where in any line of commerce in any section of the country, the effect of such acquisition may be substantially to lessen competition, or to tend to create a monopoly.
>
> No corporation shall acquire, directly or indirectly, the whole or any part of the stock or other share capital and no corporation subject to the jurisdiction of the Federal Trade Commission shall acquire the whole or any part of the assets of one or more corporations engaged in commerce, where in any line of commerce in any section of the country, the effect of such acquisition, of such stocks or assets, or of the use of such stock by the voting or granting of proxies or otherwise, may be substantially to lessen competition, or to tend to create a monopoly.
>
> This section shall not apply to corporations purchasing such stock for investment and not using the same by voting or otherwise, to bring about, or in attempting to bring about, the substantial lessening of competition.

The term "merger," as used in this chapter, means the acquisition of one company by another by any means, including the purchase of that company's stock or assets.

Mergers can be divided into three categories:

1. Horizontal mergers, in which a competitor is acquired.

2. Vertical mergers, in which a supplier or a customer is acquired.

3. Conglomerate mergers involve the acquisition of a company which is neither a competitor nor a supplier or a customer.

HORIZONTAL MERGERS

It is easy to see the problems with horizontal mergers. If company A and company B are selling the same product in the same location and competing for the same customers, a merger of the two corporations will destroy this competition. The problems here are the following:

1. The relevant market, both as regards the product line and the geographical area, must be determined.

2. It must be decided at what quantitative point the merger would have such a competitive effect as to be prohibited. (In the above example, if A and B combined represented only 5 percent of the market, the other 95 percent being held by ten other large companies, the merger should obviously be allowed. On the other hand, if A and B each have a 40 percent market share, so that between them they have an 80 percent market share, the merger would not be permitted.)

3. It must be ascertained whether or not there are any special factors which change the normal market-share approach.

Relevant Market

The basic problems here are the same as those considered in Chapter 10.

1. The market is composed of products which have a high cross-elasticity of demand (products which, though physically somewhat different, are used for the same purpose and are more or less interchangeable).

2. The relevant geographic area must be determined.

3. The possibility of a submarket must be considered.

Submarkets

The following passages from the *Brown Shoe* case illustrate the submarket concept:

> The outer boundaries of a product market are determined by the reasonable interchangeability of use or the cross-elasticity of demand between the product itself and substitutes for it. However, within this broad market, well defined submarkets may exist which, in themselves, constitute product markets for antitrust purposes. The boundaries of such a submarket may be determined by examining such practical indicia as industry or public recognition of the submarket as a separate economic entity, the product's peculiar characteristics and uses, unique production facilities, distinct customers, distinct prices, sensitivity to price changes, and specialized vendors. Because section 7 of the Clayton Act prohibits any merger which may substantially lessen competition 'in any line of commerce,' it is necessary to examine the effects of a merger in each such economically significant submarket to determine if there is a reasonable probability that the merger will substantially lessen competition. If such a probability is found to exist, the merger is proscribed.

Cross-Elasticity

The nature of the relevant-market problem precludes any exhaustive study of all the possible arguments, but the following are some factors:

1. The function of the product should be analyzed and a list of all products with a similar use or function should be gathered. Reasonable arguments based on this list can be constructed. Economic data bearing on the relevant cross-elasticity of demand is useful.

2. The sales of the product by the company and by other companies should be analyzed to construct appropriate arguments for or against the inclusion of sales to particular classes of trade or for particular purposes. For example, sales to captive companies and exports should definitely be stated separately and specifically analyzed to determine whether inclusion is appropriate. Sales to one group of customers (ultimate consumers, for example) should be separated from sales to other groups (manufacturers who incorporate the product into a different product, for example), and the same analysis should be made.

3. Not all of the indicia of a market or submarket enumerated in the *Brown Shoe* case must be present in each case. The existence of three or four of the elements may be sufficient to form a product submarket, and counsel must analyze the situation accordingly.

4. Management should be aware of the almost universal success of the government in persuading the court to adopt its view of the relevant market or submarket.

Geographic Areas

The geographic area for Clayton Act purposes is not necessarily the same as the geographic area for Sherman Act purposes. For Sherman Act purposes, the relevant area is the area of effective competition. For Clayton Act purposes, "The proper question to be asked . . . is not where the parties to the merger do business or even where they compete, but where, within the area of competitive overlap, the effect of the merger on competition will be direct and immediate." [*United States v. Phil. Nat. Bank,* 374 U.S. 321 (1963)]

For purposes of section 7, the determination of the relevant market, while important, is not strictly necessary from a legal standpoint, and the Court has been known to dismiss the defendant's objections to lack of proof of the relevant market by the government more or less out of hand. *United States v. Pabst Brewing Company* illustrates the problem. There the Supreme Court said:

> Certainly the failure of the Government to prove by any army of expert witnesses what constitutes a relevant "economic" or "geographic" market is not an adequate ground on which to dismiss a section 7 case. Proof of the section of the country where the anticompetitive effect exists is entirely subsidiary to the crucial question in this and every section 7 case which is whether a merger may substantially lessen competition anywhere in the United States.

Nevertheless, most planning situations will require a definition of both product and geographic market.

Competitive Effect

The next important question in horizontal mergers is the competitive effect of the merger.

Generally, this is resolved by an analysis of market shares. In this area, the most illuminating (though by no means the only) set of rules is the Department of Justice Merger Guidelines. These do give some indication of government enforcement policy. In substance, these guidelines provide as follows:

1. In highly concentrated markets (those in which the shares of the four largest firms amount to approximately 75 percent or more), the department will ordinarily challenge mergers between two firms accounting for approximately the following percentages of the market:

Acquiring Firm	Acquired Firm
4%	4% or more
10%	2% or more
15%	1% or more

2. In less highly concentrated markets (those where the shares of the four largest firms amount to less than approximately 75 percent), the department will ordinarily challenge mergers where the market percentages are as follows:

Acquiring Firm	Acquired Firm
5%	5% or more
10%	4% or more
15%	3% or more
20%	2% or more
25% or more	1% or more

The FTC has no guidelines of general application, but it has issued specific merger guidelines for textile-mill products, grocery products, and manufacturing, dairy, food-distribution, and the cement industries. While these guidelines deal primarily with vertical, product-extension, and conglomerate mergers, they include some reference to horizontal mergers. For example, the textile-products guidelines state that a significant question is raised by any horizontal merger in a textile-product submarket if one of the following applies:

1. The combined firms rank among the top four.
2. The firms have a combined market share of 5 percent or more of any submarket in which the four largest firms account for 35 percent or more of the market.

Courts have generally held horizontal acquisitions prima facie illegal if:

1. Although the combined companies have a small share of the market, there is a trend toward concentrations or substantial decrease in the number of suppliers of the product in question.
2. The acquisition produces a firm controlling an undue share of the relevant market and results in a significant increase in the concentration of firms in that market.
3. The merging companies are "major competitive factors," and competition between them is significantly eliminated.

While market shares are important, counsel should not use them as a hard-and-fast rule or as a substitute for a more detailed economic analysis of the actual competitive effects of a proposed merger. Naturally, any horizontal merger will, in some respects, lessen competition. However, most will also have some procompetitive effects (such as efficiency) and these effects must be weighed against the negative effects. This is a difficult but necessary exercise and one which often fails to yield a clear answer.

Two Supreme Court cases support this approach, the first being *Brown Shoe Co. v. United States*, where the Court said:

> Congress indicated plainly that a merger had to be functionally viewed, in the context of its particular industry. . . . Statistics reflecting the shares of the market controlled by the industry leaders and the parties to the merger are, of course, the primary index of market power; but only a further examination of the particular market—its structure, history and probable future—can provide the appropriate setting for judging the probable anti-competitive effect of the merger.

In another important case, the Supreme Court refused to hold the acquisition of one substantial coal company by another to be a violation of the Clayton Act, even though the markets were heavily concentrated and becoming more so, because in this particular context, the market shares of the companies in terms of past production were not as economically relevant as the amount of coal reserves possessed by the companies. Because the acquired company possessed very small mineral reserves, it was held not to be a significant factor in the future marketing of coal—which was largely limited to long-term contracts for utility companies—and its acquisition by another large coal producer was therefore held to be proper. [*United States v. Gen. Dynamics Corp.*]

VERTICAL MERGERS

In the area of vertical acquisitions, the potential evil is a little harder to see. If a manufacturer acquires a supplier or a customer, there is no immediate foreclosure of competition. However, the current theory is that before the merger, the manufacturer could have purchased his requirements from both the acquired supplier and a number of other suppliers. After the merger, the manufacturer may obtain all of his requirements from the acquired supplier. Competition between the acquired supplier and other suppliers is thereby foreclosed. The appropriate question in a vertical acquisition is the likelihood and extent of this foreclosure.

The market-share questions are similar to those discussed for horizontal mergers. Again in this area, the most illuminating set of rules for planning purposes is the Department of Justice Merger Guidelines. The department will ordinarily challenge mergers between supplier and customer firms if one of the following applies:

1. The supplier firm accounts for approximately 10 percent or more of the sales in its market, and the customer firm accounts for approximately 6 percent or more of the total purchases of the product sold by the supplier firm. The exception would be if it clearly appears that there are no significant barriers to entry into the business of the purchasing firm or firms.

2. The percentages are smaller than indicated above, but there is developing a significant trend toward vertical integration by merger which, if continued, would probably raise barriers to entry or impose a competitive disadvantage on firms not vertically integrated and the product sold by the supplying firm is a scarce or otherwise strategic commodity so that the vertical acquisition may give the integrated firm an important competitive advantage over nonintegrated firms.

The Supreme Court approved these general theories in the case of *Ford Motor Co. v. United States* and held Ford's acquisition of Autolite illegal because the acquisition would foreclose Ford as a market for Autolite's competitors.

CONGLOMERATE MERGERS

The 1960s saw an extremely large number of mergers which could not be categorized as either vertical or horizontal. Many conglomerates developed acquisition programs which were not based on any relationship between the companies or the products. These programs gave rise to the pure-conglomerate acquisition. Other companies developed acquisition programs which were only indirectly related to their existing activities. These kinds of acquisitions were sometimes referred to as "product-extension" or "market-extension" acquisitions. There arose out of these programs some new theories governing acquisitions of the conglomerate type. These new theories fall into the following four categories: (1) the potential-competition theory, (2) the theory of entrenchment, (3) the theory of reciprocity or reciprocity effect, and (4) the Department of Justice's novel aggregate concentration theory.

Potential-Competition Theory

The theory here is that if the companies in a particular market know that there is another company which may enter their market if economic conditions warrant, the companies already in the market will be more competitive (keep their prices down, for example) so that the potential entrant will not find it profitable to enter their market. This is obviously good for competition, and if the potential entrant is eliminated by being acquired by a leading company in the market, competition will be lessened by the removal of this potential entrant in the wings of the market threatening to make its entrance at any time. One of the frequently cited examples of this situation is the *Procter and Gamble* case. Although Procter had decided against entering the liquid-bleach market in which Clorox competed, the finding that it was "the most likely entrant" and exerted considerable influence on the market by being "on the edge of the industry" led to a decision striking down its acquisition of Clorox.

The potential-competition theory is properly applied only if the market in which the acquired company exists is concentrated. The *Marine Bancorporation* case illustrates and explains this proposition.

> The potential competition doctrine has meaning only as applied to concentrated markets. That is, the doctrine comes into play only where there are dominant participants in the target market engaging in interdependent or parallel behavior and with the capacity effectively to determine price and total output of goods or services. If the target market performs as a competitive market in traditional antitrust terms, the participants in the market will have no occasion to fashion their behavior to take into account the presence of a potential entrant. The present procompetitive effects that a perceived potential entrant may produce in an oligopolistic market will already have been accomplished if the target market is performing competitively. Likewise, there would be no need for concern about the prospects of long-term deconcentration of a market which is in fact genuinely competitive.

The word "toehold" is often used in connection with the potential-competition theory. Generally, a potential entrant into a market is permitted to make a toehold acquisition or enter the market on its own, whichever it deems appropriate. It is not entitled to acquire a leading competitor in a market in which it is a potential entrant.

A "toehold acquisition" is the acquisition of a small company in an industry by a large corporation not presently in that industry, with the intention of building up the small corporation using the financial, management, and other resources of the large corporation. The large corporation is, therefore, granted a toehold in the business, and competition will be increased because where before the acquired company could not compete effectively because of its small size and limited capital, the company will now be built into a substantial competitor.

The problem comes in deciding when a corporation has made a toehold acquisition and when it has acquired a leading competitor.

The Supreme Court, in the case of *United States v. Falstaff Brewing Corp.*, supported the government's potential-entrant theory, at least as applied to a market-extension acquisition.

In this case, Falstaff, the nation's fourth-largest beer producer, desirous of achieving national status, agreed to acquire the largest seller of beer in the New England market rather than enter the market *de novo*. The district court dismissed the government's resultant suit charging violation of section 7 of the Clayton Act, finding that entry by acquisition (which the court found was the only way that respondent intended to penetrate the New England market) would not result in a substantial lessening of competition. The Supreme Court, however, held that the district court erred in assuming that because respondent would not have entered the market *de novo*, it could not be considered a potential competitor. The district court should have considered whether respondent was a potential competitor in the sense that its position on the edge of the market exerted a beneficial influence on the market's competitive conditions.

The Supreme Court equated toehold acquisitions of smaller firms with internal expansion. It also asserted that even if these forms of market extension were ruled out by Falstaff, the firm still may have been positioned at the edge of the market in such a way that it exerted a beneficial influence on competitive conditions. The Court's finding seemed to give considerable support to the government's position that the question of whether or not a company is a potential competitor in a given market should be answered by looking at the objective facts of the case and not by looking at the internal records or the testimony of company officers as to whether or not the company would have entered the market by a toehold acquisition or internal expansion. The Court said that it did not mean to make the testimony of company officials on the future course of their firms irrelevant or suspicious in antimerger cases. It merely meant that this evidence was not to be taken as the last word in arriving at a conclusion about how the acquirer should be considered in terms of its status as a potential entrant.

The Court specifically said that it left for future determination the question of whether section 7 bars a market-extension merger by a company whose entry into the market would have no influence whatsoever on the present state of competition in that market. The Court said:

> We leave for another day the question of the applicability of section 7 to a merger that will leave competition in the marketplace exactly as it was, neither hurt nor helped, and that it is challengeable under section 7 only on grounds that the company could have, but did not, enter *de novo* or through a "toehold" acquisition and that there is less competition than there would have been had entry been in such a manner.

It should be noted that the acquiring company must actually have the ability to enter the market. If it does not, perhaps because of other laws regulating the industry, no potential competition problem will be present.

Theory of Entrenchment

The theory here is that if a merger raises barriers to entrants in an already concentrated industry, it forecloses the potential competition which these new entrants would provide and, therefore, is a violation of section 7. There are many reasons why an acquisition may run afoul of the entrenchment theory.

If a merger will give the resulting company a decisive competitive advantage over other companies in the same market, for example, it may drive those other companies out of the business and thereby lessen competition.

This was the theory of the *Reynolds Metals* and *Alcoa* cases, where mergers were struck down because the merged company would have vastly greater financial resources than its rivals and an opportunity to impose a price squeeze on nonintegrated competitors by maintaining raw-material prices at high levels and finished-product prices at depressed levels.

When a merged company would have vastly greater financial resources than its rivals, it may be struck down on what is referred to as the "deep-pocket" theory. Perhaps the classic application of the theory is the *Procter and Gamble* case referred to earlier. This case involved the heavily concentrated liquid-bleach industry, where Clorox had 48 percent of the market. It was found that all of the bleaches on the market were chemically identical. The only variation was the amount of advertising done. Therefore, if Procter and Gamble (which the Court found to be the nation's largest advertiser) acquired Clorox (which, by comparison, was a small company), new entrants would not come into the industry because they could not match Procter's huge advertising budget.

Theory of Reciprocity

The theory here is somewhat like the theory prohibiting vertical acquisitions. It is argued that if some of the members of a conglomerate purchase some products from an acquired company or sell to the acquired company, the acquisition will foreclose competition because the two companies will now engage in reciprocal dealing, whereas before, each would have bargained with others.

However, the reciprocity doctrine is sometimes extended to what may seem extraordinary lengths. An example is the *White Consolidated Industries* case, where the Court said, "Unlike recent cases in steel and other industries, the issue here is not overt reciprocity, but rather what the Government terms 'reciprocity effect.'" This, simply, is an alleged tendency for prospective suppliers of a firm to direct their purchases to that firm in order to maintain its goodwill. (It should be noted in the *White* case that the merger involved two companies in the top 200 manufacturing firms. The Department of Justice has already stated that it will challenge every such merger, and the sheer size of the companies involved could have affected the result.)

However, it has been held that the existence of an antireciprocity policy within a company can be very important (and indeed decisive). In one *ITT* case, the Court denied the government's motion for a preliminary injunction against an ITT acquisition largely because ITT had such a policy, backed up by organization on a profit-center basis which provided no incentive to managers to enter into reciprocal arrangements. In addition, ITT did not pass around purchasing data to its sales personnel, so transactions among the various members of the conglomerate were not widely known.

Product-extension and market-extension mergers can be attacked on the same theories as outlined above. In addition, however, these kinds of mergers can be attacked by the normal horizontal rules if the market is appropriately defined to include both the markets of the acquiring and the acquired companies. A primary example is the *Continental Can* case, where the market was determined to include both the bottles made by one company and the cans made by the other.

Most cases will involve a combination of the theories discussed above.

Aggregate Concentration Theory

In 1969, the Attorney General announced that the Justice Department might well oppose any merger involving two companies in the top 200 manufacturing firms or two firms of comparable size in other industries. Subsequent speeches by members of the Department of Justice have indicated that a merger of one firm in the top 200 and another in the top 500 might also be challenged as a matter of course. At this time, the courts have not endorsed this aggregate concentration theory.

DEFENSES

When an acquisition is proscribed by any of the above-stated rules, the only defense which has met with any success at all is the failing-company defense. The theory behind this defense is simply that there is no foreclosure of competition because if the acquired company is not acquired, it will go bankrupt. However, even this defense is rarely successful, the following passage from the *Citizen's Publishing* case illustrates the point: "Generally, the failing company defense is very strictly construed and will serve to take an acquisition out of an otherwise illegal context only in rare and unusual cases." Some other possible defenses have been suggested, such as the fact that an acquisition would give rise to economies of production or distribution or that the merger of a small company into a large one would enable it to compete more effectively. However, these defenses have met with almost universal failure in the courts.

PREMERGER NOTIFICATION

In 1976, Congress enacted legislation which required companies contemplating large mergers—where the company to be acquired has $10 million or more in sales or assets and the combined company will have more than $100 million in sales or assets—to notify the Federal Trade Commission and the Department of Justice of their intention to merge and then to wait for at least 30 days before actually consummating the merger. The waiting period can be extended for an additional 20 days if the government asks for additional information. The notification has to be presented on a fairly elaborate form which supplies a considerable amount of information on the products and sales of the two companies. In addition, the companies must turn over planning documents and documents used to brief the companies' officers and directors on the merger. Theoretically, this is *not* a preclearance procedure. The companies don't have to get the government's approval—they simply have to tell the government what they are going to do so that the government can object before the fact if it wants. As a practical matter, however, the premerger notification rules now in effect, implemented by regulations in 1978, do operate as a kind of preclearance procedure. On the one hand, if the government objects, the companies know that they are likely to be in for a long and expensive fight, and the prospect of entering into a merger with this problem hanging over their heads is not attractive. Also, in some cases, the government may be able to convince a court that government's chances of winning the lawsuit are good enough that the court should enjoin the merger until the matter is finally decided. On the other hand, if the government gets all this information from both parties to the merger and does nothing, it appears likely that a court would look with disfavor on any subsequent actions by the government to try and make the acquiring company divest the acquired company. Thus, as a practical matter, the planning for these large mergers has been somewhat simplified. You simply inform the government in accordance with the procedures and wait for its decision.

REMEDIES

The usual remedy when a merger is found to be illegal is a divestiture. Generally, there will also be an order prohibiting certain acquisitions in the future without government approval. It should be noted, however, that the court is not limited to divestiture in its remedies and can do whatever it thinks is appropriate, including requiring that a new competitor be created. Compulsory licensing of technology—and actual controls on the manufacturing activities of the offending corporation—are also possible.

It should be noted that there is no statute of limitations here. Mergers can be attacked at any time, and the *Du Pont-GM* case shows that such delayed attacks are a very real possibility. Thus the premerger notification procedure only partially insulates the parties from government attack. The government is probably effectively foreclosed from complaining for at least a few years; but after that, it could allege that the merger, which was all right when accomplished, has become anticompetitive because of changes in circumstances.

FOREIGN ACQUISITION

The acquisition of a foreign company by a United States company, or the reverse, can be attacked under United States antitrust laws. Generally, the analysis of a foreign acquisition by a United States company is done in the same way, using the same criteria, as a United States acquisition. The foreign firm's sales or potential sales in the United States market are analyzed in relation to the position of the domestic acquiring firm, and the same rules governing United States acquisitions apply.

CHAPTER FOURTEEN

JOINT VENTURES: ANTITRUST

INTRODUCTION

The term "joint venture" can be used to refer to either (1) a corporate joint venture, in which a new business is established with two or more corporate partners or (2) informal joint activity between companies (usually involving a joint project or joint research undertaking).

A corporate joint venture is the creation of a new business entity by two or more corporate partners. The new entity may operate in the same geographic location as one or more of the partners, or it may not. It may carry on the same business as one of the corporate partners, or its business may be totally different from that of any of its partners.

A joint venture is different from a merger, where two or more companies combine all of their assets to create a new entity; in the joint venture, the two companies combine less than all of their assets to create a new business. In the merger situation, the merged company usually becomes a part of the acquiring company and is operated as a subsidiary or division thereof. In the joint venture, the management is likely to be more equal.

An antitrust analysis of a corporate joint venture can conveniently be made in the following three steps.

1. First, decide whether the joint venture can be entered into at all. At this stage, it is appropriate to consider all of the theories by which a merger may be attacked. Section 7 of the Clayton Act is generally the appropriate statute.

2. Next, assuming that the joint venture can be entered into without a violation of the antitrust laws, examine all of the restrictions which are involved in

the joint-venture agreement to see if they violate section 1 of the Sherman Act. Generally, business executives feel that joint ventures should be coupled with a number of restrictions on both the joint-venture partners and the joint-venture company. These restrictions frequently involve marketing, pricing, territories, customer allocations, and other subjects which can cause antitrust problems. In fact, in the overwhelming majority of cases where joint ventures have caused antitrust problems, it has not been the joint venture itself which has been held illegal but some of the aspects of the joint-venture agreement which imposed unreasonable or anticompetitive restrictions on the parties involved.

3. Assuming that the first two hurdles can be overcome, check the arrangement for possible Robinson-Patman problems. The broad provisions of section 5 of the Federal Trade Commission Act, which condemns unfair competition or deceptive practices, should also be considered.

The major anticompetitive aspects of a joint venture are the following:

1. There can be a lessening of actual competition between the two members of the joint venture. This is obvious in the horizontal situation, where, for example, two chemical companies form a joint venture to carry on some aspect of the chemical business. However, it is also present in the vertical situation, where the partners and the joint-venture company occupy the relationship of purchaser and seller. Here the problem is market foreclosure and is similar to the problem in a vertical merger.

2. There can be a loss of potential competition. While it is true that where two or more corporations form a new business entity a new competitor is created, this new competitor may be at the expense of competition from the two partners individually or from one of the partners while the other remains a potential entrant. The theory here is similar to the theory in the merger situation. Here, it is said that the partners in the joint venture were potential entrants into the relevant market, and the creation of the joint venture lessened competition because the partners were eliminated as potential entrants when they formed the joint venture.

3. It has been suggested that if two competitors have a relationship in a joint venture, competition will automatically be foreclosed between them because it cannot be expected that they will operate as partners in the joint venture and as vigorous competitors in other areas. The logical extension of this theory would be that two competitors can never enter into any kind of a joint venture. This has not as yet been used in any case as the rationale for holding that a particular joint venture is illegal. Thus far, the inquiry has always centered around the activities of the joint venture itself rather than on the psychological impact which the participation in a joint venture may have on other unrelated activities. The source for this theory is the *Minnesota Mining* case, which involved a joint venture to establish factories abroad. The court made the following statement: "The intimate association of the principal American producers (of coated abrasives) in day-to-day manufacturing operations, their exchange of patent licenses and industrial know-how, and their common experience in marketing and fixing prices may inevitably reduce their zeal for competition *inter se* in the American market."

4. Assuming that the joint venture can be done without violation of section 7 of the Clayton Act (the same basic prenotification requirements apply to joint ventures as to mergers so the government will be of some assistance in making this judgment in the larger cases) and that the stated restrictions in the documents do not violate any antitrust law, it is necessary to analyze further how the joint venture will be managed because, in many cases, the net result will be that two companies who actually compete with the joint-venture company—or with each other—will participate on the board of directors of the

joint-venture company. This is particularly likely to be troublesome in foreign joint ventures. In these cases, it must be absolutely clear, both in the governing documents and the minds of the parties, that neither company has any authority to participate in any decisions which would have the effect of lessening competition. Such decisions include the prices at which the products would be sold, whether the foreign company would market in the United States, or develop new products to compete with those of the joint-venture partners.

Balanced against the above anticompetitive effects are various justifications for joint ventures. The following are the most important:

1. Sometimes the capital requirements for large-scale operations are so high that only a joint venture will permit smaller firms otherwise unable to enter the market to do so.

2. Sometimes the risks associated with entry into a given operation are so high that few or no existing firms would be able to assume 100 percent of the risk. The combination of two or more firms promotes entry into the business because the risks can be spread out.

3. Separate operations can be economically wasteful. This is the natural-monopoly situation. An example is a case where twenty-one companies interested in bidding for oil and gas resources in Alaska joined together to conduct joint exploratory work. In this situation, separate exploratory work would have been very expensive and would have involved heavy destruction of natural resources.

SECTION 7 OF THE CLAYTON ACT

The basic law on domestic joint ventures is contained in the case of *United States v. Penn-Olin Chemical Co.* In that case, the Penn Salt Company and the Olin-Mathieson Company formed a joint venture for the purpose of producing sodium chlorate (sodium chlorate is a white crystalline chemical used principally in bleaching pulp paper). Each company owned half of the stock of the new company, and each had an equal representation in the management. Generally, Penn-Salt operated the plant, and Olin handled sales.

The Department of Justice brought suit against the participants on the theory that the joint venture violated section 1 of the Sherman Act and section 7 of the Clayton Act. The primary objection to the joint venture was that (1) in the absence of the joint venture, both Penn Salt and Olin might have entered the relevant market or, (2) if both had not entered, at least one of the two parent companies would have entered, leaving the other as a potential entrant. It was the contention of the Justice Department that the joint venture had therefore lessened competition.

The district court apparently concluded that only if both participants would have entered the market would a section 7 violation be involved. However, the Supreme Court said that this was not the rule and that the court should have considered the possibility that one would have entered the market and the other remained lurking on the sidelines as a potential competitor. The Court's theory was that this situation would have created a more competitive atmosphere than did the joint venture.

Thus, there are two questions. The first is whether either of the participants in the joint venture would have entered the market by itself. If this question is resolved negatively, no further inquiry need be made because the formation of the joint venture could not possibly foreclose or lessen any competition. In essence, there is one new competitor where before there would have been no new competitors. However, if it is determined that one or both companies were potential entrants into the market, one must answer the second question: Will there be a substantial lessening of competition? The Supreme Court opinion in the *Penn-Olin* case does give some general guidelines on this question. It provides as follows:

> We note generally the following criteria which the trial court might take into account in assessing the probability of a substantial lessening of competition: the number and power of the competitors in the relevant market; the background of their growth; the power of the joint venturers; the relationship of their lines of commerce; the competition existing between them and the power of each in dealing with the competitors of the others; the setting in which the joint venture was created; the reasons and necessities for its existence; the joint venture's line of commerce and the relationship thereof to that of its parents; the adaptability of its line of commerce to noncompetitive practices; the potential power of the joint venture in the relevant market; an appraisal of what the competition in that relevant market would have been if one of the joint venturers had entered it alone instead of through Penn-Olin; the effect, in the event of this occurrence, of the other joint venturer's potential competition; and such other factors as might indicate potential risk to competition in the relevant market. In weighing these factors the court should remember that the mandate of the Congress is in terms of the probability of a lessening of substantial competition, not in terms of tangible present restraint.

There remains the question, however, of how one determines whether or not one of the two corporations would have entered the market by itself. This question was not resolved by the *Penn-Olin* case because of the peculiar course the litigation followed.

When the case was remanded to the lower court, the lower court determined that neither of the companies would have entered the market on its own. During this trial, the government did not produce any additional evidence, but the defendants offered the testimony of each of their presidents to the effect that his company would not have entered the market but for the joint venture. On the basis of this testimony, plus other evidence and the record in the first trial, the district court held that neither company would have entered the field on its own.

The government appealed the case again, on the theory that the court decided the question on a completely subjective basis, placing an undue amount of weight on the testimony of the presidents of the companies rather than upon the objective evidence. The Justice Department believed that the testimony of the corporation as to its intentions was less valid than what it called "objective economic evidence." The Justice Department would have the question of whether or not a corporation would have entered the field depend on such things as the company's technical ability to produce the product, its financial capability, and the incentive each company would have to enter the industry because of, among other things, the profit margins. When the second appeal got to the Supreme Court, the Court split 4 to 4 on the question of subjective versus objective intent and, therefore, left the lower court's decision standing.

Thus the question of how one determines whether or not one of two corporations would have entered a market by itself is still not absolutely clear at this time. However, in the case of *United States v. Falstaff Brewing Corp.*, the Supreme Court indicated at least a willingness to examine objective evidence as to whether or not a company was a potential entrant. The Court said that it did not mean to make the testimony of company officials on the future course of their firms irrelevant or suspicious in antimerger cases. It merely meant that this evidence was not to be taken as the last word in arriving at a conclusion about how the acquirer should be considered in terms of its status as a potential entrant. (See Chapter 13).

An analysis of some of the more significant cases and consent decrees since the *Penn-Olin* Case justifies the following generalities:

1. The combined market shares of the companies entering into the joint venture is extremely important—particularly if the share is as large as it was in the *Minnesota Mining* case.

2. If the partners in the joint venture are direct competitors, the joint venture is much more likely to be attacked than if the joint-venture partners merely supplement each other's capabilities.

3. If the joint-venture company competes directly with one or both of the joint-venture partners, it is more likely to be attacked than if the joint venture involves a new activity.

In summary, evaluating a joint venture from the section 7 standpoint is much like evaluating a merger, and the same uncertainities are present. However, in evaluating a joint venture, there are many more affirmative factors which can be taken into consideration: (1) the presence of other joint ventures in the relevant market, (2) the amount of financial resources available to each joint-venture partner separately, compared to the amount for the project, and (3) the individual technical capabilities of each company as opposed to the capabilities required for the project. In the merger area, these defenses are of limited practical value, but in the joint venture area they are important.

In evaluating a joint venture, it is also only necessary to look at the actual economic effects of the joint venture; the other, unrelated, activities of each of the joint-venture companies probably do not have to be considered. For example, if two conglomerate companies who are not competitors in the market for a particular product form a joint venture to manufacture and sell that product, it is probably not necessary to consider the fact that the companies are direct competitors in some other market, if the other market is unrelated and the joint venture is not used as a device to restrict competition or make restrictive agreements relating to that other market.

SECTION 1 OF THE SHERMAN ACT

This brings us to the next hurdle: the provisions of the joint-venture agreement. When asked to consider a proposed joint venture, management may tell counsel that it is "absolutely essential," in order for the deal to make "any business sense," that there be a number of restrictions on the independent operations of the joint-venture partners and the joint-venture company itself. Many of these restrictions will involve pricing, territories, customers, and the kinds of products each partner will make or sell. In the majority of cases, it will be these proposed restrictions which will cause the most severe antitrust difficulty.

Most joint ventures which cause antitrust difficulty do so, not because of the joint venture itself, but because of some anticompetitive effect of one of the provisions of the joint-venture agreement. This, of course, brings into play the whole body of United States antitrust law. Without going into great detail, the following comments are appropriate:

1. The joint-venture partners and the joint-venture company are independent entities. They are in no way protected by the joint-venture arrangement from the normal antitrust laws prohibiting agreements among competitors on prices, territories, and customers.

2. Assuming the joint venture to be a valid undertaking under section 7 of the Clayton Act, it is permissible to have certain restrictions which are only incidental to the conduct of the joint venture. It is only if these restraints are unreasonable that the Sherman Act is violated. This means that, for each restraint, the following must be objectively answered:

   (a) Is the restriction ancillary to carrying out the lawful primary purpose of the joint-venture agreement?
   (b) Is the scope and duration of the restriction only as broad as is necessary to support the primary purpose?
   (c) Is the restriction otherwise reasonable under the circumstances? Would a less restrictive provision accomplish the desired result?

3. Sometimes it is said that a restriction is not anticompetitive because the company restricted would never do what it is restricted from doing anyway. This, however, is a specious argument, at least in the view of government enforcement officials, who counter by asking, "If it was not a realistic restriction, why did you have it in the agreement?" The presence of these restrictions causes antitrust difficulties, and they should not be put into the agreements unless they are important.

An example of the ancillary restriction problem is *Citizens Publishing Co. v. United States*, where two daily newspapers in Tucson, Arizona, entered into a joint operating agreement. The complaint was that the operating agreement lessened competition because it contained price-fixing, market control, and profit-pooling provisions. Subsequent court decrees permitted joint activity by the newspapers but eliminated any aspect of the conduct which could lead to price-fixing, profit-pooling or market allocation, and provided that such joint activity must be conducted on an independent cost basis, with each of the two participants receiving only the revenue which was applicable to its own operations.

Another example is the *United States v. Automobile Manufacturers Ass'n* case, where the government objected to a joint venture in research in smog-control devices. In this situation, the consent decree prohibited conspiring to prevent or restrain the development of smog-control devices, the exchange of restricted information or cross-licensing patents. The effect of this order was, however, to put an end to the joint-venture research project. Mr. McLaren (then Assistant Attorney General, Antitrust Division of the Department of Justice) indicated in a speech that the action against the auto makers in the smog-control field does not necessarily indicate that all joint-research agreements among competitors are illegal per se. However, joint-research arrangements covering entire industries are suspect and will be attacked where they tend to lessen the incentive for individual firms or where they involve undue marketing restrictions.

ROBINSON-PATMAN AND SECTION 5 OF THE FEDERAL TRADE COMMISSION ACT

The first two problems discussed relating to section 7 of the Clayton Act and section 1 of the Sherman Act are the most important antitrust implications in a joint venture. However, if the joint-venture company purchases from one or both of the joint-venture partners, Robinson-Patman Act implications may be present—especially if formation of the joint venture will cause the corporate partners to become engaged in a dual-distribution program.

The broad prohibitions of section 5 of the Federal Trade Commission Act which condemn any unfair method of competition always place a premium on good judgment. Even if the arrangement does not present any other technical problems, there should be no aspects of the arrangement which are obviously unfair or predatory.

MANAGEMENT

Assuming that all of the above hurdles can be met, counsel should examine the question of whether or not the management of the joint venture should be structured to avoid possible problems under section 1 of the Sherman Act. This will probably be necessary in any case where the joint-venture partners are competitors or where the joint-venture company competes with one or more of the joint-venture partners.

Consider the following example: Company A and company B are each in the business of manufacturing synthetic textile materials. Suppose further, however, that they are not direct competitors for the following reasons:

1. Company A is located in the United States, and company B is located in Europe.

2. Company A manufactures one type of synthetic textile on which it holds patents for the process, and company B manufactures another kind of textile.

These two companies want to enter into a joint venture whereby a new company is formed in Europe to manufacture synthetic textiles of the kind company A manufactures and sells in the United States and company B does not. Company A will contribute its patents, technology, and some capital; company B will contribute its European marketing expertise and some capital.

Unless some rather unusual facts are present, it would seem that the only problem under section 7 of the Clayton Act would be the loss of potential competition from company B entering the United States market by import or the loss of potential competition from company A exporting the textiles directly. Let's assume that this hurdle can be overcome because of the economic problems the United States company would face if it had to pay the shipping charges and tariffs to export the product competitively with other European manufacturers and because of the similar economic problems the European company would face if it shipped into the United States. The fact that the European company does not now make the product would further minimize the section 7 problem.

Let's further assume that both companies understand that they cannot enter into any restrictive provision whereby they all agree on prices or on who should sell in what territory. In other words, assume they make a clean joint-venture agreement which neither restricts the United States company from selling in Europe directly if it wants to nor restricts the joint-venture company from importing into the United States if it wants to.

However, there is still a problem. Let's assume that this joint venture is going to be a 50-50 deal, with a board of directors consisting of ten people—five from each company. Let's further assume that all major marketing and pricing decisions are subject to board review and change upon majority vote. Let's assume further that a majority vote of the board of directors is needed to make certain management decisions like investing substantial amounts of new capital, going into new kinds of businesses, opening new plants, and hiring new management.

If one does nothing, an obvious problem is present because while the agreements do not contain any territorial provisions or price-fixing agreements, the United States company has a 50 percent voice in whether or not the joint venture can ship competitive products into the United States and, if so, at what price. Let's suppose the question came up at a board meeting.

The management of the joint-venture company said it thought it could penetrate the United States market because of its lower labor costs and because its facility was new and modern. Let's further assume that company A has no patent on the product, which would allow it to stop such importation. The members of the board of directors who are from company A would obviously object to the move because the joint-venture company would be competing with company A. Since any such shipment into the United States would have to be approved by a majority of the board, these members could effectively block the shipment. The result would be the same as if the joint-venture agreement had a restriction against shipping into the United States products which competed with company A—a provision which would clearly be illegal.

This situation should not be permitted. Instead, the following should be done:

1. Explain the situation to those who will serve on the board of the new company.

2. Include in the joint-venture documents themselves provisions to the general effect that decisions relating to the joint-venture company's competition with company A would not be eligible for consideration by representatives from company A. In other words, when the subject arose, they would be disqualified from discussion and voting.

Other provisions in the joint-venture agreement, such as allowing representatives of company A to block additional investments or the hiring of new management, would not cause any antitrust difficulty.

REMEDIES

Once a joint venture is attacked and either the government wins or the participants decide to enter into a consent decree, the remedies can be quite extensive.

An example is the *Phillips Petroleum* case. In this case, Phillips and another corporation (National Distillers and Chemical Corp.) entered into two joint ventures, one referred to as Alamo Industries, Inc., and another known as A.B. Chemical Corp. The consent agreement provided that National was to sell its interest in Alamo to Phillips and Phillips was to sell its interest in A.B. to National. Then Phillips, as the owner of Alamo, was required to dispose of a part of this facility to a commission-approved purchaser to the end that such divested facilities be established as a going concern and effective competitor in the marketing and manufacturing of the polypropylene resins involved. After Alamo's resin business had been sold, Phillips was obliged to build new polypropylene resin facilities to compete with the buyer of Alamo's resin-production plant. In addition, the consent agreement went on to provide for other dissolutions and divestitures of related joint ventures and acquisitions and prohibited future acquisitions and joint ventures by Phillips or National.

FOREIGN JOINT VENTURES

There has been considerable discussion as to the applicability of the various parts of the Clayton Act, section 1 of the Sherman Act, and section 5 of the Federal Trade Commission Act to foreign joint ventures. It is fairly clear that, while there may be certain jurisdictional differences among the various statutes, if the government wants to attack a foreign joint venture, one of the statutes will permit it to do so. The general rules would be the same. If the foreign joint venture would tend to lessen competition, it could be attacked. The key would be that it would tend to lessen some kinds of American competition. This does not necessarily mean competition within the United States;

it would be sufficient if the joint venture lessened competition between two United States corporations, both of which exported. Naturally, if an otherwise legal joint venture is coupled with some sort of illegal scheme or is simply used as a subterfuge for some kind of restrictive market activity, it will be declared illegal. Joint ventures cannot be used as a device or justification for price-fixing, market allocation, customer allocation, or other agreements in restraint of trade.

The case of *Timken Roller Bearing Co. v. United States* is an example of this situation. Here, U.S. Timken, British Timken, and French Timken entered into various agreements, one of which was a joint venture. However, in addition to the joint venture, the agreements allocated trade territories, fixed prices, and contained other restrictions. Timken tried to justify these restrictions as being merely ancillary to a valid joint venture, but this argument was rejected.

The following excerpt from comments by Assistant Attorney General Thomas E. Kauper, Chief of the Justice Department's Antitrust Division, to Arch N. Booth, president of the U.S. Chamber of Commerce, on the Chamber's "Task Force Report on Impact of U.S. Antitrust Laws on U.S. Business Performance Abroad" indicates the position of the government on this question. However, it should be kept in mind that (1) speeches do not bind the department—let alone successors to the speaker or private litigants, and (2) this letter was written with a view toward defending the existing antitrust laws against proposed amendments which were not supported by the Department of Justice. It is, therefore, a piece of advocacy rather than an impartial analysis. However, it appears to be a correct and realistic analysis of the government's position.

1. *The Issue of Joint Ventures and Joint Bidding.* Your Task Force Report concludes that U.S. antitrust laws discourage American participation in joint ventures and other multi-company projects which are markets for substantial exports, where the size or risks of the projects are so great that one company alone cannot undertake the project. . . . "(Report, pg. 2, No. 5)."

The report, however, does not allege that American antitrust law makes most or even many such joint ventures illegal, or even that antitrust officials have sought to discourage such foreign joint ventures. The allegation that businessmen feel discouraged goes to their state of mind and is obviously impossible to verify or to refute. On the other hand, the known facts tend to refute any concrete assertion about the inhibitory effect of the antitrust laws.

First: Neither the Antitrust Division, nor the Federal Trade Commission, nor to the best of our knowledge any private antitrust plaintiff, has prosecuted a single joint venture or bidding arrangement to sell to foreigners in at least the last two decades.

Second: Literally hundreds of foreign joint ventures have been formed and operated successfully by Americans over the last twenty years.

Third: Antitrust enforcement agencies have challenged fewer than a dozen *domestic* joint ventures in the last two decades out of the many thousands which have been formed during that period. In the opinions of the courts regarding joint ventures, such as the decision of the Supreme Court in *United States v. Penn-Olin*, 378 U.S. 158 (1964), and in the speeches of antitrust enforcement officials, it has been made crystal clear that if, in the words of your report "the size and risks of the projects are so great that one company alone cannot undertake the project," a joint venture will be held to be legal rather than illegal under U.S. antitrust law.

It is when the joint venture is proved to have been a device for suppressing individual competition which otherwise could or would have occurred or for excluding competitors that the transaction will raise serious problems under our antitrust laws.

Fourth: As to joint bidding, the Department of Justice for many years has taken the position that bona fide joint bids are permissible under the antitrust laws where there is a reasonable showing that each party to the joint bid could not singly bid for or perform the contract.

There were a series of antitrust prosecutions, primarily in the 1940's, involving foreign joint ventures and Webb-Pomerene associations, which probably provide the basis for whatever concern businessmen may have about the legality of joint operations abroad. It thus seems appropriate to examine the reasoning of those cases. In *United States v. U.S. Alkali Export Assn.,* the court held that it was illegal for an American export association to make a price agreement with its foreign competitors abroad. It is difficult to see why that holding is not correct, or why it poses any problem for American businessmen today who wish to join together to compete more effectively against foreigners.

If the American businessmen truly want to *compete* abroad, then it is certainly inappropriate for them to make anti-competitive agreements with their foreign competitors. Other major antitrust decisions of the post-war era . . . involve joint ventures not among Americans but between Americans and their leading foreign competitors as part of a broader plan to divide and allocate world markets.

These were illegal schemes which had the effect both of restricting American exports and limiting the competitive alternatives to U.S. consumers. Cases such as these, which represent the classical application of American antitrust law to U.S. foreign commerce should provide no reason for concern to Americans engaged in good faith efforts jointly to sell or bid in foreign markets.

The only other important case from that period involving activity only of Americans is *United States v. Minnesota Mining and Manufacturing Co.,* 92 F. Supp. 947 (D. Mass. 1950). There, Judge Wysanski found illegal a joint venture by companies comprising 80% of American abrasive production to build a single plant in Europe, with a side agreement that no party to the joint venture would sell individually in Europe. Clearly, this joint arrangement was much more all-encompassing in its membership and its territorial coverage than a typical joint venture between a few American businessmen in a single country or in regard to a single project.

Moreover, the agreement by the parties not to sell except through the joint venture obviously had the effect of restricting American export trade rather than developing it, and certainly is not a typical provision in most joint ventures. Thus, the peculiar facts of the *3M* case only highlight the nonapplicability of the antitrust laws to most foreign joint ventures.

In 1968, the Supreme Court decided one of the very few recent cases concerning a joint export association. The Court held, in *United States v. Concentrated Phosphate Export Assn.,* 393 U.S. 199, that it was not legal for American sellers of phosphate jointly to agree on the price of a product that would be sent to Korea and paid for by the U.S. Government as part of our foreign aid program.

The Supreme Court was careful to point out that American foreign aid legislation requires that such contracts can be awarded *only* to American sellers; foreign competitors are ineligible as bidders for such business. The Court reasoned that its holding would in no way discourage or disadvantage American exports, since by law such business must be assigned to American firms.

The Court concluded that the joint bidding would merely assure that American taxpayers paid an artificially high price for the goods used in the foreign aid program, and therefore that an antitrust exemption could not be in the national interest. Even now, it seems difficult to quarrel with this cogent reasoning, or to see how this decision in any way interferes with the ability of Americans to compete with foreigners in those areas of foreign trade open to competition.

Additional insight on Department of Justice views can be obtained from the following cases published by the department:

Case 6

A major American company wishes to enter into a joint venture with one major company from each of two European countries. They would like to build a plant in a developing South American country; this would involve sale of substantial goods and services. These companies might also operate the plant. The risk of expropriation, plus normal business risks, leads the American company to conclude that it should not undertake this project unless it can find partners to share the risks.

Case 7

Assume the same facts as case 6 except that one of the joint venturers is to be a producer of related products in the South American country. Risk of expropriation is not reasonably present. However, the government of the country insists as a matter of policy through informal channels, but not as a matter of law, that significant new manufacturing facilities must have local participation and that manufacturers of this type of product may not export from the country.

Except for the export restriction, there is again no apparent antitrust problem. Whether or not the export restriction would be valid depends primarily upon two factors (1) whether or not it had any material effect on U.S. commerce, and if so (2) whether or not the restriction in fact originated with the foreign government. The difficulty that some American firms have had in proving subsequently that a particular export restriction was indeed imposed by the foreign government could be largely alleviated through use of the department's business review procedure which would allow contemporaneous determination of whether the restriction was a prerequisite established by the foreign government.

Case 8

A number of major American construction companies seek to bid jointly on heavy construction and engineering projects overseas. In doing so, they would be in competition with other American construction companies bidding singly. Foreign companies engage in joint bidding on these same projects.

So long as the joint effort does not adversely affect the competition of other American firms, this poses no antitrust problem.

Case 9

Assume the same facts as Case 8 except that one of the joint venturers is a company domiciled in the country where the project to be bid is located.

There is again no antitrust objection on the facts as stated.*

---

* These cases are from a statement of Deputy Assistant Attorney General Walker B. Comegys before the Senate Subcommittee on Foreign Commerce and Tourism on S. 2754, the "Export Expansion Act of 1971," January 25, 1972. Mr. Comegys was testifying against this legislation.

CHAPTER FIFTEEN

ANTITRUST
PROBLEMS INVOLVING
PATENTS

Patent laws are designed to encourage science and industry by granting a benefit for inventions. However, the benefit conferred by patent laws is, in essence, a monopoly, and, since this is the very thing antitrust laws seek to prohibit, the interaction of patent and antitrust laws provides an interesting area for discussion.

PRINCIPLES OF PATENT LAW

A patent gives the right to exclude others from making, using, or selling the patented article—nothing more. In essence, it is simply the right to bring a lawsuit.

A patent consists of two principal parts: disclosures and claims. "Disclosures" are drawings, specifications, or some other description of the article in question. "Claims" are what is actually protected by the patent.

The material contained in the disclosures does not give the patentee any rights; it merely keeps others from getting a patent on anything contained therein. In patent jargon, it is said that disclosures are part of the "prior art," or "preceding technology." Anything in this category, of course, is not novel and is therefore not patentable.

Claims specify what the invention is and are the source of the patentee's power to prohibit others from using his invention. It is therefore very important that the claims be drawn correctly. If they are too narrow, the patentee will not get sufficient benefit from his invention. If they are *much* too narrow, the patentee may not get any benefit at all because anyone who wants to make, use, or sell the patented article can simply invent around the patent.

"Inventing around" is patent jargon for designing an article which does not infringe on any of the claims of the prior patent but serves substantially the same purpose as other patented products. If claims are too broad, the patent may not be granted, or, if granted, a court may strike it down if enforcement is attempted. Most patent practitioners draft a comprehensive set of claims, progressing from very broad claims to very narrow claims, to provide maximum protection to their clients against infringement on the one hand and invalidity on the other.

A patentee has the right to sue someone he thinks is infringing his patent, but the person who is sued has two defenses: (1) there is no infringement or (2) the patent is void.

A patent may be void for any number of reasons. A court has the right to second-guess the patent office. The standards of care and diligence applied in filing a patent application are not the same as the standards applied in the conduct of a lawsuit. It is therefore not at all unusual to find a court saying that the patent should not have been granted because the invention was covered by prior art. This is understandable because patent lawyers file many, many patent applications, very few of which are ever actually commercially profitable. On the other hand, if a lawsuit is involved, there is usually a significant amount of money at stake.

The only way a patent can actually be enforced is through a lawsuit. When someone is sued, he tends to look around for counterclaims in addition to defenses. If he can find an antitrust counterclaim, he has the potential for recovery of treble damages plus attorneys' fees. Much litigation in the patent/antitrust area comes about this way. A patentee sues an alleged infringer and the infringer says (1) he did not infringe, (2) the patent is invalid, or (3) the patentee is guilty of a violation of the antitrust laws and therefore is liable for treble damages.

In many, many cases, the owner of a patent does not have anything to do with the manufacture, use, or sale of the patented product. Instead, he licenses somebody else to do this. The licensee pays a royalty. However, if for some reason the licensee decides he will not, or cannot, pay the royalty and is sued by the patentee, the licensee also looks around for defenses and usually comes up with some type of antitrust claim. Thus, while it is by no means the universal rule, antitrust cases involving patents usually involve a suit by a patentee for infringement or for collection of a royalty and a defense or counterclaim against the patentee based on some antitrust theory.

RESTRICTIONS ON LICENSEES

How may the patentee be guilty of an antitrust violation? In the overwhelming majority of situations, the problem will involve something in the license agreement. In drafting the license ageement, the patentee's attorney will want to protect the position of his client to the maximum extent possible and sometimes will want to put certain restrictions on the licensee. If those restrictions fall anywhere in the following categories, great care must be taken to ascertain whether there are any antitrust problems:

- Tying Arrangements
- Grantbacks
- Postexpiration Royalties
- Package Licensing
- Field of Use

- Price-Fixing
- Territory Allocations
- Quantity Limitations

Tying Arrangements

Under either decisional law or the views of the Justice Department, tying arrangements involving patented products are illegal per se. From a theoretical standpoint, there may be rare situations where tying arrangements are not illegal. If the company is a small entrant into a new field, a tie-in may be lawful. But the only case which has indicated this actually held that the tying arrangement was unlawful because it was extended past the time needed for the protection of the new business.

Some cases have upheld tying arrangements even when patented articles were involved. In *Dehydrating Process Co. v. A. O. Smith Corp.*, the maker of patented silo unloaders refused to sell his unloader except for installation in his patented silo. The facts in this case revealed that there had been complaints about the unloader when it was installed in other companies' silos. In the *Electric Pipe Line, Inc. v. Fluid Systems* case, the defendant had a patent on a heating system and refused to supply the plans for the heating system unless the purchaser also bought the components. In this case, the court said that "where the owner of a combination patent designs the installation and guarantees its performance, it is not an unreasonable use of the patent to insist that the compontents of the patented system be obtained from it."

Grantbacks

"Grantbacks" are provisions in a patent license to the effect that the licensee must assign all improvement patents he may develop back to the licenser. Variations include provisions that the licensee must grant the licenser a license under any such improvement patents—which license may be exclusive or nonexclusive. The following paragraph from an article by the Director of Policy Planning, Antitrust Division, Department of Justice, illustrates the current state of the law and the views of the department:

> In its 1947 *Trans-Wrap* decision the Supreme Court held that unlimited grantbacks of improvement patents are not illegal *per se*. This decision has not been directly overruled despite widespread criticism. We expect to bring cases under Sherman Act Section 1 against patent licenses which require an assignment or license grantback of all improvement patents. It is our view that the right to a non-exclusive licenseback on improvements, with reasonable royalties going to the improvement patentee, may be a legitimate provision in the licensing of a basic patent. However, assignment grantbacks tend unduly to expand the patent monopoly and to stifle research and development efforts on the part of licensees, contrary to the public interest. Although we think it is distinguishable, the Supreme Court's *Trans-Wrap* decision may in some degree be questioned by this challenge. [Notes omitted.] [Donnem, *The Antitrust Attack on Restrictive Patent License Provisions*, THE ANTITRUST BULLETIN, xiv (1969), p. 749]

A similar problem results from license agreements which create a situation where no single person has the right to grant a license. The *Krasnov* case is an example of this problem. This case held that a series of licensing provisions which created a situation where neither the patentee, the assignee, nor the licensee could grant any licenses or sublicenses without the consent of the other two was anticompetitive.

Logically, this holding would cover a simple exclusive license. Here, the patentee grants a license to the exclusive licensee, and, if the license prohibits sublicenses, no one else can have any rights under the patent. In fact, the Department of Justice seems to think that this should be prohibited. However, it has not been suggested even by the department that this is the current state of the law. At the present time, exclusive licenses without the right of sublicenses are generally legal.

Postexpiration Royalties

The exaction of royalties for the use of a machine after the patent has expired is an abuse of the patent monopoly. However, this does not mean that the patentee cannot receive any royalties after the expiration of this patent. The important point is that the royalties must be for the use of the patent during its term. For example, it would be illegal to charge a royalty of 100 dollars per year for the use of a machine for 20 years if the life of the patent is only 17 years. However, it would be legal to charge a royalty of $2000 for the use of the machine for the life of the patent, with the $2000 being payable 100 dollars yearly for 20 years. This is one of those areas where the form of the transaction can determine its legality.

Package Licensing

"Package licensing" is the refusal to grant a license under one patent unless the licensee takes a license on a package of patents and pays royalties accordingly. The practice is just like a tying arrangement because the granting of a license under one patent is tied to the taking of a license under another. Accordingly, the practice is generally illegal.

If the patentee grants individual licenses, but under royalties which have the effect of tying the patents together, an unlawful package-licensing arrangement will also probably be found, unless the differential between the per-patent license rate and the package is related to the cost differences of the patentee. An example of a de facto tying arrangement is the *Hazeltine-Zenith* case, where Hazeltine charged a higher royalty for nine individual licenses than for a package containing the nine.

At times, the actual mechanics of patent arrangements become extremely complicated—to the point where a company having many patents and desiring to license another company to manufacture a specific article would have difficulty putting together a single patent or even a package of patents which would cover the article. Radios and other complex electronic equipment are examples here. In that situation, the simple expedient is to allow the manufacturer to make the article irrespective of the particular patents involved. *Automatic Radio Mfg. Co. v. Hazeltine Research* is an example of this practice. Here, if the situation is genuine and not merely a cover-up for an illegal extension of the patent monopoly, it is legal.

Closely related to this situation is one in which a package of licenses is alleged to be a single product. If the package really is a single product, there is no package-license or tying problem. The test here is whether or not any commercially feasible device can be manufactured under any one of the patents without infringing the others.

In a situation where the patents involved in a given product have different expiration dates, a package of these patents which is based on the term of the longest patent is clearly illegal unless there is a reduction in the royalty rate reflecting the expiration of the other patents.

Field of Use

Field-of-use restrictions in a license are restrictions specifying that the license can only be used in a particular field. The courts have been fairly universal in recognizing the right of a patentee to restrict his licensee to a particular field of operation. These cases started with the *General Talking Pictures* case, where the Supreme Court said, in 1938, that it was permissible to grant a license for the manufacture and sale of patented sound equipment only in the commercial sound reproduction field. Other cases have sustained the validity of (1) a license limiting use of the patented device to the inspection of railroad rolling stock, (2) two exclusive drug licenses—one for the human field and one for the animal field—and (3) a chemical license permitting use only in the commercial area—not in home gardening. In another interesting case, two steel companies each held patents effectively blocking the other from making a commercially profitable product. They exchanged licenses, with one taking the finished-product field and the other the semifinished-product field. The licenses were upheld. However, the government has recently attacked field-of-use licenses and has had some success in the drug area.

In contrast to the situation in the courts, the Department of Justice thinks there is no difference between a license which contains a positive prohibition against sales in a particular field and one which merely grants a license limited to a particular field. In addition, the department feels that the continued authority of the *General Talking Pictures Corp.* decision is extremely doubtful.

Price-Fixing

At this point in the development of the law, it is absolutely clear that it is a per se violation of section 1 of the Sherman Act for a patentee to require a licensee to adhere to any specified or minimum price with respect to the licensee's sale of the licensed products. The Department of Justice has stated its views to this effect publically, and the courts have upheld the view on a number of occasions, most notably in *United States v. General Electric Co.*, 358 F. Supp. 731 (1973). In this case, the Court finally eliminated the last vestige of any contrary argument based on an earlier Supreme Court opinion holding that General Electric's system of consigning lamps to agents allowed it to fix the resale price. The old *General Electric* case holding did not expressly restrict itself to patented articles, although G.E. had a dominant position in patents on these lamps. However, subsequent cases distinguished the old G.E. decision on the basis of those patent rights, and it was generally thought by almost all antitrust counselors that if the identical facts in the *G.E.* case were presented today, a contrary decision would result. The belief was confirmed in 1973, when the identical facts—including the same G.E. consignment system—were presented to the Court and held to be a per se violation of section 1 of the Sherman Act.

Territory Allocations

Generally, territory allocations are frowned upon under antitrust laws. However, section 261 of Title 35 of the United States Code (the patent laws) specifically allows territory restrictions. In view of this, it is unlikely that a territory restriction, standing alone, would be held illegal by the courts. However, most practitioners use territory allocations sparingly because when coupled with other restrictions, they may cause a license agreement to be found illegal.

Quantity Limitations

In the view of the Department of Justice, it is unlawful for the owner of a process patent to attempt to place restrictions on his licensee's sales of products made by the use of the patented process. However, the decided cases hold to the contrary, and most practitioners believe that quantity limitations are not illegal, despite the contrary view of the Department of Justice.

CROSS-LICENSING AND PATENT POOLING

In many cases, two companies will hold blocking patents so that neither company can make a commercially practical product without infringing on the other's patents. An example is a case where one company holds the basic patent on a product and another company holds a patent on an improvement of the product which would make it commercially successful. In this situation, it is clearly lawful for the companies to cross-license each other or to enter into a patent-pooling arrangement where both companies can use all of the patents. However, if the cross-licensing or patent-pooling arrangement is part of a device to exclude competitors, it is illegal.

An example is the *Singer* case, where Singer and a number of other companies entered into an agreement, including an agreement on patents, for the purpose of excluding Japanese competition from the United States. Any restrictions in licenses granted under pooled patents are dangerous.

The following are some questions set forth in a speech by Donald I. Baker, Justice Department Director of Policy Planning, on May 24, 1973. These questions should be answered in evaluating the legality, under the antitrust laws, of patent-pooling arrangements. The remarks were made for the *Banking Law Journal*'s Fifth Annual Institute on Licensing Law and Practices in New York City.

1.   Does the pool contain or involve price fixing features? If so, it is obviously illegal without further inquiry.

2.   Does the pool contain or involve production limitations, or customer or territorial limitations? These are also *per se* violations which will make the arrangement illegal.

3.   Does the license contain terms that would be illegal if practiced by a single owner? Naturally, such terms will also be illegal when contained in a patent pooling arrangement.

4.   Is the pooling arrangement limited to patents that are in interference with each other or are complementary, or does it extend to fully competitive patents? Why was the pooling arrangement entered into? The fact that it was entered into as a settlement of possible interference or infringement claims suggests a good business purpose and would be helpful to show. Naturally, the more limited the scope of the pooling the easier it would be to justify.

5.   Is the pooling limited to existing patents or does it cover future patents as well? If it covers future patents, it would be more difficult to justify.

6.   Will the pooling arrangement represent an aggregation of power which might be equivalent to a monopoly? If so, it will be difficult to justify because it must be shown that it was motivated by skill, industry and foresight rather than a desire to exclude competitors from the market.

7.   How many competitors are covered? If the pool arrangement covers most of the firms in a relevant line of business, it must grant reasonable access to all in that business, to present as well as prospective competitors, on substantially equal terms in order to be safe under the antitrust laws.

8.   Is there any showing of any purpose to exclude others from the industry? If so, substantial antitrust difficulties can be anticipated.

9.   Does the pooling arrangement provide sufficient incentives to individual

firms to engage in technical research and development, or is it simply an agreement to safeguard the participants from being placed at a disadvantage by innovations from others? If the arrangement lacks such incentives, it will be looked upon as an anticompetitive agreement entered into by the participants.

VIEWS OF THE JUSTICE DEPARTMENT

A speech made by Bruce B. Wilson, Deputy Assistant Attorney General in the Antitrust Division, before the Michigan State Bar in Detroit on September 21, 1972, listed nine antitrust patent licensing practices which the department considers clearly illegal and also summarized the department's view of the rule of reason by which all other restrictions should be judged. The speech does not represent any startling new theories, but it does provide a clear, concise statement of the views of the Department of Justice and probably represents a fair statement of existing case law (or the general consensus of opinion of the probable outcome of a case if one were to be decided at this time). The nine illegal areas listed by Mr. Wilson were as follows:

1. Tying unpatented materials to a license.
2. Requiring a licensee to assign back any patent issued to the licensee after the licensing arrangement is executed.
3. Restricting a purchaser of a patented product in the resale of the product.
4. Restricting a licensee's freedom to deal in products or services not within the scope of the patent.
5. Agreeing with licensees that the patentee will not grant further licenses without the licensee's consent.
6. Mandatory package licensing which is an unlawful extension of the patent.
7. Insisting as a condition of the license that royalties be paid in an amount not reasonably related to the licensee's sales of products covered by the patent; i.e., royalties on the total sales of products of the general type covered by the licensed patent.
8. Restricting a process patent licensee on the sales of products made with the process.
9. Requiring a licensee to adhere to any specified or minimum price with respect to the licensee's sale of the licensed product.

Mr. Wilson's summary of the rule of reason is as follows: "(a) the restriction must be ancillary to carrying out the lawful primary purpose of the agreement; (b) the scope and duration of the restraint must be no broader than is necessary to support the primary purpose; and (c) the restriction must be otherwise reasonable under the circumstances."

DISTRIBUTORSHIP AGREEMENTS

It should not be assumed that the patent license is the only transaction which can generate problems in this area.

The case of *Agrashell, Inc. v. Hammons Products Co.* involved the illegal extension of a patent monopoly through the use of a distributorship agreement. Two distributorship agreements were involved. In one, Agrashell set the resale prices. It attempted to rely on the old *General Electric* case, which held that a patentee does not violate the antitrust laws by fixing the price at which his agents can sell the product. However, the Court held that whatever protection would have been afforded by the *G.E.* case was not available here because the agreements extended past the life of the patent. The second agreement provided that the distributor must handle Agrashell products exclusively until the patent expired and for three years thereafter unless a competitor quoted a lower price and Agrashell did not meet that lower price. The Court held that this also illegally extended the life of the patent and was a violation of the antitrust laws. The Court said, "any attempted reservation or continuation by the patentee or those claiming under him of the patent monopoly, after the patent expires, whatever the legal device employed, runs counter to the policy and purpose of the patent laws." Therefore, it was proper for the jury to find that this distributorship agreement extended the life of the patent unlawfully and constituted a contract in restraint of trade.

It is interesting to note that this case, like so many, arose out of a patent suit by Agrashell against Hammons for infringement of the Agrashell patent. The patent was held invalid and not infringed, and Hammons' antitrust counterclaim cost Agrashell about $750,000—and the loss of its patent.

CHAPTER SIXTEEN

ANTITRUST AND INTERNATIONAL OPERATIONS

The subject of the application of United States antitrust laws to international transactions has received much attention recently. Our worldwide economy, coupled with the fact that the antitrust laws of the United States are unique, has led some to comment that United States business executives are fighting in the international ring with one hand tied behind their backs.

The U.S. Department of Justice has been leading the fight against those who advocate that our antitrust laws be liberalized at least as they apply to international trade. The department published, on January 26, 1977, an "Antitrust Guide for International Operations." The department had two motivations. The first was to inform business of its enforcement views, and the second was to counter some of the business arguments advocating relaxation of the antitrust laws. The department's theory is that much of the inhibition business executives feel on the basis of United States antitrust laws results from an incorrect understanding of those laws. If business executives understood the law correctly, there would be less of a push toward relaxation.

Their guide is very well-written, but it should be remembered that it represents only the views of the Department of Justice, and private litigants are not bound by it. Also, subsequent administrations at the department are not bound by it. The guide is certainly not perfect. It leaves many questions unanswered, and lawyers differ as to the correctness of some of its interpretations. It is reprinted in this chapter, however, because it is by far the best source available for an understanding of this complex subject, and it is a milestone in antitrust development. The department has only published one other such document, and that was their set of merger guidelines.

The actual guide contains elaborate footnotes. For purposes of brevity, we have eliminated the footnotes from this version. For anyone desiring further information or citations to the relevant authority, the footnotes from the original guide should be considered. The guide is available in all the standard legal services on antitrust.

ANTITRUST GUIDE FOR INTERNATIONAL OPERATIONS*

PART I.   INTRODUCTION

Every year, American businesses enter into thousands of international transactions which raise possible antitrust issues. These include overseas distribution arrangements; overseas joint ventures for research, manufacturing construction and distribution; patent, trademark and know-how licenses; distributorship contracts; mergers with foreign firms; and raw material procurement agreements and concessions. Likewise, American businesses frequently operate as foreign firms' distributors, licensees and joint venture partners in the United States.

Many of these transactions—indeed probably most of them—do not raise serious antitrust enforcement issues. Yet uncertainty on this score may sometimes cause businesses to abandon or limit unobjectionable transactions, or to embark upon unnecessarily restrictive transactions which would not be undertaken if the antitrust risk were more clearly perceived. Therefore, we try here to provide a working statement of government enforcement policy, illustrated by hypothetical case examples in several significant areas of business activity. This is intended to help businesses plan transactions which the Department of Justice is not likely to challenge, and to see which transactions are likely to require detailed factual inquiry by the enforcement agencies.

This paper is intended to be of assistance to—and not a substitute for—experienced private antitrust counsel. Nor is it a substitute for the Department of Justice Business Review Procedure (28 C.F.R. Sec. 506), under which the Department may issue a statement of enforcement intention with respect to a specific pending transaction. Use of the Business Review Procedure is necessary if a firm expression of Antitrust Division views is desired in regard to particular transactions which pose close or difficult antitrust questions.

Applicable Antitrust Laws

The U.S. antitrust laws are the foundation of our broad national commitment to competition based on efficiency—to providing consumers with goods at the lowest price that efficient business operation can justify, and to allowing enterprises to compete on the basis of their own merit. The most relevant provisions are still Sections 1 and 2 of the Sherman Act, enacted in 1890. Section 1 bars "every contract, combination . . . , or conspiracy, in restraint of trade or commerce among the several States, or with foreign nations. . . ." Section 2 makes it a violation of law to "monopolize, or attempt to monopolize, or combine or conspire with any other person or persons, to monopolize any

---

* Published by the U.S. Department of Justice.

part of the trade or commerce among the several States, or with foreign nations. . . ." Certain types of agreements are regarded as illegal per se—including, most notably, agreements among competitors to fix prices at which their offerings are sold, or to allocate territories or customers in order to avoid competing with each other. This is done because experience generally has established that such agreements' "pernicious effect on competition and lack of any redeeming virtue" makes an "elaborate inquiry as to the precise harm [that individual restraints] have caused or the business excuse for their use" generally not worth the effort.

Most other restraints are tested by a full factual inquiry as to whether they will have any significantly adverse effect on competition, what the justification for them is, and whether that justification could be achieved in a less anticompetitive way. This test is the so-called "rule of reason" first enunciated by the Supreme Court in 1911. The rule of reason may have a somewhat broader application to international transactions where it is found that (1) experience with adverse effects on competition is much more limited than in the domestic market, or (2) there are some special justifications not normally found in the domestic market. Either circumstance could justify a fuller factual inquiry. We emphasize, however, that the normal per se rules will be applied fully to basic horizontal restraints designed to affect U.S. market prices or conditions or to divide the U.S. market from other markets.

The antitrust laws are very different in focus and technique from many of the other legal rules with which businessmen have to deal in international transactions. The United States antitrust statutes do not provide a checklist of specific, detailed statutory requirements, but instead set forth principles of almost constitutional breadth. This broad mandate frequently requires private parties, prosecutors and the courts to consider the overall purpose and effect of business arrangements in order to evaluate them under the antitrust laws. Terms of an agreement may be permitted, despite the fact that they restrict some competition, provided that the restriction is clearly *ancillary* to some legitimate purpose and is appropriately limited in scope. Stated more broadly, the antitrust concern is very often not so much with the *particular form* of a transaction, but its surrounding circumstances. This point is frequently illustrated in the subsequent case discussions. For example, a limited non-competition restriction in a single know-how license may be justified by a showing that it is reasonably ancillary to a legitimate technology transfer agreement. On the other hand, a broad pattern of such restrictions, covering a wide variety of different products and know-how of widely differing worth, may be quite objectionable because the overall effect is to create a broad territorial allocation between the parties. This suggests the key inquiries in regard to an international trade restraint of the rule of reason variety. First, is it an anticompetitive restraint which is ancillary to a lawful main purpose? Secondly, is its scope or duration greater than necessary to achieve that purpose? Thirdly, is it otherwise reasonable, either alone or in conjunction with other circumstances?

A special antitrust exemption is provided under the Webb-Pomerene Act for acts of a collective export association of American producers, provided that the association does not (i) artificially or intentionally restrain U.S. domestic trade or affect U.S. domestic prices, or (ii) restrain the export trade of any U.S. competitor of the association. The Webb-Pomerene Act applies solely to the export of "goods, wares or merchandise" and, therefore, does not explicitly extend to service and licensing transactions. An association must be limited to domestic firms. In fact, the general policies discussed above are broadly consistent with the Webb-Pomerene Act, given its specific limitations. Therefore, we do not anticipate that transactions outside the coverage of the Webb-Pomerene Act will be subject to substantially different rules under the Sherman Act.

Enforcement Policy

Antitrust enforcement by the United States Government has two major purposes with respect to international commerce. The first is to protect the American consuming public by assuring it the benefit of competitive products and ideas produced by foreign competitors as well as domestic competitors. Competition by foreign producers is particularly important when imports are or could be a major source of a particular product, or where the domestic industry is dominated by a single firm or a few firms. An agreement or set of private agreements designed to raise the price of such imports or to exclude them from the domestic market raises most serious antitrust concerns. Antitrust enforcement can be expected against domestic firms and foreign firms subject to our jurisdiction for participation in such agreements. Moreover, the form of agreement is not controlling; an informal undertaking embodied in a single conversation may be just as punishable as the same undertaking contained in a complete contract. Any type of restraint which limits the competition offered by significant foreign competitors and products in our domestic market will be examined with great care by enforcement officials.

The second major antitrust enforcement purpose is to protect American export and investment opportunities against privately imposed restrictions. The concern is that each U.S.-based firm engaged in the export of goods, services, or capital should be allowed to compete on the merits and not be shut out by some restriction imposed by a bigger or less principled competitor. Often, the most objectionable private restrictions involve collective efforts by one group of competitors to exclude another from a particular market.

The Department of Justice is and will continue to be strongly committed to these two policies. Their status as the cornerstones of our enforcement policy leads to the general conclusion that a very large proportion of international business transactions involving American firms and/or American markets usually will not involve violations of U.S. antitrust law because such transactions will not adversely affect U.S. consumers or competitors. This is especially true of those transactions which involve the development or expansion of export markets, whether this be through the formation of foreign subsidiaries, joint ventures, licensing arrangements or distributorships.

Questions of Jurisdiction

The application of U.S. antitrust law to overseas activities raises some difficult questions of jurisdiction. First, there is the question of subject matter jurisdiction: whether United States antitrust law applies to certain overseas acts which affect U.S. commerce. The acts of U.S. citizens in a foreign nation normally are subject to the law of the country where they take place. Yet U.S. law in general, and the U.S. antitrust laws in particular, are not limited to transactions which take place within our borders. When foreign transactions have a substantial and foreseeable effect on U.S. commerce, they are subject to U.S. law regardless of where they take place. Analysis of whether there is sufficient impact on U.S. commerce to confer jurisdiction generally involves the same practical analysis of purpose and effect discussed in the preceding section on enforcement policy. Accordingly, considerations of jurisdiction, enforcement policy, and comity often, but not always, lead to the same conclusion: the U.S. antitrust laws should be applied to an overseas transaction when there is a substantial and foreseeable effect on the United States commerce; and, consistent with these ends, it should avoid unnecessary interference with the sovereign interests of foreign nations.

For example, to use the Sherman Act to restrain or punish an overseas conspiracy whose clear purpose and effect is to restrain significant commerce in the U.S. market is both appropriate and necessary to effective U.S. enforcement. By contrast, to apply the Sherman Act to a combination of United States firms for foreign activities which have no direct or intended effect on United States consumers or export opportunities would, we believe, extend the Act beyond the point Congress must have intended. This could encroach upon the sovereignty of a foreign state without any overriding justification based on legitimate United States interests. In fact, antitrust laws and enforcement programs various foreign nations have adopted (or could adopt) may offer a more direct means for redressing unreasonable trade restraints which have their primary impact on the residents of those jurisdictions, but have no significant impact on United States consumer interests and export opportunities.

Subject matter jurisdiction may sometimes be challenged through affirmative defenses such as (i) the act of state doctrine; (ii) the doctrine of foreign governmental compulsion; and (iii) other claims based on considerations of comity. These defenses often are claimed much more broadly than seems appropriate if the Department is to carry out its essential function of protecting the competitiveness of U.S. markets and export opportunities. Therefore, we seek to explain their application in the factual settings which will be found in the case material which follows.

Second, there is the question of personal jurisdiction over those who would be charged with a violation of our law. The general trend of modern history has been to expand the personal jurisdiction of our courts to reach those who transact business in a certain place, even if they are not "found" there in a traditional jurisdictional sense. The Department will utilize these principles to seek to exercise the fullest permissible jurisdiction over those who illegally cartelize our markets. Finally, the doctrine of sovereign immunity provides a defense to the personal jurisdiction of the U.S. courts, but we believe only for conduct of the sovereign acting in its "sovereign" capacity rather than in a "proprietary" capacity.

Conclusion

The Department's most important concern is to protect the U.S. domestic market against restraints on competition—restraints on entry, pricing and terms of sale. In carrying out this effort, no essential distinction is made between domestic and foreign firms. In general, foreign firms, including state-owned or controlled firms, will be expected to observe the prohibitions of our antitrust laws, and to benefit from the enforcement of those laws in the same manner as domestically incorporated enterprises.

PART II.   ILLUSTRATIVE CASES

These selected cases illustrate how U.S. antitrust enforcement is likely to apply in some representative fact situations. Some cases involve quite clear and easy answers. In others, the analysis is complex and the answers depend heavily on surrounding circumstances. The case discussions make clear that antitrust analysis usually turns heavily on facts. We constantly ask the business reason why something is being done; what benefits are being produced; and whether less anticompetitive ways exist to achieve the same benefits.

Case A: A Multinational Operation

International Action Corporation (IAC) is a large, well-known multinational corporation headquartered in New York City. IAC manufactures printing machines in New Jersey, but it does not export them except to Latin America. It relies on overseas subsidiaries to manufacture and sell its products throughout the rest of the western world. Although IAC's patents on its printing machines expired years ago, the IAC group has retained a dominant position in most markets because of superior sales and service organizations, accumulated know-how, and low manufacturing costs.

The IAC system of management involves a strong "profit center" concept, and individual subsidiaries are measured in terms of their ability to develop sales in their own assigned territories. Normally when an order comes in to one subsidiary from the assigned territory of another, the recipient will send it on, or suggest that the consumer contact directly the subsidiary assigned to the territory.

One IAC subsidiary is International Action (U.K.) Limited, which manufactures IAC products and sells them throughout the British Commonwealth, except Canada. This was a wholly-owned subsidiary when formed in 1954, but as a result of a 1964 public stock offering, 40 percent of the stock is now owned by the British public. IAC also has a wholly-owned Canadian subsidiary, Action, Ltd., which sells only in Canada.

International Action G.m.b.H., incorporated in the Federal Republic of Germany, manufactures and sells IAC products in the Common Market countries (other than Britain and Ireland) and it sells the machines in all other countries except members of the British Commonwealth, the United States and Latin America. This German subsidiary was acquired in 1951 from four large individual investors. IAC now holds 56 percent of the stock in the German company and the remaining 44 percent is evenly divided among the four original organizers.

IAC has received an offer for seven percent of the stock in the German subsidiary, which would leave it with a 49 percent stock ownership, but effective working control. Also IAC is negotiating to sell a 50 percent interest in its Canadian subsidiary to a Canadian government corporation which buys the stock of Canadian companies for investment.

Discussion

This case involves the antitrust status of territorial allocations and other practices by a fairly typical multinational corporation. It appears to be a worldwide leader in its field. It has structured its operations in such a way that each overseas subsidiary in effect has an exclusive sphere of operation.

This case involves some obvious factual parallels to the Supreme Court's important 1951 *Timken Roller Bearing Co.* decision. Yet, in the end, the situation here appears to differ in purpose and effect. *Timken* was a Sherman Act section 1 case charging a whole series of agreements, going back to 1909, between American Timken and a major foreign competitor (originally part of the Vickers group) to limit their competition in the American and worldwide markets for antifriction bearings. British Timken had evolved between 1909 and 1928 as an enterprise jointly controlled by American Timken and certain British interests which acquired the rights from Vickers. French Timken was then organized by American Timken and the British interests behind British Timken. By 1948, American Timken owned 30 percent of the stock of British Timken and 50 percent of the stock of French Timken. The District Court found that the parties maintained tight exclusive territories, fixed prices, combined together to eliminate outside competition from each other's markets, and participated in foreign cartels which restricted exports by other U.S. producers. The Supreme Court sustained the finding of violation with the statement that "common ownership or control of the contracting corporations does not liberate them from the impact of the antitrust laws," but it reversed the District Court's order of divestiture.

The IAC arrangement is quite distinguishable from the *Timken* situation. IAC has unilaterally organized its worldwide activities by setting up various subsidiaries; *Timken* involved a leading American firm eliminating competition in the United States and elsewhere from its leading foreign competitor through an agreement, and ultimately binding up this agreement in a more permanent form through stock ownership. As Mr. Justice Reed said in his opinion.

> . . . it may seem strange to have a conspiracy for the division of territory for marketing between one corporation and another in which it has a large or even major interest, but any other conclusion would open wide the doors for violation of the Sherman Act at home and in foreign fields.

That is precisely the point. The preexisting territorial agreement between the Timken and Vickers interests was clearly subject to antitrust challenge, for it eliminated potential Vickers imports into the United States, while cutting down Timken's potential overseas markets. The agreement could not be saved by a subsequent stock affiliation.

The Department of Justice has consistently accepted the view stated in the 1955 *Report of the Attorney General's National Committee to Study the Antitrust Laws:* a parent corporation may allocate territories or set prices for the subsidiaries that it fully controls. The Department's test has generally been formulated in terms of whether the parent controls a majority of the voting stock of the subsidiary. However, the same reasoning may apply to a minority position where the U.S. firm maintains effective working control.

Where majority stock control is not present, the Department may make a careful inquiry into the facts of the particular case.

Likewise, if the German subsidiary had been a major preexisting firm in the same field or a similar field, then the situation would require such factual inquiry. Such an acquisition could be challenged under Clayton Act Section 7 or under Sherman Act Section 1 if it eliminated the foreign firm as an important competitor in the domestic market, or if the foreign firm were a likely one among a small group of potential entrants into the concentrated U.S. market where IAC was a leader. This does not seem to be the case here. Potential competition issues are discussed below in Case B.

The members of the IAC group do allocate territories and reinforce that allocation with a "profit center" concept designed to encourage each to develop fully its own territory. For the majority-controlled subsidiaries, no objection arises under U.S. antitrust laws. IAC and its majority-controlled subsidiaries are treated as a single enterprise for antitrust purposes, and the enterprise is left to carry on its pricing and marketing strategies based on its judgment of its own interests.

If IAC's position was reduced to that of a minority shareholder, then the Department would have to look carefully at the relationship between IAC and the other shareholders—especially if the other shareholders constituted some sort of independent competitive interest. The test is essentially one of continued control: does IAC in fact still control the company or is the arrangement some institutionalized market-sharing arrangement? On the facts given, it would not appear that a sale of an additional seven percent in the German subsidiary to an independent investor, or a sale of 50 percent interest in the Canadian subsidiary to a Canadian government holding company, would in fact change the essential competitive situation. But such sales would cause the territorial arrangement to be more closely scrutinized by U.S. authorities, especially if it subsequently appeared that independent foreign exports into the United States were somehow being restrained.

Case B: A U.S. Firm's Foreign Acquisition

Razors, Inc. ("RI"), an American company, is the largest manufacturer of razor blades both in the United States and internationally, accounting for about half of all U.S. and world sales. RI proposes to buy Glint, a small German specialty manufacturer, which has developed a cadmium steel razor blade arguably superior to the traditional steel blades offered by RI and the other major companies here and abroad. Glint has started selling these blades in Germany (but on a low advertising budget) and still accounts for less than 1% of all razor blade sales in Germany. Its export sales to the United States are insignificant. RI independently possesses the technical capability to manufacture cadmium blades, but it has decided against doing so either in the United States or abroad.

Discussion

The basic U.S. antitrust merger provision is contained in Section 7 of the Clayton Act (15 U.S.C. 18). Section 7 bars corporate acquisitions which foreclose or eliminate substantial competition in any relevant market. The section applies to mergers between direct competitors, between potential competitors, and between customers and suppliers, among others.

It seems unlikely that Section 7 would apply here because there is no suggestion that Glint is engaged in making sales in the United States. A recent Supreme Court decision held that Section 7 requires that the acquired firm be "engaged in commerce"; it is not enough that the acquisition merely affects commerce. [*United States v. American Building Maintenance Industries.*] To be "engaged in commerce" a corporation must be engaged in the production, distribution, or acquisition of goods or services in commerce among the U.S. states or between the United States and a foreign country. The "engaged in commerce" limitation will prevent the application of Section 7 to those international acquisitions where, as here, the foreign party is small and not directly operating in the United States.

Section 7 contains geographic limitation. The section bars any merger whose "effect in any line of commerce in any section of *the country* may be substantially to lessen competition or to create a monopoly." (Emphasis added.) The focus under Section 7 is on the effect of a merger on United States markets. Where an American firm seeks to buy a foreign company that already competes directly in the U.S. market, Section 7 applies and bars any merger which has any prohibited effect in any relevant U.S. market. For example, in *United States v. Joseph Schlitz Brewing Co.*, the Department successfully challenged an acquisition by Schlitz, a leading American brewer, of a Canadian brewer which in turn controlled a California brewer that competed directly and substantially with Schlitz.

Acquisition of a foreign firm that is a major potential entrant in a U.S. market, can be challenged under the U.S. antitrust laws if the foreign firm is otherwise engaged in U.S. commerce. Here the inquiry will be whether (1) the U.S. market (or relevant local market) is highly concentrated; (2) the foreign firm is by virtue of its capability of entering the market one of a relatively small group of potential entrants; (3) the foreign firm has the incentives to enter the U.S. market; and (4) the foreign firm has the capability of entering the market or threatening to enter. If all these factors are present, a merger between such a firm and a leading American firm may well violate Section 7 of the Clayton Act—regardless of whether in form the American firm is acquiring the foreign firm (as in *Schlitz*) or the foreign firm is acquiring the American firm (as in *British Oxygen*).

In the instant case, we shall assume the relevant American razor market is indeed concentrated and potential competition might well be an important factor in present and future market structure and behavior. However, the acquired firm (Glint) does not appear to be a significant potential entrant into the U.S. market under our normal standards. It is not an industry leader abroad, and has limited size and resources. Even in its home market it has not engaged in the extensive product promotion so important to consumer products. All these factors weaken any suggestion that it has the capability to enter the U.S. market.

Glint's new product is the key factor which might separate this from the normal case. If Glint's new type of blade is shown to be clearly superior to blades now sold in the U.S., this raises some inference that Glint might enter the U.S. market to exploit the blade and that its entrance might have a significant procompetitive impact in the U.S. market. Absent such a unique asset or product, the acquisition of such a small foreign competitor would probably not be of concern to antitrust enforcement agencies.

This suggests one final variation. If Glint in fact holds U.S. patent rights to its new product, the patent might be considered an "asset" subject to Clayton Act Section 7, and business transactions dealing with Glint's U.S. patent might cause it to be regarded as "engaged in commerce." If this were so, RI's acquisition of Glint or Glint's patent could be subject to Clayton Act Section 7. However, it is more probable that, if Glint's only U.S. involvement were with its patent, the situation would be approached under Sherman Act Section 1, and the case treated as if Glint had assigned or granted an exclusive U.S. license to RI. Such a license or assignment would not be per se illegal, unless it were a part of a larger territorial allocation among significant competitors. That does not seem to be the case here.

The fact that Glint is of foreign nationality is of no special significance under U.S. antitrust law and enforcement policy. The Department's antitrust enforcement program does not discriminate against or in favor of business entities on the basis of their citizenship in this or any other antitrust situation. In U.S. antitrust enforcement, it is a firm's role in or effect on U.S. commerce that is of concern.

Case C: Joint Bidding

Several U.S. electrical equipment manufacturers and engineering firms have established a consortium for the purpose of submitting a bid on an extremely large hydroelectric project in a Latin American country. The consortium consists of the second, third, and sixth largest U.S. equipment manufacturers (the second largest being the smaller of the two U.S. hydroelectric generator manufacturers). The consortium also includes the United States' first, fifth, and eighth largest engineering firms.

The parties have formed the consortium because the project is too large for a smaller group to finance, and a smaller group would not have the technical capabilities necessary to carry out the project. Most of the manufacturers and engineers have tight capital situations and are already reasonably busy due to domestic demand and contracts made for sales and construction work in other countries. Since the project will take almost ten years to complete, the parties also are concerned with the long-run political situation in the host country.

The parties believe that they will be competing against similar consortia supported by the Japanese and British governments. Because they are anxious that U.S. firms not "cut each others' throats," several senior U.S. Government officials have been strong supporters of the proposed consortium.

The parties have not invited any other American or foreign firms to join the group; and they do not know whether other American engineering or equipment manufacturing firms know about it.

Discussion

The "joint venture" is a particularly common form of business organization in the international field, for a variety of entirely legitimate reasons. Some joint ventures are, as in this case, essentially "one shot" consortia engaged in a single venture limited in time and scope. Others may involve what are essentially permanent combinations for the production or distribution of products and services. Joint ventures may be designed for a variety of business reasons—e.g., to take advantage of complementary skills or large economies of scale, to spread large risks, or to give an international enterprise a "local" flavor. Giving a particular undertaking a "joint venture" label is not controlling for antitrust purposes. Rather, antitrust enforcers will be concerned with the reasons for a joint venture—and the availability of less anticompetitive alternatives—if the joint venture is among competitors or important potential competitors.

Any joint venture among competitors involves some antitrust risk that the cooperation may spill over into other areas. Accordingly the parties should use special care in policing the operations of a joint venture involving actual or potential competitors, to insure that the parties stick strictly to the joint venture's legitimate business. In some circumstances, such as an ongoing, long-term venture, it may be desirable that the venture have separate personnel of its own, to reduce day-to-day contact among officials of the competitor-members.

The antitrust inquiry into the legality of a particular joint venture generally involves three major issues. The first is whether the *creation* of the joint venture itself unreasonably restrains competition. The second is whether the joint venture has any unreasonable collateral restraints that must be struck down even if the venture is allowed. The third is whether the joint venture is in essence a "bottleneck monopoly" which is so important to those in the business that it must be opened to all on reasonable and nondiscriminatory terms.

The creation of a joint venture of the more permanent variety will in essence be looked at as if it were a merger between parties in the field covered by the venture. Where an overseas joint venture is involved, Section 7 of the Clayton Act frequently does not apply and the joint venture must be examined under Section 1 of the Sherman Act.

Normally, the Department would not challenge a merger or joint venture whose only effect was to reduce competition among the parties in a foreign market, even where goods or services were being exported from the United States. The rules are even less stringent where a limited "one shot" type of venture is involved creating a special limited competitor for a special limited purpose. Such short-term consortia are useful where large risks or dollar amounts are involved (as with a multiple bank loan or securities underwriting) or where complementary skills are required (as with the typical construction joint venture).

The present joint venture seems typical and legitimate. Complementary skills are involved; the project is large; the firms lack capital to do it individually; and there appear to be some political risks. These considerations do not necessarily make the joint venture legal—but they tend to justify it to the degree that they are truly significant.

In this case, there is no reason to suspect that the joint venture either would eliminate competition in the domestic U.S. market or foreclose export opportunities for U.S. firms. The venture is creating a larger, and presumably stronger joint competitive effort. Its creation appears unobjectionable, and no impermissible collateral restraints are shown.

Nor does this venture appear to be an "essential facility," exclusion from which would impose a serious handicap on other members of the industry. In general the "essential facility" or "bottleneck monopoly" doctrine has been applied only to more or less permanent joint ventures—such as those controlling a terminal railroad, a dominant national news gathering service, or a dominant stock exchange.

We have not found any application of the doctrine to short-term consortia. It is unlikely that any particular short-term consortium is an "essential facility" necessary to continued competition in the business.

The present consortium, although important, does not appear to be essential for either the non-participating engineers or equipment suppliers. Indeed it appears possible that the remaining U.S. engineers and equipment suppliers could form another consortium, either alone or with a foreign interest, to bid on the particular project. This would argue strongly against applying the essential facility doctrine to require compulsory access.

The informal encouragement from the senior government officials might assist the parties where their good faith is at issue, but it clearly is not controlling as a matter of antitrust analysis and would not convey any sort of antitrust exemption.

Case D: Joint Research

RXI, the second largest of five producers of X-metal in the United States, has entered into preliminary discussions with British Metals Ltd., one of the largest X-metal producers in the Common Market, about a research and development joint venture for the development of a process for producing X-metal from materials other than X-ore. X is available in a variety of domestic shales, but nobody has found an economic way to recover it. Several X-metal producers, including RXI and British Metals Ltd., are trying some research at the laboratory stage, but so far none has been able to develop any workable process.

The parties will form a British company, in which each would own half of the shares and appoint half the directors. The parties agree that all their research operations in this area will be conducted through the joint company. The parties have agreed that if the joint venture's research is successful, the joint company will seek to obtain patents covering its processes. RXI would be given an exclusive license to all patent rights and use of know-how in North America, while British Metals Ltd. would be given similar rights to patents in the United Kingdom, other EEC countries, and all former British colonies and dominions except Canada.

Discussion

A joint research venture, as with any joint venture, raises three questions: (1) does its creation eliminate any significant existing competition between the parties; (2) are there any unreasonable collateral restraints; and (3) is the joint venture an essential facility that must be open to all on reasonable and nondiscriminatory terms? On the facts of this case, the third issue does not appear to present any problems.

Competition clearly is important to the development and delivery of new products. While most antitrust cases concern existing product markets, antitrust enforcement also is concerned with competitive incentives to develop new products. The creation of this joint venture would in essence eliminate competition between the two partners in the development of a process for producing X-metal from sources other than X-ore. This is clearly significant. However, there is no per se rule applied to joint research agreements. One question is whether the parties would have undertaken the research on their own or whether the costs and risks are so large that the alternative to the joint venture is no research at all—in other words, less competition. If the latter could be shown, there would be no antitrust objection to the formation of the venture. Nor would there be any antitrust objection in a case where two nondominant joint venturers were but two of a considerable number of firms with the incentive and capability to do the type of research involved, for then the elimination of competition between the two in research would not be substantial in relation to the total market.

The present case involves a combination between two of a relatively small group of X-producers. That being so, a factual inquiry will be necessary to determine whether the venture is likely to restrict long-run competition in the X-industry, focusing on the costs, scope and risks of the proposed venture. The narrower the scope of the venture, in both time and subject matter, the less likely it is to limit long-run competition in the X-industry. If the capital costs and risks were shown to be so high that the project could not be carried out without the cooperation of substantial competitors, then such a research-type venture might not raise antitrust objections even though it involves the second largest U.S. producer and one of the largest foreign firms. That would be especially true if there were evidence that, but for the joint venture, neither of the parties could or would have undertaken the development. The additional fact that other leading U.S. and foreign firms will continue to parallel the efforts of the joint venture seems to assure a competitive spur on the partners' research efforts and tends to reduce any inference that the venture is in reality a device for restraining competitive research.

Based on the facts given in the problem, we believe it likely that the Department would not object to the *creation* of the RXI-British Metals joint venture. This would depend on a showing that (i) development costs and risks were high enough to make joint activity appropriate; (ii) the venture was not unduly broad in time and scope; and (iii) the venturers had continuing competitive incentives from others in the industry to develop an X-metal process on an independent basis.

Even where the creation of a joint venture is legitimate, collateral restrictions may be challenged under the Sherman Act if they unreasonably restrain competition among the parties to the joint venture. Thus, for example, while it may be legitimate for small-to-medium-sized grocers to form an association to obtain certain joint purchasing and marketing advantages, joint venture provisions which give each grocer-member an exclusive territory violate the Sherman Act. A restriction that is not per se illegal will be examined under the so-called "ancillary restraints" doctrine to see whether such restraint was reasonable in scope and truly necessary to the legitimate purpose of the joint venture. If such a restraint did not pass this test, it would violate the Sherman Act, Section 1.

In this case, the Department would focus carefully on the patent features of the joint venture, the overall effect of which is to give each party an exclusive "home" territory with respect to patents developed by the joint venture. A patent, being a grant of rights from a sovereign state, is necessarily territorial in scope, and, therefore, a territorial division created explicitly by such rights is not now regarded by the Department as being illegal *in itself* under the antitrust laws.

For example, if the holder of both U.S. and British patents on a particular product grants exclusive rights under its British patents to another company and retains its U.S. patent rights during the life of the patent, it legally may be able to protect the U.S. market from sales by its British licensee. If the licensee exports to the United States, the licensor can file a patent infringement action against the licensee or initiate proceedings before the International Trade Commission under the Tariff Act seeking exclusion of the patented article. Conversely, the British licensee can initiate legal proceedings in Great Britain to exclude articles manufactured under the United States patent whose importation into the United Kingdom would infringe on its rights under the British patents.

In the present case, if the product developed by the joint venture were itself patentable (which may be unlikely with a metal) the exclusive license grants from the joint venture to each joint venture partner would have the effect of creating exclusive territories for the sale of X-metal. Under the general rule noted above, this does not necessarily result in antitrust liability. However, inasmuch as the U.S. and foreign X-metal patents would be the consequences of joint collaboration among leading firms, there may be some circumstances when an exclusive license barring U.S. sales by the non-U.S. party would raise antitrust problems. The larger the period of exclusivity, the more serious these problems would become.

In the present problem, the joint venturers hope to produce a *process* patent relating to the production of X-metal, not a *product* patent relating to invention of the product itself. Therefore, unlike holders of product patents, the joint venturers would not be able to effect a territorial division in the X-metal market solely by enforcement of their patent rights. It was established four decades ago that a process patent conferred no rights to restrict sales of the unpatented product produced by the patented process. Congress later enacted Section 337a of the Tariff Act, which explicitly allows exclusion from the U.S. of materials covered by a U.S. process patent on the same basis as a product subject to a U.S. patent. Section 337a provides only an administrative remedy, however. The item may be embargoed only after the International Trade Commission, subject to Presidential approval, makes a number of findings, including findings that importation of the article would be an unfair method of competition or an unfair act "the effect or tendency of which is to destroy or substantially injure" an efficient U.S. industry. However, Section 337a is limited to imports and would not apply to exports of X-metal from the United States to Britain. Even in situations where Section 337a arguably may be applicable, it does not confer antitrust immunity upon the private agreement between RXI and British Metals Ltd.

An additional caveat should be noted as to the application of U.S. antitrust law in this general area. While a patentee can maintain territorial exclusivity for a patent through exercise of its legal rights under patent law, it is not necessarily protected when it agrees to allocate or exchange patents (or other industrial property) with an actual or potential competitor to achieve the same result on a broader scale. Such cases will turn on their facts. The general rule is that aggregations of patents cannot be used to create broad territorial allocations going beyond any single patent or discrete group of patents.

Finally, there is the problem inherent any time competitors collaborate: the spillover effect noted in Case C above. The Department obviously cannot police each research joint venture to ensure that production and marketing are not also discussed. Of course, in appropriate cases the Department may wish to make subsequent inquiries to confirm that the research collaboration has not extended into other areas.

Case E: Manufacturing Joint Venture and Know-how License

Hot Chip, Inc. is the third largest U.S. manufacturer of certain key transistor parts. It has about 22 percent of the domestic market. It has been unsuccessful in its attempts to market its transistor parts in Japan, one of the world's most important markets for the product. In order to surmount this difficulty, it has entered into a joint venture with Japan Manufacturing (JM), one of Japan's largest industrial combines. They will form a manufacturing joint venture, JZC, using Hot Chip know-how to produce completed transistors. Hot Chip will have 49 percent of the stock and half of the Board of Directors. JM will be responsible for the day-to-day operation of JZC. JM has not been in this particular field, but does manufacture a great deal of electronic equipment. Accordingly, the joint venture company will be operating on know-how licensed by Hot Chip.

Hot Chip is very concerned because JZC will have lower manufacturing costs than it has in the United States, and JM and JZC may be sources of disruption to Hot Chip's existing marketing arrangements in Australia, New Zealand, the Philippines, Europe, and the United States. Accordingly, Hot Chip has inserted into the agreement with JM a condition that neither JZC or JM will export the transistors to the United States or other designated markets.

Discussion

The mere creation of this joint venture does not appear to violate U.S. antitrust law. The joint venture does not appear to eliminate any direct competition. Hot Chip and JM are not direct competitors in the relevant U.S. market because JM was not producing the product. The joint venture by itself does not appear to be any part of a broader arrangement to divide world markets between JM and Hot Chip, nor does it seem in any way to prevent JM from selling *other* products in the United States. It is, on its face, supported by a legitimate factual basis, established by Hot Chip's difficulty in exporting to Japan.

However, JM might be a potential entrant into the U.S. market by virtue of its size and experience in closely related electronic products. Thus, the joint venture might eliminate potential competition, which stems from the possibility that JM would develop the relevant transistor and then directly compete with Hot Chip in the United States. If Hot Chip's leading position in the concentrated U.S. market gives it a substantial degree of market power—the ability to control competitive parameters such as pricing in its market—fear of entry by a firm in the wings of the market may be a significant constraint on its abuse of that power. Therefore, elimination of one of a small group of potential entrants could possibly give rise to an antitrust violation under Clayton Act Section 7 if the jurisdictional requirements of Section 7 are satisfied. This, however, is not clear from these facts, and further inquiry would be necessary along the lines suggested above in connection with Case B. Whether JM was capable of developing the product and entering the U.S. market would be significant in determining whether the joint venture would substantially lessen competition. The fact that JM does not now make this product anywhere does reduce its significance as a potential entrant vis-a-vis any capable foreign firms that do make it, for it introduces another level of uncertainty into the possibility that it would enter.

The more manifest problem is with the collateral restraints imposed by the venture. The limitations on export by JZC and JM constitute a territorial allocation agreement, and this would be a matter of antitrust concern, at least as to exports back to the U.S. market.

The mere existence of a technology-sharing agreement between two firms is not by itself an antitrust defense to a charge that the firms have entered into a larger agreement with the purpose or effect of restraining competition. The courts generally will permit a moderate competitive restraint if the defendants can show that the main purpose of the agreement between the parties is some legitimate business objective (such as the transfer of technology), and the restraint is "ancillary" to that main purpose—that is, the restraint is reasonably necessary if the main purpose is to be achieved. This involves a balancing of the anticompetitive effects of the restraint (to be proved by the government or other antitrust plaintiff) against the business considerations which are alleged to justify the arrangement (to be proved by the defendant).

In this case, the Department would be likely to challenge the open-ended restraint on selling transistors into the United States.

The agreement permanently preludes JZC and JM from exporting the relevant products to the United States. This exclusion probably is of substantial competitive significance because Hot Chip is a leading firm in the concentrated domestic market for the products associated with the license, and it is predicated on the fact that JZC will have lower manufacturing costs than Hot Chip. Such potential "disruption" from cost-cutting entrants is something which the antitrust laws are designed to preserve.

On the other hand, the antitrust laws permit reasonable ancillary restraints, as noted above. In order to establish that their territorial restraint is reasonably ancillary to their joint venture and licensing agreement, Hot Chip and JM must prove that the know-how being transferred is of substantial value, and that the territorial restraint is no greater in scope or duration than is necessary to prevent frustration of the underlying contract. One measure for insuring that the restraint is truly no longer in duration than necessary, is to limit an ancillary territorial restraint of this type to no longer than the time it would take for JM to develop equivalent know-how itself (the "reverse engineering" period). Where the restraint exceeds the reverse engineering period, a defendant must be prepared to bear the burden of proving the necessity of the restraint. The permanent restraint in this case would seem virtually impossible to justify. Where technology is changing as rapidly as it is in Hot Chip's field, only a short-term restriction would seem appropriate. JM's status as a very substantial firm which manufactures products technologically similar to those affected by the know-how license would be highly relevant to the determination of how much time it would require to develop equivalent know-how itself.

The fact that this is a joint venture is important to the foregoing analysis. As indicated above in connection with Case A, there might be different considerations if JZC were in fact a majority-controlled subsidiary of Hot Chip.

Case F: Know-how License

Fast Technology, Inc. (FTI) is a small Massachusetts corporation which possesses valuable unpatented technology. It enters into a 20-year know-how license with Badische Maschinenwerke A. G., a major manufacturer located in the Federal Republic of Germany, pursuant to which FTI receives a royalty. FTI is a small but growing factor in the domestic market and heretofore has not been particularly successful in the export trade. One of the presumed advantages to FTI is that it will be able for the first time economically to export its domestically produced components and equipment by selling them to the German licensee for incorporation into the latter's product or for use in the latter's manufacturing process. The licensee is a large, well-financed international company fully capable of invading the United States market once it acquires the technology. Therefore, FTI requires that the following three provisions be included in the license:

(a)   the licensee will not compete with FTI in the United States for 20 years in any product for which FTI technology is used;

(b)   the licensee will purchase and use only FTI-provided components in executing the process; and

(c)   the licensee will use the FTI trademark on all goods manufactured under the license, with appropriate quality control supervision by FTI.

FTI is also negotiating a similar agreement with a large Japanese manufacturer. The prospective Japanese licensee insists that the German licensee be barred from selling licensed products in Japan, Australia and East Asia.

Discussion

This case involves three types of know-how license restrictions: territorial allocation, product tie-in, and trademark use. Similar restrictions occur in connection with patent licensing. Because know-how licensing lacks the protections and legislative mandate of the patent system however, know-how licenses will in general be subject to antitrust standards which, if anything, are stricter than those applied to patent licenses.

The license in the instant case is subject to a number of infirmities. The first is the long-term territorial restriction preventing a major European manufacturer capable of entering the United States market from doing so. The fact that FTI is a small firm, and smaller than its licensee, may have made this particular provision slightly less objectionable than if the licensor were an industry leader, but this fact alone cannot save such an agreement. The territorial restriction here would likely be challenged if the length of the restriction (20 years) exceeded the time necessary for reverse-engineering of the technology, unless the parties could justify it as necessary to the technology sharing agreement.

If the time period were reasonable, this restraint itself would appear reasonable. It involves (i) a unilateral territorial restraint imposed by the licensor upon the licensee, (ii) a product that substantially depends upon the licensed know-how, and (iii) a single license of a specific piece of know-how. By contrast, where reciprocal territorial restraints are exchanged, where the licensing agreement is part of a continuing web of licenses and restrictions between the parties, or where the know-how is an insubstantial part of the product subject to the restriction, then the parties would have to bear a heavy burden of proof to show why such restraints were necessary. Experience has shown that reciprocal restraints, bundling of know-how licenses and continuing exchange of know-how development often encourage cartelization and permanent market division.

The above discussion dealt only with the territorial restraint. The license also contains a requirement that the German licensee use FTI-manufactured components. Assuming this license is sufficiently valuable to confer monopoly power, it is a tie-in and would be illegal per se under the Sherman Act and Clayton Act if practiced in the domestic market. In the international context, the presumption against the legality of a tie-in may not necessarily be as absolute; and the Department may, in any event, be reluctant to expend resources on international tie-ins which do not have the types of effects on U.S. commerce discussed below. However, such tie-ins may be illegal, especially in the patent licensing context, under the laws of many foreign jurisdictions. From the standpoint of U.S. antitrust law, such a tying provision would be of concern if it foreclosed other sellers engaged in U.S. commerce from competing for the tied items. The exclusion of overseas suppliers of the tied items from overseas sales normally does not constitute U.S. foreign commerce, and hence, their exclusion is not prohibited by U.S. antitrust law. Therefore, FTI ordinarily should incur no U.S. antitrust liability if it required the German licensee to procure components from U.S. sources (as opposed to any particular U.S. firm). As a practical matter, this would enable FTI to compete on its merits with other U.S. firms having similar labor costs.

It is also possible that FTI could justify a complete tying restriction on the ground that it was necessary to protect its interest in the goodwill of the licensed technology. However, such claims are not allowed except on the basis of very clear factual proof that technical specifications alone will not suffice to protect goodwill. In any event, such a tying provision might be challenged if it extended beyond an equivalent of the "reverse-engineering" period. A longer period might be justifiable if smaller competitors were involved or particularly heavy investment were present.

The requirement in the license that the German firm use the FTI trademark might be part of an attempt to exclude goods from the United States market that are produced abroad under a foreign license of the mark. Section 526 of the Tariff Act of 1930 provides such a right of exclusion even as to identical products where the U.S. trademark registrant and the foreign registrant of the same mark abroad are not in a parent/subsidiary or common control relationship. While the law in this area is very much unsettled, the Department would look with considerable suspicion upon the use of Section 526 to exclude identical German trademarked goods in this situation. FTI has not assigned the German trademark, relinquishing all control over it. Presumably, after the 20 years, the German firm loses any property right in the trademark, and the German trademark reverts to FTI. (This assumes, of course, that FTI has preserved its property right in the mark by maintaining adequate quality supervision.) Accordingly, there is a very real element of continuing control by FTI over the trademark rights in the U.S. and Germany. While this type of trademark licensing is not inherently illegal, as with other ancillary restraints it may become an antitrust violation where it has the purpose or effect of territorial allocation.

The final paragraph of the example raises the issue of foreign market allocation in the form of a territorial restraint upon the German licensee at the request of the Japanese licensee. Such a restriction, which only bars the German licensee from Japan, Australia and East Asia, would not seem to come within the subject matter jurisdiction explained in the Introduction. The result might be different if the restriction barred a significant amount of imports into the United States, or if the overseas market allocation were part of a broader scheme affecting the U.S. market.

Case G: Tying of Licensed Technology

Big Wheels Corporation, a major U.S. manufacturer, desires to do business in Country X, a less developed country, but because of restrictive local laws and regulations, finds it impractical to export to that country. In lieu thereof, Big Wheels decides to license a local company in Country X to manufacture its product under its X Country patents and using certain of its know-how. In Country X, however, royalty rates are subject to government approval and are notoriously low. Central bank currency restrictions often further limit the basis on which royalties may be calculated for purposes of remittance abroad. Thus, Big Wheels concludes that to achieve an acceptable return on the technology, it will require two things from the licensee:

(1)   A separate contract must require the licensee to buy exclusively from Big Wheels all components, supplies and equipment necessary to manufacture under the license (the components, supplies and equipment are unpatented and are sold by other manufacturers in the United States and other countries); and

(2)   The license must cover certain patents which the licensee has no desire to have or intention of using.

Discussion

This case involves two different types of tying: tying Big Wheels' unpatented goods to the patent license, and tying other patents to the primary patent. Big Wheels is simply trying to increase its effective rate of return on the patent license—and thereby reduce the impact on it of the exchange control system in Country X. In our view, such a motive does not justify the corporation in doing what would otherwise be illegal under U.S. antitrust laws.

The first aspect of the tying arrangement is exactly the same one discussed in connection with Case F. As noted there, such a tie-in would be illegal per se if practiced in the domestic market; but, in the overseas market, it is only objectionable under U.S. law to the extent that it unreasonably forecloses other U.S.-based sellers from making sales, or affects goods reexported to the United States. Of course, requiring purchase of the tied products from U.S. sources (the suggested solution in Case F) might not effectively serve Big Wheels' purpose here in increasing its effective rate of return. It can do so only through its own sales.

Yet, regardless of Big Wheels' motives, the effect of its action may be to exclude other American competitors from competing for sales of the tied product in Country X. The focus of the antitrust inquiry, therefore, must be on whether U.S. exports are possible. If they are not, no effective exclusion exists. If competing U.S. exports are effectively and unreasonably excluded, the tie-in would appear to violate U.S. antitrust law.

Big Wheels' second proposal is, in effect, package licensing of a much larger package of patents than its licensee in X desires to have, again in the hope that the government of X will allow more total royalties (even at low rates) than would otherwise be the case. The normal domestic rule is that such package licensing of the broad package of unwanted patents is a per se illegal tie-in, because it forecloses U.S. customers' effective choice in selecting the package. In *United States v. Loews Inc.*, the Supreme Court prohibited an analogous package licensing scheme for copyrighted movie films under Sherman Act Section 1. Lower courts have found mandatory package licensing of patents to be illegal in a variety of different cases. Package licensing which is limited to valid blocking patents, none of which can be used alone, may be more appropriately subject to something less than a per se prohibition.

Because Big Wheels' package licensing requirement is imposed upon a foreign customer, the Department would be unlikely to seek to invoke U.S. antitrust enforcement jurisdiction absent a belief in the case that it had some significant effect on overseas licensing opportunities for other U.S. firms or some impact on sales in the United States. The requirement involves the use of X Country patents in X's territory, within which they provide monopoly privileges. It is not apparent that the package licensing requirement will have any material effect on U.S. exports or imports, or U.S. customers' choices. The conclusion might be different if, for instance, U.S. competitors of Big Wheels found their export markets foreclosed by Big Wheels' package licensing requirement, or if the package licensing requirement were to raise the price, quality or availability of goods exported from X to the United States.

It should be noted that even if Big Wheels' licensing arrangement passes muster under U.S. laws, it may violate the laws of X because many countries, particularly developing countries, impose more stringent requirements upon licensors of technology than does the United States.

Case H: Licensing a Non-Market (State-Owned) Enterprise

An American company, FX Incorporated, has negotiated a license agreement providing for transfer of unpatented technology to an agency of X, a non-market economy country, for an extremely handsome price payable in dollars. The license covers know-how necessary to manufacture a special chemical compound. A state enterprise in Country X has exported to Western Europe automobiles manufactured under license from a Western European company which had expected (but not required) sales to be confined to Country X. Furthermore, the automobiles are rumored to have been sold at a noncompensatory price. Accordingly, FX writes into the license a prohibition against export to the United States or other Western Hemisphere countries of products produced under the license.

Discussion

The question presented by this case is the effect, if any, the fact that the licensee is a non-market, state-owned enterprise has upon the analysis otherwise used in connection with restraints ancillary to know-how licenses. In some instances, such state-run enterprises may not include the true cost of capital or other production inputs in their pricing decisions. In others, pricing decisions may be entirely divorced from true costs. Furthermore, with significant state resources at their command, state-owned enterprises may be able to engage in predatory pricing practices in selling the fruits of licensed technology back in the licensor's home market, though evidence of this actually occurring is rare.

The focus of concern here is the prohibition on reexport back to the United States of licensed products manufactured in Country X. This prohibition does affect U.S. import competition. The prohibition on reexport to other Western Hemisphere countries does not directly affect U.S. commerce and therefore probably raises no objection under U.S. antitrust law.

The absence of patent rights makes this problem more difficult. Were FX Incorporated licensing under product patents, it might have no need for this type of restriction as far as the U.S. market is concerned. U.S. sales by a Country X manufacturer of patented products might infringe the licensor's U.S. patent rights and, therefore, the Country X goods could be excluded by means of an infringement action or use of Section 337 of the Tariff Act.

Because only know-how is involved, we must face the same issues here as those discussed in connection with Cases E and F above. A know-how license may contain a limited territorial restriction which is ancillary and limited in duration to the reverse-engineering period, or some other specific period which the parties can establish is justified by the facts of their situation.

We question, however, the permanent prohibition on sales into the United States. We believe the licensor may have alternative means available to protect it from the "unfair" advantage enjoyed by its state-owned, non-market licensee. For example, it might sometimes be able to structure a licensing arrangement which provides for an increase in royalties based on increased production and sales, thereby compensating FX Incorporated even if its products were to face competition in the United States from its licensee's products. Furthermore, under the countervailing duty provision of the Tariff Act and under the Anti-Dumping Act, as amended by the Trade Act of 1974, FX Incorporated will have available remedies if the licensee in fact is exporting its products into the United States at an unreasonably subsidized or discriminatory price, thereby injuring FX Incorporated's industry.

The availability or lack of effective alternative remedies and the degree to which a U.S. enterprise is in fact at an unfair disadvantage in dealing with a nonmarket enterprise may be important in determining the legality of any competitive restraint included in an agreement between a U.S. firm and a nonmarket enterprise. These considerations may of course be brought to the attention of the Department of Justice pursuant to the Business Review Procedure.

Case I: Exclusive Grantback Licensing

American Company X has licensed a subsidiary in which it has 85 percent of the voting stock to practice certain patents and know-how in foreign Country A. X requires the foreign subsidiary to grant back title or an exclusive license on any new patents or know-how the foreign subsidiary may obtain or develop related to the licensed technology rights.

Meanwhile Company X grants a similar license (including the grantback) in Country B to a licensee in which X has a 30 percent voting stock interest, and the remaining stock is held by the public.

Finally, in Country C, X grants a similar license (including the grantback) to a leading local firm, which agrees to pay X a royalty.

Discussion

In the *Transwrap* decision of 1947, a narrowly divided Supreme Court held that exclusive grantbacks of improvements made by licensees were not illegal per se. The Supreme Court made clear nevertheless that an exclusive grantback device could raise antitrust problems:

> Conceivably the device could be employed with the purpose and effect of violating the antitrust laws. He who acquires two patents acquires a double monopoly. As patents are added to patents, a whole industry might be regimented. The owner of a basic patent might thus perpetuate his control over an industry long after the basic patent expired. Competitors might be eliminated and an industrial monopoly perfected and maintained. Through the use of patent pools and multiple licensing agreements the fruits of invention of an entire industry might be systematically funneled into the hands of the original patentee.

In short, even under *Transwrap,* the use of exclusive grantback provisions can violate the antitrust laws if such use is part of a larger monopolistic arrangement.

The Department has made clear for a number of years that it questions the need for and appropriateness of exclusive grantback provisions; and it may in an appropriate case wish to assert that an exclusive grantback requirement involving independent parties is per se illegal. An exclusive grantback tends to perpetuate a monopoly of the licensor and may discourage innovation by the licensee. Of course the licensor has a legitimate interest in assuring that it has access to improvements on its patent, but this interest, we believe, can normally be satisfied by a nonexclusive grantback, at least in the case of a non-blocking patent.

Two factors will probably influence the Department's decision whether to challenge any such exclusive grantback in a particular case. The first concerns the scope of the licensee's obligation to grant back; and the second concerns the competitive relationship between licensor and licensee.

Where the grantback obligation is narrowly defined, an exclusive grantback is in fact less likely to be anticompetitive. For example, an obligation to grant back an exclusive license on an improvement patent during the term of an original patent, where the improvement patent could not be used alone without infringing on the original patent is unlikely to change the state of competition substantially during any period the original patent remains valid and in force. This is so because by definition the holder of the original patent has the right to block the use of the improvement, if the original patent is valid and fully blocking in scope. The other extreme, an obligation of the licensee to grant back to the licensor any new patent remotely related to the field of the original patent, would impose a broad restraint on competition between them. This restraint would be doubly broad if the obligation to grant back went beyond the term of the original patent. Such broad grantback obligations are likely to be challenged if the parties to the licenses could in any way be regarded as actual or significant potential competitors in the United States market.

The relationship of the parties may be important for enforcement decisions on international grantback obligations. A main thrust of U.S. antitrust enforcement in the international field is to make sure that leading firms do not carve out for themselves broad spheres of territorial and market exclusivity affecting U.S. commerce. An obligation to grant back a U.S. patent or give an exclusive U.S. license to the U.S. licensor may isolate the U.S. market from significant import competition from a leading foreign firm. A narrowly drawn exclusive grantback in the only license between an American licensor and a foreign single licensee is less serious in competitive effect than the same grantback clause which is one of many involving the two parties. It is also less serious than where similar clauses are involved in a multiplicity of other licenses from the licensor to other licensees in other countries, covering a variety of related areas.

As pointed out above, it is the Department's position that the foregoing problems and uncertainties could be resolved by having the grantback obligations nonexclusive.

The instant case involves three different grantback license arrangements between American company X and licensees in three different countries. In the case of Country A, the licensee is a majority-controlled subsidiary. In these circumstances, the Department would treat the two parties as a single enterprise (for reasons explained above in connection with Case A). The inclusion of an exclusive grantback to the American company is therefore entirely a matter of internal organization based on tax or other business reasons. The two firms are not substantial real competitors and there would be no objection to the scheme.

Although X only owns 30 percent of the licensee in Country B, the balance of the stock is publicly held, and in these circumstances it may be that X effectively controls this licensee. This is a question on which a very careful factual inquiry will have to be made (see Case A). If in fact X does have working control of this licensee, then again the exclusive grantback arrangement is not objectionable as a matter of U.S. antitrust law. In other words, because of X's control, the licensee is not a present or likely potential competitor—directly or through licensing—in the United States market.

The situation in Country C is quite different. Here the licensee is "a leading local firm" in which X has no preexisting stock interest. The situation is broadly analogous to *Timken*. If, as may well be the case, the licensee in C is capable of competing in the United States—directly or through licensing—then a broad exclusive grantback of "any new patents or know-how . . . *related to* the licensed technology rights" is likely to be per se illegal for the reason stated above. If the exclusive grantback were limited only to newly developed blocking patents, and the exclusivity did not extend beyond the initial patent, it would be less likely to be challenged. The safer course here would be a nonexclusive grantback which would permit the licensee in C to compete in the United States domestic and export markets after the expiration of the original licensed patent.

Case J: Exclusive Distributorship

USC and GAG are substantial, but not dominant, manufacturers of machine tools in the United States and the Federal Republic of Germany respectively. Neither now makes any substantial volume of sales in the home country of the other. Their proposal is that USC will appoint GAG as its exclusive distributor in the Common Market, while GAG will appoint USC as its exclusive distributor in North America. Both appointments will be for a period of five years. A few of their products are directly interchangeable in use, but most are complementary in the sense that they can be used in conjunction with each other or have significant special features.

The parties recognize that neither distributor is likely to "push" those imports which are directly interchangeable with his own products, but each believes that the total exports promoted by use of such well-established distributors will be greater than if independent distributors are used. Under the proposed plan each distributor will pay a predetermined price (based on factory costs) and will then be free to resell the imported products at whatever level it sees fit. Additionally, USC and GAG agree that each will prohibit the other 40 distributors of its products, worldwide, from reexporting their products into either the EEC or United States markets.

Discussion

The appointment of an exclusive foreign distributor by an American firm does not by itself raise U.S. antitrust concerns. That is essentially a customer-supplier relationship which does not necessarily have a direct impact on either the U.S. domestic market or the export opportunities of other U.S. firms. However, the situation is quite different where the two parties to the agreement are both substantial manufacturers, for in these circumstances the exclusive territorial distribution agreement creates a territorial allocation between them. Each controls the local sales of its foreign competitor. This issue was involved in the *Timken* case, where, among other things, exclusive distributorship arrangements were used to create market allocations between American Timken, British Timken, and French Timken. The Supreme Court held such general territorial allocations among competitors to be per se Sherman Act Section 1 violations in *Timken,* and has reemphasized that holding since then.

We believe that such a rule would be applied to the present facts, since each party is a substantial manufacturer who can (or could) compete in the territory of the other. The Department may recognize a *limited* exception for a short-term exclusive distributorship for a new manufacturer who could not otherwise distribute its products in a new market. This issue could be raised through use of the Business Review Procedure. The USC-GAG case, however, does not qualify for any such "infant industry" exception. Therefore, the fact that the USC-GAG arrangement is for only five years (in contrast to the long-term arrangements in *Timken*), would not protect it from the general per se prohibition.

This arrangement might be treated differently if the exclusive distributorship provisions were confined to those products as to which USC and GAG do not compete, and there were no express or implied agreements not to use or allow independent distribution arrangements for the competitive products. Then the scheme would look very much less like a territorial allocation scheme among competitors. A full factual inquiry would probably be required under the rule of reason to determine whether the effect of the arrangement was significantly to promote or limit (i) market competition in the United States or (ii) U.S. firms' ability to compete abroad.

A safer course would be for the parties to appoint someone other than a competing manufacturer as an exclusive foreign distributor. Where a foreign manufacturer is used, the Department will look with particular care at the impact on U.S. commerce. It is especially important that significant foreign products which could compete in U.S. markets not be confined to exclusive channels for distribution dominated by a directly competing U.S. manufacturer already well established in the field.

Another issue is raised by the agreement to restrict exports by other distributors of each party's products so that no American products will be reexported from third countries to Europe and no German products will be reexported to the United States. This would conflict with the rule in *United States v. Arnold, Schwinn & Co.,* which holds generally that the first arms-length sale of a product exhausts the seller's right to restrain those to whom it may be resold. Therefore, this provision would violate the U.S. antitrust laws, if significant reexports to the U.S. were thereby restrained.

Case K: Price Stabilization

Sharp Oil Co., an independent U.S. refiner, purchases crude oil produced in Country A from several U.S. oil companies which operate in A. The government of A believes that Sharp's sales of various oil products in the U.S. and eastern Canada are disruptive because they are below the "going price." Accordingly, the government has issued a decree prohibiting any oil company operating in A from selling any A crude oil to this particular independent refiner.

O, a U.S. oil company, fearing the penalties A may impose, complies, without consulting any of the other oil companies. The company's lawyer in A advised that he was "at least 75 percent certain" that the decree in question is invalid under the law of A.

Additionally, government A requires O and its other distributors to United States markets to resell A's oil in those markets at a price established by A. A insists that each distributor police this requirement by monitoring the pricing conduct of its competitors and reporting price cutters back to A.

Discussion

The government of A has commanded O to take action which will have a direct anticompetitive effect within the United States.

A truly unilateral decision by O not to deal with Sharp would not violate the antitrust laws because there would be no agreement in restraint of trade between O and another person, and O is not a monopolist. But if O had entered into an agreement with its competitors, in response to the pressure of government A, not to provide oil to Sharp, O would be party to an explicit horizontal group boycott which is illegal per se. The facts here suggest an illegal boycott in which each distributor only deals directly as a boycott participant with A. Depending upon the totality of the circumstances, this may nonetheless constitute an illegal conspiracy among the distributors. While government A may be immune from antitrust liability as a sovereign, its immunity does not shield the non-immune distributor co-conspirators for their activities in the United States.

Nor may the distributors avail themselves of the act of state or sovereign compulsion defenses. The government-directed conduct here is within United States territory, not within the territory of A.

The distributor's assets in A are put at risk by violating A's command as to a product which is exported from A's territory to the United States. Such a situation, where two sovereigns' directives to a private party are in direct conflict, frequently leads the courts to balance the interests of the two sovereigns in accordance with the principles of comity. Generally, when an unresolvable and direct conflict between the laws of two countries imposes substantial hardship upon the affected party, comity may indicate that the laws of the nation with the more important national interest at stake, based upon its own laws and policies, should prevail.

We believe the United States antitrust laws represent a fundamental and important national policy. In this case, the purpose and necessary effect of A's "command"—to create a per se antitrust violation in U.S. markets—is contrary to that policy. Accordingly, we do not believe comity would require that the United States treat A's command as controlling here.

The fact that the "command" is probably illegal under the law of A also may be significant, because it reduces the "command" to what amounts to "informal encouragement" by the foreign governmental officials. While the legality under foreign law may not be controlling for U.S. antitrust purposes, it is an issue which can bear on the good faith of the defendants, and the weight to which the "command" is entitled in adjudicating private activity under it.

This problem is similar in many respects to *Interamerican Refining Corp. v. Texaco Maracaibo, Inc.*, and much of the analysis here is inconsistent with the decision in that case. The Department believes the case to have been wrongly decided to the extent that it dictates a contrary result, and will pursue the position stated in this case in making enforcement decisions.

Case L: Dealing with a Cartel

Offshore, Inc., a large multinational corporation, incorporated in Delaware, mines X-ore abroad and processes it into X-product which it sells in the U.S. and a number of other countries. Offshore owns 75 percent of a subsidiary which it organized in C to operate a large X-ore mine there.

Import Metals Company mines X-ore in five countries and it sells X-ore and X-product in a number of countries, including the U.S. Import Metals is 75 percent owned by the Natural Resources Group, a diversified investment company which appears to be mostly owned and controlled by the government of C, the Asian country where Import Metals and its parent are headquartered.

Vitamina is a European-based fruit company which sells large quantities of fruit juices in its own stores in the U.S. It recently discovered a very large X-ore deposit on one of its fruit plantations and has been selling X-ore abroad.

Import Metals, Vitamina and the four or five other foreign X-ore producers recently met in Country C to form a cartel, and agreed on quotas and prices for all X-ore production. Import Metals is the only one of these foreign producers which sells X-ore or X-product in the United States, but the others all sell substantial amounts of X-ore to foreign brokers, who resell about 25 percent of world production in the U.S. The government of C has given notice that it wants Offshore to pledge to the cartel members that it will abide by the agreed-upon quotas and prices.

Discussion

This cartel agreement would be a clear violation under the U.S. antitrust laws unless defenses peculiar to the international situation apply to particular defendants. In view of the large portion of the world X-ore market which is imported into the U.S., it is reasonably clear that the foreseeable effect of the agreement is to restrict U.S. imports. Therefore, there is subject matter jurisdiction over the transaction under the Sherman Act. Offshore and its subsidiary are the most vulnerable of the above parties if they agree to participate in the cartel. They clearly are subject to personal jurisdiction because Offshore is doing business in the U.S.

Offshore may have a defense to a U.S. antitrust action under the act of state or foreign compulsion doctrines. These defenses are subject to important limitations, however. A major limitation is territorial. Although the U.S. courts will recognize an antitrust defense for actions taken or compelled by a foreign sovereign within its territory, such recognition will not be afforded with respect to an act inside the United States. The situation in third countries is less clear. A second limitation is that the act upon which the defense is based must be the act of a truly sovereign entity acting within the scope of its powers under the law of its nationality. The valid decree of a foreign government usually meets this requirement; the action of a nongovernmental agency of a foreign government does not, at least when it is not proved that such agent clearly was authorized to perform the alleged acts of state as a delegated sovereign function. Third, the act of state defense does not apply to the "commercial" actions of a foreign government or instrumentality, but only to its public, political actions. And underlying the foreign compulsion defense is a balancing of the comity interests of Restatement Section 40 as well as the question whether the company is being reasonable in doing what it felt it had to do.

Offshore may have a sovereign compulsion defense if C, acting in conformity with its own law, requires Offshore to observe the terms of the cartel for its acts solely within C's territory. Offshore would not have such a defense if C purported to require such conduct in the United States, or if the requirement is not imposed by the government of C acting as a sovereign.

This example clearly involves the possibility of conflict between the sovereign governments of the U.S. and C. In these circumstances, Offshore may find it advantageous to seek a business review. Even if a business review letter is not sought or issued, full and candid disclosure by Offshore of its activities in connection with the cartel may serve as evidence of its intent to comply with the law, and would substantially reduce the risk that it would be charged with criminal liability.

The above discussion of subject matter jurisdiction, the act of state defense and sovereign compulsion is equally applicable to Vitamina and Import Metals, but the personal jurisdiction requirements of the Sherman Act place them in slightly different situations. Vitamina, because of its juice business in the U.S., is subject to the personal jurisdiction of the U.S. courts even in connection with matters, such as the X-ore agreement, which are totally unrelated to its juice business. Thus Vitamina can be served immediately through its U.S. agent with a subpoena, complaint or indictment. Import Metals, which has no business activities at all in the U.S., may be more difficult to reach under the U.S. antitrust laws, but the Department will try to include all appropriate defendants in every case. If Import Metals has property in the United States, it may be seized under certain circumstances to induce consent to the jurisdiction of a U.S. antitrust court. Even if personal jurisdiction and venue requirements are lacking, the United States may file indictments or other process against an absent defendant, and hold them outstanding indefinitely, or until such requirements are met. In at least one instance, such an indictment has been served—years later.

The fact that Import Metals apparently is controlled by the government of C would not provide it with a sovereign immunity defense to an American antitrust action. The sovereign immunity defense does not extend to "commercial" activity of a foreign state or of a business corporation partially or wholly owned by a foreign state.

Case M: Political Risk Insurance

Six major oil companies (four based in the United States and two in Western Europe) operate oil concessions in an African country. The four American companies also operate major concessions in a Latin American country. The companies are concerned about the long-term stability of their operations in both countries. The companies are especially concerned about continued access to low-sulphur oil from the African country, because low-sulphur oil is required to comply with environmental standards in several large American cities, and substitutes are scarce.

The companies feel that their bargaining positions vis-a-vis both governments would be strengthened if they could assure some alternative sources of supply. Therefore, they propose a joint venture to deal with the situation. Three of the American members, however, are adamant about excluding the fourth American company, Maverick Oil Co., which has been an unpredictable factor in the industry and an important source of supply to independent refiners in the United States.

Ultimately, the three American companies (A, B and C) and the two European companies (D and E) agree to form a joint venture company, incorporated in the Bahamas and called Oil Guarantee Ltd. The three American companies each own 25 percent of the stock, while D and E each own 12.5 percent. Oil Guarantee Ltd. operates only with respect to the two concession countries. Its purpose is to arrange for back-up commitments of oil from its members and from outside sources. The agreement provides for a "pool" for producer-members in each country, and guarantees each producer-member a pro-rata share of that "pool" based upon prior production percentages.

The British Government owns 50 percent of the stock of D and 16 percent of the stock of E.

Discussion

One of the regularly accepted justifications for a joint venture is the sharing of large and unusual risks. The formation of Oil Guarantee Ltd. for this purpose seems within this traditional justification; and, as long as the joint venture sticks to its assigned role, it does not threaten unreasonably to restrain U.S. foreign commerce. Nor does it appear to involve any impermissible collateral restraints on any individual member's ability to compete on an entirely individual basis. Nevertheless, since it is a limited purpose joint venture, prudence would dictate that it be given a set termination date—rather than having it remain as a forum for cooperation among its competitor-members after its original purpose has passed.

However, as noted in Case C above, there is a third antitrust concern which applies when a joint venture is found to be an "essential facility" or a "bottleneck monopoly." The basic rule is that where a group of competitors form a joint venture which (i) is important competitively to the member-competitors and (ii) cannot be reasonably duplicated, then they must grant access to such an "essential facility" to all firms in the business. While this rule originated with joint ventures controlling a key physical facility, such as a railway terminal or a fish market the concept has been much more broadly applied as it developed. Perhaps the most useful illustration is the Associated Press, which was formed as a central news gathering service by a group of major newspapers in most leading cities. The Supreme Court applied the "essential facility" doctrine to this service, requiring fair access be extended to all newspapers. Although recognizing that some wire service alternatives were available to these newspapers, the Court held that the inability to buy news from the largest, and what many regarded as the best, news service necessarily restricted the publication of competitive newspapers.

The question whether a particular joint venture is an "essential facility" is a fact question. The question may be phrased in terms of whether exclusion places the excluded firm at a serious disadvantage or whether a reasonably interchangeable alternative exists.

In the instant case, the key issue is the exclusion of Maverick Oil Co. from Oil Guarantee Ltd. If the joint venture company is indeed an "essential facility," and exclusion of Maverick Oil places Maverick at a serious disadvantage in its efforts to import oil and compete in the United States, then this exclusion of Maverick from membership would constitute a violation of Sherman Act Section 1. The question whether Oil Guarantee Ltd. is an "essential facility" will depend on how much it adds to the members' ability to bargain with the foreign governments and to enter into firm (or relatively firm) contracts for delivery of oil to U.S. customers. There appears to be no immediately available alternative to the venture because the dominant oil companies in both concession countries appear to have joined it.

Moreover, if Maverick Oil were excluded as punishment for its independent competitive tactics in the past, this exclusion would be an additional relevant factor arguing in favor of giving Maverick compulsory access to the joint venture. Certainly this fact tends to negate any "good faith" defense on the part of the existing joint venturers. If Maverick Oil must be included, it should be included on equitable terms as compared to the other members, and, accordingly, it too would have to put up a fair share of capital for the enterprise.

The mere ownership by the British government of a stock interest—even a controlling stock interest—of two Oil Guarantee members does not in any way immunize the total venture from appropriate U.S. antitrust liability. It is not clear from the facts given whether D and E, or for that matter Oil Guarantee Ltd., are engaged in U.S. foreign or interstate commerce or are subject to U.S. personal jurisdiction through presence in the United States. Even if they are not, appropriate action could still be taken against the American parties—which in fact seem to be responsible for excluding Maverick Oil—for they have agreed among themselves on this policy of exclusion. Finally, the so-called "restrictive theory of sovereign immunity" employed by the United States would allow application of U.S. antitrust law to D and E's "commercial" activities despite the fact that a foreign sovereign is a major or controlling stockholder.

Case N: Government-Imposed Restraint

A, a corporation organized under the laws of Country X, is a wholly-owned subsidiary of AUSA, a U.S. company. A manufactures and sells 25 percent of the widget market in Country X. Two of the other widget suppliers, B and C, are entirely locally owned and together account for about 20 percent of the market in X. The fourth supplier, D, is a majority-owned subsidiary of a manufacturer located in the Federal Republic of Germany, and accounts for about 30 percent of the market. The remaining 25 percent of the X market is accounted for by imports from U.S., Japanese and Swiss manufacturers.

B and C find the widget market in X unprofitable. The government of X asks A, B, C and D to form an advisory council to advise it on how to strengthen the local widget manufacturing industry. A joins B, C and D in advising the X government that the market in X is not large enough to sustain four local manufacturers plus substantial imports; and A, B, C and D suggest either a tariff increase or an embargo for a specified period. This action, if taken, would affect exports by a second U.S. manufacturer presently accounting for about six percent of the market in X. Officers of AUSA are advised of this action of A.

Discussion

The key restraint on U.S. export competition has been imposed by the government of X. A government imposition of protectionist tariffs and quotas is normally considered a sovereign function of the state within its own territory and therefore exempt from U.S. antitrust enforcement under the act of state doctrine, discussed above in the Introduction and Case L.

In 1961, the Supreme Court enunciated another exemption to antitrust prohibitions, holding that "the Sherman Act does not prohibit two or more persons from associating together in an attempt to persuade the legislature or the executive to take particular action with respect to the law that would produce a restraint or monopoly." This has become known as the *Noerr-Pennington* doctrine. There is an exception to this rule when the collective activity, ostensibly intended to get the government to impose a restraint, is in fact a "sham" which conceals a direct restraint by the parties, such as a misuse of administrative procedures. There is another exception where private parties, at least in the regulatory context, collectively lie to the government and thereby cause it to impose a restraint. A similar exception might exist for conspiracy with a licensing authority or bribery. None of these possible exceptions seems applicable here.

The only question here, therefore, is whether the *Noerr-Pennington* doctrine applies to efforts to cause a foreign government to impose restraints on U.S. commerce. While the *Noerr* case turns in part on U.S. domestic constitutional considerations, the Department does not consider it to be limited to the domestic area. The Supreme Court's discussion in *Continental Ore Co. v. Union Carbide & Carbon Corp.*, implies as much. The Court there distinguished *Noerr*—not on the ground that a foreign government was involved—but rather on the ground that the private party was directly restraining commerce itself.

Accordingly, we conclude that A's activity, joining B, C and D in the making of a recommendation that the government of X exclude another U.S. competitor, does not violate U.S. antitrust law. The fact that this activity occurred in the context of an advisory council appointed by the government of X reinforces this conclusion, but the result would be the same even if A, B, C and D had jointly initiated the idea in an informal way. Under *Noerr-Pennington*, the collective exercise of the right of political expression is protected, even where its goal is highly anti-competitive.

BUSINESS
FRANCHISING

INTRODUCTION

Franchising arrangements vary from a situation in which the franchisor supplies all physical facilities and equipment and an elaborate manual for doing business—a complete turnkey operation—to one in which the franchisor simply authorizes the use of his trademark or trade name and provides some minimal rules as to identification. Business franchising as used herein refers to the Howard Johnson, Chicken Delight, Holiday Inn-type arrangement, where a franchisor provides a franchisee with a complete, ready-to-operate business. In this kind of franchise, controls are generally the essence of the system. In order for the system to be effective and profitable, the public must be able to depend upon receiving the same product and the same services at all of the franchisor's locations. Also, for advertising purposes, there must be a high degree of similarity among all of the locations. However, controls exercised by one company over other separate and, at least technically, independent companies tend to be anticompetitive and, therefore, present potential antitrust problems. For this reason, the subject of antitrust questions in franchising can best be approached by analyzing permissible and impermissible controls.

In general, controls can be divided into (1) controls which do not directly affect the franchisor's income and (2) controls which do have an effect on his income.

Included in the first category of controls—those not directly affecting income—are such things as controls on the cleanliness of the operation, the attire of the employees, the color of the building, and the design of the menus. As a general rule, these types of controls do not present any antitrust problems. However, one must always keep in mind the antitrust maxim that the use of a proper legal right to obtain an unlawful result constitutes a violation of the antitrust laws. An example would be a franchisor who wants to make sure his franchisees buy all of their requirements from a certain supplier and, to this end, rigidly enforces indirect controls—possibly to the extent of harassment—against those franchisees who do not purchase from the designated supplier and is more lenient with those franchisees who do.

The second category of controls—those directly affecting the franchisor's income—presents extremely serious antitrust problems. These controls can be roughly divided into (1) restrictions on the pricing practices of the franchisee, (2) restrictions on the franchisee's procurement of equipment or supplies, (3) restrictions on the goods that the franchisee may sell, the area in which he may operate, or the customers to whom he may sell, and (4) restrictions on the franchisee after termination of the franchisor-franchisee relationship by way of restrictive covenants.

RELEVANT STATUTES

Before proceeding to a discussion of these controls, a brief mention of the relevant statutes is appropriate. These are as follows:

1. Section 1 of the Sherman Act prohibits any contract, combination, or conspiracy in restraint of trade.

2. Section 3 of the Clayton Act prohibits the sale of goods on condition that the buyer refrain from buying the goods of a competitor.

3. Section 5 of the Federal Trade Commission Act prohibits any unfair method of competition.

4. State antitrust legislation is not discussed herein, but it should not be overlooked because it is sometimes more restrictive than federal legislation.

It is also helpful to review the per se antitrust violations, which include (1) pricing restraints, (2) territorial allocations, (3) boycotts, (4) restraints on the resale of products sold to or made by another franchisee, and (5) tying arrangements.

In the franchise area, there are two important restrictions whose legality depends upon their reasonableness. These are (1) the total-requirements arrangement, where the franchisee is required to buy all of his supplies from the franchisor or a franchisor-designated supplier, and (2) the exclusive-dealing arrangement, where the franchisee is prohibited from selling products other than those of the franchisor.

CONTROLS

Pricing Practices

It is clear that the franchisor cannot dictate to an independent franchisee the price at which he may resell the product involved. There are certain minor exceptions to this rule, but it is submitted that in most cases, these exceptions are of academic importance only.

Procurement of Equipment or Supplies

The first of the restrictions in this category is the tying arrangement. This kind of restriction is illegal per se.

This was established in the *Chicken Delight* case, where Chicken Delight, in essence, tied its trade name to the chicken and all of the other supplies sold by its outlets. Chicken Delight introduced quite a bit of evidence to justify its arrangement, but the court held that it was a tying arrangement and therefore illegal per se.

If a patented product, process, or machine is involved, it is illegal to tie that patented article to other unpatented articles. A tying problem is present whenever one uses one's economic leverage as the supplier of one product or service or as the owner of one patent or trademark to promote or improve one's competitive position in some other area. Tying in any form is extremely dangerous because of its per se nature.

Other restrictions in this category, however, are not illegal per se. These include (1) the granting of exclusive distribution rights, (2) the imposition of sales quotas, (3) the imposition of inventory requirements, (4) restrictions as to the handling of competitive products, and (5) restrictions as to the suppliers from whom the franchisee may buy. Restrictions on competition after termination are also not illegal per se. All of these restrictions, however, are legal *only* if they are justified. Also, if another, lesser restraint would serve the same purpose, the more restrictive restraint would probably be unjustified and illegal.

Goods, Area, Customers

Territorial allocations are, of course, generally illegal. Once the franchisor has sold the product to the franchisee, the franchisee is free to sell it at whatever price to whomever and wherever he wishes. However, there are some things the franchisor may do. He may give the franchisee a primary area of responsibility, and if the franchisee does not adequately service that primary area of responsibility, the franchisor may terminate the franchise or impose other penalties. The theory here is that if the franchisor and the franchisee agree on an appropriate area of responsibility, the franchisee will be so busy servicing that area and will have to expend so much time and effort on that area that he will not be able to go into other areas. As a practical matter, this usually works pretty well, but if the franchisee has a particularly lucrative account outside of his primary area of responsibility, he may not be legally restricted from selling that account.

Another thing which may be done is to grant exclusive franchises. The franchisor cannot tell a franchisee that some other franchisee will not come into his area. However, he can tell the franchisee that he, the franchisor, will not authorize anybody else to sell in that area.

If these devices are properly used, territorial allocation can be accomplished in many areas. For example, if the franchisor of a fast-food outlet were to grant an exclusive franchise in an area of a city or town, the franchisee would be fairly well protected. Thus, in the area of the business franchise, restrictions as to area are not as important as they are in the product franchise area, where a distributor of a product in Chicago could, as a practical matter, distribute that product anywhere in the country. In this situation, the area of primary responsibility would have to be resorted to, and the justification for granting exclusive franchises in other areas of the country would simply be based on freight considerations and other economics of the situation which would make it uneconomical for the Chicago franchisee to compete with, say, the Houston, Texas, franchisee. Naturally, that is a clear case. The more difficult case is where there are two franchisees in Chicago, one on one side of town and one on the other. Here, unless transportation of the product were a real problem, the franchisees would just have to be left to fight it out. The franchisor could not divide the city and require each franchisee to stay on his side of town.

In summary, a franchisor may not impose any kind of control on the franchisee if that control could be categorized as (1) a fixing of the ultimate resale price, (2) a tying arrangement, or (3) a territorial allocation.

A franchisor can impose various noneconomic controls on the franchisee unless these are used for an improper purpose, and he can impose other controls on the franchisee which do not come under the per se antitrust rules if there is a legitimate business reason for imposing these controls.

FRANCHISE ANTITRUST BAR

Another important factor in the franchise area is the growth of a body of franchise antitrust lawyers.

There was a time when the cases of *Susser v. Carvel* and *Siegel v. Chicken Delight* were virtually the only antitrust cases in the business franchise area. Furthermore, when the *Susser* case was filed, there was only one plaintiff. After some time had elapsed, about seven or eight other plaintiffs were added. At that point, the court indicated that it thought there might be some solicitation going on and that if any more plaintiffs were added, it was going to question the plaintiff's lawyer in chambers and, if it found any evidence of solicitation, notify the bar authorities.

Now, however, the situation is quite different, principally because of the new class-action rules. In the *Siegel v. Chicken Delight* case, there were some 800 plaintiffs, and it can be expected that any future antitrust suit in the franchise area will eventually turn into a class action. Furthermore, the development of a franchise antitrust bar means that the competence of the plaintiffs' attorneys will be considerably greater.

DAMAGES

Chicken Delight tied its trademark to all of its chicken and other products. It was generally agreed that the price of these other products—which had to be purchased from Chicken Delight—was inflated and that the difference between the inflated price and the actual market value of the products would be Chicken Delight's compensation for its trademark. There was no separate charge for the trademark other than these higher prices.

The first court held that this was an unlawful tying arrangement and indicated that the measure of damages was simply the difference between the actual price and the fair market price for all of the supplies. However, the court of appeals reversed this decision and held that the value of the trademark must be taken into consideration in determining the damages.

We will have to await the final outcome of the *Chicken Delight* case to ascertain precisely how this determination is going to be made. However, the damage question is more complex than simply determining the amount of money the franchisee lost by reason of the franchisor's improper controls. Indeed, in some cases, the franchisee will not be able to show *any* damage. In the *Chicken Delight* case, for example, it is perfectly possible that the court will eventually determine that the value of the trademark exceeded the difference in the price of the products. In this event, there will, of course, be no actual monetary damages. However, if there is a violation of the antitrust laws—even a technical one—the plaintiffs can recover attorneys' fees, and, in addition, if the violation is contained in some part of the franchise agreement, there is a possibility that the entire franchise agreement—the objectionable antitrust portion and all the rest of it—will be unenforceable. The franchisor will then not be able to impose any of the restrictions contained in the agreement.

WHO CAN SUE?

An antitrust attack may come from (1) the franchisee, (2) an excluded competitive supplier, (3) the Department of Justice or the Federal Trade Commission, or (4) the state attorney general's office.

The wide variety of potential plaintiffs, coupled with the development of a franchise antitrust bar, certainly indicates that any antitrust violation in a franchise arrangement will be ferreted out by somebody and raised in litigation. In addition, there is a kind of momentum factor here. In the past couple of years, the number of cases involving substantially similar factual situations has increased from the two that existed at the time of the *Chicken Delight* case and *Susser v. Carvel* to considerably more.

CONCLUSION

Franchise agreements, like patent license agreements, provide a fertile ground for digging if one is looking for antitrust problems. The law in the area is not completely settled. The franchisor, like the patent licenser, has a great deal to lose if the agreement runs afoul of some antitrust rule. In addition to having to pay treble damages and attorneys' fees to a large number of franchisees, he may wind up having all of his previously negotiated agreements held unenforceable. However, in order for the franchise operation to be commercially successful, some measure of control is necessary. Each control should therefore be tested by the following standards:

1. Can it be characterized as a per se violation? If so, it must be stricken.

2. Would a less restrictive provision serve just as well? If so, the less restrictive provision should be used.

3. Is the restriction justified by good business reasons? If not, the restriction should be stricken.

Only if a restriction passes all three of the above tests can it be considered acceptable from an antitrust viewpoint.

CHAPTER EIGHTEEN

UNFAIR
COMPETITION

The law of unfair competition is so subjective as to defy any kind of systematic analysis. There are two bodies of this law: common law and section 5 of the Federal Trade Commission Act. According to common law, a person who is damaged in his business by the unfair actions of his competitor may recover. It is a fairly normal kind of legal action. The plaintiff goes to court and describes the unfair conduct of his competitor. If he can convince the court that his competitor's unfair conduct is actionable under the laws of that state, he then must prove that he has been damaged. If he can prove damages, he can recover those damages from the defendant. Usually, there will be attempts to recover punitive damages also, and whether this is possible will depend upon the laws of the state involved.

The two most prevalent kinds of cases under common law are (1) "palming off" and (2) improper use of a competitor's trade secrets. In a palming-off case, a competitor has attempted to pass his product off on the public as someone else's. For example, if a well-known company has designed a product which becomes successful and a new company copies that product and sells or advertises it in such a way that a reasonable person would accept it as the product of the well-known company, that would be actionable. In the trade-secret area, if a company improperly steals the trade secrets of a competitor, that can be considered unfair competition under the laws of some states. Sometimes it might be a separate tort (civil wrong) under state law, but it is always actionable if it can be proven.

Disparagement is another type of unfair competition. Generally it requires a competitor to say something which is false about your product. Another series of cases involved companies hiring away the employees of a competitor with the intention of driving the competitor out of business or reducing his competitive effectiveness. This is also actionable under the laws of almost all states, although it is sometimes covered under the state's antitrust laws.

The second body of law in the area of unfair competition is section 5(a) of the Federal Trade Commission Act. This act forbids unfair methods of competition in commerce and unfair or deceptive acts or practices in commerce. There are equivalent statutes in most states, and there are even some municipal ordinances with similar provisions. Federal Trade Commission activity in this area is not new in principle, but the magnitude and extent of its activity in the area has greatly increased in recent years.

The FTC has always been concerned with advertising, labeling, and marketing devices which are unfair. Old examples are a case which involved the labeling of part-wool underwear as "wool," which was held to be unfair to competitors who lawfully labeled such products, and cases involving merchandising by lottery, which was held to exploit the consumer's gambling instinct and to unfairly divert business from competitors.

SUBSTANTIVE LAW OF UNFAIR AND DECEPTIVE TRADE PRACTICES

Consumer Intelligence Standard

An advertisement is tested by the impression it is likely to make upon the general populace, the ordinary purchaser, or an appreciable segment of the public. The law specifies "the public—the vast multitude which includes the ignorant, the unthinking and the credulous," but an advertiser will not be held liable for every conceivable misconception—however outlandish—to which his representation might be subject among the foolish or feebleminded.

Determining the Meaning of an Advertisement

The following are the general ground rules used by the FTC to determine the meaning of an advertisement:

1. The advertisement is considered in its entirety. The total impression of the advertisement governs its meaning.

2. Literal truth will not save the advertisement if it is misleading when read in the context of the entire advertisement.

3. The advertisement is false if one of its two possible meanings is false.

4. Expressions of subjective opinion (puffery) are not actionable, but any statement subject to objective disproof will be considered to be a factual misrepresentation.

Generally the FTC has complete authority to determine the meaning of an advertisement. Dictionary definitions, consumer and expert testimony, and surveys are not necessary and not even determinative if presented. Examples of this doctrine are the *Bakers Franchise Corp.* case, where the FTC determined that the "Lite Diet" trademark for bread improperly implied dietary properties on the basis of its own authority, despite expert testimony to the contrary, and the *Liggett & Myers Tobacco* case, where an advertisement containing the word "milder" was held to promise that the cigarette would be less irritating than other cigarettes, despite the common dictionary definition of the word "milder" and the lack of any consumer testimony.

Determining the Truth of a Claim

Under older court decisions, the FTC has the burden of proving that a claim is false. The commission may rely on expert testimony, trade witnesses, surveys, and consumer testimony in reaching its conclusion. The rule of administrative law, which provides that if the FTC's determination is supported by substantial evidence the court will not reverse, makes it extremely difficult to obtain a judicial reversal of a commission finding in this area. At the present time, this particular question is the subject of a great deal of discussion because the FTC has taken the position, in some cases, that the burden is on the advertiser to support his claims, rather than on the FTC to prove they are false.

Potential Consumer Exploitation

While a tendency or capacity to deceive must be shown, no actual deception is necessary, and it is not necessary to prove any specific intent to deceive on the part of the advertiser.

SPECIFIC TYPES OF UNFAIR AND DECEPTIVE PRACTICES

The following is a brief listing of the major categories of unfair and deceptive practices which have been challenged by the FTC:

1. It is an unfair and deceptive trade practice to make a false claim of status or to use a trademark which is inherently deceptive. Examples here would be a company which advertised itself as a manufacturer when it had no manufacturing facilities and was merely a distributor or a company which adopted a name or trade name improperly suggesting some connection with the government.

2. It is deceptive to make false claims about the composition, quality, quantity, or effectiveness of a product.

3. It is deceptive to make false claims of price reductions, comparative prices, manufacturer's lists, or suggested retail prices. Bait-and-switch advertising and the use of the word "free" in a misleading situation are also unfair.

4. Guarantees and warranties must not be used deceptively.

5. Misuse of the names of cities, countries, or regions and failure to disclose the foreign origin of products which consumers might believe to be domestic are unfair.

6. Unfair interference with the operation of a competitor's business, such as false disparagement or passing off or inducing the breach of contracts, is unfair.

7. Lotteries or other practices which appeal to consumers' gambling instincts are unfair and prohibited even when not deceptive.

8. It is unlawful for a supplier to pay "push money" to a customer's employees without the knowledge of the customer, pursuant to a lottery scheme, or where the sale of competitive products is hampered or the requirements of the Robinson-Patman Act are not met. "Push money" refers to payments made by a manufacturer to a retailer's sales representatives to "push" the manufacturer's products. Some groups feel the entire practice is unfair because if a potential customer asks for a sales representative's opinion on the comparative quality and value of different brands and the sales representative recommends one brand, not because of his honest opinion on quality and value but because

he is receiving "push money" from that manufacturer, the consumer has been imposed upon.

9. It is unlawful to send unsolicited merchandise through the mail. If this is done, the consumer may retain the unordered merchandise and pay only if he decides to purchase the goods.

CURRENT EFFORTS OF THE FTC TO EXPAND ITS REMEDIAL POWERS

In 1969, "Nader's Raiders" issued a report criticizing the FTC for its failure to detect violations, establish priorities, enforce the statute vigorously, and seek sufficient statutory authority to make its work effective. This report was followed by an American Bar Association commission study which also criticized the FTC as being ineffective, lacking a unified approach based on policy planning, and insufficient to provide leadership to local enforcement agencies.

In June of 1970, the FTC was reorganized under Chairman Weinberger, and a Bureau of Consumer Protection was established. In addition, field-office responsibility was increased, federal-state task forces and consumer advisory boards were created, and the FTC's rules of practice and procedures were restudied. Since then, the FTC has engaged in a search for new and stronger remedies. Part of its effort is directed toward getting new legislation which will increase its power. Other effort is directed toward instituting selected cases and requesting new, stronger, and more appropriate relief.

Corrective Advertising

One of the current pushes of the FTC is in the area of corrective advertising. The leading case involves Listerine mouth wash, which the FTC felt was advertised unfairly because it was said to prevent colds or reduce their severity and the company was unable to prove this claim. The FTC wanted the company to state the following in all of its future advertising:

1. The product does not prevent colds or reduce their severity.

2. Advertisements in the past so stating have been false.

The federal courts held that the FTC did have the power to require corrective advertising. They held, in this case, that the first remedy was appropriate but not the second. The company will have to state that Listerine does not prevent colds, but it will not have to state that its previous claims have been wrong.

The FTC and the courts imposed this requirement on the advertisements purchased with the next funds of the company. The company cannot avoid the implications of the order simply by refraining from advertising for a period of time. The next time it advertises the product it will have to make the corrective statement.

Affirmative Disclosure

In some recent cases, the FTC has included in its proposed consent orders provisions to the effect that certain affirmative disclosures must be made in future advertising. Some of these disclosures would have the effect of destroying the company's ability to market the product. For example, in the *Du*

Pont case, the FTC proposed a disclosure that Zerex antifreeze may damage automobile radiators; in the *Fabergé* case, it proposed a disclosure that a weight-reducing belt may be physically dangerous.

Banning Products and Limiting Business

In addition to requiring affirmative disclosures which could result in discontinuance of the product or the business activity, the FTC has indicated that it might attempt to ban the product if the disclosure does not provide adequate relief. It has also limited the maximum amount of any consumer contract which a respondent is authorized to enter into in the future.

The *Du Pont* case is an example of the first situation; Zerex was going to be banned if disclosure of its damaging qualities provided insufficient relief. The *Arthur Murray* case is an example of the second situation; the FTC said that no consumer contract in excess of $1500 was authorized because of the prior unfair and deceptive activities of Arthur Murray sales representatives.

Trademarks

The commission has already received judicial authorization to require a company to discontinue the use of deceptive trademarks. However, this form of remedy is the subject of considerably increased activity. Examples are FTC attacks on Profile bread, "Welcome Newcomer" as a trade name for a credit bureau, and "Pro-Slim" as a trade name for a dietary product.

Restitution and Damages

The FTC has traditionally included provisions in its orders requiring restitution in connection with future violations. However, in addition, some recent complaints have included provisions requiring restitution for alleged past violations in the form of contract or fraud damages.

Substantiation of Product Claims

The FTC is taking the position at this time that it is inherently unfair, under certain circumstances, to make advertising representations which are unsupported by adequate and well-controlled tests. Examples are the *Du Pont* case, where the FTC claimed an absence of any test indicating that the antifreeze did not damage the auto, and the *Standard Oil* case, where the FTC claimed an absence of any test supporting antipollution claims for the gasoline.

Consumer Information

A number of proposed trade-regulation rules and three trade-regulation rules already issued appear to be based on the concept that it is unfair to deprive the consumer of product information which would assist him in making informed product choices based on price, quality, and value. Deception seems to be either not an issue at all or a secondary issue. Examples here are FTC regulations regarding the posting of minimum octane ratings on gasoline pumps and a rule requiring the disclosure of the odds of winning in games of chance in the food-retailing and gasoline industries.

Exploiting Consumer Weakness

A number of commission proceedings are currently based on the theory that it is unfair to exploit various consumer weaknesses, such as a tendency to procrastinate, financial irresponsibility, a gambling instinct, and a lack of sales resistance. Examples here are the complaint against the Reader's Digest Association and Metromedia for using the names of consumers who responded to a free-goods offer, the complaint against door-to-door sales representatives requiring a 3-day cooling-off period in any door-to-door sales situation, and the 7-day cooling-off period required in the *Arthur Murray Dance Studio* case.

Advertising Chemically Identical Products

Certain recent FTC complaints seem responsive to consumer advocate demands that advertisers disclose that their products are chemically identical to other products available on the market.

Meaningless Claims

In a number of recent cases, the FTC has challenged television demonstrations which, although true, do not allegedly support the advertising claim being made. An example here is a Krona Chrome razor blades advertisement which shows two razor blades magnified a great deal. The ad shows a competitive blade after some use with an irregular shaving edge. The edge of the Krona Chrome blade is not as irregular after the same use. The FTC alleges that while the demonstration may be true, the razor blades are magnified so much as to be misleading. The highly magnified irregularities shown on Brand X do not affect its shaving characteristics.

Advertising to Especially Susceptible Audiences

The FTC has indicated its intention to adopt stricter advertising rules in connection with advertising addressed to special audience groups, such as children or the elderly. One example is the complaint against Mattel, Inc. and Topper Corp. involving television commercials which allegedly exaggerated the appearance or performance of the toys in question. Another example is the complaint against ITT Continental Baking Co. which alleged improper exploitation of mothers' concern about purchasing nutritional products for their children.

TRADE-REGULATION RULES

One of the most troublesome current problems in the unfair-competition area is that the Federal Trade Commission now has the power to issue substantive rules specifically defining practices which are unfair or deceptive under section 5 of the Federal Trade Commission Act. The Federal Trade Commission also has authorization to seek civil penalties of up to $10,000 per day for violations of one of these trade-regulation rules if the defendant had actual or constructive knowledge of the rule as it applied to his business. Thus if the FTC issues an order against one company in an industry, another company in the same industry can be held to be in violation of the order if the FTC can show that it knew or had implied knowledge of the order. Since the orders will be published and probably distributed by various trade associations, it might be difficult for the second company to argue that it had no knowledge of the order even if that is, in fact, the case. This is very new, and at this time there have not been any prosecutions using this new power granted to the FTC in late 1974. It will, however, be an area of important future concern. What is or is not unfair will have to be considered in the light of any FTC regulations governing the industry.

CHAPTER NINETEEN

ADVANCE CLEARANCE
PROCEDURES

Both the Department of Justice and the Federal Trade Commission have procedures by which companies intending to take a course of action and concerned about its antitrust implications can ask for prior government advice. Generally, clearance from either agency is sufficient; you don't have to ask both. In most cases, you can also take your choice as to which agency you want to ask.

However, most antitrust counselors see a very limited number of situations in which these advance clearance procedures are useful. They feel that in clear cases, you don't need advance clearance, and in close cases, the government is always going to take an adverse position. This is essentially the case, and so the use of advance clearance procedures is limited. However, they can be useful in the following situations:

1. If you and your counsel feel fairly certain that a proposed course of conduct presents substantial antitrust risks while others in your company—or other parties to the proposed transaction—feel strongly about going ahead, you should consider the advance clearance procedures. If you get the go-ahead, you can put your concerns aside; if you don't, the other parties will have to take your concerns more seriously.

2. In a very large undertaking, such as a joint venture involving many companies and large sums of money, the advance clearance procedures might be an economic necessity to justify the expenditures.

3. Certain special transactions, like interlocking directorates under section 8 of the Clayton Act, present good cases for advance review. There usually isn't

any hurry about the transaction, and there is very little downside risk. If you don't get the clearance, you just don't go on the board of directors.

4. Acquisitions are one area where advance clearance is necessary, but in the case of acquisitions, you have to use the new premerger notification procedures rather than the business review procedures. When a large acquisition is involved, you have to notify the government and then wait a certain prescribed period of time before you can go ahead. The procedure is not voluntary, and the steps you have to take are spelled out in great detail in the appropriate regulations.

The Department of Justice calls its procedure "Business Review Procedure," and it issued the following amendments on February 22, 1977.

Although the Department of Justice is not authorized to give advisory opinions to private parties, for several decades the Antitrust Division has been willing in certain circumstances to review proposed business conduct and state its enforcement intentions. This originated with a "railroad release" procedure under which the Division would forego the initiation of criminal antitrust proceedings. The procedure was subsequently expanded to encompass a "merger clearance" procedure under which the Division would state its present enforcement intention with respect to a merger or acquisition; and the Department issued a written statement entitled "Business Review Procedure." That statement has been revised several times.

1.   A request for a business review letter must be submitted in writing to the Assistant Attorney General, Antitrust Division, Department of Justice, Washington, D.C. 20530.

2.   The Division will consider only requests with respect to proposed business conduct, which may involve either domestic or foreign commerce.

3.   The Division may, in its discretion, refuse to consider a request.

4.   A business review letter shall have no application to any party which does not join in the request therefor.

5.   The requesting parties are under an affirmative obligation to make full and true disclosure with respect to the business conduct for which review is requested. Each request must be accompanied by all relevant data including background information, complete copies of all operative documents and detailed statements of all collateral or oral understandings, if any. All parties requesting the review letter must provide the Division with whatever additional information or documents the Division may therefore request in order to review the matter. Such additional information, if furnished orally, shall be promptly confirmed in writing. In connection with any request for review, the Division will also conduct whatever independent investigation it believes is appropriate.

6.   No oral clearance, release or other statement purporting to bind the enforcement discretion of the Division may be given. The requesting party may rely only upon a written business review letter signed by the Assistant Attorney General in charge of the Antitrust Division or his delegate.

7.   (a) If the business conduct for which review is requested is subject to approval by a regulatory agency, a review request may be considered before agency approval has been obtained only where it appears that exceptional or unnecessary burdens might otherwise be imposed on the party or parties requesting review, or where the agency specifically requests that a party or parties request review. However, any business review letter issued in these as in any other circumstances will state only the Department's present enforcement intentions under the antitrust laws. It shall in no way be taken to indicate the Department's views on the legal or factual issues that may be raised before the regulatory agency, or in an appeal from the regulatory agency's decision. In particular the issuance of such a letter is not to be represented to mean that the Division believes that there are no anticompetitive consequences warranting agency consideration.

(b) The submission of a request for a business review, or its pendency, shall in no way alter any responsibility of any party to comply with the Premerger

Notification provisions of the Antitrust Improvements Act of 1976, 15 U.S.C. sec. 18A, and the regulations promulgated thereunder, 16 C.F.R., Part 801.

8. After review of a request submitted hereunder the Division may: state its present enforcement intention with respect to the proposed business conduct; decline to pass on the request; or take such other position or action as it considers appropriate.

9. A business review letter states only the enforcement intention of the Division as of the date of the letter, and the Division remains completely free to bring whatever action or proceeding it subsequently comes to believe is required by the public interest. As to a stated present intention not to bring an action, however, the Division has never exercised its right to bring a criminal action where there has been full and true disclosure at the time of presenting the request.

10. (a) Simultaneously upon notifying the requesting party of any Division action described in paragraph 8, the business review request and the Division's letter in response shall be indexed and placed in a file available to the public upon request.

(b) On that date or within thirty days after the date upon which the Division takes any action as described in paragraph 8, the information supplied to support the business review request and any other information supplied by the requesting party in connection with the transaction that is the subject of the business review request, shall be indexed and placed in a file with the request and the Division's letter, available to the public upon request. This file shall remain open for one year, after which time it shall be closed and the documents either returned to the requesting party or otherwise disposed of, at the discretion of the Antitrust Division.

(c) Prior to the time the information described in subparagraphs (a) and (b) is indexed and made publicly available in accordance with the terms of those subparagraphs, the requesting party may ask the Division to delay making public some or all of such information. However the requesting party must: (1) specify precisely the documents or parts thereof that he asks not be made public; (2) state the minimum period of time during which nondisclosure is considered necessary; and (3) justify the request for nondisclosure, both as to content and time, by showing good cause therefor including a showing that disclosure would have a detrimental effect upon the requesting party's operations or relations with actual or potential customers, employees, suppliers (including suppliers of credit), stockholders or competitors. The Department of Justice, in its discretion, shall make the final determination as to whether good cause for nondisclosure has been shown.

(d) Nothing contained in subparagraphs (a), (b) and (c) shall limit the Division's right, in its discretion, to issue a press release describing generally the identity of the requesting party or parties and the nature of action taken by the Division upon the request.

(e) This paragraph reflects a policy determination by the Department of Justice and is subject to any limitations on public disclosure arising from statutory restrictions, Executive Order, or the national interests.

11. Any requesting party may withdraw a request for review at any time. The Division remains free, however, to submit such comments to such requesting party as it deems appropriate. Failure to take any action after receipt of the documents or information, whether submitted pursuant to this procedure or otherwise, does not in any way limit or stop the Division from taking such action at such time thereafter as it deems appropriate. The Division reserves the right to retain documents submitted to it under this procedure or otherwise and to use them for all governmental purposes.

CHAPTER TWENTY

CRIMINAL
PENALTIES

There has been a great deal of sword-rattling recently by the Department of Justice aimed at more certain and higher jail terms for antitrust violators—particularly in the price-fixing area. The principal development is of course, the amendment of the Sherman Act making antitrust violations felonies rather than misdemeanors. The department has made an attempt to formalize its approach to requesting jail sentences by adopting recommendations for sentencing in antitrust felony cases, in the form of a memorandum from Assistant Attorney General of the Antitrust Division Don Baker to the division's attorneys. There is no reason to believe that the content of this memorandum will change with future administrations. A copy of the memorandum is included in this chapter. In fact, new Attorney General Griffin B. Bell, in an address before the *Harvard Law Review* on March 19, endorsed this memorandum.

In the case of *United States v. Alton Box Board Co.*, the U.S. District Court for the Northern District of Illinois dealt with the jail-term question in the context of an apparently elaborate price-fixing scheme in the folding-carton industry. That court imposed jail sentences harsher than prior sentences for antitrust violations but somewhat less harsh than the government wanted and less harsh than would be called for by the sentencing guides. Accordingly, it appears that the amendment to the Sherman Act giving the penalty felony status, combined with the government's push, has already yielded some increased jail terms, and it would appear that more, rather than fewer, jail terms will await future antitrust violators—although the current sentencing practice in the folding-carton case makes it clear that the jail sentences will be directly related to the degree of participation of the individuals in the price-fixing scheme. Court activity to date indicates that jail sentences will be imposed with more frequency but their magnitude may not be quite what the government would like. Of course, the matter of sentencing is so individual with each judge that any generalizations would be very difficult to justify.

TO: All Attorneys and Economists, Antitrust Division

FROM: Donald I. Baker, Assistant Attorney General, Antitrust Division

SUBJECT: Guidelines for Sentencing Recommendations in Felony Cases under the Sherman Act.

February 24, 1977

This memorandum is intended to state the policies that the Antitrust Division will use in making sentencing recommendations for persons convicted of felonies established by the Antitrust Procedures and Penalties Act of 1974. It embodies the Division's commitment to increased criminal sentences and to evenhandedness in law enforcement.

INTRODUCTION

A primary purpose of these Guidelines is to provide a means by which sentencing recommendations will be more rational and equitable. Sentencing in past antitrust cases, as with past sentencing in white collar crimes in general, can be criticized on two bases: it has been ineffective in that it has been lenient, and it has been inequitable as evidenced by disparate sentences. Congress, by increasing the maximum penalties in the Sherman Act, has given the courts a mandate for heavier sentences. In the Antitrust Procedures and Penalties Act, Congress increased the maximum penalties under the Sherman Act to a three-year maximum jail term and $100,000 maximum fine for corporations.[1] These Guidelines are designed to serve as a tool to enable our attorneys to make reasoned and consistent sentencing recommendations and to explain to the courts and the public what we are doing.

The issue of equity is a necessary first step in achieving justice that is fair and proper as well as evenhanded in application. The Judiciary has been increasingly concerned about the sentencing process, especially the lack of guidance and review.[2] Without explicit policy to structure and guide discretion, decisionmakers, whether trial attorneys, top staff, or judges, tend to function as rugged individualists, and consistency is lost. These Guidelines are designed to improve our contribution to the sentencing process—to structure our sentencing recommendation discretion without removing it. They provide an articulated foundation for an equitable sentencing policy, while retaining the

---

[1] Under prior law, the maximum sentence was one year imprisonment and a $50,000 fine for individuals, and a $100,000 fine for corporations.

[2] For example, Chief Justice Burger addressed the subject in his 1977 State of the Judiciary message. The Judicial Conference Committee on Rules of Procedure is presently holding hearings on the subject. Senator Kennedy has recently introduced legislation (S. 181) in the Senate which would, *inter alia*, establish sentencing criteria and a sentencing commission to promulgate sentencing guidelines. 123 Cong. Rec. S405 (Jan. 11, 1977).

potential for individual variation justified by the facts of a particular case. At a minimum these Guidelines help articulate the factors used—the amount of commerce involved, the duration of the conspiracy, the coercive or predatory nature of the conduct involved, the level of authority—and the weights given to them in calculating a sentence which both fits the crime and the defendant, and furthers our antitrust enforcement goals.

Undoubtedly, some will feel that the factors we have chosen are inappropriate or over- or under-inclusive. However, they are factors that have been selected after a great deal of thought and work by many experienced antitrust attorneys. Experience will show us whether and how our Guidelines need revision. If we can make what we are presently doing explicit and, thus, more consistent, we shall be better prepared to argue the merits of the factors, after we have had some experience with them.

The obvious question is what is our justification for recommending prison sentences for convicted antitrust felons. One justification is that Congress recently increased not only the maximum fine but also the maximum prison penalty for Sherman Act violations, indicating a judgment that imprisonment should play an important role in punishing antitrust crime. In the last several years, the amount of price fixing that has been uncovered continues to increase, despite the threat of single damage actions on behalf of the United States, treble damage actions by private plaintiffs and criminal fines.

A second reason is that prison sentences are uniquely effective in deterring antitrust violators (who are generally white collar businessmen) who may view a fine as a "license fee" for fixing prices[3] but who view the threat of a substantial prison term more seriously. This applies not only to deterring a convicted antitrust criminal from repeated violations (specific deterrence), but also to deterring others who may be tempted to engage in price fixing (general deterrence). Antitrust crimes, like other "white collar" crimes, have characteristics that warrant the belief they will be deterred by the threat of substantial penalties. An antitrust violation is not a crime of passion, nor is it normally committed out of need, desperation or stupidity. It is more likely to be carried out over a period of several months or years, with at least a minimum degree of coordination and planning rather than a single impulsive act. In sum, an antitrust crime is carried out by one who has a clear option to engage or not to engage in criminal activity and as such the imposition of substantial sentences can have a major effect in deterring such criminal conduct. It bears emphasizing here that the Sherman Act does not require proof of specific intent (scienter) but rather presumes that individuals are responsible for the reasonable and necessary consequences of their acts and so intend them.

The importance of deterrence as a basis for sentencing those who violate the antitrust laws is similar to the importance of deterrence as a basis for sentencing those convicted of tax violations. The functioning of our economy, as with the functioning of our tax system, depends largely upon voluntary compliance. The Antitrust Division can no more monitor the competitive behavior of every firm and industry than the IRS and Tax Division can enforce the tax laws by monitoring every citizen. Instead it is the practice of the Tax Division to always recommend prison sentences in criminal cases, thereby hoping to deter the millions of other taxpayers from attempting to evade taxes. Given the impossibility of monitoring all the businesses in the country,

---

[3] Businessmen have been quoted as admitting that they view a fine or light criminal sentence as a small price to pay for the chance to increase profits substantially as the result of a price-fixing conspiracy. *Business Week,* p. 48, June 2, 1975.

and the difficulty of detecting and proving criminal violations of the antitrust laws, the sentencing opportunities of each antitrust case must be used to the maximum advantage in deterring other violations.

The Guidelines reinforce our deterrence efforts by making clear the kinds of sentences we shall recommend for antitrust violators. By explicitly identifying the factors important to our sentencing recommendations, we put the businessman on notice of the kind of conduct that we view as clearly falling outside the law and within serious criminal sanctions.

There are several reasons why we believe it important to submit sentencing recommendations. First, antitrust sentences should be broadly consistent over time and across the country in order to achieve our national enforcement goal of general deterrence. Our recommendations will indicate to the judge (who may never have sentenced an antitrust felon before) the type of sentences we have sought elsewhere. Uneven sentencing would cause society to perceive the sentencing decision as the product of chance or unexplained decision process, and would weaken public trust in the rule of law and the enforcement process. Secondly, as the agency charged with enforcing the antitrust laws, we have expertise on the relative degree of seriousness of different fact situations, and can assist the judge in understanding why one defendant's conduct merits more or less punishment in accordance with the enforcement objectives of the Sherman Act. We also have unique access to information relevant to how well our goal of general deterrence is being achieved, as indicated by the number of pending grand jury and CID investigations. Sentencing disparities are not due to design on the part of judges but rather to their lack of familiarity with the whole picture, with the relation of this case to other cases and overall enforcement. As such, these Guidelines and our recommendations will provide the judges with tools that will assist them in the exercise of their discretion in an efficient and rational manner. Thirdly, the degree of cooperation with the government, an important mitigating factor, is something peculiarly within our knowledge. Finally, the Federal Rules of Criminal Procedure authorize us to address the court on sentencing. Rule 32 states that "[t]he attorney for the government shall have an equivalent opportunity to speak to the court" as is afforded the defendant and counsel for the defendant. F. R. Crim. P. 32(a) (1).

* * *

This memorandum is divided into three sections:

   I.   Recommended Prison Terms for Individuals;
  II.   Recommended Fines for Individuals; and
III.   Recommended Fines for Corporations.

I. Recommended Prison Terms for Individuals

This is in many ways the most difficult area of sentencing, because individual sentencing involves judgments as to the behavior of individual human beings, and imprisonment deprives people of cherished personal freedom. For that reason it is important that our sentencing recommendations be rational and uniform, and provide just punishment for the offense. At the same time, the sentence must reflect the seriousness of the offense in terms of the larger law enforcement needs of the Department of Justice and the Antitrust Division. The factors set forth below should provide a framework that will insure sentence recommendations that meet these requirements.

As discussed above, the primary reasons the Division will recommend imprisonment of antitrust criminals are general and specific deterrence—to deter all prospective violators from violating the Sherman Act and to deter a particular defendant from repeating the violation.

A.   The Impact of Parole

In calculating the prison term which best serves these goals, we must take into account the parole provisions of Title 18 of the United States Code. As discussed below, those provisions provide for parole after a portion of the sentence has been served, assuming the prisoner satisfies certain parole criteria.[4] We can assume that our white collar price fixers will generally satisfy these criteria, for they probably, for example, will have observed prison rules, will not be drug addicts, and will pose no jeopardy to the public welfare. Thus, the major consideration relevant to a parole determination for an antitrust prisoner is whether release would "depreciate the seriousness of his offense or promote disrespect for the law . . ."[5] This determination can and should be made by the court at the time of sentencing, rather than after the defendant has served some time under a somewhat open-ended sentence.

Federal law basically provides that prisoners sentenced to a definite term of more than one year shall be eligible for parole after serving one-third of the term, with additional time off for good behavior.[6] We believe this provision should be applied uniformly by the courts in antitrust cases, so that antitrust prisoners will not be eligible for parole before they have served one-third of the sentence imposed minus good time.[7] Obviously standard parole treatment is a necessary part of uniform antitrust sentencing.

The important thing to remember about the parole provisions is that they substantially reduce the amount of time served[8] and on occasion produce unintended consequences in terms of actual time served. A defendant sentenced to less than six months is not eligible for parole, and may serve more time than a defendant sentenced for a longer period but released on parole. These computations are something which should be made before recommending a sentence.

In the discussion that follows, we shall assume that the sentence imposed implicitly or explicitly provides that the prisoner will be eligible for parole after serving one-third of the sentence (less good time), unless the sentence imposed is less than six months.

B.   The 18-Month Base Sentence

The maximum prison term for a Sherman Act felony is three years, and the corresponding parole eligibility would occur after one year. The Division

---

[4] See 18 U.S.C. sec. 4206; 18 C.F.R. sec. 2.20 (41 Fed. Reg. 37316-37324, Sept. 3, 1976).

[5] *Id.*

[6] 18 U.S.C. secs. 4161, 4162, and 4205. Maximum "good time" allowances under these provisions can total eight days per month for sentences between six months and one year, and 11 days per month for sentences between one and three years.

[7] 18 U.S.C. sec. 4205 essentially provides that the sentencing court may provide for the prisoner's release "as if on parole" after serving one-third of a sentence of six months to one year, and does not provide for parole in cases where the sentence is less than six months. Additionally, the sentencing judge has the authority to prescribe a time period of less than one-third of the sentence after which the prisoner will become eligible for parole.

[8] For this reason, recommendations of early parole should be used to take into account mitigating circumstances which, though unrelated to the seriousness of the crime itself, are relevant to our enforcement efforts or the personal situation of the defendant. See discussion *infra.*

will, in appropriate circumstances, recommend this maximum penalty. In arriving at individual recommendations, we shall follow a step-by-step approach considering and applying several aggravating and mitigating factors to a base sentence of 18 months.[9] The 18 months will be the base period from which to calculate our recommendations in all criminal antitrust cases except those which involve very small, purely local conspiracies.

The 18-month base was selected as the figure which we at present perceive to best advance the enforcement needs of the Sherman Act. It may be altered in light of what experience shows us is its actual deterrent effect. As the midpoint of the sentencing range legislated by Congress, it meets the congressional concern that antitrust sentences be increased, yet leaves flexibility to increase or decrease the recommended sentence in accordance with the aggravating or mitigating factors present in a particular case. It is long enough, we hope, to deter the average individual from participating in a proffered price-fixing conspiracy. It is also long enough to bring antitrust sentences more or less in line with sentences for other white collar felonies.[10]

Since sentencing deals with an infinite variety of human behavior, it is impossible to plan for all possible fact situations in advance. Instead, the Sentencing Guidelines identify the factors that should be taken into account in recommending a sentence that will be rationally related to the offense and will deter future violations. The aggravating factors listed below should be applicable to most fact situations. The weight to be assigned to each factor will depend upon the degree to which the factor was present in the particular violation.[11] In addition, these Guidelines may well have to be adjusted over time to reflect their actual effectiveness in deterring price fixing.

Sentencing is not an exact science. Unfortunately, there is no way to calculate precisely what kind of punishment will most accurately satisfy those goals in the case of each individual defendant. Rather it is based upon broad judgments that a particular sentence (e.g. zero to three years) is the type of punishment necessary to punish and deter a particular crime (e.g. price fixing).[12]

Given that type of mandate and level of knowledge about sentencing, there is no assurance that fine-tuning a sentence to reflect every detail of a violation would provide any more effective punishment and deterrence than recommendations based upon the more flexible guideline approach outlined here.

C. Factors in Aggravation

Experience has shown that there are five factors that will almost always be relevant in determining the severity of the sentence necessary to deter antitrust violations:

---

[9] As explained above we assume that under such a sentence of 18 months, an individual would be eligible for parole after less than six months.

[10] In fiscal 1976, those convicted of securities fraud were sentenced to an average of 45.4 months imprisonment. Transportation of forged securities was punished by an average imprisonment of 45.4 months, and bank embezzlement by 22.6 months. Income tax fraud brought an average imprisonment of 15.4 months. Administrative Office of the United States Courts, *1976 Annual Report of the Director*, App. II, Table D5.

[11] We recognize that there may be special cases that will require individual treatment. The burden, however, will be on the person seeking deviation from the Guidelines to justify such special treatment.

[12] *See, e.g.*, 119 Cong. Rec. H10761, H10763 (Nov. 19, 1973) (noting that the antitrust crimes need heavier punishment).

(1) amount of commerce involved;

(2) position of the individual;

(3) existence and degree of predatory or coercive conduct;

(4) duration of participation; and

(5) previous conviction.

These factors should be considered in aggravation. Although no precise weight can be given to any of these factors, as a *general* proposition the recommended sentence should be adjusted upward from one to six months for each aggravating factor that is present.

1. Amount of Commerce Involved. The amount of commerce involved in a conspiracy is a rough measure of the potential impact it could have upon the economy. Inasmuch as the conspiracy is the aggregate result of the agreements of all its members, each member should be held responsible for the aggregate amount of commerce affected.

The base recommendation of 18 months already takes into account an "amount of commerce" factor commonly present in small or medium size conspiracies. Where the commerce affected by the conspiracy exceeds $50 million in any one year, this factor will result in an upward adjustment of the recommended sentence by one to six months. A major conspiracy, involving for example ten times that amount of commerce, would call for a six-month additional sentence on this ground. Where the amount of commerce is extremely small, as in the very smallest, local price-fixing conspiracy involving extremely small companies or "mom and pop" enterprises, the amount of commerce involved may be considered a mitigating factor for reasons discussed below.[13]

2. Position of the Individual. This element should only be considered as an aggravating factor. The 18-month base assumes a defendant is an "average" employee and a run-of-the-mill member of the conspiracy. Where the defendant serves in an executive position, e.g., sales manager, vice president, president or chairman (or any other position where the individual is largely giving orders rather than largely following directions), the 18-month base sentence recommendation should be adjusted upward from one to six months, depending upon the position of the individual. This should also be done where the individual has been the obvious linchpin or leader of the conspiracy responsible for organizing it and holding it together. By making clear that those who have positions of responsibility should receive heavier prison sentences, we hope to deter them from getting themselves and their subordinates involved in price-fixing schemes.

In considering this factor, it is important that we not slip into the practice of comparing the relative roles of activity or passivity of all the conspirators. Apart from leaders and high corporate officials, all co-conspirators should be treated equal to all others. An agreement is all that is necessary to constitute the offense, and the agreement of a passive conspirator is just as much an agreement as an agreement by a more active participant. An individual who has been indicted and convicted is sufficiently involved in the conspiracy to warrant a sentence which is strong enough to both punish him and deter him and others from similar conduct. The more marginal conspirator is per-

---

[13] See discussion *infra.*

haps the one most likely to be deterred by tougher sentences, and, if such conspirators are essential to a scheme, deterring them may be enough to prevent a conspiracy from ever being created.

3. Existence and Degree of Predatory or Coercive Conduct.   By this element we mean the use of threats, force, or economic reprisals to further the conspiracy. To be sure, a well-run conspiracy probably does not need coercion to carry out its illegal objective, and accordingly the absence of coercion is in no way a mitigating factor. However, coercion is socially undesirable conduct, from which we want to deter others, and as such justifies increasing the sentence. The presence of coercion requires an upward adjustment of one to six months to the recommended sentence, depending on the character and scope of the relevant conduct, and the power of the party doing the coercion.

Coercion might arise in a number of contexts, the most obvious being coercive price fixing, e.g., where small competitors are threatened with retaliation if they do not increase prices. Predatory conduct should be scrutinized to ascertain to what extent it is being used to coerce competitors to join in a conspiracy or course of conduct.

4. Duration of Participation.   While normally the brevity of one's participation in a short-term conspiracy should not be considered a mitigating factor, unusually lengthy participation is an appropriate factor to consider in aggravation. The fact that a defendant had participated in the conspiracy only briefly before our investigation or indictment brought it to a halt is irrelevant, for we have no way of knowing how long his participation would have continued had we not uncovered the crime.[14]

The 18-month base recommendation takes into account some minimum duration necessary to get the conspiracy operating. This will vary from conspiracy to conspiracy. In general, duration should be treated as an aggravating factor increasing our recommended sentence by one to six months where the defendant's participation has extended over a period of more than one year.

5. Previous Conviction.   In most instances a prior antitrust conviction (including a *nolo contendere* plea) should result in the maximum recommendation regardless of other factors. A prior conviction for a similar state or federal crime should result in an upward adjustment of one to six months.

D. Factors in Mitigation

There are two mitigating factors that should be considered, if present, in virtually all cases: (1) cooperation with the government and (2) personal, family or business hardship. These factors will be considered after the recommended sentence has been determined and applied, to reduce the amount of time we recommend actually be served. For example, a recommended sentence of 18 months would typically mean parole after serving somewhat less than six months (one-third of the sentence less time off for good behavior) absent mitigating circumstances. Given mitigating circumstances, we would supplement our sentence recommendation with the further recommendation that parole be granted sooner than it otherwise would be.

The practice of using mitigating factors to reduce the time served rather

---

[14] In contrast, affirmative withdrawal from a continuing conspiracy may be considered in mitigation. See discussion *infra*.

than the recommended sentence recognizes that the purposes served by imprisoning price fixers bear little or no relationship to the defendant's personal characteristics or feelings. We imprison those who fix prices largely to deter them and others from similar conduct. Deterrence requires that substantial sentences be consistently and predictably imposed upon illegal conduct. The only mitigating factors relevant to antitrust violations—cooperation with the government and business, personal or financial responsibilities—relate not to the seriousness of the crime or the degree to which society wants to punish that crime and deter others from crimes like it, but to the appropriateness of imprisoning a particular defendant because of outside factors relevant to our enforcement goals.

1. Cooperation with the Government. Cooperation, even when delayed until after indictment, is extremely important and should be encouraged and rewarded as much as possible. It is important not only because it can save the government time and money and improve the chances of convicting the guilty, but also because cooperation, to the extent that it improves our enforcement ability, may increase the deterrent effect of our enforcement efforts. Rewarding cooperation will also, we hope, deter some potential conspirators from entering into a conspiracy when they realize that if caught, their co-conspirators have an incentive to tell the whole story.[15] Where a defendant provides us with timely and full cooperation with respect to his case and, where we actually need and accept the cooperation, we should recommend that the time served be substantially reduced below that which would otherwise be served under our recommended sentence. However, we must actually *need,* receive, and accept the cooperation. Where cooperation is offered by a defendant but not accepted because it is unnecessary, significant mitigation is not justified. Such a policy should help encourage earlier cooperation, because each defendant will know that if he or she cooperates after several others, a reduced sentence is less likely.

There are obviously other factors which defendants undoubtedly will urge the court to consider in mitigation. Two that we have frequently encountered in the past are early withdrawal from the conspiracy and remorse. The former may be entitled to some consideration in mitigation; the latter is not.

Early withdrawal from an ongoing conspiracy is conduct that we seek to encourage. However, withdrawing and keeping quiet about the conspiracy falls far short of withdrawing and then bringing the illegal activity to the government's attention. Withdrawal, absent cooperation with the government, is therefore entitled to very little mitigating weight. To some extent this factor has already been considered in connection with the "amount of commerce" and "duration" aggravating factors, for the briefer the defendant's participation, the smaller those factors will be.

Remorse has no more bearing upon our goal of general deterrence than defendant's churchgoing habits or charitable contributions. It should come as no surprise that a businessman who has been indicted and convicted of a felony should feel remorse. Furthermore, if he were truly remorseful he would have cooperated with the government at an early stage, and that fact would have been considered in mitigation. Accordingly, remorse that is unaccompanied by cooperation with the government is not a factor in mitigation.

---

[15] We are dealing here with post-indictment cooperation. Valuable preindictment cooperation generally results in immunity. In the event we were to indict someone who had given us substantial and important preindictment cooperation, that cooperation would likewise be a mitigating factor.

2.   Personal, Family or Business Hardships.   These mitigating factors, best considered as a group, will be largely within the personal knowledge of the defendant. They are less within our expertise than are considerations of general deterrence or cooperation with the government.

Obviously, the defendant's age and health, family responsibilities, or extreme business hardship may in some cases present valid reasons for reducing the amount of the sentence actually to be served. The defendant should submit any facts in support of a request for mitigation to the attention of the court and the government at an early date, so that the government can determine whether to submit evidence to the contrary. We may wish to utilize FBI investigators or experts, and to hire medical experts, to investigate the substance of proffered economic or personal hardships. The judge, the probation officer and the Director of the Bureau of Prisons also have a range of powers to order and conduct presentence investigations and reports that may be used for the purpose of verifying mitigating factors raised by the defendant.[16]

Where the government attorney believes that the facts in mitigation clearly call for an early parole, that may be part of the sentence recommendation. Otherwise the burden is on the defendant to argue mitigation. A defendant also has a right to move for a reduction of sentence within 120 days of judgment.[17] Given that option, we should point out to the court that if there is any uncertainty over the ability of the defendant's health to survive prison, the court should impose a sentence without mitigation, leaving it to the defendant to make a Rule 35 motion for reduction if and when health becomes a problem.

3.   Extremely Small, Local Conspiracies.   The nature of our enforcement activities inevitably means that some of our cases will involve localized conspiracies, with relatively small amounts of commerce affected. It is important that small, local price-fixing activities are not completely ignored and, until state enforcement resources are considerably expanded, it is essential that we continue to bring prosecutions of this type. In addition, we frequently are simply presented with facts demonstrating a criminal violation, by an informant or otherwise. When that happens, the Division has traditionally felt an obligation to prosecute, even though the amount of commerce involved is small.

Once these cases are brought, however, and the defendants convicted, different considerations from the normal may well apply to sentencing recommendations in these cases. For example, business hardship may be a particularly important mitigating factor where a defendant's company is a small, local firm, largely owned and run by the defendant. In such a case, even a brief period of imprisonment may leave the firm without management and cause it to go out of business. There may be other circumstances in these cases that would call for slightly different sentencing considerations than are outlined here. In any event, in these cases, sentencing recommendations should take into consideration whatever special circumstances may exist.

II.   Recommended Fines for Individuals

Fines are usually poor alternatives to prison sentences and should be used and viewed only as a second choice.[18] Accordingly, we would prefer to recom-

---

[16] *E.g.,* 18 U.S.C. sec. 4208; F. R. Crim. P. 32(c).

[17] F. R. Crim. P. 35.

[18] By way of comparison, it has long been the policy of the Tax Division to always request the imposition of a jail sentence in addition to a fine in criminal cases. It is the position of the Department that the payment of the civil tax liability, plus a fine

mend a fine only in those circumstances where we conclude that a prison sentence is not appropriate. However, in practice we shall probably have to back up our prison recommendation with a recommended fine in the event the court should reject all or part of our prison sentence recommendation.

We should recommend prison first and make it clear that was indeed our recommendation. We should then state that, if for some reason a prison sentence was not to be imposed, the defendant should receive our recommended fine. We should also make it clear that to the extent the court imposes a prison sentence which is less than our recommendation, a compensating percentage of the recommended fine should be imposed.

The recommended fine should track the recommended prison sentence. The midpoint in the permissible sentencing range, $50,000, will be the base point, just as 18 months was the base prison sentence. $50,000 may be unduly severe for defendants with net worth below a certain figure. Accordingly, where $50,000 exceeds 25 percent of an individual's net worth, we would use the latter figure as the base point. If in fact we recommend fines only where we do not recommend and receive a prison sentence, it is important that the fine be substantial enough to in fact be a deterrent. The foregoing is based upon the assumption that the individual himself will bear the burden of the fine. If the individual is or will be indemnified, and this is known to us, we should argue this to the court as further reason for imposing a jail sentence.

The same factors in aggravation and mitigation as have already been discussed with respect to prison sentences should be applied to increase or decrease the fine. To calculate the fine, we simply translate the recommended prison sentence into dollars. This involves calculating the percentage amount by which the recommended prison term is greater or less than the 18-month base point, and increase or decrease from the fine base point (i.e., $50,000 or 25 percent of net worth) by the same percentage. To illustrate, assume that our recommended prison sentences were 20 months, two months in addition to the 18-month base. That is an increase of one-ninth or 11.1 percent over the base. We should then increase the base fine, be it $50,000 or 25 percent of net worth, by 11.1 percent also.

By tying the determination of the fine to the prison sentence, we have built in the flexibility to enable the court to impose a compensating percentage of the fine in the event our full recommended prison sentence is not imposed. For example, if our recommended prison sentence were 20 months and the judge imposed a sentence of 16 months (four-fifths of our recommendation) we would also want one-fifth of the recommended fine imposed to compensate for the one-fifth prison sentence reduction.

The fine recommendations may seem high in an individual case, especially when compared with past antitrust fines. Accordingly we must be prepared to emphasize to the court the role that the fine must play as a deterrent if no prison sentences or reduced prison sentences are imposed.

III. Recommended Corporate Fines

Corporations profit, or expect to profit, from price fixing. To the extent they are permitted to retain the fruits of their illegal activity, price fixing will persist. An appropriate penalty must at least deprive them of that profit. Given the difficulty of detection and proof of criminal violations of the antitrust

---

and suspended sentence or probation, does not ordinarily constitute a satisfactory disposition of a criminal tax case. (Lecture by Cono Namorato, Chief, Criminal Section, Tax Division, New York State Bar Association, November 5, 1976.)

laws, the fine must also impose an additional punishment beyond a simple recovery of illegally-earned profits in order to prevent subsequent violations by the same corporation and to deter other violators. However, profits are not the sole criteria, for the aim of the antitrust laws is to deter all price-fixing conspiracies, regardless of whether they were successful or profitable. Accordingly, corporation fine recommendations should be designed to include a substantial penalty, with a substantial minimum fine, perhaps $100,000, based just on the fact of participation in an illegal conspiracy.[19]

The figure we have chosen to penalize and take the profit out of price fixing is a base point of 10 percent of the corporation's total sales in the affected line of commerce by a corporation during the conspiracy. Where there is evidence that this figure is in fact low, such as in specific bid-rigging conspiracies, we shall use the actual percentage increase, and apply this figure to all members of the bid-rigging conspiracy, regardless of whether they were awarded the contract or not. We have attempted to select a figure that is high enough to serve our law enforcement goals, yet not so high as to force a corporation out of business or substantially diminish its competitive viability.

This base fine of 10% of sales (or a higher figure if price fixing raised prices more than 10%) will then be modified by the aggravating or mitigating factors present in a particular case.

In the case of a corporation, recidivism is the chief aggravating factor. Where a corporation has a prior record of antitrust violations, we should recommend a higher fine, often the maximum $1 million fine. At the present time we have not identified any other factors which should be used to increase the corporate fine in all cases. Individual cases may, however, present their own aggravating factors.

Cooperation with the government and ability to pay are mitigating factors. Cooperation in the corporate sense means truly corporate cooperation, evidenced perhaps by corporate counsel providing the government with the necessary information and offering to make all relevant officers, directors and employees available to the government for questioning and as witnesses. Individual cooperation by corporate officials will normally be taken into account in their individual indictment or sentencing decisions, and will not be double-counted in mitigation of the corporate sentence as well.

Ability to pay means whether the fine is so large relative to the corporate profits and assets that the fine would endanger the corporation's continued viability as a competitor. Any fine will injure a corporation to some degree, and put it at a competitive disadvantage. A fine is, after all, an unproductive expenditure not necessarily incurred by a corporation's competitors.[20] That is an unavoidable corollary of any punishment, and we should expect corporations to argue that our recommended fine will hurt their business. If a fine doesn't hurt, it loses its deterrent value. The Sherman Act represents a judgment that price fixing is so injurious to the economy and society that it should

---

[19] Of course, the possibility of treble damages will always exist, and some might argue that this method of calculating fines is simply the governmental equivalent of a damage action. But if economic losses for antitrust violators were limited to illicit gains, that would truly be a license fee. Fines are intended to punish, and the fact and the amount of treble damages are always uncertain. It is simply impractical to try to factor into the calculation of a recommended fine the possibility of treble damage exposure, and we do not plan to do so.

[20] To the extent that the price-fixing conspiracy gave a corporation a competitive advantage over non-conspirator competitors, the competitive disadvantage imposed by the fine establishes a sort of compensating balance.

be punished as a felony—in essence that the injury to the economy caused by price fixing outweighs the injury to the economy that results from the decreased competitive strength of convicted and fined price fixers.

The balance may tip, however, where the corporation can show that the recommended fine would impose such a burden so as to effectively remove it from the market as a viable competitor. This is a heavy burden to meet. The defendant corporation will have the burden of proving any such contention, but having done so, we should be prepared to decrease our recommended fine.

CHAPTER TWENTY-ONE

PARALLEL ACTIVITY

Parallel activity of competitors is one of the most talked-about areas of anti-trust law today. The terms being used to describe the phenomenon are "conscious parallelism," "price leadership," and "oligopoly." The government, particularly the Department of Justice, is very concerned about this activity because it views it as a new kind of price-fixing.

It might be expected that if two businesses do exactly the same thing all the time, it could be inferred that they have agreed on what they will do. In fact, the courts have indicated that while parallelism in itself is not enough to establish a conspiracy, it is a factor "to be weighed and generally to be weighed heavily" in making the determination. However, on the other side of the story, it is clear that two competitors may independently, and without collusion, refuse to do business with a third company for very similar reasons, and that competition in the sale of a homogeneous product will tend toward identical prices at any given time because price reductions will be met, and price increases, if not followed, will be rescinded. The steel industry is certainly an example of this latter point. Thus, if everyone is doing exactly the same thing, it is sometimes difficult to tell whether there is perfect competition or perfect collusion.

The government seems to be contending that competitors, instead of getting together in private to fix prices, are communicating with one another by public announcements. One company will announce, and others will follow.

Obviously, the problem is that when sufficient facts exist to provide a jury question there is no telling how the case will come out, and there is some support for the proposition that parallelism alone is enough to provide a jury question. It is therefore important to avoid situations which can give rise to the inference of an agreement.

Sending press releases to competitors before the releases are made public should be avoided, and a similar rule applies to price lists before they are published. Some counselors even avoid sending price lists to their competitors *after* announcement. It may be true that your competitor has independent access to your price list anyway, but that would not remove the danger of an improper implication from your sending it to him directly.

Under existing law, conscious parallelism, standing alone, is not a violation of the Sherman Act. However, if anything else is thrown into the picture, a definite problem results. Some of the other possible items—besides communications between competitors—are (1) a radical departure from past business practices, (2) submission of identical bids to public agencies, (3) uniform use of a delivered price system, (4) artificial product standardization, (5) raising prices in a time of surplus, and (6) anything else which would substantiate a claim that the parallel conduct resulted from an agreement rather than from business conditions or competition.

There have been many recent examples of this concern, including an article in the *Wall Street Journal* of Tuesday, September 6, 1977, stating that Alcoa omitted announcing a price increase allegedly in response to government pressure. Naturally, Alcoa, U.S. Steel, and other giant companies are in different situations than most companies. On the other hand, if there is a clear case of conscious parallelism or price leadership, the government could be expected to attack it even if it is in a very small and limited market. It appears that the government is looking for some victories to establish some good law. One way to obtain those victories is to find clear cases in small industries where the time and expense of an antitrust lawsuit would be beyond the capability of the potential defendants.

THE COURT'S VIEW

One difficulty it may run into is an increased standard of willfulness, or intent to violate the law, being imposed by the courts because of the change in status of antitrust violations from misdemeanors to felonies. It may be that federal court judges will be more reluctant to tar a business executive with the felony brush on the basis of new and novel theories than they were when the crime was a misdemeanor. Traditional applications of criminal-law principles would seem to require this result. A defendant should not be found guilty of a felony if his activity was in a doubtful area. To that extent, the Antitrust Improvements Act may actually impede the development of new theories of liability under the Sherman Act.

There are only a few recent cases on this subject. The one most people are concerned about right now (early 1978) is the case of Bogosian and Parisi versus most of the world's oil companies. The *Bogosian and Parisi* case was recently decided in the Third Circuit Court of Appeals, which is a highly repected court. That court stated the general rule with a little different twist. It said the following:

> The law has settled that proof of consciously parallel business behavior is circumstantial evidence from which an agreement, tacit or express, can be inferred but that such evidence, without more, is insufficient unless the circumstances under which it occurred make the inference of rational, independent choice less attractive than that of concerted action.

It went on to hold that the plaintiffs, who alleged only parallel activity on the part of the defendants, stated a cause of action under the antitrust laws. Like so many antitrust cases, it was decided on a motion to dismiss. This means that the case will be sent back to the lower court for additional evidence. Further cases will have to be decided before any clear rule emerges, but the existing trend seems to be toward more, rather than less, concern about conscious parallelism.

HOW TO AVOID EXPOSURE

With the hostile attitude of the government and courts and their increased attention to this subject, it might be wise to consider ways in which to avoid possible exposure for clients. Those might include the following:

1. Identify any area in which the company is selling products at a price identical to that of its competitors. The prime example is steel. Other relatively homogeneous products, such as paper, would be other examples. If the area is one in which there is a long history of parallel pricing and the product is, in fact, homogeneous, the principal area of concern would be that of following a certain price leader in certain ways. For example, if there are four companies in an industry and company A always announces a price increase first, followed by company B in 10 days and company C and company D within 20 days, that is a much more troublesome situation than one in which different companies take the initiative for price increases or reductions at different times. Naturally, a pattern of rotation is also highly suspect.

2. If your company is in a situation where parallel pricing is absolutely essential to maintaining its competitive position, there should be a relatively high degree of emphasis placed on a good antitrust compliance program—emphasizing hard-core price-fixing problems. Documentation to show the independent nature of your actions is important.

3. If possible, it is highly desirable to find some way to create differences. If there are differences in credit practices, delivery, and sales support among competitors, these facts will indicate competition and serve to negate any inference of lack of competition created by the parallel pricing.

4. If there is parallel pricing in products which are not homogeneous, there should be a very clear and cogent explanation as to why this is the case.

5. The analysis should not stop at parallel pricing—although that is certainly the most sensitive area. In fact, there is much less justification for parallel activity in other areas, and there might be a greater problem explaining why all the companies in the industry had the same practices or policies.

6. If your company has a problem with parallel activity with its competitors, there should be more attention than normal given to trade-association meetings with those competitors. Some antitrust counsel recommend against participation in trade-association meetings, and if a conscious parallelism problem is present, the troublesome trade-association problems take on an added dimension.

7. If any parallel activity is caused by any association or group rules (such as the professional engineers' rule against submitting competitive bids), the company should be advised that recent cases in this area have uniformly held that professional organizations, including bar associations, do not shield anticompetitive activity from antitrust attack.

DEPARTMENT OF JUSTICE VIEWS

The views of the Department of Justice were best stated by Attorney General Bell in a speech before the *Harvard Law Review* in early 1977. Following is a portion of that speech:

> One of the areas that I am very much interested in is the problem of shared monopoly, or oligopoly, price leadership, conscious parallelism—call it what you will.
>
> The single-firm monopolist is relatively rare in this country. But there are many industries in which a very small number of firms hold dominant positions. A large and respectable body of economic opinion attributes enormous costs to this essentially non-competitive market structure. What should we do about it?
>
> One possibility is to prosecute these situations under the antitrust laws as "shared monopolies," using Section 2 of the Sherman Act or, in the case of the FTC, Section 5 of the FTC Act.
>
> Such cases obviously present novel legal issues. But perhaps more important, they eat up a lot of resources—as many and maybe more resources than a monopolization suit brought against a single firm.
>
> Our experience with single-firm monopolization cases, in terms of speedy resolution, is not very good. FTC's more recent experience with "shared monopoly" cases is not any better.
>
> If the litigation approach is to be made workable, some procedural changes must be accomplished so that the process can run its course within the lifetime of a normal human being. This is a matter to which I am giving close attention and about which I will make a public statement at an early date. I want to develop expedited pretrial and trial procedures that will shorten the lifespan of the complicated and massive cases known to all of us.
>
> Notwithstanding the recent step-up in criminal antitrust enforcement, the word "antitrust" causes most people today to conjure up a Dickensonian image of a case such as *Jarndyce v. Jarndyce* which "still drags its dreary length before the Court, perennially hopeless."
>
> The stakes are high in structural cases—either monopoly or merger. They are the antitrust equivalent of capital cases. Accordingly, the defendants' attorneys will, as they should in our adversary system, utilize every available resource to win—or, what is often the same, to delay resolution indefinitely.
>
> In recent years, the Department has focused on conduct by firms in these oligopoly industries. It has conducted economic analyses and looked very hard for price-fixing disguised as independent, parallel action.
>
> In industries in which only a few people are required to agree to an effective scheme, it is much harder to identify the agreement. One must overcome the hurdle of "conscious parallelism"—the argument that there has been no agreement but merely independent decisions to act in a parallel manner in the independent interest of each firm involved.
>
> In industries dominated by a few large organizations, firms will undoubtedly be particularly aware of the potential reactions of their competitors to individual pricing actions. There are, under these circumstances, few incentives to lower prices across the board. The other competitors would likely match that reduction and overall profits of the industry would be lowered.
>
> On the other hand, there are tremendous incentives to follow a competitor's raises, since that means more income from the same sales. If one firm does not emulate the raise, however, competitors may well be forced to bring their prices back down to the holdout's level. Holding the priceline, therefore, probably will not mean increased sales because the price advantage will quickly evaporate.
>
> As a result, pricing in oligopoly industries tends to be done in lockstep. Price reductions—and, much more common, price increases—are followed by most or all major firms. In other words, the firms take parallel action, conscious of the likely reactions of their competitors.

Non-competitive pricing is the result. The hard question is whether such non-competitive pricing is, or ought to be, subject to antitrust attack. There are two basic difficulties with trying to deal with "conscious parallelism" through antitrust enforcement.

First, by definition, no direct communication occurs between the firms involved. Hence, there is no explicit agreement between the firms.

"Conscious parallelism" does not present us with a "smoking gun." We don't have, as we sometimes do in other circumstances, the minutes of price-fixing cabals.

Thus, we must seek to prove an agreement by inference—by arguing that the course of the conduct under attack leads inevitably to the conclusion that there must have been an agreement, however implicit, among the firms.

There is, of course, at least one perfectly rational response to such a line of argument: that the conduct in question was reasonable business behavior by each individual firm acting independently.

Under the general state of existing law today, parallel action in order to be challenged as a conspiracy must at the very least be "consistent with the individual self-interest of the concerned only if they all decided [to act] in the same way."[1]

In the absence of such a showing—and such a showing is likely to be quite rare—something more than parallel conduct is required to carry the burden of providing an agreement by inference. It is that "something more" that antitrust enforcers look for.

There is, of course, a second problem with antitrust enforcement in this area: the difficulty of obtaining intelligent and effective relief.

If the basis of the antitrust complaint is that the pricing level in the industry was set through other than independent action, the relief must logically seek to require a different method of setting prices.

But since prices have been set in this situation through independent (albeit parallel) action, what the court could require to ameliorate the "illegal" conduct is hard to discern.

One approach would be to order the oligopolists to sell their products at a competitive price—presumably marginal costs or some near equivalent.

Obviously, the supervision of such an order would place an enormous administrative burden on the courts. The courts would, in fact, become price regulatory agencies. This is not a satisfactory way to resolve whatever problems arise from oligopoly pricing—for reasons apparent to those who believe in the free enterprise system. But neither is it satisfactory to permit a few firms that dominate an industry to act as if they were one. "Shared monopoly," where it truly exists, ought to violate the antitrust laws, and judicially-controlled pricing may be an approach we may have to consider further.

"Conscious parallelism" poses, therefore, a very difficult problem. Nevertheless, I am extremely interested in pursuing innovative ways to deal with this kind of tacit collusion. The Antitrust Division will vigorously search out that "something more" whenever and wherever it can.

I should note, however, that I believe successful, pure, tacit collusion (or true "conscious parallelism" without the "something more") to be more unusual than some might think. What would occur more often, I think, is some indirect agreement used to organize an industry into an effective cartel. If several competitors behave in a way that is not to the individual benefit of each unless all of them act together, that behavior signals the possibility of a conspiracy or agreement, stated or implied.

I was interested, therefore, in the Antitrust Division's recent action proposing a modification of the old antitrust decrees outstanding against General Electric and Westinghouse. This approach may well be an important step in dealing with oligopoly pricing.

The situation was this: In 1963, in the wake of a period of overcapacity and low prices, GE announced a new—and we feel anticompetitive—pricing policy. GE promised to follow newly published price levels by quoting only book prices on

[1] *The Definition of Agreement under the Sherman Act: Conscious Parallelism and Refusals to Deal,* 75 HARV. L. REV. 655, 658 (1962).

all transactions. It adopted a "price protection clause" which promised that if GE lowered its price for any particular customer, any buyer within the previous six-month period would be given an identical retroactive discount upon request.

Finally, GE announced that it would publish all orders previously received and the quotations previously made at previous price levels. This was done to insure that any lower outstanding price quotations had, in fact, been given prior to the adoption of the new pricing policy.

Soon after GE implemented its new policy, Westinghouse began using the GE price book and GE's published multiplier to determine its prices too. The next year, Westinghouse adopted its own price book—a book based on the GE book. It also instituted a price protection policy.

After a lengthy investigation, the Antitrust Division came to the conclusion that GE and Westinghouse, through indirect—although public—price communication and signaling had maintained a price-fixing conspiracy.

The two never sat down and reached an explicit agreement. But the Antitrust Division believed that the measures they both took, such as the "price protection clause," were a manner of policing an implicit agreement through eliminating the incentive for price cuts. Theirs was not a case of unavoidable conscious parallelism: It was a case of "avoidable cooperation." Apart from their tacit agreement the two firms would not have acted in this manner.

The relief we sought was designed to eliminate these abuses. It would eliminate public statements of pricing policy; enjoin the use of policing tools such as the price protection policy; prohibit the public dissemination of price and price-related information from which a general pricing policy or strategy can be inferred; and prohibit the manufacturers from examining each other's bids to individual customers.

The *GE-Westinghouse* case presents an unusual but important situation. Normally, of course, the marketplace performs better with the free exchange of price information. But because of the made-to-order product and two-firm structure of the industry involved, different relief was appropriate.

In that sense, the case underscores the need for innovative, creative thinking in the antitrust field. More important, it breaks new ground in our effort to deal with conscious parallelism, price leadership, or whatever your label may be.

CHAPTER TWENTY-TWO

INTRACORPORATE CONSPIRACIES

Intracorporate conspiracies, or "bathtub" conspiracies, are agreements between a parent corporation and its subsidiaries or between the subsidiaries of a parent corporation. Technically, subsidiaries are separate legal entities, and so they can constitute the two entities necessary to establish a conspiracy. Obviously, if this doctrine were carried to its extreme, all enterprises operating through subsidiaries would have serious antitrust problems because they all discuss prices, territories, and customers with their subsidiaries. While there is some language in the cases which would seem to suggest this result, most antitrust counselors believe that the doctrine will be applied only if the activities of a third party are affected. Generally, this means that the doctrine will apply only if the related corporations get together to coerce another seller, supplier, or distributor. It also applies, however, if two entities engage in obviously predatory practices or mislead the public by holding themselves out as competitors.

Examples where the doctrine has been applied include (1) an agreement among commonly owned cab companies not to buy cabs from a certain company, (2) an agreement to fix prices between subsidiaries who held themselves out to be competitors, (3) an agreement among a United States corporation and its foreign subsidiaries to divide world markets, and (4) an agreement among commonly owned companies to coerce independent distributors through the use of requirements and tying contracts and the imposition of territorial and price limitations.

Unfortunately, it takes a bit of straining to get all of the intracorporate-conspiracy cases to come under the concept of coercing outsiders. For antitrust purposes, it should not be assumed that the two parties necessary for a conspiracy are lacking simply because the two corporations involved are commonly owned or are in the relation of parent and subsidiary. On the other hand, this idea cannot be carried too far or it will be impossible to do business through subsidiaries. This is a classic example of the difficulties and highly subjective nature of our antitrust laws and why such a high premium must be placed on the best possible antitrust advice. Agreements among related corporations which would be flagrant abuses of the antitrust laws should probably be avoided. Price-fixing is the most troublesome, with market divisions and boycotts close behind. Also, it is dangerous for subsidiary corporations to hold themselves out as competitors. Subsidiaries less than 100 percent owned increase the risk. A minority-owned company increases the risk further. In the international area, the Department of Justice view is very favorable, but the possibility of a private action should not be overlooked.

CHAPTER TWENTY-THREE

INTERLOCKING DIRECTORATES

THE CLAYTON ACT

Section 8 of the Clayton Antitrust Act prevents interlocking directorates. "Interlocking directorates" are generally defined to be situations where one person serves as a director of two corporations which compete with one another. Technically, the following four elements must be present in order for a violation of section 8 to exist:

1. One person must be serving as a director of two or more corporations.

2. The capital surplus of at least one of the corporations must exceed $1 million.

3. Both corporations must be engaged in interstate commerce.

4. The corporations must compete with each other.

There has not been a great deal of litigation under section 8 of the Clayton Act, and there does not seem to be a very high risk if a violation is found to exist. Almost all section 8 matters are settled by the resignation of the director plus, in some cases, the entering of an order against the person and possibly the corporation involved prohibiting a second violation of section 8. The significance of this order is that a subsequent violation is punishable by large fines (up to $10,000 per day). The order may also go beyond merely prohibiting a technical violation of Section 8; it may prohibit the director from serving as an officer of any competing corporation and require him to notify the FTC in advance of becoming a director or officer of any company.
Section 8 has been given increased attention lately because there have

been a number of attempts to amend the statute so as to broaden its application. Many people feel that section 8 is ineffective in preventing joint business decisions by virtue of interlocking directorships because (1) it is so technical and (2) it only prohibits a person from serving as a director of two corporations which compete with each other. It does not prohibit a person from serving as (1) an officer of two corporations which compete with each other or (2) a director of two corporations which have a vertical relationship.

The growth of conglomerate companies with many lines of business—some of them very small in relation to the total business—has also created a problem because many business executives have found out only after receiving letters from the Federal Trade Commission that the companies on which they serve as directors compete with one another in some small, insignificant line of business.

Section 8 is a rather technical statute where violations are not very serious, but it is also a rather easy statute to comply with. Company counsel should be asked to keep a listing of all the company's directors and the other companies on which they serve as directors. Further, the list should be kept current by asking the directors to update it periodically. Any new person who is being considered as a director for the company should be asked to disclose his other directorships, and an analysis should be made to see if there is any competition.

A closely related statute is section 10 of the Clayton Act, which prohibits persons who serve on the board of a common carrier from serving on the board of any corporation which does business with that common carrier in an amount which exceeds $50,000 a year. Because of the rather complicated politics involved in enacting section 8, this vertical relationship was only prohibited in the case of common carriers, not other business corporations.

THE FEDERAL TRADE COMMISSION ACT

Whenever an interlocking directorate is challenged by the Federal Trade Commission, section 5 of the Federal Trade Commission Act, which prohibits any unfair method of competition, is usually thrown into the list of allegations also. At this time, there are no cases which hold that section 5 can be used in any case where section 8 does not also apply, but the limited scope of section 8, plus the increased use of section 5 in cases where there is no technical violation of the antitrust laws, make this a likely area for development in the future.

CHAPTER TWENTY-FOUR

ANTITRUST COMPLIANCE PROGRAMS

Antitrust compliance programs have always been considered important by counsel and business leaders. Even before any of the recent developments strengthening the antitrust laws and increasing the penalties, many major corporations had elaborate programs aimed at educating their employees about the antitrust laws through seminars, small meetings, memorandums or manuals, statement of policy, or combinations of the above. This chapter contains some observations of how these programs might be conducted and some descriptions of various procedures which have been used successfully in the past.

A compliance program is a set of procedures and material designed to inform all company employees who may be affected by the general content of the antitrust laws of the necessity for compliance therewith. Essentially, the purpose of the program is to prevent any antitrust difficulties which might arise from the acts of employees who either did not know the prohibitions of the antitrust laws or were not fully aware of their importance and seriousness.

Another important purpose of a compliance program is to protect the chief executive officers of the company from allegations that they either were personally involved in unlawful conduct or failed to supervise their employees or exercise the proper direction over them to keep them from being involved. Obviously, no compliance program is going to save the top executive who has personally engaged in unlawful conduct under the antitrust laws. However, such a program—endorsed, sponsored, promoted, and emphasized by the chief executive officers of the company—can serve to insulate these officers, at least partially, from personal difficulty if an employee is later found to have committed a serious antitrust violation.

Obviously, the specific content of any antitrust compliance program should depend upon the nature of the company, the quantity and quality of legal resources which it has available, its past history, the business in which it is engaged, its organization (whether it is centralized or decentralized), and a great number of other factors. However, most comprehensive compliance programs consist of at least the following:

1. Some kind of written material should be a part of any compliance program. This material should (1) state that the company expects complete compliance with the antitrust laws and that failure to comply can result in discipline or discharge and (2) give whatever appropriate guidance might be required under the circumstances to inform the employees of precisely what kind of conduct is proscribed by the antitrust laws. Some companies require each employee to sign a card certifying that he has read and understands the written material. This written material is indispensable.

2. Virtually all serious compliance programs include a series of meetings and discussions between company antitrust counsel (it does not make any particular difference whether it is inside counsel or outside counsel) and any employees of the company who may be affected. These meetings and discussions range all the way from one-on-one conversations, usually between the antitrust lawyers and members of top management of the company, to more or less formal presentations given by the antitrust lawyers to groups of employees. The opportunity for questions and answers is an essential part of any meeting or discussion. If the only thing involved is a speech, the company will not have a good program.

3. The compliance program must include certain company procedures which ensure that any activity with antitrust significance is reviewed at the proper management level and that proper legal assistance and advice is obtained before the action is taken.

4. The written material, the meetings and discussions, and the company procedures are usually supplemented with some kind of audit.
   The audit can include a careful examination of the files of the top executives of the company and other persons who might be in situations where violations of the antitrust laws would be possible, such as sales managers and people who frequently attend trade-association meetings. Since trade-association meetings are, at least in the view of most antitrust counselors, the single most troublesome aspect of the important hard-core violations of the antitrust laws (including price-fixing, customer allocation, and territory allocation), the audit should also include a careful listing of all the people who attend trade-association meetings (including those where technical subjects may be discussed) and a review of the attendees' files relating to such meetings.
   If the company is subject to an existing antitrust order or consent decree, the audit will also include sufficient investigation to assure that the order or decree is being complied with.
   Most audits also include some kind of record-retention program. It is submitted that there is no legal requirement or even particularly logical or compelling reason why a record-retention program should be part of an antitrust audit. However, in a significant number of cases, record-retention programs are instituted as part of an antitrust audit. It would appear that one of the possible reasons for this procedure is that some company people (hopefully nonlawyers) generate a lot of paper which could be extremely harmful in an antitrust case. Most of this paper has no particular corporate significance, and therefore there is no reason to retain it. However, after a government investigation is started and subpoenas are received by the company, it is, of course, too late to discard damaging documents even if they are erroneous, inaccurate, or untrue. Because this problem appears to be particularly prevalent in the antitrust context, it is submitted that a good antitrust audit should include some attention to record-retention problems.

WHOM SHOULD THE PROGRAM COVER?

The question of whom the program must include depends to a considerable extent upon the organization of the company and its business. However, the following generalities may be stated:

1. It should definitely include all members of top management, including chief executive officers, executive vice presidents, and the department heads of the various staff functions. It is absolutely essential that each of these people have a comprehensive working knowledge of the antitrust laws so that appropriate assistance from company counsel can be sought where necessary. Failure at this level can be an absolute disaster because while the company may be able to disavow the acts of some lower-echelon employee who, perhaps in an overly zealous attempt to meet a sales quota or impress his boss, has engaged in an antitrust violation, this obviously cannot be done for the chief executive officers of the company, who will have to bear sole responsibility for their acts or omissions.

2. Executive people in the fields of sales, marketing, planning, and purchasing should also be covered by the program, although perhaps it might be appropriate to emphasize different aspects of the antitrust laws to these people. For example, the problems of reciprocity and section 2(f) of the Robinson-Patman Act should probably be heavily emphasized in meetings with purchasers but perhaps only mentioned in passing in meetings with the other groups.

3. The third category of people who should be covered is the one which will be the hardest to manage: everyone in the company whose actions can get the company in trouble. In most situations, this will go all the way down to the bottom rung in the areas mentioned above.

    It is the sales representative actually making the calls and writing memorandums to his boss who can cause the company most of its antitrust difficulty in the distribution area. It is the lowest-level planning man, who writes damaging memorandums about cornering the market and driving a competitor out of business, who can cause the company unfortunate antitrust complications even though it may turn out that he had no authority to carry out his recommendations and that those recommendations were disapproved of by management and therefore never carried out. This is one of the very difficult aspects of a compliance program. It is not sufficient to address the upper-level management of the company and expect that somehow this will solve the problem. Everyone who is in a position to harm the company through conduct which may be held damaging under the antitrust laws must somehow be given the word.

4. Last but not least, the company should not forget its own lawyers. It is submitted that virtually every lawyer in the company should have a fairly thorough working knowledge of the antitrust laws, even if antitrust matters are referred only to one or two corporate experts in this area. Unfortunately, this is a goal not always reached, and in some companies experienced sales executives actually have a better knowledge of the antitrust laws than do some of the company's lawyers who do not work in this area. It is particularly important for the securities and finance lawyers and the patent lawyers to have a very thorough understanding of the basic principles of the antitrust laws. In the patent area, the reason is obvious: Patents and patent licenses are themselves productive of a great many difficulties under the antitrust laws. The securities lawyers typically prepare a great many comprehensive documents, including prospectuses, registrations under the 1933 Act, and various reports under the 1934 Act, and they are in a peculiarly advantageous position to spot potential antitrust problems and point them out for consideration by the company's antitrust experts. Also, most legal departments have adopted procedures whereby news releases are reviewed by the securities lawyers—usually for

10(b)(5) reasons—and if the securities lawyers understand the basic problems and principles under the antitrust laws, they are in a position to request input from the trade-regulation lawyer where appropriate. For example, the company public relations people might want to put out a news release which contends that the company is "the world leader" in a given market. The securities lawyers may object to this if they feel that it is not supportable, and the antitrust lawyers may also have objections, particularly if the company is contemplating or has recently accomplished an acquisition in that market area.

REASONS FOR THE PROGRAM

An antitrust compliance program is going to involve some expense—even if it is conducted by house counsel on a "time available" basis. If it is done properly, it will be a continuing expense rather than a one-shot expenditure. Management must weigh the cost against the benefits which will be obtained from expending this money and effort. The antitrust compliance program can be thought of as an insurance policy aimed at minimizing the following corporate risks:

1. The first, and probably the most important, risk is that of a substantial fine or even a jail sentences for members of the top management of the company or other employees found guilty of a hard-core antitrust violation.

2. The second risk is that of disruptive litigation, large expenditures of money for attorneys' fees, a treble-damage verdict, or an injunctive action which will void existing contracts or transactions or otherwise place the company in a competitively disadvantageous position.

3. The third risk is that of a government suit, which again could cause a great deal of disruption and expense and possibly result in a sweeping decree that will place the firm at a severe competitive disadvantage.

4. The fourth risk which a compliance program is aimed at minimizing is the business risk of having employees restrict their competitive activity because of an inaccurate or incomplete understanding of the antitrust laws. For example, it appears to be commonly believed that any refusal to deal is a violation of the antitrust laws, and in some cases it is thought that it is absolutely impossible to terminate a distributor for any but the clearest economic reasons. Both of these beliefs are widely held, inaccurate, and can result in reduced business opportunities for the company if the people who hold them are not properly informed of the true state of the law.

5. The last risk in not having a compliance program is that corporate employees without legal training will act as their own lawyers in this area. The existence of a compliance program ensures that corporate employees know that some knowledgeable antitrust lawyer is available for consultation, and increases the likelihood that they will seek help from him.

There have been some contentions that there are also negative aspects to an antitrust compliance program—particularly if it is not properly done. The people who espouse this point of view generally point out that if an employee is accused of an antitrust violation and there is a written company policy which clearly explains what conduct is proscribed, the prosecution will be able to make a much clearer case for a willful violation of the antitrust laws. It is true that some antitrust trials have included testimony or cross-examination with this objective. However, at this stage of the development of the law and the constant reporting thereof in the *Wall Street Journal* as well as other popular magazines, it is submitted that it will be difficult for any corporate executive to benefit from any claim of ignorance of the law—even if the claim was only offered to provide mitigation of sentencing.

Another problem with an ineffective compliance program is that it may lull the top management of the company into thinking that all the employees are complying with the antitrust laws. Common sense as well as the law should make top management aware that a manual—no matter how attractively printed—is not sufficient to take them off the hook should an antitrust problem arise. Obviously, more is needed, and a compliance program should be conducted with a reasonable degree of efficiency and professionalism.

WHAT SHOULD THE PROGRAM COVER?

Obviously, a compliance program should cover all of the antitrust problems which a company may encounter. However, it is extremely important to break down the problems and risks into smaller areas and to limit the compliance program to the realistic problems of the group at hand. If the compliance program attempts to make antitrust lawyers out of everyone, it will be a sad failure. The program should cover hard-core antitrust problems and problems in the areas of distribution, pricing, trade associations, monopolization, and unfair competition.

Hard-Core Antitrust Problems

These are the section 1 criminal violations and are the most important part of the program. They should be covered thoroughly and completely with at least the sales and marketing people in the company (as well as, of course, top management).

Distribution Problems

Distribution problems are in one sense much less important than hard-core problems because they will, in the overwhelming majority of cases, be susceptible of rather easy settlement. However, distribution problems are also the most common antitrust problems, and if an unlawful practice in this area is carried out on a large scale, it may literally result in the bankruptcy of the company.

Distribution problems should be covered on these two levels:

1. The actual structure of the distribution arrangement should be covered. Are independent distributors or franchisees used? What is the content of the distributorship or franchise agreement? It is very important that antitrust counsel focus on these questions at a very early stage (especially where any changes are contemplated) to make sure that a disaster does not occur.

2. The day-to-day relations with the distributor should be covered. The overwhelming majority of the problems here come about in situations where distributors are either terminated or where a distributor wants to handle the company's products and the company does not want, for one reason or another, to sell its products to that distributor.

Pricing Problems

Obviously, this is a third area of considerable antitrust importance. Pricing must not only comply with Robinson-Patman Act requirements, but in some cases there are Sherman Act implications to the pricing practices of the company.

Trade Associations and Related Problems

Some antitrust lawyers advise the companies they represent to avoid trade associations completely. Most antitrust counselors do not go this far, but it does appear that in the overwhelming majority of antitrust cases involving price-fixing or other unlawful conduct between competitors, trade associations or trade-association meetings become involved. It is, therefore, absolutely essential that antitrust counsel address the problem of the trade-association meeting as well as the informal sessions which always accompany these meetings.

Monopolization Problems

If a company has a very large market share, it must be a little more circumspect in some of its competitive practices than if it does not. Antitrust counsel would be wise to point out the monopolization problems in any situation where it may be appropriate.

Unfair Competition and Deceptive Practices

These are problems regulated by section 5 of the Federal Trade Commission Act. Because the only risk here is that of a Federal Trade Commission suit and an injunction against continuing the practice, these problems are not as serious as hard-core violations, where criminal penalties may be imposed, or other antitrust violations, where private plaintiffs may obtain treble damages and attorneys' fees. However, the increased activity and power of the Federal Trade Commission dictate that these problems be given serious attention—especially if a consumer product is involved. There is always the possibility of having to enter into a consent decree or of having the commission actually bring a court case asking for an injunction, damages, and consumer redress.

Other Antitrust Problems

There are other antitrust problems which a company can face, problems which are not covered in the average compliance program. They include, for example, mergers, acquisitions, and joint ventures. These problems, while important are usually handled on a case-by-case basis, with the lawyers heavily involved. Patents and patent licensing arrangements are also usually handled on a case-by-case basis. It is generally thought inappropriate to try to cover these in any kind of manual. However, it is necessary to exercise some degree of prevention here.

For example, in the joint-venture area, it would be appropriate to announce and enforce a company policy that no joint venture, joint bidding arrangement, or other joint activity with competitors be undertaken except upon legal review, and naturally all mergers and acquisitions should be accompanied by a thorough legal review. It might also be appropriate to educate those people involved about the difficulties of improper writing and creation of materials which will in and of themselves almost guarantee antitrust problems. For example, a low-level planner who has found a company which he feels his employer should acquire is very likely to write a glowing memo describing the company to be acquired as the "leading competitor in the field" and one which, if acquired, will allow the combined companies to "dominate the market." In the overwhelming majority of cases, these kinds of statements will be far from the truth. However, they will definitely present problems if they are shown to an antitrust adviser who is later asked about the legality of the proposed transaction under section 7 of the Clayton Act. It is, therefore, appropriate to make sure that the people writing the planning documents of the company have some basic understanding of the antitrust laws and that they exercise some discretion in making these kinds of statements.

A similar approach might be taken in the patent and patent licensing area. Those people who negotiate the patent and know-how licenses for the company should be informed of the basic problems in this area so that they do not make tentative arrangements or perhaps even off-the-record arrangements which would violate the law.

Section 8 of the Clayton Act is an antitrust law involving interlocking directorates. It is not very useful to cover this kind of a problem in the normal compliance program. Instead, company counsel should be asked to keep a listing of all the company's directors and the companies on which they serve as directors. Any new person who is being considered as a director for the company should be required to disclose his other directorships, and an analysis should be made to see if there is any competition.

State law is another problem which generally does not get addressed in the antitrust compliance program per se. Instead, since the federal antitrust laws are generally more restrictive than state laws, it is usually pointed out that compliance with the federal laws will also assure compliance with most state laws. However, this is not universally true, and many states are expanding coverage of their antitrust laws, particularly those regarding franchise and distributorship arrangements.

A similar approach might be followed with foreign laws. Here, however, there is a danger of overkill. The company executives who have responsibility for running businesses in foreign countries should not be saddled with the United States antitrust laws. In many foreign countries, the existing antitrust laws are not enforced at all, and in other countries there actually are no significant antitrust laws. Further, the general European pattern of antitrust laws is to adopt a rule-of-reason approach to almost everything. Consequently, even in the case of what might be clearly illegal under United States rules, it may be possible to obtain an exemption in Europe if the appropriate authorities can be convinced of the economic merit of the conduct.

APPROACH AND MATERIAL

No matter what the specific content of an antitrust compliance program, certain steps will have to be taken and certain material will have to be prepared.

The Team of Experts

The first thing to decide in an antitrust compliance program is who is going to conduct it. It can be conducted by outside counsel, who may be familiar enough with the operations of the company, or by inside counsel, who may be able to develop a program and spend almost full time on it. Another possibility is to have each operating unit lawyer responsible for the antitrust compliance program for that operating unit. Of course, there are innumerable variations as, for example, having the responsibility shared by either inside or outside corporate counsel and the appropriate division or group counsel.

Written Material

The next task is the preparation of the written material. At a minimum, the written material should include some kind of policy statement and a brief description of the antitrust laws. Many different forms of antitrust manuals are in use. Those I have seen range from three pages through seventy-five pages, and they range from booklets elaborately printed on glossy paper together with photographs and illustrations, to 8½- by 11-inch typewritten pages stapled together. An examination of many of these manuals reveals that there is a great deal of similarity among them. Generally, they are not copyrighted, and, indeed, most of the lawyers who prepared them are very happy to exchange them and to allow any lawyer who feels that portions of them may be useful for his company to use them. Following are some comments on a good manual:

1. It appears essential to have a clear statement from top management that the antitrust laws are important and must be complied with.

2. While lawyers will certainly differ on the proper way to explain appropriate antitrust conduct, it would appear that the manuals which make at least some reasonable attempt to explain the basis of the law and the reason for the required conduct are superior to those which simply list a number of dos and don'ts without making any attempt to explain the rationale behind the rules.

3. The manual is meant to be distributed to a large number of people. Consequently, it should be written with a view to sending it not only to company people but to other lawyers or corporate executives who may be interested, and it should be anticipated that the manual will wind up in the hands of either a potential private plaintiff or a government enforcement agency. Therefore, while it should be truthful and accurate, it should also be a self-serving document without any potentially incriminating statements.

4. The manual should include the procedures discussed in this chapter (dealing with legal review of important transactions).

In addition to the manual, the following material may be useful: (1) one or more articles from popular publications, such as *Business Week, Time,* the *Wall Street Journal,* and *Barron's,* which deal either with current antitrust enforcement or with antitrust investigations into the particular industry involved, (2) a memorandum on distributorship terminations, (3) a memorandum on general antitrust laws involving distributorships, (4) a copy of the Federal Trade Commission advertising-allowance regulations, (5) a memo on trade-association problems, and (6) a copy of any particular Federal Trade Commission ruling or proposed ruling which may be appropriate to the industry.

Meetings and Discussions

In addition to the written material, counsel will need a series of speeches to be given at meetings. These speeches may range from more or less formal presentations to a few introductory remarks followed by informal discussion. Indeed, it is inappropriate for counsel to deliver any kind of prepared speech or memorized speech and fail to discuss the subject in detail with the attendees of the meeting.

If the meeting is large, counsel may have to have a prepared statement so that he can start the discussion going and cover a few basic points. Generally, the smaller the size of the group, the less formal the prepared statement should be and the more emphasis should be placed on personal conversation. However, if the meeting is a total exchange without any prepared speech, counsel must be sure to have a checklist to make sure that when the session is over, he has at least covered the basic points which he thought were appropriate.

As indicated, his remarks must be tailored to the group being addressed. In general, these groups can be broken up into (1) top-management people, (2) top-level sales marketing people, (3) general sales representatives, and (4) purchasers.

Top Management

Top management is generally not involved in the day-to-day operations of the company, such as distributorship, advertising, pricing, trade associations, and unfair or deceptive practices. Consequently, the top-management speech can be short and aimed only at hard-core problems.

Generally, it has been found useful in the past to begin a presentation to top management by suggesting that each listener draw a large black line in his mind, separating it into two compartments. In one compartment would be the hard-core antitrust violations which he must be thoroughly familiar with and avoid at all costs. In the other compartment would be the vast array of other complicated and complex antitrust laws which he should know and recognize but which he can obtain legal counsel on when the need arises.

Obviously, the distinction is in the severity of the problem. However, there is another important distinction. Problems involving hard-core violations can arise in immediate, on-the-spot contexts where it is impossible to request legal advice, such as social gatherings of competitors, meetings of trade associations, and other meetings where competitors may be present. The other kinds of antitrust problems, when they are presented to top management, will usually be in the form of some kind of a question or proposed program and it will be possible to obtain legal counsel's advice. However, in the hard-core violations, when members of top management go out into the world on their own, they must be armed with a sufficient working knowledge of the antitrust laws to avoid problems.

Obviously, top management of the company would not have attained top-management level without some basic knowledge of at least the fact that price-fixing is illegal. Accordingly, it is generally not necessary to harp too much on this point. However, what top management seldom understands is the lack of any definitive correlation between the existence of an overt act of price-fixing and a legal antitrust problem. In other words, some feel that in order for them to have a problem under the antitrust laws, they must actually agree with a competitor on specific prices. Some of the more sophisticated managers understand that the agreement may be implied and that therefore the danger is a little broader. Few of them understand, however, that their mere presence at a trade-association meeting where prices are discussed can cause them to be indicted in a criminal price-fixing case. In addition, many executives do not understand that "prices" does not necessarily mean any *specific* number, percentage or formula.

For example, in the case of *Bray v. Safeway Stores*, some supermarket executives were held to have violated the Sherman Act on the basis of a trade-association meeting where one participant made a speech to the general effect that it was time for supermarkets to stop passing lower wholesale meat prices on to consumers and to keep some of it for themselves. The court found a conspiracy to keep wholesale prices low and retail prices high.

The verdict was over $32 million, and attorneys' fees were set at $3.2 million.

Trade associations are an important part of the compliance program. The subject was discussed in chapter 8 and will not be repeated here.

In speaking to top management, the lawyer must be careful to disclose the realities of the antitrust world and to disabuse the executives of the notion that in order to have an antitrust indictment filed against them, they must actually have actively participated in specific illegal conduct. He must, instead, point out that indictments may be filed on a more-or-less blanket basis, and unless the executive is in a position to introduce some kind of affirmative evidence of his lack of involvement, he may be in for some embarrassing moments. If at all possible, executives should structure their conduct so as to avoid any kind of indictment because once an indictment is filed, much of the damage to their careers and personal reputations has already occurred—even if they are later acquitted.

In summary, the top-management speech can be limited to hard-core violations, perhaps followed by questions and answers dealing with some of the other problems. If appropriate, counsel may want to follow the hard-core speech with some kind of a brief rundown of other potential antitrust problems which may be appropriate for future consultation between him and top management.

Top-Level Sales Representatives

When addressing the top-level sales or marketing people, it is necessary not only to cover the hard-core subjects but to mention some of the other important antitrust areas because at this level, planning and policy decisions are sometimes made which may cause the company extreme difficulty if proper antitrust advice has not been obtained. Accordingly, the sales representatives' speech should also cover distributorship problems, pricing problems, and advertising problems.

General Sales Representatives

Many companies have regular gatherings of all of their salespeople, perhaps on an annual or a regional basis, for sales or marketing meetings. At this time, it is highly desirable to set aside an hour or so to cover antitrust problems.

Since this will typically be a little larger group than the top-level salespeoples' group, the formal presentation might have to be somewhat longer here and the give-and-take session might have to be a bit shorter. Also, since these sales representatives will probably not have pricing authority, it might be somewhat academic to spend too much time on hard-core price-fixing violations. They should definitely, however, be covered. The sales representatives may be more interested in—and it may be of greater benefit to the company to go into—an elaborate explanation of some distributorship problems. Distributorship terminations are both a frequent source of difficulty and a convenient context in which to explain a number of frequently misunderstood concepts.

The first point which must be made is that a distributor is an independent business executive. As such, he is free to sell his products at the price he desires in the territories he desires to the customers he wishes. Some sales representatives are under the mistaken impression that if a distributor handles their products, the company is entitled to dictate a great many things to him. This causes a great deal of trouble, and the sales representatives must be properly informed of the independent nature of the distributor.

It is then appropriate to at least list the various restrictions which may cause trouble. These include, in order of importance: (1) restrictions as to price, (2) restrictions as to territory, (3) restrictions as to the handling of competitive goods, and (4) restrictions as to customers.

1. Generally, it is well not to tread too closely to the legal boundary line when discussing price restrictions with sales representatives. While there are some cases which may suggest that certain restrictions may be permissible, it is usually more desirable, from a counseling point of view, to adopt a harder line with sales representatives. Certainly they should be strongly advised to avoid any attempt to keep distributors from cutting prices. True, some cases may indicate that "jaw-boning," or suggesting, is not a violation of the antitrust laws, but it is dangerous to allow sales representatives to engage in these activities, especially when it comes to prices. Consequently, it would appear most desirable to put prices on a list of absolutely forbidden subjects for sales-people if the intent of their conversations is to influence the price charged by a distributor.

2. Basically, the same remarks can be made about territory restrictions. However, there is a chance here to accentuate the positive. Sales representatives may strive to motivate distributors to cover adequately the territories to which they have been assigned. What they must *not* do is to *dissuade* those distributors from selling *outside* of that territory. So long as this distinction is clearly understood and observed by the sales force, there is no problem.

3. Sales representatives cannot require a distributor to refrain from handling the goods of a competitor, but they can try to persuade him to handle more of their company's goods and to promote those goods, so long as they do not directly require the distributor to refrain from handling the goods of a competitor.

4. A distributor is, of course, free to sell to whatever customers he can, and the sales representatives should be instructed not to dissuade any distributor from selling to any particular account.

After making the above observations, it would be useful for counsel to go through a typical problem with the sales representatives.

Suppose, for example, that distributor A has generally been doing a poor-to-satisfactory job in a given city. At the present time, distributor A is the company's only distributor in that city, but he does not have any contractual right to be the exclusive distributor in that city.

The sales representative reports back to the sales manager that distributor B in the city is a fine, aggressive company employing many sales representatives. The distributor is doing a fine job of selling competitive products, and it is this salesperson's recommendation that distributor A be terminated and distributor B be appointed instead so that the sales of the company's products in that area will increase.

The lawyer can say truthfully at this point that if that is all that is in the picture, the company is perfectly free to terminate distributor A, appoint distributor B, and have no fear of adverse legal consequences. However, let's suppose the sales representative sent the following memo:

> On [a certain date] I discussed this matter with [distributor B] and he indicated to me that he would be glad to handle our products if we terminated [distributor A]. However, he would not even consider handling our line unless we terminated [distributor A] because in his judgment, there was only room for one of them in [the town].

At this point, counsel is still relatively free to advise the company to go ahead with the transaction. True, there is a greater risk because it may be that distributor A, when he is terminated, will be able to allege an agreement between the company and distributor B to terminate him. Still the risk is minimal, and there are some court cases which indicate that this is not a violation of the antitrust laws. However, let's assume that counsel, upon investigating the file further, comes across this memo, dated six months earlier:

Dear Boss:
   Today I made a call on [distributor A], and I noticed that he was selling our products on a discounted basis and advertising them as "discount products." I told him that I was very unhappy about this and did not like the idea of our company's products being sold on a discount basis.

With such a memo in the file, if the company decides to terminate distributor A, and distributor A gets a lawyer and writes to the company objecting to the termination, it is virtually impossible for the company to do anything except reinstate that distributor. In other words, by the sales representative writing this kind of a memo, he has restricted the company from taking an action which it might otherwise take.

The same example could be used for territories, handling the goods of a competitor, and customer restrictions. Sales representatives must be instructed as to the appropriate things to say to a distributor and must be further instructed on the appropriate things to commit to writing.

Full-line forcing is another problem which is not clear in the minds of many sales representatives and even a good number of lawyers. Basically, the reason it is not clear is because there is usually no hard-and-fast line beyond which one transgresses the bounds of legality. Tying, the practice of refusing to sell a distributor one product unless he buys the other, is clearly illegal. On the other hand, if a company sells, for example, woodworking tools aimed at the do-it-yourself market, it is obviously entitled to require a distributor to carry a reasonably representative number of such tools and to stock a certain number of such tools. It is not clear exactly where tying begins and merely requiring adequate representation and adequate inventories ends.

While the line may be impossible to draw with any kind of precision, counsel is going to have to advise the sales representatives on at least the theory and a possible approach. Generally, that approach is to adopt what may seem to be a reasonable attitude under the circumstances and to talk to distributors about "representative products" and "adequate inventories" rather than talking to them about "full lines" or requiring them to buy product X if they want product Y.

"Substance over form" is another subject which must definitely be covered in the sales representatives' meeting. In some cases, there is an unfortunate belief that using certain magic words to characterize some activity will remove all problems. While it is certainly true that various words may place either a favorable or an unfavorable connotation on a series of activities, if one is going to terminate a distributor because he is cutting prices, the problem cannot be solved by simply announcing to the world and to the distributor that he is being terminated because "the company is realigning its distribution."

This subject is a difficult one to cover because the lawyer is telling the sales representatives, on the one hand, that words are important, that they must be careful of what they write, and that they must place the proper connotations on their activities, and, on the other hand, that whatever jargon or labels are attached to it, substance governs over form and they cannot shield themselves from problems by using the proper vocabulary.

Purchases

In preparing an antitrust speech for the purchasing department, it is necessary to make a distinction between (1) a company which is basically in a buy/sell business, such as a discount store or grocery store, where the function of purchasing is to acquire items which will be sold in exactly the same form to the customers and (2) a manufacturing company, where the function of purchasing is to acquire items which will be used by the company in the manufacture and sale of its products. For purposes of this chapter, we have assumed the latter situation. If the situation is the former, the Robinson-Patman Act will present a very great area of possible difficulty, and the act, together with all of its ramifications, should be thoroughly explored with the proper people. However, in the manufacturing area, the antitrust laws do not operate as a major hindrance to purchasing, and as a matter of fact, mistaken belief about the antitrust laws sometimes inhibits a purchaser from being able to get the best price on the products available.

It is not inappropriate to give purchasers a copy of the antitrust manual, even though it is not prepared with their function specifically in mind, because it is useful for them to know the rules by which the sellers they deal with must play. In other words, it provides a background for them. The following areas, however, should at least be mentioned in a speech to purchasers:

1. Obviously, it would be inappropriate for the purchasers for various companies to get together for some reason and boycott the products of a single seller for some anticompetitive reason. Indeed, in the purchasing context, it is difficult to think of any legitimate reason for companies to agree to boycott the products of a single seller. It may be permissible for purchasers to exchange information on the quality of the products, and it may even be permissible for them to exchange information about the seller's reliability, in terms of delivery dates and performance. (Any such exchanges should be carefully controlled by counsel.) However, there appears to be no legitimate reason why it should be necessary for purchasers of competing companies to agree that they either will or will not acquire specific products from a given company.

2. There is some theoretical debate as to whether voluntary reciprocity (that is, where two companies purchase from and sell to each other without any agreement to do so or without one of the parties exercising any coercion over the other) is legal under the antitrust laws. The Department of Justice clearly thinks it is not. Most antitrust practitioners feel that discretion is the better part of valor on this point and that reciprocity in any form should be discouraged. Many companies have codes of ethics which prohibit reciprocity, and many companies have been sued by the Department of Justice for violations of what the department believes to be a clear rule against any kind of reciprocity. Accordingly, purchasers should be instructed that procurement should be made on the basis of price, quality, service, and other items which are important to them and should in no way be based upon whether or not the proposed seller purchases products from the company. As a matter of fact, it is usually highly undesirable to allow purchasers access to this information. (Obviously, the same thing is true of sellers: They should not be granted information as to how much the company purchases from those companies who are also their customers.)

3. Purchasers should be alerted to the basic price-discrimination prohibitions of the Robinson-Patman Act, specifically section 2(f). However, they should

be cautioned that the only realistic problem in the case of normal procurement, where the items procured are either used in or incorporated into another, different product, is allowing the sellers to fill their files with incriminating documents. The typical problem here is a situation such as the one in the *Kroger v. Beatrice Foods* case, where a seller will try to make it appear as if a buyer has induced him to meet a competitive price—even when this is not the case. For example, a purchaser normally sends out requests for quotations on a given commodity and receives back such quotations. Sometimes, however, he will get the quotation back along with a covering letter which says, "This quotation is granted to you to meet competitive offers which we understand you have already obtained" or something similar. Purchasers should be wary of this kind of ploy and should simply send the bid back, along with a statement that the covering letter is erroneous and that the purchasers desire only a quotation of specific prices for specific goods and do not desire to receive from the seller any kind of information or letter written by their lawyers as legal justification for those prices. The legal problems of the sellers are their own, and purchasers are interested only in obtaining the goods the company requires at the best possible price.

Purchasers should also be made aware of the basic provisions of the Robinson-Patman Act because in many cases, they will desire a price from a seller who alleges that he cannot grant that price because of the Robinson-Patman Act. In many cases, this statement will be either inaccurate or based upon absolutely no facts or legal basis whatsoever. However, this is a very complex area, and even Robinson-Patman experts disagree as to precisely what the act means in specific situations. Accordingly, the best advice in this area is to ask the purchasers to consult with legal counsel when the problem comes up.

The above four speeches will usually equip counsel to make a fairly good presentation to the groups in question. There are many other antitrust problems, but as can be observed from the content of the speeches, the idea is not to make the recipients antitrust lawyers but to give them a working knowledge of the antitrust laws so that they can deal with antitrust problems on a day-to-day basis.

Lawyer Preparation

A great deal of preparation is necessary in order to conduct a meaningful antitrust compliance program. It is assumed that the lawyer will have a thorough understanding of the relevant substantive laws, but in addition, the following preparation is necessary:

1. Ascertain the antitrust history of the company, and learn what antitrust problems have emerged in the past.

2. Do the same for the industry. Read cases involving competitors to see what problems have been discussed.

3. Learn who the competitors are and a little about them. Get their annual reports, if available. Study the catalog of competitors and your company's catalogs so that you will understand the products.

4. Subscribe to trade publications.

All of the above is necessary for two reasons. First, it greatly aids in establishing the credibility and rapport which are necessary in order to draw potential problems out of the employees. Second, it makes the lawyer more aware of what problems might exist and where they might be found. Also, it greatly facilitates discussion between counsel and the attendees at the various meetings which he must have with company employees. As indicated, the most important part of these meetings is the question-and-answer session, and counsel must understand the questions and their implications in order to make appropriate responses.

Company Procedures

Obviously, no company is going to make all of its employees into antitrust lawyers. It is, therefore, necessary not only to alert all employees to potential problems but to provide certain company procedures by which certain matters are automatically brought to upper-level management or legal counsel for authorization or approval.

Authorization

Upper-level management, which will have at least some familiarity with antitrust laws, should be required to authorize certain actions which have potential antitrust significance but probably do not need legal approval in every case. These upper-level managers should, of course, have ready access to antitrust counsel so that they may call and discuss the matter if they have the least concern. Some of the actions which should be cleared with upper-level management are (1) any change from printed prices to meet competition, (2) any distributorship termination—even if routine, and (3) any refusal to sell.

Approval

Legal approval should be required in all of the following cases:

1. There is a change from printed prices to meet competition, and the responsible management official (who is assumed to be familiar with the basic rules) has a doubt about the legal implications of the proposed transaction.

2. There is an agreement with a distributor or a supplier. (Counsel should review the forms which are used. Thereafter, counsel need only review any situation in which there might be a modification of the printed form.)

3. There is patent or know-how agreement.

4. There is joint venture or joint bidding arrangement.

5. There is acquisition of another company—or a substantial part of the assets of any other company.

6. Counsel should approve all new memberships in trade associations. Generally, counsel should determine whether (1) the trade association is represented by competent antitrust counsel, (2) the trade association is useful for company business or is merely an excuse for socializing, and (3) the members or participants from his company are aware of potential problems in trade-association meetings.

7. All inquiries of any sort from the Department of Justice, the FTC, or any other enforcement agency should immediately be forwarded to counsel—and no response (other than a bare acknowledgement of receipt of the letter) should be made without antitrust counsel's review.

8. New marketing programs should obtain legal review before institution so all possible legal problems—including Robinson-Patman Act problems—can be evaluated.

9. In some cases, it might be desirable to establish documentation procedures for any case in which certain important action is taken. For example, it may be important to establish a rule that any time a normal price is reduced in order to meet competition, a certain form is filled out stating exactly why the action was taken and the basis for it. In another example, any time a conversation with a competitor takes place (in other than a social context), it might be desirable to completely document the conversation, including exactly when it took place, the context, and the exact discussion. Indeed, some writers even suggest forms for this purpose. This is a subject for consideration, but my view is that it causes more problems than it solves. Consequently, it is mentioned for consideration in unusual circumstances but is not necessarily recommended. (An exception would be where your company was under an existing order or consent decree and needed to document compliance.)

10. In particular businesses, counsel will probably want to add specific procedures as necessary to assure compliance with the antitrust laws in the context of the relevant business environment. For example, any company subject to an existing FTC decree would undoubtedly need elaborate and formal procedures to assure compliance.

The Audit

A fairly thorough audit is an indispensable part of the antitrust compliance program. Logically, it might appear that counsel should take all of the steps previously mentioned in this chapter before undertaking an audit, but this is not necessarily so. In fact, it might be advisable to start the whole program with a preliminary audit so that the written material, meetings and discussions, and company procedures could be responsive to the actual problems and concerns of the company. In any event, the following items are appropriate subjects for concern in the audit:

1. If company procedures have been instituted and written material has been distributed, are they being complied with? Have they been read and understood?

2. Patent, trademark, and know-how licenses should be read along with the files because in more cases than not, the signed agreement is modified either formally or informally by subsequent letters or memorandums. Even assuming counsel originally examined and approved the license, it should be included in the audit because of these frequent modifications.

3. Hopefully, joint venture and joint bidding arrangements will have been examined by counsel at the time of their execution. If not, they should be examined carefully.

4. Any area where the company may have a possible monopolization problem should be ferreted out by company counsel, the appropriate people should be informed of the situation, and the appropriate actions should be taken.

5. Counsel should have a list of all directors and a list of every other company where those directors also serve on the board. Counsel must then satisfy himself that there is no problem with section 8 of the Clayton Act. Counsel should make a similar inquiry for any new member of the board of directors.

6. If the company involves more than one separate legal entity (parent, subsidiary, or brother/sister corporations), the "bathtub" conspiracy theories should be looked at to see if they may cause a problem. If so, the appropriate people should be alerted and corrective action taken.

7. It is a good idea to have a list of all the trade associations to which the company belongs, together with a list of persons frequently attending those trade associa-

tions. Special meetings with those people and discussion of the appropriate problems might be called for.

8. The procedures the company uses to price its products and any deviation from prices to meet competition should be analyzed for appropriate comment by antitrust counsel.

9. All distribution, franchise, or other agreements—together with related documents, such as the correspondence which is used to either implement or operate the agreements—should be reviewed.

10. Major contracts with customers or suppliers should be reviewed.

The above is a very brief list of broad areas which should be reviewed in an audit. Naturally, the precise problems and the way of handling them will depend upon the particular company.

A big part of the antitrust audit will be reading files. Naturally, the question arises as to what to look for. Here the knowledge of the attorney in both the substantive area of law involved and the business of the company will have to be the primary guide, but the following are appropriate comments.

1. Whenever the files regarding an agreement are examined, it is absolutely essential to read the entire file to see how that agreement has been implemented and whether it has been modified by a subsequent understanding. In the overwhelming majority of cases involving a violation of the antitrust laws, the most significant aspect of the conduct is not the actual words of the agreement but the enforcement of that agreement by one of the parties or some later understanding regarding the agreement.

2. The files of policymaking executives are important, and there should be no such thing as personal executive files which are not examined. Even the executive's personal appointment calendar has been subpoenaed in antitrust cases to show the conduct of the executive, whom he met with, and at what times.

3. Normal corporate files, such as the minutes of the meetings of the board of directors or executive committees and SEC or public relations documents, should not be overlooked.

4. In many cases, counsel will have to do some selecting in the files examination. It is not at all unusual to prepare a list of types of files which should be examined and then to discover that there is literally a whole room full of them. Counsel should have a discussion with the executive first to see where issues might be raised. This may signal particular files to look at. If the executive keeps a chronological file, counsel should take a quick look through that first. It might point the way for further reading.

5. Certain words should signal further reading. These include such notations as "destroy after reading" (of course no one ever does), "personal and confidential," and "original—no copies." Other examples of less incriminating but still troublesome words include "aggressive," "beating," "matching," "competition," "no objection from [competitor]," and "[competitor] will go along."

The purpose of the antitrust compliance program is to assure future compliance with the antitrust laws—not to cover up past violations. Also, the audit is not an inquisition aimed at ferreting out the misdeeds of company employees so that they can be reprimanded. The audit is meant to warn company employees about possible problems before they become serious and to give top management some assurance that all employees understand and abide by the antitrust laws. True, any kind of audit does have some aspect of policing, but this should be minimized by counsel because if the employees do not cooperate and freely discuss problems and allow free access to files, the audit will probably be a waste of time. Indeed, the word "audit" itself may be changed to something less harsh like "review." Management must be sensitive to this problem to avoid hostility and a consequent reluctance on the part of company employees to discuss their problems fully.

SECTION THREE: LABOR LAWS

CHAPTER TWENTY-FIVE

DISCRIMINATION IN EMPLOYMENT

OVERVIEW

Federal and state legislation have prohibited discrimination in employment for a number of years. In the past, these requirements were applied principally to companies which deliberately discriminated against minorities. However, this is no longer the case. Discrimination in employment has become a monumental problem even for companies which have active, good faith programs to hire and promote minorities. Indeed, it has been some companies' experience that the more they try to work this problem, the deeper into trouble they get. Some people blame this on the fact that the company is "sensitizing" its employees to their rights and therefore the employees exercise their rights more aggressively in these kinds of companies. However, it is generally agreed that any problems inherent in sensitizing employees do not outweigh the advantages to be gained and trouble to be avoided by heavy attention to the subject. In order to handle the EEO problem properly, companies must fight on two fronts. The first front is the proper handling of EEO complaints filed by employees against the company, and the second is a planning, auditing, or "affirmative action" front which should be designed principally to avoid the costly kinds of discrimination which might affect large classes of people. This chapter begins by describing the basic legal framework, proceeds to a discussion of the principal problem areas, and concludes with some observations on how best to gear up to fight both fronts of the EEO battle.

SUMMARY OF THE LAWS RELATING TO DISCRIMINATION IN EMPLOYMENT

Civil Rights Act—Title VII

The basic legislation involving discrimination in employment practices is contained in Title VII of the Civil Rights Act of 1964. The two principal provisions of this law provide as follows:

(1) It is unlawful for any company to fail or refuse to hire or to discharge any individual or otherwise to discriminate against any individual with respect to his compensation, terms, conditions, or privileges of employment because of such individual's race, color, religion, sex, or national origin.

(2) It is unlawful to limit, segregate or classify employees in any way which would deprive or tend to deprive any individual of employment opportunities or otherwise adversely affect his status as an employee because of such individual's race, color, religion, sex, or national origin.

The Equal Pay Act of 1963

The Equal Pay Act of 1963 provides that no employer may discriminate against employees on the basis of sex by paying higher wages to employees of one sex than the other for equal work. There are exceptions for a seniority system, a merit system, and a system measuring earnings by quality or quantity of work.

The Age Discrimination in Employment Act of 1967

The Age Discrimination in Employment Act of 1967 provides that it is unlawful to fail to hire or to discharge any individual, or to treat employees differently in any way because of their age. The act, as amended in 1978, protects employees between the ages of forty and seventy.

Old Civil Rights Acts

There are a number of older civil rights acts on the books which were enacted after the Civil War and which could be construed to cover much of what is covered by the new legislation. In appropriate situations, these may be brought to bear against a company, but in the overwhelming majority of situations discrimination disputes will be governed by the more modern legislation because the enforcement mechanisms are better defined. However, these older laws become very important when one of the many procedural aspects of the newer laws would seem to preclude a plaintiff from recovery. A considerable number of cases indicate that where there has been discrimination, but the plaintiff is barred from using the new laws because of some technicalities, these older civil rights laws may provide a means of obtaining relief.

The National Labor Relations Act

This act also provides a possible remedy for discrimination against employees. It is generally held that discrimination by a union or employer violates the unfair labor practice provisions of the National Labor Relations Act. This is especially true if there is any connection between the discrimination and a right which is protected under the act. It is important because it gives a potential plaintiff another "bite at the apple" in pressing EEO complaints.

State Laws

In addition to the above federal laws there are innumerable state laws, some of which are even more severe than the federal laws. For example, some state laws prohibit discrimination on account of age but do not restrict their application to workers between the ages of forty and seventy. Other state laws are "restrictive" in that they impose different limitations on males and females for jobs. These are the so-called female protective statutes which, while enacted with noble motives, can cause problems because legally they are superseded by the federal law which requires equal treatment of the sexes. Even so, some states still make an occasional stab at enforcing them.

It is important to note at this point, while we are still talking about *all* companies whether or not they have government business, that the above statutes not only require the absence of any actual discrimination but they require *affirmative action* on the part of the employers to *remove any existing discrimination. This is the crux of the problem.* Being an absolutely fair-minded employer and following the law to the letter is just not enough anymore. You can get into all kinds of trouble simply by having a bad statistical profile of your work force.

Government Contractor Rules

If the company happens to be unlucky enough to have any government business, a whole host of even more burdensome rules involving affirmative action apply. The first and most significant is that any government contractor must have an "affirmative action plan," which is an elaborate written document which analyzes the work force of the company in extreme detail and then sets forth a plan of action to remedy any situations where minorities are not adequately represented. The government contractor is required to establish "goals" and to use "affirmative action" to meet those goals. The affirmative action plans are supposed to be reviewed annually by the government. There used to be innumerable government agencies involved, but now this responsibility has been centralized with the Office of Federal Contract Compliance of the Labor Department.

Affirmative action programs are required by executive order. In addition to these executive orders, two other laws apply to government contractors and require *affirmative action* in the *hiring of handicapped workers* and *veterans.* The Rehabilitation Act of 1973 requires government contractors to take affirmative action to employ and advance in employment qualified handicapped workers. The Vietnam era Veterans' Readjustment Assistance Act of 1974 (passed over a presidential veto) requires government contractors to take affirmative action to employ veterans. Thus, the list of protected people grows and grows. Happily, the administrative burdens placed upon government contractors in the handicapped and veterans areas are not as great as those placed upon them by the executive orders involving women and minorities. Nevertheless, if a company wants to engage in government business, it is going to have to play the employment game by the government's rules.

In the remainder of this chapter, the legal rules relating to employment discrimination are discussed in the following order: race discrimination; sex discrimination; age discrimination; religious discrimination; the employee selection process; record-keeping and posting requirements; affirmative action requirements for government contractors; enforcement.

After this substantive discussion, some commentary is provided on certain problems, including the following: how to handle EEO cases; what kinds of audit procedure should be established; what kinds of educational programs should be established.

PRINCIPAL PROBLEM AREAS

Race Discrimination

Assuming good faith on the part of the employer, race discrimination problems will generally arise through unintentional, seemingly innocent conduct which, because of past practices or current realities of our society, might have a discriminatory effect. A typical example was the case of an employer who maintained separate facilities (lunchroom, restroom, drinking fountains, recreational areas, etc.) for minority employees before the civil rights acts became effective. Obviously, this was illegal after those laws and the employer stopped this practice and simply announced a "freedom of choice" system. Any employee could use any facility he wanted. The Equal Employment Opportunity Commission, however, indicated that such a solution was improper, stating as follows:

> Experience has shown in somewhat analogous situations that where a pattern of compulsory segregation is replaced by "Freedom of Choice," the freedom to make a choice which would disturb that pattern is often effectively denied in subtle ways. An employer who has participated in maintaining segregated facilities prior to the effective date of Title VII, therefore, should *take positive steps* to prevent the pattern of segregation from perpetuating itself. [*EEOC Opin. Letter,* July 26, 1965]

A further problem in the race discrimination area is that the Equal Employment Opportunity Commission can find race discrimination in practices which most business people would consider to be rather commonsense practices. This is illustrated by a holding of the EEOC that a policy of rejecting applicants with lengthy arrest records was discriminatory. The logic given was that minorities were arrested more often than whites and, therefore, a rejection based upon a number of arrests was discriminatory. The applicant involved had been arrested on fourteen different occasions and there was no allegation that the employer's policy against hiring applicants with lengthy arrest records was discriminatorily applied.

Race discrimination problems—as all employment discrimination problems-generally fall into two classes. The first is the problem of complaints filed by employees or applicants with the EEOC, and subsequent investigation and negotiation of those complaints. The second is the problem of having and using an effective affirmative action plan if you are a government contractor. The problems are usually closely related, but it is useful to keep them in mind throughout Chapter 25.

The following list of examples of possible discriminatory conduct is far from complete and in reading it one must distinguish between those kinds of practices which are obviously discriminatory and which will not require the plaintiff to show any discriminatory effect and those practices which will only be discriminatory if they, in fact, have an adverse effect upon minorities.

First, the maintenance of job classifications or categories for groups (for example, the maintenance of a job classification in which only blacks are allowed to work, particularly if the job classification involves an undesirable job). This might be considered to be an obvious statement, but one must consider *the effect of statistics*. In the first place, companies may have discriminated against minorities in the past by providing job categories for minority groups. Since the Civil Rights Act is not very old, the effect of this discrimination may very well carry forward to the present. In addition, some blacks simply desire to work with blacks and whites with whites and because of this preference of the employees rather than because of the company maintenance of any discriminatory job categories, a statistical breakdown of jobs may show that whites generally fall into some categories and blacks into others. An EEOC investigator who comes across this situation is not going to accept the fact that the discriminatory effects are not the fault of the company, but is going to consider this as discriminatory conduct and require the company to remedy it. If the different jobs include different pay, the EEOC would ask for a back-pay award for the minorities, assuming they were in the lower paid jobs.

Second, a ban on conversation in a foreign language. In the case involved, a ban on conversing in Spanish was held to violate the act.

Third, the retention of a foreman who is admittedly biased or the failure of the employer to correct situations involving overt racial hostility such as employees making racially derogatory remarks to minorities. Again, the point is that it is not sufficient for company management to sit in their offices and ignore racial problems out in the plant. They have to make sure that all employees are treated fairly, and any practice which operates against minorities will be held against the company whether or not "it is the company's fault."

Fourth, a policy against hiring unwed mothers. The commission said that in the relevant geographical area, blacks comprised about 29 percent of the population but accounted for 80 percent of the illegitimate births. The hiring ban therefore had a discriminatory effect. Again, by the mere use of statistics the commission was able to prove a discrimination case against the company which had a policy never intended to operate in a discriminatory manner.

Fifth, the use of word-of-mouth recruiting when this has the effect of perpetuating past discriminatory hiring. Since only whites were hired, only acquaintances of whites—generally other whites—would hear about job openings, and the commission felt that this was discriminatory.

Sixth, the placing of an arbitrary age limit on persons eligible for promotion or training programs where this served to eliminate a disproportionate number of blacks from consideration.

Seventh, preferential treatment of relatives in hiring can be discriminatory for the same reason as given for word-of-mouth recruiting.

Eighth, a common policy of discharging employees after several garnishments. In this case, the Court held that the policy was discriminatory even though it was racially neutral and fairly applied to all employees. The rationale was that it operated statistically to exclude more blacks than whites. The Court placed a great deal of weight on the evidence which showed that the proportion of racial minorities who had their wages garnished was significantly higher than the proportion of racial minorities in the general population. Furthermore, the Court held that the business necessity rule, which provides that a practice which operates discriminatorily may nevertheless be used *if* there is *business justification,* really means that the business reason for discrimination must involve the individual employee's capability to perform the job—not inconvenience, annoyance, or the extra expenses caused by frequent garnishments. The Court also mentioned the federal Garnishment

Law, which provides that no employee may be discharged for garnishments on a single debt. The Court held that this rule had no application here and that it did not imply that it would be permissible to discharge an employee for multiple garnishments involving more than one debt. This is a further example of the complexity caused by complex and overlapping federal regulation of business.

Ninth, the maintenance of *any policy* (even where equally applied) which is not justified by business necessity and which causes a *greater than normal* rejection of minorities, or generally restricts or inhibits the advancement of a larger than normal number of minorities. (Greater than normal is generally assumed to be greater than 20 percent more rejections of minorities than nonminorities.)

Seniority

The seniority issue has at least three different aspects:

1. What kinds of seniority systems are legal and which kinds cause problems?

2. If there is a need for a reduction in the work force, can a strict seniority provision be used or will that be illegal under Title VII if it results in a disproportionate number of minorities being laid off?

3. Assuming that there has been some past discrimination, what kinds of remedies would be appropriate where seniority is involved, recognizing that giving any constructive seniority to minorities must by necessity take away from nonminorities?

Each of these three problems has produced many cases and much literature. At this point in the development of the law, however, it seems clear that the practical answers are as follows.

The usual problem with seniority systems is the maintenance of seniority lists or systems which are arranged in such a way that past discrimination is perpetuated. Generally, this is the so-called departmental seniority system wherein separate seniority lists are kept for separate departments and wherein an employee transferring between the departments cannot retain his old seniority. If there has been any discrimination in the past generating departments which are predominantly white or black, the maintenance of such a system would inhibit transfer between the departments. The most frequently cited example is in the trucking industry where companies maintained separate seniority lists for over-the-road drivers and intracity drivers. In these cases, the over-the-road drivers were predominantly white and the intracity drivers were predominantly black. Further, the over-the-road jobs were generally more desirable. There were literally hundreds of cases involving essentially this same issue in many industries. Finally, a case was brought to the Supreme Court in 1977 and the Court held, in the *Teamsters* case, that bona fide seniority systems were protected under Title VII. A company which had such a system could continue to use it even though it admittedly perpetuated past discrimination. This decision was a blow to civil rights advocates. However, it is clear under the legislative history of the law that Congress did not intend to disturb seniority systems and the Civil Rights Act of 1964 has an express statement to this effect. Accordingly, while the law on this point is very clear, it should not be extended by analogy to other areas where the legislative history is not as clear and where there is no express provision of the law saying that seniority systems are protected. It should also be noted that the EEOC intends to interpret this decision very narrowly. In their view, it should be limited to seniority systems which were established before the effective date of the Civil Rights Act.

In 1974–1975 a group of lower court cases held that it was a violation of Title VII to reduce the work force in a declining economy on the traditional seniority rules of last hired–first fired. They reasoned that the affirmative action of companies in recent years would create a situation where the minorities on the payroll would generally have less seniority than nonminorities and, therefore, would be adversely affected by the last-hired–first-fired rule. However, Title VII does contain a clear statement that it was not meant to prohibit the use of normal seniority practices, and the courts of appeal reversed all of these lower court decisions. In view of the Supreme Court's statements on seniority, this is even clearer now. Use of a traditional last-hired–first-fired rule in the context of a reduction in the work force is certainly protected under Title VII. There must, however, be a bona fide seniority system. This is not likely to be a problem in the case of any union contract, but for salaried workers the company must be able to prove a valid seniority system or practice.

In 1976 the Supreme Court held, in the case of *Franks and Lee v. Bowman Transportation Co.,* that Title VII permitted a court to grant constructive seniority to plaintiffs who alleged that they had been discriminated against because the defendant company failed to hire them sooner because of their race. The Court said that an award of seniority retroactive to the date of the individual job application was appropriate under Title VII, and that merely requiring an employer to hire the class victim of discrimination falls far short of a make-whole remedy, and a concomitant award of the seniority credit he presumptively would have earned but for the wrongful treatment would also seem necessary in the absence of justification for denying that relief. The Court also held that retroactive seniority should not be denied to the class merely because it would conflict with the economic interests of other employees of the company.

This decision certainly sounds different than the more recent *Teamsters* case described above in which the Supreme Court said in 1977 that seniority systems were protected under the Civil Rights Act. It is possible to reconcile the decisions by pointing out that the *Bowman* case involved admitted discrimination and the use of constructive seniority as a remedy, whereas the *Teamsters* case involved an allegation that the system itself was illegal and had to be changed. That seems to be the current view although the lower courts and some commentators are having some difficulty applying these two sets of rules.

Business Necessity

The business necessity rule provides that a practice which does have a discriminatory effect may continue to be used if it is justified by some legitimate business necessity. However, the business necessity defense has not met with a great deal of success. It is limited by the following:

1. The "company image" is irrelevant. For example, sending a black sales representative into an all-black territory solely because of his race would not be justified by the fact that he might have a greater acceptance and be able to produce more orders.

2. Customer preferences are irrelevant. The classic case is *Diaz v. Pan Am* which holds that the admitted customer preference for female flight attendants did not justify a refusal to consider males for that position; the holding would be identical if racial preferences were involved.

3. Preference among coworkers is irrelevant. The need to have "harmony among employees" is irrelevant. The employer must do this, but not by discriminating against minorities.

4. Inconvenience is not a business necessity. Inconvenience of the employer is not sufficient justification; e.g., the garnishment situation described above.

Affirmative Action

A word of clarification on the phrase "affirmative action" is necessary. Generally, there are two contexts in which this is used. The first is where the EEOC will require a company to take some affirmative action such as the steps mentioned above *to rectify* some situation which has created a discriminatory statistical picture. The other situation is where the government, through the power of purchasing, may dictate to companies that sell to the government additional and more elaborate steps involving affirmative action, including long and elaborate affirmative action plans. These latter are discussed in a separate section. It is important, however, that the two concepts not be confused. The government through their purchasing power can require affirmative action even when a company has not engaged in any discriminatory practice in the past. On the other hand, the EEOC *can only require affirmative action to remedy past discrimination.*

Sex Discrimination

The simple proposition of equal pay for equal work and of equal job opportunities for men and women is, in this writer's opinion, the most troublesome of all the discrimination-in-employment laws. Back in the old civil rights days of the early 1960s involving sit-ins, etc., it might have been that the idea of having blacks in "white" jobs was very difficult to get across. Now, however, it seems fair to say that the overwhelming majority of problems involving race discrimination involve the practical difficulty of finding qualified blacks to fill the jobs and the elimination of statistical problems rather than strong emotional predispositions on the part of employers to reject or fail to promote black employees.

In the sex area, however, we have not yet reached that stage and in some cases, never will. First of all, in the race area, one can argue quite strongly that blacks and whites are the same in all material respects. While there may be some residual effect of past discrimination, such as poor education which gives rise to problems in testing, and while there may be some cultural differences, no one can seriously argue that blacks and whites are fundamentally different in anything but skin color. In the sex area, however, this is simply not true. Obviously, there are differences. Obviously, both sexes should be treated equally, but also obviously they should not be treated "the same." Whenever there are differences, there are going to be differences of opinion on what is equal. While this may not be the place for detailed biological observations, some rather rudimentary comments can illustrate the problem.

1. Women have children and men do not. The issue of what benefits should be allowed for pregnancy is therefore subject to much discussion.

2. Women live longer than men. The issue of pension benefits must therefore be considered. Should the benefits or the contributions be equal?

3. Statistically, women are smaller, shorter, and lighter than men. Thus, what may be a perfectly reasonable requirement in certain jobs for physical strength, but which is stated in the form of minimum height and weight requirements, will operate to screen out more women than men.

In addition to these factors, it would be naive to assume that there are no social problems, or even prejudice, on the part of some men against women at work—particularly in the higher paying executive jobs.

There are many arguments which have been used to justify treating men and women differently for employment purposes and for placing them in different jobs. However, to make a long story short, just about the only practice which has withstood the test of time is offering separate bathrooms. In 1978, Congress enacted a law preventing employers from excluding pregnancy from their benefit programs. Generally, employers have to treat pregnancy as a disability and pay the same benefits for that as for any other kind of disability. Generally, employers cannot have any benefit plan, including a pension plan, which is based on the statistical assumption (even though valid) that women live longer than men. Therefore, employers must make sure that their pension plans do not require either different contributions or different benefits for males as opposed to females. These latter two subjects were recent developments which occurred just before this book was printed. The first was a federal law and the second was a decision of the Supreme Court in the case of *Manhart v. Los Angeles*. Consequently, there has not been sufficient interpretation of these two principles to justify discussion of the detailed implications. However, the trends are clear. Men and women must be treated as absolutely equal for purposes of employment, benefits, pay, job assignments, pensions, promotions, and every other aspect of employment. In addition, employers must be aware of the same statistical problems involving men/women as involve blacks/whites. No matter what your practices or intentions, if you have a statistical profile which looks like you discriminate against women, you are likely to run into difficulty.

Now that we have stated the problem, what can the company and its lawyers do about it? The answer is relatively easy to state, but like the problem, it will require some effort in order to implement. All the appropriate people in the company must understand the law. Not only must they understand the general rules, but they must understand the law in some detail and know exactly what kinds of practices and procedures are permissible and which are not, and they must know the kinds of situations which can frequently raise difficulties so that they can seek legal help when needed.

The Law on Sex Discrimination

Basically, the law on sex discrimination is contained in both Title VII of the Civil Rights Act and the Equal Pay Act of 1963. The relevant part of the Equal Pay Act of 1963 is reproduced below.

> No employer . . . shall discriminate between employees on the basis of sex by paying wages to employees at a rate less than the rate at which he pays wages to employees of the opposite sex for equal work on jobs the performance of which requires equal skill, effort, and responsibility, and which are performed under similar working conditions, except where such payment is made pursuant to (i) a seniority system; (ii) a merit system; (iii) a system which measures earnings by quantity or quality of production; or (iv) a differential based on any other factor other than sex: *Provided,* That an employer who is paying a wage rate differential in violation of this subsection shall not, in order to comply with the provisions of this subsection, reduce the wage rate of any employee.

The Equal Pay Act was enacted because of a general economic fact that women can usually be hired for less money than men. In today's job market, the reverse may be true in some specialized areas where the supply of women is simply not adequate to meet the demand for companies to satisfy their

EEO requirements. However, as a general proposition, in the lower level jobs a company can get women to work for a lower wage rate than men and it is very tempting for them to do so. Title VII and the Equal Pay Act (which overlap to a considerable extent) both extend to the same kinds of "statistical" discrimination described in the racial context, in order to avoid circumvention of the law through various subterfuges. For example, if a personnel man came to his supervisor and reported that in the work force he could hire women for 4 dollars an hour and men for 5 dollars an hour to serve as tellers in a bank, and the company could save a great deal of money by simply designating the women as tellers and the men as "management trainees," it would be absolutely clear that this was simply a scheme designed to get around the law. On the other hand, a bank obviously needs "management trainees," and these management trainees should spend some time at the teller window so they know how the business of the bank is really transacted. Accordingly, if the same personnel man came to company management with the same proposition, but instead of characterizing it as the way to tap the lower price female job market, he indicated that it was in the best interest of the company to have two classes of entry-level employees (those people who, in the judgment of management, would never progress any farther than the teller window and would be paid 4 dollars an hour, and those who were "management timber," and who should spend some time at the teller window in order to gain valuable experience, and would be paid 5 dollars an hour), this latter program would be perfectly legitimate.

Let's suppose the management of our hypothetical bank thought it was a good idea and told our personnel man to go ahead. Six months later the facts were that there were six female tellers and six male management trainees working at the teller windows. Under these circumstances, it is quite clear that the statistical fact that the women were in the lower paid jobs performing equal work would be enough to bring the case before a jury. On the other hand, if the facts were that there were three female and three male tellers and three female and three male management trainees, there would probably be no practical problem. The point to be made here is that statistics are a very important part of the story.

Let's examine our hypothetical example a little further to make a few more refinements. Supposing that the manager of our hypothetical bank had devised certain very objective criteria in which he would judge who was going to be a management trainee and who was going to be a teller. Let's suppose further that these were legitimate criteria prepared with the best interests of the bank in mind and, in the judgment of this manager, would produce the best quality management employees for the bank. Assume that his criteria included the following: basic ability to get along with people; demonstrated achievement through either high scholastic marks or prior job performance; ability to articulate a point of view and advocate a position; interest in the banking industry.

Let's assume that the manager carefully interviews all of the applicants for the twelve positions and makes his recommendations as to who should be a teller and who should be a management trainee.

Let's assume that the above criteria are reasonable for the purpose for which they are intended and that the interviewer rates each job applicant very objectively and it turns out that the six males score higher than the six females and are therefore placed in the management trainee slot—at the higher pay. Does the use of these admittedly valid and seemingly proper procedures in order to select the best employees for the company solve the problem?

The answer to this question now turns on whether the criteria are "valid" in a very highly technical, legal sense of the word. This is another recent development which took place in 1978 just before this book was printed. All the government agencies involved in employment discrimination matters finally got together on a set of testing guidelines which are described in a subsequent section of this chapter. Essentially, they say that since our situation involves one where a greater than normal number of females were screened out from the management trainee assignment, our personnel man must have available a *validity study* which demonstrates, under very stringent criteria, that the criteria used for the selection is job-related. If he does not have this study available, the bank will be in violation of both the EEOC and Government Contractor rules. Further, private litigants would be able to bring suit and probably get evidence of the use of this invalid selection criteria into the case. This is the subject of further discussion under "The Employee Selection Process."

The questions of equal work, equal skill, equal effort, equal responsibility, and similar working conditions are very difficult to separate and analyze. However, following are some of the major principles which have emerged in an attempt to define them.

1. If it is claimed that the jobs are unequal because the men have to perform additional work, it must be shown that all the men perform these additional tasks. It will not be enough to show that only some males are available for or actually perform additional work which is not assigned to female employees.

2. There must be a reasonable relationship between the wage differential and the economic value to the employer for the work for which the wage differential is paid.

3. In order for jobs for women to be equal with jobs for men in terms of effort, skill, responsibility, and working conditions, the work need not be identical but only substantially equal.

4. The history of the wage differential is important. If it was admittedly based on sex before the effective date of the discrimination laws, it is very suspect.

5. If the fact that men have to do additional work is asserted, that work must demand greater physical effort, require more skill, and responsibility, or be performed under substantially different working conditions, be performed over a substantial period of the work cycle, and not incidentally or occasionally, and be specifically defined and described as an employment practice and not merely be based on a verbal and vague understanding between the employer and the employee.

6. If a wage differential is based upon the fact that the one getting the higher wages is a trainee, then the following factors are important: the training program must be somewhat formalized; it must be open to both men and women; The trainee should progress from the simpler work to the more complicated jobs. Unwritten and unspecified company training programs and promotional policies will not justify any wage differential.

Another aspect of the problem is the question of equal pay. It is clear that the law covers more than simple differences in the wage rate. For example, if an employer provides greater fringe benefits of any kind, including any form of insurance, or guarantees more hours to men than women, the prohibited discrimination will result.

The problem of unequal pay has become quite complex and just about anything which is done for one sex and not the other is a potential problem area. The following is a representative but far from exhaustive list of typical problems.

First, different base rates for substantially equal jobs where women are predominantly in the lower paid classification. (Again, a statistical problem.)

Second, the starting of a woman in a job classification lower than the one men are offered. For example, a company manufactures electric motors. It has two assembly lines, one for electric motors used in the auto industry for power windows, seats, etc., and the other for standard electrical motors for general use. The standard motors are somewhat larger and heavier than the auto industry motors, but realistically the difference in weight is not material and is well within the capacity of most individuals (including most women). The company has two job classifications for winders, "light winders" and "heavy winders." The base rate for a light winder is less than that for a heavy winder. Women are predominantly hired as light winders, men as heavy winders. This practice raises an equal pay problem as well as a problem of discrimination against women under Title VII.

Another example is the classic "orderly/aide" classification. This has generated a great deal of litigation. In most hospitals, at least in the past, orderlies (men) were generally paid more than aides (women); on the other hand, the orderlies were generally required to perform certain duties which the aides were not. There are a great many complex and detailed cases involving these situations. Indeed, it is from these orderly/aide cases that many of the general principles stated above have been taken. However, in most of these cases, it has been held that the work of the orderlies was *substantially equal* to that of the aides and therefore the pay differentials were not justified.

Third, differences in pension plans. The simple problems are where the women are allowed to retire earlier or with less service than men. This is an obvious violation and the company exposes itself to a suit by the men for compensatory awards. The problem gets a little more complex, however, because in most actuarial computations, a longer life is assumed for women than for men. Accordingly, the company faces the difficult choice of whether to make the benefits equal as far as *cost* or make them equal as far as the *benefits* actually received. If the cost-equality route is chosen, the women will get a smaller pension since they live longer. On the other hand, if the benefit-equality plan is chosen and normal actuarial practices are followed, the cost to the company will be greater for women than for men. A possible solution is the use of new "unisex" actuarial tables.

Fourth, different treatment (whether or not intentional) in promotions or merit increases.

Fifth, red circle rates. Red circle rates (rates above those which the job classification would normally call for) are both a tool to solve EEO problems and a pitfall for potential EEO difficulties. Generally, the key question to ask when red circle rates are involved is the reason for the red circling. If red circling is done for no reason other than the fact that those whose rates are red circled had been receiving a higher wage because of past discriminatory practices, a problem will definitely be present. This is true because the red circling will be said to perpetuate the past discrimination and therefore continue the violation. On the other hand, if the reason is legitimate (for example, a man who might be demoted for health reasons but allowed to keep his former wage rate) there should be no discrimination because this is a "reason other than sex." Naturally, there may be a Title VII problem if similarly situated females are not granted the same treatment. Red circle rates are, on balance, troublesome. Generally, it will be best to eliminate them where possible. This might be done by a one-time "buy out" of the individual (reduce rate to normal in exchange for a lump-sum payment), upgrade or transfer the individual, or redesign the job and the rate. Also, it will generally be advisable to avoid red circle rates as much as possible in the future, so it might be desirable to establish a maximum time limit for red circle rates.

Turning from the question of equal pay to the general discrimination questions under Title VII involving a woman's right to obtain and hold a job, it is useful to look at some of the previously decided cases of the Equal Employment Opportunity Commission.

Unfortunately, even if it is assumed that an employer fully intends to comply with both the letter and the spirit of Title VII of the Civil Rights Act, there is still a potential for trouble because the EEOC can find discrimination in cases where the average reasonable man might not be able to foresee any problem. An illustration of such a situation is the holding that the furnishing of only men's bicycles for use by employees in traveling from one company building to another provided a reasonable basis for belief that the company engaged in sex discrimination. This example shows that it would be virtually impossible short of an entire volume on the subject to list all of the possible situations where a sex discrimination question might arise. The best protection against difficulty caused by inadvertent discrimination is a sensitivity to the problem and an awareness of some of the examples of situations where the question has arisen.

According to the EEOC, it is unlawful to refuse to hire a female on the grounds that state laws forbid females from engaging in certain occupations. It is unlawful to discharge a woman because of her marriage. Generally, an employer cannot discharge a female because she becomes pregnant. The fact that separate facilities will have to be provided for women is not justification for failing to hire them, nor is the employer's preference for males. Also, the fact that a job requires interstate travel is insufficient justification for the rejection of females. A rule against hiring females with pre-school age children is discriminatory. According to the EEOC, the mere asking of a female if she has any child care problems is a violation of Title VII. In the situation involved, the employer's interviewers were instructed to ask each female job applicant if she had any child care problems as a result of entering the job market. According to the EEOC, this discriminated against the females because the same question was not asked of the male applicants.

Any discrimination in insurance benefits is unlawful. This includes many items in addition to the obvious violation which would be caused by the payment of smaller sick benefits or lesser amounts of life insurance. A health plan which grants maternity benefits to wives of male employees and not to female employees is unlawful. Even a voluntary life insurance plan to which no contribution is made by an employer but which is arranged with the knowledge and implied consent of the employer, cannot discriminate because it is said to be a term or condition of employment. Of course, the fact that unequal insurance benefits are contained in the union agreement does not save them from a Title VII violation. The granting of two 15-minute breaks to females and not to males, the offering of supervisory training only to males, providing of fringe benefits (such as passes in the case of an airline) to spouses of male employees only, and the maintenance of a discriminatory profit sharing plan are also discriminatory.

Pregnancy

In 1978, Congress ended a dispute of long duration concerning the proper treatment of pregnancy in company benefit plans. The portions of the Civil

Rights Act which prohibit discrimination on account of sex were expressly amended to include disabilities relating to pregnancy. The following definition was added to the Civil Rights Act:

> The terms "because of sex" or "on the basis of sex" include, but are not limited to, because of or on the basis of pregnancy, childbirth or related medical conditions; and women affected by pregnancy, childbirth or related medical conditions shall be treated the same for all employment related purposes including receipt of benefits under fringe benefit programs, as other persons not so affected but similar in their ability or inability to work, and nothing in section 703(h) of this title shall be interpreted to permit otherwise. This subsection shall not require an employer to pay for health insurance benefits for abortion, except where the life of the mother would be endangered if the fetus were carried to term, or except where medical complications have arisen from an abortion: *Provided,* that nothing herein shall preclude an employer from providing abortion benefits or otherwise affect bargaining agreements in regard to abortion.

Thus, if the company has any medical benefit plans, or any salary continuation plans, those plans must include pregnancy just like any other disability. If the company pays for medical or hospital care for a broken leg, it would have to do so for pregnancy. If the company would continue the salary of an employee disabled with a broken leg, it would have to continue the salary of a female disabled because of pregnancy. The time limit on salary continuation because of pregnancy is a troublesome subject. It is clear that this legislation does not require the employer to have any salary continuation at all, and if the employer has a plan, it does not have to change to pay larger benefits for pregnancy—it just has to pay whatever benefits would otherwise be allowed on account of pregnancy just as for any other disability. For example, if a company has a policy of paying salary continuation for 10 days per year of service, that policy would apply to pregnancy, so a woman with 2 years of service would be covered for 20 days. Further, only the period of medical disability is covered, not voluntary child care or child rearing after delivery.

Sex as a Bona Fide Occupational Requirement

As previously mentioned, sex as a theoretical matter can be a bona fide occupational requirement. However, as a practical matter, this is a question which is best reserved for debate in law school classrooms rather than application to normal corporate situations. The following rules illustrate the problem, and the net result is that sex is a bona fide occupational requirement only in very limited and obvious situations.

1. The refusal to hire a woman because of her sex based upon the assumption of the comparative employment characteristics of women in general is illegal. For example, the assumption that the turnover rate is higher than among men is not a legitimate basis for refusing to hire women even assuming it is true. (Most of the studies show that it is not true.)

2. It is illegal to refuse to hire an individual based upon stereotyped characterizations of the sexes. Such stereotypes include, for example, that men are less capable of assembling intricate equipment and that women are less capable of aggressive selling.

3. It is illegal to refuse to hire females because of the preferences of coworkers or even customers. (This was established in the well-publicized airline stewardess cases where airlines attempted to justify their use of only females as stewardesses on the basis of customer preference. The court did not accept it.)

4. The fact that the employer may have to provide separate facilities for persons of the opposite sex is not a good enough reason to refuse to hire females.

5. Physical height and weight requirements are rarely sustained. In 1977 the Supreme Court added its weight to the many lower court cases which held that it was a violation of Title VII to establish arbitrary height or weight limitations for hiring. The problem is that these requirements, while neutral on their face, in practice, almost always operate to exclude many more women than men and the company usually has absolutely no evidence which shows that the requirement is business-related. This is an example where proper counseling could avoid the problem. The company is entitled to establish requirements as to strength. This is usually the reason the companies give for the height or weight requirement. The problem is the lack of any evidence showing a correlation between strength and height and weight. The company should evaluate what requirements are necessary (e.g., the ability to lift 50 pounds) and use that requirement. Admittedly, it's a little more troublesome and subjective, but it prevents possible costly EEO problems.

By Executive Order issued in 1978, President Carter transferred enforcement of the Equal Pay Act from the Department of Labor to the EEOC. However, since virtually everything which would have been a violation of the Equal Pay Act would also have been a violation of Title VII of the Civil Rights Act, this probably doesn't change anything. In fact, it reduces by one the number of agencies the company might have to worry about in a sex discrimination case.

Age Discrimination

When Congress enacted Title VII of the Civil Rights Act of 1964, which prohibited discrimination in employment because of race, color, religion, sex, or national origin, it directed the Secretary of Labor to make an investigation into the problem of discrimination in employment because of age. The secretary found that arbitrary discrimination based on age existed. Congress thereupon passed the Age Discrimination in Employment Act of 1967. The provisions of the act are similar to those of the other bodies of legislation involving discrimination in employment, but there are very important procedural differences which greatly affect the magnitude of the problem a company will have if it is faced with an age discrimination charge as opposed to a charge involving sex or race discrimination. Basically, the age discrimination law provides that it is unlawful for an employer to discriminate, with respect to employment, against any individual who is between the ages of forty and seventy. The law is equally applicable to corporations, unions, and employment agencies.

As is almost always the case in employment discrimination matters, it is the subtleties of the law which become important. It is assumed for purposes of this discussion that employers, unions, and employment agencies do not desire to intentionally discriminate against the protected group, but, on the other hand, there are certain normal and logical employment practices which can have this effect.

The broad provision of the act which prohibits any kind of discrimination against older employees is subject to the following three exclusions. (1) The employer is allowed to discriminate where age is a *bona fide occupational qualification*. (2) The employer is entitled to observe the terms of any bona fide *seniority* systems or bona fide *employment benefit plan* such as retirement, pension, or insurance plan which is not a subterfuge to evade the purpose of the act. This exception is qualified, however, because the existence of any such employee benefit plan cannot excuse the failure to hire any individual. (3) The act does not prohibit the discharge or other discipline of any individual *for good cause*.

Coverage

Since the law is based upon the commerce clause of the U.S. Constitution, only employers' unions and employment agencies that are engaged in industry affecting interstate commerce are covered. The act only applies to individuals who are between the ages of forty and seventy and only includes employers who have twenty or more employees.

Troublesome Areas

The following specific problems sometimes come up in the age discrimination context.

The Department of Labor believes that it is discriminatory to write help wanted notices or advertisements in ways which tend to discriminate against individuals between the ages of forty and seventy. Department of Labor regulations provide that the following phrases are not acceptable: "age 25–30"; "young"; "boy"; "girl"; "college student;" "recent college graduate;" or other similar phrases which tend to indicate the employer would not consider an applicant between the ages of forty and seventy.

Any phrase which indicates that the employer will restrict hiring to those at the other end of the scale is also prohibited. Examples are specifications such as "retired person" or advertisements which contain the phrase "supplement your pension." The statute does not prohibit an individual seeking employment from stating his age.

The request on the part of the employer for information on the application blank disclosing the age of the applicant, such as "date of birth" or "state age," is not in itself a violation of the act. However, any employer using the form with such a question must be prepared to defend it and to show that the company does not, in fact, discriminate on account of age. Furthermore, in any case where age is asked the company should include language on the form substantially like this: "The Age Discrimination in Employment Act of 1967 prohibits discrimination on the basis of age with respect to individuals who are at least forty but less than seventy years of age."

The act also recognizes that apprenticeship is an extension of the educational process to prepare young men and women for skilled employment; accordingly, the prohibitions of the act do not apply to bona fide apprenticeship programs.

Examples of Permissible Practices

The exceptions to the act which were stated above are intended to be narrowly applied and the burden of establishing that an exception is present rests upon the person claiming it, usually the employer.

There have not been a great many judicial or administrative pronouncements as to when age is a bona fide occupational qualification. Generally, only the obvious has been stated to the effect that age is a bona fide occupational qualification for airline pilots within the jurisdiction of the Federal Aviation Agency, since that agency's regulations bar pilots from engaging in carrier operations as pilots after they reach age sixty; and age is a bona fide occupational requirement in the case of an actor required for youthful or elderly characterizations or roles, or persons used to advertise or promote the sale of products designed for and directed to appeal exclusively to either youthful or elderly customers.

A requirement based on physical fitness is acceptable, but the employer is not permitted to assume that persons over a certain age cannot meet the fitness requirements.

Discrimination based on a seniority system is acceptable, but the system must be bona fide and not designed to circumvent the act. Obviously, if a new system is established giving those with longer service lesser rights, it will probably fail to meet the test. For a system to be bona fide, it must be communicated to all the affected employees and must be applied uniformly to all employees regardless of age.

Use of Statistics

Statistics may be used to show age bias or discrimination just as in the case of race or sex discrimination under Title VII.

Early Retirement—Mandatory Retirement

In 1978, Congress amended the Age Discrimination Act in two very important respects. First, it increased the protected group from ages forty to sixty-five to ages forty to seventy; and second, it modified the exception for bona fide benefit plans to eliminate mandatory retirement prior to age seventy. The increase in the protected group to age seventy is a very straightforward change, and it has been reflected in the previous discussions in this chapter. The mandatory retirement issue, however, is much more complex. It is also the area where most questions and problems will arise and therefore warrants further discussion.

The basic provision of the Age Discrimination Act which allowed mandatory retirement under the old law was the section which exempted bona fide retirement plans from the law. Thus a company could establish, in a bona fide retirement plan, any mandatory retirement age it wanted. So long as it was uniformly applied, the plan could have a retirement age of less than sixty-five. However, that section of the law has now been changed, and it is important to read the law as amended very carefully. It is quoted here with the amended portion underlined:

> Section 4(f) It shall not be unlawful for an employer, employment agency, or labor organization—
> (2) to observe the terms of a bona fide seniority system or any bona fide employee benefit plan such as a retirement, pension, or insurance plan, which is not a subterfuge to evade the purposes of this Act, except that no such employee benefit plan shall excuse the failure to hire any individual, <u>and no such seniority system or employee benefit plan shall require or permit the involuntary retirement of any individual specified by section 12(a) of this Act because of the age of such individual.</u>

It is very important to note that the basic exemption for bona fide seniority systems or benefit plans remains in the law—it is only that such a system or plan may not require or permit involuntary retirement of any person. This has many important implications.

1. The "normal retirement age" and all other provisions—except for mandatory retirement—can continue as before. Specifically, if the normal retirement age is sixty-five, for employees between the ages of sixty-five and seventy, you do *not* have to

    (a) credit service under the plan, or

    (b) pay the actuarial equivalent of normal retirement benefits to employees choosing to work past sixty-five.

2. In the case of benefit plans, it seems clear that a plan will not be in violation of the Age Act if it provides no benefits whatever for employees working past age sixty-five—so long as it is bona fide. This is because the exception for such plans is still effective except for the one factor of mandatory retirement.

In summary then, it appears that, at least according to one reading of this new law, the only thing it does is to allow an employee to continue to work until age seventy so long as the employee can still do the job. There is no requirement to pay the employee any increased benefits, and, in fact, it appears that benefits which might normally accrue to employees such as insurance and credited service under the pension plan do not have to be paid to employees between ages sixty-five and seventy.

However, according to some other views, the amendment could have a greater effect. The key is what is bona fide. The words of the statute are "*bona fide employee benefit plan such as* retirement, pension, or insurance plan . . ." (emphasis added). However, the words "such as" should not be read too broadly. For planning purposes, the exception should be limited to pension, retirement, and insurance plans. Anything which is similar and which might be included by the "such as" language should be a red flag for more careful and deliberate analysis. Only those things which are clearly almost identical would be covered. For example, if a company had a self-funded (but not insured) health plan where benefits were paid out of a trust for hospital, major medical, etc., that would probably be covered even though technically there was no "insurance." On the other hand, such employee benefit plans as tuition assistance, stock options, bonuses, or vacation plans would probably not be covered even assuming they met the bona fide test.

What Is a Bona Fide Plan? In the Court of Appeals case of *McMann v. United Airlines*, the Fourth Circuit Court of Appeals held that, contrary to some other appellate decisions, a plan was not bona fide simply because it was established before the Age Act was enacted. Previous cases had held that, since it appeared obvious that a plan could not be a subterfuge to evade the purpose of the act if it was established before the act, all plans, at least of the pension and insurance type, which were established before the Age Act was enacted were automatically bona fide. The Supreme Court reversed the *McMann* case and brought the law back into line with those other decisions. It was in response to this Supreme Court opinion that Congress changed the law. We are thus left with considerable uncertainty as to what is meant by a bona fide plan. This is crucial because, if there is no exception, almost any pension or insurance plan is going to be a clear violation of the law. Remember that the basic prohibitions are very broad. Certainly any practice which reduced an employee's pension or insurance below those to which younger employees would be entitled would be illegal discrimination were it not for the exemption.

If we assume, as apparently we must in light of the legislative history, that all plans will be either bona fide or not depending on some kind of analysis which no one has as yet articulated, we have a very high degree of uncertainty. If we analogize to other areas of discrimination law, it appears clear that a plan which in fact discriminated would be held illegal unless the employer met the burden of proving business necessity. If, on the other hand, we place on the employees the burden of showing that the plan is a subterfuge to evade the purposes of the act, almost all plans would pass muster. While this latter approach seems most logical in light of the wording of the exemption, it has unfortunately been severely eroded by the legislative history. If an employer cannot show that the plan is not a subterfuge to evade the purposes of an act which was not even in existence when the plan in question was adopted, and have that showing be conclusive, one wonders what kind of evidence will be needed to show bona fides.

The importance of this discussion relates to the desirability of amending plans. In many cases, a pension plan or insurance plan will be ambiguous as to how to treat employees between ages sixty-five and seventy. This leaves you with some possibilities:

1. Leave all documents alone and simply interpret them literally, or issue interpretations if they are completely silent or ambiguous or inconsistent with the new law, and make the interpretations consistent with the new law.

2. Examine the documents, make the choice as to what you want to do, and then amend the documents accordingly.

From a legal point of view, neither of these approaches is entirely satisfactory. Leaving the documents alone will, in many cases, create ambiguity. In other cases, a literal reading of the documents might give a very poor result, even if legal. For example, suppose you have insurance documents which simply stop coverage for all covered employees at age sixty-five. The new law probably does not prohibit this, but you may want to continue various kinds of employee insurance with the employee picking up the cost. To do this, you would probably have to amend the plan. On the other hand, amending the plan *may* have some effect on whether it is deemed bona fide. While the adoption of a plan before the Age Act is not conclusive evidence of its bona fides, certainly no one has suggested that it is not some evidence that the plan is bona fide. If you amend it, you lose whatever benefit this argument has. If you amend it now—after the Age Act amendments and with the purpose of treating older employees in the sixty-five-to-seventy age group less favorably than others, even if more favorably than they would have been treated without the amendment—the question of bona fides becomes even more uncertain. Leaving the documents alone and issuing interpretations eliminates this problem, but it is not a very efficient way of administering benefit plans.

The Bona Fide Occupational Qualification.   Another exception to the law is the bona fide occupational qualification. This section reads as follows and was not amended by the new law.

> [An employer may] take any action otherwise prohibited . . . where age is a bona fide occupational qualification reasonably necessary to the normal operation of the particular business, or where the differentiation is based on reasonable factors other than age. . . .

While the new law did not change this exception for private industry, it did have some effect by implication through the elimination of any maximum age for mandatory requirement in the government sector *except* for firefighters, law enforcement personnel, air traffic controllers, and foreign service officers. Thus by implication it may be argued that age is a bona fide occupational requirement for the civilian equivalent of these kinds of jobs.

The Senate, in considering this legislation, felt uncomfortable with the uncertainty of this. They expressed concern that litigation should not be the sole means of determining the validity of a bona fide occupational qualification. They recommended that the Secretary of Labor issue guidelines to aid employers in determining the applicability of this exception to their particular situations.

The bona fide occupational exception to the Age Act has met with some success in the courts where safety of the public was involved. In the case of *Hodgson v. Greyhound,* the Court of Appeals for the Seventh Circuit reversed a lower court decision holding that Greyhound violated the Age Discrimination Act by refusing the hire drivers over thirty-five years of age.

The case is somewhat complicated by the unusual business requirements of Greyhound and the possibility of some safety implications of having older drivers perform the extremely arduous runs typically assigned to those drivers with low seniority. For this reason, the case is of doubtful use for planning purposes, but it does illustrate that safety is an important factor in deciding the question of whether age can be a bona fide occupational qualification.

Another aspect of this problem is state law. California and Connecticut have already enacted legislation which prohibits mandatory retirement *at any age* and doesn't have the bona fide executive provisions in the federal law. Thus if a company operates in those two states, the above discussion must be supplemented with the state laws. It is clear that states do have the right to adopt laws which are more restrictive than the federal laws so long as they apply only within their own jurisdictions. If a company operates in more than one state, it may have to observe different rules in various states—unless it wants to simply adopt the rule of the most restrictive state in which it operates and use it everywhere.

The new Age Discrimination Act is very important for business because it goes to some very fundamental management philosophies. If a company wants to adopt a general philosophy of "making room for younger people," "infusing younger blood," etc., it is going to have to think a long time about this new law and possibly make some fundamental changes in its management style. The most important points involve the top executives. It would appear that the idea of allowing production and nonexempt salaried workers to stay on the job until they want to retire or until they can't produce efficiently any longer creates only one substantial problem—the unpleasantness involved in telling an older worker that he isn't performing and possibly generating a system for job evaluation to make that assessment as objectively as possible.

However, on the management side, there are additional and complex problems. The actual effect of this new law is unclear because no one yet knows for sure whether management employees in general will retire around age sixty-five anyway or will stay until the company forces them out. For large companies, it appears that there are a number of things they could do to "work the problem." The keys to the new law are "retirement" and "salary." There is nothing in the law which prevents management from reassigning people or giving them special assignments. Thus, if a vice-president is merely putting in his time with the company and, in the process, blocking more talented people, there is nothing to prevent the company from giving that vice-president a "special project" of some kind and moving the more talented person in his place even if the performance of the vice-president is not bad enough to justify letting him go or if the company doesn't want to take such drastic action. So long as the man is allowed to work at the same salary, the only complaint he could possibly have would be one alleging discrimination in status or power within the company and it is not likely that the courts are going to look with much favor on that kind of complaint. Even if they do, it is an individual case which isn't likely to cause very much of a problem for the company.

The moral of this story is that reductions in the work force or forced early retirement programs must be handled with great care in order to avoid possible legal exposure. It is not enough that the company act in the proper manner. It must document its efforts to act in the proper manner and must avoid producing documents which create legal problems. The following example illustrates this problem.

Company A has 1000 salaried employees and is suffering from poor business and desires to reduce its work force by 10 percent. Some of the company's employees are between the ages of sixty and sixty-five and pursuant to the company's pension plan an employee can retire voluntarily at age sixty-two with a reduced pension benefit. Further, the company may wish to allow employees to retire at age sixty and pay these employees some sort of financial inducement to do so, such as either a lump-sum payment or by providing a monthly benefit to them which is equal to the amount they would lose by retiring at this earlier age. The company can do a number of things, some of which are clearly legal, some of which are illegal, and some of which could fall in the gray area.

Among the clearly legal possibilities are to offer financial inducements for early retirement. The company can offer just about any kind of financial aids it would like to entice people to early retirement. As long as the program is voluntary, there should be no legal problem. However, there is a practical problem. Those enterprising people who might want to start a second career or might have some business of their own but who also do a good job for the company are very likely to snap up these financial inducements and retire, whereas the employees who are just "putting in their time" may feel that they should just put in their time a little longer and get a higher pension at age seventy. Accordingly, as a practical matter, the financial inducement route may also not solve the problem.

In order to solve the practical problem mentioned above and stay within the law, it might be possible to adopt a voluntary early retirement program and then "counsel" certain employees as to what action they should take. Obviously, if an employee is valued and the company does not want him to take early retirement, there is no reason why they can't tell him, flatter his ego a little bit, and perhaps induce him to stay. In addition, the company might indicate that if the employee stays, he would get a raise or perhaps a bonus or some other financial consideration. On the other end of the scale, the company may find employees who are actually not producing at the required level of efficiency or productivity. The company may tell these people that, in their opinion, they are not producing and it may counsel them that in their own best interest they should adopt the early retirement option because, if they do not, they would be the ones let go during a cutback because of their low efficiency or productivity. As a technical matter this is clearly a legal approach and in many cases it will work. In some cases, however, an employee will object and differ with the company as to his efficiency or productivity and then the company might find it difficult to prove its case.

Some of the dangerous things a company might do would be the following. (1) Create a series of memorandums by staff people addressed to the senior management containing such phrases as "program to induce older people to retire" or some other kind of memorandum which indicated that the company was basing its decision on who to force into early retirement on the basis of age rather than efficiency or productivity. (2) Fail to keep appropriate records or analysis or job evaluations so that if an employee did complain the company was not in a position to prove its case of lowered efficiency and productivity. (3) Choose the people who were to stay and those who were to go on an arbitrary basis rather than on some systematic basis of objective evaluation of performance. Obviously, it is very difficult to evaluate the performance of an employee when there is no objective yardstick such as number of pieces turned out per hour. However, it is possible to do this by a ranking procedure whereby management ranks all employees in terms of their efficiency and productivity on a regular basis and by accurate and honest personnel reviews of each employee and their supervisors. Generally, if all of this is done in a bona fide manner, the company will be protected by the business judgment rule and the court will not second-guess whether or not one employee was more productive than another. On the other hand, if the company is not careful to evaluate in an organized manner, a court may very likely look not at the procedures but at the statistics and, except where the layoff is by seniority, the statistics in early retirement or reduction in work force cases may be adverse to the company.

The Department of Labor has been increasing prosecution of complaints based upon age. Statistics published by the department show that the number of age discrimination complaints processed by them and the amounts of money which they collect on behalf of employees has been growing substantially in recent years. Accordingly, this subject merits attention. Obviously, the most important thing for the company to avoid is any kind of large-scale discrimination on the basis of age.

President Carter issued an Executive Order in 1978 which will transfer enforcement of the Age Act from the Department of Labor to the EEOC. The effect of this is unclear, but historically the EEOC has shown a tendency to take more unreasonable, arbitrary, and capricious actions than has the Department of Labor. Accordingly, enforcement of the new law is likely to be more troublesome than in the past. At the root of all substantial problems will be some kind of discriminatory *system* which operates against older people. This may be some kind of forced-retirement system as described above or a general practice of having a situation where older people are paid less than younger ones simply because the younger ones can command more in the job market. Unless these kinds of differences are justified by the performance of the people, they will show a discrimination on account of age and substantial recoveries are possible. Accordingly, while management must always be alert to the individual situation where one person in the protected group is discriminated against in favor of a younger person, the most important problem will be to ensure that there are no large-scale systems, practices, or sets of statistics which can be used to show that the company is discriminating against the older worker.

As in all areas, a little common sense goes a long way. Unfortunately, however, experience has shown that common sense does not always go hand in hand with employment matters. There have been instances where persons with more than thirty years of service, and who were within six months of mandatory retirement at age sixty-five, were laid off against their will even though their work performance could not be shown to be substantially worse than anyone else's. There have been situations where the individual was told during his exit interview that he was being let go in favor of younger employees. There have been memorandums breaking down the employer's work force by age and then carefully analyzing how the older ones could be disposed of in one way or another without the slightest hint of any evaluation of the performance of any individual worker. Hopefully, management can contribute some common sense to these kinds of situations and, if nothing else, at least counsel the personnel people to keep the paper work in order.

Religious Discrimination

Both the Civil Rights Act of 1964 and the executive order requiring nondiscrimination in employment by government contractors contain prohibitions against discrimination because of religion. It is therefore unlawful to refuse to hire or to discharge an employee on the basis of his religion. The principal questions involving religious discrimination arise in connection with religious holidays and observance of the Sabbath.

Legal History

In the case of *Dewey v. Reynolds Metal Company*, which was decided by the Supreme Court in 1971, Dewey was asked to work on Sundays. To accommodate those not wishing to work on Sunday, the employer permitted the use of a substitute to be furnished by the employee. However, Dewey, after providing a substitute on a number of occasions, stopped doing so, saying that his religion forbade him from encouraging anyone to work on Sundays. After giving the required warnings pursuant to the labor contract, the company fired Dewey for refusing to work on Sundays. The U.S. Court of Appeals for the Sixth Circuit indicated that the employee had no complaint under Title VII. It said that:

> Nowhere in the legislative history of the Civil Rights Act do we find any congressional intent to coerce or compel one person to accede to or accommodate the religious beliefs of another. The requirement of accommodation to religious beliefs is contained only in the EEOC regulations which in our judgment are not consistent with the act.
>
> The fundamental error of (the plaintiff) . . . is that they equate religious discrimination with failure to accommodate. We submit these two concepts are entirely different; the employer ought not to be forced to accommodate each of the various religious beliefs and practices of his employees.

The *Dewey* case was affirmed by an equally divided U.S. Supreme Court.

In 1972, however, Congress indicated a dissatisfaction with the *Dewey* case and proceeded to amend Title VII of the Civil Rights Act of 1964 by altering the definitional section dealing with religion as follows:

> The term religious includes all aspects of religious observance and practices as well as belief unless an employer demonstrates that he is unable to reasonably accommodate to an employee or prospective employee's religious observance or practice without undue hardship on the conduct of the employer's business.

The act, of course, then goes on to prohibit any discrimination in employment on the basis of religion. Another amendment to the act inserts the words "applicants for employment" in the section prohibiting segregation and classification of employees or applicants for employment in any way which would deprive or tend to deprive any individual of employment opportunities or otherwise adversely affect his status as an employee because of such individual's race, color, religion, sex, or national origin.

The majority of the recent decisions on the question of religious discrimination involves situations relating to Seventh Day Adventists who refuse Saturday work. Generally, it seems as though normal manufacturing-type operations find it extremely difficult to substantiate their failure to make an accommodation to Seventh Day Adventists. The EEOC and the overwhelming majority of court cases hold that firing Seventh Day Adventists because of failure to accept Saturday work is discriminatory.

On the other hand, if there really is a business necessity for the Saturday work, and it really does cause a substantial problem to make the reasonable accommodations, a discharge will be allowed.

Supreme Court View

The Supreme Court, in 1977, addressed the question of the extent to which an employer must accommodate the religious beliefs of its employees. That case held that the employer's duty of accommodation was very limited. Specifically, the Court said in the case of *Trans World Airlines, Inc. v. Hardison* that the employer is under no obligation to (1) pay overtime in order to accommodate the religious beliefs of an employee; (2) alter any seniority system for that reason; and (3) make changes in work assignments which decrease the effectiveness of the other departments in order to have someone work in place of the employee. Examples include the processing engineer who was required to be on call twenty-four hours a day, seven days a week, and the seasonal worker who was only needed at harvest time for whom it was impossible to find a person to do the Saturday work for the one and one-half month period which was involved.

As would be expected, the mere assertion of the business necessity of the employer's actions will be insufficient. The employer must submit specific evidence of the hardship which would be caused by requiring him to make accommodation to the religious needs of his employees. Other examples from older cases include the following:

1. If an employer decides to grant religious holidays, he must do so without discrimination. However, absolute mathematical uniformity is not required. An employer does not discriminate by giving one religious group one or two paid holidays while giving another none, but a ratio of six for one group and one for the other might be discriminatory.

2. Discrimination against atheists violates Title VII to the same extent as discrimination against any particular religious group.

3. In most cases decided under the National Labor Relations Act and the Railway Labor Act, it is generally held that in the union shop situation an employee cannot refuse to pay union dues on the grounds that his religion does not permit any union affiliation. There are, however, a few contrary decisions.

The Employee Selection Process

Introduction

In most cases, the employee selection process is comprised of three parts: (1) advertising; (2) preemployment inquiries; e.g., application forms, interviews, etc.; (3) testing.

Advertising

The rules on advertising have been briefly mentioned in the preceding sections dealing with specific kinds of discrimination. Generally, it is illegal to discriminate in an advertisement, just as it is illegal to discriminate in hiring.

1. Advertisements which indicate a sex preference are illegal. This includes advertisements under column heads such as "help wanted—female" or advertisements which indicate a particular gender. The only exception would be a case where sex is bona fide occupational requirement, but these cases are extremely rare under the strict interpretation placed on this exception by the EEOC and the courts.

2. Advertisements which indicate preference for a particular age are illegal. These include advertisements with adjectives such as "young," "recent college graduate," or at the other extreme, "elderly," or "pensioner."

3. Advertisements indicating a preference for a particular race or color are prohibited. There are no exceptions here.

4. Advertisements indicating a preference for a particular religion are prohibited unless a particular religion is a bona fide occupational requirement.

Preemployment Inquiries

There is no provision in Title VII of the Civil Rights Act of 1964 prohibiting preemployment inquiries concerning a job applicant's race, color, sex, religion, or national origin. Further, the legislative history of this statute is silent as to the congressional intent on the subject. However, the EEOC has said that it looks with disfavor on preemployment inquiries and unless they are otherwise explained they would weigh significantly on the commission's decision as to whether or not Title VII had been violated. The following illustrates their position:

> Accordingly, in the investigation of charges alleging the commission of unlawful employment practices, the Commission will pay particular attention to the use by the party against whom charges have been made of pre-employment inquiries concerning race, religion, color or national origin, or other inquiries which tend directly or indirectly to disclose such information. The fact that such questions are asked may, unless otherwise explained, constitute evidence of discrimination, and will weigh significantly in the commission's decision as to whether or not Title VII has been violated. [*EEOC Guidelines on Preemployment Inquiries*]

It should be noted, however, that there are direct prohibitions against preemployment inquiries on race in some state laws.

Inquiry of an applicant's age is permissible if it is not used for discriminatory purposes. The Department of Labor says that if age is asked on the form, the form should say: "The Age Discrimination in Employment Act of 1967 prohibits discrimination on the basis of age with respect to individuals who are at least forty but less than sixty-five years of age." The same basic rule applies to date of graduation. It is all right to ask, but the information must not be used for discriminatory purposes and the form must expressly so state.

Asking for arrest or criminal records is also risky under recent interpretation of the EEOC.

It is useful to look at the company's employment application forms very critically to find out what information is actually needed. It appears to have been the practice in the past to ask for all kinds of information which the company had no business asking, on the theory that "the company might want to know some day." Under present law, this is a very dangerous position to take. If the company gets into EEO difficulty, the questions on the application form can become evidence, in court, against the company. Following are examples of some things which many companies have asked in the past but which, under the more modern view, are not useful information and which are possibly discriminatory.

1. The maiden name of female applicants

2. Whether or not the applicant owns or rents his home

3. Whether the applicant owns an automobile

4. Prior arrest records of the applicant

5. Any other kind of personal information which may have a disparate effect upon minorities

The question about child care discussed in the sex discrimination section is a typical example of 5. The question mentioned above on whether or not the applicant owned his own home would undoubtedly be held against the company in any case where this was shown to have been a factor in hiring. In such a case, the EEOC or the private plaintiff would almost certainly be able to show that statistically more whites than blacks own their own homes, and it would be virtually impossible for the company to prove that this question related to whether or not the person could perform the job. Accordingly, if personnel people persist in asking these kinds of irrelevant questions, they are unduly jeopardizing the position of their company in the EEO area.

Credit Reporting

If the company uses credit reports as a means of employee selection, the Fair Credit Reporting Act provides that if a company orders an "investigative consumer report" on a job applicant the company must disclose to that job applicant that such a report will be made and that it will include information as to his character, general reputation, personal characteristics, and mode of living. The notice must (1) be made in writing and mailed or otherwise delivered to the applicant; (2) be issued not later than 3 days after the report is ordered, and (3) include a written statement that, upon written request by the applicant, additional disclosure concerning the scope of the investigation will be supplied to him. This disclosure must be made within 5 days after receipt of the applicant's request for such information.

If employment is rejected because of the adverse report, this information must be disclosed to the applicant and the applicant must be supplied the name and address of the reporting agency.

It should be noted that the liability of noncompliance (both willful and negligent) also applies to the user of a consumer credit report.

The use of any credit information in the employee selection process can also cause a problem if it causes disproportionate rejections of minority groups or women. Government contractors should be especially careful of this problem and cover it in their affirmative action programs.

Testing

In 1978, the various government agencies in charge of enforcing the employment discrimination laws finally got together, after many years of negotiation, and issued a set of uniform guidelines on employee selection. This is a very important step and requires management of both government contractors and nongovernment contractors to take steps to analyze their employee selection procedures, identify them, identify which have an adverse impact on minorities, and either validate or discontinue any such test. Test is defined broadly to include not only the paper and pencil variety, but *any criterion* which is used to make hiring or promotion decisions.

The uniform guidelines are complex and technical, but by way of very rough summary, they provide for the following.

80% Rule. There is an 80 percent rule-of-thumb definition for adverse impact. That is, if any selection procedure, or if the selection procedures for a job taken as a whole, select 80 percent as many minorities as nonminorities, as a general rule, the enforcement agencies will not consider the selection procedures to be discriminatory. It is clear that this is only a rule-of-thumb guide for the discretion of the enforcement agencies, but it nevertheless provides a useful starting point.

Bottom Line Concept. The guidelines continue the "bottom line concept" which, in essence, says that a company is entitled to group all of the selection procedures together for any one job and determine whether, taken as a whole, they have an adverse impact. There are, however, some important exceptions to this bottom line concept. These exceptions are: (1) where the individual factor restricts promotional opportunities for minorities, or (2) where there are court decisions holding that the individual practice is discriminatory.

Validation. The general rule is that if a selection procedure has an adverse impact, it can only be continued if there is some "business necessity," and "business necessity" is defined to be one of the specific kinds of validation studies. Validation is a very complicated procedure. There are three basic types of validation.

A *criteria-related* validation study is a study showing a statistical relationship between scores on a test or other selection procedures and measures of job performance. The key here is the statistical relationship. This makes a criteria-related validation study quite complicated.

A *content validity* study is a procedure justified by showing that the test represents the same tasks which are required in the job. A typing test for secretaries is the classic example.

Construct validity involves identifying some psychological trait (the construct) which underlies successful performance on the job and then devising a selection procedure to measure that trait. An example is a test of leadership ability where that is necessary for the job. Construct validity is extremely complicated and difficult.

While criteria-related studies and construct validity are very complicated statistical procedures involving the necessity for statisticians and psychologists, it seems that content validity studies are possible to do in certain cases with lawyers and personnel people.

Technical Requirements Are Important—Common Sense Is Not. According to the government, common sense does not have much of a role in this subject. One of the draft questions and answers issued by the Department of Justice, which is supported by the content of the regulations, provides as follows:

Q. Is the demonstration of a rational relationship between a selection procedure and the job sufficient to meet the validation requirements of the guidelines?

A. No. The mere demonstration of a rational relationship between a selection procedure and the job does not meet the requirements of Title VII of the Civil Rights Act of 1964. . . . All three validity strategies called for by these guidelines require evidence that the selection procedure predicts or measures actual performance on the job. [Draft Q&A No. 26.]

We are thus faced with a situation where our federal government calls rationality a "mere demonstration of a rational relationship" and says that it is irrelevant. The clear implication is that selection procedures are going to have to be looked at carefully by persons who have become *very familiar* with these regulations and who have good judgment as to what to do—not withstanding the fact that the government may lump good judgment along with rationality and dispute its relevancy.

Definition of "Selection Procedures." The regulations define "selection procedure" very broadly to include not only paper and pencil tests for initial hires, but *any selection criteria* which are used for *hiring or promotion.*

Records. The regulations contain an important and serious affirmative duty to have and maintain records concerning the selection procedures. Thus, affirmative action plan compliance reviews are likely to have as an important element a review by the compliance officer of these records. This is a very serious provision because the regulations also contain a statement that if the records are not kept and made available to the compliance officer, there may be an adverse implication that the selection procedures are discriminatory.

Informal Tests Discouraged. The area of informal testing presents another implication shown by these rules. The guidelines contain a very important paragraph which says, in substance, that where an informal or unscored selection procedure is used, you had better either make sure that it does not have an adverse impact or change it to a formal scored or quantified measure. Read literally, this means that the normal job interview and gut feeling that most people use in the majority of hiring decisions either must be administered so that it does not have an adverse impact or must not be used any more and be replaced by a formal test. In short, then, these guidelines have both imposed a great degree of complexity and detail into the testing area and effectively precluded any informal or unscored procedures (unless there is no adverse impact).

Statistical Validity. Criteria-related validity tests and construct-related validity tests appear to be too complicated for most companies because the statistical studies would necessitate more time and energy and imply the existence of more employees than the normal company would have for any given job. However, the new guidelines do offer a little help here. The help comes in section 7, entitled "Use of Other Validity Studies."

Section 7 of the new guidelines provides that under certain circumstances it is possible to use validity studies which were done either by the publisher of a test or by other companies. To be sure, a company must have its own study to show that it is reasonably likely that the test done by the publisher or the other company would apply to the circumstances existing at the company, but this test is again the narration kind of a test described in the content validity studies. In short, if you are using a test which is put out by a publisher who has already done a validity study, all you have to do is write up a narration as to why that study is applicable to your company. You do not have to have a separate statistical correlation study done. Again, the analysis has to be in good faith, and you may run into a dispute with the reviewing officer, but it seems as though you would be in a much better position having made a good faith stab at justifying the use of a publisher's or another company's validity study than by having nothing in the record whatsoever.

The area of testing has already generated a whole new industry of consultants to companies, and it can be expected that in the future there will be many more tests with validity studies already done than there are at present. Much work is already under way. At this time, the number of tests which might fall into this category are limited, but the new guidelines do offer an invitation to this new burgeoning industry to do more work and market these tests to companies that do not want to do their own studies but do want to have relatively formal testing.

Testing Guidelines in Context of Affirmative Action.   These testing guidelines have to be taken in the total context of affirmative action plans for government contractors. The whole idea behind affirmative action plans is for government contractors to take affirmative action to increase the pool of applicants, and further, to direct those actions where the increase is likely to be an increase in minority applicants. If, however, you are successful in increasing the pool of applicants, and the increase comes mostly from minorities, a higher number of minorities are going to be involved in any selection procedure, and it is going to be more difficult to satisfy the 80 percent requirement. This, then, is how the whole thing fits together. The affirmative action plan taken as a whole requires the contractor to go out and get minorities into the pool of applicants, and these selection criteria effectively require the government contractor to hire at least 80 percent as many of those minorities as nonminorities in every job classification.

It appears that this means that companies should discriminate in getting applicants. In short, they should be reasonably assured that they are going after qualified applicants. To the extent that the pool of applicants contains all qualified people, the application of the 80 percent rule should not result in any more than a mechanical record-keeping problem. On the other hand, if you have a situation where the applicant pool consists of a certain number of qualified people and many unqualified people who you have just gone out and encouraged to apply for purposes of the other sections of the affirmative action regulations, these new testing rules will cause a substantial problem.

Technically, there is a defense to this problem in section 4(d). Section 4(d) contains a statement that "greater differences in selection rate may not constitute adverse impact where the differences are based on small numbers and are not statistically significant, or where special recruiting or other programs cause the pool of minority or female candidates to be atypical of the normal pool of applicants from that group." However, as a practical matter, this exception will be possible to use successfully in only the clearest of cases.

It should also be noted that the phrase "statistically significant" is not given its technical meaning by the government. Normally, "statistically significant" is followed by some percentage—usually 95 percent—and the meaning is that, in accordance with recognized statistical computations (elaborate formulas in most cases), the differences being evaluated would occur by chance only five times out of one hundred. Thus any differences are 95 percent likely to be "real" rather than the result of chance. The government, however, in their draft questions and answers, takes the position that "statistically significant" is not to be given this technical meaning, but instead has some kind of commonsense meaning. This problem may be resolved as the drafting of these question-and-answer guides progresses, but at present it would seem a little risky to use the phrase "statistically significant" in its technical sense.

This is important because the formula used to evaluate statistics is heavily influenced by the size of the sample. In other words, the more people in the sample, the smaller the differences which can be shown to be statistically significant. Conversely, in a small sample, the formula will not produce a statistically significant result even if there is a large difference. To take a simple example, if you have one hundred applicants, a large sample, and select fifty people out of these one hundred applicants for a specific type of job, it would be likely that differences of only two or three persons in the various classifications of minorities could be shown to be statistically significant in the technical sense. On the other hand, if you have only ten applicants and select five people, it would be almost impossible to show any "significant difference" in the technical sense even though perhaps all five people you selected were nonminorities.

One practical implication of these guidelines will be to force those companies which do not already have it to acquire some expertise in statistics, at least enough to perform a basic statistical comparison to see if differences in rejection rates are statistically significant. While this might not be determinative in the negative sense, it probably is in the positive sense. That is, if a rejection ratio is statistically significant (at the 95 percent level) to a greater extent than the 80 percent or four-fifths allowed, you probably need a validation study of some kind or else you should stop using the test or change it.

Posting, Record Keeping, and Reporting

There is no place in the law where the overlapping and cumbersome federal regulatory process is more apparent than in the posting requirements under the Equal Employment Opportunity laws. A look at almost any company bulletin board where the company is making a reasonable attempt to comply with these rules reveals a new form of American graffiti which has been developed in an attempt to inform employees of their rights under these laws.

Virtually every one of the federal laws has its own requirement for posting a separate notice, usually a prescribed one, often large and colorful, printed by the government in order to inform the employees of their rights under these laws. Only two agencies, the EEOC and OFCC, have issued a joint poster which will satisfy the requirements of more than one law.

The EEOC and the OFCC each require the posting of an approved notice announcing that discrimination in employment because of race, sex, religion, or national origin is against the law. The notice must be posted in conspicuous places available to employees, applicants, and union members or representatives. A willful violation of the posting requirement is punishable by a fine of up to 100 dollars for each separate offense.

The Age Discrimination in Employment Act of 1967 also requires the posting of a notice. Again, the notice must be posted in conspicuous places on the premises of the employer, agency, or union and generally provides that discrimination against employees between the ages of forty and sixty-five is prohibited by law. This is a separate poster. It is available from the local offices of the Wage and Hour Division of the Department of Labor.

The Equal Pay Act is part of the Fair Labor Standards Act and is, therefore, subject to the posting requirements of that act. Those requirements are contained in regulations which provide that employers covered by the act must post and keep posted an approved notice in a place where the employees can readily observe it on the way to or from their places of employment. Generally, the notice sets forth the facts that (1) federal law prescribes a certain minimum wage; (2) federal law requires equal pay for equal work without regard to sex; and (3) federal law contains certain restrictions on the employment of minors.

In addition to these, there are almost always state law posting requirements.

Each of the principal laws dealing with discrimination in employment has its own set of record-keeping requirements. The most important requirements are contained in Title VII of the Civil Rights Act of 1964 and Executive Order 11246.

Each employer of 100 persons or more is required to file an annual report on Form EEO-1. The employer must also retain a current copy of the report and show it upon request to an agent of the EEOC. If an employer has more than one establishment, he must file a separate report for each establishment, plus a combined report.

The EEOC has not adopted any requirement that records be made or kept by employers, beyond the EEO-1 reports mentioned above. Their regulation on records as to the racial or ethnic identity of employees, however, is important to note. It provides as follows:

> Sec. 1601.13. Records as to Racial or Ethnic Identity of Employees. — Employers may acquire the information necessary for completion of Items 5 and 6 of Report EEO-1 either by visual surveys of the work force, or at their option, by the maintenance of post-employment records as to the identity of employees where the same is permitted by State law. In the latter case, however, the Commission recommends the maintenance of a permanent record as to the racial or ethnic identity of an individual for purpose of completing the report form only where the employer keeps such records separately from the employee's basic personnel form or other records available to those responsible for personnel decisions, e.g., as part of an automatic data processing system in the payroll department.

If the employer does make or keep records, however, the following retention periods are called for. (1) Six months for any personnel or employment record made or kept by an employer (including but not necessarily limited to application forms submitted by applicants and other records having to do with hiring, promotion, demotion, transfer, layoff or termination, rates of pay or other terms of compensation, and selection for training or apprenticeship). Also, records involving involuntary termination should be kept for 6 months from the date of such termination. (2) If there is any unfair employment practice charge filed, the employer must keep any relevant records until disposition has finally been made of the charge.

The record-keeping and reporting requirements for government contracts are contained in Order No. 4. The most important are the records related to employee selection mentioned under "Testing."

The Age Discrimination in Employment Act of 1967 has an elaborate set of regulations on record keeping in 29 CFR 850. Generally, these regulations provide that employers subject to the act are required to keep records for each of their employees which contain at least the following information; name, address, date of birth, occupation, rate of pay, and amount of pay earned each week. To the extent that the employer makes other records, he is generally required to keep them for 1 year. Naturally, when an investigation is commenced, records must be kept until it is completed.

There are no specific reporting requirements.

Since the Equal Pay Act is part of the Fair Labor Standards Act, the record-keeping requirements of that act apply. Generally, those requirements are contained in 29 CFR 516. No particular form of records is required, and there are no specific reporting requirements.

The records must, however, include the following for each nonexempt employee: name, address, date of birth if under nineteen, sex and occupation in which employed, the time of day and day of week on which the employee's workweek begins, the regular hourly rate of pay, hours worked each workday and total hours worked each workweek, total daily or weekly straight-time earnings or wages, total overtime excess compensation for the workweek, total additions to or deductions from wages paid each pay period, total wages paid each pay period, and the date of payment and the pay period covered by the payment.

In other words, employers must keep sufficient payroll records to show compliance with the requirements of the act. The regulations also require records to be kept for exempt workers (although not as detailed) so that the legality of their exempt status can be audited.

Retention periods of either 2 or 3 years are called for, depending on the records involved. Payroll records and plans or written agreements are required to be kept for 3 years.

Probably the most significant document for Equal Employment Opportunity purposes is Form EEO-1—especially the table which shows the total employees and minority-group employees for each of nine categories. This table from the EEO-1 form is reproduced on the following page.

AFFIRMATIVE ACTION PLANS

The following statement of the Department of Labor sets forth the definition and purpose of an affirmative action plan.

> An affirmative action program is a set of specific and result-oriented procedures to which a contractor commits himself to apply every good faith effort. The objective of those procedures plus such efforts is equal employment opportunity. . . . An acceptable affirmative action program must include an analysis of areas within which the contractor is deficient in the utilization of minority groups and, further, goals and timetables to which the contractor's good faith efforts must be directed to correct the deficiencies and, thus to achieve prompt and full utilization of minorities and women at all levels and in all segments of his work force where deficiencies exist.

The present guidelines for developing affirmative action programs are contained in Order No. 4. This order provides the necessary guidance for the preparation of affirmative action programs. However, it is subject to interpretation, and different reviewing officers have placed different interpretations on its provisions. The order should be used as a guide only, but should be followed closely as to format. Under current procedures, affirmative action programs may have to be tailored to the wishes of the particular reviewing officer. However, unless the plan follows the correct format in typical bureaucratic fashion, one is almost certainly going to be in for trouble during a review.

Who Must Have an Affirmative Action Program?

Each prime contractor or subcontractor with fifty or more employees and a contract of $50,000 or more must develop a written affirmative action compliance program *for each of its establishments* (even if only one establishment has government contracts) within 120 days of the commencement of the contract. (The provisions of Order No. 4 apply only to nonconstruction contractors. Construction contractors are subject to their own set of requirements.)

Section D — EMPLOYMENT DATA

Employment at this establishment--Report all permanent, temporary, or part-time employees including apprentices and on-the-job trainees unless specifically excluded as set forth in the instructions. Enter the appropriate figures on all lines and in all columns. Blank spaces will be considered as zeros.

NUMBER OF EMPLOYEES

JOB CATEGORIES	OVERALL TOTALS (SUM OF COL. B THRU K) A	MALE						FEMALE					
		WHITE (NOT OF HISPANIC ORIGIN) B	BLACK (NOT OF HISPANIC ORIGIN) C	HISPANIC D	ASIAN OR PACIFIC ISLANDER E	AMERICAN INDIAN OR ALASKAN NATIVE F		WHITE (NOT OF HISPANIC ORIGIN) G	BLACK (NOT OF HISPANIC ORIGIN) H	HISPANIC I	ASIAN OR PACIFIC ISLANDER J	AMERICAN INDIAN OR ALASKAN NATIVE K	
Officials and Managers													
Professionals													
Technicians													
Sales Workers													
Office and Clerical													
Craft Workers (Skilled)													
Operatives (Semi-Skilled)													
Laborers (Unskilled)													
Service Workers													
TOTAL													
Total employment reported in previous EEO-1 report													

(The trainees below should also be included in the figures for the appropriate occupational categories above)

| Formal On-the-Job trainees | White collar | | | | | | | | | | | | | |
| | Production | | | | | | | | | | | | | |

1. NOTE: On consolidated report, skip questions 2-5 and Section E.
2. How was information as to race or ethnic group in Section D obtained?
   1 ☐ Visual Survey   3 ☐ Other—Specify ....
   2 ☐ Employment Record ....
3. Dates of payroll period used –

4. Pay period of last report submitted for this establishment

5. Does this establishment employ apprentices?
   This year?   1 ☐ Yes   2 ☐ No
   Last year?   1 ☐ Yes   2 ☐ No

What Is the Effect of Not Having a Plan, or Having an Inadequate Plan?

If a contractor does not have a plan at all, or has an unacceptable plan, it is unable to comply with the Equal Employment Opportunity Clause in all government contracts. The effect of this can be that (1) the company cannot be awarded any new contracts, and (2) the company's existing contracts can be canceled.

What Should an Affirmative Action Plan Contain?

An affirmative action program should follow the outline contained in Order No. 4.

The following are some comments on the contents of affirmative action plans which have been obtained from experience with past reviews.

First, since Order No. 4 took effect, compliance review officers have been very much more demanding in what constitutes an acceptable affirmative action plan. The general trend has been to demand very literal conformance with the statements and sequences of Order No. 4, but the emphasis given to various elements of the order varies among the review officers.

Meetings with supervisors to explain and discuss the program are a valuable element of internal dissemination of policy and of the importance in developing attainable goals plus the commitment for their achievement. Meetings with union leaders to request their support and citation of any segments of the union contracts which emphasize equal employment principles are very desirable. Company publications should carry articles featuring minority employees and in all respects give a balanced representation of the work force.

In some compliance reviews, exception has been taken to the fact that sources such as the National Alliance of Businessmen and the Office of Economic Opportunity have not been contacted and requested to refer minorities for positions. This should be done, but with an important proviso: the basic premise of equal employment opportunity is equal opportunity for those with equal ability. Goals and timetables are set for the employment of minorities at all levels, including management, on the assumption that with diligent effort fully qualified minority candidates can be located. This is the case in most instances, and affirmative action commitments are based on this fact. Employment of the disadvantaged is an entirely different matter. It is equally important in a corporation's responsibilities as a good citizen, and commitments should be undertaken to employ the disadvantaged when there are requirements and provisions to provide the necessary training. Where this is done, the minority members of the disadvantaged group hired would certainly count toward the affirmative action commitments. However, the equal employment opportunity commitment should not include provisions for hiring the disadvantaged.

Finally, analysis by job categories based on the nine categories from Form EEO-1 is generally unacceptable. A more detailed job-category breakdown is required, as indicated by the following paragraph from Order No. 4:

> (a) Workforce analysis which is defined as a listing of each job classification as it appears in applicable collective bargaining agreements or payroll records (not job group) ranked from the lowest paid to the highest paid within each department or other similar organizational unit including departmental or unit supervision. If there are separate work units or lines of progression within a department a separate list must be provided for each such work unit, or line, including unit supervisors. For lines of progression there must be indicated the order of jobs in the line through which an employee could move to the top of the line. For each

job classification, the total number of male and female incumbents, and the total number of male and female incumbents in each of the following groups must be given: blacks, Spanish-surnamed Americans, American Indians, and Orientals. The wage rate or salary range for each job classification should be given. All job classifications, including all managerial job classifications, must be listed.

Establishment of Goals

Commitment must be made to goals which represent significant progress in the attainment of a balanced work force. No compliance review officer is going to be willing to settle for token goals. On the other hand, Order No. 4 specifically states that the goals and timetables should be *attainable* in terms of the contractor's analysis of his deficiencies and his entire affirmative action program. Thus, in establishing his goals and timetables, the contractor should consider the results which could be reasonably expected from his good-faith efforts to make his overall affirmative action program work. If he does not meet his goals and timetables, the contractor's good-faith efforts shall be judged by whether he is following his program and attempting to make it work toward the attainment of his goals.

As a rough rule of thumb, the ultimate goal will match the percentage of qualified minorities available for the job—taking into account whatever geographical area is appropriate for the job in question. This creates some substantial statistical problems, as it is often difficult to reach agreement on the number of minority engineers, technicians, lawyers, accountants, etc.

It is preferable to express goals in percentages. The advantages of this are as follows. (1) If shrinking business eliminates the potential openings, the percentage goal goes to zero along with the number of potential openings. (2) If unanticipated business expansion increases the number of potential openings, the company can enhance its stand in equal employment opportunity by hiring more minorities. (3) When dealing with small job categories, good business judgment prohibits establishing a commitment to the effect that the first opening which occurs will necessarily be filled with a minority member. Until the opening occurs, the requirement, the urgency, the number of qualified candidates from within the corporation who might take precedence, etc., are all unknown. Nonetheless, it is necessary to somehow establish a commitment to change the minority representation in such categories as rapidly as possible and the percentage goal can express this commitment.

The best possible documentation of good-faith efforts is qualified minorities on the payroll as pledged. Failing this, the efforts to attain the goal should be most carefully documented.

Freedom of Information Act

Some federal courts hold that the affirmative action plans of government contractors are available to the public under the Freedom of Information Act. Others hold that at least certain parts of such plans cannot be disclosed to private parties by the government. Counsel is thus in a position of being unable to assure his clients that material contained in affirmative action plans will remain confidential and, therefore, should consider the following.

1. Attempt to omit any information which might be considered harmful to the company in a competitive sense. This includes any references to proposed business expansion or contraction or reorganization.

2. If it is necessary to include any such information, separate it from the body of the plan and clearly mark it "trade secret" or "commercial and financial information—privileged and confidential."

3. Attempt to keep individual career development plans and similar information out of the plan.

4. Keep in mind that in order to have any chance of substantiating a claim of confidentiality, you must be able to tell a convincing story on precisely why the information in question can hurt your company. You must, therefore, be restrictive in labeling confidential information. Simply stamping everything "confidential" or "secret" is self-defeating.

REVERSE DISCRIMINATION

Reverse discrimination is a very emotional subject. Generally, it refers to the practice of favoring minorities over whites for affirmative action purposes. From a legal point of view, it is clearly illegal. The Supreme Court and several lower courts have held that it is just as illegal to favor minorities because of their race or sex as it is to discriminate against them for that reason. If a white male can show he was discriminated against, he will have a cause of action. The fact that the discrimination occurred under an affirmative action plan where the company was trying to satisfy the government contract authorities will not make any difference. However, it is useful to look at the decided cases to see how this problem arises.

In the *McDonald v. Santa Fe* case, the Supreme Court held that white employees who were disciplined had a cause of action for discrimination against the company because black employees guilty of the same offense were not disciplined the same way. This, of course, is the typical kind of case usually brought and won by minorities. In the *McDonald* case, three employees were caught stealing cargo; two of them were white and one black. The two white employees were fired and the black employee was not. There is no discussion in the opinion about any difference in the degree of guilt among the three employees, and it is implicit in the opinion that all three were guilty of the same offense in the same degree.

The reason for the discharge of the whites and retention of the black is not clear, but it can be assumed that it dealt with Santa Fe's affirmative action concerns. The white employees sued and won. In other cases, companies have instituted affirmative action programs which were based on quotas or express numbers. For example, the company would say that one-half of its training program would be open to all qualified people on some nondiscriminatory basis and the other half would emphasize minorities. In the case of a college, they might say that a certain number of seats were reserved for minorities. These quota systems have been held to be illegal discrimination.

Let's look at these cases more closely, however. In the *McDonald* case, employees with different skin colors were treated differently in a definite dispute where all three were guilty of the same thing. This is hardly a very good case. The company had absolutely no justification for treating the employees differently because of any difference in conduct. In the other cases decided so far, there have been express numbers used to designate opportunities reserved in one way or another for blacks. In short, the blacks have been singled out, identified, and granted a specific preference over whites. This is not affirmative action, it is discrimination. Further, it is very easy to prove.

If companies would limit their affirmative action to increased efforts to seek out qualified minorities and good-faith efforts to hire them without doing it "by the numbers," there would be far fewer problems. This whole area is still developing, but intelligent management can solve most of the legal problems. The emotional problems should not be allowed to cloud the picture and interfere with good solid affirmative action efforts where those are needed.

In 1978, the Supreme Court issued its famous Bakke decision which held, in substance, that the program of the University of California Medical School by which 16 out of 100 slots were held for minorities was discriminatory. The Bakke decision was very confusing, with almost all of the Justices writing a separate opinion. Basically, the Court said that while the numerical approach used by the University of California was illegal, a subjective approach accomplishing basically the same thing used by Harvard was not. Harvard could, by a process of judgment in each case, make decisions taking into account the desirability of having a balanced student body. Thus they could take the applicant's race, sex, or age into account, and could also consider his location. Bakke has been written about at length and will continue to be written about in the future. There are those who think the difference between the University of California approach and the Harvard approach is one of semantics only, but nevertheless that is the basis of the Court's decision. There is another case involving an employment situation on its way to the Supreme Court (*Kaiser Aluminum*), but that too involves stated numbers. In that case, 50 percent of the apprenticeship jobs was reserved for minorities for affirmative action purposes. Thus it is possible that this issue will not be resolved in the context of a "normal" affirmative action plan for quite some time. As a practical matter, it is clear that companies should go ahead with normal affirmative action efforts and should avoid the rigid kinds of numerical systems in *Bakke* and *Kaiser Aluminum*.

AFFIRMATIVE ACTION FOR VETERANS

The Vietnam Era Veterans Readjustment Assistance Act of 1974 (Public Law 93-508, December 3, 1974) requires government contractors to exercise affirmative action to hire and promote veterans. That act amended section 2012 of Title 38 of the U.S. Code (Chapter 42) to read as follows:

Sec. 2012. Veterans' Employment Emphasis under Federal Contracts. (a) Any contract in the amount of $10,000 or more entered into by any department or agency for the procurement of personal property and non-personal services (including construction) for the United States, shall contain a provision requiring that the party contracting with the United States shall take affirmative action to employ and advance in employment qualified disabled veterans and veterans of the Vietnam era. The provisions of this section shall apply to any subcontract entered into by a prime contractor in carrying out any contract for the procurement of personal property and non-personal services (including construction) for the United States. In addition to requiring affirmative action to employ such veterans under such contracts and subcontracts and in order to promote the implementation of such requirement, the President shall implement the provisions of this section by promulgating regulations within 60 days after the date of enactment of this section, which regulations shall require that (1) each such contractor undertake in such contract to list immediately with the appropriate local employment service office all of its suitable employment openings, and (2) each such local office shall give such veterans priority in reference to such employment openings. (b) If any disabled veteran or veteran of the Vietnam era believes any contractor has failed or refused to comply with the provisions of his contract with the United States, relating to the emploment of veterans, such veteran may file a complaint with the Veterans' Employment Service of the Department of Labor. Such complaint shall be promptly referred to the Secretary who shall promptly investigate such complaint and shall take such action thereon as the facts and circumstances warrant consistent with the terms of such contract and the laws and regulations applicable thereto.

AFFIRMATIVE ACTION FOR HANDICAPPED WORKERS

The Rehabilitation Act of 1973 requires government contractors and subcontractors to take affirmative action to employ and promote qualified handicapped individuals. This act was amended, effective February 6, 1975, to greatly expand the definition of handicapped persons. The term handicapped individual now means any individual who has a physical or mental impairment which substantially limits one or more of such person's major life activities, has a record of such impairment, or is regarded as having such an impairment.

There are regulations spelling out the details of the affirmative action plan and required practices, and records. Following are general rules:

1. A plan for the handicapped is required from all companies and facilities with plans for minorities.

2. The elaborate statistical analysis required in the case of minorities is not required for handicapped.

3. The plan for handicapped workers should be separate—it should not be a part of the company's affirmative action plan under Order No. 4.

4. In almost all cases, contractors and subcontractors will have to sign certifications to the effect that they have a plan and follow it.

THE ENFORCEMENT PROCESS

The mechanics involved in enforcing the EEO laws either by the government or by private parties depend upon the particular law under which they are proceeding. It is, therefore, impossible to describe only one enforcement process; instead, the enforcement process for each of the relevant laws must be described.

Title VII of the Civil Rights Act

In 1972 Title VII of the Civil Rights Act of 1964 was amended to change the enforcement procedures to give the EEOC power to institute a lawsuit against the company. Before that time, they did not have this power. The new procedures can be summarized as follows.

Filing of the Charge

The procedures are all started by an employee filing a charge claiming that he has been discriminated against. (It is also possible for a member of the commission to file a charge.) The charge must be filed within 180 days of the alleged unlawful practice. This 180-day rule is very important and it is probably the single procedural device most used by companies to limit the number of claims. Essentially, the company can forget about anything that happened more than 180 days ago unless someone has filed a complaint. The Supreme Court focused on this problem in 1978 and said, in effect, that even if the past violation has a continuing effect, that continuing effect will not extend the 180-day period. This is a very important concept because it says to management, "Put your EEO house in order and you can forget about any problems based on vague allegations of the continuing effect of past practices." The charge filed by the employee is very simple. A sample form is reproduced on the next two pages. Typically, the employee goes to the EEOC

(PLEASE PRINT OR TYPE)

APPROVED BY GAO	CHARGE OF DISCRIMINATION	CHARGE NUMBER(S) (AGENCY USE ONLY)
B—180541 (RO511) Expires 1-31-81	IMPORTANT: This form is affected by the Privacy Act of 1974; see Privacy Act Statement on reverse before completing it.	☐ STATE/LOCAL AGENCY ☐ EEOC

Equal Employment Opportunity Commission and
_____(State or Local Agency)

NAME (Indicate Mr., Ms. or Mrs.)	HOME TELEPHONE NUMBER (Include area code)
STREET ADDRESS	
CITY, STATE, AND ZIP CODE	COUNTY

NAMED IS THE EMPLOYER, LABOR ORGANIZATION, EMPLOYMENT AGENCY, APPRENTICESHIP COMMITTEE, STATE OR LOCAL GOVERNMENT AGENCY WHO DISCRIMINATED AGAINST ME. (If more than one list below).

NAME		TELEPHONE NUMBER (Include area code)
STREET ADDRESS	CITY, STATE, AND ZIP CODE	
NAME		TELEPHONE NUMBER (Include area code)
STREET ADDRESS	CITY, STATE, AND ZIP CODE	

CAUSE OF DISCRIMINATION BASED ON MY (Check appropriate box(es))

☐ RACE ☐ COLOR ☐ SEX ☐ RELIGION ☐ NATIONAL ORIGIN ☐ OTHER (Specify)

DATE MOST RECENT OR CONTINUING DISCRIMINATION TOOK PLACE (Month, day, and year)

THE PARTICULARS ARE:

I will advise the agencies if I change my address or telephone number and I will cooperate fully with them in the processing of my charge in accordance with their procedures.	NOTARY — (When necessary to meet State and Local Requirements)
	I swear or affirm that I have read the above charge and that it is true to the best of my knowledge, information and belief.
	SIGNATURE OF COMPLAINANT
I declare under penalty of perjury that the foregoing is true and correct.	SUBSCRIBED AND SWORN TO BEFORE ME THIS DATE (Day, month, and year)
DATE: _____ CHARGING PARTY (Signature)	

EEOC FORM 5B JAN. 78   PREVIOUS EDITIONS OF ALL EEOC FORM 5'S ARE OBSOLETE AND MUST NOT BE USED

NOTICE OF NON-RETALIATION REQUIREMENT

Section 704(a) of the Civil Rights Act of 1964, as amended, states:

It shall be an unlawful employment practice for an employer to discriminate against any of his employees or applicants for employment, for an employment agency to discriminate against any individual, or for a labor organization to discriminate against any member thereof or applicant for membership because he has opposed any practice made an unlawful employment practice by this title, or because he has made a charge, testified, assisted, or participated in any manner in an investigation, proceeding, or hearing under this title.

Persons filing charges of employment discrimination are advised of this Non-Retaliation Requirement and are instructed to notify the Equal Employment Opportunity Commission if any attempt at retaliation is made.

PRIVACY ACT STATEMENT

(This form is covered by the Privacy Act of 1974, Public Law 93-579 Authority for requesting and uses of the personal data are given below.)

1. FORM NUMBER/TITLE/DATE
   EEOC Form 5B, Charge of Discrimination, Jan. 78.

2. AUTHORITY
   42 USC 2000e 5(b)

3. PRINCIPAL PURPOSE(S) The purpose of the charge, whether recorded initially on Form 5B or abstracted from a letter, is to invoke the Commission's jurisdiction.

4. ROUTINE USES. This form is used to determine the existence of facts which substantiate the Commission's jurisdiction to investigate, determine, conciliate and litigate charges of unlawful employment practices. It is also used to record information sufficient to maintain contact with the Charging Party and to direct the Commission's investigatory activity. A copy of the charge will be served upon the person against whom the charge is made.

5. WHETHER DISCLOSURE IS MANDATORY OR VOLUNTARY AND EFFECT ON INDIVIDUAL FOR NOT PROVIDING INFORMATION. Charges must be in writing, signed under penalty of perjury, setting forth the facts which give rise to the charge of employment discrimination and be signed by or on behalf of a person claiming to be aggrieved. However, use of EEOC Form 5B is not mandatory. Technical defects or omissions may be cured by amendment.

office and explains what happened. The EEOC people then help the employee fill out the charge. The employee does not need a lawyer at this stage.

Deferral to State Agencies

At this point, a rather curious procedural twist takes place, with the EEOC deferring to any appropriate state agencies (the majority but not all of the states have appropriate civil rights agencies) and allowing that state agency to try and solve the problem for a certain period of time. At this point, the state procedures take over; they will not be discussed herein except to note that whether or not the state "solves the problem" is irrelevant from the point of view of the EEOC. If the employee is still unhappy with the result, even though the state may have determined that he doesn't have any just cause to believe he was discriminated against, the EEOC can still proceed. See the section "The Practicalities of Enforcement" later in this chapter for further development of this problem.

Notice of the Charge

The commission must serve a notice of the charge on the employer. The notice must include the date, place, and circumstances of the alleged unlawful employment practice and must be served within 10 days.

Investigation

The commission then makes an appropriate investigation. In making the investigation, the commission has all of the authority of the National Labor Relations Board. That authority is spelled out in the National Labor Relations Act and includes the power to examine documents, summon witnesses, take testimony under oath, and obtain court aid in compelling production of evidence in the attendance of witnesses.

Determination

After the investigation, the commission either determines that there is no probable cause to believe there is a violation or that there is such probable cause. If their determination is that there is no such cause, the case is dismissed and the charging party then has a right to institute a civil suit if he desires. If there is probable cause, the commission must endeavor by conciliation, conference, etc., to eliminate the unlawful practice. The commission must make a determination as to the existence of probable cause within 120 days from the time the charge is filed.

Court Action

If conciliation fails, the commission may institute suit against the employer. The commission also has authority to request a temporary injunction if it concludes that prompt judicial action is necessary to carry out the purposes of the act. If the commission does not desire to sue, it will issue a "right to sue" letter to the employee who may then institute a suit himself, either individually or as a representative of a "class." Since attorneys may recover the fees from the defendant if they win, there is some incentive to do this.

Relief

The relief that may be granted by the court includes injunction, reinstatement, and back pay, but is not limited to these. The court may grant any equitable relief it deems appropriate. Back-pay liability, however, may not accrue from a date more than 2 years prior to the date of filing of a charge with the commission, and interim earnings or amounts earnable with reasonable diligence by the person or persons discriminated against, must be used to reduce these back-pay awards. Unfortunately, however, this 2-year period is somewhat misleading because the 2 years starts from the time the employee files the charge and it is sometimes 3 or 4 years before the charge finally gets resolved. Consequently, if the company is found to have discriminated and back pay is awarded, the time period can be 5 or 6 years rather than 2. If the case is appealed through the courts, the time period can even be longer.

Enforcement under the Equal Pay Act

Procedurally, the provisions for enforcement of the Equal Pay Act are not as favorable to employees or their attorneys—particularly when there is a possibility of a class action—as those under Title VII of the Civil Rights Act. In addition, almost everything which would constitute a violation of the Equal Pay Act would also constitute a violation of the Civil Rights Act. However, there may be some cases where a plaintiff would find it advantageous to bring suit under the Equal Pay Act either independently or as part of a suit, alleging violation of the Civil Rights Act also.

If the Department of Labor is given notice of a violation, they may sue directly until October 1, 1979 at which time the EEOC assumes enforcement of this law.

Basically, the enforcement provisions of the Equal Pay Act (being those for the Fair Labor Standards Act, of which it is a part) are as follows.

Suits by Employees

An employee may sue an employer in any court of competent jurisdiction on behalf of himself or on behalf of himself and other employees similarly situated. However, no employee shall be a party plaintiff to any such action unless he gives his consent in writing to become such a party and such consent is filed in the court in which the action is brought.

The employee or employees may recover any amounts due them and an additional equal amount as liquidated damages. They may also be awarded attorney fees.

The right provided the employee to sue, however, terminates if the Secretary of Labor brings an equivalent action.

Suits by the Government

When the employee notifies the Secretary of Labor of a possible liability under the Equal Pay Act, the secretary may bring an action to recover the appropriate amount on behalf of the employee. The secretary may also obtain affirmative injunction relief against an employer.

Enforcement under the Age Discrimination in Employment Act of 1967

Like the Equal Pay Act, the Age Discrimination in Employment Act of 1967 adopts the enforcement procedures of the Fair Labor Standards Act. However, important modifications to that procedure are contained in the Age Discrimination in Employment Act.

Section 7 of the Age Discrimination in Employment Act makes the following modifications to the Fair Labor Standards Act procedures.

1. Liquidated damages may be obtained only in the case of a willful violation. (Under the Fair Labor Standards Act, liquidated or punitive damages in an amount equal to the actual recovery may be obtained.)

2. Before instituting an action, the Secretary of Labor must attempt to eliminate the discriminatory practice and to effect voluntary compliance through informal methods of conciliation, conference, and persuasion.

3. Any person aggrieved may bring a civil action in any court of competent jurisdiction for such legal or equitable relief as will effectuate the purposes of the act, but (a) the right of such person to bring such action terminates upon the commencement of an action by the secretary to enforce the rights of such employee; and (b) the individual must give the secretary 60 days'

written notice of his intention to file suit, and such notice must be filed within 180 days of the alleged violation.

Section 14(b) of the act requires plaintiffs to defer to appropriate state agencies for 60 days before bringing suit in the federal courts. Naturally, the requirement is only applicable where there is a state law prohibiting discrimination in employment because of age and a state authority which can seek relief. The EEOC will assume enforcement of this law October 1, 1979.

The Practicalities of Enforcement

Now that we have gone through the legalistics of the enforcement procedure, let's examine some types of hypothetical cases to see what actually happens.

First, let's take one hypothetical complaint and see how many different avenues of enforcement are available.

The Union Grievance Procedure

If the employee is governed by a collective bargaining agreement and believes that he has been discriminated against, he may file a complaint under the grievance procedure of the union contract and have it processed in the normal way. This, however, will not bar him from also instituting procedures under Title VII if the union grievance procedure does not produce a satisfactory result.

City or Local Agencies

Many cities have local human rights agencies which may be involved in discrimination matters. Sometimes these agencies become involved only when the city is dealing with the company; other times they are "general" and will handle any complaint arising within their jurisdiction. Again, the use of these procedures does not preclude the use of any other procedures.

State Agencies

As indicated above, the majority of the states have civil rights agencies which can process individual complaints.

The Equal Employment Opportunity Commission

Complaints under the Equal Employment Opportunity Commission are handled as above.

The Courts

If all of the administrative agencies fail, the courts are the employee's next step and here there are various levels. Complaints are initially brought in the federal district court and then can be appealed to the circuit courts of appeals.

The Department of Labor and Government Contractors

If an employee of a government contractor believes he has been discriminated against, he may complain to the Department of Labor which will investigate in much the same way as a company being examined for compliance with Order No. 4.

Hypothetical Example

From the above list, it is clear that a person who believes he has been discriminated against has a great many avenues of potential relief. Further, these relief avenues are not mutually exclusive. The employee can proceed down many of them simultaneously and if he loses at any stage he is not precluded from continuing further until all his remedies have been exhausted. This multiplicity of remedies presents one of the major complicating factors in the enforcement process.

The second major complicating factor is that the complaint of any individual employee does not necessarily have anything to do with the final problem the employer might be confronted with. In many cases, for example, an employee will file a complaint with the EEOC. The commission will investigate that complaint and find that the employee had no reasonable grounds to believe that he had been discriminated against, but during the course of the investigation, it often finds information, usually statistical in nature, which indicates that the company might have discriminated against minorities in one or more employment practice. The commission will, therefore, dismiss the individual's complaint but pursue the company for other violations which it discovered during the course of its investigation. Two examples will show how these complicating factors influence the progress of an employment discrimination problem and provide some important background for the final section of this chapter ("Suggestions for Procedures") wherein the procedures a company should use to minimize its problems or to handle complaints are discussed.

In our first example, let's assume a situation where two black employees were discharged for fighting. Assume each files a complaint with the EEOC, which in turn defers to the appropriate state agency. The state agency then investigates the charge. Assume for this discussion that the state agency comes to the conclusion that one or both of the employees have reasonable cause to believe he had been discriminated against, perhaps because of statistics which might indicate that previous cases involving employee fights did not result in discharge. In fact, both the state and federal EEO agencies are generally very zealous in their enforcement and, unless the company can show quite clearly that the action taken was not discriminatory, it is very likely that the civil rights agency involved will hold that it was. Sometimes this whole thing merely amounts to a finding that the employer has not satisfied its burden of proof to show that the action was not discriminatory; in other words, the employer is presumed guilty until he proves himself innocent.

Suppose that in order to settle this case with the state civil rights agency, the employer agrees to reinstate the employee who was least to blame for the particular fight. Let's further assume that this does, in fact, settle the matter with the state agency and the reinstated employee starts back to work—with or without any back pay that might have been agreed upon— but the other employee continues to pursue his remedies with the EEOC. The EEOC then investigates the matter and the company attempts to defend the case on the grounds that it has already been investigated by the state civil rights agency and settled in a manner satisfactory to that agency. This "defense" will not even get to first base with the EEOC. In short, the company will have to go through the whole procedure again, and the fact that they had reached an agreement with the state civil rights agency will not have any substantial bearing on the negotiations between the company and the EEOC. Obviously, the lesson to be learned from this is clear: at the state level, a company should not give anything away in the hope that the matter will be "settled," because it really won't be.

To illustrate the second point, assume the case of a black female who was promoted from the position of secretary to administrative assistant and then discharged from that position when she was found incapable of handling the increased duties. Assume that the employee filed a complaint and it was determined that her complaint had no merit because her discharge was for a cause, the company having satisfied its burden that she did not perform her duties in a satisfactory way and that white employees were treated equally.

These are the essential facts of an actual case where the following determination letter was received from the EEOC. Naturally, the names have been changed and some minor editing has been done, but, in essence, this is an actual and typical determination letter from the EEOC.

> Jennifer J. Johnson
> (address)
>> Charging Party
>> v.
> Franklin Corporation
>> Respondent
> *Determination*
> The Commission has completed the investigation of the subject charge. Having considered the entire record and pursuant to Section 1601.19(b) of the Commission's Procedural Rules (27 Fed. Reg. 70165, September 27, 1972), I issue, on behalf of the Commission, the following determination as to the merits of the subject charge.
>
> Respondent is an employer within the meaning of Title VII and the timeliness and all other jurisdictional requirements have been met.
>
> Charging Party alleges that Respondent engaged in unlawful employment practices in violation of Title VII of the Civil Rights Act of 1964, as amended, by denying her adequate training and discharging her because of her race (Black) and by denying promotional opportunities into the higher positions to Black employees.
>
> It is undisputed that Charging Party was hired on March 3, 1969 as a senior secretary that she was promoted to pricing cost data technician on January 29, 1972, and that she was terminated on April 21, 1972. It is also undisputed that Charging Party filed a grievance on her discharge which was ultimately rejected by Respondent and that she was offered a senior secretary position in lieu of discharge which she rejected.
>
> I. Training/Discharge
> Charging Party contends that she had been a satisfactory employee for three years but that when she moved into the new position, she received insufficient training and poor supervision. She asserts that her supervisor resented her because he was forced to select her and that he inquired of her former supervisor whether she was arrogant and uppity.
>
> Respondent denies the charge and contends that Charging Party received the same adequate on-the-job training as other pricing data technicians. Respondent asserts that Charging Party was a good employee in her former position but that she demonstrated poor performance, poor attitude and inflexibility in the pricing data technician position after repeated counselling.
>
> Charging Party's personnel file and testimony of her former supervisor confirm that she was considered an above average employee while a senior secretary and well qualified for the technician position. Her former supervisor denies that he was asked whether she was uppity or arrogant and states that he was only asked about her abilities.
>
> Charging Party's supervisor who recommended her discharge testifies that he (and not someone else) selected her for the position, that her attitude was unsatisfactory with respect to taking constructive criticism and responding to deadlines and that a White female technician had similar problems and was also discharged.

The senior pricing technician stated that Charging Party was unaccustomed to a pressure position and that she was unwilling to adjust her schedule to such a position.

Charging Party's replacement in the position, also Black, states that she has received adequate training and that it seemed as if Charging Party could not accept constructive criticism. She and two other pricing technicians confirm that training for the position is on-the-job.

The investigation confirmed that a White female technician was also terminated at the same time as Charging Party and for the same reason. The investigation also disclosed that Respondent has discharged two White males for unsatisfactory performance.

Based on the foregoing evidence, especially that White males and a female have been discharged for the same reasons and that Charging Party was offered and declined a senior secretary position in lieu of discharge, we conclude that Charging Party's race was not a factor in her training and discharge, as alleged.

II. Promotional Opportunities

Charging Party alleges that Respondent fails to promote and hire Black employees into the higher level professional and managerial positions because of their race.

Respondent's employment statistics as of the end of December 1971 indicate that for the facility in question, it employed 51 officials and managers, of whom 2 (4%) were Black. There were 154 persons classified as professionals, of whom 3 (2%) were Black. Its total workforce was 12% Black. The 1970 Census statistics reflect that the relevant metropolitan area is approximately 25% Black.

Title VII permits the use of statistical probability to infer the existence of a pattern or practice of discrimination. It is not necessary to decide whether the statistics cited are to be regarded as conclusively showing a violation of the Act or whether they establish a *prima facie* case of discrimination with respect to the employment opportunities of Blacks. Suffice it to say that the pattern of racial discrimination depicted by these statistics has not been rebutted by Respondent. Accordingly, we conclude that Respondent has restricted and limited the employment opportunities of Blacks as a class in violation of Title VII.

Having determined that there is reasonable cause to believe that Respondent has engaged in unlawful employment practices the Commission now invites the parties to join with it in a collective effort toward a just resolution of this matter. We enclose an information sheet entitled "Notice of Conciliation Process" for the attention of each party. A representative of this office will be in contact with each party in the near future to begin the conciliation process. If you are definitely unwilling to enter into conciliation at this time, please so notify this office within 10 days of receipt of this letter and we shall process the case under the Commission's Procedural Regulations, Section 1601.25.

On behalf of the Commission:

Deputy Director

_____ District Office

This letter shows two things. First, it shows what kind of a case a company is going to have to prove in order to get the individual's charge dismissed and, second, it shows that, even assuming it satisfies this proof, the EEOC is very likely to continue with its findings which are set forth under part II of the above letter.

This particular determination letter is a fairly good one because the EEOC has limited their charges to situations which are reasonably related to the complaint filed by the individual (promotional opportunities in the higher levels of employment) and has also told the company the evidence on which it is basing its charges. All EEOC determination letters are not this narrow. In some cases, they go on to cite practices which are not at all related to the individual's charge and they cite discriminatory practices by the company over a very broad range of areas without going into the specific evidence which justifies these findings. Accordingly, this determination letter is not a "horrible example" but in fact is a rather good example of relatively reasonable treatment on the part of the EEOC.

The next step of the enforcement process is "conciliation."

Conciliation is a noun which is derived from the verb conciliate which means (1) to gain goodwill or favor by pleasing acts; (2) to cause to agree; make compatible; (3) to win over; to gain the goodwill of; to make friendly. A synonym is "pacify" and an antonym is "antagonize." Apparently, the EEOC uses a slightly different version of conciliation by which they have assumed that the antonym antagonize applies to them and the synonym pacify applies to everyone else. Accordingly, their procedures seem to be to antagonize the defendant to a sufficient extent that the defendant will pacify the commission. To show what we mean, the following letter is only a slightly abridged version (again, the names were changed and some minor editing was done) of the letter actually received from the EEOC as their invitation to conciliate in the same case as in the above determination letter.

> Re: Jennifer J. Johnson v.
>   Franklin Corporation
> Mr. W. T. Colegrove
>   Counsel
>   Franklin Corporation

Dear Mr. Colegrove:

In accordance with Commission procedures, you are invited to enter into settlement discussions in an effort to resolve the issues which were found to be discriminatory employment practices in the Commission Determination issued in the above cited charge on July 16, 1975.

In order to resolve the cause finding of the Commission's Determination, conciliation will have to deal primarily with the establishment and the implementation of percentage goals for the hiring and upgrading of Blacks into the higher level professional and managerial positions so as to insure that Blacks will have equal representation in all positions in these classifications within a two-year timetable.

Commission procedures further require that I point out that conciliation discussions must be confined to a mutual setting forth of settlement terms to be incorporated into a Conciliation Agreement which must meet the Commission's Minimum Guidelines for Conciliation and is acceptable to all parties.

Therefore, it is important that all concerned parties are made aware that during our settlement discussions we will not include aspects of the investigation which served as the foundation for the Commission Determination, nor will we debate the findings of the Determination upon which the Conciliation Agreement must be based. The Commission regards the Determination as a final document and not subject to revisions.

Should you decide to avail yourself of the opportunity to close this case by entering into a Conciliation Agreement, please advise me of your interest, in writing, within ten (10) days of receipt of this invitation.

Thank you for your attention to this matter.

> Sincerely,
> Mary A. Smith
> Conciliator

Of particular interest are paragraphs two and three of the letter. Apparently, the commission is saying that while they would like the company to conciliate they are not willing to discuss any of the facts; they are going to presume the company guilty, and the only way the company can engage in conciliation is if it will pacify the commission by agreeing to whatever they feel is appropriate remedial action, irrespective of the fact of existence of any discrimination in the first place.

Nevertheless, most counsel have developed a reasonably acceptable way of handling this kind of a problem. They send the EEOC a response to their "invitation to conciliation" which is essentially a restatement of the good points of the case. Assuming the company has legitimate arguments to make in support of its position, these arguments, made in this response, then become part of the record. Whether or not the matter can be successfully conciliated, the company is not placed in the adverse position of refusing to conciliate and, at the same time, the EEOC records and files are supplemented with the company's side of the story. Thus those people higher up on the ladder who will eventually make the decision of whether or not to institute a suit against the company, have both sides of the story. If the company's story is a good one, EEOC lawyers are not likely to file suit because they don't like to waste their time and lose cases just as company attorneys don't. Accordingly, the procedure seems to work about as well as anything which could be designed given the posture of the EEOC.

In this case, for example, it should be noted that the figures the EEOC are using are 1971 figures even though the date of the letter is 1975. This is necessary from their point of view because of the fact that the charge was filed in 1972 and they can't very well use 1975 figures for this charge because it is possible that they might be overlooking three years of discrimination. However, it is also possible that the company has made sufficient progress since 1971 to achieve good representation in these areas as of 1975 and in this situation, the EEOC's charges might be moot.

There are a number of other typical arguments which a company could make. For example, the EEOC has used the minority population of entire metropolitan areas, and the particular location in question was actually a rather distant suburb of the city. Accordingly, the relevant population statistics are subject to a considerable amount of debate. Usually, the EEOC will use whatever statistics give them the best case and the company, of course, will do the same. Obviously, the right thing to do is to use the statistics from the area in which the company actually does its recruiting. For some jobs, this may be national; for some it may, in fact, be a large metropolitan district, but for most it is going to be the area within a reasonable commuting distance of the facility. This is the position which would probably be used by most courts.

Another typical problem is that the total minority work force might not be a relevant statistic. For example, if the company involved was a high-technology company and the positions of managers, professionals, etc., required a technical degree, the total number of minorities in the work force would not be a relevant statistic—the relevant statistic would be the total number of minorities in the work force in the relevant population which actually had the required qualifications.

In summary, the EEOC generally presents a one-sided view of their case and it is up to the company to present the other side. If the company feels that the EEOC "investigation" is objective and fair, or even if the EEOC is attempting to be objective and fair, it is unfortunately sadly mistaken. This may be a sad commentary on the use of our tax dollars, but it is a fact of life which companies and their counsel and management must keep in mind.

Up to this point, we have discussed the practicalities of the enforcement process up to the point the case gets to court. If and when the case does get to court, some new considerations emerge. If the case is filed on behalf of an individual claimant alleging treatment involving that person, it will rarely present a substantial financial liability to the company. Often it could be settled for a modest amount of money, perhaps less than the costs of defending it. However, this presents two problems. The first is the employee relations aspect of paying a person who presents a charge which the company considers to be without merit and the second is that the company cannot let itself get the reputation of being an easy mark so that any minority employee can simply file a charge and eventually extract one or two thousand dollars from the company in settlement. Also, there will, of course, be emotional aspects to the case. There is no "right" or "wrong" approach to handling individual cases.

However, cases which might develop into class actions are an entirely different matter. Here, there is no room whatsoever for emotions or principle. Management and counsel must realistically evaluate the merits of the case and, if the plaintiff and the class the plaintiff could represent have a legitimate complaint, settlement should be carefully considered. On the other hand, the company cannot panic and throw good judgment to the winds whenever they receive a legal document threatening a class action. From management's point of view, however, the words "class action" should be a red flag which should cause careful supervision of the matter and insistence on the proper quantity and quality of legal attention. Also, it is a management problem in the sense that an adverse judgment could cost a lot of money and thrust the company into a legal war with all the costs in the form of drained management attention and legal fees which are involved in such an important confrontation.

The same situation would exist if the EEOC itself rather than a single private plaintiff were to institute suit. In either of these situations, the company should give the matter top priority and should first endeavor to resolve the conflict short of all-out war, and, if this is not possible, the company must be sure to commit whatever legal and management resources are necessary to properly fight that war. The potential for sizable judgments against the company, not to mention burdensome requirements to hire and promote given numbers or percentages of minorities in the future, are grave risks indeed and "war" is not too strong a term to use in this context.

Suggestions for Procedures

It should be apparent that the EEO area requires attention from both management and the lawyers on a continuing basis. Following is a discussion of some of the factors which might be considered in deciding just what that management and legal participation should be at given levels.

The Complaint Process

The first question companies must address is the stage in the complaint process at which counsel should personally take an active role in the problem. It is useful to make a few general observations, some of which contradict each other in terms of their implications regarding the question of legal involvement.

First, in many cases, employees who may be aggrieved on the basis of some EEO question may be able to be satisfied by some relatively simple action on the part of the company, perhaps involving nothing more than common sense or good employee relations. To bring a lawyer into this kind of situation obviously increases the chance of the other parties doing the same, which increases the chance of escalating a minor problem into a big one.

Second, almost all EEO cases involve a considerable number of stages of the enforcement process, usually state enforcement bodies first, the EEOC next, and then the courts. Therefore, it is very difficult to judge the seriousness of any complaint at the early stages because literally any complaint can be escalated into a serious class action, possibly even in cases where the complainant himself has not even been the victim of any discriminatory conduct. Therefore, there is no such thing as a nonserious EEO case, even though the implications of some particular cases, when they are being discussed at the state or local level, may not seem too important.

Third, as in all legal matters, record building is very important. Experience has shown two things to be present in the overwhelming majority of EEO matters. (1) There are two sides to the story: Very rarely in this day and age does a company discharge or refuse to hire or promote people because of their minority status. The problem is almost always one step more complicated, involving some action which was taken against a minority and which may not have been taken in similar circumstances with nonminorities or which, while not discriminatory on its face, may have a discriminatory effect. This, in turn, means that the company will almost always have some good arguments which it can make in justifying the actions it took in a particular situation, and this is exactly the kind of thing lawyers are trained for and personnel people are not. (2) The EEOC or other investigatory body will almost always want to go far beyond the facts involved in the original complaint and, if this is done, there are almost certainly some statistical facts somewhere in the facility which will seem to present some discrimination question. As a practical matter, it is very unlikely that a company can completely satisfy all EEO requirements.

Fourth, some EEOC personnel and other compliance enforcement people in this area have a very unfortunate attitude somewhat reminiscent of the old witch-hunt days of Joe McCarthy and the Communists. These people convey the impression that unless the company agrees to anything they suggest, the company must be guilty of bigotry in the extreme. This impression has two unfortunate implications: (1) it is intimidating to personnel people who are not used to dealing in this kind of atmosphere; and (2) if the company has the temerity to get the lawyers involved (even though almost all EEOC compliance officers are lawyers or at least have legal training), the EEOC feels particularly insulted, especially if the lawyers resist them at all in the normal legalistic manner of good-faith negotiations on various points.

Fifth, one theory is "it doesn't matter who does it—just make sure it's done right." Logically, the handling of EEO complaints should be done in a rather careful manner which builds the best record possible and, hopefully, does not antagonize people so that the matter is continued "on principle" rather than on the merits. Theoretically, it should not matter whether the person handling the problem has a law degree or not. However, experience has shown that somehow the lawyers must get involved in complaints at an early stage if they are to be handled in a manner which will provide any kind of useful record in subsequent proceedings. The outcome of any EEO case depends heavily on behind-the-scenes work which the lawyers can supervise. While it may sound good to say that the lawyers will simply write a policy of how EEO matters are to be handled and then the personnel people will actually do it until the matter gets into court, something will be lost in this process, and it is exactly this tradeoff we are talking about: is it best to have the best possible legal approach from the beginning or is it best to sacrifice some legal content in order to reduce legal fees, reduce the "confrontation" atmosphere which is sometimes created by legal involvement, and to maximize the personnel relations aspects of the problem rather than the legal implications?

What this all boils down to is a situation where legal involvement can be either beneficial or detrimental to the company, and it is sometimes very difficult to know just when and how lawyers should participate in the front lines of an EEO battle. If the lawyers do not participate until the matter actually gets to court, they risk having the company steamrollered into completely unrealistic and unnecessary consent orders with the EEOC, possibly including back-pay awards, and, in addition, possibly having a poor record created in the agency proceedings. If the lawyers come in at the very first stages, they may increase the legal costs and, in addition, run the risk of escalating a matter which might be settled in a friendly manner into a full-scale battle which drains the resources of the company, increases legal fees, and may even come out worse than the initial settlement proposals.

With the benefit of the above comments, following are some specific observations on what legal involvement might be appropriate for each of the stages listed above.

Internal Company Grievance Procedure   The lawyers should have assisted in drafting and planning the internal company grievance procedure so that it assures the employees a meaningful chance to present their side of any argument. At the same time, the lawyers should have participated in the education of company people who are handling the grievance so that they present fairly and honestly the company's side of the story and do not take the position that either the matter is entirely within the company's discretion and the employee is somehow "out of line" by using the grievance procedure (if this is the attitude, you should not have an internal grievance procedure) or the attitude that the employee's feelings must not be hurt. Part of the grievance procedure must be an understanding by the employee that he will be told the truth about his performance and the reasons for any action that was taken, and possibly will be less than pleased to hear all of this.

In summary, at the stage of internal company grievance procedures, it would seem that the lawyers should not be involved in the front lines, but should be involved behind the scenes in establishing and adjusting the procedures as necessary, in training the personnel people, and in making sure that the grievance procedure is a meaningful tool. If the lawyers feel that the procedure is there only "for show" they should counsel strongly against having any internal grievance policy at all because it is bound to create hostility.

Union Grievance Procedure   Employees have the right to present EEO complaints to their union and have the matter resolved through normal grievance procedures. Generally, the same comments would seem to be applicable to a union procedure as to a company procedure, except that there is no choice on whether or not to have one at all, so the lawyers must make sure union grievances in the EEO area are fairly heard and considered in good faith. Again, however, it would seem appropriate to have the lawyers stay behind the scenes at this stage.

Local Enforcement Agencies   Some cities have local agencies which work in the EEO area. Some of these local agencies are "general" in that they will handle complaints from any employee within their jurisdiction, and others are limited to making sure that contractors who do business with the city satisfy the relevant EEO requirements.

The question of whether or not to get a lawyer involved in the front lines of this kind of a proceeding depends on all the facts. Generally, it would seem that it would not be necessary to have legal counsel represent the company in a matter where the local enforcement is general and the complaint can be handled by the personnel people who have been properly counseled and where there is no legal record made which might have weight with a higher enforcement body. However, there should be some consideration given to legal representation at any hearings or at least legal review of any material to be presented at the hearings by the personnel people. The choice should be on a case-by-case basis.

State Enforcement Agencies   At a stage where state enforcement agencies are involved, EEO problems must be considered to be not only serious, but to have a significant degree of legality involved. Basically, this is because if there is a state enforcement agency, the EEOC is required by law to defer to that state agency and allow them to try to make an acceptable agreement for the complainant. Also, many state enforcement agencies have considerable enforcement authority in their own right. In addition to all of that, many state enforcement people are themselves lawyers, and the process tends to take on more of a legal tone at this stage. Accordingly, it would seem appropriate to have legal counsel involved in any EEO complaint which was being considered by the relevant state enforcement body.

If counsel is not involved the record in the state enforcement proceeding might be less than adequate, and the state enforcement might include future state court action which would be prejudiced by the bad record in the enforcement agency. More likely, a bad record in the state enforcement agency might cause the people in authority to decide to bring a court case in a situation where, had the record been better, no court action would have been brought at all. This latter point is very important and is equally applicable in the context of the EEOC. Generally, both state and federal EEOC investigators do not have authority to bring a suit against a company. Instead, they are limited to investigation and attempts to reach a conciliation. The decision on whether to bring suit rests with higher people. These higher people are going to base their decision of whether or not to bring suit on two things, the recommendation of the investigator and the file. Furthermore, it is these higher level people who are generally going to have to personally try the case or be responsible for its outcome. Since we can assume that lawyers generally do not like to lose cases, it is probable that if the file shows a good defense on the part of the company, the higher level people in the enforcement agency are going to be more reluctant to bring a lawsuit than if the record or file is very skimpy and all they have to go on is the recommendation of the investigating officer. In summary, counsel's main job in these investigatory processes is to *make sure the record contains all the good points he can make.*

Should you be tough or conciliatory? Basically, it seems to be generally agreed that, since a resolution of the matter at the state level is not often going to be the end of the matter anyway, it is not a good idea to give away anything at this level just to settle the case, because it will not really be settled. However, within this broad guideline there is considerable disagreement as to whether it is best to negotiate in a friendly conciliatory manner, without giving up anything unjustified, or to take a very tough attitude. Generally, this decision will depend on the temperament and style of the parties, and there is no one approach which is "better" than another. However, it is suggested that management be wary of attorneys who take the same posture in all cases. Generally, the best procedure is to carefully evaluate the case, the opponent, and then take whichever approach seems to be most likely to produce the desired result.

Equal Employment Opportunity Commission   Much of what was said above goes also for the EEOC with the exception of the following: generally, the settlement of the matter with the EEOC will dispose of the case, unlike the lower stages where settlement only disposes of the particular agency, not the entire case.

At this level, it is therefore necessary to carefully weigh the trial risks, and this is generally best done by lawyers. Therefore, it is submitted that the lawyer in charge supervise any dispute with the EEOC although it is proper, in some cases, to have the personnel people continue the actual negotiations. Another thing to keep in mind is that the EEOC enforcement powers are substantial. Almost all of their investigators are lawyers, and if your company enters this area unarmed with some good legal talent, it is almost bound to come out with some substantial wounds. Again, there is the question of whether one should be tough or conciliatory or use the two approaches in some kind of combination. Essentially, however, when the EEOC enters the picture, careful consideration must be given to good-quality legal attention because otherwise a simple matter can get out of hand in short order. The example of the secretary discussed under "the enforcement process" illustrates the problem.

OFCC and Other Government Contractor Problems   EEO matters relating to government contractors are entirely different from those which are handled by the EEOC or state enforcement officials.

The consequences of an adverse finding can be extremely disastrous to a substantial government contractor. Therefore, the company's affirmative action plans and the process for handling review of them by government compliance officers are very important. The considerations are essentially nonlegal; therefore, it would seem that the appropriate way to handle government reviews of the company affirmative action programs is through the personnel department rather than the legal department, with the caveat that the legal department should be responsible for educating those responsible for handling the government review of the legal implication involved. Following are some comments on the laws and practicalities.

A finding of noncompliance at any plant can cut off the entire corporation from government contracts until the matter is resolved. Consequently, the subject is equally important for all plants within the company, not just those engaged in government work.

Generally, the compliance review will start with a review of the company's affirmative action plan, and the compliance reviewer should be depended upon to say that the plan is entirely inadequate. Quite frankly, many of them are and the compliance officer is correct. An examination of Order No. 4 and a comparison with many affirmative action plans reveals that they simply lack a large number of essential components. Sometimes a company will have an affirmative action plan which does have all the necessary ingredients, but not in the order or format required by Order No. 4. The company will then resist a claim that their plan is not adequate and attempt to show how it really does satisfy all the requirements. This procedure violates two fundamental principles in dealing with bureaucrats.

1. Make their job of reviewing your plan easy by putting the right provisions in the right place, numbering them properly and referencing the paragraphs of Order No. 4 in the same sequence as contained in Order No. 4.

2. When a bureaucrat objects to the form of your plan, it is usually far easier in the long run to simply redo the plan in the form called for by Order No.

4 than to fight with him. The compliance officer is almost always going to have his own personal interests and will want these taken care of in the plan. Since the regulations are so detailed and complex, even a plan which passes a review by one compliance officer one year may run into substantial difficulties the next year if another compliance officer reviews it.

In the overwhelming majority of cases, the compliance officer will give the company only a short time to fix the plan to his satisfaction, and the company people will almost always feel that they are being unnecessarily pushed around by the compliance people in this regard. This, however, is a fact of life which they should just learn to live with, and they should expend whatever efforts are required to bring their plan into compliance in the short interval allowed. Generally, it is better in the long run to spend this effort in one intensive session than to drag it out. One technique which is useful is to have the compliance officer out a day or so before the final version of the plan is typed so that he can review what you have done to that point. This shows that you are genuinely trying to do what is required and also saves a possible last-minute confrontation where the risk of a show cause letter is increased.

The compliance officers will ask for a great deal of information in a certain form and many times will keep on asking for more information in slightly different forms. In some cases, this may seem like a never-ending process. The more information you give, the more they want. However, experience has shown that if company people take a realistic view of the information a compliance officer should have, supply him all of that information, and then stand their ground when additional requests for unnecessarily detailed or irrelevant information are made, the matter can be resolved to the satisfaction of both parties, and the compliance officer will back off from requests for additional information if he cannot show the need for it.

Basically, the review of an affirmative action plan by government agencies and the handling of that process by company people involves the art of negotiation. People should be assigned accordingly. It does no good to lose one's temper, to be unresponsive or defensive, nor to unnecessarily aggravate a compliance officer who admittedly may not be the world's most amiable individual himself. On the other hand, if one does not stand one's ground when warranted, one is likely to be steamrollered by a compliance officer into the following adverse situations: (1) having a plan with goals which are not realistically attainable, thus causing a problem the next time the plan is reviewed, and (2) having a plan which contains unnecessarily self-incriminating statements about affected classes, thus giving the government and possible private plaintiffs grounds for legal action involving back pay. (Remember that the question of the availability of the company's affirmative action plan to private parties is far from settled, and many cases under the Freedom of Information Act have held that at least parts of the plan are available to the public.)

In preparing the affirmative action plan, there should be a very specific attempt to comply with the literal wording of the regulations. Sometimes there is a tendency to think that the regulations could be "improved upon," but this is generally not a good idea. There is the typical bureaucratic tendency to judge affirmative action plans on the mechanical comparison of the plan with the regulations on a paragraph-by-paragraph basis, and if the plan does not "track," some unnecessary problems might be presented.

In preparing the substantive aspects of the plan (the goals and timetables) care must be taken not to promise too much because you may later have to defend your failure to achieve those goals, and you may be accused of "bad faith" if you fall too far short of your goals. Also, if you "try too hard" you might run into the reverse discrimination problem. Of course, this can be used in negotiations with the government compliance officers. Goals must be realistic and attainable, and if the compliance officer forces you into unrealistic goals, the only way you will be able to attain them is to engage in reverse discrimination. This can be pointed out, perhaps in writing, and used as a negotiation point. The thrust is, "Of course the compliance officer does not want you to engage in reverse discrimination—does he?"

A very important part of drafting affirmative action plans is to avoid admissions. The regulations invite admissions, and these can be disastrous in litigation. This is a very important point—personnel people must be informed of the fact that affirmative action plans must be judged as *litigation documents* because they frequently wind up in the hands of the EEOC or private litigants. At least most of a company's affirmative action program will probably be available under the Freedom of Information Act (or normal discovery rules). For example, affirmative action plans which contain provisions like, "We acknowledge that traditional attitudes held by management have played a role in preventing hiring and/or promotion of females and minorities" may sit very well with the compliance officer, but this would cause substantial difficulties in litigation at a later time because you have admitted that your management has attitudes which cause discrimination. Also, statements like, "We acknowledge that seniority systems of the company have inhibited transfers of females to higher paying jobs" should be avoided because they tend to establish an "affected class" and are very difficult to rebut in court.

Instead, statements in the affirmative action plan should be made as positive as possible. For example, one should state in a case where improvement may be indicated something like: "While we have engaged in affirmative action to recruit minorities for the (insert job classification), we find that the number of minorities in this classification is less than we would like, and we, therefore, plan to increase our efforts in the future to recruit additional minorities for this classification." In other words, make the statements positive attempts at affirmative action rather than admissions of discrimination or discriminatory treatment in the past.

Affirmative action plans should have legal department review because lawyers are trained in this area of party admissions, and it is very difficult to spot all such statements, even with a lawyer looking over the plan. Many companies will routinely send all contracts over $10,000 to the legal department for review, but an affirmative action plan which may involve many millions of dollars in government contracts, back pay, or other problems will be prepared without any legal attention whatsoever. This would appear to be an improper allocation of priorities and should be changed.

There are also benefits to be derived from including participation of the legal department in on-site reviews. Compliance officers are accustomed to throwing their weight around a little, and the company personnel people may not be as thoroughly familiar with the regulations as the compliance people, so they will have no practical choice but to take the compliance officer's word on what something means, what is required, what the plan should say, etc. Accordingly, having a lawyer who can look at the regulation, read it, and speak with some authority as to what it means is sometimes helpful.

A *complete record* should be maintained of everything the reviewing officer says and everything copied by the reviewing officer. This is important because sometimes the reviewing officers will go back to their boss or rethink the problem later and come to a different conclusion and want to "remake the record." Therefore, if the reviewing officer asks for something, it is desirable to make a memorandum as to exactly what he asks for so that you do not have to depend on memory at a later time.

Communication should be a two-way street. It should be observed that the regulations *require* the compliance officers to work with the company to get an acceptable affirmative action program. Accordingly, if you make them spell out exactly what they require, in terms of a written memorandum or letter, this is helpful. For example, if the compliance officer wants additional data or further elaboration on some point, it is useful to write the compliance officer a letter and make him explain precisely what he wants.

Companies should make a complete attempt to provide data which are requested and to avoid apologies for failure to achieve goals. Naturally, there are limits here, and the compliance officers sometimes request duplicate data, data which have already been supplied in another form, or data which really are not relevant. While there are some limits, it would appear that if a company has to compromise on something, it should be in this data area. There are regulations which require the compliance officer to ask for data in the form that the company usually maintains them (as opposed to requiring the company to "create" data), and compliance officers are only entitled to ask for necessary information. On the other hand, there are no administrative tools which the company can use because the compliance officers are entitled to any data they ask for. If there is a question involving whether or not they are entitled to the data, the company's only remedy is to supply what is requested and then object. This is not entirely a fruitless endeavor because if the company objects, the data are considered a part of an "investigation file" and are not public, whereas if the information is supplied without any objection, it may be made available to a private plaintiff, to the EEOC, or otherwise under the Freedom of Information Act.

Companies should be firm in their insistence that the compliance agency specify any areas about which there are questions. They should make a written record of their belief that they think they are in compliance and their willingness to cooperate, but should adhere to their right to have explained to them *exactly* what the agency believes they are doing or not doing in violation of the regulations. Accordingly, if there are negotiations on an on-site review which are troublesome, the company should not hesitate to write a letter and ask the agency to explain clearly what they want done. It is helpful to start the letter by setting forth a willingness to cooperate and the necessity for having the views of the agency in order to cooperate. This traces the regulations which impose a burden on the agency to negotiate with the company, and the agency will have difficulty saying that they negotiated if they cannot produce a writing which says what they wanted done.

The first thing to do is to ascertain exactly what set of rules is in operation. Basically, there are two: one is the preaward clearance procedure and the second is the normal affirmative action plan reviews. The difference is quite substantial because in a preaward clearance procedure, the company is much more at the government's mercy than in a normal compliance review. The preaward compliance review procedure is contained in section 60–1.20(d), which provides as follows:

> (d) Each agency shall include in the invitation for bids for each formally advertised nonconstruction contract or state at the outset of negotiations for each negotiated contract, that if the award, when let, should exceed the amount of $1 million or more, the prospective contractor and his known first-tier subcontractors with subcontracts of $1 million or more will be subject to a compliance review

before the award of the contract. No such contract shall be awarded unless a pre-award compliance review of the prospective contractor and his known first-tier $1 million subcontractors has been conducted by the compliance agency within 12 months prior to the award. If an agency other than the awarding agency is the compliance agency, the awarding agency will notify the compliance agency and request appropriate action and findings in accordance with this subsection. Compliance agencies will provide awarding agencies with written reports of compliance within 30 days following the request. In order to qualify for the award of a contract, a contractor and such first-tier subcontractors must be found to be in compliance pursuant to paragraph (b) of this section, and with Part 60–2 of these regulations.

The situation is, then, that before an award of a new contract over $1 million can be made, the government is entitled to have a preaward compliance review, and it does not appear that it is incumbent on them to use *either* the administrative procedures set forth in the appropriate regulations or the detailed show cause procedures which are set forth in the amendments to Order No. 4. Instead, they are operating under the above paragraph which says that, "In order to qualify for the award of a contract, a contractor . . . must be found in compliance pursuant to paragraph (b). . . ." That paragraph simply says that, "Where deficiencies are found to exist, reasonable efforts shall be made to secure compliance through conciliation and persuasion. Before the contractor can be found to be in compliance with the order, it must make a specific commitment, in writing, to correct any such deficiencies." There are no "due process" safeguards in any of the provisions applicable to a preaward clearance.

Assuming, however, that one is in the position of having a normal ongoing compliance review rather than a preaward clearance, the contractor is entitled to various administrative and due process procedures in the regulations and has a set of options open to him. A useful procedure for analyzing these options would be to look at a recent case which can illustrate most of the problems. This is the case of *Timken Co. v. Vaughan* (11 EPD par. 10,906 N.D. Ohio, 1976). (As background, it is useful to note that the government dropped their appeal of the *Timken* case and stated publicly that it was a case that never should have been brought in the first place. On the other hand, we are using the *Timken* case for illustrative purposes, not necessarily to discuss the specific facts of the case, although it concerns a problem which we understand occurs with some degree of frequency.)

Essentially, the problem in the *Timken* case was a difference of opinion between Timken and the government on the proper geographic area which Timken should use for recruiting its employees. The government contended they should use an area which included a nearby city which greatly increased the minority population, and Timken said that they should use the area from which they actually recruited their employees. Obviously, Timken's argument was reasonable. The government should require the company to use the statistics from the geographic area from which they actually do recruit their employees, and the government should not be entitled arbitrarily to pick whatever geographic area they would like to impose on the government contractor irrespective of the actual recruitment area. The U.S. District Court of Ohio so held on May 4, 1976. It is useful to back up a bit, however, and put ourselves in Timken's position when the government made this assertion. The compliance officer was acting upon an internal government directive which provided essentially that compliance officers should use whatever area gave the maximum minority population. Timken then had the following options:

1. Accede to the government; e.g., use the government-imposed geographic area and then try to meet the very high goals which would be imposed by using these numbers for the next year.

2. Fail to reach any agreement with the government and allow them to issue a show cause letter and proceed with the normal show cause procedures, and if those show cause procedures did not result in a solution satisfactory to Timken, appeal them to the court. This is, in fact, the course of action which Timken used.

3. Attempt to have the matter dealt with at a hearing within the meaning of section 1.26 and the rules of practice which were described above.

4. Change the plan as required by the government and then file another request for a hearing, after the fact, under the provisions of section 60–1.24(c)(4), which provides as follows:
    When a prime contractor or subcontractor, without a hearing, shall have complied with the recommendations or orders of an agency or a director and believes such recommendations or orders to be erroneous, he shall, upon filing a request therefore within ten days of such compliance, be afforded an opportunity for a hearing and review of the alleged erroneous action by the agency or the director.

(This procedure is also referenced in paragraph 60–60.6 under Order No. 14 which establishes uniform reviewing practices for government contractors.)

There may be some other options. Under some circumstances it might be possible to get into court before the government has actually declared the company to be either nonresponsible or to have failed to satisfy the show cause requirements; but, given the normal practice of most courts to require exhaustion of administrative remedies before they will entertain a discussion of the merits of the case, it would seem that this kind of a procedure would be difficult to use unless it was apparent from the beginning that the government was really acting in an almost outrageous manner.

Each of the above alternatives has its advantages and disadvantages. It would appear, however, that in most cases, the fourth option has a great deal of merit. Proceeding down the list, it seems that the options have the following aspects.

The first option of simply caving in does not really have any problem at all for one year. It is one year later when the compliance reviewer comes back and you have not met the goals where you have the problem. However, at that point, the problem may be very severe because if you have allowed the compliance officer to talk you into goals which you have failed to meet by a wide margin, you may have an allegation of bad faith, which would be difficult to refute, in addition to perhaps "accelerated goals" for the year after. In other words, caving in the first time may eliminate the problem temporarily, but you are likely to be digging yourself a rather large hole, depending upon future events.

The show cause procedure has a tremendous amount of practical difficulty because, during the show cause proceedings, each agency must continue to determine whether the company is in compliance with the equal opportunity requirements. Given the general bureaucratic state of affairs, one can imagine how likely it is to be awarded a contract where he is on the show cause problem list. A government official sitting in his office with a choice between a bid which has no problems and one which requires him to stick his neck out and say that the contract is awardable in the face of a show cause proceeding which has already been instituted is more likely to simply avoid that problem and issue the contract to the competitor without the show cause problem. Further, you may not even be able to show that this is happening.

In most cases, the issuance of a contract is somewhat subjective, and the government usually has a fairly wide latitude on issuing contracts where the bids are fairly close. In addition, if you press the matter, the awarding officer may simply state that he is unable to show that you are in compliance, and therefore, he is unable to award you the contract. *At best, delays* in the issuance of contracts can be expected.

The hearing procedures of section 60–1.26 and the appropriate rules of practice are at this point an untried set of rules, and it is not clear how they will work in practice. As indicated, the problem with government regulations in this area has never been their precise wording. Even show cause practices would seem to be fair on their face; it is only in their implementation that they become arbitrary and unreasonable. On the one hand, the hearing process "seems fair" and you are entitled to a hearing before any adverse action is taken. On the other hand, given the normal bureaucratic problems in this area, it would appear at this point that this is a conclusion which cannot be stated with any degree of certainty. It must be observed that this whole hearing process takes place in the context of an elaborate network of government communications between and among the agencies that the company has an EEO problem. Thus, the issuance of new contracts and the issuance of changes or modifications to existing contracts may be delayed. In extreme cases, contracts which the company may have obtained may actually be given to a competitor during this process simply because of government officials being afraid to enter into any kind of arrangement which might later be questioned when there is a "safe" alternative. In most cases, costly delays will be the largest problem.

We then get down to the fourth option, which is essentially cave in and complain about it. However, as we have seen by discussion of option one, the only problem with caving in is that you are going to get into trouble during the next compliance review. Accordingly, if you can cave in and not get into trouble a year later when the compliance officer comes back, you would seem to have avoided all of the problems, not to mention a great deal of time, energy, and attorney's fees. The after-the-fact hearing may, in fact, provide this result. If you win the hearing, you would appear to be on safe ground. If you lose the hearing, you would appear not to be in any worse position than had you undertaken any of the other alternatives. After all, if you do have a decision on the merits, which was reached in a reasonable way after a proper hearing, always subject to court review if you want it, you really do not have very much to complain about. If, on the other hand, you have asked for a hearing and have not received it, or have received notice that you will be awarded a hearing but do not have a final result from that hearing when the next compliance review process occurs, it would appear that you have at least protected yourself to the maximum extent possible, and you are in no worse position than had you exercised one of your more drastic alternatives of allowing the show cause to proceed or requesting the hearing. This latter point is not at all unlikely because asking for a hearing does not mean you will get one, and if you do get one, it is not at all clear that you will get a timely one.

Pending the hearing, the company should, of course, exercise all reasonable affirmative action efforts and *document those efforts*. Many times, the affirmative action efforts exercised by a company do not yield the benefits they should in a compliance review because the company is unable to document those efforts. When you know you are going to have a hearing, the personnel people ought to have a stronger incentive to exercise good affirmative action efforts and take the time to document them.

One thing does appear clear, and that is that the incidence of "problems" in affirmative action compliance reviews is getting high enough that counsel really should have a list of alternatives available for application in any given situation before a problem arises. Accordingly, it would appear that a thorough analysis of the new regulations, and a reevaluation of the provisions which are carried over from the old ones, together with some discussion between counsel and the company as to what its policies ought to be, is appropriate. It would also appear that a reexamination of the question of when and to what extent counsel should participate in the affirmative action compliance review process would be appropriate.

Litigation

When the matter gets to court, there is no doubt that it should be handled by the lawyers, and the only question is of the use of in-house or centralized counsel as opposed to the use of local counsel in each area or a combination of the two. That question will, therefore, be addressed at this point.

To begin with, a distinction might be drawn between individual claims and class actions potentially involving large sums of money. Obviously, there is a big difference, but the question of what this difference means depends to a considerable extent on the organization of the company, its legal department, and the desires and abilities of the company's lawyers in the EEO area.

In any event, one thing is abundantly clear. Each company should have one lawyer who is responsible for all EEO matters. Whether this is a lawyer employed by the company or whether it is outside counsel depends on the size of the company and the number of problems it has. Also, whether this lawyer takes an active part in the handling of each claim depends on the desires of the lawyer, the company, and the abilities of the lawyer. However, management must have one central source where they can go to ascertain the status of all pending EEO complaints, who is handling them, what the likely outcome might be, and whether they are being handled in an efficient way for the company.

Starting with the assumption that the company is going to have one lawyer in overall charge of its EEO matters, the next question is whether individual EEO complaints are best handled by salaried company lawyers, the company's general law firm, or by local lawyers in the cities involved. Naturally, the volume of complaints and the diversity of the company's operations are going to be relevant factors in this decision, and no single approach is going to be best for every company. However, unless the company has plants in only one city, it would appear that the following generalities lead to only one conclusion.

1. If the plants are widely diversified in many jurisdictions, local counsel can make a good contribution because of his knowledge of the local courts and local EEOC enforcement people. Also, simple logistics dictates the need for local counsel in this context.

2. No local counsel is going to be entirely familiar with the company's overall situation, including other possible problems at other plants, and, therefore, one central lawyer is going to have to keep track of what is going on and advise local counsel of any other claims which might be made in other jurisdictions which might be similar to the one he is handling.

Therefore, it seems clear that most companies are going to require the services of both centralized and local lawyers. The only question is the degree to which the company wants to commit its centralized lawyers to the EEO front. It is submitted that if the volume of work warrants it (and in most larger companies, it certainly will), it is highly advantageous to have one EEO lawyer participate in as many EEO claims as possible for the following reasons.

First, as pointed out above, almost all EEO claims start out at the state enforcement level, and these state proceedings are not overly technical or detailed and the company's lawyer can do a pretty good job of representing the client, especially if he does all the spade work, prepares the necessary documents, etc., and then gets local counsel to appear with him to contribute local counsel's knowledge of the procedures, the people, and to avoid the "local versus out-of-towner" atmosphere.

When the matter gets to the EEOC, there is no reason why centralized company counsel cannot handle the matter with the help of the company's personnel people. If the company's lawyers do a good job and the personnel people are properly used and trained, the overall defense of EEO matters will be superior to having it done by local counsel in various different cities without a coordinated approach.

When the matter gets to court, the defense should be handled *principally* by the local lawyers who should be familiar with the local rules, etc., but supported by company counsel again to provide the coordinated approach.

A frequent mistake made by large companies is to look upon EEO complaints as any other local case and assign outside counsel to "defend" it before the state, federal, and court bodies. The company's central counsel then keeps a file and docket sheet on all of these cases and "hopes for the best." This approach has the following drawbacks.

First, if the volume of EEO litigation is large, it is very costly. Local counsel is going to have to do a lot of work in investigating files, preparing affidavits, etc., that the company lawyers or personnel people could do at less cost. Further, if the company lawyers or personnel people were doing it, they would have a much better understanding of the problem. It would not be looked upon as something unavoidable.

Second, if the company lawyers or personnel people are doing their jobs right, they should be looking for potential trouble spots where EEO compliance might really be a problem. Outside counsel, on the other hand, is simply out to defend the case, and while they may point out some attitudinal problems in passing, they generally view their charter quite properly, as one of doing the assigned job, which is to defend the case. The company's central lawyer should, however, have a different approach and, while defending the case is paramount, he should make note of any possible attitudinal problems or other discriminatory practices and make sure appropriate corrective or training action is taken.

Third, if outside counsel is not brought in until the court stage, frequently outside counsel will be a very seasoned and very busy trial lawyer who will present the company's position in court, but who may not be in the best position to pry the necessary facts out of the local people. This is a difficult problem because the local company employees may not fully realize what is expected of them and, in some cases, may be less than 100 percent candid with the lawyer who is defending the case.

Fourth, some law firms divide EEO and trial work so that different people handle EEO cases when they are before state enforcement agencies or the EEOC than when they are in court. This further fragments the defense and, while in those law firms it may be the best approach, from the company's viewpoint, it further shows the need for a central lawyer to follow and coordinate everyone's efforts.

Audits

Any program of information, any policy, or any affirmative action program is of doubtful effectiveness if it is not accompanied by some kind of audit. In the case of government contractors, the audit is often done by the government agencies themselves, although not on a systematized and total basis. Even government contractors of substantial size may have plants in the country which have never had a government EEO or affirmative action plan audit. It would, therefore, seem appropriate for each company to adopt some procedure for auditing EEO compliance. At a minimum, the EEO-1 forms should all be sent to a central person for evaluation. A more meaningful audit should, however, be much more extensive, including at least the following.

1. Evaluation of all employee selection processes, including especially tests and the employment application form itself.

2. Analysis of the work force in much more detail than is shown on the EEO-1 forms. For this purpose, the government evaluation procedures set forth in Order No. 14 could serve as a rough guide, although for nongovernment contractors, it would not seem appropriate to go to this extreme.

3. Evaluation of all employee benefit programs, including vacation, sick leave, pension, life insurance, to see that they are nondiscriminatory.

4. Evaluation of all labor contracts; while it may seem unbelievable, labor contracts dated 1975 have been known to call for separate treatment for males and females in express terms. (These contracts were generally ones where older language, probably from some state female protective legislation, was incorporated many years ago and not changed. However, the practices followed the contract and are, therefore, just as illegal as if specifically drafted now.)

5. Evaluate all pay scales in some way which will assure compliance with the Equal Pay Act.

6. Adopt procedures which make certain that personnel people know where legal advice is available and will seek it in appropriate situations such as proposed changes in the labor contract, substantial reductions in the work force, or similar situations which can give rise to EEO concerns.

7. Examine retirement policies to ensure there are no discrimination problems.

Educational Programs

The lawyers in many companies neglect the role of educator. Those not familiar with the legal process cannot be expected to realize the importance of "party admissions," "building a record," and other things which are very important in many aspects of EEO/affirmative action plan work. Also, the laws are very technical and change rapidly. Lawyers who do not make a good-faith effort to provide regular programs where all interested people in the company are briefed on legal developments and the rapidly changing administrative law environment are not discharging one of their most important duties. On the other hand, management and those who are "on the firing line" (typically personnel people) have an obligation to make sure they have access to the latest and best information available. If the lawyers don't provide it on their own, they should be specifically requested to do so.

CHAPTER TWENTY-SIX

THE OCCUPATIONAL SAFETY AND HEALTH ACT OF 1970

INTRODUCTION

The Occupational Safety and Health Act of 1970 (hereinafter "act") is intended to assure all workers a safe and healthful job environment. This is accomplished by requiring all employers to (1) *eliminate recognized hazards*, (2) comply with numerous and detailed occupational safety and health *standards* promulgated under the act, (3) submit to inspections by government health and safety inspectors, and (4) comply with certain *record-keeping* and *reporting* requirements.

The act covers every employer engaged in a business *affecting* interstate commerce. There is no *requirement* that the employer have a certain *number of employees*, or a certain *number of locations*. However, certain very small employers are exempted from some of the record-keeping requirements.

The basic requirements of the act are contained in section 5, which provides as follows:

Section 5(a) Each *employer*—
(1)   shall furnish to each of his employees employment and a place of employment which are free from *recognized hazards* that are causing or are likely to cause death or serious physical harm to his employees; and
(2)   shall comply with occupational safety and health *standards* promulgated under this Act.
(b)   *Each employee* shall comply with occupational safety and health standards and all rules, regulations, and orders issued pursuant to this Act which are applicable to his own actions and conduct. [Emphasis added.]

GENERAL DUTY REQUIREMENT

The first requirement is the so-called commonsense, or good-faith, general duty requirement. It means that the employer must eliminate any hazard which can readily be detected on the basis of the human senses. Hazards which require technical or testing devices to detect them are not intended to be within the scope of the general duty requirement, but if these hazards are recognized in the industry or actually known they are covered. The very nature of the General Duty Clause makes it impossible to spell out exactly the kinds of things which might be covered and those which would not. However, the following discussion should provide significant guidance in analyzing problems under this section.

Elements of the General Duty Clause

From the reading of the clause itself, it is evident that there are three elements: (1) there must be a "recognized hazard"; (2) that recognized hazard must be causing or be likely to cause death or serious physical harm; (3) the harm must be caused to employees of the employer, not the public at large or any other persons.

Recognized Hazards

The "recognized hazard" language has generated a great deal of discussion among those concerned with enforcement of the act. The problem is that Congressman Steiger (who played a leading role in the enactment of the statute) explained in the *House Conference Report* that "such hazards (that is, Recognized Hazards) are the type that can be detected on the basis of the human senses. Hazards which require technical or testing devices to detect them are not intended to be within the scope of the General Duty Requirement." On the other hand, the Occupational Safety and Health Administration (OSHA) and the Occupational Safety and Health Review Commission take a more expanded view of the language and generally indicate that it includes not only those things which can be detected by the senses but those things which are generally recognized as hazards in a particular industry, even if it requires instrumentation to detect them. The usual example is concentrated substances in the air which may not be detectable by the senses but which would be detectable by instruments and which in the particular industries involved are generally regarded as presenting health hazards. The position of OSHA is indicated by the following:

> A hazard is "recognized" if it is a condition that is (a) of common knowledge or general recognition in the particular industry in which it occurs, and (b) detectable (1) by means of the senses (sight, smell, touch, and hearing), or (2) is of such wide, general recognition as a hazard in the industry that even if it is not detectable by means of the senses, there are generally known and accepted tests for its existence which should make its presence known to the employer. [*OSHA Compliance Operations Manual*]

The Occupational Safety and Health Review Commission generally takes the same view. The review commission has established that a recognized hazard is that which is commonly found in a given industry and from which serious injury or death is reasonably foreseeable, based upon the number of employees exposed to the hazard for the length of time involved. The probability that an accident will result from the hazard is irrelevant for the purpose of establishing a violation of the General Duty Clause.

The position of the courts is generally the same: actual knowledge will satisfy the requirement that the hazard by "recognized"; and if the hazard is recognized in the industry, this will also satisfy the requirement.

The following language from one court's opinion illustrates their position.

> Even a cursory examination of the Act's legislative history clearly indicates that the term "recognized" was chosen by Congress not to exclude actual knowledge, but rather to reach beyond an employer's actual knowledge to include the generally recognized knowledge of the industry as well. [*Brennan v. Vy Lactos Laboratories, Inc.* (8th Cir. 1974)]

The precise scope of recognized hazard does give rise to a great deal of theoretical debate along the lines indicated above, but as a practical matter for planning purposes, it is obvious that business must take the view that a hazard is recognized if it is known, whether by senses, common knowledge in the industry, or otherwise.

Prudent business people must also take into consideration that in many cases involving the General Duty Clause, the question of whether a recognized hazard is present is put before the commission, review commission, or courts in the context of an accident which has already happened. While the mere fact that an accident happened does now show a violation of the General Duty Clause, the psychological effect of a victim who has been killed or seriously injured cannot be ignored.

Causing Death or Serious Physical Harm

The second requirement of the General Duty Clause is that the recognized hazard must be "causing or likely to cause death or serious physical harm." Two phrases in this quote need clarification. One is the meaning of "likely to cause" and the other is the meaning of "serious physical harm."

The statute does not define serious physical harm, but OSHA has defined the term as follows:

> Serious physical harm is that type of harm that would cause permanent or prolonged impairment of the body in that (1) a part of the body would be permanently removed (e.g., amputation of an arm, leg, finger; loss of an eye), or rendered functionally useless or substantially reduced in efficiency on or off the job (e.g., leg shattered so severely that mobility would be permanently reduced), or (2) a part of an internal bodily system would be inhibited in its normal performance to such a degree as to shorten life or to cause reduction in physical or mental efficiency; e.g., lung impairment causing shortness of breath. On the other hand, breaks, cuts, bruises, concussions or similar injuries . . . would not constitute serious physical harm. [*OSHA Compliance Operations Manual*]

Fault

The employer need not be at fault in causing the unsafe condition. This is particularly important in the construction area where there are many different "employers" working on the site. Examples of this doctrine include the following. (1) A situation where a contractor was held responsible for failure to support a concrete wall, where the contractor contended that the fault was with the architectural design. (2) A situation where a subcontractor was held responsible for failure to provide proper lighting, even though the responsibility for providing such lighting was specifically assigned to the contractor in a written contract between the parties. (3) And, perhaps the most extreme example, a situation where an employer who merely lent employees to work on a job was held responsible for violation of various standards because he exposed the employees to the hazards.

Specific Standards Control

The General Duty Clause cannot be used in a situation where there is a specific safety standard. In fact, the regulations specifically provide that an employer who is in compliance with a specific safety and health standard shall be deemed to be in compliance with the General Duty Clause insofar as it applies to hazards covered by specific standards.

With the promulgation of more and more specific standards, the significance of the General Duty Clause, at least in terms of frequency of use by OSHA, will probably decrease. However, the point where all possible safety hazards are covered by a specific standard will probably never be reached, and the General Duty Clause will always operate to require employers to use judgment and common sense in maintaining a safe workplace.

STANDARDS

The heart of the act is the standards which are promulgated thereunder. These standards range all the way from commonsense provisions, such as the requirement for barricading holes in the floor through more costly but still readily understandable provisions such as those requiring that all electrical outlets be grounded, to very elaborate provisions which can only be understood and applied by engineers, such as those dealing with toxic substances and containing elaborate chemical formulas.

Naturally, a safety officer at a plant would have to be thoroughly familiar with all of the standards which might be applicable to his plant, or at least have access to an outside consultant or assistant who was familiar and could apply them.

However, from the point of view of the business executive only a minimal knowledge of the standards is necessary. The executive must be aware, however, of the scope of the standards, the interaction of those standards, and how they might apply to business activity. The following points regarding standards are generally sufficient to provide a business executive with a sufficient working knowledge to plan and seek expert advice where appropriate.

Most Cited Violations

In spite of the almost endless nature of the standards which now comprise literally volumes of printed material, a much more limited number of standards are those most often cited in inspections of general industry or construction operations. OSHA lists the twenty-five most cited violations during various 6-months periods. While these naturally vary, the list on page 26–5 is illustrative.

Interaction of the Standards

One must not take an overly narrow view of the kinds of standards which might be applicable to his operations. This is especially true in the normal manufacturing operation where the construction standards should not be overlooked. One would not consider the normal manufacturing operation as being part of the construction business, but on those occasions when one is involved in remodeling or expanding the plant, the construction standards would be applicable.

THE TWENTY-FIVE MOST OFTEN CITED VIOLATIONS OF
THE OCCUPATIONAL SAFETY AND HEALTH ACT

GENERAL INDUSTRY: Part 1910		CONSTRUCTION: Part 1926	
Section Cited	Subject of Section	Section Cited	Subject of Section
1910.309	National Electrical Code	1926.500	Guardrails, handrails, and covers
.219	Mechanical power transmission apparatus	.451	Scaffolding
.157	Portable fire extinguishers	.450	Ladders
.212	General requirements for all machines	.350	Gas welding and cutting
.213	Woodworking machinery	.401	Grounding and bonding
.23	Guarding floor and wall openings and holes	.550	Cranes and derricks
.22	General requirements, walking and working surfaces	.25	Housekeeping
.252	Welding, cutting, and brazing	.152	Flammable and combustible liquids
.215	Abrasive wheel machinery	.400	General electrical
.178	Powered industrial trucks	.402	Electrical equipment installation and maintenance
.265	Sawmills	.150	Fire protection
.37	Means of egress, general	.652	Trenching
.106	Flammable and combustible liquids	.601	Motor vehicles
.141	Sanitation	.100	Head protection
.107	Spray finishing using flammable or combustible liquids	.552	Materials hoists and personnel hoists and elevators
.242	Hand and portable power tools and equipment, general	.50	Medical services and first aid
.176	Handling materials, general	.501	Stairways
.36	General requirements, means of egress	.300	General requirements, hand and power tools
.179	Overhead and gantry cranes	.651	Excavation
.25	Portable wood ladders	.51	Sanitation
.95	Noise exposure	.28	Personal protective equipment
.151	Medical services and first aid	.102	Eye and face protection
.132	Personal protective equipment, general	.302	Power operated hand tools
.133	Eye and face protection	.351	Arc welding and cutting
.27	Fixed Ladders	.105	Safety nets

Source: United States Department of Labor

The Scope and General Content of Most of the Standards

Business executives should be aware of the scope and general content of most of the standards so they can ascertain what effect these standards may have on the general business operation of the company outside of its safety problems. For example, if the company sells an item (such as fire extinguishers) which is governed by specific OSHA standards, business executives must be aware of this and make sure that the product complies with the standards. On the other hand, they must be aware that most of the standards govern the *use* of the product rather than its *specifications*; therefore, a company selling an item should not be allowed to warrant that "it is in compliance with all OSHA regulations," because such compliance can only be achieved by the user. As a corollary to the same point, business executives should be aware of anything purchased which may be governed directly or indirectly by an OSHA standard, and should, of course, be sure that the appropriate people in the purchasing department are aware of the existence of the relevant standard and exercise all efforts to make sure that the product complies.

Affirmative Action

The next important point which must be considered in the standards area is that the standards do more than simply require certain kinds of protective equipment and guards. In many cases, they impose an *affirmative duty* on the employer to conduct a specific program.

Examples (but far from an exhaustive list) are as follows:

1. Some standards require the conducting of a training program.

2. Education in first aid for various employees may be required.

3. The employer may have to develop and use various kinds of labels or other appropriate forms for warning the employees of all hazards to which they may be exposed.

4. The employer may have to prescribe and affirmatively require that all employees use certain protective equipment.

5. The employer may have to engage in monitoring programs to measure employee exposure to hazards.

6. The employer may have to provide certain medical examinations or other tests for employees exposed to hazards.

Outline of the Standards

The standards applicable to general business can be divided into seven sections as follows:

1. Workplace standards

2. Machines and equipment standards

3. Materials standards

4. Employee standards

5. Power source standards

6. Process standards

7. Administrative standards

The basic concept supporting these categories is that one starts evaluating a hazard potential from a base point, the workplace or work location, and then, as other production elements are added, considers additional hazard potentials. Related hazards are found in one category. These categories apply individually and collectively as follows.

Workplace Standards

There are certain basic safety and health standards which apply strictly to the workplace, a building, *or other work location.* These include safety of floors or other working sufaces, protection of floor and wall openings, access and exit requirements, sanitation, and fire and emergency protection.

Machines and Equipment Standards

When machines and equipment are added to the workplace, new elements of risk come into play. Standards are included for risks involving machine guarding, operational techniques, special safety devices, inspection and maintenance, mounting, anchoring, grounding, and other protection.

Materials Standards

Materials which are utilized, processed, or applied on the job add to the hazards. There are standards covering materials which yield dangerous or toxic fumes or mists, ignitable and/or explosive dusts, and other atmospheric contaminants. There are standards for safe storage and handling of compressed gases and flammable and combustible liquids as well as more stable materials used in production processes.

Employee Standards

When the employee is added to the workplace, other variables and related technical standards become important. What medical and first aid services are required? What personal protective equipment and devices must be provided? Are licenses or other accreditation documents required? What about special training or educational requirements?

Power Source Standards

The power source utilized creates additional hazards. there are standards for electrical, pneumatic, hydraulic, steam, explosive actuated, and other sources of power.

Process Standards

Some standards cover a special process or a special industry. Welding, cutting and brazing, spray finishing, abrasive blasting, and utilization of dip tanks are hazardous processes. Special standards exist for textile and bakery operations, sawmills, pulpwood logging, and agriculture.

Administrative Standards

In addition to the safety and health standards in part 1910, there are administrative requirements in parts 1903, 1904, 1905, 1911, and 1912 for all employers, whatever the size of the work establishment. Every employer must display an OSHA poster stating the rights and obligations of employees and employers; keep injury, illness, and exposure records; report fatalities and multiple hospital injury cases (five or more); and post an annual summary of injuries and illnesses.

The government has published a useful checklist to assess the application of the standards to general industrial plants and that checklist is reproduced on pages 26-8 through 26-15.

General Industry Safety and Health Checklist

Note: The following checklist covers approximately 90 percent of OSHA's general industry standards but should not be regarded as a substitute for the Federal Register. The checklist soon will be available as an OSHA pamphlet. Watch Job Safety & Health *for further details.*

1. Abrasive Blasting

a. Blast cleaning nozzles shall be equipped with an operating valve which must be held open manually (deadman control). A support shall be provided on which the nozzle may be mounted when not in use.

b. The concentration of respirable dust or fumes in the breathing zone of the abrasive-blasting operator or any other worker shall be below the levels specified in 1910.93.

c. Blast-cleaning enclosures shall be exhaust ventilated in such a way that a continuous inward flow of air will be maintained at all openings in the enclosure during the blasting operation.

d. The air for abrasive-blasting respirators shall be free of harmful quantities of contaminants.

2. Abrasive Grinding

a. Abrasive wheels shall be used only on machines provided with safety guards, with the following exceptions:

* Wheels used for internal work while within the work being ground;
* Mounted wheels, used in portable operations, two inches and smaller in diameter; and
* Type 16, 17, 18, 18R, and 19 cones, plugs, and threaded hole pot balls where the work offers protection.

b. All abrasive wheel bench and stand grinders shall be provided with safety guards which cover the spindle ends, nut, and flange, except:

* Safety guards on all operations where the work provides a suitable measure of protection to the operator may be so constructed that the spindle end, nut, and outer flange are exposed;
* Where the nature of the work is such as to entirely cover the side of the wheel, the side covers of the guard may be omitted; and
* The spindle end, nut, and outer flange may be exposed on machines designed as portable saws.

c. An adjustable work rest of rigid construction shall be used to support the work on fixed base, offhand grinding machines. Work rests shall be kept adjusted closely to the wheel with a maximum opening of ⅛ inch. The work rest shall be securely clamped after each adjustment. The adjustment shall not be made with the wheel in motion.

d. Every establishment performing dry grinding shall provide suitable hood or enclosures that are connected to exhaust systems to control airborne contaminants.

e. Machines designed for a fixed location shall be securely anchored to prevent walking or moving.

3. Accident Recordkeeping Requirements

a. Within 48 hours after its occurrence, an employment accident which is fatal to one or more employees or which results in the hospitalization of five or more employees shall be reported by the employer, either orally or in writing, to the nearest OSHA Area Director.

b. Records as prescribed in the Recordkeeping Requirements booklet shall be kept for all accidents that result in a fatality, hospitalization, lost workdays, medical treatment, job transfer or termination, or loss of consciousness.

4. Air Receivers, Compressed

a. Air receivers should be supported with sufficient clearance to permit a complete external inspection and to avoid corrosion of external surfaces.

b. Air receivers shall be installed so that drains, handholes, and manholes are easily accessible.

c. Every air receiver shall be equipped with an indicating pressure gauge so located as to be readily visible, and with one or more spring loaded safety valves.

5. Air Tools

a. For portable tools, a tool retainer shall be installed on each piece of utilization equipment, which, without such a retainer, may eject the tool.

b. Hose and hose connections used for conducting compressed air to utilization equipment shall be designed for the pressure and service to which they are subjected.

6. Aisles and Passageways

a. Where mechanical handling equipment is used, sufficient safe clearance shall be allowed for aisles at loading docks, through doorways, and whenever turns or passage must be made.

b. Aisles and passageways shall be kept clear and in good repair with no obstructions across or in aisles that could create hazards.

c. Permanent aisles and passageways shall be appropriately marked.

7. Belt Sanding Machines (Woodworking)

a. Belt sanding machines shall be provided with guards at each nip point where the sanding belt runs onto a pulley.

b. The unused run of the sanding belt shall be guarded against accidental contact.

8. Boilers

Boilers are not covered by present OSHA standards. These are good practice procedures and might be incorporated into future OSHA standards.

a. Boiler inspection and approval, on an annual basis, by a recognized boiler inspection service is satisfactory evidence of acceptable installation and maintenance.

b. A valid boiler inspection certificate, bearing the signature of the authorized inspector and the date of the last inspection, shall be conspicuously posted.

c. All boilers shall be equipped with an approved means of determining the water level such as water column, gauge glass, or try cocks. Gauge glasses and water columns shall be guarded to prevent breakage.

9. Calendars, Mills, and Rolls

a. A safety trip-type bar, rod, or cable to activate an emergency stop switch shall be installed on calendars, rolls, or mills to prevent persons or parts of the body from being caught between the rolls.

b. A fixed guard across the front and one across the back of the mill, approximately 40 inches vertically above the working level and 20 inches horizontally from the crown face of the roll, should be used where applicable.

10. Chains, Cables, Ropes, Etc. (Overhead and Gantry Cranes)

a. Chains, cables, ropes, slings, etc., shall be inspected daily, and defective gear shall be removed and repaired or replaced.

b. Hoist chains and hoist ropes shall be free from kinks or twists and shall not be wrapped around the load.

c. All U-bolt wire rope clips on hoist ropes shall be installed so that the U-bolt is in contact with the dead end (short or nonload carrying end) of the rope. Clips shall be installed in accordance with the clip manufacturer's recommendation. All nuts or newly installed clips shall be retightened after one hour of use.

11. Chip Guards

Protective shields and barriers shall be provided, in operations involving cleaning with compressed air, to protect personnel against flying chips or other such hazards.

12. Chlorinated Hydrocarbons

a. Carbon tetrachloride or other chlorinated (halogenated) hydrocarbons shall not be used where the airborne concentration exceeds the Threshold Limit Value (TLV) listed.

b. Degreasing or other cleaning operations involving chlorinated hydrocarbons shall be so located that vapors from these operations will not reach or be drawn into the atmosphere surrounding any welding operations.

13. Compressed Air, Use of

Compressed air used for cleaning purposes shall not exceed 30 psi and then only with effective chin guarding and personal protective equipment.

14. Cone Pulleys (Mechanical Power Transmission Equipment)

The cone belt and pulleys shall be equipped with a belt shifter so constructed as to adequately guard the nip point of the belt and pulley. If the frame of the belt shifter does not adequately guard the nip point of the belt and pulley, the nip point shall be further protected by means of a vertical guard placed in front of the pulley and extending at least to the top of the largest step of the cone.

15. Conveyors

a. Conveyors installed within seven feet of the floor or walkway shall be provided with cross-overs at aisles or other passageways.

b. Where conveyors seven feet or more above the floor pass over working areas, aisles, or thoroughfares, suitable guards shall be provided to protect personnel from the hazard of falling materials.

c. Open hoppers and chutes shall be guarded by standard railings and toeboards or by some other comparable safety device.

16. Cranes and Hoists (Overhead and Gantry)

a. All functional operating mechanisms, air and hydraulic systems, chains, rope slings, hooks, and other lifting equipment shall be inspected daily.

b. Complete inspection of the crane shall be performed at intervals depending on its activity, severity and environment.

c. An overhead crane shall have stops at the limit of travel of the trolley, bridge and trolley bumpers or equivalent automatic services, and rail sweeps on the bridge trucks.

d. The rated load of the crane shall be plainly marked on each side of the crane, and if the crane has more than one hoisting unit, each hoist shall have its rated load marked on it or its load block, and this marking shall be clearly legible from the ground or floor.

17. Cylinders, Compressed Gas, Used in Welding

a. Compressed gas cylinders shall be kept away from excessive heat, shall not be stored where they might be damaged or knocked over by passing or falling objects, and shall be stored at least 20 feet away from highly combustible materials.

b. Where a cylinder is designed to accept a valve protection cap, caps shall be in place except when the cylinder is in use or is connected for use.

c. Acetylene cylinders shall be stored in a vertical, valve-end-up position only.

d. Oxygen cylinders, in storage shall be separated from fuel-gas cylinders or combustible materials (especially oil or grease) a minimum distance of 20 feet or by a non-combustible barrier at least five feet high having a fire-resistance rating of at least ½ hour.

18. Dip Tanks Containing Flammable or Combustible Liquid

a. Dip tanks of over 150 gallons capacity, or 10 square feet in liquid surface area, shall be equipped with a properly trapped overflow pipe leading to a safe location outside the buildings.

b. There shall be no open flames, spark producing devices, or heated surfaces having a temperature sufficient to ignite vapors in or within 20 feet of any vapor area. Electrical wiring and equipment in any vapor area shall be of the explosion-proof type. There shall be no electrical equipment in the vicinity of dip tanks, associated drain boards, or drying operations which are subject to splashing or dripping.

c. All dip tanks, except hardening and tempering tanks, exceeding 150 gallons liquid capacity or having a liquid surface area exceeding four square feet shall be protected with at least one of the following automatic extinguishing facilities: water spray system, foam system, carbon dioxide system, dry chemical system, or automatic dip tank cover. This provision shall apply to hardening and tempering tanks having a liquid surface area of 25 square feet or more or a capacity of 500 gallons or more.

19. Dockboards

a. Dockboards shall be strong enough to carry the load imposed on them.

b. Portable dockboards shall be anchored or equipped with devices which will prevent their slipping. They shall have handholds or other effective means to allow safe handling.

c. Positive means shall be provided to prevent railroad cars from being moved while dockboards are in position.

20. Drains for Flammable and Combustible Liquids

a. Emergency drainage systems shall be provided to direct flammable liquid leakage and fire protection water to a safe location.

b. Emergency drainage systems for flammable liquids, if connected to public sewers or discharged into public waterways, shall be equipped with traps or separators.

21. Drill Presses

The V-belt drive of all drill presses, including the usual front and rear pulleys, shall be guarded to protect the operator from contact or breakage.

22. Drinking Water

a. Potable water shall be provided in all places of employment.

b. The nozzle of a drinking fountain shall be set at such an angle that the jet of water will not splash back down on the nozzle, and the end of the nozzle shall be protected by a guard to prevent a person's mouth or nose from coming in contact with the nozzle.

c. Portable drinking water dispensers shall be designed and serviced to ensure sanitary conditions, shall be capable of being closed, and shall have a tap. Unused disposable cups shall be kept in a sanitary container, and a receptacle shall be provided for used cups. The common drinking cup is prohibited.

23. Elevator

Elevators are not covered by present OSHA standards. These are good practice procedures and might be incorporated into future OSHA standards.

a. All elevators shall be inspected annually by a competent inspection service or inspector.

b. All hoistway openings shall be protected by doors or gates that are interlocked with the controls, so that the car cannot be started until all gates or doors are closed, and so that gates or doors cannot be opened when the car is not at the landing.

24. Electrical Installations

Every new electrical installation and all new utilization equipment installed after March 15, 1972, and every replacement, modification, repair, or rehabilitation after March 15, 1972, of any part of any electrical installation or utilization equipment installed before March 15, 1972, shall be installed or made and maintained in accordance with the provisions of the 1971 National Electrical Code, NFPA 70—1971; ANSI C1—1971 (Rev. of 1968).

25. Emergency Flushing, Eyes and Body

Where the eyes or body of any person may be exposed to injurious corrosive materials, suitable facilities for quick drenching or flushing of the eyes and body shall be provided within the work area for immediate emergency use.

26. Exits

a. Every building designed for human occupancy shall be provided with exits sufficient to permit the prompt escape of occupants in case of emergency.

b. Where occupants may be endangered by the blocking of any single egress due to fire or smoke, there shall be at least two means of egress remote from each other.

c. Exits and the way of approach and travel from exits shall be maintained so that they are unobstructed and are accessible at all times.

d. All exits shall discharge directly to the street or other open space that gives safe access to a public way.

e. Exit doors serving more than 50 people, or at high hazard areas, shall swing in the direction of travel.

f. Exits shall be marked by readily visible, illuminated exit signs. Exit signs shall be distinctive in color and provide contrast with surroundings. The word "EXIT" shall be of plainly legible letters, not less than six inches high.

27. Explosives and Blasting Agents

a. All explosives shall be kept in approved magazines.

b. Stored packages of explosives shall be laid flat with top side up. Black powder, when stored in magazines with other explosives, shall be stored separately.

c. Smoking, matches, open flames, spark-producing devices, and firearms (except firearms carried by guards) shall not be permitted inside of or within 50 feet of magazines. The land surrounding a magazine shall be kept clear of all combustible materials for a distance of at least 25 feet. Combustible materials shall not be stored within 50 feet of magazines.

28. Eye and Face Protection

a. Protective eye and face equipment shall be required where there is a reasonable probability of injury that can be prevented by such equipment.

b. Eye and face protection equipment shall be in compliance with ANSI Z87.1—1968, Practice for Occupational and Educational Eye and Face Protection.

29. Fan Blades

When the periphery of the blades of a fan is less than seven feet above the floor or working level, the blades shall be guarded. The guard shall have openings no longer than ½ inch. The use of concentric rings with space between them, not exceeding ½ inch, is acceptable, provided they are adequately supported.

30. Fire Doors

Fire doors are not completely covered by present OSHA standards. These are good practice procedures and might be incorporated into future OSHA standards.

Fan blades—When a fan is less than seven feet above the floor or working level, the blades must be guarded. The guard must have openings no longer than one-half inch.

a. Fire doors shall not be blocked or tied in an open position.

b. Fusible links for fire doors shall be located so as to properly function in case of fire and shall not be painted.

c. Three three-inch diameter vent holes, cut through the metal only, are required for tin-clad fire doors up to nine feet in height. (An additional vent hole is required for door from nine feet to 12 feet four inches in height.) The metal covering around the opening shall be secured with small nails, and the exposed wood thoroughly painted.

d. A closing device shall be installed on every fire door except elevator and power-operated dumbwaiter doors equipped with electric contacts or interlocks.

31. Fire Protection

a. Portable fire extinguishers suitable to the conditions and hazards involved shall be provided and maintained in an effective operating condition.

b. Portable fire extinguishers shall be conspicuously located and mounted where they will be readily accessible. Extinguishers shall not be obstructed or obscured from view.

c. Portable fire extinguishers shall be given maintenance service at least once a year with a durable tag securely attached to show the maintenance or recharge date.

d. In storage areas, clearance between sprinkler system deflectors and top of storage varies with the type of storage. For combustible material stored over 15 feet but not more than 21 feet high in solid piles, or over 12 feet but not more than 21 feet high in piles that contain horizontal channels, the minimum clearance shall be 36 inches. The minimum clearance for smaller piles or for noncombustible materials shall be 18 inches.

32. Flammable Liquids Incidental to Principal Business

a. Flammable liquids shall be kept in covered containers when not actually in use.

b. The quantity of flammable or combustible liquid that may be located outside of an inside storage room or storage cabinet in any one fire area of a building shall not exceed:

- 25 gallons of Class IA liquids in containers;
- 120 gallons of Class IB, IC, II, or III liquids in containers; or
- 660 gallons of Class IB, IC, II, or III in a single portable tank.

c. Flammable and combustible liquids shall be drawn from or transferred into containers within a building only through a closed piping system, from safety cans, by means of a device drawing through the top, or by gravity through an approved self-closing valve. Transferring by means of air pressure shall be prohibited.

d. Inside storage rooms for flammable and combustible liquids shall be of fire resistive construction, have self-closing fire doors at all openings, four-inch sills or depressed floors, a ventilation system that provides at least six air changes within the room per hour, and in areas used for storage of Class I liquids, electrical wiring approved for use in hazardous locations.

e. Outside storage areas shall be graded in such a manner to divert spills away from buildings or other exposures, or be surrounded with curbs or dikes at least six inches high with appropriate drainage to a safe location for accumulated liquids. The area shall be protected against tampering or trespassing, where necessary, and shall be kept free of weeds, debris, and other combustible material not necessary to the storage.

f. Areas where flammable liquids with flashpoints below 100 degrees F are used shall be ventilated at a rate of not less than one cubic-foot-per-minute per square foot of solid floor area.

33. Floors, General Conditions

a. All floor surfaces shall be kept clean, dry, and free from protruding nails, splinters, loose boards, holes, or projections.

b. Where wet processes are used, drainage shall be maintained, and false floors, platforms, mats, or other dry standing places should be provided where practicable.

34. Floor Loading Limit

In buildings used for mercantile, business, industrial, or storage purposes, all floors shall be posted to show maximum safe floor loads.

35. Floor Openings, Hatchways, Open Sides, Etc.

a. Floor openings requiring access by personnel, such as stairway openings and ladderway openings, shall be guarded by a standard railing on all exposed sides except at the access point. Access to ladderway openings shall be further guarded so that a person cannot walk directly into the opening. Other floor openings shall be guarded by a suitable covering, and further guarded when the covering is removed by a removable standard railing, or shall be constantly attended by someone. Skylight openings shall be guarded by a standard skylight screen or fixed standard railing on all four sides.

b. Open-sided floors, platforms, etc., four feet or more above the adjacent floor or ground level shall be guarded by a standard railing on all open sides, except where there is an entrance to a ramp, stairway, or fixed ladder.

36. Foot Protection

Safety-toe footwear shall meet the requirements of ANSI Z41.1—1967, Standard for Men's Safety-toe Footwear.

37. Forklift Trucks

a. All new forklift trucks acquired and used after February 15, 1972, shall comply with ANSI B56.1—1969, Power Industrial Trucks, Part II. Approved trucks shall bear a label indicating approval.

b. High lift rider trucks shall be equipped with a substantial overhead guard unless operating conditions do not permit.

c. Fork trucks shall be equipped with a vertical load backrest extension when the type of load presents a hazard to the operator.

d. The brakes of highway trucks shall be set and wheel chocks placed under the rear wheels to prevent the truck from rolling while they are boarded with forklift trucks.

e. Wheel stops or other recognized protection shall be provided to prevent railroad cars from moving while they are boarded with forklift trucks.

38. General Duty Clause

Hazardous conditions or practices not covered in an OSHA standard may be covered under Section 5(a)(1) of the Act which states: "Each employer shall furnish to each of his employees employment and a place of employment which are free from recognized hazards that are causing or are likely to cause death or serious physical harm to his employees."

39. Guards, Construction of

Guards for mechanical power transmission equipment shall be made of metal, except that wood guards may be used in the woodworking and chemical industries, in industries where atmospheric conditions would rapidly deteriorate metal guards, or where temperature extremes make metal guards undesirable.

40. Head Protection

Head protective equipment shall meet the requirements of ANSI Z89.1—1967, Requirements for Industrial Head Protection.

41. Hand Tools

Each employer shall be responsible for the safe condition of tools and equipment used by employees, including tools and equipment which may be furnished by employees.

42. Hooks, Cranes, and Hoists, Etc. (See Cranes and Hoists, No. 16)

43. Housekeeping

All places of employment, passageways, storerooms, and service rooms shall be kept clean and orderly and in a sanitary condition.

44. Jointers (Woodworking)

a. Each hand-fed planer and jointer with a horizontal head shall be equipped with a cylindrical cutting head. The opening in the table shall be kept as small as possible.

b. Each hand-fed jointer with a horizontal cutting head shall have an automatic guard which will cover the section of the head on the working side of the fence or gauge.

c. A jointer guard shall automatically adjust itself to cover the unused portion of the head and shall remain in contact with the material at all times.

d. Each hand-fed jointer horizontal cutting head shall have a guard which will cover the section of the head back of the gauge or fence.

45. Ladders, Fixed

a. All fixed ladders shall be designed for a minimum concentrated live load of 200 pounds.

b. All rungs shall have a minimum diameter of ¾ inch, if metal, or if the ladder is constructed of metal rungs embedded in concrete and exposed to a corrosive atmosphere, the rungs shall have a minimum diameter of one inch. Wooden ladders shall have rungs with a minimum diameter of 1⅛ inch. All rungs shall be spaced uniformly, not more than 12 inches apart, and shall have a minimum clear length of 16 inches.

c. Metal ladders shall be painted or treated to resist corrosion or rusting when the location demands.

d. Cages, wells, or ladder safety devices for ladders affixed to towers, watertanks, or chimneys shall be provided on all ladders more than 20 feet long. Landing platforms shall be provided each 30 feet of length, except where no cage is provided, landing platforms shall be provided for every 20 feet of length.

e. Tops of cages on fixed ladders shall extend 42 feet above top of landing, unless other acceptable protection is provided, and the bottom of the cage shall be not less than seven feet nor more than eight feet above the base of the ladder.

f. The side rails of through or side-step ladder extensions shall extend 3½ feet above parapets and landings. For through ladder extensions, the rungs shall be omitted from the extension and shall have not less than 18 nor more than 24 inches clearance between rails. For side-step or offset fixed ladder sections, at landings, the side rails and rungs shall be carried to the next regular rung beyond or above the 3½ feet minimum.

46. Ladders, Portable

a. The maximum length for portable wood ladders shall be: step-ladders 20 feet; single straight ladders 30 feet; two section extension ladders 60 feet; sectional ladders—60 feet; trestle ladders—20 feet; platform step-ladders—20 feet; painter's step-ladders—12 feet; and mason's ladders—40 feet.

b. The maximum length for portable metal ladders shall be: single straight ladders—30 feet; two section extension ladders—48 feet; over two section extension ladders—60 feet; step-ladders—20 feet; trestle ladders—20 feet; and platform step-ladders—20 feet.

c. Step-ladders shall be equipped with a metal spreader or locking device of sufficient size and strength to securely hold the front and back sections in open position.

d. Ladders shall be maintained in good condition, and defective ladders shall be withdrawn from service.

e. Non-self-supporting ladders shall be erected on a sound base at a 4-1 pitch and placed to prevent slipping.

f. The top of a ladder used to gain access to a roof should extend at least three feet above the point of contact.

g. Wooden ladders should be kept coated with a suitable protective material.

h. In general industrial use, portable metal ladders may be used in areas containing electrical circuits, if proper safety measures are taken.

47. Lighting

Lighting is not covered by OSHA standards for general industry. These are good practice procedures and might be incorporated into future OSHA standards:

Adequate illumination, depending upon the seeing tasks involved, shall be provided and distributed to all areas in accordance with ANSI Standard A11.1. (Requirements vary widely, but a good rule-of-thumb is 20 to 30 foot candles for services, and 50 to 100 foot candles for tasks).

48. Lunchrooms

a. Employees shall not consume food or beverages in toilet rooms or in any area exposed to a toxic material.

b. Covered receptacles corrosion resistant to disposable material shall be provided in lunch areas for disposal of waste food. The cover may be omitted where sanitary conditions can be maintained without the use of a cover.

49. Machine Guarding

One or more methods of machine guarding shall be provided to protect the operator and other employees in the machine area from hazards such as those created by point of operation, in-going nip points, rotating parts, and flying chips or sparks.

50. Machinery, Fixed

Machines designed for a fixed location shall be securely anchored to prevent walking or moving.

51. Mats, Insulating

Where motors or controllers operating at more than 150 volts to ground are grounded against accidental contact only by location, and where adjustment or other attendance may be necessary during operations, suitable insulating mats or platforms shall be provided.

52. Medical Services and First Aid

a. The employer shall ensure the ready availability of medical personnel for advice and consultation on matters of plant health.

b. When a medical facility for treatment of injured employees is not available in near proximity to the workplace, a person or persons shall be trained to render first aid.

c. First aid supplies approved by the consulting physician shall be readily available.

53. Noise Exposure

a. Protection against the effects of occupational noise exposure shall be provided when the sound levels exceed those shown in Table G-16 of the Safety and Health Standards. Feasible engineering and/or administrative controls shall be utilized to keep exposure below the allowable limit.

b. When engineering or administrative controls fail to reduce the noise level to within the levels of Table G-16 of the Safety and Health Standards, personal protective equipment shall be provided and used to reduce the noise to an acceptable level.

c. Exposure to impulsive or impact noise should not exceed 140 dB peak sound pressure level.

d. In all cases, where the sound levels exceed the values shown in Table G-16 of the Safety and Health Standards, a continuing, effective hearing conservation program shall be administered.

e. Table G-16—Permissible Noise Exposures

Duration per day, hours	Sound level dB(A) slow response
8	90
6	92
4	95
3	97
2	100
1½	102
1	105
½	110
¼ or less	115

54. Personal Protective Equipment

a. Proper personal protective equipment, including shields and barriers, shall be provided, used, and maintained in a sanitary and reliable condition where there is a hazard from processes or environment that may cause injury or illness to the employee.

b. Where employees furnish their own personal protective equipment, the employer shall be responsible to assure its adequacy and to ensure that the equipment is properly maintained and in a sanitary condition.

55. Portable Electric Tools (See Hand Tools, No. 41)

56. Power Transmission, Mechanical

a. All belts, pulleys, chains, flywheels, shafting and shaft projections, or other rotating or reciprocating parts within seven feet of the floor or working platform shall be effectively guarded.

b. Belts, pulleys, and shafting located in rooms used exclusively for power transmission apparatus need not be guarded when the following requirements are met:

- The basement, tower, or room occupied by transmission equipment is locked against unauthorized entrance;
- The vertical clearance in passageways between the floor and power transmission beams, ceiling, or any other objects is not less than five feet six inches;
- The intensity of illumination conforms to the requirements of ANSI A11.1—1965 (R 1970);
- The footing is dry, firm, and level;
- The route followed by the oiler is protected in such a manner as to prevent accident.

57. Pressure Vessels, Portable Unfired

Pressure vessels are not covered by present OSHA standards. These are good operating procedures and might be incorporated into future OSHA standards.

a. All portable unfired pressure vessels should be designed and constructed to meet the Standards of the American Society of Mechanical Engineers Boiler and Pressure Vessel Code, Section VIII.

b. Portable unfired pressure vessels not built to code should be examined quarterly by a competent person and subjected yearly to a hydrostatic pressure test of 1½-times the working pressure of the vessel. Records of such examination and tests should be maintained.

c. Relief valves on pressure vessels should be set to the safe working pressure of the vessel, or to the lowest safe working pressure of the system, whichever is lower.

58. Punch Presses

a. It shall be the responsibility of the employer to provide and ensure the usage of "point-of-operation guards" or properly applied and adjusted point-of-operation devices on every operation performed on a mechanical power press. This requirement shall not apply when the point-of-operation opening is ¼ inch or less.

b. A substantial guard shall be placed over the treadle of foot-operated presses.

c. Pedal counterweights, if provided on foot-operated presses, shall have the path of the travel of the weight enclosed.

59. Radiation

a. Employers shall be responsible for proper controls to prevent all employees from being exposed to ionizing radiation in excess of acceptable limits.

b. Each radiation area shall be conspicuously posted with appropriate signs.

c. Every employer shall maintain records of the radiation exposure of all employees for whom personnel monitoring is requested.

60. Railings

a. A standard railing shall consist of top rail, intermediate rail, and posts, and shall have a vertical height of 42 inches from upper surface of top rail to floor, platform, etc.

b. A railing for open-sided floors, platforms, and runways shall have a toeboard whenever persons can pass beneath the open side, or there is moving machinery, or there is equipment which could be struck by falling materials.

c. Railings shall be of such construction that the complete structure shall be capable of withstanding a load of at least 200 pounds in any direction on any point on the top rail.

d. A stair railing shall be of construction similar to a standard railing, but the vertical height shall be not more than 34 inches nor less than 30 inches from upper surface of top rail to surface of tread in line with face of riser at forward edge of tread.

61. Rail Sweeps (See Cranes and Hoists, No. 16)

62. Revolving Drums

Revolving drums, barrels, or containers shall be guarded by an interlocked enclosure that will prevent the drum, etc., from revolving unless the guard enclosure is in place.

63. Saws, Band (Woodworking)

a. All portions of band saw blades shall be enclosed or guarded except for the working portion of the blade between the bottom of the guide rolls and the table.

b. Bandsaw wheels shall be fully encased. The outside periphery of the enclosure shall be solid. The front and back shall be either solid or wire mesh or perforated metal.

64. Saws, Portable Circular

All portable power-driven circular saws having a blade diameter greater than two inches shall be equipped with guards above and below the base plate or shoe. The lower guards shall cover the saw to the depth of the teeth, except for the minimum arc required to permit the base plate to be tilted for bevel cuts, and shall automatically return to the covering position when the blade is withdrawn from the work. This provision does not apply to circular saws used in the meat industry for meat cutting purposes.

65. Saws, Radial (Woodworking)

a. Radial saws shall be constructed so that the upper hood shall completely enclose the upper portion of the blade down to a point that will include the end of the saw arbor. The upper hood shall be constructed in such a manner and of such material that it will protect the operator from flying splinters, broken saw teeth, etc., and will deflect sawdust away from the operator. The sides of the lower exposed portion of the blade shall be guarded to the full diameter of the blade by a device that will automatically adjust itself to the thickness of the stock and remain in contact with stock being cut to give maximum protection possible for the operation being performed.

b. Radial saws used for ripping shall have non-kickback fingers or dogs.

c. Radial saws shall be installed so that the cutting head will return to the starting position when released by the operator.

66. Saws, Swing or Sliding Cut-Off (Woodworking)

a. All swing or sliding cut-off saws shall be provided with a hood that will completely enclose the upper half of the saw.

b. Limit stops shall be provided to prevent swing or sliding type cut-off saws from extending beyond the front or back edges of the table.

c. Each swing or sliding cut-off saw shall be provided with an effective device to return the saw automatically to the back of the table when released at any point of its travel.

d. Inverted sawing or sliding cut-off saws shall be provided with a hood that will cover the part of the saw that protrudes above the top of the table or material being cut.

67. Saws, Table (Woodworking)

a. Circular table saws shall have hoods over the portion of the saw above the table, so mounted that the hood will automatically adjust itself to the thickness of and remain in contact with the material being cut.

b. Circular table saws shall have a spreader aligned with the blade, spaced no more than ½ inch behind the largest blade mounted in the saw. The provision of a spreader in connection with grooving, dadoing, or rabbitting is not required.

c. Circular table saws used for ripping shall have non-kick-back fingers or dogs.

d. Feed rolls and blades of self-feed circular saws shall be protected by a hood or guard to prevent the hands of the operator from coming in contact with the in-running rolls at any point.

68. Scaffolds

a. All scaffolds and their supports shall be capable of supporting the load they are designed to carry with a factor of at least four.

b. All planking shall be scaffold grade, as recognized by grading rules for the species of wood used. The maximum permissable spans for 2 x 9 inch or wider planks are shown in the following table:

	Full thickness undressed lumber		Nominal thickness lumber	
Working load (p.s.f.)....	25	50	75	25	50
Permissible span (ft.)....	10	8	6	8	6

The maximum permissible span for 1¼ x 9 inch or wider plank of full thickness is four feet, with medium loading of 50 p.s.f.

c. Scaffold planks shall extend over their end supports not less than six inches nor more than 18 inches.

d. Scaffold planking shall be overlapped a minimum of 12 inches or secured from movement.

e. Railings and toeboards shall be installed on all open sides and ends of platforms more than 10 feet above the floor except for scaffolds covering an entire interior floor with no exposure to floor openings or needle-beam scaffolds used in structural iron work. There shall be a screen with maximum ½ inch openings between the toeboard and the top rail where persons are required to pass or work under the scaffold.

69. Spray Finishing Operations

a. All spray finishing shall be conducted in spray booths or spray rooms.

b. Spray booths shall be substantially constructed of steel, not thinner than No. 18 U.S. gauge, securely and rigidly supported, or of concrete or masonry; except that aluminum or other substantial noncombustible material may be used for intermittent or low volume spraying. Spray booths shall be designed to sweep air currents toward the exhaust outlet.

c. There shall be no open flame or spark-producing equipment in any spraying areas nor within 20 feet thereof, unless separated by a partition.

d. Electrical wiring and equipment not subject to deposits of combustible residues but located in a spraying area shall be of an explosion-proof type approved for Class I, group D locations or for Class I, Division 1, Hazardous Locations. Electrical wiring, motors, and other equipment outside of but within 20 feet of any spraying area, and not separated therefrom by partitions, shall not produce sparks under normal operating conditions and shall otherwise conform to the provisions for Class I, Division 2, Hazardous Locations.

e. All spraying areas shall be provided with mechanical ventilation adequate to remove flammable vapors, mists, or powders to a safe location and to confine and control combustible residues so that life is not endangered.

f. Electric motors driving exhaust fans shall not be placed inside flammable materials spray booths or ducts. Belts or pulleys within the booth or duct shall be thoroughly enclosed.

g. The quantity of flammable or combustible liquid kept in the vicinity of spraying operations shall be the minimum required for operations and should ordinarily not exceed a supply for one day or one shift.

h. Conspicuous "NO SMOKING" signs shall be posted at all flammable materials spraying areas and storage rooms.

70. Stairs, Fixed Industrial

a. Standard railings shall be provided on the open sides of all exposed stairways. Handrails shall be provided on at least one side of closed stairways, preferably on the right side descending.

b. Stairs shall be constructed so that rise height and tread width is uniform throughout.

c. Fixed stairways shall have a minimum width of 22 inches.

71. Stationary Electrical Devices

All stationary electrically powered equipment, tools, and devices, located within reach of a person who can make contact with any grounded surface or object, shall be grounded.

72. Storage

a. All storage shall be stacked, blocked, interlocked, and limited in height so that it is secure against sliding or collapse.

b. Storage areas shall be kept free from accumulation of materials that constitute hazards or pest harborage. Vegetation control will be exercised when necessary.

c. Where mechanical handling equipment is used, sufficient safe clearance shall be allowed for aisles, at loading docks, and through doorways.

73. Tanks, Open-Surface

When ventilation is used to control potential exposures to employees, it shall be adequate to reduce the concentration of the air contaminated to the degree that a hazard to employees does not exist.

74. Toeboards

a. Railings protecting floor openings, platforms, scaffolds, etc., shall be equipped with toeboards whenever persons can pass beneath the open side, there is moving machinery, or there is equipment which could be struck by falling material.

b. A standard toeboard shall be at least four inches in height and may be of any substantial material, either solid or open, with openings not to exceed one inch in greatest dimension.

75. Toilets

a. Every place of employment shall be provided with adequate toilet facilities which are separate for each sex. Water closets shall be provided according to the following: 1-15 persons, one facility; 16-35 persons, two facilities; 36-55 persons, three facilities; 56-80 persons, four facilities; 81-110 persons, five facilities; 111 to 150 persons, six facilities; over 150 persons, one for each additional 40 persons.

b. Each water closet shall occupy a separate compartment which should be equipped with a door, latch, and clothes hangers.

c. The requirements of (a) and (b) above do not apply to mobile crews or normally unattended locations, as long as employees working at these locations have transportation immediately available to nearby toilet facilities.

d. Adequate washing facilities shall be provided in every toilet room or be adjacent thereto.

e. Covered receptacles shall be kept in all toilet rooms used by women.

76. Toxic Vapors, Gases, Mists, and Dusts

a. Exposure to toxic vapors, gases, mists, or dusts at a concentration above the Threshold Limit Values, contained or referred to in Safety and Health Standards, shall be avoided.
b. To achieve compliance with paragraph (a), administrative or engineering controls must first be determined and implemented whenever feasible. When such controls are not feasible to achieve full compliance, protective equipment or any other protective measures shall be used to keep the

exposure of employees to air contaminants within the limits prescribed. Any equipment and/or technical measures used for this purpose must be approved for each particular use by a competent industrial hygienist or other technically qualified person.

77. Trash

Trash and rubbish shall be collected and removed in such a manner as to avoid creating a menace to health and as often as necessary to maintain good sanitary conditions.

78. Washing Facilities

a. Adequate washing facilities shall be provided in every place of employment and maintained in a sanitary condition. For industrial establishments, at least one lavatory with adequate hot and cold water shall be provided for every 10 employees up to 100 persons, and one lavatory for each 15 persons over 100.
b. A suitable cleansing agent, individual hand towels or other approved apparatus for drying hands, and receptacles for disposing of hand towels, shall be provided at washing facilities.

79. Welding (See also Cylinders, Compressed Gas, No. 17)

a. Arc welding equipment shall be chosen for safe application to the work and shall be installed properly. Workmen designated to operate welding equipment shall have been properly instructed and qualified to operate it.
b. Mechanical ventilation shall be provided when welding or cutting:
* beryllium, cadmium, lead, zinc, or mercury;
* fluxes, metal coatings, or other material containing fluorine compounds;
* where there is less than 10,000 cubic feet per welder;
* in confined spaces.

c. Proper shielding and eye protection to prevent exposure of personnel from welding hazards shall be provided.
d. Proper precautions (isolating welding and cutting, removing fire hazards from the vicinity, providing a fire watch, etc.) for fire prevention shall be taken in areas where welding or other "hot work" is being done.
e. Work and electrode lead cables shall be frequently inspected. Cables with damaged insulation or exposed bare conductors shall be replaced.

80. Woodworking Machinery

a. All woodworking machinery such as table saws, swing saws, radial saws, band saws, jointers, tenoning machines, boring and mortising machines, shapers, planers, lathes, sanders, veneer cutters, and other miscellaneous woodworking machinery shall be effectively guarded to protect the operator and other employees from hazards inherent to their operation.
b. A power control device shall be provided on each machine to make it possible for the operator to cut off the power from each machine, without leaving his position, at the point of operation.
c. Power controls and operating controls should be located within easy reach of the operator while he is at his regular work location, making it unnecessary for him to reach over the cutter to make adjustments. This does not apply to constant pressure controls used only for setup purposes.
d. Each operating treadle shall be protected against unexpected or accidental tripping.

ADOPTION OF STANDARDS

Section 6(b) of the act sets forth the procedures which must be followed in adopting a standard. Generally, the procedure is that the Secretary of Labor, either on his own initiative or on the basis of information submitted to him by someone else, promulgates a standard. The standard is published in the *Federal Register* and comments are invited. A hearing is held, and the secretary then publishes the final standard. The final publication of the standard may contain a 90-day familiarization period. Whenever possible, standards should be expressed in objective criteria. The secretary may also issue a *temporary emergency standard* which becomes effective immediately upon publication in the *Federal Register*, if the secretary determines (1) that employees are exposed to grave danger from exposure to substances or agents determined to be toxic or physically harmful or from new hazards, and (2) that such emergency standard is necessary to protect employees from such danger.

VARIANCES

Section 6 of the Occupational Safety and Health Act provides for the permanent variance and the temporary variance. Of these, the temporary variance will probably be the one most often considered by employers.

A permanent variance may be granted where an employer can show that his method of dealing with a given problem is just as effective as compliance with the appropriate standard from which he seeks the variance. An example would be a variance from a safety color-coding requirement if the employer had his own previously existing color-coding system which could be shown to be effective. In fact, in this situation, requiring the employer to change from a previously existing color-coding system to a new one would likely cause more accidents because of the confusion of employees who would be used to the old one. From a practical standpoint, however, it will be rare where the employer will have such a system which is equally as good as the one from which he seeks a variance. Most of the time, the employer will want a temporary variance from a standard on the grounds that he cannot comply with it in the time required.

Both the criteria for ascertaining when the variance should be granted and the procedure for asking for it are outlined in section 6(b)(6) of the act, which provides as follows:

> Any employer may apply to the Secretary for a temporary order granting a variance from a standard or any provision thereof promulgated under this section. Such temporary order shall be granted only if the employer files an application which meets the requirements of clause (B) and establishes that (i) he is unable to comply with a standard by its effective date because of unavailability of professional or technical personnel or of materials and equipment needed to come into compliance with the standard or because necessary construction or alteration of facilities cannot be completed by the effective date, (ii) he is taking all available steps to safeguard his employees against the hazards covered by the standards, and (iii) he has an effective program for coming into compliance with the standard as quickly as practicable. Any temporary order issued under this paragraph shall prescribe the practices, means, methods, operations, and processes which the employer must adopt and use while the order is in effect and state in detail his program for coming into compliance with the standard. Such a temporary order may be granted only after notice to employees and an opportunity for a hearing: *Provided*, That the Secretary may issue one interim order to be effective until a decision is made on the basis of the hearing. No temporary order may be in effect for longer

than the period needed by the employer to achieve compliance with the standard or one year, whichever is shorter, except that such an order may be renewed not more than twice (I) so long as the requirements of this paragraph are met and (II) if an application for renewal is filed at least 90 days prior to the expiration date of the order. No interim renewal of an order may remain in effect for longer than 180 days.

(B)   An application for a temporary order under this paragraph (6) shall contain:

(i)   a specification of the standard or portion thereof from which the employer seeks a variance,

(ii)   a representation by the employer, supported by representations from qualified persons having firsthand knowledge of the facts represented, that he is unable to comply with the standard or portion thereof and a detailed statement of the reasons therefor,

(iii)   a statement of the steps he has taken and will take (with specific dates) to protect employees against the hazard covered by the standard,

(iv)   a statement of when he expects to be able to comply with the standard and what steps he has taken and what steps he will take (with dates specified) to come into compliance with the standard, and

(v)   a certification that he has informed his employees of the application by giving a copy thereof to their authorized representative, posting a statement giving a summary of the application and specifying where a copy may be examined at the place or places where notices to employees are normally posted, and by other appropriate means.

A description of how employees have been informed shall be contained in the certification. The information to employees shall also inform them of their right to petition the Secretary for a hearing.

(C)   The Secretary is authorized to grant a variance from any standard or portion thereof whenever he determines, or the Secretary of Health, Education and Welfare certifies, that such variance is necessary to permit an employer to participate in an experiment approved by him or the Secretary of Health, Education, and Welfare designed to demonstrate or validate new and improved techniques to safeguard the health or safety of workers.

The following are some practical observations on variance applications. First, if there is a false statement contained in any petition, the petitioner is subject to a fine of up to $10,000 and/or 6 months in prison. Therefore, the plant manager, safety director, or other qualified employees who are employed at the installation and who have firsthand knowledge of the facts should be the one to sign the petition.

Obviously, the sections of the petition dealing with the procedures which will be used to maintain safety to the greatest extent possible are the heart of the petition and should be given most attention by the drafters. Generally, it should be drafted by or at least under the direction of safety and health specialists who possess the required technical expertise. It should also include an accident or employee health history relating to the specific problem.

Third, if the information in the petition will disclose trade secrets, one may apply for confidential treatment as to that particular part of the petition in accordance with section 15 of the act. It is necessary to exercise some restraint here and to request confidential treatment only for those portions which really require it. All confidential information should be clearly marked as such, and there should be a legend on all of it specifying that it should not be copied or communicated to third parties or other agencies.

Fourth, the items required to be included with the application should not be considered exhaustive. If there is other information which is necessary to argue your case or put the matter in perspective, it should obviously be included.

Finally, when the application is ready, six copies of it must be filed with the Department of Labor. In some cases, this is the end of the process and, if the application has been properly drafted and merits approval, it might be approved without any further action. In other cases, the Department of Labor may request additional information, sometimes orally, sometimes in writing. However, if any affected employer or employee files a notice of hearing, then a very formal proceeding must continue. This procedure is spelled out in the regulations.

Following are some practical considerations in deciding whether or not to ask for the variance in the first place. If an application for variance is filed and is not granted, it is likely that the employer will have made admissions which would indicate that the standard had been violated, which may in turn give rise to subsequent inspections or fines. Also, while the application is pending, the employer is still subject to inspection and citation for failure to comply with any appropriate standard.

Second, if the variance is something which might be appropriate for an industrywide approach, the possibility of filing a joint application along with other employers in the industry or the area should be considered. Trade association participation might also be useful.

A number of applications for variance have already been filed and ruled upon. Accordingly, there is a substantial body of law on this point, and business executives should make sure their counsel are aware of this law and its possible relevance to the problems of the company. It is possible that either a similar request for variance has already been filed and acted upon which could provide useful guidance to the company, or a similar request for variance has already been filed and denied, thus calling into question the advisability of spending the time and effort to try again.

Finally, the obvious effects on employee-management relations must also be considered. It must be kept in mind that the employees must be notified and that the maximum efforts must be used to obtain the maximum safety possible during the interim period. This may require, for example, the wearing of protective gear or the shifting around of employees on a relatively frequent basis, so that they are not exposed to concentrations of toxic substances or noises for long periods of time.

INSPECTIONS

Inspections will be made according to priorities which OSHA publicly announces. These change from time to time, but employers should know whether they are involved in high priority or low priority activity. Currently, the emphasis is on toxic or hazardous substances and employee health. It should be noted that any employee or employee representative who believes that a violation of a safety or health standard exists which threatens physical harm or presents an imminent danger may request an inspection. Generally, the inspector will arrive without warning. The act gives the inspector power to enter without delay and at reasonable times any establishment subject to the act, and to inspect and investigate during regular working hours and at other reasonable times, and within reasonable limits and in a reasonable manner, any such place of employment and all pertinent conditions, structures, machines, apparatus, devices, equipment, and materials therein. Also to question privately any such employer, owner, operator, agent, or employee. In addition, the act requires certain record keeping, and these records must be made available to the inspector.

In 1978, the Supreme Court announced in the *Barlows* case that OSHA inspectors did *not* have the right to enter into a plant unannounced to conduct an inspection without a search warrant. The Court said that the provision of the Occupational Safety and Health Act authorizing this was unconstitutional. However, the Court also said that OSHA did not have to show probable cause that there was a violation in order to get a search warrant. OSHA merely had to show the court that the plant to be inspected was chosen pursuant to a reasonable administrative procedure which could, for example, include a procedure to inspect certain types of plants on a random basis. Further, the Court said that the employer did not have to be given notice so the surprise nature of the inspection could be preserved. Thus the case really didn't change any of OSHA's substantive rights—it just made them go through a little more paperwork. In response, OSHA said that, at least until industry in general took a "hard line" and refused to allow the inspectors access to the plant, they would not use their administrative resources to get search warrants but instead would rely on the voluntary admission of their inspectors to plants. It appears that most of industry is voluntarily letting OSHA inspectors in without a warrant because they fear that making them get a warrant will just get them mad and make them conduct a more nit-picking investigation.

Generally, the procedure will be that the inspector will arrive, show his credentials, and ask to see the person in charge of operations for that location. He will then ask to meet the employee representative. (The act gives the employees a right to have a representative accompany an inspector on his tour through the plant.) If there is no employee representative, the inspector will inform the location manager of his duty, under the act, to talk with various individual employees about safety and health questions during his inspection. The inspection will then begin. It is a so-called "walk-through" inspection, with the inspector walking through the entire plant. The compliance officer is in complete charge of the inspection and he may question employees, review records, inspect any machine or area, take environmental samples of air or water, take photographs, and employ any other reasonable investigative technique. However, he is supposed to avoid unnecessary disruption of production, and he must comply with all safety and health regulations observed by the plant. The compliance officer decides which employee representative should accompany him, and he may have an outside third party, not an employee, accompany him. If he wants to see an area involving a trade secret, he can be informed of the secret nature of the area and be requested to observe confidential trade secret treatment. This means that all photographs and environmental samplings in this area will be protected. Naturally, a company is entitled to insist that any employee or other person accompanying the inspector be authorized to enter the area. It is important to note here, however, that confidential treatment must be *affirmatively requested.*

In a typical inspection, the inspector may examine the fire extinguishers, use a meter measuring noise level in various parts of the plant, use other equipment to measure exhaust velocity where exhaust fans are used, take air samples in areas where there are potentially toxic substances, take radioactivity readings where appropriate, observe the use of safety glasses, examine barricades around construction work being done on the premises, and generally conduct a thorough investigation. The inspector will generally have been given a fairly thorough training, and will probably be familiar with all general safety hazards as well as those likely to exist in a given location or industry.

Types of Problems

After the walk-around inspection is completed, and after the inspector has either talked with the employee representative or, if no representative accompanies him, has talked with individual employees, the inspector will then talk with the location manager. At this time, the inspector will disclose any violations or potential violations which he has discovered, and a short period of "negotiation" will begin. Generally, there will be four principal areas of discussion.

Simple and Obvious Safety Violations

The inspector may have noticed a few simple and obvious safety problems which can be corrected without delay before the inspector leaves the premises. Examples would be the failure to erect a barricade around a particular piece of sidewalk which is being repaired, or the existence of an oily rag on an electrical connection box. These should create no problem.

Violations Which Take Some Time to Correct

The inspector may observe some things which management agrees are potential safety hazards, but which cannot be corrected immediately. An example would be an improper guard on a particular machine. Here, the area of negotiation would be the time which was to be allowed to solve the problem.

Enumerated Violations Which Management Feels Improper

The inspector may feel that there is a violation in a case where management does not agree a violation exists. In this situation, management will try to convince the inspector that he is wrong.

Serious Safety Hazards

The fourth and most serious area will be the situation where the inspector feels that he has discovered a serious violation of a safety or health standard which must be corrected immediately. If the problem is such that it cannot be fixed before the inspector leaves, the employer will have no choice but to suspend operations of the particular machine or operation involved until corrective action can be taken. If the employer does not agree that a violation exists, or that it is serious enough to warrant suspension of operations, the inspector has the right to petition the district court for an appropriate injunction. The inspector, however, has no authority to shut down a machine or order any other conduct without such court order.

After this negotiation period (and assuming no serious problem of the type indicated in the "Serious Safety Hazards" section exists), the inspector will return to his office and discuss the inspection with his Area Director. In our example above, assuming that the inspector was not convinced by management that no violation existed in a particular case, he would discuss this problem with his Area Director. Then, assuming the Area Director also thought a violation existed, the matter would be sent to the regional solicitor who would prepare a *citation*. The citation would then be sent to the employer by certified mail. The citation would *cite the violation*, give the employer a certain *time* to correct it, and fix a *penalty*.

A citation is merely an *allegation* that a violation exists. In many respects, it is similar to a traffic ticket. However, the act provides that when the employer receives a citation, it must be *posted* in the area of the alleged violation for *3 days* or until the violation is abated, whichever is longer. Even if the violation is corrected immediately, the citation must remain posted for the minimum 3-day period.

If the employer disagreed with either the existence of the violation, the time to remedy it, or the amount of the penalty, he would be given 15 days to contest any of these items. The citation will say where to send the letter of objection. Generally, this will be to the Area Director.

When a violation has no direct or immediate relationship to safety and health, a de minimus notice may be issued. This kind of notice does not have to be posted and no penalty is involved.

If the employer contests the citation, the Area Director will forward the employer's letter of objection to the regional solicitor who will, in turn, forward it to the commission. The employer and the employees will then be notified of the fixing of a hearing date at which either may present their views. The employer can indicate his objection to either the existence of the violation, the time for abatement, or the size of the penalty. The employees are also permitted to present their case if they feel that a safety problem exists and that the time allowed by the inspector for abatement is excessive. The hearing examiner will thereafter render his decision. The decision of the hearing examiner will be communicated to the employer, and will become final in 30 days. Before the hearing examiner renders his decision, he will send it to the reviewing commission. If the reviewing commission assumes jurisdiction, it will hear the case and hand down its own decision.

If the employer still feels that he has a complaint, he has a right to appeal either the hearing examiner's decision or the decision of the reviewing commission to the federal courts under the procedures contained in section 11 of the act. Generally, the entire body of law dealing with appeals to the courts from administrative agencies will apply here, including the rule that the decision of the agency will be affirmed if supported by *substantial evidence*, and that no objections or evidence can be introduced in court which were not put before the commission.

PLANNING FOR INSPECTIONS

In considering the enforcement process, it is helpful to divide it into three separate categories: (1) matters to be taken into account before an inspection; (2) the actual inspection process; and (3) decisions to be made and actions to be taken after the inspection is completed.

Before the Inspection

As in many areas, the key to a successful OSHA inspection is in advance planning. To some extent, advance planning is simply a matter of common sense. The following items, however, should be considered and an appropriate decision made by all manufacturing establishments subject to the act.

In the overwhelming majority of cases, the compliance officer will arrive unannounced. It is therefore important that the receptionist, or other person who typically greets visitors, knows precisely what to do when the compliance officer arrives. Generally, this simply means knowing to have the compliance officer talk to the chief of operations of the plant. It may be desirable in some locations to have an alternate person available in case the chief of operations is not available when the compliance officer arrives.

The goal of the Occupational Safety and Health Act is to have all plants in 100 percent compliance with all standards at all times. This, however, is probably an unrealistic goal for most locations, especially where the first inspection is involved. Accordingly, in most situations, one must anticipate that the inspecting officer is going to find some deficiencies, and it is important to maintain a very good relationship with the inspecting officer so that his initial impressions of the plant are of good-faith efforts to comply with the act. This should be done in at least the following three ways. (1) While it may be an obvious statement, it is important to keep the plant in a good state of order at all times so that the compliance officer does not have a bad impression of the plant when he first walks in. (2) The compliance officer will want to see the records which are required to be kept by the employer under the Occupational Safety and Health Act. Keeping these records neat, orderly, and up-to-date will avoid the negative reaction which the officer may have if he finds that the records are either not kept at all or kept in an inadequate or disorganized way. (3) In many cases, the plant will have some programs or particular things which were done to enhance its safety, and these could be pointed out to the compliance officer at the very early stages. In order to do this, the person who would be showing the compliance officer around the plant should have clearly in his mind in advance the plus factors which he wants to make sure he points out.

The Occupational Safety and Health Act provides protection for trade secrets of the employers. However, in order to take advantage of this protection, the trade secrets must be specifically pointed out to the compliance officer. It is, therefore, encumbent upon the employer representative to make sure in advance that he knows precisely what areas of his plant and what operations he considers to be trade secrets. He should identify these areas to the compliance officer at an early stage and then reidentify them when they are approached during the walk-around inspection.

Do not make any admissions, especially if the admission would show prior knowledge. For example, if the inspector points to something which he considers a hazard and the employer representative says, "Oh, yes, we know about that and we are going to fix it," it would have established his prior knowledge and may turn a nonserious violation into a serious one. Also, an admission may support a violation of the General Duty Clause, even if no standard is applicable. An admission may also cause the inspector to consider the possibility of a willful violation.

In some cases, a plant will have had a prior inspection by its own safety people or insurance carrier to identify potential safety problems. This should not be disclosed to compliance officers. While they are generally instructed to not ask for this material and not to use it to identify problems, there is no point in asking for trouble by volunteering that the plant has had a mock OSHA inspection by an insurance company or other persons. (Obviously, the employer representative should not lie to the compliance officer, and if he asks whether or not there has been such an inspection, and as a matter of fact there has, the representative should answer affirmatively but should refuse to show a copy of the report to the compliance officer.)

Finally, do not attempt in any way to interfere with or restrict the inspection. The compliance officer is in complete charge of the inspection; he may go anywhere in the plant, and he may talk to any employee.

The Actual Inspection

As indicated above, the beginning of an Occupational Safety and Health Act inspection is usually the unannounced arrival of the compliance officer. He will generally arrive at the main plant entrance and ask for the person in charge of operations at that plant. It is at this point that the planning referred to above will begin to pay off. Generally, the following points and steps should be observed and kept in mind.

Be sure to ask the compliance officer for his credentials. He will probably volunteer to show them and they should be carefully examined to make sure they are legitimate. It may also be appropriate, if there is any doubt, to call the Area Director to verify that this person is an OSHA inspector. This is not done to harass the inspector or to delay the matter, but is simply recognition of the unfortunate fact that, in some prior cases, industrial espionage has been accomplished through the ruse of having an impostor pose as a compliance officer and thereby having a complete tour of the plant. As a general proposition, if the plant contains any significant trade secrets or secret processes, it would be well worth the telephone call to verify the identity of the compliance officer.

The inspection will usually begin with an opening conference, during which the compliance officer examines the safety records of the plant. During the opening conference, the compliance officer will also find out whether the employees are represented by a union and whether or not they have previously designated an employee representative. If they have designated an employee representative, the compliance officer will naturally want to meet that representative.

It is during the opening conference that the compliance officer's initial reaction to the company will be formed. It is, therefore, important that the employer's representative demonstrates a good attitude concerning safety and an awareness of the rules and regulations under the Occupational Safety and Health Act. Obivously, the employer representative must also have a good knowledge of the employer's safety programs. He must also be able to communicate this knowledge to the compliance officer and it is, therefore, important that the employer representative be someone who is fairly articulate.

At the conclusion of the opening conference, the walk-around inspection will begin. The act does specifically say that a management representative has the right to accompany the compliance officer during this walk-around inspection. However, a decision of the Occupational Safety and Health Review Commission has indicated that if the employer representative is unavailable and the inspection is conducted without him, this will not be grounds for later objection. This is the reason, as indicated above, it would be appropriate to have an alternate employer representative in case the compliance officer arrives at a time when the principal employer representative is not available.

The employees are also entitled to have a representative accompany the inspecting officer. Generally, if the plant is represented by a union, there will be such a designated person. If it is not represented by a union, management will probably have to decide whether or not to recommend to the employees that they designate some person. If they do not designate some specific employee representative, the compliance officer is supposed to confer with various employees as he tours the plant.

The compliance officer will generally make extensive notes and may even take photographs during his inspection. The employer representative should not simply stroll around and watch what is going on. He should be very active in recording as much information as he can during the inspection process. For example, he should carefully note the activities of the compliance officer, specifically the times spent in various areas of the plant (e.g., if the compliance officer spent 5 minutes looking around a particular machine very carefully, that should be noted). Generally, however, there should not be any tape recording, and the use of photographic equipment should only be under-taken if the compliance officer decides that he wants to take photographs. If the compliance officer does decide to photograph something, the employer's representative should be prepared to take similar photographs, though per-haps from a different or more favorable angle.

Generally, an initial inspector will not be an expert industrial hygienist. The initial inspector will usually only be able to identify normal safety hazards in the particular plant. However, he will probably not carry with him elaborate measuring devices for noise or toxic substances in the air. If he notes that there may be a problem in this regard, the company can generally expect a subsequent investigation from a qualified industrial hygienist. In this event, the company probably will have some advance warning, and it would be appro-priate to have its own industrial hygienist and inspection or monitoring equip-ment available so that the tests can be done "in parallel" with those of OSHA. For example, the OSHA test on noise or concentrations of toxic substances in the air may be done at peculiar times or locations and show a bad result; whereas, other tests at other times in other locations would show a result much more favorable to the plant. Obviously, if the employer simply relies on the OSHA inspector, he will not have these more favorable data to help his case. If the employer cannot conduct tests in parallel with OSHA, he should do so at the earliest possible time thereafter.

If the inspector should arrive during a work stoppage or other labor dis-pute, management should be very careful to explain this problem to the compli-ance officer. The compliance officer will understand that in this kind of an environment there may be more employee complaints and allegations of safety defects than there might be in a normal work atmosphere. In some cases, the compliance officer will say that he will come back at another time. If, however, he insists on going through the plant anyway, it might be appropriate to call the Area Director to request a reconsideration of this position. If it finally turns out that the inspection does take place during a period of labor unrest, this point should definitely remain part of the record for possible use in any subsequent proceedings.

Employers should probably not allow the inspector to take pictures in any area where a trade secret is located; if the inspector insists, the Area Director should be consulted. If the Area Director also insists, the employer may still refuse to allow the pictures to be taken. The inspector then has the option of obtaining a court order if he feels the inspections really require the pictures. However, in many cases he will not go to this extent; but, if he does get a court order, it may be possible to require the pictures to be held in confidence.

The closing conference should probably be considered to be part of the inspection, and is very important because it will generally show any areas of substantial disagreement.

In the closing conference, the inspector will disclose all conditions or practices which, in his opinion, may constitute a safety hazard and all applica-ble sections of the standards which may have been violated. The inspector will also leave copies of the standards which he thinks may have been violated. He will also indicate that citations may be issued and monetary penalities proposed, and he will request the views of the employer on a proper time for abatement of the alleged violation.

This is the point where the employer representative must be on his toes and advocate his position. Generally, the best approach is to lay all the cards on the table and explain fully to the compliance officer any appropriate difficul-ties which will be encountered in abatement. If the problem is simple (for example, installing a better guard rail or a more appropriate machine guard), the abatement period can be relatively short. (In fact, some safety hazards can be abated on the spot by simply making some minor change, perhaps while the compliance officer is there.) On the other hand, there may be serious problems, such as the required guard may not be available, the abatement may require the hiring of additional personnel, engineering studies may have to be conducted, or new equipment may have to be purchased. There is always the problem of money, but, generally, cost is not an extenuating circumstance that will buy much time with the compliance officer.

If the employer representative adequately advocates his position, there is a good chance that when the entire record is reviewed by the Area Director, he may allow an abatement period of sufficient time to comply, and the necessity of contesting the citation will have been avoided.

Finally, immediately following the inspection and the closing conference, the employer representative should be careful to compile all of his notes and, perhaps at that time, dictate a full memorandum as to precisely what took place from beginning to end. Again, it is more advisable to take full notes and dictate a memorandum immediately after the inspection than to have any tape recorders or other recording of the conversations.

After the Inspection

After the inspection, the compliance officer will prepare his report and review it with his Area Director. If there is any violation, a citation or a notice of de minimus violation will probably be issued. A notice of de minimus violation will probably not cause the employer any substantial problem, as there are no penalties attached to it and, by the very nature of the notice, it is not a serious problem. However, if the employer gets a citation, he will immediately have to analyze it very carefully to ascertain the appropriate course of conduct. Since the periods for objection are very limited, time is of the essence.

The employer must also note that if a citation is received, it must be posted at the area where the alleged safety violation exists. This is true even though the violation is contested. If the employer desires, he can post his own notice next to it stating that he does not believe there is a safety violation and is going to contest the citation. The citation must be posted until the hazard is abated or for three working days, whichever is later.

The first step in looking at the citation is to examine what important problems it raises. Generally, the citation will give notice of an alleged violation and set forth a proposed penalty. In the overwhelming majority of cases, the proposed penalty will be a very modest amount of money, certainly far less than the attorney's fees which would be generated by any kind of objection. In addition, however, the citation will set forth a proposed period of abatement, and this may cause serious problems for the company.

There are generally two kinds of situations. One is a situation where the citation simply states that a machine lacks a guard which could be fairly readily installed or that a certain railing is not of the proper construction or height. In these situations, even though management many not feel that the citation is justified, it may be appropriate to simply accomplish the desired change because the cost and time involved in objecting to it would be more than the cost involved in making the change. In other cases, however, the citation will cause a real problem to management. For example, a citation may require the placing of a guard on a machine in such a way that the machine could not be operated. Another objection may be to noise levels or levels of toxicity which (a) the company does not have the technology to improve upon or (b) the company could improve upon but only at great cost. It is these latter cases in which the citation will have to be contested.

Following are some of the more important factors to consider in deciding whether or not to contest the citation. The employees will have to be given notice of the fact that a citation has been issued and contested. The plant will obviously have to take into account labor relations problems which this may cause.

If the abatement period is so short that the plant cannot remedy the problem in the time allotted, a reinspection at a later time may give rise to additional and more severe penalties for failure to abate the alleged violation.

The effect of the citation must be considered in the light of its future possible implications. To some extent, the situation is like building a criminal record. It may be easy to get off rather lightly on the first conviction, but thereafter the penalties become more severe. If a company "pleads guilty" to a citation which it feels is not justified, it may find that it has needlessly compromised its record and created a potential for future problems with OSHA.

Finally, the effect on possible litigation must be considered. In the case of a citation which is issued as a result of an employee accident where someone has been injured, the effect of accepting a citation alleging a safety hazard on any possible litigation against the company by the injured employee or other person, or their heirs, must be considered. In some respects, it is like pleading guilty in traffic court where there has been an accident. It may be that the simplest way to get rid of the traffic violation is to plead guilty and pay the modest fine, but an admission of guilt in traffic court might be used against the defendant in later civil action for much more substantial monetary damages. The same principle might apply for a violation of the Occupational Safety and Health rules. To some extent, the implications are less because most injuries will be covered under the workmen's compensation statutes. However, the variations among the workmen's compensation rules still make this consideration important. It is especially important if someone besides an employee has been injured. Also relevant would be the state's evidentiary rules. A plea of "guilty" might be admissible in a subsequent civil action as an admission against interest; whereas, a finding of "guilty," if the citation was contested, might not be admissible.

In summary, deciding whether or not to contest the citation will rarely, if ever, revolve around the modest fine. Most of the time, the decision will revolve around the implications of the citation or problems which the company would have in abating the alleged hazard.

It must be kept in mind that a citation must be contested within fifteen working days from the time it is received. Time is, therefore, of the essence. Legal assistance is an absolute necessity; however, the decision is not purely one for the lawyers. Indeed, except in a case where the Occupational Safety and Health Act problems may have some direct bearing on pending or possible litigation against the company, the decision will be based upon the technological and cost factors involved in abating the alleged safety hazard.

As indicated above, a citation will generally contain three parts: the statement of an alleged safety hazard; a proposed penalty; and a period of abatement. It is possible to object to only the period of abatement. However, this is a legal trap for the unwary. A simple objection to the period of abatement will not stay the period; a notice of contest to the citation will. It is, therefore, recommended by most attorneys that if the employer feels that the abatement period will cause a significant problem and is unreasonably short, he should contest the whole citation within fifteen days, even if the real purpose of the contest is simply to object to the period of abatement. The act does say that the period of abatement will be stayed only if the citation is contested in good faith and not simply for delay. As a practical matter, however, it would usually be very difficult to prove that a citation was contested only for delay where there were serious questions over the proper period of abatement.

After a citation is received, the employer may request a conference to discuss the matter with the OSHA. Generally, these conferences are very useful and, in many cases, it is possible to reach an acceptable settlement of the matter by this means. However, it is important to note that, as a legal matter, the 15-day period in which to contest the citation is not suspended while the conference is taking place. Time is, therefore, of the essence.

For planning purposes, the employer must always assume that if a citation is issued, it will receive a follow-up inspection. Follow-up inspections are only mandatory for serious, willful, or repeated violations and in imminent-danger situations. However, these inspections are discretionary with the Area Director for nonserious violations. If the follow-up inspection discloses that the hazard has not been abated, the employer faces serious penalties (up to $1000 per day).

It is possible to both contest a citation and, at the same time, to ask for a variance. Sometimes this is an advantageous procedure, especially where the employer believes he can establish grounds for a variance.

The Occupational Safety and Health Act *does not* make the employer a guarantor of the employees' safety. All that is required is that employers provide their employees with a safe place of employment.

However, as indicated in the section "General Duty Requirement" at the beginning of this chapter, the fact that an employer is not at fault in creating the hazard is *not* a defense. The fact that the employee may have been negligent himself will generally not be a defense for the company. The fact that another employee was negligent in causing the accident will also generally not be a defense.

If, however, the employer does establish safety measures for the protection of the employees, and diligently enforces those safety practices, the deliberate disregard of these safety practices may be a defense. However, this is true only if the employer made these safety practices known to the employees and adequately enforced them. The mere fact that they existed will not save the employer from liability.

Complete unforeseeability has sometimes been used successfully as a defense. However, these cases generally involve rather clear facts for the employer. Examples include a case where an experienced and well-qualified employee in a research laboratory failed to enclose the energized terminals of capacitors on which he was working, and a case where the employer had work procedures which conformed to those generally used in the industry and an accident occurred anyway.

PENALTIES

Along with the citation, or shortly after, the Area Director will advise of any penalty which may be involved. The amount of the penalty will be based on the size of the company, the type of violation involved, and the good-faith history of the company. Any previous violations would also influence the penalty.

For a serious violation, a mandatory penalty of up to $1000 will be assessed. A serious violation is defined as one in which there is a substantial probability that death or physical harm could result. For nonserious violations, a penalty of up to $1000 *may* be assessed. If the violation is not corrected, additional penalties of up to $1000 per day may be assessed. Willful or repeated violations may result in penalties of up to $10,000 for each violation. Any willful violation which causes death will, upon conviction, be punished by a fine of not more than $10,000, or by imprisonment for not more than 6 months, or both. For subsequent offenses, the punishment level becomes $20,000, one year, or both.

Precisely who goes to jail is not yet clear. Possibilities are (1) the plant manager, (2) the individual at the plant who is in charge of compliance with safety standards, and (3) the individual who was directly responsible for the particular violation.

RECORD KEEPING, POSTING, AND REPORTING

The Occupational Safety and Health Act enumerates many areas in which employers *may* be required to maintain records and furnish reports. However, to date OSHA has taken a very realistic attitude regarding paper work and has only instituted requirements which are very reasonable.

Record Keeping

There are only three records which *must* be maintained, all of which can be done on forms supplied by OSHA: (1) A log of occupational injuries and illnesses, (2) a supplementary record of information on each separate injury or illness, and (3) an annual summary of injuries and illnesses. All of these records must be retained for 5 years. The annual summary of injuries and illnesses must be posted in the establishment annually for 30 days beginning no later than February 1. All of these records must be maintained at the work site and be made available to an inspector upon request. There is no requirement that any of these records be sent or any information reported to OSHA.

Posting

Posting requirements include the requirement that the employer post a notice to keep employees informed of their rights and duties under the act (an approved poster is available from OSHA), and a requirement that the employer post a copy of any citation which it may receive from an OSHA compliance officer.

Reporting Requirements

The only affirmative reporting requirement is one which requires the employer to notify the nearest OSHA Area Director of any accident which gives rise to a fatality or the hospitalization of five or more employees.

The complete regulation is as follows:

> Section 1904.8 Reporting of Fatality or Multiple Hospitalization Accidents.—
> Within 48 hours after the occurrence of an employment accident which is fatal to one or more employees or which results in hospitalization of five or more employees, the employer of any employees so injured or killed shall report the accident either orally or in writing to the nearest office of the Area Director of the Occupational Safety and Health Administration, U.S. Department of Labor.

The reporting may be by telephone or telegraph. The report shall relate the circumstances of the accident, the number of fatalities, and the extent of any injuries. The Area Director may require such additional reports, in writing or otherwise, as he deems necessary, concerning the accident.

If requested, an employer must respond to an annual survey on occupational injuries and illnesses. This is the so-called OSHA Form 103. However, this is not a routine, recurring form, but rather one which is specifically requested by OSHA.

EMPLOYEE RIGHTS

Section 11(c) of the act provides as follows:

(c)(1) No person shall discharge or in any manner discriminate against any employee because such employee has filed any complaint or instituted or caused to be instituted any proceeding under or related to this Act or has testified or is about to testify in any such proceeding or because of the exercise by such employee on behalf of himself or others of any right afforded by this Act.

(2) Any employee who believes that he has been discharged or otherwise discriminated against by any person in violation of this subsection may, within thirty days after such violation occurs, file a complaint with the Secretary alleging such discrimination. Upon receipt of such complaint, the Secretary shall cause such investigation to be made as he deems appropriate. If upon such investigation, the Secretary determines that the provisions of this subsection have been violated, he shall bring an action in any appropriate United States district court against such person. In any such action the United States district courts shall have jurisdiction, for cause shown to restrain violations of paragraph (1) of this subsection and order all appropriate relief including rehiring or reinstatement of the employee to his former position with back pay.

(3) Within 90 days of the receipt of a complaint filed under this subsection the Secretary shall notify the complainant of his determination under paragraph 2 of this subsection.

This is a form of "Bill of Rights" for the employees, and regulations have been issued to expand and clarify the implications of this section. In summary, the employees have the following rights:

1. The right to require a federal or state safety inspection

2. The right to have citations posted

3. The right to confer with inspectors

4. The right to receive reports from inspectors

5. The right to be informed regarding appeals

6. The right to be involved in the standards-setting process

7. The right to refuse to expose himself to unreasonable safety hazards

8. The right to be protected from discrimination by management for his exercise of any of these rights

STATE PLANS

Section 18 of the Occupational Safety and Health Act provides that any state which at any time desires to assume responsibility for development and enforcement therein of Occupational Safety and Health standards relating to any Occupational Safety and Health issue, with respect to which a federal standard has been promulgated, shall submit a state plan for the development of such standards and their enforcement.

The act then goes on to provide that the Secretary of Labor shall approve the plan or such modification thereof which provides for adequate development and enforcement of safety and health standards in the state and which contains provisions that are at least as effective as those in the federal act. The act also contains provisions allowing the federal government to make financial grants to the states to encourage them to develop these kinds of plans.

From a practical point of view, the state plans have the following significance. If the establishment in question is located in a state which has an approved plan, that establishment must obviously comply with all of the requirements of that plan and cannot feel that compliance with the federal requirements is sufficient. As a practical matter, most of the state plans are almost carbon copies of the federal system. Accordingly, the general principles and most of the standards set forth in the federal Occupational Safety and Health Act will be appropriate to a given location, even if there is a state plan in existence.

There is some possibility of dual enforcement of a state and federal plan. Under section 18(e) of the act, the federal agency does maintain a dual jurisdiction with the state agency for a period of at least 3 years after the approval of the state plan. However, as a practical matter, given the shortage of inspectors at both the federal and state levels, such dual enforcement is not very likely.

A book such as this cannot go into the particular provisions of all state plans. However, it must be pointed out and constantly kept in mind that states may (and have) adopt plans which substantially, if not completely, supersede the federal regulatory scheme. It is, therefore, essential that anyone in charge of a plant safety program or anyone advising a company maintain an awareness of which states have operative plans and the content of those plans.

ASSISTANCE

Department of Labor

In typical government style, the Department of Labor publishes a tremendous amount of material on OSHA. Generally, it is very good, and it is also either free or sold at a very low cost. The principal problems are that it is sometimes not as up-to-date as that published by the commercial publishing houses, and it is not well advertised, so it is sometimes difficult to know just what is available.

In addition to the hundreds of small pamphlets on particular aspects of OSHA, a magazine entitled, *Job Safety and Health*, published by the U.S. Department of Labor, Occupational Safety and Health Administration, would be worthwhile for those involved in this area (both attorneys and safety officers). *Job Safety and Health*, published monthly, is the official magazine of OSHA. It is available by subscription from the Superintendent of Documents, U.S. Government Printing Office, Washington, D.C. 20402.

Monthly Labor Review, also a Department of Labor publication, sometimes contains some useful OSHA articles or information.

Commercial Sources

There are a multitude of commercial organizations which sell various kinds of OSHA information. From a lawyer's viewpoint, the best are the ones from the recognized legal publishing houses. CCH, BNA, and Prentice-Hall are the ones most widely used.

From a management point of view, there are a number of companies which attempt to assist businesses in complying with their OSHA requirements. Some are good; others, frankly, are, frauds. Management should be certain of precisely what the requirements are, and that the company selling the service actually has the expertise to perform the job. With the vast amount of assistance available from the other sources listed in this chapter, companies should probably carefully consider all their alternatives before spending their money for "independent" assistance from unknown firms in the OSHA area.

Trade Associations

Trade association publications sometimes contain useful information on OSHA matters. They are particularly useful to counsel because they will point out problems in the industry of which he may not have been aware. They are also useful for those actually handling the safety function, because many times the trade association will do a better job of analyzing a new standard and getting a copy of it into the hands of their members than the publishing companies who sell OSHA material. Also, trade association material generally has the advantage of being free to the members of the association.

National Institute for Occupational Safety and Health (NIOSH)

A great deal of technical assistance is available from the National Institute for Occupational Safety and Health (NIOSH) in the form of an almost endless list of publications. Some are technical, others are nontechnical; most are either free or available for a very nominal cost.

General questions concerning the work of NIOSH and requests for publications should be directed to either of the following addresses: Office of Public Information (Headquarters), National Institute for Occupational Safety and Health, Room 10-A-22, 56 Fishers Lane, Rockville, Maryland 20852; or Office of Public Information (Cincinnati Office), National Institute for Occupational Safety and Health, 1014 Broadway, Cincinnati, Ohio 45202.

Following is a list of nineteen of the products available from NIOSH. There are many, many others.

1. *Kit of Basic NIOSH Reference Materials.* Basic materials concerning the Occupational Safety and Health Act of 1970 and the NIOSH program. Contains article reprints, fact sheets, and related summary material.

2. *Films and Filmstrips on Occupational Safety and Health* (28 pages). Listing of occupational safety and health films and filmstrips compiled to provide interested individuals and groups with a current reference to *loan-free* audiovisual aids. Included also is a listing of organizations that offer rental and purchase of occupational safety and health films and filmstrips.

3. *Occupational Disease—The Silent Enemy.* General pamphlet covering various aspects of occupational diseases.

4. *Working with Industrial Solvents* (8 pages). For use by workers using organic industrial solvents. Pamphlet includes a discussion of the nature of solvents,

health problems, control of exposure, and the actions of employers and employees.

5. *Working with Lead in Industry* (6 pages). Informational pamphlet for lead workers. Discusses the health aspects of their work, lead usage, health hazards, proper controls, and possible action by employers and employees.

6. *Welding Safely* (8 pages). Informational pamphlet for welders. Discusses the health aspects of welding operations. Pamphlet includes a discussion of health hazards, control methods, and possible actions by management and workers.

7. *Working with Cutting Fluids* (5 pages). Discusses what cutting fluids are, how they are used, how they may affect the worker, and methods for control.

8. *Directory of Governmental Occupational Safety and Health Personnel.* Annual listing of local, state, and federal agencies engaged full- or part-time in occupational safety and health activities.

9. *Working with Silver Solder* (5 pages). Pamphlet covering potential health hazards to workers using silver solder.

10. *Preventing Dermatitis If You Work with Epoxy Resins* (19 pages). Intended for the worker and includes recommended precautions for handling epoxy resins. Discusses plant housekeeping procedures and personal hygiene practices.

11. *Occupational Health and Safety Legislation* (360 pages. Revised edition). Consists of citations and excerpts or digests of state laws and regulations dealing with occupational safety and health. This publication is intended primarily as a guide to state legislation and regulations dealing with the health and safety of workers and their places of employment.

12. *Annual List of Toxic Substances—1972* (572 pages). A listing of potentially hazardous materials. Serving as a guide for research needed in setting new occupational health standards. Publication required annually by the Occupational Safety and Health Act of 1970.

13. *The President's Report on Occupational Safety and Health.* A report on the year's progress by the Department of Labor (OSHA) and the Department of Health, Education, and Welfare (NIOSH) in implementing the Occupational Safety and Health Act of 1970. Available in single copies only.

14. *Annual Report of the Federal Coal Mine Health and Safety Act.* This annual report describes the activities of NIOSH (DHEW) in carrying out health responsibilities under the Federal Coal Mine Health and Safety Act of 1969.

15. *The Hazard Evaluation Program of NIOSH* (12 pages). Explains the NIOSH program of conducting hazard evaluations in places of work when requested by employee and employer representatives under the Occupational Safety and Health Act of 1970.

16. *Research and Demonstration Grants.* Describes the research and demonstration projects currently supported by NIOSH grants.

17. *Training Grants.* Describes NIOSH-supported training-grant programs underway in colleges and universities across the nation.

18. *The Toxicology of Beryllium* (50 pages). Summarizes the current state of knowledge of beryllium toxicity, and discusses how beryllium and its compounds can be used safely with proper engineering and medical control measures.

19. *On-The-Job Safety Rules for Power Tools* (4 pages). A joint publication of the Power Tool Institute, Inc., National Association of Home Builders, the United Brotherhood of Carpenters and Joiners of America, and NIOSH. Presents through drawings and narration the rules for power tool use in occupational settings.

Insurance Companies

A great deal of assistance in understanding and complying with the detailed standards under OSHA is available from most large insurance companies. Important points about this information are the following. In many cases, companies are paying for assistance whether they take advantage of it or not. That is, the cost of much of this assistance is built right into the premium. Some insurance companies view the failure of a company to avail itself of this assistance as an indication of a lack of concern with OSHA, and may take this into account as a negative factor when rating that company.

The kind of assistance available, of course, depends on the insurance carrier, but the following items, which are made available by Travelers Insurance Companies, are illustrative. (This is only a small part of the assistance which is made available by Travelers; even the booklets just listing the available assistance are many pages long.)

1. A virtually unlimited number of different well-written and well-printed publications on particular safety problems.

2. Training films and training programs for a company's safety people.

3. Films for showing to the employees on various aspects of safety.

4. Special consultation on special engineering safety problems.

5. "Mock OSHA inspections." (Depending on the situation, there may be a charge for special mock OSHA investigations.)

6. Assistance in developing forms to avoid duplicate record keeping for federal and state purposes.

Occuptional Safety and Health Administration

OSHA also provides a substantial amount of assistance, either free or at a very low cost. Following is a brief description of that information as it appeared in *Job Safety and Health*, December 1974.

Training Programs

OSHA has developed and made available courses on everything from crane safety to shoring and trenching to voluntary compliance. These courses are offered all over the country, and again, your area office has the schedule of those available near you. In addition, OSHA has developed the following courses and related materials, which are for sale from the National Audiovisual Center, Washington, D.C. 20409.

1. "Employer-Employee Rights and Responsibilities under the Occupational Safety and Health Act." A comprehensive package of instructional materials designed to explain OSHA and the rights and responsibilities of both employer and employee. Includes instructor's guide and set of 189 color slides. ($30 per set)

2. "A Guide to Voluntary Compliance." A course that provides guidelines for setting up self-inspection procedures to help employers correct workplace deficiencies. Includes student manual, instructor's guide, and set of 174 color slides. ($55 per set)

3. "Construction Safety and Health Training." A 30-hour course designed to train supervisory personnel and employees in safe work practices on construction jobs. Covers all phases of construction safety and health. Package of five manuals and 466 color slides.

OSHA's Technical Data Center

OSHA's Technical Data Center at 1726 M Street, N.W., Washington, D.C., is open to the public weekdays from 8:15 to 4:45. Under the Freedom of Information Act, the center is required to maintain a library of information on the Occupational Safety and Health Act which anyone may use. This library includes a large collection of technical safety and health reference materials; federal, state, and foreign standards regulations; training materials; and other data essential to OSHA activities. Files of public hearings, standards, variances, congressional committee reports, the *Federal Register*, American National Standards Institute (ANSI) standards—everything connected with the act—can be found in the library. The center also has photographs, magazines, books, microfilms, tapes, and slides.

Recently, lawyers involved in litigation over responsibility for the collapse of a high-rise building under construction in Virginia, in which several workers were killed, came to Washington to use the center's files because all information on the disaster, including news clippings, was there.

Speakers

OSHA is eager to educate the public about the law, and so its employees speak at hundreds of meetings per month throughout the country. Trade associations, labor unions, adult education classes, private businesses, professional organizations—OSHA addresses them all. Since many of these sessions are held at night, a number of OSHA representatives regularly devote their own time, without remuneration, to help inform the public.

OSHA speakers will talk about whatever aspect of job safety and health the audience wants to hear about. At first, most speech requests were for information on how the act affected different industries, but now audiences want specific information on details of the law.

If you want a speaker, check with your OSHA area office. Whether you have an audience of 125,000, like the Building Modernization Convention in Chicago, or two dozen tunnel workers at a local union headquarters, OSHA can find somebody to speak to you.

OSHA has more than a dozen exhibits which it sends to conventions, seminars, and meetings across the country, and also offers photographs, pamphlets, and slide presentations. If you can use any of these materials at your meeting, write to Public Liaison, OSHA, U.S. Department of Labor, Washington, D.C. 20210.

Films

Realizing that visual aids make a subject easier to understand, OSHA has produced a 26-minute color film, *This is OSHA*, which is available free to interested organizations. It reports on the agency's first 2 years of operation and gives an overview of how standards are set, what inspections are like, and how to achieve voluntary compliance with the act. The only cost for use of the film is the return postage. Write Modern Talking Picture Service, 2323 New Hyde Park Road, New Hyde Park, N.Y. 11040.

Loans

If you need to make improvements in your plant or equipment in order to comply with safety and health standards, contact your area office for information on loans available through the Small Business Administration. Among other advantages, these loans have a lower interest rate than commercial loans. For more information, ask for the pamphlet *OSHA Fact Sheet for Small Businesses on Obtaining Compliance Loans.*

Advisory Inspections

For the first few years of OSHA's existence, it was not permitted to send an inspector to your plant for an advisory inspection. If you did ask for an inspection, an inspector would be required to give you a citation for any violations he found. Obviously, no one asked for inspections.

In 1977, however, this aspect was changed, and now OSHA not only can inspect voluntarily but is willing to do so. The inspector will spend a reasonable amount of time in your facility counseling you on potential safety problems. He will not give you any citations even is he observes a violation of a standard. However, if the inspector observes what he believes to be an imminently dangerous situation, he would be obliged to take some action, even if it meant shutting down the operation in question.

IMPORTANCE OF THE OCCUPATIONAL SAFETY AND HEALTH ACT IN OTHER CONTEXTS

The Occupational Safety and Health Act may affect the operations of a corporation in the following indirect ways.

Labor Negotiations

Before the enactment of the Occupational Safety and Health Act, it was fairly standard practice to cover the safety question in a labor contract by including a phrase to the effect that: "the corporation will provide the employees with a safe and healthful place of employment." In some cases, this is still the approach that is taken. However, with increasing frequency, the unions are requesting and management is agreeing to more comprehensive treatment of the safety and health question in the collective bargaining process.

An illustration of some of the kinds of things which may be requested by a union are the following:

The corporation will provide:
—sampling and monitoring equipment to the local committees for measuring noise, carbon monoxide and air flow;
—protective equipment and clothing at no cost to employees;
—training programs, in cooperation with the union, for specialized plant personnel and educational programs for all workers;
—adequate and competent staff and medical facilities. It will also provide, without cost to the individual workers, medical services, physical examinations and other tests as often as necessary to determine whether his health is being affected by exposure to toxic agents;
—complete and accurate reports to each worker or his personal physician, upon request, of any such medical examinations related to an occupational hazard;
—comprehensive reports to the union for each of the plants covering the same data which it is already required to report to the federal government.
The Corporation's health and safety staff will make regular surveys of each plant. It will also make special surveys, when requested by either plant management or the union. Survey findings will be reported to the International Union upon request.
The International Union's health and safety staff representatives will have

access to all plants and locations where members of the union are employed, so that they can make health and safety inspections.

The company will disclose to the union the identity of any potentially harmful physical agents or toxic materials to which workers may be exposed. It will also disclose the antidotes and remedies for these materials.

The corporation and the union agree to designate two representatives each at the International level who will constitute an International Health and Safety Committee. This committee will meet at least quarterly to review policy and implement and promote an effective corporation-wide health and safety program.

The company and the union also agree to a similar joint union-management committee at the plant level, with one representative from each side, which will meet at least once a month, review special problems and make recommendations for changes. This committee will also make regular weekly inspections of the plant.

Union representatives will be notified in advance of plant inspections by government officials and will be able to accompany these officials on their inspections.

The union retains the right to strike over health and safety issues.

Obviously, the thrust of negotiations on safety problems will vary at each location. The central points to keep in mind are as follows. One, the people negotiating the contract should be fully prepared to respond to union requests for increased union participation in the safety program. In other words, the company's policies and positions on this matter should be well-thought-out before the matter comes to negotiation.

Two, the company should consider what steps it may take to "keep the employees happy." This might include such things as a stepped-up safety program, or an announcement of certain projects which the company is undertaking to make the workplace a more safe and healthful place.

Three, in deciding what to do on the labor relations—safety front, some companies sometimes consider that increased participation and publicity of their actions may simply make the employees more aware of their rights and increase, rather than decrease, the likelihood of the union raising the problem during negotiations and asking for extensive participation in the safety process. Naturally, this is a decision which would have to be made by each unit which faced the problem, but generally the publicity of Occupational Safety and Health Act requirements through other means is such that the company is probably fooling itself if it feels that employees are not already aware of the problem. Newspaper articles and other coverage of the Occupational Safety and Health Act makes it more than likely that almost all employees, and certainly all union representatives, are aware of both the Occupational Safety and Health Act and employers' responsibilities thereunder.

The Purchase and Sale of the Company's Products

In some cases, the company will be requested to warrant to those to whom it sells its products that those products "comply with OSHA requirements." In other cases, the purchaser will want to be assured that the products it purchases comply with OSHA requirements. As a general rule, it would seem unwise for a company to make any kind of a general warranty about its products complying with Occupational Safety and Health Act requirements, because so many of those requirements depend on the method of using the particular product rather than on its design. There is also the timing problem in that the standards change, and the company certainly would not want to warrant that its products will be in compliance with standards when it doesn't know what those standards might be in the future.

On the reverse side of the coin, the company should constantly strive to make sure that the products it purchases are safe and, to the extent appropriate, that they comply with the physical characteristics mandated by the standards under the Occupational Safety and Health Act. However, it is suggested that the best way to accomplish this is to have all of the people in purchasing aware of the problem and to know what requirements are present, and to be assured that the products, in fact, do satisfy those requirements. It would not seem sufficient to simply structure the company's purchasing orders with the phrase that "all products comply with OSHA standards," because this would only open the way to a lawsuit against someone if it were found later on by an OSHA inspector that a particular machine or other product did not comply. It would certainly in no way limit the liability of the company for any fines or penalties under an OSHA inspection.

However, some companies may either desire or be forced to deal with this problem specifically in terms of written contractual provisions. In that event, the following points should be kept in mind. One, if you are the seller, make sure that your warranty is tied into some specific date. This can either be the date of manufacture or the date of delivery, but in no event should the warranty be open-ended. Two, if you are the seller, any warranty that your products do comply with the Occupational Safety and Health Act of 1970 and all regulations and standards promulgated thereunder should certainly be followed by another provision which removes any liability for the way the product is used.

The following is some language which has been observed on some documents which seems adequate for the seller's purposes:

> Seller shall not be responsible for any failure to comply with the requirements of the Occupational Safety and Health Act of 1970 or the regulations or the standards promulgated thereunder which result from the location, operation, use or maintenance of the equipment or from alterations of the equipment by persons other than the seller or from an option or accessory to the equipment which was available to the buyer but omitted at the buyer's direction or from design or instructions furnished by the buyer or his agents.

The seller should probably limit his liability to the maximum extent possible to remove any liability for consequential damages, loss of profits, or any fines or penalties which the buyer may incur. Again, the following language has been observed and would appear to be adequate:

> The seller's responsibility for the products sold to the buyer is limited to modification or replacement of the equipment so that the equipment conforms to the applicable regulation or standard. Or at the seller's option to the return of the equipment and the refund of the purchase price, less an allowance for normal depreciation. In no event will the seller indemnify the buyer for any fines or penalties nor be responsible for loss due to delay or consequential damages of any nature whatsoever.

In some cases, additional consideration will have to be given to the contract. Particularly troublesome are the noise standards. Some people deal with these separately and provide in the contract that any standard promulgated with respect to noise is specifically excluded. If noise is a real problem in the particular item in question, the seller may consider offering a separate warranty, perhaps at an additional cost, relating to noise standards.

If the seller or buyer has knowledge that the equipment is going to be used in a coal mine or any other application which is governed by a specific set of standards other than the general industry standards, those standards should be taken into consideration and appropriate modifications made in the contract, if desired.

From the buyer's point of view, the following would be a representative (but not ncessarily complete) list of the kinds of things a purchasing agent should make sure comply with applicable OSHA regulations:

1. Equipment related to walking or working surfaces, such as, ladders, scaffolding or manually propelled mobile ladders, scaffolds, or towers. Also included under this category would be any kind of powered platform, manlift, or vehicle-mounted work platform.

2. Any device or commodity which in any way emits any kind of radiation.

3. Any kind of compressed gas, including acetylene, hydrogen, oxygen, and nitrous-oxide, and also including the containers in which they are shipped, stored, or used.

4. Any kind of highly flammable or combustible liquids, including the containers in which they are shipped, stored, or used.

5. Any kind of personal protective equipment, including eye protection, respiratory protection, head protection, foot protection, or electrical protection devices.

6. Any kind of medical or first aid kits or fire extinguishers.

7. Any kind of materials-handling or storage equipment, including lift trucks.

8. Any kind of powered machine tools, including woodworking machinery, metalworking machinery, abrasive wheel machinery, power presses, forging machines, mechanical power transmission apparatus.

9. Any kind of hand or portable power tools, portable electric saws, drills, etc.

10. Any kind of apparatus for welding, cutting, or brazing.

The above list is not an all-inclusive list nor are the requirements on any item very detailed. For example, the only requirement that the purchaser should be aware of when purchasing fire extinguishers is that they must operate between 40° and 120°. All of the rest of the detailed regulations involving fire extinguishers apply to their use, placement, labeling, periodic inspection, etc., and are the responsibility of the safety officer of each plant rather than of the purchasing agent. This same principle applies to many of the other regulations cited above.

Negligence

As a general rule of negligence law, the failure to live up to a standard of conduct which is set forth in any law or regulation may be evidence of negligence. Indeed, under most state laws, this failure would create a presumption of negligence. There are, of course, numerous "standards of conduct" which are inherent in the various standards promulgated under the Occupational Safety and Health Act. In appropriate cases, these may be used by a plaintiff in a lawsuit alleging negligence. To this date, there have not been a great many instances of this kind of suit because most injuries that would be caused by a failure to comply with a standard would be governed by the applicable workmen's compensation laws. However, in the future it is possible that the detailed and elaborate standards of conduct set forth in the standards for the Occupational Safety and Health Act may be used in some negligence cases.

Private Cause of Action

The Occupational Safety and Health Act *does not* give use to a direct private cause of action for the injured employee.

CURRENT PROBLEMS

There are so many possible problems in the area of occupational safety and health that a company is well-advised to spend its money where it will do the most good. Lawyers can serve a useful function here by advising on the areas where most of the litigation seems to be taking place. Trade associations can also be useful for this purpose. At this time, the two most important areas for concern are noise and toxic substances. The OSHA noise standard will require many significant changes in equipment design, manufacturing procedures, and monitoring. A good hearing-conservation program involving employee testing is probably a good idea. OSHA is also concerned with substances used in the workplace which may be harmful to employees, particularly those which might be carcinogens. At future times, other areas of concern might be more important, but right now, companies would be well-advised to spend their OSHA money on these matters.

OSHA AND THE COURTS

At this time, the courts have been rather unsympathetic to OSHA. They have held, first of all, that unannounced inspections are unconstitutional. (Inspections pursuant to employee complaints or in response to accidents would not be included in this ruling. In those cases, OSHA would have probable cause for getting a warrant to enter the facility.)

Some courts have held that walk-around inspection pay is not required. OSHA still thinks it is necessary in order to achieve the purposes of the act.

Also, some courts have held that employees have no right to refuse to work in areas where they feel there is a serious hazard. If the employees refuse to work, and are disciplined by management, these courts hold that they are not protected by the Occupational Safety and Health Act. OSHA thinks they should be protected and that disciplining an employee who believes in good faith that he should not do a particular job for safety reasons is a violation of the portions of the act prohibiting discrimination against employees.

Finally, many court cases have vacated OSHA citations because OSHA inspectors have not followed proper procedures.

These kinds of cases indicate that lawyers should be consulted anytime management feels they are being unfairly imposed on by OSHA. Legal help in the form of court action may be a solution to the problem.

CHAPTER TWENTY-SEVEN

EMPLOYEE RETIREMENT INCOME SECURITY ACT OF 1974

BACKGROUND

Beginning about 1972, there was a considerable amount of publicity concerning employees who worked for companies for many years but, for one reason or another, did not get the pension they thought they would be entitled to. The reasons included misunderstanding by the employee about the pension coverage, unfair plan provisions restricting benefits, "bad faith" acts of employers such as firing the employees just before their pensions vested or just before they reached retirement age, "dishonest" acts by persons operating the pension funds so that there were insufficient funds to pay pensions when they became due, and unfortunate economic problems which caused the company or plan to become financially embarrassed. This publicity gave rise to a number of congressional hearings and investigations, and the Employee Retirement Income Security Act of 1974 is the result.

The Employee Retirement Income Security Act of 1974 (hereinafter referred to as ERISA) enacts some fundamental changes in laws relating to private pension plans as well as other types of employee benefit plans. Generally, these changes (1) establish elaborate procedures for *reporting the contents of* "plans" (which include both pension and some other non-pension plans) and their operation *to the government*, and of *disclosing* the contents of these plans and the benefits they provide to the *participants*, (2) establish important rules about the *operation* of certain plans, including *restrictions* on the *investment* these plans may make in stock or real property *of the employer* and other rules of *prudent conduct* which must be observed *by the plan fiduciaries*, and (3) establish a number of important *substantive rules* providing that pension plans must meet certain *minimum requirements* for *funding, participation of employees, benefit accruals, vesting,* and *benefits.*

ERISA defines two different kinds of plans, *welfare* benefit plans and *pension* plans, and provides greatly different rules for each.

The first kind of plan covered by ERISA is the so-called "welfare benefit plan." When Congress first passed ERISA, there was substantial concern about these kinds of plans because the law seemed to say that virtually all plans which provided any kind of benefit to the employee were covered by this definition (including vacation pay, holiday pay, arrangements for paying employees on jury duty, etc.) and because the burdens placed on these kinds of plans were unreasonable in light of the benefits to be obtained by the employee. These plans had to be reduced to a rather formidable legal document and an elaborate set of reporting and disclosure rules applied. However, subsequent regulations of the Department of Labor took a much more realistic view of this situation and defined welfare benefit plans as only those kinds of plans which were not paid out of the general funds of the company, like insurance plans (where the insurance contract could serve as the basis of the written plan).

The second kind of plan is a "pension" plan. However, within the category of pension plans, there is a large disparity in the effect of ERISA between the so-called "defined benefit" plan, where a certain dollar amount of benefits is promised the employee upon his retirement (e.g., a certain percentage of his average salary for his last 5 years of employment), and other kinds of "money purchase" plans, which merely deposit funds into a qualified plan and provide that the employee receives what is in the account when he retires, without making any specific promise as to how much this will be. (The typical profit sharing plan falls into this latter category, although the typical profit sharing plan would technically be a pension plan under ERISA because it pays benefits upon retirement.)

OUTLINE OF THE NEW LAW

ERISA is an extremely long act, covering almost 250 pages in the *Conference Report* version. It is divided into four parts as follows.

1. *Protection of Employee Benefit Rights:* This section deals with the basic changes mentioned above. It repeals the Welfare and Pension Plans Disclosure Act and substitutes its own set of reporting and disclosure requirements; it provides certain rules which fiduciaries must observe; and it establishes certain substantive requirements for pension plans. This Part can be said to be the heart of the new law.

2. *Amendments to the Internal Revenue Code:* Part II of the law makes numerous amendments to the parts of the Internal Revenue Code dealing with private pension plans and their tax-exempt status. Generally, Part II includes conforming amendments so that the provisions of the Internal Revenue Code expressly include those requirements set forth in Part I. However, other important tax implications are contained in this bill.

3. *Jurisdiction, Administration, and Enforcement:* This section provides for a congressional study and other housekeeping or routine matters.

4. *Plan Termination Insurance:* This part of the law establishes the Pension Benefit Guaranty Corporation which will generally operate as an insurance company to insure the solvency of private benefit plans.

REPORTING AND DISCLOSURE

Title 1 of ERISA repeals the Welfare and Pension Plans Disclosure Act (including the infamous D-1 and D-1s forms previously required) and substitutes its own system of filing reports with the government and communicating the provisions of the plan to the employees. Unfortunately, these provisions are at least as complex and burdensome as the old D-1s forms they replace. Generally, each company with a covered plan will have to do the following.

First, appoint an "administrator" of each of his employee benefit plans. (The following requirements are actually the responsibility of the plan administrator.)

Second, *prepare a summary of* the plan and cause it to be *furnished to each covered employee* and to each beneficiary who is receiving benefits under the plan. There are elaborate and extensive requirements for this summary, and it must be "written in a manner calculated to be understood by the average plan participant and . . . sufficiently accurate and comprehensive to reasonably apprise such participants and beneficiaries of their rights and obligations under the plan." In this complex area, this is indeed a formidable task.

Third, *file an annual report with the Secretary of Labor* and keep that report reasonably current. It should be noted that this report must contain a statement by a qualified public accountant and an actuary. Each plan must, therefore, have these two advisors; if they do not, the secretary can hire them, cause them to prepare the required reports and statements, and charge the plan the fee.

Fourth, *furnish to any plan participant or beneficiary*, who so requests in writing, a *statement* indicating, on the basis of the latest available information, *the total benefits accrued* and *the nonforfeitable pension benefits*, if any, which have accrued, or the earliest date on which benefits will become nonforfeitable.

Fifth, *allow any participant* or beneficiary to *examine the trust agreement, annual report, or other relevant instruments* in the office of the administrator and in such other places as may be necessary to make available all pertinent information to all participants.

SUBSTANTIVE REQUIREMENTS

In addition to the above reporting and disclosure provisions, the new law contains a number of substantive provisions which all *pension* plans will have to meet. The most important of these are listed as follows.

Participation

No pension plan may require, as a condition of participation in the plan, that an employee complete a period service with the employer or employers maintaining the plan extending beyond the later of the following dates: (1) the date on which the employee attains the age of twenty-five, or (2) the date on which he completes 1 year of service.

Vesting

Every pension plan must provide for one of three different minimum vesting schedules. The plan need only satisfy one of these three schedules.

1. Twenty-five percent vested at the end of 5 years, with an additional 5 percent per year for years six thru ten, an additional 10 percent per year for the next 5 years, so that 100 percent vesting is achieved after 15 years.

2. One hundred percent vesting after 10 years.

3. A combination of age and service, such that the sum of the person's number of years of service and chronological age determines his vesting. The formula starts out at forty-five with 50 percent and ends at fifty-five with 100 percent. The plan can provide for a minimum of 5 years of service before any vesting, but must allow 50 percent vesting within 10 years and at least 10 percent per year additional vesting for each additional year of service after ten.

Benefit Accrual Requirements

Another important aspect of ERISA is the substantive rules on accrual of benefits. These rules are technical and complex. In substance, however, they are aimed at some plans which had provisions that had the effect of placing a very large premium on the later years of service (so-called "backloading"). For example, a plan might provide that a person was entitled to a "normal" benefit after 30 years of service and having reached age sixty-five. However, the person would only be entitled to a very small percentage of his normal benefit if he had perhaps 25 years of service.

ERISA permits an unlimited amount of "frontloading" (allowing as much credit as desired for the earlier years of service), but restricts the backloading in that each plan must comply with one of three stated formulas.

Joint and Survivor Annuity Requirements

The new bill provides that if a pension plan provides for the payment of benefits in the form of an annuity, such plan *must* allow for the payment of a joint and survivor annuity. Any plan which does not so provide will have to be amended accordingly. A qualified joint and survivor annuity is an annuity for the life of the participant with a survivor annuity for the life of his spouse which is not less than one-half of, or greater than the amount of the annuity payable during the joint lives of the participant and his spouse and which is the actuarial equivalent of a single life annuity for the life of the participant. The provisions of ERISA dealing with this mandatory joint and survivor option are theoretically simple because there is no requirement that the plan provide any greater benefits than the normal straight life annuity. In other words, the plan does not have to subsidize the joint and survivor option. However, the joint and survivor option is the "normal" benefit, and the covered employees have the right to elect instead a straight life annuity or perhaps other forms of benefits which might be allowed by the plan. This election can be made by the employee after the employee has received a written explanation of the terms and conditions of the joint and survivor annuity and the effect of an election not to take it.

This condition opens up some fairly complicated actuarial problems involving adverse selection because it may involve an opportunity for an employee to delay selection of the form of his payment until the last minute when he will know the state of his health and that of his spouse. In addition, if the plan provides for benefits before "normal" retirement age, a participant must be allowed a reasonable time to elect the qualified joint and survivor annuity form for the period beginning at the time he could have retired under the plan's optional retirement provisions (but there is a 120-month maximum limitation on this requirement). Again, the theory is simple but, in practice, adverse selection becomes a possibility.

While the joint and survivor requirement is simple to state, it is important to carefully evaluate all the possibilities before finalizing the provision because the simplicity is deceiving if it is desired to keep the plan costs the same. Naturally, if the plan or the company wants to underwrite the cost of adverse selection, less care is required.

Funding

Funding refers to the amounts of money placed in the plan to satisfy the obligations of the plan. Generally, when the word "funding" is used, it will be in the context of the "past service liability." (For example, suppose a plan is established today providing for full pension of 40 percent of final pay for each employee with 30 years of service who has attained the age of sixty-five. Obviously, there would have been no contributions before today to pay for this obligation; therefore, the obligations attributable to all current employees will be a "past service liability" of the plan.) Prior to this bill, there were only very limited restrictions on funding for past service liability. Generally, it was funded on the basis of 40 years (the entire past service liability was computed and then an amount equal to one-fortieth of that was contributed).

There were some instances where plans were not adequately funded at a time when the employer discontinued operations (or discontinued the plan) and employees did not get the benefits they should have been entitled to. ERISA attempts to solve this problem by providing for a somewhat more rigorous funding schedule. In the case of any *new plan*, a 30-year period must be used to fund past service liability. However, in the case of existing plans, the old 40-year rule is retained. These funding requirements are also very detailed, and each plan should be checked to make sure it complies with them. The new funding requirements mean that many companies will have to make larger contributions than they would have made in the past, particularly if a plan is adopted or amended after the effective date of the new legislation.

COVERAGE REGULATIONS

ERISA has issued final coverage regulations which do a pretty good job of removing the ridiculous amount of paper work which would have been required by literal compliance with the law. Generally, these final regulations on coverage provide that only real "plans" which are funded with a trust or insurance policy are defined as "employee welfare benefit plans" under ERISA; therefore, other kinds of arrangements do not have to comply with *any* of the other parts of ERISA, including the requirement that the plan be reduced to writing. In other words, the following kinds of normal programs are completely free from any ERISA complications.

1. Payments on account of work performed in excess of the normal working hours such as overtime pay, shift premiums, and holiday premiums.

2. Normal sick leave pay; however, the point where normal sick leave pay stops and a formal disability plan (which is covered) starts is not clear. Most commentators are taking the view that the former includes programs involving only the discretion of the employer (in other words, informal arrangements) and that wherever the arrangement is formalized by providing for a certain number

of weeks pay for a certain number of years service, for example, the plan is a disability plan.

3. Payments for time when the employee is not working because of normal absences such as vacations, military duty, jury duty, or training.

4. Holiday gifts.

5. Normal employee discount policies for the company's products.

6. Certain group insurance plans where the company plays no part and the employees pay the premiums—but the wording of this one is tricky—the employer cannot endorse the program.

The regulations go on to exempt certain other arrangements which might be deemed pension plans under the wording of the act itself. This is even more disastrous than having a plan which is merely a welfare benefit plan, because if the plan is characterized as a pension plan, it must be funded, with a trustee, and satisfy a horrendous number of other requirements. These other plans which are exempted from the definition of pension plan *may* be welfare benefit plans, however, and if this is the case, the rules of reporting and disclosure for welfare plans must be observed. The kinds of plans which are exempt from the definition of pension plan but which may or may not be exempt from the definition of a welfare plan, include severance pay plans and bonus plans. The regulations also contain an exemption for plans covering fewer than 100 participants. A plan falling into this category will be exempt from just about all requirements except that it be in writing.

FIDUCIARY RESPONSIBILITY

Another very important aspect of the act is the establishment of both *civil* and *criminal penalties* for violation of a set of fairly strict fiduciary responsibilities. These fiduciary responsibilities are detailed, but, in general, are those rules that would apply to an ordinary trustee, including an absolute prohibition against most transactions between the fiduciary and the plan.

The first part of this new section provides that each plan must be established and maintained pursuant to a written instrument which must name one or more fiduciaries who jointly or severally shall have authority to control and manage the operation and administration of the plan. The section then goes on to provide for certain fiduciary duties which include operating the plan for the *exclusive purpose* of *providing benefits* to the participants and defraying reasonable expenses of administration; operating the plan with the *care, skill, prudence,* and *diligence,* under the circumstances then prevailing, that a prudent man acting in a like capacity and familiar with such matters would use in the conduct of an enterprise of like character and with like aims; and *diversifying* the investments of the plan so as to minimize the risk of large losses.

The act then lists some prohibited transactions which include just about any kind of transaction between the plan and a "party in interest," except for the holding by the plan of stock or real property of the employer corporation. Even this latter exception is limited severely by a 10 percent rule, restricting the plan from having more than 10 percent of its assets in the stock or real property of the employer. (A party in interest includes any fiduciary and any person providing services to the plan, as well as the employer.)

The problem of fiduciary liability is of greatest concern to business executives. In analyzing the question of fiduciary liability, the first step is obviously to decide who the fiduciaries are. Generally, there are two criteria. The first is that *any person* who has certain responsibilities or takes certain actions may be a fiduciary, and the second is that certain persons who are either named as fiduciaries or occupy some other named positions may be defined as fiduciaries in the act.

Under the first category of persons whose actions or authority cause them to be fiduciaries are the following:

1. persons who render investment advice to the plan. It is important to note that the person who renders this advice does not have to have any authority over the plan assets, and it is not necessary to have any requirement that the advice be followed. Consequently, the normal broker who merely renders free advice to his plan client may be a fiduciary, even though there is no obligation to follow the advice and even though the advice is, in fact, not followed.

2. persons who, in fact, exercise discretionary control over the plan's assets. This is a realistic and rational category—persons who, in fact, exercise discretion over the plan's assets should be fiduciaries.

3. persons who exercise any authority or control with respect to the management of the plan. Discretion is not an element in this category. An employer who determines how the assets of the plan should be allocated upon termination or a plan custodian who gives no investment advice may both be fiduciaries.

4. persons who have discretionary authority or responsibility respecting administration of the plan. This may include the discretion to name the trustee, in which case the company and its board of directors are probably fiduciaries because they have this authority.

5. persons designated as a fiduciary in the plan.

In the second category, those whose title may cause them to be fiduciaries, the following might be included:

1. the plan trustee
2. the custodian of the plan
3. the investment manager
4. any employer who establishes a plan and reserves the right to amend it, to terminate it, and to select the trustee or to make certain allocations and delegations of responsibility
5. persons named in the plan as having discretionary control over the management of the plan (a typical example would be where the board of directors is given the right to amend the plan)
6. under certain circumstances, actuaries, brokers, and attorneys

The lists overlap somewhat; however, the point to be made is that a person or group may be a fiduciary either because of the authority or discretion they actually have and exercise or because of their right to exercise such discretion or control or because of their title or because they act, even gratuitously, in a manner which causes them to become fiduciaries (like the broker who gives investment advice or attorneys or others who, by course of conduct, have assumed responsibility for discretionary acts, like investment of plan assets).

TAX PROVISIONS

Generally, the amendments to the Internal Revenue Code contained in ERISA could be considered merely conforming amendments to bring the tax law and the general rules regarding pension plans into specific conformity with each other. However, the following sections of the act amend the tax law in several other important respects.

Penalty Tax

If the employer fails to adequately fund the plan as required by the new law, a tax of 5 percent of the amount of the accumulated funding deficiency is imposed. In addition, if the employer fails to correct the accumulated funding deficiency, an additional tax equal to 100 percent of this funding deficiency (to the extent that it has not been corrected) is imposed.

Spendthrift Clause

The tax law now expressly requires that, in order for a plan to be qualified, it *must* contain a spendthrift clause. This is required by a new paragraph 13 which has been added to section 401(a) of the Internal Revenue Code, which provides as follows:

> (13) A trust shall not constitute a qualified trust under this section unless the plan of which such trust is a part provides that benefits provided under the plan may not be assigned or alienated. For purposes of the preceding sentence, there shall not be taken into account any voluntary and revocable assignment of not to exceed 10 percent of any benefit payment made by any participant who is receiving benefits under the plan unless the assignment or alienation is made for purposes of defraying plan administration costs. For purposes of this paragraph a loan made to a participant or beneficiary shall not be treated as an assignment or alienation if such loan is secured by the participant's accrued nonforfeitable benefit and is exempt from the tax imposed by section 4975 (relating to tax on prohibited transactions) by reason of section 4975(d)(1). This paragraph shall take effect on January 1, 1976, and shall not apply to assignments which were irrevocable on the date of the enactment of the Employee Retirement Income Security Act of 1974.

Self-employed Plans

The act makes an important and long overdue change in the restrictions regarding self-employed plans, and generally makes these plans much more attractive by increasing the amount which can be contributed to them.

The act increases the maximum deductible contribution on behalf of self-employed persons to the lesser of 15 percent of earned income or $7500 (the prior limits were 10 percent and $2500). The same change is made as to excludable contributions on behalf of Sub-chapter S corporations. In applying the percentage limitation, not more than $100,000 of earned income may be taken into account. Self-employed persons (but not shareholder employees) are permitted to set aside up to $750 a year out of earned income without regard to the percentage limitation. The act also authorizes the Treasury regulations to allow self-employed persons and shareholder employees in effect to translate the 15 percent/$7500 limitations on contributions into approximately equivalent limitations on benefits which individuals can receive under a defined benefit plan.

The act contains a table (based on certain interest and mortality rates) which will serve as a guideline for the regulations. The act also contains technical rules to prevent an individual from obtaining unintended high benefit accruals late in his career merely by establishing a "token plan" early in his career. A plan which covers owner employees is not permitted to use the defined benefit provisions unless it provides benefits for all participants on a nonintegrated basis (i.e., without taking social security benefits into account).

Individual Retirement Accounts

An employee whose employer does not have any qualified pension, profit sharing, or similar plan is entitled to set up his own plan. Contributions up to the lesser of 15 percent of the employee's compensation or $1500 may be contributed to an individual retirement account, annuity, or bond program and may be excluded from the employee's gross taxable income. Earnings on these accounts are to be tax-free. Distributions from such accounts because of retirement after age 59½ or disability at any age are to be taxed as ordinary income. A 10 percent excise tax is levied on premature distributions. The employee and the trustee (who must be a bank or other qualified person) must guard against the fund engaging in certain prohibited transactions. These plans may not purchase life insurance, but certain endowment-type contracts to the extent of their non-life insurance elements are permissible investments.

Limitations on Benefits and Contributions

The act provides that pension, profit sharing, self-employed, and all other tax-qualified plans are now subject to certain overall benefit and contribution restrictions. Generally, a pension plan may not provide benefits greater than $75,000 per year. Contributions on behalf of an individual to a profit sharing or other defined contribution plan are limited to the lesser of $25,000 or 25 percent of compensation. All plans of the employer are combined for the purpose of testing these limitations. A lower limit equivalent to 140 percent of the limit under one plan is applicable when an individual is a member of both a defined benefit and defined contribution plan. The above dollar limitations are to be increased with the cost of living.

These limitations are very important but also very technical. The following language from the *Conference Report* is the best explanation of them in nontechnical terms.

> *Application to defined benefit plans*—Under the conference substitute, in general, the highest annual benefit which can be paid (in the form of a straight-life annuity) out of a defined benefit plan to a participant is not to exceed the lesser of (a) $75,000, or (b) 100 percent of the participant's average compensation in his high-three-years of employment. (Both of these ceilings are to be adjusted to reflect cost-of-living increases.)
>
> In the event of retirement before age 55, the $75,000 ceiling (but not the 100 percent ceiling) is to be scaled down on an actuarial basis (but not below $10,000). In general, there is no required scale down for preretirement ancillary benefits (such as medical, death and disability), but there would have to be an adjustment for post-retirement ancillary benefits, such as term-certain annuities, post-retirement death benefits, or a guaranteed payment for a period of years.
>
> If a benefit were paid in the form of a joint and survivor annuity for the benefit of the participant and his spouse, the value of this feature would not be taken into account unless the survivor benefit were greater than the joint benefit.
>
> Upward adjustments in the benefit schedule would be permitted to reflect any employee contributions to the plan, including roll-over contributions from another qualified plan or from an individual retirement account.
>
> Also the substitute would provide a *de minimus* rule, which would allow a qualified plan to pay an annual retirement benefit of up to $10,000 per annum, notwithstanding the 100-percent limitation, or the required adjustment for certain ancillary benefits, to any employee who had not participated in a qualified defined contribution plan of the employer.
>
> As a further adjustment to the rules described above, the maximum allowable

defined benefit would have to be scaled down proportionately for an employee with less than 10 years of service.

Application to defined contribution plans—In the case of a defined contribution plan, the annual additions for the year are not to exceed the lesser of $25,000 (subject to an annual cost-of-living increase) or 25 percent of the participant's compensation from the employer. The term "annual additions" means the sum of (a) the employer's contributions, (b) the lesser of (i) one-half of all the employee's contributions, or (ii) the employee's contributions in excess of 6 percent of his compensation, and (c) any forfeitures which are added to the employee's account. Annual additions do not include rollovers from a qualified plan or individual retirement account. If forfeitures for a particular year could cause the plan not to meet these requirements with respect to a particular employee, these forfeitures must be reallocated to other participants in the plan (i.e., they may not be held in a suspense account), but regulations are to provide for the situation where none of the employees in the plan are eligible to receive forfeitures.

For purposes of the overall limitation, target benefit plans (i.e., plans where the employer establishes a target benefit for his employees, but where the employee's actual pension is based on the amount in his individual account) are to be treated as defined contribution plans. If the plan is a hybrid, i.e., part target benefit and part defined benefit, the plan will be treated as a defined contribution plan, for purposes of those rules, to the extent that benefits under the plan are based on the individual account of the participant. In the case of other plans which have characteristics both of a defined benefit plan and a defined contribution plan (such as a defined contribution plan with a guaranteed benefit, or certain variable annuity plans) the Secretary or his delegate may prescribe regulations applying the limitations to the defined benefit of the plan, and the part of the plan in which benefits are based on individual account balances.

Lump-Sum Distributions

Prior to the 1969 Tax Reform Act, lump-sum distributions from qualified pension or profit sharing plans were generally accorded favorable capital gains treatment. The 1969 Tax Reform Act changed this and substituted a 7-year average rule which generally provided that a lump-sum distribution was to be taxed at ordinary income rates, but there was a 7-year averaging provision to mitigate the fact that the money would be received in one year. This was apparently unworkable, and ERISA provides a new limitation, again imposing ordinary income but averaging it out over a period of 10 years. The *Conference Report* describes this new treatment.

General Rule

Both the House bill and the Senate amendment treat the post-1973 taxable portion of a lump-sum distribution from a qualified pension, profit-sharing or stock bonus plan as ordinary income taxed under an averaging device which treats it as if it were received evenly over a period of years. Under the House bill, this special averaging treatment provides the treatment which would be applicable if the amount were spread over a period of 10 years, while the Senate amendment provides the treatment which would be applicable if it were spread over 15 years. Both the House and Senate versions treat the portion of the payment attributable to the pre-1974 period as long-term capital gain.

The conference substitute accepts the 10-year averaging period provided under the House bill. Both the House bill and the Senate amendment compute the ordinary income portion under the same general type of averaging device and this same general procedure is used in the conference substitute. The ordinary income portion is to be computed without regard to the taxpayer's other income (i.e., in effect it is taxed entirely separately as if this were the only income received by the individual). The tax rate schedule to be used in this separate-treatment approach is the schedule provided in the Code for unmarried individuals (whether or not the taxpayer is married). If the plan participant has service both before 1974 and after 1973, the amount attributed to the post-1973 service is the total taxable distribution times a fraction, the numerator of which is calendar years of active participation after 1973 and the denominator of which is total years of active participation. It is understood that the Treasury Department will provide regulations for allocating fractions of years for plan participants who have both pre-1974 and post-1973 value in lump-sum distributions.

The taxable portion of a distribution is to be the portion of the distribution attributable to employer contributions and to income earned on the account. The portion of the distribution representing the employee's contributions remains nontaxable.

Indemnification

Section 410 of the act provides that, with certain exceptions, any agreement or instrument which purports to relieve a fiduciary from responsibility or liability for any responsibility or obligation or duty under the act will be voided against public policy.

The Labor Department has issued *Interpretive Bulletin 75-4* which does permit certain indemnification agreements, provided these indemnification agreements do not relieve the fiduciary of responsibility but simply allow another party to satisfy and liability incurred by the fiduciary in the same manner as insurance. The bulletin gives the following two examples: (1) indemnification of a plan fiduciary by an employer any of whose employees are covered by the plan, or an employee organization any of whose members are covered by the plan, and (2) indemnification by a plan fiduciary of the fiduciary's employees who actually perform the fiduciary services.

The complete text of *Interpretive Bulletin 75-4* follows:

ERISA INTERPRETIVE BULLETIN 75-4

Issued June 4, 1975

The Department of Labor today announced its interpretation of section 410(a) of the Employee Retirement Income Security Act of 1974, insofar as that section relates to indemnification of fiduciaries. Section 410(a) states, in relevant part, that "any provision in an agreement or instrument which purports to relieve a fiduciary from responsibility or liability for any responsibility, obligation, or duty under this part shall be void as against public policy."

The Department of Labor interprets this section to permit indemnification agreements which do not relieve a fiduciary of responsibility or liability under part 4 of Title I. Indemnification provisions which leave the fiduciary fully responsible and liable, but merely permit another party to satisfy any liability incurred by the fiduciary in the same manner as insurance purchased under section 410(b)(3), are therefore not void under section 410(a).

Examples of such indemnification provisions are:

Indemnification of a plan fiduciary by (a) an employer, any of whose employees are covered by the plan, or an affiliate (as defined in section 407 (d)(7) of the Act) of such employer, or (b) an employee organization, any of whose members are covered by the plan; and

(2) Indemnification by a plan fiduciary of the fiduciary's employees who actually perform the fiduciary services.

The Department of Labor interprets section 410(a) as rendering void any arrangement of indemnification of a fiduciary of an employee benefit plan by the plan. Such an arrangement would have the same result as an exculpatory clause, in that it would, in effect, relieve the fiduciary of responsibility and liability to the plan by abrogating the plan's right to recovery from the fiduciary for breaches of fiduciary obligations.

While indemnification arrangements do not contravene the provisions of section 410(a), parties entering into an indemnification agreement should consider whether the agreement complies with the other provisions of part 4 of Title I of the Act and with other applicable laws.

PENSION TERMINATIONS AND INSURANCE

The *Congressional Record* recites a great many specific situations where long-term employees had been denied a pension after many years of service because the assets of their pension plan were not sufficient to pay the benefits which had been promised. Largely as a result of these kinds of situations, Congress devoted an entire section of ERISA to the attempted solution of this problem. Basically, their solution was to (1) establish a federal insurance company which would provide mandatory insurance for all private pension plans, and (2) enact substantive provisions which prevent a company from limiting its pension liability to the assets of its pension plan trust fund and instead require the employer to stand back of pension promises to the extent of 30 percent of the company's net worth.

The new law establishes a Pension Benefit Guaranty Corporation (PBGC) which, in substance, is a federal insurance company which will insure benefits from private pension plans. Generally, all defined benefit plans will be required to participate in this program and pay the established premium. (The so-called individual account plans, including most profit sharing, money purchase, thrift plans, and stock bonus plans are not required to participate. In these plans, the employee is given an account to which contributions are made, and his benefit is simply the balance in that account at the time of his retirement plus or minus any appreciation or depreciation.)

The PBGC will be a part of the Department of Labor and will be directed by the Secretaries of Labor (who will be the chairman), Treasury, and Commerce. There is also a seven-member advisory committee which will be appointed by the president.

The PBGC will insure that, up to certain maximums, the pensions which have been promised the participants in the plan will actually be paid, irrespective of the availability of the assets in the fund to pay those pensions. The limitations are basically that only vested benefits are insured, and the insurance covers benefits only up to the lesser of $750 a month or 100 percent of the average wages during the participant's highest 5 consecutive years of participation.

Insurance coverage is available only if the benefit has been provided under the plan for 5 years. For younger plans or plans which have been improved, the insurance coverage will be phased in at the rate of 20 percent per year until the plan or benefit is fully covered.

Premiums

Initially, the premiums for a single-employer plan will be $1 for each participant. (The premium is 50 cents for each participant in a multi-employer plan.) After the first 2 years, the PBGC may revise these premiums but not above these levels.

There is an alternative premium calculation for the second full plan year whereby the premium may be composed of (1) 0.1 percent of the unfunded insured benefits for a single-employer plan and 0.25 percent for multi-employer plans, and (2) a percentage to be determined by the PBGC of total insured benefits, provided that the total premium under this alternative arrangement cannot be less than 50 cents per participant in a single-employer plan and 25 cents for each participant in a multi-employer plan.

Reportable Events

Within 30 days after the plan administrator knows or has reason to know of any event which might indicate the need to terminate the plan, he must notify the PBGC. The following are specifically listed as reportable events:

1. If the plan administrator is notified by the Secretary of Labor that the plan is not in compliance with Title I of the act. (Title I sets forth the various detailed requirements on funding, vesting, and participation previously described.)

2. When any amendment which decreases the benefits is adopted.

3. When the number of active participants is less than 80 percent of the number of such participants at the beginning of the plan year, or is less than 75 percent of the number of such participants at the beginning of the previous plan year.

4. When the Secretary of the Treasury determines there has been a termination under the IRS rules.

5. When the plan fails to meet the minimum funding standards of the new law.

6. If the plan is unable to pay benefits thereunder as they become due.

7. If there is a distribution under the plan to a participant who is a substantial owner and such distribution is (a) $10,000 or more, (b) not made by reason of the death of the participant, or (c) immediately after the distribution, the plan has nonforfeitable benefits which are not funded.

8. When the plan merges, consolidates, or transfers its assets.

9. When any other event occurs [PBG] which the corporation determines may be indicative of a need to terminate the plan.

Plan Termination

The plan administrator must notify the PBGC at least 10 days before terminating any plan, and then for a period of 90 days after the date of termination the plan administrator shall not pay any benefits out of the plan unless such payments are specifically approved by the PBGC. In addition, the PBGC may itself institute proceedings to have a plan terminated if it determines that the plan has not met the minimal funding standards or that the plan is unable to pay benefits when due or that any of the reportable events described above have taken place or that "the possible long-run loss of the [PBG] corporation with respect to the plan may reasonably be expected to increase unreasonably if the plan is not terminated."

The PBGC has issued regulations which describe precisely what benefits are guaranteed and exactly what information must be included in the notice of intention to terminate an insured plan which must be sent to the PBGC *10 days before* the termination. It is necessary to be aware that these regulations exist and to have ready access to them because they become very important in the context of some corporate transactions such as mergers or liquidations. They are important for both the buyer and seller of a corporate business because the buyer may be deemed a successor employer and, if the plan is terminated, may find itself liable for large amounts of money, depending on the financial picture of the plan. For this reason, all applicable corporate transactions should include as one item in the procedure an analysis of a recent actuarial report of any pension plans so that any of these problems can be brought to light while there still may be a chance to take appropriate planning actions to negotiate exactly which party would be responsible for any liability and to reflect this decision in appropriate documents. Also, the transaction should be appropriately structured so that any plan termination takes place at the proper time (before the change in ownership or thereafter, depending on how the negotiations on liability come out). In addition, there are timing implications because it is possible that if the notice to the PBGC shows large unfunded liabilities, there might be unanticipated delays while pension matters are straightened out.

Allocation of Assets

The law requires the allocation of existing assets in a plan upon termination to take place as follows:

1. voluntary employee contributions

2. mandatory employee contributions

3. all benefit payments which had actually commenced or could have commenced if the beneficiary had retired at least 3 years before the termination (provided that these benefits must have been based upon a plan provision in effect for at least 5 years before the termination)

4. other guaranteed benefits (up to the insurance limitations mentioned above)

5. other nonforfeitable benefits

6. all other benefits

Recapture of Certain Benefits

Certain "excess payments" which are made during the 3-year period just preceding the time when the plan is terminated may be recovered. Generally, these excess payments will be anything over $10,000 a year, except for payments made on account of death or disability.

Contingent Employer Liability

It is no longer possible to have a provision in the plan to the general effect that the liability to the employee/participants is limited to the assets in the plan. Instead, the procedure now is that upon termination of a plan, the assets in the plan are, of course, applied to the liabilities as indicated above. However, if those assets are insufficient to pay all of the liabilities of the plan, the PBGC then takes over, and to the extent of the maximum insurance limitations mentioned above, actually makes the payments to the employees/participants. Then, however, the law provides that the employer is liable to the PBGC for any payments which it might have made by reason of inadequate funds in the plan limited only to 30 percent of the net worth of the employer.

Insurance will be provided for this liability also and, in addition to the premiums mentioned above, employers will be required to pay an additional amount to cover this liability insurance. This additional amount will be determined by the PBGC at a later date. The PBGC is instructed in the act to attempt to work with private insurance carriers to provide for this additional coverage.

Termination of One Facility

A question which sometimes arises in the context of plans covering employees at more than one facility is, "What happens if one facility is shut down with the work being done at that facility either being discontinued or transferred to some other operation in the company?" ERISA provides for this contingency in part 4 with the following provision (section 406(2)(e)):

> If an employer ceases operations at a facility in any location and, as a result of such cessation of operations, more than 20% of the total number of his employees who are participants under a plan established and maintained by him are separated from employment, the employer shall be treated with respect to that plan as if he were a substantial employer under a plan under which more than one employer makes contributions and the provisions of sections 406(3), 406(4) and 406(5) shall apply.

These sections thereupon go on to say that if one employer in a multi-employer plan withdraws, the plan administrator must notify the PBGC and request that corporation to determine the liability of the withdrawing employer. The withdrawing employer may have to post a bond to cover the liability or he may have to actually pay that liability into the plan.

RECORD KEEPING

Records and record keeping are still problems. Not only do these regulations require that detailed records be kept on hours of service after the effective date of the plan, but they require that the company use whatever records it may have to recalculate hours of service for periods before the effective date of the plan. The following paragraph points up the problem:

> (c) *Determination of pre-effective date hours of service.* For purposes of determining hours of service completed prior to the effective date of part 2 (see section 211 of the Act), a plan may use whatever records may be reasonably accessible to it and may make whatever calculations are necessary to determine the approximate number of hours of service completed during such prior period or periods. For example, if a plan or an employer maintaining the plan has, or has access to, only the records of compensation of employees for prior years, it may derive the pre-effective date hours of service by using the hourly rate for the period or the hours customarily worked during such compensation period. If accessible records are insufficient to make an approximation of the number of pre-effective date hours of service for a particular employee or group of employees, the plan may make a reasonable estimate of the hours of service completed by such employee or employees during the particular period. For example, if records are available with respect to some employees, the plan may estimate the hours of other employees in the same job classification based on these records. [Department of Labor regulations under ERISA]

Business executives should ascertain what steps are being taken to keep track of the appropriate information necessary for ERISA in a systematized manner. Because of the detailed requirements for computation of hours of service, for breaks in service, and the many other complicated calculations which are going to have to be made in many situations, there does not seem to be any alternative for large multi-facility companies than an elaborate computer-based data bank for all of its employees.

PLANNING

Business executives should be sure that there are systematized methods in place to comply with ERISA and to have the effects of the new law included in analyses of proposed business and employee benefit programs. Following is a discussion of the essential elements of ERISA compliance and planning.

Administrative

The precise means by which a company complies with this new legislation will depend on the company's organization, the personnel it has available, the number and complexity of its benefit plans, and its relations with and use of outside counsel and other advisors. In all cases, however, it will be desirable for a company to have specified a team of people responsible for complying with the law, taking advantage of available flexibility, and minimizing administrative cost and disruption of existing personnel policies. One important function of counsel will be to make sure the company has such a team and that enough capability is assigned to adequately cover all the points mentioned in this checklist. In most cases, this will mean at least the following:

1. fixing responsibility for *preparing plan inventory*

2. fixing responsibility for *preparing and distributing all the material needed to comply with the reporting and disclosure requirements*

3. fixing responsibility for complying with *insurance requirements*

4. fixing responsibility for *revising all plans and making all necessary amendments*

5. fixing responsibility for seeing that *the other miscellaneous items* in the checklist set forth herein are covered (the biggest problem will probably come from the new record-keeping requirements)

Following is a checklist for satisfying other requirements of the new law which relate directly to plans or their administration.

Fiduciary Duties

As pointed out above, most plans are required to have a fiduciary named in the plan instruments. Following is a checklist of substantive requirements relating to fiduciaries and their duties.

1. The fiduciary must act *solely* in the interest of plan participants and beneficiaries and for the *exclusive* purpose of providing benefits and defraying administrative costs.

2. All acts must satisfy the prudent-man rule.

3. Investments must be *diversified.*

4. There must be no prohibited transactions.

5. Any transaction with the party in interest must be carefully checked.

6. Any holding of securities or real estate of the employer must be checked.

Bonding

Generally, any person who handles funds must be bonded in accordance with section 412.

Maximum Benefits

Certain limits are placed on the maximum benefits which may be payable to any participant. Generally, the maximum benefit is $75,000 or 100 percent of the highest 3 years pay, if that is less. (Section 200(4) of act. Section 415 of Internal Revenue Code. Generally, plan years beginning after December 31, 1975.)

Plan Termination Insurance

Generally, the new act requires every defined benefit plan to participate in a federal insurance program and to pay the requisite premiums. The plan administrator will have to evaluate his choices for premium payments and make any necessary elections. The corporation will have to ascertain its contingent liability under section 406(2) and then take appropriate action on insuring it, if required, as described in section 402(3).

Plan Accountant

Every benefit plan must have a CPA, unless exempted by section 110.

Enrolled Actuary

Every pension plan must have an enrolled actuary, unless exempted by section 110.

GENERAL CHECKLIST

Following is a list of other items which may require attention because of the new act.

Additional cost factors should be computed and worked into budgets and the company's cost structure.

The new law provides for some additional record-keeping rules in sections 107 and 209. This is likely to be one of the biggest problems with the new law.

Almost every paragraph of the new act calls for attention in terms of drafting future plans. For example, there are many optional or alternative rules which should be considered in future plans. The new plans will usually have to be "new models," redrafted "from the ground up," by experts in the field.

Many people are going to have to know many new things because of this new bill, and counsel must consider what corporate legal education is necessary and appropriate. For example, sections 510 and 511 make it unlawful to interfere with any rights of the new law by discharging or discriminating against anyone who attempts to exercise those rights. Second, people in the personnel department are going to have to be able to answer questions about employees' rights under the law and the company's plans. Third, employers are going to have to become familiar with the new reporting and disclosure requirements and how to deal with them. Also, plan administrators, named fiduciaries, and parties in interest are going to have to become aware of the detailed rules applicable to them. And, fifth, special rules requiring detailed reports on plan terminations and certain "reportable events" will have to be understood and observed.

There are many planning implications to this law. Some obvious examples follow:

1. Should pension plans be expanded or should alternatives in the form of profit sharing or other programs be considered instead?

2. If a company or location was thinking of putting in a new pension plan, should other alternatives be considered?

3. Should contributory plans be reevaluated?/emphasized?

4. Should individual account plans be reevaluated?/emphasized?

5. Are plant closings possible now under the same economic facts as before?

6. What about a potential acquisition? Certainly any contingent pension liability should be considered.

7. What is the effect of the law on forthcoming labor negotiations?

In addition to direct insurance by the plan for vested benefits and corporate insurance for employer contingent liability, the act raises the following insurance-related questions. One, should *private* coverage (as opposed to Pension Benefit Guaranty Corporation coverage) be considered for the employer's contingent liability coverage as either a replacement (if this is legally permissible) or supplement to the mandatory program? Two, should additional insurance coverage for corporate people who serve as fiduciaries, experts, or advisors be obtained?

The law includes many portions directly affecting employees' actions regarding retirement. Examples are the provisions dealing with lump-sum distributions and electing alternate forms of benefits. Consideration should be given to whether, or to what extent employees should be informed of these provisions or counseled as to their elections.

ACCURACY OF INFORMATION

There is certain to be considerable controversy over the accuracy of information distributed to employees. This controversy is almost built into the act by the requirement that the company distribute a summary plan description and the corollary requirement that the summary plan description be simple enough to be understood by the average worker. Many commentators are warning against being overly simplistic, and counseling that it is better to be on the conservative side and have a more detailed document and risk a court or Department of Labor order that it be re-prepared in a simpler fashion than to give information to the employees which may be inaccurate and which may later form the basis for a costly lawsuit. At the same time, the labor department is warning that these summary plan descriptions are going to have to be easy to understand and that they are not going to accept documents which are merely abbreviated versions of the plan and which contain too much legalese for the average person to understand it.

The courts have shown a willingness to protect people from the most obvious and extreme kinds of misleading information, but the law on this point is still in a state of development. In fact, there is really only one case, and that one has caused considerable disagreement among the experts.

The case is *Daniel v. Teamsters,* where a court of appeals held that the interest of a beneficiary (Mr. Daniel) in a pension plan was a security within the meaning of the securities laws; therefore, the beneficiary was entitled to recover from the plan and its sponsor if there were inaccurate statements describing the benefits he would obtain. Mr. Daniel had a very strong case. He was a member of a Teamsters local which had a pension plan that required 20 years of continuous service in order to get any pension at all. Mr. Daniel worked about 25 years, but at one point during this period he was laid off for a few months. The administrators denied him any pension under the plan because he did not have the required 20 years of *continuous* service. There were, however, statements made to him and others, both orally and in writing, which strongly led him to believe that he would be entitled to a pension. Because of these statements, the court held that he was entitled to a pension irrespective of the fact that the plan would not have allowed him one. At this time, the case is on appeal to the U.S. Supreme Court, and their opinion should be a very important one for business.

The case raises the question of what must be disclosed to pension beneficiaries. The technical requirements of ERISA may not be sufficient in all cases. If the interest of a pension beneficiary is a security within the meaning of those laws, a whole new set of rules would be applicable, and those rules are somewhat different from the ERISA rules. At this writing, it would be unfair to generalize too much from this one court opinion, but it should be kept in mind in deciding how to disseminate information about pension plans. Other factors which might be considered include the following. One, have the summary plan description state that one person in the company (described by position) is allowed to explain the plan's benefits to the employees. This would reduce the chance of well-meaning lower level advisors misrepresenting the actual content of the plan. Second, if your plan covers a significant number of employees who speak a language other than English, you might have to have a summary plan description prepared in one or more other languages. Third, make carefully structured presentations to the employees so that you know exactly who is saying what about your plan. And, fourth, give careful attention to explaining this problem to all appropriate people in the company so that well-meaning volunteers don't unintentionally misrepresent the plan. Also, careful attention to proper training of employees who are authorized to explain the plan is important.

There seems to be some debate on whether or not a loose-leaf notebook could be used by companies to satisfy their ERISA disclosure obligations. The advantage to the company and the employees would be obvious. Once the loose-leaf book is printed, changes could be accomplished by distributing additional or substitute pages, and the employees would always have, in one readily accessible place, the entire summary plan descriptions for all the company's plans. Although the corporation would have to spend a little more initially because the binders would be more costly than simple pamphlets, the costs thereafter, of keeping the employees' information up-to-date would be greatly reduced and the process simplified.

However, as a practical matter, the employees are very likely to do a less than adequate job of supplementing their notebooks, and eventually they may have a hopelessly confused and out-of-date set of summary plan descriptions.

Before counsel advises his company to use the loose-leaf approach, it would be advisable to ascertain that the Department of Labor will accept this approach. Informally, some of their people have indicated that they might not.

OFFICER AND DIRECTOR LIABILITY UNDER ERISA

The directors and some officers of the company may be fiduciaries under ERISA regarding the company pension plan because they have ultimate power to determine how the assets of the plan shall be managed. The degree of this power depends, of course, on the relationship between the officers and directors and the actual management of the fund. It seems to be the general consensus of opinion, however, that the directors are fiduciaries under ERISA because they, at least, have the power to name the trustee, and some officers may be fiduciaries because they may have the power to designate actual investments. In some situations, officers or directors may actually make some of the investment decisions and this, of course, makes it certain that they would be deemed fiduciaries. This point is rather important because ERISA clearly provides that a fiduciary is personally liable for any loss which is incurred because of a breach of his "fiduciary duty," and both "fiduciary duty" and "fiduciary" are broad and vague terms under ERISA. Accordingly, it is not at all impossible that a court would hold a fiduciary personally liable for poor investments in a pension or profit sharing plan.

This personal liability for fiduciaries has created a considerable amount of concern but, at least at this point, there does not seem to be a sufficiently clear body of law for counsel to answer all the questions. Following are some observations which may, however, by useful. First, in the case where the directors of a company are deemed to be fiduciaries simply because they have the power to select the trustee, but, in fact, it is the trustee which makes all the investment decisions, it seems a little remote that the directors of a company would ever be held personally responsible for poor investment performance provided the directors appoint a qualified trustee (for example, a large bank) and make it clear that the trustee has investment authority and the directors monitor the performance of the trustee in light of the state of the economy and the performance of other trustees. In other words, if the directors discharge their initial duty to pick competent trustees and they discharge their continuing duty to make sure the trustee is doing a good job, there should be little problem.

Second, in some larger companies involving multiple trust funds, it may be appropriate to have more than one person or firm in charge of trust investments and then compare the performance of these various investment advisors. If there are a number of investment advisors managing different trust funds, and one is doing substantially worse than the others, the directors may have a duty to replace the poor performer.

Third, if the persons who are making investment decisions are the officers or directors of the company themselves, there does not seem to be any way to avoid liability for a poor decision, always keeping in mind that the merits of the decision must be judged at the time it was made. The investment advisors are not guarantors of the performance of the stocks in the fund. At this point, there is an important uncertainty in the law. Do you judge the investments one by one or as a whole? For example, if there were a $1 million pension fund invested in various common stocks, preferred stocks, bonds, notes, etc., and all of these investments performed satisfactorily except for a single investment of $20,000 in a small closely held company which went bankrupt, would you judge the trustee by the total performance, which was good, or would you pick the bad investment and impose personal liability for $20,000? This is a key issue, because if courts choose the latter approach smaller amounts are going to be available for new enterprises. A fiduciary may feel justified in "risking" $20,000 out of $1 million if the chances for profit in that $20,000 investment are very high, but not if the fiduciary is exposing himself to personal liability in the process. There are differences of opinion on this question. Unfortunately, there is no government regulation or case which clearly answers it, and those pieces of authority which come close do point to the one-at-a-time type of analysis.

Fourth, the directors should make sure that the diversification requirements of ERISA are complied with. This may mean not only diversification with respect to stocks, but diversification with respect to various kinds of investments, including stocks, bonds, and real estate mortgages.

Fifth, it would seem that the liability question depends on the kind of plan one has. If it is a defined benefit pension plan, the liability of the fiduciaries would seem to arise only if (1) the plan went broke, and (2) the company went broke. On the other hand, liability in a money purchase–profit sharing plan could seem to be predicated on just about any investment which turned sour. Under traditional trust law, a beneficiary is not required to wait until the trustee-fiduciary wastes all the assets of the trust before bringing suit. If it appears as though things are going badly, an employee may have the standing to bring a lawsuit, even if he is not yet entitled to any distribution under the plan.

Sixth, the prudent man standard (the one pursuant to which investments are judged) seems to be essentially the same as the prudent man standard under common law trust principles which have been in effect for many years. Unfortunately, it is an uncertain and vague standard and the plain truth is that, except in the case of the most conservative of investments, it's impossible to tell if an investment was "prudent" until after a court has ruled on it. This makes advance planning and guidance on anything other than a very conservative basis difficult.

Finally, it appears that, in the case of larger companies with already established pension or profit sharing plans, the personal liability problems of the officer or directors have been a little overplayed. Naturally, the validity of this opinion will have to await subsequent developments, but it would appear unjustified to assume that courts will take unreasonable approaches under ERISA and hold officers or directors personally liable for poor investment performance unless there is some legitimate reason to do so. If the officers and directors delegate the investment decisions to qualified people and then keep a watch on what is going on, their liability should be minimized.

On the other hand, for the small business person thinking of establishing a pension or profit sharing plan for his employees, the personal liability provisions are indeed significant. Why should he essentially risk everything he has built up over the years by establishing a pension or profit sharing plan for his employees? True, the tax incentives may be substantial, but the weight on the other side of the scale seems substantial indeed. It would appear that these personal liability provisions, added to all the other complications of ERISA, may serve to dry up the pension and profit sharing plans for many new small companies and, therefore, deprive a significant number of American workers of the benefits they might otherwise obtain. Instead, they will have to rely on the social security system. Even if the chances of personal liability are small, counsel advising the establishment of a new pension or profit sharing plan for a small, closely held business would have to point out to management the possibility, and the chilling effect of this constant threat is certainly going to be enough to slow the growth of these smaller plans.

CHAPTER TWENTY-EIGHT

PRIMER ON THE FAIR LABOR STANDARDS ACT

INTRODUCTION

The Fair Labor Standards Act contains a great many detailed requirements the explanations for which fill two volumes of the most popular lawyer's service. The same company which publishes the service also publishes a summary which in 1976 was 344 pages long.

The Fair Labor Standards Act presents a problem for lawyers because the questions presented by the personnel men in this area typically involve extremely small amounts of money, while the laws and regulations which govern these questions are technical, lengthy, and detailed. Accordingly, except in the case of a labor law specialist—and perhaps even then—it is not likely to be profitable for corporate counsel to acquire and maintain the degree of expertise in the wage-and-hour field that would be necessary to answer all or even most of the questions which might be presented. Yet, the problem cannot be ignored because the laws are enforced, and they do allow for private actions by employees who have not been paid as required. In addition, some of the portions of the wage-and-hour laws are "social" in nature, such as child labor and payment of people who do work at home, so the company could receive some bad publicity if it was found to have violated these portions of the law even if the monetary amounts were small.

The following is an attempt to make management aware of the major problems in the wage-and-hour law to provide some discussion of the problems which frequently occur. At the same time, these "problems" present planning opportunities which might be considered. For example, while the rules on employing child labor should be complied with, the rules do allow employment of minors at wages less than the minimum wage which, if the company's operations permit, may present a cost savings for the company and a good opportunity for minors to gain valuable work experience when they would otherwise not be able to get any jobs at all.

DIFFERENCES IN LAWS FOR PRIVATE AND GOVERNMENT BUSINESS

One of the difficulties of summarizing the wage-and-hour laws is that there have developed two almost entirely parallel, but somewhat different, sets of rules for business which are engaged in selling products or services to the government and those which are not. Accordingly, if one is going to prepare a summary of the wage-and-hour laws, he must at least list and briefly describe all of these various laws. There are so many of them, however, that the listing and description alone take up a considerable amount of space. For purposes of this discussion, we have lumped all of the wage-and-hour laws together because, for most large companies, both sets of laws will apply and *both* will have to be complied with. Essentially, the differences are in *overtime pay* and *minimum wage requirements*. In private industry, the Fair Labor Standards Act requires overtime pay *only* for hours worked in excess of 40 hours in one week, while the Walsh-Healey Act, which applies to government contracts, requires overtime pay for hours worked in excess of 8 per day. The Fair Labor Standards Act establishes fixed minimum wages for all workers, and the Walsh-Healey Act establishes minimum wages which are established periodically by regulation and which depend on comparable pay in private industry in similar jobs and in similar locations.

The Applicable Laws

As stated above, one of the complicating factors in discussing wage-and-hour laws is that there are so many of them. In addition, some of these separate laws (like the Equal Pay Act) are really parts of the Fair Labor Standards Act, only they have generated their own body of law and are usually described and explained separately. (This summary will not discuss Equal Pay Act problems.)

The two most important laws relating to wages and hours are the Fair Labor Standards Act, as frequently amended, and the Walsh-Healey Act. The Portal to Portal Act is also significant because it defines exactly when compensable time starts and stops.

The Important Parts of These Laws

Excluding the Equal Pay Act, the following are the important implications of the wage-and-hour laws which should be kept in mind by management.

1. The acts require certain *minimum wages* to be paid to all covered workers.

2. The acts require *overtime* to be paid for hours worked in excess of 40 hours per week, or 8 hours per day in the case of a government contract worker.

3. The acts provide rules on when employees must be paid for commuting or other travel time as well as when compensable worktime starts and stops.

4. The acts impose restrictions on the employment of minors and people doing work for the company in their own homes.

5. The acts impose restrictions on the amount of wages which may be garnisheed.

Minimum Wages.   The minimum wage requirements of the Fair Labor Standards Act are fairly straightforward. The provision relating to general industry is as follows:

> (b) Every employer shall pay to each of his employees . . . who in any workweek is engaged in commerce or in the production of goods for commerce, or is employed in an enterprise engaged in commerce or in the production of goods for commerce . . .
> (1)   not less than $2.65 an hour beginning Jan. 1, 1978
> (2)   not less than $2.90 an hour during the year beginning January 1, 1979
> (3)   not less than $3.10 an hour beginning January 1, 1980, and
> (4)   not less than $3.35 an hour beginning January 1, 1981

The minimum wage requirements for government contractors are not so straightforward. First of all, one must decide which statute is applicable. This determination will usually depend on the kind of work which is being done. The applicable statutes are the following: (1) The most widely applicable statute is the Walsh-Healey Act; the requirements of this statute will be covered herein; (2) the Davis-Bacon Act covers minimum wages paid to workers engaged in public works contracts; this is the act usually applicable in the construction industry; (3) the Service Contract Act covers workers employed by government contractors and subcontractors who provide services to the United States.

Unfortunately, the technical requirements of each of these laws differ, and space does not permit a complete listing of all the requirements of each act. However, the general thrust of the minimum wage laws in government contracts is that there are *no set minimum figures in the statute.* Instead, the minimum wages are *fixed periodically by the administrative agency* and *published in the Federal Register.* Further, in many cases, the minimum wages are *different* depending on the *industry* and the *geographical location.* The following section of the Walsh-Healey Act states the general principle.

> 41 U.S.C. 35(b).   That all persons employed by the contractor in the manufacture or furnishing of the materials, supplies, articles, or equipment used in the performance of the contract will be paid, without subsequent deduction or rebate on any account, not less than the minimum wages as determined by the Secretary of Labor to be the prevailing minimum wages for persons employed on similar work or in the particular or similar industries or groups of industries currently operating in the locality in which the materials, supplies, articles, or equipment are to be manufactured or furnished under said contract.

Coverage of workers under the government contract provisions requiring minimum wages is the same as that for overtime purposes, which is explained in the following subsection, "Overtime."

Overtime.   The general rule regarding overtime is that a company must pay workers one and one-half times their regular rate for hours worked in excess of 40 hours per week (or 8 hours per day in the case of government contracts). The difficulty comes in defining "regular rate" under the Fair Labor Standards Act and its equivalent "basic hourly rate" under the Walsh-Healey Act. (The two have the same meaning.)

Regular rate is not necessarily the normal hourly rate at which people are paid, nor even their hourly rate computed by dividing their weekly salaries by the number of hours actually worked. In most cases, either of the above would be "approximately" correct, but not necessarily absolutely correct. It should be noted that while the Fair Labor Standards Act does talk in terms of hourly rate, it is not necessary to pay workers on an hourly basis; they can be paid weekly, daily, twice a month, monthly, or whatever other period suits the employer. However, for purposes of computing their regular rate, the whole thing must be factored down to an hourly figure.

Another problem in the overtime area is deciding exactly who is covered. The Fair Labor Standards Act and the Walsh-Healey Act contain the concept of "exempt" employees and "nonexempt" employees, and it is only the nonexempt group which must be paid overtime. Exempt people include, of course, the administrative and executive and professional members of the business, and nonexempt people include the hourly paid people and the salaried people who do not meet the requirements of being exempt. It is easy to get into considerable legal difficulty by failing to pay overtime to people who the company thinks are exempt, but who are later termed nonexempt after an analysis of their duties. Typically, the problem will arise when someone who has been classified as exempt either becomes disenchanted or gets fired and sues for back pay. There will then be an elaborate analysis of the person's duties to ascertain whether the employee was exempt and, if he was not, the company will have to make up for any lack of overtime pay. In larger cases involving more people, the Department of Labor may itself initiate suit. The concept of regular rate and exempt versus nonexempt employees deserves further elaboration because these are the cornerstones of the wage-and-hour laws.

Regular Rate and Bonuses.   The employee's regular rate is the basis for computation of overtime payments and is, therefore, very important. The trouble usually comes in nonstandard payments. Beginning with simple examples, an employee who is paid a certain amount per hour for a normal workweek and receives no other form of compensation would have a regular rate equal to his hourly rate. Similarly, a typical secretary who works 40 hours a week for a certain number of dollars per week would have as a regular rate the weekly pay divided by 40 hours.

The trouble will come when some nonstandard payment is made either in the form of cash or otherwise. The regular rate includes all of the employee's compensation, not just the "base" compensation. Thus, if the employees are paid a formula-type bonus in addition to the weekly or hourly rates, this formula-type bonus would have to be factored into the employee's regular rate. For example, suppose that a company decided to institute an incentive program and would pay all the workers a bonus of 25 dollars a week if the company made certain sales or profit levels for that week. In that case, the 25 dollars bonus would have to be included in the regular rate and, if the employee worked overtime, his overtime pay would have to be based upon a regular rate which was augmented by that bonus. Thus, the employer could be in a position of having paid what he thought was a legitimate bonus only to find that he must recompute every nonexempt employee's wage and make an additional payment to those who might have worked overtime during the relevant period.

Fortunately, there are a number of statutory exclusions which minimize this problem. The following kinds of payments are completely excluded when computing the regular rate:

1. gifts, including Christmas bonuses

2. idle-time payments for holidays and absences

3. reimbursements for expenses

4. discretionary bonuses (the bonus must be completely discretionary—this will be elaborated upon below)

5. profit sharing and savings plan payments (these are also technical and will be elaborated upon below)

6. various forms of premium pay for hours worked in excess of 8 a day (the Fair Labor Standards Act requires overtime only for work in excess of 40 hours per week, not work in excess of 8 hours a day)

The above list is only a small sample of the many exclusions, but it covers the most important ones. The ones that usually cause the trouble are discretionary bonuses and profit sharing plans. In order for a discretionary bonus to be excluded, it must be truly discretionary on the part of the employer; if it is not discretionary but, instead, is based upon some kind of agreement or formula, it must be included. The same thing is true with profit sharing and savings plans. They are excluded only if they fall within the technical definitions of such plans as contained in the act.

One of the important points one must remember then is that any time any bonus or profit sharing plan or year-end gift or bonus is considered, someone must check the wage-and-hour rules to make sure that the payment falls within the statutory exclusions. If it does not, a problem will result in the computation of the regular rate for anyone who has worked overtime during the relevant period. In the case of annual bonuses which may fail to qualify for either profit sharing or discretionary bonuses, this problem could become quite complicated and costly if it were ignored. A typical example is a company that desires to use some form of incentive payment for its workers. In order for the incentive to be meaningful, it must be objective and will, therefore by definition, fail to qualify under the discretionary bonus rules.

Fortunately, however, there is a rather simple way to avoid this problem. If a company desires to make incentive payments, it should simply base them upon the employee's total compensation, overtime payments included. This will automatically take care of any wage-and-hour problem, because the payment itself will be based upon a calculation already made which included the overtime requirements. If the company desires to make the payment on a per capita basis—that is, an equal payment to everyone in the company irrespective of their compensation—a definite problem in this area will result.

Production Rates.   There are special provisions for employees who are paid on the basis of production rather than a set hourly rate, although the same general principles apply. If the employee is required to work more than 40 hours a week, he must be paid at one and one-half times the piece rate. Naturally, the exact computations can become complex, especially where there is a combination wage-and-piece rate or an incentive-compensation schedule. However, the general principles of time and one-half for work in excess of 40 hours per week will apply to all nonexempt people, irrespective of the way in which their compensation is computed. Still, the act in no way proscribes the way in which compensation must be paid, and companies are free to establish any kind of pay scale or incentive-compensation system they desire, provided they observe the time and one-half principle where employees work overtime.

Overtime Coverage.   The Fair Labor Standards Act does not require overtime or premium pay for work performed on Saturdays, Sundays, or holidays. Also, it does not require premium pay for work performed for the sixth or seventh days in a week as such. The only requirement is for overtime for work in excess of 40 hours for the workweek: overtime is required only if the Saturday, Sunday, holiday, or sixth or seventh day work causes the total work to exceed 40 hours in a workweek. Naturally, many union agreements and company practices are different, but these are not requirements of the Fair Labor Standards Act.

The overtime requirements for persons working on government contracts are essentially the same, except that the workers must be paid time and one-half for work in excess of 8 hours a day or 40 hours a week, whichever gives them the most money, and this rule applies only to those workers who are actually working on a government contract subject to the Walsh-Healey Act. Employees who are exempt (under the same definition as in the Fair Labor Standards Act) and those who do not work on the government contract are not covered. *On the other hand, there is a presumption that everyone in the plant which has the contract is covered unless separate records are kept.*

An important difference between the 8-hour-day base and the 40-hour-workweek base occurs in situations where employers want to go to a 4-day, 40-hour week or some similar arrangement which calls on the employees to work more than 8 hours per day but not more than 40 hours per week. Indeed, this requirement is one of the principal legal difficulties with the 4-day, 40-hour week.

The coverage provisions sometimes become important, particularly in the case of larger companies which may have more than one plant but government business at less than all of its plants. There are two major coverage requirements: (1) the contract itself must be covered, and (2) the workers must be those who are working on the contract.

The contract will be covered if it is for the furnishing of materials, supplies, articles, and equipment to the government in any amount exceeding $10,000.

The coverage of the workers is a little more complicated. Only those workers working on the government contract are subject to the Walsh-Healey rule. Following is the text of the portion of the ruling which spells out some of the details. [Walsh-Healey Act, 41 C.F.R. Part 50-200 et seq.]

> Section 35.   In General.—(a) All employees (except those in bona fide executive, administrative, or professional capacities and office, custodial, and maintenance employees) who, after the date of the award, are engaged in any operation preparatory to or necessary to or in the performance of the Government contract are subject to the Act.
>
> (b) The application of the Act to a given employee depends upon the work performed by him, and is not governed by the classification or title that he may have, and is not affected by the manner or method of payment to such employee except as provided in section 39(a) below. The determination as to whether a specific employee is subject to the Act is a question for decision by the Department of Labor in the light of the specific circumstances surrounding the employment of the given individual.
>
> Section 36. Employees Covered by the Act—In General.—(a) The stipulations shall be deemed applicable only to employees engaged in or connected with the manufacture, fabrication, assembling, handling, supervision, or shipment of materials, supplies, articles, or equipment required under the contract, and shall not be deemed applicable to employees performing only office or custodial work, nor, to any employee employed in a bona fide executive, administrative, or professional capacity, as those terms are defined and delimited by the Regulations, Part 541, applicable during the period of performance of the contract under section 13(a)(1) of the Fair Labor Standards Act.
>
> (b) If no separate records for employees engaged on Government work are maintained, all employees in the plant or department where the work is performed

are presumed, until affirmative proof is presented to the contrary, to be engaged on Government work.

Section 37. Employees Covered by the Act—In Particular Occupations.—The following employees have been held to be employees engaged in or connected with the performance of the Government contract, unless they meet the qualifications of executive, administrative, or professional employees:

(a) Technical workers closely associated with the productive processes involved in the manufacture of goods or commodities required by the Government.

(b) Employees who clean machines or who remove waste and other accumulations resulting from the operation of the machinery or other equipment used in the performance of the contract, in order to permit the efficient or continued use of such machines or equipment in the performance of the Government contract.

(c) Employees who prepare instructions for assembly, erection, maintenance, or repair to accompany a commodity required under the contract.

(d) Foremen supervising the performance of work on the Government contract, and instructors of employees performing such work. Such employees are covered where their work is directed to the performance of the Government contract, even though they do not operate machines, handle materials, or otherwise perform manual operations in the production of the commodities called for by the Government contract.

Section 38. Employees Not Covered by the Act—In General.—(a) The stipulations are considered not to apply to employees who are not engaged in or directly connected with the manufacture, fabrication, assembling, handling, supervision, or shipment of materials, supplies, articles, or equipment required under the Government contract.

(b) The stipulations are not considered applicable to employees engaged exclusively on commercial work if such employees are actually segregated and separate records are kept for employees engaged on Government work.

Section 39. Employees Not Covered by the Act—In Particular Occupations.— The stipulations are not considered applicable to the following employees:

(a) Executive, administrative, or professional employees meeting the qualifications set forth in Part 541 of the Regulations issued under section 13(a)(1) of the Fair Labor Standards Act. . . .

(b) Office employees engaged exclusively in office work relating generally to the operation of the business and not engaged in the production of materials, supplies, articles, or equipment required by the Government contracts.

(c) Custodial employees whose duties are directed to the maintenance of the plant and who do not perform work on the commodities required by the Government, such as electricians, engineers (engine-room employees), firemen, repair-shop crews, watchmen, maintenance men, telephone operators, and cleaners.

(d) Foremen who meet the qualifications of executive, administrative, or professional employees as defined in section 39(a), above.

(e) Service men who service the contractor's product after delivery to the Government has been completed, and the product has been accepted by the Government.

(f) Workers engaged in general experiments not specifically related to the production of the materials, supplies, articles, or equipment specified in the contract.

(g) Instructors who meet the qualifications of executive, administrative, or professional employees as defined in section 39(a), above.

(h) Employees engaged exclusively in preparing material orders and requisitions and routing orders through the plant.

Exempt Employees

Another important concept in the Fair Labor Standards Act is that of the exempt employee. The general rule is that executive, administrative, and professional employees are exempt from the minimum wage and overtime provisions of the Fair Labor Standards Act. The appropriate definitions are as follows.

An *executive* is one whose primary duty (generally agreed to be 50 percent or more of his time) is in managing an enterprise or department or subdivision thereof. He must customarily and regularly direct work of two or more other employees and must be able to hire and fire or suggest changes in status of other employees. He must customarily and regularly exercise discretionary powers.

An *administrative employee* is one whose primary duty (generally agreed to be 50 percent or more of his time) is in performing office or nonmanual work relating to the management policies or general business operations of the company. An administrative employee is one who regularly and directly assists a proprietor or executive or another administrative employee, or who works only under general supervision along specialized or technical lines requiring special training, experience, or knowledge, or who executes only under general supervision special assignments and tasks. An administrative employee must customarily and regularly exercise discretion and independent judgment.

A *professional employee* is one whose primary duty (generally 50 percent or more of his time) is in performing work requiring scientific or specialized study, as distinguished from apprentice training and training for routine work, or who performs original and creative work in a recognized artistic endeavor depending primarily on the invention, imagination, or talent of the employee, or who teaches, tutors, instructs, or lectures in the activity of imparting knowledge and is employed and engaged in this activity as a teacher. A professional employee must perform work which is predominately intellectual and varied (as opposed to routine) and which cannot be standardized in point of time. He must consistently exercise discretion and judgment, and his nonexempt work must be less than 20 percent of his total hours worked.

The act contains certain presumptions about compensation. If an executive, administrative, or professional employee's compensation is above a certain base level, he is presumed to satisfy the requirement. This presumption will take care of most of the clear situations. It should be noted that there are also minimum rates below which it will be presumed that the person is not an executive, administrative, or professional employee. The exact dollar amounts of these rates are changing rapidly because this is a politically sensitive area. At the present time, the figures are as follows:

1. Executives must make $155 per week, and are presumed executive if they make $250 or more a week.

2. Administrative employees must make $155 per week, and are presumed administrative if they make $250 or more a week.

3. Professional employees must make $170 per week, and are presumed to be professional if they make $250 or more a week.

It should be noted, of course, that these are only presumptions, and the mere fact that someone makes over the maximum amounts stated above does not automatically qualify them as an executive, administrative, or professional employee; they must still satisfy the substantive requirements. The law and regulations on the subject of exemptions are reproduced below.

> Section 13.   (a) The provisions of sections 6 (except section 6(d) in the case of paragraph (1) of this subsection) and 7 shall not apply with respect to—
> (1) any employee employed in a bona fide executive, administrative, or professional capacity (including any employee employed in the capacity of academic administrative personnel or teacher in elementary or secondary schools) or in the capacity of outside salesman (as such terms are defined and delimited from time

to time by regulations of the Secretary, subject to the provisions of the Administrative Procedure Act, except that an employee of a retail or service establishment shall not be excluded from the definition of employee employed in a bona fide executive or administrative capacity because of the number of hours in his workweek which he devotes to activities not directly or closely related to the performance of executive or administrative activities, if less than 40 per centum of his hours worked in the workweek are devoted to such activities); . . .

REGULATIONS

Section 541.1   Executive.

The term "employee employed in a bona fide executive . . . capacity" in section 13(a)(1) of the Act shall mean any employee:

(a)   Whose primary duty consists of the management of the enterprise in which he is employed or of a customarily recognized department or subdivision thereof; and

(b)   Who customarily and regularly directs the work of two or more other employees therein; and

(c)   Who has the authority to hire or fire other employees or whose suggestions and recommendations as to the hiring or firing and as to the advancement and promotion or any other change of status of other employees will be given particular weight; and

(d)   Who customarily and regularly exercises discretionary power; and

(e)   Who does not devote more than 20 percent, or, in the case of an employee of a retail or service establishment who does not devote as much as 40 percent of his hours of work in the workweek to activities which are not directly and closely related to the performance of the work described in paragraphs (a) through (d) of this section: *Provided*, That this paragraph shall not apply in the case of an employee who is in sole charge of an independent establishment or a physically separated branch establishment, or who owns at least a 20-percent interest in the enterprise in which he is employed; and

(f)   Who is compensated for his services on a salary basis at a rate of not less than $155 per week (or $130 per week, if employed by other than the Federal Government in Puerto Rico, the Virgin Islands, or American Samoa), exclusive of board, lodging, or other facilities: *Provided*, That an employee who is compensated on a salary basis at a rate of not less than $250 per week (or $200 per week, if employed by other than the Federal Government in Puerto Rico, the Virgin Islands or American Samoa), exclusive of board, lodging, or other facilities, and whose primary duty consists of the management of the enterprise in which the employee is employed or of a customarily recognized department or subdivision thereof, and includes the customary and regular direction of the work of two or more other employees therein, shall be deemed to meet all the requirements of this section.

Section 541.2   Administrative.

The term "employee employed in a bona fide . . . administrative . . . capacity" in section 13(a)(1) of the Act shall mean any employee:

(a)   Whose primary duty consists of either:

(1)   The performance of office or nonmanual work directly related to management policies or general business operations of his employer or his employer's customers, or

(2)   The performance of functions in the administration of a school system, or educational establishment or institution, or of a department or subdivision thereof; in work directly related to the academic instruction or training carried on therein; and

(b)   Who customarily and regularly exercises discretion and independent judgment; and

(c)(1)   Who regularly and directly assists a proprietor, or an employee employed in a bona fide executive or administrative capacity (as such terms are defined in the regulations of this subpart), or

(2)   Who performs under only general supervision work along specialized or technical lines requiring special training, experience, or knowledge, or

(3)   Who executes under only general supervision special assignments and tasks; and

(d)   Who does not devote more than 20 percent, or, in the case of an employee of a retail or service establishment who does not devote as much as 40 percent, of his hours worked in the workweek to activities which are not directly and closely related to the performance of the work described in paragraphs (a) through (c) of this section; and

(e)(1)   Who is compensated for his services on a salary or fee basis at a rate of not less than $155 per week ($130 per week, if employed by other than the Federal Government in Puerto Rico, the Virgin Islands, or American Samoa), exclusive of board, lodging, or other facilities, or

(2)   Who, in the case of academic administrative personnel, is compensated for services as required by paragraph (e)(1) of this section, or on a salary basis which is at least equal to the entrance salary for teachers in the school system, educational establishment, or institution by which employed: *Provided,* That an employee who is compensated on a salary or fee basis at a rate of not less than $250 per week ($200 per week if employed by other than the Federal Government in Puerto Rico, the Virgin Islands, or American Samoa), exclusive of board, lodging or other facilities, and whose primary duty consists of the performance of work described in paragraph (a) of this section, which includes work requiring the exercise of discretion and independent judgment, shall be deemed to meet all the requirements of this section.

Section 541.3   Professional.

The term "employee employed in a bona fide . . . professional capacity" in section 13(a)(1) of the Act shall mean any employee:

(a)   Whose primary duty consists of the performance of:

(1)   Work requiring knowledge of an advanced type in a field of science or learning customarily acquired by a prolonged course of specialized intellectual instruction and study, as distinguished from a general academic education and from an apprenticeship, and from training in the performance of routine mental, manual, or physical processes, or

(2)   Work that is original and creative in character in a recognized field of artistic endeavor (as opposed to work which can be produced by a person endowed with general manual or intellectual ability and training), and the result of which depends primarily on the invention, imagination, or talent of the employee, or

(3)   Teaching, tutoring, instructing, or lecturing in the activity of imparting knowledge and who is employed and engaged in this activity as a teacher in the school system or educational establishment or institution by which he is employed; and

(b)   Whose work requires the consistent exercise of discretion and judgment in its performance; and

(c)   Whose work is predominantly intellectual and varied in character (as opposed to routine mental, manual, mechanical, or physical work) and is of such character that the output produced or the result accomplished cannot be standardized in relation to a given period of time; and

(d)   Who does not devote more than 20 percent of his hours worked in the workweek to activities which are not an essential part of and necessarily incident to the work described in paragraphs (a) through (c) of this section; and

(e)   Who is compensated for services on a salary or fee basis at a rate of not less than $170 per week ($150 per week, if employed by other than the Federal Government in Puerto Rico, the Virgin Islands, or American Samoa), exclusive of board, lodging, or other facilities: *Provided,* That this paragraph shall not apply in the case of an employee who is the holder of a valid license or certificate permitting the practice of law or medicine or any of their branches and who is actually engaged in the practice thereof, nor in the case of an employee who is the holder of the requisite academic degree for the general practice of medicine and is engaged in an internship or resident program pursuant to the practice of medicine or any of its branches, nor in the case of an employee employed and engaged as a teacher as provided in paragraph (a)(3) of this section: *Provided further,* That an employee who is compensated on a salary or fee basis at a rate of not less than $250 per week (or $200 per week, if employed by other than the Federal Government in Puerto Rico, the Virgin Islands, or American Samoa), exclusive of board, lodging, or other facilities, and whose primary duty consists of the performance either of work described in paragraph (a)(1) or (3) of this section, which includes work requiring the consistent exercise of discretion and judgment, or of work requiring invention, imagination, or talent in a recognized field of artistic endeavor, shall be deemed to meet all of the requirements of this section.

In addition to the law and regulations, there are two other extremely useful references explaining the Department of Labor's views on the subject of exemptions and overtime payments: *Explanatory Bulletin on "White Collar" Regulations* and *Authorization of Established Basic Rates for Computing Overtime Pay.* These are quite lengthy and detailed explanations of the rules and would be useful for reference. They are too lengthy, however, to reproduce here, but they are available from the Department of Labor.

Waivers

Any waiver of employees' rights under the wage-and-hour laws is not valid unless supervised and approved by the Department of Labor.

THE PORTAL TO PORTAL ACT

The Portal to Portal Act generally provides that workers need not be paid for transportation from their home to their place of work. Thus, in a normal case, one computes hours worked from the time the worker actually starts work until the time he actually stops, and the time he spends going to and from his home or washing or walking from the plant door to his work station is not counted. Of course, this general rule can be altered by custom or contract. However, when one sends a nonexempt employee out of town, or requires the nonexempt employee to travel during working hours, the rules become a little more complicated. Generally, if the employee is required to travel during working hours, that time must be included as work time. If a nonexempt employee is sent out of town, he need not be paid for the travel time to and from his home, to the railroad, bus, or plane terminal, but he must be paid for all other travel time except that which is spent eating during transportation.

Where employees travel overnight on business, they must be paid for all their time spent in traveling except for meal periods during their normal working hours or on their nonworking days such as Saturdays, Sundays, and holidays. They need not be paid for traveling outside of those hours, except for any time they might spend actually performing duties for the employer.

CHILD LABOR

The law on child labor is as stated in the Fair Labor Standards Act as follows:

THE LAW

Section 12.   (a) No producer, manufacturer, or dealer shall ship or deliver for shipment in commerce any goods produced in an establishment situated in the United States in or about which within thirty days prior to the removal of such goods therefrom any oppressive child labor has been employed: *Provided,* That any such shipment or delivery for shipment of such goods by a purchaser who acquired them in good faith in reliance on written assurance from the producer, manufacturer, or dealer that the goods were produced in compliance with the requirements of this section, and who acquired such goods for value without notice of any such violation, shall not be deemed prohibited by this subsection: *And provided further*, That a prosecution and conviction of defendant for the shipment or delivery for shipment of any goods under the conditions herein prohibited shall be a bar to any further prosecution against the same defendant for shipments or deliveries for shipment of any such goods before the beginning of said prosecution.

(b)   The Secretary of Labor, or any of his authorized representatives, shall make all investigations and inspections under section 11(a) with respect to the employment of minors, and, subject to the direction and control of the Attorney General, shall bring all actions under section 17 to enjoin any act or practice which is unlawful by reason of the existence of oppressive child labor, and shall administer all other provisions of this Act relating to oppressive child labor.

(c)   No employer shall employ any oppressive child labor in commerce or in the production of goods for commerce or in any enterprise engaged in commerce or in the production of goods for commerce.

(d)   In order to carry out the objectives of this section, the Secretary may by regulation require employers to obtain from any employee proof of age.

REGULATIONS

The regulations governing child labor are long and detailed. Generally, they provide as follows:

1.   Employers can protect themselves from unintentional violations by getting a certificate, as prescribed in the regulations, that the person is above the minimum age allowed for the job. The certificate should always be obtained where the minor claims to be only one or two years above the minimum age, or where the appearance of the minor suggests the desirability of getting the certificate. Unless the employer has the certificate, there is no defense merely because the employer did not know the child was under age.

2.   Minors between 14 and 16 can, in accordance with various regulations, be employed in the following jobs:

(1)   Office and clerical work, including the operation of office machines;

(2)   Cashiering, selling, modeling, art work, work in advertising departments, window trimming, and comparative shopping;

(3)   Price marking and tagging by hand or by machine, assembling orders, packing and shelving;

(4)   Bagging and carrying out customer's orders;

(5)   Errand and delivery work by foot, bicycle, and public transportation;

(6)   Clean up work, including the use of vacuum cleaners and floor waxers, and maintenance of grounds, but not including the use of power-driven mowers, or cutters;

(7)   Kitchen work and other work involved in preparing and serving food and beverages, including the operation of machines and devices used in the performance of such work, such as but not limited to, dish-washers, toasters, dumb-waiters, popcorn poppers, milk shake blenders, and coffee grinders;

(8)   Work in connection with cars and trucks if confined to the following: Dispensing gasoline and oil; courtesy service; car cleaning, washing and polishing; and other occupations permitted by this section, but not including work involving the use of pits, racks, or lifting apparatus, or involving the inflation of any tire mounted on a rim equipped with a removable retaining ring.

(9)   Cleaning vegetables and fruits, and wrapping, sealing, labeling, weighing, pricing and stocking goods when performed in areas physically separate from those where the work described in paragraph (b)(7) of this section is performed;

Minors between 14 and 16 cannot be employed in the following aspects of retail, food service, and gasoline service establishments:

(1)   All occupations listed in section 570.33 except occupations involving processing, operation of machines and work in rooms where processing and manufacturing take place which are permitted by paragraph (a) of this section.

(2) Work performed in or about boiler or engine rooms;

(3) Work in connection with maintenance or repair of the establishment, machines or equipment;

(4) Outside window washing that involves working from window sills, and all work requiring the use of ladders, scaffolds, or their substitutes;

(5) Cooking (except at soda fountains, lunch counters, snack bars, or cafeteria serving counters) and baking;

(6) Occupations which involve operating, setting up, adjusting, cleaning, oiling, or repairing power-driven food slicers and grinders, food choppers, and cutters, and bakery-type mixers.

(7) Work in freezers and meat coolers and all work in the preparation of meats for sale except as described in paragraph (a)(9) of this section;

(8) Loading and unloading goods to and from trucks, railroad cars, or conveyors;

(9) All occupations in warehouses except office and clerical work.

Subject to extensive explanation contained in the regulations, employment of minors between sixteen and eighteen years is restricted (but not totally prohibited) in the following areas:

1. manufacture or storage of explosives

2. motor vehicle driver and outside helper

3. coal mine occupations

4. logging occupations

5. woodworking occupations

6. exposure to radioactive substances

7. operation of power-driven hoisting apparatus

8. operation of power-driven metal-forming, punching, and shearing machines

9. occupations in connection with mining, other than coal

10. slaughtering and meat packing establishments and rendering plants

11. operation of power-driven bakery machines

12. operation of power-driven paper products machines

13. manufacture of brick, tile, and kindred products

14. operation of circular saws, band saws, and guillotine shears

15. wrecking, demolition, and shipbreaking operations

16. roofing operations

17. excavating operations

This area is so complicated and technical that specific legal advice on virtually every type of job for which a person under 18 might be employed should be discussed with counsel.

GARNISHMENTS

Garnishments are another point of annoyance. The Fair Labor Standards Act restricts the amount of wages which can be garnisheed. Accordingly, the payroll department must be informed of these rules and must be instructed to comply with legitimate garnishment orders only up to the maximum extent required by law.

The federal garnishment law limits the amount of wages subject to garnishment to 25 percent of the worker's "disposable earnings," which are generally defined as his earnings remaining after withholding for taxes and other amounts required by law, or the amount by which his weekly disposable earnings exceed by thirty times the Fair Labor Standards Act minimum wage, whichever is less. Since the minimum wage is going up, the amounts which can be garnisheed change every time they do so.

Also, the federal garnishment law does prohibit the discharge of an employee because his earnings have been garnisheed for "any one indebtedness." The meaning of "any one indebtedness" is not entirely clear, but it should be noted that it is definitely different than any single garnishment. Accordingly, the mere fact that an employee has had his wages garnisheed more than once does not mean he can be discharged.

In addition, it should be observed that equal employment opportunity laws provide that a policy of discharging employees with excessive garnishments can violate those laws if the policy operates discriminatorily, and, statistically speaking, one is very likely to find this to be the result. Accordingly, the garnishment rules are something which a company is going to just have to live with, and, while it can certainly counsel its employees, it will be the rare and unusual case where the company will be justified in discharging an employee because of frequent garnishments.

RECORD KEEPING

Employers subject to the Fair Labor Standards Act are required to keep fairly detailed records concerning their employees. Records must be kept for both exempt and nonexempt employees, although the records for nonexempt employees are more detailed. The reason for the records on the exempt employees is to allow the government to make a reasonable audit to see that they were, in fact, exempt; the reason for the records on the nonexempt employees is to allow for checks on whether or not the provisions of the act have been complied with. The company does not have to keep these records in any special format, as long as that format does not make audits difficult or impossible. Generally, records must be kept to show the following:

1. name of the employee
2. home address
3. date of birth if the employee is under nineteen
4. employee's sex and occupation in which employed
5. time and name of the day on which the workweek begins
6. the regular hourly rate and the basis on which wages are paid
7. hours worked each day and week
8. daily or weekly straight-time earnings
9. weekly overtime excess compensation
10. deductions from or additions to wages
11. wages paid each pay period
12. the date wages are paid and the period covered by such payment

The text of the important record-keeping provisions, showing the record retention periods, follows:

Section 516.1 Form of Records; Scope of Regulations.—(a) *Form of Records.* No particular order or form of records is prescribed by the regulations in this part. However, every employer who is subject to any of the provisions of the Fair Labor Standards Act of 1938, as amended (hereinafter referred to as the "Act"), is required to maintain records containing the information and data required by the specific sections of this part.

(b) *Scope of Regulations.* (1) The regulations in this part are divided into two subparts. Subpart A of this part contains the requirements applicable to all employers employing covered employees, including the general requirements relating to the posting of notices, the preservation and location of records, and similar general provisions. This subpart also contains the requirements applicable to employers of employees to whom both the minimum wage provisions of section 6 and the overtime pay provisions of section 7(a) of the Act apply. As most covered employees fall within this category, employers, in most instances, will be concerned principally with the recordkeeping requirements of Subpart A of this part. Section 516.3 thereof contains the requirements relating to executive, administrative, and professional employees (including academic administrative personnel or teachers in elementary or secondary schools), and outside sales employees.

(2) Subpart B of this part deals with the information and data which must be kept with respect to employees (other than executive, administrative, etc., employees) who are subject to any of the exemptions provided in the Act, and with special provisions relating to such matters as deductions from and additions to wages for "board, lodging, or other facilities," industrial homeworkers, employees dependent upon tips as part of wages, and employees subject to more than one minimum wage. The sections in Subpart B of this part require the recording of more, less, or different items of information or data than required under the generally applicable recordkeeping requirements of Subpart A of this part.

Section 516.2 Employees Subject to Minimum Wage or Minimum Wage and Overtime Provisions; section 6 or sections 6 and 7(a) of the Act.—(a) *Items Required.* Every employer shall maintain and preserve payroll or other records containing the following information and data with respect to each and every employee to whom section 6 or both sections 6 and 7(a) of the Act apply:

(1) Name in full, and on the same record, the employee's identifying symbol or number if such is used in place of name on any time, work, or payroll records. This shall be the same name as that used for Social Security record purposes,

(2) Home address, including zip code,

(3) Date of birth, if under 19,

(4) Sex and occupation in which employed (sex may be indicated by use of the prefixes Mr., Mrs., or Miss),

(5) Time of day and day of week on which the employee's workweek begins. If the employee is part of a work force or employed in or by an establishment all of whose workers have a workweek beginning at the same time on the same day, a single notation of the time of the day and beginning day of the workweek for the whole work force or establishment will suffice. If, however, any employee or group of employees has a workweek beginning and ending at a different time, a separate notation shall then be kept for that employee or group of employees,

(6)(i) Regular hourly rate of pay for any week when overtime is worked and overtime excess compensation is due under section 7(a) of the Act, (ii) basis on which wages are paid (such as $2 hr."; "$16 day"; "$80 wk."; "$80 wk. plus 5 percent commission on sales over $800 wk."), and (iii) the amount and nature of each payment which, pursuant to section 7(e) of the Act, is excluded from the "regular rate" (these records may be in the form of vouchers or other payment data),

(7) Hours worked each workday and total hours worked each workweek (for purposes of this section, a "workday" shall be any consecutive 24 hours),

(8) Total daily or weekly straight-time earnings or wages, that is, the total earnings or wages due for hours worked during the workday or workweek, including all earnings or wages due during any overtime worked, but exclusive of overtime excess compensation,

(9) Total overtime excess compensation for the workweek, that is, the excess

compensation for overtime worked which amount is over and above all straight-time earnings or wages also earned during overtime worked,

(10)   Total additions to or deductions from wages paid each pay period. Every employer making additions to or deductions from wages shall also maintain, in individual employee accounts, a record of the dates, amounts, and nature of the items which make up the total additions and deductions,

(11)   Total wages paid each pay period,

(12)   Date of payment and the pay period covered by payment.

(b)   *Records of Retroactive Payment of Wages.* Every employer who makes retroactive payment of wages or compensation under the supervision of the Administrator pursuant to section 16(c) of the Act, shall:

(1)   Record and preserve, as an entry on his payroll or other pay records, the amount of such payment to each employee, the period covered by such payment, and the date of payment.

(2)   Prepare a report of each such payment on the receipt form provided or authorized by the Wage and Hour Division, and (i) preserve a copy as part of his records, (ii) deliver a copy to the employee, and (iii) file the original, which shall evidence payment by the employer and receipt by the employee, with the Administrator or his authorized representative within 10 days after payment is made.

(c)   *Employees Working on Fixed Schedules.* With respect to employees working on fixed schedules, an employer may maintain records showing instead of the hours worked each day and each week, as required by paragraph (a)(7) of this section, the schedule of daily and weekly hours the employee normally works, and

(1)   In weeks in which an employee adheres to this schedule, indicates by check mark, statement, or other method that such hours were in fact actually worked by him, and

(2)   In weeks in which more or less than the scheduled hours are worked, shows the exact number of hours worked each day and each week.

Section 516.3   Bona Fide Executive, Administrative, and Professional Employees (Including Academic Administrative Personnel and Teachers in Elementary or Secondary Schools), and Outside Sales Employees as Referred to in Section 13(a)(1) of the Act—Items Required.—With respect to persons employed in a bona fide executive, administrative or professional capacity (including employees employed in the capacity of academic administrative personnel or teachers in elementary or secondary schools), or in the capacity of outside salesman, as defined in Part 541 of this chapter (pertaining to so-called "white collar" employee exemptions), employers shall maintain and preserve records containing all of the information and data required by section 516.2(a) except subparagraphs (6) through (10) thereof, and, in addition thereto the basis on which wages are paid in sufficient detail to permit calculation for each pay period of the employee's total remuneration for employment including fringe benefits and prerequisites. (This may be shown as "$725 mo. * * * $165 wk. * * * $1,200 mo. plus 2 percent commission on gross sales * * * on fee basis per schedule no. 2" with appropriate addenda such as "plus hospitalization and insurance plan A," "benefit package B," "2 weeks' paid vacation," etc.).

Section 516.4   Posting of Notices.—Every employer employing any employees who are (a) engaged in commerce or in the production of goods for commerce or (b) employed in an enterprise engaged in commerce or in the production of goods for commerce, and who are not specifically exempt from both the minimum wage provisions of section 6 and the overtime provisions of section 7(a) of the Act, shall post and keep posted such notices pertaining to the applicability of the Act, as shall be prescribed by the Wage and Hour Division, in conspicuous places in every establishment where such employees are employed so as to permit them to observe readily a copy on the way to or from their place of employment.

Section 516.5   Records to be Preserved Three Years.—Each employer shall preserve for at least three years:

(a)   *Payroll Records.* From the last date of entry, all those payroll or other records containing the employee information and data required under any of the applicable sections of this part, and

(b)   *Certificates, Agreements, Plans, Notices, etc.* From their last effective date, all written:

(1) Collective bargaining agreements relied upon for the exclusion of certain costs under section 3(m) of the Act,

(2) Collective bargaining agreements, under section 7(b)(1) or 7(b)(2) of the Act, and any amendments or additions thereto,

(3) Plans, trusts, employment contracts, and collective bargaining agreements under section 7(e) of the Act,

(4) Individual contracts or collective bargaining agreements under section 7(f) of the Act. Where such contracts or agreements are not in writing, a written memorandum summarizing the terms of each such contract or agreement,

(5) Written agreements or memoranda summarizing the terms of oral agreements or understandings under section 7(g), or 7(j) of the Act, and

(6) Certificates and notices listed or named in any applicable section of this part.

(c) *Sales and Purchase Records.* A record of (1) total dollar volume of sales or business, and (2) total volume of goods purchased or received during such periods (weekly, monthly, quarterly, etc.) and in such form as the employer maintains in the ordinary course of his business.

Section 516.6   Records to be Preserved Two Years.—(a) *Supplementary Basic Records.* Each employer required to maintain records under this part shall preserve for a period of at least two years:

(1) *Basic Employment and Earnings Records.* From the date of last entry, all basic time and earning cards or sheets of the employer on which are entered the daily starting and stopping time of individual employees, or of separate work forces, or the individual employee's daily, weekly, or pay period amounts of work accomplished (for example, units produced) when those amounts determine in whole or in part the pay period earnings or wages of those employees.

(2) *Wage Rate Tables.* From their last effective date, all tables or schedules of the employer which provide the piece rates or other rates used in computing straight-time earnings, wages, or salary, or overtime excess computation, and

(3) *Work Time Schedules.* From their last effective date, all schedules or tables of the employer which establish the hours and days of employment of individual employees or of separate work forces.

(b) *Order, Shipping, and Billing Records.* Each employer shall also preserve for at least two years from the last date of entry the originals or true copies of any and all customer orders or invoices received, incoming or outgoing shipping or delivery records, as well as all bills of lading and all billings to customers (not including individual sales slips, cash register tapes or the like) which the employer retains or makes in the course of his business operations.

(c) *Records of Additions to or Deductions from Wages Paid.* Each employer who makes additions to or deductions from wages paid shall preserve for at least two years from the date of last entry:

(1) Those records of individual employee accounts referred to in section 516.2(a)(10),

(2) All employee purchase orders, or assignments made by employees, all copies of addition or deduction statements furnished employees, and

(3) All records used by the employer in determining the original cost, operating and maintenance cost, and depreciation and interest charges, if such costs and charges are involved in the additions to or deductions from wages paid.

(d) Each employer shall preserve for at least two years the records he makes of the kind described in section 516.32 which explain the basis for payment of any wage differential to employees of the opposite sex in the same establishment.

Section 516.7   Place for Keeping Records and Their Availability for Inspection.—(a) *Place of Records.* Each employer shall keep the records required by the regulations in this part safe and accessible at the place or places of employment, or at one or more established central recordkeeping offices where such records are customarily maintained. Where the records are maintained at a central recordkeeping office, other than in the place or places of employment, such records shall be made available within 72 hours following notice from the Administrator or his duly authorized and designated representative.

(b) *Inspection of Records.* All records shall be open at any time to inspection and transcription by the Administrator or his duly authorized and designated representative.

Section 516.8   Computations and Reports.—(a) Each employer required to maintain records under this part shall make such extension, recomputation, or transcription of his records and shall submit to the Wage and Hour Division such reports concerning persons employed and the wages, hours, and other conditions and practices of employment set forth in his records as the Administrator or his duly authorized and designated representative may request in writing.

The Fair Standards Act has the typical enforcement procedures which allow the government (the Department of Labor or the Wage and Hour Administration) to bring suit against any employer who is found to have violated any of the provisions and to obtain injunctive relief, plus back-pay awards to employees who were not paid the proper overtime or minimum wages.

In addition, the employees themselves have this right. They can bring suit directly and, if they are successful, they can recover attorneys' fees and, if they can show a willful violation, they can also recover an amount equal to their actual damages as "liquidated damages." There can be a class action brought by one or more employees representing all employees similarly situated, but it is important to note that this class action is a specially defined one under the Fair Labor Standards Act and not the general kind of class action. The essential difference is that in the fair-labor-standards-type action, employees have to be notified and to "opt in." In a general class action case, everyone described by the class action is automatically in unless they "opt out." The legislative provisions are in section 16(a), (b), (c), and (e) of the act, as reproduced below. (Paragraph (d) deals with American Samoa and other overseas areas and is not reproduced.) Section 17 allows the injunctive proceeding by the government.

Section 16.   (a) Any person who willfully violates any of the provisions of section 15 shall upon conviction thereof be subject to a fine of not more than $10,000 or to imprisonment for not more than six months, or both. No person shall be imprisoned under this subsection except for an offense committed after the conviction of such person for a prior offense under this subsection.

(b)   Any employer who violates the provisions of section 6 or section 7 of this Act shall be liable to the employee or employees affected in the amount of their unpaid minimum wages, or their unpaid overtime compensation, as the case may be, and in an additional equal amount as liquidated damages. Action to recover such liability may be maintained against any employer (including a public agency) in any Federal or State court of competent jurisdiction by any one or more employees for and in behalf of himself or themselves and other employees similarly situated. No employee shall be a party plaintiff to any such action unless he gives his consent in writing to become such a party and such consent is filed in the court in which such action is brought. The court in such action shall, in addition to any judgment awarded to the plaintiff or plaintiffs, allow a reasonable attorney's fee to be paid by the defendant, and costs of the action. The right provided by this subsection to bring an action by or on behalf of any employee, and the right of any employee to become a party plaintiff to any such action, shall terminate upon the filing of a complaint by the Secretary of Labor in an action under section 17 in which restraint is sought of any further delay in the payment of unpaid minimum wages or the amount of unpaid overtime compensation, as the case may be, owing to such employee under section 6 or section 7 of this Act by an employer liable therefor under the provisions of this subsection.

(c)   The Secretary is authorized to supervise the payment of the unpaid minimum wages or the unpaid overtime compensation owing to any employee or employees under sections 6 or 7 of this Act, and the agreement of any employee to accept such payment shall upon payment in full constitute a waiver by such employee of any right he may have under subsection (b) of this section to such unpaid minimum wages or unpaid overtime compensation and an additional equal amount as liquidated damages. The Secretary may bring an action in any court of competent jurisdiction to recover the amount of the unpaid minimum wages or overtime compensation and an equal amount as liquidated damages. The right provided by subsection (b) to bring an action by or on behalf of any employee and of any employee to become a party plaintiff to any such action shall terminate upon the filing of a complaint by the Secretary in an action under this subsection in which a recovery in sought of unpaid minimum wages or unpaid overtime compensation under sections 6 and 7 or liquidated or other damages provided by this subsection owing to such employee by an employer liable under the provision of subsection (b), unless such action is dismissed without prejudice on motion of the Secretary. Any sums thus recovered by the Secretary on behalf of an employee pursuant to this subsection shall be held in a special deposit account and shall be paid, on order of the Secretary, directly to the employee or employees affected. Any such sums not paid to an employee because of inability to do so within a period of three years shall be covered into the Treasury of the United States as miscellaneous receipts. In determining when an action is commenced by the Secretary under this subsection for the purposes of the statutes of limitations provided in section 6(a) of the Portal-to-Portal Act of 1947, it shall be considered to be commenced in the case of any individual claimant on the date when the complaint is filed if he is specifically named as a party plaintiff in the complaint, or if his name did not so appear, on the subsequent date on which his name is added as a party plaintiff in such action.

(e) Any person who violates the provisions of section 12, relating to child labor, or any regulation issued under that section, shall be subject to a civil penalty of not to exceed $1,000 for each such violation. In determining the amount of such penalty, the appropriateness of such penalty to the size of the business of the person charged and the gravity of the violation shall be considered. The amount of such penalty, when finally determined, may be—

(1) deducted from any sums owing by the United States to the person charged;

(2) recovered in a civil action brought by the Secretary in any court of competent jurisdiction, in which litigation the Secretary shall be represented by the Solicitor of Labor; or

(3) ordered by the court, in an action brought under section 15(a)(4), to be paid to the Secretary.

Any administrative determination by the Secretary of the amount of such penalty shall be final, unless within fifteen days after receipt of notice thereof by certified mail the person charged with the violation takes exception to the determination that the violations for which the penalty is imposed occurred, in which event final determination of the penalty shall be made in an administrative proceeding after opportunity for a hearing in accordance with section 554 of title 5, United States Code, and regulations to be promulgated by the Secretary. Sums collected as penalties pursuant to this section shall be applied toward reimbursement of the costs of determining the violations and assessing and collecting such penalties, in accordance with the provisions of section 2 of an Act entitled "An Act to authorize the Department of Labor to make special statistical studies upon payment of the cost thereof, and for other purposes" (29 U.S.C. 9a).

Enforcement of the Walsh-Healey Act is through the government's exercise of its power to award contracts. Extreme violations can result in money loss, contract termination, or blacklisting.

SUMMARY

In summary, the wage and hour rules are very lengthy and technical. However, they are also very old and are covered well in publications received by those in charge of operating the company's payroll. Also, the amounts involved in any single problem are usually small, disputes are usually fairly easy to settle, and suits are rare. On the other hand, the amounts involved in total can be large, and the public relations factor can't be ignored. Management's job is to get the right amount of legal assistance for the situation. Obviously, the problems are such that at least one lawyer could be kept busy full time doing nothing but making decisions as to exempt status, computations of regular rate, and keeping records. Equally obviously, the problems usually won't warrant this except in the case of the largest corporations and even then only if all the payroll operations are done centrally. By the same token, if no lawyer in the company is at all familiar with these rules, and if the people in the personnel/payroll departments haven't become experts themselves, it would seem that there is a more than average potential for a troublesome problem which could easily be avoided by minimal legal attention.

Most lawyers don't like wage and hour work. But management is entitled to a lawyer's assurances that all the company's practices and procedures are adequate and that exceptional cases are brought to the attention of someone with a working knowledge of these regulations and the reference materials to look up the complex rules as necessary. This doesn't have to be a lawyer—and many times should not be a lawyer. But a lawyer should be available for the occasional complex question.

CHAPTER TWENTY-NINE

VETERANS' EMPLOYMENT RIGHTS

INTRODUCTION

Various federal statutes in effect since about 1940 guarantee veterans certain employment rights when they return from service in the armed forces. Generally, these laws require employers to rehire ex-servicemen and women and to make sure that their benefits, status, and seniority are the same as if they had not left their jobs. There are a number of government publications and cases which elaborate on the provisions of these laws. The government publications generally do a good job of stating who is covered, what the mechanical requirements are, and answering some of the most common questions. Two government publications which are particularly good are included with this chapter.

However, the right of the veteran to be hired "with full benefits, status and seniority as if the serviceman had not left his position" is a little more complicated and requires additional explanation. This right is the so-called escalator principle. The leading case describes it as follows:

> . . . [The] veteran does not step back on the seniority escalator at the point he stepped off. He steps back on at the precise point he would have occupied had he kept his position continuously during the war. . . . He acquires not only the same seniority he had; his service in the armed services is counted as service in the plan so that he does not lose ground by reason of his absence. But we would distort the language of those provisions if we read it as granting the veteran an increase in seniority over what he would have had if he had never entered the armed services. [*Fishgold v. Sullivan Drydock*, 328 U.S. 275 (1946)]

This concept was incorporated in the applicable statutes as follows: "[The veteran must be restored or reemployed] in such a manner as to give such person such status in his employment as he would have enjoyed if such person had continued in such employment continuously from the time of such person's entering the Armed Forces until the time of such person's restoration to such employment."

Prior to induction or enlistment, the veteran must have been a permanent employee. Part-time or seasonal employment is considered permanent so long as it is not limited to a specific, brief, and nonrecurrent period. Probationary, apprenticeship, and trainee positions are likewise considered permanent, as the parties ordinarily enter into these types of employment relationships contemplating a continuing or recurrent employment.

The employee must have left his job for the purpose of entering or being examined for military service or training, and although the statutes are liberally construed, the circumstances must indicate that this was the primary intent in leaving employment. Military service or training, however, do not have to be the sole reasons for leaving employment, and employees on strike, leave of absence, or layoff with recall rights who enter military service are entitled to reinstatement rights. No notice to the employer of the specific intent is required except in the case of reservists or National Guardsmen.

If the employer's circumstances have changed so that the particular job no longer exists, he is required to offer another job of similar pay, status, and seniority. The cases indicate that an offer of a job of similar pay, status, and seniority, but requiring retraining, will satisfy the statute. No offer need be made if, due to "changed circumstances," such offer would place an "unreasonable or impossible" burden on the employer. The impossibility or unreasonableness must apply not only to the position the veteran left but also to any similar position he would have attained but for his military service. Reorganization, incorporation, sale, transfer, or merger of the preservice employer does not normally constitute grounds for refusal to reinstate on the basis of "changed circumstances." A mere change in the title, minor involuntary changes in duties, decline in business volume, or union organization are likewise insufficient "change of circumstances" grounds for denial of reinstatement rights.

If the position is currently filled, it must be given to the returning veteran unless the current position holder is of higher seniority. Where two returning soldiers of equal seniority desire reinstatement to the same position, the one who first entered the service has higher reinstatement priority. The veteran is not entitled to *any* or *every* position; consequently, the employer is not required to create a position if the type and level of position has been abolished through the normal progress or exigencies of business.

In addition to the above, the veteran must meet the following prerequisites. One, application for reinstatement within 90 days of regular separation or within 90 days of release from hospitalization, if service-connected hospitalization extends beyond regular separation, up to a limit of 1 year's such hospitalization. The deadlines apply only to application for reinstatement. There is no time limit as to when the veteran must actually return to work. The application may be oral or written, may be made to the employer or his agents, and may be made before the veteran's separation from service. Of course, in the last case, the 90-day period begins to run at actual separation. The time runs even though the employer is shut down, on strike, vacation, or for other reasons. Two, receipt of a certificate or other document from the particular branch of the service evidencing satisfactory completion of the period of service ("honorable," "general," "under honorable conditions";

most medical and hardship discharges are considered satisfactory). Three, a period of service not exceeding a statutory maximum (currently 5 years). Four, qualification to perform the duties of the former or a similar position, except if disqualified by reason of service-connected disabilities (in which case the right to be rehired attaches to any other similar position which the veteran is qualified to perform. Five, no actions in the nature of a waiver of rights or which are felonious or reprehensible to a degree making the veteran an undesirable employee under any circumstances. Also, a veteran may not be removed, demoted, or otherwise disadvantaged in his employment, except for good cause, nor have his reinstatement rights abridged for one year following his rehiring.

PAY, STATUS, AND SENIORITY

Generally, regarding pay, status, and seniority, an employer is expected to treat a reinstated veteran as it would any other employee who had been on furlough or leave of absence. The object of the legislation is not to give the veteran exceptional advantage over other employees such as a greater increase in seniority, status, pay, or other incidents of his position than he would have had had he remained on the job, but to make his reentry into the work force as equitable as possible. Any increases in pay, improvements of status, benefits, or moves up the seniority ladder which would have occurred automatically if the veteran had not entered the service are considered incidents of the position to which the veteran is entitled. No rights, other than those established by normal business custom or through collective bargaining are created. Rather, the statutes seek to preserve such rights where they exist.

Reinstated veterans are entitled to their former position at a pay rate equal to that which the position currently commands. The pay rate obviously then includes all general, automatic, or cost-of-living pay increases occurring during the veteran's absence. In addition, the equal-pay requirement of the statutes has been interpreted under the "escalator principle" to include military time in the calculation of layoff and unemployment benefits and severance pay. All elements of the total compensation, such as traveling expenses, drawing accounts, bonuses, and shift premiums, as well as salary and commissions, must be considered. Thus, a veteran's rights would be violated if the reinstated pay *rate* were correct but the job assigned yielded less total pay than the veteran would have received had he remained in his former position.

On the other hand, increases which are based solely on the abilities and skills of the particular person occupying the position, on the performance over a specific period of time by a particular person, or upon completion of training and acquisition of certain skills are not part of the reinstatement rights. If the circumstances indicate that the veteran would have been promoted had he been present to acquire certain skills or training, he has a right to be reemployed at the highest level for which he is actually qualified, to be given the opportunity to acquire the necessary skills or training, and upon acquiring same, to be promoted to the position he would have acquired but for the military service. On promotion, if there is an established seniority system in the position, the veteran's seniority must be adjusted to give him the rank he would have had had he not entered the service.

Although the effect of the provision requiring reinstatement to a position of equal status is uncertain, generally the administrative interpretation of status includes the features, attributes, and incidents pertaining to the job. "Status" encompasses pay and seniority, rank, duties, working conditions, and privileges. It may also cover such benefits as pension rights, place of employment, and insurance. Depending on the circumstances, status may bear some relationship to a reinstated employee's morale, happiness, and general well-being.

At a very minimum the statutes require that the position afford the same "chance to employ one's particular skills and abilities, to make use of one's past trade or professional experience and the opportunity to discharge the duties and responsibilities of a specific type of position. . . ."

Seniority is an abstract right used as a measurement of relative rank or standing of one employee in relation to his fellow workers in the same category. Seniority rights protected by the present act are only those which exist by virtue of custom or collective bargaining. They are not created by the act. Likewise, the law does not insulate the veteran from adverse occurrences, such as in the case where contract provision or custom terminate seniority and recall rights if layoff status extends beyond a certain period of time and the veteran would have been in such status had he not been in the military.

The reconstruction of a position of equal seniority must be done according to a standard of probability and reasonable certainty created by the courts. All of the cases together indicate that it is necessary to consider, along with the particular circumstances of each case, preservice employment history, the formal rules in effect, and actual practices followed during the veteran's absence, the actual statements of the veteran and his employer at the time of his return. All in-service time must be credited for purposes of seniority except in cases of skill seniority when working time is required for the purpose of acquiring and enhancing a skill, as in most apprenticeship programs.

PENSIONS, VACATION, AND OTHER BENEFITS

The legislative intent of the reinstatement rights statutes is to hold open, wherever possible, a veteran's job so as to make his readjustment into civilian life as rapid and painless as possible. To that end, the courts will imply a continuing employer-employee relationship between the veteran and his former employer. Certain benefits accrue to an employee, either by custom or agreement, based on or calculated from his length of service, longevity, or similar bases. A benefit so calculated is determined by the courts to be a perquisite of seniority. Therefore, if by express language, past custom, or judicial interpretation, the right to a benefit or the amount of the benefit is deemed a "seniority right," qualified military service must be fully credited.

Congress did not, on the other hand, intend to give the returning veteran an extra bonus of pay for hours he did not work. The law states in part:

> Any person who is restored to or employed in a position in accordance with the provisions of clause (A) or (B) of subsection (a) of this subsection shall be considered as having been on furlough or leave of absence during such person's period of training and service in the Armed Forces, shall be so restored or reemployed without loss of seniority, shall be entitled to participate in insurance or other benefits offered by the employer pursuant to established rules and practices relating to employees on furlough or leave of absence in effect with the employer at the time such person was inducted into such forces. . . . [38 U.S.C. 2021]

This subsection had been interpreted to mean that where a benefit is based on hours actually worked, wages actually paid and received, or similar bases, whatever treatment would have been afforded employees on leave of absence or furlough at the time the veteran entered the service, would be applied to the veteran on his return with respect to benefits such as insurance, vacation, or pension. This is true whether the question relates to eligibility or extent of participation in the benefit.

The leave-of-absence provision is intended to add to the veteran's protection, not to take away from him any protection to which he is entitled under the escalator provision. In all respects, the escalator provision places him basically in the position, on and after reinstatement, that he would have occupied if his employment had continued without interruption by military service. The leave-of-absence provision does not detract from this, but makes it clear that the military absence does not constitute a break in the employment relationship and assures the veteran of the additional right to be treated no worse than other employees on nonmilitary leaves of absence would be treated with respect to benefits.

In 1977 the U.S. Supreme Court addressed this subject in the context of a veteran and a pension plan. In *Alabama Power Co. v. Davis*, the Court held that a veteran was entitled to credit for military service under a pension plan. The problem in the *Alabama Power Co. v. Davis* type of situation was that some benefits, pension credits being one of them, have a dual nature. Partly they are based on seniority; partly they are based on actual pay received or actual hours worked. Traditionally, the analysis has been that for benefits based on seniority, the veteran is entitled to application of the escalator principle, but for benefits based on actual pay or actual hours worked, he is not. In *Alabama Power Co. v. Davis*, the Supreme Court said that, in these kinds of dual-nature benefits, one looks at the predominant factor. On that basis, the Court held that seniority was the predominant factor in a pension plan and the veteran was entitled to credit for his military service.

NONCOMPLIANCE: REMEDIES AND ENFORCEMENT

If a veteran is refused proper reemployment, the U.S. District Attorney of the district wherein the employer maintains a place of business may appear as the veteran's attorney in connection with amicable settlement of a veteran's claim for reinstatement of employment rights or in bringing an action to enforce the same, if the U.S. District Attorney is satisfied that the veteran is entitled to such rights. (A veteran may, of course, employ private counsel.)

The veteran need not exhaust union or NLRB grievance procedures before instituting suit. He must exercise diligence in seeking to enforce his rights and avoid delay in so doing.

The U.S. District Court is empowered to grant reimbursement for any loss of wages or benefits by reason of an employer's illegal conduct. In addition, the district court has further and separate jurisdiction to direct the employer to comply with the law. The court has jurisdiction over all individuals entitled to benefits under the reemployment statutes. Decisions are split, however, as to whether the employer may properly request declaratory judgment action to determine the veteran's rights.

Administration of the statutes is vested in the Secretary of Labor, who gives assistance to veterans through the Office of Veteran's Reemployment Rights.

GOVERNMENT CONTRACTORS

In addition to the reemployment rights requirements, government contractors are also required by law to institute affirmative action programs to hire qualified disabled veterans and Vietnam veterans, whether or not they are disabled. The section states, in relevant part:

(a)   Any contract in the amount of $10,000 or more entered into by any department or agency for the procurement of personal property and nonpersonal services (including construction) for the United States, shall contain a provision requiring that the party contracting with the United States, shall take affirmative action to employ and advance in employment qualified disabled veterans and veterans of the Vietnam era. The provisions of this section shall apply to any subcontract entered into by a prime contractor in carrying out any contract for the procurement of personal property and nonpersonal services (including construction) for the United States. In addition to requiring affirmative action to employ such veterans under such contracts and subcontracts and such requirement, the President shall implement the provisions of this section by promulgating regulations within sixty days after the date of this section, which regulations shall require that (1) each such contractor undertake in such contract to list immediately with the appropriate local employment service office all of its suitable employment openings and (2) each such local office shall give such veterans priority in referral to such employment openings.

New language in the relevant laws sets up a system for giving employment priority to Vietnam veterans and other eligible persons. The system works through a special Veterans' Employment Representative assigned to work with each state's employment service to secure maximum training and employment opportunities for the Vietnam era or disabled veteran and other eligible persons.

KEY ANSWERS ABOUT JOB RIGHTS

for National Guardsmen, Reservists, and Their Employers
U.S. Department of Labor
Labor-Management Services Administration
Office of Veterans' Reemployment Rights
Washington, D.C. 20210

National Guardsmen and reservists take part in weekly, weekend, monthly, and annual training sessions to keep current with their military responsibilities.

Almost all trainees need time off from employment for the training. Absences, lasting from a few hours to a few weeks, call for temporary adjustments by the trainee and his employer.

The U.S. Department of Labor's Office of Veterans' Reemployment Rights offers answers to questions most often asked by the employee and his employer.

Q.   Is an employer required to excuse a worker for military training duty?
A.   Yes. Chapter 43 of Part III of Title 38 U.S. Code places responsibilities on the employee and his employer—one must go and the other must let him.

Q.   May an employer discharge an employee because of his reserve membership or his participation in reserve activities?
A.   No.

Q.   How about an employee's pay for time lost from work because of military training?
A.   Employers are not required to pay for lost time because of training. Some do as a matter of policy or contract; others do not.

Q.   May the employer deny the request for leave?
A.   No. The law requires the employer to grant the leave.

Q. How about vacation time? Can the military leave be charged against it?
A. No. Whatever vacation rights an employee has, he keeps without loss because of training time.

Q. Then an employee who has accrued paid vacation time of so many days when he begins his training has that amount still to his credit when he returns?
A. Yes.

Q. Is it possible that accrual of vacation time may continue even during an employee's absence on leave?
A. Yes. He is entitled to such vacation as he would have had if he had not been absent for military training. He would therefore return from training with such additional vacation time as he would have accrued if he had not been absent.

Q. Suppose there is no regular shift or schedule of work, as in the case of a sales worker?
A. Since reporting for work is the normal way of ending leave of all kinds, it is enough and appropriate that the employee notify the employer and begin work on the day that would be his normal workday.

Q. Does the trainee lose his right to return to work if he delays reporting beyond the time prescribed under the law?
A. No. But he will be subject to the conduct rules of the employer pertaining to explanations and discipline with respect to absence from scheduled work.

Q. Are any other employment rights or benefits protected by the law?
A. Yes. The employee cannot be denied promotion or any other benefits or advantages of employment because of his reserve obligation.

Q. Are all employees in all kinds of employment covered by this federal law?
A. Yes. Except those who hold temporary positions. Coverage now extends not only to employees in private industry and the federal government, but also to employees who worked for state and local governments.

Q. What is the employee's responsibility?
A. He should return to work as soon as his training has ended.

Q. May the employer demand to know exactly when the employee will return?
A. No. It is reasonable to want this information but sometimes impossible for the trainee to furnish. The law says the trainee should report for work following training at the beginning of his next regularly scheduled working period after the end of the last day necessary for him to travel from the place of training to his place of employment, or within a reasonable time thereafter if he is delayed by factors beyond his control.

Q. Does the branch of service make any difference?
A. None. Job protection extends alike to members of all branches of service and to all kinds of military training.

Q. Is the employee required to inform his employer?
A. Yes. He must request leave for the training period. No particular form is needed. When the reservist or National Guardsman is told of his training dates, he should in turn tell his employer. In effect, the employee requests leave to participate in the training.

Q. Is a formal application for reemployment required?
A. No. An employee on leave for training is not "out of work" in the sense that he is "reemployed" on his return. It is more correct to say he simply returns to *his* job.

Q. What if an employee is disabled during training and is unable to perform his old job?

A. In most cases, disability extends the length of time an employee is allowed to return to work. Where the disability turns out to handicap the employee more or less permanently, there are still employer responsibilities. Each case should be reviewed with a representative of the Labor Department's Office of Veterans' Reemployment Rights.

FACTS ABOUT VETERANS' JOB RIGHTS

U. S. Department of Labor
Labor-Management Services Administration
Office of Veterans' Reemployment Rights
Washington, D.C. 20210

1. *What the law says. . . .* Chapter 43 of Part III of Title 38 U.S. Code provides a reemployment rights program for men and women who leave their jobs to perform training or service in the Armed Forces. The Office of Veterans' Reemployment Rights has the responsibility for informing veterans and employers of the reemployment program and assisting them in connection with any problems they may have. The purpose of this law is to ensure that those who serve their country in the interest of national defense do not lose their jobs and other employment benefits because of such services.

2. *Who is eligible?* To be entitled to reemployment rights a veteran must:
   (a) Leave a position (other than a temporary position) with a private employer, the federal government, or a state or local government for the purpose of entering the Armed Forces, voluntarily or involuntarily. Part-time and seasonal positions are not necessarily temporary positions.
   (b) Serve for not more than 4 years after August 1, 1961, *plus* a 1 year additional voluntary extension of active duty *(5 year total)** if this is the request and for the convenience of the government (plus any involuntary service). Only active military service entered from employment to which restoration is claimed is to be included in computing the time limitations on service.
   (c) Satisfactorily complete the period of active duty and have a certificate to that effect.
   (d) Be qualified to perform the duties of his position. If he is disabled during military service and cannot perform the duties of his old job, he may be entitled to the nearest comparable job he is qualified to perform.
   (e) Make timely application for reemployment after release from military training or service or from hospitalization continuing after discharge for a period of not more than 1 year. Application must be made within 90 days after completion of military service; within 31 days after completion of initial active duty for training of not less than 3 months.

3. *Employer's obligations.* The employer's obligations are to:
   (a) Reemploy the veteran, within a reasonable time after he makes application, in the position he would have occupied if he had remained on the job instead of entering military service. This could be the same position, a superior position, an inferior position, one of like seniority, status, and pay, layoff status, or no position at all, depending upon collective bargaining agreements, nondiscriminatory personnel policies and practices, or changes in the employer's business during the veteran's absence which may make it impossible or unreasonable to reemploy him.
   (b) Restore the veteran without loss of seniority. There are, however, some conditions under which the adjustment of seniority incident to a missed

---

* Reservists recalled after a period of service since August 1, 1961, may retain a longer protected period.

opportunity may be deferred until after the veteran has been reemployed and has met a special work requirement under a collective bargaining agreement or established practice. Where, under a collective bargaining agreement or established practice, the employer requires an employee to meet a special work requirement, the veteran's seniority should be adjusted upon completion of the work requirement so that his period of military duty does not cause him to lose ground to other employees who continued in their employment. Once having completed the work requirement, he is entitled to a seniority date which takes into account time spent in military service. One of the most important features of the reemployment program is the protection it gives the veteran against the loss of seniority due to military service, since seniority or length of service often determines job assignments, pay, status, vacation, pension rights, and other benefits.

The length of service or seniority a reemployed veteran has with his preservice employer generally includes: (1) his employment before military service; (2) a reasonable period between leaving his job and entering military service; (3) the entire period of his military service; (4) the period between his release from the service and his return to work.

(c)   Pay the veteran at the level he would have attained had he not left for military service. This usually includes all general, cost-of-living, and length-of-service increases, but may not include merit increases based on performance standards prescribed by contract or established practice.

(d)   Restore the veteran to the status he would have enjoyed with respect to such working conditions as choice of job shifts and place of employment, particularly where they are governed by length of service.

(e)   Allow the veteran to participate in insurance, pension, and other such benefits maturing after his reinstatement to the same extent he would be participating if his employment had continued without interruption by military service, and treat him according to rules and practices affecting other employees on leave of absence as far as such benefits maturing during his military absence are concerned.

(f)   Retain the veteran in employment for a period of not less than 1 year, unless he is discharged for cause or there is a layoff which reaches him in seniority order in accordance with a contract or established practice. Retain the reservist who returns from initial active duty for training in his employment under the same conditions for a period of 6 months.

CHAPTER THIRTY

LABOR RELATIONS LAW

PART 1 OVERVIEW

The law of labor relations is a vast body of statutory and common law dealing with the employment of individuals by businesses, the working conditions of the employees, and the rights of business and employers to engage in certain types of activities. Part 1 will provide an overview of this vast expanse of law. Subsequent parts of the chapter will discuss particular subjects in more detail.

BASIC TYPES OF LABOR LAW

Following is a catalogue of the various types of labor law.

Local Law

While this book deals only with federal laws, it must be remembered that many local ordinances and state laws apply to many labor problems. Examples include municipal ordinances which govern permissible activity on public streets and apply to union picketing and handbilling activities. Various types of state labor laws, including so-called right-to-work legislation, can also be important.

Constitutional Law

Labor problems often become complicated with Constitutional issues. The first amendment freedom of speech provision is the issue most often involved with labor problems.

Ancillary Laws

Labor problems often are related to certain ancillary laws such as the antitrust laws. The Sherman Antitrust Act in particular has become involved in many labor cases, even though it does not specifically deal with labor problems.

Federal Statutes

There are federal laws directly applying to union organization, collective bargaining, wages and hours of employment, conditions of employment, and discrimination in employment. It is this fourth category of federal laws which is most important in the majority of cases. The fourth category can be further broken down into the following catalogue of federal labor statutes.

The Occupational Safety and Health Act

While not specifically a labor law, the Occupational Safety and Health Act has application to the workers' environment and provides generally that all employers governed by the act must exercise some efforts to see that workers are provided a safe and healthful place to work. This act is discussed in more detail in Chapter 26.

Fair Employment Statutes

There are a considerable number of statutes specifically directed to fair employment practices. These include the Age Discrimination in Employment Act which prohibits certain discrimination on the basis of age, the Equal Pay Act which provides for equal pay for equal work for men and women, and the Civil Rights Act of 1964, as amended, which provides generally that any discrimination in employment on the basis of race, religion, sex, or national origin is prohibited. These laws are discussed in more detail in Chapter 28.

The Labor-Management Relations Act of 1947 (The Taft-Hartley Act)

This act, the most infamous in the eyes of organized labor, establishes certain rules for the mediation and conciliation of labor disputes affecting interstate commerce and provides for postponements of strikes and lockouts which would imperil the national health or safety.

The Norris-La Guardia Act

This statute limits the circumstances in which the federal courts may issue injunctions where such injunctions are sought by private parties in labor disputes. Generally, this statute provides that strikes, picketing, and boycotts may not be enjoined by a federal court in situations where they arise out of a labor dispute.

The Anti-Racketeering Act (The Hobbs Act)

This statute prohibits robbery and extortion in interstate commerce.

Labor-Management Reporting and Disclosure Act of 1959 (Landrum-Griffin Act)

This statute was passed in 1959 in reaction to certain union abuses involving funds and administrative procedures which had been discovered in congressional investigations. The statute in general provides that unions must file certain periodic reports of their financial activities and their organization, including copies of their bylaws, constitution, and administrative policies.

The Employee Retirement Income Security Act of 1974

This statute deals with workers and their pension benefits and is more fully explained in Chapter 27.

The National Labor Relations Act (The Wagner Act)

This is probably the most important labor statute. It is the statute which expressly sets forth the unfair labor practices (of both employers and unions) which so often become the subject of controversy.

It should also be noted that all the statutes set forth herein are closely tied together. The National Labor Relations Act of 1935 was amended by the Taft-Hartley Act, which was in turn amended by the Landrum-Griffin Act. As used in this book, the National Labor Relations Act will refer to the current law as amended, and the Taft-Hartley Act and Landrum-Griffin Act will refer only to the separate and additional material added by those statutes.

OUTLINE OF THE NATIONAL LABOR RELATIONS ACT

The National Labor Relations Act can be divided into three basic kinds of provisions:

1. Those provisions establishing certain *substantive* laws governing the conduct of unions and employers

2. Those provisions which may be said to be *procedural*, in that they establish procedures for representative elections, determining the bargaining unit, etc.

3. Those provisions which may be said to be *administrative*, such as the establishment of the National Labor Relations Board, and the various provisions for investigations, compelling testimony, serving process, etc.

Summary of Major Provisions of the NLRA

The real heart of the federal labor law is sections 8 and 9 of the National Labor Relations Act. These sections provide the basic laws relating to unfair labor practices and for representatives elections. These sections are so important that they are set forth below, with only slight editing.

UNFAIR LABOR PRACTICES

[Employer Unfair Labor Practices—]
Section 8(a)   It shall be an unfair labor practice for an employer—

(1)   to interfere with, restrain, or coerce employees in the exercise of their rights to organize and bargain collectively;
(2)   to dominate or interfere with the formation or administration of any labor organization or contribute financial or other support to it;
(3)   by discrimination in regard to hire or tenure of employment or any term or condition of employment to encourage or discourage membership in any labor organization: Provided, That nothing in this Act, or in any other statute of the United States, shall preclude an employer from making an agreement with a labor organization (not established, maintained, or assisted by any action defined in section 8(a) of this Act as an unfair labor practice) to

require as a condition of employment membership therein on or after the thirtieth day following the beginning of such employment or the effective date of such agreement, whichever is the later, (i) if such labor organization is the representative of the employees as provided in section 9(a), in the appropriate collective-bargaining unit covered by such agreement when made, and (ii) unless following an election held as provided in section 9(e) within one year preceding the effective date of such agreement, the Board shall have certified that at least a majority of the employees eligible to vote in such election have voted to rescind the authority of such labor organization to make such an agreement: Provided further, That no employer shall justify any discrimination against an employee for nonmembership in a labor organization (A) if he has reasonable grounds for believing that such membership was not available to the employee on the same terms and conditions generally applicable to other members, or (B) if he has reasonable grounds for believing that membership was denied or terminated for reasons other than the failure of the employee to tender the periodic dues and the initiation fees uniformly required as a condition of acquiring or retaining membership;

(4)   to discharge or otherwise discriminate against an employee because he has filed charges or given testimony under this Act;

(5)   to refuse to bargain collectively with the representatives of his employees, subject to the provisions of section 9(a).

[Union Unfair Labor Practices]
Section 8(b)   It shall be an unfair labor practice for a labor organization or its agents—

(1)   to restrain or coerce (A) employees in the exercise of the rights to organize and bargain collectively: Provided, That this paragraph shall not impair the right of a labor organization to prescribe its own rules with respect to the acquisition or retention of membership therein; or (B) an employer in the selection of his representatives for the purpose of collective bargaining or the adjustment of grievances;

(2)   to cause or attempt to cause an employer to discriminate against an employee or to discriminate against an employee with respect to whom membership in such organization has been denied or terminated on some ground other than his failure to tender the periodic dues and the initiation fees uniformly required as a condition of acquiring or retaining membership;

(3)   to refuse to bargain collectively with an employer, provided it is the representative of his employees subject to the provisions of section 9(a);

(4)(i)   to engage in, or to induce or encourage any individual employed by any person engaged in commerce or in an industry affecting commerce to engage in, a strike or a refusal in the course of his employment to use, manufacture, process, transport, or otherwise handle or work on any goods, articles, materials, or commodities or to perform any services; or (ii) to threaten, coerce, or restrain any person engaged in commerce or in an industry affecting commerce, where in either case an object thereof is—

(A)   forcing or requiring any employer or self-employed person to join any labor or employer organization or to enter into any agreement which is prohibited by section 8(e);

(B)   forcing or requiring any person to cease using, selling, handling, transporting, or otherwise dealing in the products of any other producer, processor, or manufacturer, or to cease doing business with any other person, or forcing or requiring any other employer to recognize or bargain with a labor organization as the representative of his employees unless such labor organization has been certified as the representative of such employees under the provisions of section 9: Provided, That nothing contained in this clause (B) shall be construed to make unlawful, where not otherwise unlawful, any primary strike or primary picketing;

(C)   forcing or requiring any employer to recognize or bargain with a particular labor organization as the representative of his employees if another labor organization has been certified as the representative of such employees under the provisions of section 9;

(D)   forcing or requiring any employer to assign particular work to employees in a particular labor organization or in a particular trade, craft, or class rather than to employees in another labor organization or in another trade, craft, or class, unless such employer is failing to conform to an order or certification of the Board determining the bargaining representative for employees performing such work:

Provided, That nothing contained in this subsection (b) shall be construed to make unlawful a refusal by any person to enter upon the premises of any employer (other than his own employer), if the employees of such employer are engaged in a strike ratified or approved by a representative of such employees whom such employer is required to recognize under this Act: Provided further, That for the purposes of this paragraph (4) only, nothing contained in such paragraph shall be construed to prohibit publicity, other than picketing, for the purpose of truthfully advising the public, including consumers and members of a labor organization, that a product or products are produced by an employer with whom the labor organization has a primary dispute and are distributed by another employer, as long as such publicity does not have an effect of inducing any individual employed by any person other than the primary employer in the course of his employment to refuse to pick up, deliver, or transport any goods, or not to perform any services, at the establishment of the employer engaged in such distribution;

(5)   to require of employees covered by an agreement the payment, as a condition precedent to becoming a member of such organization, of a fee in an amount which the Board finds excessive or discriminatory under all the circumstances. In making such a finding, the Board shall consider, among other relevant factors, the practices and customs of labor organizations in the particular industry, and the wages currently paid to the employees affected;

(6)   to cause or attempt to cause an employer to pay or deliver or agree to pay or deliver any money or other thing of value, in the nature of an exaction, for services which are not performed or not to be performed; and

(7)   to picket or cause to be picketed, or threaten to picket or cause to be picketed, any employer where an object thereof is forcing or requiring an employer to recognize or bargain with a labor organization as the representative of his employees, or forcing or requiring the employees of an employer to accept or select such labor organization as their collective bargaining representative, unless such labor organization is currently certified as the representative of such employees:

(A)   where the employer has lawfully recognized in accordance with this Act any other labor organization and a question concerning representation may not appropriately be raised under section 9(c) of this Act,

(B)   where within the preceding twelve months a valid election under section 9(c) of this Act has been conducted, or

(C)   where such picketing has been conducted without a petition under section 9(c) being filed within a reasonable period of time not to exceed thirty days from the commencement of such picketing: Provided, That when such a petition has been filed the Board shall forthwith, without regard to the provisions of section 9(c)(1) or the absence of a showing of a substantial interest on the part of the labor organization, direct an election in such unit as the Board finds to be appropriate and shall certify the results thereof: Provided further, That nothing in this subparagraph (C) shall be construed to prohibit any picketing or other publicity for the purpose of truthfully advising the public (including consumers) that an employer does not employ members of, or have a contract, with a labor organization, unless an effect of such picketing is to induce any individual employed by any other person in the course of his employment, not to pick up, deliver or transport any goods or not to perform any services. Nothing in this paragraph (7) shall be construed to permit any act which would otherwise be an unfair labor practice under this section 8(b).

[Free Speech]

Section 8(c)   The expressing of any views, argument, or opinion, or the dissemination thereof, whether in written, printed, graphic, or visual form, shall not constitute or be evidence of an unfair labor practice under any of the provisions of this Act, if such expression contains no threat of reprisal or force or promise of benefit.

[Duties of Parties in Collective Bargaining]

Section 8(d)   For the purposes of this section, to bargain collectively is the performance of the mutual obligation of the employer and the representative of the employees to meet at reasonable times and confer in good faith with respect to wages, hours, and other terms and conditions of employment, or the negotiation of an agreement, or any question arising thereunder, the execution of a written contract incorporating any agreement reached if requested by either party, but such obligation does not compel either party to agree to a proposal or require the making of a concession: Provided, That where there is in effect a collective-bargaining contract covering employees in an industry affecting commerce, the duty to bargain collectively shall also mean that no party to such contract shall terminate or modify such contract, unless the party desiring such termination or modification—

(1)   serves a written notice upon the other party to the contract of the proposed termination or modification sixty days prior to the expiration date thereof, or in the event such contract contains no expiration date, sixty days prior to the time it is proposed to make such termination or modification;

(2)   offers to meet and confer with the other party for the purpose of negotiating a new contract or a contract containing the proposed modifications;

(3)   notifies the Federal Mediation and Conciliation Service within thirty days after such notice of the existence of a dispute, and simultaneously therewith notifies any State or Territorial agency established to mediate and conciliate disputes within the State or Territory where the dispute occurred, provided no agreement has been reached by that time; and

(4)   continues in full force and effect, without resorting to strike or lockout, all the terms and conditions of the existing contract for a period of sixty days after such notice is given or until the expiration date of such contract, whichever occurs later:

The duties imposed upon employers, employees, and labor organizations by paragraphs (2), (3), and (4) shall become inapplicable upon an intervening certification of the Board, under which the labor organization or individual, which is a party to the contract, has been superseded as or ceased to be the representative of the employees subject to the provisions of section 9(a), and the duties so imposed shall not be construed as requiring either party to discuss or agree to any modification of the terms and conditions contained in a contract for a fixed period, if such modification is to become effective before such terms and conditions can be reopened under the provisions of the contract. Any employee who engages in a strike within the sixty-day period specified in this subsection shall lose his status as an employee of the employer engaged in the particular labor dispute, for the purposes of sections 8, 9, and 10 of this Act, as amended, but such loss of status for such employee shall terminate if and when he is reemployed by such employer.

[Hot Cargo Contracts]

Section 8(e)   It shall be an unfair labor practice for any labor organization and any employer to enter into any contract or agreement, express or implied, whereby such employer ceases or refrains or agrees to cease or refrain from handling, using, selling, transporting or otherwise dealing in any of the products of any other employer, or to cease doing business with any other person, and any contract or agreement entered into heretofore or hereafter containing such an agreement shall be to such extent unenforcible and void.

REPRESENTATIVES AND ELECTIONS

Section 9(a)   Representatives designated or selected for the purposes of collective bargaining by the majority of the employees in a unit appropriate for such purpose, shall be the exclusive representatives of all the employees in such unit for the purposes of collective bargaining in respect to rates of pay, wages, hours of employment, or other conditions of employment: Provided, That any individual employee or a group of employees shall have the right at any time to present grievances to their employer and to have such grievances adjusted, without the intervention of the bargaining representatives, as long as the adjustment is not inconsistent with the terms of a collective-bargaining contract or agreement then in effect: Provided further, That the bargaining representative has been given opportunity to be present at such adjustment.

Section 9(b)   The Board shall decide in each case whether, in order to assure to employees the fullest freedom in exercising the rights guaranteed by this Act, the unit appropriate for the purposes of collective bargaining shall be the employer unit, craft unit, plant unit, or subdivision thereof: Provided, That the Board shall not (1) decide that any unit is appropriate for such purposes if such unit includes both professional employees and employees who are not professional employees unless a majority of such professional employees vote for inclusion in such unit; or (2) decide that any craft unit is inappropriate for such purposes on the ground that a different unit has been established by a prior Board determination, unless a majority of the employees in the proposed craft unit vote against separate representation or (3) decide that any unit is appropriate for such purposes if it includes, together with other employees, any individual employed as a guard to enforce against employees and other persons rules to protect property of the employer or to protect the safety of persons on the employer's premises; but no labor organization shall be certified as the representative of employees in a bargaining unit of guards if such organization admits to membership, or is affiliated directly or indirectly with an organization which admits to membership, employees other than guards.

(c)(1)   Whenever a petition shall have been filed, in accordance with such regulations as may be prescribed by the Board—(A) by an employee or group of employees or any individual or labor organization acting in their behalf alleging that a substantial number of employees (i) wish to be represented for collective bargaining and that their employer declines to recognize their representative as the representative defined in section 9(a), or (ii) assert that the individual or labor organization, which has been certified or is being currently recognized by their employer as the bargaining representative, is no longer a representative as defined in section 9(a); or (B) by an employer, alleging that one or more individuals or labor organizations have presented to him a claim to be recognized as the representative defined in section 9(a); the Board shall investigate such petition and if it has reasonable cause to believe that a question of representation affecting commerce exists shall provide for an appropriate hearing upon due notice. Such hearing may be conducted by an officer or employee of the regional office, who shall not make any recommendations with respect thereto. If the Board finds upon the record of such hearing that such a question of representation exists, it shall direct an election by secret ballot and shall certify the results thereof.

(2) In determining whether or not a question of representation affecting commerce exists, the same regulations and rules of decision shall apply irrespective of the identity of the persons filing the petition or the kind of relief sought and in no case shall the Board deny a labor organization a place on the ballot by reason of an order with respect to such labor organization or its predecessor not issued in conformity with this Act.

(3)   No election shall be directed in any bargaining unit or any subdivision within which, in the preceding twelve-month period, a valid election shall have been held. Employees engaged in an economic strike who are not entitled to

reinstatement shall be eligible to vote under such regulations as the Board shall find are consistent with the purposes and provisions of this Act in any election conducted within twelve months after the commencement of the strike. In any election where none of the choices on the ballot receives a majority, a run-off shall be conducted, the ballot providing for a selection between the two choices receiving the largest and second largest number of valid votes cast in the election.

(4)   Nothing in this section shall be construed to prohibit the waiving of hearings by stipulation for the purpose of a consent election in conformity with regulations and rules of decision of the Board.

(5)   In determining whether a unit is appropriate for the purposes specified in subsection (b) the extent to which the employees have organized shall not be controlling.

PART 2   UNFAIR LABOR PRACTICES

INTRODUCTION

The previous section set forth the various types of laws governing labor relations and the text of sections 8 and 9 of the National Labor Relations Act, the heart of federal labor law. Section 8 is divided into two parts, part (a) listing five types of activities which are defined as unfair labor practices *of employers,* and part (b) listing seven types of activities which are defined to be unfair labor practices *of unions.* These twelve items constitute most of the substance of federal labor law and will be discussed in this and subsequent parts of the chapter.

While the above division is a useful organizational approach to the subject because it follows the pattern of the statute, it should not be thought that any one activity can violate only one section or that the sections are mutually exclusive. In many cases, a given activity may violate more than one section. For example, prohibiting union representatives from distributing literature on plant premises in the absence of a uniformly enforced rule against distribution of any literature may violate section 8(a)(1), which provides that it is unlawful to *restrain* or *coerce* employees in their rights to organize, and section 8(a)(3), which provides that it is unlawful to *discriminate* against employees on the basis of union activities.

Generally the problems discussed in this chapter come up in the context of a union attempt to organize a plant. The union supporters will attempt to convince the employees that they can achieve more pay, better benefits, and more job security by joining the union; and the company will attempt to show why a union is not necessary or may not even be in the best interests of the employees. However, this does not always have to be the context. Decertification, where the employees are trying to discard an existing union, or proceedings to change unions, can also generate problems. Also, the problem can present itself where there is no organizational question involved.

EMPLOYER UNFAIR LABOR PRACTICES: INTERFERENCE, RESTRAINT, AND COERCION

First on the list of employer unfair labor practices is section 8(a)(1), which provides that it shall be an unfair labor practice for an employer "*to interfere with, restrain, or coerce employees in the exercise of the rights guaranteed in section 7* [emphasis added]."

Section 7 contains the basic rights of employees to organize. It provides as follows:

> Sec. 7. Employees shall have the right to self-organization, to form, join, or assist labor organizations, to bargain collectively through representatives of their own choosing, and to engage in other concerted activities for the purpose of collective bargaining or other mutual aid or protection, and shall also have the right to refrain from any or all of such activities except to the extent that such right may be affected by an agreement requiring membership in a labor organization as a condition of employment as authorized in section 8(a)(3).

Section 8(a)(1) presents a good example of the interaction between the various sections of the National Labor Relations Act (NLRA) because an employer will violate this section when he commits any unfair labor practice under any other section of the act. However, there are a number of activities which can be an independent violation of section 8(a)(1). The obvious intent of the section is to prohibit employers from threatening employees with discharge, loss of benefits, etc., if they join the union, or from promising them some benefit if they refuse to join the union. These overt types of coercion are obvious. However, the section has been held to extend far beyond this type of overt activity. The problems can be categorized as follows:

1. What type of threats or other negative activity will constitute unlawful coercion?

2. What types of promises or other positive activity will constitute unlawful coercion?

Threats—Negative Activities

Any activity which may constitute a threat to employees in order to dissuade them from joining a union, to remove a union, or otherwise to interfere with their right to organize and bargain collectively is an unfair labor practice. Threats of physical violence, discharge, or other overt acts fall into this category. However, more subtle acts can also be unlawful. For example, extensive surveillance of employees engaged in union activities can violate the act. Also, threats of adverse economic consequences generally violate the section. Threats to eliminate certain benefits or privileges, or to close down the plant generally, fall into this category.

Threats to move the plant from one location to another—the so-called runaway shop—can also violate the act. This problem presents special difficulties in some situations because management often assumes that decisions as to whether to move the plant or to close it down are purely within management's prerogative. However, if it can be shown that the motive for such action is to thwart union activity, these management acts can be unlawful.

Interrogation of employees regarding union activity can also present a problem. A recent Second Circuit Court of Appeals case sets forth some guidelines on this important question. The important passages from that case follow:

> (3) Under our decisions interrogation, not itself threatening, is not held to be an unfair labor practice unless it meets certain fairly severe standards. These include:

(1) The background, i.e., is there a history of employer hostility and discrimination?
(2) The nature of the information sought, e.g., did the interrogator appear to be seeking information on which to base taking action against individual employees?
(3) The identity of the questioner, i.e., how high was he in the company hierarchy?
(4) Place and method of interrogation, e.g., was employee called from work to the boss's office? Was there an atmosphere of "unnatural formality"?
(5) Truthfulness of the reply.

(4) Examination of the record, interpreted in the light most favorable to the Board, indicates that the interrogation involved here did not in any realistic sense meet the tests set forth.

(1) There is very little to show any pattern of employer hostility and discrimination.
(2) The information sought was quite general. "How is the union doing?"; "Are the employees for the union?" rather than specifically "Who are the ring leaders?" "Who has joined?" etc.
(3) The principal interrogation was by low-ranking supervisors.
(4) The employees were interrogated informally while at work.
(5) In general the replies were truthful, i.e., there was no evidence that the interrogation actually inspired fear.

One troublesome question is the employer's right to predict adverse economic developments if the employees join a union. Typically, the employer will desire to convey the message that if his labor costs increase, the customers may find other sources of supply and he may have to lay off some employees or even curtail operations. From a theoretical legal point of view, the legality of these statements depends on whether they are simply expressions of opinion or a prediction; or a threat or statement of inevitable result. Naturally, motives and semantics become very important on this question. The act itself provides in section 8(c) that:

> The expressing of any views, argument, or opinion, or the dissemination thereof, whether in written, printed, graphic, or visual form, shall not constitute or be evidence of an unfair labor practice under any of the provisions of this Act, if such expression contains no threat of reprisal or force or promise of benefit.

The cases are conflicting. Some indicate that this kind of statement constitutes an implied threat of loss of employment, and some indicate that it is protected free speech.

Promises—Positive Activities

A troublesome question is the awarding of increased benefits during an organization attempt. The theoretical legal principles are clear: an employer cannot award increased benefits after a union begins an organization drive, but an employer who has previously planned an increase may put it into effect even if this happens right in the middle of the organization drive. The problem comes up where the employer has done some planning but has not made a final announcement, or where the benefit is a regular or expected benefit which probably would normally be granted anyway. Again the cases are conflicting, and minor differences in motives, history of past discrimination, and semantics can be very important. The problem of increases in benefits which would normally have been granted often puts the employer on the horns of a dilemma. The granting of increased benefits during an organization drive can be a violation; the withholding of normally scheduled benefits can also be a violation; and there is no universal agreement on precisely what kinds of increases are normal or scheduled. The employer must often make this decision at his peril.

Responsibility of a Company for Acts of Employees

Since a corporation can act only through its employees, the question of the responsibility of the corporation for acts of employees which, if performed by the corporation, would be unfair labor practices becomes important. The problem is complicated by the fact that questioned activities often take place at foreman or first-level supervisory activity. Clearly, speeches by officers of the company or those high in management are generally acts of the company. The problem arises out of actions of well-meaning but over-eager supervisors who, with the best of intentions, attempt to dissuade employees from unionizing by means which can violate the act. The problem is further complicated by the fact that not all the general rules of agency apply. Section 2(13) of the act states that "in determining whether any person is acting as an agent of another person so as to make such person responsible for his acts, the question of whether the specific acts performed were actually authorized or subsequently ratified shall not be controlling."

The employer can relieve himself of this problem by notifying all supervisors to remain neutral and notifying all employees that they must not be threatened or coerced, and immediately and positively repudiating any contrary acts which come to his attention. However, a serious threat or other coercion by a supervisor may not be capable of being negated by a management repudiation even if it turns out that the supervisor was acting from personal motives.

An employer may also be held responsible for the acts of inhabitants of a town if they are inspired by the company. This situation sometimes arises in smaller towns where the officials or inhabitants will campaign strongly against a union which they feel is neither socially nor economically desirable.

PART 3   DOMINATION AND ASSISTANCE OF UNIONS

Section 8(a)(2) of the National Labor Relations Act provides as follows:

> It shall be an unfair labor practice for an employer—(2) to *dominate* or *interfere* with the *formation or administration* of any labor organization or contribute financial or other support to it; provided, that, subject to rules and regulations . . . an employer shall not be prohibited from permitting employees to confer with him during working hours without loss of time or pay. [Emphasis added.]

The practice by some companies of forming company-dominated unions in order to circumvent the collective bargaining process provided the reason for this section. These so-called company unions were merely the pawns of management, and there was no real collective bargaining in any meaningful sense.

The act obviously prohibits the company from dominating a union, by financial support or otherwise, in such a manner as to make the union less than independent. However, as usual, the act goes far beyond this, and many decisions have held that activities which might at first glance seem innocuous have been sufficient to justify a charge of company domination of a union.

It should be noted that there are two aspects to this problem: one is unlawful domination; the other is unlawful interference or assistance. Unlawful domination is usually fairly easy to spot and avoid. It results from employers' prescribing the nature, structure, and functions of the collective bargaining organization or from supervisors' actually taking part in meetings or activities of the union. It can also be present if the union never develops any real form, has no meetings, no constitution, no bylaws, and no assets and generally serves only as an entity to accept a contract granted by the employer.

Unlawful assistance, however, is another matter. Unlawful assistance can arise in many situations, but it usually comes about where two rival unions are attempting to organize a plant or where one incumbent union is being threatened by a rival union. In many cases, the contest will be between an independent union and a local branch of a national union. *Generally, management must maintain complete neutrality in these contests.* The company must not actively support either of the unions and must not interfere in the contest in any way. It must not coerce employees into the favored union, nor assist the favored union in solicitation of membership nor provide any direct financial assistance.

The use of company facilities also creates problems. The company may not grant the use of its facilities such as bulletin boards, stenographic services, legal services, office space, or printing facilities unless it does so on a uniform basis. Discriminatory treatment in this regard may result in a finding that one union is dominated and controlled or supported by the employer. It should be kept in mind that this sort of activity can be self-defeating. If the employer really prefers one union over the other, and if it supports the union preferred, even if that union ultimately wins an election and is determined to represent a majority of the employees, the NLRB may order a new election because of the company's activities.

The check-off procedure—where the company collects the union dues by means of payroll deduction and forwards them to the union—is generally legal and does not result in unlawful support or domination if it is done pursuant to written consent of the employees and such consent is not given irrevocably for more than one year. The check-off will be valid if it is done pursuant to a union contract which provides for a checkoff.

If two rival unions attempt to organize a plant and the company bargains with one and not the other, it has obviously supported the union it bargains with. However, if the situation involves an existing union's being challenged by a new rival, the company which has already been bargaining with the existing union is not obliged to bargain with the rival unless the rival shows, to the satisfaction of the company, that it, in fact, represents the majority of the employees. If the rival union produces authorization cards of a majority of employees and the company then refuses to bargain with it and continues to bargain with the old union, it probably violates both section 8(a)(2) for unlawful assistance and section 8(a)(5) for refusal to bargain.

Generally, if a unit of employees is already represented by a union, the employer must continue to bargain with that union until the rival union shows the employer that it now represents a majority of the employees. If the rival union makes this showing, the company must bargain with it. If there is a legitimate question, the company can demand an NLRB certification election.

In the situation where two rival unions are attempting to organize a plant at the same time, the company must remain in a position of complete neutrality until such time as one union shows the company that it represents a majority of the employees, or until such time as an NLRB certification election establishes one union.

The company may adopt reasonable rules for solicitation or distribution of handbills or wearing of union pins on company premises. However, it must not enforce these rules discriminatorily when rival unions are involved. For example, it would be an unlawful employment practice for an employer to allow solicitation of members for one union and not to allow representatives of the opposing union to solicit members on company premises.

It should be observed that this is one of the many areas where practice and technical labor law do not coincide exactly. In fact, many companies deal with their employees on a day-to-day basis in discussing programs to increase productivity, and the overwhelming majority of these dealings are never challenged. On the other hand, if you seek legal advice in this kind of arrangement—as you should—the lawyers are likely to advise you that establishment at company suggestion of a committee of employees to discuss work problems creates a labor organization within the meaning of the National Labor Relations Act, and in many cases, dealing with this committee on company time will amount to unlawful domination of that committee (and therefore a labor organization) by the company and at least a technical violation of the National Labor Relations Act.

Section 8(a)(2) is a very troublesome section for employers desiring to work with their employees to increase productivity. A typical arrangement might be that companies ask their employees to get together and discuss among themselves how their work could be better organized, the plant better run, etc., in order to increase productivity. The employees would then sit down with management, discuss the suggestions, and try and reach a mutually agreeable program. If there is a labor organization in the picture, everything will be fairly trouble-free from a legal point of view, because the labor organization itself will be one in charge of negotiations with management on behalf of their employees. Even if the employees participate directly, it will at the behest of their union rather than of the company. On the other hand, if there is no union representing the employees, management is likely to be creating a company-dominated union within the meaning of section 8(a)(2), because the establishment of these committees and the dealing with them on company time creates a technical problem.

PART 4   DISCRIMINATION IN EMPLOYMENT BASED ON UNION ACTIVITY

Section 8(a)(3) of the National Labor Relations Act provides that it is an unlawful labor practice for an employer by discrimination in regard to hire or tenure of employment or any term or condition of employment to encourage or discourage membership in any labor organization. The full text is as follows.

. . . (3) by discrimination in regard to hire or tenure of employment or any term or condition of employment to encourage or discourage membership in any labor organization: Provided, That nothing in this Act, or in any other statute of the United States, shall preclude an employer from making an agreement with a labor organization (not established, maintained, or assisted by any action defined in section 8(a) of this Act as an unfair labor practice) to require as a condition of employment membership therein on or after the thirtieth day following the beginning of such employment or the effective date of such agreement, whichever is the later, (i) if such labor organization is the representative of the employees as provided in section 9(a), in the appropriate collective-bargaining unit covered by such agreement when made, and (ii) unless following an election held as provided in section 9(e) within one year preceding the effective date of such agreement, the Board shall have certified that at least a majority of the employees eligible to vote in such election have voted to rescind the authority of such labor organization to make such an agreement: <u>Provided further,</u> That no employer shall justify any discrimination against an employee for nonmembership in a labor organization (A) if he has reasonable grounds for believing that such membership was not available to the employee on the same terms and conditions generally applicable to other members, or (B) if he has reasonable grounds for believing that membership was denied or terminated for reasons other than the failure of the employee to tender the periodic dues and the initiation fees uniformly required as a condition of acquiring or retaining membership.

Most discrimination problems can be divided into two kinds:

1. Discrimination involving a situation where a previously nonunion plant is undergoing a union organization drive

2. A situation involving a strike or other labor dispute at a plant already having a union

PROBLEMS INVOLVING INITIAL UNION ORGANIZATION

It is very clear that section 8(a)(3) prohibits an employer from refusing to hire an employee or from discharging an employee *where the motivation for such action relates to the individual's union activity.* The following is a brief list of the more important points which must be kept in mind in this area.

1. In most cases, it is held that a discharge of an employee that results from mixed motives violates the act. It therefore does the employer little good to make up a reason for the discharge even if the reason can be at least partially justified. For example, if the employer discovers that one employee is engaging in union activities which it disapproves of, the employer may not find minor violations of company rules by that employee, such as being late for work, or failing to report for work on certain past occasions, and use this as a basis for discharging the employee.

2. In order for the employer to violate this section, the employer must have some knowledge of the union activities of the employee. However, the knowledge may be inferred if the situation makes it obvious that the employer must have had such knowledge. This is generally true in a small plant or a small community where the organizational activities become well known.

3. In spite of the above, the employer is not prohibited from uniformly enforcing valid company rules. In addition, proof that a rule is flexible does not amount to a proof of discrimination in a case where it is applied strictly if there is reason for strict application in the particular case.

4. Even though the employer does have reasonable rules directed at maintaining discipline in its plant during working hours, it may not distort enforcement of those rules and apply them to thwart a union organization attempt.

5. Discrimination does not always involve something as drastic as a discharge. It may involve an assignment to less desirable work or shifts or a failure to allow the employee to participate in overtime. This raises the problem of the so-called constructive discharge. However, discriminatory conduct does not have to be so severe as to cause the employee to quit. There are many

cases on the constructive discharge subject recognizing that employees may be constructively discharged by such things as demoting them to positions of lesser pay or authority or poorer working conditions. An employee can be constructively discharged without a reduction in pay, and a constructive discharge can occur by harassment of the employee, surveillance, or deliberate accumulation of complaints.

6. Generally, an employer must be able to justify its actions on the basis of economics. While the theoretical legal principle provides that the employer's action is only illegal if it is based on a motivation to influence the employee's union activities, as a practical matter, economic reasons are generally necessary in order to overcome the inference present when an employee active in union affairs is discharged or assigned less desirable work or otherwise penalized.

7. The discrimination rules apply to a *refusal to recall* for discriminatory reasons even though the employee might have originally been laid off for economic reasons.

8. In evaluating the motives of the employer, the following is the controlling principle announced in the Supreme Court's opinion in the *Great Dane Trailers* case:

From this review of our recent decisions, several principles of controlling importance here can be distilled. First, if it can reasonably be concluded that the employer's discriminatory conduct was "inherently destructive" of important employee rights, no proof of an antiunion motivation is needed and the Board can find an unfair labor practice even if the employer introduces evidence that the conduct was motivated by business considerations. Second, if the adverse effect of the discriminatory conduct on employee rights is "comparatively slight," an anti-union motivation must be proved to sustain the charge *if* the employer has come forward with evidence of legitimate and substantial business justifications for the conduct. Thus, in either situation, once it has been proved that the employer engaged in discriminatory conduct which could have adversely affected employee rights to *some* extent, the burden is upon the employer to establish that he was motivated by legitimate objectives since proof of motivation is most accessible to him.

PROBLEMS INVOLVING STRIKES

There are three basic kinds of strikes:

1. Legal economic strikes

2. Legal unfair labor practice strikes

3. Strikes which are neither of the above

A legal economic strike is one called solely for enforcing demands for improved wages, hours, and other terms and conditions of employment and one which is not in violation of any contractual no-strike clause, which does not have any other improper motivation, and for which the proper notice to the employer has been given under section 8(d) of the NLRA.

A legal unfair labor practice strike is one where the employees are objecting to some unfair labor practice of the employer.

The general rules applicable to these kinds of strikes are:

1. If the employees engage in a legal economic strike, the employer cannot discharge them because of their union activities and must reinstate them when they have unconditionally offered to return to work unless the employer has already hired a *permanent* replacement. If such a permanent replacement

has been hired, the employer is not required to discharge the permanent replacement to make way for the returning striker.

2. If the employees have been found to be engaging in a legal unfair labor practice strike, the employer must reinstate all the strikers even if this means discharging the employees who have been hired to replace them during the strike.

3. Generally, if the strike does not fall under one of the above categories, it is not protected, and the employer may discharge striking employees. For example, if the strike is in violation of a no-strike clause, the employer may discharge the strikers. Also, even if the strike starts out to be a legal strike, the employees may engage in activity which causes them to forfeit their rights to reinstatement. Such activities include destruction of company property; violence to visitors, customers, or workers during the strike; or other illegal activities.

If a strike is a legal economic strike, the employer is subject to certain restrictions as to how he treats strikers versus nonstrikers. For example, in the *Great Dane Trailers* case, from which the above basic law on determination of employer motivation was taken, the employer was held to have discriminated against legal strikers when it decided to give vacation pay to those employees who were working on a certain day during the strike and not to those employees who were striking at that time. Generally, the employer may not discriminate against legal economic strikers by refusing to reinstate the strike leaders when the strike is over, or by discharging the strikers before permanent replacements have been hired, or by adopting procedures which treat those who stayed at work and did not go on strike differently from the strikers (as was done in the *Great Dane Trailers* case).

The following are some additional points which frequently arise in a strike situation:

1. If several employees refuse to cross a picket line, this is generally concerted protected activity under the act. However, if, for example, some employees refuse to cross a picket line and the employer discharges those employees in order to use others who, for a valid business reason, such as to preserve a business relationship with the struck employer, do cross the picket line, there will be no violation if there is no antiunion attitude.

2. If strikers engage in violence or other misconduct, they may be discharged or the employer may refuse to reinstate them. Generally, mass picketing and the attempted prevention of anyone from entering the employer's place of business will justify the employer in discharging or refusing to reinstate anyone engaging in such activity. However, it should be noted that violence or misconduct must be substantial in order to justify such discharge.

3. If a strike starts out as an economic strike and then turns into an unfair labor practice strike because of some unfair labor practice of the employer, the strike is considered an unfair labor practice strike and the employer must reinstate all the strikers.

4. An employer may not adopt a "return-to-work-or-else" policy. That is, the employer may not say to the strikers that if they have not returned to work by a certain date, they will be discharged, and then immediately after that date, discharge those strikers who have not returned to work, unless they have been permanently replaced by other people.

YELLOW-DOG CONTRACTS

A yellow-dog contract is one in which the employee must promise not to join any labor union, must renounce existing memberships, and must refrain from union membership while employed. Such contracts were used extensively in the earlier days of American labor relations, but today are prohibited expressly by the Norris-La Guardia Act and the Railway Labor Act, and indirectly by section 8(a)(3) of the National Labor Relations Act. A minor variation, which is equally illegal, is the so-called Balleisen-type contract, which provides that the employee will not demand a closed shop or a signed agreement by his employer with any union.

PART 5   SYMPATHY STRIKES—INJUNCTIONS

In the early days of the development of labor law, many problems revolved around the ability of a union to organize workers in a plant. During these times, one of the weapons used by management was to ask federal courts to issue an injunction against certain activities, including strikes and picketing, in which unions and their prospective members were engaged in order to force the company to recognize the union as the bargaining agent of the employees and to bargain collectively.

Congress determined that this was improper and enacted the Norris-La Guardia Act in 1932. The Norris-La Guardia Act (or anti-injunction act) provides essentially that federal courts are not allowed to issue injunctions in labor disputes. The theory of the act is that instead of having such disputes resolved in a court by having the court decide the question of whether it should issue an injunction, the dispute should be resolved by the arbitration process.

The next major chapter in the strike/injunction saga was the *Boys Market* case, decided by the Supreme Court in 1970. In the *Boys Market* case, the Supreme Court overruled some prior decisions and held that an injunction should be issued if the union was engaged in a strike which was in violation of a no-strike clause. The facts in *Boys Market* were essentially that the union demanded that supervisory employees cease performing tasks which the union claimed to be union work. The demand was rejected, and the union struck. The dispute was susceptible to the grievance and arbitration clauses contained in the collective bargaining agreement, and it was clear that the strike violated the no-strike clause which accompanied the arbitration provisions. The Supreme Court held that the union could be enjoined from striking over a dispute which it was bound to arbitrate. The rationale of the decision was that a contrary holding would deprive the company of "the benefit of its bargain." The theory was that the company had bargained for certain concessions in the contract, and the union had agreed in exchange therefore to refrain from striking. If the union could strike during the arbitration process (which in many cases could be rather lengthy) and if the employer was not allowed to have an injunction against this admittedly improper strike, the company would be deprived of the benefit of its bargain and, in the long run, according to the rationale of the *Boys Market* decision, the collective bargaining process would be eroded rather than promoted.

Accordingly, after the *Boys Market* case, the general rule appeared to be that a court could not issue an injunction against a strike which arose out of a labor dispute *unless* the dispute was governed by a collective bargaining agreement which had an arbitration provision covering the dispute in question and which also had a no-strike clause.

Consistent with this opinion, the Supreme Court decided the case of *Gateway Coal Company v. United Mine Workers* in 1974. The *Gateway Coal* case is frequently discussed in the context of the Occupational Safety and

Health Act because it involved a safety dispute. However, the essential rationale and discussion of the case involves the Norris-La Guardia Act/*Boys Market* exception problem.

In the *Gateway Coal* case, the Supreme Court held that a safety dispute was subject to arbitration and, therefore, when the union members refused to work on the grounds of this safety dispute, the company was entitled to an injunction against this work stoppage. The facts of the *Gateway Coal* case are rather interesting because it appears that the holding was quite broad, and in addition, it appears that the "equities" of the case seemed to be at least somewhat on the side of the union members. There was an admitted safety problem—the collapse of a ventilation structure. The situation involved admittedly hazardous mining activity, and there appeared to be some falsification of safety-related records by management. Even in the face of all of this, however, the Supreme Court held that since the collective bargaining agreement covered the safety dispute, the union is obliged to arbitrate any dispute it has with management rather than strike without such arbitration.

Another interesting fact in the *Gateway Coal* case was that the application of the arbitration clause to the safety dispute was certainly not express. The court was basing its decision on the arbitration clause which required the union and the company to arbitrate the disputes "about matters not specifically mentioned in this agreement" and "any local trouble of any kind arising at the mine." The court held that this arbitration clause was sufficiently broad to encompass a safety dispute.

We now come to the current issue: the application of all this to a "sympathy strike."

In the *Buffalo Forge* case, the facts at issue were very clear. The employer sought an injunction against a sympathy strike which was called by its production and maintenance workers in order to support the attempts of clerical and technical workers to negotiate a contract. The production and maintenance workers' contract included a no-strike pledge and a general arbitration clause. Both the employer and the union agreed that the issue of whether the sympathy strike violated the no-strike pledge was, and should be, subject to arbitration. The only point of dispute was whether a federal court could issue an injunction against the sympathy strike pending an arbitrator's decision interpreting the no-strike pledge.

Unlike the *Gateway Coal* case, which was a unanimous opinion, the *Buffalo Forge* decision was a severe 5-4 split of the Supreme Court. The majority opinion held that the Norris-La Guardia Act governed the situation and the *Boys Market* exception did not apply. The majority opinion based this holding on the fact that the strike was not over any dispute between the union and the employer that was even remotely subject to the arbitration provisions of the contract. In order to reach this conclusion, however, the Supreme Court had to ignore the fact that there was a broad arbitration provision and a general no-strike clause. Certainly the union engaged in a sympathy strike was not involved in any negotiations or dispute with the employer. However, taking the contract as a whole, it did have a no-strike clause in it which was definitely subject to arbitration. Accordingly, as both sides agreed, the question of whether the sympathy strike was valid was arbitrable, but since the dispute was not over any of the actual terms or conditions of employment between the striking parties and the company, the court held that it was not over any dispute which was subject to the arbitration provisions of the contract and, therefore, the general rule of the Norris-La Guardia Act governed.

The rationale of the *Buffalo Forge* case, especially coming only about three years after a unanimous opinion in the *Gateway Coal* case, seems a little doubtful. As a practical matter, it cannot be disputed that when the employer and the union negotiated the contract, one of the key elements the employer wanted was a no-strike clause, and it is evident from the opinion that the no-strike clause and the arbitration provisions were drafted very broadly. To state that the employer was not "deprived of the benefit of its bargain" by allowing the union to engage in a sympathy strike simply because the reason they were striking involved other employees rather than the employees in their own bargaining unit seems to be stretching the point a little. This of course was observed by the dissenting opinion, which also observed that all the justices on the present court joined in the *Gateway Coal* opinion, which said that the *Boys Market* rationale allowing an injunction ought to apply to "any dispute which the union was obliged to arbitrate."

To summarize, it appears that the following three rules have been announced:

1. The *Boys Market* rule is that if the union is striking over terms or conditions of employment which are covered by a collective bargaining agreement having an arbitration clause and a no-strike clause which are applicable, the company may obtain an injunction if the union strikes before exhausting the arbitration process.

2. The *Gateway Coal* opinion says expressly that a safety dispute, even if not expressly contained in a contract, is of the type contemplated by the *Boys Market* exception.

3. The *Buffalo Forge* opinion holds clearly that a sympathy strike (generally agreed to be one where the union members are striking on behalf of other workers and the striking members do not have an actual dispute themselves) is not subject to the *Boys Market* exception but is instead covered by the general Norris-La Guardia Act, which prohibits federal courts from issuing injunctions arising out of labor disputes.

Unfortunately, the holdings of both the *Gateway Coal* and the *Buffalo Forge* cases appear to be quite broad, and they point in opposite directions. The *Gateway Coal* holding seemed to imply that the *Boys Market* exception was going to be rather liberally construed and an injunction would be allowed whenever the union was engaged in a strike over a dispute which it was obligated to arbitrate. The *Buffalo Forge* opinion could be read two ways. The first is to read it narrowly and hold that it applies only to a sympathy strike the governing factor of which is that there really is not any dispute over the terms or conditions of employment of the people doing the striking. On the other hand, it could be read broadly to the general effect that unless the union was striking over something which it had clearly agreed to arbitrate and that dispute involved the terms or conditions of employment of the same people doing the striking, an injunction would not issue. The board reading is certainly inconsistent with *Gateway Coal* and even the narrow reading seems to be stretching *Gateway Coal.* Obviously the problem is subject to differing interpretations, as evidenced by the strong 5-4 dispute in the Supreme Court.

PART 6   DISCRIMINATION AGAINST NLRB WITNESSES

Section 8(a)(4) of the National Labor Relations Act provides that "it shall be an unfair labor practice for an employer . . . to discharge or otherwise discriminate against an employee because he has filed charges or given testimony under this Act."

The number of cases under this section is very small, and its meaning is fairly plain from a simple examination of the statute. Cases under this section establish the following gloss:

1. Discrimination in any form is covered, such as discharge, layoff, failure to rehire or recall, or transfer. In this sense, section 8(a)(4) is interpreted very much as is section 8(a)(3).

   Even though a supervisor is not an "employee" as defined in the act, the board has the duty to protect the supervisor if he is subpoenaed and gives testimony as a witness in an NLRB case and is subsequently discriminated against by an employer because of that testimony.

2. In the case of *NLRB v. Scrivener*, the Supreme Court held that the words in 8(a)(4) "has filed charges or given testimony under this Act" cannot be interpreted too literally and, in fact, include giving a statement in preparation for giving testimony. Accordingly, an employer who discharged three employees for having given such written statements to a board field examiner violated section 8(a)(4). In *Sinclair Glass Co. v. NLRB*, this was extended to the filing of an affidavit with the board agent.

PART 7   THE DUTY TO BARGAIN COLLECTIVELY

Section 8(a)(5) of the National Labor Relations Act provides as follows:

> Sec. 8(a).   It shall be an unfair labor practice for an employer—
> . . . (5) to refuse to bargain collectively with the representatives of his employees, subject to the provisions of section 9(a).

Section 9(a) states as follows:

> Representatives designated or selected for the purposes of collective bargaining by the majority of the employees in a unit appropriate for such purpose, shall be the exclusive representatives of all employees in such unit for the purposes of collective bargaining in respect to rates of pay, wages, hours of employment, or other conditions of employment: Provided, That any individual employee or a group of employees shall have the right at any time to present grievances to their employer and to have such grievances adjusted, without the intervention of the bargaining representative, as long as the adjustment is not inconsistent with the terms of a collective-bargaining contract or agreement then in effect: Provided further, That the bargaining representative has been given opportunity to be present at such adjustment.

This may be considered the heart of the National Labor Relations Act. Unfortunately, it is also the area which has caused the greatest concern and confusion. There are literally hundreds of cases.

Both the company and the union are under a duty to bargain in good faith. This chapter will consider the problem from the viewpoint of the company.

While there are innumerable ways to organize and present the vast body of law which deals with section 8(a)(5), the following outline, containing three basic units, is thought to be one of the better approaches and is used herein:

1. Discussion of the circumstances and point in time at which the company is subjected to the duty to bargain with the union in good faith.

2. Discussion of what topics must be bargained about.

3. Discussion of the way in which the duty is discharged

WHEN THE DUTY TO BARGAIN ARISES

The employer is under a duty to bargain with a union only when the employer has reasonable grounds to believe that that union does, in fact, represent a majority of the workers in the bargaining unit. Basically, there are two contexts in which the problem can arise. The first is the context of a nonorganized bargaining unit which is in the process of being organized, and the second is the context of an organized unit which is undergoing an organization drive by a rival union or where the employees are seeking to force the existing union out and continue in an unorganized fashion.

New Organization

The usual method by which a union organizes a company is to solicit all the employees to sign a union authorization card. There are many different kinds of cards; some authorizing an election, some simply designating a union as the representative of the employees, and some doing both. Generally, an election is then held, which election is certified by the NLRB, and, depending upon the results of the election, it is clear whether the union does or does not represent a majority of the employees, and, therefore, whether or not the employer does or does not have to bargain collectively with that union.

   However, problems do arise. Under former law, if the union simply presented the company with a number of authorization cards signed by a majority of the work force, the employer was then under a duty to bargain with that union unless it entertained a reasonable doubt as to whether or not the union, in fact, represented a majority of the employees. Such doubt was said to be reasonable where the employer had reason to believe that coercion was used in obtaining the cards, where the employees did sign them but subsequently revoked their authorization, or where there was any other good faith reason. However, the Supreme Court, in the case of *NLRB v. Gissel Packing Co.,* changed this rule, and at this time, an employer is entitled to insist upon an NLRB-certified election before he bargains with any union, provided, however, that if the union does solicit cards from a majority of the employees and the employer then conducts an act of unfair labor practice which would inhibit the conduct of a free and open election, the employer will, at that point, be under a duty to bargain with the union even though the election may not have been held yet. An employer's good faith doubt is now largely irrelevant, and the key to the question of whether or not he must bargain with the union is the commission of a serious, unfair labor practice that would interfere with the election process and tend to preclude the holding of a fair election.

   An employer's duty to bargain does not arise until the union makes a demand upon the employer. While it is not necessary that the demand be in any particular form, or even in writing, it is necessary that the demand be made at a time when the union, in fact, possesses signed authorizations from a majority of the employees in the bargaining unit.

   The current rule can be summarized in the following quotation from the *Gissel* case:

> When confronted by a recognition demand based on possession of cards allegedly signed by a majority of his employees, an employer need not grant recognition

immediately, but may, unless he has knowledge independently of the cards that the union has a majority, decline the union's request and insist on an election, either by requesting the union to file an election petition or by filing such a petition himself under section 9(c)(1)(B). If, however, the employer commits independent and substantial unfair labor practices disruptive of election conditions, the Board may withhold the election or set it aside, and issue instead a bargaining order as a remedy for the various violations. A bargaining order will not issue, of course, if the union obtained the cards through misrepresentation or coercion or if the employer's unfair labor practices are unrelated generally to the representation campaign.

In some extreme cases, the NLRB may issue a bargaining order even though the employer may have reasonable doubt as to the union's majority status. This is the kind of case where the employer has engaged in rather severe unfair labor practices that are designed to destroy the union's majority status.

After a union is approved by an NLRB-certified election, it is conclusively presumed to represent a majority of the employees for one year. However, after that year, events may show that the union no longer does represent a majority of the employees, and in this event, the employer's duty to bargain with that union may terminate. Ordinarily, the doubt is raised by a petition filed by a rival union asking for an NLRB-certified election. Generally, such a petition will relieve the company of the duty to bargain with either union (even though almost all employees continue the dues check-off to the incumbent union) and furthermore may obligate the employer to refrain from bargaining with the incumbent union.

ON WHAT SUBJECTS MUST THE COMPANY BARGAIN?

Sections 8(a)(5) and 8(d) taken together establish the duty to "confer in good faith with respect to wages, hours, and other terms and conditions of employment." Interpreting this language, the Supreme Court, in its decision in *NLRB v. Wooster Division of the Borg-Warner Corp.*, established that there was an obligation of the employer and the representative of its employees to bargain with each other in good faith with respect to "wages, hours and other terms and conditions of employment," but that the duty was limited to those subjects and within that area neither party was legally obligated to make any concessions to the other. The Court went on to say, however, that as to other matters, each party is free to bargain or not to bargain, to agree or not to agree.

Thus, there has emerged a distinction between mandatory and permissive subjects of collective bargaining. There is a third category of illegal subjects for collective bargaining, which includes those items which would be illegal for the company and the union to agree upon—such as an agreement discriminating against one group of employees on account of their race.

The importance of this distinction is that a party has a statutory obligation to bargain about a mandatory subject of collective bargaining, and a refusal to bargain about such a mandatory subject is, even without a finding of any kind of bad faith, a violation of the act. In addition, any unilateral action taken with respect to a mandatory subject of collective bargaining may be a per se violation of the act. Conversely, if the subject involves only a permissive subject of collective bargaining, a party not only need not bargain about it, but also has no right to insist upon bargaining by the other party. In other words, the proponent of a subject of permissive subject of bargaining cannot insist upon inclusion of any clause involving that permissive subject as a prerequisite to his agreement on the contract. Furthermore, the insistence upon incorporation of a permissive bargaining subject does not have to be the sole cause for an impasse in order to establish that the person doing the insisting has engaged in a violation of his duty to bargain.

It should be noted that section 8(d) of the act specifically provides that there is no duty upon either party to agree or to make any concessions even with respect to a mandatory subject. Therefore, there is no violation of the act even if a party insists to the point of deadlock on a proposal relating to a mandatory subject (assuming that the party has, in fact, bargained in good faith about that subject).

With the above background, it is possible to make lists of mandatory, permissive, and illegal subjects of collective bargaining. However, within the mandatory list, it is necessary to establish a subheading of conditional subjects of mandatory bargaining. These are the kinds of subjects which, while *generally* subject to the duty of mandatory collective bargaining, may not be in a particular case.

Mandatory Subjects of Collective Bargaining

The first broad category of mandatory subjects of bargaining is wages, rates of pay, or any other kind of compensation paid for services rendered. Within this broad category, the following are included: overtime pay, shift differentials, paid holidays, paid vacations, severance pay, piece rates and incentive plans, pension and other welfare plans, profit sharing plans, stock purchase plans, merit wage increases, company houses, meals, discounts and services furnished to the employees, and generally any other item which, fairly considered, represents compensation to the employee for services rendered.

A second broad category of subjects of mandatory bargaining is the hours worked. This includes the particular hours of the day, the days of the week, whether the hours fall in daytime, nighttime, or on Sunday, etc. The problem of hours worked and its related aspects has not generated a great deal of litigation or difficulty.

A third category of mandatory subjects may simply be termed "other terms and conditions of employment," as that phrase is used in the statute. This category includes such things as the grievance procedure, arbitration, layoffs, discharge, workloads, vacations, holidays, sick leave, work rules, use of bulletin boards by unions, change of payment from a salaried base to an hourly base, definition of bargaining unit work and performance of bargaining unit work by supervisors, bargaining about employees' physical examinations, the duration of the collective bargaining agreement, seniority, promotions and transfers, compulsory retirement age, union shop check-off, agency shop and hiring hall provisions, management rights clauses, plant rules, safety, and the no-strike clause.

Conditional subjects for mandatory bargaining include the following:

Bonuses

Bonuses are generally a subject of mandatory bargaining, because only in the case where the bonus is termed to be a gift is it not a form of wages or salary. Therefore, if the bonus is paid with any degree of regularity, it will usually be determined to be a subject of mandatory bargaining even though there may be no legal obligation on the part of the company to pay that bonus.

Subcontracting

Subcontracting is generally a subject of mandatory bargaining, but there may be exceptions, and the application of this rule must be tempered with some reasonableness. There are very clear cases where the employer desires to subcontract a lot of work which is currently being done in the bargaining unit. In this situation, the subcontracting work is naturally a subject of mandatory bargaining. However, there are also de minimus kinds of subcontracting, such as the subcontracting out of the installation, on a one-time basis, of a new machine which is being installed in the plant. In this latter situation there is some doubt as to whether or not subcontracting is a mandatory item of collective bargaining, and unilateral action on this regard may be appropriate. As a practical matter, the problem is usually solved by a paragraph in the collective bargaining agreement which clearly sets forth the circumstances under which management may, in their sole discretion, subcontract work.

Permissive Subjects of Bargaining

A catalogue of permissive subjects of bargaining includes the following:

1. Definition of the bargaining unit. (Generally, the board decides the appropriate unit, but even in this case, the parties are free to bargain about it.)

2. Supervisors and agricultural labor. The act is not applicable to supervisors or agricultural workers. The parties may bargain about their inclusion but not insist to the point of impasse on the matter.

3. The parties to the agreement. Generally, only the company and the union are parties, but the parties may negotiate on whether or not others—such as the international union as well as the local, or an employer association—should be included.

4. Performance bond. Requiring the union to post bond to secure performance or requiring employer to post bond to assure payment of wages.

5. Legal liability clauses, subjecting the union to liability for violation of a strike clause. The board's view follows the Fourth Circuit Court ruling that says that the company may insist to the point of impasse.

6. Internal union affairs. This includes such things as providing that nonunion employees will have the right to vote on a contract or that the union must take a strike vote before calling a strike.

7. The union label.

8. Industry promotion funds.

9. Settlement of unfair labor charges as part of the agreement.

Illegal Subjects

While there are not many decisions showing precisely what constitutes an illegal provision in a collective bargaining agreement, the following are generally agreed to be illegal:

1. A provision for a closed shop

2. A hot cargo clause in violation of section 8(e)

3. Any provision which is inconsistent with the duty of fair representation owed by the union to the employees

4. Any provision which requires discrimination against employees on the basis of race, or separation of employees on the basis of race

5. Any provision which violates the antitrust laws, such as an agreement by the employer and the union to impose a particular wage scale on another unrelated bargaining unit

HOW IS THE DUTY DISCHARGED?

The duty to bargain collectively is discharged by bargaining in good faith.

As lawyers observe in many different contexts, a statutory duty which is phrased in general terms such as "good faith" is always extremely difficult to apply and generates a great deal of conflicting and confusing authority in the form of many decisions by both the courts and the board which are not always capable of reconciliation.

There are three basic concepts in the area of bargaining in good faith. These are as follows:

The Totality of the Conduct Governs

Except in some rather unusual and clear cases (such as insistence upon an illegal provision in a contract), there will be no single act of either the employer or the union which is held to violate a duty of good faith. Instead the court and the NLRB will examine in detail the history and progress of the negotiations, and on the basis of the totality of conduct of one of the parties will decide whether that party has or has not been bargaining in good faith.

Bargaining Techniques

While there has been a great deal written on the subject, and much criticism of the position of the board and the courts, as a practical matter, in collective bargaining, you must "play the game right." "Right" means that there must be bilateral bargaining and that a company or a union cannot simply adopt one position, no matter how reasonable that position may be, and insist on that provision without agreeing to modifications or changes.

The leading case on this point is *NLRB v. The General Electric Co.,* and the key word is "boulwarism." In the *General Electric* case, GE, after a great deal of research, formulated a single offer that anticipated the union's demands. Basically, the company then simply insisted upon this offer and refused to negotiate from it (although it did make some minor changes before the contract was eventually signed). The company was charged with a violation of sections 8(a)(1), 8(a)(3), and 8(a)(5).

A complete reading of the *General Electric* case does disclose some limitations on its express holding. The following two quotations technically serve to limit the case to the precise facts of the GE situation and are worthy of note.

> We do not today hold that an employer may not communicate with his employees during negotiations. Nor are we deciding that the "best offer first" bargaining technique is forbidden. Moreover, we do not require an employer to engage in "action bargaining," or, as the dissent seems to suggest, compel him to make concessions, "minor" or otherwise.
>
> . . . .
>
> Our dissenting brother's peroration conjures up the dark spectre that we have taken a "portentous step" [but] paints over with a broad stroke the care we have taken to spell out the bounds of our opinion. We hold that an employer may not so combine "take-it-or-leave-it" bargaining methods with a widely publicized stance of unbending firmness that he is himself unable to alter a position once taken. It

is this specific conduct that GE must avoid in order to comply with the Board's order, and not a carbon copy of every underlying event relied upon by the Board to support its findings. Such conduct, we find, constitutes a refusal to bargain "in fact." . . . It also constitutes, as the facts of this action demonstrate, an absence of subjective good faith, for it implies that the Company can deliberately bargain and communicate as though the Union did not exist, in clear derogation of the Union's status as exclusive representative of its members under section 9(a).

However, as a practical matter, the take-it-or-leave-it approach or best-offer-first approach is almost bound to generate a great deal of legal difficulty in the collective bargaining process if the union does not feel that the offer of the company is fair or appropriate, and they seldom will.

Elements of Good Faith

As indicated above, it is the totality of the conduct of the parties which answers the question as to whether or not they have bargained in good faith. In judging this totality of conduct, the board and the courts, throughout their opinions, rely on a number of catch-phrases and concepts which can be considered under the broad heading of "elements of good faith," or, alternatively, "elements of bad faith." The concept here is similar to the old concept of "badges of fraud" under the common law.

These elements of good or bad faith can be very briefly categorized as follows:

Surface Bargaining

Neither the NLRB nor the courts will tolerate a situation where one party makes an unreasonable proposal or a series of unreasonable proposals even though both sides may meet quite frequently to discuss the matters openly and make various concessions to the other party. On the other hand, the fact that extensive negotiations do not produce a contract does not justify an inference that one of the parties is engaged in surface bargaining. As in most areas, there is a fine line between legality and illegality, and a premium is placed on the good judgment of the people involved.

Among the specific items which have sometimes been held to constitute surface bargaining are:

1. Arbitrary scheduling of the times of the meetings

2. The failure to designate a bargaining agent with sufficient authority to make reasonable concessions and accept reasonable proposals

3. A predetermined and inflexible position toward matters of importance

Failure to Make Concessions

Although the act specifically says that it does not require either party to accede to the demands of the other, the fact remains that the board or the court must judge the good faith of the parties on the basis of objective facts rather than the subjective statements or states of minds of the parties. Accordingly, if one or the other of the parties refuses to make any concessions, or makes only insubstantial or minor concessions, this fact will be taken into consideration and may be held to be an indication of bad faith.

The Advancement of Proposals

In some cases the company refuses to make any specific proposal to the union, and this has been held to be an indication of lack of good faith. Generally, the company must make some proposal even though that proposal may be predictably unacceptable. However, if the proposal is too harsh or patently unreasonable it may be held to be an indication of bad faith as an attempt to frustrate agreement. Again, the lines may be fine, and a premium is placed on judgment and discretion.

Arbitrary Positions

The taking of arbitrary positions, or the taking of positions which are based not on economics but on the employer's unwillingness to do anything to help the union, have sometimes been held to be an indication of lack of good faith. An example is the *H. K. Porter* case, where the company refused to consider a check-off provision solely on the grounds that it did not want to give aid and comfort to the union.

Insistence on a Broad Management Rights Clause

A number of problems arise in the context of the management rights clause. As a general proposition, the courts are much more favorable to the company in this area than is the NLRB. The board, generally, views any insistence on a very broad management rights clause which may have the effect of undermining the union's ability to adequately represent the employees as an element of bad faith. An obvious example would be a management rights clause insisting upon unilateral control of wages, hours, or terms of employment.

Generally, however, the courts and sometimes the board will uphold insistence on fairly broad management rights clauses which reserve power in the company to assign work, subcontract, and grant individual merit increases and reserve for the company the final decision in a grievance procedure.

Dilatory Tactics

Obviously, any conduct of the employer which can be determined to be a dilatory tactic will be considered as an element of bad faith.

Imposing Mandatory Conditions Precedent

If the company imposes conditions precedent on its willingness to bargain, this will generally be determined to be an element of bad faith. For example, if the company refuses to bargain unless the employees cease their strike, that would be an element of bad faith.

Unilateral Changes or Conditions

Any unilateral action taken by an employer which affects the employees' compensation during bargaining is a strong indication that the employer has not bargained in good faith. Generally, any unilateral action of the employer taken during bargaining is suspect as an indication of bad faith. On the other hand, the employer may make unilateral changes after the end of the certification year if there are reasonable grounds to believe that the certified union has lost its majority support. However, there is some authority for the idea that the company is placed at its peril here, and its belief must be not only reasonable but also accurate. The employer may also grant unilateral wage increases after a bona fide impasse has been reached (except if the impasse was caused by the employer's lack of good faith).

The employer may put into effect or continue traditional payments which have already been promised to the employees, and there are a number of cases raising this point. For example, if the employer has traditionally been granting Christmas benefits of one kind (merchandise or money) and there happen to be negotiations going on during one Christmas period at a time when such benefit is normally given or paid, the employer may continue to give or pay this benefit. Also, if some arrangement has been planned before the union goes on strike and is scheduled for implementation at a time when the union *is* on strike, it may be implemented by the employer.

Attempts to Bypass the Representative

Any attempts to bypass the union as the representative of the employees and deal directly with the employees is an element of bad faith.

Unfair Labor Practices

Obviously, the commission of any unfair labor practice under any other provision of the act will be considered to be an element of bad faith on the part of the employer.

Failure to Furnish Information

The assertion by the company of some grounds for objection to a union proposal requiring substantiation from company records and the refusal of the company to supply the information from such records is generally considered an element of bad faith. For example, if the company alleges that it cannot pay the union request for increased wages because of its precarious financial condition, it must provide information supporting that statement.

PART 8   THE LOCKOUT

As used herein, "lockout" means the employer's equivalent to the strike. In this context, it must be contrasted with:

1. The *permanent* closing of all or a substantial part of the employer's business
2. The discharge or layoff of *less than all* of the employees

Generally, courts hold that a lockout is not unlawful per se. As in most areas of labor law, the legality of the lockout depends upon the motivation of the employer. If the motivation is to strengthen his bargaining position, and the lockout is not applied discriminatorily (as by locking out only union members), the lockout is probably legal. On the other hand, if the lockout arises out of an antiunion bias, it is generally illegal even if it also has the effect of strengthening the employer's bargaining position. For this reason, an employer who desires to use the lockout must carefully weigh his actions and conduct so as not to give rise to any implications of antiunion bias, and to demonstrate the relevance of the lockout to his economic position.

The NLRB, however, does not always follow this pattern. Many times, they decide that the lockout is unlawful because it operates to coerce the employees and is discriminatory.

In the *American Ship Building* case, the employer locked out the workers after it had bargained to an impasse. The reason for the walkout was that the impasse occurred at the employer's slack season, and the employer felt that his bargaining position would be better if a work stoppage occurred during a slack season than if it occurred during the busy season. The Supreme Court held that the lockout was lawful. The following passages from the opinion illustrate the holding:

> To establish that this practice is a violation of section 8(a)(1), it must be shown that the employer has interfered with, restrained, or coerced employees in the exercise of some right protected by section 7 of the Act. The Board's position is premised on the view that the lockout interferes with two of the rights guaranteed by section 7: the right to bargain collectively and the right to strike. In the Board's view, the use of the lockout punishes employees for the presentation of and adherence to demands made by their bargaining representatives and so coerces them in the exercise of their right to bargain collectively. It is important to note that there is here no allegation that the employer used the lockout in the service of designs inimical to the process of collective bargaining. There was no evidence and no finding that the employer was hostile to its employees' banding together for collective bargaining or that the lockout was designed to discipline them for doing so. It is therefore inaccurate to say that the employer's intention was to destroy or frustrate the process of collective bargaining. What can be said is that it intended to resist the demands made of it in the negotiations and to secure modification of these demands. We cannot see that this intention is in any way inconsistent with the employees' right to bargain collectively.
>
> Moreover, there is no indication, either as a general matter or in this specific case, that the lockout will necessarily destroy the union's capacity for effective and responsible representation. The unions here involved have vigorously represented the employees since 1952, and there is nothing to show that their ability to do so has been impaired by the lockout. Nor is the lockout one of those acts which are demonstrably so destructive of collective bargaining that the Board need not inquire into employer motivation, as might be the case, for example, if an employer permanently discharged his unionized staff and replaced them with employees known to be possessed of a violent antiunion animus. . . . The lockout may well dissuade employees from adhering to the position which they initially adopted in the bargaining, but the right to bargain collectively does not entail any "right" to insist on one's position free from economic disadvantage. Proper analysis of the problem demands that the simple intention to support the employer's bargaining position as to compensation and the like be distinguished from a hostility to the process of collective bargaining which could suffice to render a lockout unlawful. . . .
>
> The Board has taken the complementary view that the lockout interferes with the right to strike protected under sections 7 and 13 of the Act in that it allows the employer to pre-empt the possibility of a strike and thus leave the union with "nothing to strike against." Insofar as this means that once employees are locked out, they are deprived of their right to call a strike against the employer because he is already shut down, the argument is wholly specious, for the work stoppage which would have been the object of the strike has in fact occurred. It is true that recognition of the lockout deprives the union of exclusive control of the timing and duration of work stoppages calculated to influence the result of collective bargaining negotiations, but there is nothing in the statute which would imply that the right to strike "carries with it" the right exclusively to determine the timing and duration of all work stoppages. The right to strike as commonly understood is the right to cease work—nothing more. No doubt a union's bargaining power would be enhanced if it possessed not only the simple right to strike but also the power exclusively to determine when work stoppages should occur, but the Act's provisions are not indefinitely elastic, content-free forms to be shaped in whatever manner the Board might think best conforms to the proper balance of bargaining power.
>
> Thus, we cannot see that the employer's use of a lockout solely in support of a legitimate bargaining position is in any way inconsistent with the right to bargain

collectively or with the right to strike. Accordingly, we conclude that on the basis of the findings made by the Board in this case, there has been no violation of section 8(a)(1).

Section 8(a)(3) prohibits discrimination in regard to tenure or other conditions of employment to discourage union membership. Under the words of the statute there must be both discrimination and a resulting discouragement of union membership. It has long been established that a finding of violation under this section will normally turn on the employer's motivation. . . . Thus when the employer discharges a union leader who has broken shop rules, the problem posed is to determine whether the employer has acted purely in disinterested defense of shop discipline or has sought to damage employee organization. It is likely that the discharge will naturally tend to discourage union membership in both cases, because of the loss of union leadership and the employees' suspicion of the employer's true intention. But we have consistently construed the section to leave unscathed a wide range of employer actions taken to serve legitimate business interests in some significant fashion, even though the act committed may tend to discourage union membership. . . . Such a construction of section 8(a)(3) is essential if due protection is to be accorded the employer's right to manage his enterprise. . . .

But this lockout does not fall into that category of cases arising under section 8(a)(3) in which the Board may truncate its inquiry into employer motivation. As this case well shows, use of the lockout does not carry with it any necessary implication that the employer acted to discourage union membership or otherwise discriminate against union members as such. The purpose and effect of the lockout were only to bring pressure upon the union to modify its demands. Similarly, it does not appear that the natural tendency of the lockout is severely to discourage union membership while serving no significant employer interest. In fact, it is difficult to understand what tendency to discourage union membership or otherwise discriminate against union members was perceived by the Board. There is no claim that the employer locked out only union members, or locked out any employee simply because he was a union member; nor is it alleged that the employer conditioned rehiring upon resignation from the union. It is true that the employees suffered economic disadvantage because of their union's insistence on demands unacceptable to the employer, but this is also true of many steps which an employer may take during a bargaining conflict, and the existence of an arguable possibility that someone may feel himself discouraged in his union membership or discriminated against by reason of that membership cannot suffice to label them violations of section 8(a)(3) absent some unlawful intention. The employer's permanent replacement of strikers, . . . his unilateral imposition of terms, . . . or his simple refusal to make a concession which would terminate strike—all impose economic disadvantage during a bargaining conflict, but none is necessarily a violation of section 8(a)(3).

To find a violation of section 8(a)(3), then, the Board must find that the employer acted for a proscribed purpose. Indeed, the Board itself has always recognized that certain "operative or economic" purposes would justify a lockout. But the Board has erred in ruling that only these purposes will remove a lockout from the ambit of section 8(a)(3), for that section requires an intention to discourage union membership or otherwise discriminate against the union. There was not the slightest evidence and there was no finding that the employer was actuated by a desire to discourage membership in the union as distinguished from a desire to affect the outcome of the particular negotiations in which it was involved. We recognize that the "union membership" which is not to be discouraged refers to more than the payment of dues and that measures taken to discourage participation in protected union activities may be found to come within the proscription. . . . However, there is nothing in the Act which gives employees the right to insist on their contract demands, free from the sort of economic disadvantage which frequently attends bargaining disputes. Therefore, we conclude that where the intention proven is merely to bring about a settlement of a labor dispute on favorable terms, no violation of section 8(a)(3) is shown.

In *National Labor Relations Board v. John Brown,* the Supreme Court held that a lockout in a multi-employer retail store group was lawful. One store was struck, and the others locked out all the employees represented by the union and continued business with temporary employees. The Court held that the motivation for the lockout was simply to preserve the multi-employer group and that this was a legitimate objective.

PART 9   SUCCESSOR EMPLOYERS

THE GENERAL PROBLEM

When one company takes over another and continues to employ some of the existing workers, a question arises as to the extent of the obligations of the new employer under any existing collective bargaining agreement covering the employees.

Generally, there are three essential questions:

1. Is the new employer bound by the terms of the existing labor contract?
2. Is the new employer obliged to bargain with the existing representative?
3. What wage rates or other terms or conditions of employment may be offered to the existing employees?

The case of *NLRB v. Burns International Security Systems* sheds some light on each of these questions.

Is the New Employer Bound by the Terms of the Collective Bargaining Agreement?

The new employer will be bound by the terms of a collective bargaining agreement covering the existing employees only in two situations:

1. Where it has *expressly agreed* to be bound by such contract
2. Where the particular terms of some *express law* impose the terms on a successor (i.e., a statutory merger) or where, because of the form of the transaction, it is either obvious that the employer *must have agreed* to those terms along with all the other terms and conditions involved, or where the particular *contracting entities* have not changed (as in a stock acquisition)

The *Burns* case makes it clear that the succeeding employer will not be bound by the terms of an existing labor contract simply because it proceeds to hire the former employees and conduct the same business operation previously conducted by the old employer. In this situation, the successor employer will be obligated to bargain with the existing representative, but will not, as a matter of federal labor law, be bound to the terms of the existing employment contract.

The following provision from the *Burns* case illustrates the Supreme Court's holding:

> Adoption of Contract
> It does not follow, however, from Burns' duty to bargain that it was bound to observe the substantive terms of the collective-bargaining contract the union had negotiated with Wackenhut and to which Burns had in no way agreed. Section 8(d) of the Act expressly provides that the existence of such bargaining obligation does not compel either party to agree to a proposal or require the making of a concession. Congress has consistently declined to interfere with free collective bargaining and has preferred that device, or voluntary arbitration, to the imposition of compulsory terms as a means of avoiding or terminating labor disputes. In its report accompanying the 1935 Act, the Senate Committee on Education and Labor stated:

The Committee wishes to dispel any possible false impression that this bill is designed to compel the making of agreements or to permit governmental supervision of their terms. It must be stressed that the duty to bargain collectively does not carry with it the duty to reach an agreement, because the essence of the collective bargaining is that either party shall be free to decide whether proposals made to it are satisfactory.

The Supreme Court opinion points out that the recent Board interpretation that a successor company may be bound by the substantive terms of an existing employment contract is a new development which is not justified by the National Labor Relations Act.

The Duty to Bargain

In many situations, a successor employer will have the duty to bargain with the representative of the existing employees. This will almost certainly be the case in a situation where the existing union has been recently certified and where the new employer hires most of the employees involved in the old unit and where substantially the same duties are performed by the new employees and where the composition and organization of the successor employer does not require the definition of a new unit or the inclusion of the acquired employees in some preexisting unit. However, if any of these elements is lacking, a successor employer may not even have the duty to bargain with an existing union. The following paragraph from the Supreme Court *Burns* opinion illustrates the general rules involved:

The Board, without revision, accepted the trial examiner's findings and conclusions with respect to the duty to bargain, and we see no basis for setting them aside. In an election held but a few months before, the union had been designated bargaining agent for the employees in the unit and a majority of these employees had been hired by Burns for work in an identical unit. It is undisputed that Burns knew all the relevant facts in this regard and was aware of the certification and of the existence of a collective-bargaining contract. In these circumstances, it was not unreasonable for the Board to conclude that the union certified to represent all employees in the unit still represented a majority of the employees and that Burns could not reasonably have entertained a good-faith doubt about that fact. Burns' obligation to bargain with the union over terms and conditions of employment stems from its hiring of Wackenhut's employees and from the recent election and Board certification. It has been consistently held that a mere change of employers or of ownership in the employing industry is not such an "unusual circumstance" as to affect the force of the Board's certification within the normal operative period if a majority of employees after the change of ownership or management were employed by the preceding employer.

The Terms and Conditions Offered to the New Employees

In the *Burns* case, the Board was of the opinion that when Burns employed the new employees under changed terms and conditions, Burns engaged in an unlawful employment practice because it unilaterally changed the terms and conditions of employment without consulting the appropriate bargaining representative. The Supreme Court indicated that this was not the case because, although Burns offered employment at different terms and conditions, Burns did no change any of *its* terms and conditions which it had offered to *its former employees*. The following paragraph from the *Burns* case illustrates the general rule involved:

Although Burns had an obligation to bargain with the union concerning wages and other conditions of employment when the union requested it to do so, this case is not like a section 8(a)(5) violation where an employer unilaterally changes a condition of employment without consulting a bargaining representative. It is difficult to understand how Burns could be said to have *changed* unilaterally any pre-existing term or condition of employment without bargaining when it had no previous relationship whatsoever to the bargaining unit and, prior to July 1, no outstanding terms and conditions of employment from which a change could be inferred. The terms on which Burns hired employees for service after July 1 may have differed from the terms extended by Wackenhut and required by the collective-bargaining contract, but it does not follow that Burns changed *its* terms and conditions of employment when it specified the initial basis on which employees were hired on July 1.

However, caution is dictated here because the Court did point out that there were situations where the employer was not free to set initial terms on which it would hire the employees of a predecessor. The following paragraph illustrates those conditions:

Although a successor employer is ordinarily free to set initial terms on which it will hire the employees of a predecessor, there will be instances in which it is perfectly clear that the new employer plans to retain all of the employees in the unit and in which it will be appropriate to have him initially consult with the employees' bargaining representative before he fixes terms. In other situations, however, it may not be clear until the successor employer has hired his full complement of employees that he has a duty to bargain with a union, since it will not be evident until then that the bargaining representative represents a majority of the employees in the union as required by section 9(a) of the Act, 29 U.S.C. section 159(a). Here, for example, Burns' obligation to bargain with the union did not mature until it had selected its force of guards late in June. The Board quite properly found that Burns refused to bargain on July 12 when it rejected the overtures of the union. It is true that the wages it paid when it began protecting the Lockheed plant on July 1 differed from those specified in the Wackenhut collective-bargaining agreement, but there is no evidence that Burns ever unilaterally changed the terms and conditions of employment it had offered to potential employees in June after its obligation to bargain with the union became apparent. If the union had made a request to bargain after Burns had completed its hiring and if Burns had negotiated in good faith and had made offers to the union which the union rejected, Burns could have unilaterally initiated such proposals as the opening terms and conditions of employment on July 1 without committing an unfair labor practice.

PART 10   UNFAIR LABOR PRACTICES OF THE UNION

The previous list of unfair labor practices fell within the general category of unfair practices of the employer. There is a similar and even longer list of unfair labor practices by a union which are set forth in the very same section of the National Labor Relations Act. As indicated initially, those matters which deal with unfair practices of an employer are in subparagraph (a) of Section 8, and those paragraphs which deal with unfair labor practices of the union are in subparagraph (b). Following is a section-by-section—but very much abbreviated—discussion of the unfair labor practices of a union.

GENERAL UNFAIR PRACTICES

The first unfair labor practice of a union is contained in paragraph 8(b)(1), which provides as follows:

(b) It shall be an unfair labor practice for a labor organization or its agents—
(1) to restrain or coerce (A) employees in the exercise of the rights guaranteed in section 7: <u>Provided,</u> That this paragraph shall not impair the right of a labor organization or prescribe its own rules with respect to the acquisition or retention of membership therein; or (B) an employer in the selection of his representatives for the purposes of collective bargaining or the adjustment of grievances.

A union which is recognized or certified as the majority representative has a duty to represent all the employees in the bargaining unit. Accordingly, the union cannot favor one group over another. This can come about in a number of ways. Sometimes the discrimination alleged might be racial. This is dealt with in Chapter 25 of this book. Essentially, the union has a duty to represent all of its members, black or white, male or female, on an equal basis, and if it does not do so, it is subject to the same sanctions as an employer who discriminates on this basis. If a union member feels he or she is being unfairly represented because of race or sex, the grievance procedure can be used.

Another problem which arises under this section concerns union fines against its own members. Typically, the pattern will be that there is a work dispute and a union member will be favorably disposed towards management's side of the question or will want to resign from the union and continue working and cross the union's picket lines. The question of when and to what extent the union may fine such a member is usually governed by the constitution of the union and whether the member has been informed of the fact that he may be fined under certain circumstances. Without going into all the technicalities, however, the general principle seems to be that the union may fine its members for activity which is legitimately against the interest of the union so long as the member has notice of the fact that he may be fined if he engages in this kind of activity, but the union may not fine members if it appears under all the circumstances that the fine was levied to *punish* the union member because of some activity which the union didn't like or if the fine was levied against the union member *in his capacity as a supervisor* rather than his capacity as a worker. In some cases, union members may also be supervisors, and this is a very touchy area because the union then is dealing with a person who wears, so to speak, two hats. On the one hand, the union may discipline the member and require dues from him in his capacity as a worker, but it may not discriminate against him because he is also a member of the management team. The classic example is where the union may fine or discipline a supervisory member for performing rank-and-file work during a strike but may not discipline the same person for performing supervisory work during the strike.

Section 8(b)(2) provides essentially that it is an unfair labor practice for a union to try to force an employer to discriminate against employees with respect to whom membership in the union has been denied or terminated on some ground other than their failure to pay standard dues and initiation fees. This means that a union may not discriminate against workers in an arbitrary way but must instead establish uniformly enforced rules and apply them to everyone. Generally, the only requirement for joining a union must be the payment of reasonable dues and initiation fees, although in some cases—notably the construction industry—there may be training, apprenticeship, or other waiting period requirements which are lawful.

This brings up the whole question of union security, closed shops, agency shops, etc. Generally, "closed shop" is a term used to refer to a contract provision which would prohibit employers from hiring anyone except union members, and this is generally unlawful. This is contrasted with a "union shop," which generally is lawful and requires all new employees to become members of the union after some period of employment—usually thirty days—and in the case of a company which becomes unionized requires all employees to join the union within thirty days after the union shop clause is first agreed to.

There is also the "agency shop," which requires everyone in the bargaining unit to pay dues to the union but may not require them to actually become members. Section 8(f) of the act generally allows the "hiring hall" practices engaged in in the construction industry and may be considered somewhat of an exception to the general rules.

Section 8(b)(3) contains the counterpart to the company-refusal-to-bargain section and states that it is an unfair labor practice for the union to bargain collectively with an employer. For example, if the union refuses to bargain with the attorney of the employer and insists on bargaining instead with the employer, this may be a refusal to bargain if it is not based upon economic grounds. (This of course assumes that the attorney has authority to bargain for the employer.) The usual question here, however, is *when the union may strike*. The union must give notice to the employer sixty days prior to the expiration date of the contract and must also notify the Federal Mediation and Conciliation Service, and if there is a state mediation agency, it must also notify that. The notification must generally indicate the union's desire to meet and bargain over changes in the contract. If the union does not do any of these things before the contract expires, it cannot strike, and if it does so, it violates section 8(b)(3).

Section 8(b)(4) is perhaps the most important section of the labor unfair practices law. The most important portion of this section deals with "secondary boycotts." In practice, secondary boycott problems usually arise in connection with "hot cargo" problems, and so both of these problems are discussed together in Part 2 of this chapter. In addition to the secondary boycott problems, section 8(b)(4) contains a paragraph which provides that it is unlawful for any union organization to attempt to require the employer to recognize or bargain with anyone other than the certified representative. Thus, in the case of a company which has a certified union and an attempted organization drive by a second union, it would be illegal for the second union to take any action to attempt to make the company deal with it rather than with the already certified union.

The last proviso of section 8(b)(4) is the so-called work assignment problem. This is subparagraph (D), which says that it is unlawful for a union to "[force] the employer to assign particular work to employees in a particular labor organization or in a particular trade, craft, or class rather than to employees in another labor organization or in another trade, craft or class unless such employer is failing to conform to an order or certification of the Board determining the bargaining representatives for employees performing such work." This section has its own enforcement procedure in section 10(k) of the act. Essentially, section 10(k) says that whenever the parties have a dispute over work assignment and they are unable to resolve it within ten days, the board will resolve it for them pursuant to procedures set forth in the act.

Work assignment disputes usually come about when a company has workers who belong to more than one union. The rules are technical, and all management really needs to know is that in this kind of case there are rules which must be complied with and they cannot simply reassign work on their own among people who are members of different unions. Some of the typical examples of problems which come up will be where a company goes from manual to automated or computerized procedures, in which case the company will desire to assign the new work to a group other than the one doing the old work because of its different nature. These kinds of cases will typically be determined by the particular facts of the situation and historical practices.

Sections 8(b)(5) and 8(b)(6) deal respectively with excessive and discriminatory fees and featherbedding. Section 8(b)(5) is rather self-explanatory; and the only troublesome question in the featherbedding section is "standby" work. Featherbedding applies only where payments are requested for no work at all. It does not apply where the workers involved are committed to be at the employer's place of business or to stand by even if, in fact, they don't do any work. Accordingly, it is not featherbedding for a union to demand payment for musicians to stand by even though they don't actually perform any work. Naturally, it must be a legitimate standby, and the musicians must be ready, willing and able to provide competent services if requested.

PICKETING

Section 8(b)(7) deals with picketing and states that it is illegal for a union to picket an employer with intent to cause that employer to recognize the union (as opposed to mere informational picketing) when the following circumstances hold true:

1. Where another union has been certified under the act

2. Where there has been a union certification election within the past twelve months

3. Where there has been no petition filed within thirty days from the commencement of the picketing (the petition must be filed with the board stating what the labor dispute is)

These kinds of picketing are illegal because they frustrate the purposes of the act, which are to promote collective bargaining. Allowing a union to picket when another union has already been certified as the bargaining agent would be inconsistent with the purposes of the act. Another purpose of the act is to eliminate frequent and repetitive labor disputes; hence, the second proviso: no picketing if an election has been held within the past twelve months. Similarly, since there should not be any picketing unless there has been negotiation and discussion of the issue, the board requires a notice to be filed within thirty days before the picketing starts, and if there is no notice, the picketing is illegal.

Picketing is a subject which crosses many areas of labor law. Usually picketing will occur in the context of a strike or when the union wants to be recognized as the collective bargaining agent for the employees.

A Strike

During a strike the employer can expect pickets. This is the so-called primary picket line, and it is perfectly permissible so long as the pickets do not engage in any forcible activity such as throwing stones or physically prohibiting those who desire from crossing the picket line. The strike picketing question, however, branches off into two other areas. The first is whether the employees who are on strike against the primary employer may go off and picket the employer's customers or other associated businesses; and the second is whether the employees of the struck employer's suppliers or customers will cross the primary picket line.

The first question is the gist of the secondary boycott issue, which is discussed in Part 2. The second point—whether employees of customers or suppliers can cross a primary picket line—is subjective. It appears that an employer has no right to automatically discharge an employee who refuses to cross a primary picket line, but by the same token, he does have a right to discharge and replace an employee who refuses to do so if it is necessary to continue his business. For example, if a company were supplying a struck employer with products and the delivery truck driver refused to cross the primary picket line but it appeared that it was not essential for the products to be delivered then, it would appear that the employer would not have sufficient cause to discharge the employer. On the other hand, if the employer's business was performing repair work on machinery and a repair employee refused to cross the primary picket line and this in turn resulted in a disturbance to the employer's work because he could not perform the repairs and obtain the revenue, there would be a much better cause for discharging this employee and replacing him with another who would cross the picket line.

Picketing for Organizational or Recognition Purposes

Picketing for organizational or recognition purposes is different from picketing a labor dispute. This was alluded to in the discussion of section 8(b)(7) above. The rights of a union to picket for organizational or recognition purposes are very restricted. Accordingly, if the purpose of the picketing is to force the employer to recognize a union, that picketing will be illegal if it is proscribed under the rules of section 8(b)(7).

On the other hand, if none of these prohibitions apply, a union may picket a company for recognition or organizational purposes, again with the limitation that there can be no violence, coercion, or intimidation.

Even assuming the picketing for recognition or organizational purposes is not prohibited by some other clause, it is still limited by a reasonable time requirement. It is not possible to picket for this purpose forever, and generally thirty days is determined to be a reasonable time period.

Because of the tendency of many union members to refuse to cross any picket line at all, and because of the wording of the statute which does allow truthfully advising the public in informational picketing, the act suggests the concept of a picket line which may not be designed to have an illegal effect but which nevertheless does have one. In this case, the picketing can be stopped. Unfortunately, the exact point at which the illegal effect begins is not clear, and here is where there are many conflicting decisions and approaches. In theory, however, if the interruptions of deliveries or the work stoppages create a significant impact on the employer's business, it is possible that he can cause the pickets in this context (as opposed to pickets in the strike context) to be removed.

Injunctions

If a company believes that it is being unlawfully picketed, the National Labor Relations Act authorizes the NLRB to seek injunctions in three kinds of situations:

1. In order to prevent any change in the position of the parties during proceedings to enforce an NLRB order

2. Against any unfair labor practice (against either a company or a union) after a complaint of such practice has been issued by the board

3. Where the picketing or other coercive activity involves section 8(b)(4)(D) (the work assignment part of the unfair labor practices section described above), because that section has its own enforcement procedure

In addition to those three cases where the board *may* seek an injunction, the act says that the board *must* seek an injunction even before an unfair labor practice complaint is issued if the board has reasonable cause to believe that there is an unlawful labor action relating to any of the following:

1. Strikes to induce an employer to enter into a hot cargo agreement or to force any employer or self-employed person to join a labor organization

2. Picketing to force anyone to stop doing business with any other person

3. Forcing an employer to bargain with a union in defiance of another union's certification

4. Forcing an employer to recognize an uncertified union

In general, therefore, unless there is some violence present, an employer will not be able to directly enjoin any picketing and must go to the board and prevail upon it to do so under one of the theories listed above.

Damage Suits

Unlike injunctions, however, a private party may bring a damage suit for a violation of most of the provisons of the labor laws. If an employer is injured by an unlawful practice under section 8(b)(4), that party may institute suit in federal district court under the normal rules and may recover damages plus costs.

PART II   SECONDARY BOYCOTTS AND HOT CARGO PROVISIONS

"Secondary boycotts" is a term used to refer to activity by a union against a company which does not have a labor dispute with the employees it is representing. An example would be picketing of a company which purchased goods from or supplied goods to a company where there was a legal economic strike. The union could picket the company where the employees worked concerning the economic problems, but it could not picket the suppliers or customers of that company, with certain exceptions. The "activity" is usually picketing or refusal to do a certain kind of work, but any kind of activity aimed at coercion of a "neutral" employer is included.

A "hot cargo provision" is an agreement by which the union and company agree that the union members will not handle goods which are not made by union members.

In the older days of labor law, these were two very separate issues. The secondary boycott issue was clearly a kind of conduct (whether or not there was an agreement) which could be separately analyzed, and the hot cargo problem was usually raised in the context of the legality of a provision of the union contract. Now, however, there are very few clear hot cargo provisions and very few secondary boycotts which are clearly aimed at coercing a neutral employer. The problems usually are more complex and quite frequently interact. In fact, the leading Supreme Court authorities link both considerations, and hence, the two are considered together in this discussion.

WORK PRESERVATION

Many of today's problems occur in the context of work preservation concerns. The typical pattern is that a union and a company will enter into some clause which is aimed at preserving the work for the employees of that company. A typical clause is one where a company agrees to abide by certain work rules established by the union. Then something will happen which causes a problem; there will be a picket line, a work stoppage, or a refusal to install a particular item, and the parties will be off to the NLRB or the court. There have been many cases involving essentially these facts. The first major one was the Supreme Court opinion in the case of *National Woodwork Manufacturers Assoc. v. NLRB*, in which the Supreme Court upheld a union's right to insist on the observance of a work rule which prevented its members from hanging pre-hung doors. The rationale of that decision was that the basic work rule was designed to safeguard the work of the employees of the general contractor, and there was no intention to satisfy union objectives elsewhere. The court held that the hot cargo provision did not prohibit the union from negotiating a clause which was aimed at *preserving work traditionally done* by those employees. Accordingly, there was no violation of section 8(b)(4) of the National Labor Relations Act by observations of the work rule, and the work rule itself was not an illegal hot cargo provision.

After the *National Woodwork Manufacturers Assoc.* case, there were a number of decisions which attempted to deal with this kind of problem. Some courts based their decisions on whether the employer whose employees were striking or refusing to work were under control of the matter in question. In other words, could the employer do anything about the problem? If not, it was usually held that this was strong evidence that the real objectives of the union were something besides a legitimate dispute with the employer and hence an illegal secondary boycott. If, on the other hand, the employer was under control of the situation—he could refrain from using the pre-hung doors—union picketing or refusal to work was legal.

Many other courts refused to apply this test and used various others. There were splits among the circuits, and the Supreme Court agreed to address the problem in the case of *NLRB v. Plumbers Local 638*. In this case, the court upheld the right-to-control test as being essentially proper although observing that it should not be blindly followed in all cases.

The Law on Secondary Boycotts

Secondary boycotts are proscribed by section 8(b)(4)(B) of the National Labor Relations Act which, when read in its entirety with all the provisos, is as follows:

> 8(b)   It shall be an unfair labor practice for a labor organization or its agents—
> . . . (4)(i) to engage in, or to induce or encourage any individual employed by any person engaged in commerce or in an industry affecting commerce to engage in, a strike or a refusal in the course of his employment to use, manufacture, process, transport, or otherwise handle or work on any goods, articles, materials, or commodities or to perform any services; or (ii) to threaten, coerce, or restrain any person engaged in commerce or in an industry affecting commerce, where in either case an object thereof is—
> . . . (B) forcing or requiring any person to cease using, selling, handling, transporting, or otherwise dealing in the products of any other producer, processor, or manufacturer, or to cease doing business with any other person, or forcing or requiring any other employer to recognize or bargain with a labor organization as the

representative of his employees unless such labor organization has been certified as the representative of such employees under the provisions of section 9: <u>Provided,</u> That nothing contained in this clause (B) shall be construed to make unlawful, where not otherwise unlawful, any primary strike or primary picketing; . . . <u>Provided,</u> That nothing contained in this subsection (b) shall be construed to make unlawful a refusal by any person to enter upon the premises of any employer (other than his own employer), if the employees of such employer are engaged in a strike ratified or approved by a representative of such employees whom such employer is required to recognize under this Act: <u>Provided further,</u> That for the purposes of this paragraph (4) only, nothing contained in such paragraph shall be construed to prohibit publicity, other than picketing, for the purpose of truthfully advising the public, including consumers and members of a labor organization, that a product or products are produced by an employer with whom the labor organization has a primary dispute and are distributed by another employer, as long as such publicity does not have an effect of inducing any individual employed by any person other than the primary employer in the course of his employment to refuse to pick up, deliver, or transport any goods, or not to perform any services, at the establishment of the employer engaged in such distribution.

As might be expected, drawing the line between actions taken by a union that are primary and secondary has given rise to a considerable number of cases. Many of these are in the construction industry where, because of the sharing of the work site by many employers, the problems are magnified. However, manufacturing companies can have problems also.

Following are some of the general principles which have emerged in the course of many decisions pertaining to this problem.

Informational or Consumer Picketing

Picketing which is purely informational is protected by the Constitutional guarantee of freedom of speech. Consequently, even though a union may have absolutely no dispute with a company, it may picket the company to inform customers or others of the union's dispute with a third party. The classic example is the case of *NLRB v. Fruit and Vegetable Packers & Warehousemen,* where the Supreme Court held that the union could picket a supermarket with which it had no dispute provided that the picketing was peaceful, did not disrupt the normal operations of the supermarket, and clearly noted the fact that the dispute was not with the supermarket but with the supplier of apples sold by that supermarket. The picketing was in the form of requests that customers not buy those apples. Thus, in order to qualify for this exception, the picket signs must say that the dispute is with a third party—generally by identifying the product which is involved. Naturally, the picketing must be orderly, peaceful, and otherwise reasonable. There are a whole line of cases to this effect in the newspaper industry, where the board consistently requires the union to identify the struck product when it is picketing the newspaper which advertises the product.

Reasonableness of the Picketing

As might be expected, the question of reasonableness has also generated much law. The main case, however, is still *Sailors Union of the Pacific (Moore Dry Dock Co.).* In that case, the board held that picketing must satisfy four requirements:

1. The picketing must be strictly limited to times when the situs of dispute is located on the secondary employer's premises.

2. The picketing must be engaged in at the time the primary employer is engaged in its normal business at the situs.

3. The picketing must be limited to places reasonably close to the location of the situs.

4. The picketing must disclose clearly that the dispute is with the primary employer.

The Supreme Court has affirmed these criteria, but held that they should not be applied mechanically, in *Electrical Workers Local 761 v. NLRB (General Electric)*. The court said that, even though the union mechanically complied with the *Moore Dry Dock* criteria, there was a violation because of the union's intention to cause the employer's customers to cease doing business with the employer.

The Ally Doctrine

Another exception to the general secondary boycott rule is the ally doctrine, which provides that a union can picket an ally of the company with which it has the primary dispute. The problem here is determining who is an ally. In theory, an ally is a company which performs work in place of the struck company during the labor dispute that it would not normally do. In other words, a company which manufactured wood products and entered into an agreement with another wood products manufacturer to do some of its work during a strike would create an ally out of that second company, and the union could picket that company also. The problem, of course, is that normal business relations develop, and the situation is not likely to be that clear cut. The first company will probably have a second company which, during normal business, handles overflow or other work which the first company cannot do. During a strike, this activity may continue normally without creating an ally out of the other company, but the exact definition of what is normal in this kind of situation is difficult.

Damages

Someone subjected to illegal secondary activity must be able to show damages in order to bring a law suit against the union. If all the company wants is an injunction, that will not be granted by the court unless there are some damages. One could go to the NLRB, because its jurisdiction is not so limited.

Hot Cargo

Turning to the hot cargo question, the relevant law is section 8(e) of the National Labor Relations Act, which provides as follows:

> 8(e) It shall be an unfair labor practice for any labor organization and any employer to enter into any contract or agreement, express or implied, whereby such employer ceases or refrains or agrees to cease or refrain from handling, using, selling, transporting or otherwise dealing in any of the products of any other employer, or to cease doing business with any other person, and any contract or agreement entered into heretofore or hereafter containing such an agreement shall be to such extent unenforceable and void: <u>Provided,</u> That nothing in this subsection (e) shall apply to an agreement between a labor organization and an employer in the construction industry relating to the contracting or subcontracting of work to be done at the site of the construction, alteration, painting, or repair of a building, structure, or other work: <u>Provided further,</u> That for the purposes of this subsection

(e) and section 8(b)(4)(B) the terms "any employer," "any person engaged in commerce or an industry affecting commerce," and "any person," when used in relation to the terms "any other producer, processor, or manufacturer," "any other employer," or "any other person" shall not include persons in the relation of a jobber, manufacturer, contractor, or subcontractor working on the goods or premises of the jobber or manufacturer or performing parts of an integrated process of production in the apparel and clothing industry: Provided further, That nothing in this Act shall prohibit the enforcement of any agreement which is within the foregoing exception.

The leading cases are *National Woodwork Manufacturers Assoc. v. NLRB* and the recent *Plumbers* case.

As pointed out earlier, in today's climate you are not likely to run across the standard hot cargo clause in labor contracts. What you will find many times, however, is a work preservation clause of one kind or another. It may be a union work rule, as in the *National Woodwork* case, or it may be a clause requiring certain work to be done on site and/or by members of the bargaining unit. The facts involving the *Woodwork* and *Plumbers* cases are very similar, but the status of the parties was different. Hence, the cases came to different conclusions.

In the *National Woodwork* case, a general contractor agreed with the Carpenters' International Union to be bound by the rules and regulations agreed upon by local unions with contractors in areas where the general contractor had operations. The general contractor then got a job to act as contractor for a Philadelphia housing project where the local collective bargaining agreement provided that no union member would handle any prefitted doors. The court held that, in this case where the preservation of work traditionally performed by job site carpenters was the objective of the agreement, it did not constitute an illegal hot cargo clause. Further, the court held that the actual refusal to handle those doors was not illegal activity under the secondary boycott provisions of the act. Again, the union's objective was the key: job preservation. It is important to note, however, that a very important aspect of the case was that the company which employed the members of the union had the power to use or not to use prefitted doors. It was the company's own decision to do this, not something imposed upon it by a third party.

The facts in the *Plumbers* case were very similar. There was an applicable work rule which provided that cutting and threading would be done by members of the union on the job site. In this case, however, the way the problem arose was that the employees of a *subcontractor* refused to install air conditioning equipment which had cutting and threading already done at the factory. The general contractor was a third and unrelated party, and the specifications for the job expressly included air conditioning of the type which was procured for the job and which had the cutting and threading work already done. The union members *of the subcontractor* refused to install the equipment, and the contractor went to the NLRB because the job was being held up. The administrative law judge and the board agreed with the contractor, but the Court of Appeals for the District of Columbia did not. The case went to the Supreme Court and it was reversed. The Supreme Court opinion ended the ten-year split which existed among the circuits on how to decide when this kind of activity was a violation of the secondary boycott rules. The Supreme Court held that the fact that the employer whose employees were refusing to do the work—the subcontractor—was not in control of the situation showed that the union must have had some objective other than influencing the actions of that employer.

The court also addressed the legality of the work rule under the hot cargo section (section 8(e)) and said, in a footnote, that it appeared legal but was applied in a way that violated the secondary boycott provisions. Footnote 8 provided as follows:

8.   The validity of the will-not-handle provision in this case was not challenged by the charging party, and the Board referred to it as a valid provision. Because the scope of the prohibitions in sections 8(b)(4)(B) and 8(e) are essentially identical, except where the proscriptions in sec. 8(e) are limited by the provisos in that section, the Court of Appeals regarded as anomalous that a valid provision in a collective-bargaining contract could not be enforced through economic pressure exerted by the union. This conclusion ignores the substance of our decision in *Sand Door.* Even though a work preservation provision may be valid in its intendment and valid in its application in other contexts, efforts to apply the provision so as to influence someone other than the immediate employer are prohibited by sec. 8(b)(4)(B). . . .

Nor does the Board's decision undermine the collective-bargaining process as the Court of Appeals suggests. In appropriate circumstances, the Board has not found the lack of control to be determinative . . . and the Board has declared its intention to continue to eschew a mechanical application of its control test in order to ascertain whether the struck employer is truly an unoffending employer.

PART 12   THE REPRESENTATION PROCESS

Unlike unfair labor practices and related matters described above, the representation and election process provided for by the act will normally not apply to the kind of crisis situation where management may be compelled to act without benefit of legal counsel or where legal counsel might have to be consulted almost simultaneously with the action taken. Also, by its very nature, the representation and election process will be an area where the desirability and indeed necessity for competent legal involvement will be obvious and management will not need to be involved in all the technicalities. On the other hand, for purposes of completeness, there should be at least a brief discussion of the process so that everyone understands what is going on.

To begin with, it should be observed that it is not necessary to get the National Labor Relations Board involved in the question of whether a union represents a majority of the members of the work force. On the other hand, it is a rare case, indeed, where this will not happen. Typically, the pattern is that a union will allege that it represents a majority of the appropriate work force and ask that management bargain with it and enter into a contract for all the members of the bargaining union. Management then will deny that the union represents a majority of the work force—or at least allege that this is in question—and request the board to conduct an election.

The union can also request the NLRB to conduct an election if it can show that the work force has a substantial interest in being represented by the union. Generally, this means thirty percent. The means by which the union will attempt to get the employees to indicate an interest is the so-called authorization card. Depending on the facts, the union may either go directly to the company and show that it has a majority of the members of the bargaining unit who have already signed authorization cards or go to the board and ask for an election because it has signatures of thirty percent of those employees. The board will then conduct an election pursuant to a rather elaborate set of rules.

There are a tremendous number of cases on exactly who can say what during this period. However, the long and the short of it is that those cases are absolutely irreconcilable among themselves, and in addition the board decisions are irreconcilable with the court decisions. This is one of the biggest reasons why most knowledgeable members of management will insist on a labor lawyer with extensive experience. The maxim that "the life of the law is not logic but experience" is nowhere more graphically illustrated than in the labor area—particularly in the context of a union's organization drive and a company's efforts to fight it. A literal reading of the cases—assuming one believes everything that one reads in all cases—can lead to only one conclusion: that the company must sit on its hands and say nothing during the whole procedure. Obviously this conclusion is not justified by a fair reading of all of the cases, and accordingly one must apply judgment and experience. If one takes too restrictive a view and essentially adopts the position that the company should do nothing that has ever been held prejudicial, even by the NLRB, one will conclude that the company may do nothing. If the company takes the opposite view and says it will do everything that is not absolutely proscribed by a Supreme Court decision, it is likely to be in a no-win situation, because if its activities are successful, the union will probably be able to have the election set aside because of the employer's illegal activities. That essentially is the judgment question: How much and what kind of activity can and should an employer engage in during a union recognition drive in order to maximize its communications with its employees but minimize the union's chances of winning the almost certain unfair labor practice charge if they should happen to lose the election?

The principal problem in this area is threats. The company cannot threaten the employees and say that if they vote for the union they will be fired or lose their jobs. On the other hand, the company, along with everyone else in the country, does have a right of free speech and can exercise that by saying quite clearly and explicitly that it does not believe it is in the employees' best interest to vote for the union. Unfortunately, when one gets down to an analysis of what kinds of statements are permissible and what kinds of statements are not permissible, it is absolutely impossible to set forth any meaningful guidance except to get a thoroughly experienced labor lawyer whose judgment you respect. In fighting a union organization drive it may be unwise even to rely on the company's general counsel, whether or not that general counsel is an experienced labor lawyer. Lawyers who may have at one time possessed a great deal of knowledge, expertise, and judgment in the labor law area but who have since risen to higher and more responsible administrative posts covering more than labor law may not have kept up on the labor area. Management must be aware of this possibility.

As one would expect, the detailed rules of exactly how the election is conducted, when, what kind of notices must be given, and who can vote are exceedingly lengthy and complex—even in summary form—and for that reason will not be described herein.

NEGOTIATING THE CONTRACT

Assuming that the union wins the election or that the company is already represented and the contract is about to expire, there are a number of questions that relate to negotiating the contract. Most of these can be grouped under the duty of both parties to bargain in good faith and therefore are discussed in the foregoing section-by-section analysis in this chapter.

The Duty to Furnish Information

The duty to bargain in good faith includes the duty to furnish relevant information. Generally, relevant information is anything which the union might legitimately need in order to adequately represent its employees at the negotiation table. The union must demand the information before it can complain that it wasn't supplied, and the information must of course be relevant. One of the most interesting cases is one where the company claimed an inability to pay higher wages and the Supreme Court held that in such a situation that claim had to be backed up by furnishing the union sufficient information regarding the financial status of the company. Accordingly, if a company is going to claim inability to pay higher wages, it must be in a position to support that claim and must be willing to disclose that information to the union. Information must be given to the union promptly and in a reasonably useful form.

ADMINISTRATION OF THE CONTRACT

After a contract has been entered into, some questions can arise as to its administration. The heart of the administration process is the so-called grievance procedure. This is sometimes called the arbitration procedure. It has been described as being at the very heart of the system of industrial self-government. In the words of one Supreme Court case, "arbitration is the means of solving the unforeseeable by molding a system of private law for all the problems which may arise and to provide for their solution in a way which will generally accord with the varying needs and desires of the parties. The processing of disputes through the grievance machinery is actually a vehicle by which meaning and content is given to the collective bargaining agreement."

Accordingly, whenever the collective bargaining agreement doesn't cover some point or the parties disagree on the interpretation of the bargaining agreement, the procedure will be that the union, on behalf of one or all of its members, will file a grievance and then, depending upon the internal mechanisms provided in the contract, will discuss the problem fairly informally with the company. If the union and the company cannot agree on a proper interpretation of the contract, the matter will then be submitted to arbitration before an NLRB arbitrator. This will be a semiformal hearing where each side will present its arguments and the arbitrator will then render a decision. The decision of the arbitrator is enforceable by the courts, and the function of the court is essentially only to ascertain whether:

1. The question was one which was proper for arbitration.

2. The arbitrator had some reasonable basis for deciding as he did.

All doubts should be resolved in favor of the arbitration, and the court must enforce the arbitrator's decision, even if the court would decide the matter differently itself, so long as the arbitrator's decision is based upon some reasonable basis and upon the evidence.

The arbitration grievance process can be long and complicated, and there are many technical rules. However, for the reasons stated above, these are not really essential for management to have its fingertips. Accordingly, they will not be described in detail herein.

SECTION FOUR:
FEDERAL INCOME TAXATION

CHAPTER THIRTY-ONE

GENERAL
CONSIDERATIONS

The subject of federal income taxation of corporations is much too complex to deal with in a handbook such as this if the objective is to make the reader even fundamentally conversant with the substantive rules. However, in the context of informing the reader of the kinds of considerations which are important, the basic methodology involved, and some considerations in obtaining tax advice, the subject is manageable.

To begin with, the corporate executive must recognize the complexity of federal income tax laws, their constantly changing provisions, and the ever-increasing number of interpretations issued by the Internal Revenue Service and the courts. This means that no corporate executive, even one who has a good tax background, should attempt to serve as his own tax adviser. This is courting disaster but, unfortunately, seems to be an occupational hazard of tax people. "Once a tax man, always a tax man" seems to be more the rule than the exception, even though the executive may have moved into the ranks of management and not kept up on the vast amount of reading necessary to maintain a good knowledge of this area of the law. The purpose of this chapter is not to teach tax law, but merely to show the kinds of considerations which are important and, in some of the more frequently recurring transactions, to serve as a very basic reference tool for the executive to use before talking to his tax expert so that they can communicate more effectively.

The importance of tax planning should also be well understood by management. Following are some important factors.

1. State and local taxes have risen even more rapidly than federal taxes.

2. In addition to the tax payout, a company must consider the cost of compliance—especially in the area of state and local taxes, where a company operating

in all states might have to fill out more than 1000 tax returns annually. This includes the salaries, overhead, etc., attributable to those actually doing the tax work, and also travel, research materials, publications and services, data processing and record storage, and the time of the management supervising this whole effort.

3. Penalties for failing to file returns—even negligently—can be quite high. Individually, however, the dollar amounts may be small. There is sometimes a tendency to disregard these penalties in tax planning and to "leave well enough alone," in the sense of refraining from conducting comprehensive studies to see where the company should be filing or where it is not. When such studies are neglected, however, the odds seem to be that sooner or later those taxing authorities which have not been paid their due will find out about it and assess not only the back taxes but also penalties.

After recognizing that tax is very important and one of the most specialized of all the specialties, the executive must clear a couple of other hurdles. The first is the ever-present debate between lawyers and accountants as to who is best qualified to deal with a corporation's tax problems from a *planning* standpoint. There is no doubt that the tax accounting and the filling out of the tax returns are best left to the accountants—of course with assistance in interpretation from the company's lawyers as needed. However, when one is talking of tax planning, this problem always seems to arise, even if the company has very good people in each department who normally do not engage in corporate politics. The problem is that the accountants feel that they are in the best position to do tax planning because they fill out the tax returns and have a better knowledge of where and how the company is spending its tax dollars. They further point out that it is demotivating to their people to be simply "form completers" and that, in order to attract and keep good tax accountants, planning has to be a part of their function. The lawyers typically do not disagree, but argue that the training of lawyers in tax law makes them well qualified to aid in the corporation's tax planning, and they point out that they have the same motivation problems as the accountants. If the only time the lawyers see a tax problem is after the accountants have filed all the returns and the IRS auditors have asserted a deficiency, they become mere negotiators or litigators, so that keeping good tax planners becomes hard.

The decision on which department is best qualified to deal with tax planning will have to be made on a company-by-company basis depending on the people available. It will be the rare situation where one department is given the responsibility for tax planning to the total exclusion of the other and, if that is the situation, business executives should reexamine it to make absolutely sure it is best for their company. The businessperson is faced with the problem of keeping some relative peace in the family and at the same time keeping both departments properly motivated. Generally, this means recognizing the contribution of both in such a way that neither feels cheated. Healthy competition between the two departments in the tax planning field is something which is not necessarily bad. The fact that there may be some duplication of effort and an occasional spat about who first thought of a good idea is the price which will have to be paid for a healthy competitive atmosphere where each department is diligently trying to minimize the company's tax payments. If this healthy competition does exist, executives should be extremely conscious of two problems.

First, there should be increased attention to the motivation questions so that the competition does not degenerate into an unhealthy situation. Essentially, an unhealthy situation is that in which one department tries to discredit the ideas of the other rather than either rendering constructive criticism or thinking of additional ideas for tax savings.

Second, there should be a careful watch over the question of tax evasion. Whenever there is competition, whether it be between two divisions, two companies, or two departments within a company, there is danger of overzealous competition, in which some party takes liberties with the law in order to achieve a good result and save the company money. There is a fine line between tax minimization, which is not only proper but necessary for business survival in a competitive economy, and tax evasion, which may involve false record keeping or reporting fictitious book entries or other questionable practices in order to save taxes. Sometimes it will be hard for executives to tell the difference. For example, if a company is selling products to a foreign subsidiary, or buying those products from a foreign subsidiary, those products must be bought or sold at a "fair price" so that the proper taxes are paid in the proper country. The question of fair prices, however, is very subjective and this is where the tax planning comes in. Unfortunately, it can also be where the question of tax evasion or tax fraud arises. While executives will necessarily have to rely on their tax accountants and lawyers for advice as to where one stops and the other starts, it *must* be made clear that the line has to be drawn and not crossed, and it must be made clear by word and deed.

There are many ways to handle the tax function, and management must be sure to do so according to the talent available. It is suggested that the best approach is to fit the structure to the team, not the other way around. If your lawyers are good tax lawyers, make sure that you use them and that you don't let the accountants keep them out of the picture. If your accountants are good tax planners, don't let the lawyers shut them out.

One problem will be in recognizing an accountant or lawyer who merely talks a good game or is very able at corporate politics but who really doesn't have the necessary substantive capability. You will also run into the opposite: a lawyer or accountant who is substantively very capable but who does not have the skills to deal with top management or to handle the people he has to supervise or work with. This is an age-old management problem, but the dollar effect of this one is direct and rather easy to see. If a business operates on a 4 percent after-tax profit rate, it must generate 25 dollars of sales to make a dollar. If it saves a dollar by saving taxes, the profit is increased by this amount—less only the administrative effort that went into the activity that saved the dollar.

STAFFING

Another question which arises is how to staff and evaluate the tax function or functions. Here we are talking about what amount of staff is most cost-effective. From the above discussion, we should not give the impression that management should allow the people running the tax function to hire all the tax lawyers or accountants they want. There is, of course, a law of diminishing returns, and the proviso above, that the dollar in tax saved is a dollar of profit "less only the administrative effort that went into the activity that saved the dollar," is very important.

What size staff is most cost-effective? At one extreme one could take the view that the absolute minimum staff necessary to fill out all the tax returns in a reasonably acceptable manner and handle routine audits would be appropriate because the cost of additional staff would not be outweighed by the tax savings. On the other extreme one could staff the function(s) with enough people to fully examine every possible avenue for tax savings and achieve maximum tax savings on the theory that, overall, the tax savings would be more than the cost of the staff. Neither extreme is likely to be most effective, but the appropriate middle ground is apt to be hard to pinpoint.

STATE AND LOCAL TAXES

Following are some observations which might be considered: State and local taxes are taking a larger and larger bite out of the corporate till, and because there are so many of them, a rather large staff is likely to be required to deal with all the problems. In the past, state and local taxes were less important, and many corporations simply had a staff of clerks who merely filled out state and local tax returns by copying information from the previous year's return, updating certain figures from the company's financial statements, and paying the bill. Many times the old tax return did not reflect adequate tax planning, or perhaps was even erroneously prepared to the detriment of the company. An adequate staffing in the tax function must include a realization of the importance and growth of state and local taxes, and there must be adequate staff both for compliance and for review and planning. On the other hand, every single state and local tax return does not have to be reviewed for maximum tax effectiveness at the same time. If a corporation does this, its staff is likely to be too large after the initial project. Accordingly, one should staff the function so that there is a meaningful program of auditing, reviewing, and analyzing the entire state and local tax picture over a continuing period of time so that the corporation both complies with the state and local tax rules and takes maximum advantage of opportunities.

EMPLOYMENT TAXES

The same things which were said about state and local taxes apply to employment taxes. Social security alone has mushroomed in the past few years, and other employment taxes, including unemployment taxes and workmen's compensation premiums (which may not technically be a tax but can be looked at at the same time) take a large part of the corporate dollar. The staff must be more than sufficient to simply keep up with the paperwork; there must be enough people, and the people must be competent enough, to do a good job of analyzing, reviewing, and planning. An example: Is your company paying the social security tax on sick pay? If so, it is wasting money, because it is not required to. Example: Do you review workmen's compensation and unemployment claims to make sure they are legitimate? If not, you are probably passing up a good cost-saving opportunity.

FEDERAL TAXES

Federal taxes are, of course, the single biggest problem because of their magnitude and complexity. However, because they are and always have been a big problem, the company is likely to have a good system in place for dealing with them, and the job here may be more one of fine tuning. The staff must include very good people who have the time for planning. Tax people must be smart people. The law is much too complicated and the stakes too high to compromise on quality here. The state and local and employment tax jobs can be done by people who are good organizers and hard workers, good at detail and follow-up. Federal income tax planners must be all that, but, in addition, a company should get the best lawyers and accountants, with the best academic records and experience, it can possibly afford. The investment will pay off in the long run.

TAX EXPERTISE

The tax law is so large and complicated that subfields of the profession have developed, sometimes to the extent that practitioners specialize in the application of a single section of the code. Almost any business can benefit from the knowledge of these superspecialists, but few can afford to employ them full-time, because the need for their expertise is limited. Therefore, even assuming you have an adequate tax function, you are going to require outside help. A number of questions will arise. Should you get the expert help from an accounting firm or a law firm? Should you use a large law firm with a good tax department or should you use a smaller firm which specializes in tax law? How do you find out which firms specialize in tax law?

These questions have no easy answers, but good management dictates that they be carefully considered—with the help of the people in the tax function. Remember that on a day-to-day basis, it will be the people in the tax function who will be the clients of these outside experts. Don't short-circuit them by going directly to the tax experts yourself when you think you see a problem. This is the single most prevalent complaint of in-house professionals—and one which is 100 percent valid. If you don't have enough confidence in your in-house people to involve them in the process, you need new in-house people. If you do have this confidence and short-circuit them, you are making a definite management mistake.

CHANGING THE GUARD

One of the most difficult situations involved in examining the tax function will arise when you come to the conclusion that the problem is at the top. You have decided that neither your lawyers nor your accountants have the technical/managerial leadership abilities to steer your corporation through the troubled tax waters. Here, you must hold firm and get a good captain for the ship. One of the worst mistakes you can make is to swell the staff with bright young attorneys and accountants and leave the leadership to someone less competent. Your bright young people will be frustrated and their tenure will be short; your company will suffer because they will not have the guidance from the top they need to be fully effective; and, in extreme cases, their ideas will be stifled by the leader who either fails to see their merit, is too timid to implement them, or is afraid to admit that one of his subordinates has had a better idea than he.

The best advice is to seek help from the best tax or accounting firm you can to find a new department head, bring him in at a high management level, and give him authority, within certain corporate bounds, to shape up the department. Make sure, however, that your new leader applies an even and just hand. Remember that management must be concerned with the morale and performance of the whole company, and if a new boss comes in and cleans house in a harsh or arbitrary manner, you may wind up with a better tax function but with morale problems elsewhere in the corporation. On the other hand, if you require your new department head to keep the poor performers already in the department, you will be wasting your effort. A balanced approach is always necessary.

INVOLVE YOUR TAX PEOPLE EARLY

One of the most frequent frustrations of good tax experts is that they are presented with transactions which have been structured in such a way that taxes are not minimized. There is no reason why the transaction could not be restructured to minimize taxes, but the whole endeavor has already been cast in concrete because the progress of the negotiations has been so extensive that, as a practical matter, nothing can be done. Tax planning requires early involvement in all corporate matters. This means having someone with a fairly good knowledge of tax law present when corporate transactions are being discussed. As a practical matter, this means making very sure that the corporate general counsel or chief financial officer has enough knowledge of the tax law to recognize where study is needed and to get help from the appropriate sources. You don't need the experts in on the "general" sessions; indeed this would probably be a waste of time at best and a bad mistake at worst. On the other hand, if both your general counsel and chief financial officer are weak in tax law (a frequent situation), you should make sure that this deficiency is remedied by having the capability supplied in some other way. Just how is going to depend on the structure of the company, but recognizing that the problem exists is the first step. Another problem is the general counsel who thinks he is a tax expert or won't admit that he is weak in the area. This is a very frequent situation. It will be the *very* rare situation in which a general counsel can maintain a good working knowledge of the tax law, even assuming he starts out with one. There are too many other problems and administrative duties involved to keep up with the reading, and the human mind forgets what it does not use frequently. Management must recognize and deal with this problem. If a problem comes up, *ask for a written answer*. This will force your general counsel to make sure the proper experts focus on the problem. If a planning opportunity is being discussed, *force a written tax discussion*. This will help you to evaluate your tax function as well as to make certain that you get the best advice available.

A complete book could be written about how to manage the tax function. One writer has suggested that a good method to evaluate the tax function is to have all the tax people keep time on what they do and then to match the effort spent on what that writer termed the "proper balance." This is certainly a scientific way of going about the problem, but one could expect great difficulty in getting the lawyers and accountants to keep time with any degree of accuracy and consistency, and then there is the problem of exactly what the proper balance should be. It is clear, however, that the tax function—whether viewed as legal or accounting—includes the following:

1. Compliance activity. The existing laws must be complied with.

2. Reviewing or auditing. It is safe to say that no one in the company should ever file any tax return without taking the time to ask the question "How can we save some money in this area?" Miracles will not happen every day. Not every idea your tax people have will be good, and they will not often be able to slash great chunks off your tax dollars by asking this question, but it certainly is preferable to the procedure used by many tax compliance people of simply taking out the last year's return and inserting the current year's figures.

3. Reviewing major transactions for tax implications.

4. Making sure that the administration of the compliance function is effective so that penalties don't "nickel and dime" the company to death.

5. Making sure the company has access to good outside help. No in-house tax function can handle all problems. Outside consultants—either lawyers or accountants—are a must, and there must be a good way to handle tax litigation.

6. Making sure the company has a good way to handle IRS audits. I suggest team work between the lawyers and the accountants.

7. Making sure the tax function is structured in such a way as to assure that the good people find challenging work and are compensated accordingly.

8. Making sure that the tax people insert themselves into the planning stages of business. As mentioned so many times in this book, management must manage. They should not sit back and criticize the tax function when an opportunity is missed because they did not speak up in time. Management should insist on active and early involvement of the tax people.

The list could be expanded. Some commentators suggest that the tax people should get involved in proposed legislation and proposed regulations. If your people have the capability *and the inclination*, this is desirable. However, this is one thing which cannot be pushed down from the top. All that management can do here is to indicate its willingness to let the tax people do this, even though in most cases the time will not produce anything concrete. If they desire to get involved in proposed legislation or proposed regulations, it will generally provide the company with a more balanced, knowledgeable, and capable function. On the other hand, it is not essential, and if the people are not personally inclined to do it, it would be a mistake to force the issue. There is one exception. Tax people should be responsible for monitoring significant federal proposals and advising management on any which would substantially affect their company in an unusual way. The keys are "substantially" and "unusual." If your company will be affected just like everyone else—as in the case of a general rate hike—there probably isn't much you can say that the legislators don't know. On the other hand, some tax provisions may have a substantial and unusual impact on your company or industry which may be unintended. In this case, the company, either independently or through its trade association, should make sure the problem is known and suggest constructive alternatives.

THE TAX LAW

It would be impossible to set forth any complete explanation of the federal tax law as it applies to corporations in a handbook like this, but it is possible to set forth some typical corporate transactions and some typical tax problems and the general principles involved. The purpose is not to make the business executive into a tax lawyer but instead to provide a useful check on the tax advice. By "check" we don't mean determining whether the advice is accurate but instead seeing if it has been provided in the best way. For example, in this section we will list various types of corporate reorganizations as they are classified by the tax laws and the relative non-tax and tax advantages of each. If you are buying a company and your tax lawyers provide you a memorandum which lists each of these basic types of reorganization and explains the advantages and disadvantages of each as applied to that transaction, we think you can be fairly sure you are on the right track in your tax function. On the other hand, if you tell your tax lawyer that you want to acquire a small company and he says immediately, "We can do that by a statutory merger and there will be no problem," you either have one of the most astute tax lawyers in the world or you have a careless one who has not taken the time to carefully consider and evaluate all the alternatives and make a carefully thought-out recommendation. As another example, suppose you are conducting a number of businesses in the form of separate subsidiaries and think that there might be some economies of administration by folding them into the parent company, or suppose one is operating at a loss and you want to close it down. There are a number of ways to do this which are discussed in the "liquidation" chapter of this section. If your tax lawyers present a memorandum analyzing each alternative and reach a conclusion, you probably are progressing properly.

The second purpose of this section is to illustrate the standard tax problems which arise again and again so that business executives are aware of at least the principal areas which have tax implications so severe that they almost dictate the form of the transaction. Almost all transactions have tax implications, but corporate reorganizations and liquidations have such important tax considerations that they tend to be the moving force behind the whole deal. Similarly, the tax law principles of installment sales, stock dividends and recapitalizations, and all forms of deferred compensation tend to present the kind of overwhelmingly important tax considerations that overshadow most of the other aspects of the transaction. Accordingly, those are the areas which are briefly described herein.

In addition to these kinds of overwhelmingly important considerations, there are a host of very significant problems which are not dealt with at all, but which are simply left to management and their lawyers to best apply to the company using the principles set forth herein. These include the best depreciation system to use, whether property should be purchased or leased, whether existing property should be sold to a third party and leased back, whether proper records are being kept to support all the corporate deductions which are claimed, and whether the proper allocations are being made between capital items which must be depreciated over a period of time and expenses which can be deducted in the year incurred.

CHAPTER THIRTY-TWO

CORPORATE
REORGANIZATIONS

This chapter will discuss tax-free corporate reorganizations in the context of the acquisition of one corporation by another. The first part of the chapter will list the various methods by which one corporation can acquire another, give a brief description of each, and briefly discuss the most important non-tax factors which are common to all types of acquisitions. The next part of this chapter will list and briefly discuss the common tax factors.

METHODS OF ACQUISITION

There are seven basic methods by which one corporation can acquire another. These can be listed and grouped as follows (different writers may give longer or shorter lists depending on the writer's classification method but they should all be essentially the same):

Two-party taxable transactions.

1. The purchase of all of the assets of the corporation for cash

2. The purchase of all of the stock of the corporation for cash

Two-party tax-free transactions. These are the transactions commonly referred to as the "A," "B," and "C" reorganizations because they are described in sections 368(a)(1)(A), 368(a)(1)(B), and 368(a)(1)(C) of the Internal Revenue Code.

3. A *statutory merger* or consolidation: the "A" reorganization

4. The acquisition of the stock of the acquired corporation, in exchange for the

stock of the acquiring corporation: the "B" reorganization, or the *stock-for-stock* transaction

5. The acquisition of all the assets of the acquired corporation in exchange for the stock of the acquiring corporation: the "C" reorganization, or the *stock-for-assets* transaction

The newer, three-party acquisitions.

6. The *subsidiary merger,* in which the company to be acquired is merged into a newly formed subsidiary of the acquiring corporation

7. The *reverse subsidiary merger* (sometimes called the reverse merger, the reverse triangular merger, or the left-handed merger), whereby a newly formed subsidiary is merged into the company to be acquired

In these subsidiary mergers, the usual procedure is for the acquiring corporation to form a new corporation immediately before the merger into which it transfers its own stock. Then, in the case of a subsidiary merger, the company to be acquired is simply merged into the subsidiary, so that the company to be acquired disappears but its business is carried on in corporate form as a subsidiary of the acquiring company. The mechanics are the same as in any merger except that, by the terms of the merger agreement, the shareholders of the company to be acquired are given the parent company stock which was previously transferred into the subsidiary for that purpose. In the reverse subsidiary merger, the new subsidiary is merged into the company to be acquired, so that the new subsidiary disappears. The shareholder of the new subsidiary—the acquiring parent—will receive the stock of the company to be acquired, and by the terms of the merger agreement, the shareholders of the company to be acquired will receive stock of the parent company. The newly acquired company ends up as a subsidiary. Generally, these three-party transactions are used in place of a stock-for-stock transaction where the technical requirements of that type of transaction would be difficult to meet, in place of tender offers, and in place of a statutory merger when it is desired to operate the newly acquired company as a subsidiary rather than as simply an unincorporated division.

The relative merits of each of the above methods depend upon all the facts of each situation. The advantages or disadvantages of each method often depend upon whether the transaction is viewed from the point of view of the seller or that of the purchaser. The decision as to which method would be most appropriate usually depends upon two sets of factors. One set is the *non-income tax factors*; the other set is the *tax factors*.

CORPORATE ACQUISITIONS: NON-TAX FACTORS

The following is a list of the most important and most usually relevant non-tax factors which should be considered before deciding which method is best.

Contingent Liabilities

Sometimes, a company to be acquired may have certain unknown or contingent liabilities which are not disclosed on its balance sheet. Further, these liabilities may be completely unknown and unascertainable at the time of the acquisition. These unknown or potential liabilities can include such things as income tax claims by the federal government or personal injury or product liability claims by private parties. Generally, a purchaser of the *assets* of the corporation—whether the assets are purchased for stock or cash—will not be subject to unknown or contingent liabilities. However, if the *stock* of a company is acquired either for cash or stock, or if the company is acquired by a statutory merger or consolidation, the acquiring company will generally be liable for these unknown or contingent liabilities. To some extent this risk can be minimized by obtaining warranties of the selling shareholders and/or placing some part of the purchase price in escrow, or by providing for the issuance of additional stock (sometimes called contingent stock) at a future time. These, however, create considerable complexity and offer, at best, only partial protection.

Liabilities of the Purchaser for the Debts of the Seller

Generally, the purchase of the *assets* of a corporation for cash or in exchange for stock will *not* give rise to the imposition of liability on the acquiring corporation for the debts of the acquired corporation *unless* there is some violation of the Bulk Sales Act or unless the purchase price is paid to the selling shareholders rather than to the selling corporation, or unless the assets are purchased for stock and the particular state involved has the de facto merger doctrine. In a stock deal, that is, the acquisition of the stock of the selling corporation either for cash or in exchange for the stock of the acquiring corporation, the acquiring corporation will be liable for the debts of the acquired corporation, *but only to the extent of the value of the stock*. In a statutory merger, or a consolidation, the acquiring corporation will *automatically* become liable for all the liabilities of the acquired corporation.

Bulk Sales

Generally, the state Bulk Sales Acts provide that the purchaser must demand and receive a list of the seller's creditors and their addresses and the amounts owed to each, and must notify each creditor a certain time in advance before taking possession of the acquired assets. If the Bulk Sales Act, together with all its technical requirements, is not complied with, the purchaser may wind up paying for assets which can be foreclosed on by creditors.

Purchase Price Paid to Shareholders

Another potential problem here is that if the purchase price for the assets is paid directly to the selling shareholders, there may be an assertion that the acquiring corporation has enabled the selling corporation to defraud its creditors by virtue of the acquisition of substantially all of its assets and the payment of the purchase price to the shareholders rather than to the corporation. Generally, therefore, it is advisable in both taxable and tax-free transactions to pay the purchase price for assets directly to the selling corporation.

De Facto Merger

If the stock of a selling corporation is acquired for the stock of the acquiring corporation, the net effect of the transaction is almost identical to that of a statutory merger—at least as far as creditors are concerned. There has, therefore, arisen the doctrine of the *de facto* merger, which provides in substance that in such a case, the transaction will be deemed a de facto merger, which means that the acquiring corporation will automatically become liable for all the debts of the acquired corporation. The de facto merger doctrine is applicable in some states and not in others.

The Mechanics of the Transfer

The stock transaction or a statutory merger (whether of the simple two-party or newer three-party type) is relatively easy to carry out from a mechanical standpoint. However, the acquisition of the *assets* of a corporation may be extremely difficult, depending on what is involved. If there are many parcels of real estate or many items of personal property, and if different locations are involved, the paperwork in a transaction involving the acquisition of assets may be significant.

Restrictions in Existing Agreements

If the acquired corporation has some major contracts, it should be ascertained whether these are assignable. License agreements, loan agreements, mortgages, labor contracts, and virtually all other documents having an important effect on the acquired company must be examined for provisions regarding transfer of assets or stock or statutory mergers. Sometimes a particular provision in an important contract or agreement will be so significant that it will be determinative of the entire question of what form the transaction should take. An example would be a corporation which is manufacturing a product under a license which provides that it is not assignable and cancelable if the corporation disposes of substantially all of its assets. If a satisfactory solution to this problem cannot be negotiated, a simple two-party statutory merger or an acquisition of assets may be ruled out. The only possibilities will be the acquisition of the stock of the company or the reverse subsidiary merger, where the corporate entity of the acquired company remains intact.

The Dilution Factor

In a tax-free transaction, the acquiring corporation generally must issue voting stock. If voting common stock is issued, both the equity and voting interest of the existing shareholders will be diluted. The dilution of the equity can be avoided, if it can be agreed upon, by the issuance of a voting *preferred* stock or by simply using cash. The issuance of preferred stock in a reorganization can create serious problems under sections 305 and 306 of the Internal Revenue Code. However, in no event is it possible to avoid the dilution of voting interest of a purchasing corporation's shareholders in a tax-free stock or asset transaction.

Shareholder Approval

If one or both of the corporations involved has a large number of shareholders, there can be some potential problems. From the acquired corporation's point of view, the transfer of all its assets or a merger or a consolidation will usually require shareholder approval. If there are many shareholders involved or if the company is publicly held, this can be a costly and highly burdensome requirement. In addition, this sort of transaction usually gives rise to a shareholder's right of dissension and his right to force the corporation to redeem his shares at fair market value. If the corporation is not publicly held, the question of fair market value can be troublesome.

State corporation law statutes and the company's articles of incorporation will generally provide different rules for shareholder approval for different forms of transactions. Sometimes these requirements will have a strong influence on the form of the acquisition. With respect to the acquiring corporation, shareholder approval must generally be obtained in any situation where the articles of incorporation must be amended, where more than a certain percentage of the acquiring company's stock will be issued, or where the acquiring corporation is going to issue its own stock and does not have a sufficient amount of authorized but unissued stock or treasury stock.

In a stock transaction, there is generally no form of approval necessary unless the acquiring corporation is going to issue its own stock and has to amend its articles of incorporation. Any shareholder who wishes to sell his stock simply does so—there is no need to act through the corporation—and any shareholder who does not wish to sell his stock is not given any kind of appraisal right. This, however, is assuming that the articles of incorporation or other relevant documents do not contain any restrictions on the right to transfer shares. If there are such restrictions, they must be examined with this problem in mind.

Minority Stock Interests

In a stock transaction, the purchaser of the stock runs the risk of not being able to convince all of the selling shareholders to sell at a reasonable price. He may, therefore, wind up with only a portion of the stock, and outstanding minority shareholders may cause some harassment and administrative difficulties.

Securities Law Problems

There are two sets of securities regulations, the state securities laws and the federal securities laws.

The state securities laws should be examined to ascertain their exemptions and other requirements. If the acquiring corporation is going to issue stock or securities in the acquisition, there might be some state securities law registration requirement, and, because of the typical state securities law pattern of allowing the relevant authorities to investigate and pass on the fairness of a transaction, some substantive requirements may be present.

The federal securities laws must also be observed. If there is no exemption, the complete process of registration and proxy solicitation must be undertaken. If either company is listed on an exchange, the requirement of the exchange must also be satisfied.

In some situations, the necessity for compliance with state and federal securities laws may favor one form of transaction over another.

Preemptive Rights

Where the acquiring corporation issues additional shares, the preemptive rights question may be applicable. Some states provide that preemptive rights do not exist where stock is issued for consideration other than cash. In such a situation, there will probably be no problem, but the particular state statutes involved must be checked, and the preemptive rights question may influence the form of the transaction.

State and Local Tax Problems

Sometimes state and local tax considerations will favor conducting operations in a given state in the form of a separately incorporated subsidiary rather than a division, or vice versa. Naturally, this will affect the form of the transaction.

CORPORATE ACQUISITIONS: TAX FACTORS

Following is a brief listing of the more important federal income tax factors which are common to all types of corporate acquisitions:

Tax-free versus Taxable Transactions

The first question which must be addressed in any corporate acquisition is the question of whether or not the acquisition should be tax-free. There are three basic possibilities:

1. The transaction may be *fully taxable*. In this event, the seller will incur a taxable gain or a deductible loss which will generally be measured by the difference between his tax basis and the value of the consideration received in the transaction and which will generally be at the capital gains rate.

2. The transaction may be *completely tax-free*. If the transaction is structured in such a way as to satisfy all the technical requirements of the relevant provisions of the Internal Revenue Code, neither the selling corporation nor its shareholders will incur any tax in the transaction. Thus, if a transaction is properly structured, it is possible that the shareholder or shareholders of a small, closely held corporation whose tax basis in their stock is less than the fair market value of the corporation can completely sell out and receive in exchange marketable securities of a publicly traded corporation and pay no tax currently on the transaction. Of course, their basis in their new, publicly traded stock will be very low (generally equal to the basis of their stock in their old, closely held company), and when this new, publicly traded stock is sold, an appropriate capital gains tax must be paid.

3. The transaction may be *partly tax-free and partly taxable*. This type of transaction is not simply a combination of a tax-free transaction and a taxable transaction. Rather, it is a transaction which would be tax-free except for the fact that the selling shareholders receive something in addition to the voting stock of the acquiring corporation. This cash or other property is usually called "boot" in the tax jargon. In this situation, any shareholder who receives boot will have to pay a tax on the value of the boot to the extent of any gain inherent in the transaction. In addition, in some situations this tax will be assessed at ordinary income rather than capital gains rates. Sometimes boot is used intentionally in order to provide cash for one or more parties to the transaction. However, it can also arise contrary to plans on the fringe of the transaction. A frequent source of unintentional boot is the payment by the acquiring corporation of the expenses properly attributable to the shareholders of the selling corporation.

   Intentional boot can be illustrated by the acquisition of a small, closely held company by a larger company. Assume that the small, closely held company is owned by two shareholders, each of whom has a basis of $10,000 in his stock. The value of the company is currently $200,000. The acquiring corporation issues one of the shareholders $100,000 worth of its stock, and to the other shareholder it issues $95,000 of its stock and $5000 in cash. Assuming that all the other requirements of a tax-free reorganization are satisfied, the first shareholder, who received only stock, will not have to pay any tax at that time. The second shareholder, however, will have received $5000 in cash, and this amount will be taxable to him currently, possibly at ordinary income rates.

   One point which must be kept in mind in evaluating the three possibilities is that in many cases, boot will be taxed at ordinary income rates, whereas, in a completely taxable transaction, the capital gains rates will apply. It is possible, therefore, that a partly tax-free and partly taxable transaction will result in a greater tax than a completely taxable transaction.

Basis Problems

As a corollary to the tax-free nature of a tax-free reorganization, the basis of all the property involved (from which subsequent gain and depreciation will be figured) remains the same. This means that the seller receives a "substituted basis" for the shares which he receives in exchange for his old company's shares. That is, the seller's basis in the new stock which he receives will be the same as his basis in the old stock. Conversely, the acquiring corporation in this kind of transaction obtains a "carry-over basis" for the stock or assets which it acquires. In the case of stock, any gain upon a subsequent sale will be based on this carry-over basis. In the case of assets, all future depreciation will be based on this lower basis, resulting in a reduction of the depreciation which would otherwise be available.

From the purchaser's point of view, the tax-free nature of a transaction is generally a detriment because of the increased gain upon subsequent disposition of stock or assets and the smaller depreciation base available. In addition, even if the transaction is fully taxable, the purchaser will not have to pay any tax, the tax being imposed upon the seller. For this reason, the acquiring company will often be willing to pay a higher price if the transaction is taxable than if it is tax-free. If the transaction is partly tax-free and partly taxable, the purchasing corporation obtains a carry-through basis, but it will be increased by the amount of the gain recognized by all of the sellers.

Loss Carryovers

Where a corporation has incurred losses, these losses can generally be carried back to the three prior years to offset taxable income realized in those years. However, if after carrying back such losses there is still an amount remaining, the excess can be carried *forward* to the next seven years to offset future operating profits. These losses which are available as offsets against future profits are called operating loss carryovers. These operating loss carryovers may be extremely valuable if they can be used. However, there are a number of complicated rules which provide that the losses cannot be used in certain situations. Before amendments were made by the Tax Reform Act of 1976, the availability of these net operating loss carryovers and the restrictions on their use often, to a large part, dictated the form of any acquisition. However, extensive changes made in the law relating to loss carryovers in corporate acquisitions by the Tax Reform Act of 1976 have effectively reduced the availability of net operating loss carryovers in future corporate acquisitions to such an extent that this is not likely to be a substantial planning factor.

Following are the basic rules involving the carryover of net operating losses:

General Rule

The general rule is that in certain corporate transactions, the net operating loss carryover can be used by the surviving corporation. However, this rule is limited by the provisions of other sections of the Internal Revenue Code. The 1976 Tax Reform Act provides that:

1. The sole criterion for determining whether a loss company may continue to use its loss carryovers is whether the ownership of its stock has changed hands. Whether the loss company continues to carry on the same trade or business is irrelevant. (Under previous law this distinction was important.) Under the new law a change in stock ownership of at least 60 percent occurring over a three-year period will result in a cutback in the right of a loss company to carry over losses from prior years and for the year of change. The loss carryovers will be cut back on a pro rata basis as the change in ownership increases 60 percent to 100 percent. From 60 percent to 80 percent the cutback is 3½ percent for each percentage-point change in ownership, and from 80 percent to 100 percent the cutback is 1½ percent for each percentage-point change in ownership.

2. A parallel cutback provision is provided for in the case of the acquisition of the business of a loss company in a tax-free reorganization. Under the old law the availability of the loss carryovers is cut back unless the stockholders of the loss company acquire at least 20 percent of the stock of the acquiring company. Under the new law, which applies to tax-free reorganizations occurring on or after January 1, 1978, the threshold percentage is increased from 20 percent to 40 percent. For each percentage point by which the stockholders of the loss company wind up owning less than 40 percent of the stock of the acquiring company there is a cutback in the loss carryover available to the loss company after the reorganization. From 40 percent to 20 percent the cutback is 3½ percent for each percentage-point decrease, and from 20 percent to 0 the cutback is 1½ percent for each percentage-point decrease.

3. Under the old law, the ownership of the stock of a loss company can be changed in a stock-for-stock exchange qualifying as a "B" reorganization without the loss or cutback in the availability of loss carryovers. Under the new law, the acquisition of the stock of a loss company in a "B" reorganization is subject to the tax-free reorganization rules with the same cutback in the availability of the loss carryovers as would exist in an asset acquisition.

Since the normal business situation involves the acquisition of all the stock or assets of a loss company by an acquiring company, the amendments made by the new law and applicable to taxable reorganizations would seem to eliminate any advantage in acquiring the stock or assets of a loss company for the purpose of utilizing its loss carryovers. Accordingly, all the old lore about loss carryovers in corporate reorganizations is now obsolete.

Installment Reporting

In any taxable transaction, the availability of the installment-reporting sections of the Internal Revenue Code must be considered. Generally, in a sales transaction, the seller must report the entire amount of his gain in the year of the sale—even if what he actually receives is simply stock or a promissory note rather than cash. Of course, if the cash-basis seller receives a promissory note which is payable in installments over a number of years, he is entitled to discount that note and report gain on only its present value. However, this is still quite likely to result in a very high tax at a time when the seller has received no cash with which to pay it. If the transaction is properly structured, however, the seller may elect to report his gain as it is received under the installment-reporting sections of the code. In a very simplified example, a seller who sold an item in which his basis was $1000 and received a promissory note for $2000 payable in ten equal annual installments of $200 each would be able to report his $1000 gain over the period of the next ten years at the rate of $100 per year. In order to qualify for the installment-reporting method, the seller may not receive more than 30 percent of the sale price in the year of sale.

This presents some pitfalls. One is that the seller will receive almost 30 percent of the price in cash and some other indirect payment which had not been thought of which will push the total over 30 percent and destroy the installment election. An example would be the purchasers' agreeing to pay the seller's legal or accounting fees. Another pitfall is that the seller may receive a negotiable promissory note which, for purposes of the Internal Revenue Code, will be treated as if the seller had received cash. Generally, this will be the case in any situation where the note the seller receives is payable on demand, readily tradable, or otherwise immediately convertible into cash. If the note could easily be discounted at a local bank, for example, a problem would be present. A final pitfall in installment reporting is that a portion of the purchase price may be treated by the IRS as unstated interest under a section of the tax law which imputes interest where none is stated in the transaction if the situation warrants it. This could result in a reduction in the purchase price so that the seller may have received more than 30 percent of the sale price in the year of the sale. It is important therefore that the sale contract provide for adequate interest.

In an attempt to limit conglomerate acquisitions, the Tax Reform Act of 1969 amended the traditional rules of installment reporting as applied to corporate acquisitions. The section provides generally that receipt of bonds payable on demand or corporate obligations with interest coupons attached or in registered form will take the transaction out of the installment-reporting section. Before this new law was enacted, a taxable transaction using corporate bonds redeemable only after a long period—say 15 or 20 years—could have given the selling shareholders a "free ride" for a long time while giving the purchasing corporation a stepped-up basis in the stock or assets.

Depreciation Recapture

In taxable transactions, the depreciation-recapture sections of the code must be considered. These are extremely complicated, and there are different rules for personal and real property. The depreciation-recapture rules provide in substance that if property which has been the subject of depreciation is disposed of within a certain time, at a price greater than the adjusted basis (which is simply the cost less depreciation), the amount of this depreciation which the seller has now "recaptured" by virtue of the sale will have to be reported at ordinary income rates. In a greatly simplified example, if the taxpayer sells an item of personal property for $10,000 for which he previously paid $12,000, and has since taken $4000 as depreciation, he will have to report $2000 as ordinary income. (The $12,000 cost less the $4000 depreciation gives an adjusted basis of $8000, and the sale price of $10,000 exceeds this by $2000, which, if subject to the depreciation-recapture rules, would be taxed at ordinary income rates.)

The Use of Preferred Stock

Sometimes it will be desirable to give the shareholders of the company to be acquired preferred stock of the acquiring company as either part or all of the consideration. In this event, special problems are created under section 306 of the Internal Revenue Code, which provides that, in certain situations, the redemption or other disposition of the preferred stock will give rise to ordinary income. Generally, preferred stock which is received as a stock dividend will be characterized as section 306 stock and forever tainted so that upon a subsequent redemption or other disposition ordinary income will be realized. A similar problem can arise in a reorganization. Generally, however, in a properly structured transaction, the problem can be avoided.

Stock Dividends

The Tax Reform Act of 1969 amended section 305 of the Internal Revenue Code, dealing with stock dividends. Section 305 always provided that stock dividends were not taxable; however, there is now a section 305(b) which imposes substantial limitations and complications on this formerly simple rule. Generally speaking, if some shareholders have an *election* to receive stock or property, or if the *proportionate interests* of the shareholders are altered, a section 305 problem will be present. If section 305 applies, it will usually operate to impose an ordinary income tax on some or all of the participants in the transaction.

Code Section 279—Interest in Indebtedness Incurred by a Corporation to Acquire Stock or Assets of Another Corporation

In response to general concerns over the extent of conglomerate acquisitions, Congress enacted new code section 279 in the Tax Reform Act of 1969, *disallowing* a deduction for the interest payments on certain debt securities issued by a corporation in connection with the acquisition of the stock or assets of another corporation. Generally, the section applies only to certain bonds or debentures which have some *characteristics of equity*—such as convertibility or subordination. The section applies only if the interest exceeds $5 million.

CORPORATE REORGANIZATIONS: THE "A" REORGANIZATION

Perhaps the simplest and most straightforward way of combining two corporations in a tax-free reorganization is the "A" reorganization, or the statutory merger or consolidation. Mechanically, the transaction is accomplished by compliance with the relevant state statutes. Almost all states have relatively simple, straightforward procedures pursuant to which two companies may be combined. Generally the procedure is simply to draft articles of merger (or an agreement of merger) which, in some states, become the articles of incorporation of the surviving or consolidated company. Each corporation then approves the agreement of merger as necessary according to state law, and the agreement is filed with the appropriate state official—generally the secretary of state. In the simplest form of statutory merger, the shareholders of the company to be acquired trade in their shares in the old company for new shares in the surviving company at an agreed-upon exchange ratio. When the mechanics of the transaction are completed, the surviving corporation and the acquired company will comprise one neat corporate entity. This surviving corporation will own all the assets and be liable for all of the debts of the acquired company.

In a simple merger, even cautious tax counsel will sometimes advise that no ruling be requested. If a ruling is requested, it is generally one of the easiest to obtain. In addition to being one of the simplest forms of tax-free reorganization, it is also one of the most flexible. There is no "solely-for-voting-stock" requirement as there is in a "B" reorganization, and it is possible, with certain qualifications, for the shareholders of the company to be acquired to be given nonvoting stock, securities, or other property, including cash, without destroying the tax-free nature of the reorganization. Of course, if the shareholders receive cash or other property, a boot distribution problem will be present, and they may receive ordinary income to the extent of the distribution of cash or other property. However, unlike the rules in "B" or "C" reorganizations, the use of nonvoting stock or other property will not destroy the tax-free nature of the entire transaction but will only impose income tax on the particular shareholder who receives the cash.

Another point which adds to the flexibility is the ability in an "A" reorganization to transfer all or any portion of the assets which are acquired to a controlled subsidiary. Thus, a statutory merger with a subsequent transfer of the assets into a controlled subsidiary can achieve the same result as the complex and very restricted "B" reorganization and the mechanically complex "C" reorganization.

There is no requirement that substantially all the assets of the target company be acquired. In a "C" reorganization, this requirement is present, and if the target company has substantial assets which are not desired, these cannot be stripped off immediately before the acquisition as they can in an "A" reorganization.

Potential Problems

While the "A" reorganization is relatively simple and flexible, it does have certain potential problems. These can be briefly listed as follows:

Potential Liabilities

From a business point of view, perhaps the largest single problem with a statutory merger is that the surviving company will automatically, as a matter of law, become completely liable to the extent of all the assets of the combined companies for all the debts and liabilities—both known and unknown, fixed and contingent—of the company to be acquired. On the other hand, in a properly structured "C" reorganization, the surviving company can acquire only the assets of the company to be acquired and be completely free from any unwanted debts or liabilities. In a "B" reorganization, if the stock of the selling company is acquired and the selling company is operated as a subsidiary, the extent of the acquiring company's liability for debts and liabilities of the selling firm is limited to the assets of the acquired firm.

Possible Boot

Another potential problem with an "A" reorganization is the question of whether a particular item is an *assumption of a liability* on the one hand or *additional consideration* on the other. Of course, if it is not an assumption of liability but an additional consideration, it will be considered boot and taxed to the recipient, generally as ordinary income. The payment by the purchasing corporation of the selling corporation's expenses of reorganization is one item which sometimes generates this question. If an "A" reorganization is involved, all that will be at stake will be the potential tax, possibly at ordinary income rates, on the particular disputed item. However, in a "B" or "C" reorganization, it is possible that the characterization of a particular item as the payment of additional consideration will destroy the tax-free nature of the entire transaction.

The Business-Purpose Requirement

This requirement, as its name implies, requires some kind of legitimate business purpose for the transaction. In most situations, this will not present any problem. However, if the transaction really does not accomplish anything, has as its principal motive some kind of tax-avoidance scheme, is really a sham for something else, or is otherwise some kind of device which merely uses the form of corporate reorganization as a disguise, the tax-free nature of the transaction may be destroyed.

Continuity-of-Interest Requirement

The continuity-of-interest requirement provides, in substance, that in order for the transaction to be tax-free, the shareholders of the company to be acquired must have some kind of continuity of interest with the surviving corporation. In the simple situation where the shareholders of the acquired corporation are given stock in the new corporation, the continuity-of-interest requirement is clearly met. However, under at least some state laws, there is no requirement that the shareholders of the company to be acquired be given stock, *or any equity interest at all,* in the surviving corporation. Instead, they can be given bonds, part cash and part bonds, or some other form of short term note or security. In this event, the Supreme Court has held that the continuity-of-interest rule is not satisfied and the shareholders of the acquired company become mere creditors of the surviving corporation. The continuity-of-interest rule does not apply to each shareholder, but instead applies to the shareholders as a group, and generally, if the shareholders as a group retain at least 50 percent of the value of the disappearing corporation's outstanding stock in some form of equity interest in the surviving corporation, the rule will be satisfied. It is not necessary that the equity interest be common stock. It can be preferred stock or nonvoting common stock.

The continuity-of-interest requirement must be met both at the time of the reorganization and for some reasonable period thereafter. If the transaction is structured in such a way as to satisfy the continuity-of-interest requirement immediately after the reorganization, and then, pursuant to some previously planned scheme, all the shareholders immediately sell their equity interests, the requirement will not be met and there is a danger that the tax-free nature of the merger may be retroactively destroyed. This rule, however, is only applicable in rather severe cases. Generally, it is a real danger where there is some preexisting plan for a rather prompt subsequent disposition of the stock acquired by the selling shareholders. It is clear that minor sales of stock acquired pursuant to the statutory merger will not destroy the tax-free nature of the transaction if there is some change of circumstances or legitimate business reason for the subsequent sales.

Step-Transaction Doctrine

As in all areas of the tax law, transactions cannot be fragmented into "steps," even if those steps standing alone would satisfy all the technical requirements of the tax laws. Instead, if what is obviously a single transaction is so fragmented, it will be restructured by the Internal Revenue Service into its proper single transaction and taxed accordingly. However, since there is no requirement in an "A" reorganization that the acquisition be solely for voting stock, that substantially all the assets of the target company be acquired, or that the acquiring corporation end up in control of the acquired corporation following the transaction, the step-transaction doctrine will seldom, if ever, be applicable to a statutory merger, at least in the sense of destroying its tax-free nature. In some cases, however, the step-transaction doctrine might operate *in reverse* to characterize what might be otherwise a group of taxable transactions into a tax-free "A" reorganization.

Depreciation Recapture

Since a statutory merger is a tax-free transaction, the depreciation-recapture sections will not generally apply. However, if property which would otherwise be subject to depreciation recapture is distributed as boot to the shareholders of the disappearing corporation, then the depreciation-recapture sections do apply.

Carryovers

A statutory merger is one of the transactions in which the net operating loss carryover can be used by the surviving corporation if all the appropriate requirements previously discussed are met.

Section 306 Stock

Since it is possible in a statutory merger to use preferred stock, it is possible for the preferred stock to be section 306 stock. If it is, the proceeds received by any shareholder upon a subsequent redemption or sale may be treated as ordinary income. Generally speaking, the section 306 stock problem can be avoided in a statutory merger. If the stock of the issuing corporation is widely held and the section 306 stock by its terms is not redeemable for a period of at least five years from the date of issuance, a ruling can usually be obtained which will remove the section 306 stock danger.

Mergers of Related Corporations

For purposes of this discussion, it is assumed that the two companies involved are unrelated companies. It is possible to have a merger of a subsidiary into a parent or of a parent into a subsidiary or a merger between two brother-sister corporations. These types of mergers between related parties have all the problems of mergers between unrelated parties plus certain additional complications.

The general problem with a merger between a subsidiary and a parent corporation concerns the solvency of the subsidiary and the question of whether the transaction is a merger or a liquidation. Generally, the IRS treats the merger of a subsidiary into a parent as a liquidation rather than as a merger—even though for state law purposes the transaction may take the form of a statutory merger.

If the corporation to be acquired must be stripped of some of its assets, and it is determined that the appropriate method to accomplish this is a tax-free spin-off or some other divisive reorganization under section 355 (discussed in Chapter 35), certain additional problems are present. Generally, however, these problems involve only the status of the divisive reorganization. Subject to some qualification, it is generally possible to couple a tax-free divisive reorganization under section 355 and a tax-free "A" reorganization without destroying the tax-free nature of either transaction. However, the only question in this regard involves the tax-free status of the divisive reorganization. The rule is sometimes contrary if the tax-free divisive reorganization is followed by a "C" reorganization.

Summary

In spite of all the new and sophisticated developments under section 368 which permit reverse mergers, subsidiary mergers, and all kinds of variations on these, the simple two-party statutory merger in which the target company is merged into the acquiring company still has a lot of advantages. It is one of the most flexible forms of corporate reorganization; it is mechanically very simple; it is generally easily understood by all the parties involved, and it is generally very easy to get a ruling on the transaction. It can be made complex by the use of contingent stock, escrowed stock, section 306 stock, and the distribution of other property including cash. However, it can also be a very simple mechanical surrender of the common stock of one company for the common stock of another.

CORPORATE REORGANIZATIONS: THE "B" REORGANIZATION

The "B" reorganization, or the stock-for-stock transaction, is defined in section 368(a)(1)(B) of the Internal Revenue Code as

> the acquisition by one corporation, in exchange *solely* for all or a part of its *voting stock* (or in exchange solely for all or a part of the voting stock of a corporation which is in control of the acquiring corporation), of stock of another corporation if, immediately after the acquisition, the acquiring corporation has *control* of such other corporation (whether or not such acquiring corporation had control immediately before the acquisition). [Emphasis added]

This definition raises two problems: the solely-for-voting-stock requirement, and the requirement that "control" of the acquired corporation be obtained. Also, the use of *contingent stock*, a triangular merger involving a subsidiary of the acquiring company, and the liquidation of a newly acquired company into the parent generate certain additional problems. In addition to these problems, which have their principal application to a "B" reorganization, all the other problems previously mentioned as common to reorganizations in general will be relevant to the "B" reorganization.

The Solely-for-Voting-Stock Requirement

The solely-for-voting-stock requirement has two aspects: the *definition* of voting stock, and the problem of *additional consideration*. In general, the term "voting stock" means any kind of stock which normally carries the right to vote in the election of the directors. The stock will not qualify as "voting stock" if its voting rights are conditioned on some future developments, such as the amount of earnings or dividend payments. A typical problem is with preferred stock which carries the right to elect directors only if the dividends thereon are in arrears. This kind of stock is certainly not voting stock if the dividends are not actually in arrears at the time in question, and there is even some question as to whether it would be considered voting stock if the dividends were actually in arrears.

The actual voting power of the stock (as opposed to voting rights) is usually not relevant. It is therefore possible to have two classes of voting stock, one having the actual power to control the corporation, and the other, while having the right to vote, not having any actual power because the voting rights are diluted. But the stock probably does have to have a right to a *significant* participation in the management of the company.

Of course, the stock in question must actually be stock, and if it is merely termed stock but is really a debt instrument, it will not satisfy the requirements. This would probably be the case in a situation where a class of stock was created which did have voting rights but had no rights to any dividends or to assets upon liquidation of the company.

Convertible bonds do not constitute voting stock.

Consideration in Addition to Voting Stock

The general rule in a "B" reorganization is that the acquiring corporation may pay, and the acquired corporation's shareholders may receive, *only* voting stock. This requirement is very strictly construed and there are only minor and limited exceptions. Generally, the basic transaction can be easily structured to provide for a simple stock-for-stock exchange. However, difficulties arise on the fringe of the transaction and in certain other ancillary transactions. Generally, there will be a problem where the acquiring corporation pays something which can be characterized as a liability *of the selling shareholders* or where the stock-for-stock acquisition is accompanied by some other side deal which amounts to a sale of a small asset for a large price. The following is a list of some of the troublesome areas:

Fractional Shares

In a genuine situation, cash may be paid by the acquiring corporation in a "B" reorganization in lieu of the issuance of fractional shares. However, this must be limited to the rounding off of the fractional shares for accounting purposes.

Expenses Incidental to the Reorganization

In addition to the purchase price, a corporate reorganization generally involves a substantial amount of expenses. These may include brokers' fees or finders' fees, legal fees, accounting fees, and state stock transfer taxes. Extreme care must be exercised in the payment of these expenses, because the acquiring corporation cannot pay any expenses considered directly attributable to the shareholders of the acquired corporation; and the Internal Revenue Service's published statements on this issue should be strictly followed. If this rule is violated, there is a potential that the shareholders of the acquired corporation will have received something in addition to the voting stock, and the entire tax-free nature of the reorganization will be destroyed.

If reorganization expenses directly attributable to the acquired corporation's shareholders are paid not by the selling shareholders or by the acquiring corporation but instead by the acquired corporation, there is a possibility that such payment will be deemed a constructive dividend to the shareholders of the acquired corporation.

Registration of Stock

In some cases, the acquiring corporation will be issuing stock which has not been previously registered with the Federal Securities and Exchange Commission. If such stock is not registered, its marketability is extremely restricted, and the selling shareholders may be reluctant to accept this kind of stock. In such a case, it is sometimes agreed that at some future time, the acquiring corporation will cause the stock to be registered. This will generally cost a substantial amount of money, and it might be argued that since it is for the benefit of the shareholders of the acquired corporation, they have received something in addition to voting stock. However, the Internal Revenue Service agrees that a covenant to register stock will not be additional consideration to the selling shareholders in a "B" reorganization.

Employment Contracts

In many situations, the acquiring corporation will desire to retain the services of key employees of the acquired corporation, and those employees may also want the security of an employment contract with the acquiring corporation. To the extent that these employees are shareholders of the acquired corporation, a problem may result because, in addition to receiving voting stock, they will have received an employment contract. Theoretically, the "B" reorganization and the employment contract should be different and unrelated transactions. However, if the employment contract calls for an unreasonably large compensation to be paid in the light of the services to be performed, the two transactions may be put together, and it will be contended by the IRS that the shareholder does receive consideration in addition to voting stock.

Stock Options

Generally, the assumption by the acquiring corporation of the stock options previously granted by the acquired corporation will not cause the tax-free nature of a "B" reorganization to be destroyed.

Control

The second problem raised by the definition of a "B" reorganization is the acquisition of *control*. There can be no tax-free "B" reorganization unless the acquiring corporation acquires control of the acquired corporation. Control is defined by the Internal Revenue Code as at least 80 percent of the stock representing the voting power of a corporation and at least 80 percent of the total number of shares of all other classes of stock. This latter phrase has been interpreted to mean 80 percent of the total number of shares of each of the other classes of stock of the corporation.

This raises the problem of "creeping control." It is clear that the control requirement may be satisfied in stages; thus, it is possible to acquire 80 percent of the ownership of a company by various steps over a reasonably limited period of time and pursuant to a common plan. However, this does raise certain problems. The first question is, "What time period would be permissible?" Here the regulations suggest twelve months. The next problem is that the acquisitions must be made pursuant to a single preexisting plan. Each of the series of acquisitions must somehow be fitted into this single preexisting plan. However, this is complicated by the fact that each step must satisfy the solely-for-voting-stock requirement if it is part of the single preexisting plan. In the event that some acquisition of shares is made for cash or in some other manner which would not satisfy the requirements of the "B" reorganization, this part of the series must be removed from the single preexisting plan. As an example of this situation, it would probably be permissible for a corporation independently and without any intention of acquiring control of a certain corporation to purchase 5 percent of the shares of that corporation, and at some point substantially later in time and after a plan of acquisition had been formulated, to acquire control of the acquired corporation. In this event, if all other requirements incident to a "B" reorganization were satisfied, the transaction would probably be tax-free. On the other hand, if it could be shown that the initial acquisition of 5 percent for cash was made as a part of or as a prelude to acquisition of control of the company, this would destroy the tax-free nature of the transaction.

This sort of theory can also operate in reverse in the context of a later cash acquisition. If the corporation enters into a "B" reorganization transaction and acquires 80 percent of the voting stock of the company to be acquired and then subsequently purchases some additional shares for cash, there is a danger that these two transactions will be lumped together, destroying the tax-free nature of the transaction.

The attribution rules do not apply to the acquisition of control of the acquiring corporation. Thus, it is necessary that control must be acquired by one corporation, not by two or more corporations, even if they are related under traditional attribution-of-ownership rules.

Thin Incorporation

Where the acquired corporation is closely held and where it is possible that some of the loans made by the shareholders to the corporation are really equity securities, an obvious problem will be presented if a "B" reorganization is attempted. In this situation, if a company were to acquire all the outstanding stock in a stock-for-stock transaction, and it were later determined that some of the "debt" was really equity, it may turn out that the acquiring corporation had failed to acquire the requisite 80 percent of the voting stock.

General Problems

As in any tax-free reorganization, the business-purpose requirement is applicable to a "B" reorganization. Because of its technical requirements, however, the continuity-of-interest problem is not usually presented. The concept of boot has no application to a "B" reorganization. Generally, if there is boot, there is no "B" reorganization. Also, since only stock is involved, the depreciation-recapture rules are not applicable to a "B" reorganization except to the extent that the potential recapture inherent in the acquired corporation's assets may affect the value of the consideration to be received by the acquired corporation's shareholders.

Section 306 Stock

It is possible in a "B" reorganization for the acquiring corporation to give voting preferred stock in exchange for the stock of the company to be acquired. Thus, there may possibly be a section 306 stock problem in connection with a "B" reorganization. However, in a properly structured transaction, the section 306 problem can be avoided and a ruling obtained from the Internal Revenue Service that the preferred stock will not be considered section 306 stock.

Carryovers

As previously noted, the Tax Reform Act of 1976 amended the net operating loss carryover rules to include a "B" reorganization even though the same corporate entity remains intact. Therefore, under the new rules, the acquired corporation will lose its operating loss carryovers if the ownership changes.

Contingent Stock

In some cases, it is useful to provide for the issuance of additional shares of stock upon certain events. Examples are situations where the acquired company has certain unliquidated or contingent liabilities or where the acquired corporation contends that its future operations would be more profitable than the acquiring corporation is willing to concede at the time of the acquisition. Contingent stock can also be used in a situation where the stock of the acquiring company is alleged to be depressed. Thus, the parties may agree that additional stock will be issued if the market price of the stock of the acquiring company does not reach a certain value by a certain time. The rules on the use of contingent stock are complex, but there is a Revenue Procedure which sets forth rather clearly the conditions upon which an advanced ruling will be granted, and if these conditions are satisfied, it is possible to use contingent stock in a "B" reorganization.

Triangular "B" Reorganizations

In some situations, a simple two-party "B" reorganization may not be desirable. An example would be a case where the acquired corporation might have substantial undisclosed or contingent liabilities. In this event, it might be desirable to have a subsidiary corporation hold the stock of the company to be acquired. This can be done in two ways: the acquiring corporation can transfer all or a portion of the stock acquired to a control subsidiary; or a subsidiary may be created, the stock of the parent transferred to it, and the "B" reorganization accomplished directly between the subsidiary and the company to be acquired.

Liquidation of the Acquired Corporation after a "B" Reorganization

After a "B" reorganization is completed, the parties will generally end up in the relation of parent and subsidiary, and at a future time it may be desired that the subsidiary be liquidated into the parent. Normally, this could be done as a simple tax-free liquidation of the subsidiary, and all the rules incident to such a liquidation of the subsidiary would be applicable. However, if a "B" reorganization is followed by a liquidation of the subsidiary into the parent, the IRS would probably take the position that the transaction was, in reality, a stock-for-assets transaction (or a "C" reorganization), which would be tax-free, if at all, according to the requirements for such a "C" reorganization. Generally, the characterization of a transaction as a "C" reorganization rather than a "B" reorganization will not destroy its tax-free nature because, at least to some extent, consideration other than voting stock can be given in a "C" reorganization while this is not possible in a "B" reorganization. However, there are some situations where the characterization of a transaction as a "C" reorganization would destroy its tax-free nature. This may be the case where liabilities of the acquired corporation are assumed or where there have been redemptions prior to the reorganization. It is possible in a "B" reorganization to redeem some of the shareholders out before the "B" reorganization is accomplished, and the assumption of liabilities of the acquired corporation in a "B" reorganization is usually not material. However, in a "C" reorganization, the assumption of liabilities does create some problems, and if there have been a substantial number of redemptions prior to the transaction, it may be held that the acquiring corporation did not acquire substantially all of the assets of the acquired corporation because it did not acquire the assets which were used to redeem the stock of the acquired corporation.

CORPORATE REORGANIZATIONS: THE "C" REORGANIZATION

A "C" reorganization is defined as the acquisition by one corporation, in exchange *solely* for all or part of its *voting* stock, of substantially all the *properties* of another corporation. In many respects, a "C" reorganization is similar to a statutory merger and is, in fact, sometimes referred to as a "practical merger." In a simplified example of a "C" reorganization, the assets of the transferor or acquired corporation simply become a part of the assets of the acquiring corporation, and the acquiring corporation's stock is transferred to the shareholders of the acquired corporation, either directly or by issuance of stock to the transferor corporation, which in turn makes the distribution to its shareholders. The end result is, therefore, very similar to a merger, where substantially the same mechanical steps take place. However, there are certain fundamental differences. One difference is that in the merger, the assets become a part of the acquiring corporation as a matter of law, and there is no need to actually physically transfer each asset by a bill of sale, a deed, or other appropriate means. In a "C" reorganization, on the other hand, each asset must be transferred to the acquiring corporation. Obviously, in a situation where there are a great many motor vehicles, parcels of real estate, or other items of property which require some sort of mechanical transfer, this can be a significant problem. Another fundamental difference is that in a "C" reorganization, all that is generally acquired is *the assets* of the selling company; if any liabilities are assumed, they are limited to *known* liabilities. On the other hand, in a statutory merger, or "A" reorganization, all of the assets together with all of the liabilities (known or unknown) of the acquired corporation are folded into the acquiring corporation.

These differences suggest the principal kinds of situations where a "C" reorganization will be desirable. Generally, a "C" reorganization will be desirable when, and only when, there is an overriding desire to acquire only assets and to avoid the acquisition of any kind of liabilities of the acquired corporation—particularly unknown or hidden liabilities.

The definition of a "C" reorganization raises two principal problems. These are the substantially-all-of-the-properties requirement and the solely-for-voting-stock requirement.

The Solely-for-Voting-Stock Requirement

The solely-for-voting-stock requirement in a "C" reorganization is substantially the same as that in a "B" reorganization, and substantially the same kinds of problems are presented. These problems include the question of when stock is voting stock and when consideration in addition to the voting stock will be involved. As in a "B" reorganization, consideration in addition to the voting stock may be found on the fringe of the transaction in the form of an assumption of a liability or the payment of an expense which is properly attributable to the shareholders of the acquired corporation or in various ancillary transactions where assets are purchased or services performed with payments greatly in excess of their real value. Two of the principal problem areas are employment contracts and the payment of attorneys' fees, accounting fees, or other expenses incurred on behalf of shareholders in connection with the reorganization. However, there is one important addition to the solely-for-voting-stock requirement when applied to a "C" reorganization. This is the so-called 20 percent rule described in section 368(a)(2)(B) of the Internal Revenue Code. This rule provides that a corporation whose assets are being acquired in a "C" reorganization can receive, in addition to voting stock, cash or other property without destroying the nontaxable nature of the transaction if the property for which the voting stock was transferred has a value of at least 80 percent of the fair market value of all the transferor corporation's properties. This 20 percent rule is substantially limited by the additional requirement that, in determining whether the 80 percent test is met, liabilities assumed by the acquiring corporation, or liabilities attaching to the property received by it, are treated as if they constituted cash paid to the transferor corporation. Thus, if additional consideration, however small, is paid, liabilities are then treated as cash for purposes of making the 20 percent statutory computation. If there is no additional consideration, liabilities are simply not considered, even though they represent a substantial percentage of the corporation's assets. In a simplified example, if one corporation were to acquire all the assets of another corporation, valued at $500,000, in exchange for voting stock valued at $400,000 and $100,000 in cash, the acquisition would qualify as a "C" reorganization as long as the acquiring corporation neither assumed any liabilities of the acquired corporation nor took any of its property subject to any of the liabilities. However, if the acquiring corporation assumed even $1 of liabilities in this transaction, or took property subject to any liabilities, the transaction would fail to qualify as a "C" reorganization, because any such liabilities would be treated as additional cash pushing the total over 20 percent.

The Substantially-All-of-the-Properties Requirement

The second definitional problem of the "C" reorganization is the substantially-all-of-the-properties requirement. The IRS uses a percentage-of-assets test for ruling purposes and defines the substantially-all requirement to mean at least 90 percent of the fair market value of the gross assets held by the transferor corporation immediately preceding the transfer. Note that it is the fair market value of the assets and not their basis or cost which is controlling and that intangible assets including good will are considered. Because of the substantially-all requirement, it is difficult to carry out a tax-free "C" reorganization where the corporation whose assets are acquired has assets which are unwanted by the acquiring company. Dividends and redemptions occurring within a reasonable period of time before the reorganization might be attacked as attempts to dispose of assets unwanted by the acquiring company, and this might be held a violation of the substantially-all requirement.

Operating Assets

Recent judicial decisions indicate that only the operating assets of the business are considered in making the substantially-all computations. Thus, where a corporation has "investment" assets, such as real estate or other unrelated securities, these—at least according to the courts—can be excluded from the computation.

Assets Retained to Pay Liabilities

The courts have also indicated that the substantially-all requirement is applied to those assets which remain after a retention of a sufficient amount to pay the liabilities which are not assumed by the acquiring corporation. The IRS appears to agree with this position. Of course, the assets retained must not be excessive in relation to the liabilities involved.

The various requirements set forth above can create some rather difficult problems in a "C" reorganization. An example would be a corporation having gross assets of $1 million and liabilities of $900,000. If the acquiring corporation were to refuse to assume any liabilities, it could acquire only $100,000 of assets. In one case involving substantially this situation, the court (with Internal Revenue Service support) indicated that this would probably not come within the definition of a "C" reorganization. In this kind of situation, the acquiring corporation might have to take the assets subject to the liabilities and discharge the liabilities with the assets required. This might seem a bit inconsistent with the general theory of using the "C" reorganization only where assets alone are wanted and it is not desired to assume any liabilities. However, in most situations it is not the *known* liabilities which create the problems; it is the *unknown* or the *contingent* liabilities. In a "C" reorganization, certain known liabilities, such as mortgages or outstanding loans secured by personal property, can be specifically assumed and discharged with the assets acquired without creating an undue risk on the part of the acquiring corporation of assuming some kind of unknown, contingent, and potentially very large unanticipated liability.

If the Selling Company Stays Alive

According to one theory, the substantially-all requirement is applied more strictly if the transferor corporation continues in existence (as it is entitled to do in a "C" reorganization) and its assets are retained. The theory here seems to be that the company to be acquired must, at least as a practical matter, go out of business, or otherwise it would be possible to create a divisive reorganization without complying with section 355 of the Internal Revenue Code, which specifically applies to divisive reorganizations. Thus, if the acquired company retains assets which would be sufficient to run a business, a problem is presented. Under this theory, not only the percentage of assets but also their total dollar amount is significant.

The Use of a Subsidiary

Triangular "C" reorganizations are permissible. This can involve either a "C" reorganization between two companies with a subsequent transfer of the assets so acquired into a subsidiary of the acquiring corporation formed before the reorganization, or the contribution by the parent of the parent's stock into the subsidiary and the acquisition of the assets of the company to be acquired in exchange for the parent company's stock directly from the subsidiary.

Acquisition of a Partly Owned Company

Where the acquiring corporation has already obtained some of the stock of the company to be acquired, a "C" reorganization must be handled with extreme care. The biggest problem here is that if the acquired corporation is liquidated after the "C" reorganization, the acquiring corporation may be said to have acquired part of the transferor's assets in *liquidation* rather than solely for voting stock so as to destroy the "C" reorganization. It is possible that this difficulty may be avoided by simply keeping the transferor corporation alive or by using the control subsidiary device. It is also possible that the 20 percent boot-relaxation rule indicated above might serve to protect the acquiring corporation if it owns a small part of the transferor's stock.

General Tax Problems

The general tax problems incident to all corporate reorganizations have been previously mentioned in connection with "A" and "B" reorganizations, and few, if any, special problems are presented if a "C" reorganization is used.

SUBSIDIARY MERGERS

While the previously described transactions are sometimes referred to as "simple" reorganizations, there are many situations where an acquisition can be made very complicated, if not impossible, if the "simple" two-party method must be used. Examples of such situations include those that involve companies which have important nontransferable assets such as contracts, franchises, permits, or licenses; or companies which have many contracts which may not all be assignable or would require a large amount of paper work to accomplish any assignment. In addition, some companies have potentially large contingent liabilities or engage in businesses where potential uninsurable liabilities can be very large. In these situations, a simple two-party reorganization can present difficulties and problems which are often insurmountable. In most of the cases a three-party reorganization involving the acquired company, the acquiring company, and a specially formed subsidiary will solve most of the problems.

As an example of the above discussion, assume that a conglomerate company wishes to acquire a company which has as its principal business advantage a very large and favorable contract which either is unassignable or requires consent for assignment, which consent would be impossible or expensive to obtain. In addition, the company engages in a business which involves substantial exposures to large liabilities which are difficult to insure. Examples would be offshore oil well drilling, operation of oil tankers (the danger being that an oil spill would cause expensive damage) or the manufacture of critical parts for large aircraft, the malfunction of which could cause the loss of many lives. The following would be relevant factors in determining the best type of reorganization:

1. Quite obviously, the corporate existence of the corporation to be acquired must remain intact. This rules out a merger into the parent or into a subsidiary of the parent. Thus a normal "A" reorganization can be ruled out.

2. The company could not sell all of its assets, because of the provision against assignment of the contract. Thus a "C" reorganization can be ruled out.

3. In many situations involving the above factors, it would be theoretically possible to accomplish the acquisition by a "B" reorganization. However, the technical requirements for a "B" reorganization generate many significant problems, including the requirement for affirmative action by 80 percent of the acquired company's shareholders, more than either an "A" or "C" reorganization; the fact that some of the shares will probably not be exchanged, thus preserving a group of minority shareholders; and the need to meet a very strict solely-for-voting-stock test.

Therefore, in the above situation, neither an "A" nor a "C" reorganization will be possible, and it would be very advantageous to find a suitable alternative to a "B" reorganization. A possible solution to this problem is what is referred to as a reverse triangular merger, or simply a reverse merger.

The mechanics are substantially as follows. The acquiring company forms a new subsidiary and transfers its stock to the subsidiary in exchange for all the shares of the subsidiary. The newly formed subsidiary is then merged into the company to be acquired, and the company to be acquired issues its stock to the stockholder of the subsidiary (the acquiring parent corporation). Thus the company to be acquired winds up as the surviving corporation, with its shares being owned by the acquiring parent. (The exact procedure can be varied considerably and must satisfy the relevant state law. Some states have merger statutes which may inhibit or prohibit subsidiary mergers, and this point should be checked early in the planning.) This accomplishes the following objectives:

1. The corporate existence of the company to be acquired is not changed, and so there is no problem with transferring any contracts.

2. To the maximum extent possible, the parent company has limited its exposure to the liabilities of the company to be acquired. The acquiring parent is simply the stockholder of the company to be acquired, and, subject to the general rules on liability of a parent corporation for the liabilities of its subsidiary, it should have accomplished its objective of limiting liability for problems created by the subsidiary to the assets of the subsidiary and not exposed the assets of the parent to these dangers.

The above transaction is accomplished by means of a statutory merger of the newly formed subsidiary into the company to be acquired. If the corporate existence of the company to be acquired need not be maintained but it is desired to operate the acquired company as a subsidiary rather than as a division, the transaction can be reversed, with the target company merging into the newly formed subsidiary.

Background

It is only recently that the above, relatively simple and advantageous procedures were sanctioned by the Internal Revenue Code. The subsidiary acquisition (that is, the merger of a company to be acquired into a subsidiary of the parent) was possible in a "C" reorganization under the 1954 Code, and in a "B" reorganization under the Revenue Act of 1964. However, the difficulties with a "B" reorganization have already been mentioned, and a "C" reorganization in which the acquired assets end up in a subsidiary is an extremely complicated transaction.

There were some roundabout ways to accomplish a subsidiary merger and a reverse subsidiary merger, but they depended upon structuring the transaction very carefully and qualifying them under the provisions for "B" and "C" reorganizations. Therefore, the strict rules of "B" and "C" reorganizations still had to be met.

However, because of technical problems with the Internal Revenue Code, a subsidiary merger (either forward or reverse) was impossible because of some old cases which held that in such a situation, the parent corporation was not a party to the merger and therefore the transfer of its stock was not tax-free. This problem was partially solved in 1968 with the addition of section 368(a)(2)(D) to the Internal Revenue Code, which made a forward subsidiary merger possible. The problem was further relieved by the addition of section 368(a)(2)(E) to the code in 1971, allowing the reverse subsidiary merger.

Unfortunately, the statement that a merger of a company to be acquired into a subsidiary, or a reverse merger of the subsidiary into the company to be acquired, is now allowed as a modified "A" reorganization is oversimplified and misleading. From a theoretical standpoint, there is absolutely no reason why the above-mentioned amendments could not have simply allowed as a tax-free "A" reorganization a subsidiary merger of either the forward or reverse type. However, instead of doing this, the code provisions created for these subsidiary mergers certain qualifications and extra requirements which are not required in a regular two-party merger and which are somewhat difficult to understand in that they do not seem to plug any "loopholes" or to otherwise further any legitimate tax objective. As a result, instead of simply having the three types of reorganization previously mentioned ("A," "B," and "C") with the added proviso that any could be accomplished by the use of a subsidiary, we now really have two additional types of reorganization which, while depending upon compliance with state corporate merger requirements, are really different from a standard two-party merger. It is probably substantially accurate to say that the technical differences between a standard two-party merger and a subsidiary merger (forward or reverse) will not be particularly significant in most situations. However, in certain situations, the slight differences that do exist can be very important, and in all transactions it is important to make certain that all the technical requirements of the subsidiary merger are met.

CHAPTER THIRTY-THREE

CORPORATE REORGANIZATIONS: POST-CLOSING ADJUSTMENTS

POST-CLOSING ADJUSTMENTS IN THE TRANSACTION

On occasion, it will be impossible or impractical to make a final deal in a corporate acquisition. There may be fundamental disagreements as to the earning potential of one or both companies. The acquired company may not be willing to assume that the current market price of the stock of the acquiring company will represent the real value of the stock—especially if the market price has been volatile in the past. There may be undefinable or unascertainable contingent liabilities, or there may be an attack on the transaction by a government agency dictating a recision of the deal—for example, an attack on the basis of a violation of the antitrust laws. In these and other situations, it is possible to build some post-closing flexibility into the transaction. The following are the basic working tools; of course, infinite variations are possible.

1. Contingent Stock. The acquiring corporation offers to issue additional stock to the shareholders of the acquired corporation if certain favorable subsequent events occur, such as increased earnings or favorable resolution of contingent liabilities; or if certain unfavorable events occur, such as a sharp drop in the market price of the stock of the acquired company.

2. Escrowed Stock. Some of the stock which is issued is placed into escrow to be released only on certain future conditions. For example, a certain number of shares could be placed into escrow to be released if earnings of the acquired corporation were to reach a certain level by a certain time. If earnings did not reach the desired level at the indicated time, the stock would revert back to the acquired company.

3. Rights of Recision or Other Modification Built into the Agreement. By this tool, the acquisition agreement itself provides that the deal can be canceled after certain occurrences, such as an allegation by the Federal Trade Commission or the Department of Justice that the proposed merger violates the anti-trust laws. Generally, if this sort of provision applies only before the actual exchange of stock, it creates no problems. However, if it applies after the exchange, so that "the egg must be unscrambled," serious questions are raised.

4. Warranties or other undertakings may be obtained from the selling shareholders.

5. Convertible preferred stock may be issued with the conversion rates tied to subsequent events.

The following is a brief discussion of the fundamentals of these procedures.

Contingent and Escrowed Stock

There are elaborate Internal Revenue Service policies on the use of contingent and escrowed stock as a means of adjusting a reorganization after the fact. However, these rules are generally quite reasonable, and since they are stated clearly, it is generally possible to have an agreement which calls either for the issuance of contingent stock (perhaps if the acquired company meets certain profit goals) or for the holding of stock in escrow for issuance to the shareholders of the acquired company later, possibly as a means of protecting against contingent liabilities. For example, a certain number of shares could be placed in escrow for a period of time, and if no unanticipated claims were presented against the acquiring company, they would be issued to the shareholders of the acquired company.

Warranties

Of course, it is possible for the acquiring corporation to obtain all sorts of warranties from the selling shareholders, or for the selling shareholders to obtain warranties from the acquiring corporation or its shareholders. The practical problems here are presented in providing a workable procedure to make the warranties meaningful. In the context of publicly held corporations, this generally means putting at least some of the stock into escrow for a certain period of time, as there is almost no other practical method of collecting on the warranties if they are breached. In smaller transactions where there are a small number of financially responsible shareholders, the straight warranty procedure without any escrow might be of some use.

Convertible Preferred Stock

Most of the problems of both contingent and escrowed stock can be solved by the use of convertible preferred stock. By this procedure, convertible preferred stock would be issued, and the conversion feature would be based upon the same future event as would give rise to the necessity for the use of contingent or escrowed stock. For example, the conversion could be increased by a certain number of common shares if the earnings attributable to the acquired company increased to a certain level by a certain time.

CHAPTER THIRTY-FOUR

CORPORATE LIQUIDATIONS: TAX CONSEQUENCES—AN OVERVIEW

The purpose of this chapter is to provide a brief explanation of the general tax implications of corporate liquidations, a list of potential problems, and a description of the alternatives available under various sections of the Internal Revenue Code. It will begin by setting forth some of the actual situations in which corporate liquidations may arise, proceed to a discussion of the various types of liquidations specifically described in the Internal Revenue Code, and conclude with a list of potential problems in any corporate liquidation.

CIRCUMSTANCES INVOLVING CORPORATE LIQUIDATIONS

Corporate liquidations are not restricted to the situation where an existing business is "calling it quits." In certain situations, the liquidation of a corporate entity may constitute part of a reorganization of an existing business with full intent that business operations will continue but perhaps under a different structure (for example, as a division). Following is a brief list of some of the more common situations where a corporate liquidation may be used as a tool to facilitate the conduct of the business.

Changes from Corporate to Noncorporate Form

In some instances, the decision to incorporate a business proves to have been unwise. In other situations, a change of circumstances may indicate that a business formerly conducted in corporate form can best be conducted in noncorporate form. This will be an unusual situation, but it can come about, especially if losses are realized and subchapter S, for some reason, cannot be elected and the shareholders have other income which the losses can be used to offset currently.

Liquidation as Part of an Acquisition

A corporate liquidation may be an integral part of an acquisition. A typical example is the purchase of the stock of a corporation followed by a liquidation of that corporation into the parent. If this is done properly, the acquiring corporation can accomplish the acquisition by a stock purchase and receive the same tax treatment as if the assets were acquired directly. This procedure is sometimes useful where an acquisition of assets is desired but for some reason is impractical or impossible to do directly. In this case, if the stock can be acquired in a simple stock purchase transaction and the acquired corporation can be liquidated within two years, the acquiring corporation can obtain a tax basis for depreciation purposes in the assets equal to the purchase price of the stock.

Merger of Parent and Subsidiary

Completely apart from the acquisition context, it may be that a previously existing parent-subsidiary relationship between two corporations is no longer necessary or desirable. For example, it may have been desirable in the past to conduct a part of the corporation's business in the form of a separate subsidiary, or for tax reasons an acquired corporation may have continued in existence as a subsidiary. If the reasons for the existence of the separate corporate entity cease to exist, it will generally be advisable to avoid the extra administrative and clerical problems generated by this separate entity by merging it into the parent. This can be done by simply liquidating it. The simplification can also be accomplished by a statutory merger of the wholly owned subsidiary into the parent. If a subsidiary is to be liquidated, the transaction is governed by a special section of the Internal Revenue Code (section 332) and can generally be accomplished completely tax-free to all parties concerned. A tax-free merger would also accomplish the same objective. However, whatever mechanism is employed, the Internal Revenue Service generally takes the position that this kind of combination is governed by section 332, even though it may be cast in the form of a merger. Consequently, the detailed timing and other rules of section 332 must be observed in any case.

TYPES OF LIQUIDATIONS

There are four types of liquidations specifically provided for in the Internal Revenue Code. The first and most common is the standard liquidation involving the distribution of all assets of the corporation to the shareholders thereof. The tax treatment of this type of liquidation is set forth in section 331 of the Internal Revenue Code, which provides that the transaction is treated as an exchange of the stock for the assets, which exchange is accorded capital gains treatment. In essence, the shareholder pays a capital gains tax on the difference between his cost basis in his stock and the fair market value of the assets he receives in exchange for that stock.

The second type of liquidation is the subsidiary liquidation described above. It is covered in section 332 of the code. Generally, a subsidiary can be liquidated into the parent corporation tax-free. The two principal requirements are that the parent own 80 percent of the stock of the subsidiary and that the liquidation be accomplished within three years of the close of the taxable year in which the first distribution is made, or within the taxable year of adoption of a plan of complete liquidation by the shareholders.

The third type of liquidation is the so-called one-month liquidation. This type of liquidation may be elected in certain situations generally involving closely held companies. The tax treatment is a bit complicated, but in substance, the shareholder generally computes his gain in the same manner as for the standard liquidation but is taxed at ordinary income rates and only to the extent of the earnings and profits of the corporation. Generally, then, the shareholder pays a higher tax on a smaller part of his gain. Whether or not this has any advantage in a given situation depends on all the facts, the most important of which is the amount of earnings and profits of the company to be liquidated. Since the treatment is elective, the shareholders should not be hurt by it.

The fourth major type of liquidation is the 337 liquidation, or one-year liquidation. In this type of liquidation, the rule for tax treatment *of the shareholders* is the same as the general rule provided in section 331: they are taxed at capital gains rates on the difference between the basis in their stock and the value of the assets or cash they receive in liquidation. However, if the corporation adopts a resolution of liquidation and then proceeds to sell all of its assets within one year, it will generally not have to pay any tax at the corporate level on any gain it realizes. The section 337 liquidation is perhaps the most usual form of liquidation when a business is being terminated because it allows the corporation to sell the assets without any tax at the corporate level. It is particularly useful where the assets have a low book value in relation to their market value, or where the corporation desires to sell some of its assets and distribute others to the shareholders in kind.

LIQUIDATION PROBLEMS

Following is a listing of the major problems frequently encountered in corporate liquidations.

Collapsible Corporations

The most serious problem in corporate liquidations is the collapsible-corporation problem, which is applicable to stock sales as well as to liquidations. When a collapsible corporation is liquidated or its shares sold, the gain realized by the shareholder may be taxed as ordinary income rather than as capital gains. Collapsible-corporation rules are among the most complex contained in the Internal Revenue Code. However, the basic reason for the rules is easy to see. The collapsible-corporation rules were put into the code in 1950 to plug a loophole which allowed some businessmen to convert ordinary income to capital gains. The procedure was particularly useful in the construction and movie industries and generally went something like this. Assume a taxpayer has a parcel of land to be developed for single-family residences. If the taxpayer simply did this in noncorporate form, the profit on the sale of the houses would be ordinary income, if we assume he was in the business of developing and selling real estate. If the taxpayer incorporated, again the profits would be taxed to the corporation at ordinary income rates. However, if the taxpayer put the land into the corporation, had all the houses built, and then liquidated the corporation before these houses were sold, he would receive capital gains treatment on the difference between his cost and the fair market value of the houses. In other words, by the simple expedient of liquidating the corporation before the houses were sold instead of after, he obtained capital gains treatment on the profits from the venture. Since the taxpayer received a stepped-up basis in each house, he could then proceed to sell them at little or no gain. Section 341 was added to the Internal Revenue Code to attempt to solve this problem. It did this by defining a collapsible corporation as any corporation formed or availed of principally for the manufacture, production, etc., of property with a view to the sale or exchange of the stock of the corporation before the profits were realized.

For purposes of this discussion, it should be pointed out that the statute goes far beyond the clear situation set forth above, and careful attention to the problem is necessary in any corporate liquidation or any sale of a substantial amount of the shares of any corporation.

Valuation Problems

Another very significant problem in most liquidations is the value of the property distributed to the shareholders. As indicated above, the general tax treatment of a liquidation is a capital gains tax on the difference between the basis of the stock and the fair market value of the assets distributed. The question of the fair market value of assets often becomes quite complex and subjective. However, it is clear that it should not be assumed that the fair market value of assets is simply the value on which they are carried on the books of the corporation.

Shareholder Indebted to Corporation

Some technical problems exist if a corporation is liquidated at the time a shareholder is indebted to the corporation. The problem is particularly apparent if there is only one shareholder. Generally, the problems are:

1. If the debt is not repaid before the liquidation, there may be an allegation that the original loan was not bona fide, that there never was any intention of paying it back, and, therefore, that it was really a dividend. This problem is significant where the year in which the loan was made is still "open."

2. If the debt is not repaid before liquidation, there may be a technical forgiveness of the debt by the corporation, giving rise to ordinary income to the shareholder.

Generally, loans to shareholders should be repaid before liquidation even if some interim borrowing from an outside source is required to do it. This is a simple way of avoiding the problem, and the net effect to the shareholder is the same except possibly for some interest charge if borrowing is necessary.

Basis Questions

Generally, basis of the assets in question is stepped up if the transaction is taxable, so that the shareholders obtain a new basis on the assets equal to the fair market value of the assets. In the case of a one-month liquidation which is partially taxable and partially tax-free, there is an allocation making the new basis equal to the old basis plus the amount of gain actually taxed whether at capital gains or ordinary income rates. In the case of the liquidation of a controlled subsidiary shortly after its acquisition, the basis of the assets is the same as the basis of the stock (provided the liquidation takes place within two years and satisfies the other detailed requirements for this type of transaction). In a "standard" liquidation of a controlled subsidiary, the transaction is tax-free, and so the parent simply receives a substituted basis in the assets equal to the basis which the subsidiary had before the liquidation.

Problems of the Liquidating Corporation

Generally, a corporate liquidation which is taxable to shareholders will of itself have no tax effects on the liquidating corporation. There are, however, two principal exceptions to this rule. The first is the distribution of installment obligations. Generally, if a corporation has an installment obligation and distributes it before it has been paid for all the installments, it must report income on the unpaid installments at the time of the liquidation. The second exception refers to the depreciation-recapture rules. The liquidation is treated as a disposition of depreciable property for purposes of these rules, and the corporation must add back the depreciation previously taken.

Reserve for Bad Debts

In some situations, a bad debt reserve might have to be added back to the corporation's income upon liquidation. This would probably be the case if all the debts of the corporation were liquidated for their full value before liquidation. If the debts are simply distributed in kind to the shareholders, the question of the bad debt reserve is still uncertain, but it is certainly arguable that no add-back is necessary (assuming the reserve is reasonable). Generally, the bad-debt-reserve question will not be significant in the liquidation of a controlled subsidiary. In a "standard" liquidation of a subsidiary where the stock had not been acquired in the past two years, no add-back is necessary. If the liquidation takes place within two years of the acquisition, an add-back is necessary, but the parent corporation should be able to obtain a corresponding addition to its bad debt reserve (again assuming the existing reserve is reasonable).

Earned but Unreported Income

In some situations a corporation may have to add to its income and pay tax on income which it has previously earned but which it has not yet reported. This problem is quite complicated and depends principally on the method of accounting used by the corporation. For example, some methods of accounting call only for reporting of income upon the completion of a contract (completed-contract method) or when the company is actually paid for a job (cash method).

At any given time, a company may have substantial amounts of earned income resulting from the performance of services or the sale of products which has not yet been reflected in income by its accounting method. On liquidation, this creates some problem because it may be that, upon liquidation, the earned but previously unreported income will have to be reported even if such reporting is inconsistent with the method of accounting previously used by the company.

NON-TAX FACTORS

In many situations, non-tax factors will govern the form of the transaction. In cases like these, the number of alternatives will be greatly reduced and evaluation of the possibilities simplified. For example, it may be impractical to distribute assets in kind, and impossible to find a single buyer to purchase the stock of the company. In this case, it will almost universally be appropriate to use the 337-type liquidation and have the corporation sell the assets to various buyers as appropriate and then distribute the cash to the shareholders within one year. In other situations, the purchasing corporation will have such a dominant bargaining position that, as a practical matter, the choice of the form of the transaction will not be negotiable. In still other situations, the corporation to be liquidated may have appreciated assets but no earnings or profits, in which case the 333 election is clearly suggested. However, in many cases, at least two different elections with differing tax consequences will be possible, and proper planning may generate a substantial tax saving.

TAX FACTORS

In order to evaluate the various liquidation possibilities, one must have at least the following facts:

1. The *value* of the assets and their *basis*

2. The *earnings and profits* of the corporation

3. The *operating loss carryover* situation

4. The existence of any *installment obligations* owned by the corporation to be liquidated

5. The *accounting method* of the company to be liquidated and the amount of earned but unreported income

6. Any potential for *collapsible-corporation* treatment

7. The *depreciation situation,* which enables the effects of the depreciation-recapture provisions to be evaluated

Naturally, in order to intelligently consider liquidation problems, one must have a working knowledge of each of the four basic types of liquidations, but that discussion is beyond the scope of this book. The foregoing, however, should enable a business executive to ask the right questions to make sure that the tax people have done a thorough job.

CHAPTER THIRTY-FIVE

CORPORATE SEPARATIONS

From time to time, it becomes necessary or desirable to divide a corporate enterprise. It may be that a corporation which formerly conducted two separate businesses now desires to separate those businesses and have one group of shareholders conduct one enterprise and another group the other. It may be that several shareholders have had a falling-out and, in order to settle the dispute, it is necessary to divide the corporation so that its former activities which were conducted by the shareholders together will now be conducted separately.

> **EXAMPLE:** A and B are each 50 percent owners of corporation XYZ. The corporation has two separate businesses of equal worth. A and B have a falling-out, and it is decided to distribute one business to A, the other to B, so that thereafter each will conduct his business separately.

The problem is that while there is certainly no reason to tax the above transaction, it could be used as a device to pull earnings out of a corporation at capital gains rates. For that reason, the provisions under which the above division could be accomplished tax-free are circumscribed with many technicalities so that the device cannot be abused. Unfortunately, sometimes these technicalities will operate to impose a tax on a transaction even where there is no tax-avoidance motive.

> **EXAMPLE:** Assume that in the above transaction, A and B did not have a falling-out, but simply decided that their two busi-

nesses, which were formerly conducted by a single corporation, should now be conducted by two separate corporations. A corporate division could be accomplished by simply putting one of the businesses into a separate corporation with A and B as 50 percent shareholders. However, suppose that immediately after this corporate division was made, A and B sold their stock in the new corporation or liquidated it. Generally, such a sale or liquidation would be entitled to capital gains treatment, and A and B could have gotten out a substantial amount of earnings from the corporation without paying a dividend, thereby avoiding the double tax incident to the usual dividend.

PROCEDURE

Corporate divisions are generally referred to as *spin-offs*. However, from a mechanical point of view, there are really at least three separate kinds of corporate divisions, as follows:

1. *Spin-off.* "Spin-off" refers to a transaction in which the stock of a subsidiary of the parent corporation is distributed to the parent's shareholders without any surrender of stock by them.

2. *Split-off.* "Split-off" refers to a transaction where the stock of a subsidiary is distributed to some or all of the shareholders of the parent corporation in exchange for some or all of their stock in the parent corporation.

3. *Split-up.* "Split-up" refers to a transaction where stock of two or more subsidiaries is distributed to the shareholders of the parent corporation in complete liquidation of the parent corporation.

Today, all these kinds of transactions are treated alike for tax purposes and are generally lumped together under the term "spin-off." As used herein, the term "spin-off" will be used to include all types of corporate divisions mentioned above.

Generally, the form of the transaction will depend on whether the shareholders will continue their respective percentage ownerships in all corporations after the division. In the first of our two examples (with A and B going their separate ways), the form would be a split-off. A separate subsidiary would be formed, one business contributed to it in exchange for all of its stock, and then one shareholder would exchange his stock in the old corporation for stock in the new subsidiary. After the transaction, each shareholder would be the sole owner of a separate corporation. On the other hand, in the second transaction, there would be no need for any stock exchange. A new subsidiary could be formed, one business contributed to it, and the stock of that subsidiary distributed pro rata to the shareholders: 50 percent each to A and B in our case. After the transaction, A and B would each be 50 percent owners of two separate corporations.

Obviously, it is the second type of transaction which creates the greatest possibility for tax avoidance. Consequently, the Internal Revenue Service has announced that the detailed requirements of section 355 and the regulations thereunder will be applied more stringently to that type of pro rata spin-off than to non-pro rata split-offs. In fact, any spin-off creates substantial possibilities for tax avoidance, because the shareholders will have a direct interest in at least two corporations, one of which may be liquidated or sold. It is, therefore, highly desirable to obtain an advance ruling from the Internal Revenue Service before undertaking a spin-off.

The Ingredients of a Tax-free Corporate Division

Following are the basic ingredients of a tax-free division:

1. There must be a distribution to a shareholder with respect to his stock or to a security holder in exchange for his securities.

2. The distribution must be of stock or securities that a corporation controls immediately before the distribution.

3. The transaction must not be used principally as a device for the distribution of earnings and profits of the distributing corporation.

4. Each corporation must be engaged in an active business which it has actively conducted for the past five years.

CHAPTER THIRTY-SIX

EMPLOYEE STOCK OWNERSHIP PLANS

Employee Stock Ownership Plans (ESOPs) and trusts are tools of corporate finance and compensation which are being discussed and used extensively in a wide variety of situations. While they are not new, certain recent changes in the tax law and some helpful provisions in ERISA have called attention to them and eliminated a few but not all of the technical problems.

BACKGROUND

An ESOP (the acronym will be used herein to refer to both the plan and the trust) is essentially a qualified stock bonus plan which has been recognized by the Internal Revenue Code for many years. A "qualified plan" is simply a tax term to refer to a kind of plan which is described in the Internal Revenue Code and which will allow employers to make contributions for employees and deduct those contributions *when made* while providing a benefit to the employees for which they will have to pay no tax until they *actually receive* a distribution from the plan. Also, contributions under a qualified plan must be made to a trust which is exempt from taxes on the money it earns. The most typical qualified plans are pension and profit sharing plans. In order to achieve this favorable tax treatment, the plans have to be "qualified," in the sense that they have to meet many detailed requirements contained in the Internal Revenue Code. These requirements are very technical, and if the plan does not meet any one of them, it will lose its qualified status and the employer may lose all the tax deductions it has claimed for contributions to the plan, the employees may be taxed on all the money allocated to them under the plan, and the trust may be taxed on its income. Hence, a failure to meet any one of the numerous technical requirements for a qualified plan would be a disaster of large proportion.

Under a typical ESOP, the employer establishes the qualified plan and trust. The rights of the employees, when they could participate, to what extent, when their interest would vest, etc., would all be spelled out in these two documents. For the sake of illustration, let's assume a small company is involved and all of the employees are participants. The company could then make a contribution, in cash, which would be deductible by the corporation in the year it was contributed, and use that cash to purchase its own stock. As an alternative, it could make a contribution of the stock directly and claim a deduction for the value of the stock. The employees would then have an interest in the company through their interest in the plan. Generally, the amount of this interest would depend upon the amount of stock contributed to the plan and the size of the interest any particular employee had in the plan, which in turn is usually based upon his or her compensation. In a typical plan, the employee's interest is expressed as a fraction, the numerator of which is his annual compensation and the denominator of which is the total compensation of all the employees involved. For example, if there were ten employees, each making $10,000 per year, each one would have a one-tenth interest in the plan.

From an economic point of view, the net effect of an arrangement like this is that the employer and the employee become "partners in capitalism." A number of years ago, a man named Louis Kelso became a strong advocate of ESOPs, and as a result of his own activity and writing the device was widely adopted on the West Coast. It was not extensively used in other parts of the country. Then, however, Mr. Kelso succeeded in convincing Senator Long of the desirability of this kind of plan, and two things happened: (1) The Tax Reduction Act of 1975 included a provision allowing corporations to claim an extra 1 percent investment credit for certain contributions to ESOPs; and (2) ERISA was drafted to specifically recognize the unique nature of ESOPs and to allow them, in spite of the fact that an ESOP will invest entirely in stock of the employer and will, therefore, not meet the normal diversification requirements of ERISA. Since that time, Mr. Kelso has become famous; articles on ESOPs have appeared in the *Wall Street Journal, Barron's, U.S. News and World Report, Forbes,* and many other business periodicals; and many tax seminars and tax publications have included discussions of the ESOP. Additional legislation to make ESOPs even more attractive continues to be considered. This chapter will try to discuss ESOPs in an impartial way and to set forth their advantages and disadvantages in a number of situations where corporations might find that an ESOP is an appropriate tool for accomplishing the desired objective. First, however, it is necessary to spend a little time on the "ESOP atmosphere."

The ESOP craze has so thoroughly convinced a number of people that the ESOP is the best tool for solving all the problems discussed herein and possibly others that no matter what the question happens to be, the answer is "Form an ESOP." Other people are, to be frank, out to make a buck out of the ESOP. Corporations and their counsel must examine any material generated by ESOP specialists and be very critical of it if it does not do two things:

1. Explain both the advantages and disadvantages

2. Explore the alternatives

This is absolutely essential, because if there is one universal truth in this area, as in all others, it is that there are alternatives to the ESOP and that the ESOP does have certain disadvantages and risks.

On the other side of the coin, there are those who, perhaps in reaction to those who have oversold the ESOP, have tended to resist its use in any situation because it is new and all the rules of the ESOP game are not yet thoroughly understood. Also, to be quite practical, the ESOP is new, and many business advisers (both legal and other) have never used one and do not have one in their file. A business counselor considering an ESOP as a possible solution to a problem may have to start from scratch in:

1. Drafting the plan and trust

2. Getting it qualified with the Internal Revenue Service

3. Learning about the new provisions in the Tax Law Act and ERISA

4. Figuring out the mechanics

5. Explaining the whole thing to the trustee—typically, a bank—which, unless it is very large or on the West Coast, may not have acted before as the trustee for or lender to an ESOP

6. Explaining the whole transaction to the employees and company management

Some businessmen will, therefore, be faced either with advisers who feel that the ESOP is the answer no matter what the question, or with advisers who attempt to throw cold water on the whole idea by pointing out only the potential problems which the first group has failed to mention.

DISCUSSION OF THE ESOP

It would seem logical to begin discussion of an ESOP with a definition or description. However, an ESOP is many things simultaneously to different people. Beyond the brief description given in this chapter, it is generally not useful to discuss ESOPs in the abstract, because the purpose for which they are going to be used plays a substantial part in determining the form they take, the mechanics involved, and the relative advantages and disadvantages.

With that caution, however, it may be useful to describe a typical ESOP and some fairly standard variations so that the advantages of this tool can be easily shown.

As stated at the beginning of the chapter, a typical ESOP simply involves placing employer securities in a tax-qualified trust for employees. The advantages are that the employer gets a deduction for the value of the stock placed in the trust and that the employees receive a benefit partially subsidized by the federal tax laws. Accordingly, in an oversimplified situation, a company could, for example, contribute $10,000 worth of stock to an ESOP and obtain a tax benefit which (assuming a net 50 percent effective tax rate) would amount to $5000. The employees would have a benefit of $10,000 on which they would have to pay no tax until they actually received a distribution, and the employer would in effect have a $5000 increase in cash with which to purchase additional equipment or to do anything desired.

Subject to some of the problems discussed later in this chapter, which could probably be handled by competent attorneys and accountants, this simple device would appear to create no substantial legal difficulties. However, the utility of the device, at least in terms of the dollars which could be generated for the company, could be increased substantially if, instead of simply contributing cash or stock and being content with a 50 percent tax benefit, the company sold the stock to the trust. Then, instead of having a $5000 net benefit from our above transaction, the company would have the entire $10,000 in cash to use to purchase additional equipment or for anything else. Obviously, someone would have to supply the money to pay the company the $10,000, and, hence, the bank would usually be brought into the picture. The employer would sell the stock to the trust for the $10,000 and the trust would then pledge the stock with the bank, which would loan the trust the $10,000 to pay the employer. The employer would then make future contributions to the trust in order to allow the trust to repay the loan. These future contributions would be deductible by the corporation. Since the qualified trust is a tax-exempt entity, the trust would pay no tax on the money it received from the company but could instead use all of it to repay the bank loan.

The net effect of all this paperwork is that the company would, in essence, be paying off a bank loan through a qualified trust, and this, in turn, means that the entire payment is deductible. On the other hand, assuming that the corporation simply went to the bank directly to borrow the money and then paid it back in periodic installments, the only amounts which would be deductible would be those attributable to interest. Using an ESOP, the company would get a deduction not only for the interest but for the principal as well. Thus, in principle, the ESOP can be used in order to raise capital much more expeditiously than a simple direct loan.

PROBLEMS IN THE USE OF ESOPs

Unfortunately, at the present time, there are a host of problems in using ESOPs in this kind of transaction, some of which don't have very good solutions and others of which don't have any solution at all. Following is a brief catalogue of some of those problems.

To begin with, the plan must qualify under the detailed provisions of the Internal Revenue Service. This means that the employees who are going to benefit from the plan and trust cannot be limited to officers or highly paid employees but instead must be a reasonable cross section of employees. This is one of the many prices which must be paid for the favored "qualified" status.

Second, when the plan or trust makes distribution to the employers, it must make that distribution in the form of employer stock. If the employer stock does not have a readily ascertainable market value, or if it cannot be sold by the employees, there are problems of valuation and problems of providing the employees with some kind of benefit they can use. Generally, this can be solved by simply giving the employee the right to require the ESOP to purchase the stock back from him at some value; however, this in turn creates a considerable number of problems, because the ESOP trustee must operate prudently and it may not be prudent at any specific time to purchase stock back from employees. In addition, the value at which the stock must be repurchased would be subject to dispute, and about the only sure way of handling that would be to have annual appraisals, which would be a costly and troublesome undertaking.

A third problem is that the trust must be for the exclusive benefit of the employees and their beneficiaries and the tax law surrounding this subject is very uncertain, especially in the context of the newer applications of the ESOPs. If the ESOP is used for some kind of leveraged financing the real reason for which is to allow the company to raise capital to buy new equipment or to buy out a stockholder or for any of a number of other possible applications, there is substantial doubt as to whether the Internal Revenue Service would consider that the exclusive-benefit rule has been satisfied.

A fourth problem is that the ESOP must meet all the technical requirements of ERISA except those involving diversification, which are expressly held to be inapplicable to ESOPs. However, some of the other requirements of ERISA would be very difficult for an ESOP to meet. For example, ERISA requires that the ESOP trustee act prudently, and it may not be prudent to invest in stock of a small company which is not publicly held.

One advantage an ESOP has over a normal profit sharing plan is that contributions do not have to be made from profits. They can be made on the basis of any desired formula if they do not exceed the maximum allowable contribution, which is 15 percent of the compensation of the employees. Therefore the amounts involved are limited by the payroll of the covered employees. (This 15 percent limitation is, like almost everything in the Internal Revenue Code, complicated and involves some useful carry-forward and carry-back provisions which would allow the contribution to go as high as 25 percent in some years.)

Like most of the tax-favored qualified plans, the ESOP must involve "continuing contributions." While there is some uncertainty as to exactly what this means, the ESOP should be structured in such a manner that continuing contributions are made and that these continuing contributions are recurring and substantial and not merely single or occasional.

One of the basic theories for congressional approval of ESOPs in the recent tax and ERISA legislation is that they are supposed to facilitate employee ownership of American business and make employees more productive. Unfortunately, the correlation between the ESOP and employee productivity has yet to be proved. Whether or not an ESOP really has any demonstrable effect on the work performance of employees is going to be debated for many years, but the theory sounds good, and the difficulty of obtaining any empirical evidence of the validity of the concept may not be a stumbling point.

Complication and cost are two things which are bound to accompany an ESOP. Someone is going to have to draft a plan and a trust which comply with very complicated provisions of the Internal Revenue Code and ERISA; there is going to have to be some kind of explanation of the whole program in accordance with the requirements of ERISA; and all the continuing requirements of ERISA for welfare benefit plans will apply to the ESOP.

Aggravation is going to be another constant companion of an ESOP. This is especially true if a company is going to go from a very small shareholder group to a larger one by virtue of selling a stock to an ESOP. There will be subsequent problems with stock transfer, stock valuation, shareholder records, shareholder relations, and many other forms of aggravation which will always haunt the ESOP and those who are trying to manage it.

Perhaps the largest single problem is uncertainty. The IRS has not issued detailed ESOP regulations, and the ERISA rules are far from clear. The economic disasters which would accompany any mistake in this area make it very difficult to justify an ESOP except in cases where the ESOP is going to be relatively simple and where it is not used as some form of complicated corporate financing scheme so that the exclusive-benefit rule casts a shadow over the whole thing. The ESOP area is a rapidly developing one, and some of the technical problems which are alluded to in this chapter may be eliminated by the time it finds its way into print. Unfortunately, this is one of those areas where it may be anticipated that new technical problems will arise at a rate that exceeds the solution of the old ones. Accordingly, on the technical front, we simply have to call attention to some of the basic problems and point out that expert advice must be obtained if an ESOP is to be considered. On the practical side, however, the observations made in this chapter are likely to remain valid for quite some time. The essential financial advantage is likely to be the repayment of capital with tax-deductible dollars; and the essential disadvantages are likely to be a myriad of technical problems which the lawyers and accountants may or may not be able to solve in a particular situation, and a substantial amount of increased complexity, cost, aggravation, and uncertainty which are going to accompany any scheme involving distribution of stock to employees. Accordingly, the evaluation should involve a weighing process with the financial advantages placed on one side and the technical uncertainties and business complexities and aggravations placed on the other.

CHAPTER THIRTY-SEVEN

EXECUTIVE COMPENSATION

EXECUTIVE COMPENSATION

For many years before 1969, the field of executive compensation was relatively stable. The inventory of basic tools to compensate top management included:

1. A salary

2. Usually some form of bonus

3. A qualified stock option

4. A deferred-compensation contract

5. The inclusion of executives in normal pension and profit sharing plans

After 1969, however, there were a number of developments which changed this whole picture, and the field of executive compensation became greatly more complicated. To highlight these developments, they included the following:

1. In 1969, the tax rates were changed very significantly. The maximum tax rate on earned income (salary) was reduced from 70 percent to 50 percent and at the same time the maximum effective rate for capital gains tax was increased from 25 percent to 35 percent. This, of course, had the effect of greatly diminishing the relative value of any kind of compensation technique which depended upon capital gains to reward the executive. A qualified stock option was the primary example.

Congress finished the job on qualified stock options in 1976 when it completely eliminated them, subject to certain transitional rules.

2.   The Employee Retirement Income Security Act was passed in 1974, and it limited the amount of money which could be paid to any individual employee out of a pension plan. Thus, certain highly paid people had to be covered by new "excess-benefit plans" to make up for this ERISA gap.

3.   In addition to the changes in the law, the stock market became much less attractive during this period, and as a general proposition, compensation techniques which based their value to the employee on the prospect that the company's stock might rise in the future lost a great deal of their appeal because of the stock market performance.

4.   The accountants also complicated the picture by issuing a number of interpretations which changed the normal accounting treatment of deferred payments.

5.   The ever-changing SEC rules continued their gradual developments to complicate any executive compensation program which depended on the issuance of securities or options.

In summary then, the field of executive compensation became very much more complicated. Almost any technique of compensating executives has to be considered from a number of angles.

1.   What are the tax implications?

2.   What are the Pension Reform Act implications?

3.   What are the actual economic implications (stock market, inflation, etc)?

4.   What are the accounting implications?

5.   What are the securities law implications?

I have placed the executive compensation chapter in the tax section of this book because in the overwhelming majority of cases, the tax aspects of the program will outweigh the others in importance. However, these other factors are very important, and management must realize that all of them must be evaluated. This is particularly significant in a company which has separate departments and people for tax, securities law, personnel, and general law. Management must make sure they all work together in the area of designing executive compensation packages for the company.

As in substantially all the subjects dealt with in this book, the executive compensation area is changing rapidly, and the material contained in this chapter may be out of date by the time you read it. On the other hand, the basic concepts contained herein are likely to remain true for a considerable period of time. Every executive compensation plan deserves an analysis which includes all the factors mentioned above, plus answers to the additional nonlegal questions:

1.   Are the traditional compensation devices (salary and traditional qualified plans and traditional fringes) adequate? It would seem inappropriate to give too much consideration to the exotic forms of executive compensation if the basic foundation is weak.

2.   What are the particular objectives to be achieved? Is it simply to put more money in the executive's pocket, to take advantage of some tax situation, or to create an incentive for the executive? It is suggested that these kinds of executive compensation programs ought to accentuate the last purpose: creat-

ing an incentive for the executive. They should, therefore, be appropriately designed to accomplish that objective.

3. What are the actual economic effects of the proposal from the standpoint of both the employee and the employer? Does the program take into account the effects of inflation, income yield, other plans, and the whole tax picture? This means considering the deduction to the company, as well as the employee's tax.

As mentioned above, the 1969 Tax Reform Act changed the basic tax rules considerably. The three basic changes are described below.

Earned Income

The Tax Reform Act of 1969 established a new maximum marginal tax rate of 50 percent on earned taxable income for taxable years beginning after December 31, 1971. Earned income includes wages, salaries, professional fees, and compensation for personal services. The spread between the value of stock at the time of acquisition and the option price, capital gains, and some deferred compensation payments is *not* considered earned income. Indeed, the option spread and the deductible half of capital gains are *tax-preference items*, which have the effect of *reducing* the amount of earned income subject to the new 50 percent maximum. The problem is clear. Previously, an employee benefiting from a stock option was in a very favorable situation; the maximum tax rate on his salary was 70 percent and the maximum tax rate on the capital gains treatment of his gains under the stock option plan was 25 percent. Now, the maximum marginal rate on his salary is 50 percent and the capital gains may be subject to a 35 percent effective maximum. Furthermore, his option spread and the deductible half of his capital gains will be deemed preference income and will reduce the amount of his salary sheltered by the 50 percent rule.

Tax Preferences

Tax preferences were alluded to above. As far as executive compensation is concerned, two types of income are so-called preference income. These are:

1. The bargain element in stock options. (With respect to a qualified stock option, this means the amount by which the fair market value of the stock at the time of exercise exceeds the option price.)

2. The deductible one-half of long-term capital gains.

The effect of having tax preference income is that it is subject to a 15 percent minimum tax and that it reduces the amount of earned income sheltered by the new 50 percent maximum.

The 10 percent minimum tax on preference income is mitigated by a de minimus rule providing that the tax applies only to the preference income in excess of $10,000 or one-half the taxpayer's regular tax, whichever is greater. Thus, if a taxpayer had a $10,000 tax bill for a given year, he could have $40,000 of preference income without incurring any minimum tax. There is a similar rule applying to the reduction of income sheltered by the 50 percent rate. If you have preference items greater than the amounts stated above, some of your earned income may not be subject to the 50 percent maximum rate, and you may have to pay a tax at higher rates, up to 70 percent.

Capital Gains

Previously, an individual having capital gains could include one-half of these gains in his ordinary income, or as an alternative computation, could merely pay a tax of 25 percent of the amount of the capital gain. Obviously, for an individual whose tax bracket exceeded 50 percent, this alternative tax computation has been eliminated for individuals with capital gains over $50,000 (for married individuals filing joint returns; $25,000 for a single person). The calculations are somewhat complex, but in essence, an individual who has more than $50,000 of capital gains pays a tax of 25 percent on the first $50,000 and includes one-half the remainder in his ordinary income, which is taxed at ordinary income rates. Capital gains are not earned income, and so the 50 percent ceiling does not apply. Instead, the ordinary rate ceiling of 70 percent applies, and so, for capital gains in excess of $50,000, the maximum effective rate is 35 percent.

Summary

It can be seen that the changes brought about by the Tax Reform Act have substantially complicated the picture, especially as applied to persons with sufficient economic wealth to be affected by the capital gains and tax-preference provisions of the new act. At the same time, it decreased the current income tax burden of these same people by providing for the 50 percent maximum rate on earned income.

The net effect of all this has been the growth of a trend to make available to the executive a package of benefits with differing tax consequences, so that an employee can choose those which will benefit him most. Furthermore, in order to enable the executive to make such an analysis, corporations have turned to professional economic advisers, including attorneys, analysts, accountants, and financial consultants, and they have in effect made these professionals available to the executives at company expense. This is currently being done only in large corporations and only for top management. However, the principle of tailoring the executive pay package to fit the circumstances of the recipient is sound in smaller corporations as well. Coordination among corporate counsel, personnel, and the accountants can generate a pay package which still has many advantages over a simple increase in current compensation.

THE FACTORS IN EXECUTIVE COMPENSATION

At this time, a good analytical way of looking at the executive compensation picture is to list the various compensation factors and make a few comments about each. We will be using the following list:

1. Salary
2. Bonuses
3. Perquisites
4. Nonqualified Stock Options
5. Stock Appreciation Rights
6. Shadow-Stock Plans
7. Deferred-Compensation Plans
8. Excess-Benefit Plans

Salary

Not much can be said about salary, other than that the obvious should not be overlooked: the corporate salary structure has to be on a sound foundation before you start building exotic things on top of it.

Bonuses

Bonuses are fairly straightforward, and not much is usually said about them. It could be that the very simplicity of a bonus is its principal drawback. Perhaps the specialists and consultants hesitate to recommend anything so simple and obvious. It would appear, however, that almost all the objectives of executive compensation could be achieved by judicious use of bonuses, and since they are so simple, a company could save a lot of legal, accounting, tax, securities, and compensation time if it adopted this technique as its basic means of rewarding executives. A bonus does not have to be the traditional kind of discretionary bonus paid at year-end. That, of course, is a very good technique and is often used. However, the discretionary aspect can be a drawback if you want to motivate the employee and he feels that having a bonus paid at the discretion of his boss would not necessarily motivate him to do the best job for the company. This means that you would need some kind of bonus plan. It could be based upon the objectives of the company. Much of the current literature describing "participating units" or "performance units" is really nothing more than bonus plans which have been reduced to writing and which base the bonus on objective criteria. In these kinds of arrangements, the company simply establishes a formula for paying bonuses. The formula is entirely independent of the stock market, and the payments are not necessarily annual. They could, for example, be based on two-, three-, and five-year programs. "Participating units" is a name which evolved because some of the plans start with a base unit of some kind and calculate the payments on the change. For example, if a subsidiary has profits of $100,000 per year and if management thinks that should be doubled in three years, executives may be given a "unit" which is equivalent to the existing profit. After each year, the units would be adjusted to reflect results. For example, the unit may be 1.5 if the goal is halfway met during the second year. This type of plan is particularly useful for divisions, subsidiaries, or other units where the stock of the company might not be a good indication of the executive's performance.

Before the company spends a lot of money in registering stock option plans with the SEC and drafting elaborate arrangements which may have to be approved by the shareholders, the question of whether all the objectives could be achieved by the use of a simple bonus should be asked. Naturally, a bonus can be a part of a plan which includes all of these techniques.

Perquisites

The question of executive perquisites is currently receiving a great deal of attention. The Securities and Exchange Commission is carefully investigating companies to make sure that all of the compensation, including the value of these perquisites, is reported in the proxy material for the top executives. The Internal Revenue Service is auditing returns of top executives very closely to make sure that they pay tax on the value of everything they should. Congress and the administration are currently talking about changes in the laws which govern the taxability and deductibility of noncash payments to executives. The thing to watch in this area is this increased government attention.

Nonqualified Stock Option Plans

Since qualified stock option plans have been eliminated from the Internal Revenue Code, nonqualified plans have become the standard form of executive incentive compensation. Most people seem to agree that they really do not provide any meaningful incentive, because the executive's performance in his job is related only indirectly and remotely, if at all, to the price of the stock. On the other hand, they are used by almost all the major companies which have publicly traded stock, and they do represent the only realistic kind of incentive which does not have any upper limit. There is always the possibility, however remote, that the stock will increase greatly in value and the executive will become rich.

The tax treatment of nonqualified stock options can become a bit complicated. Technically, the timing and amount of the tax due with respect to the receipt of nonqualified options depends upon whether the *option* (not the stock) has "a readily ascertainable fair market value" at the time it is granted, and whether such stock option is subject to "a substantial risk of forfeiture." Most options do not have a readily ascertainable market value because they are not transferable by the employee. In this case, the employee is not subject to any income tax at the time the option is granted. However, when the option is exercised, the employee will have ordinary income (subject to the maximum 50 percent rate) in an amount equal to the spread between the market value of the stock and his option price. Thereafter, if he sells the stock at a profit, he will have capital gains on the difference between the market value at the time he received the stock and its subsequent sale price.

It is possible for an option to have a readily ascertainable fair market value at the time it is granted. In this case, the executive would be subject to a tax in the amount of that value. However, any subsequent gain realized at the time the stock is sold would be taxed as capital gains. The trade-off then is a relatively larger amount of ordinary income later when the option is exercised and no tax when the option is granted, or a small tax when the option is granted versus the possibility of capital gains later when the gain is realized.

Options Subject to a Substantial Risk of Forfeiture

Even if an option has a readily ascertainable market value at the time it is granted, a tax will not be imposed (unless the employee elects to the contrary) if the option is subject to a substantial risk of forfeiture. Generally, where the future performance of services is required for the full enjoyment of the option, a substantial risk of forfeiture is present. Thus, for example, an option granted to an employee which requires continued employment for it to be exercisable is subject to a substantial risk of forfeiture, and the option is not subject to taxation at the time it is granted. If the employee exercised the option, there would be a tax applicable to the spread between the market value and the option exercise price.

On the other hand, for options without a readily ascertainable fair market value, a substantial risk of forfeiture has no effect on the timing of the tax.

Elections

The most uncertain area of the new scheme for taxing stock options is the ability of the employee to elect to include in his gross income the value of an option which apparently has no readily ascertainable market value or to include the value of an option which is subject to a substantial risk of forfeiture. Much of this ambiguity is caused by the amendments made to the Tax Laws in 1976. During the debate on these tax amendments, the Senate proposed to amend the law to allow an employee the right to elect to have the option valued at the date of its grant despite the absence of an active market for the option. However, this was not done, and instead, the legislative history provides instructions to the Internal Revenue Service that they should "make every reasonable effort to determine a fair market value for an option . . . where an employee irrevocably elects (by reporting the option as income on his tax return) to have the option valued at the time it is granted."

This is a very uncertain area of the law. The legislative history provides some instructions to the Internal Revenue Service, and it goes on to give them some guidance as to how they might establish a fair market value in the absence of a traded quotation price. The IRS is understandably upset with this method of legislation, and about all that can be said at this time is that the whole area of valuing stock options which do not have a traded market is unclear.

Conclusions

The above rules have created an elaborate set of possibilities in the nonqualified stock option area. You can grant options which have a fair market value or options which do not have a fair market value. The options can or cannot be subject to a risk of forfeiture; the underlying stock can or cannot be subject to a risk of forfeiture; the recipient of the stock either can or cannot choose to exercise the available elections. It appears that most of the larger companies are sticking with the nonqualified stock option with no readily ascertainable market value and the stock is not subject to any risk of forfeiture. In short, they are simply substituting a nonqualified stock option for essentially the same kind of option which previously was a qualified option. The grant is usually at fair market value, just as the old qualified options were, but in many cases, the new options are for ten years rather than five.

In addition to the basic grid work of possibilities, there are a lot of esoteric kinds of devices being recommended in the literature. Seesaw, or inverse variable, options and performance shares are two examples. In a seesaw option, the exercise price is decreased for every dollar of increase of the underlying stock. For example, a company whose stock is being traded at $25 per share might grant one of these options to an executive at the then fair market value. Assuming the stock went to $35 per share, the option price would decrease by $10. The executive would then have an option to purchase stock with a market value of $35 and an option price of $10. The advantage, of course, is that it greatly increases the benefit to the executive if the stock does go up in value. It does not change the tax rules.

"Performance shares" is simply the grant of actual stock to the executives as opposed to the issuance of options. For example, if the company attains stated sales of earnings at a specific time, shares may be awarded to the executive. If the goal is not met, the awards can either be scaled down or forfeited altogether.

Still another variation is a deferred stock bonus. This has also been described as the opposite of a restricted-stock plan. In a restricted stock plan, the employee is given stock right away, with the stock subject to restrictions which impose a substantial risk of forfeiture. If any of these restrictions occur (for example, if the employee quits before a specified date), he forfeits the right to full ownership of the stock. In a deferred-stock plan, the award is made right away, but the stock is not given until a later time. For example, the employee might be given an award of 1000 shares of stock to be delivered to him in five years, if he is still employed. At the time the stock is delivered, the employee should have ordinary income (protected by the 50 percent maximum tax rate) and the employer should have a deduction in the same amount.

Stock Appreciation Rights

One very popular variation on the nonqualified stock option is called a "stock appreciation right." Generally, the stock appreciation rights are contained in a key employee stock option plan and allow the company to grant the rights in connection with the stock option at their discretion. This is not required, however, and the stock appreciation rights could exist independent of any other option plan. Essentially, the stock appreciation right allows the employee to simply swap the stock option for the spread at the time. Suppose, for example, that an employee is granted a nonqualified stock option with a stock appreciation right for 100 shares of the company stock at $25 per share. Suppose that a few years later the stock has gone up to $40 per share. If the employee had the stock appreciation right, along with his option, he could simply surrender his option to the company for $15 per share, or $1500. In the alternative, he could exercise the option by actually paying the company $2500 and getting the stock. If the employee wanted to sell the stock immediately, it would be advantageous to exercise the stock appreciation right because this would help him avoid all the brokerage commissions, the trouble, the possible borrowing cost of coming up with the initial $2500, and most securities problems. On the other hand, if the employee wanted to keep the stock, he could exercise his normal option.

The Securities and Exchange Commission has issued an elaborate set of regulations on these plans. Essentially, those regulations provide reasonable guidance and will allow the operation of most stock appreciation rights. However, it is a very technical area, and the Securities and Exchange Commission Rules have to be checked out.

Also at this time, the Internal Revenue Service has not issued any express approval of the normal stock appreciation right. The IRS view thus must be considered at least somewhat questionable.

Shadow-Stock Plans

Shadow-stock plans afford the executive the benefits of stock ownership without any disadvantages through the risk of market decline or initial capital outlays. The plan typically creates accounts in the name of the covered executive to which participation units are transferred. Each unit is equivalent to a share of stock in the company, and it is assigned a value equal to the fair market value (or book value) of a share of stock at the time of the transfer. Thereafter, the accounts are credited with dividend equivalents attributable to the stock represented by the unit. These dividend equivalents are equal to the dividends actually paid on outstanding stock. In addition, at some time in the future when the employee exercises his right to the shadow-stock plan account, he receives not only the dividend equivalents but also the amount of appreciation in the value of the stock represented by the unit. Thus, a "participation unit" entitles the employee to the amount of dividends paid on the equivalent number of shares during the period of his unit account and the appreciation in the value of the stock represented by the unit.

Shareholder Approval

While it is not necessary to obtain shareholder approval for a shadow-stock plan, in many cases the corporation will not want active shareholder resistance to its compensation plans. High salaries and stock options which deplete corporate earnings and dilute the value of stock do not have much appeal to the shareholders. However, since the typical shadow-stock plan depends on *dividends*, there is generally no shareholder resistance.

Deferred Compensation

In a deferred-compensation agreement, an employee agrees to work for a current compensation less than his services could otherwise command, and in return, his employer agrees to pay him additional amounts in the future, usually after retirement. The principal advantage of the arrangement lies in its potential income tax savings. For example, if an executive is receiving current compensation in the 50 percent bracket and defers receipt of some of this compensation until after retirement when his bracket will be lower, a tax saving will result. Deferred compensation arrangements were much more commonplace when the top income bracket for salary was 70 percent. Now that it has been reduced to 50 percent, there is considerably less incentive to use this form of compensation.

A thorough economic analysis of the facts in any given situation is necessary in order to justify recommending a deferred compensation plan. This can usually be accomplished by listing advantages and disadvantages of the plan and seeing how they apply to the situation at hand.

Possible Advantages

The first and most important advantage is the possible income tax savings. In addition, however, the following advantages are sometimes cited:

1. The corporation will have the use of the deferred funds until they are actually paid.

2. The deferred compensation arrangement provides a certain amount of retirement security.

3. The arrangement can serve to reduce executive turnover because the payments are usually forfeitable in the event of premature resignation.

4. The necessary papers are simple and relatively inexpensive to draft.

5. Last but not least, there is always the psychological advantage of having a personal deferred-compensation arrangement.

Possible Disadvantages

The following factors must be placed on the other side of the scale:

1. Beyond mere deferment, there is no special tax advantage to the arrangement; there is no possibility of capital gains; the payments will always be ordinary income to the executive, and the corporation will receive a deduction only when the funds are actually paid to the employee.

2. Since the employer's deduction will be deferred, there is always the possibility that it may fall in a year in which there are either no profits or insufficient profits against which to offset the deduction.

3. Since the arrangement usually takes the form of a mere promise to pay in the future, there is always the risk that the corporation may be unable or unwilling to make the future payments.

4. The accounting regulations currently provide, in substance, that if an employee is to be paid deferred compensation after he retires, it should be accrued during the employee's period of active employment. Thus, for accounting purposes, it may not be possible to defer the effect on the profit-and-loss statement.

5. Last but perhaps most important, considering all the facts, the plan may result in an overall net economic loss to the very employee it was designed to benefit. The following are some of the financial factors to consider in evaluating this potential disadvantage.

    (a) *Progressive income tax rates*   While it is true that present tax rates are progressive, it is important to note that the progression decreases in the higher income tax brackets. Since the Tax Reform Act of 1969 was passed, the actual progression of the earned income rates has stopped at 50 percent. The obvious effect is that the higher the executive's current compensation is, the smaller will be the relative tax savings to be achieved by deferring part of it.

    (b) *Effect on other benefits received by employees*   Many typical *qualified* pension and profit sharing plans base their benefits on the participant's current compensation. Therefore, if the participant's current compensation is only a part of his total compensation, he receives less under these qualified plans than he would have received if all his compensation had been paid currently.

    (c) *Loss of investment yield*   If the executive is paid the compensation currently, he will be able to invest the after-tax increases and obtain a yield on the investment. While the yield will also be subject to tax, most of it might be at the capital gains rates, and there may be a substantial net yield to the executive. However, with the maximum rate on earned income at 50 percent and the other rates at 70 percent, and the 10 percent tax on preference income, the actual calculation of this additional investment yield would be a formidable task, necessitating a careful individual evaluation of the particular executive's financial picture.

    (d) *Inflation*   The establishment of a fixed amount of cash on the basis of today's dollars to be paid later in dollars worth substantially less because of inflation has an obvious disadvantage to the executive. The amount of this loss will depend upon how the inflation spiral progresses and upon how long the payments are deferred. Offsetting this factor is the probability that the corporation will be willing to commit a larger amount if it is to be deferred than if it is to be paid currently.

At this time, the tax effects of a deferred compensation contract are unclear. The Internal Revenue Service has issued a proposed ruling which will make many of the normal kinds of deferred compensation arrangements unattractive because, according to this position, the IRS will assume that the deferred payments are available to the employee while he is working and therefore he will be taxed on those amounts on a constructive-receipt theory. About all that can be said at this time is that this is a problem which should be looked at carefully when the occasion arises.

Excess-Benefit Plans

The kinds of deferred compensation contracts to which the above discussion is directed are characterized by individuality. Each contract is tailored to the specific circumstances of the executive. There is, however, a very close cousin to the deferred-compensation contract which was born out of the necessity for dealing with the limitation on benefits from qualified plans imposed by ERISA. ERISA established a lid of $75,000 per year on benefits which people could receive out of a qualified pension plan. This was to be indexed upward to the cost-of-living index, and as of 1976, the $75,000 limit had been indexed up to $80,475. The maximum benefit limitation is somewhat complicated. However, for purposes of this discussion, it is sufficient to note that if a company has one or more executives who would receive more than the maximum amount allowed under their pension or profit sharing plans (it should be noted that the limitation is an aggregate one; it is not $75,000 per year per plan), something will have to be done to provide the executives with the difference. The popular name for a program to provide executives with this difference is an "excess-benefit plan." Since it applies only to the very top management of the company, the plan is exempt from most of the detailed and burdensome ERISA requirements. Naturally, these kinds of plans do not receive any special tax benefits, and the tax treatment is governed by normal rules and is not affected by the fact that the intention of the plan is to provide benefits which would not be allowed under ERISA. Most excess benefit plans simply provide for the payment of cash after retirement and are, therefore, very much like a deferred compensation contract. In most cases, the tax treatment will simply be that the corporation gets a deduction when the amounts are actually paid and the individual receives ordinary income when the amounts are received. There are, however, some differences between a typical excess-benefit plan and a deferred-compensation contract. These differences arise out of normal practice rather than legal requirements. In other words, the differences simply reflect ways corporations have dealt with the excess-benefit problem.

The first difference is that the excess-benefit plan will normally provide benefits for the lifetime of the executive while a deferred-compensation contract will normally provide a stated amount of benefits. Typically, a company pension plan will provide, for example, a retirement benefit of 60 percent of the average of the highest five years of compensation. In an excess-benefit plan designed to supplement this pension, the normal approach would be simply to have the executive to be covered promised a benefit under the excess plan of 60 percent of the final five years' compensation and then have that benefit reduced by benefits actually paid under the company's other qualified plans. It is possible, of course, to reduce the benefit by payments received from social security or other sources if that is desired.

Another difference is that the excess-benefit plan usually covers more than one person and imposes a set of relatively standard rules which apply to this group of people who would be affected by the excess-benefit rule. In short, the excess-benefit plan is really a private pension plan for the benefit of top management, even though it takes the form of a nonqualified deferred-compensation arrangement. The provisions of the excess-benefit plan are likely to be much more like a pension plan than is a normal deferred-compensation contract. The benefit is likely to be referred to as a normal retirement benefit, and there are likely to be the same kinds of provisions as contained in a pension plan for adjusting that benefit for early retirement, a surviving spouse, etc.

Since the whole arrangement is, by definition, exempt from any substantive requirements, it is not necessary to follow any prescribed set of rules. For example, you do not have to base the benefit on the same formula that is used in the pension plan. Some companies have based the benefit of these executives on the highest three rather than the highest five years of compensation, and it is possible to credit the executive with more years of service than his actual employment with the company for purposes of this kind of excess-benefit plan. It is also possible to completely disregard the pension plan and establish a whole new set of ground rules for benefits.

An excess-benefit plan is usually directed toward solving the problems imposed by the ERISA limitations on benefits, but it can also be used to solve certain other problems which sometimes arise out of using a broad-based pension plan to fit the needs of a very select group of top management. These might include the following:

1. to include specific provisions to deal with the problem of managers recruited in mid-career who may be close to retirement and who would not be able to obtain a full benefit under the company's pension plan

2. to replace or phase out individually negotiated arrangements with a consistent program

3. to solve the early retirement problems which are unique to senior management

Excess benefit plans have also been attacked by shareholders. The typical approach is to introduce a shareholder proposal along the following lines:

RESOLVED: That the stockholders of the Corporation, assembled in annual meeting in person and by proxy, hereby request that there shall be a fixed dollar ceiling on amounts payable to any executive in excess of the limitations provided for under the Employee Retirement Income Security Act of 1974.

This excess benefit plan discussion is included here only for completeness and because some other commentators include this subject in similar discussions. Actually, it does not really belong in a discussion of incentive compensation because it takes a considerable stretching of reality to find a great deal of incentive in a plan which is devised principally, if not solely, to provide executives with what they had before that was taken away by the Employee Retirement Security Act of 1974.

SECTION FIVE: FEDERAL SECURITIES LAWS

CHAPTER THIRTY-EIGHT

SECURITIES REGULATION: AN OVERVIEW

PERSPECTIVE

A business executive's first job in learning about securities regulation is to establish a good sense of perspective of exactly what it is he should know. He must know about those aspects of securities regulation which affect his company directly—particularly insider trading—and should have a good understanding of the general framework in which securities lawyers operate and the importance of the application of securities laws to all aspects of the company's business. On the other hand, once certain relatively simple procedures are in place, there should be no reason why businesspeople cannot feel confident that the securities area is being well handled by their company's lawyers.

Unlike antitrust and some aspects of labor relations, the securities area is not one where executives must sometimes operate without legal guidance. *In SEC matters, legal guidance should be involved in virtually every transaction.* The timing of most securities regulation problems is such that proper guidance can easily be obtained if the right procedures are in place. This chapter is relatively short because many very important aspects of securities regulation have been deliberately glossed over as being the province of lawyers. The business executive should obtain from this chapter:

1. A basic understanding of the securities law framework so that he can communicate better with his lawyers and ask the right questions at the right time

2. A basic understanding of some of the important problems and why legal reviews must be built into the kinds of corporate situations which can create securities law problems

As further explained in this chapter, the executive should make sure that he and his company are obtaining correct and adequate guidance in their affairs to stay clear of securities problems. This will generally include the following:

1. Involvement of legal counsel in all important business decisions, and attendance of legal counsel at meetings of the board of directors, meetings of executive committees, and management meetings. The purpose is not to let the lawyers run the company but to keep them informed of the business progress of the company, so that they can advise management on the aspects of corporate disclosure further described in this chapter.

2. Legal review and involvement of public announcements. Again, the purpose is not to let the lawyers take over the public relations function, but merely to make sure that corporate news dissemination does not create a problem for the company.

3. Legal review of all stock purchases by insiders. This should assure compliance with rule 10(b)(5) (insider trading) and section 16(b) (short swing profits). The method of this legal review can be informal and flexible—perhaps having all insiders have a conversation with legal counsel before purchasing or selling any of the company stock or that of any of its affiliates.

4. A review by management of how the lawyers are discharging the routine requirements imposed on the company by the various securities laws. Even if management simply asks the question of the lawyers, it will make the lawyers examine their own procedures, and they will have to give some thought to how these routine matters can be handled in the most efficient and economical way for the company. As a practical matter, the management review is likely to be simply a meeting with the senior company lawyer where he or she reports on how this is being accomplished. On the other hand, it is a costly item, and management should focus on this cost just as on any other and require the company's lawyers to justify the costs in terms of other available alternatives.

5. A review with counsel of the officer and director liability question, in which the company lawyer is asked for recommendations on handling potential problems.

OVERVIEW

The regulation of corporate activity by the various securities laws has been so extensive that many practitioners now refer to these laws as "The Federal Corporation Law." These laws reach into almost all corners of corporate activity, and it is the rare business transaction of any magnitude which is not affected in some way by them. From a corporate point of view, there are two important federal securities laws. These are the Securities Act of 1933 and the Securities Exchange Act of 1934.

THE SECURITIES ACT OF 1933

The Securities Act of 1933 regulates any transaction which involves the offering for sale of any security. The act was passed in order to safeguard the investing public against being duped into buying worthless securities. The act is a so-called disclosure statute. In other words, it does not impose any standard of fairness or make any economic judgments as to any security; it simply provides that before any security can be sold to the public, either (1) it must be registered with the Securities and Exchange Commission by providing the Securities and Exchange Commission with a great deal of information, which is then available to the public, and also by the creation of a prospectus, which is filed with the Securities and Exchange Commission and which must be supplied to any prospective purchaser of the new stock; or (2) one of the various exemptions from the securities laws must be found.

Registration of an offering of securities with the SEC and the corresponding preparation of a prospectus is a big job requiring many thousands of dollars of legal and accounting time plus a great deal of administrative effort by the management of the company. The legal implications of this procedure are crucial. If it isn't done right, anyone who signs the registration statement will be liable to the investing public for any loss sustained, and if the prospectus is in any way misleading, the company and those people who signed the registration statement can be liable to people who bought the stock.

The following problems fall under the 1933 Act and should be understood by management:

1. Problems relating to the *public offering* of securities and the possible ways to sell securities under one of the various exemptions. If securities are sold either via a public offering registered with the SEC or under one of the exemptions, there are two possible things that can happen. Either the stock will go up in value, in which case it doesn't really matter whether or not there was any legal problem in the whole procedure, or the stock will go down in value, in which case some purchasers are going to scour every single piece of paper involved in that sale in order to ascertain whether or not there is anybody they can sue to recoup their losses. Accordingly, in order to safeguard themselves from the downside risk, management must make sure that the legal work involved in any sale of securities is not only substantially correct but that it is absolutely and totally without any legal defect at all. This is one of the reasons why the whole process is so time-consuming for both lawyers and accountants. Everyone must check, double-check, and triple-check everything to make sure that there is no possibility of any mistake which a prospective purchaser could seize upon in order to have the transaction rescinded and get his money back. Since the likelihood of suit would be from a lawyer who would also be asking for attorney's fees, a class action asking for substantial recoveries could be expected if a defect in the process was present.

2. Problems relating to *business combinations* where the stock of one company will be given to shareholders of the other. Before 1972, the normal business combination was exempt from any securities regulation on the theory that the exchange of stock between one company and the shareholders of the other was not really a sale of stock. However, this approach was changed in 1972, and the normal business combination will now be subject to SEC rules and must comply with the registration requirements prescribed for such a situation. Again, lawyers must make sure that the entire transaction is completely proper, because if the recipients of the company stock become disenchanted for any reason, one can depend upon a thorough examination of all the documents in order to seize upon any possible defect to rescind the transaction.

3. Problems related to restricted stock where a person obtains shares which were not registered in a normal public offering and, therefore, cannot be sold like normal shares. When shares are not registered with the SEC and are sold in something other than a regular public offering, they are known as "restricted." Typical examples include shares which are obtained in a merger or shares which are obtained in a private offering or intrastate offering, either of which is exempted by the 1933 Securities Act. People who have this kind of stock are subject to elaborate regulation as to what they can do with it. Generally, the amount of such stock which can be redistributed is small, and there are prescribed holding periods.

Each of these problems is discussed in the following sections.

THE SECURITIES EXCHANGE ACT OF 1934

The second important piece of legislation in the securities area is the Securities Exchange Act of 1934. The principal difference between the 1934 Act and the 1933 Act is that the 1934 Act is aimed at providing continuing information to the investing public for certain registered companies, which are generally those companies traded on a national securities exchange or heavily traded in the over-the-counter market. It is the developments under the 1934 Act—particularly section 10(b) and rule 10(b)(5)—which cause the assertion that the federal securities laws now govern corporate transactions so much that they are really a "Federal Corporation Law."

While much of the 1934 Act is technical and of interest only to securities lawyers, the following areas are important for executives to understand, at least enough to spot potential problems and consult counsel where appropriate.

Insider Trading or Deceptive Practices

Section 10(b) of the 1934 Act prohibits any unfair or deceptive practice in the purchase or sale of securities. This rather innocuous sounding phrase has given rise to literally thousands of cases. In some cases, plaintiffs have used this section of the securities law in order to question the management of the corporation in a certain transaction, and in other cases people who bought securities, only to find that they later decreased in value, asserted that those who sold the securities were trading on the basis of "inside information" and, therefore, the transaction should be rescinded. Virtually any kind of business transaction which involves the purchase or sale of securities has been the subject of litigation. Section 10(b) has given rise to more cases and more writing in the legal journals than any other aspect of the federal securities laws—perhaps more than any other single section of any law except section 1 of the Sherman Act.

Short Swing Profits

Another provision of the 1934 Act is section 16(b), which deals with so-called short swing profits. This section prohibits any officer or director or 10 percent shareholder of a company from profiting through two successive trades of the stock of his company made within any six-month period, *irrespective of whether or not that person either knew or used inside information.* If any officer or director or 10 percent shareholder does engage in any such short swing trading, he or she must pay back any profit to the company, and the rules relating to the computation of this profit can actually impose liability in circumstances where money is lost in dealing with the company stock!

Proxy Rules

The 1934 Act provided that it was unlawful to solicit any proxy unless the proxy-soliciting material complied with numerous detailed and technical requirements. This is why the solicitation of proxies for the normal annual meeting of the company is such a legally intensive affair. Again, however, the problem has become complicated because the proxy-solicitation rules are very detailed and if a shareholder of the company either doesn't like what is happening or feels that he was improperly induced to vote for a specific business transaction, he may sue the company under the proxy rules and try to have that transaction rescinded. Again, the problem is that if the business transaction doesn't work out well, or if there is a minority group of shareholders whose views are against the proposed business transaction, there is bound to be a very detailed examination of the proxy-solicitation material, and if there is any problem in it, the company will be sued and will run the risk of having the transaction set aside. In addition, if anyone is damaged, the company might have to pay damages.

Periodic Reporting Requirements

The 1934 Act provides numerous and detailed periodic reporting requirements. The actual content of these reporting requirements is of interest only to securities specialists; however, management should be aware of the broad scope of these requirements and the amount of legal and accounting work which is necessary to comply with them and keep up with the ever-changing rules.

Officer and Director Liability

Both the 1933 and 1934 Securities Acts create many situations which can give rise to personal liability of the officers and directors of the company. This subject is discussed in Chapter 65.

THE SECURITIES ACT OF 1933 AND ITS REGISTRATION REQUIREMENTS

The Securities Act of 1933 was passed by Congress after the Great Depression because it became apparent that, in hindsight, one of the causes of the tremendous stock market decline was a considerable amount of abuse in the securities industry. Stock was sold to the public where no information about the company was available to the public, where the public had no means of finding out such information about the company, and where there was no control over information which a company did disclose. Except for the basic rules of common law fraud, a company could disclose any information it wanted, any time it wanted, and color that information to just about any shade it wanted.

Congress thought that one way of preventing this problem in the future was to provide that any time any company wanted to sell stock to the public it would be required to register that stock by providing certain detailed information about the stock and the company. The 1933 Act started out, and remains, essentially a *disclosure statute*. That is, the Securities Exchange Commission, which is the agency established by Congress to administer the Securities Acts, *makes no value judgments* about the stock. However, the SEC does require detailed information to be supplied by the company, and this information is available to the investing public. Further, the company must solicit the public to buy the stock only by means of a prospectus, which is a document governed by elaborate provisions of the 1933 Act and rules of the SEC all aimed at providing the investor with all the knowledge he should have in order to make an intelligent investment decision. Thus, if a company files the proper registration statement with the SEC and uses a proper prospectus to sell the stock to the public, the requirements of the 1933 Securities Act have been completely satisfied, and there is no federal government stamp of approval on the stock in the sense of an approval that the offering price is fair. In fact, the SEC requires a statement on the face of the prospectus expressly stating that the commission does not "approve" the transaction in the sense of pronouncing on the fairness of it.

Thus, if you or I wanted to raise money from the public, we could simply form a corporation and sell stock to the public at $10 per share (or any other figure we wanted), and the only requirements would be that we filed the registration statement and prepared and used a proper prospectus. In fact, during the market frenzy of the late 1960s, that's just about what happened in a number of situations. Someone with a "hot" scientific or electronic idea who needed capital would simply form a company with a very small amount of his own capital and then sell shares to the public to raise additional capital to conduct research and development to find out if his idea would work and if the product could be sold. All of this was clearly stated in the prospectus—along with statements like "This is a highly speculative security" and financial statements showing that the company had almost no assets and no sales, but investors still snapped up the shares as fast as the underwriters could peddle them. More often than not, most of these highly speculative issues of new companies resulted in financial loss to the people who bought the shares, but it wasn't because all the relevant information wasn't made available to them.

When a company wants to "go public" or when an established company wants to issue additional shares to raise new capital, it will need a great deal of technical legal and accounting help, and it is not the purpose of this chapter to explain all the details of this complex process. However, it does help if management is aware of the legal basis for all the frenzied activity which takes place during a public offering, and some of the pitfalls and planning opportunities which should be explored.

In order to understand the legal activity, some awareness of the rather unusual securities rules and definitions is necessary. The following problems are worthy of some discussion:

1. The legal significance of the registration statement and what it must contain

2. The legal significance of the prospectus and what it must contain

3. Some of the exemptions which may be used to avoid the tremendously cumbersome and costly registration process

Registration

The theory of the 1933 Act is based on the idea that the public can make informed investment decisions if all the relevant information about a company is made available to it. Further, the theory goes, if the company submits that information to the government, which then makes it available to anyone who simply goes to Washington, D.C., parades through the maze of SEC offices until he finds the public filing room, waits a bit in line, attempts to explain to a clerk what he wants, waits a bit more, and then is supplied with a stack of paper 3 inches high but no place to sit down and read it, all investment decisions will be made intelligently.

Even back in 1933, the government had some intimation that each and every person who desired to buy a share of stock might not go to this effort, and so in addition to the registration statement, which is all the material filed with the SEC, the government announced that all stock must be sold pursuant to a prospectus, which is a document designed for the public containing some but not all the material in the registration statement and supposedly understandable by the average investor. The theory of the statute was that the investing public would be provided with a prospectus, given the chance to read it, and then would make the decision on whether to buy the stock.

Obviously, theory and practice do not go hand in hand in the securities area. However, while it is certainly appropriate to poke a little fun at the statute, the securities industry has developed in such a way that the theory really does work just about as set forth above, with one important exception: It isn't the investor who is doing the reading and analysis; rather, the broker or investment adviser has stepped in to accomplish this function.

What will usually happen is something like the following. The company will decide it wants to sell common stock and will select an underwriter. The underwriter will then form a syndicate of other underwriters, and the underwriters will buy the stock from the company at a discount from the public offering price. The underwriters and all the members of the syndicate will then sell the stock to the public. The syndicate is typically quite large, involving a number of brokerage houses each of which has a number of account representatives, known to us all as stockbrokers. The underwriters usually also have research people who do analyze things like registration statements and prospectuses. Thus the original theory of the 1933 Act does work in a permuted sort of way because the underwriters, researchers, and stockbrokers will read all this material, make a decision on which stocks to recommend, and then call their customers with the recommendation. The customer is then relying on the judgment of the stockbroker, and, in many cases, the first time the actual investor ever sees the prospectus is when it comes with his confirmation slip telling him that he has already bought the stock by virtue of the telephone conversation with his broker.

Again, however, certain practicalities tend to get in the way of pure theory. Remember the procedure above: the underwriter bought *all* that stock from the company, and unless he can sell it to the public, he is going to be stuck with it. Therefore, when the stockbroker calls you and says that such and such a company is having a public offering, and that you can buy some of this stock without any commission, what that means is one of the following:

1. The broker has carefully analyzed your investment requirements and the merits of this stock and feels that there is a match and is offering you the chance to buy stock on which the *company* has paid the commission (in this case the underwriting discount).

2. The broker has been told that his quota of stock for such and such a company is so many shares and he had better unload all of it, and your telephone number is one that came up.

This, of course, is true any time a broker calls. You never really know if he legitimately feels that he is presenting you with a special investment opportunity (and assuming he believes this, neither of you really knows if he is right) or whether he is simply trying to peddle some stock. Thus, the universal recommendation to all investors: Know your broker and his reputation.

When you are dealing with large companies already publicly traded and national brokerage houses, the risk of getting taken too badly on some absolutely worthless stock is low. On the other hand, for local brokerage houses handling new ventures, there is a greater degree of risk, and all the SEC filings in the world won't change this. In summary, then, the theoretical protection provided by the availability of all this information is of questionable value. The value of the information itself, however, is very great. The SEC documents are usually absolutely correct, complete, and honest. Hence if you want objective information about a company, that is the place to start. The cost implications of providing all of this information are indeed significant for all companies and will be elaborated on later.

In summary, then, the information made available to the SEC is good

information; there may be too much of it for any average investor to understand or wade through; the mechanisms for getting that information to the
investor may not be good in practice, but there is no doubt considerable merit
in having this complete, accurate, and honest information available. The key
is the complete and honest factor. What makes the information complete
and honest? It is the liability sections of the Securities Act of 1933, which
must be understood by all businesspeople.

Liability

The Securities Act places liability on certain people if the registration statement or prospectus "contains any untrue statement of a material fact or
omits to state a material fact which is necessary for the registration statement
not to be misleading." Congress, of course, could not have said that material
submitted to the SEC had to be accurate, complete, and honest; the elaborate
phraseology used above had to be drafted. Nevertheless, in this book we will
simply use the phrase "honest and complete" with the understanding that
it corresponds to the legalese quoted above.

The persons on whom liability is imposed are the following:

1. The issuer

2. Everyone who signs the registration statement

3. Every director

4. Every person who is named as being about to become a director

5. Every accountant, engineer, or appraiser, or any person whose profession gives
    authority to a statement made by him, who has with his consent been named
    as having prepared or certified any part of the registration statement

6. The underwriter

Note carefully that the drafters of the law (lawyers, of course) carefully
omitted mentioning lawyers in this section. There are some cases which hold
lawyers liable for deficiencies in the registration statement but these involve
cases of rather severe negligence or misconduct. Generally, lawyers are subject
to a lower standard of care because they aren't specifically mentioned in
the statute.

Defenses

Except for the issuer itself, there is a defense to liability if the person accused
can show that "he had, after reasonable investigation, reasonable ground to
believe and did believe, at the time such . . . registration statement became
effective, that the statements therein were true and that there was no omission
to state a material fact required to be stated therein or necessary to make
the statements therein not misleading." In other words, if the accused did
his homework and generally tried to do the best job he could to assure that
the information was complete and honest, he will not be held liable, even if
it is later determined that the information was not complete and honest.
This is sometimes referred to as the "due diligence" defense. This accounts
for the honesty and completeness of the information filed with the SEC.

An example should make the point clear. A company is about to offer
stock to the public, and a registration statement is prepared by the company's
lawyers and accountants. It turns out that the stock is offered to the public

at $30 per share. Shortly after the offering there is news that the company has suffered an embezzlement which will cause a write-down of a material amount, and the stock drops to $25 per share. The persons who bought at the public offering price of $30 are going to be unhappy, and they may allege that the company failed to disclose all material relevant facts in the prospectus. There would then be an elaborate inquiry in order to determine the exact status of the embezzlement at the time of the public offering. Following are some possibilities:

1. The first sign of the embezzlement occurred one week after the public offering. In this situation, there would be no liability on anyone's part. This is the risk inherent in buying stock.

2. The first sign of the embezzlement occurred one week after the public offering, but had the company's auditors exercised proper audit procedures, it would have been discovered before the offering. Here, the auditors would be liable because they were negligent.

3. The first sign of the embezzlement occurred one week before the public offering but management deliberately kept it from the auditors and lawyers so that the bad news wouldn't hurt the offering. Obviously, everyone who participated in the cover-up would be liable. The liability of the directors (assuming they had no knowledge of the embezzlement) would depend on whether they exercised due diligence to make sure the registration statement was accurate.

To whom are these people liable and for how much? In our case, the typical answer would be that these people are jointly and severally liable (meaning that each one is liable for the entire amount of the loss) to all the people who bought the stock at $30 per share, and the damages will most likely be $5 per share because that is the difference in price the stock sold for when knowledge of the embezzlement was made known.

There are, of course, an infinite variety of examples and situations which could be given, but the essential point is that, when you are filing documents with the SEC, management must be sure it has done everything in its power to make sure that the information is correct. If it does not, it runs the risk of personal liability for huge amounts.

One problem in the SEC area is that of the so-called expert, which in this context can mean an accountant and, arguably, in some situations a lawyer. An expert is placed in the same class as a director or principal officer of the company for purposes of SEC liability, and if the attorneys and accountants don't do a good job (judged of course in hindsight by a court after a problem has been discovered) they will be held liable unless they can show the court that they exercised due diligence in the preparation of their respective parts of the registration statement and prospectus. This accounts for the frenzied activity and the checking, cross-checking, and interviewing that goes on during the preparation of a registration statement and also accounts for a considerable amount of the costs involved, at least in terms of legal and accounting time. Naturally, it aids in the completeness and accuracy of the finished product, and without this potential liability, the SEC documents would not be prepared with the same care they are.

A Word about SEC Forms

SEC forms are unlike those used by most other government agencies. They are not really forms in the sense of income tax forms, and one doesn't really fill them out. Instead, the SEC forms are elaborate guides which have as their base a set of questions which the registrant must address. The amount of space necessary to spell out the required information and the exact way it is provided varies among different practitioners, and experienced SEC lawyers will have elaborate sets of "forms" in the sense of prior registration statements which have been approved by the SEC. Since all information must be submitted to the SEC in essentially the style that the person preparing it wants, and since the SEC has the ability to require you to state the information in the style *it* wants, the usual practice is to submit information in ways which parallel past submissions as closely as possible, and most SEC registrations start out as "cut-and-paste jobs." This, however, is a potentially troublesome problem, because management sometimes gets the impression that the lawyers are simply cutting up an old registration statement or prospectus, changing a few figures and dates, and using it for the new registration. In some cases, this may be true, but this would be done only after the lawyer had elaborately checked every point to make sure that all required information was submitted accurately and completely. The fact that the language may look very much the same from prospectus to prospectus means only that lawyers tend to use what has been previously used and not (if they are doing their job properly) that they simply sat down in their office and cut up an old prospectus to use for your offering.

Using the Underwriters' Counsel

The preparation of the registration statement will involve the underwriters to a substantial degree because their interest in the transaction is essentially the same as management's—to present an honest, error-free document—because they have the same liabilities as management if something goes awry. Consequently, they will be represented by their own counsel, who, in most cases, will be a partner from one of the larger law firms who specialize in SEC work. One of management's jobs should be to make sure that their own counsel uses underwriters' counsel to the maximum extent possible and does not let the preparation of the registration statement turn into some kind of contest between management's lawyers and underwriters' counsel to see who can do the most work. If management uses outside counsel, this will run the bill up considerably. If the company is large enough to have in-house capability in this area, the underwriters' counsel should be used to provide a legal overview and to supplement the work of the in-house counsel, who may not have the same breadth of experience because he has not handled registrations with the same degree of regularity. One of the items for negotiation between the company and the underwriters in the initial transaction will be who is paying the underwriters' legal fees. If the underwriters are paying, the company may as well make use of this free legal help. On the other hand, if part of the deal is that the company will pay these fees, management should make sure it doesn't get "double-barreled" on everything.

Alternatives to a Public Offering

Even assuming that a company is already publicly traded, there is so much time, effort and expense that must go into a public offering that it is worth considering alternatives. Some of the alternatives are in the kind of stock which will be offered (preferred, common, bonds, etc.). These are financial alternatives and, from the point of view of the registration process, aren't very different, because it takes just about equal effort to register an offering of common stock, preferred stock, or bonds. All of these are securities, and essentially the same rules apply to all.

However, the SEC rules discussed above apply only if a company is offering its securities to the public in interstate commerce. If the offering is private, or if all the offerees are resident within one state, different rules apply. Unfortunately, there has developed another complete set of rules involving these so-called private and intrastate offerings, so that while it is fair to say that the time and expense involved will be less than for a public offering, there will still be the necessity for substantial legal work.

I mention the subject of exemptions because it would appear appropriate any time management wants to raise money through a stock offering, or to use a stock offering in a business combination, to ask the lawyers to present an analysis of the possible exemptions so management can be sure that it isn't missing out on a possible tool which would save a lot of money and trouble. In many cases, there will be some legal reason why none of the exemptions apply, but the only way management can be sure that they have been considered adequately is to ask the lawyers for a discussion.

BUSINESS COMBINATIONS: RULE 145

Background

For many years, the SEC had a rule (Rule 133) that, in the case of mergers and some similar corporate reorganizations, there was no need to comply with the registration requirements of the Securities Act of 1933. The rule did this by providing that in such cases, the exchange of shares of one company for the shares of the other did not constitute a sale. The rationale for this rule was that the transaction was not really individual action but rather action by the shareholders of the corporation as a group (in approving the merger, for example). The result of this rule was that in some cases extremely large amounts of securities could be issued to relatively large numbers of persons without the filing of any registration statement or other document with the SEC. For example, a large, publicly held company could acquire a smaller company and issue an unlimited number of its shares to an unlimited number of people without making any filings with the SEC. Naturally, if the acquired company required the approval or consent of its shareholders and it was a registered company, the acquired company itself would have to comply with the proxy-solicitation rules, and the proxy materials would contain a considerable amount of material on the acquiring company. However, if the company to be acquired was not subject to the proxy rules, no SEC filings were needed in the case of the typical merger.

In addition to the above, there were some unfortunate and confusing exceptions to Rule 133, the most important of which was the negotiated-transaction exception, which provided, in substance, that if the company to be acquired had only a few shareholders, all of whom were active in the merger negotiations, the rule did not apply, because each shareholder really had something to say about the matter. Also, the question of the status of the shares obtained in the merger was subject to question. Were the persons who obtained the shares of the acquiring company free to sell those shares or not? Rule 133 itself contained some "leakage" provisions, which provided that small amounts of shares acquired pursuant to a Rule 133 transaction could be sold, but even these provisions were subject to some differences of opinion as to their applicability on a continuing basis.

Rule 133 lead a stormy life. Many persons both within and without the commission advocated its repeal. The following were the principal objections to the rule:

1. Its basic logic was thought by some to be incorrect: the individual shareholder did act individually and was not necessarily dragged into a merger by the will of the majority.

2. The provisions of the rule itself—particularly those involving subsequent distribution of shares acquired in a Rule 133 transaction and the negotiated transaction problem—created practical problems because of their ambiguity.

3. As a practical matter, some persons were funneling large amounts of unregistered securities into the public by use of Rule 133 and publicly held shell corporations. In some cases, companies actually went public by simply merging with a shell corporation which was publicly held. Publicly held shell corporations became valuable for this purpose, and it was possible to effect a distribution of a large amount of stock and obtain a public market in the securities of a company by this method without ever filing a registration statement with the SEC.

The solution to the above problems was promulgated by the SEC in the form of Rule 145.

What the Rule Does

Basically, Rule 145 simply repeals Rule 133 and provides that a typical merger is not an exempt transaction just because no sale is involved; rather, it must be registered with the SEC (unless, of course, another exemption applies). In some cases, this really has very little practical business significance. These are the cases where:

1. The company to be acquired is already publicly held, so that the proxy-solicitation rules would have to be complied with anyway. Here, the new rule simply provides for a very short registration form which is little more than a few items of information in addition to the proxy statement.

2. The company to be acquired is very small. In this case, it is likely (though by no means certain) that another exemption might be applicable. The most likely candidates for another exemption are the private offering exemption and the intrastate offering exemption. It should be noted that in many cases, the intrastate offering exemption will not be applicable because the state of incorporation of the acquired company, the principal place of business of the acquired company, the state of incorporation of the acquiring company, and the principal place of business of the acquiring company may all be different. The private offering exemption may not be clearly applicable in many cases. It is, therefore, possible that even a very small acquisition will necessitate a registration statement.

In all other cases, the new rule will necessitate the filing of a registration statement with the SEC. There is a new form for this purpose (Form S-14), and substantially the same kinds of information would have to be filed with the SEC and given to the persons who will become shareholders of the new company, as in a public offering.

Sale of Shares Acquired in a Rule 145 Transaction

The status of shares acquired in a merger under the prior Rule 133 "no sale" rule was a little unclear, some practitioners taking the view that such shares were "free" and could be resold at will and others taking a more restricted view. Under Rule 145, the ability of a person to resell the shares he acquires in a Rule 145 transaction depends upon that person's status under the securities law concept of "affiliate." If the person is not an affiliate, the shares he obtains are apparently free of any restriction on resale. On the other hand, if the person is an affiliate (defined as a person controlling, controlled by, or under common control with the acquired company) the following rules are applicable:

1. The person can sell his shares only in nonpublic transactions or pursuant to a registration statement (Form S–14).

2. The affiliate may resell in compliance with Rule 144 (discussed infra), which provides for the sale of smaller quantities of stock without registration, except that the two-year holding period of Rule 144 is not applicable, and Form 144 need not be filed.

RESTRICTED STOCK

When a person acquires stock which has not been registered, that stock will be called "restricted stock," and it cannot be sold by that person except in compliance with the terms of the SEC rules on selling restricted stock. Formerly, these rules were very subjective and ambiguous. Often the answer to the question of whether stock acquired in a private placement, an intrastate offering, or a merger (the three prime examples of situations where stock was not registered) could be sold depended on the lawyer you asked. There were even many jokes about "opinion shopping." This opinion shopping resulted only in part from differences in integrity of various lawyers. The principal problem was the ambiguity involved in these rules and the legitimate differences of opinion among the members of the securities bar. While all of these differences and ambiguities have not been removed, the SEC took a giant step in this direction by promulgating Rule 144, which provides the rules for the sale of restricted stock.

Background

Under the prior law, after a private placement, intrastate offering, or merger, the question of how and when the person who acquired the shares issued in that transaction could sell them depended principally on three factors. These were:

1. Elapse of time

2. Change of circumstances

3. The fungibility concept

The Time Requirement

It had been thought by the commission and the securities bar that restricted stock could be sold by the holder only after it had been held for a certain period of time. Unfortunately, there was no agreement on what this time period was. Further, it was not any fixed time, but it seemed to depend upon all the circumstances of the situation. Some people even denied that there was any specific amount of time the passing of which by itself justified the sale of restricted stock without a registration.

The Change-of-Circumstances Doctrine

When a person bought securities under the private placement exemption he represented that he was taking them "for investment," and the technical legal question was whether or not he was taking them for investment at the time when he took them. If he was taking them for investment initially, it technically shouldn't have made any difference whether he sold them the next day. Unfortunately, if he did, there might be some justifiable question as to whether or not he was really telling the truth when he said he was taking them for investment. There therefore emerged the change-of-circumstances doctrine, which was basically a tool by which an investor could say with some legitimacy that while he took the securities for investment when he bought them, the facts were now different and he was entitled to sell them. The time requirement is also, of course, based upon this theory. His intention at the time of the acquisition was to hold for investment, but his intent changed after the requisite period of time. Unfortunately, there was no agreement between the commission and the securities bar, or among members of either group, as to precisely what constituted a change of circumstances which would justify the sale of unregistered securities.

Further, there seemed to be a nebulous but nevertheless very important interaction between the time requirement and the change-of-circumstances doctrine. The theory was very simple: The longer the time requirement, the less the need for a change in circumstances, and vice versa. Again, however, the actual application of this doctrine depended to a considerable extent upon the degree of persuasiveness of the individual investor, the competence and sophistication of the lawyer, and, as some less-than-charitable critics have suggested, the value of the client to the lawyer and the fee to be charged by the lawyer for his opinion letter that the proposed sale could take place.

The Fungibility Doctrine

The fungibility doctrine is another one of those theories which made the sale of the restricted securities an extremely complicated matter. If an individual bought registered securities in a public offering and then acquired securities of the same company in a transaction which did not constitute a public offering—i.e., restricted securities—he could not sell any stock, even that stock acquired in the public offering, because, since some of his stock was restricted stock, it was all governed by the rule for restricted stock. The general consensus of members of the securities bar was that this theory would not stand up in court, but since the commission used it for purposes of issuing "no-action letters" and deciding when to prosecute, it presented a problem.

In addition, a person who was in control of an issuer had a similar problem, because a control person could not make a distribution of stock and the question of what constituted a distribution (which was forbidden without a registration) as opposed to mere trading (which is expressly permitted by the Securities Act) was very complex. Generally the question depended upon the amount of the securities sold and the frequency with which they were sold.

The above state of the law was highly unsatisfactory from the standpoint of both the commission and the securities bar, principally because of its uncertainty. Beginning approximately 1969 and continuing through a later series of proposals by the commission and discussions with the securities bar, these rules were evaluated and new ones proposed. Rule 144 represents the results of these discussions. Rule 144 is now the "Bible" on the sale of restricted stock. Generally Rule 144 provides that a person who holds restricted stock can sell it under the following circumstances and conditions:

1. There must be available a certain minimum amount of current public information concerning the issuer. If the company is one which is subject to the 1934 Act and files all its proper reports, this requirement will be satisfied. If the company is not registered under the 1934 Act and does not file all the required reports, the rule gives a long list of things which must be publicly available but does not greatly elaborate on what "publicly available" means. Consequently there may be some problem in the application of Rule 144 in a company which is not registered under the 1934 Act. On the other hand, if a company is registered under the 1934 Act there is a premium on filing all the required reports on time so that those people who may hold restricted stock can sell it.

2. There must be a minimum holding period. Generally this is two years. Again, however, there are some elaborate technical requirements. For example, the person must have been a beneficial owner and the full price must have been paid for the stock for the two-year period.

Limitation on Amounts of Securities Which Can Be Sold

There are basically two limitations on the amount of restricted stock which the holder may sell. The first is any limitation contained in an express promise. In other words, if the purchaser promised to retain the stock for a certain period, say one year, or to refrain from selling that stock to any person not a resident of a certain state, those are contractual commitments which are, of course, binding. The second is the arbitrary maximum amounts imposed by Rule 144 so that persons who obtain restricted stock can only sell small amounts of it at any one time. Thus, for example, if a person obtained a large amount of stock in a private placement, intrastate offering, or merger, that person could only "dribble out" the stock pursuant of these Rule 144 maximum amounts. Generally, the maximum amounts depend on the trading in the stock. The higher the trading volume, the more that can be sold. In summary, the rule is the following:

During any three-month period a person holding restricted stock can sell only the greater of

1. 1 percent of the shares outstanding if the stock is not publicly traded

2. An amount equal to the average weekly trading volume in the preceding four weeks before the sale if the stock is publicly traded

Manner of Sales

Sales of stock under Rule 144 may be made in brokers' transactions but the seller may not solicit or arrange for the solicitation of orders or make any payments other than the normal brokerage commission. The broker must do no more than execute the order as agent for the seller and receive no more than the usual broker commission. The broker is under the duty of reasonable inquiry to make sure that the seller is complying with all requirements.

Filing the Notice

At the same time the order is placed with the broker upon reliance on Rule 144 the seller must file three copies of Form 144 with the SEC unless sales during any six-month period will not exceed 500 units or $10,000.

Attribution Rules

In making the necessary computations under Rule 144, the following rule must be taken into consideration: A "person" is defined to include his or her spouse and all relatives in the same household, any trust or estate in which such person has a 10 percent beneficial interest or serves as trustee or executor, and any other organization in which the seller has a 10 percent or more equity interest. Sales by any of the following must be aggregated and attributed to all of them:

1. Pledgor, pledgee and purchaser of pledged securities during two years after default

2. Donor and donee during two years following donation

3. A trust and its settler during two years after acquisition of securities by the trust

Rule 144 Not Exclusive Method of Selling Restricted Stock

Rule 144 is not the exclusive method of selling restricted stock. However, the following statement of the commission on this point should be kept in mind:

> A number of persons have commented that it is not clear whether the rule, as proposed, was intended to be the exclusive means for selling restricted securities without registration under the Securities Act. In this connection, certain commentators asserted that the Commission does not have the statutory authority to adopt such an exclusive rule while others stated that the Commission had such power and urged it to adopt an exclusive rule. The Commission does not believe it is necessary to reach these questions relating to its statutory authority at this time, since the rule as adopted is not exclusive. However, persons who offer or sell restricted securities without complying with Rule 144 are hereby put on notice by the Commission that in view of the broad remedial purposes of the Act and of public policy which strongly supports registration, they will have a substantial burden of proof in establishing that an exemption from registration is available for such offers or sales and that such persons and the brokers and other persons who participate in the transactions do so at their risk.

Change-of-Circumstances Doctrine

The commission has put all persons on notice that the change-in-circumstances concept should no longer be considered as one of the factors in determining when restricted stock may be sold.

Time Factor in Non-Rule 144 Cases

The commission has also said that, with respect to restricted securities acquired after the effective date of the rule but not sold pursuant to the provisions of the rule, the commission hereby gives notice that in deciding whether a person is an underwriter, the length of time the securities have been held will be considered, but the fact that securities have been held for a particular period of time does not by itself establish the availability of an exemption from registration.

Fungibility

The SEC announcement adopting Rule 144 provides that the fungibility doctrine will not apply to transactions covered by the rule. The clear implication
is that it will apply to any transaction not specifically covered by the rule.

Practicalities and Paperwork

As is evident from the foregoing discussion, proper compliance with Rule
144 can be complicated, and prudent business executives as well as brokers
will want to document the fact that the rule is being complied with. This
means generating a considerable amount of paperwork, usually including the
following:

1. Form 144. Form 144 should be properly filled out and mailed to the commission
    and any appropriate stock exchanges.

2. Prudent counsel will generally want a letter from the client covering at least
    the following points:

    (a) Affiliation to the issuer
    (b) The applicability of any attribution rules
    (c) The transaction by which the securities were acquired and how long they
        have been held
    (d) A representation that no solicitation or payment besides customary bro-
        kers' commissions will be made by the seller
    (e) The seller's bona fide intention to sell the securities

3. A letter from the issuer stating that it has filed all the required SEC forms
    (or otherwise satisfied the public-availability-of-information requirement) and
    that it authorizes the transfer if the other requirements of Rule 144 are met.

4. Seller's letter to his broker (generally covering the same items as the letter
    to his attorney).

5. The broker will generally want the opinion letter to cover all the various
    points set forth in Rule 144 and to contain a statement that it may be relied
    upon by the issuer and the transfer agent.

6. Other considerations.

    (a) If any shares are not sold, a certificate for those unsold shares should
        probably have the restrictive legend placed on them and a stop order
        issued to the transfer agent before the certificate is returned to the seller.
    (b) If appropriate, the seller must file the Form 4 (required of officers, directors
        and 10 percent shareholders under section 16(a)) within ten days after
        the end of the month in which the sale took place.

This is an extremely technical area, and business executives should seek
legal advice when sailing in these deep waters. They should also insist that
their counsel keep enough abreast of developments and any relevant facts
to provide constructive advice and guidance before problems arise.

CHAPTER THIRTY-NINE

INSIDER TRADING

Section 10(b) and Rule 10(b)(5)

Section 10(b) of the 1934 Securities Act provides in pertinent part as follows:

> It shall be unlawful for any person . . . to use in connection with the purchase or sale of any security . . . any manipulative or deceptive device or contrivance in contravention of such rules and regulations as the Commission may prescribe as necessary or appropriate in the public interest or for the protection of investors.

The relevant regulation is rule 10(b)(5) of the Securities and Exchange Commission, which provides as follows:

> It shall be unlawful for any person, directly or indirectly by the use of any means or instrumentality of interstate commerce, or of the mails, or of any facility of any national securities exchange
>
> (a) to employ any device, scheme, or artifice to defraud,
> (b) to make any untrue statement of a material fact or to omit to state a material fact necessary in order to make the statements made, in the light of the circumstances under which they were made, not misleading, or
> (c) to engage in any act, practice, or course of business which operates or would operate as a fraud or deceit upon any person, in connection with the purchase or sale of any security.

The principal development in the 10(b) area occurred in 1947, when it was held that the section, as elaborated on by the rule, created a *private right of action.* Because of the broad working of the section and the rule, there has been a veritable flood of litigation concerning them, and entire books have been devoted to this body of law.

Analysis of Rule 10(b)(5)

Rule 10(b)(5) establishes the following requirement:

> Anyone in possession of material inside information must either disclose it to the investing public or abstain from trading. Further, where the corporation is concerned, the duty to disclose may exist in certain cases even if the corporation is not trading in its own securities.

The theory of the rule is that it is inherently unfair for a person who has material inside information to enter into a transaction, either buying or selling, with a person who does not have this information. Also, this type of activity does not promote public confidence in a free and open securities market.

Following are some points which add to the above description of the rule:

Securities Covered

The rule applies to all transactions in securities even if the transactions are in shares of a closely held company.

Persons Covered

The category of persons owing a duty under rule 10(b)(5) is virtually unlimited. Of course, it includes the corporation itself and the officers, directors and majority shareholders. However, the prohibitions of rule 10(b)(5) extend to anyone in possession of material inside information, even including those who are not connected in any way with the corporation, such as brokers. A person receiving a "tip" may be covered by the rule. Such persons must not trade on the inside information they receive. It is not clear precisely how far this doctrine goes. At this point persons tipped by those already tipped are probably covered, but the extent of this chain is not yet known.

Privity

There is no requirement of privity in a 10(b) case. The rule can reach market transactions where the buyer and seller do not deal directly with each other. A plaintiff can maintain an action against original sellers of securities although he did not purchase directly from them, and a plaintiff can establish a claim against a corporation even though the corporation did not engage in any transaction in its own shares.

Materiality

Most 10(b)(5) cases involve either misrepresentation or nondisclosure of a material fact. The question of precisely what is a material fact is, of course, ultimately decided by the trier of fact. The courts hold that a conservative standard is not appropriate, that speculators and chartists of Wall Street are also deserving of protection, and that insider trading activity itself is "highly pertinent evidence" of materiality.

The concept of materiality is limited only by the imagination of the SEC, plaintiff's lawyers, Congress, and other groups who sometimes try to use the securities laws for purposes for which they were never intended. For example, the concept of materiality can be extended to the character of the officers and directors of the company, because it is assumed investors would not want to invest in companies whose officers and directors made illegal political contributions, questionable foreign bribes, etc. The concept can extend to social questions, such as employment discrimination and pollution. To its credit, the SEC has thus far tended to use a fair amount of discretion in confining the concept to the kind of financial materiality which was originally intended; but it has required disclosure of financially immaterial political contributions because they are illegal, and it does require disclosure of environmental litigation, even for small cases.

Interaction of Inside Information and Other Factors

In some cases involving alleged insider trading, the defendant will try to cloud the issue of possible misuse of inside information by pointing out that there were a number of other factors which influenced his decision to buy or sell. Also, the defendant may say that, while he had certain information, this information was so uncertain and subject to so many contingencies that it was too remote to give rise to liability.

These contentions will not remove possible liability. The case of *SEC v. Shapiro* is illustrative. In this case, the defendants were financial consultants who were trying to arrange a merger between two companies. The proposed merger was not public information, but the defendants nevertheless purchased stock of one of the companies and tried to escape from subsequent liability by contending that the merger information was not material because the actual possibility of a merger was too remote and was subject to many contingencies. The court, however, did not accept any part of this argument.

> Defendants claim that their purchases were based on an evaluation of criteria independent of the merger negotiations. We reject that claim since the timing of the purchases clearly suggests that they were based on the knowledge of the proposed merger and the effect it would have on the value of Harvey's stock. Even though other factors may have been evaluated, their insider knowledge must be considered the key and motivating element in their decision to buy.

There are some very difficult problems in this area which are not yet adequately resolved. For example, what is the status of a financial analyst who assembles data, most of which is public but some not, simply because no one bothered to print it?

Reliance

It is sometimes said that in order for a plaintiff to succeed in a 10(b)(5) case, there must be some form of reliance. However, this is generally limited to cases involving some actual misrepresentation. In misrepresentation cases, the test of reliance becomes clouded with the issue of materiality. For example, one court has indicated that "the test of reliance is whether the misrepresentation is a substantial factor in determining the course of conduct which results in [the plaintiff's] loss." In nondisclosure cases, the reliance requirements seem to be entirely subsidiary to the materiality requirement. The Supreme Court has indicated, in *Affiliated Ute Citizens v. United States*, that reliance is not a requirement for recovery in nondisclosure cases. In that case, the Court said:

Under the circumstances of this case, involving primarily a failure to disclose, positive proof of reliance is not a prerequisite to recovery. All that is necessary is that the facts withheld be material in the sense that a reasonable investor might have considered them important in making his decision.

In the proxy situation, it has already been held that reliance was satisfied by a showing of materiality. In the case of *Gilbert v. Nixon*, the court stated that reliance is not a condition for recovery under rule 10(b)(5), but held that "evidence of reliance when presented does bear upon the issue of materiality if that reliance is determined to be reasonable."

Causation

Causation is another element which technically must be present but, in most cases, courts are willing to assume its presence. For example, in the *Affiliated Ute Citizens* case, the Court said:

This obligation to disclose and this withholding of a material fact establish the requisite element of causation in fact.

Intent Requirement

Some of the early cases in the 10(b) area questioned whether or not any criminal state of mind was necessary. The cases tended to talk in terms of "negligence" or something that the defendant "should have known" or lack of "due diligence." However, the Supreme Court laid all these arguments to rest in 1976 in the case of *Ernst & Ernst v. Hochfelder*, where it read the language of rule 10(b)(5) fairly literally and said that, in order to recover damages, the plaintiff had to prove that the defendant deliberately engaged in some deceptive practice. Mere negligence was not enough.

Standing to Sue

In the *Birnbaum* case, a lower court expressed the proposition that the plaintiff must be a purchaser or seller of securities. This so-called Birnbaum limitation has been frequently followed. It has been much criticized by many writers but, in the words of one case, "bloody but unbowed, Birnbaum still stands." The Birnbaum holding was sustained by the Supreme Court in 1975, and so there is no doubt about its validity. This "purchaser-or-seller" rule is quite troublesome because it admittedly creates inequities. If someone deliberately misleads the public into refraining from selling shares by saying good things about the company so that the shareholders hold their stock, they cannot recover. Yet if the same statements induce a new shareholder to purchase stock, he can. On the other hand, a contrary holding would create an administrative nightmare and a horrendous liability. Every time a company was accused of sending out a misleading press release, everyone in the world could claim that he either held his shares, or did not buy shares, because of this and was therefore damaged. Consequently, the purchaser-or-seller rule is really one of administrative convenience.

Damages and Injunction Questions

In face-to-face transactions, the damage problem is not particularly complicated. Plaintiffs can have a recision of their transaction even if this results in a windfall to them, or they can collect their actual damages or lost profits. However, the damage question in market transactions is considerably different, particularly in class actions against a single defendant or group of defendants. In this case, the basic securities law principles of compensation and deterrence must be balanced against considerations of fairness.

1. If liability is limited to those who can trace their transactions to the insider, the plaintiffs who recover will be receiving a windfall because of the accident that their transactions could be traced to insiders. Deterrent value will be small.

2. If defendants are required to pay all who traded during the period of their trading activities, they may be financially destroyed.

3. If recovery is limited to defendant's profits and either distributed evenly among all plaintiffs or given to the corporation, the deterrent value will again be small and injured parties will not be compensated for their injuries.

In the damage area, there is probably a distinction between misrepresentation cases and simple negligent nondisclosure cases. In misrepresentation cases involving market trading by the defendant or those in which the defendant has engaged in deliberate or reckless conduct, it may be fair to make him pay damages to everyone injured.

It is clear that *punitive damages* are not allowed.

Where misleading, incomplete, or incorrect information is disclosed to the public, the theory of damages seems to be that the defendants ought to be able to recover the difference between the price at which they bought or sold and the price that the stock would have reached had correct information been disclosed. In the most frequently cited case squarely raising this point, *Texas Gulf Sulphur*, there was a corrective press release issued shortly after the incorrect press release, and the courts have thus far used various formulas for determining a price based on the corrective press release. One court used the mean average price of TGS common stock on the day following publication of the corrective press release, and another court chose the average of the highest daily sales for the twenty days after the corrective press release came out.

Tipping

The *Texas Gulf Sulphur* case also required one defendant to pay an amount equal to his "tippee's" profits. In *Shapiro v. Merrill Lynch Pierce Fenner & Smith*, the Second Circuit Court of Appeals has laid down some rather harsh laws on the liability of tippers and tippees in securities cases. This case arose out of an underwriting for Douglas Aircraft done by Merrill Lynch in 1966. Basically, the facts were that Merrill Lynch, in its capacity as underwriter, learned of some very substantial adverse information regarding Douglas Aircraft. This information included sharply reduced earnings from earlier periods and reduced projections for the next year's earnings. Merrill Lynch then proceeded to tell this information to some of its institutional customers, who then sold. The price of Douglas's common stock dropped over 20 points in nine days because of the selling activity of these tippees. When the whole story of the reduced earnings and lower projections was finally made public, the stock dropped some more.

There were a number of cases filed and decided, with the obvious result. The following rules were established:

1. There is no legal distinction (at least for this purpose) between the nontrading tippers and the trading tippees.

2. The trading tippees are liable, not only for damages to those who purchased their stock but to all those who traded in Douglas common during the relevant time (the problem is that the transactions all took place on national securities exchanges, and it would be almost impossible to trace specific purchaser/seller relationships. A contrary holding would have greatly reduced the practical liability of the trading tippees).

3. Of course, the tippers also violated the law, and this has been clear since the basic *Texas Gulf Sulphur* litigation.

Injunction

The SEC has injunctive power under sections 20(b) of the 1933 Act and 20(e) of the 1934 Act. There have been uses of this from time to time, including a use in the *Texas Gulf Sulphur* case where the Second Circuit Court ordered cancellation of stock options issued to insiders.

Corporate Disclosure

As far as the corporation is concerned, Rule 10(b)(5) poses two major questions:

1. What should be disclosed, when should disclosure be made, and to whom should disclosure be made?

2. Under what circumstances may the corporation purchase or sell its own shares?

From a day-to-day operating standpoint, the first question is perhaps the more serious. The rule is very simple to state: A corporation should make prompt disclosure to the public of all material facts affecting the corporation. However, in practice, it is very difficult to determine precisely what is a material fact, and it is also difficult to determine precisely at what time a development should be disclosed to the public. In addition, some companies have a question of how to disclose information. In large, publicly held companies traded on a national exchange, it is fairly easy to make disclosure through a press release. However, in smaller companies, the newspapers are simply not interested in having press releases dealing with a lot of things, even those which the corporation probably should disclose. In this situation, the corporation just has to think of another way to disseminate information. Possible solutions are letters to shareholders and paid space in newspapers.

Another question which the corporation always faces is the particular wording of the news release. This was apparent in the *Texas Gulf Sulphur* case. Everyone seemed to realize that a press release had to be issued, but the first press release was judged by the court to be too conservative and therefore misleading. In the 10(b)(5) area, the corporation must walk a tightrope between nondisclosure and too much disclosure, and between disclosure which is too pessimistic and disclosure which is too optimistic.

The Texas Gulf Sulphur press release illustrates the problem. In the *Texas Gulf Sulphur* case, the corporation had made one test drill in Timmins, Ontario, and had removed a sample core which showed a very, very high mineral content. Texas Gulf Sulphur felt very strongly that it had made a good find, and it proceeded to acquire many leases in the area of the test drill. When it had substantially completed its acquisition of leases, there were many rumors about a high mineral find, and Texas Gulf Sulphur decided that it had to make a press release. The first press release which it made attempted to play down the find on the theory that it was really only one test drill and not too much emphasis could be placed on a single drill. However, a few days later, after some additional drilling, Texas Gulf put out a much brighter looking press release. In the meantime, it appeared that many Texas Gulf employees had purchased stock when they had never purchased stock before, and indeed had even purchased calls in some cases where they had never before purchased anything in the stock market. This activity all tended to cloud Texas Gulf's contention that its first press release was merely an innocent misrepresentation.

The SEC policy on corporate disclosure is well stated in a 1970 announcement:

For RELEASE Thursday, October 15, 1970
SECURITIES AND EXCHANGE COMMISSION
Washington, D.C. 20549

SECURITIES ACT OF 1933
Release No. 5092
SECURITIES EXCHANGE ACT OF 1934
Release No. 8995
INVESTMENT COMPANY ACT OF 1940
Release No. 6209

TIMELY DISCLOSURE OF MATERIAL CORPORATE DEVELOPMENTS

The Securities and Exchange Commission today reiterated the need for publicly held companies to make prompt and accurate disclosure of information, both favorable and unfavorable, to security holders and the investing public. Companies subject to the reporting requirements of the Securities Exchange Act of 1934 are, at the present time, generally required to file annual reports within 120 days after the end of their fiscal years, semi-annual reports within 45 days after the end of the 6-month period and current reports within 10 days after the end of the month in which a reportable event has occurred. . . . In this regard, the Commission has noted that certain reporting companies from time to time have been delinquent in filing periodic reports under the Securities Exchange Act and the Investment Company Act. The Commission emphasized its concern about such delinquent filings, and hereby reminds reporting companies of their obligations to file reports on a timely basis as required by the Commission's rules.

Notwithstanding the fact that a company complies with such reporting requirements, it still has an obligation to make full and prompt announcements of material facts regarding the company's financial condition. The responsibility for making such announcement rests, and properly so, with the management of the company. They are intimately aware of the factors affecting the operations of the business. Management of non-investment companies are cognizant of factors affecting profits and losses, such as curtailment of operations, decline of orders, or cost overruns on major contracts. They are also cognizant of liquidity problems such as a decreased inflow of collections from sales to customers, the availability or lack of availability of credit from suppliers, banks, and other financial institutions, and the inability to meet maturing obligations when they fall due. . . .

Not only must material facts affecting the company's operations be reported; they must also be reported promptly. Corporate releases which disclose personnel changes, the receipt of new contracts, orders and other favorable developments but do not even suggest existing adverse corporate developments do not serve the public needs and may violate the anti-fraud provisions of the Securities Exchange Act of 1934, and in the case of a registered investment company or other issuer making a continuous offering of its shares may also violate the Securities Act of 1933 if the prospectus is not appropriately updated.

The policy of prompt corporate disclosure of material business events is embodied in the rules and directives of the major exchanges. It should be noted that unless adequate and accurate information is available, a company may not be able to purchase its own securities or make acquisitions using its securities, and its insiders may not be able to trade its securities without running a serious risk of violating Section 10(b) of the Securities Exchange Act of 1934 and Rule 10(b)(5) thereunder.

Corporate managements are urged to review their policies with respect to corporate disclosure and endeavor to set up procedures which will insure that prompt disclosure be made of material corporate developments, both favorable and unfavorable, so that investor confidence can be maintained in an orderly and effective securities market.

Corporate disclosure can arise in another situation—usually referred to as "gun jumping" or "market conditioning." This is the situation where a company is "in registration" (generally defined to be the period after a registration statement is filed with the SEC and before the distribution of those securities has been completed and all market stabilizing activities have ceased). This situation has given rise to a specific SEC release stating the circumstances under which disclosure should be continued even during this period of registration. By implication, that release would seem to have some relevance to standard 10(b)(5) disclosure because it provides that certain disclosures should be made even if the company is in registration, therefore making it probable that the SEC would view such disclosures to be appropriate if the company was not in registration. The text of that release is reproduced below.

Text of SEC Act Release No. 5180 (August 16, 1971)

GUIDELINES FOR THE RELEASE OF INFORMATION BY ISSUERS WHOSE SECURITIES ARE IN REGISTRATION

The Commission today took note of situations when issuers whose securities are "in registration" may have refused to answer legitimate inquiries from stockholders, financial analysts, the press or other persons concerning the company or some aspect of its business. [Editor's note: "In registration" is used herein to refer to the entire process of registration, at least from the time an issuer reaches an understanding with the broker-dealer that is to act as managing underwriter prior to the filing of a registration statement and the period of forty to ninety days during which dealers must deliver a prospectus.] The Commission hereby emphasizes that there is no basis in the securities acts or in any policy of the Commission which would justify the practice of non-disclosure of *factual* information by a publicly held company on the grounds that it has securities in registration under the Securities Act of 1933 ('Act'). Neither a company in registration nor its representatives should instigate publicity for the purpose of facilitating the sale of securities in a proposed offering. Further, any publication of information by a company in registration other than by means of a statutory prospectus should be limited to factual information and should not include such things as predictions, projections, forecasts or opinions with respect to value.

A basic purpose of the Act and the Securities Exchange Act of 1934 is to require dissemination of adequate and accurate information concerning issuers and their securities in connection with the offer or sale of securities to the public, and the publication periodically of material business and financial facts, knowledge of which is essential to an informed trading market in such securities. It has been asserted that the increasing obligations and incentives of corporations to make timely disclosures concerning their affairs creates a possible conflict with statutory restrictions on publication of information concerning a company which has securities in registration. As the Commission has stated in previously issued releases this conflict may be more apparent than real. Disclosure of factual information in response to inquiries or resulting from a duty to make prompt disclosure under the antifraud provisions of the securities acts or the timely disclosure policies of self-regulatory organizations, at a time when a registered offering of securities is contemplated or in process, can and should be effected in a manner which will not unduly influence the proposed offering.

Statutory Requirements In order for issuers and their representatives to avoid problems in responding to inquiries, it is essential that such persons be familiar with the statutory requirements governing this area. Generally speaking, Section 5(c) of the Act makes it unlawful for any person directly or indirectly to make use of any means or instruments of interstate commerce or of the mails *to offer to sell* a security unless a registration statement has been filed with the Commission as to such security. Questions arise from time to time because many persons do not realize that the phrase "offer to sell" is broadly defined by the Act and has been liberally construed by the courts and Commission. For example, the publication of information and statements, and publicity efforts, made in advance of a proposed financing which have the effect of conditioning the public mind or arousing public interest in the issuer or in its securities constitutes an offer in violation of the Act. The same holds true with respect to publication of information which is part of a selling effort between the filing date and the effective date of a registration statement.

Section 5(a) of the Act makes it unlawful to sell a security unless a registration statement with respect to such security has become effective. Section 5(b) makes it unlawful to make use of any means or instruments of transportation or communication in interstate commerce or of the mails to transmit a prospectus with respect to any security as to which a registration statement has been filed unless such prospectus contains the information specified by Section 10 of the Act. Pitfalls may be encountered because the term *"prospectus"* has a broad meaning. The Act defines prospectus to include any notice, circular, advertisement, letter or communication written or by radio or television, which offers any security for sale except that any communication sent after the effective date of a registration statement shall not be deemed a prospectus if prior to or at the same time with such a communication, a written prospectus meeting the requirements of Section 10 of the Act was sent or given.

Guidelines The Commission strongly suggests that all issuers establish internal procedures designed to avoid problems relating to the release of corporate information when in registration. As stated above, issuers and their representatives should not initiate publicity when in registration, but should nevertheless respond to legitimate inquiries for factual information about the company's financial condition and business operations. Further, care should be exercised so that, for example, predictions, projections, forecasts, estimates and opinions concerning value are not given with respect to such things, among others, as sales and earnings and value of the issuer's securities.

It has been suggested that the Commission promulgate an all-inclusive list of permissible and prohibited activities in this area. This is not feasible for the reason that determinations are based upon the particular facts of each case. However, the Commission as a matter of policy encourages the flow of factual information to shareholders and the investing public. Issuers in this regard should

1. Continue to advertise products and services.
2. Continue to send out customary quarterly, annual and other periodic reports to stockholders.
3. Continue to publish proxy statements and send out dividend notices.
4. Continue to make announcements to the press with respect to factual business and financial developments; i.e., receipt of a contract, the settlement of a strike, the opening of a plant, or similar events of interest to the community in which the business operates.
5. Answer unsolicited telephone inquiries from stockholders, financial analysts, the press and others concerning factual information.
6. Observe an "open door" policy in responding to unsolicited inquiries concerning factual matters from securities analysts, financial analysts, security holders, and participants in the communications field who have a legitimate interest in the corporation's affairs.
7. Continue to hold stockholder meetings as scheduled and to answer shareholders' inquiries at stockholder meetings relating to factual matters.

In order to curtail problems in this area, issuers in this regard should avoid:

1. Issuance of forecasts, projections, or predictions relating but not limited to revenues, income, or earnings per share.
2. Publishing opinions concerning values.

In the event a company publicly releases material information concerning new corporate developments during the period that a registration statement is pending, the registration statement should be amended at or prior to the time the information is released. If this is not done and such information is publicly released through inadvertance, the pending registration statement should be promptly amended to reflect such information.

The determination of whether an item of information or publicity could be deemed to constitute an offer—a step in the selling effort—in violation of Section 5 must be made by the issuer in the light of all the facts and circumstances surrounding each case. The Commission recognizes that questions may arise from time to time with respect to the release of information by companies in registration and, while the statutory obligation always rests with the company and can never be shifted to the staff, the staff will be available for consultation concerning such questions. It is not the function of the staff to draft corporate press releases. If a company, however, desires to consult with the staff as to the application of the statutory requirements to a particular case, the staff will continue to be available, and in this regard the pertinent facts should be set forth in written form and submitted in sufficient time to allow due consideration.

Private Trading—Conclusions

From a trading standpoint, it is clear that if the corporation knows of some factor which would influence the value of the stock, it should not trade in its stock unless this factor (1) is disclosed and (2) has had sufficient time to reach the public. (It should be noted that rule 10(b)(6) prohibits the company from purchasing any of its own shares irrespective of any inside information involved at a time when a distribution of those shares is being made. This prohibits the obviously manipulative practice of a company's making an artificial market in its own shares at a time when it is having a public offering.) The tipping problem is also important for companies because it appears that if a corporate insider discloses material inside information for a proper purpose and takes adequate precautions to see that the tippee does not improperly use or further disclose the information, he is not subject to liability even if that tippee actually does improperly use or disclose that inside information.

From an individual trader's point of view, whether he is a corporate insider or an individual who has inside information but no connection to the corporation, rule 10(b)(5) would stand for the proposition that such an individual should not trade in the shares of the subject corporation until this information has been disseminated to the public. This has been held in the *Texas Gulf Sulphur* case to prohibit an insider from receiving a stock option at a time when he had undisclosed inside information even though the committee which granted him the stock option did not have such information. If a person who receives material inside information discloses that information to a second tippee and that second tippee profits by the information, it has been held that the disclosing insider is liable for the second tippee's profits *even though the tippee did not personally profit from the transaction.* As of this time, this is as far down the chain as this theory has gone. However, if the tippee happens to be a brokerage house which passes the information on to its customers, as in the Merrill Lynch–Douglas Aircraft situation, the tippee problem could generate a veritable avalanche of liability.

CHAPTER FORTY

SHORT SWING
PROFITS

INTRODUCTION: Section 16(b) of the Securities Exchange Act of 1934

Section 16(b) of the 1934 Securities Exchange Act provides that *any profit realized by insiders from transactions within any six-month period involving securities of their company shall be recoverable by their company.* Prior to the enactment of section 16(b), it was a generally accepted practice for corporate insiders to profit from "sure thing" speculation in the stock of their corporations. For example, one reported case involved a situation where the president of a corporation and his brothers controlled a company with a little over 10 percent of the shares. Shortly before the company passed a dividend, these insiders disposed of their holdings for more than $16 million and later repurchased them for about $7 million, showing a profit of approximately $9 million on the transaction. Section 16(b) was enacted to prevent this type of conduct by corporate insiders who used confidential information for their personal gain at the expense of the investing public.

To implement the law, section 16(a) provides that insider transactions must be reported to the Securities and Exchange Commission, which in turn publishes them. In addition, potential 16(b) liability must be revealed in proxy statements. Suit can be brought by any shareholder whether or not he was a shareholder at the time the violation occurred, even though he purchased his shares for the purpose of bringing the suit, and reasonable attorney's fees are awarded where funds are recovered for the issuer, even if the principal motive for instituting the suit is to recover attorney's fees. Thus there has grown a body of persons who can be depended upon to examine the SEC reports and ascertain violations of the short swing profits section and take appropriate action.

Who Is Subject to the Law?

Section 16(b) applies to three classes of persons:

1. Beneficial *owners* of more than 10 percent of any class of equity security of a company which is registered under section 12 of the Securities Exchange Act of 1934. (Generally, companies with more than $1 million of assets and 500 shareholders are required to register.)

2. A *director* of such a company.

3. An *officer of* such a company.

Who Is an Officer?

The normal SEC definition of "officer" applies to short swing transactions, and this provides as follows:

> The term "officer" means a president, vice-president, treasurer, secretary, comptroller, and any other person who performs for an issuer whether incorporated or unincorporated, functions corresponding to those performed by the foregoing officers.

The SEC and the courts have taken a functional view of the question of who is an officer. In other words, it is the actual duties performed by the person that will govern the question rather than the title the person has or whether the person is listed as an officer in the corporation's annual report or bylaws. Accordingly, it is possible that a person might be termed an officer of the company in the company's publications but might not be covered by 16(b) because he really did not perform the duties of such an officer. (A typical example would be a person designated as a vice-president who really did not perform any important duties for the company.) On the other hand, designation of a person as an officer has an obvious prima facie effect. This gives rise to the problem of whether or not a person designated as an officer of a division would be covered by 16(b). For example, suppose an executive was given the title of president of the truck division of Allied Motors Corporation. Even though the person would be designated as a president, it is probable that if that person's duties were limited to the truck division, as opposed to corporate duties, he would not be covered by section 16(b).

On the other hand, the reverse situation could apply. An executive could have a very modest title and perhaps even be called an "assistant," a title which normally would exempt him from the application of 16(b). However, if that person actually performed the duties of an officer, he would be covered. Furthermore, it would not appear necessary for the person to perform the duties of the officer at all times. For example, suppose an executive was given the title of "assistant to the president" and actually performed as assistant until the president became ill, and then for a period of six months performed the duties of the president. For this six-month period, such a person should be considered an officer for 16(b) purposes. One case indicates that the term "officer" includes an employee "performing important executive duties of such character that he would be likely, in discharging those duties, to obtain confidential information about the company's affairs that would aid him if he engaged in personal market transactions." This is not the approach taken by the SEC and would probably not be the approach taken by most courts today. However, many cautious company counsel believe that individuals who would be included in this category should be informed of the basic provisions of section 16(b) and advised that a violation, if discovered, might cause them and the company some embarrassment and legal expenses. Such persons are clearly subject to 10(b)(5) restrictions.

Who Is a Director?

This rule is analogous for directors: it is a functional definition. A director includes any person who performs the duties of a director and, if a director is *designated* by an organization to act on its behalf, the designator may also be a director for 16(b) purposes. This is particularly significant for investment firms, which sometimes designate one of their members to act as a director in companies in which they have an interest. In this situation, the investment company may itself be deemed a director.

The deputization problem is frequently discussed in the 16(b) literature. The first important case to raise it was *Blau v. Lehman.* While this case pointed out the theory, it actually held that the director in question was acting individually. There was a strong dissent. The case of *Feder v. Martin Marietta Corporation* involved two business corporations rather than the financial community. This case actually held that the Sperry Rand Corporation was the director, and the individual actually serving as a director was merely a deputy of Sperry Rand. There was considerable evidence to support this finding.

The counseling point is very clear, especially in the business context. If there is any doubt about whether the corporate employee is serving in his own capacity or in that of an agent of his employer, both should refrain from short swing transactions.

A person who *becomes* a director or officer between two transactions within six months is probably subject to the rule, and, in the time since the *Martin Marietta* case, a person who *ceases* to be a director or officer between two transactions within six months can be held subject to it. However, liability cannot be imposed on a *former* officer or director of a company who purchases and sells within six months even if this is done shortly after he terminates his employment.

It might be assumed that, as a practical matter, the application of section 16(b) could be limited to those who, in fact, report their transactions in the issuer's stock under 16(a) and, if a restrictive approach as to who should report under 16(a) is taken, the application of 16(b) will be limited accordingly. However, reporting under 16(a) is not an admission of status under 16(b), and a specific disclaimer of status under 16(b) can be, and often is, included in the 16(a) report. *Also, a failure to report under section 16(a) will probably have the effect of tolling the two-year statute of limitations for the assertion of a claim under 16(b).* It is, therefore, dangerous to fail to report on the assumption that if you do not, "no one will ever know."

In addition, the SEC has successfully prosecuted a corporate officer for failure to file a report, and has censured a company whose officers and directors were repeatedly late in filing. If a person is damaged by an officer's or director's failure to file a report, civil liability might result. However, by far the most serious problem would be a willful violation of section 16(a), either by not filing where it was required or by misstating information on the report. In this event, section 32(a) of the Exchange Act would apply, and it provides criminal penalties.

Careful monitoring of the section 16 area is in order for business executives and corporate counsel. The problem simply cannot be ignored, because all the reports are published, and there are a substantial number of "professional plaintiffs" who carefully review these reports in order to find cases where they might recover attorneys' fees, which are generously awarded because of the congressional intent to have this law enforced not only by the SEC but by these private plaintiffs.

Who Is a 10 Percent Owner?

Section 16(b) applies to a 10 percent shareholder only if he is such both at the time of purchase *and* at the time of sale. However, these terms are slightly ambiguous because it is not entirely clear whether the precise purchase by which one either becomes or ceases to become a 10 percent shareholder is counted. There is conflicting authority on these points. The most logical approach, which was recently announced in the Seventh Circuit Court in the case of *Allis-Chalmers Mfg. Co. v. Gulf & Western Industries, Inc.*, seems to be to refrain from adopting any hard and fast rule on this point, but to look instead at whether or not the purchase by which one acquired his 10 percent interest was one in which there was any possibility for insider abuse. The *Allis-Chalmers* case goes into considerable detail on this point and discusses the conflicting authority and the legislative history of section 16(b). However, in the facts of that case (which involved an initial purchase of more than 10 percent in a tender offer), the court held that such a purchase should not be counted because there was no possibility for abuse of insider information. The courts, especially in the tender offer situation, are making increasing use of this "equitable" approach to 16(b) even though it was originally drafted as a hard and fast rule to be applied irrespective of actual misuse of inside information. However, the rule was originally promulgated with more or less "normal" trading by individual insiders in mind, and these tender offer situations create entirely different situations involving very different equities. Accordingly, the cases which allow an equitable approach to section 16(b) interpretation are very strong in the area of tender offers, but it may be dangerous to attempt to generalize them to other situations.

It appears at present that the owner of more than 10 percent of a company who wants to divest his ownership without waiting out the statutory six-month period can do so in stages and avoid liability for the last stage of the transaction when he is no longer a 10 percent shareholder. An insider with 13 percent of a company can sell slightly more than 3 percent in one transaction, which will be governed by 16(b), and then sell the remaining slightly-less-than-10 percent without any 16(b) liability. The Supreme Court has sanctioned this approach.

The purchase and sale must take place within the six-month period, and a purchase in the final day of a six-month period beginning with the date of a previous sale is not considered a prohibited short swing transaction. The six-month period is started at 12:01 A.M. on the first day and ends at midnight on the day two days prior to the corresponding date in the sixth succeeding month. As an example, an insider who made a sale on April 17 would not be liable for a subsequent purchase unless it occurred on or before October 15.

Following are some points on calculating 10 percent ownership in cases where the individual involved is deemed to own more shares than those registered in his name. It should be noted that many of these points are covered in the context of *reporting* under 16(a) rather than *liability* under 16(b). The mere fact of being required to report under 16(a) will not automatically give rise to liability under 16(b), but the reverse is probably true: if there is no reporting requirement under 16(a) there will be no liability under 16(b). Hence, while the analogies to 16(a) rules for 16(b) purposes may be less than perfect, they are very useful.

1. SEC Release 34–7733 (1966) provides that stock owned by a person's spouse and minor children will generally be regarded as beneficially owned by him, but the presumption is rebuttable. In one illustrative case where the presumption was rebutted, the person's wife maintained a separate trading account for many years—her funds were kept segregated, her trades were made without her husband's knowledge, and purchases were made entirely with her own money.

2. The SEC presumes stock owned by the relative of a person in the same household is beneficially owned by him, but beneficial ownership can be disclaimed on Form 4.

3. In some cases, stock owned by a partnership or a trust will be deemed owned by the individual.

4. If convertible stock is involved, the 10 percent is determined by assuming conversion.

Definition of Equity Security

An equity security encompasses far more than just the common stock of the company and includes securities which may be converted into common stock. Again the general Exchange Act definition contained in rule 3(a)(11) applies:

> The term "equity security" is hereby defined to include any stock or similar security, certificate of interest or participation in any profit sharing agreement, preorganization certificate or subscription, transferable share, voting trust certificate or certificate of deposit for an equity security, limited partnership interest, interest in a joint venture, or certificate of interest in a business trust, or any security convertible, with or without consideration into such a security, or carrying any warrant or right to subscribe to or purchase such a security or any such warrant or right, or any put, call, straddle, or other option or privilege of buying such a security from or selling such a security to another without being bound to do so.

Class of Security

The 10 percent rule applies separately to every class of security. A class of securities includes all those which have substantially the same character and rights attached to them, but different series of stock which call for different dividend rates, redemption prices, or sinking fund provisions are not considered separate classes.

TO WHAT TRANSACTIONS DOES 16(B) APPLY?

Section 16(b) applies to *purchases* and *sales* of an equity security. A purchase or sale includes any contract or agreement to acquire or dispose of a security, and conversions, mergers, reclassifications, corporate simplifications, acquisitions, stock dividends, and stock splits have also been defined as purchases and sales for this purpose by the courts. These types of transactions can become quite complex and their characterization as a purchase or sale depends on all the facts. However, it is relatively clear that if there is in fact any potential for insider abuse, the transaction is very likely to be characterized as a purchase or sale for 16(b) purposes.

Conversions are a troublesome area. Here, the courts have tended to say that 16(b) should not be applied automatically in any case where there is no possibility of unfair insider trading. The comment is made that such an automatic application would be purposeless harshness. Thus, at least in the conversion context, if the convertible security and the underlying common stock are economic equivalents and there is no change in the insider's investment risk, the conversion will probably not be characterized as a purchase or sale, or if so characterized, the court is likely to refuse to impose any liability because of the lack of realization of any profit.

Corporate reorganizations must be examined closely to determine whether or not the particular exchange involved can be coupled with another within six months to give rise to an unforeseen liability. Recent court cases have tended to take a subjective approach here and hold that there is a purchase or sale involved only where there is at least some possibility of abuse of inside information. However, there are many cases where liability has been imposed and extreme caution is dictated.

Traditional 16(b) rules apply to the employee benefit area. The granting of the typical stock option is not a purchase or sale, nor is the accrual of the right to exercise the option. Of course, the actual acquiring of the shares under the option is a purchase.

Section 16(b) has no application to bona fide gifts, even though the insider may receive a tax benefit by giving the stock to a charitable donee, or an emotional gratification by giving the stock to a noncharitable donee. If the gift is not bona fide (for example, if it is made to the insider's controlled foundation, which immediately sells the stock), a problem could result.

Puts and calls may not be equity securities *of the issuer* because they are typically not issued by the company, but rather are written by individual shareholders. However, put-and-call transactions can generate some rather complicated factual situations and some significant litigation. In addition, this is a particularly sensitive area with some commentators because the tremendous leverage inherent in put-and-call transactions makes the possibility of flagrant insider abuses in this area very significant. Therefore, put-and-call transactions should be considered as a potential source for 16(b) difficulty and analyzed accordingly. Rule 16(a)(6) requires reporting of puts and calls, but this does not entirely dispose of the liability question.

Computation of 16(b) Liability

Liability is computed by matching the highest sales with the lowest purchases during the appropriate six-month period. Purchases and sales during different six-month periods and possibly even during overlapping six-month periods can be matched in the same suit. For example, in the same suit, a May purchase could be matched with a September sale, and an October sale with a December purchase. The periods could probably be overlapped to match the May purchase and the October sale and the September sale and the December purchase. There can be no matching of certificates in the sense that this is permitted for federal income tax purposes; and no first in–first out rule, average cost rule, or any other method yielding a lesser liability can be used.

In the case of stock acquired under an option, the purchase price is deemed to be the *higher* of (1) the market value of the stock at the date on which the option first became exercisable, or (2) the lowest market price within six months before or after the sale (note that this gives the insider the right to use the rule providing the least recovery). This rule has little logic but is a reasonable compromise between providing that the purchase price is the actual purchase price under the option, and thus penalizing the insider for the increase in value of the stock over a long period of time, and providing that the purchase price is the market value on the date of exercise, thus yielding no recovery even in the case of obvious abuse.

If dividends are declared on the insider's shares during the period he is holding them, the dividends can also be recovered unless they are too inciden-tal. A dividend will be incidental where (1) it is small in relation to the value of the stock, or (2) there is no possibility of insider manipulation of the dividend.

Interest on the profits can be awarded at the discretion of the court, and usually is. The expenses of the transaction (e.g., brokerage commissions and transfer taxes) can be deducted from the recovery. However, if the individual has borrowed money to purchase the shares, it is not clear that the interest paid for the use of this money is deductible from the recovery. (Of course, it is deductible for federal income tax purposes.)

If an insider engages in a series of transactions, some of which produce an economic loss, it is clear that he cannot deduct those losses from the profits made on the other transactions. Furthermore, it is possible that each transaction would produce a loss but, considered together, a gain for 16(b) purposes would occur. For example, if an insider bought some shares at $10 and sold them at $5, and bought additional shares at $20 and sold them at $15, he would have a loss on each transaction, but the high sale price of $15 would be matched against the low purchase price of $10 to give a 16(b) liability of $5 with no offset for any losses. Profit is realized, and hence the period of the statute of limitations begins, on the date the order giving rise to the profit is executed. The fact that the particular shares in question represented a controlling block can be taken into consideration by the plaintiff to increase the amount of the recovery. This is an equitable concept designed to accomplish the objective of the statute. However, it is difficult to use the concept the other way and attempt to deduct a "control premium" from the sale price so as to eliminate what would otherwise be a short swing profit.

Possible Defenses

Once all the elements of a 16(b) case are shown, the application of the rule *is automatic.* There are no defenses. A settlement of a 16(b) liability between the corporation and the insider does not bind any security holder not a party to it, irrespective of the wisdom of bona fides displayed by the corporation. In addition, the insider cannot raise the defense of estoppel against the corporation, even if the insider sold the stock at the issuer's suggestion and had the sale approved by all the issuer's then shareholders. The insider may not discharge his obligation to the corporation by giving the corporation a promissory note. He must immediately pay the profits back in cash. Since the corporation and the employee are at least theoretically in a conflict of interest situation where 16(b) is involved, it is probably inappropriate for company counsel, either outside or inside, to give advice to insiders concerning their personal liability under 16(b). Also, it is possible (although it has not yet been held) that an employee who receives inadequate or inaccurate advice from his employer on a 16(b) problem may have a cause of action against the employer.

Federal Income Tax Treatment of 16(b) Payment

There is a division of opinion between the tax court and the federal courts on the question of the deductibility of payments made by an employee to his employer under section 16(b). The typical pattern of the cases is that the employee pays the employer the profit and attempts to claim an income tax deduction because the payment was an ordinary and necessary expense of his trade or business (of being an employee). The trouble is, this "profit" which he is paying back to the corporation may have previously been reported as a capital gain (where he was permitted to deduct one-half the total gain or pay a maximum rate of 25 percent) and if a deduction from ordinary income is allowed, there will, in effect, be a double deduction. It is, therefore, argued that when these profits are paid back to the corporation, they should retain the same character as when they were originally taxed and treated only as a long term capital loss, which, of course, is much less favorable under the income tax laws.

At the present time, the tax court usually holds that there is no integral connection between the original sale at a profit and the required payback to the corporation under 16(b) and, therefore, the payment under 16(b) is deductible as an ordinary and necessary business expense. However, the federal courts of appeals almost universally hold to the contrary and reverse the tax court.

OTHER RELATED RULES

Section 16(c) of the Securities Exchange Act of 1934 makes it unlawful for any insider to engage in a short sale or a "sale against the box" of any equity security of his issuer. A short sale is a sale of a borrowed security, where the seller has no inventory of such security. A sale against the box is a sale of a borrowed security where the seller does have an inventory of such security but chooses not to deliver it at the time of sale. If an insider owns a security in his company which he is selling, he must deliver it within twenty days or place it in appropriate delivery channels (like the mails) within five days of the sale.

The New York Stock Exchange has issued an announcement dealing with insider trading on companies listed thereon. The announcement says that it would seem appropriate for officials to buy or sell stock in their companies for a thirty-day period commencing one week after the annual report has been mailed to stockholders and otherwise broadly circulated, or after quarterly reports or other wide dissemination of information, such as a proxy statement or prospectus, has been made, or where there is a relative stability in the company's operations and the market for its securities. The announcement specifies only guidelines, and the New York Stock Exchange Manual itself provides that "in the final analysis, directors and officers must be guided by a sense of fairness to all segments of the investing public."

The 10(b) problem is closely related to short swing profits. However, there is a fundamental difference between rule 10(b)(5) and section 16(b). Rule 10(b)(5) requires some sort of manipulative practice. The perimeters of rule 10(b)(5) are still being drawn, but it is clear, at least at this point, that there must at least be an allegation of some sort of deception or failure to disclose, or some other conduct which is in some way "bad" even if only negligent. However, section 16(b) has no such requirement. Its provisions operate automatically once the required elements are shown, and actual possession of inside information, use of inside information, disclosure, or the care taken by the insider to deal fairly and honestly, are all completely irrelevant.

PRACTICAL ADVICE AND PROBLEMS

The above is a general discussion of the various 16(b) rules, and the following are some of the possible applications of those rules in certain problem situations.

Dividend Reinvestment Programs

Many companies have dividend reinvestment programs by which shareholders may have the dividends they would normally receive automatically reinvested for them in company stock—usually with some advantage. The advantage may be either the lower commissions charged on the basis of the higher volume purchases or the company's picking up the tab for all or part of the commission. In addition to the possible monetary advantage, there is a certain convenience factor for shareholders who want to increase their holdings in the company and, according to some financial advisers, the "dollar averaging" which results from purchasing shares with a given amount of money at periodic intervals is a good investment technique.

There is certainly nothing wrong if an officer or director or 10 percent shareholder participates in a dividend reinvestment program. However, the following problems are present:

1. Usually the program calls for purchases of stock every three months. The insider is, therefore, purchasing stock all the time, and it is virtually impossible for him to sell any at any time without a 16(b) problem unless he terminates his participation in the dividend reinvestment plan and waits six months. The problem is present even if the purchases are made annually, because the 16(b) requirements apply both six months before and six months after a given transaction. If purchases are made annually, any sale is bound to be within six months of one of the purchases.

2. A purchase of stock on behalf of an officer or director in a dividend reinvestment plan is not exempt from the reporting requirements. Therefore, the officer or director has to file a Form 4 report for each purchase made on his behalf through the program. This is not a significant problem, but it can be a minor nuisance, particularly if the amounts involved are small.

Officers and directors and 10 percent shareholders must weigh the problems against the advantages of the dividend reinvestment program to see if they want to participate. In many cases, the answer will be that they do not.

Stock Options

Rule 16(b)(3) provides that the granting of a stock option is not reportable under 16(b) and does not cause any other 16(b) implications. However, rule 16(b)(3) goes on for about three pages, and businessmen should get specific advice from their counsel in this area.

The exercising of the stock option, however, is definitely a purchase of stock under section 16(b), and this is perhaps the single most troublesome aspect of the rule. In the first place, even officers or directors who are attuned to the normal application of 16(b) forget about reporting the exercise of stock options because it is not a normal purchase and usually does not lend itself to the possibility of abuse of inside information. However, it is absolutely clear that the transaction is reportable, and the officers and directors of the company who have stock options should be kept informed of this problem. Since the officers and directors in many companies change frequently, this is an ongoing duty.

The second problem is more important, however. Since the exercise of the option is a *purchase,* the officer or director should neither sell any stock six months before or after he exercises his option nor exercise his option within six months of selling any shares.

In many cases, this problem will be overlooked by officers or directors, and they will wind up in violation of section 16(b). It is particularly troublesome for the executive whose principal asset is stock of the company and who, in order to raise the money to exercise his options, must sell company stock. There are many ways to handle this problem if it is discovered in time.

1. The executive can solve the problem on his own by simply remembering to sell the stock needed to raise the money six months before he wants to exercise the option.

2. The executive can borrow the money to exercise the option for six months and then sell the company stock to repay the loan. If the loan is personal, there is no problem. If the stock is pledged for the loan or if the loan is made for the purpose of buying the stock (through the exercise of the option), the normal margin rules are applicable and the individual might not be able to borrow the entire amount he needs, depending on the value of the stock and the option price at the time.

3. It would appear that the executive could borrow the money to exercise his stock option through a loan which was secured by a pledge of company stock (rule 16(a)(6)), but this would be treading on some fairly thin ice because, while the pledge itself, if bona fide, would not be a sale, the sale of the pledged stock would be. Therefore, if the executive did not pay off the loan properly and the pledgee sold the stock before six months, a problem would result, and if the pledgee sold the stock just after the six months, the bona fides of the pledge might be questioned.

4. Many stock options can be exercised periodically. In other words, an executive may have an option for 5000 shares which may be exercised at the rate of 1000 shares each for the next five years. Here, the same problems mentioned in connection with the dividend reinvestment plan exist. If the executive is buying stock at one-year intervals, there is virtually no point at which he can sell any without running afoul of 16(b). This is the classic case where good advance planning is necessary because, if the executive has such an option, and it is valuable, and he wants to reap the benefits from it as they become available, he is going to have to carefully plan his sales and exercises unless he happens to have enough money to exercise the options without selling any company stock.

Gifts

A bona fide gift of securities to a legitimate charity is not a sale of securities for the purpose of 16(b). However, this is subject to two problems:

1. If the donee is not a bona fide charity, but is instead the insider's spouse, minor child, or controlled organization, the sale within six months by such a donee would probably cause 16(b) questions, although the ultimate result would depend on the original bona fides of the gift. For example, if an executive needed to raise money for his child's college and could not sell stock because of another purchase within six months, and simply gave the stock to the child and told him to sell it, a problem might result.

2. If the insider makes a pledge in a *dollar* amount and then satisfies it by giving shares, some commentators (no courts to my knowledge) have suggested that this is just like selling the shares for cash and using the cash to satisfy the pledge, and should be treated for 16(b) purposes as such. The moral of this problem is clear: if one wants to donate company stock to a charity, he should decide at the outset and make the pledge in the form of a certain number of shares rather than stating it in a dollar amount.

Reporting Problems

The reporting rules under 16(a) are a little complex, and they present a number of cases where officers and directors can and should be educated as to the requirements.

Timing

Within 10 days after becoming an officer or director, one must file a Form 3. This form shows the officer's or director's interests in the company at that time. It does not show any changes in ownership. Form 4 is the one which shows the changes, and it is a more important one. It must be filed before the tenth day of the calendar month in which any change occurs. (An officer or director has to file a Form 4 during the first six months after becoming an officer or director and must show all changes in ownership during the preceding six months, not merely those changes that occurred since he filed his Form 3. Form 4 must, of course, be filed all the while the individual is an officer or director—but only when changes occur—and, in addition, it must be filed for six months after he ceases to be an officer or director. Therefore, a retiring officer or director must still keep on filing for six months and should still observe the insider trading prohibitions for this period of time.

What Must Be Reported?

The reporting requirements are very broad and include just about any imaginable change in the officer's or director's ownership in the company stock and many transactions which *might* result in such a change. It is this latter concept which is the problem. The reporting requirements cover not only stock registered in the name of the officer or director and beneficially owned by him, but they cover stock which may be in the name of his family members, in a trust for family members, owned by him as trustee, or owned by any other person or business where he has a beneficial interest. On the other hand, just because the insider has to report the transaction, it does not mean it is governed by 16(b). This is where counsel can and should educate the officers and directors as to how to report so that the true facts are reflected.

Stock Held by Family Members

One of the most troublesome areas is stock held by family members. The SEC's position on beneficial ownership of shares held by family members is contained in Release No. 34-7793 (1966), which provides in part as follows:

Generally a person is regarded as the beneficial owner of securities held in the name of his or her spouse and their minor children. Absent special circumstances such relationship ordinarily results in such person obtaining benefits substantially equivalent to ownership, e.g., application of the income derived from such securities to maintain a common home, to meet expenses which such person otherwise would meet from other sources, or the ability to exercise a controlling influence over the purchase, sale or voting of such securities. Accordingly, a person ordinarily should include . . . securities held in the name of a spouse or minor children as being beneficially owned by him.

A person also may be regarded as the beneficial owner of securities held in the name of another person, if by reason of any contract, understanding, relationship, agreement, or other arrangement, he obtains therefrom benefits substantially equivalent to those of ownership. Accordingly, where such benefits are present such securities should be reported as being beneficially owned by the reporting person. Moreover, the fact that the person is a relative or relative of a spouse and sharing the same home as the reporting person may in itself indicate that the reporting person would obtain benefits substantially equivalent to those of ownership from securities held in the name of such relative. Thus, absent countervailing facts, it is expected that securities held by relatives who share the same home as the reporting person will be reported as being beneficially owned by such person.

A person also is regarded as the beneficial owner of securities held in the name of a spouse, minor children or other person, even though he does not obtain therefrom the aforementioned benefits of ownership, if he can vest or revest title in himself at once, or at some future time.

Generally, the officer or director should report all shares owned by family members, but if the officer or director believes that he is not the beneficial owner of such shares, he should disclaim such beneficial ownership as permitted by the regulations (rule 16(a)(3)). In other words, while the shares should be reported, the method of reporting depends on whether or not there really is any beneficial ownership. For example:

1. If shares are held by the spouse, but the officer or director feels he or she is the beneficial owner, those shares should be listed separately, but with the notation in column 9 "by spouse."

2. If the officer or director feels that the spouse is the real owner, the shares again should be listed separately, but a footnote should include the following statement or its equivalent:
   "Beneficial ownership of the _____ shares held by my spouse is disclaimed."

Stock Held in a Trust

Rule 16(a)(8) sets forth the rules on shares in a trust. In many cases, the officer or director will be deemed the beneficial owner of such shares, and this should be reflected in the Form 4 report. A common and frequently used device to reduce income tax is to place the company stock in a ten-year trust for the benefit of minor children so that the dividends will not be taxable to the officer or director. This is an example of a situation where the shares in the trust should be reported on Form 4.

Employee Stock Savings Plans

Many companies have programs whereby employees are allowed to purchase stock in an employee stock savings plan. Some plans include some form of company contribution, which makes participation desirable. In this case, the officer or director will usually have an account in the plan which will provide that he is the beneficial owner of a certain number of shares. The exact mechanics vary, but the company usually solves any 16(a) reporting problems this might cause by filing a separate report for the plan itself disclosing the interests of officers or directors. In this event, the officer or director should, to be 100 percent safe, include a reference to this report on his own personal Form 4. Something like the following would suffice:

I am a participant in the _____(plan) which holds company stock. Reference is made to the latest annual report _____
[refer specifically to the plan's report, giving the name of the plan]. This report does not include any shares in such plan which may be attributable to my account.

Another aspect of these kinds of plans is that generally the stock received from the plan at the periodic distribution intervals must be reported but is not a purchase. Therefore, when stock so received is reported, it is important to note that it came from one of these kinds of plans. A legend something like the following might be appropriate:

These shares were received in a distribution from _____ [name of the company plan].

These shares, however, are not ignored for 16(b) purposes, and a subsequent sale of them could be matched with another purchase to yield a 16(b) liability.

FORMAL CORPORATE DISCLOSURE

The Securities Exchange Act establishes an elaborate system for formal disclosures which, in many publicly traded companies, can keep one lawyer busy for enough time to justify putting one on salary. Following is a brief rundown of the mass of paperwork which is generally required of a company with publicly traded stock. Taken with the normal advice which must be given and other work related to stock transfer questions, stock exchange matters, and other related aspects of securities regulation, it justifies an evaluation of the most productive means of obtaining this legal work. Management should keep in mind that most of this work which is done in corporate law firms is actually done by senior associates or junior partners (three to seven years' experience). While it may sound a little complicated at first, it is relatively easy to master. In addition, the staff of the SEC is one of the most helpful in all the regulatory agencies. Accordingly, while the traditional lawyers' observation that "it all depends on the facts" must be made here, it would seem that in-house legal attention to securities regulation and related problems could save money and provide a better result and should therefore be looked into.

Highlights of Formal SEC Reporting Requirements

Form 8-K

Form 8-K must be filed within ten days after the end of a calendar month in which any of the specified events occur. Events which currently trigger the report include the following:

1. Certain organizational changes, such as a company's becoming a wholly owned subsidiary or ceasing to be a subsidiary of another company

2. The acquisition or disposition of a significant amount of assets otherwise than in the ordinary course of business

3. The institution of legal proceedings if the outcome would be material to the registrant, or the termination of any previously reported legal proceeding

4. Any change in the instruments defining the basic rights of the security holders, such as the articles of incorporation

5. Any change in the security for registered securities (for example, changes involving security for bonds issued by the company)

6. Any material default with respect to the company's indebtedness

7. Any increase or decrease in the amount of outstanding securities or grant of options for more than 5 percent of the company's securities

8. Any extraordinary charges against income or credits, or in general, any material charges

9. Any material additions to income

10. Any material and unusual credits to income or provision for loss

11. The submission of any matter to the vote of security holders

12. Any change in the registrant's certifying accountant

Form 8-K further defines the above events and sets forth the information to be supplied in connection with each.

Forms 10-Q and 10-K

Forms 10-Q and 10-K must be filed quarterly and annually, respectively, disclosing a great deal of information. These forms are routine in the sense that they have to be filed even if there has been no material event during the period.

In addition to the specific information asked for in the above reports, there is the additional general duty relating to all SEC reports contained in rule 12(b)(20):

> In addition to the information expressly required to be included in a statement or report, there shall be added such further material information, if any, as may be necessary to make the required statements . . . not misleading.

In addition to the periodic reporting requirements, the following relatively formal SEC paperwork is involved in complying with the 1934 Act:

1. Proxy solicitation requirements for the annual meeting, even if the meeting is a routine one, are detailed.

2. The annual report to shareholders, while relatively free from regulation, still requires legal review because there are some technical requirements.

3. The reporting requirements in connection with section 16(b) on short swing profits.

4. State securities law reports. Many states have securities laws, sometimes called "blue sky laws," which impose reporting or registration requirements.

5. Both the American Stock Exchange and the New York Stock Exchange have reporting requirements in the sense of required notification of them for certain major corporate transactions.

In addition to all the above, there are numerous accounting developments which are taking place with great rapidity. Generally, these are the domain of the accountants, but it may also be desirable to have corporate counsel participate in analyzing these accounting requirements and helping ascertain their effect on the company.

Stock Transfer

If the company acts as its own transfer agent, it must be registered with the SEC, and this, of course, entails a substantial amount of legal paperwork.

CHAPTER FORTY-ONE

FOREIGN CORRUPT PRACTICES

During the latter part of 1976 and almost all of 1977, Congress considered various approaches for legislation directed toward the "improper payments" question in the context of multinational corporations and payments to foreign officials.

The outcome of this discussion was the Foreign Corrupt Practices Act of 1977, which was signed by the President on December 20, 1977.

The Foreign Corrupt Practices Act does two things:

1. It imposes some new accounting standards.

2. It imposes some specific prohibitions against improper payments to foreign officials by United States nationals and imposes stiff penalties including fines and possible jail sentences.

ACCOUNTING STANDARDS

The accounting standards which were ultimately enacted are much less burdensome than those which were proposed by various other pieces of legislation. The law requires a company to make and keep books, records, and accounts which, in reasonable detail, accurately and fairly reflect the transactions and dispositions of the assets of the issuer; and to devise and maintain a system of internal accounting control sufficient to provide reasonable assurances that

1. transactions are executed in accordance with management's general or specific authorization

2. transactions are recorded as necessary to permit preparation of financial statements in conformity with generally accepted accounting principles and to maintain accountability for assets

3. access to assets is permitted only in accordance with management's general or specific authorization

4. the recorded accountability for assets is compared with the existing assets at reasonable intervals and appropriate action is taken with respect to any differences

The duty to make and keep books is directed at off-the-books "slush funds." The words "in reasonable detail" were inserted by the House-Senate conference committee "in light of the concern that such a standard, if unqualified, might connote a degree of exactitude and precision which is unrealistic. The amendment makes clear that the issuer's records should reflect transactions in conformity with accepted methods of recording economic events and *effectively prevent* off-the-books slush funds and payments of bribes." (Conference committee report.)

Since it is difficult to see how any system of accounting could allow an off-the-books slush fund, it is difficult to understand the actual effect which this new law might have on a company which had previously developed a good system of accounting. In a very large company, however, the words, "in reasonable detail" could conceivably connote a little more detail in some accounting records than might exist at this time. Accordingly, in light of this new law, it might be a good idea to examine any accounting practices or criteria which could allow for de minimus or immaterial amounts "off the books" and to eliminate any such practice if it exists.

The second accounting requirement is to "devise and maintain a system of internal accounting controls." Obviously, all companies already have a system of internal accounting controls, and any reasonable system would provide assurances against all the things mentioned in the statute. On the other hand, it is possible that existing systems of internal accounting controls might have to be reexamined and possibly restated in order to *expressly* cover these items. In light of this specific requirement, it is probably desirable to have a standard practice instruction of some kind which uses the same words as the statute and imposes upon all the appropriate financial, accounting, and auditing people in the company an express duty to maintain the controls set forth in the statute.

ACTUAL PROHIBITIONS

The actual prohibitions contained in this new law appear clear and reasonably straightforward. They are contained in a new section 30(A) of the Securities Exchange Act of 1934.

The prohibitions are essentially as follows:
It shall be unlawful for any company or for any officer, director, employee or agent of such company, or any stockholder thereof, to make use of the mails or any means or instrumentality of interstate commerce corruptly in furtherance of an offer, payment, promise to pay, or authorization of the payment of any money, or offer, gift, promise to give, or authorization of the giving of anything of value to—

(1)   any foreign official political party or candidate for purposes of—
    (A)   influencing any act or decision of such foreign official in his official capacity, including a decision to fail to perform his official functions; or
    (B)   inducing such foreign official to use his influence with a foreign government or instrumentality thereof to affect or influence any act or decision of such government or instrumentality,
in order to assist the company in obtaining or retaining business for or with, or directing business to, any person.

In addition to the normal words contained in statutes imposing a criminal penalty, such as "for the purpose of," "knowingly," etc., it is interesting to note that all the specific prohibitions are prefaced by the requirement that the payment be made "*corruptly* in furtherance of an offer, payment, promise to pay." (Emphasis added.) It appears that the statute makes it reasonably clear that only those kinds of payments which are probably recognizable by the average person as bribes would be covered. Further, all the specific prohibitions are followed by the phrase "in order to assist the issuer in obtaining or retaining business for or with, or directing business to, any person." This would seem to mean payments made on some kind of a "quid pro quo" basis, involving the actual negotiation of a contract, as opposed to payments to customs officials to *facilitate* entry of materials into a country, etc.

This latter problem created quite a bit of discussion during the passage of the legislation because it appears that it is fairly normal business practice in some countries to make relatively small payments to customs officials to facilitate entry of goods into the country. The conference committee report points out that the term "foreign official" was defined to mean "any officer or employee of a foreign government . . . or any person acting in an official capacity for or on behalf of such government." The term does not include employees whose duties are primarily ministerial or clerical. This definition, coupled with the other portions of the law requiring a corrupt payment as a quid pro quo, would seem to make it reasonably clear that so-called grease payments made to induce people to take ministerial duties sooner rather than later were not intended to be covered.

Payments for Services

Most of the foreign bribes which have been brought to the attention of Congress have been in the form of payments for services. Further, the payments were coupled with admittedly legal and proper payments. For example, a law firm which charged $1000 for a piece of work might be paid $2000 instead, the extra $1000 going to some foreign official; commissions might be increased over the normal; advertising expenses might be padded; insurance payments might be irregular. In some of these cases, the people involved knew what they were doing, but others higher up in the corporation were effectively kept in the dark because of the highly subjective amounts of these kinds of fees.

One problem this new statute presents is how companies should audit admittedly proper payments to make sure they do not contain improper elements. What duty does the corporation have to make sure its foreign law firm is not padding its fees so that it can bribe a foreign official? What about commissions to foreign sales agents? What kind of system does the company need to make sure that commissions are paid only for legitimate services? No one is quite sure yet, but there should be some effort to determine this.

At a minimum, there ought to be the consideration of issuing a memo summarizing this new statute to everyone in the company who is in charge of paying these kinds of fees so that such people are required to satisfy themselves that the fees are proper and to make inquiries about any unusual charges. For example, if an agent suddenly increases his commission from 5 percent to 8 percent, there should be something in the file reflecting that the company investigated the reason and was satisfied that it was legitimate. In some cases, it might be prudent to consider a letter to everyone performing these kinds of services for the company that the company policy is to abide by his new law and not to pay any bribes. It may also be prudent to have the recipients sign a copy of the letter and return it to verify the fact that all charges are only for services rendered. As an alternative, you might want to have these people include a legend on all their statements, or you might want to include a letter with all your checks, saying (quite truthfully) that your intention is merely to comply with the requirements of the new United States law on foreign corrupt practices. The new law makes it quite easy to bring up this delicate subject.

PENALTIES

The penalty section is quite severe and imposes fines of up to $1 million for the company and up to $10,000 or imprisonment of not more than five years for officers or directors who willfully violate section 30(a).

The new law also contains the following provision:

> Whenever a fine is imposed . . . upon any officer, director, stockholder, employee, or agent of an issuer, such fines shall not be paid directly or indirectly by such issuer.

JURISDICTION

One of the troublesome problems dealt with during the enactment of this legislation was the question of jurisdiction. The Foreign Corrupt Practices Act covers only United States companies and individuals who are subject to the jurisdiction of the United States. It defines "domestic concern" as follows:

> (1) The term "domestic concern" means (A) any individual who is a citizen, national, or resident of the United States; or (B) any corporation, partnership, association, joint-stock company, business trust, unincorporated organization, or sole proprietorship, which has its principal place of business in the United States, or which is organized under the laws of a State of the United States or a territory, possession, or commonwealth of the United States.

Using normal principles of law, the clear cases are easy to describe.

1. The act probably reaches domestic concerns and individuals subject to the jurisdiction of the United States if they plan a bribery operation in this country and simply have the actual cash delivered by a foreign subsidiary or a foreign national not subject to the jurisdiction of the United States.

2. A bribery scheme wholly conceived and carried out by a legitimate subsidiary of a United States company is probably not reached by this statute, even if the stock were 100 percent owned by a domestic concern.

Superimposed on all this, of course, is the requirement that interstate commerce be involved. The statute says expressly that interstate commerce means:

trade, commerce, transportation, or communication among the several States or between any foreign country and any State or between any State and any place or ship outside thereof. Such term includes the intrastate use of (A) a telephone or other interstate means of communication, or (B) any other interstate instrumentality.

SEC REGULATIONS

It is understood that the SEC is considering issuing either rules or interpretive releases under the accounting rules described above. To date, however, it has not done so. On the other hand, the legislative history of the existing law shows that a number of provisions favored by the SEC were ultimately eliminated. One of the most controversial provisions made it a crime for a corporate official to "knowingly" falsify records or "knowingly" lie to an accountant who is auditing the firm's records. Some proposals did not even include the word "knowingly," so that *any* falsification of records or lie to an accountant would be a crime. The SEC favored the latter approach and objected to the "knowingly" language because it felt that this would raise very difficult problems of proof, particularly in injunction actions. Also, some congressmen *and* the SEC disagree with the Supreme Court's stand on the scienter requirement under 10(b)(5) as announced in the case of *Ernst & Ernst v. Hochfelder* (1976). There is, therefore, some movement in the SEC to issue rules to cover those provisions which were not enacted in the final version of the law.

COMPLIANCE PROGRAM

Management ought to insist on some kind of compliance program for the Foreign Corrupt Practices Act. It must have at least two parts. One part would be all the procedures necessary to assure that the company people did not pay any illegal bribes, and the other part would be to assure that the company had the proper internal auditing controls.

As to the first part—the illegal bribes—the program should include discussion of the statute with the appropriate people, communication of the requirements to all affected people in the company, emphasis on compliance by top management, and documentation of all this so you can show your good faith compliance efforts if a problem is ever presented.

As to the program for the internal auditing controls, the best current authority (as of late 1978) is the proposal by the American Institute of Certified Public Accountants on what kinds of controls should be acceptable under this statute. The AICPA undertook the task of designing an appropriate system of internal controls and published their first draft for comment. They are scheduled to publish the final version in early 1979 and that should serve as a useful guide.

The Foreign Corrupt Practices Act is unlikely to be enforced by itself. Instead, it is likely to be used as an additional enforcement tool when the SEC discovers what they believe to be illegal activity. That has been the pattern of the first three reported cases. The SEC has alleged violation of the disclosure rules along with the Foreign Corrupt Practices Act accounting provisions. Their current attitude seems to be that if you have made an improper payment, your internal controls must be inadequate.

Management is likely to be subjected to the "Ping-Pong" treatment when they request a compliance program. The lawyers are likely to say it's an accounting problem and the accountants are likely to say it's a legal problem.

In fact, the problem also involves the companies internal auditors, those responsible for computer security, the audit committee of the board of direo-tors (or the full board if there is no audit committee) and management. Everyone must work together to put together a reasonable balanced program to assure compliance, and a good record of the steps taken to achieve that compliance.

CHAPTER FORTY-TWO

PROXY
SOLICITATION

Every year public companies will have to go through the ritual of soliciting proxies for the annual meeting. In addition, if there are special transactions, such as a merger, proxies will have to be solicited for that purpose. Solicitation of proxies is just as technical as any of the other SEC requirements, and it is not really necessary to go through in detail all of the fine points on how this must be done. It is important, however, to understand that there are many fine points; if you run afoul of any of these technicalities, you can wind up with the potential for an invalid meeting and personal liability on the part of the directors. For example, if you have a material error or omission in the proxy material, it could subject to attack the election of directors or any other business transacted at the annual meeting (including approval of stock option or other compensation programs).

Another problem which frequently arises in connection with the annual meeting and the proxy solicitation is the question of how to deal with shareholder proposals. The securities laws require that a company make reasonable availability of its proxy machinery for shareholders to make proposals. These, again, are very technical.

THE PROXY MATERIALS

The proxy rules constitute a very important part of the current statutory disclosure scheme. The three basic forms of disclosure called for in the SEC Laws are:

1. The registration statement, including the prospectus which is filed whenever a company issues stock.

2. Various periodic reports required to be filed with the 10-K from time to time, such as the annual report 10-K, which must be filed every year, and

monthly 8-K reports, which must be filed whenever certain important things happen.

3. The proxy rules.

Of these three forms of disclosure, the proxy rules are the only ones generating material which generally gets into the hands of investors. The registration statement and prospectus are not even sent to most investors because it is necessary for individuals to be in possession of them only when there is an offering of the company stock. After the initial distribution, during the trading period, there is no need to keep the registration statement or the prospectus current. In addition, even during the initial offering, the prospectus is not read by many investors. Typically, stock is sold by a call from the broker who simply sends the prospectus with the confirmation slip.

The various reports which are required by the SEC are read by only a very small fraction of the investing public. These reports are read in some detail by investment advisers, researchers, analysts, and some brokers, and hopefully, much of the information ultimately finds its way to the investing public via recommendations from these people.

The annual report to shareholders is a very important document, but it is not governed by many SEC rules. At least at this time, the annual report is one place where management can do a little boasting, give the shareholders pretty pictures of the company's products and plants, and so on.

The proxy materials, on the other hand, are subject to SEC regulation and are sent to every shareholder of record of the company. These materials are typically short enough and simple enough to be read and understood by the majority of them.

Proxy materials are generally very similar from year to year. So are the procedures for developing them. This has the rather unfortunate connotation that the whole operation is simply a "cut-and-paste job" and that anyone can do it. Unfortunately, this is not the case. The rules are very technical, and everything has to be done according to rather elaborate procedures. Otherwise, management can be criticized and even held liable for any misstatements that might be included in the proxy materials. Management must be sure that the people handling the preparation of the proxy materials are familiar with both the law and the facts. Familiarity with the law can be assumed if you are dealing with competent lawyers, but familiarity with the facts cannot, particularly if those lawyers are members of outside law firms. Usually, the question of how to get the data to complete the proxy statement is resolved by sending out questionnaires to the officers and directors of the company. The form and content of these questionnaires depends upon the circumstances and the relation of counsel to the client. However, there are many published forms which provide helpful starting points. The purpose of the questionnaire is to enable counsel to prepare an appropriate proxy statement which contains all of the material required by the regulations and the schedules. The questionnaire should, therefore, be fairly comprehensive to minimize the possibility of material information being omitted or misrepresented. It will also help to protect counsel if it later turns out that something might have been omitted or misrepresented in the proxy. Remember, however, that it is very imprudent to depend upon any form or standard procedure to safeguard against lawsuits for negligence. Forms and standard procedures are necessary, but they are not sufficient by themselves; and if management gets the impression that the whole annual meeting and proxy solicitation process is being done "mechanically," they should definitely intervene and ask for an explanation.

ANNUAL REPORT

The proxy material must be accompanied or preceded by an annual report. Formerly, the annual report was not subject to any direct regulation and was one of the very few places remaining where company management could do a little boasting. This is still true, but there are now some regulations. The annual report to shareholders retains its status as a "nonfiled" document so it will not subject management to liability in the event of technical misstatements. However, there are some technical requirements governing the financial statements, a description of the business done by the company during the year, etc., and you must comply with these.

There is a great deal of lore about the form of proxy, the form of proxy statement, exactly how the proxy card ought to be laid out, the requirements for the mailing envelope, and so forth. All of these, however, are best left to the SEC specialists. They will not be discussed here. The one exception is the necessity for stating the annual compensation of the highest-paid directors and officers. This is a very important subject at this point. The proxy materials must disclose the total annual compensation, including perquisites, and if the perquisites are furnished "in kind," they must be reasonably valued and the value must be put in the proxy statement. All you need is a total figure; you do not have to itemize everything. But this is a very touchy subject, and it is important for management to make certain that the files are complete in the sense of itemizing every conceivable benefit and making appropriate disclosure.

The reason we mention this touchy problem here is not that it will necessarily continue to be especially important. In fact, chances are it won't be more important a few years from now than any other item in the proxy statement. Similarly, "questionable payments" were very important a few years ago and now are probably just about as important as any other part of the proxy process (but no more so). The point is that there will almost always be one or two "sensitive" points—either because of government concern or a development within the company. This sensitive point is where management should place its effort. Leave the design of the proxy card, the type sizes, and the punctuation to the lawyers (just be sure you have good ones). Put your time in questioning the lawyers as to how they have handled the sensitive parts.

PROXY STATEMENT LIABILITY

From management's point of view, the key problem is that if the proxy statement is not prepared right, the company and certain officers and directors can be held personally liable. Technically, the rule is that a proxy statement will give rise to liability if it contains any statement

> which, at the time and in the light of the circumstances under which it is made, is false or misleading with respect to any material fact, or which omits to state any material fact necessary in order to make the statements therein not false or misleading.

As might be expected, there are pages and pages—indeed volumes and volumes—of material as to exactly what constitutes a material misleading statement. However, as the phrase is defined, the standard is very low. The most recent Supreme Court announcement on materiality is that

An omitted fact is material if there is a substantial likelihood that a reasonable investor would consider it important in deciding how to vote. . . .

Put another way, there must be a substantial likelihood that the disclosure of the omitted fact would have been viewed by the reasonable investor as having significantly altered the 'total mix' of information available.

The trouble is that this materiality concept is not limited to financial materiality. There is not any dollar test. Certainly, if an item is material from the financial point of view because it involves a lot of money, it is obviously a material statement. On the other hand, there are a number of other things which are material only in the sense of the character of management and other such vague things. Accordingly, if a company makes illegal political contributions and fails to disclose that fact in the proxy statement, the SEC feels that that is a material omission because it adversely reflects upon the character of management and their ability to manage, irrespective of the size of the contribution.

In summary, then, management's best protection against problems arising out of improperly solicited proxies is not to become SEC lawyers themselves, but rather to understand that this is a very technical area and make sure that the proper resources are devoted towards preparing the company's proxy materials. They should make sure that all of the directors of the company and all of its principal officers fully cooperate with counsel and that counsel does whatever seems reasonably required to gather all of the necessary facts. Also, all of the members of the management team, as well as all of the directors, should *read the proxy statement carefully* so that they can be sure for themselves that there is nothing inaccurate or omitted. If there are any questions, they should, of course, be discussed with counsel.

SECTION SIX: PRODUCT SAFETY, WARRANTY, AND LIABILITY

CHAPTER FORTY-THREE

THE MAGNUSON-MOSS WARRANTY ACT

On January 4, 1975, the President signed Public Law 93-637, which is generally known as the Magnuson-Moss Warranty–Federal Trade Commission Improvement Act. This piece of legislation does two things:

1. It provides new federal rules relating to warranties for consumer products.

2. It provides some important new powers for the Federal Trade Commission.

This chapter describes the warranty provisions of this legislation.

BRIEF SUMMARY OF THE NEW LAW

The warranty law does the following:

1. It requires that any company making a consumer product which is warranted in any way must fully and conspicuously disclose in simple and readily understood language all the terms and conditions of such warranty.

2. It introduces the distinction between a *full warranty* and a *limited warranty* and further provides certain minimum federal standards for any warranty which is to be called a full warranty.

3. It provides restrictions against disclaimer of warranties.

4. It provides procedures which a manufacturer may use to allow the seller of its products (a distributor, for example) to assist in carrying out the terms of the warranty.

5. It provides a mechanism whereby a company can establish an informal claims procedure for resolving warranty disputes, and it further provides that if such a procedure is established, no consumer may sue the company on the basis of a breach of warranty before going through this informal procedure.

6. It provides for enforcement by the Federal Trade Commission of the provisions of the law and permits the FTC to enjoin the use of any deceptive warranty.

7. It provides that a consumer may sue for breach of any warranty and recover not only damages but also expenses and attorney's fees.

DISCUSSION OF THE SUBSTANTIVE PROVISIONS OF THE NEW LAW

The act applies only to a "consumer product," which is defined as follows:

Sec. 101. For the purposes of this title:

(1) the term "consumer product" means any tangible personal property which is distributed in commerce and which is normally used for personal, family, or household purposes (including any such property intended to be attached to or installed in any real property without regard to whether it is so attached or installed).

The act specifically does not require a company to give any warranty on any consumer product or any of its components.

Sec. 102(b)(2). Nothing in this title . . . shall be deemed to authorize the Commission to prescribe the duration of written warranties given or to require that a consumer product or any of its components be warranted.

Further, if any warranty is given, the law contains no requirement as to the duration of that warranty. However, if any warranty at all is given regarding a consumer product, that warranty (to the extent required by rules of the commission) must fully and conspicuously disclose in simple and readily understood language its terms and conditions. The act provides that the rules which will be promulgated by the commission may cover any of the following items, among others:

1. The clear identification of the warrantors by name and address

2. The identity of the party or parties to whom the warranty is extended

3. The products or parts covered

4. A statement of what the warrantor will do in the event of a defect, malfunction, or failure to conform with the written warranty; at whose expense; and for what period of time

5. A statement of what the consumer must do and what expenses he must bear

6. Exceptions and exclusions from the terms of the warranty

7. The step-by-step procedure which the consumer should take in order to obtain performance of any obligation under the warranty, including the identification of any person or class of persons authorized to perform the obligations set forth in the warranty

8. Information respecting the availability of any informal dispute settlement procedure offered by the warrantor and a recital, where the warranty so provides, that the purchaser may be required to resort to such procedure before pursuing any legal remedies in the courts

9. A brief, general description of the legal remedies available to the consumer

10. The time at which the warrantor will perform any obligations under the warranty

11. The period of time within which, after notice of a defect, malfunction, or failure to conform with the warranty, the warrantor will perform any obligations under the warranty

12. The characteristics or properties of the products, or parts thereof, that are not covered by the warranty

13. The language of the warranty, which must not mislead a reasonable, average consumer as to the nature or scope of the warranty

The act further requires that the commission shall prescribe rules which require that the terms of any written warranty of a consumer product be made available to the consumer *prior to the actual sale*.

On December 31, 1975, the Federal Trade Commission issued regulations following the statute fairly closely on these points.

FULL AND LIMITED WARRANTIES

Section 103 of the act requires that any written warranty be labeled either a full warranty or a limited warranty. A full warranty is defined as one which meets the standards set forth in section 104(a) of the act as follows:

Sec. 104(a). In order for a warrantor warranting a consumer product by means of a written warranty to meet the Federal minimum standards for warranty:

(1) such warrantor must as a minimum remedy such consumer product within a reasonable time and without charge, in the case of a defect, malfunction, or failure to conform with such written warranty;

(2) notwithstanding section 108(b), such warrantor may not impose any limitation on the duration of any implied warranty on the product;

(3) such warrantor may not exclude or limit consequential damages for breach of any written or implied warranty on such product, unless such exclusion or limitation conspicuously appears on the face of the warranty; and

(4) if the product (or a component part thereof) contains a defect or malfunction after a reasonable number of attempts by the warrantor to remedy defects or malfunctions in such product, such warrantor must permit the consumer to elect either a refund for, or replacement without charge of, such product or part (as the case may be). The Commission may by rule specify for purposes of this paragraph, what constitutes a reasonable number of attempts to remedy particular kinds of defects or malfunctions under different circumstances. If the warrantor replaces a component part of a consumer product, such replacement shall include installing the part in the product without charge.

A limited warranty is any warranty which fails to meet any of these requirements.

The new law provides that *no implied warranty can be disclaimed* if any written warranty is given. Implied warranties are defined to be those which arise under state law, and in most cases, will probably be the implied warranties of merchantability and fitness for purpose as defined in sections 2-314 and 2-315 of the Uniform Commercial Code. Those two code sections are reproduced on the next page.

Sec. 2-314. Implied Warranty: Merchantability; Usage of Trade.

(1) Unless excluded or modified (section 2-316), a warranty that the goods shall be merchantable is implied in a contract for their sale if the seller is a merchant with respect to goods of that kind. Under this section the serving for value of food or drink to be consumed either on the premises or elsewhere is a sale.

(2) Goods to be merchantable must be at least such as

   (a) pass without objection in the trade under the contract description; and

   (b) in the case of fungible goods, are of fair average quality within the description; and

   (c) are fit for the ordinary purposes for which such goods are used; and

   (d) run, within the variations permitted by the agreement, of even kind, quality and quantity within each unit and among all units involved; and

   (e) are adequately contained, packaged, and labeled as the agreement may require; and

   (f) conform to the promises or affirmations of fact made on the container or label if any.

(3) Unless excluded or modified (section 2-316) other implied warranties may arise from course of dealing or usage of trade.

Sec. 2-315. Implied Warranty: Fitness for Particular Purpose. Where the seller at the time of contracting has reason to know any particular purpose for which the goods are required and that the buyer is relying on the seller's skill or judgment to select or furnish suitable goods, there is unless excluded or modified under the next section an implied warranty that the goods shall be fit for such purpose.

The general rule of the Uniform Commercial Code (as stated in section 2-316) is that any of these warranties can be excluded, provided that the exclusion is done in a clear conspicuous manner and that it is not unconscionable.

Sec. 2-316. Exclusion or Modification of Warranties.

(1) Words or conduct relevant to the creation of an express warranty and words or conduct tending to negate or limit warranty shall be construed wherever reasonable as consistent with each other; but subject to the provisions of this Article on parol or extrinsic evidence (section 2-202) negation or limitation is inoperative to the extent such construction is unreasonable.

(2) Subject to subsection (3), to exclude or modify the implied warranty of merchantability or any part of it the language must mention merchantability and in case of a writing must be conspicuous. Language to exclude all implied warranties of fitness is sufficient if it states, for example that "There are no warranties which extend beyond the description on the face hereof."

(3) Notwithstanding subsection (2)

   (a) unless the circumstances indicate otherwise, all implied warranties are excluded by expressions like "as is," "with all faults" or other language which in common understanding calls the buyer's attention to the exclusion of warranties and makes plain that there is no implied warranty; and

   (b) when the buyer before entering into the contract has examined the goods or the sample or model as fully as he desired or has refused to examine the goods there is no implied warranty with regard to defects which an examination ought in the circumstances to have revealed to him; and

   (c) an implied warranty can also be excluded or modified by course of dealing or course of performance or usage of trade.

(4)   Remedies for breach of warranty can be limited in accordance with the provisions of this Article on liquidation or limitation of damages and on contractual modification of remedy (sections 2-718 and 2-719).

The federal law is inconsistent with this. Accordingly, it would seem that a company is placed in the position of either having to exclude absolutely all warranties, including express warranties, or being forced to include the code warranties of merchantability and fitness for purpose if any express warranty at all is given. The new law defines the term "written warranty" very broadly as follows:

Sec. 101(6). The term "written warranty" means:

(A)   any written affirmation of fact or written promise made in connection with the sale of a consumer product by a supplier to a buyer which relates to the nature of the material or workmanship and affirms or promises that such material or workmanship is defect free or will meet a specified level of performance over a specified period of time, or

(B)   any undertaking in writing in connection with the sale by a supplier of a consumer product to refund, repair, replace, or take other remedial action with respect to such product in the event that such product fails to meet the specifications set forth in the undertaking, which written affirmation, promise, or undertaking becomes part of the basis of the bargain between a supplier and a buyer for purposes other than resale of such product.

Related definitions in the new law making clear that the manufacturer of the consumer product is included are the definitions of "supplier" and "warrantor," which are as follows:

Sec. 101(4). The term "supplier" means any person engaged in the business of making a consumer product directly or indirectly available to consumers.

Sec. 101(5). The term "warrantor" means any supplier or other person who gives or offers to give a written warranty or who is or may be obligated under an implied warranty.

The new law does, however, permit limitation of the *duration* of the implied warranty so that it can correspond with the duration of any express warranty.

Sec. 108(b). Implied warranties may be limited in duration to the duration of a written warranty of reasonable duration, if such limitation is conscionable and is set forth in clear and unmistakable language and prominently displayed on the face of the warranty.

The warrantor may designate representatives to perform his duties under any written or implied warranty, provided that the warrantor makes reasonable arrangements for compensation of the designated representative. However, no such designation will relieve the warrantor of his direct responsibilities to the consumer or make the representative a co-warrantor (section 107).

ENFORCEMENT

The act contains a very interesting enforcement mechanism. It provides in section 110(a)(1) that "Congress hereby declares it to be its policy to encourage warrantors to establish procedures whereby consumer disputes are fairly and expeditiously settled through informal dispute settlement mechanisms." That section then goes on to provide that if a warrantor establishes an informal dispute settlement procedure which meets the rules of the commission, the consumer may not commence any action against the manufacturer until he has gone through these procedures. However, the FTC has issued such detailed regulations on how this kind of procedure works that in many cases it is impractical.

If the consumer has gone through any available informal procedures and is still not satisfied he may bring suit against the manufacturer in court, and if the consumer finally prevails in any such action he may be allowed by the court to recover as part of the judgment his damages and attorney's fees.

The consumer's action under this act is limited to recovery under a written warranty and apparently will not allow recovery of attorney's fees in case of the breach of an oral warranty. (This is expressly pointed out in the legislative history.) In addition to providing a procedure for private consumers, the act provides that it will be a violation of section 5 of the Federal Trade Commission Act to fail to comply with any of the requirements of this new law and the attorney general or the Federal Trade Commission may bring appropriate actions against a company which violates the law. In addition, the law includes a provision allowing the Federal Trade Commission to obtain an injunction against any "deceptive warranty," which is defined as follows:

> Sec. 110(c)(2). For the purposes of this subsection, the term "deceptive warranty" means (A) a written warranty which (i) contains an affirmation, promise, description, or representation which is either false or fraudulent, or which, in light of all of the circumstances, would mislead a reasonable individual exercising due care; or (ii) fails to contain information which is necessary in light of all of the circumstances, to make the warranty not misleading to a reasonable individual exercising due care; or (B) a written warranty created by the use of such terms as "guaranty" or "warranty," if the terms and conditions of such warranty so limit its scope and application as to deceive a reasonable individual.

Various provisions of section 110 of the act recognize that a class action may be brought on the basis of a breach of any of the provisions of the act.

CONCLUSION

In addition to keeping a close watch on the regulations which are going to be issued under this act, the following precautions are appropriate:

1. **Evaluate the importance of warranties** An examination should be made of any warranties which are given in connection with any consumer product and some thought given to a determination of the commercial importance of such warranties. In other words, it is important to know exactly how important those warranties are so that an intelligent decision can be made whether to comply with all of the detailed requirements or simply to sell the product without any warranties at all.

2. **Consider the informal dispute procedure** While the new regulations make informal dispute settlement procedures complicated and costly, they may be desirable in some cases. Accordingly, they should be evaluated.

3. **Evaluate the cost of warranties** While it may not be possible to put a precise amount on the cost of new warranty procedures, it is desirable to

give some thought, for the purpose of future pricing, to the expenditures which might be necessary to comply with this new act. In this connection, note that many existing warranties are probably given without any thought to their actual cost. The new law will make this carelessness more dangerous.

4. **Examine existing warranties**   Some things are already clear under the new law. An example is the restriction against the disclaiming of implied warranties if any express warranty is given. Accordingly, the existing warranties of consumer products should be examined so that this problem can be dealt with. Obviously, any warranty which is potentially deceptive should be avoided.

5. **Use of a representative**   The law allows the designation of a representative to perform warranty functions, and it might be desirable to do some advance planning about this possibility. It would be possible, for example, to designate the distributors as being in charge of performing the warranty services. However, the distributors will have to be compensated for this service, and this procedure will not relieve the company from ultimate responsibility.

6. **Consider the options for use of a full or a limited warranty**   A decision will have to be made whether the product, if warranted at all, will have a full or a limited warranty.

CHAPTER FORTY-FOUR

THE CONSUMER PRODUCT SAFETY ACT

The Consumer Product Safety Act was signed into law by the President on October 27, 1972. The basic purpose of the act was to establish an independent regulatory agency with extremely broad powers to protect consumers from unreasonable risk of injury from hazardous products. The agency is headed by five commissioners serving 7-year terms. Each is appointed by the President and confirmed by the Senate. The agency has the authority to set safety standards for consumer products and ban those products showing evidence of undue risk of injury. (Note the similarity to the Occupational Safety and Health Act, under which the commission promulgates safety standards and can shut down a machine or plant if it finds it dangerous to the employees.) The act also establishes a fifteen-member Product Safety Advisory Council, which includes representatives of the business community, the consumer community, and federal, state, and local government agencies.

PRODUCTS COVERED

The act covers consumer products, but it defines a consumer product very broadly as any article or *component part thereof*— whether American-made or imported—manufactured or distributed (1) for sale to a consumer for use *in or around* a permanent or temporary residence or a school, in recreation or otherwise; or (2) for the personal use, consumption, or enjoyment of a consumer *in or around* a permanent or temporary household or residence or a school, in recreation or otherwise.

The following points should be noted:

1. Component parts are included.

2. The act covers not only manufacturing, but also distribution and retailing.

3. The Consumer Product Safety Commission is taking a very broad view of "consumer product," as evidenced by the advisory opinions issued by its general counsel:
   (a) In Advisory Opinion 181, traffic control signals and fire alarm equipment sold to municipalities were held to be consumer products.
   (b) In Advisory Opinion 182, elevators intended for use by consumers were held to be within the definition of consumer products.
   (c) In Advisory Opinion 128, it was held that copying machines were consumer products if they were manufactured to be coin-operated.

In Advisory Opinion 126, the commission indicated its position on the troublesome question of components of a consumer product. After pointing out that a product need not be directly used by a consumer but merely ultimately consumed to fall within the commission's jurisdiction, the commission's general counsel stated the following:

> Where the finished product is discovered to contain a substantial product hazard, manufacturers, distributors and retailers of components thereof are advised to ascertain the extent to which the component may be involved and to report the problem to the Commission. Responsibility would be determined on a case-by-case basis, with a view toward assessing the causal connection between the component part and the defective aspects of the end product that primarily contributed to, or may be responsible for, the injury or risk of injury.

Exclusions

There are, however, significant exclusions from the act. The most important general exclusion is of any article not customarily produced and distributed for sale for the use, consumption, or enjoyment of a consumer. The other exemption is for products covered under other federal regulatory agencies whose authority has not been transferred to the commission. These include (but are not limited to) the following:

Tobacco and tobacco products

Motor vehicles and motor vehicle equipment

Firearms

Aircraft and aircraft engines, propellers, and appliances

Boats

Drugs, devices, and cosmetics

Food

DEVELOPING STANDARDS

The act contains provisions which are aimed at assuring maximum consumer and public participation in the development of standards. Any time the commission finds that standards are necessary to prevent or reduce the risk of injury through use of a product, it may promulgate standards. The commission has broad information-gathering powers to aid it in determining whether to initiate the standard-setting process. In addition, the commission must entertain petitions from all interested persons to set safety standards, and a petitioner may institute a suit to require the setting of a standard if the commission refuses. The pattern envisioned by the act is basically as follows:

1. After the commission determines that a standard is necessary by either con-
    ducting its own investigation or acting on a petition, it should publish a notice
    in the *Federal Register* which:
    (a) identifies the product and the nature of the risk of injury associated with
         the product
    (b) states the commission's determination that a standard is necessary
    (c) includes any known information about existing standards
    (d) invites offers of any person, including the manufacturer or distributor
         of the product, to develop the proposed standard

2. Within 210 days after making the above announcement, the commission must
    either propose a standard or else withdraw its proceeding or declare the product
    to be a "banned hazardous consumer product."

3. During the next 60 days, the commission must hold hearings on its proposed
    standard, and after 60 days, it must promulgate the standard or withdraw
    the applicable notice of proceeding.

What the Standard Will Contain

Generally, the standard will be a so-called *performance standard*. The act provides that the standards are to consist of

one or more of any of the following types of requirements:

(a) Requirements as to performance, composition, contents, design, construction,
     finish, or packaging of a consumer product.
(b) Requirements that a consumer product be marked with or accompanied by
     clear and adequate warnings or instructions, or requirements respecting the
     form of warnings or instructions.

Judicial Review

The act contains the normal judicial review procedure for standards which are felt to be objectionable by any person. Within 60 days after promulgation of a consumer product safety standard, any person adversely affected thereby may petition for a review by the appropriate court of appeals.

WHAT HAPPENS WHEN A SAFETY PROBLEM IS PRESENTED

The event which triggers most of the action in this area is the awareness by the commission of a consumer product containing a possible safety defect. This may come from any number of sources, including the requirement of section 15 that a manufacturer or seller of a consumer product must notify the commission when it obtains knowledge that there may be a defect which presents a substantial risk of serious injury to consumers; from the commission's "hot line" (the lengthy and heavily contested proceedings involving a trouble light which had a serious defect that could cause electrocution were started by a telephone call from a consumer informing the commission of the fact that a man had been electrocuted using the light); or from virtually any other source. When the commission does become aware of a problem, the actions it will take depend upon two things:

1. The seriousness of the hazard

2. The kind of product involved

The Seriousness of the Hazard

The seriousness of the hazard is by far the more important factor, because the other one—the kind of product involved—really only determines the particular statute which the commission will proceed under and the other statutes in question have remedies which are similar to those of the Consumer Product Safety Act.

Basically, the alternatives open to the commission, from the least severe to the most, are the following:

1. Proceeding under section 15, which allows the commission a broad set of remedies in any case where it appears that there is a substantial product hazard. These remedies range from simply requiring a notice or warning, to having the product recalled.

2. Proceeding under sections 8 and 9, which is the normal way to ban a hazardous product.

3. Proceeding under section 12, which is the imminent hazard section and where the commission can, without hearing or other process, go into court and request an order immediately forbidding the manufacture or sale of the product and even seizing it.

Section 15 Procedure

Under section 15, when it appears to the commission that a product which has been sold in commerce either fails to comply with a given standard or else has a defect which—because of the pattern of defect, the number of defective products distributed, the severity of the risk, or other reason—creates a substantial risk of injury to the public, the commission may, after affording interested persons a reasonable hearing, order one or several of a number of remedies including:

1. Requiring the manufacturer or the distributors or retailers to give notice of the defect by (a) public announcement, (b) mailing individual notices to others in the chain of distribution, or (c) mailing individual notices to the ultimate consumers

2. Requiring the manufacturer or the distributors or retailers to bring the product into conformity with the standard or repair the defect

3. Replacing the product with an equivalent product without the defect

4. Refunding the purchase price

5. Submitting a plan to the commission for satisfactorily carrying out the required action

The commission may apply to a federal court for an injunction prohibiting manufacture or sale of the product pending the outcome of the administrative proceedings.

Sections 8 and 9 Procedure for Banning Hazardous Products

In sections 8 and 9 proceedings, the commission must conduct a hearing as provided for in the Administrative Procedure Act. These procedures require publication of a notice of the proposal in the *Federal Register* and a public hearing at which interested parties may appear and present their views, either orally or in writing. Generally, the commission must first issue a proposed ban, and then within 60 days it must either make it effective or withdraw it. (The 60 days may be extended for good cause.)

In order to justify making the proposed ban effective, the commission must make appropriate findings with respect to:

1. The degree and nature of the risk of injury

2. The approximate number of consumer products or types or classes thereof subject to the ban

3. The need of the public for the products subject to the ban

4. Any means of achieving the objective while minimizing adverse effects on competition or disruption or dislocation of manufacturing and other commercial practices

The commission may not make the ban effective unless it finds that:

1. The ban is necessary to eliminate or reduce an unreasonable risk of injury associated with the product to be banned.

2. The ban will be in the public interest.

3. No feasible consumer product safety standard under the act would adequately protect the public from the unreasonable risk of injury associated with the product.

After these proceedings have been completed, the commission may issue a ban which is effective immediately. After the effective date of the ban, the manufacture or sale of the product is subject to criminal and civil sanctions. The ban may be applied to products that are already in the chain of distribution and even on the retailers' shelves.

Section 12: Imminent Hazard

The provisions for designating a "banned hazardous product" are the ones which must be used if there is no imminent hazard. If there *is* an imminent hazard, the commission may use other, more drastic provisions contained in section 12 of the act. Section 12 defines an "imminently hazardous consumer product" as one which presents an imminent and unreasonable risk of death, serious illness, or severe personal injury. If the commission finds such a risk to exist, it may file in United States district court an action:

1. Against the product for seizure

2. Against any person who is a manufacturer, distributor, or seller of the product

3. Against both

The commission may file this action notwithstanding the existence of any standard or the pendency of any other proceeding.

The court may impose whatever equitable remedy is necessary or appropriate to adequately protect the public from the imminent hazard, including orders for recall, replacement, repair, or refunds. The commission may exercise its emergency power to file an action in an appropriate U.S. district court to seize and condemn the product.

The Kind of Product Involved

In addition to the seriousness of the problem, the kind of product involved will determine the procedures to be used. Section 30 of the Consumer Product Safety Act transfers enforcement of a number of other federal statutes to the Consumer Product Safety Commission. These other statutes include:

1. The Federal Hazardous Substances Act
2. The Poison Prevention Packaging Act of 1970
3. The Flammable Fabrics Act

Further, section 30(d) of the Consumer Product Safety Act provides that if any risk of injury is associated with a consumer product which is covered by any of the above-mentioned acts, and can be eliminated or reduced to a sufficient extent by action taken under one of those acts, such action must be taken. In other words, the provisions of those other acts will take precedence over those of the Consumer Product Safety Act if they can adequately solve the problem.

NEW PRODUCTS

Section 13 of the Consumer Product Safety Act is also potentially troublesome. It provides that the commission may, by an appropriate rule, require that the manufacturer of any new consumer product furnish notice and a description of such product to the commission before its distribution into commerce. For the purpose of the act, a "new consumer product" is one which incorporates a design, material, or form of energy exchange (1) which has not previously been used substantially in consumer products and (2) about which there is not adequate information to determine its safety in use by consumers.

The House report contains the following explanation of this provision:

> This section is designed to provide the Commission with a means of keeping abreast of new products entering the market place so that it can head off imminently hazardous products in the courts or promptly institute a proceeding to ban or develop standards for products which it determines are unreasonably hazardous. *It is not intended that the Commission's rulemaking powers under this section be used to require premarket clearance of new consumer products. Thus, the Commission would not have authority under this section to require a manufacturer to postpone distribution of a new product until the Commission has had an opportunity to run tests on the product or make an analysis of its potential for harm.* [Emphasis added.]

The potential trouble, of course, is in the way this provision will work out in practice. If the maker of a new product notifies the commission and the commission voices even an informal objection, the potential liabilities coupled with the obvious marketing problems may serve as a practical bar to the manufacture, distribution, or sale of the product. Also, distributors may be reluctant to handle new products unless they have some reasonable assurances that the commission does not feel they contain any potential safety hazard.

NOTIFICATION REQUIREMENTS

An important provision of the act requires that a company which finds a substantial safety hazard in its product must notify the commission. Some companies have already notified the commission of potential safety hazards in consumer products, and the commission feels that this is a very important aspect of the act and is emphasizing its enforcement.

The relevant provisions of the act are as follows:

Sec. 15(b). Every manufacturer of a consumer product distributed in commerce, and every distributor and retailer of such product, who obtains information which reasonably supports the conclusion that such product—

(1) fails to comply with an applicable consumer product safety rule, or
(2) contains a defect which could create a substantial product hazard as described in subsection (a)(2),

shall immediately inform the Commission of such failure to comply or of such defect unless such manufacturer, distributor, or retailer has actual knowedge that the Commission has been adequately informed of such defect or failure to comply.

The substantial product hazard defined in section 15(a)(2) is as follows:

(2) a product defect which (because of the pattern of defect, the number of defective products distributed in commerce, the severity of the risk, or otherwise) creates a substantial risk of injury to the public.

Even before these new regulations were adopted, some manufacturers submitted notices to the Consumer Product Safety Commission of possible serious safety hazards in their products. The various specialized services reporting on this act periodically contain reports of notices sent by manufacturers of television sets and other consumer products to the commission. Now, however, such notifications are required:

1. To be made within 24 hours
2. To be made in the particular form called for by the regulations

The most important sections of these very important regulations are reproduced below.

Sec. 1115.1 Purpose—
The purpose of this part 1115 is to set forth the Consumer Product Safety Commission's (Commission's) interpretation of the reporting requirements imposed on manufacturers (including importers), distributors, and retailers by section 15(b) of the Consumer Product Safety Act, as amended and to indicate the actions and sanctions which the Commission may require or impose to protect the public from substantial product hazards, as that term is defined in section 15(a) of the CPSA.
Sec. 1115.2 Scope and Finding.—
(a) Section 15(a) of the CPSA defines "substantial product hazard" as either (1) a failure to comply with an applicable consumer product safety rule, which failure creates a substantial risk of injury to the public, or (2) a product defect which (because of the pattern of defect, the number of defective products distributed in commerce, the severity of the risk, or otherwise) creates a substantial risk of injury to the public.
(b) Section 15(b) of the CPSA requires every manufacturer (including an importer), distributor, or retailer of a consumer product distributed in commerce who obtains information which reasonably supports the conclusion that the product either fails to comply with an applicable consumer product safety rule or contains a defect which could create a substantial product hazard immediately to inform the Commission, unless the manufacturer (including an importer), distributor, or retailer has actual knowledge that the Commission has been adequately informed.

This provision indicates that a broad spectrum of safety-related information should be reported under section 15(b) of the CPSA.

(c)   Sections 15(c) and 15(d) of the CPSA empower the Commission to order a manufacturer (including an importer), distributor, or retailer of a consumer product distributed in commerce that presents a substantial product hazard to give various forms of notice to the public of the defect or the failure to comply and/or to order the subject firm to elect either to repair, to replace, or to refund the purchase price of such product. However, information which should be reported under section 15(b) of the CPSA does not automatically indicate the presence of a substantial product hazard since what must be reported are failures to comply with consumer product safety rules and defects that could create a substantial product hazard. (See section 1115.12.)

(d)   The provisions of this part 1115 deal with all consumer products (including imports) subject to regulation under the Consumer Product Safety Act, as amended (CPSA), and the Refrigerator Safety Act (RSA). In addition, the Commission has found that risks of injury to the public from consumer products subject to regulation under the Flammable Fabrics Act (FFA), the Federal Hazardous Substances Act (FHSA), and the Poison Prevention Packaging Act of 1970 (PPPA) cannot be eliminated or reduced to a sufficient extent in a timely fashion under those acts. Therefore, pursuant to section 30(d) of the CPSA, manufacturers (including importers), distributors, and retailers of consumer products which are subject to regulation under provisions of the FFA, FHSA, and PPPA must comply with the reporting requirements of section 15(b).

Sec. 1115.3   Definitions.—

In addition to the definitions given in section 3 of the CPSA, the following definitions apply:

(a)   "Adequately informed" under section 15(b) of the CPSA means that the Commission staff has received the information requested under sections 1115.12 and/or 1115.13 of this part insofar as it is reasonably available and applicable or that the staff has informed the subject firm that the staff is adequately informed.

(b)   "Commission meeting" means the joint deliberations of at least a majority of the Commission where such deliberations determine or result in the conduct or disposition of official Commission business. This term is synonymous with "Commission meeting" as defined in the Commission's regulation issued under the Government in the Sunshine Act.

(c)   "Noncompliance" means the failure of a consumer product to comply with an applicable consumer product safety rule issued under the CPSA.

(d)   A "person" means a corporation, company, association, firm, partnership, society, joint stock company, or individual.

(e)   "Staff" means the staff of the Consumer Product Safety Commission unless otherwise stated.

(f)   "Subject firm" means any manufacturer (including an importer), distributor, or retailer of a consumer product.

Sec. 1115.4   Defect.—

Section 15(b)(2) of the CPSA requires every manufacturer (including an importer), distributor, and retailer of a consumer product who obtains information which reasonably supports the conclusion that the product contains a defect which could create a substantial product hazard to inform the Commission of such defect. Thus, whether the information available reasonably suggests a defect is the first determination which a subject firm must make in deciding whether it has obtained information which must be reported to the Commission. In determining whether it has obtained information which reasonably supports the conclusion that its consumer product contains a defect, a subject firm may be guided by the criteria the Commission and staff use in determining whether a defect exists. At a minimum, defect includes the dictionary or commonly accepted meaning of the word. Thus, a defect is a fault, flaw, or irregularity that causes weakness, failure, or inadequacy in form or function. A defect, for example, may be the result of a manufacturing or production error; that is, the consumer product as manufactured is not in the form intended by, or fails to perform in accordance with, its design. In addition, the design of and the materials used in a consumer product may also result in a defect. Thus, a product may contain a defect even if the product is manufactured exactly in accordance with its design and specifications, if the design presents a risk of injury to the public. A design defect may also be present if the risk of injury occurs as a result of the operation or use of the product or the failure of the product to operate as intended. A defect can also occur in a product's contents, construction, finish, packaging, warnings, and/or instructions. With respect to instructions, a consumer product may contain a defect if the instructions for assembly or use could allow the product, otherwise safely designed and manufactured, to present a risk of injury. To assist subject firms in understanding the concept of defect as used in the CPSA, the following examples are offered:

(a)   An electric appliance presents a shock hazard because, through a manufacturing error, its casing can be electrically charged by full-line voltage. This product contains a defect as a result of manufacturing or production error.

(b)   Shoes labeled and marketed for long-distance running are so designed that they might cause or contribute to the causing of muscle or tendon injury if used for long-distance running. The shoes are defective due to the labeling and marketing.

(c)   A kite made of electrically conductive material presents a risk of electrocution if it is long enough to become entangled in power lines and be within reach from the ground. The electrically conductive material contributes both to the beauty of the kite and the hazard it presents. The kite contains a design defect.

(d)   A power tool is not accompanied by adequate instructions and safety warnings. Reasonably foreseeable consumer use or misuse, based in part on the lack of adequate instructions and safety warnings, could result in injury. Although there are no reports of injury, the product contains a defect because of the inadequate warnings and instructions.

(e)   An exhaust fan for home garages is advertised as activating when carbon monoxide fumes reach a dangerous level but does not exhaust when fumes have reached the dangerous level. Although the cause of the failure to exhaust is not known, the exhaust fan is defective because users rely on the fan to remove the fumes and the fan does not do so.

However, not all products which present a risk of injury are defective. For example, a knife has a sharp blade and is capable of seriously injuring someone. This very sharpness, however, is necessary if the knife is to function adequately. The knife does not contain a defect insofar as the sharpness of its blade is concerned, despite its potential for causing injury, because the risk of injury is outweighed by the usefulness of the product which is made possible by the same aspect which presents the risk of injury. In determining whether the risk of injury associated with a product is the type of risk which will render the product defective, the Commission and staff will consider, as appropriate: The utility of the product involved; the nature of the risk of injury which the product presents; the necessity for the product; the population exposed to the product and its risk of injury; the Commission's own experience and expertise; the case law interpreting Federal and State public health and safety statutes; the case law in the area of products liability; and other factors relevant to the determination. If the information available to a subject firm does not reasonably support the conclusion that a defect exists, the subject firm need not report. However, if the information does reasonably support the conclusion that a defect exists, the subject firm must then consider whether that defect could create a substantial product hazard. (See section 1115.12(f) for factors to be assessed in determining whether a substantial product hazard could exist.) If the subject firm determines that the defect could create a substantial product hazard, the subject firm must report to the Commission. Most defects could present a substantial product hazard if the public is exposed to significant numbers of defective products or if the possible injury is serious or is likely to occur. Since the extent of public exposure and/or the likelihood or seriousness of injury are ordinarily not known at the time a defect first manifests itself, subject firms are urged to report if in doubt as to whether a defect could present a substantial product hazard. On a case-by-case basis the Commission and the staff will determine whether a defect within the meaning of section 15 of the CPSA does, in fact, exist and whether that defect presents a substantial product hazard. Since a consumer product may be defective even if it is designed, manufactured, and marketed exactly as intended by a subject firm, subject firms should report if in doubt as to whether a defect exists. Defect, as discussed in this section and as used by the Commission and staff, pertains only to interpreting and enforcing the Consumer Product Safety Act. The criteria and discussion in this section are not intended to apply to any other area of the law.

. . .

Sec. 1115.10   Persons Who Must Report and Where to Report.—

(a) Every manufacturer (including importer), distributor, or retailer of a consumer product that has been distributed in commerce who obtains information that such consumer product contains a defect which could create a substantial risk of injury to the public shall immediately notify the Product Defect Correction Division, Consumer Product Safety Commission, Washington, D.C. 20207 (telephone: 301-492-6608), or such other persons as may be designated. Manufacturers (including importers), distributors, and retailers of consumer products subject to regulation by the Commission under provisions of the FFA, FHSA, PPPA, as well as consumer products subject to regulation under the CPSA and RSA, must comply with this requirement.

(b) Every manufacturer (including importer), distributor, or retailer of a consumer product that has been distributed in commerce who obtains information that such consumer product fails to comply with an applicable consumer product safety standard or ban issued under the CPSA shall immediately notify the Commission's Product Defect Correction Division or such other persons as may be designated. A subject firm need not report a failure to comply with a standard or regulation issued under the provisions of the RSA, FFA, FHSA, or PPPA unless it can be reasonably concluded that the failure to comply results in a defect which could create a substantial product hazard. (See section 1115.10(a).)

(c) A distributor or retailer of a consumer product (who is neither a manufacturer nor an importer of that product) is subject to the reporting requirements of section 15(b) of the CPSA but may satisfy them by following the procedure detailed in section 1115.13(b).

(d) A manufacturer (including an importer), distributor, or retailer need not inform the Commission under section 15(b) of the CPSA if that person has actual knowledge that the Commission has been adequately informed of the defect or failure to comply. (See section 15(b) of the CPSA.)

Sec. 1115.11   Imputed Knowledge.—

(a) In evaluating whether or when a subject firm should have reported, the Commission will deem a subject firm to have obtained reportable information when the information has been received by an official or employee who may reasonably be expected to be capable of appreciating the significance of the information. (See section 1115.14(b).)

(b) In evaluating whether or when a subject firm should have reported, the Commission will deem a subject firm to know what a reasonable person acting in the circumstances in which the firm finds itself would know. Thus, the subject firm shall be deemed to know what it would have known if it had exercised due care to ascertain the truth of complaints or other representations. This includes the knowledge a firm would have if it conducted a reasonably expeditious investigation in order to evaluate the reportability of a death or grievous bodily injury or other information. (See section 1115.14.)

Sec. 1115.12   Information Which Should Be Reported; Evaluating Substantial Product Hazard.—

(a) General—Subject firms should not delay reporting in order to determine to a certainty the existence of a noncompliance or a defect and the substantiality of a possible hazard. The obligation to report arises upon receipt of information from which one could reasonably conclude the existence of a noncompliance or of a defect which could create a substantial product hazard. Thus an obligation to report may arise when a subject firm receives the first information regarding a potential hazard or noncompliance. (See section 1115.14(c).) A subject firm in its report to the Commission need not admit or may specifically deny that the information it submits reasonably supports the conclusion that its consumer product is noncomplying or contains a defect which could create a substantial product hazard within the meaning of section 15(b) of the CPSA. After receiving the report, the staff will preliminarily determine whether the noncompliance or defect presents a substantial product hazard. This determination can be based on information supplied by a subject firm or from any other source. If the matter is adjudicated, the Commission will ultimately make the decision as to substantial product hazard or will seek to have a court make the decision as to imminent product hazard.

(b)   Failure to Comply.—Information indicating that a consumer product fails to comply with an applicable consumer product safety standard or ban issued under the CPSA must be reported.

(c)   Death or Grievous Bodily Injury.—Information indicating that a noncompliance or a defect in a consumer product has caused, may have caused, or contributed to the causing, or could cause or contribute to the causing of a death or grievous bodily injury (e.g., mutilation, amputation/dismemberment, disfigurement, loss of important bodily functions, debilitating internal disorders, severe burns, severe electrical shocks, and injuries likely to require extended hospitalization) must be reported, unless the subject firm has investigated and determined that the information is not reportable.

(d)   Other Information Indicating a Defect or Noncompliance.—Even if there are no reports of a potential for or an actual death or grievous bodily injury, other information may indicate a reportable defect or noncompliance. In evaluating whether or when a subject firm should have reported, the Commission will deem a subject firm to know what a reasonable and prudent manufacturer (including an importer), distributor, or retailer would know. (See section 1115.11.)

(e)   Information Which Should Be Studied and Evaluated.—The following are examples of information which a subject firm should study and evaluate in order to determine whether it is obligated to report under section 15(b) of the CPSA:

(1)   Information about engineering, quality control, or production data suggesting the existence of a noncompliance or of a defect which could create a substantial product hazard.

(2)   Information about safety-related production or design change(s) suggesting the existence of a noncompliance or of a defect which could create a substantial product hazard.

(3)   Product liability suit(s) suggesting the existence of a noncompliance or of a defect which could create a substantial product hazard.

(4)   Information from an independent testing laboratory suggesting the existence of a noncompliance or of a defect which could create a substantial product hazard.

(5)   Complaint(s) from a consumer or consumer group indicating the existence of a noncompliance or of a defect which could create a substantial product hazard.

(6)   Information received from the Commission or another governmental agency indicating the existence of a noncompliance or of a defect which could create a substantial product hazard.

(7)   Information received from other firms, including requests to return a product or for replacement or credit, indicating the existence of a noncompliance or of a defect which could create a substantial product hazard. This includes both requests made by distributors and retailers to the manufacturer and requests from the manufacturer that products be returned.

(f)   Evaluating Substantial Risk of Injury.—Information which should be or has been reported under section 15(b) of the CPSA does not automatically indicate the presence of a substantial product hazard. On a case-by-case basis the Commission and the staff will determine whether a defect or noncompliance exists and whether it results in a substantial risk of injury to the public. In deciding whether to report, subject firms may be guided by the following criteria the staff and the Commission use in determining whether a substantial product hazard exists:

(1)   Hazard Created by Defect.—Section 15(a)(2) of the CPSA lists factors to be considered in determining whether a defect creates a substantial risk of injury. These factors are set forth in the disjunctive. Therefore, the existence of any one

of the factors could create a substantial product hazard. The Commission and the staff will consider some of all of the following factors, as appropriate, in determining the substantiality of a hazard created by a product defect:

(i) Pattern of Defect.—The Commission and the staff will consider whether the defect arises from the design, composition, contents, construction, finish, packaging, warnings, or instructions of the product or from some other cause and will consider the conditions under which the defect manifests itself.

(ii) Number of Defective Products Distributed in Commerce.—Even one defective product can present a substantial risk of injury and provide a basis for a substantial product hazard determination under section 15 of the CPSA if the injury which might occur is serious and/or if the injury is likely to occur. However, a few defective products with no potential for causing serious injury and little likelihood of injuring even in a minor way will not ordinarily provide a proper basis for a substantial product hazard determination.

(iii) Severity of the Risk.—A risk is severe if the injury which might occur is serious and/or if the injury is likely to occur. In considering the likelihood of any injury the Commission and the staff will consider the number of injuries reported to have occurred, the intended or reasonably foreseeable use or misuse of the product, and the population group exposed to the product (e.g., children, elderly, handicapped.)

(iv) Other Considerations.—The Commission and the staff will consider all other relevant factors.

(2) Hazard Presented by Noncompliance.—Section 15(a)(1) of the CPSA states that a substantial product hazard exists when a failure to comply with an applicable consumer product safety rule creates a substantial risk of injury to the public. Therefore, the Commission and staff will consider whether the noncompliance is likely to result in injury when determining whether the noncompliance creates a substantial product hazard. As appropriate, the Commission and staff may consider some or all of the factors set forth in Section 1115.12(f)(1) in reaching the substantial product hazard determination.

Sec. 1115.13   Content and Form of Reports; Delegations of Authority.—

(a) Written Reports.—The chief executive officer of the subject firm should sign any written reports to the Commission under section 15(b) of the CPSA unless this responsibility has been delegated by filling a written delegation of authority with the Commission's Product Defect Correction Division. Delegations of authority filed with the Commission under section 1115.9 of the previous regulations interpreting section 15 of the CPSA will remain in effect until revoked by the chief executive officer of the subject firm. The delegation may be in the following form:

DELEGATION OF AUTHORITY

(Name of company) _____.

I _____ hereby certify that I am Chief Executive Officer of the above-named company and that as such I am authorized to sign documents and to certify on behalf of said company the accuracy and completeness of information in such documents.

Pursuant to the power vested in me, I hereby delegate all or, to the extent indicated below, a portion of that authority to the person listed below.

This delegation is effective until revoked in writing. Authority delegated to:

(Name)   _____

(Address) _____

(Title)   _____

(b) Distributors and Retailers.—A distributor or retailer of a possibly defective or noncomplying consumer product (who is neither a manufacturer nor an importer of that product) satisfies the initial reporting requirements either by telephoning or writing the Product Defect Correction Division, Consumer Product Safety Commission, Washington, D.C. 20207; by sending a letter describing the defective or noncomplying product to the manufacturer (or importer) of the product and sending a copy of the letter to the Commission's Product Defect Correction Division; or by forwarding to the Commission's Product Defect Correction Division reportable information received from another firm. A distributor or retailer who receives reportable information from a manufacturer (or importer) shall report to the Commission unless the manufacturer (or importer) informs the distributor or retailer that a report has been made to the Commission. A report under this subsection should contain the information detailed in Section 1115.13(c) insofar as it is known to the distributor or retailer. Unless further information is requested by the staff, this action will constitute a sufficient report insofar as the distributor or retailer is concerned.

   (c)   Initial Report.—Immediately after a subject firm has obtained information which reasonably supports the conclusion that a product fails to comply with an applicable consumer product safety rule or contains a defect which could create a substantial risk of injury to the public, the subject firm should provide the Product Defect Correction Division, Consumer Product Safety Commission, Washington, D.C. 20207 (telephone: 301-492-6608), with an initial report containing the information listed below. This initial report may be made by any means; but if it is not in writing, it should be confirmed in writing within 48 hours of the initial report. (See Section 1115.14 for time computations.) The initial report should contain, insofar as is reasonably available and/or applicable:

   (1)   An identification and description of the product.
   (2)   The name and address of the manufacturer (or importer) or, if the manufacturer or importer is not known, the names and addresses of all known distributors and retailers of the product.
   (3)   The nature and extent of the possible defect or the failure to comply with an applicable consumer product safety rule.
   (4)   The nature and extent of the injury or risk of injury associated with the product.
   (5)   The name and address of the person informing the Commission.
   (6)   To the extent such information is then reasonably available, the data specified in Section 1115.13(d).

   (d)   Full Report.—Subject firms which file initial reports are required to file full reports in accordance with this subsection. Retailers and distributors may satisfy their reporting obligations in accordance with 1115.13(b). At any time after an initial report, the staff may modify the requirements detailed in this section with respect to any subject firm. If the staff preliminarily determines that there is no substantial product hazard it may inform the firm that its reporting obligation has been fulfilled. However, a subject firm would be required to report if it later became aware of new information indicating a reportable defect or noncompliance, whether the new information related to the same or another consumer product. Unless modified by staff action, the following information, to the extent that it is reasonably available and/or applicable, constitutes a "full report," must be submitted to the staff, and must be supplemented or corrected as new or different information becomes known:

   (1)   The name, address, and title of the person submitting the "full report" to the Commission.
   (2)   The name and address of the manufacturer (or importer) of the product and the addresses of the manufacturing plants for that product.
   (3)   An identification and description of the product(s). Give retail prices, model numbers, serial numbers, and date codes. Describe any identifying marks and their location on the product. Provide a picture or a sample of the product.
   (4)   A description of the nature of the defect or failure to comply with an

applicable consumer product safety rule. If technical drawings, test results, schematics, diagrams, blueprints, or other graphic depictions are available, attach copies.

(5)   The nature of the injury or the possible injury associated with the product defect or failure to comply with an applicable consumer product safety rule.

(6)   The manner in which and the date when the information about the defect or noncompliance (e.g., complaints, reported injuries, quality control testing) was obtained. If any complaints related to the safety of the product or any allegations or reports of injuries associated with the product have been received, copies of such complaints or reports (or a summary thereof) shall be attached. Give a chronological account of facts or events leading to the report under section 15(b) of the CPSA, beginning with receipt of the first information which ultimately led to the report. Also included may be an analysis of these facts or events.

(7)   The total number of products and units involved.

(8)   The dates when products and units were manufactured, imported, distributed, and sold at retail.

(9)   The number of products and units in each of the following: in the possession of the manufacturer or importer, in the possession of private labelers, in the possession of distributors, in the possession of retailers, and in the possession of consumers.

(10)   An explanation of any changes (e.g., designs, adjustments, additional parts, quality control, testing) that have been or will be effected to correct the defect or failure to comply and of the steps that have been or will be taken to prevent similar occurrences in the future together with the timetable for implementing such changes and steps.

(11)   Information that has been or will be given to purchasers, including consumers, about the defect or noncompliance with a description of how this information has been or will be communicated. This shall include copies or drafts of any letters, press releases, warning labels, or other written information that has been or will be given to purchasers, including consumers.

(12)   The details of and schedule for any contemplated refund, replacement, or repair actions, including plans for disposing of returned products (e.g., repair, destroy, return to foreign manufacturer).

(13)   A detailed explanation and description of the marketing and distribution of the product from the manufacturer (including importer) to the consumer (e.g., use of sales representatives, independent contractors, and/ or jobbers; installation of the product, if any, and by whom).

(14)   Upon request, the names and addresses of all distributors, retailers, and purchasers, including consumers.

(15)   Such further information necessary or appropriate to the functions of the Commission as is requested by the staff.

Sec. 1115.14   Time Computations.—

(a)   General.—Weekends and holidays are excluded from the computation of the time periods in this part.

(b)   Imputing Knowledge.—In evaluating whether or when a firm should have reported, the Commission shall impute to the subject firm knowledge of product safety related information received by an official or employee of a subject firm capable of appreciating the significance of the information. Under ordinary circumstances, 5 days should be the maximum reasonable time for information to reach the Chief Executive Officer or the official or employee responsible for complying with the reporting requirements of section 15(b) of the CPSA. The Commission will impute knowledge possessed by the Chief Executive Officer or by the official or employee responsible for complying with the reporting requirements of section 15(b) of the CPSA simultaneously to the subject firm.

(c)   Time When Obligation to Report Arises.—The obligation to report under section 15(b) of CPSA may arise upon receipt by a subject firm of the first information regarding a noncompliance or a potential hazard presented by a product defect. Information giving rise to a reporting obligation may include, but is not limited to, complaints, injury reports, quality control and engineering data. A subject firm should not await complete or accurate risk estimates before reporting under section 15(b) of CPSA. However, if information is not clearly reportable, a subject firm may spend a reasonable time for investigation and evaluation. (See section 1115.14(d).)

(d) Time for Investigation and Evaluation.—A subject firm may conduct a reasonably expeditious investigation in order to evaluate the reportability of a death or grievous bodily injury or other information. This investigation and evaluation should not exceed 10 days unless a firm can demonstrate that a longer period is reasonable. The Commission will deem that, at the end of 10 days, a subject firm has received and considered all information which would have been available to it had a reasonable, expeditious, and diligent investigation been undertaken.

(e) Time to Report.—Immediately, that is, within 24 hours, after a subject firm has obtained information which reasonably supports the conclusion that its consumer product fails to comply with an applicable consumer product safety rule or contains a defect which could create a substantial risk of injury to the public, the firm should report. (See Section 1115.13.) If a firm elects to conduct an investigation in order to evaluate the existence of reportable information, the 24-hour period begins when the subject firm has information which reasonably supports the conclusion that its consumer product fails to comply with an applicable consumer product safety rule or contains a defect which could create a substantial product hazard. Thus, a firm could report to the Commission before the conclusion of a reasonably expeditious investigation and evaluation if the reportable information becomes known during the course of the investigation. In lieu of conducting an investigation, the firm may report the information immediately.

If one is going to prepare a notice to the Consumer Product Safety Commission, obviously it will be the exceptional case when all of the requested information can be supplied within the time limits. In order to minimize this problem, managers should give some advance thought to the problem so that counsel and management can establish responsibility for preparing the notice and delegate responsibility for digging out the needed information before the problem arises. If this is done, time will not be wasted on preliminaries. (Note the formal delegation requirement in the notification regulations.) It might be useful to designate a team and make sure that each member is up to date on the rules. The team might include members from the following departments:

1. Engineering, to evaluate design or manufacturing problems

2. Legal, to draft the report

3. Public relations, to draft press releases

4. Sales/marketing, to inform on the marketing or distribution of the product

5. Purchasing, to contribute necessary information if the problem is caused by a purchased component

6. Top management, to make necessary policy decisions

Public Availability of the Information Submitted

With the recent amendments to the Freedom of Information Act, companies must assume that virtually anything submitted to the Consumer Product Safety Commission will be public information. The submission should be prepared accordingly. If it is absolutely essential to furnish any information which is competitively significant or which discloses a trade secret, this information should be *physically separated* from the main body of the report and clearly labeled that it is exempt from disclosure under the Freedom of Information Act (see Chapter 62).

RIGHTS OF THE COMMISSION TO INVESTIGATE AND OBTAIN INFORMATION

The act gives the Consumer Product Safety Commission the following rights to obtain information:

1. The commission or its staff may conduct investigative hearings or "other inquiry" anywhere in the United States.

2. The commission may order reports and answers to questions under oath, subpoena testimony of witnesses and production of documents, and conduct depositions. (These can be enforced in court.)

3. The commission may, by rule, require a company to provide it data relating to performance and safety of a consumer product which it manufactures.

4. The commission, through its employees, has certain inspection powers, including the right to enter at reasonable times any premises where products are manufactured or held, the right to inspect such premises in a reasonable manner, and the right to inspect books and records and papers relevant to determining compliance.

CERTIFICATION OF CONFORMANCE WITH STANDARDS

Manufacturers and private labelers must provide to their distributors or retailers certificates specifying applicable standards, affirming the product's conformance to those standards, and stating the name of the manufacturer and place of manufacture. If the original shipment is broken up for delivery to more than one retailer, it is sufficient to send copies of the original certificates to all parties within the distribution chain. In the case of a product with more than one manufacturer or private labeler, the commission may issue appropriate rules designating the person responsible for issuing the certificate.

The commission may also, in its discretion, promulgate rules dealing with the labeling of any consumer products, including products not subject to a safety rule. The act gives the commission authority to require that consumer products bear labels identifying the manufacturer or private labeler and the date and place of manufacture. Not that the comparable provisions of the Fair Packaging and Labeling Act, which had more limited application because of that act's more limited definition of consumer product, may be superseded by this requirement.

GENERAL PROHIBITIONS

The act has a very broad prohibition making it unlawful for any person to manufacture for sale, or offer for sale, distribute in commerce, or import any consumer product which is not in conformity with an applicable safety standard or which has been banned by the commission.

The act contains the usual provisions in this type of legislation making it unlawful to refuse the commission access to records, to fail to furnish infor-

mation or technical data, to fail to provide the required certificate of conformance, to falsify any such certificate, or to fail to comply with any commission
remedial order. The act also provides for inspection of the premises by the
commission, and requires the maintenance of such records as the commission
may by rule require.

PRIVATE ACTIONS

In a provision which is almost bound to create another entire body of law—
not to mention another body of lawyers—the act provides that:

1. If a product violates a rule, private parties may sue for damages sustained
   and recover attorneys' fees.

2. Private parties may enforce the provisions of the act (after appropriate notice
   to the commission and the attorney general) and recover attorneys' fees for
   such effort.

3. Any private remedy a person may have had before is not abrogated by the
   act, even if the product in question complies with all applicable standards.

RECORD-KEEPING REQUIREMENTS

At the present time, there are no specific record-keeping requirements. However, section 16(b) of the Consumer Product Safety Act authorizes the commission to issue such regulations, and they have been issued in proposed form.
The proposal is quite burdensome, because it requires that the records be
kept for 5 years, that they apply to products regulated under the transferred
acts as well as to consumer products, and specifically that all records of product
safety complaints and the written or oral responses and lawsuits be kept,
by product, for 5 years.

VIOLATIONS AND PENALTIES

The Consumer Product Safety Act sets forth specific prohibited actions (section
19), specific civil penalties for violating those prohibited actions (section 20),
and criminal sanctions for knowingly violating those prohibited actions (section 21).

Prohibited Actions

The following actions are declared to be in violation of the act:

1. To manufacture, offer, distribute, or import for sale any product that fails
   to conform to a safety standard or has been banned as a hazardous product

2. To refuse access to or copying of records or to refuse to permit inspection of
   records or facilities or products

3. To fail to comply with a commission order dealing with repair, replacement,
   or refund

4. To falsify compliance certificates or fail to furnish them

5. To stockpile a product in order to circumvent the purpose of a safety rule

Civil Penalties

There is a fine of $2000 for any section 19 violation. Each failure or each day of violation is a separate offense. Total penalties for a series of related offenses cannot exceed $500,000.

Criminal Penalties

Any person who knowingly and willfully violates any provision of section 19 after receiving notice of noncompliance from the commission may be fined not more than $50,000 or sentenced to prison for not more than 1 year, or both. A director, officer, or agent of a corporation who knowingly and willfully authorizes, orders, or performs prohibited acts is subject to the same criminal penalties.

COMMENTARY

At this stage, it appears that the Consumer Product Safety Commission has acted fairly and reasonably in *most* cases. However, it also appears that one cannot depend on this fair and reasonable treatment in *all* cases. The case of *Marlin Toy Products, Inc.* is a harrowing example. In this case, the Food and Drug Administration informed Marlin that the toy plastic balls it sold were potentially unsafe because they contained plastic butterflies and colored pellets which could be swallowed by a child *if* the top broke open. The company had never recieved any complaint of harm from the toys since their introduction in 1962. However, at a cost of $96,000, the company recalled the balls and removed the pellets in order that the toys could be redistributed with the approval of the FDA. In 1973, anticipating big holiday sales, the company made a large quantity of the toys. In the meantime, however, the Consumer Product Safety Commission, which had taken over regulation of toys, published a banned products list including the toys Marlin had redesigned. The agency admitted its error, but by that time, stores which had ordered the toys cancelled the order, costing Marlin about $1.2 million. Marlin sold its toy lines, which accounted for 85 percent of its revenue, and laid off all but ten of its employees.[1]

SUMMARY OF REQUIRED ACTIONS IN THE AREA OF PRODUCT SAFETY

Ascertain Which Laws Govern Your Products

The Consumer Product Safety Act, of course, applies only to consumer products as defined therein. There are, however, many other statutes which have similar but not identical implications, and there are many products which are still not covered by any specific legislation at all. The first step is to ascertain which products made by your company are governed by which statutes (not overlooking OSHA), so that you know what rules to comply with.

Adopt Appropriate Procedures and Make Appropriate Plans

Depending on the circumstances, some planning should be considered. For example, if a company manufactures a product covered by the Consumer Product Safety Act, it should have at least:

---

[1] *U.S. News and World Report,* June 30, 1975, p. 28.

1. An awareness program to teach lower-level employees to report possible safety defects at early stages

2. A "safety team," including legal counsel, to determine what actions are appropriate and to carry them out

3. A delegation appointed by the chief executive officer of the company that has the authority to make a notification to the commission while the CEO is absent

CHAPTER FORTY-FIVE

PRODUCT LIABILITY

The questions of product safety, product warranty, and product liability are all deeply entangled in a maze of federal and state laws. These are among the most serious issues for business executives today and are also issues where much benefit can inure from thorough and expert application of the available legal medicines.

Simply stated, the problem is that any company manufacturing anything may be found liable for any personal injury which that product causes, even though the injury may occur many years after the product has been made and under circumstances in which the manufacturer could not reasonably have anticipated that injury might occur. It is absolutely essential for companies to have insurance against exposure to this liability, but ultimately the company is going to bear the liability through increased insurance premiums. To complicate the matter, new federal laws, principally the Consumer Product Safety Act, have added the distinct possibility that defective products might have to be recalled from the market and that, in addition to private lawsuits, companies can expect costly litigation with the federal government if there is a consumer product liability problem.

There have always been general principles of negligence providing in substance that when the negligence of one party causes injury to another party, the negligent party is liable for damages to the injured party. Applying these principles to the manufacturing area was generally impossible, because a potential plaintiff had the burden of proving negligence of the manufacturer, which was extremely difficult at the very least. In addition, the so-called privity doctrine required the plaintiff to have some direct relationship with the defendant, e.g., having purchased goods from the defendant. In many cases, the injured party had no relationship to the manufacturer and therefore was unable to recover damages even in a case where he was injured by a clearly defective product.

Gradually, the law developed to provide that (1) if a product was shown to be defective, liability would be imposed on the manufacturer on some ground, such as presumption of negligence, a breach of warranty, or strict tort liability; and (2) if the plaintiff was anyone who could reasonably be expected to be injured by the product, he could recover damages even without privity. In addition to this evolution of the law itself, there has developed a "plaintiff's bar," which is expert in prosecuting these personal injury cases and obtaining very large awards from juries. Of course, the fact that the cases usually involve a plaintiff who has really been injured—perhaps grotesquely—and a defendant which is a business corporation contributes to the large settlements which are sometimes awarded: it may be sympathy for the plaintiff and the belief that the corporation and its insurance company can pay, rather than any substantial product defect, that motivate juries.

THEORY OF LIABILITY

Following is a brief discussion of the grounds on which a seller may be held liable for a defective product.

Strict Tort Liability

Perhaps the origin and best statement of the theory of so-called strict liability is section 402(a) of the Restatement of Torts. That section provides as follows:

(1) One who sells any product in a defective condition—unreasonably dangerous to the user or consumer or to his property—is subject to liability for physical harm thereby caused to the ultimate consumer or user or to his property, if
   (a) the seller is engaged in the business of selling such a product, and
   (b) if it is expected to and does reach the user or consumer without substantial change in the condition in which it is sold.
(2) This rule . . . applies although
   (a) the seller has exercised all possible care in the preparation and sale of his product, and
   (b) the user or consumer has not bought the product from or entered into a contractual relation with the seller.

The manufacturer can raise the following defenses:

1. The plaintiff misused the product. That is, the plaintiff used it for an unintended purpose, used it with knowledge of the danger involved, used it in disregard of an appropriate warning, used it contrary to instructions, or abused it.

2. The defect involved did not cause the injury complained of. This is really saying something else caused the plaintiff's injury, usually the negligence of the plaintiff himself or a third person.

3. The manufacturer has no duty to make an absolutely foolproof product. Therefore, while there might have been some danger, it was not unreasonable.

4. The defect involved was obvious. This defense is a variation on the basic assumption-of-risk doctrine. The plaintiff should have seen the obvious defect and not used the product.

5. There was really no defect. Generally this is complicated to prove.

6. There *was* some danger involved in the use of the product, but such danger was disclosed by an adequate warning.

Breach of Express Warranty

Naturally, if a manufacturer makes an express warranty which is then breached, the breach of that warranty may give rise to liability. Generally, the plaintiff must show:

1. There was an express warranty.
2. The warranty was breached.
3. The warranty concerned a material fact.

In most jurisdictions, the plaintiff does not need to show that he *relied* on the express warranty. If he *knew* it was false, however, he cannot use the argument of reliance to justify his suit.

Following is the general law on express warranties in sales transactions as contained in the Uniform Commercial Code in effect in most states:

UCC Sec. 2-313.   Express Warranties by Affirmation, Promise, Description, Sample.

(1) Express warranties by the seller are created as follows:
  (a) Any affirmation of fact or promise made by seller to the buyer which relates to the goods and becomes part of the basis of the bargain creates an express warranty that the goods shall comform to the affirmation or promise.
  (b) Any description of the goods which is made part of the basis of the bargain creates an express warranty that the goods shall conform to the description.
  (c) Any sample or model which is made part of the basis of the bargain creates an express warranty that the whole of the goods shall conform to the sample or model.

(2) It is not necessary to the creation of an express warranty that the seller use formal words such as "warrant" or "guarantee" or that he have a specific intention to make a warranty, but an affirmation merely of the value of the goods or a statement purporting to be merely the seller's opinion or commendation of the goods does not create a warranty.

Breach of Implied Warranty

In many states, the courts talk in terms of warranty liability rather than strict tort liability. Technically there is some difference, but generally the result is more formal than substantive: the manufacturer is usually liable.

The Uniform Commercial Code provides for two implied warranties:

1. The warranty of merchantability. This says that the goods are of at least as good quality as similar goods passing through the marketplace and are generally fit for the purpose for which they are intended.
2. The warranty of fitness for a particular purpose. This says that the goods are of a sufficient quality and are suitable for the particular purpose for which the buyer intends to use them—if the seller is aware of that particular purpose.

These two warranties have their basis in the following two sections of the Uniform Commercial Code.

UCC Sec. 2-314.   Implied Warranty: Merchantability; Usage of Trade.

(1)   Unless excluded or modified (Section 2-316), a warranty that the goods shall be merchantable is implied in a contract for their sale if the seller is a merchant with respect to goods of that kind. Under this section the serving for value of food or drink to be consumed either on the premises or elsewhere is a sale.

(2)   Goods to be merchantable must be at least such as
  (a)   pass without objection in the trade under the contract description; and
  (b)   in the case of fungible goods, are of fair average quality within the description; and
  (c)   are fit for the ordinary purposes for which such goods are used; and
  (d)   run, within the variations permitted by the agreement, of even kind, quality and quantity within each unit and among all units involved; and
  (e)   are adequately contained, packaged, and labeled as the agreement may require; and
  (f)   conform to the promises or affirmations of fact made on the container or label if any.

(3)   Unless excluded or modified (Section 2-316) other implied warranties may arise from course of dealing or usage of trade.

UCC Sec. 2-315.   Implied Warranty: Fitness for Particular Purpose.
Where the seller at the time of contracting has reason to know any particular purpose for which the goods are required and that the buyer is relying on the seller's skill or judgment to select or furnish suitable goods, there is unless excluded or modified under the next section an implied warranty that the goods shall be fit for such purpose.

Problems in Warranty Cases

One question involved in product liability cases based on warranty, either express or implied, is the question of privity, of contract. The Uniform Commercial Code itself has removed the privity requirement as applied to the purchaser's immediate family or guests. The code itself does not change the privity rules as applied to all others but leaves that to developing case law. A fair summary of that developing case law is that the privity requirement has been so substantially eroded by one means or another that it is probably safe to make the assumption, at least for planning and risk-exposure analysis, that privity is no longer a requirement. It should be noted, however, that this is not to say that even under the most liberal versions anyone can sue when a defective product causes injury. There is still the basic rule of the "unforeseeable plaintiff" which holds that a manufacturer is liable only for injuries which could reasonably be anticipated, and while cases have been very liberal in imposing liability, there are some boundary lines.

Another basic problem in the warranty area is that it is quite clear that a manufacturer of a car, for example, cannot escape liability for a defect by proving that the defect occurred in some part which he bought from someone else and simply installed in the car, e.g., brakes or steering gears. This is true even if it can be clearly shown that the defect was in the product at the time it left the original maker's plant and that the auto maker was not negligent in handling or installing the article.

On the other hand, it is also clear that the manufacturer of a component part is liable himself for any defects in parts which he sells. This has given rise to a troublesome situation for manufacturers of component parts. The following rules apply to any manufacturer of parts which are incorporated into another product.

Joinder   When someone sues the manufacturer of a finished product on the basis of a defective part, many times the alleged manufacturer of the defective part, if known to the plaintiff, is *joined* as a co-defendant. Often the plaintiff is wrong and investigation discloses that the defendant named did not make the component part in question. If the defendant is not careful here, it may expend a considerable amount of time and effort defending a part it did not even manufacture.

When a product manufacturer and one of its suppliers are so joined as codefendants, a conflict of interest will ensue between the two. This conflict greatly complicates the defense of the lawsuit.

Vouching In   The Uniform Commercial Code has a section dealing with a suit against a manufacturer for a problem caused by one of its suppliers. That section provides that if a company is sued for breach of warranty or other obligation under circumstances where one of that company's suppliers is ultimately liable, the company sued may give that supplier written notice of the litigation. If the notice states that the supplier shall be allowed to defend itself or else be bound by any determination of fact, the supplier will be so bound. As an example, if a plaintiff sues General Motors for a defective steering mechanism which caused an accident in a Chevrolet and General Motors had purchased that steering mechanism from a supplier, General Motors can "vouch in" that supplier by giving the supplier notice of the lawsuit and stating that the supplier should come in and defend itself. If the supplier does not do so, and if the judge or jury determines that the steering gear was in fact defective, that question cannot again be litigated in a subsequent suit by General Motors against the supplier for reimbursement of any damages it has to pay. Since the only question of substance involved in product liability is whether the product is defective, vouching in amounts to forcing the supplier to either defend the case or rely on the client corporation to defend the case, recognizing that it might not defend it too strongly if it can collect from the supplier, or notify the insurance company and let both firms' insurance companies negotiate the procedure for defending the case.

Workmen's Compensation Cases   Another thorny procedural problem involves companies that make products used by other manufacturing companies, such as metal-stamping equipment or machine guards. When an employee is hurt on the job, his remedy against the employer will usually be provided by state workmen's compensation laws, which provide fairly speedy but very low recoveries. Generally, these workmen's compensation laws provide that the recovery is exclusive, irrespective of the negligence of the employer, the employee, or fellow employees. However, if the employee is hurt on a defective machine, most courts will allow the plaintiff to sue the manufacturer of the machine, and the manufacturer will not be protected by these workmen's compensation laws. A recent development is that some courts are now allowing the manufacturer of the equipment to sue the employer, or forcibly join him as codefendant, if the employer was negligent in maintaining the equipment or in allowing employees to use it improperly or while it was in a defective condition. Some of these cases are quite bizarre and have been reported in business periodicals. They may involve the manufacturer of a piece of equipment made in the late 1800s or early 1900s, sold and resold many times, and improperly used or maintained by its various owners. If an employee is injured on such a machine, he can sue the manufacturer who—depending on the state law—may or may not be able to join the employer as codefendant. The prospect of such suits has caused the product liability insurance of these capital equipment manufacturers to skyrocket even faster than medical malpractice insurance, and many manufacturers are in serious financial condition as a result.

In summary then, by one means or another, in the overwhelming majority of cases a plaintiff who has been injured by a defective product is able to recover damages from the manufacturer of that product. Furthermore, given the practicalities of our imperfect jury system, a manufacturer may have liability imposed upon it if someone is injured even under circumstances where the product was not defective, or where if it was defective, the defect was not what caused the plaintiff's injury.

MANAGING THE PRODUCT LIABILITY PROBLEM

From a management's point of view, product liability should be considered in two contexts. The first is the liability for personal injury to anyone using the product, and the second is liability for damages other than personal injury. For example, if a company manufactures steering gears for heavy trucks, it will have two risk exposures. The first is the liability for personal injury which might befall the driver or other people if the steering gear fails, and the second is the possible damage to the truck and its contents if the steering gear fails. From a legal point of view, it is necessary to keep these two questions separate, because they must be dealt with in different ways.

Personal Injury

No matter what kind of contracts you write or forms you use in the sale of your product, if that product is defective and causes personal injury, your company can be liable irrespective of any contrary provision in any contract. For example, pursuing our steering-gear/truck example, if the steering gear manufacturer enters into a contract with the truck manufacturer stating that if the steering breaks and causes personal injury to the driver or any other person, the steering gear manufacturer will not be liable, that contract is not binding in any way on anyone actually injured; an injured party may sue the steering gear manufacturer without regard to the contract. Of course, the steering gear manufacturer might, if the contract has been properly drafted, have a right of action against the truck manufacturer for indemnification.

Property Damage

The property damage part of the product liability problem is not so severe, because awards for items of tangible property are usually of relatively minor amounts when compared with personal injury awards. On the other hand, property damage can be substantial. In the case of our truck example, it is not unreasonable to assume that the truck containing the steering gear could be worth $20,000 and the cargo $10,000. Accordingly, if the steering gear malfunctions, a total loss of $30,000 is possible. Further, we might assume that the trucking company would lose revenue by having this truck out of operation for a period of time. To carry the example to the extreme, the trucking company may default on or lose a large contract because this truck is not available—all because of the faulty steering gear. These kinds of property and consequential damages are generally recoverable if they can be proven.

In this area, the rule on contractual protection is different. Between merchants (which is a magic phrase used by the Uniform Commercial Code to describe business as opposed to consumer transactions) it is permissible to enter into *any kind of deal desired.* The only restriction is against "unconscionable" contracts. While liability for personal injury may not be limited, liability for all other damages may, at least between merchants. Accordingly, one of the ways to manage the product liability problem is to minimize by contract any liability for property damage, consequential damages, lost profits, or any other kind of damages that might occur by reason of a product failure. This is particularly useful for companies which manufacture something used in a manufacturing process. Suppose, for example, a company manufactures a piece of equipment used on an assembly line and that equipment malfunctions. If the equipment is shut down for a long period of time, a great deal of production might be lost and there might be a large claim for lost profits or other consequential damages. These kinds of damages can and should be limited by contract.

There is a great deal of law on the question of just how one goes about limiting liability by contract. The general rule is that any language clear enough to limit liability is permissible, but the courts seem to look with extreme disfavor on these limitations and use all manner of theories to get around them. The best approach is to thoroughly study the law applicable to the jurisdictions where the product is sold and comply with all the technical requirements. For larger companies, it is best to structure the contract forms to deal with all the problems presented in myriad state law decisions.

One of the principal difficulties is that the courts tend to say that a limitation-of-liability clause—which generally provides that the sole liability of the manufacturer is to replace any defective part and that the manufacturer is not liable for damage to the completed product or consequential damages—is qualified by the general legal theory that a company cannot exempt itself from liability for its own negligence unless it does so clearly in the contract, and sometimes not even then. Accordingly, unless the limitation clause uses the word "negligence" and in some jurisdictions the word "tort" the court may say that if a plaintiff can prove that the product was negligently manufactured, the contract limitation does not apply. Further, the court might go on to help the plaintiff by presuming that if the product malfunctioned in the ordinary course of operation it was negligently manufactured. After all is said and done, however, if management insists that its lawyers do a proper job of limiting liability by contract, or if the lawyers appreciate all the problems and take it upon themselves to do a good job, a manufacturer can generally reduce or even eliminate its liability for property damage to other "merchants."

Once a manufacturer has done this, however, it is faced with the next element of the problem: how to balance the legal considerations with the marketing and customer-relations ones. The trouble is that the language limiting liability is likely to be at cross-purposes with the sales department. Where sales language is meant to draw an appealing picture of the product, the limitation language is likely to be in bold print and to imply that the product was thrown together from whatever raw materials were available and that the customer takes it "as is." The method of resolving this conflict has to be determined on a case-by-case and company-by-company basis, but it is a step which must be undertaken by management, with the understanding and cooperation of both the sales department and the legal department.

Tools of the Trade

Indemnification

One of the ways to manage the product liability problem is to get indemnification from your customers. This is a very good technique if your company is a manufacturer of component parts, but it doesn't work very well if your company manufactures and sells the completed product.

Indemnification might at first seem to be wishful thinking, but it should not be so considered, because it is very useful, if properly approached. The proper way to approach a risk exposure under product liability claims is to assess the cost involved. Pursuing our steering-gear/truck example above, let's assume that a truck manufacturer wants to procure steering gears from outside sources and asks for quotations on a given set of specifications. One of the principal cost factors in the quotation is likely to be product liability. In other words, if the truck manufacturer itself is willing to indemnify the parts manufacturer, it will be able to procure those parts at a substantially lower price. On the other hand, if the parts manufacturer has to pay for the insurance and assume liability, it will have to build this cost into the price structure. Accordingly, from a logical point of view, it is simple to assess which party could more advantageously and economically defend any product liability lawsuits. Usually, it is the manufacturer of the finished product, because such a company is typically larger than a parts manufacturer, that can obtain broader insurance coverage, can insure itself, and is responsible for the performance of the entire product and can more efficiently defend product liability cases, many of which will allege a multitude of defects rather than a single defect.

In our above example, which party should bear the cost of product liability was a simple matter of business negotiation. Of course, if either of the parties doesn't read the contracts carefully, it could wind up behind the eight ball. Suppose, for example, that the steering manufacturer receives a quotation request on a form printed by the truck maker that states on the back that the supplier is to be held responsible for the product. If the steering gear manufacturer is unaware of this provision, it might very easily fall into the trap of pricing the product on the basis of manufacturing costs without including this product liability factor. Of course, the converse is also true: if the truck manufacturer thinks it is passing the problem off on the steering gear maker but the contract does not adequately reflect this, the truck manufacturer could be the one which ultimately has to absorb the costs.

Warnings

In some cases, a manufacturer's liability to the consumer can be greatly reduced by proper warnings. In many cases, a manufacturer will be liable for damage caused by a product *unless* there are appropriate warnings; if there *are* appropriate warnings, the manufacturer may be able to avoid liability where the product is used in disregard of that warning. Generally, any time a company sells a product which might be termed "unreasonably dangerous," there should be appropriate warnings. In the chemical industry, any product which can cause burns or which is flammable or caustic requires warnings, and there are special statutes applicable to these kinds of products. Other unreasonably dangerous products include such things as explosives and firearms.

On the other hand, there are many products which are not unreasonably dangerous but which can cause substantial injury if they are used improperly. The law in this area is almost comical, but some of this comedy can mean the difference in a product liability suit between large recoveries against a manufacturer and a successful defense. Take the case of an ordinary stove, for example, with the kind of front oven door that pulls down from the top. One might reasonably expect that the maker of such a stove should not have to warn consumers not to stand on this door to clean the kitchen ceiling. Not so. Why? Because the company often knows that these kinds of injuries occur. In the case of an injury of first impression—the first time anyone is injured by standing on a stove door to clean the kitchen ceiling—it might be persuasively argued that such an occurrence was unforeseeable and there was no duty to warn the customer not to stand on the oven door. On the other hand, after a number of such occurrences have come to the attention of the manufacturer and the manufacturer knows that people are likely to stand on the oven door to clean the ceiling, no matter how ridiculous this might seem, there may be a duty to warn of this danger.

Thus, companies must consider warnings to be one of the tools of the trade by which they can reduce product liability exposure, and if they know that their products are misusable or unreasonably dangerous, a good warning program should be undertaken.

A good warning program requires a little bit of good legal work, and a large amount of crystal ball work. Some of the legal propositions include the following. The warning, to be effective, must address itself to the danger of personal injury. If the warning does not tell the whole extent of the danger, or if it is so evasive that it seems to refer to a danger other than personal injury, it is not effective. For example, a company that manufactured baseball pitching machines labeled its product with the warning "Stay clear of throwing arm at all times." The throwing arm remained in a cocked position when the machine was at rest, and a plaintiff reported that he was injured severely and permanently when the throwing arm struck him as he was standing near it when it was at rest. The courts held the manufacturer liable for failing to warn specifically that the machine was still dangerous when at rest. "All times" was not clear enough.

As another example, a company stated that a product used in roofing should not be heated over an open flame because its waterproofing qualities would be impaired. It was held that this was not a warning that explosive gases would be emitted if the material was heated in an enclosed space. Similarly, "Keep in a cool place" was not sufficient notice of the explosive nature of a bleach when exposed to heat. In another interesting case, a fingernail polish carried the warning "Do not use near heat or fire." The user was injured when she used the product while smoking and it ignited her clothing. The court said that the company should have specifically warned against the flammable danger of the fumes.

Obviously, a warning must be conspicuous enough to come to the user's attention. This is a rule-of-reason approach. The labeling requirements under the Federal Hazardous Substances Act can be used as a good checklist for warnings on products that are not covered by the act as well as on those that are. Following is a checklist for the Federal Hazardous Substances Act:

1. The name of the hazardous substance

2. The "signal" word, such as "Danger" or "Warning"

3. An affirmative statement of the principal hazard or hazards, such as "Flammable" or "Causes burns"

4. Precautionary measures describing the action to be followed or avoided, such as "Use only in a well-ventilated room"

5. Instructions for first aid treatment, where applicable

6. Special handling or storage instructions, when necessary, such as "Heat above 120°F may cause bursting"

7. A statement equivalent to "Keep out of the reach of children," where applicable

In summary, the warning is a tool which can be used to manage the product liability problem in many cases besides those which involve unreasonably hazardous products.

Insurance

Wherever appropriate, companies should, of course, have product liability insurance coverage. That does not mean that it is prudent to simply rely on the insurance company to defend all product liability cases, except possibly for smaller companies which do not have the legal resources to assist the insurance company. A major reason why this is important is that most larger companies are moving towards self-insurance, a system in which the insurance company is usually involved in litigation and sets the premium on a retrospective basis so that the company ultimately pays the cost of product liability suits.

If a company has a substantial liability exposure, it can probably save money by heavily participating in the defense of product liability suits. Generally, this means having engineers or other technical experts participate in the defense of the lawsuit and having the company's lawyers oversee the conduct of the case to be sure that proper attention is given it, that the insurance company is not compromising or improperly settling the case, and that any long range implications—such as an assertion of design defects which might affect many of the company's products—are properly evaluated. Of course, such active participation costs money, and management must question whether the benefit is outweighed by the cost. Since the cost is certain and measurable and the benefit uncertain and hard to measure, this is a difficult analysis. A rule-of-reason approach, however, suggests that a middle-of-the-road posture would be productive. It would probably be too costly to assume a major role in handling the defense of *all* company product liability claims, but it would be foolish to abandon the whole area to the insurance company—especially if the insurer had an arrangement whereby it simply billed the company for the amounts paid out, usually with a percentage added to cover administrative costs in handling claims.

Vouching In

As another tool of the trade for managing the product liability problem, the vouching-in sections of the Uniform Commercial Code described above should be used to the best advantage possible. If you manufacture a completed product, you should carefully consider the vouching-in sections when a suit alleges a defect in a component which you have procured from someone else. If you manufacture component parts and are frequently faced with vouching-in notices, you should have some kind of legal procedure to handle them; either an overriding agreement with the manufacturer that the manufacturer will handle the problem, as in the indemnification discussion above; or else a clear method of evaluating claims to know whether it is useful for you to go in and defend, either through your own counsel or through your insurance carrier. It goes without saying that a good legal procedure includes efficient and competent legal assistance in handling any product liability problem.

It should, of course, be recognized that the legal aspect of product liability is only part—and perhaps a small part—of the whole story. The solution is in quality control. The best way to avoid liability for defective products is simply not to make defective products. We must all recognize, however, that we do live in an imperfect world and so even if we have good quality control procedures, we are still going to need some good legal assistance for the problems which will undoubtedly arise.

SECTION SEVEN: INDUSTRIAL PROPERTY

CHAPTER FORTY-SIX

PATENTS

Of all the areas of the law which affect corporations, patent laws are perhaps the most specialized. Actually, the patent law itself is rather simple. However, it becomes entwined with technical, mechanical, electrical, or chemical questions; therefore, patent lawyers tend to have engineering degrees and perhaps even some practical experience in engineering work.

Patent laws are all federal; there is one United States patent law which applies in all jurisdictions, and there are no state patent systems. There are, however, numerous foreign patent systems. The United States patent law provides essentially that any person who invents something can obtain a patent on that product or process. The two principal kinds of patents are product patents, which cover actual physical products, and process patents, which govern the process by which products are made. A given article might be subject to both a product patent governing the finished product and a process patent governing the manufacturing process.

The holder of a patent has the right to exclude any other person from copying the invention disclosed by the patent. Thus, if you have a patent on a product, you have the right to exclude others from making an identical product; and if you have a patent on a certain manufacturing process, you have the right to exclude others from using it.

As is readily apparent, there are a number of questions which can arise under the patent laws. For example, what kind of invention will justify a patent? Most courts state that there must be something *new* and *substantially different* from the "prior art" in order to justify a patent. How much is substantially different? The criterion seems to be that what would have been readily apparent to a craftsman is not new or novel but something that goes beyond that is. Obviously, this is a subjective area.

Another question is, If you have a patent on an article, may somebody else manufacture one which is only a little bit different? Again, this is a subjective area, and the test is whether the difference in the product which is alleged to infringe your patent is substantial. Obviously, if you make a certain product and paint it red and a competitor makes the same product and paints it green, the mere fact that one is red and one is green will not protect the competitor from a claim of infringement. On the other hand, if the competitor changes the product in a way which makes it substantially different from yours, he will not be guilty of infringement. If he changes the product in a way which does not substantially change it from yours but improves it, it is possible that he can get an improvement patent. Thus, you will have a situation where you have the basic patent and the competitor has the improvement patent, and if the improvement is something substantial which makes the device commercially feasible, it may be necessary for one party to license the other. Perhaps you could not make the product commercially feasible without his improvement, and he could not use his improvement without a license from you on the basic patent.

PATENT RIGHTS OF CORPORATE EMPLOYEES

Patents are usually issued originally in the name of one or more individual inventors, but they can then be assigned to anyone, including a corporation. In the case of employees who are hired with the reasonable expectation that they may invent something useful for the company, there should be an agreement which spells out the rights of the parties. Typically, this kind of agreement will provide the following:

1. The employee will assign to the company all rights to any invention made during the course of his employment.

2. The employee will prosecute or assist in the prosecution of any patent application. The agreement usually provides that the company will pay all expenses.

3. If any patents are issued, the employee will assign them.

Some companies have *all* their employees sign this kind of agreement upon hiring. For example, even though I work as a corporate attorney, I was required to sign such an agreement for my company when I was hired. This is good practice, because it is sometimes difficult to know in advance which employees will come up with patentable ideas. The employee agreement must be reasonable or it will not be enforceable. It must limit its application to inventions and patents made during the course and scope of the employee's work. It cannot cover *all* inventions including those made on the employee's own time. This can be a troublesome area, because sometimes employees get their corporate and personal work so mixed up with each other that it is difficult to tell whether an invention was made on company time using company equipment or on the employee's personal time.

If this problem is not covered in a contract, it will be left to the general legal rules. These provide that in the case of an employee who was hired to invent, such as a research engineer, the law will impute an agreement substantially like that stated above so that all inventions made during employment which relate to what the employee was hired to do for the company will have to be assigned to the employer. If, on the other hand, the employee was not hired to invent, this will not be the case; the invention will belong to the employee but will be subject to a shop right for the employer. A shop right is the right of the employer to use the invention without infringing even if the employee is later granted a patent. If the employee invents something entirely on his own time using his own equipment and facilities, the invention and any subsequent patents belong entirely to him, and the corporation has no greater right than anyone else to those inventions.

Obviously, the subjectivity inherent in all of this, plus the likelihood that the precise facts (Did the invention occur during company time? On company property? Was it the kind of thing the employee was hired to do?) will be less than 100 percent clear in most cases, dictates the desirability of preparing for this problem by the use of properly drawn and executed invention agreements.

VIOLATIONS OF PATENT LAW

Infringement

Infringement is simply the unauthorized use of an invention. It is not necessary that the infringer know he is infringing; ignorance of the law is not a valid excuse with the patent office. Indeed, that is perhaps the biggest advantage of a patent over a trade secret. However, there are two additional concepts which are worth mentioning. These are *inducing infringement* and *contributory infringement.*

Inducing infringement is just what the name implies. The law provides that "whoever actively induces infringement of a patent shall be liable as an infringer."

Contributory infringement refers to the sale of parts or components of a patented product. The law provides that whoever sells a component of a patented product constituting a material part of the invention, knowing the same to be especially made for use in an infringement of a patent, shall be liable as a contributory infringer.

Misuse

Generally, patents are practiced either by the person to whom they were issued (or assigned) or by someone obtaining a license from the owner. The person owning the patent may sue anyone using it unless the use is authorized. However, this is limited by the concept of misuse. Misuse is an equitable defense when asserted by someone who has been sued for infringing a patent. It provides that the patent owner should not be allowed to assert his patent if and when he has misused it. The most usual grounds for misuse are antitrust violations. If, for example, you license a patent on the condition that the licensee purchase some other, unpatented product from you, this is an illegal tying arrangement under the antitrust laws and also a misuse of patent. Therefore, if you are found to have done this and if you sue an infringer, both of the following are likely to occur:

1. The defendant will counterclaim for the antitrust violation and recover three times his actual damages plus attorney's fees.

2. He will allege patent misuse to preclude you from recovering any damages from him on account of his infringement.

Fraud on the Patent Office

Another kind of misuse is fraud on the patent office. Generally, an inventor is more familiar with prior art in the field of his invention than patent examiners. The United States patent procedures rely heavily on voluntary disclosure to the patent examiners by the person applying for the patent of all prior art. If you fail to make such disclosure and a patent is issued, that failure can cost you heavily. The fraud will be grounds for any person infringing the patent to avoid liability, and depending on the facts, it may even give rise to liability for damages against you.

THE QUALITY OF A PATENT

In popular thought, a patent is a patent. Unfortunately, it is not so simple. All patents look alike in the sense that they have a disclosure and a set of claims. However, there is considerably more to it than that. The patent lawyer must be able to judge exactly what to disclose and what to claim. The disclosures must not be too broad but must be broad enough. The claims must not be too broad but must be broad enough. The disclosures and the claims must match up so that a patent is claimed on everything disclosed. In short, it is simply not good enough to know that you have "a patent" on something. You must know how strong that patent is, how broad it is, and whether it is something that is easy to circumvent.

All these subjects are very complicated and subjective and are best left to patent lawyers. The purpose of this chapter is not to discuss the intricacies of patent law but to explain a little about how it fits into the corporate scheme of things.

USING PATENTS

There is a distinction between patents and trade secrets. That matter will be discussed in Chapter 49. However, it is necessary to understand that you have two choices if you have an invention: to keep it secret, or to patent it. In deciding between the two, the first step is to ask whether or not your company has anything worth patenting. In most cases, this first step will have already been taken, because most manufacturing companies have at least some basic patents.

This leads to the second step, which is to decide exactly how much patent protection the company ought to have. Some companies have a great many patents plus pending applications on products which are generically the same; other companies manufacture a wide variety of products and have very few patents. It depends partly upon the industry—electronics and chemical companies tend to have a lot of patents—and partly upon the philosophy of the company and the kinds of products it makes. Still, it is necessary to apply organization and management to the patent function. Sometimes a company will feel that it needs a number of patents and will simply hire a patent lawyer or will engage an outside law firm to deal directly with its engineers.

A haphazard approach in this area is very dangerous. It may result in an extremely costly patent function or one which does not cover all the products and processes which should be covered. The company may want to turn the matter over to a good inside patent counsel or even a good outside patent counsel, if it has one or the other; but management should not simply assume this is adequate unless it has some kind of master plan or framework for the patent function. If you let your engineers deal directly with outside patent counsel without any overall supervision, it is likely that you will wind up spending a great deal of money on patent applications, and you may not have comprehensive coverage of all your inventions.

It seems that the best approach is to have one or more patent lawyers who report to a general counsel; then the whole patent function, along with the rest of the legal functions in the company, is managed and organized by the general counsel under the direction of top management. In large companies, this is the rule; some even have assistant general counsels for patents. In smaller companies, the closer this system can be approached, the better.

The next thing to do in the patent area is to give some thought to what you are going to do with the patents. It does not make a great deal of sense to pay a lot of money for patents merely for the right to sue somebody infringing one of them. If you do have valuable patents, it is worthwhile exploring how they can be licensed to others. For example, if you have a good product or process patent in the United States but your company cannot exploit it abroad, you may find it profitable to license it to overseas companies. Obviously, in order to do this, you will need a set of foreign patents corresponding to the United States patent, and obtaining these will be a substantial undertaking. You will need patent counsel in foreign countries, and you count on several thousands of dollars per patent for any kind of broad coverage, even if you limit yourself to the highly industrialized countries.

Another use of patents is as a marketing tool. This works particularly well in the automotive industry. You get a good product or improvement and then sell it to a manufacturer of the motor vehicle. Since they will usually want alternative sources, you can license them or other companies. Thus by the sale of the product, or by licensing royalties, or by both, you can help market the company's products by sound use of patents.

If you decide to license the patents, the role of the patent lawyer becomes very important. In many companies, the patent lawyer or the general counsel also acts as the person primarily in charge of negotiating patent licenses or the arrangements whereby the technology is licensed to another company. In other companies, all of this is done by management, the lawyers simply drafting up the documents. Either approach works if you have the right people in the right places.

PATENT VALIDITY

In the United States, a large portion of litigated patents are eventually determined to be invalid. A brief look at the process by which patents are issued shows why this is the case. In order to obtain a patent, you have to file an application that discloses the invention. This then goes to the patent office, which has one of its examiners look over the prior art, which is a combination of previously issued patents and material published in technical journals. If the patent examiner does not find any prior art, he will issue your patent. Usually, there is a process of negotiation whereby the patent examiner and the patent applicant negotiate what kind of patent might be available and what claims ought to be allowed. A patent consists essentially of two parts. One is the disclosure of the invention, and the other is the set of claims. Naturally, the broader your claims, the better your coverage. However, if your claims are too broad, the likelihood is enhanced that a court will determine that your invention really did not justify the claims and, therefore, the patent was invalid.

All this applies to every patent. Of all the patents issued, only a small fraction turn out to be commercially valuable. Thus, when you file a patent application, in most cases you really do not know how much the patent will be worth to you if and when it is issued, and therefore it is a little difficult to judge how much time and effort to expend in preparing the application.

What really does show up the validity and the value of a patent is litigation. If a patent is important enough to be in litigation, it must be a very valuable one. Patent litigation is one of the most expensive kinds of litigation; it involves many, many hours of legal time in finely combing all of the prior art and generally flyspecking the whole process. This kind of all-out effort is bound to turn up things which were not turned up in the original patent application; therefore, a great many patents are, upon court scrutiny, determined to be invalid.

To point is, If the patents you have are of dubious validity (statistically your odds are about 50-50 in court), do they really do you any good? Can you really sue someone for infringing your patent? Remember, one of the most prevalent sources of antitrust counterclaims is patent suits in which one company alleges that another company infringed a patent and the defendant company counterclaims for many millions of dollars on the basis of an antitrust violation. Thus, if you sue someone for infringing your patent, you risk a multimillion-dollar counterclaim, plus the possibility that your patent may be termed invalid.

There really is no hard and fast rule as to when you should sue and when you should not. However, some of the reported cases tend to indicate that companies do not always thoroughly evaluate this question before filing lawsuit. Some of the cases seem to show—at least after the fact—that the company should have known that the patent was of dubious validity and that its antitrust risk outweighed the possibility of any advantage from winning the patent suit. In short then, the use of patents—especially suing under them—is something that should receive top management attention, and management ought to be sure that it has not only the patent counsel's opinion but also the general counsel's opinion as to the advisability of instituting any patent suit.

PATENT COUNSEL

Another problem which management ought to be aware of is the proper place of patent counsel in the corporate hierarchy. Again, there are no hard and fast rules, but it is something which should not be left to chance. The general counsel ought to be asked periodically to report on not only the patent function but the personnel as well. Patent lawyers are sometimes neglected in the overall corporate personnel planning effort, and if this happens, eventually the company will wind up with a very ineffective and very costly patent function.

SUMMARY

What then, should management know about patent law? Following are some suggested items for attention:

1. Do you have a list of all your patents?

2. Do you have a list of all your patent licenses (both where you are the licensor and where you are the licensee)?

3. Do you have someone generally in charge of managing the patent function (which should also include trade secrets, copyrights, and trademarks), or is the matter left to chance?

4. Do you have someone supervising the patent attorney's interaction with the engineers so that you have a relatively efficient way of handling the costly patent application process?

5. Do you have a good program for attracting and keeping good people in this complex area?

6. Have you done everything appropriate for your company in covering possible disputes about employee inventions, including signing agreements between the corporation and the employees?

7. Do you have a good system for making sure you are getting the maximum benefit from your patents—perhaps by licensing, perhaps by assignment, or perhaps just by practicing the inventions yourself?

8. Do you have a good system for making sure you get a thorough and complete review of any patent infringement lawsuit your company is considering filing so that this highly explosive area does not turn into a disaster for you?

9. Do you have some idea of which are your key patents and how valid they are?

10. Do you have some program for making sure your company does not infringe other patents? If you are using new processes or making new products which you are not going to patent, do you still check the prior art to ascertain what patents you might be infringing?

11. Do you periodically get reports on how much the patent function is costing the company?

CHAPTER FORTY-SEVEN

COPYRIGHTS

The federal copyright law protects the ownership of written material and, since it was amended substantially as of January 1, 1978, of just about any other mode of recorded information, including tapes, phonograph records, cable television, and works of art and music. Generally, all you have to do to protect your ownership interest in these kinds of tangible mediums of expression is to affix the proper copyright notice and publish the work. That will provide copyright protection, but before you can use the copyright in court to sue for infringement, you will also have to register the work with the copyright office. This chapter will deal only with written materials. However, the new copyright law also covers virtually any tangible medium of communication, whether now known or later developed. The only significant difference is that different mediums require different forms of copyright notices.

Although copyright protection can be obtained for anything in writing (or recorded in any other medium), the copyright extends only to the writing. It does not protect the idea, procedure, process, system, method of operation, concept, principle, or discovery.

QUESTIONS AND ANSWERS ABOUT COPYRIGHTS

How Do You Claim a Copyright?

In the case of written material, you claim the copyright by simply including the copyright notice. That has three elements:

1. The copyright symbol (ⓒ), the word "copyright," or the abbreviation "copr."
2. The year of first publication
3. The name of the copyright owner

Before the new copyright law went into effect, there were some other very important technicalities. The copyright notice had to be on the page immediately following the cover page, and if it was omitted from even one issue, the copyright would be lost. Now, however, these technicalities have been greatly relaxed. The copyright notice can appear any place in or on the work where it will reasonably inform the reader that it is copyrighted, and if the notice is omitted from no more than a relatively small number of copies, the copyright protection will not be lost. An innocent infringer, however, who copies the work unaware of the copyright because the notice wasn't included is protected from liability for infringement.

How Do You Register?

You can register your copyrighted material with the copyright office by depositing a copy, paying a modest fee, and filling out its appropriate registration forms. There is a registration procedure for written materials, and there are other procedures and forms for other items such as phonograph records.

What Does a Copyright Give the Owner?

A valid copyright gives the owner the exclusive right to use the work and to do or authorize others to do the following:

1. Reproduce it
2. Prepare derivative works based on the copyrighted work
3. Distribute copies to the public by sale, lending, or otherwise
4. In the case of literary, musical, dramatic, and similar works, to perform them for profit or display them publicly

Also, of course, it gives the owner the right to sue anyone who infringes the copyright.

How Long Does the Copyright Last?

Under the old law, a copyright lasted for 28 years. Now, however, it has been extended to last for the life of the author plus another 50 years.

What Are the Remedies for Infringement?

The possible remedies for infringement are severe indeed. They include, of course, an injunction to make the infringing party stop infringing, and damages for past infringement. They also include lost profits which the copyright owner might have obtained, possible impounding of infringing articles, costs and attorney's fees, and, in extreme cases, criminal penalties.

FAIR USE

One of the most difficult questions raised by the copyright law is the concept of fair use. The proliferation of copying machines is, of course, the cause for most of the concern. Indeed, one of the principal items of discussion during the legislative debates was the extent to which photocopying should be allowed. Since the old law was enacted long before these machines were invented, there was no provision dealing with the problem. The new law attempts to codify the law of fair use as it emerged in several cases decided under the old laws. Unfortunately, most of the cases involving the fair use question don't involve normal corporate operations. Also the law's statement of what constitutes fair use is not very easy to apply to any actual situation. The law says that fair use is permitted in section 107, which provides as follows:

> Notwithstanding the provisions of section 106 [the portion of the law which gives the copyright owner the exclusive right to reproduce his work] the fair use of a copyrighted work, including such use by reproduction in copies or phonorecords or by any other means specified by that section, for purposes such as criticism, comment, news reporting, teaching (including multiple copies for classroom use), scholarship, or research, is not an infringement of copyright. In determining whether the use made of a work in any particular case is a fair use the factors to be considered shall include:
>
> (1) the purpose and character of the use, including whether such use is of a commercial nature or is for nonprofit educational purposes;
> (2) the nature of the copyrighted work;
> (3) the amount and substantiality of the portion used in relation to the copyrighted work as a whole; and
> (4) the effect of the use upon the potential market for or value of the copyrighted work.

In summary, it seems that, within some broad guidelines, we have a rather straightforward, commonsense test of fair use. While this is very flexible, it also presents difficulties for planning purposes, because different people are obviously going to have different ideas of what is fair. In the context of corporate use of published materials, the possibilities appear to run from a very clear case of infringement where the corporation buys one subscription to a service and then makes copies for several of its employees on a routine basis, to a clear case of fair use where a corporation buys one subscription for its library and on an irregular and infrequent basis various employees will make single copies of single articles from the publication for their use or research. Obviously, it is the cases in between which present possible problems, and at this time there are no clear guidelines.

Libraries

There are some specific provisions dealing with libraries in the new law. These require libraries to provide persons ordering copies with special forms which inform them of the copyright limitations. Also, notices on coin- or self-operated photocopy machines are required. Some corporate libraries might fit the definition of "library" and therefore might want to comply with these rules also.

SOME CORPORATE IMPLICATIONS

Some corporate documents cost a lot of money to generate and cannot be protected as trade secrets because they have to be published. Catalogues and booklets containing specifications are prime examples. Corporations should, of course, make sure that these kinds of things are copyrighted. Also, the converse is true: corporations should be very careful about using material from competitors because remedies for infringement can be very severe.

In order to detect infringement, corporations should consider including "traps" in their material. For example, if you have put together a catalogue for something which required much time and effort for gathering information, you might want to include some false material in several places so that if someone copies your catalogue, you can prove that the material was not original but was a copy of yours. Without these traps, proof of infringement would be difficult if not impossible. Obviously, the converse is also true: if you want to put out a catalogue like your competitor's, you had better make sure you generate all the information yourself and don't simply copy his catalogue, for there might be traps in it.

Copyright protection is only part of a broader spectrum of devices to protect industrial property. Trade secrets and registered trademarks are often related to copyright protection. In the catalogue situation, you cannot rely on trade secret protection and so copyright protection is all that is available. In other cases, however, trade secret protection is available. For example, if you have specifications or drawings for your products, these probably qualify as trade secrets and should be handled accordingly. On the other hand, if you have to publish them in order to get any value from them or to sell the products, you might have to rely only on copyright protection. Of course, you might have patent protection available for the product itself.

CHAPTER FORTY-EIGHT

TRADEMARKS

The federal trademark law is the Lanham Act, sometimes called the Trademark Act, which was adopted in 1946. While it has been amended on several occasions, it would be fair to say that the law is generally the same now as then.

Essentially, the pattern of the legislation is that it provides for a federal registration system for trademarks used in interstate commerce in something called the "Principal Register" and then provides that any trademark which is registered in the Principal Register, and the person registering it, has the following benefits:

1. The registration puts everyone else on notice that the trademark is claimed by the person registering it.

2. The registrant has the right to bring suit in the federal courts against an infringer without the necessity for proving the other usual requirements for bringing a suit in federal court (diversity of citizenship of all the parties and a minimum amount in controversy).

3. If the registrant is successful in the lawsuit, he can get an injunction against the infringer, damages, and in some cases triple damages and the destruction of infringing labels.

4. The registration in the Principal Register is prima facie evidence of the validity of the registration and the registrant's ownership of the mark and is sufficient proof of this in court. The defendant can prove that the registrant does not own the mark or that it is an invalid mark.

5. The registrant may obtain relief against products which are imported bearing an infringing trademark. This is true even if the court doesn't have jurisdiction over the foreign company actually applying the infringing mark. The relief can include seizure of the goods.

If a mark cannot be registered in the Principal Register, there is also a "Supplemental Register," which is used for marks which are capable of distinguishing goods or services but for some reason are not registerable in the Principal Register. Registration in the Supplemental Register is of considerably less value than registration in the Principal Register, but if registration in the Principal Register cannot be obtained, there are some benefits in registering in the Supplemental Register.

DEFINITIONS

Before proceeding further, it is useful to define a few terms.

A *trademark* means any word, name, symbol, or device or any combination thereof adopted and used by a manufacturer or merchant to identify his goods and distinguish them from those manufactured or sold by others.

In addition to trademarks, there are a number of other marks which are afforded the same protection under the Trademark Act as a normal trademark.

A *service mark* is a mark used in the sale or advertising of services to identify the services of one person and distinguish them from the services of others. Titles, character names, and other distinctive features of radio or television programs may be registered as service marks.

The term *certification mark* means a mark used upon or in connection with the products or services of one or more persons other than the owner of the mark to certify regional or other origin material, motive, quality, accuracy, or other characteristics of such goods or services, or that the work or labor on the goods or services was performed by members of a union or other organization.

The term *collective mark* means a trademark or service mark used by the members of a cooperative, an association, or other collective group or organization and includes marks used to indicate membership in a union, an association, or other organization.

Generally, for business planning purposes, all of these different marks can be lumped together, because essentially they are afforded the same protection under the Trademark Act.

A trade name is technically different from a trademark. However, there is obviously also a great deal of similarity, and some writers have even referred to trade names as "quasi trademarks." Some examples will serve to clarify the distinctions.

In some cases, a single name may be the name of a corporation, a trademark, and a trade name. Typical examples are IBM and Xerox. In some cases, the corporate name, the trade name, and the trademark can be different even though closely related. An illustrative example is the case of Sears Roebuck and Co., where "Sears Roebuck and Co." is the corporate name but the trade name is "Sears" and there are many trademarks under which their products are sold, including "Kenmore" and "Craftsman."

Legally, there is an important distinction between a trade name and a mark because it is only marks which are registrable. Trade names are not. However, as a practical matter, trade names can be thought of in the same category as marks because usually the trade name and trademark will be very close and, even though the trade name cannot be registered, much of the protection afforded trademarks is available in the case of trade names. Accordingly, for purposes of the remainder of this chapter, all marks and trade names will be included in the single term trademark except where distinctions are specifically mentioned.

REGISTERING A TRADEMARK USED IN INTERSTATE COMMERCE

There is an important difference between patent and copyright law and trademark law because the Constitution specifically authorizes Congress to enact laws relating to patents and copyrights but not trademarks. This has given rise to a situation where the federal laws relating to patents and copyrights have entirely preempted the field and states cannot pass patent or copyright laws. On the other hand, the federal trademark law applies only to trademarks *used in interstate commerce* and does not preempt the field. Accordingly, almost all states have their own trademark law, and if a trademark is to be used entirely within one state, the only means of protection is registration under that state's trademark law. Unfortunately, there is a great deal of difference among the various state trademark laws. For purposes of this chapter, only the federal law will be discussed.

It is important to note that a mark must be *used* in interstate commerce before it can be registered. Accordingly, you must design and use a mark before you can register it, and this means that you will want to have maximum assurance that, after you spend the effort and money to do this, you can in fact register it and it won't infringe someone else's trademark. Therefore, before using a trademark, you should search through the available public records to be as sure as possible that no one else has a prior right to it. Fortunately, there are a number of legal tools through which lawyers can provide management with substantial assurance that any given mark is or is not available for registration or has or has not been used previously. Unfortunately, this legal assurance cannot be absolute because the search system is not perfect. In the first place, there is no necessity for registering a trademark. Accordingly, if someone has used a trademark without registering it, he probably has common law rights in the use of that mark which could not be preempted by someone else registering it later. Also, there is, of course, the gray area where someone might have used a mark which is similar but not identical to the one being proposed.

As a practical matter, however, the state of the art on trademarks is such that management can feel relatively certain that it can use a trademark if it has obtained the proper trademark search and gotten a clean bill of health. On the other hand, cavalier use of a mark without going through this step is dangerous. It may subject the company to damages, and there may be a great deal of money wasted in advertising and goodwill buildup which has to be abandoned if someone has a prior right to the mark.

This is quite important because the trademark does not exist in the abstract but must be connected with some product or service. One cannot simply think up an abstract mark and have it registered in the Principal Register. Instead, like copyrights, it must be shown that the trademark is identified with a particular product or service and that it must either by itself or by association point distinctly to the origin or ownership of that article to which it is applied.

As common experience would note, there does not have to be anything in the trademark which shows what product it might be applied to. For example, the name "Kodak" has no intrinsic significance, but it has now acquired an association with photographic products. Essentially then, the use must come before the registration. As a practical matter, the two can take place in a fairly close period of time, but the trademark search is necessary because the prima facie validity of the mark obtained by registry in the Principal Register will take place only after it has been applied to goods and becomes associated with them. Thus, there will be substantial planning, management, advertising, and possible risk of infringement before the mark is actually registered.

LOSS OF TRADEMARKS

The two principal ways a trademark can be lost are by abandonment and by any other course of conduct, including lack of enforcement, which causes the mark to lose significance as an indication of origin.

Abandonment is fairly obvious. The patent law provides that a trademark shall be abandoned "when its use has been discontinued with intent not to resume." Intent not to resume may be inferred from the circumstances. Nonuse for two consecutive years shall be prima facie abandonment.

The second problem, nonenforcement, is a little more troublesome. The statute provides that a mark shall be deemed abandoned "when any course of conduct of the registrant, including acts of omission as well as commission, causes the mark to lose its significance as an indication of origin."

For some very successful trademarks, there is a substantial problem in this area because the trademark itself can be associated with something other than the *origin* of the goods and can indeed become a *generic name* for a kind of product. Coca-Cola for example has an elaborate procedure for enforcing its trademark "Coke" and indeed will bring a lawsuit against people who sell Pepsi Cola or other carbonated cola drinks in response to a request for a "Coke." Many beverage dispensing establishments, for example, will handle only one kind of carbonated cola, and if that doesn't happen to be Coca-Cola and a person comes in to ask for a "Coke," the merchant will routinely, if properly counseled (and perhaps previously visited by a representative of Coca-Cola), inform the purchaser that what it can provide is "Pepsi" or something else. Coca-Cola has a number of people who go around to these kinds of establishments and ask for a "Coke," and if they are supplied something else, they promptly object. Because of the success of the trademark "Coke" this enforcement is probably essential for Coca-Cola to keep possession of its trademark.

Xerox is in a similar situation. At the time this book is being written, for example, there are many full page advertisements in national magazines pointing out the difference between the trademark "Xerox" and the word "xerox" meaning the reproducing procedure used in the xerographic process. Again, the Xerox trademark has been so successful that this kind of admonitory advertising needs to be done in order to prevent loss of the trademark.

In one legal article, the following list of very valuable trademarks was listed as being lost into the generic-term category because of improper use and lack of enforcement:

1. Aspirin

2. Cellophane

3. Celluloid

4. Escalator

5. Kerosene

6. Lanolin

7. Linoleum

8. Milk of Magnesia

9. Shredded Wheat

10. Thermos

Essentially, what happened with all of these words is that they started out with an arbitrary trademark significance but their meanings changed in the minds of consumers and they became ordinary words of the English language, and because of the way they were understood, they lost any association with the company which originally adopted them.

PROPER USE OF TRADEMARKS

It would be good practice to have all of a company's trademarks identified and their use monitored by legal counsel to make sure that it is proper. Fundamentally, there are two rules.

The first and more important rule is simply to make sure that the trademark is not used in place of the generic name of the product. One writer has suggested that a simple test to apply to advertising copy is to ask the question "Would a complete thought be expressed if the trademark were omitted from the sentence?" If the answer is in the affirmative, the trademark is probably being used in an acceptable fashion. If it is not, the trademark is probably being used as a noun instead of an adjective, generally one of the causes for trouble.

The second rule is to inform the public that a trademark is involved by stating that fact, or, more commonly, using the trademark symbol® immediately above and after the trademark. Another good practice is to print the trademark, if possible, in some special type or graphical form. Specially constructed letters, slanted letters, and letters in a particular relationship with one another are all techniques which can be used.

"PRIMARILY MERELY A SURNAME"

A problem which frequently arises is that the Trademark Act provides that it does not cover a name which is "primarily merely a surname." Whether a name is primarily merely a surname is a matter of judgment, but generally, this is interpreted fairly reasonably by the patent office; even though a name like "Douglas" may be primarily merely a surname, because of its well-known association with Douglas Aircraft it still can be registered.

LABELS AND COPYRIGHTS

There is an important interaction and distinction between trademarks, copyrights, and labels.

The copyright statutes include among the items which may be copyrighted prints and pictorial illustrations, including prints or labels used for articles of merchandise. On the other hand, the enforcement which may be obtained under the copyright statutes is much more limited than that which can be obtained under the Trademark Act and in addition, the requirements for obtaining a substantial enforcement under the copyright law for violation of a label are very strict because any minor change in the label may be enough to take it out of copyright even though for all purposes the label carries the same message. Accordingly, it is necessary to make a distinction between the trademark and the label, and generally it is better to rely on trademark protection than on copyright protection. In constructing a label it is, therefore, necessary to make sure that if the trademark appears on the label, it appears properly and includes the use of the "registered" symbol; and for advertising purposes, the emphasis should be on the trademark rather than on the label.

UNFAIR COMPETITION

The laws relating to unfair competition extend across almost the entire legal framework; however, one important segment of those laws has to do with trademarks and trade names.

The part of unfair competition law in this area has to do with "palming off," which is a term used to describe the attempt by one company to deceive the public into believing that the products it sells were actually manufactured by another. It is very important to remember that this violation is the attempt at deception and not the copying of another company's product. If another company's product is not patented, there is no legal restriction against another company's copying it exactly and selling it provided it does not attempt to palm off its version of the product *as that of the other company.*

The leading and illustrative case in this area is that of *Sears Roebuck v. Stiffel.* This case involved the sale of lamps by Sears Roebuck and Co. identical to those designed by Stiffel. The Stiffel design was not patented. The court held that Sears Roebuck had a right to copy the Stiffel design so long as it did not palm its version off as a lamp actually made by Stiffel.

The test appears to be whether the public will be misled. Obviously, this is very subjective and depends upon all the facts. It places a premium on a detailed analysis of the entire situation, and the maximum effort from legal counsel is required to estimate whether a company can be found to have deceived the public. Similarity in appearance of products is a large factor to consider, as are similarity of advertising, similarity in the place or facilities of business, similarities in advertising slogans or words, or in trademarks or packaging.

Another interesting difference between infringing a trademark and unfair competition is in the cases that hold that the use of a competitor's trademark on something other than the product—such as on an advertising circular or letter—does not infringe the trademark but may be an unfair method of competition, depending upon the purpose, effect, and circumstances.

When an article is sold used and repaired or rebuilt, even though it may have been rebuilt by someone other than the company that originally made it or has the trademark, it may nevertheless be sold without removal of the trademark. Therefore, garages may rebuild Ford automobiles and sell them without removing the Ford trademark. Similar situations, of course, exist in the area of office equipment and machinery.

The fact that the federal trademark law does not preempt the state versions must be kept constantly in mind. Also, the doctrine that the person who first used the trademark is entitled to continue to use it and to foreclose new people from using it is important. Thus, if someone has used a trademark in, for example, the state of California and someone else has used the same trademark in the state of New York, the two may continue to use their trademarks in their respective states; the person to use the trademark first in California can continue to do so there and the person to use the trademark first in New York can continue to do so there. The question of which state trademark acquired its significance first becomes irrelevant because the significance is limited only to the state in question. Once a trademark is placed in the "Principal Register," however, it achieves priority from that time throughout the United States.

CHAPTER FORTY-NINE

TRADE SECRETS

In the 1973 case of *Kewanee Oil Co. v. Bicron Corporation*, the Sixth Circuit Court of Appeals held that the federal patent laws preempted state trade secret laws.

The implication of the case was that secret information on anything which was patentable must be patented in order to be protected and companies did not have the option of protecting this kind of information under trade secret laws. The ruling was in conflict with several others from other circuits and was widely criticized by industry, trade associations, and the patent bar. It was appealed to the United States Supreme Court and, fortunately, was reversed. Accordingly, it is now quite clear that companies have the option of protecting their business secrets *either* by use of the patent system *or* through the trade secret system of simply keeping the information confidential. This is sometimes referred to as the "patent or padlock" dilemma, and that phrase is descriptive of the problem. The purpose of this chapter is to first set forth a list of considerations which should be considered in making the "patent or padlock" decision and then, assuming the "padlock" is chosen, to list some of the important considerations in maintaining the trade secret.

THE OPTIONS

The choice facing the holder of a trade secret is, as stated above, either to get a patent or to keep the secret. However, this choice deserves a little more elaboration. The choice must be made during the first year after the discovery is made. The patent laws provide that a patent can be obtained only if the invention in question has not been in public use for more than 1 year before the application is filed. Furthermore, use by the inventor, even in secret, for commercial purposes is considered public use. Accordingly, during this 1-year period, the inventor must make his selection of how the secret is to be protected and, if the trade secret method is elected, the patent is probably foreclosed forever. Companies should observe appropriate caution in computing the 1-year period, because the exact date when the new process or invention is "discovered" is rarely easy to pin down.

The other option—to get a patent—is also exclusive. By definition, the patent must include a full disclosure of precisely what was invented. Indeed, the patent will only cover what is disclosed, and the price paid for the 17-year period of exclusive use is that the public will be able to use all the disclosures when the patent expires. Accordingly, it is not possible to get a patent and at the same time keep some aspect of the invention secret so that competitors will not be able to make use of it. However, it is worth noting that patent *applications* are not public information, and an applicant may withdraw a patent application at any time before the patent issues without any public disclosures. Accordingly, if the patent is elected, it only becomes irreversible when the letters patent are issued, and in most cases this is a number of years after the application is filed. Furthermore, it is clear that during the period the application is pending, trade secret protection is available to the applicant.

Which Protection Is More Beneficial?

The following is a discussion of the essential differences between the patent and the trade secret protection devices and serves as a checklist of the various factors which counsel should consider in making the decision as to which is better in any given case.

The Subject Matter of Trade Secrets and Patents

Sometimes the decision of which option to use will be made as a matter of law because the secret in question may not be patentable. This may be true in two situations:

1. The level of invention may not be adequate for a patent. While there may be some uncertainty, the level needed for a patent is definitely higher than that which is required to support a trade secret.

2. The subject matter may be one that is not patentable. The patent law provides that any new and useful process, machine, manufacture, or composition of matter, or any new and useful improvement thereof, may be patented. Separate statutes provide for patenting designs and plants. But some things do not fall into any of these categories and are, therefore, not patentable. Trade secrets, however, encompass all of the above plus intangible or commercial secrets, such as business information, customer lists, lists indicating special customer interests or preferences or characteristics, cost and pricing data, market research, new product plans, sources of supply, systems or methods of production or operation, and computer software—none of which are patentable. All that is necessary for consideration of something as a trade secret is that it must lend a competitive advantage, must in fact be treated as a secret by the enterprise, and must not be generally known within the industry.

In summary, the subject matter of the particular trade secret will sometimes dictate the method of protecting it.

Disclosure of Discoverer

One unfortunate aspect of the patent law is that the *individual* (not the corporation he or she works for) who made the invention must be disclosed on the application. In some cases, the identity of this person may be of interest to competitors who would like to hire away the inventor. While hiring the inventor would obviously not give the competitor any greater rights regarding the patent, it might be extremely useful in related lines of business or for developing alternatives or "inventing around" the patent.

Cost

The costs of obtaining a patent are relatively high. Generally, if the patent is significant, applications will have to be filed in more than one country, and it has been estimated that the cost of obtaining more or less normal patent protection in most major commercial countries is about $15,000 per patent. The costs of keeping a matter secret range from almost nothing to quite considerable, depending on the programs and number of people involved. Generally, however, there will be hidden costs in maintaining an adequate program for reasonably safeguarding trade secrets. Companies should, therefore, analyze the cost factors quite carefully before jumping to the conclusion that patents are more expensive than trade secrets.

Duration of Protection

Patents run from the date the letters patent are issued for 17 years. Trade secrets can protect valuable information from their inception and can extend indefinitely.

Potential Loss of Rights

Generally, patent rights may be asserted against any infringer whether infringement is intentional or not. In the trade secret area, however, the advantage may be lost forever if it is disclosed unintentionally by the owner in some unprotected way, or if it becomes generally known, or if it is discovered independently by a competitor.

Tax Problems

Generally, patents and trade secrets are accorded similar tax treatment and in the context of a license or sale, both can generate capital gains if the owner disposes of substantially all of his interest in the patent or trade secret. Tax treatment in the context of depreciation, depreciation recapture, and investment credit is complicated but is substantially the same for trade secrets and patents.

Antitrust Problems

Generally, antitrust problems involving patents and trade secrets are similar. There may be some differences which favor patents because of express provisions in the patent laws permitting territorial and field-of-use restrictions. There are also some differences favoring trade secret law in that the patent antitrust interaction has produced some per se illegality rules involving tying arrangements which do not seem to be present, at least at this stage of the law, in the trade secret context. However, these minor differences do not seem substantial enough to make the antitrust question very important in deciding which type of protection to choose.

Availability of Relief, Theoretical

Theoretically, there is very little difference in the availability of relief for companies that choose patents and those that choose trade secrets. In appropriate cases, both damages and injunctive relief can be obtained in either case. It may be a little easier to recover attorney's fees in a trade secret case, but this is not a significant factor in the original decision of which to choose.

Availability of Relief, Actual

In the real world, however, actual relief in a patent case has proved very difficult to obtain. In 1968, the *Wall Street Journal* published an article which said that during the prior decade, 80 percent of all U.S. patents considered by our courts on appeal were held invalid or unenforceable. It would not appear that subsequent cases have materially changed this statistic. However, the patent office has done its own study, with the following results, as stated by Patent Commissioner C. Marshall Dann on June 6, 1974, at the FBA-BNA Briefing Conference in Washington, D.C.:

> I should mention that the batting average of patent owners in the courts apparently is not as bad as has been generally believed. The Patent Office has compiled data showing that the rate of holdings of invalidity—taking into account district courts as well as courts of appeals—is around 50 percent, rather than the figure of 70 percent commonly quoted in the past. One can argue that 50 percent is exactly what the figure should be, regardless of the merits of issued patents generally, since parties will not go to court unless they think they have a chance to win, and plaintiffs and defendants on the average will each be right half the time.
>
> In addition to published decisions, the Patent Office studies took into account unpublished decisions reported to the Patent Office by the clerks of the federal courts as required by 35 U.S.C. 290. We cannot be sure that we have counted all decisions; the clerks may have inadvertently failed to report some. However, we believe the results are based on more complete data than any previous study.
>
> When a patent is held invalid, it has become fashionable for the court to make some disparaging reference to the lower standard of patentability which is said to prevail in the Patent Office than in the courts. Considering that over 1,000,000 U.S. patents are in force, that well under 1 percent are ever litigated, half of which are upheld, and that the particular court has usually only one or two patents before it, any such criticism would seem to be a broader generalization than is justified statistically.
>
> I have noticed that once a court has made such an observation, on whatever basis, other courts like to quote it and seem to feel that the oftener it is repeated the truer it gets.

Thus, we have a system where the courts are openly hostile to patents, and the patent commissioner himself publicly proclaims that there is nothing wrong with a system where the validity of a patent is sustained only 50 percent of the time.

Because of this unfortunate problem, many business executives feel a certain uneasiness about relying on patent protection entirely. For larger technological companies, there is still another problem with suing a potential infringer of a patent. That problem is that a patent suit by a large company almost invariably draws a counterclaim, usually on the basis of the antitrust laws, for many millions of dollars. This operates as a strong deterrent in the consideration of whether or not to sue a patent infringer. While antitrust counterclaims are certainly conceivable in trade secret litigation, they do not seem to be almost automatic as they are in patent litigation.

On the other hand, it should be observed that if a trade secret is stolen or otherwise unlawfully obtained, the technicalities of the legal process and burden of proof questions might mean that a legal remedy is not practically available. This is especially true if the secret is stolen by a company with limited financial resources. The original holder may have a perfectly good legal remedy against the original thief but may not be able to collect enough money to make the remedy substantial.

Disclosure

In order to get a patent, substantial and complete disclosures must be made, and these disclosures may indicate to skilled technicians or engineers a way to invent around the patent so that substantially the same result can be achieved by an article or process which does not infringe the original patent. In some cases, these attempts to invent around may actually involve some improvement or means of reducing cost so that the original inventor is at a disadvantage. If this is a realistic possibility, trade secret protection will generally be advantageous.

On the other hand, sometimes the mere sale of the article will tell all there is to know about any secrets involved. If a competitor can simply buy a sample article and reverse-engineer it, patents will be the best course of protection.

The problem of disclosure is especially troublesome in the area of *processes* (as opposed to substances or articles). In many cases, it will be impossible to tell upon examining a product whether the secret process has been used in the manufacture of that product. This is especially true if the secret process does not affect the quality or appearance of the finished article but only enables it to be produced in a more efficient and profitable manner. Thus, if the secret process is disclosed in a patent, it will be virtually impossible to ascertain whether a competitor is using it in his own plant. Thus, in the process area, trade secret protection has a distinct advantage.

Economic Use

Theoretically, the holder of a trade secret should be able to license that secret just as the holder of a patent. However, as a practical matter, it is much easier to license a patent. Licensees generally will pay royalties more easily for a patent license. Also, a patent license is much easier to draft, administer, and police than a pure know-how license.

While there may be additional factors important in some special cases, the above considerations will generally cover the significant differences between patent and trade secret protection and, if each is considered, companies and their counsel should be able to make an intelligent recommendation on which to choose in any specific case.

Assuming that a client/company has or desires to have some program of trade secret protection, the following considerations on implementing it become important.

CONTRACTUAL PROTECTION

It is probably obvious that many situations involving possession of company trade secrets can and should be dealt with by specific contractual provisions between parties, but since state law principles also provide some protection, and since the necessity of these contractual provisions is sometimes questioned, it is useful to briefly list the advantages which inure to a company which uses a good program of contractual restrictions governing trade secrets instead of merely relying on general legal principles.

Arguments in Favor of Contractual Protection

Experience

While statistics do not necessarily prove anything, there is a certain safety in numbers, and the companies which use contractual means to protect trade secrets are in the overwhelming majority. In one widely quoted study it was reported that 83 out of 86 companies used some kind of contractual provisions to protect their trade secrets.

Notice

Using a contractual provision puts the other party to the contract on notice that you think your trade secrets are important, and that he should be both honest and careful in his disclosures. Whether the contract is with employees, suppliers, purchasers, or others, the notice aspect of the provision is a great practical aid in avoiding problems and obtaining legal (particularly injunctive) relief if the need arises.

Broader Protection

Generally, contracts can be drafted to provide broader relief than general principles of law would allow. Injunctions are easier to obtain where a contractual provision precludes an activity. Also, a contract may more broadly define the scope of the information considered a trade secret than a court will define it.

Clarification

There is always the opportunity in well-drafted contracts to clarify for the benefit of both parties, and the court if necessary, exactly what trade secrets are involved, and what use may be made of those trade secrets.

Possibility of an Arbitration Clause

A contract can include an arbitration clause, but this can be a mixed blessing. There is considerable disagreement on whether arbitration clauses are desirable at all and even more disagreement on whether they are desirable in a trade secret agreement, or an employment agreement which includes restrictions on the employees' disclosure of trade secret information. However, for those who prefer arbitration, a written contract gives the opportunity to include an appropriate arbitration clause.

Choice of Law

State laws vary widely on the permissible extent to which an employee's future employment can be restricted. While a company operating only in California, hiring a California resident, may not state in a contract that Ohio law will govern the contract, there are some cases where national companies may be able to choose among different laws to their advantage. (California's law on restraining an employee is more restrictive to the employer and more liberal to the employee than Ohio's.)

Arguments against Contractual Protection

To give the full story, some of the arguments raised against using contractual provisions include the following—none of which seem too convincing.

If an agreement is drafted too broadly, it may be unenforceable altogether. (A properly drafted agreement will provide for this contingency by saying that if it is unenforceable as written, the court should enforce it to the maximum extent it deems it enforceable.)

If it is drafted too narrowly, it might restrict rights the company would otherwise have. (Counsel's job is to make sure it is drafted broadly enough to accomplish the necessary result.)

A contract might change a tort action to a contractual action and run into some procedural limitations under state law, such as the admissibility of certain evidence under the parol evidence rule, which provides that a written contract can't generally be contradicted by oral evidence. (A scholarly but not very impressive argument.)

There is a possible employee-relations problem. The thought here is that if a long-term employee is asked to sign an agreement restricting disclosure of confidential information, he may take it as a personal affront to his integrity. The problem, if there is one, will arise only once, because after the program is started, employees should be asked to sign the contract as soon as they are hired. Furthermore, if it is handled right, the approach should be to remind the long-term employee of his privileged situation in knowing about these trade secrets and his responsibilities as a result of them. If there is any personal affront, it is because the matter is being handled clumsily or the employee is overly sensitive.

Areas Where Protection Is Needed

Following is a list of the kinds of things, both contractual and otherwise, which can and should be used to protect trade secrets. Obviously, not all of the items will be appropriate in all cases. The fundamental proposition is this:

> The protection accorded the trade secret holder is against the disclosure or unauthorized use of the trade secret by those to whom the secret has been confided under the express or implied restriction of nondisclosure or nonuse. The law also protects the holder of a trade secret against disclosure or use when the knowledge is gained, not by the owner's volition, but by some "improper means" which may include theft, wiretapping, or even aerial reconnaissance. A trade secret, however, does not offer protection against discovery by fair and honest means, such as by independent invention, accidental disclosure, or by so-called reverse engineering. . . . [Supreme Court opinion in the *Kewanee Oil* case.]

The company's job in each of the following areas is to make sure that when disclosures are made, they are accompanied by a restriction, express and clear, of nondisclosure or nonuse, and to the maximum extent practicable, to safeguard against disclosures which are not accompanied by such restrictions or which may be accidental.

Contracts with Employees

Undoubtedly the most important area for protecting trade secrets is in the contracts or other agreements with employees. In some cases, it will be appropriate for the employees to have an employment agreement containing both restrictions on disclosure of confidential information and restrictions against competition after employment. In other cases, all that is needed is a simple nondisclosure agreement.

Suppliers

Vendors and suppliers may need access to your trade secrets to adequately service your needs. However, they should not be given unlimited access without restriction. Their access should be only to those areas where there is a legitimate need to know, and you should have a written agreement protecting your company from unauthorized disclosure.

Customers

The same comments hold true for customers. Many times a close working relationship with a customer is necessary from a business point of view, but if the customer will have access to your trade secrets, it should be only on a limited need-to-know basis with proper contractual safeguards.

Licensees

You may want to sell your know-how or intentionally make it available to a licensee or potential purchaser of your business. Naturally, this should be done with extreme care, and great attention must be given to restrictions on the licensee's handling of your proprietary information. Don't be afraid to be strict and precise in these kinds of agreements. Include detailed provisions:

1. Setting forth precisely what is secret information.

2. Spelling out precisely what the other party may or may not do with it—that documents may not be copied, that documents will be returned upon expiration or termination of the agreement, etc.

3. Detailing the procedures for transferring the information. If there are to be meetings, make them scheduled and keep detailed minutes of who is present and what is disclosed.

4. Detailing the specific persons in your organization from whom information may be obtained and specifically limiting the persons in the other organization who may obtain it.

Personnel Turnover

Employment practices are important. Make sure employees know your practices and policies when they are hired and that, on termination, they are aware of their responsibilities. Exit interviews are useful.

Accurate Registry

Don't forget the obvious: in order to protect trade secrets or know-how, you must know clearly what you consider to be proprietary. This means establishing a master register of what is proprietary information and precisely who has access to which information. Also, the people who have access to confidential information must know precisely what is proprietary. Employee education and motivation are important. Many trade secrets can be lost through simple ignorance of their importance to the company or from inadvertent disclosure.

Employee Morale

Be aware of the compensation picture of all employees, but particularly those who have access to company proprietary information. Use a little extra effort to make sure they are treated fairly. This includes the usual technique of salary surveys to make sure your employee compensation arrangements are in line with those generally prevailing in the community and in the trade. A competitor may seek out your key employees and entice them away with unduly high offers, but there is no use in *driving* them away through inattention to employment environment, fringe benefits, and compensation.

Security

Adopt procedures to keep unauthorized visitors out of the plant area. Authorized visitors to the plant need not be granted access to the *entire* plant. If there is a trade secret operation involved, try to keep it limited in terms of area and restrict access to that area.

Division of Labor in Sensitive Areas

Try to avoid having the entire trade secret process or body of know-how available to any single employee. Arrange the job descriptions so that it is divided up as much as possible.

Handling of Documents

Do not be afraid to use such devices as special covers marked "company proprietary" or such equivalent to designate confidential material and establish firm written procedures for handling this kind of information. These should be reasonable and should be enforced.

Receiving

If you purchase chemicals from outside sources, ask your source to deliver them in containers which use only your code name or some other name which does not disclose the chemical composition of the contents. No use in displaying the chemicals you use to everyone—particularly if they are not specially formulated for you and could be readily obtained by competition.

Extramural Activities

Screen technical articles by employees. Some employees, in their zest to advance themselves professionally or impress their colleagues, give away trade secrets innocently through publications or delivery of papers to professional associations. This activity should be carefully monitored where this risk is present.

Intercorporate Hiring

Clear employees who come from a competitor. A company should not leave itself open for attack by another company for hiring away technical people and taking trade secrets. Also, as a practical matter, this activity tends to lead to retaliation to the detriment of both companies. An employee coming from a competitor should be carefully questioned to see that he would not be using trade secret information in his new job which would be prejudicial to his former employer, and where some doubt exists, the company might consider getting an express approval on whatever terms seem appropriate from the former employer. Employees coming from government agencies should also be questioned, because they sometimes have had access to competitor's trade secrets.

Antitrust

Last but not least—watch out for antitrust problems. Many times arrangements involving transfers of trade secrets may be characterized by the court as joint ventures. Also, restrictions in agreements can create antitrust problems, particularly if they involve restrictions on the use the recipient can make of the articles he makes using the trade secrets. Particularly troublesome are restrictions on the places where he may resell the product, the customers he may sell it to, or the price at which he may sell it.

A TYPICAL STATE LAW

Trade secret laws are state laws and, of course, each state's law should be checked before relying on the general principles contained herein. However, most industrial or commercial states do have state trade secret laws in both statutory and case law form. The statutory law will generally not be extensive; the following section of the Ohio Revised Code is reasonably representative:

Ohio Revised Code sec. 1333.51.   [Theft or conversion of trade secret.]

   (A) As used in this section:
      (1) "Article" means any object, material, device, or substance, or copy thereof, including any writing, record, recording, drawing, sample, specimen, prototype, model, photograph, blueprint or map.
      (2) "Representing" means describing, depicting, containing, constituting, reflecting, or recording.
      (3) "Trade secret" means the whole or any portion or phase of any scientific or technical information, design, process, procedure, formula, or improvement, or any business plans, financial information, or listing of names, addresses, or telephone numbers, which has not been published or disseminated, or otherwise become a matter of general public knowledge. Such scientific or technical information, design, process, procedure, formula, or improvement, or any business plans, financial information, or listing of names, addresses, or telephone numbers is presumed to be secret when the owner thereof takes measures designed to prevent it, in the ordinary course of business, from being available to persons other than those selected by the owner to have access thereto for limited purposes.
      (4) "Copy" means any facsimile, replica, photograph, or reproduction of any article, or any note, drawing, or sketch made of or from an article.
   (B) No person shall, with intent to deprive or withhold from the owner thereof the control of a trade secret, or with the intent to convert a trade secret to his own use or the use of another, obtain possession of or access to an article representing a trade secret.
   (C) No person, having obtained possession of an article representing a trade secret or access thereto with the owner's consent, shall convert such article to his own use or that of another person, or thereafter without the owner's consent make or cause to be made a copy of such article, or exhibit such article to another.
   (D) No person shall, by force, violence, threat, bribe reward, or offer of anything of value on or to another person or member of his family, obtain

or attempt to obtain from such other person an article representing a trade secret.

(E) No person shall, without authorization, enter upon the premises of another with intent to obtain possession of or access to an article representing a trade secret.

R/C sec. 1333.99.   [Penalties.]

(E) Whoever violates section 1333.51 of the Revised Code shall be fined not more than Five Thousand Dollars, imprisoned not less than one or more than ten years, or both.

SPYING

While it may seem a little "cloak-and-daggerish," companies cannot afford to entirely dismiss the possibility of corporate spying, particularly in high technology areas. An article in the *Harvard Business Review*, November–December 1974, cites three examples:

1. A plot to steal IBM disc designs worth about $600 million

2. An international plot where a Ford employee attempted to sell a Ford process for liquid-mercury glass to a Rumanian for $250,000

3. Attempts to get a valuable Du Pont chemical process by aerial photography during plant construction

PRESENTATION OF IDEAS

A discussion of the subject of protecting trade secrets is not complete without some mention of the problem of presentation of ideas to a company. Consider the following example.

EXAMPLE: Company T manufactures and sells toys for children. It has a development department to design new toys. The department has almost completed the design of a new toy based on a map of the world which is divided into many compartments of different shapes. There are also pieces of different shapes representing various natural resources such as oil, coal, and gold. It is a puzzle designed so that the child fits the different shapes into the corresponding compartments and, in the process, learns which natural resources exist in which parts of the world. The idea for this new toy (before marketing, of course) would qualify as a trade secret, and if an employee took the idea to a competing toymaker and the competing toymaker introduced it into the market first, a clear cause of action would arise in favor of the original developer against the disloyal employee.

However, a problem could arise in another way. Suppose that about a month before the toy is to be introduced through a program of national television advertising, company T receives a call from a Mr. Z saying that he has just developed a "great new toy" that the company might like to look at. Suppose further that the company says yes and arranges a meeting for the next week, and when Mr.

Z arrives, he tells about his great new idea for a map of the world with various compartments in which shapes representing natural resources are inserted, etc. Maybe he even brings a model which is almost exactly like the one back in the development section of the company. Unless Mr. Z can be clearly convinced that the company thought of the idea first, he is very likely to pay a visit to his lawyer when he is turned down at this meeting and then turns on his television three weeks later only to see a national advertisement based on "his" toy.

Thus problems in the trade secret area can arise not only through carelessness or disloyalty, but through an innocent program of accepting unsolicited ideas without the proper safeguards.

Many companies have a firm policy against accepting any unsolicited suggestion and elaborate programs which are aimed at preventing problems in this area. Many companies prohibit employees from receiving *any* ideas or suggestions *in confidence* except upon approval of the company's lawyers.

Generally, the problem can be solved by simply refraining from accepting unsolicited suggestions for new products, improvements in your products, etc., unless the suggestor has an appropriate agreement with your company on compensation. Generally, such agreements take the form of a letter something like the following:

Dear Sir:

Thank you for offering to show us your idea. As I am sure you must realize, our company receives many such suggestions, and experience has shown us that in most of these cases, the idea presented has already been considered by us. Accordingly, we are unable to accept your proposal unless you are willing to agree to the following conditions:

1. [If appropriate, provide that samples cannot be returned to the submittor.]
2. [Provide that compensation will be paid only if the company, in its sole discretion, deems it appropriate, and only then in such amounts as the company, in its sole discretion, deems appropriate.]
3. [Provide that the company accepts no responsibility for holding any information in confidence.]

The above sounds a little harsh, but anything less creates a possible problem for a company. Since it is very rare that an unsolicited idea is both new and good, the risk of anything less than the complete protection suggested above is not worth taking.

SECTION EIGHT: ENVIRONMENTAL LAWS

CHAPTER FIFTY

ENVIRONMENTAL LAW:
AN OVERVIEW

Between 1970 and 1978 environmental laws rose in importance to the point where they are now on a par with antitrust, securities, tax, and labor laws for corporations which are affected. The environmental laws are lengthy and complex. The regulations are even more lengthy and complex. Chapters 51 through 54 discuss the four major environmental laws in more detail: air pollution, water pollution, solid waste disposal, and toxic substances. Chapter 55 discusses the necessity for a corporate compliance program for the environmental laws. The present chapter will provide a brief discussion of some of the more general problems and a specific discussion of some of the important federal environmental laws which are not covered in the four subsequent chapters.

SPECIAL ENVIRONMENTAL PROBLEMS

Environmental laws present several special problems which make this area considerably different from other federal laws affecting business. Some of the more important of these problems follow.

Complexity, Length, and Specificity

The environmental laws are probably the most complicated and lengthy pieces of federal legislation affecting business outside the Internal Revenue Code. They present all the drawbacks both of laws which are general and give broad authority to the regulatory agencies, and laws which are so specific that the regulatory agencies have little discretion. Environmental laws contain provisions which fall into both of these categories. The Clean Air and Water Acts contain much specific language which strongly implies that Congress did not trust the regulatory agencies to do a good job of enforcing the law. Examples are the effective dates for various types of technology where no discretion is left to the agency. On the other hand, broad and important areas are left totally to agency rulemaking—such as the designation of hazardous substances. Thus when you read the law you see many provisions which constrict agency flexibility—and therefore your ability to negotiate with them—and other provisions which do not give any guidance at all except to tell the agency to issue regulations.

There Are Many Environmental Laws

There are so many environmental laws that merely listing them all takes quite a bit of space. There are laws which regulate specific industries—nuclear being the prime example—and old laws which still have considerable effect (the Rivers and Harbors Act of 1899 is the primary example of this type of law). Following is a brief listing of the major environmental laws, which illustrates this problem.

1. The National Environmental Policy Act, which requires environmental impact statements for government projects

2. The Environmental Quality Improvement Act of 1970, which establishes the Office of Environmental Quality to provide professional and administrative help in the environmental area

3. The Environmental Education Act, which establishes an environmental education office to provide programs for schools, education of teachers, etc.

4. The Energy Supply and Environmental Coordination Act of 1974, to meet the country's energy needs without sacrificing environmental quality

5. The Fish and Wildlife Coordination Act, to help preserve fish and wildlife and provide research and development for that purpose

6. The Ports and Waterways Safety Act of 1972, which contains provisions to prevent pollution during the loading and unloading of ships

7. The Marine Protection Research and Sanctuaries Act of 1972

8. The Safe Drinking Water Act, which contains provisions to prevent the contamination of underground water

9. The Deep Water Port Act of 1974, which contains environmental provisions in the context of development of ports

10. The Aircraft Noise Abatement Regulation Act

11. The Federal Environmental Pesticide Control Act of 1972

12. The Surface Mining Control and Reclamation Act of 1977

13. The Coastal Zone Management Act of 1972, which requires management programs for coastal zone areas

14. Conservation laws, such as the Marine Mammal Protection Act, the Endangered Species Act of 1973, the Wild and Scenic Rivers Act, and the Soil and Water Resources Conservation Act of 1977

15. The Noise Control Act

In addition to all of these there are executive orders, securities laws, and tax laws which bear upon environmental matters.

It should be noted that this broad listing of laws omits the most important ones, which are discussed in the next four chapters.

Effective Dates and Delays

All of the important environmental laws contain mandatory effective date provisions which usually depend upon the Environmental Protection Agency's issuing regulations. For example, the Clean Air Act requires certain technology to be used by certain dates but leaves the definition of that technology to the EPA. As a matter of course the EPA fails to meet the statutory deadlines for issuing the regulations required, and by wide margins. There is usually no corresponding stay of effective dates for industry. This problem runs consistently through all the environmental laws. The statutory rules may seem reasonable on their face, but the way they are implemented by the EPA industry is put into a situation where noncompliance is virtually assured.

Economic Benefits from Noncompliance

The Clean Air Act Amendments of 1977 contain an elaborate penalty system which is aimed at taking the economic benefit of noncompliance out of the law by establishing mandatory penalties in the amount which a company would save by not installing the required equipment. Just how this will work is not clear, but until it was enacted the fact was that in many cases it really didn't matter how much money you spent on air pollution. Given the state of technology and the enforcement procedures there were many situations where your choice was to spend a lot and be in noncompliance or not to spend very much and be in noncompliance. In the water area the same problem exists. This makes conscientious counseling very difficult.

Technical Aspects of the Law

In some cases the law and the regulations recognize that the technology necessary to accomplish the stated objectives is simply not available. In the air situation it is just simply impossible to achieve the required air quality levels. A law which has the practical effect of placing everyone in noncompliance and therefore subject to the whim of the regulatory agency in negotiations about how to fix this problem offends many lawyers and business executives.

The Laws Are New

On the list of environmental laws the first thing which appears is that the dates of virtually all of this vast body of legislation are after 1970. When you have laws this long and technical which are so new that the agencies themselves don't fully understand all the implications, problems are bound to persist.

The Laws Have a Political Aspect

Many people call these "anti-pollution laws." People or companies who violate them are "polluters." Companies which operated in full compliance with all laws for dozens of years suddenly found themselves in a situation where they were violating pollution laws and there was no practical way to stop short of closing down. It was not simply a matter of getting a license, changing some employment practices, making certain disclosures, amending pension plans prospectively, or refraining from taking certain anti-competitive actions. Normal business operation simply was not possible without spending substantial sums on pollution equipment which, in some cases, was either ineffective or not available at all.

The Laws Have a Very Beneficial Objective

It is impossible for good citizens to argue with the intentions of these laws. The facts are that industry has in general used more than its fair share of the country's natural resources and something should be done to assure future generations that these resources will be available to them. It is a delicate balancing problem between this desirable objective and the economic facts of life in an industrialized society.

The Federal Laws Do Not Preempt State or Local Laws

The laws are quite clear in establishing the federal regulations described herein as minimal requirements. State and local governments are free to establish more stringent requirements. Further, the basic pattern of the air, water, and solid waste laws is to require states to adopt their own implementation plans. As a practical matter, manufacturing facilities will be governed by state or local laws administered by state or local people. Thus you have all the complications of different systems of requirements in each of the states, even though there are certain federal common denominators.

THE IMPORTANT ENVIRONMENTAL LAWS

Besides the air, water, solid waste, and toxic substances laws discussed in Chapters 51 through 54, there are a number of other important environmental laws; those listed above are the primary examples. Two of them deserve a little further discussion: The National Environmental Policy Act and The Noise Control Act.

The National Environmental Policy Act is remarkably short—less than three 8½- by 11-inch printed pages. The act states its purpose in section 2 as follows:

> To declare a national policy which will encourage productive and enjoyable harmony between man and his environment; to promote efforts which will prevent or eliminate damage to the environment and biosphere and stimulate the health and welfare of man; to enrich the understanding of the ecological system and natural resources important to the nation; and to establish a Council on Environmental Quality.

The basic provisions of the National Environmental Policy Act require environmental impact statements for all federal projects. As indicated, however, the act is very short. Beyond requiring the preparation of these impact statements (the act doesn't even expressly use those words) and creating a Council on Environmental Quality to review them, there is absolutely no guidance given. Accordingly there has grown a large body of regulations promulgated by the council itself and other federal agencies on exactly what must be contained in the environmental impact statement, how it must be prepared, whom it must be filed with, etc. The catch in the whole thing is that the act directs that the impact statements shall be made available to the public, and the courts have held that the public, therefore, has the right to institute suit to have these environmental impact statements reviewed to make sure that they take everything into account they are supposed to. Since it is not now and never has been very clear exactly what it is they are supposed to take into account, and since this lawsuit device has been used by many organizations as a device to slow down controversial projects such as nuclear generation of electricity, the list of environmental cases dealing with environmental impact statements is lengthy. While it would take a very large volume to analyze all of the decisions, it takes only three words to explain what they add up to: time, money, and uncertainty.

The point of this is that if your company is about to undertake any project which may require an environmental impact statement, either because it is asking for a federal grant, is using federal property, or is undertaking the project for some agency program, you had better know about it long in advance, budget a substantial number of dollars for helping the government agency prepare the statement, and take into account the fact that even if you do all this you will not be sure the project will be allowed to go ahead.

Noise Pollution

Noise pollution is defined as either excessive sound or unwanted sound. It is somewhat different from the other forms of pollution in several important respects. It typically does not produce lasting or serious effects (although there is some argument about this) and it is not a silent killer or a difficult thing to recognize. The technology to reduce sound to acceptable levels exists—at least in most cases—but it can be expensive, and there is a debate about the cost-benefit analysis. The technology to measure sound is not very well developed. There is such a bewildering array of terminology that the science is complex and confusing even to engineers.

Noise shares one thing with the other pollutants: a federal statute to regulate it. The Noise Control Act of 1972 establishes a fairly complex federal system to regulate noise, although the statute is nowhere near as complex and thorough as that for air, water, and solid waste. The Noise Control Act doesn't mandate any state implementation plans, and there are no effective dates for the requirements of the act. Thus, unlike the Clean Air and Water Acts, which provide that certain levels of accomplishment are to be attained by certain dates, the Noise Control Act simply establishes a federal system for investigation and research and provides for specific federal regulation in some limited cases.

The Noise Control Act authorizes regulations to be issued in four areas (but doesn't set a timetable):

1. Noise emission standards for four categories of sources (construction equipment, transportation equipment, motors or engines, and electrical equipment)

2. Labeling of any product which emits noise capable of affecting adversely the public health or welfare and which the buyer may choose on the basis of its noise level

3. Aircraft noise and sonic boom

4. Noise emission regulation for other transportation sources (railroads and motor carriers)

The enforcement provisions are fairly weak. There are prohibitions against tampering with any noise control device or using a product after such a device has been rendered inoperative, and for removing any notice or label relating to a product's noise-level rating. However, the only sanction is an injunction against continuing or repeating the violation. There are prohibitions for distributing any product manufactured in violation of the noise emission standard, for distributing a product which doesn't conform to the labeling requirements, for importing products which don't comply, and for failing to obey a compliance order. These are subject to fines.

The statutory authorization for regulations for each product which is a major source of noise in the categories listed above is quite broad. It probably includes just about all the equipment used in a normal manufacturing facility. In addition to these mandatory regulations, there is also a provision allowing noise standards for any other product for which noise emission standards are feasible and are requisite to protect the public health and welfare.

The standards are supposed to be performance standards. The administrator should prescribe the results but leave the decision as to how to achieve those results to industry.

At this time, except for those companies manufacturing a few items subject to a noise standard, the OSHA emphasis on noise as a worker health problem is more important than the Noise Control Act of 1972.

CHAPTER FIFTY-ONE

THE CLEAN AIR ACT

BACKGROUND

The existing law on air pollution is the Clean Air Act of 1970 as substantially amended in 1977. To understand the law, it is useful to run briefly through the predecessor legislation.

The Air Pollution Control Act of 1955

The Air Pollution Control Act of 1955 was the first major piece of federal air pollution legislation. This act defined the federal role as being confined to research and, upon request, assistance to the states with technical problems. The act clearly said that the responsibility for air pollution control was with the states, and this theory continues, although with substantially more federal involvement.

The Clean Air Act of 1963

The next statute was the Clean Air Act of 1963, which slightly enlarged the federal involvement. The act contained a statement of purpose to achieve the prevention and control of air pollution, but the details were not spelled out. The federal involvement was based not on a state request, as in the 1955 Act, but instead on a finding that the pollution problems of one state affected another state.

The Air Quality Act of 1967

The Air Quality Act of 1967 was the first attempt at a comprehensive and detailed regulatory scheme. The act contained four basic steps:

1. The establishment of atmospheric areas and air quality control regions (A-QCRs)

2. The issuance of air quality criteria and control techniques reports

3. The adoption of ambient air standards by the states within the air quality regions

4. The development of state plans (by the states) to deal with the problem

Pursuant to the 1967 Act, the Department of Health, Education, and Welfare designated eight atmospheric areas covering the contiguous forty-eight states plus two others for Alaska and Hawaii. An atmospheric area is a geographical area where climate, meteorology, and topography (the factors influencing concentrations of air pollution) are relatively homogeneous. Also, a number of air quality control regions were designated. A region is a group of communities that should be treated as a unit for purposes of setting and implementing air quality standards. This designation takes into account not only meteorological and topographical considerations but political boundary lines also. Today there are about 250 of these air quality control regions, most of which were established under the 1967 Air Quality Act.

THE CLEAN AIR ACT OF 1970

The Clean Air Act of 1970 is a comprehensive regulatory scheme to deal with air pollution. Some of the principal features of this legislation are the following.

Section 101 contains a very broad statement of purpose which has been used in subsequent cases and legislation to support a general policy of non-degradation (no significant deterioration of existing air is allowed).

The heart of the statute establishes a system for dealing with pollution that is theoretically fairly simple. It involves the following steps:

1. Air quality control regions are designated.

2. Air quality criteria and pollution control techniques for major pollutants are published.

3. National ambient air quality standards (NAAQSs) for major pollutants are established.

4. The states prepare implementation plans.

5. The federal government reviews those plans against the minimum standards set forth in the statute.

6. The states enforce their programs, subject to federal supervision and enforcement if the state enforcement is inadequate.

The Regions

Most of the air quality regions established under the Air Quality Act of 1967 still remain in existence. Under the new law, the question of whether the air quality in a region is above or below standard is important because different standards apply.

The Criteria and Control Techniques

This is essentially the government's research and development (R&D) function. The importance of all this material is in presenting evidence in administrative or judicial proceedings. These criteria and control technique documents have not had a great influence in the courts. They become obsolete very fast and represent only summaries of views of other parties.

The Air Quality Standards

After designating the regions and issuing the criteria and control technique documents, the administrator of the EPA is directed to establish *primary* and secondary national ambient air quality standards for each "criteria pollutant." A criteria pollutant is simply one which has been listed as such. When the 1970 Act was passed, there were already five pollutants for which air quality criteria had been issued. These were sulfur oxides, particulates, carbon monoxide, hydrocarbons, and photochemical oxidants. Since 1970, the EPA has added nitrogen oxides and has been forced by a citizens' suit to add lead.

There are two kinds of standards. The primary ambient air quality standards are those which affect the public health, and the secondary ambient air quality standards are those which affect the general welfare (but not health) of the public and plants, animals, and visibility. Primary standards for these pollutants were to be met by July 1, 1977, and the only limit for the secondary standards was a reasonable time.

The primary standards in many areas were not met by July 1, 1977, and the EPA issued a set of regulations to allow some construction and development in these areas by a program of trade-offs. Essentially, companies could add pollution if they took more pollution out of the same area from someplace else.

State Implementation Plans

The means to attain the primary ambient air quality standards is through state implementation plans (SIPs). The statute, however, establishes a set of required items for these plans. Those provisions are the key to the program and are reproduced below.

> Sec. 110(a)(2). The Administrator shall, within four months after the date required for submission of a plan under paragraph (1), approve or disapprove such plan for each portion thereof. The Administrator shall approve such plan, or any portion thereof, if he determines that it was adopted after reasonable notice and hearing and that:
>
> (A) except as may be provided in subparagraph (I)(i) in the case of a plan implementing a national primary ambient air quality standard, it provides for the attainment of such primary standard as expeditiously as practicable but (subject to subsection (e)) in no case later than three years from the date of approval of such plan (or any revision thereof to take account of a revised primary standard); and (ii) in the case of a plan implementing a national secondary ambient air quality standard, it specifies a reasonable time at which such secondary standard will be attained;
>
> (B) it includes emission limitations, schedules, and timetables for compliance with such limitations, and such other measures as may be necessary to insure attainment and maintenance of such primary or secondary standard, including, but not limited to, transportation controls, air quality maintenance plans, and preconstruction review of direct sources of air pollution as provided in subparagraph (D);
>
> (C) it includes provision for establishment and operation of appropriate devices, methods, systems, and procedures necessary to (i) monitor, compile,

and analyze data on ambient air quality and (ii) upon request, make such data available to the Administrator;

(D) it includes a program to provide for the enforcement of emission limitations and regulation of the modification, construction, and operation of any stationary source, including a permit program as required in parts C and D and a permit or equivalent program for any major emitting facility, within such region as necessary to assure (i) that national ambient air quality standards are achieved and maintained, and (ii) a procedure, meeting the requirements of paragraph (4), for review (prior to construction or modification) of the location of new sources to which a standard of performance will apply;

(E) it contains adequate provisions (i) prohibiting any stationary source within the State from emitting any air pollutant in amounts which will (I) prevent attainment or maintenance by any other State of any such national primary or secondary ambient air quality standard, or (II) interfere with measures required to be included in the applicable implementation plan for any other State under part C to prevent significant deterioration of air quality or to protect visibility, and (ii) insuring compliance with the requirements of section 126, relating to interstate pollution abatement;

(F) it provides (i) necessary assurances that the State will have adequate personnel, funding, and authority to carry out such implementation plan, (ii) requirements for installation of equipment by owners or operators of stationary sources to monitor emissions from such sources, (iii) for periodic reports on the nature and amounts of such emissions; (iv) that such reports shall be correlated by the State agency with any emission limitations or standards established pursuant to this Act, which reports shall be available at reasonable times for public inspection; (v) for authority comparable to that in section 303, and adequate contingency plans to implement such authority; and (vi) requirements that the State comply with the requirements respecting State boards under section 128;

(G) it provides, to the extent necessary and practicable, for periodic inspection and testing of motor vehicles to enforce compliance with applicable emission standards;

(H) it provides for revision, after public hearing, of such plan (i) from time to time as may be necessary to take account of revisions of such national primary or secondary ambient air quality standard or the availability of improved or more expeditious methods of achieving such primary or secondary standard; or (ii) except as provided in paragraph (3)(C), whenever the Administrator finds on the basis of information available to him that the plan is substantially inadequate to achieve the national ambient air quality primary or secondary standard which it implements or to otherwise comply with any additional requirements established under the Clean Air Act Amendments of 1977;

(I) it provides that after June 30, 1979, no major stationary source shall be constructed or modified in any nonattainment area (as defined in section 171(2)) to which such plan applies, if the emissions from such facility will cause or contribute to concentrations of any pollutant for which a national ambient air quality standard is exceeded in such area, unless, as of the time of application for a permit for such construction or modification, such plan meets the requirements of part D (relating to nonattainment areas);

(J) it meets the requirements of section 121 (relating to consultation), section 127 (relating to public notification), part C (relating to prevention of significant deterioration of air quality and visibility protection); and

(K) it requires the owner or operator of each major stationary source to pay to the permitting authority as a condition of any permit required under this Act a fee sufficient to cover—
   (i) the reasonable costs of reviewing and acting upon any application for such a permit, and
   (ii) if the owner or operator receives a permit for such source, whether

before or after the date of enactment of this subparagraph, the reasonable costs (incurred after such date of enactment) of implementing and enforcing the terms and conditions of any such permit (not including any court costs or other costs associated with any enforcement action).

Essentially, the above boils down to a system of state regulation of all new construction and modification of existing facilities where there is any substantial discharge of any of the pollutants.

THE TECHNOLOGY OF POLLUTION CONTROL

Discussion of environmental problems usually centers around technical matters. Most of it involves "modeling" and discussion of the "relevant technology."

Modeling

An air quality model is a simulation scheme by which pollution discharges from a specific source can be traced to other nearby sources and the effects of the source pollution on the nearby areas can be determined. It is a very complicated and technical undertaking, and very subjective. It is, however, the essential link between the actual emission and the standards that actual emission is supposed to meet. The model will contain many assumptions about weather and other things, and a minor change in any of them can affect the outcome drastically.

Best Technology

The *best technology* principle is usually applied to new sources. Technically, it is "best available control technology" and is abbreviated BACT. The 1977 Amendments, discussed later, introduce LAER (lowest achievable emission rate), which is an even stricter level and means at least the strictest limit achieved in practice anywhere for such a source.

The statutory language which relates to BACT is in section 111 and provides as follows:

A standard for emissions of air pollutants which reflects the degree of emission limitation achievable through the application of the best system of emission reduction which (taking into account the cost of achieving such reduction) the Administrator determines has been adequately demonstrated.

In the case of *Portland Cement Ass'n v. Ruckelshaus,* the court examined some of the components of this wording. The holding was startling. The court said in effect that "adequately demonstrated" did not mean that it had to be in existence, and the cost language did not require any cost benefit analysis.

On the demonstration point, the court said:

We begin by rejecting the suggestion of the cement manufacturers that the Act's requirement that emission limitations be adequately demonstrated necessarily implies that any cement plant now in existence be able to meet the proposed standards. Section 111 looks toward what may fairly be projected for the regulated future, rather than the state of the art at present, since it is addressed to the standards for new plants.

On the cost point the court said:

> However desirable in the abstract, such a requirement would conflict with the specific time restraints imposed on the Administrator. The difficulty, if not impossibility, of qualifying the benefit to ambient air concentrations, further militates against the imposition of such an imperative on the agency. Such studies should be considered by the Administrator, if adduced in comments, but we do not inject them as a necessary condition of the action.

In short then, when you apply for a permit to construct a new source, you must demonstrate that you have used the best available pollution control technology, and cost is a very minor (if relevant at all) consideration. Further, "available" does not seem to mean that it has to be in existence any place.

This problem persists throughout the environmental law. As a general rule, it is very difficult to find good judicial authority to support a realistic criterion for cost effectiveness or for requiring use of realistically available technology. This, in turn, puts companies at a disadvantage in negotiating with the agency. You know that if you appeal the agency's decision to the courts on the basis of cost or technology, the odds are against you.

HAZARDOUS AIR POLLUTANTS

There is a second set of procedures under the Clean Air Act for hazardous pollutants. Essentially, these regulations and provisions parallel those for conventional pollutants: new sources have to be approved, there must be a determination of hazardous pollutants, existing sources are given time to comply, etc. An existing source of a hazardous pollutant must meet the limitations established by regulation (or obtain necessary waivers or delays). The existing hazardous pollutants are asbestos, beryllium, mercury, and vinyl chloride.

CONTROL OF MOBILE SOURCES

The Clean Air Act of 1970 also contains numerous provisions aimed at controlling emissions from the automobile, including both the level of emissions from the individual car and concentrations of emissions in major metropolitan areas. Indeed, one of the biggest and most socially disruptive forces in this law is the concept of substantial changes in commuting patterns in the large metropolitan areas in order to achieve compliance with the standards. The basis for the transportation control aspect of the regulation is in section 110 (the state implementation plan section) which says that a state implementation plan must include emission limitations, schedules and timetables for compliance, "and such other measures as may be necessary to insure attainment and maintenance of the primary and secondary standards, including, but not limited to, land-use and transportation controls."

The difficulties with transportation and land-use controls have led to a situation where very little is actually done. The transportation-related pollutants (CO, NO_x, HC, and photochemical oxidants) are over the limits in many areas. The transportation control plans have used devices which do not directly affect too many people in a direct way. They have tended to be the kinds of things which encourage mass transit rather than outright bans on driving. Following are some of the techniques states have used to try to reduce transportation-related pollutants:

1. Bus and car-pool priority treatment (special lanes on the busy highways)
2. Mass transit improvements
3. Car-pooling (voluntary and incentive measures as opposed to mandatory ones)
4. Management of the parking supply
5. Vehicle-free zones
6. Bicycle lanes

THE CLEAN AIR ACT AMENDMENTS OF 1977

The air quality standards under the 1970 Act were not being met on schedule and, in late 1977, the Clean Air Act Amendments were enacted to deal with the problems of attaining the goals and at the same time dealing responsibly with the necessity for growth and construction. There were three basic amendments to the Clean Air Act which dealt with the basic stationary source problems:

1. There were specific statutory provisions dealing with the prevention of significant deterioration (PSD).
2. There were new regulations for areas which failed to meet the standards (nonattainment areas).
3. There were new enforcement techniques—delayed compliance orders (DCO), noncompliance penalties (NCP)—and some changes in the civil penalty provisions.

Prevention of Significant Deterioration (PSD)

In response to a court decision requiring the EPA to require PSD provisions in state implementation plans, the amendments to the statute now require such provisions. These are rather extensive provisions which establish three land classifications for allowable increases of particulates and SO_2 in areas where air quality is cleaner than required by ambient air quality standards. All clean air areas would initially be designated Class II, with the exception of certain national parks, which would be Class I. There would be a third class which is less restrictive: Class III. The states, after consulting with the federal land manager, could redesignate Class II areas Class I or the less restrictive Class III. Allowable increments of pollution above baseline concentrations are set by statute for sulfur dioxide and particulates. Within two years, states must submit plans establishing allowable increments or other means of preventing significant deterioration from nitrogen oxides, hydrocarbons, carbon monoxide, and oxidants. The EPA must approve the plan within 4 months if it meets applicable requirements; otherwise, it must propose a plan for the rejected state within 4 months of the disapproval.

There is a special section which provides visibility protection for federal Class I areas (parks) to prevent any future, or remedy any existing, impairment of visibility in a mandatory Class I area which results from industrial and automotive air pollution. The secretary of the interior is to identify all such Class I areas where visibility is an important value and publish a list.

The administrator is required to report to Congress, within 18 months, the results of a study to: (1) establish methods for determining and measuring visibility impairment; (2) establish modeling techniques or other methods for determining contribution of air pollution to visibility impairment; (3) report on methods for controlling air pollution which results in visibility impairment; and (4) identify categories of sources and types of air pollutants which may reasonably be anticipated to cause or contribute significantly to impairment of visibility.

Within 24 months the administrator is required to promulgate regulations to assure reasonable progress toward meeting the national goal. The regulations shall provide guidelines to the states for the revisions of implementation plans taking into account the recommendations of the report to Congress on techniques and methods for implementing this section. Each state will identify the sources that impair visibility and fall within the requirements of this section.

For sources which significantly affect visibility in federal Class I areas, the states must require the "best available retrofit technology," taking into account the cost of compliance, energy impacts, and existing controls at the source, and establish the appropriate emission limitation on a source-by-source basis. The EPA will provide guidelines for best available retrofit technology for all power plants over 750 megawatts.

Regulations for Nonattainment Areas

The new regulations for nonattainment areas can be summarized as follows:

1. After July 1, 1979, states must revise their SIPs to assure that areas will meet national ambient air quality standards for all pollutants by December 31, 1982, or by December 31, 1987, for photochemical oxidants or CO if the 1982 date cannot be met using all reasonably available measures. A second plan revision must be submitted by July 1, 1982, to require the implementation of enforceable measures to ensure attainment by 1987; such measures include a mandatory inspection and maintenance program.

2. The SIP revision must specify the amount of new source growth which will be permitted; new sources must achieve the lowest achievable emission rate, reflecting the most stringent emission limitation which is contained in the SIP of any state for such class or category or source or the most stringent emission limitation which is achieved in practice, whichever is more stringent. The SIP must require reasonably available control technology (RACT) for existing sources which will result in annual incremental reductions in emissions sufficient to attain the applicable NAAQS by the specified attainment date. The SIP would also have to contain emission limitations, schedules, and other measures to assure compliance by the applicable dates.

3. Within 6 months after enactment, for each AQCR which would not attain CO or photochemical oxidant standards by July 1, 1979, the state and elected officials of affected local governments must jointly determine which elements of the revised SIP will be planned and implemented by the state and which by the local governments or regional agencies, and which by a combination thereof. The local governments have 6 months from enactment to designate an organization and get it certified by the state to carry out the planning; if no such designation is made within the 6 months, the governor shall designate an area wide agency or a state agency to do the planning. Preference is expressed for local planning, and it is also preferred that the local planning organization be the agency handling area wide transportation planning or air quality planning, or both. There also is a requirement for coordinating and interrelating air quality planning and transportation planning.

4. The EPA may make 100-percent grants to local government agencies with transportation or air quality planning responsibilities to pay for the cost of transportation control planning, to supplement funding already available from federal programs.

5. There are sanctions for noncompliance: a state would lose its highway funds (except for transit, safety, or air quality–related transportation projects) where the governor did not submit a revision by July 1, 1979, or where reasonable

efforts toward submitting such an SIP were not being made; this also applies to the 1982 SIP revision. Where the state or local governments are not implementing an SIP, they cannot receive any grants under the act. There is a requirement for federal agencies not to take any action, including making any grant, that does not conform to an approved SIP, nor can any transportation planning agency give approval to anything which does not conform to the SIP. Priority must be given, for purposes of programs with air quality/transportation consequences, to the implementation of SIPs necessary to achieve and maintain air quality standards.

6. Nonattainment states may adopt California car standards, provided that California and such states adopt such standards at least 2 years before the model year, in accordance with EPA regulations.

7. Within 9 months of enactment, the EPA has to publish guidance documents to assist states in implementing the requirements regarding lowest achievable emission rates; these must be revised at least every 2 years.

Enforcement Changes

In order to remove any economic incentive from noncompliance, the statute contains the new concept of mandatory noncompliance penalties. This penalty would be calculated by the EPA on the basis of the costs a noncomplying source avoids by delaying compliance. Specifically, the calculation of the noncompliance penalty must consider the capital costs of compliance and debt service over a normal amortization period not to exceed 10 years, operation and maintenance costs forgone, and any additional economic value of a delay. In essence, the penalty would reflect financial savings realized by the firm as a result of noncompliance with the law.

The EPA is also authorized to issue orders prohibiting construction or modification of a major stationary source in a nonattainment area and to authorize the courts to impose civil penalties up to $25,000 per day for a violation of the act.

In an effort to make reasonable progress in areas where complete compliance with standards is not possible, the new law specifically authorizes a delayed compliance order. In essence, the delayed compliance order is a negotiated agreement where the source will come into compliance as rapidly as possible in exchange for enforcement based on the negotiated conditions. If the source violates the conditions, there will be enforcement based on a breach of the order.

Some of the other important aspects of air pollution regulation brought about by the 1977 Amendments are the following:

1. After July 1, 1979, *construction in nonattainment areas is prohibited* unless the state has revised its SIP to meet the requirements of the 1977 Amendments. That SIP must provide for the attainment of the primary standards not later than December 31, 1982.

2. There is a requirement in the new law that emissions *from existing sources* be reduced by use of reasonably available control technology (RACT) at a minimum.

THE PROBLEMS OF AIR POLLUTION REGULATION

The problems presented by the Clean Air Act can usefully be divided into two classes: problems for existing sources and problems for new sources. Following are some of the most important aspects of these problems.

Existing Sources

If the existing source is new, there may be requirements in the construction permit which include continuous monitoring or pre-start-up notification.

For existing sources in nonattainment areas, the state implementation plan revisions which must be in effect by July 1, 1979, must require reasonably available control technology.

Existing sources less than 15 years old which impair visibility in a Class I area may be required to install best available retrofit technology.

The act contains very broad record-keeping and reporting requirements.

If there is a malfunction, there is a duty to minimize emissions during that malfunction, and the SIP or operating permit may specify criteria for notification of the malfunction.

If the facility is subject to a delayed compliance order (DCO), there will be specific requirements to be met. DCOs are probably somewhat limited because, except for facilities using innovative technology or involved in coal conversion, the final compliance date is no later than July 1, 1979.

Existing sources are subject to mandatory penalties if they are not in compliance on July 1, 1979. These new mandatory penalties will be equal to the economic value of the delay in compliance.

Existing facilities are subject to inspection. This presents the typical kinds of problems associated with random inspections (like those of OSHA), and the problems and procedures involved in preparing for an OSHA inspection would be relevant here also. Specifically, facilities which might be inspected should be identified and the appropriate management people alerted to this fact. There should be standard procedures for conducting the inspection including:

1. Make sure the inspector presents adequate identification to assure that he really is who he says he is.

2. Determine the nature of the inspection. There should be something more specific than simply a general air pollution inspection. The inspector should state what he is inspecting and why.

3. Escort the inspector at all times. Take notes of everything the inspector does. Note areas where the inspector appears to have a special interest.

4. Make concurrent observations of everything the inspector does. If he makes opacity observations, you should also—at least if you have reason to believe there might be a problem.

5. There should be a complete record of the inspection and notes, and this should be forwarded to appropriate management or legal people in the company. (The same is true for all contacts with regulatory agencies.)

New Sources

The problems for new sources are more severe because, in some cases, environmental restrictions will actually be so severe as to prevent the construction. "New sources" includes modifications of existing sources if the modification would result in an increase in the amount of air pollution emitted or in the emission of any new type of pollutant. Reconstruction of existing facilities (even if it is the same kind of facility, with no increase in pollutant emission) is a new source if the cost of reconstruction exceeds 50 percent of the cost of replacing the facility with a new one.

Under the existing law, the governing laws are the 1977 Amendments and the EPA Interpretive Ruling published in the *Federal Register* of December 21, 1976, which announced the offset rule. Under this rule, new sources in or near nonattainment areas can be constructed only if:

1. The emissions to be emitted are more than offset by reductions in existing sources.

2. Reasonable further progress toward the air quality is achieved.

3. Technology up to the LAER (lowest achievable emission rate) is employed.

4. All sources owned by the company in the air quality control region are in compliance or on an approved compliance schedule.

The 1977 Amendments basically continue this rule until July 1, 1979, when SIP revisions are due, except that the baseline for determining emission offset credits is SIP regulation in effect at the time the permit application is submitted (instead of reasonably available control technology). For example, if you have an existing source which emits 20 pounds of pollutant and you reduce that to 10 pounds in a new source but the SIP allows only 15 pounds' emission, the reduction credit under the amendment would be only 5 pounds rather than 10, even assuming the initial 20 was achieved by using RACT.

After July 1, 1979, construction in nonattainment areas is prohibited unless the state has revised its SIP to meet the requirements of the 1977 Amendments which provide for the attainment of primary standards not later than December 31, 1982.

Thus, if you are planning a new source in a nonattainment area, it will be necessary to make sure any pollution is offset by reductions elsewhere, since if you cannot, the source simply cannot be constructed.

There are many unanswered questions in the offset program. These include the type of control measures which are required by LAER, the ratio of offsets to be provided—they must be greater, but the amount of the difference is unclear and probably subject to negotiation—and the type of offsets which will be counted. These points are quite interesting and might result in a "market" for offsets. If a plant closes down for economic reasons, it may be possible to "sell" the amount of decreased pollution to someone else, but this is unclear at this time.

The new rules on PSD (prevention of significant deterioration) also establish rules for constructing new sources in areas where there is currently no air pollution problem. These rules provide essentially that no new source can be constructed in or near an attainment area unless the emissions from the source plus any anticipated growth will not cause a violation of the increments specified in the 1977 Amendments (spelled out in detail in the *Federal Register* of November 3, 1977).

Thus, in almost every case of new construction, there is going to have to be a preconstruction review which includes the following:

1. A public hearing

2. An air quality analysis (an emission modeling study)

3. A demonstration that the projected emissions will not exceed the maximum allowable increments or ambient standards for particulates or SO_2 more than once per year

4. Satisfaction of the state or federal authorities that the source will employ the best available control technology (BACT) for all pollutants regulated under the act with a *potential* emission rate in excess of 100 tons per year

5. An analysis of the growth impacts associated with the construction of the source

6. A 1-year preconstruction monitoring program which demonstrates compliance

Then you will have to negotiate the actual permit (and the emission limits) on a case-by-case basis.

COMMENTARY

Where does all this leave us? The facts are that almost all of the urban areas of the country do not satisfy existing ambient air quality standards. In fact, the *Federal Register* of March 3, 1978, points out that just in the case of photochemical oxidants, 103 of the 105 urban areas in the United States with populations greater than 200,000 have a problem. (Honolulu, Hawaii, and Spokane, Washington, are the two single exceptions.) Further, in many areas of the country—and the ones where most of the people are—there is no realistic possibility of attaining these standards in the foreseeable future without measures that society will not accept, such as shutting down plants and prohibiting cars.

A second fact is the complexity of these regulations. The laws are complex, but they are the simple part. The technology involved is not only complex but in some cases is also unavailable or very subjective.

A third fact is the expense. Expense is an emotional subject, particularly with the regulators. They say that we should have clean air without regard to the cost. However, the kind of expense they are usually talking about is the expense of the pollution control equipment. That is only one of the problems. If business was simply told that all new facilities had to incorporate certain kinds of equipment which cost money—even if the amount was large—they could deal with the problem. However, in addition to the equipment costs, there are the substantial legal and engineering costs associated with the regulatory process, plus the substantial costs of the uncertainty and delay.

A fourth fact is that the regulators are placed in an impossible position. They have a law which requires standards which cannot be met short of politically and socially unacceptable actions in an industrial society. Yet they cannot simply ignore the law.

It appears that this all boils down to a no-growth or very-limited-growth situation. The regulators are going to have to concentrate on new sources because this is the only politically acceptable thing to do. They simply cannot close down plants or ban cars from cities under current conditions. Perhaps some disaster or cancer scare might change the public's attitude, but right now, the public is simply not willing to stop driving or give up jobs to have cleaner air.

Also, the regulations mean increased costs. They apply to existing as well as new sources, and so companies are going to have to spend the time to become familiar with the rules, hire technical experts, and expend considerable time and effort just to maintain the status quo.

CHAPTER FIFTY-TWO

THE CLEAN WATER ACT

The principal law dealing with water pollution is the Federal Water Pollution Control Act as amended in 1972 and 1977.

The Clean Water Act is extremely long and complicated and is divided into five titles. Title I contains a declaration of goals and establishes the national water pollution policy. It also deals with research and demonstration projects. The goals established in Title I are important. The highlights are as follows:

1. The discharge of pollutants into navigable waters shall be eliminated by 1985—the no-discharge rule.

2. Water shall be fishable and swimmable by 1983.

3. The discharge of toxic pollutants in significant amounts shall be prohibited.

The basic concept of the act is that any discharge of pollutants into the waters of the United States is unlawful unless done pursuant to a permit. There are two basic kinds of standards: water quality standards and effluent limitation standards. The basic water quality standards play a secondary role in the Clean Water Act. To that extent, it is fundamentally different from the Clean Air Act, where ambient air standards are the primary control mechanism. In the Clean Water Act, the primary control is in the effluent limitations. There are several important concepts in the Clean Water Act which should be kept in mind.

JURISDICTION: NAVIGABLE WATERS

For historical reasons, the act still uses the term "navigable waters" in the main text. However, in the definitions, "navigable waters" is defined to include the waters of the United States. The legislative history and numerous cases make it very clear that all waters of the United States are covered, whether or not navigable. Feeder streams and wetlands are included. In fact, normally dry streams where water *may* flow are covered.

Point Sources

The act, taken as a whole, covers all pollution, but the heart of the act— the permit system—covers only discharges from point sources. Further, the point source must discharge directly into waters of the United States. This broad ruling does not include indirect discharges, like those into sewers. Those discharges are governed by different rules.

A point source means any discernible, confined, and discrete conveyance, including but not limited to any dike, ditch, channel, tunnel, conduit, well, discrete fissure, container, rolling stock, concentrated animal feeding operation, or vessel or other floating craft from which pollutants are or may be discharged. Thus, for example, if fertilizer or insecticide is spread on farm land and washes into a neighboring river, this is not a discharge from a point source. However, if the farmer digs a system of drainage ditches so that one ultimately goes into the river, that would be a point source. Similarly, if an industrial complex uses materials which end up as dust around the plant and rain washes that pollutant into a river, it is not covered. If on the other hand, the facility establishes a system of drains which catch the rain water and then carry it to a river, that is covered.

Pollutants

Unlike the Clean Air Act, which lists relatively specific pollutants, the Clean Water Act defines pollutants very broadly. It means dredged spoil, solid waste, incinerator residue, sewage, garbage, sewage sludge, munitions, chemical wastes, biological materials, radioactive materials, heat, wrecked or discarded equipment, rock, sand, cellar dirt, and industrial, municipal, and agricultural waste discharged into water.

There is another definition for *toxic* pollutants. Toxic pollutants are those pollutants which, after discharge and upon exposure, ingestion, inhalation, or assimilation into any organism, either directly from the environment or indirectly by ingestion through food chains, will, on the basis of information available to the administrator, cause death, disease, behavioral abnormalities, cancer, genetic mutations, physiological malfunctions, or physical deformations.

THE PERMIT SYSTEM

The heart of the Clean Water Law is the permit system. The 1972 Act established a National Pollutant Discharge Elimination System permit (NPDES). These permits are issued by either the federal Environmental Protection Agency or the states where state plans have been adopted and approved by the EPA.

The first deadline for obtaining NPDES permits was December 31, 1974, and so any discharge not covered by a permit is now unlawful.

The permit will probably contain numerous limitations and restrictions. It is essentially a negotiated document in which the government tries to get as many provisions as possible which make the discharge as inoffensive as possible and the applicant tries to have provisions which are reasonable in terms of cost and technology. Sometimes the permits will have a series of limitations, some going into effect at a later time. For most of these the later effective date was July 1, 1977, because that was a key date under the 1972 Amendments.

Permits are valid for a maximum of 5 years, and there must be a renewal application 6 months prior to the expiration. The EPA takes the position that permit violations are strict liability offenses, and malfunctions, breakdowns, or acts of God do not constitute a defense. In some cases, however, it may be possible to negotiate specific language in the permit to mitigate this harsh result.

The general rule under the 1972 Act was that industrial sources had to achieve effluent limitations which require application of the best practicable control technology (BPT) currently available by July 1, 1977. This is a level of technology which is established by the EPA for the particular industry pursuant to an elaborate series of technical guidelines. In general, BPT means the average of the best technology currently used in the industry. There is some consideration given to costs, but it is limited.

The EPA and most courts took the position that this July 1, 1977, date could not be extended by the agency. Therefore, all the NPDES permits show July 1, 1977, as the deadline for compliance with this requirement. In some cases, the EPA issued enforcement compliance schedule letters (ECSL), a technical way around this problem for sources which legitimately could not comply. These letters did not technically extend the date but, on the basis of prosecutorial discretion, constituted an agreement by the EPA not to sue so long as the schedules in the letter were carried out. The validity of this was doubtful, but the 1977 Amendments seem to make the issue moot.

Under the 1977 Amendments, some industrial sources may obtain limited extensions for BPT until April 1, 1979. The extension, however, is only from the federal BPT requirement and would not affect any more stringent state or local requirement. In essence, then, companies either should have complied with the BPT requirement at this time or be sufficiently along the road to compliance (having started construction of the necessary facilities) to get an extension.

The second phase of the 1972 Clean Water Act contemplated the achievement by industry for point-source discharges of the best available control technology economically achievable (BAT) not later than July 1, 1983. The precise meaning of BAT is unclear, but it seems apparent that it is something more than BPT.

The 1977 Amendments, however, made some significant changes. Pollutants were divided into three classes: conventional, toxic, and nonconventional.

Congress apparently felt that BAT should not be required for conventional pollutants. Instead, a new standard was established and, by not later than July 1, 1984, industrial sources must achieve effluent limitations which require application of the best conventional pollutant control technology (BCT). BCT will be established by the EPA using the statutory criteria on an industry-by-industry basis. One of the key criteria is the cost and level of reduction at a publicly owned treatment works as compared to the cost and level of reduction using industrial technology. BCT appears to be somewhere between BAT and BPT, but which it is closer to is subject to some disagreement.

Toxic Pollutants

The emphasis in water pollution regulation has changed toward toxic pollutants. The basis for this change was the *NRDC v. Train* litigation, which culminated in the so-called Flannery Order (named after the judge). The Flannery Order requires the EPA to promulgate BAT effluent limitations for twenty-one major industries (listed in the order) covering 65 toxic substances (which are further broken down to produce a total of 129 substances.)

The 1977 Amendments to the Clean Water Act essentially adopted this approach of requiring BAT toxic effluent limitations on an industry-by-industry basis. It also, however, preserved the possibility of adopting all-inclusive toxic effluent standards in certain cases.

Best available technology (BAT) is required for toxic effluent limitations. The Flannery Order is basically incorporated into the new law and so, under the new law and Flannery, the EPA must promulgate BAT effluent limitations for the 21 industrial categories and 65 (or 129) pollutants by July 1, 1980, and compliance must be achieved not later than July 1, 1984. The *Federal Register* of January 31, 1978, provided the official listing of the 65 pollutants, but additional ones can be added later.

Most commentators feel that the development of BAT for toxic pollutants will be a much more difficult task than BPT or the BAT guidelines developed to date. Thus, there is doubt that the EPA can meet the statutory schedule. There is no corresponding delay for industry, however.

Another concept introduced in the 1977 Amendments was "best management practices" (BMP). (That exact term is not used in the statute.) Best management practices were resisted by industry but were eventually accepted as a trade-off for some of the other provisions of the 1977 Amendments. These BMP regulations are to control plant-site runoff, spillage, or leaks, sludge or waste disposal, and drainage from raw material storage.

The statute provides that there can be no waivers or variances from the toxic effluent limitations.

The third and last kind of pollutants are the nonconventional pollutants. This is a catchall category defined as pollutants not specified as "conventional" or "toxic." The EPA must promulgate BAT effluent guidelines for nonconventional pollutants, but no deadline is set. The industries must achieve compliance within 3 years of the date the limitations are set, but in no event later than July 1, 1987.

New Sources

The definition of a "new source" is one for which construction is started after publication of proposed regulations which would be applicable. The EPA is required to establish standards of performance for new sources for at least twenty-seven specified categories of industries. The standard of performance means a standard for the control of the discharge of pollutants which reflects the greatest degree of effluent reduction achievable through application of the best available demonstrated control technology, process, operating methods, or other alternatives including, where practicable, a standard permitting no discharge of pollutants (BADT). BADT is difficult to describe generally. Conceptually, it probably falls somewhere between BAT and BPT, but even this can be disputed.

The Clean Water Act contains a provision which says that any new source which is constructed to meet all applicable standards for performance shall not be subject to any more stringent standard of performance for a period of 10 years.

Pretreatment Standards

The 1972 Act requires the EPA to publish regulations establishing pretreatment standards covering discharges by industrial plants to publicly owned treatment works (POTW). These regulations are designed to prevent industry from discharging things into the municipal sewer which cannot be treated by the treatment works, or which interfere with the operation of the treatment works. Those regulations were published in 40 C.F.R. 128. The regulations point out that the 1977 Amendments to the Clean Water Act modified it to require local pretreatment programs to enforce national pretreatment standards as a condition of municipal NPDES permits. Congress added a new section (309(f)) to provide that violations by industrial users of national pretreatment standards should be enforced by the POTW. If after 30 days' notification of a violation the POTW does not commence appropriate enforcement action, the EPA or the NPDES state may bring a civil action against the POTW. In these cases, the violating industrial user shall be made a party to the action. In addition, the EPA retains authority under section 309 to bring criminal charges against industrial users who violate national pretreatment standards and against POTWs who violate the terms of the permit. Accordingly, all industrial concerns which discharge effluent into a POTW will have to be concerned with pollution control to substantially the same degree as those which discharge directly into the waters of the United States, except that the discharges into the POTW do not require a permit directly to the industrial discharger.

ENFORCEMENT

Inspections, Monitoring and Entry

Section 308 of the Clean Water Act gives the EPA broad authority to inspect facilities; require them to make reports and keep records, install, use, and maintain monitoring equipment or methods; and sample effluents. States also have similar rights where they have approved plans.

Liability for Spills or Discharges of Oil or Hazardous Substances

The Clean Water Act contains a separate section for liability for discharge of oil or hazardous substances into or upon the waters of the United States. The key distinction between this and the other sections discussed previously is that this liability is focused upon one-time spills rather than ongoing discharges. Naturally, however, it is possible to discharge oil or hazardous substances either in a one-time spill or in conjunction with other discharges. In the latter case, the discharger will be liable not only under the special hazardous substances section but also under the normal permit liabilities. This is especially important under the reporting provisions because such an event would have to be reported twice—once under the special hazardous substance section and once under the provisions of the permit.

Oil is broadly defined, and the harmful-quantity requirement is any quantity which would cause a film or sheen upon or discoloration of the surface of the water or adjoining shorelines or cause a sludge or emulsion to be deposited beneath the surface of the water or upon an adjoining shoreline.

Hazardous substances are specifically listed in the *Federal Register* of March 13, 1978. The harmful quantities are also spelled out.

There are special reporting requirements for an oil spill or discharge of a hazardous substance. An oil spill must be reported to the Coast Guard and any other spill must be reported to the EPA.

The penalties are quite severe. Failure to report as required is subject to fine or imprisonment. The actual spill can give rise to a fine of up to $5000 for each offense. In addition, however, there are specific penalties which depend on whether the substance is actually removable or not, and if not, how toxic it is.

If the substance is not actually removable, there is a schedule of additional penalties based on toxicity, degradability, and dispersal characteristics of the substance, and how much of it was discharged. In other words, this is a subjective penalty based on how bad the spill was.

If the substance is actually removable, the liability is the actual cost of cleaning it up.

For any source which has discharged, or because of its location could reasonably be expected to discharge, oil in harmful quantities, there must be a spill prevention control and countermeasure plan (SPCC plan) filed with the EPA. Failure to have such a plan can give rise to a fine even if there was never any spill.

In summary then, the 1977 Amendments, the prior law, regulations, and cases provide just as complicated a maze under the Water Act as the Clean Air Act. For each facility, there should be data on the following points:

1. Is a *permit* needed? If so, has one been obtained? What does the permit say, when will it expire, what are the likely problems on renewal?

2. Does any location discharge a *hazardous substance* as defined in the *Federal Register* of March 13, 1978?

3. What are the implications of the *pretreatment* regulations as they appear in the *Federal Register* of June 26 for all locations discharging into a POTW?

4. Does the location need a SPCC?

5. Is the location *adequately monitoring* discharges if appropriate, and has there been discussion about how to handle visits from the EPA or state inspectors?

6. Is there a clear understanding of all applicable *reporting requirements?* All pollution laws—but especially the Clean Water Act—contain reporting requirements, and most of the severe civil cases, and all the criminal cases, involve failure of the company to report data that should have been reported.

CHAPTER FIFTY-THREE

THE SOLID WASTE LAW

The laws relating to solid waste disposal are newer than those relating to air and water—at least in the context of a detailed federal regulatory scheme. The federal law is the Resource Conservation and Recovery Act of 1976. Unlike the Clean Air and Water Acts of 1977, this is really a new law, in that it creates a federal regulatory scheme for solid waste where none existed before. The new law starts out with a qualified prohibition against open dumping:

> Any solid waste management practice or disposal of solid waste or hazardous waste which constitutes the open dumping of solid waste or hazardous waste is prohibited, except in the case of any practice or disposal of solid waste under a timetable or schedule for compliance established under this section.

The act then goes on to establish essentially the same kind of regulatory scheme as for water. The states are directed to develop plans and programs, and there are specific rules for these plans. The EPA provides approval of the plans, enforcement in the absence of a state plan, and money.

The portions of the Resource Conservation and Recovery Act of 1976 (RCRA) which apply to nonhazardous waste are principally directed to municipal dumps, although a private establishment that constitutes a dump could also be covered. For corporate planning purposes, however, it can be assumed that, except in the case of hazardous substances, the solid waste disposal problem will be only indirect. Federal regulation of the dumps will undoubtedly cause some of them to close and the costs of all of them to rise, but corporations should be able to count on dumps or sanitary land fills to be available, and there is no obligation on the part of the corporation to get any permits or do any pretreatment of its solid wastes. It must be noted, however, that the fact that this law is very new and is not based on substantial previous federal regulation makes prediction of its ultimate implications very difficult.

The situation is a little different with hazardous wastes. A hazardous waste is a solid waste, or combination of solid wastes, which, because of its quantity, concentration, or physical, chemical, or infectious characteristics may:

1. Cause, or significantly contribute to, an increase in mortality or an increase in serious irreversible, or incapacitating reversible, illness

2. Pose a substantial present or potential hazard to human health or the environment when improperly treated, stored, transported, or disposed of, or otherwise managed

The EPA is charged with publishing a list of solid hazardous wastes. While it has not yet done so, it can be expected that the hazardous items listed under the Clean Water and Air Acts would be prime candidates.

After a substance is designated as hazardous, the disposal, storage, or treatment of it will be prohibited except under a permit. All these terms are broadly defined so, for example, storage would include temporary storage by industry pending hauling the substance to a disposal site. Disposal is also broadly defined, and just about any conceivable private disposal of a hazardous substance would be covered.

In order to get a permit, it is necessary to show the EPA (or state agency) that the reporting and record-keeping requirements will be satisfied, that there is a contingency plan to minimize damage if there is a problem, and that the disposal will comply with criteria for disposal of the substance published by the EPA.

The Resource Conservation and Recovery Act gives the EPA authority to set standards for generators and transporters of hazardous waste. The act proceeds according to the following pattern:

1. There will be regulations applicable to generators of hazardous wastes which will establish requirements for record-keeping practices, labeling practices, use of appropriate containers for hazardous waste, furnishing information on the general chemical composition of the waste, use of a manifest system, and submission of reports setting out the quantities and dispositions of all hazardous waste generated during a given time period.

2. There will be regulations for transporters of hazardous waste which will include record keeping and a fairly elaborate set of requirements to safeguard against spills or accidents during transport.

3. There will, of course, be elaborate regulations for the landfills or treatment facilities.

4. There will be a permit system.

5. There will be provisions to authorize state implementation plans.

6. There will be regulations governing a preliminary report to the EPA of hazardous waste generators and transporters and operators of waste-management facilities.

It has been said that this framework constitutes a cradle-to-grave system for watching over hazardous wastes. The manifest system will require that each hazardous waste load must be accompanied by a manifest filled out by the generator of the waste. On this manifest, the generator designates the facility to which the waste must be taken. The manifest goes with the load to the facility and a copy of it is returned to the generator by the facility. The generator is responsible for maintaining these manifests as evidence that he has properly managed his hazardous wastes.

The facilities receiving the hazardous wastes (including the generator's own facilities, if he elects to handle his own hazardous waste) must meet strict standards for technical soundness and financial responsibility in order to obtain a permit.

Taken altogether, these regulations will provide a system of federal regulation for hazardous waste from the time they are generated to the time they are disposed of, including the transportation of them between points. In practice, this should ultimately produce a well-run system, but in the short run, it will probably close some waste-management facilities (of the open-dump variety) and will create some problems for industry. According to the EPA, the two biggest problems with this system are siting and capacity. "Siting" refers to where good facilities can be located. There are a number of constraints; some are technical—improper soil, too close to rivers, etc.—and others are political—local citizen opposition to new facilities. At this time, these regulations are not in final form (many of them are not even in proposed form). However, when operative, industry will have to do at least the following:

1. Ascertain if it generates any hazardous waste as that term is defined and as the hazardous waste substances are listed by the EPA.

2. If so, notify the EPA.

3. If the location does not manage the problem itself and ships the hazardous waste away, institute the manifest system and record-keeping procedures.

4. Find an acceptable location (one having a permit or at least approval from the EPA to operate on a temporary basis).

These regulations will undoubtedly increase the costs of waste management for hazardous wastes. The EPA itself has provided the following general estimates:

1. A secure landfill costs about ten times as much as an open dump.

2. Controlled incineration can be thirty times as expensive as an open dump.

3. The total annualized incremental cost of sound hazardous-waste management for those industries directly affected might be about 1 percent of the value of their shipments.

CHAPTER FIFTY-FOUR

THE TOXIC SUBSTANCES CONTROL ACT

The Toxic Substances Control Act was signed by President Ford on October 11, 1976, and became effective January 1, 1977. The purpose of the act was to attempt to bring some order and understanding to the vast number of new substances consumed or used by the American public about which little safety information was available. Newspaper accounts that rather common substances possibly caused cancer, sterility, or genetic problems were probably the biggest cause for passage of this act.

The act is much more troublesome to chemical companies than it is to other manufacturing companies, and most of the act and the regulations issued to date apply either solely or chiefly to chemical companies. Nevertheless, the act does have some incidental effects on manufacturing companies, and the indirect effect of the act can also be significant.

SUMMARY OF THE ACT

The act is long and complicated, but essentially it provides the following:

1. There will be an inventory which attempts to identify virtually all of the substances manufactured or processed in the country. It is the "or processed" aspect of the act which may make it applicable to non-chemical companies.

2. After the creation of the inventory, the Environmental Protection Agency (the lead agency designated to implement the Toxic Substances Control Act) will identify fifty chemicals from this inventory for further study. In addition, any "new" chemical (meaning any chemical which is not on the inventory)

will have to be cleared with the Environmental Protection Agency before it can be manufactured or used. Thus, after the creation of the inventory, the EPA will be dividing its efforts between analysis, testing, and development of regulations for a certain set of identified chemicals which they believe may be hazardous, and the analysis, testing, and evaluation of "new" chemicals.

Inventory

For immediate purposes, the inventory is the most significant aspect of the act. Section 5 of the act provides as follows:

(a) In General.—

   (1) Except as provided in subsection (h), no person may:
      (A) manufacture a new chemical substance on or after the 30th day after the date on which the Administrator first publishes the list required by section 8(b), or
      (B) manufacture or process any chemical substance for a use which the Administrator has determined, in accordance with paragraph (2), is a significant new use, unless such person submits to the Administrator, at least 90 days before such manufacture or processing, a notice, in accordance with subsection (d), of such person's intention to manufacture or process such substance and such person complies with any applicable requirement of subsection (b).
   (2) A determination by the Administrator that a use of a chemical substance is a significant new use with respect to which notification is required under paragraph (1) shall be made by a rule promulgated after a consideration of all relevant factors, including:
      (A) the projected volume of manufacturing and processing of a chemical substance,
      (B) the extent to which a use changes the type or form of exposure of human beings or the environment to a chemical substance,
      (C) the extent to which a use increases the magnitude and duration of exposure of human beings or the environment to a chemical substance, and
      (D) the reasonably anticipated manner and methods of manufacturing, processing, distribution in commerce, and disposal of a chemical substance.

Accordingly, it is essential that both chemical companies and industry put on the inventory all of the chemicals which they sell or use, or else they will have to get EPA clearance for continued use of these chemicals.

One of the items of current concern is the mechanics for gathering this inventory. Initially, the EPA published a long and elaborate set of regulations which would have required almost every company in the country to submit data on chemicals manufactured or used. In response to criticism that this was not a very effective way of creating the inventory, the EPA withdrew these regulations and substituted another set which applied only to chemical companies. It is likely that after the initial reporting from the chemical companies, the EPA will require some input from the manufacturing segment of the economy, but it is likely that this will be much reduced by virtue of the chemical company reporting.

The reports filed by the chemical companies have to disclose every chemical they make and sell, the plant where they make it, and the amount of that chemical manufactured at that plant. One of the items of concern is the protection that this information would be given by the government. The chemical companies claim that it is a trade secret and highly sensitive from a competitive point of view, and that the government may be unable or unwilling to protect that information against disclosure under the Freedom of Information Act or against "leaks." The government claims that it recognizes the confidentiality problem and can adequately protect the information.

Testing

The act calls for testing of chemicals (both new and old) but with an important twist: the testing has to be done at the expense of industry. The act contains a rather elaborate attempted explanation of how these testing expenses are going to be apportioned among the companies manufacturing essentially the same chemical, and it is likely that this is going to be an item of some concern and dispute in the future. It is clear, however, that the act places the ultimate burden of the cost of testing on private industry.

Priority List

The determination of which chemicals from the inventory will be given priority and selection for testing and study will be done by a committee which will consist of members from other government agencies. This committee is responsible for developing a list of fifty priority substances to be given further study.

Record Keeping

The act requires the administrator to develop what appears to be a rather elaborate set of reporting and record-keeping procedures, but these have not been implemented as yet. Therefore, it is hard to say whether or not they will be overly burdensome.

Relation to OSHA

Perhaps one of the biggest implications of the Toxic Substances Control Act is its interaction with OSHA. OSHA has greatly increased its emphasis on occupational health, including exposure to harmful chemicals—mostly carcinogens—and the information obtained by the EPA under the Toxic Substances Control Act will, of course, be shared by OSHA. Also, OSHA will have an input for placing items on the priority list, and undoubtedly one of the important factors will be the prevalance of suspected chemicals in manufacturing processes.

Processing

Counsel for most manufacturing companies will probably want to focus on the definition of "process," which is as follows:

Sec. 3 (10).
The term "process" means the preparation of a chemical substance or mixture, after its manufacture, for distribution in commerce:
    (A)   in the same form or physical state as, or in a different form or physical state from, that in which it was received by the person so preparing such substance or mixture, or
    (B)   as part of an article containing the chemical substance or mixture.

Some of the normal manufacturing operations which may be affected by the Toxic Substances Control Act because of this definition are the following:

1. Any process where lubricants are used or where a lubricant is placed on the finished product (as oil and grease are on many steel products)

2. Any plating operation where metal is placed on another metal

3. Any item which is dusted or coated with any chemical substances

4. Any item which contains a lubricant (such as pumps and some motors)

RESTRICTION OF DEVELOPMENT

One of the implications of the Toxic Substances Control Act which many people fear is its inhibition of research and development. Some people point to changes in the Food and Drug Act in the early 1960s which required essentially the same procedures for food and drugs as the new act requires for chemical substances. They claim that those procedures inhibited the development of new drugs. They feel that this same thing might happen in the case of chemicals. Whether or not this is true remains to be seen, but it is, of course, very clear that chemical companies are going to have to pay very close attention to the problem, and even manufacturing companies which use chemicals in their processing are going to have to be aware of it. Some of the procedures by which manufacturing companies work with chemical companies to develop new products for use in their processes will definitely have to include notifying the Environmental Protection Agency and testing, both involving quite a bit of time and trouble before the chemicals can be used.

PRESIDENTIAL AND WHITE HOUSE STATEMENTS ON THE ACT

A copy of former President Ford's statement on signing the Toxic Substances Control Act on October 11, 1976, and the White House Fact Sheet issued October 12, 1976, follow.

Statement by the President

I have signed S. 3149, the "Toxic Substances Control Act." I believe this legislation may be one of the most important pieces of environmental legislation that has been enacted by the Congress.

This toxic substances control legislation provides broad authority to regulate any of the tens of thousands of chemicals in commerce. Only a few of these chemicals have been tested for their long-term effects on human health or the environment. Through the testing and reporting requirements of the law, our understanding of these chemicals should be greatly enhanced. If a chemical is found to present a danger to health or the environment, appropriate regulatory action can be taken before it is too late to undo the damage.

The legislation provides that the Federal Government through the Environmental Protection Agency may require the testing of selected new chemicals prior to their production to determine if they will pose a risk to health or the environment. Manufacturers of all selected new chemicals will be required to notify the Agency at least 90 days before commencing commercial production. The Agency may promulgate regulations or go into court to restrict the production or use of a chemical or to even ban it if such drastic action is necessary.

The bill closes a gap in our current array of laws to protect the health of our people and the environment. The Clean Air Act and the Water Pollution Control

Act protect the air and water from toxic contaminants. The Food and Drug Act and the Safe Drinking Water Act are used to protect the food we eat and the water we drink against hazardous contaminants. Other provisions of existing laws protect the health and the environment against other polluting contaminants such as pesticides and radiation. However, none of the existing statutes provide comprehensive protection.

This bill provides broad discretionary authority to protect the health and environment. It is critical, however, that the legislation be administered in a manner so as not to duplicate existing regulatory and enforcement authorities.

In addition, I am certain that the Environmental Protection Agency realizes that it must carefully exercise its discretionary authority so as to minimize the regulatory burden consistent with the effective protection of the health and environment.

The Administration, the majority and minority members of the Congress, the chemical industry, labor, consumer, environmental and other groups have all contributed to the bill as it has finally been enacted. It is a strong bill and will be administered in a way which focuses on the most critical environmental problems not covered by existing legislation while not overburdening either the regulatory agency, the regulated industry, or the American people.

The White House Fact Sheet

The President today signed S. 3149—The Toxic Substances Control Act. This Act provides, for the first time, comprehensive authority for the Federal Government to regulate all substances or the use of all substances that may produce toxic effects.

Highlights

This new law will better enable us to minimize the risk of unknown hazards to health or the environment from toxic substances while permitting us to continue to reap the benefits which these substances can contribute.

The bill contains some 53 pages of intricate regulatory material.

Generally speaking, the bill gives authority to the EPA Administrator to:

require private industry to provide test data and supply detailed information on specified substances;

prevent, or place limitations on, the marketing of new substances which the Administrator believes harmful; and

ban or limit continued marketing of existing substances.

The Toxic Substances Control Act is designed to prevent problems. By allowing early and selective regulation of only those uses that are likely to be hazardous, the Act minimizes adverse regulatory impacts on the chemical industry. In addition, this preventive approach should help reduce the need for regulations under other laws which hurt important industries such as fishing, food processing, and many other manufacturers who rely on chemical products.

Background

New chemical substances are being formulated rapidly and new commercial applications are being found almost daily. The production of metals, metal compounds and synthetic organics, which has been growing at a rate of 10 to 15% over the past 20 years, will continue to provide many new benefits to our society. For example, organic chemicals, which can be tailored in structure and properties to fit almost any imaginable need, are being used in ever-increasing quantities to produce dyes, pigments, flavors, perfumes, plastics, rubber products, detergents, pharmaceuticals, and so on. Yet, substances which in some applications have been extremely useful have been found in other applications to cause unanticipated and undesirable side effects on the environment and human health. Examples are vinyl chloride, polychlorinated and polybrominated biphenyls, kepone, fluorocarbons, and lead.

There presently exists a number of statutory authorities to regulate toxic substances. Among these are the:

—Federal Food, Drug, and Cosmetic Act which regulates substances which are used as foods, drugs, or cosmetics;

—Occupational Safety and Health Act which regulates contact with substances in the work place;

—Consumer Product Safety Act which regulates dangers from consumer products;

—Federal Insecticide, Fungicide, and Rodenticide Act (FIFRA) which regulates substances used as pesticides;

—Safe Drinking Water Act which regulates the level of toxic substances that can be present in drinking water supplies;

—The Federal Water Pollution Control Act which provides for State and Federal regulation over industrial discharges of toxic pollutants into the Nation's waters.

However, there are certain important gaps in the regulatory framework. For example, there is presently no effective way to regulate PCB's until and unless their dispersion into the environment affects water supply. This type of situation will be subject to control under various provisions of the bill.

CHAPTER FIFTY-FIVE

ENVIRONMENTAL COMPLIANCE PROGRAMS

The complexity of the environmental laws, plus the fact that criminal penalties are possible, seems to indicate that most corporations would be well advised to have a relatively comprehensive and formal program to assure compliance with these laws. The kind of program we are referring to might be termed a "first-level" program, in the sense that it contemplates a system whereby top management issues policies or instructions which require those in the company who are directly responsible for plant operations to assure that they are in compliance with all the environmental laws. This should be distinguished from a program designed by engineers and lawyers for a specific plant to actually control the emissions and discharges. That kind of program is necessary but it is so specific and technical that top management would probably not have the necessary expertise to establish it.

ASCERTAIN THE COMPANY'S NEED

The first step would be to ascertain the needs of the company. This in itself is actually the start of the compliance program. If management can show that they are aware of the company's environmental problems and are taking steps to correct them, any allegations of bad faith or assertions that there should be criminal penalties in case of an accident will be avoided. (Conversely, if there were a serious accident resulting in a bad discharge, and management could not even show a systematic procedure for maintaining a knowledge of the company's environmental problems, it might precipitate more stringent enforcement activity.)

Answers to the following questions for each of the company's principal facilities appear to be required.

1. Designation and address of the location.

2. The name of the person at that establishment responsible for environmental matters.

3. The approximate amount of time that person has devoted to the problem and his other responsibilities.

4. A basic description of the operations carried out at the location.

5. A list of all the discharge permits which the location has, and a description (or better yet, a copy) of those permits, for:
    (a) water
    (b) air

6. A listing of every toxic or hazardous substance at the location, including:
    (a) toxic air pollutants
    (b) toxic water pollutants
    (c) toxic substances used in the manufacturing process
    (d) substances identified by OSHA as being toxic
    (The intention here is to ascertain if the location uses any known toxic substances out of the already published lists.)

7. A description of any complaints against the location—either formal from a government agency or informal by neighbors—which relate to pollution (keeping in mind that formal environmental litigation must be disclosed in SEC documents even if it is not material in the normal financial sense).

8. Does the facility discharge into a POTW, and if so:
    (a) What does it discharge?
    (b) What are the effects of that discharge on the POTW?

9. Does the facility have any storage capacity for oil or any other hazardous substance? If so, does it have a spill prevention/control plan which is formally filed as required? If so, get a copy of the plan.

10. Does the facility have written instructions or plans to deal with inspectors? The following inspections should be included:
    (a) smoke or air pollution
    (b) water pollution
    (c) OSHA (for toxic substances affecting workers)

11. Does the facility have a formal plan for notifying the government (or top management) of information relating to harmful substances as per the Toxic Substances Control Act, the Air and Water Acts, or other environmental laws?

12. What kind of solid wastes are created and how are they disposed of?

13. Is there a noise problem?
    (a) In the context of noise emissions from the plant as a whole.
    (b) In the context of noise exposure to the employees. (The latter problem, if present, should be dealt with in the context of OSHA.)
    (c) In the form of design of the company's products.

14. Brief description of the principal pollution control equipment installed to date, including approximate costs. Also include a brief description of presently planned pollution control equipment.

15. Is there any plan to expand or add to the facility? If so, what considerations have been given to environmental requirements for permits or renewals?

16. Discussion of the AQCR in which the plan is located and whether it is an attainment or nonattainment region.

Of course, this is only an illustrative list, but it does show some of the information which will be required and highlights some of the things which should be considered.

On the legal side, there are two important aspects: the federal laws and the state laws. Chapters 50 to 54 have highlighted the important federal laws and, in the case of the air, water, and solid wastes acts, it was pointed out that the pattern of the regulations was to establish a general set of federal regulations and then require state implementation plans for states to actually carry them out. Many states have such programs. The federal laws constitute minimum requirements. The states—and even local subdivisions—can have stricter requirements and often do. Therefore, it is very difficult for corporate counsel in company headquarters to prepare an accurate description of the laws applicable to any facility. One technique which has been suggested is to prepare manuals for each location. The manual would have all the things counsel and the engineers thought necessary, and, in sections dealing with legal requirements, it would have the state laws relevant to that plant. The manual would thus be different for each plant, but the people in the plant using the manual would be assured of having the proper laws without wading through the lengthy and expensive commercial sources themselves.

USE A TEAM APPROACH

In most cases, management would be well advised to avoid depending on one discipline to deal with the company's environmental problems. A team consisting of lawyers and engineers will be required in almost every case. It is not too important which person takes the lead role; lawyers or engineers could do it equally well. The relevant factors would be the abilities of the people to manage; the compliance program is largely a management rather than a technical effort. The fact that you need a team doesn't mean you need a full-time team. While you need lawyers and engineers, if you have a limited number of problems, part-time efforts will be sufficient.

You are also probably going to require consultants. Even in large companies with good in-house legal and engineering staffs, the environmental problems are usually so technical and specific that consultants may be required. This is particularly true if there is any air pollution problem.

REPORT TO TOP MANAGEMENT

The next logical step would appear to be a report by the staff to top management. The objectives are to:

1. Inform top management of the situation—either that there is no problem or that there is some work yet to be done.

2. Suggest some actions on the part of top management:
   (a) a policy statement
   (b) other form of communication
   (c) financial support if necessary
   (d) additional staff support if necessary

The report should discuss the approximate situation at each of the major locations in terms of compliance with the relevant pollution standards, and inform management whether the problem seems to be well in hand. Any conclusions would then be supported in the normal way.

ESTABLISH A COMPLIANCE PROGRAM

Even if the company is in good shape, there should be a relatively formal compliance program to assure that the company remains in good shape *and* to assure that management can show they did their job, if that is ever necessary.

A good compliance program will have to be tailored to each company. It is probably not necessary to tailor the program for each location because we are talking here about systems, procedures, and reports rather than specific items of equipment.

Following are some things which a good compliance program should consider. Most of them, in one form or another, are probably necessary for a reasonably effective program.

A Company Policy Statement

A good company policy statement should contain the following items. It is possible to have these items covered in some other kind of communication, but a policy statement seems most appropriate.

1. A statement of the objectives or the basic policy of the company regarding environment.

2. A statement of whom the policy is directed to. The policy might be directed to the persons in charge of the major operating facilities. It would appear appropriate to direct it to the people who are in charge of doing whatever is called for: the plant managers, attorneys, and engineers.

3. A statement of delegation is important. One of the reasons for having the policy statement is to make it clear that the persons who are running the entire company—the chief executive officers—appreciate the problem but have delegated compliance to the operating managers. It also makes it clear to the operating managers that they have the responsibility.

4. A statement of follow-up activity is important. There may be a requirement for each operating manager to report back on how the responsibilities have been discharged.

5. A statement of how the performances are to be audited is necessary.

6. A statement of exceptions, procedures for requesting them, and the general criteria on which they will be granted seems to be a good consideration.

7. Some discussion of how the policy is to be interpreted, by whom, and when it should be reviewed is necessary.

As an illustration, the following sample policy statement is included. It is suitable for a large, decentralized company with no special problems.

ENVIRONMENTAL POLICY STATEMENT

Objectives
The Company desires to comply with all relevant laws relating to the environment and to conduct its operations in a way which prevents significant pollution or interference with the environment. Environmental factors shall be taken into consideration in each new plant location, for each new product, and for each substantial modification of additional facilities.

[Note: I suggest avoiding going beyond the law because the legal provisions are already so detailed and extensive. I have so limited this statement. However, it is possible to draft the statement to say that the company desires to respect the environment and comply with the letter *and spirit* of the pollution laws, if that seems appropriate for a given company.]

Delegation

The responsibility for operating the Company's facilities in compliance with the environmental laws rests with the operating manager of each such location [or with the Executive Vice-President for each major operating unit, who may in turn delegate that responsibility to the plant managers]. Each operating manager, or his designee, shall, within 90 days of receipt of this statement, provide either a report as to how this policy has been implemented or a status report stating the progress of implementation and an anticipated completion time. Such reports shall be sent to the General Counsel's office. Each location shall have a specific program for compliance with the environmental laws in a form which has been approved by the General Counsel. [If there is a Chief Engineer or manufacturing staff Vice-President, he might be placed in charge of approving plans rather than the General Counsel, or both could do it together.]

Audit

The General Counsel shall be responsible for auditing the existence and form of all written environmental compliance programs and [the chief manufacturing engineer] shall be responsible for auditing the actual implementation of such plans and the sufficiency of their technical content.

Reports

All complaints received by any location from any state or federal agency alleging that the Company is not in compliance with any environmental law or any permit issued under any environmental law shall be promptly communicated to the General Counsel.

[Note: This is a minimum procedure necessary to comply with SEC reporting rules. It may be desirable to have other reports forwarded for management purposes.]

[The following might be required:]

Each operating location shall submit to _____ within 90 days a report covering the following:

[Insert as many of the items in the questionnaire as appropriate. If you use the questionnaire first, this portion of the policy statement can be used to require updated information. It is also possible to issue the policy statement first and use it to get the information.]

Review

The General Counsel shall review this policy annually. Suggested changes should be submitted to the Chief Executive Officer.

Interpretation

The General Counsel will interpret any portions of this policy statement as they may apply to specific situations.

Preparation of Environmental Compliance Manual

It shall be the responsibility of each of the operating units which discharge pollutants into the air or water, or which generate solid wastes, or which are otherwise subject to environmental laws, to create and maintain an Environmental Compliance Manual in a form satisfactory to the General Counsel [and the Chief Engineer]. Such manual shall, at a minimum, contain the following:

1. Copies of all of the laws and regulations which affect that operating unit, including state and local laws and regulations.

2. Copies of any necessary permits, applications, variances or other documents issued to the location by any agency having responsibility for enforcing environmental laws.

3. Copies of management summaries of any engineering or planning documents which relate to the establishment's compliance with environmental laws.

4. The names and titles of the persons in the facility responsible for environmental matters.

5. Any emergency, contingency, or malfunction programs which have been established to deal with environmental problems.

A Centralized Staff of Experts

There should be serious consideration to a centralized staff of experts in environmental matters. Someone is going to have to catalogue the information and make recommendations for appropriate actions, and this is likely to be a time-consuming chore. In some cases, depending on whether the company is basically centralized or decentralized, it may even be necessary to have enough expertise to actually work the environmental problem, including the procurement/design of the necessary equipment, the financing of it, and the negotiation of the necessary permits.

Consultants

In the majority of situations, outside consultants will be necessary for specific problems. The team should be put together, or at least coordinated, centrally so that various units of the company do not each independently do a lot of work trying to solve the same problems. Outside consultants will be necessary where the company does not have all the expertise necessary in house (or the in-house expertise is committed to other projects), where outside research and development work is needed, or where independent stack testing or effluent analysis is appropriate.

Environmental Compliance Manual

There should probably be an environmental compliance manual for each division. Whether it is prepared by the division or the corporate staff would be a management decision, but if it is prepared by the division, there should be a copy forwarded to the corporate headquarters.

SECTION NINE:
COMMERCIAL LAWS

CHAPTER FIFTY-SIX

THE BATTLE OF
THE FORMS

Most commercial contracts are accomplished through exchanges of more or less standard forms rather than individually negotiated. Many times, the boilerplate on these forms is not read by either party to the transaction.

The Uniform Commercial Code creates somewhat of a lawyer's paradise where if one party is on his toes and/or the other is asleep at the switch, an extremely advantageous (or disadvantageous) contract can be created merely by the exchange of appropriate forms without either party's negotiating or even thinking about most of the terms.

ENFORCEABLE CONTRACTS

The situation is created by the following provision of the Uniform Commercial Code, which has been adopted substantially as indicated herein by almost all states.

Section 2-207. Additional Terms in Acceptance or Confirmation.
   (1)   A definite and seasonable expression of acceptance or a written confirmation which is sent within a reasonable time operates as an acceptance even though it states terms additional to or different from those offered or agreed upon, unless acceptance is expressly made conditional on assent to the additional or different terms.
   (2)   The additional terms are to be construed as proposals for addition to the contract. Between merchants such terms become part of the contract unless:
      (a)   the offer expressly limits acceptance to the terms of the offer;
      (b)   they materially alter it; or

(c) notification of objection to them has already been given or is given within a reasonable time after notice of them is received.

(3) Conduct by both parties which recognizes the existence of a contract is sufficient to establish a contract for sale although the writings of the parties do not otherwise establish a contract. In such case, the terms of the particular contract consist of those terms on which the writings of the parties agree, together with any supplementary terms incorporated under any other provisions of this Act.

Basically, this provision was designed to accomplish two objectives. The first was to make certain that there was in fact an enforceable contract when normal business procedures were intended to create an enforceable contract. The provision was necessary because, under the older common law, unless the acceptance was almost a mirror image of the offer, there was simply no contract. Since the offeror's form was usually substantially different from the buyer's acceptance form, many situations arose where business executives thought they had negotiated a deal only to have the lawyers tell them there was no enforceable contract.

The second objective was to establish certain ground rules to determine precisely what the terms of this deal were where the documentation was inconsistent. That is the basic problem—and the opportunity.

An examination of the above statute reveals that paragraphs (1) and (3) address the question of establishing an enforceable contract. Paragraph (2) establishes precisely what the terms of the contract are in the event the forms are inconsistent.

Generally, the effect of this provision is that the additional terms contained in a response to an offer (either an offer to sell or an offer to buy) become part of the contract. This happens automatically unless the offer expressly limits acceptance to the terms of the offer; the additional terms materially alter the offer; or the offeree objects to those terms.

Naturally, a busy purchaser or seller cannot possibly read, evaluate, and make necessary objections to every form that comes across his desk. However, unless he does so, he is very likely to wind up with a contract unfavorable to his company. Here is where the forms come in. If the company personnel have an adequate arsenal of appropriate forms and a knowledge of their importance and their use, this problem can be minimized and, in many cases, turned into a distinct advantage for the company. Following is a suggested technique to achieve this corporate advantage.

FORMS

Forms are the basic weapon in this battle. Naturally, anyone participating in the fight must have ammunition. Following are the four basic forms which every corporate purchaser or seller should have.

Purchaser	Seller
Request for quotation	Quotation
Purchase order	Sales form

The object of the forms is to make sure the contract is on your company's terms, not the other party's. Therefore, you must use a form which establishes that the only deal is the deal you propose and that if the other party proposes additions or changes, those additions or changes are of no effect and your deal governs.

The "Magic" Language

Following are two suggested clauses which will usually accomplish the desired objective. The UCC does not provide that any specific words be used. Any phraseology which makes the same point would be acceptable. However, the words should probably be conspicuous on the form, not buried in the fine print.

Terms for Buyer's Documents

Vendor's commencement of work on such goods or shipment of such goods, whichever occurs first, shall be deemed an effective mode of acceptance of purchaser's offer to purchase contained in this purchase order. Any acceptance of this purchase order is limited to acceptance of the express terms of the offer contained on the face and back hereof. Any proposal for additional or different terms or any attempt by vendor to vary, in any degree, any of the terms of this offer in vendor's acceptance shall not operate as a rejection of this offer, unless such variance is in the terms of the description, quantity, price, or delivery schedule of the goods, but shall be deemed a material alteration thereof, and this offer shall be deemed accepted by vendor without said additional or different terms. If this purchase order shall be deemed an acceptance of a prior offer by vendor, such acceptance is expressly conditional on vendor's assent to any additional or different terms contained herein.

Terms for Seller's Documents

Any acceptance of the offer to sell contained herein is limited to acceptance of the express terms of such offer contained on the face and back hereof. Any proposal for additional or different terms or any attempt by buyer to vary, in any degree, any of the terms in buyer's acceptance by purchase order or otherwise shall not operate as a rejection of this offer to sell unless such variance is in the terms of the description, quantity, price, or delivery schedule of the goods, but shall be deemed a material alteration thereof, and this offer shall be deemed accepted by buyer without said additional or different terms. If this document shall be deemed an acceptance of a prior offer by buyer, such acceptance is expressly conditional on buyer's assent to any additional or different terms contained herein.

When Do You Use the Form?

In many situations, the offeree will do one of the following:

1. Expressly accept the offer or accept by a course of conduct (such as starting work)

2. Send an expression of acceptance by a writing which does not include the proper language to make acceptance conditional on acceptance of any additional terms, i.e., the magic language

If he does either of these, the first offeror has his way entirely.

If the offeree is on his toes and sends an acceptance with the above-mentioned magic language, which makes the acceptance expressly conditional on acceptance of his additional terms, there is a square conflict. Then what happens? The rule is that the inconsistent terms simply cancel each other out, and the parties are left with the terms which they agree upon or which are not inconsistent and such other terms as are generally imposed by law.

Therefore, if you play the game right, you may wind up with your desires entirely; the worst that can happen is that you wind up with as many of your terms as are not inconsistent with the other party's terms and the remainder of the contract is governed according to general principles of law. If you either do not play the game at all or play it wrong, you may wind up with a contract almost entirely on the terms of the other party.

What Should the Forms Contain?

After going through all the above to make certain that your forms govern the transaction, it is essential that those forms provide you with a good deal. Naturally, no single form is adequate for all uses. However, the following list of important items should be considered when you set forth your best deal.

Warranties

This is probably the most important provision in most situations. From a business standpoint, when you sell a product, you want to give as limited a warranty as possible, and when you buy a product, you want the broadest warranty coverage you can get. In selling a product, you certainly want to limit any warranty to replacement of the defective part—to exclude consequential damage. In many cases, the form may not achieve the desired result if the matter goes to litigation, but the words in writing are generally helpful.

Shipment and Risk of Loss

It is generally helpful to expressly fix the point at which risk of loss passes from the seller to the buyer. Naturally, the seller will want that point to occur as soon as possible, preferably as soon as the product leaves his plant. The buyer will want the risk to remain on the seller for the maximum time, preferably until the buyer actually receives delivery at his plant.

Patents

Section 2-312(3) of the code provides for an implied warranty by a merchant-seller that the goods are delivered free of rightful claims of third persons by way of infringement or the like. Where the goods are made according to the buyer's specifications, however, this section makes the buyer responsible for infringement claims arising out of compliance with such specifications. Section 2-607(5)(b) requires the buyer to notify the seller of an infringement claim and permits the seller to assume control of the litigation. Sellers and purchasers will want to review these provisions to determine whether it is desirable to define in greater detail each party's responsibility in respect to infringement.

Force Majeure

The UCC, in section 2-615, provides the following on this question:

> UCC 2-615. Excuse by Failure of Presupposed Conditions. Except so far as a seller may have assumed a greater obligation and subject to the preceding section on substituted performance:
>
> (a) Delay in delivery or non-delivery in whole or in part by a seller who complies with paragraphs (b) and (c) is not a breach of his duty under a

contract for sale if performance as agreed has been made impracticable by the occurrence of a contingency the non-occurrence of which was the basic assumption on which the contract was made or by compliance in good faith with any applicable foreign or domestic governmental regulation or order whether or not it later proves to be invalid.

(b) Where the causes mentioned in paragraph (a) affect only a part of the seller's capacity to perform, he must allocate production and deliveries among his customers not then under contract as well as his own requirements for further manufacture. He may allocate in any manner which is fair and reasonable.

(c) The seller must notify the buyer seasonably that there will be delay or non-delivery and, when allocation is required under paragraph (b), of the estimated quota thus made available for the buyer.

The seller or purchaser will want to consider whether to enumerate more specifically the circumstances which will excuse a delay or failure in performance.

Cancellation or Change

If cancellation or change orders are to be accepted, a seller or purchaser may want to establish appropriate procedures therefor in the form. Any additional charges might also be spelled out.

Dies, Patterns, Special Tooling, and the Like

If such terms are involved in a given situation, either the buyer or the seller will want to consider the responsibility for them.

Choice of Law

The UCC permits the parties to choose the law applicable to their contract within wide limits, and this should be done.

Modification and Waiver

Under the code, a modification of a contract needs no consideration to be binding. Parties often try to limit the possibility of unauthorized (and perhaps fraudulent) claims of modification by requiring modifications to be in writing and signed by an authorized person.

Integration Clause

Parties may incorporate in their agreement all provisions by which they intend to be bound and provide that the written agreement supersedes all prior understandings, agreements, and representations. Many contracts include these express provisions, and they are generally desirable from the point of view of the seller, but not for the buyer. Generally, the questions involve exaggerated claims or assurances made in the selling process which the buyer desires to rely on.

Taxes

Many forms explicitly allocate the burden of sales, use, and excise taxes required to be paid or collected in connection with the transaction. Generally, this point should be considered by each party and appropriate language placed in his form.

Returns

Questions sometimes arise on the conditions, if any, under which goods are returnable. This point should be considered by each party, and a provision suitable to that party's desire should be placed in the contract.

Other Bargained-for Provisions

Generally, the following terms are bargained for in most contracts and are typed or written onto the printed form. If, in a particular situation, the term is standard or if a party desires to make it appear to be standard, it can, of course, be preprinted.

> Description of goods.
>
> Quantity.
>
> Price and other credit terms.
>
> Delivery schedule.
>
> Particular currency in which payment may be made, if not in U.S. dollars.
>
> Price increases—generally applicable if the contract calls for performance in installment. Is the price to be firm or to be subject to change to reflect prices then in effect?
>
> Special handling, boxing, crating, etc. Generally any special terms here should be individually spelled out. If the business warrants, this term may be preprinted.

OVERRIDING AGREEMENT

It is possible to completely avoid the problem of "the battle of the forms" by entering into an overriding agreement with a supplier or customer to the general effect that all transactions between them should be governed by the terms set forth in the overriding agreement. Sometimes this is advantageous, particularly in situations where you have a fairly good bargaining position, because it prevents possible slip-ups in the battle. However, where your bargaining position may not be as good, you would probably be better off engaging in the battle than entering into negotiations on all of the points mentioned herein and possibly others. If you fight the battle right, you might win your own terms completely, and if you have the best ammunition (forms) possible, you can at least reduce the deal to the provisions which would be implied by law, which are generally fairly equally weighted between the buyer and the seller.

CHAPTER FIFTY-SEVEN

PURCHASING LAW

THE NEED TO EDUCATE PURCHASERS

The amount of legal advice rendered to purchasers is not proportionate to the tremendous amount of the company's money they spend. This is not entirely inappropriate, because the dollar amounts involved do not necessarily indicate the degree of legal complexity. However, business executives must have an understanding of the strong interrelationship between purchasing and the law and the pitfalls and lost opportunities that can result in lost profits if lawyers fail to render proper advice to purchasers.

Purchasers operate in the same legally complex climate as all other businesspeople, this means that they must have appropriate training in how the law applies to their profession. The following discussion will show what knowledge is needed in the specific context of purchasing.

Management should consider having its lawyers conduct training programs so that this information is supplied to all purchasers. In addition, there are various commercial courses which purchasers can take, and of course there is a vast amount of writing on all of these subjects. The key thing to keep in mind is that in order to educate purchasers, top management support and effort is required. Management cannot assume that the purchasers will do this homework on their own, even though purchasers should realize that expenditure of effort in this area would further their own careers.

Neither the executive nor the lawyer should overplay the emphasis on the legal aspects of purchasing. Instead, it should be realistically pointed out that it is merely one piece of a very complex machine. It should also be pointed out, however, that just as most machines will not function properly if any part is not in working order, so a purchaser cannot function properly if he has either an incorrect or insufficient understanding of the legal framework in which he must operate.

An overall caution is in order. Any program directed at informing the purchasers of the legal aspects of their profession should expressly state that it is not meant to make purchasers into their own lawyers and that legal counsel should be sought where appropriate. The corollary to this is that management must provide the purchasing function access to competent legal counsel.

SUBSTANTIVE COMMERCIAL LAW

Purchasers must clearly understand the substantive commercial laws of agency, contract (particularly contracts of sales under the Uniform Commercial Code), and forms and their proper use. This chapter will not go into a full discussion of all of these areas. However, the following observations will be made.

Basic commercial law is adequately explained in a great number of commercially available sources. In addition, there are various periodicals, such as the *Purchasing Executive's Bulletin* and the magazines *Purchasing World* and *Purchasing Magazine*, which devote some of their space to legal problems, generally in the context of the implications of the various provisions of the sales chapter of the Uniform Commercial Code. It is not necessary for the company to generate all of its own training materials unless it desires to do so. However, it should also be observed that almost all of these commercial sources are limited in their scope to basic commercial law. They do not contain very much discussion of the other factors which are mentioned in this chapter, and therefore the company must supplement these commercially available sources with its own work.

AGENCY

Purchasers should clearly understand the general law of agency, because in many cases purchasers make serious mistakes by either exceeding their own authority or depending upon representations by unauthorized agents of sellers and later finding that these representations are untrue and that their company has no legal recourse. Consider, for example, the purchaser who is charged with the obligation of procuring some nonstandard item which, because of certain requirements of his company, must have especially high quality and performance characteristics. He calls in a number of suppliers, all of whom present stock items which are not meant for the unusual application but which the sales representatives, of course, assure the purchaser will perform adequately. Since the ordinary manufacturer's representative or salesman is not authorized to give any other warranty than that which is expressly stated in the written material supplied by the manufacturer, a purchaser must understand that he cannot rely on these oral representations and instead must go further and obtain the necessary specific promises from authorized officers of the selling company.

FORMS AND THEIR USE

Forms and their use is a very important subject frequently misunderstood by purchasers. In many face-to-face conferences, some of them with purchasers who have been in the business for years, it has become painfully obvious that they have used forms which they have never even read. It is even more obvious that many of the provisions in the forms are not understood by the purchasers who have taken the trouble to read them. The battle of the forms about which so much has been written is not even understood by all lawyers, let alone all purchasers. Conscientious management cannot let this problem exist in its company.

WARRANTIES AND PRODUCT LIABILITY

The question of warranties and product liability deserves separate attention. Again there is a great deal of writing available so that the company does not have to spend the money to have its inside or outside counsel create the educational material.

It is submitted that the best general approach to the warranty/product liability problem is to do two things. The first, of course, is to make sure that both company counsel and the purchasers and sellers understand it, and the second is to consider it simply to be a matter of evaluating the economics. That is, if the company wants to sell a product with a good warranty and to assume the risk of liability in the event it is defective, it should charge a higher price than if it sells the product without any warranties. Likewise, in the purchasing function, if the company desires to have assurances from the sellers of the various items which it purchases that free the company from any warranty or product liability obligation, it should be willing to pay more for these products than if it purchases them and assumes these liabilities itself. Generally, the lawyer's function is not to say either that purchasers must in all cases insist on complete indemnification from the sellers or that the selling people in the company must in all cases insist on a provision to the general effect that products are sold without any warranty, but rather to insist that the purchasers and the sellers carefully consider the warranty/product liability question and make whatever management decisions involving pricing or other terms of the transaction seem appropriate in the light of the risks which are assumed. Naturally the company's insurance coverage will play a big part in making this determination.

COMMERCIAL ARBITRATION

In educating the purchasers, it is necessary to make some mention of commercial arbitration so that purchasers are aware of this avenue for resolving disputes.

GOVERNMENT CONTRACTS

Even in a basically commercial company, the rules involving government procurement should at least be mentioned so that the purchasers know, if nothing else, that there are detailed rules and regulations whenever the government gets into the picture.

INTERNATIONAL PURCHASING

Since trade is ever more international, purchasers will want to consider foreign sources for some procurement. The international law area is extremely complex and ever-changing. It is, therefore, even more essential for purchasers to have access to adequate legal advice if national boundaries are to be crossed in obtaining products. At the present time, an American purchaser is basically free of most restrictions on overseas investments either in the form of direct procurement on a purchase-and-sale basis or investment in foreign companies made with a view toward acquiring an overseas source of supply. However, this picture can change overnight, and in addition, there are complex tariff and duty problems which can arise and should be carefully analyzed before any transaction is entered into. If purchasing is done on an international basis, company executives will want to make sure that their counsel has evaluated the possible effect of at least the following laws:

1. The Anti-Dumping Act of 1921. This statute is aimed at preventing the importation into the United States of commodities at prices lower than those in effect in the country where the commodity was made.

2. The Tariff Act of 1930 (countervailing duties). This statute provides that whenever any foreign country or business organization thereof "shall pay or bestow, directly or indirectly, any bounty or grant upon the manufacture or export of any article or merchandise," there shall be levied and paid upon it, upon importation, in addition to the regular duty, an additional one "equal to the net amount of such bounty or grant, as estimated by the Secretary of the Treasury."

3. The Buy-American Act of 1933.

4. The Trade Reform Legislation.

5. Various customs and Federal Trade Commission requirements directing that imports must be properly labeled with their country of origin.

ANTITRUST

Purchasers should be aware of the basic antitrust laws for two reasons. The first, obviously, is to keep out of trouble themselves, but the second is to make sure that the company is not taken advantage of either by violation of the antitrust laws by other companies or through improper assertions of the application of those laws to justify higher prices to the company.

A frequently recurring problem under the antitrust laws as they apply to purchasers is the Robinson-Patman Act. Unfortunately, this has proven to be an extremely difficult problem. Admittedly, it is a complex law, but considerable experience in this area has indicated that it is almost universally misapplied and misunderstood by purchasers. To apply the Robinson-Patman Act realistically, purchasing transactions should be divided into two kinds. The first are those where the purchaser is buying something that the company is going to resell *in its same form*. This is typical of the supermarket or other retail company which is simply procuring an item for resale to the consuming public in the exact same form in which it was purchased. Purchasers in this situation must be highly conscious of the Robinson-Patman Act, particularly section 2(f), which imposes penalties upon any company which induces or receives a discriminatorily low price. On the other hand, a purchaser for a manufacturing company which is procuring items to be used in the manufacturing process or to be incorporated in a larger finished product is in a much different position and, as a practical matter, need not be highly concerned with section 2(f) of the Robinson-Patman Act. The reason for this is so simple it seems unexplainable that it is so often forgotten. The Robinson-Patman Act says in substance that it is illegal to grant different prices to different customers who compete with one another where the difference in price might cause a substantial effect on competition. Generally, the act places this limitation on sellers, but section 2(f) adds the thought that it is unlawful for a *purchaser* to induce or ask for a discriminatorily low price; the concept of some effect on competition is the same. In the typical grocery store situation, it is very easy to see how a store which, for example, purchases milk at 2 or 3 cents a gallon less than another competing store can obtain a substantial competitive advantage. It can either advertise the milk at a lower price while maintaining the same profit margins or it can sell at the same price but keep the higher profit margins to use elsewhere in the business. Indeed, it is the grocery store operation which Congress had in mind when it enacted this law. It was moved by the thought that large chains could purchase at lower prices and thereby drive the small grocers out of business.

Turning, however, to the typical manufacturing context, let's assume that your company makes automobile parts and desires to purchase typewriter ribbons in quantity for office use. Suppose it deliberately induces a manufacturer to grant a price for typewriter ribbons which is materially lower than that paid by the company's competitor making a similar auto part. Is it realistic to think this will have a substantial effect on the competition between the two companies? Obviously not. The above is an extreme case, but the principles are equally applicable when purchasing products which, considered by themselves, are not a material part of the finished product.

There is another reason why purchasers in other than straight buy-sell operations do not have to be overly concerned with the Robinson-Patman Act. This is the fact that as a practical matter the only person who could complain about a violation would be a competitor, and because of the complexity of proving lost profits and competitive effects, it is very unlikely that one could think of a realistic situation where a competitor could show substantial damages. To be sure, it is possible; it has even happened. However, it is this separation between the theoretically possible and the actually practical which some corporate counsel are guilty of neglecting. To counsel against aggressive buying on the grounds that it is theoretically possible that a Robinson-Patman problem might present itself is not good corporate counsel in this context. While management should make sure that the company, in both the purchasing and the selling areas, complies with the Robinson-Patman Act, it should also make sure that an overly restrictive view of the Robinson-Patman Act does not inhibit aggressive bargaining and result in lost opportunities to procure the necessary goods at the lowest possible prices.

Exactly the opposite is true for purchasers purchasing goods for resale such as through a distributorship operation or in a retail situation. Here it is necessary to observe the basic principles of the Robinson-Patman Act.

Another frequent problem which arises is that a purchaser will attempt to arrange his purchases either by combining all the requirements of various different plants or by placing an order on an annual basis so that he can get a lower price by buying a larger quantity. In some cases these efforts are met by a seller with the response that he cannot grant a lower price, because of the Robinson-Patman Act. In some cases this assertion may be true. However, in others it may simply be a device used by the seller to resist cutting prices. A good purchaser will understand this possible device and obtain proper legal advice from his own counsel as to whether or not the Robinson-Patman Act really would prohibit his receiving a lower price.

Other antitrust questions for specific coverage include group buying and boycotts. Purchasers, however, should also have a rudimentary knowledge of all general antitrust laws, including those normally applicable to the marketing people, because these problems are often a mirror image of those presented to purchasers and, as indicated above, antitrust violations by sellers can often result in higher prices to purchasers. The antitrust laws and the Robinson-Patman Act are explained in more detail in Section 2 of this book.

THE OCCUPATIONAL SAFETY AND HEALTH ACT

Any purchaser purchasing anything which is used by employees should be aware of the implications of the Occupational Safety and Health Act. Generally, this act places obligations on employers to provide a safe working environment and does not directly apply to purchase and sales transactions. However, it does have certain indirect applications which are very important.

From the purchaser's point of view, the company should constantly strive to make sure that the products it purchases are safe and, to the extent appropriate, comply with the physical characteristics mandated by the standards under the Occupational Safety and Health Act. However, it is submitted that the best way to accomplish this objective is to have all of the people in the purchasing function aware of the problem and to have them know what requirements are present and be assured that the products, in fact, do satisfy those requirements. It is not sufficient to simply structure the company's purchase orders to include the phrase that "all products comply with OSHA standards," because all this would do is give rise to a lawsuit against someone if it were found later by an OSHA inspector that a particular machine or other product did not comply. It would certainly in no way limit the liability of the company for any fines or penalties in an OSHA inspection. On the other hand, it should be pointed out that this is a subject of some disagreement among purchasers and lawyers and many of them do prefer to have the purchase orders include this phrase on the theory that it can't do any harm.

From a purchaser's point of view, the following would be a representative (but not necessarily complete) list of the kinds of things a purchasing agent should be sure comply with applicable OSHA regulations:

1. Equipment related to walking or working surfaces, such as ladders, scaffolding, or manually propelled mobile ladders, scaffolds, or towers. Also included under this category would be any kind of powered platform, manlift, or vehicle-mounted work platform.

2. Any device or commodity which emits any kind of radiation.

3. Any kind of compressed gas, including acetylene, hydrogen, oxygen, and nitrous oxide, and also the containers in which it is shipped, stored, or used.

4. Any kind of highly flammable or combustible liquids and the containers in which they are shipped, stored, or used.

5. Any kind of personal protective equipment, including eye protection, respiratory protection, head protection, foot protection, and electrical protection devices.

6. Any kind of medical or first aid kits or fire extinguishers.

7. Any kind of materials-handling or -storage equipment, including lift trucks.

8. Any kind of powered machine tools, including woodworking machinery, metal-working machinery, abrasive-wheel machinery, power presses, forging machines, and mechanical power transmission apparatus.

9. Any kind of hand or portable power tools, such as portable electric saws and drills.

10. Any kind of apparatus for welding, cutting, or brazing.

This list is not an all inclusive list, nor are the requirements on any item very detailed. For example, the only requirement that the purchaser should be aware of when purchasing fire extinguishers is that they must operate between 40 and 120°F. All the rest of the detailed regulations involving fire extinguishers apply to their use, placement, labeling, periodic inspection, etc., and are the responsibility of the safety officer of each plant rather than the purchasing agent. This same principle applies to many of the other items cited above.

THE CONSUMER PRODUCT SAFETY ACT

Any purchaser purchasing anything which is a consumer product as defined by the Consumer Product Safety Act must obviously be aware of that act's implications and how best to protect his company.

PATENTS, INDUSTRIAL SECRETS, AND CONFIDENTIALITY

Purchasers must understand the patent system and must know what their rights and duties are regarding not only their own company's trade secrets but also those of other companies with whom they deal. Appropriate patent indemnification clauses should be in *all* procurement documents.

BANKRUPTCY AND PURCHASING FROM FINANCIALLY UNSTABLE SELLERS

Purchasers should be aware of some of the fundamental principles of bankruptcy law, including the right of the trustee in bankruptcy to disavow most executory contracts. (Executory contracts are those where one party has not completed performance.) Purchasers should also be made generally aware of the various kinds of bankruptcy and reorganization proceedings. As far as the purchaser is concerned, these laws generally stand for the proposition that no matter what contracts are written or what safeguards are entered into, "you can't get blood out of a turnip," and it is, therefore, risky to purchase from financially unstable sellers. Again, the role of the lawyer should be merely to alert the purchasers to the problem, not to say that they can't purchase from a company which has a questionable financial statement. It is a matter of risk. If a company is faced with a choice of purchasing a given item at a low price from a small, possibly financially unstable seller or purchasing the same item at perhaps a higher price from a large company, it is a management decision as to which to choose. The lawyer's role is generally to point out that there is a risk involved in purchasing from the financially weak seller. In some cases, the lawyer can help minimize this risk by creative contract drafting and possibly by some other legal means, such as making sure that title to any special tooling involved remains with the company and not with the financially weak seller. Again, however, many of these legal techniques may work in theory and may in fact be sufficient to win a court case. However, the best approach is generally to stay out of court, and business should endeavor to get advice from counsel that will prevent trouble rather than merely opinions on what the outcome of a court case might be.

PURCHASING FROM MINORITY BUSINESS AND OBSERVING EEO REQUIREMENTS

Purchasers should be aware of the basic EEO requirements in most government business.

LAW AND ETHICS

All purchasers should adhere to the code of ethics of the National Association of Purchasing Management. This commonsense conduct will prevent many legal problems and in the long run is good business.

LEASING AS AN ALTERNATIVE TO PURCHASING

In today's market, almost anything that can be purchased can be leased. However, the state of the art in leasing is at a much less developed plateau than that of purchasing. Basically, leasing transactions, particularly if large items are involved, are done on an individually negotiated basis involving a considerable amount of paperwork and having complex tax, legal, and financial reporting implications. Business executives should make sure that their purchasers are aware of the following points:

1. Leasing is almost always an alternative to a direct purchase.

2. It is always necessary to make economic comparisons to see which is best for the company.

3. If leasing is chosen, it is very important that proper coordination be effected between the legal, tax, and financial reporting people.

SHORTAGES/BREACH OF CONTRACT

The problem of breach of contract and a shortage economy should be understood by all purchasers, because it is almost bound to be a recurring problem in one form or another.

RECEIVING AND PAYING

The purchasing job is not really finished until the right goods are delivered on time at the right place in an undamaged condition and an invoice at the proper price is sent.

Proper procedures should be established to assure that when the goods are received by the company, any objections are made in a proper and timely manner. This might include:

1. Stamping cartons "Received subject to inspection and count"

2. Making sure that procedures are adopted to inspect and count the goods promptly, as failure to do so might waive rights to object

3. Making sure that the person doing the inspecting knows precisely what was supposed to be delivered

4. Adopting a procedure and perhaps a set of forms to notify sellers of any shortage, damage, or other problem with its goods

5. Making sure that the accounts payable people are informed of any problems so that they do not pay any bills which may be in dispute

In addition, purchasers should know that they have the right under the Uniform Commercial Code to "cover," which basically means that if defective products are shipped or if the products are not shipped at all, the purchasers have the right to go out and procure other products and then make a claim against the original defaulting seller for any increased price which the purchaser has to pay.

PROCUREMENT OF SERVICES

In some cases, purchasers will be asked to procure a service rather than a product. For example, a company may make a product which has to be plated when the company itself does not have a plating operation. Accordingly, the company will make the product, send it to a subcontractor to accomplish the plating, and then have it returned for either further processing or sale to the customer. In these situations, purchasers have unique problems, because in a sense they actually become part of the manufacturing process. If their link in the chain breaks down, it is just as serious as if one of the company's own manufacturing processes breaks down, and disastrous consequences can result. In addition, in many cases a company will have very expensive parts sent out to have an inexpensive operation performed on them. For example, in some businesses it is not unusual to send out a $50,000 part to a plater who will perform a plating service with a value of less than $500. The following problems might result:

1. The product might be damaged through the fault of the plater.

2. The plating operation might be done improperly or defectively.

3. The plating operation might not be done on time.

It is up to the purchaser to make sure that he protects his company to the maximum extent possible. Most of the protection will be practical; that is, the purchaser should make sure that he selects someone who is capable of doing the job, who is reliable, careful, and likely to be in business for a number of years, and who would value the company's business and do a good job and stand behind it. However, there are also certain legal aspects to the problem:

1. Purchasers should make sure that their insurance covers them to the desired degree. Generally, the insurance should cover them from the time the product leaves their shop to the time it returns. In order for this insurance to be at all economical there must be a deductible amount, but at least the company's risk will be minimized.

2. It is possible to structure the company's forms to protect it, and this should be done so that the company is in a good bargaining position should damage to its products occur. Essentially, this means going over all forms which may be used for this purpose and making sure that the word "services" is included in each place where it might be appropriate. For example, in the case of a form which says that the seller warrants the goods furnished to be free of all defects, etc., the words "and services" should be added. Generally, this should be done when the form is printed, but if this has not been done, the words can be put in the appropriate contracts manually.

Purchasers should, however, be realistic. If they are shipping a $500,000 part to a plater for a $500 plating operation, they must realize that the plater's profit is just not going to be sufficient for him to incur a risk for the entire $500,000 part. Here is where the purchaser's judgment, coupled with his knowledge of the fundamental legal principles, comes in. If the purchaser considers the problem and tries to protect his company to the best of his ability, he has done his job. If he sends the part out to an unknown or unproven plater and hopes for the best, he has shirked his responsibility. In summary, possibilities for company protection against this problem include:

1. Procurement of insurance by the company.

2. Agreeing to pay a higher price to the plater so that he can procure the insurance.

3. Building the possible risk of loss into the price. The insurance cost would be built into the price anyway, and so this is essentially a decision to self-insure.

PROCUREMENT OF COMBINATIONS OF MACHINERY AND SERVICES

In many cases, purchasers will be asked to procure some nonstandard item used in the manufacturing process, such as special materials-handling equipment or special equipment to perform various machinery operations. The purchaser will then enter into a contract involving both the sale of goods and the performance of services, because the selling company will probably have to engineer the equipment specifically for the buyer. It is clear that such a contract is covered under the Uniform Commercial Code, so that all of the normal contract principles apply. However, it is also clear that most people don't conduct business on a technical legal basis (and of course they probably shouldn't), and in many cases when the equipment is delivered and found to be less than adequate, the company will give the vendor the chance to make whatever changes or alterations are necessary in order to make the equipment useful. Unfortunately, a common problem is that in many cases the vendor will be unable, despite diligent efforts, to make the equipment perform to the satisfaction of the buyer and at some point will simply give up trying and say that it has performed its part of the contract by providing the machinery and equipment and the company owes it the purchase price. To complicate the matter further, the company may have paid all or part of the purchase price. This is a constantly recurring problem and a troublesome one for the lawyers. In theory the answer is simple. When the machines arrive and they don't comply to the buyer's specifications or perform according to the agreed-upon performance criteria, they should simply be rejected. In this case it would be absolutely clear that, assuming the company was right in its contention that the machines were noncomplying, there would be no obligation to pay for them. However, this will rarely happen, because both parties will probably be under the legitimate belief that the problems can be corrected and it will only be after a great deal of time and money has been spent that one or the other might come to the conclusion that the equipment is just not suitable.

Purchasers should protect their company in this context by making sure that, in any such case, *performance criteria* are clearly specified. This may not be a cure-all, but it is a good procedure to maximize the company's bargaining position.

In summary, a great portion of the laws relating to federal business activity are very important in the purchasing function; however, purchasers need only become familiar with relatively small parts of those laws, and it is therefore not a very difficult task. A complete program of educating purchasers on all aspects of the law which may be applicable to them has been conducted by this writer in a 2-day seminar, and there was plenty of time for considerable discussion between lawyers and purchasers on all legal questions which they had. It would appear that this time was very well spent. Purchasers who attended recommended that the program be mandatory for all the company's purchasers. While a 2-day session will not make a purchasing agent into a lawyer, it does sensitize the purchasers to the legal problems and provide an avenue of communication between the purchasers and the lawyers, and if both parties do their jobs, it would seem certain that some problems are bound to be avoided.

CHAPTER FIFTY-EIGHT

ARBITRATION

For many years, there have been two basic means of settling disputes: the courts and the arbitration process. The discussion of labor laws contained in this book even points out that some statutes contain as their basic method of resolving disputes a form of the arbitration process. However, this discussion is not directed at arbitration in the labor law sense (although it is very similar), but arbitration in the context of resolving commercial disputes. Further, it is limited to domestic arbitration, although with the exception of the fact that the enforceability of arbitration decisions in the international context is somewhat more complicated than in the domestic, the general principles are the same.

Arbitration refers to a process where each party by mutual agreement (it has to be by mutual agreement) agrees that disputes will be settled by either a single arbitrator or a panel of arbitrators and that the decision of the arbitrator will be final. Neither party will go to court unless it feels that the arbitrator's decision was capricious or the arbitrator was biased. The value of arbitration is that it saves a great deal of time and money and it is more private than a court proceeding. If two parties to a commercial agreement have a difference and go to court, it might be very expensive for both; the cost and delays inherent in processing that difference in our court system are legendary. On the other hand, theoretically, if each party agreed to arbitration, the dispute could be resolved rather promptly with much less cost to either side, especially in attorneys' fees.

There is a rather substantial difference of opinion as to the desirability of arbitration in a general sense. In fact, the issue can get very emotional. Those people who favor arbitration tend to accuse lawyers who resist it as doing so for their own mercenary motives because it cuts down their fees. Those people who are against arbitration tend to accuse those in favor of it of oversimplifying the problems and failing to point out that arbitrators as well as lawyers receive fees for their services, fees that are sometimes quite substantial. Accordingly, it is difficult to find an impartial discussion of the subject. One thing, however, is usually clear, and that is that it is usually apparent that arbitration for a specific client is either good or bad *in a specific case.* Accordingly, once a dispute arises, it is usually to one party's relative advantage to have it resolved via the arbitration process and to the other's to have the dispute resolved in court.

On the other hand, you have to decide whether to put an arbitration clause in your contracts before you know the context of the particular dispute. At that time, you simply are taking a chance and guessing whether the problems that are likely to arise are likely to be best settled from your standpoint through arbitration or litigation. Unfortunately, arbitration is usually one of the very last things thought about in a contract. In fact, it is usually the last paragraph in the contract, or if it is not the last, the only things following it are very routine provisions, such as stating where notices should be sent. Sometimes the traditional placement of the arbitration clause at the end can cause it to be put in or left out without much thought. This is unfortunate, because the subject, while controversial, is important.

The arbitration process is generally very much like an informal trial before a judge. Each party is entitled to be represented by counsel, and each party is entitled to present evidence to support his side of the dispute. In an arbitration procedure the rules of evidence are much more liberal than in a trial, although even in the arbitration process they are not unbounded. In the arbitration process you will not get the familiar, television-style objections; however, even in the arbitration area, counsel is expected to submit only evidence which is relevant to the particular dispute at hand and which is, to the best of counsel's ability, the best evidence that can be submitted. In other words, if the witnesses to the particular transaction are available, *they* should be called to testify, not other people in the company who may have gotten the information secondhand. The difference is that in a court proceeding, anyone getting information secondhand could probably be completely excluded under the hearsay rule, whereas in an arbitration proceeding this secondhand information would be admitted and the arbitrator would, by whatever process he felt appropriate, give that evidence whatever weight it deserved.

Typically, an arbitration proceeding is rather small and takes place rather quickly. The parties select an arbitrator (or in some cases a panel of arbitrators consisting of three—one chosen by each side and then one chosen by mutual agreement of the two people selected by each side, and each party presents its side of the argument. The arbitrators then adjourn, consider all the evidence, and render an opinion in much the same manner as a judge would. The arbitrators are supposed to be knowledgeable in both the substance of the dispute and in the elements of the law. There is no jury, and so theoretically there isn't any value in theatrics or showmanship and the whole thing should be a relatively businesslike affair.

In summary, the theory of arbitration sounds eminently reasonable and certainly desirable in most cases. Since essentially the same thing happens in an arbitration procedure as in a court proceeding where there is no jury, it saves a great deal of time and expense and eliminates all of the legal pitfalls of "hearsay information" or information which may not be admissible under some other technical rule of evidence. In addition, it saves all of the theatrics which typically go along with a jury trial and the uncertainty involved when a number of people who perhaps know nothing about the law, nothing about the businesses involved, nothing about the people involved, and nothing about the commercial dispute involved are asked to render a verdict.

On the other hand, a close reading of the summary shows that it has definite advantages and disadvantages once you know what the commercial dispute is going to be. For one thing, time and expense generally operate to the advantage or disadvantage of one or the other party to a dispute. Consequently, once you know what the dispute is, you are in a position to assess whether your side would be advantaged by a long and expensive procedure or a short and quick procedure.

Time can also be deceiving. In some cases, depending upon the jurisdiction in question and how crowded the courts are as well as how many arbitrators are available and how crowded their agendas are, there may not be an appreciable time difference between going to court and going to the arbitration process. Accordingly, time is not always a factor in favor of arbitration.

Expenses can also be deceiving. The arbitrator's fees must be considered. If a dispute is important, you are likely to wind up spending just as much management and legal effort to prepare your case in front of the arbitrator as you would in front of a judge, and so it is somewhat misleading to say that you are going to save money simply by staying out of the courtroom. Most of the lawyer's time is spent in preparation, analysis, and interviewing witnesses, and the actual court time is in most cases not a great deal different from the time spent in the arbitration process. Accordingly, the classic argument that arbitration is less costly than court proceedings isn't usually as significant as it might at first appear.

The basic problem with arbitration, however, is that the arbitrator's decision doesn't necessarily have to follow the law. The arbitrator can make an "equitable" disposition of the matter. Thus, consider a commercial dispute in which one party claims that services which were supposed to be performed were not performed in accordance with the contract and, therefore, the other party is guilty of a breach of contract and is not only entitled to no payment for the services rendered but indeed owes the company some money for damages for breach of the contract; and in which the party performing the services alleges that the services were rendered properly in accordance with the contract, etc., and demands payment. A court decision will usually yield a decision either one way or the other. The party rendering the services will either get its money or not. In an arbitration case, however, this is very unlikely to be the result. The arbitrator will look at all of the facts, and since by definition there are probably arguments on each side, he would find it unfair to deny the party performing the services any money but also find it unfair to make the recipient of the services pay the entire amount when the services were not performed properly. He is very likely to "split the difference."

Accordingly, one of the big factors in determining whether arbitration is desirable is whether you have a strong legal case on your side. If you do, arbitration probably isn't the route to go because the arbitrator is usually going to render a decision which keeps both parties somewhat happy. On the other hand, if your legal position is weak but your equitable position is a little stronger, arbitration is desirable. Naturally, once a dispute arises, both parties will know pretty much what their legal and equitable positions are and whether it is favorable to go to arbitration. It is less likely that the parties will agree after the fact.

Assuming you do have an arbitration proceeding and the arbitrator's judgment is rendered, it is enforceable in court. The only exception is where the arbitrator's decision is unreasonable or capricious or where there has been a showing that the arbitrator was not in fact impartial (e.g., one party finds out that the arbitrator was a business associate or relative or friend of the other party).

The desirability of arbitration clauses is subject to much dispute, and I believe that the general counsel of the company is in the best position to make determinations as to whether arbitration provisions should be included as a general matter or only in specific cases. In the overwhelming majority of cases, this decision should be made pretty much on a case-by-case basis, although when you start getting down to printing forms you are going to have to make it in a more general sense.

Following are some general observations on the desirability of arbitration:

1. A large company with a good legal staff which typically transacts business in a "legal" way and is able to finance extended litigation if necessary is generally better off without an arbitration clause than with one. The contrary is true of a small corporation or an individual. The classic example of a disagreement would be an employment contract between one person and a large company. Typically, the large company would be better off without the arbitration clause but the individual would be better off with one.

2. The kind of business in which you are involved can play an important part. One of the advantages of arbitration is that the arbitrators are usually familiar with the business involved and if there is any technology, they are familiar with that also. The American Arbitration Association provides a very large pool of qualified arbitrators and, of course, since the typical clause provides that each party can select his own arbitrator anyway, the parties can usually be assured of a hearing before someone who knows what he or she is talking about. Consequently, if the subject matter is at all technical or if patents, trade secrets, or rather unusual business arrangements are involved, one might be better off in arbitration than before a judge or jury who may have to be educated about some pretty basic things.

3. If the company is involved in a specialized industry, arbitration may be more desirable than a court determination, for the same reasons. Specialized industries would generally be those which are either regulated by a set of statutes or where there is a great deal of custom and usage in the trade which is taken for granted by insiders but which a judge or jury may not recognize.

The main point of this whole discussion is that management and its lawyers should communicate on the arbitration question and decide on some general approaches. The usual procedure, however, is either for the lawyers to make the determination on their own without explaining the differences to management or in some cases for contracts to be negotiated without any consideration at all on either side about an arbitration clause. From a management point of view, certainly questions to the lawyers which ask them their position on arbitration, which kinds of agreement they put the clause in, which kinds they don't put it in, etc., are not out of order. With today's high cost and complexity of litigation, coupled with the fact that in some jurisdictions there are substantial time and money savings in the arbitration process, management is certainly entitled to an answer to these questions and by merely asking them forces the lawyers to focus on the problem and make conscious and intelligent decisions.

CHAPTER FIFTY-NINE

CREDIT LAWS

Like so many of the federal laws discussed in this book, the credit laws are creatures of the 1970s. The credit laws described in this chapter apply only to consumer transactions. The laws resulted from a number of situations where Congress felt that consumers had been unduly imposed upon. There are five principal problems which Congress sought to remedy—and hence five major laws.

1. Congress perceived that there was discrimination in credit, because some women and minorities had trouble getting independent credit even though their ability to make payments was equivalent to that of white males who had credit. Congress reacted with the Equal Credit Opportunity Act.

2. Congress felt that many consumers were being deceived about the true interest rate and that many of the forms consumers were asked to sign were virtually incomprehensible. They reacted with the Truth in Lending Act.

3. The rise of credit cards and the vast amount of billing on open-end credit gave rise to a number of errors. Congress thought that consumers ought to have a fair and equitable means of causing these errors to be redressed and reacted with the Fair Credit Billing Act.

4. The need of credit grantors to ascertain the credit worthiness of consumers gave rise to a great expansion in credit bureaus and the automation of many credit bureaus. Consumer reports were issued which in some cases contained errors. Congress felt that consumers ought to have fair access to their consumer files in order to remedy any errors and that consumer credit companies ought to be regulated to prevent abuse. The Fair Credit Reporting Act accomplishes this.

5. In 1977 Congress became aware of a number of debt collection practices which they thought were unfair. They reacted with the Fair Debt Collection Practices Act of 1977.

All of these laws are extremely complex. Indeed credit law, as is the case in so many other areas discussed in this book, has spawned a new legal specialty, and many lawyers are engaged full-time either in drafting and creating the necessary forms for consumer-oriented companies to use, or in bringing lawsuits against companies by consumers who feel that they have a complaint. The following summary is a rather rough oversimplification of these laws, but it does highlight the scope of federal regulation of consumer credit.

THE EQUAL CREDIT OPPORTUNITY ACT

The Equal Credit Opportunity Act prohibits discrimination in any aspect of the credit transaction because of sex, marital status, race, national origin, religion, or age. It also prohibits discrimination against people who receive payments from public assistance programs, such as social security or Aid to Families with Dependent Children. All creditors who regularly extend credit are covered by the act, including banks, small loan and finance companies, retail and department stores, credit card companies, and credit unions. The act outlaws any kind of discrimination but does not prohibit a credit grantor from determining credit worthiness by considering such factors as the income, expenses, debts, and reliability of the applicant.

Creditors are prohibited from discouraging persons from applying for credit because of their sex, marital status, age, religion, race, or national origin or because they have public assistance income.

When a person applies for credit, the creditor is not allowed to require certain information. For example, a creditor must not:

ask the applicant's race, sex, national origin, or religion. (But a creditor may ask the applicant to voluntarily disclose his or her sex, marital status, race, or national origin if the applicant is applying for a real estate loan to purchase a residence. The rationale is that this information helps federal agencies in enforcing anti-discrimination laws. A creditor may also ask the immigration or residence status of the applicant.)

ask the applicant about his or her marital status if the applicant applies for a separate, unsecured account, unless the applicant lives in a community property state.

ask whether the applicant is divorced or widowed.

ask for information about the applicant's spouse, unless the spouse is living with the applicant, the spouse will be allowed to use the account, or the applicant is relying on the spouse's income or on alimony or child support income from a former spouse, or the applicant resides in a community property state.

ask about the applicant's plans for having or raising children.

ask whether the applicant receives alimony, child support, or separate maintenance payments unless the creditor first informs the applicant that he/she does not have to disclose such income unless the applicant wants to rely on it to get credit.

In deciding whether to grant credit, creditors are prohibited from considering sex, marital status, race, national origin, or religion. Also, it is generally not permitted to consider age unless the applicant is too young to sign contracts (generally under age 18).

In evaluating the income which an applicant does disclose, a creditor must not refuse to consider reliable public assistance income and must not discount income because of the applicant's sex or marital status (it is illegal, for example, for a creditor to count a man's salary at 100 percent and a woman's at 75 percent). Also, a creditor may not assume that a woman of childbearing age will stop work to have or raise children. A creditor cannot discount or refuse to consider income because it is derived from part-time employment or from a pension, annuity, or retirement benefit program. Also, a creditor may not refuse to consider consistently received alimony, child support, or separate maintenance payments. A creditor may, however, ask for proof that this income has been consistently received.

Individuals have a right to have credit in their own name (including their maiden name), to get credit without a cosigner if they meet the creditor's standards, to have a cosigner other than the spouse if a cosigner is necessary, or to keep their own accounts after they change their name or marital status or reach a certain age or retire.

The act imposes certain time requirements. Applicants have a right to know within 30 days whether their application has been accepted or rejected, and if their application is rejected, they have the right to know why. The creditor must either immediately give you the specific reasons for the rejection or tell you that you have the right to the specific reasons if you make a request within 60 days. Examples of specific reasons are that the applicant's income is too low or that the applicant has not had his or her present job for long enough. However, statements such as "the applicant didn't meet the minimum standards" or "didn't receive enough points on our credit scoring system" are too vague and do not comply with the law.

Credit histories are a problem for some married women, and the Equal Credit Opportunity Act doesn't do a great deal to solve this problem. A good credit history is often necessary to obtain credit. Unfortunately, many married, separated, divorced, and widowed women do not have credit histories in their own names, even though they have used credit. The reason for this is that women often lose their own credit histories when they marry and change their names and creditors typically report the credit histories on accounts shared by married couples in the husband's name only.

In one attempt to solve this problem, the Equal Credit Opportunity Act requires (as of June 1, 1977) that creditors who report histories to credit bureaus must report information on accounts shared by both spouses in the name of both spouses. Women have the right to require a creditor to report information on accounts they share with their spouses in both names. In addition, the Equal Credit Opportunity Act provides that a creditor cannot:

1. Use unfavorable information about an account a woman shared with her husband or former husband if the woman can show that the bad credit rating does not accurately reflect her willingness to repay

2. Refuse to consider the credit history of the prior joint account if the applicant can show that this does present an accurate picture of her willingness and ability to repay

The Equal Credit Opportunity Act provides the normal spectrum of remedies, including the ability to sue in federal district court and recover actual damages, punitive damages of up to $10,000, and reasonable attorney's fees and court costs. It is also possible to file a class action and recover punitive damages for the class of up to $500,000. People who feel they have been discriminated against can also file complaints with the Federal Trade Commission.

THE TRUTH IN LENDING ACT

The Truth in Lending Act is a very complex piece of legislation which requires disclosures to consumers concerning the various details of credit transactions. The theory is rather simple, but the practice has created a whole new set of detailed federal regulations and a substantial number of reported cases. The high points of the Truth in Lending Act are the following.

The Determination of the Finance Charge

The act contains an elaborate set of provisions which spell out how the finance charge must be determined. Essentially the finance charge includes the sum of all charges which the consumer must pay for the privilege of borrowing money. This includes fees, service charges, carrying charges, interest, points, or even premiums for insurance if that is required by the lender.

The Annual Percentage Rate

The key to the Truth in Lending Act is the determination and disclosure of the annual percentage rate. Essentially the annual percentage rate is the effective interest rate. Technically, however, it is the effective interest rate as computed by a very elaborate set of statutory rules.

Rules for Open-End Consumer Credit Plans

Open-end consumer credit plans present special problems for calculating interest and fees. The typical open-end plan (the credit card or charge account) can have the interest or fees computed in a wide variety of ways, and the act requires that the method of computing the interest be spelled out to the consumer.

Liability of the Holder of the Credit Card

The Truth in Lending Act also contains the statutory limit on the liability of the holder of the credit card to $50 for unauthorized use of the card.

Credit Advertising

The act contains numerous requirements for disclosures in credit advertising.
    The Truth in Lending Act also contains the Fair Credit Billing Act and the Fair Debt Collection Practices Act, which are discussed below.

THE FAIR CREDIT BILLING ACT

In 1975 Congress enacted the Fair Credit Billing Act as an amendment to the Truth in Lending Act. This act sets up a billing dispute settlement procedure which allows the customer to question what he believes to be billing errors on his periodic statements. The creditor must acknowledge the inquiry and promptly correct any errors or explain why it believes the statement is correct. In addition, the act imposes certain other requirements on the creditor to insure fair and prompt handling of credit accounts.
    The Fair Credit Billing Act applies only to open-end credit plans. For purposes of the act, "open-end" covers all consumer credit extended by the use of a credit card as well as most other types of revolving credit, including

department store charge cards and line-of-credit plans such as overdraft checking. The act does not apply to installment loans or purchases (such as cars or homes) which must be paid according to a set schedule of installments.

The procedures required by the act cover only disputes relating to billing errors on the periodic statement, such as:

1. Charges the customer alleges he did not make, or charges made by a person not allowed to use the account

2. Charges billed with the wrong description, amount, or date

3. Charges for property or services which the customer did not accept or which were not delivered as agreed

4. Failure to credit the customer's account for payments or for goods the customer has returned

5. Accounting errors, such as arithmetic mistakes in computing finance charges

6. Billings for which the customer requests an explanation or written proof of purchase

7. Failures to mail or deliver a billing statement to the current address, provided the customer gives at least 10 days' notice of any change of address

Disputes over the quality of goods or services are not billing errors under this act and are not subject to the dispute procedure. However, the act does provide that if a customer purchases unsatisfactory goods or services on a credit card, even if the card was not issued by the seller (as a bank credit card is not), the customer can assert against the credit card company any claims or defenses which he might have against the seller. This means, for example, that if a customer has a right to withhold payment from the seller for faulty merchandise, under certain circumstances the customer may also withhold payment for that merchandise from the credit card account. The act does not help the customer settle this type of dispute but it does allow him to hold his money up while it is being settled. That right is described more fully in paragraph 7 of the Fair Credit Billing Act notice which is printed below.

The heart of the act is a requirement that the creditors tell customers about the dispute procedure. Credit grantors must give a notice summarizing the dispute procedure to all active account holders. After the first notice additional copies must be provided every 6 months. Alternatively, creditors may send a shortened version with each monthly statement, but if they do so they must also provide the full notice at the customer's request and whenever a dispute is filed.

The act actually contains the full text of the notice the creditor is required to give the customer. It has seven separate paragraphs which tell the customer:

1. How to notify the creditor of a billing error

2. What the creditor must do

3. How the customer is protected from collection and bad credit reports

4. What happens if the dispute is settled

5. What happens if the dispute is not settled

6. How the creditor can be penalized for not following the procedure

7. When the customer may withhold payment for faulty goods or services purchased with a credit card

Following is the Statutory text of the required statement:
In Case of Errors or Inquiries about Your Bill

The Federal Truth in Lending Act requires prompt correction of billing mistakes.
1. If you want to preserve your rights under the Act, here's what to do if you think your bill is wrong or if you need more information about an item on your bill:
    a. Do not write on the bill. On a separate sheet of paper write (Alternate: Write on the bill or other sheet of paper) (you may telephone your inquiry but doing so will not preserve your rights under this law) the following:
        i. Your name and account number (if any).
        ii. A description of the error and an explanation (to the extent you can explain) why you believe it is an error. If you only need more information, explain the item you are not sure about and, if you wish, ask for evidence of the charge such as a copy of the charge slip. Do not send in your copy of a sales slip or other document unless you have a duplicate copy for your records.
        iii. The dollar amount of the suspected error.
        iv. Any other information (such as your address) which you think will help the creditor to identify you or the reason for your complaint or inquiry.
    b. Send your billing error notice to the address on your bill which is listed after the words: 'Send Inquiries To:' or similar wording. (Alternate: Send your billing error notice to: (creditor's name and address).))
        Mail it as soon as you can, but in any case, early enough to reach the creditor within 60 days after the bill was mailed to you. If you have authorized your bank to automatically pay from your checking or savings account any credit card bills from that bank, you can stop or reverse payment on any amount you think is wrong by mailing your notice so the creditor receives it within 16 days after the bill was sent to you. However, you do not have to meet this 16-day deadline to get the creditor to investigate your billing error claim.
2. The creditor must acknowledge all letters pointing out possible errors within 30 days of receipt, unless the creditor is able to correct your bill during that 30 days. Within 90 days after receiving your letter, the creditor must either correct the error or explain why the creditor believes the bill was correct. Once the creditor has explained the bill, the creditor has no further obligation to you even though you still believe that there is an error, except as provided in paragraph 5 below.
3. After the creditor has been notified, neither the creditor nor an attorney nor a collection agency may send you collection letters or take other collection action with respect to the amount in dispute; but periodic statements may be sent to you, and the disputed amount can be applied against your credit limit. You cannot be threatened with damage to your credit rating or sued for the amount in question, nor can the disputed amount be reported to a credit bureau or to other creditors as delinquent until the creditor has answered your inquiry. However, you remain obligated to pay the parts of your bill not in dispute.
4. If it is determined that the creditor has made a mistake on your bill, you will not have to pay any finance charges on any disputed amount. If it turns out that the creditor has not made an error, you may have to pay finance charges on the amount in dispute, and you will have to make up any missed minimum or required payments on the disputed amount. Unless you have agreed that your bill was correct, the creditor must send you a written notification of what you owe; and if it is determined that the creditor did make a mistake in billing the disputed amount, you must be given the time to pay which you normally are given to pay undisputed amounts before any more finance charges or late payment charges on the disputed amount can be charged to you.
5. If the creditor's explanation does not satisfy you and you notify the creditor

in writing within 10 days after you receive his explanation that you still refuse to pay the disputed amount, the creditor may report you to credit bureaus and other creditors and may pursue regular collection procedures. But the creditor must also report that you think you do not owe any money, and the creditor must let you know to whom such reports were made. Once the matter has been settled between you and the creditor, the creditor must notify those to whom the creditor reported you as delinquent of the subsequent resolution.

6. If the creditor does not follow these rules, the creditor is not allowed to collect the first $50 of the disputed amount and finance charges, even if the bill turns out to be correct.

7. If you have a problem with property or services purchased with a credit card, you may have the right not to pay the remaining amount due on them, if you first try in good faith to return them or give the merchant a chance to correct the problem. There are two limitations on this right:
    a. You must have bought them in your home State or if not within your home State within 100 miles of your current mailing address; and
    b. The purchase price must have been more than $50. However, these limitations do not apply if the merchant is owned or operated by the creditor, or if the creditor mailed you the advertisement for the property or services.

In order to start the Fair Credit Billing Act's dispute settlement procedure, the customer has to send a written notice of the billing error to the creditor. The written notice must reach the creditor within 60 days after the first billing statement containing the error is made to the customer's current address. The customer may withhold payment of the amount in dispute pending the investigation. However, amounts not in dispute must be paid as normally required. Also, while the investigation is being conducted, no collection threats or actions to get the disputed amount are allowed. If the investigation shows that the bill was correct, the customer has to pay for any finance charges which accumulated on the amount while it was not paid. When it turns out that the creditor was wrong, the customer must be allowed the same amount of time to pay the correct amount due without any finance charges or late fees as is normally allowed for undisputed bills. If the investigation does not settle the dispute, both sides retain their rights and remedies under state contract law.

If the creditor does not follow the dispute settlement procedure, the creditor may not collect the first $50 of the disputed amount, even if the bill turns out to have been correct. The customer may also sue the creditor for damages which result from its failure to comply with the act, and these damages include a minimum statutory award of $100 and reasonable attorney's fees.

In addition to this dispute procedure, the act contains a number of other features. These also apply only to open-end creditors.

Open-end creditors must:

1. Give customers a statement of their account for each billing period in which they have a credit or debit balance greater than $1

2. Where the customer is given a time period within which to pay the bill without a finance charge, mail or deliver the bill to the customer at least 14 days before the end of the period

3. Credit a customer's account with payments as of the date they are received, unless not doing so would not cause extra charges (to insure prompt crediting, creditors may specify a time, manner, and place of payment)

4. Promptly credit any customer overpayment to the account and, if requested by the customer, promptly refund the overpayment

5. Where the merchant accepts returns, credit a customer's account promptly for any refunds on returns

6. Not offset a customer's credit card debts for money held on deposit with the creditor unless the customer had previously authorized that this be done periodically as a method of payment

7. Allow merchants if they wish to grant discounts to customers for paying by cash instead of by credit cards

THE FAIR CREDIT REPORTING ACT

The Fair Credit Reporting Act was passed on April 25, 1971, to protect consumers against the circulation of inaccurate or obsolete information and to insure that consumer credit reporting agencies exercise their responsibilities in a manner that is fair and equitable to consumers. Under this law consumers can take steps to protect themselves if they have been denied credit, insurance, or employment, or if they believe they have had difficulties because of a consumer report which did not contain adequate information.

Under the Fair Credit Reporting Act consumers have the following rights:

1. To be told the name and address of the consumer reporting agency responsible for preparing a consumer report that was used to deny them credit, insurance, or employment or to increase the cost of credit or insurance.

2. To be told by a consumer reporting agency the nature, substance, and sources (except investigative sources) of the information (except medical) collected about them.

3. To take anyone of their choice with them when they visit the consumer reporting agency to check on their file.

4. To obtain within 30 days after their interview all information to which they are entitled, free of charge, when they have been denied credit, insurance, or employment. After 30 days, the reporting agency is permitted to charge a reasonable fee for giving the information.

5. To be told who has received a consumer report on them within the preceding 6 months, or within the preceding 2 years if the report was furnished for employment purposes.

6. To have incomplete or incorrect information reinvestigated, unless the request is frivolous, and, if the information is found to be inaccurate or cannot be verified, to have such information removed from their file.

7. To have the agency notify free of charge those they name who have previously received the incorrect or incomplete information, that this information has been deleted from their file.

8. When a dispute between the consumer and the reporting agency about information in the consumer's file cannot be resolved, the consumer has the right to have his version of such dispute placed in the file and included in future consumer reports.

9. To request the reporting agency to send the consumer's version of the dispute to certain businesses for a reasonable fee.

10. To have a consumer report withheld from anyone who under the law does not have a legitimate business need for the information.

11. To sue a reporting agency for damages if it willfully or negligently violates the law and, if successful, to collect attorney's fees and court costs.

12. To have no adverse information reported after 7 years. One major exception is bankruptcy, which may be reported for 14 years.

13. To be notified by a business when it is seeking information about the consumer which would constitute an "investigative consumer report."

14. To request from the business that ordered an investigative report more information about the nature and scope of the investigation.

15. To discover the nature and substance (but not the sources) of the information that was collected for an investigative consumer report.

If a consumer wants to know what information a consumer reporting agency has collected about him, he can either arrange for a personal interview at the agency's office or call in advance for an interview by telephone. The consumer and credit reporting agencies are obliged to grant this interview. The consumer may request the agency to reinvestigate and correct or delete information that was found to be inaccurate, incomplete, or obsolete. The consumer may also follow up to determine the results of the reinvestigation. If the reinvestigation still produces information which the consumer feels is incorrect, he may insert his version of the facts in the file.

The Fair Credit Reporting Act also contains elaborate requirements placed directly upon the credit reporting company. These requirements are such that credit companies should really be classified as regulated businesses. The requirements include elaborate timetables for how old the information in the credit file may be, who is entitled to ask for the information, how the inquiries from consumers are to be handled, etc. About the only thing the regulations don't cover is how much the agencies may charge for the credit reports.

THE FAIR DEBT COLLECTION PRACTICES ACT

In 1977 Congress reacted to some abuses in the debt collection business with a statute to regulate how debts could be collected. Some of the highlights of that legislation are the following:

1. The way debt collectors may acquire information about where the debtor is located is limited. The collectors must identify themselves, state that the consumer owes a debt, etc. The use of subterfuges is generally not allowed.

2. The communications directly with the debtor are limited. Collectors are prohibited from communicating with the debtor at any unusual time or place which they know, or should know, is inconvenient to the consumer. In the absence of actual knowledge, debt collectors are presumed to know that it is inconvenient to contact consumers before 8:00 A.M. or after 9:00 P.M.. If the debt collector knows the debtor has an attorney, the debt collector is obliged to deal with that attorney.

3. Certain harassment or abusive techniques are prohibited. Specifically, debt collectors may not:
    (a) Use threats of violence or other criminal means to harm the physical person, reputation, or property of any person
    (b) Use obscene or profane language
    (c) Publish a list of consumers who allegedly refuse to pay debts
    (d) Use repeated or harassing telephone calls or place telephone calls without disclosing the caller's identity

Taken as a whole the consumer credit laws establish a whole new requirement for those companies which either sell directly to consumers through credit transactions or finance those transactions. This is a highly technical area of the law, and management ought to be sure that if it engages in any consumer credit transactions it has adequate counsel to steer it through this regulatory maze.

SECTION TEN: MISCELLANEOUS

CHAPTER SIXTY

CORPORATE
POLITICAL
ACTIVITY

CORPORATE SOLICITATION

The legal problem with political activity is that corporations may not give their corporate funds to candidates or political parties at the federal level, or in many states at the state and local levels. *This has been the law for many years and continues to be the law.* With Watergate many years from being forgotten, business must constantly keep this basic prohibition in mind and carefully guard against not only making any illegal political contributions in the form of direct payments of cash, *but also against using corporate funds or facilities in any manner which may be deemed to be a political contribution.* While the relevant statutes have been amended to allow substantial activity on the part of corporations in this area, executives must not let these amendments obscure the basic prohibition.

On the other hand, at the same time this restriction against corporations exists, Congress is busily enacting laws which substantially affect corporations and drastically increase both direct costs in conducting corporate affairs and the general cost of government. To add to the problem, Congress itself has changed drastically since Watergate. At this writing, we have a very strongly antibusiness Congress. In addition to all that, the rules by which Congress operates have themselves changed. The old power structure is no longer present to the same extent it was before. All members now have a voice in what goes on. The days when the committee chairman simply listened to everyone, nodded respectfully (or perhaps even disrespectfully) and then did as he chose are gone. There are many members of Congress who are really interested in doing a good job for their constituents. (The U.S. Chamber of Commerce,

NAM, MAPI, and other business associations are not their constituents.) There is, therefore, both a problem and an opportunity. The problem is that it is very difficult to know just how to make your views known (i.e., lobby), but the opportunity is that there are many such possibilities: all candidates will have to stand for reelection, and in order to be reelected, they will need two things—votes and dollars.

Another problem is the past approach of business to relations with government, which has been, to be generous, about 30 years behind that of organized labor. The following problems have been present:

1. Many business leaders have equated "lobbying and politics" with "sin and sex" and, therefore, felt that:
   (a) It is bad.
   (b) It should only be done in private with great secrecy.
   This frame of mind is absolutely and unequivocally wrong and should be changed. Congress members welcome the views of their constituents, particularly if their constituents happen to be executives of companies that employ substantial numbers of people (voters). They are willing to listen to their views (to be lobbied) and, in fact, have on many past occasions heavily criticized business for failing to lobby.

2. The typical executive's attitude has been that he is not in a position to strongly express his views for or against legislation and, instead, the various trade associations can do it much better. Generally, he is right; most trade associations do an excellent job. The trouble is that trade associations do not vote. The net result of all this is that an inarticulate chief executive of a substantial employer in a congressional district can go to Washington, drop in to see his representative, and explain the beneficial or detrimental effects of a piece of legislation on his business and its employees, and have a much greater impact than the entire expert and articulate staff of his trade association.

3. The third problem is that business leaders have felt that making political contributions to elected officials was somehow "buying" them. In today's climate where all contributions are restricted in amount and the amount which a representative or senator can spend on an election is limited, this is absolutely ridiculous—if it was not indeed ridiculous before the new law. However, the plain and simple fact of life in Washington is that you need votes to get reelected and you need money to get votes. Consequently, senators and representatives must be just as cognizant of the fund-raising problem as the executive is of his bottom line. They must, therefore, have fund-raising dinners, and they must send out periodic requests for political contributions. Accordingly, while you certainly cannot buy a member of Congress for $500, if you can cause this amount to be contributed to his campaign, it will make it much easier for you or your deputies in Washington to get to see him. This is not to say that if you do not make a political contribution your representative will not talk to you, nor is it to say that if you do make a contribution, he will vote the way you like. However, if you have someone in Congress who shares at least some of your views, who is not antibusiness, and whom you feel relatively comfortable having as your representative in Washington, you can help him stay there by supporting him financially. Also, representatives and senators are very busy, and access is a relative thing. Depending on how many times you want to talk with your elected representatives, financial support might greatly increase your access to them.

In summary, federal laws enable you to take an active part in contacting your elected officials and supporting them or their opponents in the next election, in terms of both financial support and activities back home to get votes. The caveat is that there are some rather detailed and technical rules which must be followed, or your company, its top officials, and possibly its lawyers are liable to wind up on the wrong side of a federal criminal statute. The remainder of this chapter discusses this problem in more detail and explains at some length exactly what corporations and their employees may and may not do. Some of these techniques may be appropriate for some businesses; some or all of them may not. Executives must be aware that there are those that are in the business of selling one or more of these tools for various reasons. These people, while well-intentioned, sometimes take liberties with the law which may involve an element of risk. They tend to justify many of their activities on the "practical" or "everybody's-doing-it" theory, which has never been too convincing, although they are usually right: the actions they recommend are usually being done by many other people. Further, they are usually able and very willing to document this to you, and your lawyer will be the "bad guy" who has to stand up and be counted when he cannot justify a proposed action on the basis of existing law. Good corporate counsel, however, will do just that. That is what he is paid for. If he cannot write an opinion letter based on statutes, cases, or rulings which will clearly justify the proposed action, he should counsel against it. If he is not sure where the boundaries of legality are, he will probably stay well within them.

The Federal Election Law starts out by saying that it is illegal for any corporation to make any contribution or expenditure in connection with any federal election. The opening sections define "contribution" and "expenditure" very broadly. The statute, however, then goes on to say that the terms "contribution" and "expenditure" do not include any of the following:

(1) communications by a corporation to its stockholders and executive and administrative personnel and their families or by a labor organization to its members and their families on any subject,
(2) non-partisan registration and get-out-the-vote campaigns by a corporation aimed at its stockholders and executive or administrative personnel and their families, or by a labor organization aimed at its members and their families, and
(3) the establishment, administration, and solicitation of contributions to a separate segregated fund to be utilized for political purposes by a corporation, labor organization, membership organization, cooperative, or corporation without capital stock.

Another section of the law makes it clear that these rules also apply to government contractors.

Immediately following the above permissible activities, however, there is a paragraph providing that it shall be *unlawful* to do any of the following:

(1) obtain money by use of force, job discrimination, threat of force, forced dues, etc.,
(2) neglect to inform employees of the political purpose of the fund at the time of any solicitation, and
(3) neglect to inform the employee at the time of solicitation of his right to refuse to contribute without any reprisal.

Thus, in the case of a corporation which wants to have a fund for its executive or administrative personnel, the only substantial legal rule is that the corporation cannot force people to contribute money to the fund. There are a number of other practical problems, because the fund will be considered a political committee under this law, and it will have to register and file numerous reports. However, these are purely mechanical and should create no problem other than increased administrative expense.

Immediately following the rules quoted above, however, the law goes on to say that it is unlawful for a corporation to solicit contributions to a fund *from any person other than administrative and executive personnel, its stockholders and their families* except in compliance with the following rules:

1. There can only be two solicitations during any calendar year.

2. The solicitation may be made only by mail and addressed to the stockholders or executive or administrative personnel, and must be mailed to the employee's residence.

3. The program must be so designed that the corporation cannot determine who makes a contribution of $50 or less as a result of this solicitation and who does not make a contribution.

This latter requirement is a substantial impediment to the operation of a fund because it prohibits a corporation from using the payroll deduction process. If a corporation uses the payroll deduction process, it obviously knows who participates and to what extent, and this is now illegal.

There are limits on the amount of money a corporate separate, segregated fund can give to any one political candidate or committee, but those limits are rather substantial and are generally $5000 per candidate per election with maximums of $15,000 per year to national political party committees, $5000 per year to other political committees, and no limit at all for the total aggregate contributions. There is a limit of contributions to a corporate political fund, but again it is very substantial: $5000 per year.

A corporate political fund is technically referred to as a "multi-candidate committee" in the regulations, and in order to qualify, it must be registered for 6 months, have received contributions from more than fifty persons, and have made contributions to five or more federal candidates. Before that time, a corporate political fund would be subject to smaller limits of $1000 per candidate per election. If a corporate political fund was small enough that it could not meet these requirements, it would also be subject to these smaller limits.

In general, it would seem that any corporation that was inclined to do so could rather easily maintain a corporate political action fund provided that the fund was limited to shareholders and executive and administrative people. Extending the fund to a larger group than that would be a bit troublesome from a mechanical point of view, and it would take a rather large amount of legal, accounting, planning, and other administrative work.

UNION SOLICITATION

The new law contains the following section relating to making solicitation methods available to unions:

Notwithstanding any other law, any method of soliciting voluntary contributions or of facilitating the making of voluntary contributions to a separate segregated fund established by a corporation, permitted by law to corporations with regard to stockholders and executive or administrative personnel, shall also be permitted to labor organizations with regard to their members.

The implication of this provision is that if the company has a political action fund and allows executives to use payroll deduction for making their contributions, the company will be required to allow the union to use payroll deduction to facilitate contributions to their political fund—but only from the union members. Also, the corporation will be able to charge the union for this. The amount must only be sufficient to cover the corporation's costs though. As a practical matter, the union will undoubtedly have good procedures to solicit contributions from their own members and will not be interested in using any corporate procedures, particularly if they have to pay for them. However, if the company solicits nonmanagement people, this gives the union the right to solicit nonunion people in the company and this can get very complicated and have many labor relations implications. For example, if the company solicited even a small group of secretaries for participation in the corporate political action fund, the union would be allowed to solicit all the employees in the company, not just the union members and not just the employees in the same unit as the secretaries. Also, the company would have to make these names available either to the union or to an independent mailing company. Thus almost universally corporations limit solicitations to management people only when seeking contributions for their corporate political action fund for use in federal elections. The state laws are different and these must be evaluated on a state-by-state basis. In many states, it is possible to solicit all employees for corporate contributions without any problem so long as it is clear that the funds are separate and the state money is not used either in any federal election or in any state where it would be illegal.

GOOD-GOVERNMENT ACTIVITY

Many corporations desire to sponsor political activity other than fund raising. The two most usual kinds of activities are candidate visits and registration and get-out-the-vote drives. Again, there are a few technical problems if candidate visits and registration and get-out-the-vote drives involve more than shareholders, executives, and administrative people. In the case of registration and get-out-the-vote drives, if the availability of the registration procedure is extended past shareholders and administrative and executive employees, it must be done by a civic organization and it must be jointly sponsored by the union and the company. Similarly, in the case of candidate visits, if the candidate is allowed to speak to employees as a group including nonexecutive and nonadministrative people, the premises of the company must be available on similar terms to all opposing candidates for the same office.

INDIVIDUAL POLITICAL CONTRIBUTIONS

The basic limit on individual political contributions is $1000 per candidate per election. The $1000 limitation applies to each person, and a husband and wife may each give $1000 per candidate per election.

The law, however, has a very broad definition of "contribution" to include not only money but anything of value, and the definition of "contribution" in the law has certain exceptions which illustrate several pitfalls.

"Contribution" is defined to *exclude* the following:

1. The value of services provided without compensation by individuals who volunteer a portion or all of their time on behalf of a candidate or political committee

2. The use of real or personal property and the cost of invitations, food, and beverages voluntarily provided by an individual to a candidate, and rendering voluntary personal services on the individual's residential premises for candidate-related activities

3. The sale of any food or beverage by a vendor for use in a candidate's campaign at a charge less than the normal comparable charge if such charge for use in a candidate's campaign is at least equal to the cost of such food or beverage to the vendor

4. Any unreimbursed payment for travel expenses made by an individual who in his own behalf volunteers his personal services to a candidate

All of the above, however, except for the personal-service time exemption, are subject to a maximum $500 limitation with respect to any election. Thus, if an executive wanted to give a party for a candidate, the entire cost of the party would be counted as a political contribution unless the party was conducted at the executive's residence, and if it was conducted at his residence, he could only exclude $500 of the cost of the party. Naturally, this assumes that the executive is paying for the cost out of his personal funds. If he attempted to put it on his expense account and have the corporation pay, this would be an illegal political contribution.

The question of what kinds of parties are covered is not entirely clear, but it would seem that common sense would provide a reasonable guide. If candidates are invited to a social gathering and do not make any formal presentations, and if the primary purpose of the gathering is social, it would not seem to cause a problem. On the other hand, if the real purpose of the gathering is to introduce the candidate to other people in attendance, simply calling it a social gathering would not take it out of the definition of a political contribution.

Other limitations are that no person may make contributions to multicandidate committees, such as a corporate political action committee, of over $5000 per year. There is an overriding $25,000 limitation which provides that no individual shall make contributions aggregating more than $25,000 in any calendar year.

As a result of a Supreme Court case declaring it unconstitutional, the old limitation on the amount of money an individual could expend to voice his political views on the merits of the election of any given candidate has been removed from the law, and so theoretically there is no limit on the amount of money one can spend on one's own to advocate the election or defeat of any candidate. However, as a practical matter, this may be illusory, because the definition of a contribution includes the following:

(1) Expenditures made by any person in cooperation, consultation or concert with or at the request or suggestion of a candidate, his authorized political committees, or their agents shall be considered to be a contribution to such candidate.
(2) The financing by any person of the dissemination, distribution or republication in whole or in part of any broadcast or any written, graphic or other form of campaign materials prepared by the candidate, his campaign committees, or their authorized agents shall be considered an expenditure for purposes of this paragraph.

In other words, unless the activity engaged in by the individual is done entirely on his own and there is no consultation with the candidate or his political committee, and unless the advertisement or handbill or other message is not one prepared by the candidate or in consultation with the candidate or approved by the candidate, the amounts expended would be covered by the law and would be subject to the above limitations.

The subject of when a corporate employee can work for a candidate without taking an unpaid leave of absence also is governed by a rule-of-reason approach. Proposed regulations under the new law make it clear that the rule of reason is very restrictive and that any substantial activity would be deemed a corporate contribution. For example, the proposed regulations say that:

1. If an employee of a corporation makes several local phone calls on his or her office phone to friends suggesting that they contribute to or vote for a particular federal candidate, the employee is not required to make any reim-

bursement, since the use is occasional and incidental and the overhead costs of the corporation are not increased.

2. If an official of a labor organization makes several long distance phone calls on his or her office phone to friends suggesting that they contribute to or vote for a particular federal candidate and the cost of the calls is billed to the official's office phone, the official is required to reimburse the labor organization for the cost of the calls, since the corporation's overhead costs were increased by this amount.

3. If an employee of a corporation spends several nights a week making numerous phone calls on his or her office phone to friends suggesting that they contribute to or vote for a particular federal candidate, the employee is required to reimburse the corporation at the normal and usual charge for all long distance phone calls, a pro rata cost of the monthly service charge per phone, pro rata federal and state tax, the equivalent deposit, and a commercial rate for installation of the phone used as well as the normal and usual charge for the use of the office space and utilities.

LOBBYING

Federal lobbying laws have remained the same for a number of years, but they are currently undergoing a revision in the form of numerous pieces of proposed legislation. Accordingly, these comments may be substantially outdated in a short period of time.

There are both federal and state statutes which govern lobbying activity. Under the federal lobbying rules, two kinds of activity can give rise to a reporting requirement:

1. Communications to congressional representatives

2. Receiving or soliciting contributions or making expenditures to influence legislation

The federal statutes generally provide that any person who "engages himself for pay or for any consideration for the purpose of attempting to influence the passage or defeat of any legislation by the Congress of the United States" must register with the clerk of the House of Representatives and the secretary of the Senate and thereafter must file certain periodic reports disclosing his receipts and expenditures relating to his lobbying activities. There are similar requirements for receiving or soliciting contributions or making expenditures to influence legislation.

The following statute governs the persons to whom this requirement is applicable:

Sec. 266.   Persons to whom chapter is applicable.

The provisions of this chapter shall apply to any person (except a political committee as defined in the Federal Corrupt Practices Act, and duly organized State or local committees of a political party), who by himself, or through any agent or employee or other persons in any manner whatsoever, directly or indirectly, solicits, collects, or receives money or any other thing of value to be used principally to aid, or the principal purpose of which person is to aid, in the accomplishment of any of the following purposes:

(a) The passage or defeat of any legislation by the Congress of the United States.

(b) To influence, directly or indirectly, the passage or defeat of any legislation by the Congress of the United States.

The principal case construing the lobbying legislation on the federal level is *United States v. Harriss*, which held in substance that:

(1) The "person" must have solicited, collected or received contributions.
(2) One of the *main purposes* of such person or one of the main purposes of such contributions, must have been to influence the passage or defeat of legislation by Congress.
(3) The intended method of accomplishing this purpose must have been through *direct communication with members of Congress*.

The general practice in this area seems to be to consider that the rule of the *Harriss* case is satisfied only if 5% or more of the person's time is spent in *direct* lobbying. The Department of Justice seems to concur, at least informally. Furthermore, in computing the time, one figures only the time spent actually conferring directly with members of Congress on specific legislation—and excludes the taxi ride to and from the office, time spent in preparation for the meeting or the analysis of the results, waiting time, time spent following or analyzing legislation, and informal nonbusiness contacts with Congressmen.

CONCLUSION

From the standpoint of the federal lobbying legislation as applied to activities of corporate employees, the problem seems to be susceptible to a fairly mechanical solution. Simply compute the time spent by a person in direct communications with members of Congress on legislative matters, and if that percentage exceeds 5%, registration is in order. If the percentage is less than but close to 5%, or if future anticipated activities may take it over the 5% mark, registration should be considered as a safeguard, but probably is not required, at least until the 5% figure is actually exceeded. If the time spent in direct lobbying activities is substantially less than 5%, there should be no registration problem under the lobbying legislation at the federal level. There is no specific time period over which the 5% must be computed, but since reports must be filed quarterly, use of that period would seem reasonable.

From the point of view of the individual states, the problem is much more complex because of the great number of different statutes. State legislation generally falls into three categories:

1. The most common type is basically comparable to the federal statutes. This type requires registration of the lobbyist (and sometimes his employer) and *periodic filing of reports*.

2. Some states prohibit only certain kinds of bad conduct, such as employing a lobbyist on a contingent fee basis or other kinds of corrupt lobbying. There is no reporting or registration for straightforward lobbying activity.

3. Some states have no direct legislation on the point.

Naturally, of most concern will be the first type. Most of the major industrial states have this kind of statute. Some states have relatively simple, straightforward legislation. Other states have very detailed and elaborate systems for registration and reporting of lobbying activities.

Following are typical of some of the provisions which may be found in state laws:

1. Some states require the registration of the employer as well as the employee.

2. Some states require a fairly frequent registration, sometimes before each session of the legislative body, and frequent filing of reports (every month).

3. Almost all states absolutely prohibit the payment of any kind of contingent compensation for a lobbyist.

4. Some states require a person to have a certificate of some type before talking to any legislator or legislative committee.

The question of the constitutionality of many of these state statutes is uncertain. Also, they are interpreted differently in different states. It should not be assumed that just because there is no problem under the federal rules, there will be no problem in all states. There is much new state legislation in this area. The business executive should always take the precaution of having legal counsel check the latest state statutes on a particular problem.

CHAPTER SIXTY-ONE

PRIVACY LAW

The subject of privacy law has received a great deal of attention lately, but no one has really attempted to realistically assess the effects of various courses of action on private industry.

The legal aspects of privacy begin as "a right to privacy," which, subject as usual to a great deal of legal qualification, can be summarized as the right to be left alone. This is not the kind of privacy we are talking about. Since that original "right to privacy" was recognized by our courts around the beginning of the twentieth century, the privacy issue has progressed from an interesting but fairly irrelevant subject (unless your company happens to be a publisher) into a rather troublesome problem, because the right to privacy has now been extended to information contained in data banks. By definition, a "data bank" is not limited to compilations of information in a computer but can be simply a manual set of files, as for example, a company's personnel files.

The beginnings of this problem were foreshadowed in the Privacy Act of 1974, which was aimed at assuring individuals in the country that there would be no "big brother" system by which information on virtually all aspects of their lives was stored in some master computer and someone with evil intentions could press a magic button and have a computer print out information about everyone, including all of the money he had ever earned, all the money he had ever deposited in any bank, his health, any criminal records, all of the jobs he had ever held, all of the motor vehicles he had ever owned, etc. The Privacy Act of 1974 accomplished this by requiring all federal agencies to adopt reasonable procedures to assure that the vast amount of information that they must collect on people in order to administer their agencies properly is kept private. As a normal incident to this, it was decided that it was inappropriate for all of the federal agencies to use the social security number as the primary identifying vehicle for all of the people. The theory apparently was that if all agencies used the social security number, there would some day be one great computer with all the information from all the agencies in it and the key would be an individual's social security number: anyone who had access to the computer either legitimately or illegitimately could obtain vast amounts of information about anyone by simply punching in that person's social security number. It was thought to be much more difficult if the identifying systems were different and there were no great central compilation of all of these data.

In the context of the federal government, this did make some sense, although it also caused a great deal of trouble and expense. Unfortunately, the same concept is spreading to private industry in the form of proposed federal legislation and a multitude of proposed state laws which also have the effect of prohibiting a company from creating master files on its employees using the social security number as the primary identifying vehicle. Further complicating the situation is the fact that the social security number *is* the single best way to identify people. Even a casual glance at any metropolitan telephone book will show that the names of people are certainly not a good way to identify them, and even if you couple names with elaborate systems of addresses, ages, places of employment, etc., you wind up with something which is less perfect than the already existing social security system. Also, we do have the Social Security Administration and we do have to report individuals' earnings to it, and the social security system must operate. To further complicate matters, so many of the federal government tax rules are keyed into the social security number that industry must maintain this information whether it wants to or not.

At this time, all we have is a federal privacy law which if extended to the private sector would amount to a minor disaster, plus a multitude of proposed state pieces of legislation, some of which have been enacted, which amount at this time to minor annoyances but which if enacted in some of the forms in which they are proposed could amount to a monumental disaster, especially for companies trying to do business in more than one state.

While it is impossible to give any legal guidelines at this time because there are no federal laws which apply to the private sector and the state laws are somewhat of a hodgepodge, it does appear that some generalities are worth mentioning. First of all, the issue of privacy is very politically motivated and it can be depended upon to produce an avalanche of proposed pieces of legislation both at the federal and the state level. In addition, it is a subject which companies should be concerned about, because from a moral point of view their employees do have a right to privacy about their personal lives. However, the company must for compliance with its own legal requirements, pension plans, policies, etc., maintain a great deal of data on employees which is private. It would appear, therefore, that in the absence of express legislation, the best thing to do would be to take a commonsense but rather active approach to the problem. It should not simply be ignored, because we can virtually bank on some kind of legislation; the only question is what kind it will be. We know enough about the subject to make sure any new computer programs, any new systems, or any new personnel policies are designed to assure the employees a right to the maximum amount of privacy possible, given the necessity of business to maintain the information in the first place.

One of the best general statements of the purposes of privacy legislation is contained in a bill which was introduced in Congress in 1974 but which was never passed. That bill contained the following ideas.

1. There should be no personnel information system whose very existence is kept secret from the people who are covered.

2. No information should be collected unless there is a need for it and that need has been clearly established in advance. In other words, companies should not collect information on their employees just because it may be interesting to them or because for some unknown and unstated reason they may need it some day.

3. Information should be appropriate and relevant to the purposes for which it has been collected. The equal opportunity area is a prime example of this. Companies should take a realistic and rather restrictive attitude on the information which is collected, and the information should bear some relevance to the reason for gathering the information in the first place.

4. Information should not be obtained by fraudulent or unfair means. This would seem to be generally agreed upon by everyone.

5. Information should not be used unless it is accurate and current. This is a rather substantial problem, as has been shown under the Fair Credit Reporting Act. In principle, it is sound, but human beings and machines being what they are, there is *some* possibility for error, and an absolute prohibition against using inaccurate information or perhaps criminal sanctions for distributing information which is inaccurate or not current is unreasonable and operates to the detriment of the vast number of people who do pay their bills and are not worried about the small risk of being wrongly identified.

6. There should be a prescribed procedure for an individual to know the existence of information stored about him, the purpose for which it has been recorded, and particulars about its use and dissemination, and to examine that information. Again, this seems like a rather laudable objective, but when it is applied to personnel files, there are obviously contrary arguments. If one is going to maintain a personnel file, it may or may not be in the best interest of either employer or employee to let the employee have access to it. This depends on one's philosophy of management. If one's philosophy is to be open and candid, there is probably nothing wrong with letting the employee see his file. On the other hand, if this employee is considered unpromotable (even if he is happy in his present job and does it well), it would seem to be an unnecessary complication of a satisfactory situation to have the employee find something in a file which proved he would not be promoted.

7. There should be a clearly prescribed procedure for an individual to correct, erase, or amend inaccurate, obsolete, or irrelevant information. Again, the theory is good but sometimes the practice creates a problem. The credit situation is a prime example. Credit companies have in response to the Fair Credit Reporting Act adopted elaborate procedures for allowing people to examine their credit files and make corrections, but the overwhelming majority of the public has paid for this vast amount of overhead in the form of increased cost of credit reports as reflected in increased prices of the goods, etc.

8. Any organization collecting, maintaining, using, or disseminating personal information should assure its reliability and take precautions to prevent its misuse. Again, a very laudable objective; the only question is degree. If the word "reasonable" is included, even if it is interpreted rather restrictively, it is a good idea. On the other hand, if people who gather information are somehow insurers of its accuracy, very unfortunate problems can result.

9. There should be clearly prescribed procedure for an individual to prevent personal information collected for one purpose from being used for another purpose without his consent—again, a good idea.

61-4   MISCELLANEOUS

10. Federal, state, and local governments should not collect personal information except as expressly authorized by law—again, a reasonable requirement.

One of the problems in the privacy area is that no one quarrels with the theory. It is the practice and the means by which the end result is to be accomplished which causes the trouble. Again, the key seems to be the social security number. That, plus the violent reaction of some people when you say that the employees can have access to their personnel files, is probably the most important area of privacy problems. From a legal point of view, it is also troublesome to envision a maze of fifty different state laws governing a company which operates in all fifty states and requires different provisions for keeping data on its employees. It is to be hoped that, by the time the law is finally clarified on this subject—which is likely to be a couple of years away—some rationality will be injected into the whole discussion and:

1. There will be one piece of federal legislation which preempts all the state legislation in the area.

2. The social security number will be recognized for what it is—the best way to identify people—and instead of banning the use of a social security number, legislation will instead prohibit unauthorized use or misuse of information contained in a data bank and provide severe penalties for people who deliberately disregard the rights to privacy of employees and the public and also penalize those companies and institutions that do not take reasonable precautions to assure that data—once collected—are kept current and used properly.

CHAPTER SIXTY-TWO

THE FREEDOM OF INFORMATION ACT

The Freedom of Information Act (FOIA) was enacted in 1966 and amended in 1974 to establish a procedure by which private citizens could better evaluate the performance of government agencies. The thought was that if substantially all documents of government agencies were open to the public, the performance of these agencies could be better evaluated by the public, and the agencies would be motivated to do a good job and to administer the laws fairly and uniformly. At the time, most corporate leaders and their lawyers took only passing notice of the statute. However, the FOIA has now turned into a significant device which can greatly aid those who might wish to attack a private corporation. It can also be used by a company to find out information about its competition in general or about a specific competitor. The 1974 Amendments to the act, the almost paranoid attitude toward disclosure in today's political atmosphere, a trend on the part of the courts to liberally construe the act towards disclosure, and the increased awareness of the act and its usefulness by business executives and their lawyers have intensified this problem. To top it all off, the notorious "leak" has crept into the picture and the federal courts have been known to ignore good faith agreements between government and business requiring the government to hold information confidential. For these reasons, executives and their lawyers must realize that information submitted to the government may be made public and should be aware of the policies and practices which they can use to protect their confidential and proprietary information to the maximum extent possible.

The current situation is that almost all businesses of any size are required to submit extensive information to many different government agencies regarding a host of different laws. In a growing number of cases, this information is of great value to:

1. Private litigants seeking to enforce some claim against the corporation (e.g., EEO or product liability complaints)

2. Public interest organizations seeking to establish some principle of the law or to have certain antibusiness legislation enacted, or perhaps just to disclose for the sake of disclosure

3. Competitors seeking to strengthen their competitive position

The problem from the corporate point of view is that the information is in the hands of the government and so the government is going to have control of exactly what is disclosed, when, and to whom, and the drafting of the Freedom of Information Act is such that the starting point is that *everything* in the agencies' files is subject to disclosure to *anyone* who asks for it without restriction as to its subsequent use. Of course there are certain important exceptions, but business is placed on the defensive because it often has to prove that the material it does not want disclosed comes within one of the exceptions.

The 1974 Amendments to the FOIA intensified the problem by placing severe burdens on the government, including the following:

1. Each agency of the government must adopt and publish regulations as to how requests for information will be processed.

2. Requests for material under the Freedom of Information Act must generally be answered by the government within 10 days.

3. There is a possibility of disciplinary proceedings against any employee who is found to have withheld information improperly.

4. The government agency can be assessed attorney's fees if it is found to have withheld information improperly.

In the past, the government really never did have any great incentive to resist disclosure of information obtained from industry. The only incentive it had was the general philosophy that if it did not, business might not cooperate with it and data might be more difficult to get. However, to give credit where it is due, government agencies in the past exercised a great deal of effort to make sure that any information obtained in confidence was kept in confidence. If a company and the government made an agreement that certain information would be supplied on a confidential basis, business could be reasonably sure that the government would do everything in its power to honor its side of the bargain. There would be no second-guessing as to whether the information was really a trade secret or whether it was sufficiently out-of-date to justify disclosure. This attitude was already beginning to change shortly before 1974, but now the case is almost the opposite. Government agencies can no longer be depended upon to expend any substantial effort to resist disclosure except in the clearest of cases or where the disclosure request involves their own information. In fact, corporations are doing a very good job if they even find out about the proposed disclosure of their confidential data before it is already an accomplished fact.

The opportunity, of course, is the other side of the coin. If a company wants to do a little intelligence work itself, it can probably get some fairly useful information about its competitors by raiding the government's files.

THE ACT AND ITS EXEMPTIONS

Following is a very brief discussion of the important aspects of the FOIA from the business standpoint:

The starting point of the Freedom of Information Act is the following provision:

> Each agency, upon any request for records which (A) reasonably describes such records and (B) is made in accordance with published rules stating the time, place, fees (if any), and procedures to be followed, shall make the records promptly available to any person.

In other words, everything is available to anybody who asks for it. There are, however, a number of important exceptions set forth in the act, the most important of which for business purposes are the following:

(b)(3) specifically exempted from disclosure by statute;
   (4) trade secrets and commercial or financial information obtained from a person and privileged or confidential; . . .
   (7) investigatory records compiled for law enforcement purposes, but only to the extent that the production of such records would (A) interfere with enforcement proceedings, (B) deprive a person of a right to a fair trial or an impartial adjudication, (C) constitute an unwarranted invasion of personal privacy, (D) disclose the identity of a confidential source and, in the case of a record compiled by a criminal law enforcement authority in the course of a criminal investigation, or by an agency conducting a lawful national security intelligence investigation, confidential information furnished only by the confidential source, (E) disclose investigative techniques and procedures, or (F) endanger the life or physical safety of law enforcement personnel.

"Specifically Exempted from Disclosure by Statute"

In many cases, material supplied to the government will be specifically exempt from disclosure under the statute requiring that information be supplied. Primary examples are the income tax laws. However, it should be noted that the exception applies only to materials specifically restricted by statute. In many cases, particularly those involving the newer requirements of the government for submission of information on lines of business and in the areas of government procurement, the specific statutory protection is inadequate.

"Trade Secrets and Commercial or Financial Information Obtained from a Person and Privileged or Confidential"

This is by far the most important exemption for business. It is the basis for the practical advice contained in the remainder of this chapter.

"Investigatory Records Compiled for Law Enforcement Purposes"

This exception is of great importance when a government investigation of a company whose information you are after is being conducted or has been conducted. Important points to keep in mind are:

1. The exemption seems to apply only to a specific investigation of a company which was being conducted to see if some law has been violated. If the investiga-

tion was not done for law enforcement purposes but merely to provide data for use by the agency, the exemption would not seem to be applicable even if it showed a possible violation of some law.

2. Some agencies have time periods beyond which these investigatory files are no longer held confidential. From a competitive point of view, however, the information may remain extremely sensitive for longer periods of time.

3. When information is submitted to a government agency in the course of an investigation, consideration should be given to a stamp or legend to the effect that the information is exempt from disclosure under the Freedom of Information Act (and possibly other statutes or regulations). In addition, if at all possible, it is a good idea to negotiate an agreement with the agency about the confidentiality of the information. While the courts may not enforce such an agreement, it is still a useful tool and definitely recommended where it can be obtained.

THE TRADE SECRET–INFORMATION EXEMPTION

The trade secret exemption quoted above was not changed by the 1974 Amendments to the FOIA and remains the same as the original language drafted in 1966. The legislative history of this section would, therefore, be appropriate authority, but unfortunately this legislative history does not add very much to the clarification of some of the problems presented. Further, even assuming that the purpose and intent of the law is clear, there are many problems in application.

What Is Protected?

The theory of what is protected is fairly easy to understand by closely reading the statute, a few cases, and some of the standard law on trade secrets. Each word of the exemption—admittedly poorly drafted—is important.

> . . . Trade secrets and commercial or financial information obtained from a person and privileged or confidential . . .

The operative disjunctive is the first "and." In other words, two things are protected:

1. Trade secrets

2. Information which is
    (a) Commercial or financial
    (b) Obtained from a person
    (c) Privileged or confidential

This construction of the exemption was set forth in a Consumer's Union case where the Consumer's Union wanted access to records relating to federally tested hearing aids. These records apparently rated the hearing aids as to effectiveness, and the Consumer's Union wanted to publish this information. The court said that these data were neither obtained from a person nor confidential and so the exemption did not apply. The court also drew a distinction between information which was generated at the expense of private industry and that generated by the government at taxpayers' expense and said that the public clearly had a right to the latter.

Trade Secrets

The definition of the kinds of trade secrets which are protected appears to be the standard trade secret law definition, which is generally very broad. The definition is usually contained in state laws, but most state laws are based upon the old common law definition, and the Ohio statute is typical:

> "Trade Secret" means the whole or any portion or phase of any scientific or technical information, design, process, procedure, formula, or improvement, or any business plans, financial information, or listing of names, addresses, or telephone numbers, which has not been published or disseminated, or otherwise become a matter of general public knowledge. Such scientific or technical information, design, process, procedure, formula, or improvement, or any business plans, financial information, or listing of names, addresses, or telephone numbers is presumed to be secret when the owner thereof takes measures designed to prevent it, in the ordinary course of business, from being available to persons other than those selected by the owner to have access thereto for limited purposes.

A reading of the definition reveals two important things:

1. The definition can be very broad.
2. It will generally require the holder to take some affirmative measures *before the disclosure* is requested to have the information treated confidentially.

This latter point is very important. If a company resists disclosure of information on the ground that it is a trade secret, it will greatly help the case if the company can show steps which it has taken to protect the information. (See Chapter 49.) On the other hand, if the information is treated in a cavalier manner until someone asks the government for it under the FOIA, and then all of a sudden the company raises loud cries of "trade secrets," the company's protestations are likely to fall on deaf ears in the agencies or courts.

In summary, trade secrets can be just about anything your company wants to keep secret, but you have to identify them and take steps to protect their confidentiality *before* the question arises.

Commercial or Financial Information

Exactly what information will meet the requirements of the second part of the exemption is not quite as clear. However, a fairly good operative definition, at least for planning purposes, is that it includes any information which your company reasonably considers private. The words "commercial or financial" seem broad enough to cover just about all corporate information, and all that remains is the establishment of the privileged or confidential requirement. The same basic consideration as above would seem to apply. If your company makes the determination that the information is privileged or confidential at the time it is submitted to the government, it will, at least, put the government on notice that the exemption may be applicable. This simply means labeling the information.

It is generally agreed that the kind of information which is intended to be covered by this exemption is any information which would not customarily be released to the public by the person from whom it was obtained, but there is a difference of opinion among the courts as to whether or not that is the end of the matter. Some cases indicate that in addition to being the kind of information which would not be released to the public, the court must determine whether or not the release of the information would harm the person submitting it. In other words, there is a subjective weighing of the need for the person requesting the information versus the harm which might be caused to the person who supplied it in the first place.

Is the Exemption Mandatory or Permissive?

Another question which can arise is whether or not, assuming the information falls within the exemption, the agency nevertheless has discretion to release it. This question is very difficult to answer. From a purely legal approach, it would appear that the FOIA exemptions are not discretionary with the agency, and there is sound judicial support for this argument.

However, there are some contrary cases and a number of practical problems. In the first place, as a matter of mechanics, the request is made from an outside party to the government, and it is the government which must make the determination in the first instance of whether or not to disclose the information. As indicated above and as evidenced by the decided cases, the government was generally fairly conscientious in doing this, partly because of its concern regarding future business cooperation and partly because, until recently, the path of least resistance was generally to refuse disclosure. In addition, there is a federal criminal penalty imposed upon government officials who disclose private trade secret information. Thus, the government had nothing to gain by disclosing the information and a considerable amount to lose, particularly if the criminal statute was applicable, by disclosing it.

The facts have now changed; today, anyone who refuses to disclose anything is automatically suspected of being involved with big business as part of some scheme which must be covered up, and while the criminal statute referred to above is still in effect, the Freedom of Information Act was amended to provide for disciplinary action for government employees who failed to disclose information which the court said they should have disclosed.

With this threat hanging over them, as well as the criminal statute problem, government employees are going to have to keep on their toes when requests for information under the FCIA are received. With the current judicial trend toward interpreting the statute to provide for liberal disclosure, employees would seem to lean more towards disclosing information than not disclosing it in most cases.

Another practical problem is that the government has the information. Thus, you can argue all you want about whether the exemption is mandatory or permissive, but the fact remains that the situation is not unlike that of the catcher and the pitcher. The catcher may have the right to call pitches but the pitcher is the one throwing the ball and, therefore, has considerable voice in what is actually going to happen. Nevertheless, there are cases which provide good authority that government agencies must respect the FOIA exemptions, and this brings up the timing problem. If you do not label your information confidential and do something to assure that the government will tell you when someone has requested it, you are likely to find out only after the fact that your information has been disclosed. This is especially true in the context of congressional inquiries, where agencies feel that they must immediately provide any information Congress requests. In many cases, agencies will inform the company whose information is being sought, but the agencies generally take the position that this is done only out of the goodness of their hearts and there is no general obligation to do it. This, again, raises the desirability of a nondisclosure agreement with the agency. If you have such an agreement requiring a certain number of days of prior notice before disclosure, your chances of having notice in time to do something are increased.

Promise of Confidentiality

As mentioned above, one possible approach to the problem of giving the government confidential information is to obtain a confidentiality agreement from it providing that it will not release the information to outside parties, or if such a broad agreement is not negotiable, at least providing that it will not release the information to any outside party without giving the company some advance notice. The company then has the chance to try to talk the agency out of the proposed disclosure, or if it is unsuccessful, the company can apply to the federal courts for an injunction against the agency prohibiting it from disclosing the information. In negotiations with the agency, the criminal statute providing liability for disclosing trade secret information should, of course, be brought to its attention.

Unfortunately, the courts have not looked with great favor on confidentiality agreements with the government and, as a matter of fact, have dismissed them out of hand. Accordingly, the confidentiality agreement, while a good idea and generally desirable, cannot be used as a cure-all.

SUMMARY AND PRACTICAL COMMENTS

The Freedom of Information Act is well known and used by private businesses. It has been covered extensively in the news media and analyzed and commented upon in national news magazines and business journals. Many of these articles point out that business itself is one of the biggest users of the act—to request information about competition.

In many cases, a government agency will promise, perhaps even in writing, not to release data it has obtained from companies subject to its jurisdiction. In some cases, the forms on which the data is submitted contain such a promise or undertaking. These promises may not be sufficient in all cases, and the mere inclusion of such an agreement should not be looked at as the end of the matter if truly confidential information is involved.

All government submissions should be carefully analyzed by appropriate people in the company to determine precisely what is really confidential, and these portions of the submissions should be separated and very clearly labeled with some appropriate label. "Commercial and financial information, privileged and confidential" is one label which has been used. In labeling information, however, it is appropriate to keep in mind that not everything is truly confidential. There does appear to be some predisposition by industry to consider almost everything confidential, and this is unrealistic and self-defeating. Almost all decided cases on this matter which restrict disclosures are based on the ability of the company whose data are sought to identify which information is proprietary and explain precisely why it is proprietary. Further, only information which is proprietary or a trade secret is exempted, and if it is possible to provide the data and delete the trade secret information, this should be done.

In order for the Freedom of Information Act considerations to arise, information must be submitted to the government and a private party must request that information. Generally, this will put the government in a position of having to act on the private party's request. Business should keep this in mind and when submitting information to the government should:

1. Make it easy for the government to resist disclosure by specifically pointing out and labeling which information is proprietary

2. Conspicuously label and identify all proprietary information so that it is not inadvertently disclosed

Realistic business managers should recognize that the only way to substantially benefit their company is to have the government on their side. They must, therefore, not alienate the government by making unsupported or overextended requests for confidential treatment. Confidential treatment should be requested only where it is absolutely necessary and where the necessity can be supported by some understandable explanation.

Business executives and their lawyers should be aware of and take advantage of the particular rules of the agency which may be aimed at securing confidential treatment. Almost all agencies have such procedures, and business should make maximum use of them.

As a last resort, business executives and their lawyers should be ready to go to court to ask for an injunction against improper disclosures and to use the criminal statute as leverage against the government if it will not cooperate.

The Freedom of Information Act seems to be of particular use to competitors in the context of government procurement, and companies submitting bids to the government should be particularly careful to protect their secret information as well as they can.

The affirmative action plan of companies is another extremely sensitive area both from the standpoint of competitors obtaining useful information and from the standpoint of private litigants obtaining possible material for civil rights cases.

The obvious should not be overlooked. Freedom of Information Act problems will not apply at all if you keep the confidential information out of the hands of the government either by not giving it up in the first place (perhaps the government would be content to examine it on your premises) or by doing everything you can to get it back after the government's reason for having it ends.

CHAPTER SIXTY-THREE

RECORD RETENTION:
LEGAL ASPECTS

Record retention is one very narrow portion of records management, and, as its name implies, records management is a management problem. On the other hand, there is a rather elaborate scheme of federal requirements governing the period for which companies must maintain records and in some cases establishing exactly what records must be maintained. Accordingly, records management has some legal overtones, as do most other areas of business.

The federal requirements on document generation and retention are lengthy and detailed; however, they are conveniently collected once each year by the United States Government Printing Office and published in a separate issue of the *Federal Register*. It takes approximately 100 pages of this *Federal Register* fine print to set forth all of these details, but at least they are gathered in one place. On the other hand, when you go through this guide item by item, it becomes apparent that the overwhelming majority of the requirements are very particular or special in nature and the requirements applicable to most businesses are much more limited. For purposes of this discussion, we will not go through a detailed list of the kinds of records businesses must generate and the length of time they must keep them, but the following general observations should illustrate some of the problems.

Federal law expressly requires the creation and maintenance of many different kinds of records. Sometimes the federal requirements are lengthy and specific, other times they are very general and subjective. Records relating to employment taxes, including withholding records and records relating to social security and the federal unemployment tax are required to be kept for 4 years after the due date of such tax or the date tax is actually paid, whichever is later.

Numerous requirements provide record retention periods for government contractors, the normal period being 3 years.

There are numerous specific requirements for tax records. The general retention period, however, is subjective: as long as the contents thereof may become material in the administration of any Internal Revenue law.

ERISA requirements are substantial and complicated. The Occupational Safety and Health Act, the environmental laws, the Consumer Product Safety Act, the Securities Exchange Act, the Civil Rights Act, and many other laws contain their own specific requirements as to which records must be generated and how long they must be kept.

STATUTES OF LIMITATIONS

Another way that the law relates to records management is in statutes of limitations. The statutes of limitations should be considered when constructing a record retention policy; however, they should not necessarily be controlling. Following are general comments on statutes of limitations as they relate to record retention policies:

1. The Uniform Commercial Code provides for a general 4-year statute of limitations on sales contracts.

2. Various state laws provide for statutes of limitations, as for example the following list from the Ohio Revised Code:

Written contracts (except for sales)	15 years
Title or real possession of property	21 years
Contract not in writing	6 years
For the torts of trespass, recovery of personal property, fraud, or other injury	4 years
Bodily injury	2 years
Libel, slander, assault, battery, malicious prosecution, false imprisonment	1 year
Unpaid minimum wages and overtime	2 years
For other matters not specifically listed	10 years

Statutes of limitations refer to the period during which an action may be brought for an alleged wrong. Unfortunately, the period when the statute of limitation starts is sometimes not clear. In the case of bodily injury or assault and battery, the event which gives rise to the cause of action is clear, but in other cases it may be subjective. For example, in the case of a written contract which is going to take 3 years to perform, the 15-year period may start not from the time the contract is executed but instead from the time someone defaults on it. In other words, if the contract is performed adequately for 2 years and then someone breaches it, the 15-year period may start from then. Also, in the case of latent defects, fraud, or other faults which would make it inequitable to bar someone's suit on the basis of an arbitrary time limit, the courts may extend that time limit by measuring it not from the time the event occurred but from when the aggrieved person found out about the event. Libel and slander are prime examples. For example, if someone published a libel statement about someone else but the other party did not find out about it until some time later, the court might very well measure the 1-year period from the time the person found out about the libel statement rather than from the time it was issued.

Besides all that, it is not absolutely essential that documents be kept for the period of the statute of limitations. Record retention and records management involves a balance between keeping everything you may ever conceivably need and throwing out things you might wish you had kept. Also, the magnitude of the contract or other problem is important. For example, it may be appropriate to retain contracts over a certain amount for 15 years, whereas contracts under that amount would not necessarily need to be retained for the entire 15-year period.

MICROFILM

In some cases, a document retention program will involve microfilming of documents in order to save space or perhaps to provide disaster protection through the creation of a duplicate set of important documents kept in a separate facility. Again, the legal input is small but very important. Generally, any business record which would be admissible in court in its original form will be admissible if it is on microfilm *provided*:

1. The microfilming program is done in the regular course of business.
2. The microfilming is done in good faith.
3. The microfilm can be properly identified.

In other words, a microfilm program will generally not create any legal problems if it is properly established and maintained; but if it is done in a haphazard and random fashion, the company runs the risk that the microfilm records might not be admissible in court because the court may say that they weren't kept in the regular course of business, or it may be very difficult to identify the microfilm because of the lack of any uniform procedures for the process.

The law on this subject is contained in the federal statutes and a number of state statutes which have substantially similar provisions. The federal statute provides as follows:

> If any business, institution, member of a profession or calling, or any department or agency of government, in the regular course of business or activity has kept or recorded any memorandum, writing, entry, print, representation or combination thereof, of any act, transaction, occurrence or event, and in the regular course of business has caused any or all of the same to be recorded, copied, or reproduced by any photographic, photostatic, microfilm, microcard, miniature photographic, or other process which accurately reproduces or forms a durable medium for so reproducing the original, the original may be destroyed in the regular course of business unless its preservation is required by law. Such reproduction, when satisfactorily identified, is as admissible in evidence as the original itself in any judicial or administrative proceeding whether the original is in existence or not, and an enlargement or facsimile of such reproduction is likewise admissible in evidence if the original reproduction is in existence and available for inspection under direction of court. The introduction of a reproduced record, enlargement, or facsimile does not preclude admission of the original. This subsection shall not be construed to exclude from evidence any document or copy thereof which is otherwise admissible under the rules of evidence.

Some state statutes, however, are slightly more restrictive, and they should be checked before starting a microfilm program.

Microfilming of certain kinds of records has become extremely common. Generally, if some record or group of records has the following characteristics, microfilming should be carefully considered:

1. The records would take a lot of space if they were not microfilmed.

2. The records generally take the form of pieces of paper which are all the same size and can easily be put in some logical sequence.

3. The records will probably not have to be frequently referred to.

The following kinds of records generally satisfy these characteristics and are commonly microfilmed:

1. Canceled checks of all kinds.

2. Dividend registers, shareholder lists, or similar items which take the form of a large volume of computer printout paper.

3. Routine payroll and tax forms.

Commercial microfilming equipment has progressed quite substantially in recent years, and there are now pieces of equipment which not only show the microfilm on a reader but can print out a printed copy, so if you want a printed copy to work from you can get it easily on the same machine you use to read the microfilm.

Generally, papers which do not take a lot of space and which in many cases involve sheets of various sizes which may be stapled together are usually only microfilmed by companies which have fairly elaborate and extensive microfilming facilities of their own. Examples include:

1. Articles of incorporation or amendments thereto of the company and its affiliates.

2. Insurance policies.

3. Miscellaneous contracts, patents, etc.

4. Nonstandard size engineering and accounting records.

SUBPOENA POWER

Companies must remember that all documents retained, whether in microfilm or otherwise, are subject to subpoena by private litigants and the government. This is true even if the company is not directly involved in the litigation. The efforts and expense incident to these subpoenas, which are issued very frequently in today's litigious atmosphere, are cogent reasons for implementing a meaningful document retention program—which of course is merely another name for a document destruction program.

LEGAL IMPLICATIONS OF DOCUMENT DESTRUCTION

Destruction of documents pursuant to a formal legal document retention program is both legal and ethical, but in some cases there can be problems. One of the legal inputs to the records retention program and the records management program must be to make certain that the program incorporates a method whereby it can be interrupted if the company becomes involved in an investigation or litigation. There is nothing more disastrous for a company in litigation than to have to admit that it destroyed documents after it had reason to believe someone would submit a claim for which those documents would be relevant.

One of the more usual areas where this arises is in the field of antitrust. Indeed, some articles which tell lawyers how to do an antitrust audit contain as an integral part of the recommendation a document retention program.

In many companies the trade regulation lawyer is assigned the task of establishing, revising, or supervising a document retention program.

Generally, the destruction of documents pursuant to a normal document retention policy will create no legal or ethical problems. However, the following situations may be exceptions to this:

1. After the service of process requiring the production of documents, it is illegal to destroy those documents which may be relevant.

2. During the course of alleged voluntary cooperation with government authorities, it may be illegal or at best imprudent to destroy documents.

3. Possibly even after learning of a relevant inquiry but before being contacted by the authorities, destruction of documents could create embarrassment, if not some legal and ethical problems.

In these situations, it is submitted that companies should suspend the operation of their document retention program pending resolution of the problem.

ELECTRONIC DATA PROCESSING (EDP)

Information is increasingly stored on electronic data processing equipment. This is especially true of data relating to federal income taxes. There are a number of Internal Revenue Service rulings and procedures on this point, generally to the effect that if properly done, data can be stored on magnetic tape and comply with IRS rules. Generally, the procedure is to individually negotiate procedures with the IRS and then have a letter setting forth the agreement. Generally, the retention period for these so-called machine-sensible records is the earliest of:

1. The completion of the computer-assisted auditing techniques for the taxable year

2. The expiration of the statute of limitations for the taxable year

3. The release by mutual consent

Sometimes, the company is expressly required to retain the hard copy so that the "audit trail" will be maintained.

PERSONNEL INVOLVED

It is probably not very economical to charge counsel with the complete job of establishing and administering a record retention program. However, counsel should play some part in that program because of its legal implications. In addition, it is clear that a record retention program and a records management program are horses of different colors. A record retention program or policy can be done by lawyers in writing; but a records management program which includes procedures for actually calling forth documents for examination and possibly destroying them after the relevant periods, and for filing documents in a way that they can be found and for storing them, is a complex and in some cases very costly and complicated program. Also, the system generally doesn't work without the cooperation of everyone, including the persons who put the paper into this system in the first place. Those people must designate at least initially the period of retention so that the records can be called forth at the end of that period and a decision made as to whether they should be kept further, microfilmed, or thrown out. A program which is pushed down from the top seems to be doomed to early failure, although top management's support is required, because money is usually required. To be successful, those people who will actually use the system must be convinced of its value. In most cases, this means the expenditure of a great amount of time and effort on educating the people who will operate this system as well as those who will use and be responsible for it.

THE RETENTION PERIODS

The retention periods are generally a function of administrative decision by company management rather than legal requirements; however, the company should make sure that any document retention program at least corresponds with the legal requirements referred to above. The writing of a record retention program (especially the listing of documents and the period of retention) is a difficult and complex job. Furthermore, in examining a number of schedules from published sources and those which have been made available from private companies, there appears to be a great deal of difference of opinion as to the proper periods of record retention.

Another problem is the organization of the guide. Generally, there are two approaches. One is a simple, alphabetical listing by the name of the document. The other is some kind of functional grouping. It appears that the functional grouping is a little better because it seems easier to use and understand.

Another problem is the question of whether to list every single document which may be found in the company's files or to condense the list down to one page of general categories or to hit some compromise in between. Each approach has been observed and in the appropriate context each can be workable. It would appear, however, that a reasonable compromise would usually be the best.

The record retention periods should assume a reasonable business risk. It should be recognized that some documents may be discarded in a case where it would have been better to keep them. This is the price one pays for the savings and space and increased efficiency which should be generated by the program.

As a rough guide and as a sample of what a guide could look like, the following chart of various kinds of documents and suggested record retention periods is set forth. As in all legal matters, it should not be implemented by any specific company without thorough analysis by the appropriate people to make sure that it is workable, useful, and appropriate. It does, however, show the kinds of things which should be considered and is intended to be the compromise approach referred to above. The list of kinds of documents could be made much longer, or in the alternative, documents could be grouped together under headings and the guide could be greatly shortened.

RECORD RETENTION GUIDE

Abbreviations
P—Permanent
AT—After Termination
SUP—Until Superseded
OBS—Until Obsolete
AC—After Completion
AF—After End of Fiscal Year

GUIDELINES FOR RETENTION OF CORRESPONDENCE AND INTERNAL
MEMORANDUMS

General correspondence should normally be retained as follows:

I. *Letters to be destroyed immediately and never filed.*
   A. Unimportant letters and notes which require no acknowledgment or follow-up, such as notes of appreciation, congratulations, letters of transmittal and plans for meetings.
   B. Form letters which require no follow-up.
   C. Other letters of inconsequential subject matter or which definitely close correspondence to which no further reference will be necessary.
   D. Copies of interdepartmental or other company correspondence where another copy of the same letter will be in the file.

II. *Letters to be filed temporarily (30 days to 12 months).*
   A. Letters of general inquiry and replies which complete a cycle of correspondence and have no value after possible reference from the correspondent within a reasonable period of time.
   B. Letters requesting specific action such as name or address change or complaints, which have no further value after changes are made or action taken.
   C. Similar letters of various types which might be referred to shortly after they are received or written but which soon cease to have value unless further immediate correspondence ensues.

III. *Letters to be kept from 1 to 5 years.*
   A. Letters relating to establishing credit. Letters applying for employment with the company.
   B. Memorandums and reports about expense accounts which have limited value after the voucher is approved.
   C. Letters explaining but not establishing company policy.
   D. Collection letters which have limited value after the account is paid.
   E. Quotation letters where no contract results.
   F. Letters to which a customer might make reference a year or two later.
   G. Other letters to which some reference might be helpful as late as 1 to 5 years after date.

IV. *Letters to be kept indefinitely or for the life of the principal document which they support.*
   A. Letters pertaining to patents, copyrights, licensing agreements, bills of sale, permits, etc.
   B. Letters which constitute all or a part of a contract or which are important in the clarification of certain points in a contract.
   C. Letters denying liability of the company.
   D. Other letters which the company might need to produce in court to disprove liability or to enforce rights of the company.

GUIDELINES FOR RETENTION OF OTHER DOCUMENTS OR RECORDS*

I. *General corporate records including documents processed or received by the Office of the Corporate Secretary.*
   General Principle
   The Office of the Corporate Secretary shall be responsible for establishing adequate record retention programs and policies for all documents normally handled by that office. The Office of the Corporate Secretary shall keep indefinitely all documents which may be legally required or which may have business signifi-

---

* Figures at right refer to number of years.

cance, and, in addition, shall keep or provide for the retention of such other documents as may have historical value.

A. All SEC and SEC-related material and all financing documents, credit agreements, loan agreements, commitments, etc. . . . .   P
B. Records of incorporation, code of regulations and amendments thereto. . . . .   P
C. Meetings of directors, shareholders and the Executive Committee. .   P
D. Annual reports, quarterly reports and proxy material . . . .   P
E. Proxies for any meeting of shareholders for meetings for other than solely election of directors . . . .   P

II. *Shareholder records.*
General Principle

The Shareholder Records Department shall be responsible for establishing and maintaining a record retention program which will protect the interests of the company in this area.

The Shareholder Records Department shall keep such records as will enable the company to ascertain who its existing shareholders are, who its shareholders were at any time in the past and whether or not any person was ever a shareholder of the company. The Shareholder Records Department shall also keep an adequate record of the payment of all dividends so that the company's dividend liability to any shareholder or group of shareholders can be ascertained.

A. Stock transfer and stockholder records . . . .   P
B. Stock savings plan records. . . . .   P
C. Dividend checks . . . .   P
D. Dividend register . . . .   P

III. *Tax records.*
General Principle

All corporations required to file a tax return of any kind must keep such permanent books of account or records, including inventories, as are sufficient to establish the amount of gross income, deductions, credits, or other matters required to be shown by such person in any such return.

These documents and records should be kept for as long as the contents thereof may become material in the administration of an Internal Revenue law.

The corporation should keep sufficient records to compute its earnings and profits permanently.

A. Depreciation schedules . . . .   P
B. Tax bills and statements . . . .   P
C. Tax returns (all) . . . .   P
D. Social security tax records. . . . .   P
E. State property tax records . . . .   P
F. State income tax records . . . .   P
G. Unemployment tax records   ⎤ Until Statute
                                                               ⎟ of
H. Sales and use tax records   ⎬ Limitation
                                                               ⎟ on tax
I. Excise tax records   ⎦ has expired

Work papers for each of the above should be kept for corresponding periods.

IV. *Pension documents and supporting employee data.*
General Principle

Pension documents and supporting employee data shall be kept in such manner and for such periods that the company can establish at all times whether or not any pension is payable to any person and if so the amount of such pension.

A. Pension plans and all amendments thereto . . . .   P
B. Records of employee service and eligibility for pension (including hours worked and any breaks in service) . . . .   P

C. Required personal information on employees and former
employees. (name, address, social security number,
period of employment, pay, hourly or salaried) .... P
D. Records of plan administrator setting forth authority to pay .... P
E. Records of pension paid to employees or their   6 after
beneficiaries   death of payee
F. Reports of pensions or pension plans filed with the Department
of Labor or Internal Revenue Service .... P

V. *Accounting and finance.*
A. All ledgers 20
B. All balance sheets and other financial statements .... P
C. Estimates, projections, planning, memos, etc. 10
D. Banking records, including deposit and withdrawal records,
bank statements 20
E. Checking records, including account statements, check register
and canceled checks 20
F. Expense accounts, approvals, petty cash records, sales
personnel commission records 10

VI. *Patents and trademarks.*
A. Original patents and trademarks, related docu-   Life of the patent
ments, work papers, correspondence, memos, etc.   or trademark, plus
5 years
B. Royalty records ....   Life of the patent
or trademark, plus
5 years

VII. *Plant and property records.*
A. Depreciation schedules .... P
B. Inventory records .... P
C. Maintenance & repair, building 10
D. Maintenance & repair, machinery 5
E. Plant account cards, equipment .... P
F. Property deeds, easements, licenses, rights of   10 years after
way   disposal of
property
G. Purchase or lease records of plant facility ....   10 years after
property ceases
to be occupied
H. Space allocation records 1
I. Mortgages ....   5 years after recording of cancellation
J. Property insurance ....   10 years after
disposal of property

VIII. *Personnel.*
A. Applications (nonemployees)   1
(employees) ....   3 AT
B. Attendance records (general)   3
C. Commissions/bonuses, incentives, awards, etc. (general) ..   6
D. Earnings records (general) ....   P
E. Education and training records (general) ....   10 AT
F. Garnishments (general)   3
G. Fingerprints (general) ....   10 AT
H. Job evaluations   3
I. Medical histories ....   P
J. Safety or injury frequency reports   10
K. Testing (general)   10
L. Time cards and time sheets   4
M. Individual contracts of employment ....   6 AT

N.   Fidelity bonds 10
O.   Insurance records (employees) .... 11 AT
P.   Job descriptions .... 2 SUP
Q.   Training manuals .... P
R.   Union agreements .... 3 (1 copy P)
S.   Affirmative action programs .... 1 SUP
T.   EEO-1 3
U.   Employees' personal records, including application forms, individual attendance records, medical history, performance evaluations, termination papers, exit interview records, withholding information, garnishments, test results (individual), etc.
        Hourly .... 4 AT
        Salaried (nonexempt) .... 4 AT
        Salaried (exempt) .... 6 AT
V.   Invention assignment forms .... P

IX.   Printing and duplicating.
A.   Copies reproduced, technical publications, charts .... 1 or OBS
B.   Negatives 5
C.   Photographs 1
D.   Production records .... 1 AC

X.   Manufacturing.
A.   Bills of material 2
B.   Drafting records .... P
C.   Drawings 15
D.   Inspection records 15
E.   Lab test reports .... P
F.   Memos, production .... AC
G.   Product tooling, design, engineering, research, experiment & specs records 20
H.   Production reports.................................... 3
I.   Quality reports .... 1 AC
J.   Reliability records .... P
K.   Stock issuing records .... 3 AT
L.   Tool control .... 3 AT
M.   Work orders 3
N.   Work status reports .... AC

XI.   Office supplies and service.
A.   Inventories .... 1 AF
B.   Office equipment records .... 6 AF
C.   Requests for services................................. 1 AF
D.   Requisitions for supplies .... 1 AF

XII.   Quality control and inspection.
A.   Customer service records 15
B.   Equipment and instrument calibration records 15
C.   Inspection and test records 15
D.   Material substitution records 15
E.   Supplier quality data 15
F.   X-ray films... 15

XIII.   Sales and marketing.
A.   Customer order file (O.E. business)
     (Customer order files for replacement type or off-the-shelf products may be retained for only 3 years after becoming inactive.)

     1. Correspondence .... Active + 5
     2. Cost estimates .... Active + 5
     3. Customer purchase order .... Active + 15
     4. Quotations .... Active + 5
  B. Sales invoices .... 1 after payment
  C. Market investigations and reports 7
  D. Presentations and proposals 7
  E. Sales analysis reports 5
  F. Sales expenses 5
  G. Market research data 7

XIV. *Public relations.*
  A. Master copies of annual reports, quarterly reports, financial
      publications .... P
  B. Mailing lists .... Active + 5
  C. Publicity clippings 5
  D. Photographs and artwork .... P**
  E. Employee publications .... Active + 1
  F. Corporate/division brochures 3
  G. Corporate identity guides & style sheets 10
  H. Examples of trademark/logo use 5
  I. Product/program information 3
  J. Corporate/group films/slides (master copies) ...... P*
  K. Corporate calendar/lithograph files .... P

XV. *Credit relating to customers.*
  A. Application for credit, approval forms, qualification
      reports .... Active + 1***
  B. Correspondence—collection 2
  C. Customer financial statements 3
  D. Guarantees and subordination agreements .... Active + 3
  E. Security agreements & financing statements .... Active + 3
  F. Trade clearances 3
  G. Marginal accounts .... ****
  H. Disputed accounts .... ****
  I. Embarrassed debtors .... ****

XVI. *Contracts—commercial customer & government.*
  A. Contracts—commercial customer .... 10 years after expiration or termination
  B. Contracts—government (prime and subcontract)† 6 years after expiration or termination‡
     Might include:
        Contracts & correspondence
        Material requisitions
        Production records
        Purchase orders

** Weeded out periodically to retain only items with historical value.
*** Retain for 1 year after becoming inactive.
**** Files to be retained at the discretion of the credit manager.
† While the contract is in effect, the packet should be continually reviewed and duplicates destroyed. After termination, all non-essential papers should be destroyed prior to filing contract in storage.
‡ Records pertaining to outstanding exceptions, unsettled clams, incomplete investigations, cases pending or under litigation shall be retained until final clearance or settlement.

Receiving records
Shipping records
Shop orders
Work orders
Vendor invoices—contract and modifying documents
Security requirements
Cost & pricing data
Consent to subcontract or purchase
Performance bond
Purchase orders issued
Notice to proceed and start or stop orders
Insurance policies or certificates of insurance
Documents supporting advance or progress payments
Production records
Progress or status reports
Advice of delays and corrective actions
Delivery and production completion documents
Quality assurance and quality control
    1) Quality program & review reports
    2) Subcontract inspection records
    3) Inspection & test reports
    4) Authority to ship and acceptance documents

XVII. *Traffic & transportation.*
    A. Aircraft operating and maintenance .... P
    B. Bills of lading, waybills .... 2 after delivery
    C. Employee travel .... 1 AF
    D. Freight bills .... 3 after payment
    E. Freight claims .... 2 after settlement
    F. Household moves.................................... 3 after move
    G. Motor operating & maintenance 2
    H. Rates and tariffs .... SUP
    I. Receiving documents 2–10
    J. Shipping and related documents 2–10

XVIII. *Security.*
    A. Classified material violations .... P
    B. Courier authorizations .... 1 mo after trip
    C. Employee clearance lists .... SUP
    D. Employee case files 5
    E. Fire prevention program .... P
    F. Protection—guards, badge lists, protective devices 5
    G. Subcontractor clearances .... 2 AT
    H. Visitor clearance 2

ESSENTIAL-DOCUMENT PRESERVATION

For certain documents, it is essential to preserve the original or a copy admissible in court. Contracts, some tax records, and some accounting and business records are examples. One of the lawyer's responsibilities in the record retention area should be to identify those documents which the corporation *must* retain and protect from theft, willful destruction, fire, etc. Generally, the only way to assure this is to have a duplicate (perhaps in the form of microfilm) stored in some other place besides the corporate offices. EDP records may also fall into this category. Some EDP records in the form of magnetic tapes or discs may have to be duplicated and stored in another location to assure the company's continued ability to operate in the event of a disaster.

On the other hand, one need not go overboard on this concept, because some documents naturally find their way into two separate places; the most numerous are those filed with the government. For example, a company should protect copies of all documents filed with the SEC via duplicate storage, but this is accomplished automatically, because the documents are available at the SEC and if all the company's SEC documents happened to be destroyed by fire, the company could get duplicates by going to the SEC (although this might be time-consuming and expensive). The same thing is true for patents, trademarks, and copyrights, although in some cases there may be some ancillary documents not filed with the patent office that need disaster protection.

Another source of possible document duplication is outside counsel's office. Management should make certain its general counsel knows which documents are where and that there are duplicates where it makes sense to have duplicates. Remember that counsel's office is subject to disaster also and so the duplication procedure should run both ways. Essential documents which are only in outside counsel's files should be duplicated in-house and vice versa.

Disaster protection can be accomplished via microfilm, but the precautions about "regular course of business" must be observed. It would be dangerous to use a random microfilm procedure to preserve essential documents, because they may fail the requirements for admissibility in court when they are needed.

There are many firms which specialize in this area—both in consulting and in actually providing the space for storage of the duplicate documents. It does cost money, but it would seem that some disaster-protection system would be prudent business management and that the lack of any procedure at all could be viewed as a possible subject of a corporate mismanagement claim if a situation arose where the company's essential documents were destroyed and substantial financial detriments were incurred. In other words, some system may be necessary to protect top management from a shareholder suit in the event of a disaster.

CHAPTER SIXTY-FOUR

STATE CORPORATION LAW

Since the mid 1970s (principally arising out of the large number of cases which seemed to show that corporations had made illegal political contributions, bribes, etc.), there has been a push at the federal level to enact statutes which will require the nation's largest corporations to be federally chartered. Essentially, this would mean that the large corporations would operate under a set of uniform rules established and enforced by the federal government. However, at the present time, this is not the case, and all corporations from the largest to the smallest operate under *state* corporation laws. All of these corporations have corporate charters which are issued by the state, not the federal government, and the rules governing corporate rights, duties, and procedures are state laws rather than federal laws.

Obviously, there are many exceptions to this statement. Indeed, those exceptions are the basic reason for this book. Today, there is so much federal regulation of business that the old texts on business law, which discussed state corporate laws, contract rights, agency, and similar subjects, simply do not deal with the kinds of problems corporate executives face today. The principal exception to the rule that corporations are governed by state law is that any time securities are issued in interstate commerce, the securities acts take effect, and some commentators have characterized the intervention of federal securities laws into corporate activity as significant enough to warrant the characterization of these laws as a new "federal corporation law."

While it is certainly true that federal regulation of business has been so substantial as to justify the assertion that there really is a federal corporation law, it is important to note that, technically at least, corporations are still creatures of state law. They are created under a set of rules established by the state, and the rights and duties of the various constituencies (shareholders, officers, and directors) are still largely governed by state corporation law.

Lawyers are taught in law school that state corporation laws differ rather substantially among the states. However, these differences are very technical, and from a business point of view they are usually not significant. Some years ago, there was a battle among the various states to make their corporation laws attractive so that companies would incorporate there and the states could in turn obtain the taxes the corporations paid. Delaware led the fight by liberalizing its corporate laws so that some of the archaic and cumbersome rules were eliminated. New Jersey joined the battle by doing the same thing, and in fairly short order many of the nation's largest corporations were chartered under the laws of either Delaware or New Jersey. Delaware and New Jersey corporate laws are still very favorable, and there are many large companies chartered in these two states. However, many other large companies are chartered in other states, and the differences between state corporation laws is generally not a substantial factor in business planning today.

This is not to say that state *tax* laws are not a substantial business factor. In fact, state taxes have substantially overshadowed the importance of state corporate laws for purposes of determining which states companies or their various subsidiaries want to be chartered in.

Almost all the state corporation laws have the following pattern. First, there is a system for establishing a corporation. In the progressive states, it is rather simple to do, and one individual can do it. This facilitates the one-person corporation, which is sometimes useful in the professions or for small businesses. In other states, it may be that two or three or more incorporators are necessary; but in all states, the procedures for forming a corporation are so simple that in most cases it is not even necessary to have a lawyer do it. Further, in most states, the required paperwork to maintain the corporation can be done by anyone who takes the time to learn a few simple requirements.

All corporation laws then proceed to provide in one way or another that the shareholders elect the directors, who in turn elect the officers. There are, thus, these three constituencies in all corporations, and state corporation laws go into considerable detail in regulating the details, rights, duties, and obligations of these groups.

THE SHAREHOLDERS

The shareholders own the corporation, but they do not have the right to participate in the day-to-day management of the corporation. The shareholder's main right is to elect the directors. Almost all state corporate statutes require the corporation to hold an annual meeting at which the shareholders elect the directors. On the other hand, the laws almost always allow a "staggered board," so that the shareholders elect only some directors each year. It is thought that a staggered board inhibits an unfriendly takeover offer, because even if some group were successful in getting all of the shares of the company, it would have the right to elect only a percentage of the directors for any one year, and it would take 2 or 3 or perhaps more years to replace the entire board of directors.

Many state laws also provide for "preemptive rights." This means that the shareholders are allowed to purchase any new stock issued by the corporation up to the percentage they own already. This prevents the corporation from reducing the percentage interest of certain shareholders by simply issuing more stock. For example, if a corporation has three shareholders each owning one-third of the stock, then if there were no preemptive rights, two-thirds of the shareholders could authorize the corporation to issue an additional block of stock which would, for all practical purposes, operate to reduce the other shareholder's interest to almost nothing.

Another right often granted shareholders is the right to vote their shares cumulatively. Cumulative voting is a mechanism whereby a shareholder is assured that if he owns a certain percentage of the company, he will be able to elect a certain percentage of the directors. If cumulative voting were not available, an individual who owned more than half the stock could elect the entire board. If shareholders have cumulative voting, an individual who owns slightly less than half the stock will at least be assured some representation on the board. The exact figures are complicated, and they depend upon how many directors are on the board, whether the board is staggered, and what percentage of stock is owned by the individual desiring to vote cumulatively.

Preemptive rights and cumulative voting are important subjects for small businesses, but they are not very important in large, publicly held corporations. In larger companies, the shareholders are really not concerned with their percentage of interest or ownership—it is usually so small as to be insignificant—and even under cumulative voting, they could not elect any of the directors.

Shareholders also, however, have the right to examine the books of the corporation, and this can be important in large as well as small companies. The right to examine books is fairly technical, and there are a lot of limitations, depending upon the jurisdiction involved. However, the Ohio statute is typical, and it provides the following:

1. Any shareholder at a meeting of shareholders can demand to see a list of all the other shareholders (there is some question under many state laws whether the shareholder is entitled to copy that list).

2. Any shareholder, "upon written demand stating the specific purpose thereof," shall have the right to examine in person or by agent and for any reasonable and proper purpose the articles of the corporation, its regulations, its books and records of account, and minutes and records of shareholders. This portion of the Ohio statute specifically allows the shareholder to "make copies or extracts thereof."

The right of shareholders to examine the books of the company does not seem to be exercised too much in large companies, but it does in smaller ones. The principal reason to do so is to ascertain the value of the company. In the case of a large company where the stock is publicly traded, the marketplace will fix the value of the stock, and if a shareholder wants to either buy or sell shares, the market information plus the information the company must file with the SEC will usually satisfy his needs. In the case of a smaller company, however, about the only way a shareholder who does not have direct access to management could ascertain the true value of the company would be to use this right to examine its books and records.

The right to examine the shareholder list can become troublesome even in a large company, because the availability of the shareholder list can be used in a tender offer situation. The Ohio statute does not seem to expressly allow someone to make a complete copy of the shareholder list. At least in Ohio, therefore, this would not seem to be a problem. On the other hand, you would have to make sure that the shareholder list was available at the annual meeting in case someone wanted to see it.

Shareholders are entitled to vote by proxy, and most of them do. In most large companies, the proxy rules are governed by the SEC laws rather than by state corporate laws, and those are discussed in Chapter 42.

THE DIRECTORS

The right to manage the company is vested in the board of directors. The Ohio statute is typical. It says that:

> Except where the law, the articles, or the regulations require action to be authorized or taken by shareholders, all of the authority of a corporation shall be exercised by its directors.

The Ohio law, like that of most states, authorizes the directors to do the following:

1. Rely upon the books and records of the corporation or upon reports made to the corporation by an officer or other employee selected "with reasonable care"

2. Establish committees of the board of directors, including an executive committee that can take any action the entire board can take

3. Elect the officers of the company

In addition, there are some other points of corporate law which people serving on the board of directors should be aware of. The most important is the state laws relating to conflict of interest in transactions with the corporation in which the director has a personal interest. Most state laws do allow the corporation to transact business with a director even though the director may have a personal stake in the deal. On the other hand, almost all of these kinds of statutes require full disclosure on the part of the director, and they also require the director to abstain from voting on the transaction.

The common law of most states also requires that the directors act prudently and use "reasonable business judgment." This business judgment rule is very important to the directors, because it provides essentially that if they do use good judgment, the fact that a particular transaction might turn out badly and cost the corporation and its shareholders money is not grounds to sue them individually. On the other hand, if the directors do not act in a reasonably prudent fashion and do not exercise good business judgment, they can be held personally liable for corporate losses which arise out of their imprudent conduct.

In addition to these general laws, there are some unusual state laws which impose liability in specific cases. In Ohio, for example, there is a specific statute which imposes personal liability upon a director for a corporate loan to any officer, director, or shareholder of the corporation. Thus, if an Ohio corporation loans money to an employee who also happens to be either an officer, director, or shareholder, the board of directors is personally liable for any losses the corporation might sustain if the employee does not repay the loan.

THE OFFICERS

The officers of a corporation are usually the president, a secretary, a treasurer, and if desired, a chairman of the board or one or more vice-presidents and other assistant officers. The Ohio rule on the authority of officers is typical and provides as follows:

All officers, as between themselves and the corporation, shall have such authority and perform such duties as are determined by the directors.

Thus, the officers are practically under the complete control of the board of directors. Naturally, this does not mean that the board could get out of a contract which the officers had entered into with apparent authority to execute. The words "as between themselves and the corporation" make it clear that we are talking about the rights of the corporation, the officers, and the directors, and not third parties who might have relied upon the apparent authority of an officer. Except for the rights of third parties, however, the officers must account to the board of directors, and they can be removed by the directors at will (they might have contract rights for damages, but they can still be removed).

THE CAPITAL STRUCTURE OF THE CORPORATION

Most state statutes allow almost unlimited flexibility in the capital structure of a corporation. The company can have common stock, preferred stock, or a wide variety of different classes of common or preferred stock. Almost all of the state statutes are very liberal in this regard, and so long as the proper documents spell out the rights of each class, a corporation can divide its ownership just about any way it wants.

Statutes usually provide that the common stock shall exercise all of the voting power of the corporation. However, there can be different classes of common stock, and it is possible to use voting trusts or proxy arrangements to concentrate the voting power and control of a corporation in a very small group, even if there might be many different common shareholders.

The preferred stock is usually stated to be nonvoting, with the possible exception that in some cases it may be voting stock if the corporation does not pay the preferred dividends for a certain period. Preferred stock dividends may be cumulative or noncumulative. A cumulative preferred stock requires the company to make up any missed dividends, and a noncumulative one does not.

Preferred stock may also be convertible into common stock on any basis that the corporation desires. A corporation may issue bonds (straight debt securities) and these can also be convertible.

In short, most corporation laws will allow just about any kind of capital structure that management or the financial people feel would be desirable.

DISSENTING RIGHTS

In certain major transactions where the shareholders as a whole may exercise authority to approve the transaction or not, those who dissent may have a right to be bought out at the market value of their stock. Usually, the statutes create a right to have the stock appraised by an independent appraiser, and sometimes these dissenting rights are also referred to as "appraisal rights." Statutes differ on the precise kinds of transactions which will give rise to dissenting or appraisal rights. Usually, only major and fundamental actions give rise to this right. In Ohio, for example, there are three situations which give rise to appraisal rights. They are (1) a merger, (2) a sale of all the assets of the corporation, and (3) amendments to the articles of incorporation which change the purpose of the corporation or adversely affect the rights of the class of shares owned by the person asking for the appraisal right.

Dissenting rights also have greater importance to small, nonpublic corporations than they do to public ones. If the stock is publicly traded, that serves as the independent appraisal, and in most situations, a shareholder would be hard pressed to say that any offer at market or above was unfair and, therefore, get a higher price pursuant to a dissenting or appraisal right statute.

DERIVATIVE LAWSUITS

One of the most important rights a shareholder has is to bring a lawsuit on behalf of the corporation—usually against the board of directors or an officer of the corporation. The theory here is that the shareholder is suing "derivatively" because the directors or officers will not cause the corporation to take a required action. The most prevalent example of a derivative lawsuit is in the area of short swing profits, where it might be alleged that a director or 10-percent shareholder has illegally profited from a short swing transaction (see Chapter 40 for a more detailed discussion). If the corporation will not bring suit against the director or officer in order to recover these profits, the shareholder can bring such a suit derivatively. The recoveries, of course, would inure to the benefit of the corporation, but the shareholder would be entitled to his attorney's fees, and that is usually the motive behind these derivative lawsuits: most of them are brought by attorneys.

In other cases, it may be that the shareholders feel that the directors have acted against the interest of the shareholders—perhaps in a merger or other corporate reorganization—and they may bring a derivative suit, again, essentially on the same theory—the corporation is suing the director on the grounds that he did not discharge his obligation to the shareholders of the company to make the best deal possible. The corporate-reorganization-type derivative lawsuit, however, usually involves securities, and therefore the suit is usually brought under one of the federal securities laws, because that is generally more advantageous procedurally to a plaintiff than a state law derivative suit.

INDEMNIFICATION

State corporation laws almost always allow the corporation to indemnify officers or directors who may be sued for actions they have taken on behalf of the corporation. Most of these statutes also expressly allow the corporation to procure insurance to either pay the officers directly or reimburse the corporation for any indemnification payments it makes. This is a highly technical area where the state statutes do differ. Even a difference of a few words in a statute can mean the difference between a situation where a director can be indemnified and one where he cannot. (Indemnification is also discussed in Chapter 65.)

The above is a gross oversimplification of state corporate law. It is included herein more for the purpose of illustrating the basic premise of this book: in today's modern corporations, it is the multitude of new federal laws which have the most substantial effect on corporate activity. State corporation laws are certainly very important. However, they have remained essentially unchanged for a long time, and almost everyone who is affected by them knows their basic content. For the business executive, the principal importance of state law is how it affects his possible personal liability. If he is a director, the state statutes which establish the authority of the board of directors and enable him to rely on others in the corporation and to be indemnified are important.

CHAPTER SIXTY-FIVE

MANAGEMENT LIABILITY

There are a substantial number of situations where management can incur personal liability on the basis of actions taken in their capacity as corporate officers, directors, or even management employees. We are talking here about incurring personal liability during the course of conducting corporate business in good faith. We are excluding the obvious situation where corporate employees can incur personal liability by virtue of fraudulent or dishonest acts relating to their corporate employment.

Even assuming the best of intentions, however, it is possible to incur personal liability in a wide variety of circumstances. Personal liability can be either civil or criminal. Criminal personal liability is discussed in Chapter 66. This chapter is limited only to situations where civil liability can be imposed. Civil liability generally means liability for monetary penalties. However, in some cases, it also includes injunctions or decrees personally obligating the corporate officers or directors to take or refrain from taking certain actions.

There has been a great deal written about protecting officers and directors from personal liability. Lately, the trend is to take a very broad look at the whole spectrum of laws which can give rise to this personal liability and make sure that appropriate people know about the laws and that there are appropriate programs to assure corporate compliance. The program also includes insurance and indemnification so that officers or directors or other employees who might happen to make a good faith mistake while acting in the best interests of the corporation can still be indemnified or reimbursed for any fines or penalties they might have to pay.

LAWS WHICH CAN GIVE RISE TO PERSONAL LIABILITY

The biggest source of personal liability for officers or directors is the securities laws. The 1933 Securities Act, which governs the issuance of securities, imposes an absolute liability on directors who sign the registration statement. Generally, during a public offering, if there are any misstatements or omissions in any of the SEC documents, there is a good chance that the officers or directors can incur personal liability if the stock which is sold during the public offering later goes down in value. This is one of the reasons for the elaborate and frantic activity which goes on during the sale of stock.

The proxy rules can impose personal liability if there is a mistake or omission in the proxy statement.

Section 16(b) imposes personal liability for officers or directors who purchase or sell a company's stock within 6 months and receive a profit, and section 10(b) imposes personal liability upon officers or directors who are found to have engaged in any kind of insider trading.

The antitrust laws can impose civil and criminal liability on executives at all levels.

State corporation laws can impose personal liability if the officers or directors are found to have engaged in mismanagement or negligent management.

The environmental laws can impose civil and criminal liability.

Each of these laws has been discussed in more detail in the chapter specifically dealing with it, and the substantive discussion will not be repeated here.

The purpose of including this chapter is to make management aware that there are a large number of situations where personal liability can be imposed and that there are a number of things the company should do in order to deal with this problem. Following are some of them.

WAYS TO DEAL WITH PERSONAL LIABILITY

Officer- and Director-Liability Insurance

The primary weapon in dealing with potential personal liability is officer- and director-liability insurance coupled with good internal indemnification provisions. Typically, a corporation will have a provision in the relevant documents (bylaws or code of regulations, depending on the state law) which says in effect that any corporate employee who has been subjected to personal liability may be reimbursed for that liability by the corporation if the board of directors determines that the employee acted in the best interest of the corporation without any knowledge that the activity he was engaging in was illegal. Indemnification statutes vary slightly among the states. Consequently, the indemnification provisions used by corporations also vary. However, almost all major corporations have such provisions in order to provide some protection to officers or directors dealing with the complicated federal system of regulations which they must steer the company through.

Many companies—particularly the largest ones—also purchase officer- and director-liability insurance. The old forms of officer- and director-liability insurance required two policies: one policy directly covered the officers or directors, and the other policy was issued for the benefit of the corporation and in effect reimbursed the corporation if it had to reimburse the officers or directors. Officer- and director-liability insurance is a complicated subject, and different counselors disagree as to its real value. There are many exceptions in the policy, it is usually expensive, and in some cases—particularly for smaller companies—it may even be impossible to obtain. The prevailing opinion seems to be that where you can get it, you ought to, if for no other reason than to be able to attract good people to your board of directors and top management team.

There are a growing number of situations, however, where it is illegal to indemnify (either by insurance or through direct indemnification) officers or directors. For example, the Foreign Corrupt Practices Act provides that if a corporate officer or director engages in an illegal bribe, it is illegal for the corporation to indemnify him against any fines he has to pay. The SEC considers that indemnification of corporate officers or directors for securities law liability would be against public policy, although it appears that the commission does not feel that it would be against public policy to provide insurance coverage for such liability. Essentially then, while officer- and director-liability insurance and indemnification are very good tools and are useful in most cases, they do not provide 100-percent protection.

Informing Officers and Directors of Liability

Another tool which is used to help protect officers and directors from personal liability is various forms of educational programs. The complexities of federal regulation are such that in some cases, merely telling the officers or directors that they can incur personal liability in a given situation will alert them to problems and enable them to avoid any cases where it might arise. The primary example here is section 16(b). Many short swing profit cases arise out of inadvertent violations. The most usual one is where an executive will want to exercise a stock option and will sell stock in the company in order to obtain the money to exercise the option to purchase additional shares. This simply cannot be done within a 6-month period. The executive has to make sure that all purchases and sales—including those under stock option plans, stock savings plans, or dividend reinvestment programs—are arranged so that there is at least a 6-month interval between them.

Committees of the Board of Directors

There are also a number of structural considerations which apply mostly to the board of directors. The biggest item here is the growing use of committees of the board of directors. There have been many recent situations where the SEC has criticized corporate directors for not being sufficiently involved in the business of the company to know about mismanagement or other improper activities. The Penn Central litigation, where the SEC heavily criticized the Penn Central board, is perhaps the most publicized example. In order to deal with this problem, there has been an increasing awareness of the necessity for directors to actually do a good job directing the affairs of the company. The days when the board of directors occupied a ceremonial role and simply rubber-stamped everything that the top management presented to it are now over. If the board of directors is to do a good job, it generally must divide itself into committees, because it would be impossible for the board to keep on top of all the things it is responsible for unless the responsibility were divided up. In fact, the New York Stock Exchange has now established a requirement that companies have an independent audit committee.

There are a number of other committees of the board of directors which are becoming very popular. The litigation committee is one which has received some attention from a number of lawyers. A litigation committee would be a committee of the board of directors which made a determination whether the company ought to sue an employee (usually an officer or other director) who had engaged in improper conduct. For example, if the company president is found to have used corporate funds to make an illegal political contribution, the board of directors probably ought to establish a litigation committee of independent directors (those neither involved in the transaction nor reporting to the president) in order to make a determination as to whether it would be in the best interest of the company to sue the president to require him to reimburse the company for the illegal use of funds. In one case it was held that if an appropriately independent litigation committee makes this decision, the courts will not second-guess it.

The nominating committee is also becoming popular. The days when the corporate president simply picked his friends to serve on the board now appear to be numbered, and directors are chosen because of their ability and because they can bring something to the board which is needed by the company.

Most boards have an executive committee, which is usually established in order to transact day-to-day business between formal board meetings. The usual reason for establishing an executive committee is convenience. Certain actions must be taken by the board, and most state statutes allow the board to delegate its responsibilities to a committee. These executive committees normally have the power to do everything that the full board does.

A procedures committee is one which is supposed to recommend and establish board policies and procedures. It is usually charged with the responsibility of coordinating the activities of the other various board committees. One of its specific duties is usually to insure that procedures exist within the corporation to facilitate moving information up and down to satisfy the disclosure requirements and to make sure that the board is kept informed of everything that it should be kept informed of.

Almost all companies with publicly traded stock also have compensation committees. The principal duty of the compensation committee is to establish the compensation of the chief executive officers, including stock options. There may also be disclosure-practices committees, executive-selection and -review committees, conflict-of-interest committees, corporate-responsibility committees, and ad hoc committees of various types.

Which committees you need will depend upon your particular company. It appears, however, that an audit committee will be necessary for almost all companies—it is definitely necessary at this time for those listed on the New York Stock Exchange—and a compensation committee also seems to be almost a necessity. As a practical matter, an executive committee is also needed in most cases. It would appear that the presumption is in favor of having at least these three committees. On the other hand, the desirability of other committees seems to depend upon the company. General Motors, for example, has the following six board committees:

1. Salary and Bonus

2. Executive

3. Audit

4. Finance

5. Public Policy

6. Nominating

Keeping the Board Informed

Another very important factor in minimizing director liability is to make sure proper attention is given to how the board actually operates. Again, there is certainly no shortage of writing on this subject. However, it is important that the board itself make sure that it gets all the information it wants and needs and that items be brought to its attention sufficiently in advance to allow it to make meaningful decisions.

Delegation of Responsibility

Company policy statements are still another tool which can be used to insulate management from liability. The theory here is that when a company policy statement specifically delegates responsibility to someone, the person doing the delegating ought to be off the hook if the person to whom the responsibility is delegated makes a mistake, provided, of course, that the person doing the delegating has selected the corporate employees with due care. For example, if the president of a company signs a policy statement which delegates environmental compliance to the vice-president for manufacturing, it would appear that if there is a problem at one of the company's facilities, it would be very difficult to impose any personal liability on the president unless it could be shown that he was somehow personally involved in the actual oil spill, air pollution problem, or whatever. Obviously, this has exactly the opposite effect on the vice-president for manufacturing. He has been specifically delegated the authority and responsibility for this problem, and therefore the existence of this kind of policy statement would make it easier for someone to impose personal liability on him. The pros and cons of policy statements, particularly those containing these kinds of express delegations, are subject to debate, and quite a bit depends upon which people you are trying to protect.

To summarize then, management should ask its lawyers for an analysis of what personal liability exposure it may have and what steps the lawyers are taking to minimize this exposure. When the lawyer reports back, you should look for an analysis of director- and officer-liability insurance and indemnification. If you are a member of a board of directors, you should have a complete report on how the board acts to avoid personal liability of its members—which essentially means, How does the board of directors actually do its job? Common sense is still the best guide, but the standards are getting very high. More and more cases are being litigated which involve admittedly well-intentioned and competent directors who simply did not ask enough questions or give enough direction to the affairs of the company. The view of the SEC is that the directors are under an affirmative obligation to protect the interests of the shareholders and that if they just sit around doing very little and the affairs of the company turn bad, liability is going to be asserted.

If you are not a director of any company, your risks are smaller. However, there are still some things you ought to know about, and as a member of the management team you do not have to let the lawyers spend all their efforts taking care of the directors. You should be thinking yourself about which chapters in this book affect your job or responsibilities, and you should ask the company's lawyers about any circumstances where personal liability might be asserted.

CHAPTER SIXTY-SIX

FEDERAL CRIMINAL LAWS APPLICABLE TO BUSINESS

In addition to the *civil* liabilities mentioned in numerous other places in this book, there is an increasing trend towards imposing *criminal* liabilities on management of corporations in certain situations. The antitrust, securities, tax, and pension laws all contain criminal penalties. The criminal penalties in the antitrust laws have been in effect for a long time and have been rather diligently enforced. Actual criminal sentences imposed have, however, been infrequent and of modest severity. In the case of the securities laws, criminal sanctions are generally imposed only in cases where the facts seem to dictate quite clearly that there has been fraud, and some of those cases have involved rather lengthy criminal penalties. In the case of the tax laws, criminal penalties against executives of a large company are unlikely. Most of the cases involving criminal penalties for corporate taxes against individual executives involve smaller corporations where the executives were among a small group of owners who actually committed tax fraud using the corporate device. In the case of the pension laws, the criminal sanctions are new, and there has been very little activity in this area.

The major activity in criminal liability against executives has been in the area of improper payments. This ranges all the way from illegal political contributions to foreign bribes. It is interesting to note, however, that in the overwhelming majority of criminal prosecutions, the actual criminal prosecution is under an ancillary statute rather than for the main crime. For example, in one case, an executive was going through Kennedy Airport with a suitcase full of cash on his way to making an illegal payment in a foreign country, and he was apprehended and prosecuted not for bribery but for failure to comply with the foreign exchange requirements, which require you to file papers with the Treasury Department when you take substantial amounts of United States currency out of the country. There are many of these ancillary statutes. They are usually general, and prosecution is usually easier under these statutes than under the one dealing with the main crime. Following is a basic list of the kinds of statutes which impose general criminal penalties in connection with some other more specific criminal statutes.

1. Accessory after the fact. Imposes criminal penalties on anyone who assists in any way or prevents apprehension of someone else who has committed a crime.

2. Misprision of felony. Imposes criminal penalties for anyone who conceals a crime.

3. Conspiracy. This is perhaps the most severe statute of all, as it imposes criminal penalties if two or more persons conspire to commit any crime.

4. Making false statements. It is a crime to make any false statement to the government in connection with any investigation.

5. Mail fraud. It is a crime to use the mails to commit any crime or participate in any fraudulent activity.

6. Obstruction of justice. It is a crime to take any action which obstructs officers from getting testimony in the case of a crime or finding the criminal or apprehending him.

Of course, the above is only a very brief summary of some rather technical and lengthy statutes, but it serves to illustrate the basic point. Executive criminal liability is often founded on these kinds of ancillary statutes rather than on any specific crime involving something which is clearly illegal, such as bribery or fraud.

The specific substantive federal laws which contain criminal penalties will be briefly summarized in this chapter. However, before proceeding, it is useful to list some general considerations which apply to all of these special federal statutes.

1. There appears to be an increasing trend towards criminal prosecution of individuals in all cases of federal criminal law. Antitrust laws seem to be the most well publicized, but environmental laws and securities laws are also experiencing this trend.

2. In many cases, these new special federal laws—particularly the environmental ones—generate a lot of emotion and political pressures to "get the polluters" or "get the makers of unsafe or unhealthy consumer products."

3. Many federal agencies in charge of enforcing these new laws are coming under criticism for lax enforcement. Where a good criminal case presents itself, they may feel they have to prosecute it for political reasons, even if there may be circumstances which otherwise might persuade them to use only civil enforcement.

4. Many of these federal laws—again the environmental laws are the prime example—are now more mature. People understand what they prohibit, there is less uncertainty, business has had a fairly long period to comply, and the claim that a corporate official was unaware of the law will be more difficult to sustain.

5. Many of these cases involve withholding information in the face of a clear legal requirement to disclose it. Withholding of information is a very sensitive area today.

6. Many cases are judged in hindsight—perhaps after a rather significant unfortunate event (e.g., a large oil spill, discovery of an unusually high incidence of cancer as a result of some chemical, some deaths from an unsafe work place condition). This can color a case to the point where it could change from a civil to a criminal matter.

FEDERAL LAWS CONTAINING CRIMINAL PENALTIES

Following is a representative listing of the more important areas of federal law containing criminal penalties.

Antitrust Laws

Antitrust laws are still the biggest source of criminal liability. Price fixing leads the list by a wide margin.

Securities Laws

The federal securities laws provide the second most frequent source of criminal liability. Fraud in the sale of securities leads the list, but the Foreign Corrupt Practices Act is new, and prosecutions under this statute have not started yet.

Political Contributions

Illegal political contributions were a big source of criminal liability, but it would appear that corporations have now gotten the message on this point, and there have been very few prosecutions recently.

Bribery

The federal laws prohibiting bribery of public officials are very difficult to enforce, and there have been very few prosecutions. Typically, the problem is that, even in fairly clear cases, the government cannot prove that the payments were made with the requisite intent to influence the official act of the government officials.

Private bribery cases (the most usual is the bribery of a purchasing agent by a vendor) are usually subject to state rather than federal law.

Bribery of foreign officials has only recently been covered by a specific United States law (the Foreign Corrupt Practices Act), and future enforcement is uncertain.

The Toxic Substances Control Act

The Toxic Substances Control Act provides that any person who manufactures, processes, or distributes in commerce a chemical substance or mixture and who obtains information which reasonably supports the conclusion that such a substance or mixture presents a substantial risk of injury to health or the environment must immediately inform the administrator of the Environmental Protection Agency of such information. If he fails to do so, there is a criminal penalty. Also, there are criminal penalties for failure to maintain adequate records or to distribute a chemical in violation of the other provisions of the act.

The Occupational Safety and Health Act

The principal criminal penalty of the Occupational Safety and Health Act imposes criminal liability for anyone who willfully violates any standard, if that violation causes a death to any employee. There is also a criminal penalty for failing to file the required documents or for making false statements.

The Consumer Product Safety Act

The principal criminal penalty of the Consumer Product Safety Act applies only if the person knowingly and willfully violates an order of the Consumer Product Safety Commission. Thus, it is almost impossible to incur criminal liability under the Consumer Product Safety Act without being on notice of some violation.

Environmental Laws

Most of the laws relating to the environment have criminal penalties, and there have been increased incidents of criminal prosecution under these laws. State laws relating to the environment are often similar or even harsher in the context of personal liability. The principal environmental laws are the Clean Air and Clean Water Acts. Both of these laws contain criminal liability provisions.

The Clean Water Act contains a possible criminal penalty for any person who willfully *or negligently* violates provisions of the act. Also, there are criminal penalties for any person who knowingly makes a false statement or falsifies records relating to this statute.

The key here is the word "negligently." This is one of the few statutes where negligent conduct can give rise to criminal liability.

The Clean Air Act also contains criminal penalties, but in order for the criminal penalty to be applicable, a person must knowingly violate one of the provisions of the Clean Air Act. Also, any person who knowingly makes false statements or falsifies records relating to the Clean Air Act can incur criminal liability.

It is important that the word "knowingly" be understood in the criminal context. It does not mean that you have to know that the conduct you are engaging in is illegal. It only means that you have to know that the particular action you are taking is likely to produce a specific result. Also, it must be kept in mind that whether your action was taken knowingly or not will be the subject of a determination by a judge or jury after the fact. For example, in a prosecution for criminal liability under the Clean Air Act where the allegation is that you knowingly made a false statement or falsified a record, it is only necessary to show that you knew or should have known that the statement you made was false. It is not necessary to show that you knew that it was a violation of the law.

The Arab Boycott

In 1977, Congress enacted certain amendments to the Export Administration Act which made specific types of conduct relating to the Arab Boycott a crime. It appears, however, that in the overwhelming majority of cases, criminal penalties would not be imposed in this context.

SPECIFIC STATUTES

In addition to these general kinds of laws which affect all businesses, there are some specific laws which regulate particular businesses and have more stringent penalties. For example, the Food and Drug Act contains a strict-liability criminal penalty, and in one case the president of a large food chain was held criminally liable for a violation at one warehouse which allowed the food at that warehouse to be contaminated. The court recognized that this was a harsh result but said that the interest of the public in having pure foods and drugs outweighed the harshness to the defendant of imposing criminal liability, even though it was acknowledged that he had absolutely nothing to do with the violations at the specific warehouse.

PROPOSED LAWS

Beginning in the early 1970s and progressing at least through 1978, the Senate and the House of Representatives have been considering various bills to reform all of the federal criminal laws. At this time, this major reform project has not yet been completed, and it is uncertain when or if it will be. Most of the proposed laws, however, do contain the rather interesting concept of making it a crime for a corporate officer to fail to adequately supervise the employees under his control if that failure allows those employees to commit a crime. For example, under these proposed rules, if a sales employee was guilty of price fixing under the antitrust laws, it could also be alleged that his boss was guilty of failure to supervise him properly, even though the boss might have not participated at all in any of the price fixing conversations.

COMPLIANCE PROGRAMS

The reason for including this chapter in this book is to show the importance of compliance programs. Any statute which imposes criminal liability on top management ought to be the subject of a rather elaborate compliance program by which top management can be reasonably assured that the company and all of its employees are complying with the relevant laws. At a minimum, there ought to be antitrust and environmental compliance programs. These are difficult areas, because both of them involve a wide spectrum of corporate employees. The securities laws are also important. However, the issuance of corporate securities is usually closely controlled in the corporation, and it is difficult to envision how someone could fraudulently issue corporate securities and escape top management's attention. The same thing is true in the case of tax and pension laws. Also, if a company is governed by a specific statute (such as the federal Food and Drug Act) or if it has specific problems (as, for example, a company which is involved in nuclear activity or which must have hazardous working conditions or which manufactures dangerous products), other specific compliance programs are necessary. Obviously, a food or drug maker ought to have an elaborate program to assure compliance with the Food and Drug Act, a mining company ought to have a program to insure compliance with the Occupational Safety and Health Act, and companies making lawn mowers, ladders, or other consumer products which have proved hazardous ought to have compliance programs relating to the Consumer Product Safety Act.

LEGAL REPRESENTATION

Another important point relating to criminal statutes is that in criminal proceedings it is very easy to have a conflict of interest (or at least divergent interests) between the corporation and the individuals over legal representation. In most cases, criminal liability will be imposed only where someone in the company did something which he knew was illegal. To be sure, there may be exceptions, but the overwhelming majority of criminal prosecutions will allege that some specific actions took place which corporate executives knew to be illegal. Even under the conspiracy statute, the persons indicted are likely to be connected in some clear way with the illegal activity. Thus, for any individual defendant, one avenue of defense was that the actions taken by others in the company were done without his knowledge. In a criminal price fixing case against a division manager, the president of the company will certainly want to be able to show that the company has a clear policy against antitrust violations and that the division manager took his illegal and unauthorized actions on his own. On the other hand, the division manager might want to try to show (or at least strongly imply) that his actions were taken at the instigation and suggestion (or at least acquiescence) of top management, so that he will appear to be less of a "bad actor" and will possibly receive a less severe sentence. The examples are limitless, but the point should be clear: if you are involved in a criminal matter in any way, it is essential to consider the question of how representation is to be accorded all the parties involved, and it is usually a very bad idea to have the company's lawyers represent both the company and the individuals in this kind of case.

To some extent, the comments on legal representation could also be applicable in civil cases, but representation of the corporation and the individual officers, directors, or employees by the same law firm is usually less objectionable in civil cases. Any allegation of criminal conduct should be a red flag to both the company and the employees to strongly consider getting individual and independent representation. Most lawyers will be careful of this and will advise having other counsel at the slightest hint of any potential conflict of interest. However, like everything else discussed in this book, the subject is usually too important to be left solely to the lawyers. Management needs to be aware of the problem to be sure the lawyers are dealing with it effectively.

CHAPTER SIXTY-SEVEN

INTERNATIONAL BOYCOTTS (THE ARAB BOYCOTT)

OVERVIEW

"The Arab Boycott" is a term which is used to refer to all the activities of the Arab countries to discourage Arab states and those doing business with them from dealing with Israel or Israeli companies. The Arab Boycott dates all the way back to 1922. The Arab League itself was founded in 1944, and one of its principal purposes was to establish a boycott against "Zionist" products. Originally the boycott was designed as a primary boycott, which was simply a boycott of direct trade between Arab countries and Israel. However, in the early 1950s, the concept expanded to a secondary boycott, and more recently, to a tertiary boycott. The terms "secondary" and "tertiary" are not used in the same context by all people. The Arab Boycott has expanded, however, from a simple boycott against direct trade with Israel to a boycott of Israeli products (which some people refer to as a "secondary boycott") and in some cases a boycott of companies which trade with Israel (some people refer to this as a "tertiary boycott"). The names "secondary" and "tertiary," however, are not particularly important, because they are not used in any statutes or regulations. The important fact is that the Arab Boycott expanded from a simple, direct boycott against a country into a situation where at least the United States felt that the Arab countries were improperly dictating the conditions on which United States companies could do business.

The classic objection was to a requirement that in order to sell products to Arab countries, a United States company would have to refrain from dealing with Company X (even for non-Arab-related business) if Company X was on the Arab Boycott Blacklist because perhaps it had Jews on its board of directors or did business in a way which the Arabs thought aided the Israeli economy. In a reaction to what Congress thought was an over-extension of Arab sovereignty, two important pieces of legislation were passed. The first is the Tax Reform Act of 1976, which says, in substance, that if American companies (including their overseas subsidiaries) did anything which amounted to "participation in or cooperation with any international boycott" (meaning, of course, the Arab Boycott of Israel) they would lose tax benefits in a way described by the act. The second piece of legislation is the Export Administration Act Amendments of 1977, which provide that if a company engages in certain, enumerated activities, it will be guilty of a violation of that act and, therefore, subject to a revocation of its export license or, in extreme cases, civil or criminal penalties.

In normal American fashion, the tax laws and the Export Administration Act Amendments contain not only substantive rules but detailed reporting requirements. Accordingly, in addition to the substantive implications of these laws, counsel must consider the virtual blizzard of paperwork which they create. Attendant to this paperwork, which is in the form of reports filed with the Internal Revenue Service and the Department of Commerce, counsel must consider procedures and policies which will assure compliance with these laws, and counsel must also consider ways to educate those people in the company about the meaning of these laws and what can and cannot be done. In the area of international boycotts, this is a particularly troublesome problem, because both of these laws have implications for foreign subsidiaries and affiliates, and most companies run their foreign operations in a decentralized fashion. Furthermore, the American concern with protecting our companies against unwarranted interference by the Arabs is not universally shared abroad, and the American propensity to tack an elaborate reporting form on its substantive legal requirements is distressing to many foreign operating managers.

To further complicate the picture, the tax laws and the Export Administration Act are not even talking about the same thing or the same people. In other words, their respective definitions of prohibited acts and of people to whom those prohibitions apply are different.

Type of Participation or Cooperation

Under the tax laws you may lose tax benefits if you "participate in or cooperate with" an international boycott, and that phrase is defined as follows:

(1) As a condition of doing business directly or indirectly within a country or with the government, a company, or a national of a country to:
   (i) Refrain from doing business with or in a country which is the object of an international boycott or with the government, companies or nationals of that country.
   (ii) Refrain from doing business with any United States person engaged in trade in a country which is the object of an international boycott or with the government, companies, or nationals of that country.
   (iii) Refrain from doing business with any company whose ownership or management is made up, all or in part, of individuals of a particular nationality, race, or religion, or to remove (or refrain from selecting) corporate directors who are individuals of a particular nationality, race, or religion.
   (iv) Refrain from employing individuals of a particular nationality, race, or religion.

(2) As a condition of the sale of a product to the government, a company, or national of a country, to refrain from shipping or insuring products on a carrier owned, leased or operated by a person who does not participate in or cooperate with an international boycott.

Prohibitions and Exceptions

On the other hand, the Export Administration Act contains a rather lengthy set of prohibitions, which are in turn followed by an equally lengthy set of exceptions. Essentially, the Export Administration Act prohibitions are as follows:

1. Refusing to do business with a boycotted firm or in a boycotted country

2. Refusing or requiring any other person to refuse to employ or otherwise discriminate against any United States person on the basis of race, religion, sex, or national origin

3. Furnishing information with respect to the race, religion, sex, or national origin of any United States person

4. Furnishing information about whether any person has had or proposes to have business relationships within a boycotted country

5. Furnishing information concerning charitable or fraternal organizations which support a boycotted country

6. Paying a letter of credit which does any of the above

The exceptions to the above are as follows:

1. A boycotting country must be allowed to prohibit the importation of goods from the boycotted country.

2. Companies must be able to comply with the unilateral selection by boycotting countries of carriers, insurers, and suppliers.

3. Companies must be able to comply with import and shipping document requirements with respect to the country of origin.

4. Companies must be able to comply with export requirements of boycotting countries relating to shipments or transshipments of exports to the boycotted country.

5. Companies must be able to comply with the immigration or passport requirements of any country.

6. Companies must be able to comply with foreign laws which apply only to activities within that foreign country.

While there is a great deal of overlap, it is certainly obvious that the tax laws and the Export Administration Act prohibit different kinds of conduct.

Coverage is also a problem. The tax laws apply to all United States companies and their foreign subsidiaries. In fact, for reporting purposes, the tax laws even apply to foreign affiliates where the United States company owns 10 percent or more of the stock.

The Export Administration Act applies, of course, to United States taxpayers and to foreign subsidiaries, but only in situations where the subsidiary is engaged in United States commerce. Affiliates may also be covered under the Export Administration Act if the parent controls the affiliate. Further, it would appear that the Export Administration Act applies only to the activity which affects United States commerce. In other words, a foreign subsidiary could be covered by the Export Administration Act Amendments in one set of transactions and not in another set of transactions.

On the antitrust front, the principal problem occurs where two United States companies agree to boycott a third United States company. There must, at least at the present time, be some agreement. The agreement, however, can probably be between the United States company and the Arab country. Accordingly, if a United States company agrees not to do business with another United States company by reason of a request from an Arab country, that may constitute a violation of the antitrust laws. On the other hand, if an Arab country requires the United States company to use a particular component which is produced by a firm friendly to the Arabs (as opposed to a component which may be produced by a blacklisted firm), the United States company is apparently within its rights under both the antitrust laws and the Export Administration Act to agree to this request if it desires to do so.

The laws relating to discrimination in employment must also be considered. The principal problem would be the refusal of a United States company to hire a person of the Jewish religion because the job required travel to an Arab country and the Arab country would not allow that person to enter.

On the SEC front the application is a little less direct; it usually involves improper corporate payments. The implications are ones of disclosure, and there is no particular relationship between improper corporate payments and the Arab Boycott except that in some cases the improper corporate payments have been made in order to induce Arab countries to do business with a United States company or to have a United States company removed from the blacklist, or some similar purpose. In some situations, the normal disclosure rules could apply. If a company's Middle Eastern or Israeli operations are themselves material, there might have to be some disclosure of this fact to investors. If the application of the tax rules or the Export Administration Act might have a material effect on company operations, this would have to be disclosed. In short, the normal disclosure rules dealing with "hard" data like material financial implications might necessitate disclosure, and some "soft" data like improper payments in the Middle East or management's worries about loss of Middle East business might necessitate disclosure, although the test of materiality in the latter situation is still very vague.

On the state law front, it appears that the Export Administration Act has preempted any state law which directly attempts to regulate corporate activity on the basis of compliance with an international boycott. On the other hand, many of these state laws have been phrased in terms of amendments to the Antitrust or Civil Rights Acts, and, therefore, the state laws would not necessarily be preempted by the Export Administration Act. This is still a developing area, and it is not clear to what extent the Export Administration Act will nullify state laws which were passed in order to react to what the state perceived as unwarranted Arab interference with state businesses, even though the state laws may have been cast in the form of antidiscrimination or antitrust laws. There are also constitutional issues dealing with the preemption question. Since the Arab Boycott involves United States export commerce, it seems very likely that Congress would have a right to preempt any state legislation based on the antitrust laws, but the constitutionality of preempting state legislation aimed at preventing discrimination within a state against citizens of that state is less clear.

HOW THE BOYCOTT WORKS

The Arab Boycott is not a coherent body of law but is instead a rather informal set of practices which are imposed both individually by certain Arab countries and collectively by the Arab League. To further complicate matters, the application of the principles of the Arab Boycott depends upon which country you are talking about and the particular circumstances of the country. Apparently, the Arab countries do not stand on principle quite as much as Americans tend to, and in many cases, the decision as to whether and under what circumstances the Arab countries will purchase products from a company which either does business with Israel or refuses to comply with one or more Arab requests depends to a considerable extent on how badly each country needs the American company's products and what alternative sources are available, if any. Accordingly, it is very difficult to set forth a description of the Arab Boycott in any concrete terms. Instead, that description must be subjective, and readers must understand that the American format of reducing everything to writing—even if the writings are lengthy and complex—is not necessarily used in other countries.

The main force behind the Arab Boycott is the Arab League Central Boycott Office, which is located in Damascus. This office is supposed to monitor observance of the boycott and maintain liaison among the various league members. At the present time, the following countries are members of the Arab League:

Algeria*	Oman
Bahrain	Qatar
Egypt	Saudi Arabia
Iraq	Somalia*
Jordan	Sudan*
Kuwait	Syria
Lebanon	Tunisia*
Libya	United Arab Emirates†
Mauritania*	Yemen Arab Republic
Morocco*	People's Democratic Republic of Yemen

* The formal IRS list does not include these countries.
† This is a federation of seven emirates: Abu Dhabi, Sharja, Dubai, Ajman, Fujaira, Umm al-Qaiwan, and Ras al-Khaimah.

In addition to this central office, however, each member state has its own national boycott office. Thus, in reality there are twenty-one Arab Boycott offices; one general one, and twenty others for the member countries.

Following is a list of the kinds of activities which, at the present time, may subject a company to blacklisting by the Central Boycott Office:

1. Establishing a main or branch factory in Israel

2. Establishing an assembly plant in Israel

3. Exporting component parts or units of equipment from any third country to Israel in sufficient quantities to permit an Israeli company to assemble an end product 50 percent or more of which is attributable to such parts or units

4. Maintaining general agents or head offices for Middle Eastern operations in Israel

5. Granting trade name or trademark rights to an Israeli company

6. Making an equity investment in any Israeli company

7. Transferring technology or know-how to an Israeli company

8. Refusing to answer questions submitted to it by boycott officials

9. Importing Israeli goods into third countries for the purpose of selling them in commercial quantities

10. Acting as agent for importers of Israeli goods

11. Acquiring rights or licenses to manufacture products of boycotted companies

12. Using products of boycotted companies in excess of certain percentages in the production of its own products

13. Entering technical-assistance agreements with boycotted companies

14. Having as a controlling person someone deemed to have Zionist sympathies

15. Acting for the account of Israel or its interests

16. Constructing or selling ships or tankers to Israel or Israeli companies

17. Transporting cargo to Israel

18. In the case of a bank, having financial dealings with Israel which are deemed to strengthen the economy and industry of Israel

19. Maintaining aircraft service to Israel

20. In the case of an insurance company, participating in industrial or commercial companies in Israel

21. Selling factories to Israel

It should be noted, however, that the Arab Boycott offices (both the central one and those in each individual country) do not operate under our traditional American procedures of spelling everything out in writing and acting according to published procedures. In fact, most of the proceedings of the Central Arab Boycott Office and of those for each individual country are secret, and the list of items referred to above should be considered representative rather than exhaustive or complete. Some member countries do not adhere to all of these requirements, while other member countries have additional ones which will subject a company to boycotting, such as:

1. Membership in a foreign Israeli chamber of commerce

2. Prospecting for natural resources in Israel

In addition, it should be noted that many of these criteria are somewhat subjective. Note for example, number (14), which might put a company on the blacklist because it has as a controlling person someone who is deemed to have Zionist sympathies. Generally, a Zionist sympathizer is one who:

1. Is a member of an association which acts in the interest of Zionism or Israel

2. Engages in activities benefiting Zionism or Israel

3. Engages in propaganda activities supporting Israel and Zionism or attacking Arab countries

Also, a company can become blacklisted because of its relationship with other companies which are themselves blacklisted. Note for example, items (13) and (15) on the list. These will subject to blacklisting a company which enters into a technical-assistance agreement with boycotted companies or acts for the account of Israel or its interests.

Two examples appearing in a *Wall Street Journal* article on the Arab Boycott illustrate some of the principles. In the first example, Coca-Cola was blacklisted because it opened a bottling plant in Israel. The Arab spokesman said that Coca-Cola could have exported all the Cokes it wanted to Israel without being blacklisted, because this would have used Israel's valuable foreign exchange. However, when the company helped the Israeli economy with the bottling plant, it was blacklisted. A similar situation exists in the case of Ford Motor Company, which presumably could have sold all the cars it wanted in Israel without being blacklisted; because of its manufacturing facilities in Israel, it is blacklisted. In another illustrative example, Elizabeth Taylor's movies are blacklisted, because she has given substantial amounts of financial aid to Israel, reportedly through the purchase of bonds.

The Boycott Procedure

As indicated above, the boycott procedure does not operate with our traditional American formalism. However, there are certain generalities which can be stated. The first is that the procedure generally starts when a company commences to do business in one of the Arab states. At this time, the company will usually be checked against that particular state's version of the general principles stated above, and in addition the company may be sent a questionnaire. If the company fails to answer the questionnaire after a certain period (the period may range from 6 weeks to 3 months or even longer, depending upon the country involved), the failure to respond will itself subject the company to blacklisting.

If the company does answer the questionnaire, the evaluation of the responses will then be made, and if the company makes admissions which the particular state feels come within its general principles, it will be blacklisted unless the company explains them away. Naturally, once a company is blacklisted by any one of the states, the chance of its blacklisting spreading to other countries through the Central Boycott Office is significant, because it is the very purpose of this Central Boycott Office to accomplish this kind of coordination. If a company decides that it must answer a questionnaire which will show on its face that the company should be blacklisted, it may decide to explain why it should not be blacklisted. Generally, this kind of explanation is not as futile as it may at first appear, and in some cases a persuasive explanation can end the investigation. If a company is charged with activities which will cause it to be blacklisted, it may deny those charges and enter into negotiations with the state in question to persuade it not to blacklist the company. Generally, denials or explanations must take the form of notarized statements of an officer of the company, and this statement must be authenticated by an Arab consular official. Frequently, however, whenever any question arises, there is a long and elaborate investigation which may take years, and at this point, outside guidance from local agents or attorneys is usually required.

If a company is on the blacklist, getting off of it is subject to the same formal and lengthy procedures as an investigation. Getting off the blacklist depends, to a considerable extent, on the country in question, the reason the company was put on the blacklist in the first place, and the nature of the products the company wants to sell. As a general proposition, getting off the Central Arab Boycott list is a little more difficult than getting off a national list and, of course, more time-consuming.

A further factor which complicates the Arab Boycott is that there are hard-line Arab countries and soft-line countries. These are phrases which characterize how strictly the countries adhere to the boycotts. A hard-line country will absolutely refuse to do any business at all with any company on its boycott list, will put a company on the boycott list for any suspicion of Zionist sympathies, and will only reluctantly take a company off its boycott list. A soft-line country will take a more subjective approach, and the economic result sometimes depends on the country's need for the product, alternative sources, or the reason for any possible problem.

NOTE: How the boycott will actually work now that the Export Administration Act makes it a crime to furnish almost any information to an Arab Boycott office remains to be seen.

COMPARISON OF THE TAX AND EXPORT LAWS

While the Export Administration Act Amendments of 1977 and the Ribicoff Amendment to the tax laws of 1976 were each drafted to prevent American companies from complying with the secondary or tertiary aspects of the Arab Boycott, the laws are, unfortunately, different in a number of important respects. Essentially, those differences are:

1. The *coverage* is different.

2. The *penalties* are different.

3. The *specific conduct* which is prohibited is different.

Coverage

One of the most troublesome differences between the tax law and the Export Administration Act is the difference in coverage. Naturally, both laws cover United States companies and all of their establishments here. The trouble comes in the context of foreign subsidiaries. The tax law covers, in the substantive prohibitions, "all controlled foreign subsidiaries," which is defined as subsidiaries of which the parent company owns 51 percent of the stock. The tax law *reporting provisions* also include subsidiaries of which the company owns only 10 percent of the stock, but the actual substantive prohibitions do not extend down that far.

Under the Export Administration Act, foreign subsidiaries will be included in the coverage of the law if they are "controlled in fact," and there are a number of presumptions which will effectively sweep under the law all foreign subsidiaries where the parent owns 51 percent or more of the stock, plus certain other presumptions. On the other hand, these foreign subsidiaries will only be covered by the export law for transactions in the interstate commerce of the United States. There are elaborate and detailed regulations defining exactly what is and what is not in United States commerce in the context of a foreign subsidiary. However, the thrust of those regulations is that the activity of foreign subsidiaries which are substantially independent is not in United States commerce. Therefore, in giving instructions to the foreign subsidiaries, it is necessary to explain to them that they will be in violation of the tax law if they enter into any agreement to participate in or cooperate with the boycott, no matter what the transaction (whether or not it is in United States commerce), but there must be concern with the Export Administration Act requirements only in cases where the particular transactions in question are deemed to be in United States commerce. It would appear that this may be the single most difficult aspect of the boycott laws. Each of the laws and regulations is very complex, and when you superimpose the two along with the complex initial determination as to which laws apply, it is almost inconceivable that anyone could prepare a reasonably short, understandable explanation which could be used and applied by laymen.

The obvious implication is that some procedure is required whereby any transaction which either calls for the signing of any boycott certification or the furnishing of any boycott-type information should be reported to one central point of expertise, which would make these kinds of determinations and advise the foreign operating units. In order to conduct business reasonably efficiently, it would appear that at least the initial point of determination has to be closer to the operating unit than the United States. In a large company, perhaps there could be one such point of expertise in each country.

Penalties

The penalties for violation of the Export Administration Act can include both civil and criminal penalties as well as loss of the company's export license. On the other hand, penalties in the tax law are simply the denial of certain tax benefits. Accordingly, any company is well within its legal and moral rights to make an economic analysis of any given transaction and determine whether it will enter into it even if it is a violation of the tax laws. This is a further complicating factor in this area, and unless the company wants to take a posture of absolutely refraining to enter into any transaction which violates either the tax or the Export Administration Act, this difference introduces a further level of complexity to the analysis of any specific problem.

Differences in the Activity Which Is Prohibited

The tax laws generally prohibit any *agreement* to participate in or cooperate with the Arab Boycott. While an agreement can be inferred under any one of a great many circumstances set forth in the regulations, there must be in existence either an implied or an express agreement. In the Export Administration Act, no agreement is necessary, and even the furnishing of boycott-related information is prohibited.

Employment Discrimination

Both laws prohibit discrimination in employment. Each law also has elaborate regulations on this point. It appears clear, however, that the emphasis given to this matter in the regulations is grossly disproportionate to the number of problems which actually arise. As a generalization, it would appear that all of this material has been inserted in the law out of theoretical concern for possible discrimination as opposed to any actual evidence that the Arab Boycott would require any religious discrimination on the part of American companies. It is likely that during all of the discussion of this problem over the past years, there have been isolated instances of religious discrimination. However, that does not appear to be one of the major problems being faced by American companies, and the Arabs strongly deny that their boycott is connected in any way with religious discrimination.

Furnishing Information

As indicated above, the tax laws do not directly prohibit the furnishing of information. In fact, they state clearly that furnishing information does not constitute an agreement, unless, of course, it is coupled with other factors which might constitute a course of conduct. On the other hand, the Export Administration Act, in three of its six basic prohibitions, deals with furnishing information.

Letters of Credit and Shipping Documents

The current regulations under the tax laws provide that letters of credit and shipping documents are to be included as part of the basic transaction, and a provision in a letter of credit to the effect that the company will not ship the goods on a blacklisted vessel, for example, would be an agreement, even though such provision was not included in the actual contract. Under the tax laws then, a letter of credit or other shipping document is looked upon merely as a piece of the contract, and the governing fact is whether the documentation, taken as a whole, shows that there has been an agreement.

However, the exceptions in the Export Administration Act allow a company to agree to comply with requirements prohibiting the shipment of goods through the boycotted country, on a carrier of the boycotted country, or by a route other than that prescribed by the boycotting country or recipient of the shipment. Also, it is permissible to comply or agree to comply with import and shipping document requirements with respect to the country of origin, the name of the carrier, and the route of the shipment, and the name of the supplier of the shipment. This latter point is qualified by a requirement that most such certifications cannot be stated in the negative after 1 year from the date of enactment.

Unilateral Selection

The tax laws do not contain any specific reference to unilateral selection. However, under most circumstances, it is clear that if the Arab customer selected a contractor, subcontractor, or supplier, there would be no basis upon which to infer any kind of agreement to participate in or cooperate with the boycott. The tax regulations do prohibit the use of a "whitelist," because under their interpretation, this would be an implied agreement.

The unilateral selection requirements of the Export Administration Act are, however, very detailed, and they are probably more stringent than those under the tax laws. Under the Export Administration Act, the selection has to be both unilateral and specific, and there are many regulations which spell out what the "specific" means. It is also coupled with the concept that the goods must be identifiable when they enter the Arab country, which precludes the use of the exception for any situation where the goods to be purchased become a part of the finished product. The example usually given is the case of a tractor, in which it would be possible to make a unilateral and specific selection of the company to supply the tires but impossible to do so in the case of the supplier of the paint on the tractor.

Except for this unilateral selection concept, both the Export Administration Act and the tax laws would preclude any company from refusing to do business with another company for boycott reasons.

Complexity

One area in which both the tax laws and the Export Administration Act appear almost identical is the level of complexity. Form is almost always exalted over substance. Typically, this means that in many cases, a transaction will be legal under the Export Administration Act and present no problem under the tax laws if structured in one way, whereas the opposite will be true with a fairly minor variation.

SUGGESTIONS FOR COMPLIANCE

It is very difficult to provide precise instructions for compliance with a body of law which is as complicated and imprecise as the Arab Boycott laws. On the other hand, the complexity itself suggests one of the important elements of a compliance program: except in very unusual cases, it will be necessary to allow the operating people to take only very limited action without advance approval of an expert. Further, since the laws are so complex, it would appear best to keep the number of experts in either the law firm or corporate legal department to a minimum. While the law is complex, it is a relatively easy subject for a lawyer to master. A day or two with the appropriate regulations will make a lawyer a fairly efficient expert in this area. The same can be said for any competent business executive who takes the day or two necessary to master the regulations and has enough occasions to use the material to keep the intricacies in his mind and to keep up on changes. The problem is in getting more than a very few executives to take this time, and that will mean that a lawyer is going to have to do it in almost all cases. I believe almost every company will want at least the following:

1. A fairly accurate and complete assessment of the problem
2. A company policy statement
3. A relatively comprehensive set of operating procedures
4. A short and simple operating guide for distribution to the first line of defense: the persons who receive documents with boycott language

Following is a more complete discussion of these points, with the obvious caveat that they must be carefully tailored to specific circumstances.

Assessment of the Problem

Counsel should advise management of at least the following aspects of this problem:

1. What are the financial risks?
    (a) Tax penalties
    (b) Loss or interruption of export privileges
    (c) Fines
2. How much legal time and effort/expense is likely to be required to keep the company in compliance?
3. How much administrative time and expense is likely to be required to keep the company in compliance?

Following are some of the things you will have to know in order to accurately answer these questions.

1. How many boycotting countries do you do business in?
   (a) Operations (sales)
   (b) Locations
   (c) Joint ventures, licensing arrangements, etc.

2. How much commerce is involved?
   (a) In total
   (b) In various segments
       (1) By country
       (2) By subsidiary

3. How is the business done? What is the role of freight forwarders, agents, etc.? What documents are usually involved? How are the goods shipped? (The practices and, therefore, the documents involved in shipping by sea are different from those in shipping by land.)

4. How many different managements are involved? If your organization has a decentralized management, you may have either a very complicated problem or a much simpler problem, depending on how many operating units do business in the Middle East.

The Company Policy

Most companies will want at least a brief policy statement relating to the Arab Boycott. This will be true even if they already have a policy on "Legal and Ethical Conduct" or something similar which says that all company employees must comply with the law. Further, this policy statement must be distributed to the management and employees of the foreign operations, and this might mean translating it into other languages. Some of the reasons why a corporate policy statement is important include the following:

1. Both the tax and export laws contain the concept of "intent" and "inadvertent violation." Both laws require boycott actions to be taken with some degree of intent, and both contain examples where boycott actions were not violations because they were done inadvertently by persons who either failed to notice the boycott language or did not appreciate its significance. A good corporate policy statement might make the difference in a close case where some document was accepted or certification made. The policy would bolster any argument that low-level employee actions inconsistent with the policy were inadvertent or that any given action was not taken with the requisite intent. This, however, should not be overplayed. It is likely that it would make a difference only in a very close case.

2. A corporate policy statement can focus management's attention on some of the complexities and perhaps greatly simplify the compliance problem. For example, if management were to allow counsel to simply prohibit any corporate action which could cause a tax problem, compliance on that front would be much simpler than weighing various actions against potential loss of tax benefits.

3. The policy statement presents an opportunity to spell out the various roles of company people—management, the general counsel, the tax department, etc.

A sample company policy statement is included at the end of this chapter.

Procedures

Closely related to the question of a company policy statement is the question of the appropriate company procedures. There are fairly elaborate reporting requirements under both the Export Administration Act Amendments and the tax laws, and there must, of course, be some procedure to make sure that these reporting requirements are met. Beyond that, however, there is the same "intent/inadvertent violation" question which militates strongly in favor of good procedures. Conversely, the lack of good and relatively formal procedures for handling boycott matters could be turned against the company. Following are some comments on procedures to deal with these problems.

1. It is necessary to know all the places where boycott language could be received by the company and where boycott certifications could be made. This is not the whole picture, because, as pointed out above, problems can arise in places other than the order desk. However, the order desk or the quotation desk is where most of the problems are likely to arise.

   Locations outside the company should also be considered. Freight forwarders, customs agents, warehouse operators, and agents are persons who could execute documents on behalf of the company. There should be appropriate instructions to all of these people.

2. There should be procedures for actually dealing with boycott requests. Following are some possibilities:
   (a) Have every document containing any boycott language forwarded to someone who is expressly charged with knowing all about the boycott laws.
   (b) Draft a list of preapproved certifications which can be made at the order-desk level. These would be such things as positive certificates of origin, which present no problem under either the tax laws or export act. Anything other than the preapproved language should be forwarded to someone who is knowledgeable about the boycott laws.
   (c) Adopt an education program for a relatively large number of company people. For example, you could identify the operations which frequently did business in the Middle East and then require someone from each operation to become a boycott expert.

3. There should be an express document retention program so that files can be examined, the export act and tax law reports filled out and audited if necessary, and the express document retention requirements of each law satisfied. It would appear that a general 6-year retention period would be best for most situations, although this is longer than expressly required.

4. There should be coordination with tax law and export act reporting. The tax report must be filed annually, and the export act report must be filed periodically as requests are received. Records must be kept of all boycott requests received. There might be some advantage in coordinating the approval procedures with these reporting requirements. Since all requests would have to be reported, it might be less of a burden to have them reported as received to a central location which would both advise on what should be done and be responsible for the necessary reports.

   The time delays inherent in this kind of process in a large company would weigh against it unless there were very good communication facilities between all the locations.

5. Education of company people is necessary. There are some rather unusual provisions in these regulations which call attention to problems that might not be apparent at first examination. This would seem to mean that counsel should go through each of the regulations and identify the people in the company who should be advised of the general rules and the specific rules which may be applicable. Following are some examples:
   (a) The regulations note that patent procedures in some Arab countries re-

quire certifications which might be illegal or might cost tax benefits. Therefore, the company's patent counsel and everyone who works for him (including outside counsel) should be informed of the problem if the company
registers or licenses any patents in the Middle East.

(b)   The company's sales force should be informed of the problems to the extent
they make calls on Arab customers. This is compounded by the fact that
the Export Administration Act prohibitions are against furnishing information—even information stating that the company does business in Israel
and intends to continue to do so.

6.   The regulations are complex, and procedures must be sophisticated. The differences between legal and illegal activities are *very fine* in both sets of regulations. One example in the Export Administration Act is the comparison between two situations under the unilateral-selection regulations involving
aircraft. Those examples are as follows:

(a)   A, a United States aircraft manufacturer, is negotiating to sell aircraft
to boycotting country Y. During the negotiations, Y asks A to identify
the company which normally manufactures the engines for the aircraft.
A responds that they are normally manufactured by United States engine
manufacturer B. B is blacklisted by Y. In making the purchase, Y specifies
that the engines for the aircraft should be supplied by United States engine
manufacturer C.

A may comply or agree to comply with Y's selection of C because
Y's selection is unilateral and specific.

(b)   A, a United States aircraft manufacturer, has an order to supply a certain
number of planes to boycotting country Y. In connection with the order,
Y asks A to supply it with a list of qualified aircraft tire manufacturers
so that Y can select the tires to be placed on the planes. This is a highly
unusual request, since, in A's worldwide business operations, choice of
tires is customarily made by the manufacturer, not the customer. Nonetheless, A supplies a list of tire manufacturers, B, C, D, and E. Y chooses
tire manufacturer B because B is not blacklisted. Had A, as is customary,
selected the tires, company C would have been chosen. C happens to be
blacklisted, and A knows that C's blacklist status was the reason for Y's
selection of B.

A's provision of a list of tire manufacturers for Y to choose from
destroys the unilateral character of Y's selection, because such a preselec-
tion service is not customary in A's worldwide business operations.

These complexities, which often exalt form over substance, present a big
problem in the procedure area. On the one hand, you can structure your
business operations to avoid violating the laws, but on the other hand, it
would be very easy for these structuring operations to run afoul of the evasion
provisions, particularly those in the export act. The implication appears to
be that a premium is placed on good, innovative legal advice at the right
time and place, and it is very difficult to systematize the procedures to deal
with these complexities. Thus it appears that any procedures must be supplemented with ad hoc legal counsel, which must usually be rendered before
the fact if it is to be useful for avoiding problems.

Operating Guide

Following is a sample operating guide.

ARAB BOYCOTT GUIDE

United States law requires all units of the Company, including foreign subsidiaries
in which the Company owns a majority of the stock, to take certain actions with respect

to dealings in the Middle East. Those actions are summarized in this memorandum. Please contact your operating unit counsel for more specific guidance.

I. *Identify All Boycott Requests*

Any document received by the company, whether pursuant to a specific contract or not, and irrespective of whether the Company responds, which contains *any* boycott language should be identified and separated. Examples of such language include the following:

Certify that these goods are not of Israeli origin.
Certify that these goods are not shipped on a blacklisted vessel.
Certify that you have no dealings with Israel.
Certify that you have no operations in Israel.

Certain language is exempted from this requirement. Following are some examples of permissible certifications. These exceptions are the only ones allowed except on specific approval of operating unit counsel.

Certify that these goods are solely of _____ origin [i.e., a positive certificate of origin].
Certify that these goods will not be shipped on a vessel which is scheduled to call at an Israeli port before discharging at _____ [i.e., a war risk or confiscation certificate].
The carrier is _____ [i.e., a positive statement of the identity of the carrier].
The goods will not be shipped on a carrier which flies the flag of Israel or is owned or operated by nationals or residents of Israel [another war risk certification].

After identifying the boycott-related request, there must be a determination as to whether it is received in a transaction in connection with United States commerce. If it is, it must be forwarded immediately, along with a copy of the document on which it was contained, to _____. The request will be in United States commerce either where the transaction involves goods from the United States or where the purpose of the request is to qualify the recipient to do business in a boycotting country. If the request does not involve United States commerce, it must be reported once each year.

II. *File Retention*

It is necessary to maintain identifiable files on all transactions which relate to the boycott and on all transactions which do not relate directly to the boycott but which involve business transacted in a boycotting country. These files should be retained for a period of at least 6 years. Whether these files are kept physically separate or whether there is simply an index so that they can be specifically located is up to the operating unit.

III. *No Action*

No action should be taken in connection with any request containing boycott language (except for the excepted types of certificates listed above) without having such action approved, in advance, by operating unit counsel.

A SAMPLE STATEMENT OF POLICY

STATEMENT OF POLICY
INTERNATIONAL BOYCOTTS

Various United States laws impose obligations on the Company in connection with our relations with customers of countries engaging in international boycotts. Principally, the laws relate to the Arab Boycott of Israel. In order to assure the Company's complete compliance with all of these laws, including the avoidance of any tax penalties, the following policy is established. This policy applies to all employees of the Company and to all if its subsidiaries throughout the world.

I. *Statements or Certifications*

Every employee shall make sure that any statements or certifications made in connection with any Company transactions comply with all applicable laws and regulations. Every employee shall consult with legal counsel in any case where he is uncertain as to the application of the boycott laws to the certification or statement he intends to make. Following are some brief, general statements as to the basic rules applicable at this time. However, each employee involved in transacting international business is responsible for maintaining an awareness of the laws as they may apply to the Company from time to time, and for consulting with legal counsel in cases where the application of such laws is unclear or unknown to the employee.

A. *Permissible Certifications*

The Company is permitted to certify as to the following in connection with business transactions—including transactions with or in a boycotting country:
1. The fact that the goods will not be shipped on a carrier owned or operated by, or which flies the flag of, Israel. (This is the only negative-type certification or statement which is allowed.)
2. A request to name the carrier on which the goods will be shipped or identify the route to be used by the carrier.
3. A positive statement as to the origin of the goods or any component of the goods.
4. A positive statement as to the identity of the supplier of the goods.

B. *Impermissible Certifications*

Following are certifications or statements which cannot be made by any employee—including employees of the Company's foreign subsidiaries—except on prior approval of legal counsel:
1. A negative certification of origin (e.g., "These goods are not of Israeli origin").
2. A negative statement as to the identity of the carrier (e.g., "The goods will not be shipped on a blacklisted carrier").
3. A certification or any statement relating to business dealings with or in Israel. This includes positive statements as well as negative statements (e.g., it is not permitted to say that the Company does have dealings with or in Israel).
4. It is not permissible to answer any boycott questionnaires.
5. It is not permissible to furnish any information to the Central Boycott Office.

II. *Actions by the Company or Its Employees*

Following are various actions which may not be taken by the Company or any employee. The list is illustrative only; it is not comprehensive.
A. The Company may not enter into any agreement, express or implied, to participate in or cooperate with the boycott. Agreements include all aspects of a transaction, including the contract, the shipping documents, letters of credit and oral understandings.
B. The Company may not refuse to do business with any company as a result of a request for such refusal from any customer for boycott reasons.
C. The Company may not furnish any information concerning the Company's business dealings with third parties in connection with a request for such information from a boycott office. Generally, the Company may not answer any request for any information from a boycott office with any statement other than one which says that United States laws prohibit answering the questionnaire.
D. The Company may not base the selection of suppliers on any blacklist or whitelist.

E. The Company may not discriminate against any person in employment on account of such person's religion or national origin.

F. The Company may not engage in any conduct or transaction which is designed to circumvent the above-stated rules. The anti-evasion sections of all the applicable laws are very broad. All employees of the Company are instructed to refrain from discussing transactions or practices designed to circumvent the boycott laws without prior consultation with the Company's lawyers to make certain that such discussions or procedures are not prohibited.

III. *Responsibilities*

A. The operating manager of every operating unit shall be responsible for establishing and maintaining adequate procedures to see that all of the applicable laws and regulations dealing with international boycotts are observed. For purposes of this requirement, these laws include all the statutes, regulations and other relevant authority as identified by the Company's lawyers. Specifically, procedures shall be instituted which will assure that every document received by the Company in the normal course of business from any boycotting country is examined to see if there is any boycotting language, and that no action is taken with respect to such document except on prior approval of the Company's lawyers.

B. The general counsel of the company shall be responsible for identifying all boycott laws which might affect the Company's business and for notifying the operating unit managers of such laws.

The general counsel shall establish and maintain procedures to assure that all relevant reports are properly filed except for reports under the United States Internal Revenue Code, which shall be the responsibility of the director of federal income tax. The general counsel shall be responsible for providing legal counsel in connection with such tax report.

C. The senior-group operating lawyer shall be responsible for distributing information relating to all such laws which may apply to units in his group. He shall also be responsible for answering any specific questions relating to boycott matters.

D. Every employee of the Company who is engaged in any aspect of the Company's business shall be responsible for obtaining and maintaining a working knowledge of the portions of these laws which apply to such employee's duties and for consulting with the Company's lawyers in all cases where the employee is uncertain as to the exact application of those laws or desires clarification of the laws.

IV. *Files*

All units of the Company having operations with or in any boycotting country (this includes selling goods to customers located in a boycotting country) shall be responsible for maintaining complete and accurate records on all transactions with any country engaging in any boycott. For purposes of this Policy Statement, this includes all transactions with any Arab country, or any other country which the general counsel shall determine, or which the operating unit personnel have reason to know engages in any international boycott. Such files shall contain all documents relating to any contract, as well as all requests for quotations or correspondence. This policy does not require retention and separation of correspondence of a purely technical nature having to do with the performance or specifications for products, provided such documents have no boycott language in them.

V. *Cooperation*

All units of the Company shall cooperate with the Company's legal and tax staffs in responding to requests for information which is needed to file the required tax and Department of Commerce reports.

CHAPTER SIXTY-EIGHT

TENDER OFFERS

Before 1968 (the date when the securities laws were amended to partially regulate tender offers), there were a significant number of tender-offer situations which struck some people as a form of legalized looting of corporations. These occurred during the late 1950s and in the 1960s. "Tender offer" is a term which is usually used to refer to any situation where someone outside of the management of a company makes a public announcement that he will purchase shares tendered at a specific price. Usually, the person selects a price which offers a substantial premium over the market price so that there is an incentive for those people holding the shares to tender them. On the other hand, the prices are also less than what the offeror believes to be the fair value of the shares.

There are two basic ways to look at tender offers. One is as the equivalent of a raid on the corporation or a prelude to looting. Senator Williams, the author of the SEC takeover law, analyzed the problem when he introduced his legislation with the following words:

> In recent years, we have seen proud old companies reduced to corporate shells after white-collar pirates had seized control with funds from sources which are unknown and in many cases, then sold or traded away the best assets, later to split up most of the loot among themselves. The ultimate responsibility for preventing this kind of industrial sabotage lies with the management and the shareholders of the corporation that is so threatened, but the leniency of the laws places management and shareholders at a distinct disadvantage in coming to grips with the enemy.

Some of the commentators, in analyzing the same phenomenon in Great Britain, stated the British feeling in characteristically British terms by stating that there was a feeling that such things "are just not done by the best people."

Support for these criticisms was generally found by looking over old tender-offer situations where some of the people who desired to acquire control of the companies had previous criminal records or a history of violating the securities laws. Also, there was some feeling that the origin of the money used in these cash tender-offer situations was questionable and that some of it might have had illegal origins.

There is, however, another view towards tender offers. Essentially, that view is that they are a desirable device to have in our society in order to regulate management. According to this theory, there really is not any objective way of measuring managerial efficiency. Accordingly, if we have the potential for takeovers, there will be some assurance of competitive efficiency among corporate managers and this will ultimately inure to the benefit of small, noncontrolling shareholders.

Still another view of takeovers is that they are simply another form of corporate reorganization. This, however, really applies only to the "friendly" takeover. Certainly, if two companies decide they want to merge, one of the ways of doing so is simply to make a cash tender offer for the shares of the company to be acquired.

In 1968, the federal securities laws were amended to provide that certain minimal requirements would apply to takeover situations. Essentially, these requirements are that a company engaging in a tender offer has to file a statement, together with a lot of information, with the SEC. This then, of course, becomes public, and the target company, the shareholders, and the public will have access to a great deal of information about the people involved in the takeover. There are also a significant number of technical provisions which prevent prior abuses. For example, a person making a tender offer has to pay the highest price offered during the course of the tender offer, no matter when the shares are tendered. Thus, if there is a tender offer at $35 per share and through subsequent bidding contests or negotiations that price is raised to $40 two weeks later, the people who tendered their shares at $35 for the first 2 weeks would, nevertheless, receive the $40 price.

Part of the statement that has to be filed with the SEC requires the person making the tender offer to disclose the purpose of the tender offer. Generally, there are two cases. One is where the tender offer is made for investment and where the person making the offer has no intention of acquiring a controlling interest. The other extreme, of course, is where the tender offer is made with the intention of acquiring a controlling interest in the company. Any time someone acquires more than 5 percent of the outstanding shares of any class of stock, a statement must be filed with the SEC. This prevents the silent takeover, where someone simply purchases stock in the market until he owns a substantial block and then forces a merger or has a takeover bid for the remainder of the stock.

Tender offers have good and bad points in accomplishing a corporate reorganization. Generally, you can acquire control by purchasing a smaller number of shares. You can put a limit on the amount of stock you will accept in the tender offer, and this can be a number which will give you effective control—51 percent in some cases.

Generally, the documentation, agreements, and legal and accounting details involved in a tender offer are less than in a negotiated merger. On the other hand, this has its drawbacks, because you do not have an elaborate merger agreement together with warranties and the full opportunity to analyze business financial statements and potential liabilities of the company to be acquired. Also, in a tender-offer situation, you are likely to wind up with minority shareholders, whereas this can be avoided in a merger.

Still another group of laws which applies to tender offers is state tender offer statutes. A number of states (twenty-three by one recent count) have statutes which restrict the ability of a person to make a tender offer by surprise. Typically, the statutes require some kind of a waiting period after the initial filing disclosing the intention to make a tender offer. The waiting period gives the management of the company to be acquired a chance to react; and generally, since the existing management has a number of advantages in communicating with shareholders, since it knows the financial condition of the company and its plans, this is a very substantial advantage.

Still another law which regulates tender offers is the 1976 Antitrust Amendments (the Hart-Scott-Rodino Amendments). One provision of these laws requires that in a larger merger (one where the acquired company has assets or sales of more than $10 million and the acquiring company has assets or sales of more than $100 million) there must be a filing with the Department of Justice and the Federal Trade Commission and a waiting period. The waiting period is generally 15 days between the time the government is first notified and the time when the merger may be consummated, unless the government wants additional information, and then it is another 10 days. Thus, as a practical matter, the new law will impose a 25-day delay period in almost all mergers with any antitrust implications at all.

For purposes of management liability, tender offers are an important subject, because it is very easy to incur liability during the course of an unfriendly tender offer. From the point of view of the tender offeror, liability can be incurred by making inaccurate or misleading statements to the shareholders or in the documents filed with the SEC. The existing management can also incur liability on the same grounds; and in addition it can incur liability by acting in a way which the shareholders feel is not protective of the shareholder interest.

One of the principal reasons given by those who support tender offers for encouraging them and minimizing the red tape is that management typically has a vested interest in keeping its jobs and will, therefore, fight any kind of merger or takeover even if it is in the best interests of the shareholders. In short, these people allege that there is an inherent conflict of interest between management and the shareholders in most tender-offer situations. The shareholders will be offered a premium price for the stock and, therefore, be favorably disposed towards the tender offer, whereas management will be in the position of losing high-paying, powerful jobs if the offer goes through and will, therefore, resist it. The implications of this for purposes of this chapter seem to be that management ought to have some previously thought-out arrangements to deal with tender offers. These arrangements can be grouped into two classes. The first is arrangements which generally ought to be made in order to avoid the risk of an unfriendly takeover, and the second is a set of contingency plans on how to react to one if it should occur.

The most popular step for dealing with unfriendly tender offers on the prevention side is to have a staggered board of directors. This means one where not every member of the board is up for election every year. For example, if you have a fifteen-member board, you can have a system whereby the terms of five expire each year for a period of 3 years so that during any year only five members of the board are up for election. The second way to deal with hostile takeover offers is to have a provision in the governing documents of the corporation (usually the articles of incorporation) that provides that a merger can only be effected upon approval of at least two-thirds of the voting shares (or such other percentage as may be allowed by the state law). This makes it necessary for the tender offeror to acquire more shares than would otherwise be legally required.

The most important step which can be taken in terms of preparing a contingency plan is to make sure you have access to very good legal, accounting, and financial counseling. Your in-house lawyers ought to have some expertise and awareness of the laws relating to tender offers, but they cannot have, and perhaps should not be expected to have, a sufficiently detailed knowledge of how these kinds of laws work in order to represent the company adequately during this kind of crisis situation. One recent estimate of the legal fees (including both sides) in a contested tender offer was $2 million (this was a 1976 estimate, and no doubt inflation has taken its toll on this as on everything else). The costs involved in one of these kinds of operations are large, but more importantly, the cost shows the intense and frantic activity of a large number of people. There is no way that corporations can justify preparing for a tender offer and having this kind of capability in-house. They must rely on outside counsel. If your company happens to be represented by one of the major corporate law firms, undoubtedly you will have this facility available. On the other hand, if you happen to be represented by a small or even medium-sized law firm, it is probably necessary to do a little candid discussing of this problem with your lawyers, accountants, and financial representatives. Perhaps they need to have a contingency arrangement whereby they can turn to some large corporate law firm in this kind of circumstance. Again, it is a matter of economics. You probably ought not to ask a small corporate law firm to acquire the expertise to deal with this kind of problem if you are the only client that is going to be benefited, because you will have to pay for it. On the other hand, if your corporate law firm represents a number of companies of similar size, it should have some arrangements to deal with unfriendly tender offers.

The law is not the only discipline involved. The accountants will have to be involved, because there will probably have to be financial statements to either file or examine, and financial advisers will be crucial, because the key to the whole thing is the real value of the company and the relationship of the offered price to that real value. If a financial consulting firm or an investment banker or other recognized financial person is able to represent to your shareholders that even though the offered price is above the market value, it is still less than the true value of the company stock, you at least have a talking point and can use it to ask the shareholders to refrain from making an immediate tender.

On the other hand, you have to have a firmly thought-out plan, because if the price is high enough, you are very likely to incur personal liability by resisting it. Therefore, you ought to have some feel, or at least a means of getting a quick feel, for what price would be acceptable for the company stock. When the stock market is performing very well and your company happens to be in a highly regarded group of securities, the stock market will take care of this itself. On the other hand, if the reverse is true and you happen to be in a situation where the market is low and your company is in a disfavored group of securities, you may be a prime candidate for a tender offer because a premium could be offered over market and still represent less than the value of the company—in some cases, perhaps even less than the book value.

You should also have some specific plans or procedures for handling an unfriendly takeover. For example, existing management can communicate to shareholders because it has the list of shareholders. You can also note who owns large blocks and can or should be contacted individually. You probably have some strong allies—banks where you keep your deposits, insurance companies where you place your business, suppliers, and customers. You ought to know which ones you can count on.

There is a rather ironic twist in this area as far as banks are concerned, and some recent articles have pointed out situations where banks have financed unfriendly tender offers against companies which do a substantial amount of business with the bank. The mere fact that you have an account—even a substantial one—at a bank does not mean that it won't agree to loan somebody money to make a tender offer for your stock.

Another avenue is to have in mind a group of friendly suitors. One of the initial reactions to an unfriendly tender offer is that management doesn't care who gets the company so long as it is not the person who made the first unfriendly tender offer. This reaction can also give rise to some personal liability, because if it is later shown that the merger actually made with a friendly suitor was less advantageous to the shareholders than the one made by the first tender offeror, some liability can result. Obviously, in the case of a cash offer where there was simply a bidding contest, there would not be any liability based on inadequate consideration, so long as the highest price was received by the shareholders. However, if the shareholders could later show that the individual officers or executives negotiated favorable personal arrangements with the friendly suitor, that might give rise to some personal liability.

Management hostility to a takeover offer can also increase the price paid by the original or subsequent bidders. Thus, you may be in a situation where if you do not resist the original takeover offer, you could incur personal liability because the shareholders might allege that management should have resisted this offer in order to force higher offers from the same person or from other suitors. In this case, evidence that management had negotiated favorable individual deals with the first tender offeror would also serve to characterize the transaction and perhaps tilt the scales one way or another on the personal liability question.

In short, there really is not any hard and fast way to deal with tender offers to avoid personal liability. You can incur personal liability by either fighting them or going along with them. This is a problem which is unique to top management—principally the board of directors of the company. On the other hand, it is a specific situation where advance thought and planning and some contingency arrangements are very necessary in most cases. Some companies are just obviously not going to be taken over. It is a little difficult to envision an unfriendly takeover offer against one of the top 50 companies in the Fortune 500—perhaps even one of the top 100 or 200 such companies. On the other hand, the overwhelming majority of companies in this country are potentially subject to takeover offers, because the stock market is such a fickle barometer of worth. While your stock may currently be selling at a high premium, there is no indication at all that this will be the situation a year or two from now. The bottom line then is that you need some contingency arrangements for tender offers, but in most cases, the economics of the situation will be that the way you ought to do this is to have a list of outside people who can come to your rescue promptly. This is a highly technical and specialized area, and events move very rapidly, even in states where there is protective legislation and in mergers which are subject to the waiting period of the antitrust laws. If you wait until that time to start lining up good lawyers, accountants, and financial consultants, you have a problem. Furthermore, the fact that you may already have very good people in these areas does not really help you much if your existing people do not have experience with tender offers. In other words, while you may have the very best small law firm in the country, if that small law firm has to gear up to deal with a tender offer situation for you, you have substantial problems, because there just is not time to educate everyone adequately. You must find people with prior experience and expertise.

INDEX TO CASES

INDEX TO LAWS

INDEX

Procurement:
  of franchising equipment, 17-3
  of services, 57-9 to 57-10
Product:
  banning of, 18-5
  legal-statute approach, 1-29
  new, 44-6
  safety, warranty, and liability, 1-22 to 1-23,
    43-3 to 43-9, 45-1 to 45-11, 57-3
Productivity of employees, 30-12
Professional employees, 28-8 to 28-10
Profit:
  passover technique, 11-15
  short-swing, 1-14, 6-3, 38-6, 40-1 to 40-14
  unfair, 10-5
Profit sharing, 1-17, 28-5, 37-1
Property, industrial, 1-20
Property damage, 45-6
Protection of information given to government,
  1-28
Protective order, 1-28
Proxy:
  rules, 38-6 to 38-7
  solicitation, 42-1 to 42-4
Purchasing:
  ethics in, 57-8
  forms for, 56-4, 57-2
  from minority business, 57-8
Purchasing agents, 1-24
Purchasing departments, 24-13 to 24-14
Purchasing law, 1-24, 57-1 to 57-11
Push money, 18-3

Qualitative substantiality, rule of, 11-5 to 11-6
Quantitative substantiality, rule of, 11-5 to
  11-6
Quantity limitations, patent, 15-3, 15-6
Quotas, sales, 17-3
Quotation, request for, 56-4

Race discrimination, 25-6
Railway Labor Act, 25-26
Reason, rule of, 7-6, 11-1, 11-4, 11-18, 15-7, 16-3
Recalls, 1-23
Recidivism, 20-12
Reciprocity, 11-2, 13-6, 13-8
Records:
  for Consumer Product Safety Act, 44-13
  employee, 25-33 to 25-34
  for ERISA, 27-15
  for Fair Labor Standards Act, 28-14 to 28-18
  for OSHA, 1-19, 26-28
  for Toxic Substances Control Act, 54-3
Records retention, 1-26, 6-9, 24-2, 63-1 to 63-13
Red circle rates, 25-14
Refusals to deal, 11-10
Refusals to sell, 11-6
Registration:
  requirements under Securities Act, 38-7 to 38-
    10, 39-8
  of trademarks, 1-21, 48-3 to 48-4
Regulations:
  accounting, 1-15
  for air quality standards, 51-8
Rehabilitation Act of 1973, 25-5, 25-40

Relatives, preferential treatment of, 25-7
Reliance, 39-3
Religious discrimination, 25-25, 67-9
Reorganizations:
  "A," 32-1, 32-10 to 32-11
  "B," 32-2, 32-14 to 32-18
  "C," 32-2, 32-18 to 32-21
  corporate, 32-1 to 32-24
  liability in, 32-11
  post-closing adjustments, 33-1 to 33-2
  tax-free, 1-15
  (See also Acquisitions; Mergers)
Reporting:
  of contents of plans, 1-17
  credit, 1-28, 25-28
  engineer's, 3-7
  for ERISA, 27-1 to 27-3, 27-13
  installment, for IRS, 32-8
  for OSHA, 1-19, 26-1, 26-28 to 26-29
  securities regulation, 38-7, 40-13 to 40-14
Representatives of manufacturers, 11-10
Requirements contracts, 11-4
Research:
  applied, 9-6
  basic, 9-6
  and development, 8-4, 9-3, 9-6
  foreign, 16-12 to 16-16
Reserves:
  for bad debts, 34-5
  contingency, 5-6 to 5-7
Resource Conservation and Recovery Act of
  1976, 53-1 to 53-3
Restitution for FTC violations, 18-5
Restrictions:
  on distributors, 11-14
  on franchisees, 17-2
  government-imposed, 16-28
  joint-venture, 14-5, 14-9
  licensing, 1-20, 15-2, 15-7
  price, 11-14, 17-2, 17-4
  territory and customer, 11-15
  on trade, 7-3
Retirement, mandatory, 25-19, 25-24
Return of goods, 56-8
Reverse discrimination, 25-38 to 25-39
Risk:
  corporate, 24-2
  of loss, 56-6
  trial, 11-19
Risk analysis (legal), 3-3 to 3-5
Robinson-Patman Act, 1-12, 3-4 to 3-5, 7-4 to
  7-5, 10-2, 11-11, 12-1 to 12-18, 14-2, 14-6,
  24-5, 24-13, 57-5 to 57-6
Royalty on patent, 15-2, 15-4
Rule of reason, 7-6, 11-1, 11-4, 11-18, 15-7, 16-3

Safe Drinking Water Act, 50-4, 54-6
Safety:
  product, 1-22, 44-1 to 44-19
  standards for, 9-2, 44-2 to 44-3
Safety hazards, 26-20 to 26-21, 44-3 to 44-6
Salary (see Wages)
Sales:
  direct, 11-10
  forms for, 56-4
  quotas for, 17-3

Hancock, William A.
Executive's guide to business law

DATE DUE

MY 15 '92			
MY 1 4 93			

DEMCO 38-297